Seventh Edition

EDUCATIONAL PSYCHOLOGY

Windows on Classrooms

PAUL EGGEN
University of North Florida

DON KAUCHAK
University of Utah

PEARSON

Merrill
Prentice Hall

W9-BXN-666

Upper Saddle River, New Jersey
Columbus, Ohio

Library of Congress Cataloging in Publication Data

Eggen, Paul D.
    Educational psychology: windows on classrooms / Paul Eggen, Don Kauchak.--7th ed.
      p. cm.
    Includes bibliographical references and index.
    ISBN 0-13-172448-7 (pager)
    1. Educational psychological--Study and teaching (Higher)--United States. 2. Learning,
Psychology of--Case studies. I. Kauchak, Donald, P., II. Title.

LB1051.E463 2007
370.15--dc22

                                     2006043243

Vice President and Executive Publisher: Jeffery W. Johnston
Assistant Vice President and Publisher: Kevin M. Davis
Development Editor: Autumn Benson
Editorial Assistant: Sarah Kenoyer
Production Editor: Sheryl Glicker Langner
Design Coordinator: Diane C. Lorenzo
Cover Design: Ali Mohrman
Cover Image: Fotosearch
Photo Coordinator: Valerie Schultz
Production Manager: Laura Messerly
Director of Marketing: David Gesell
Marketing Manager: Autumn Purdy
Marketing Coordinator: Brian Mounts

This book was set in Life BT by Carlisle Publishing Services. It was printed and bound by Courier Kendallville, Inc. The cover was printed by Phoenix Color Corp.

Photo Credits: Photo credits are on page xxiii.

Pearson Education Ltd.
Pearson Education Singapore Pte. Ltd.
Pearson Education Canada, Ltd.
Pearson Education–Japan

Pearson Education Australia Pty. Limited
Pearson Education North Asia Ltd.
Pearson Educación de Mexico, S.A. de C.V.
Pearson Education Malaysia Pte. Ltd.

10 9 8 7 6 5 4 3 2 1
ISBN: 0-13-172448-7

This book is dedicated to our parents.
They taught us our most important lessons in life.

PREFACE

NEW TO THIS EDITION

As we prepared the seventh edition of *Educational Psychology: Windows on Classrooms* we attempted to make our book, already the most applied text in the field, even more usable and reader friendly. To reach this goal we have adopted a *Guided Learning System.* The *Guided Learning System* is a feature designed to maximize students' understanding of the text content. Grounded in basic principles of learning and teaching, it provides learners with structure, opportunities to actively process the chapter content, feedback, and reviews, each an essential factor for learning from both text and classroom activities.

The *Guided Learning System* has the following features:

- *A specific learning objective* is written for each major section of each chapter.
- A set of *"Checking Your Understanding" questions* directly aligned with the learning objective is then included at the end of the section.
- *Feedback* for the "Checking Your Understanding" questions is provided in Appendix B at the end of the text.
- *"Knowledge Extension" questions* that help learners relate the content to topics they've already studied are provided on the book's Companion Website (CW). Feedback for the questions is included on the CW.
- *"Meeting Your Learning Objectives" review sections* that restate the learning objectives are provided with bulleted summaries of the topics covered in that section.

In addition to the *Guided Learning System,* the following features are new to this edition:

- **Learning and Teaching in Urban Environments:** A rapidly increasing number of our nation's students attend urban schools, and it is likely that your first job offer will be in an urban environment. Integrated sections in Chapters 1, 3, 8, 11, 12, 13, and 15, in addition to thematic emphasis in Chapter 4, directly address the unique challenges and rewards related to social development, learning, motivation, classroom management, instruction, and assessement that exist in urban environments.
- **New Chapter:** *Learning and Instruction and Technology:* Technology is now an integral part of our lives, and it is having an increasing impact on teaching and learning. Chapter 14 relates technology to theories of learning and provides readers with descriptions of instructional applications of technology.
- **"Analyzing Classrooms"DVDs:** Two DVDs that are packaged with the book inlcude 25 episodes that provide real-world examples of various aspects of the teaching-learning process. Margin notes in each of the chapters refer readers to the episodes.
- **Expanded Coverage of Social Constructivism:** Increasing attention is being placed on the social construction of knowledge in the learning-teaching process. Expanded coverage of social constructivism in Chapter 8 includes detailed discussions of cognitive apprenticeships, situated learning, sociocultural learning theory, and classrooms as learning communities.

- **Thematic Coverage of Teacher Professionalism:** Teacher professionalism is increasingly emphasized in education today. Professionalism and the role of professional knowledge in learning to teach is now a theme for the text.
- **Connections to Prentice Hall's *Teacher Prep* Website:** Prentice Hall's *Teacher Prep* website provides a variety of resources for text users, and each chapter of the text identifies links to the *Teacher Prep* website in its *Exploring Further* feature.
- **Increased Integration of Case Studies.** Instead of merely presenting a beginning-of-chapter case study, the content of each chapter begins with a series of questions that provide a bridge from the case to the topics in the chapter. The questions are specifically addressed as the content is presented, and the case study is elaborated and integrated with the content, making the theory and research presented in the chapter concrete, meaningful, and applicable.
- **Increased Coverage of Instructional Principles and Models of Instruction:** Each chapter includes sections that provide principles of instruction for applying the content of the section in classrooms. *Principles of Instruction* sections are included for each major topic of the book. In addition, detailed coverage of models of instruction, including *Direct Instruction, Lecture Discussion, Guided Discovery,* and *Cooperative Learning* sections are presented in Chapter 13.

Integrated Companion Website. The book's Companion Website at *www.prenhall.com/ eggan* is now more closely integrated with each of the chapters in the text. It includes:

- *Integrated Online Cases.* An online case integrated with the content of each chapter gives students additional experience with applying the chapter's topics to the real world of learning and teaching. Multiple-choice and short-answer questions similar to those found on the PRAXIS™ exam are included with the case study.
- *"Exploring Further" Topics.* The "Exploring Further" feature allows students to study selected topics in greater depth. At least one of the "Exploring Further" topics in each chapter is linked to Prentice Hall's *Teacher Prep* website.
- *Feedback for Short-Answer Questions Following the End-of-Chapter Cases.* The feedback provides students with ideal answers consistent with the requirements of the PRAXIS™ exam.
- *Knowledge Extensions.* The "Knowledge Extension" questions and feedback that are part of the *Guided Learning System* are on the Companion Website.
- *Practice Quiz and Essay Questions:* Practice quiz items in multiple-choice format and essay questions, both in the *Self-Assessment* module of each chapter, help students study for quizzes and exams. The practice quiz and essay questions are similar to those found on the PRAXIS™ exam.
- *Portfolio Activities.* Suggested portfolio activities help students begin the process of preparing a professional portfolio.

In addition to the features new to this edition, we have retained the best features of earlier editions. The following pages illustrate the features of the text.

EXCEPTIONALLY APPLIED

A central goal of *Educational Psychology: Windows on Classrooms* is to help its readers be able to use educational psychology as teachers. To capture the real world of learning and teaching, we capitalize on the use of case studies, video clips, and a number of features that help students connect content to classrooms.

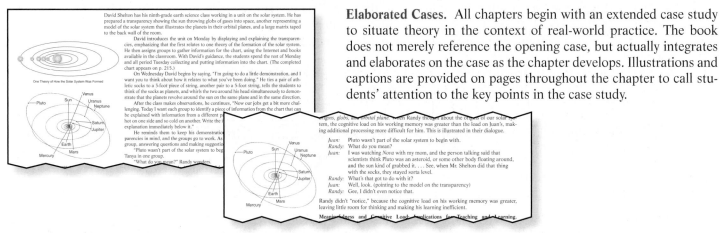

Elaborated Cases. All chapters begin with an extended case study to situate theory in the context of real-world practice. The book does not merely reference the opening case, but actually integrates and elaborates on the case as the chapter develops. Illustrations and captions are provided on pages throughout the chapter to call students' attention to the key points in the case study.

Analyzing Classrooms DVD. New to this edition is a two set DVD that allows students to observe real children and classrooms. The video clips on the DVDs are integrated throughout the text and allow students to analyze the clips relating to the concepts and principles discussed in the text. Viewing videos and discussing and analyzing them not only deepens understanding of concepts presented in the book, but also builds skills on observing and analyzing children and classrooms.

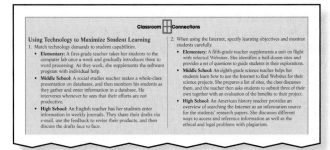

Classroom Connections at the Elementary, Middle School, and High School Levels. These boxes in each chapter offer strategies for applying content to specific learning and teaching situations. Each strategy is illustrated with a classroom example, derived from the authors' experiences, at the elementary, middle and junior high, and high school level.

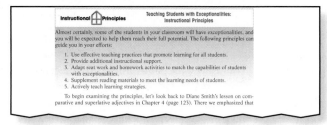

Instructional Principles. *Instructional Principles* sections lay out guidelines for applying key chapter content. These sections, which are situated in case studies throughout the text, explicitly show teachers' efforts to apply instructional principles derived from educational psychology.

Developing as a Professional. Since the PRAXIS™ exam continues to emphasize case-based questions, the entire text prepares students for the PRAXIS™ by helping them become familiar and comfortable with responding to the type of case-based questions they will find on the exam. Short-answer questions following each end-of-chapter case parallel the type of questions on the PRAXIS™ to provide students with experiences in responding to items similar to those they will find on the exam. In addition, many questions provided in the *Test Bank* are similar to the questions on the PRAXIS™ and require students to apply their understanding of chapter content.

CLEARLY IDENTIFYING AND REINFORCING KEY IDEAS IN EVERY CHAPTER

The text's new pedagogical structure clearly identifies core concepts and helps students focus on every chapter's big ideas. This *Guided Learning System* maximizes students' understanding of the text content by matching learning objectives to the chapter outline, reinforcing the main ideas with *Checking Your Understanding* questions at the end of every section, and organizing the summary around the learning objectives.

Clear Alignment of Learning Objectives and the Chapter Outline. Like the previous edition, the seventh edition begins every chapter with learning objectives. However, in this edition, the specific learning objectives are linked to each of the major headings in the chapters. By aligning the learning objectives and the chapter outline, the key ideas of the chapter are clearly presented and highlighted to help students identify the key concepts and maximize their learning.

Chapter Outline		Learning Objectives
		After you have completed your study of this chapter, you should be able to
Problem Solving	**1**	Identify examples of ill-defined and well-defined problems, and describe the role of deliberate practice in solving them.
Well-Defined and Ill-Defined Problems • A Problem-Solving Model • Expert-Novice Differences in Problem-Solving Ability • Helping Learners Become Better Problem Solvers: Instructional Principles • Problem-Based Learning		
The Strategic Learner	**2**	Explain differences between effective and ineffective strategies in studying behaviors.
Metacognition: The Foundation of Strategic Learning • Study Strategies • Developing Strategic Learning in Students: Instructional Principles		
Critical Thinking	**3**	Define critical thinking, and identify its characteristics in classroom activities.
The Challenge of Critical Thinking • Elements of Critical Thinking • Developing Critical Thinking: Instructional Principles		
Transfer of Learning	**4**	Identify factors that influence transfer in classroom learning activities.
General and Specific Transfer • Factors Affecting the Transfer of Learning		

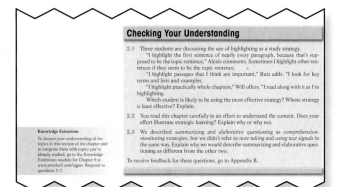

Checking Your Understanding. *Checking Your Understanding* questions at the end of every major section are directly aligned with the learning objectives and reinforce the big ideas of that section. These *Checking Your Understanding* questions provide students with an opportunity to actively process the chapter content and maximize their learning. Students can assess their understanding of the chapter content with the feedback provided in Appendix B.

Meeting Your Learning Objectives. The end-of-chapter *Meeting Your Learning Objectives* review section restates the learning objectives and provides a bulleted summary of the most important topics covered. By organizing the chapter summary around the concrete learning objectives, students are reminded of the key ideas presented in the chapter and the most important information is, once again, reinforced.

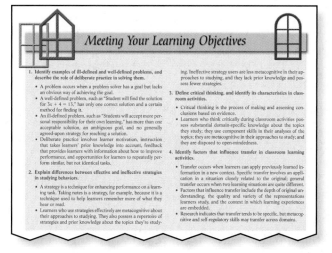

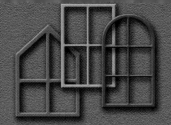

TEACHER PREP

**MERRILL
PRENTICE HALL**

AUTOMATICALLY PACKAGED WITH EACH NEW COPY OF THIS TEXT.

We invite you to explore our new, innovative and engaging website and all that it has to offer you, your course, and tomorrow's educators! Organized around the major courses pre-service teachers take, the Teacher Preparation Classroom site provides media, student/teacher artifacts, strategies, research articles, and other resources to equip your students with the quality tools needed to excel in their courses and prepare them for their first classroom.

This ultimate on-line education resource is available at no cost, when packaged with a Merrill text, and will provide you and your students access to:

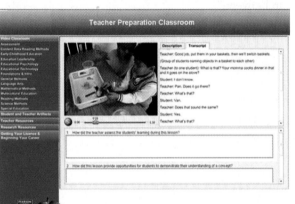

Online Video Library. More than 150 video clips—each tied to a course topic and framed by learning goals and PRAXIS-type questions—capture real teachers and students working in real classrooms, as well as in-depth interviews with both students and educators.

Student and Teacher Artifacts. More than 200 student and teacher classroom artifacts—each tied to a course topic and framed by learning goals and application questions—provide a wealth of materials and experiences to help make your study to become a professional teacher more concrete and hands-on.

Research Articles. Over 500 articles from ASCD's renowned journal *Educational Leadership.* The site also includes Research Navigator, a searchable database of additional educational journals.

Teaching Strategies. Over 500 strategies and lesson plans for you to use when you become a practicing professional.

Licensure and Career Tools. Resources devoted to helping you pass your licensure exam; learn standards, law, and public policies; plan a teaching portfolio; and succeed in your first year of teaching.

The Teacher Prep site is integrated throughout the text in many of the "Exploring Further" margin notes. When readers go to the Exploring Further module on the Companion Website, they will often be directed to resources on the Teacher Prep site.

Supplementary Materials

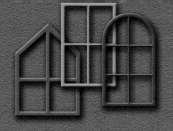

For Students

Where the Web Meets Textbooks for Student Savings!

SafariX Textbooks Online is an exciting new choice for students looking to save money. As an alternative to purchasing the print textbook, students can subscribe to the same content online and save up to 50% off the suggested list price of the same text. With a SafariX WebBook, students can search the text, make notes online, print out reading assignments that incorporate lecture notes, and bookmark important passages for later review. The ISBN for the SafariX WebBook for this text is 0-13-172447-9.

VangoNotes

Attention Students: You're busy. We get it. With *VangoNotes* you can study "in between" all the other things you need to get done. *VangoNotes* gives you the confidence you need to succeed in the classroom. They're **flexible;** just download and go. And, they're **efficient.** Use them in your car, at the gym, walking to class, wherever. Visit *www.VangoNotes.com* to get yours today and start studying.

The Student Study Guide

The *Student Study Guide* (0-13-173615-9) includes chapter outlines, overviews, and objectives. More importantly, several additional features, such as application exercises, involve students in applying teaching and learning concepts.

Teacher Preparation Classroom

All copies of the seventh edition come automatically packaged with access codes for this new interactive website offering students a wealth of course-specific resources and activities to enrich and deepen their preparation as a teacher. Organized around the major courses pre-service teachers take, the Teacher Prep site provides more then 150 video clips—each tied to a course topic and framed by learning goals—and PRAXIS-type questions, more than 250 student/teacher artifacts—each tied to a course topic and framed by learning goals and application questions, over 500 strategies and lesson plans, over 500 *Educational Leadership* research articles, and other resources to equip students with the quality tools needed to excel in their courses and prepare them for their first classroom.

Analyzing Classrooms DVDs

New to this edition, this two-set DVD allows students to observe real children and classrooms. The edited video clips on the DVDs are integrated throughout the text and provide students the opportunity to analyze the clips relating to the concepts, principles, or strategies discussed in the text, building skills on observing and analyzing children and classrooms. The DVDs are automatically packaged with every text.

Companion Website

The *Companion Website* for this text found at *www.prenhall.com/eggen* serves students as an interactive study guide, providing *Practice Quiz* and *Essay Questions* with self-assessment and feedback. In addition, feedback for the *Developing as a Professional: PRAXIS Practice* questions posed in the book's closing case studies is provided in the *Practice for PRAXIS* module. The *Exploring Further* module provides students with additional content to deeper delve into chapter topics. Rounding out the site are *Knowledge Extension* questions that help students integrate chapter topics with topics they've already studied.

Simulations in Educational Psychology and Research CD-ROM, Version 2.1

This problem-solving simulation CD-ROM (0-13-113717-4) allows students to experience and explore (1) Piaget's developmental stages, (2) misconceptions and the role of prior knowledge in learning, (3) schemas and the construction of meaning, (4) Kohlberg's stages of moral development, and (5) mental models and assessment.

FOR PROFESSORS

Multimedia Presentation Software

The *Multimedia Presentation Software* (0-13-175318-5) is a series of DVDs that contain materials from the ancillaries offered with the text and organized around PowerPoint presentations. This technology enables professors to use available ancillaries in a classroom setting and to show appropriate video clips or present examples, scenarios, or problems to help facilitate classroom discussion or to supplement lectures. Professors can also create their own PowerPoint presentations or modify existing ones.

Instructor's Manual and Media Guide

The *Instructor's Manual and Media Guide* (0-13-172449-5) includes chapter overviews and objectives; listings of PowerPoint slides available on the Instructor Resource Center; and presentation outlines and teaching suggestions for each chapter. In addition, it contains directions for using the *Multimedia Presentation Software,* directions for using the Simulations CD (for students), information for using the text's Companion Website, information for using the Teacher Prep classroom site, and descriptions of the 10 videos that accompany the text, along with questions for discussion and analysis including feedback.

Test Bank and TestGen

The *Test Bank* (0-13-172450-9) contains approximately 1500 test items, providing a comprehensive but flexible assessment package. Test items fall into two categories: lower-level items in the form of multiple-choice and true-false questions, and higher-level items that require students to apply what they know in mini-cases and essay questions. The computerized test bank software *(TestGen)* (0-13-172454-1) gives instructors electronic access to the test questions printed in the *Test Bank* and allows them to create and customize exams. *TestGen* is available in both Macintosh and PC/Windows versions.

Online PowerPoint Slides

The *Online PowerPoint Slides* (0-13-172453-3), available on the Instructor Resource Center at *www.prenhall.com*, highlight key concepts, summarize content, and illustrate a number of key figures and tables from the text. To access the Online PowerPoint Slides, go to *www.prenhall.com* and click on the Instructor Support button and then go to the Download Supplements section. Here you will be able to login or complete a one-time registration for a user name and password.

OneKey Course Management

OneKey is Prentice Hall's exclusive new resource for instructors and students. OneKey is an integrated online course management resource featuring everything students and instructors need for work in or outside of the classroom, including *Analyzing Classroom Video* DVDs, *Student Study Guide,* Companion Website material, *Instructor's Manual and Media Guide, Test Bank,* and *Online PowerPoint Slides.* OneKey is available in the nationally hosted CourseCompass (0-13-172457-6) platform, as well as WebCT (0-13-172458-4) and BlackBoard (0-13-172456-8). The ISBNs for the OneKey Student Access Kits are: CourseCompass Student Access Kit (0-13-222314-7), Web CT Student Access Kit (0-13-228440-5), and BlackBoard Student Access Kit (0-13-243211-0). For more information about OneKey, instructors should contact their local Prentice Hall representatives prior to placing their textbook order.

The Video Package

The extensive video package that has accompanied previous editions is being offered, including *Looking Through Classrooms Windows: Tape One* (0-13-110890-5), *Looking Through Classrooms Windows: Tape Two* (0-13-110892-1), *Concepts in Classrooms* (0-13-026405-9), *Insights into Learning: Finding Area in Elementary Math* (0-13-095277-X), *Insights into Learning: Using Balance Beams in Fourth Grade* (0-13-095278-8), *Insights into Learning: Designing Experiments in Seventh Grade* (0-13-095279-6), *A Private Universe* (1-55981-515-9), *Double-Column Addition: A Teacher Uses Piaget's Theory* (0-13-751413-1), *Windows on Classrooms* (0-13-579948-1), *Educational Psychology Video Package I* (0-02-389496-2), and *Educational Psychology Video Package II* (0-02-331703-5).

ACKNOWLEDGMENTS

Every book reflects the work of a team that includes the authors, the staff of editors, and the reviewers. We appreciate the input we've received from professors and students who have used previous editions of the book, and gratefully acknowledge the contributions of the reviewers who offered us constructive feedback to guide us in this new edition: Ronna F. Dillon, Southern Illinois University; Oliver W. Edwards, University of Central Florida; Leena Furtado, California State University, Dominguez Hills; Robert L. Hohn, University of Kansas; Anne N. Rinn, Western Kentucky University; Rayne A. Sperling, Penn State University; Nancy Vye, University of Washington; and Glenda Wilkes, University of Arizona.

In addition, we acknowledge with our thanks, the reviewers of our previous editions. They are Kay S. Bull, Oklahoma State University; Jerome D'Agostino, University of Arizona; Thomas G. Fetsco, Northern Arizona University; Newell T. Gill, Florida Atlantic University; Dov Liberman, University of Houston; Hermine H. Marshall, San Francisco State University; Luanna H. Meyer, Massey University–New Zealand; Nancy Perry, University of British Columbia; Jay Samuels, University of Minnesota; Gregory Schraw, University of Nebraska, Lincoln; Dale H. Schunk, Purdue University; Rozanne Sparks, Pittsburgh State University; Karen M. Zabrucky, Georgia State University; Patricia Barbetta, Florida International University; David Bergin, University of Toledo; Scott W. Brown, University of Connecticut; Barbara Collamer, Western Washington University; Betty M. Davenport, Campbell University; Charles W. Good, West Chester University; Tes Mehring, Emporia State University; Evan Powell, University of Georgia; Robert J. Stevens, Pennsylvania State University; and Julianne C. Turner, Notre Dame University.

In addition to the reviewers who guided our revisions, our team of editors gave us support in many ways. Kevin Davis, our Publisher, continues to guide us with his intelligence, insight, and finger on the pulse of the field. Autumn Benson, our development editor, helped us make the book accessible to our readers. Luanne Dreyer Elliot, our copy editor, has been thoroughly professional in her efforts to make the content of the book as clear and understandable as possible. Sheryl Langner, our production editor, has been with us for five editions; in each she has been supportive and flexible, and the professionalism and commitment to excellence that she consistently demonstrates are appreciated more than we can say.

Our appreciation goes to all these fine people who have taken our words and given them shape. We hope that all our efforts will result in increased learning for students and more rewarding teaching for instructors.

Finally, we would sincerely appreciate any comments or questions about anything that appears in the book or any of its supplements. Please feel free to contact either of us at any time. Our e-mail addresses are: peggen@unf.edu and kauchak@ed.utah.edu.

Good luck.

Paul Eggen
Don Kauchak

CONTENTS

Chapter 8
Constructing Knowledge   232

Chapter 9
Complex Cognitive Processes   262

Part 3: Classroom Processes

Chapter 10
Theories of Motivation   296

Chapter 11
Motivation in the Classroom   334

Chapter 12
Creating Productive Learning Environments: Classroom Management   366

Chapter 13
Creating Productive Learning Environments: Principles and Models of Instruction   404

Chapter 14
Learning and Instruction and Technology   442

Chapter 15

Assessing Classroom Learning   472

Chapter 16

Assessment Through Standardized Testing   508

Appendix A

Using This Text to Practice for the Praxis™ Principles of Learning and Teaching Exam   A-1

Appendix B

Feedback for "Checking Your Understanding" Questions   A-9

SPECIAL FEATURES

Instructional Principles

PHOTO CREDITS

Paul Conklin/PhotoEdit Inc., pp. 2, 361, 461; Bill Aron/PhotoEdit Inc., pp. 5, 15, 248; Will Hart/PhotoEdit Inc., pp. 9, 87, 113 (top), 275, 360, 430, 432, 436; Anthony Magnacca/Merrill, pp. 16, 37 (left and right), 81, 146, 153, 266, 290, 339, 343, 466; Laura Bolesta/Merrill, pp. 20, 168, 421, 452; Jonathan A. Meyers/The Stock Connection, p. 28; , Richard Hutchings/PhotoEdit Inc., pp. 31, 36, 418; Stockbtyte, p. 40; Michael Newman/PhotoEdit Inc., pp. 42, 46, 78, 150, 187, 214, 232, 251, 313, 380, 384, 428, 502; Scott Cunningham/Merrill, pp. 49, 107, 112, 113 (bottom), 118, 133, 155, 209, 375, 490, 497; Eddie Lawrence © Dorling Kindersley, pp. 52, 370; Will & Deni McIntyre/Photo Researchers, Inc., pp. 60, 94, 140; Patrick White/Merrill, pp. 63, 65, 75, 442; EyeWire Collection/Getty Images–Photodisc, pp. 68, 457; Gail Zucker/Gail Zucker Photography, p. 71; David Grossman/The Image Works, p. 72; Mary Kate Denny/PhotoEdit Inc., pp. 83, 88, 350, 394, 477; Todd Yarrington/Merrill, pp. 98 (left and right), 135, 144 (right); David Young-Wolff/PhotoEdit Inc., pp. 100, 235, 415, 512; Valerie Schultz/Merrill, pp. 101, 410; KS Studios/Merrill, pp. 104, 392 (bottom); Robert Kusel/Getty Images Inc-Stone Allstock, p. 130; Spencer Grant/PhotoEdit Inc., pp. 136, 166; James L. Shaffer, p. 144 (left), 355, 487; Tony Freeman/PhotoEdit Inc., p. 151; Bill Bachmann/PhotoEdit Inc., p. 162; Krista Greco/Merrill, pp. 165, 517; Britt J. Erlanson-Messens/Getty Images Inc.–Image Bank, p. 174; Larry Hamill/Merrill, p. 175; Patrick White/Merrill, pp. 181, 182; Alan Oddie/PhotoEdit Inc., p. 198; Tom Watson/Merrill, pp. 204, 256, 273, 392 (top); Frank Siteman/Creative Eye/MIRA.com, p. 212; Peter Skinner/Photo Researchers, Inc. p. 216; Bob Daemmrich/The Image Works, p. 225; Bill Bachmann/Photo Researchers, Inc. p. 250; Bill Bachmann/Creative Eye/MIRA.com, p. 262; Steve Skjold/PhotoEdit Inc., p. 267; Liz Moore/Merrill, pp. 278, 328, 448; Frank Siteman/PhotoEdit Inc., p. 283; Steve Shott © Dorling Kindersley, p. 296; Jim Pickerell/Stock Boston, p. 301; Mary Kate Denny/Getty Images Inc.–Stone Allstock, p. 304; Stockbyte, pp. 309, 450; Ellen Senisi/The Image Works, p. 322; Antonio Mo/Getty Images Inc.–Taxi, p. 334; Laima Druskis/PH College, pp. 344, 345, 359; Jose L. Pelaez/Corbis/Stock Market, p. 353; Bob Daemmrick/Stock Boston, p. 366; David R. Frazier/Photo Researchers, Inc.,. p. 377; Chip Henderson/Getty Images Inc.–Stone Allstock, p. 390; Elena Rooraid/PhotoEdit Inc., p. 398; F. Pedrick/The Image Works, p. 404; Scott Teven/The Stock Connection, p. 416; Pearson Learning Photo Studio, p. 423; Lawrence Migdale/PhotoResearchers, Inc., p. 446; A. Ramey/PhotoEdit Inc., p. 455; Cleve Bryant/PhotoEdit Inc., p.465; Jeff Greenberg/Photoedit Inc., p. 472; David Buffington/Getty Images, Inc.–Photodisc, p. 484; Getty Images, Inc.–Photodisc, p. 492; Spencer Grant/Photo Researchers, Inc., p. 496; Jim Pickerell/The Stock Connection, p. 499; Jose Luis Pelaez, Inc./Corbis/Bettman, p. 508; © Bob Daemmrich/PNI, p. 513; Mark Burnett/Stock Boston, p. 518; Steve Lyne, Rex Interstock/Stock Connection/Picture Quest, p. 526; Photos.com, p. 528; Kathy Kirtland/Merrill, p. 531.

Additional Credits: "Family Circus" cartoon on p. 20 reprinted with special permission of King Features Syndicate.

CHAPTER 1

Educational Psychology:
Developing a Professional
Knowledge Base

Chapter Outline	Learning Objectives

After you have completed your study of this chapter, you should be able to

Educational Psychology and Becoming a Professional

Characteristics of Professionalism

1 Describe the characteristics of professionalism, and identify examples of the characteristics in teachers' actions.

Professional Knowledge and Learning to Teach

Knowledge of Content • Pedagogical Content Knowledge • General Pedagogical Knowledge • Knowledge of Learners and Learning • The INTASC Standards: States Respond to the Need for Professional Knowledge • Changes in Education: Reform and Accountability • Learning Contexts: Teaching and Learning in Urban Environments

2 Describe the different kinds of knowledge professional teachers possess, and identify examples of professional knowledge in teachers' actions.

The Role of Research in Acquiring Knowledge

Descriptive Research • Correlational Research • Experimental Research • Action Research • Conducting Research in Classrooms: Instructional Principles • Research and the Development of Theory

3 Describe different types of research, and analyze applications of these types.

The Use of Case Studies in Educational Psychology

4 Explain how using case studies to place educational psychology in real-world contexts makes it meaningful.

E xpert teaching requires a great deal of decision making based on a foundation of professional knowledge. As you read the following case study, think about the decisions the teachers make and the knowledge on which those decisions are based.

"Hi, Keith. How's it going?" Jan Davis, a veteran seventh-grade math teacher, greets Keith Jackson, a first-year teacher at Lakeside Middle School. "You look deep in thought."

"Okay, I guess. My last period class is getting to me, though," Keith replies. "The students are okay when we stick to mechanics, but they hate word problems. They always try to take the easiest way out . . . memorize a formula, and if the next problem is even the teeniest bit different from the first, they can't do it.

"I thought I was going to be so great when I got here. I have a really good math background, and I love math. I just knew the kids would love it too, but I'm not so sure anymore. . . . And there are a few who sit in the back of the room like they're comatose. . . . No one prepared me for this.

"Then, there's Kelly. She disrupts everything I do. I've tried everything. Ignored her talking, given her referrals, called her mother. . . . Nothing works. And I don't think she's really a bad kid. I even took her aside and asked her straight out why she was giving me such a hard time. . . . Actually, I think she's a bit better lately."

"You're in the process of becoming a real teacher," Jan smiles. "There aren't many easy answers for what we do. Very little in teaching is cut-and-dried. . . . But then, that's part of the fun, and challenge, of it.

"Like working with Kelly. You said it helped when you took her aside. She might not have another adult she can talk to, and she may simply need someone to care about her. . . . And there's no question that kids' personal needs influence their learning.

"About the quiet ones in the back of the room: This is a problem for me, too, and I'll tell you what works for me. First, I move them up to the front, and I tell them, 'I want you to learn, and I want you up close where I can work with you.' Then I make it a point to call on all of them as equally as possible. One of my university instructors had us read some research indicating how important it is to call on all the kids, so I practice it in my classes. Once they get used to it, they really like it. It's one of the most important things I do."

"How about the math part?" Keith asks. "I've tried explaining the stuff until I'm blue in the face."

"I understand your concern, and I've had the same kinds of troubles in the past. As it happens, I'm taking another course, and it's changing my thinking. It emphasizes involving the kids, and then we practice the ideas with our own students.

"Here's an example. We've been reviewing decimals and percents, so at the beginning of class, I brought in a 12-ounce can, a 16-ounce bottle, and a 6-pack of soft drinks with price tags on them. I put the kids into pairs and told them to figure out a way to determine which one was the best buy. Some of them struggled trying to figure out whether they should find the price per can or price per ounce and what to do about liters, but I helped them along. We created a table, the groups computed their answers, and we compared them. Now they're beginning to see how math relates to their day-to-day lives.

"I learned from it. In some cases I jumped in too soon when they could have figured it out for themselves, and at other times I let them stumble around too long and they wasted time. But, they learned a lot more than they would have if I had simply stood up and lectured to them."

"I hate to admit this," Keith says, "but some of my university courses suggested just what you did. It was fun, but I didn't think it was *real* teaching."

"You couldn't relate to it at the time. You didn't have a class with live students who 'didn't get it.'

"Hang in there," Jan continues. "The fact that you're thinking about it means you really care about what you're doing. That's what we need in teaching—professionals."

Let's begin our study of educational psychology with three questions. (1) What does it mean to be a "professional"? (2) What characteristics did Jan and Keith demonstrate that suggested they are professionals? (3) How can educational psychology contribute to your professional growth? We address these and other questions in this chapter.

EDUCATIONAL PSYCHOLOGY AND BECOMING A PROFESSIONAL

Teacher professionalism and its impact on student learning are receiving increasing attention in American education. Raising standards for teachers has been called for, and teachers are being asked to know and do more (Bransford, Darling-Hammond, & LePage, 2005; Darling-Hammond & Baratz-Snowdon, 2005).

Let's see what *professionalism* means.

Characteristics of Professionalism

The first two questions of the three we just posed about professionals focus on the relationship between professionalism and teaching. We try to answer them in this section.

Definitions of professionalism vary, but most include the following characteristics (Ingersoll, 2003):

- A commitment to learners that includes a code of ethics
- The ability to make decisions in complex and ill-defined contexts
- Reflective practice
- A body of specialized knowledge

These characteristics answer the first question we asked: What does it mean to be a professional? The characteristics of professionalism are outlined in Figure 1.1 and discussed in the following sections.

Concepts learned in educational psychology help teachers understand the complexities of classroom life.

Commitment to Learners

Let's take another look at Keith's and Jan's conversation. Keith began by describing his concerns about both his last-period class and his student Kelly; that is, why the class hated word problems and why one student was giving him such a hard time. Keith was committed to his students and their learning. A less-committed teacher may have abandoned word problems and written Kelly off as incorrigible, doing whatever it took to eliminate her distractions and letting it go at that.

Jan was equally committed, and because of her experience, her response was more sophisticated than Keith's. For instance, she modified her instruction to increase student involvement and motivation, and she attempted to grow professionally by studying and taking extra courses.

Some authors describe this commitment as *professional caring*. "A professional doesn't view his or her profession as just a *job,* but rather sees it as a *calling* that is all about caring for children. The ability to make personal connections with students is an identifiable trait of a successful teacher" (Kramer, 2003, p. 23).

Exploring Further:

The National Education Association, a prominent professional organization, has created a code of ethics that guides teachers in their commitment to students. To see this code, go to the "NEA Code of Ethics" in the *Exploring Further* module of Chapter 1 at *www.prenhall.com/eggen.*

Figure 1.1 Characteristics of professionalism

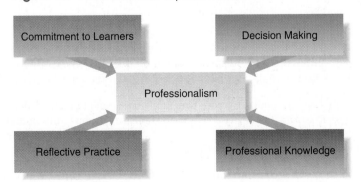

Decision Making

The ability to make decisions in complex and ill-defined situations is another essential characteristic of professionals. This ability is one of the differences between a professional and a **technician,** someone who uses specific skills to complete a well-defined task, such as an electrician wiring an outlet. As Jan commented to Keith, "There aren't many easy answers for what we do. Very little in teaching is cut-and-dried. . . . But then, that's part of the fun, and challenge, of it."

For instance, Jan made decisions with regard to the following:

- The learning objectives for her lesson on decimals and percents
- The strategy she used to help the students reach the objectives
- The examples she selected
- The sequence of activities for the lesson
- Which students to call on and in which order
- The specific questions she asked
- Her response to students after they answered or failed to answer

The number of decisions teachers must make is staggering. Some historical research suggests that they make as many as 800 decisions per day (Jackson, 1968). Further, they are on their own in making the decisions, and more significantly, expert teachers make the decisions routinely and efficiently (Berliner, 1994, 2000).

Reflective Practice

Teachers make an enormous number of decisions, but how do they know if their decisions are valid and wise? This is a tough question, because they receive little feedback about the effectiveness of their work. Administrators observe teachers only a few times a year at most, and teachers receive only vague, sketchy, and uncertain feedback from students and parents. In addition, they get virtually no feedback from their colleagues, unless the school has a peer-coaching or -mentoring program (Darling-Hammond, 1996, 1997). To improve, teachers must be able to assess their own classroom performance.

The ability to conduct this self-assessment can be developed, but it requires that teachers are inclined to critically examine their actions. This is the essence of a simple, yet powerful notion called **reflective practice,** the process of conducting a critical self-examination of one's teaching. "Reflective practice is a deliberate pause . . . [to examine] beliefs, goals, and practices, to gain new or deeper understandings that lead to actions to improve learning for students" (York-Barr, Sommers, Ghere, & Montie, 2001, p. 6).

Professional Knowledge

Professionals make decisions in ill-defined situations and reflect on these decisions afterward to refine and improve their practice. But how does a teacher like Jan make and refine these decisions? She didn't make them based on intuition, whim, or emotion; her decisions were grounded in a deep understanding of professional knowledge (Hogan, Rabinowitz & Craven, 2003). For example, her decision to call on all her students as equally as possible was based on research indicating that this practice increases student achievement. And her decision to use the containers of soft drinks as the framework for her lesson on decimals and percents was based on learning and motivation theory indicating that real-world applications increase both. In addition, the fact that Keith was less knowledgeable helps explain some of his struggles. Making decisions based on knowledge is the essence of a professional teacher. This is the reason you're studying educational psychology, and this answers the third question we asked at the beginning of the chapter: Educational psychology contributes to your professional growth by contributing to a knowledge base that will allow you to make the kinds of decisions expected of a professional.

> The accumulation of richly structured and accessible bodies of knowledge allows individuals to engage in expert thinking and action. In studies of teaching, this understanding of expertise has led researchers to devote increased attention to teachers' knowledge and its organization. (Borko & Putnam, 1996, p. 674)

We examine this knowledge base in more detail in the next section.

Exploring Further:
To see some suggestions for furthering your professional development go to "Increasing Your Professionalism" in the *Exploring Further* Module of Chapter 1 at www.prehall.com/eggen.

Technician. Someone who uses specific skills to complete a well-defined task

Reflective practice. The process of conducting a critical self-examination of one's teaching

Checking Your Understanding

1.1 Describe and explain the characteristics of professionalism.

1.2 Identify at least three ways in which Keith demonstrated the characteristics of professionalism in his conversation with Jan.

1.3 Explain how Jan demonstrated each of the characteristics of professionalism in her conversation with Keith.

1.4 Using the characteristics of professionalism as a basis, describe the primary difference between Keith's and Jan's level of professional behavior.

To receive feedback for these questions, go to Appendix B.

PROFESSIONAL KNOWLEDGE AND LEARNING TO TEACH

In the previous section, we emphasized the importance of knowledge as an essential element of professionalism. Now, we want to examine this knowledge in more detail.

To begin, complete the following Learning and Teaching Inventory, designed to provide a brief introduction to the different kinds of knowledge needed to understand students, ourselves, and the way learning occurs. Mark each item true or false.

Learning and Teaching Inventory

1. The thinking of children in elementary schools tends to be limited to the concrete and tangible, whereas the thinking of middle and high school students tends to be abstract.
2. Students generally understand how much they know about a topic.
3. Experts in the area of intelligence view knowledge of facts (e.g., the answer to "On what continent is Brazil?") as one indicator of intelligence.
4. Effective teaching is essentially a process of presenting information to students in succinct and organized ways.
5. Preservice teachers who major in a content area, such as math, are much more successful than nonmajors in providing clear examples of the ideas they teach.
6. To increase students' motivation to learn, teachers should praise as much as possible.
7. Teachers who are the most successful at creating and maintaining orderly classrooms are those who can quickly stop disruptions when they occur.
8. Preservice teachers generally believe they will be more effective than teachers who are already in the field.
9. Teachers primarily learn by teaching; in general, experience is the primary factor involved in learning to teach.
10. Testing detracts from learning, because students who are tested frequently develop negative attitudes and usually learn less than those who are tested less often.

Let's see how you did. The answer and an explanation for each item are outlined in the following paragraphs. As you read the explanations, remember that they describe students or other people in general, and exceptions will exist.

1. *The thinking of children in elementary schools tends to be limited to the concrete and tangible, whereas the thinking of middle and high school students tends to be abstract.*
   False: Research indicates that middle school, high school, and even university students can think effectively in the abstract only when they are studying areas in which they have considerable experience and expertise (P. Alexander, 2006; Serpell, 2000; Thornton & Fuller, 1981). When we examine development of students' thinking in Chapter 2, you'll understand why and how your understanding of this idea can improve your teaching.

2. *Students generally understand how much they know about a topic.*
   False: Contrary to what we might think, learners in general, and young children in particular, often cannot assess what they know (Hacker, Bol, Horgan, & Rakow, 2000; Schommer, 1994). Students' awareness of how they learn and what they already know strongly influences understanding, and cognitive learning theory helps us understand why. (We discuss cognitive learning theory in Chapters 7 to 9.)

3. *Experts in the area of intelligence view knowledge of facts (e.g., the answer to "On what continent is Brazil?") as an indicator of intelligence.*
   True: The Wechsler Intelligence Scale for Children—Fourth Edition (Wechsler, 2003), the most popular intelligence test in use today, has several items very similar to the example. Is this an effective way to measure intelligence? Theories of intelligence, which are analyzed in Chapter 4, examine this and other issues related to learner ability.

4. *Effective teaching is essentially a process of presenting information to students in succinct and organized ways.*
   False: As we better understand learning, we find that simply explaining information to students often is not effective in promoting understanding (Bransford, Brown, & Cocking, 2000; Greeno, Collins, & Resnick, 1996; R. Mayer, 2002). Learners construct their own understanding based on what they already know, and their emotions, beliefs, and expectations all influence the process (Bransford et al., 2000; Bruning, Schraw, Norby, & Ronning, 2004; R. Mayer, 2002). (We examine the processes involved in constructing understanding in Chapter 8.)

5. *Preservice teachers who major in a content area, such as math, are much more successful than nonmajors in providing clear examples of the ideas they teach.*
   False: One of the most pervasive myths in teaching is that knowledge of subject matter is all that is necessary to teach effectively. In one study of teacher candidates, math majors were no more capable than nonmajors in effectively illustrating and representing math concepts in ways that learners could understand (National Center for Research on Teacher Learning, 1993). Knowledge of content is essential, but understanding how to make that content meaningful to students requires an additional kind of knowledge (Darling-Hammond & Baratz-Snowdon, 2005). (We discuss in detail ways of making knowledge accessible to learners in Chapters 2, 6–9, and 13.)

6. *To increase students' motivation to learn, teachers should praise as much as possible.*
   False: Although appropriate use of praise is important, overuse detracts from its credibility. This is particularly true for older students, who discount praise they perceive as unwarranted or invalid. Older students may also interpret praise given for easy tasks as indicating that the teacher thinks they have low ability (Emmer, 1988; Good, 1987a). Your study of motivation in Chapters 10 and 11 will help you understand this and other factors influencing students' desire to learn.

7. *Teachers who are the most successful at creating and maintaining orderly classrooms are those who can quickly stop disruptions when they occur.*
   False: Research indicates that classroom management, one of the greatest concerns of preservice and beginning teachers (Borko & Putnam, 1996), is most effective when teachers prevent management problems from occurring in the first place, instead of responding to problems when they occur (Emmer, Evertson, & Worsham, 2003; Evertson, Emmer, & Worsham, 2003; Kounin, 1970). (Classroom management is discussed in detail in Chapter 12.)

8. *Preservice teachers generally believe they will be more effective than teachers who are already in the field.*
   True: Preservice teachers (like yourself) are often optimistic and idealistic. They believe they'll be very effective with young people, and they generally believe they'll be better than teachers now in the field (Borko & Putnam, 1996). They are also sometimes "shocked" when they begin work and face the

challenge of teaching completely on their own for the first time (Borko & Putnam, 1996; S. Veenman, 1984). Keith's comments in the opening case study illustrate the experience of many beginning teachers: "I thought I was going to be so great when I got here. I have a really good math background, and I love math. I just knew the students would love it too. I'm not so sure anymore. . . . No one prepared me for this." The more knowledge you have about teaching, learning, and learners, the better prepared you'll be to cope with the realities of your first job. Keith's conversation with Jan helped him acquire some of that knowledge.

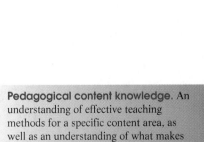

Pedagogical content knowledge allows teachers to represent difficult-to-teach concepts in meaningful ways.

9. *Teachers primarily learn by teaching; in general, experience is the primary factor involved in learning to teach.*
   False: Experience is essential in learning to teach, but it isn't sufficient by itself. In many cases, experience can result in repeating the same actions and procedures year after year, regardless of their effectiveness (Putnam, Heaton, Prawat, & Remillard, 1992). Knowledge of learners and learning, combined with experience, however, can lead to high levels of teaching expertise (Cochran & Jones, 1998).

10. *Testing detracts from learning, because students who are tested frequently develop negative attitudes and usually learn less than those who are tested less often.*
    False: In comprehensive reviews of the literature on assessment, experts concluded that frequent, thorough assessment is one of the most powerful and positive influences on learning (P. Black & William, 1998a; Bransford et al., 2000; Stiggens, 2005). (We discuss assessment and its role in learning in Chapters 15 and 16.)

The items you've just examined give a brief sampling of the different kinds of knowledge teachers need to help students learn. Let's examine those in more detail.

Research indicates that four different kinds of knowledge are essential for expert teaching:

- Knowledge of content
- Pedagogical content knowledge
- General pedagogical knowledge
- Knowledge of learners and learning (Darling-Hammond & Baratz-Snowdon, 2005; Shulman, 1987)

Knowledge of Content

We can't teach what we don't understand. This self-evident statement has been well documented by research examining the relationships between what teachers know and how they teach (Bransford, Darling-Hammond, & LePage, 2005; Darling-Hammond & Baratz-Snowdon, 2005; Shulman, 1986). To effectively teach about the American Revolutionary War, for example, a social studies teacher must know not only basic facts about the war but also how the war relates to other aspects of history, such as the French and Indian War, the colonies' relationship with England before the Revolution, and the characteristics of the colonies. The same is true for any topic in any content area.

Pedagogical Content Knowledge

Pedagogical content knowledge is an understanding of effective teaching methods for a specific content area, as well as an understanding of what makes specific topics easy or hard to learn (Shuell, 1996; Shulman, 1986). In addition, some authors suggest that understanding student motivation and emotions is also a part of pedagogical content knowledge (Brophy, 2004; McCaughtry, 2004).

Knowledge of content and pedagogical content knowledge are closely related. For example, content knowledge is an understanding of a particular topic (e.g., factors leading

Pedagogical content knowledge. An understanding of effective teaching methods for a specific content area, as well as an understanding of what makes specific topics easy or hard to learn

to the American Revolution); pedagogical content knowledge is the ability to effectively represent that topic. The two are inseparable for making the topic meaningful (Loughran, Mulhall, & Berry, 2004; Segall, 2004).

As an illustration, do the following activity. Fold a sheet of plain 8½ × 11 paper into thirds, and draw shading lines across the center one third of the paper, as shown:

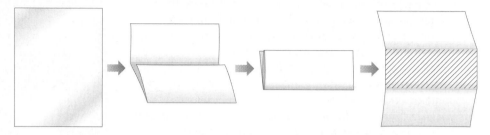

Refold your paper so that the shaded third is exposed:

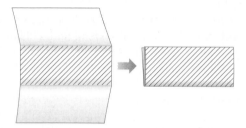

Now fold the paper in half, and in half again, so that one fourth of the shaded one third is visible. On that portion, draw lines across the original lines. Then unfold the paper, as shown:

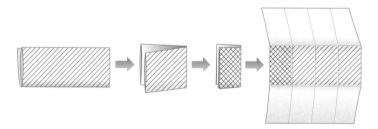

You've just prepared a concrete example demonstrating that ¼ × ⅓ = ¹⁄₁₂ (the cross-hatched portion of the paper). Intuitively, it doesn't make sense that multiplying two numbers results in a smaller number, so many students mechanically perform the operation with little understanding. The concrete example helps students understand the idea and also helps them apply their understanding in real-world settings (R. Mayer & Wittrock, 1996). This is why pedagogical content knowledge is so important. Without examples, students grasp what they can, memorize as much as possible, and little understanding develops (Bransford et al., 2000; Donovan & Bransford, 2005).

Greater pedagogical content knowledge would help Keith understand why his students are "okay when we stick to mechanics," but "they hate word problems." It is likely that he has relied primarily on verbal explanations ("I've tried explaining the stuff until I'm blue in the face") to help his students understand problems. Unfortunately, this isn't very effective (Bransford et al., 2000). In contrast, Jan used real-world examples—the containers of soft drinks—to illustrate her abstract topic, demonstrating her more advanced pedagogical content knowledge.

Representations of content exist in a variety of forms:

- *Examples.* A fifth-grade math teacher, DeVonne Lampkin, uses pieces of chocolate to illustrate equivalent fractions (opening case study, Chapter 15). An eighth-grade physical science teacher, Karen Johnson, compresses cotton in a drink cup to illustrate the concept *density* (opening case study, Chapter 2).
- *Demonstrations.* First-grade teacher Jenny Newhall uses water to demonstrate that air takes up space and exerts pressure (closing case study, Chapter 2). A

ninth-grade earth science teacher, David Shelton, demonstrates that planets revolve around the sun in the same direction and in the same plane by swinging socks tied to strings (opening case study, Chapter 7).

■ *Case studies.* Case studies are used throughout this text to illustrate the topics you're studying. Along with vignettes (short case studies), they are effective ways to illustrate complex and difficult-to-represent topics. For instance, an English teacher illustrated the concept *internal conflict* with this brief vignette: "Andrea didn't know what to do. She was looking forward to the class trip, but if she went, she wouldn't be able to take the scholarship-qualifying test." In addition, analysis of video cases, such as the ones that accompany this text, helps teachers think about connections between teaching and student learning (Siegel, 2002).

■ *Metaphors.* A world history teacher uses her students' loyalty to their school, their ways of talking, and their weekend activities as metaphors for the concept *nationalism.* Kathy Brewster, another history teacher, uses her class's "crusade" for extracurricular activities as a metaphor for the actual Crusades (opening case study, Chapter 10).

■ *Simulations.* An American government teacher creates a mock trial to simulate the workings of our country's judicial system, and a history teacher has students role-play delegates in a simulated Continental Congress to help his students understand forces that helped shape our emerging country.

■ *Models.* A science teacher uses a model of an atom to help students visualize the organization of the nucleus and electrons. The model in Figure 7.1 (on page 203) helps us think about the ways we process and store information in memory.

From the preceding list, we can see why item 5 on the Learning and Teaching Inventory is false. Majoring in math does not ensure that a teacher will be able to create examples like the one involving the multiplication of fractions, and majoring in history does not ensure that a social studies teacher will think of using the students' school activities as a metaphor for the Crusades. The ability to do so requires both a clear understanding of content and pedagogical content knowledge. If either is lacking, teachers commonly paraphrase information in learners' textbooks or provide abstract explanations that aren't meaningful to their students.

General Pedagogical Knowledge

Knowledge of content and pedagogical content knowledge are domain specific; that is, they are related to knowledge of a particular content area, such as multiplying fractions, the concept *density,* or the Crusades. In comparison, **general pedagogical knowledge** involves an understanding of essential principles of instruction and classroom management that transcends individual topics or subject matter areas (Borko & Putnam, 1996).

Instructional Strategies
Regardless of the content area or topic, teachers need to know how to use instructional strategies that involve students in learning activities, check their understanding, and keep lessons running smoothly. Jan applied an important strategy when she called on all her students as equally as possible (Good & Brophy, 2003; McDougall & Granby, 1996). She was teaching math, but the ability to involve students is important for teaching any topic. Similarly, teachers must communicate clearly, provide feedback, and perform a variety of other skills to maximize learning for all students. We examine these aspects of general pedagogical knowledge in detail in Chapter 13.

Classroom Management
Teachers must also know how to create classroom environments that are orderly and focused on learning (Emmer et al., 2003; Evertson et al., 2003). To succeed at keeping 30 or more students engaged and working together in learning activities, teachers must know how to plan, implement, and monitor rules and procedures; organize groups; and intervene when misbehavior occurs. The complexities of these processes help us see why item 7 in the Learning and Teaching Inventory is false. It is virtually impossible to maintain an orderly classroom if we wait for misbehavior to occur. Classroom environments must be designed to prevent, rather than stop, disruptions. Chapter 12 is devoted to a discussion of this topic.

General pedagogical knowledge. The type of professional knowledge that involves an understanding of general principles of instruction and classroom management that transcends individual topics or subject matter areas

Knowledge of Learners and Learning

Knowledge of learners and learning is essential, "arguably the most important knowledge a teacher can have" (Borko & Putnam, 1996, p. 675). Let's see how this knowledge can influence the way we teach.

Knowledge of Learners

Items 1, 2, and 6 in the Learning and Teaching Inventory all involve knowledge of learners, and each has important implications for the way we teach. For instance, we learned from item 1 that students need to have abstract ideas illustrated with concrete examples, and this is true for older as well as for younger students. Chapter 2, which focuses on cognitive development, describes how understanding learners increases our pedagogical content knowledge and helps us provide meaningful representations, such as in the example of multiplying fractions.

Item 2 suggests that learners often aren't good judges of either how much they know or the ways they learn. Chapter 7, which discusses the development of metacognition, helps us understand how to guide our students to become more knowledgeable about themselves and more strategic in their approaches to learning (Bruning et al., 2004).

Item 6 has implications for the ways we interact with our students. Intuitively, it seems that providing as much praise as possible is not only desirable, but effective. However, both research and theories of motivation, which we examine in Chapters 10 and 11, help us understand why this isn't always the case.

Knowledge of Learning

As we better understand the ways people learn, we can understand why item 4 on the Learning and Teaching Inventory is false. For example, evidence overwhelmingly indicates that people don't behave like tape recorders; they don't simply record in memory what they hear or read. Rather, they interpret information personally and idiosyncratically in an effort to make sense of it (Bransford et al., 2000; R. Mayer, 2002). In the process, meaning can be distorted, sometimes profoundly. For instance, look at the following statements, actually made by students:

> "The phases of the moon are caused by clouds blocking out the unseen parts."
> "Coats keep us warm by generating heat, like a stove or radiator."
> "A triangle which has an angle of 135 degrees is called an obscene triangle."

Obviously, students didn't acquire these ideas from teachers' explanations. Rather, students interpreted what they heard, experienced, or read, related it to what they already knew, and attempted to make sense of both.

These examples help us see why "wisdom can't be told" (Bransford, 1993, p. 6) and why "explaining the stuff until I'm blue in the face" usually isn't enough. Effective teaching is much more complex than simply explaining, and expert teachers have a thorough understanding of the way learning occurs and what they can do to promote it. (We examine learning in detail in Chapters 6 to 9.)

We now can also understand why item 9 is false. Experience is essential in learning to teach, and no one suggests that it isn't necessary. However, we can already see that teachers won't acquire all the knowledge needed to be effective from experience alone. Acquiring this knowledge is one reason you're studying educational psychology.

Analyzing Classrooms Video
To examine teachers' knowledge in classroom settings, go to Episode 1, "Demonstrating Knowledge in Classrooms," on DVD 1, accompanying this text.

The INTASC Standards: States Respond to the Need for Professional Knowledge

In response to a growing recognition of the importance of professional knowledge in teaching, a number of states collaborated to create the Interstate New Teacher Assessment and Support Consortium (INTASC), an organization whose goal is to increase the professionalism of beginning teachers. INTASC has set rigorous standards in each of the areas of teacher knowledge discussed in the previous sections. The standards describe what teachers should know and be able to do and are organized around the 10 principles outlined in Table 1.1. The portfolio activities at the end of each chapter in this text are aligned with the standards from INTASC.

Table 1.1 The INTASC principles

Principle	Description
1. Knowledge of subject	The teacher understands the central concepts, tools of inquiry, and structures of the discipline(s) he or she teaches and can create learning experiences that make these aspects of subject matter meaningful for students.
2. Learning and human development	The teacher understands how children learn and develop, and can provide learning opportunities that support their intellectual, social, and personal development.
3. Adapting instruction	The teacher understands how students differ in their approaches to learning and creates instructional opportunities that are adapted to diverse learners.
4. Strategies	The teacher understands and uses a variety of instructional strategies to encourage students' development of critical thinking, problem solving, and performance skills.
5. Motivation and management	The teacher uses an understanding of individual and group motivation and behavior to create a learning environment that encourages positive social interaction, active engagement in learning, and self-motivation.
6. Communication skills	The teacher uses knowledge of effective verbal, nonverbal, and media communication techniques to foster active inquiry, collaboration, and supportive interaction in the classroom.
7. Planning	The teacher plans instruction based upon knowledge of subject matter, students, the community, and curriculum goals.
8. Assessment	The teacher understands and uses formal and informal assessment strategies to evaluate and ensure the continuous intellectual, social, and physical development of the learner.
9. Commitment	The teacher is a reflective practitioner who continually evaluates the effects of his/her choices and actions on others (students, parents, and other professionals in the learning community) and who actively seeks out opportunities to grow professionally.
10. Partnership	The teacher fosters relationships with school colleagues, parents, and agencies in the larger community to support students' learning and well-being.

Source: Principles from Model Standards for Beginning Teacher Licensing and Development: A Resource for State Dialogues, by Interstate New Teacher Assessment and Support Consortium, 1993, Washington, DC: Council of Chief State School Officers. Reprinted with permission.

Exploring Further:

To see more information about INTASC and the INTASC standards, go to "INTASC" in the *Exploring Further* module of Chapter 1 at *www.prenhall.com/eggen*.

Changes in Education: Reform and Accountability

The focus on knowledge and professionalism is part of a broader emphasis on **reforms,** suggested changes in teaching and teacher preparation intended to increase the amount students learn. We see this emphasis in federal legislation, such as the well-known and somewhat controversial No Child Left Behind Act passed in 2001, a major provision of which is a call for improved teacher quality. According to the act, by 2005–2006, all teachers were to be fully qualified (Hardy, 2002). This provision is a direct result of research indicating that teachers have a powerful effect on student achievement and that poor, minority, and urban students are often taught by underqualified teachers (Darling-Hammond & Baratz-Snowdon, 2005).

Reforms. Suggested changes in teaching and teacher preparation intended to increase the amount students learn

An important aspect of the reform movement is increased emphasis on **accountability,** the process of requiring learners to demonstrate that they possess specified knowledge and skills as demonstrated by standardized measures and making teachers responsible for student performance. Widespread in the P–12 sector of education, accountability is becoming more prominent in teacher preparation as well. For example, a report prepared by a panel of educational leaders and sponsored by the National Academy of Education called for a national teacher test with results incorporated into state licensing requirements (Bransford et al., 2005). Many states already require teachers to pass tests before they're licensed.

The Praxis™ Exam

The most widely used teacher test is the Praxis Series™ published by the Educational Testing Service (*Praxis* means putting theory into practice). Forty-three states plus the District of Columbia, Guam, and the U.S. Virgin Islands use this series (Educational Testing Service, 2005).

An important part of the Praxis Series is the Principles of Learning and Teaching (PLT) tests, four tests specifically designed for teachers seeking licensure in early childhood, or grades K–6, 5–9, and 7–12. The PLT tests are closely aligned with the INTASC standards we discussed in the previous section, and this book addresses most topics covered on the tests. A discussion of the Praxis exam and a correlation matrix linking test and text topics appear in Appendix A.

Exploring Further:

To see information about each of the PLT tests, go to "The Praxis™ Exam" in the *Exploring Further* module of Chapter 1 at *www.prenhall.com/eggen.*

Each of the grade-level–specific PLT tests has two parts (Educational Testing Service, 2005). The first consists of multiple-choice questions similar to those in the test bank that accompanies this text. The second part presents case histories that you will be asked to analyze. The PLT case histories are similar to the case studies you will find at the beginning and end of each chapter of this text. You will then be asked to respond to short-answer questions related to the case histories (Educational Testing Service, 2005). We have designed this text to help you succeed on the Praxis PLT test by designing multiple-choice questions that require you to apply your understanding to real-world learning and teaching events and by giving you practice with short-answer questions that parallel the short-answer questions on the Praxis PLT tests. The case studies and short-answer questions are found at the end of each chapter in the section entitled "Developing as a Professional: Praxis Practice."

The significance of the reform movement lies in its focus on professional knowledge. At no point in the history of education has the role of knowledge been more strongly emphasized. Helping you acquire this knowledge is the goal of this text.

Learning Contexts: Teaching and Learning in Urban Environments

For a number of years, researchers have expressed a great deal of concern about the education of students in urban environments. Consider the following statistics (L. Hoffman, 2003; B. Young, 2002):

- The 100 largest school districts in the nation represent less than 1 percent of all districts, but they are responsible for the education of 23 percent of all students. These districts are overwhelmingly urban, and the New York City Public Schools and the Los Angeles Unified School District, the two largest in the nation, each have enrollments greater than the total enrollments of 27 states.
- The 100 largest districts employ 22 percent of the nation's teachers.
- Sixty-nine percent of urban students are minorities, and some urban schools have enrollments that are more than 95 percent minority.
- More than half of all urban students are eligible for free or reduced-price school lunch.

In addition, research indicates that in urban schools,

Children are often taught by teachers who are the least prepared; children are less likely to be enrolled in academically challenging courses; they are too often treated differently in what they are expected to do and the kinds of assignments they are given and teachers often lack the resources need to teach well. (Armour-Thomas, 2004, p. 113)

Accountability. The process of requiring learners to demonstrate that they possess specified knowledge and skills as demonstrated by standardized measures and making teachers responsible for student performance

Unquestionably, teaching in urban schools differs from teaching in other settings. Urban schools are large, they have great numbers of students from diverse backgrounds, and they present challenges to both teaching and learning (Armour-Thomas, 2004; R. A. Goldstein, 2004, Rubinson, 2004).

In addition, many negative stereotypes about urban students exist, ranging from "All urban kids are in gangs" to "Urban children are mostly from poor, dysfunctional homes, homeless shelters, or foster homes and come to school 'just to grow up' and then drop out" (R. A. Goldstein, 2004, pp. 43–44). These stereotypes are then exacerbated by events such as the school riots that occurred in the urban schools in Los Angeles in June of 2005.

These stereotypes and events tend to create fear in people not familiar with the situation. This fear can then lead to actions that are damaging to everyone.

Urban environments present both challenges and opportunities for teachers who understand these instructional contexts.

> When I was in high school, we had the chance to host a group of students from the suburbs. . . . So, this girl comes with her friends, and they pair us up. Later on I find that they [the students from the suburbs] were told not to wear any jewelry or nice clothes or bring any money with them so they wouldn't get robbed. . . . All they saw when they visited us were people who might rob them. (R. A. Goldstein, 2004, p. 47)

Being a successful teacher in an urban environment isn't as simple as ignoring stereotypes or caring about and being committed to kids (Kincheloe, 2004). It takes specific knowledge that directly addresses essential aspects of teaching and learning, such as the influence of the social environment on learning and development, ways of organizing urban classrooms to promote learning, and teaching strategies that promote learning and motivation in urban students. We address these issues in special sections of Chapters 3, 4, 8, 11–13, and 15.

Checking Your Understanding

2.1 Describe and give an example of each of the different kinds of knowledge that professional teachers possess.

2.2 Identify the statement Keith made in the opening case study that best indicates his lack of pedagogical content knowledge in trying to teach problem solving to his students. Explain why the statement shows that he lacks this knowledge.

2.3 A life science teacher holds up a sheet of bubble wrap and then places a second sheet of bubble wrap on top of the first to help her students visualize the way that cells are organized into tissue. What kind of knowledge does the teacher's demonstration best indicate? Explain.

To receive feedback for these questions, go to Appendix B.

Knowledge Extensions

To deepen and integrate your understanding of the topics in this section, go to the *Knowledge Extensions* module for Chapter 1 at *www.prenhall.com/eggen*. Respond to questions 1 and 2.

THE ROLE OF RESEARCH IN ACQUIRING KNOWLEDGE

In the previous sections, we considered the different kinds of knowledge teachers need to help their students learn. Where did this knowledge originate, how does it accumulate, and how can we acquire it?

One answer is experience, sometimes called "the wisdom of practice" (Berliner, 1994, 2000; Munby, Russel, & Martin, 2001; Richardson & Placier, 2001). Effective teacher

Research provides valuable information that teachers can use in their instructional decision making.

education programs help people like you acquire the beginnings of "the wisdom of practice" by integrating clinical experiences in schools with the topics you study in your classes.

A second source of teacher knowledge is **research,** the process of systematically gathering information in an attempt to answer questions. It is the process all professions use to develop a body of knowledge (Gall, Gall, & Borg, 2003). For example, in an effort to answer the question "How does teacher questioning influence student learning?" researchers have conducted a great many studies examining the numbers of questions, the patterns in their questioning, and the types of questions teachers ask (Good & Brophy, 2003). The influence of teacher questioning on student learning is part of the body of knowledge of educational psychology. Jan drew from it when she made her comment about the changes she's made in her classroom based on "research studies indicating how important it is to call on all the kids." Jan is a veteran teacher, but she continues to grow professionally by staying up-to-date on current research.

Research exists in many forms. In this chapter, we consider four of the most common:

- Descriptive research
- Correlational research
- Experimental research
- Action research

Descriptive Research

Descriptive research, as the term implies, uses interviews, observations, and surveys to describe opinions, attitudes, or events. In one study, for example, researchers interviewed urban students in an attempt to understand their perceptions of good teachers. Here are two of their comments:

> "A good teacher takes time out to see if all the kids have what they're talking about and cares about how they're doing and will see if they need help."
> "The teachers are real at ease. They take the time, you know, go step-by-step. We learn it more. It seems like they got the time to explain it all. We don't have to leave anyone behind." (Corbett & Wilson, 2002, p. 20)

Interviews can provide valuable insights into both students' and teachers' thoughts.

Observations have also been used in descriptive research. Perhaps most significant is the work done by Jean Piaget (1952, 1959), a pioneer in the study of cognitive development, one of the cornerstones of educational psychology. Piaget studied the way learners' thinking develops by making detailed observations of his own children. Because of his observations, and a great deal of research conducted by others, we realize, for example, that 10-year-olds don't simply know more than 5-year-olds; they think differently. We understand these differences in children's thinking because of Piaget's and other researchers' systematic descriptive research. (We examine Piaget's work in detail in Chapter 2.)

Surveys are a third important source of descriptive information. For instance, when asked to name schools' biggest problems, teachers cite classroom management as one of their most challenging problems (L. C. Rose & Gallup, 2004). In another descriptive study, researchers administered the popular Myers-Briggs personality test to 4,483 university students who were considering majoring in education. They later checked the students' records to see who graduated and their majors (Sears, Kennedy, & Kaye, 1997). The researchers found that elementary education majors tended to fit a profile described as "warm, sociable, responsible, and caring about people" (p. 201), whereas secondary majors tended to be "oriented to the theoretical, disposed to investigate possibilities and relationships, and drawn to complexity, innovation, and change" (p. 201). The knowledge generated by this research may have implications for both teacher educators and people considering teaching as a career.

Research. The process of systematically gathering information in an attempt to answer questions

Descriptive research. Research that uses interviews, observations, and surveys to describe opinions, attitudes, and events

Evaluating Descriptive Studies

A great deal of research exists, and teachers need to become proficient at evaluating different studies, not only for their validity but also for their applicability to specific teaching situations. In the case study at the beginning of the chapter, Jan noted to Keith that a university instructor referred to "a number of research studies." This information is significant: Several studies reporting similar results provide information that is more likely to be valid than a single, or even a few, studies.

For descriptive studies, two additional aspects are important. First, the subjects and instruments used should be well described (McMillan, 2004). For instance, the previously mentioned study conducted by Sears et al. (1997) identified the number and characteristics of the population studied (4,483 undergraduate university students considering an education major) as well as the instrument used (the Myers-Briggs personality test). This information allows the reader to judge how applicable the findings are to other similar (and dissimilar) populations.

Second, readers must be careful not to predict future behavior based on descriptive studies (McMillan, 2004). For example, predicting that secondary teachers would respond more positively to innovation and change than would elementary teachers, based on the Sears et al. (1997) study, would not be valid. Nor would it be valid to predict, from the study reported by Corbett and Wilson (2002), that students taught by teachers that fit the students' descriptions would be more motivated or would achieve higher than students taught by teachers with different attributes. Additional research is needed to make such predictions.

Finding relationships between variables leads us to correlational research.

Correlational Research

Consider the following questions:

Does a relationship exist between

- Students' grade point averages and their scores on the Scholastic Aptitude Test (SAT)?
- Students' absences and their grades in school?
- Students' heights and high school grade point averages?

A **correlation** is a relationship, either positive or negative, between two or more variables. In our examples, the variables are *grade point averages and SAT scores, absences and grades, height,* and *high school grade point averages.* In the first case, the variables are positively correlated: In general, the higher students' grade point averages, the higher their SAT scores. In the second case, the variables are negatively correlated: The more school students miss, the lower their grades will be. No correlation exists in the third: Height and high school grade point averages are not related.

Much of what we know about learning and teaching is based on **correlational research,** the process of looking for relationships between two or more variables that enables researchers to predict changes in one variable on the basis of changes in another variable without implying a cause–effect relationship between the variables. A great deal of this research attempts to find relationships between teachers' actions and student achievement. For example, researchers have found positive correlations between the number of questions teachers ask and their students' achievement (Shuell, 1996). They have also found negative correlations between achievement and the time teachers spend in noninstructional activities, such as taking roll, passing out papers, and explaining procedures (Brophy & Good, 1986). These relationships are diagrammed in Figure 1.2.

Correlations are represented quantitatively and can range from a perfect positive correlation of 1 to a perfect negative correlation of -1. As a simple example, speed and distance have a correlation of 1. For each mile per hour faster we travel, there is a corresponding increase in the distance we cover in the same amount of time. Most correlations are less than a perfect 1 or -1. For instance, the correlation between the number of questions teachers ask and student achievement is about .5, and the correlation between time spent in noninstructional activities and achievement is about $-.4$ (Good & Brophy, 1986; Shuell, 1996).

Correlational research is valuable because it allows us to make predictions about one variable if we have information about the other (B. Johnson & Christensen, 2004;

Correlation. A relationship, either positive or negative, between two or more variables

Correlational research. The process of looking for relationships between two or more variables that enables researchers to predict changes in one variable on the basis of changes in another variable without implying a cause–effect relationship between the variables

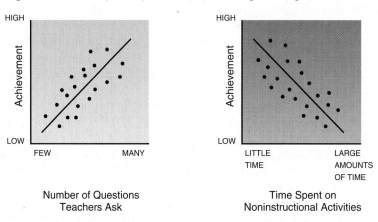

Figure 1.2   Examples of positive (left) and negative (right) corrections

McMillan, 2004). For instance, because a positive correlation exists between teacher questioning and student achievement, we can predict that students will learn more in classrooms where teachers ask many questions than those where teachers primarily lecture.

Evaluating Correlational Research

As with descriptive research, correlational studies have limitations. Most important, correlational studies describe relationships between variables, but they do not suggest that one variable *causes* the other (Gall et al., 2003; McMillan, 2004). Consider the relationship between grade point average and SAT scores. Obviously, a high grade point average doesn't cause a high SAT score. Other factors, such as time spent studying, effective study strategies, and general intelligence are likely to be causes of both. The same kind of reasoning applies to our negative correlation example. Being absent, per se, doesn't cause low grades. Instead, missing opportunities to learn topics, not completing homework assignments, and losing chances to interact with peers are some likely causes.

Experimental Research

Whereas correlational research looks for relationships in existing situations (e.g., the existing relationship between grade point averages and SAT scores), **experimental research** systematically manipulates variables in attempts to determine cause and effect. Experimental studies commonly build on correlational research. For example, let's look again at the relationship between teachers' questioning and student achievement.

In an extension of earlier correlational studies, researchers randomly assigned teachers to a treatment and a control group. **Random assignment** means that an individual has an equal likelihood of being assigned to either group, and it ensures that the two groups are comparable. The researchers trained teachers in the treatment group to provide prompts and cues when students initially failed to answer a question; the researchers attempted to consciously manipulate the variable *frequency of teachers' prompts* through training. Teachers in the control group received no training; they taught as they normally did. Researchers compared the reading scores of the students in both groups at the end of the year. Students taught by teachers in the treatment group scored significantly higher on an achievement test than did students taught by teachers in the control group (L. Anderson, Evertson, & Brophy, 1979). In this case, researchers concluded that the ability to provide prompting questions and cues causes increases in achievement.

Evaluating Experimental Research

As with both descriptive and correlational studies, teachers should read experimental studies with a critical eye. Factors to consider include

- Comparability of experimental and control groups
- Maximum control of extraneous variables
- Sample size
- Clearly described manipulation of the independent variable

Experimental research. Research that systematically manipulates variables in attempts to determine cause and effect

Random assignment. A process used to ensure that an individual has an equal likelihood of being assigned to any group within a study

For instance, let's consider the L. Anderson et al. (1979) study again. It would be possible to conclude that prompting caused higher reading achievement only if the treatment and the control groups were similar. If, for example, the students who received prompts had higher initial ability than students in the control group, conclusions about the effectiveness of the prompts would be invalid. Similarly, if the teachers who were trained to provide prompts had higher initial levels of expertise than teachers in the control group, conclusions about prompting would also be invalid.

Using random assignment and an adequate sample size also help ensure that experimental and control groups are comparable. For instance, if 20 teachers each have been randomly assigned to experimental and control groups, concluding that teacher expertise has been controlled is more valid than it would be if only 5 teachers existed in each group.

Finally, experimental research must clearly describe the treatment of the experimental group. The questioning study gave explicit details about how researchers trained the teachers in the experimental group to provide cues and prompts. This clear description not only allows the reader to evaluate the research but also allows other researchers to replicate it, which is another way to increase validity.

Action Research

Earlier in the chapter, we saw that teachers' being knowledgeable is an essential element of professionalism. Understanding and critically examining others' research is one way to increase teacher knowledge. Another is for teachers to conduct research in their own classrooms. **Action research** is a form of applied research designed to answer a specific school- or classroom-related question (Gall et al., 2003; A. P. Johnson, 2005). It can be conducted by teachers, school administrators, or other education professionals and can include descriptive, correlational, or experimental methods. When they conduct action research projects (and share the results with others), teachers learn about research and begin to understand how self-assessment and reflection can link theory and practice (Sagor, 2000). The primary intent in action research is to improve practice within a specific classroom or school (McMillan, 2004). It also increases the professionalism of teachers by recognizing their ability to contribute to the growing body of knowledge about learning and teaching (Bransford et al., 2000).

Online Case Book

To analyze professional knowledge and research in a classroom case study, go to the *Online Case Book* for Chapter 1 at *www.prenhall.com/eggen*.

Instructional ⊞ Principles   **Conducting Research in Classrooms:
Instructional Principles**

If you decide to conduct action research in your classroom, the following principles can be a guide in planning and conducting your studies (A. P. Johnson, 2005):

1. Identify and diagnose a problem that is important to you.
2. Systematically plan and conduct a research study.
3. Implement the findings to solve or improve a local problem.
4. Use the results of the study to generate additional research.

Let's see how Tyra Forcine, an eighth-grade English teacher, attempts to implement these principles in her classroom.

> Tyra is sitting in the teachers' lounge after school with a group of colleagues who are discussing problems they're having with homework. "My kids won't do it," Kim Brown laments. "A third of them blow it off on some days."
>
> "I solved that problem. . . . I simply don't assign homework," Bill McClendon responds. "I give them a seat-work assignment, we do it after the lesson, and that's it. . . . I'm tired of fighting the homework battle."
>
> "I've heard teachers say that homework doesn't help that much in terms of learning, anyway," Selena Cross adds.
>
> "That doesn't make sense to me," Tyra counters. "It has to help. The more kids work on something, the better they have to get at it."
>
> "Well, I'm not sure," Selena shrugs.
>
> The conversation bothers Tyra. She consistently gives her students homework and checks to see that it's done, but because of the conversation, she decides to take a more

Action research. A form of applied research designed to answer a specific school- or classroom-related question

Action research allows teachers to investigate connections between their instruction and student learning and share their findings with other teachers.

systematic look at its effects. She starts digging around but is surprised that she can't find a clear answer, so she decides to do her own research.

She begins her study a week later, which is the start of the third grading period. She collects homework every day and gives the students 2 points for having done it fully, 1 for partial completion, and 0 for minimal effort or not turning it in. As part of her daily routine, she discusses the most frequently missed items on each assignment. On Fridays she quizzes the students on the content discussed Monday through Thursday, and she also gives a midterm test and final exam. She then tries to see if a relationship exists between students' homework averages and their performance on the quizzes and tests.

At the end of the grading period, Tyra summarizes the results. Each student has a homework score, a quiz average, and an average on the two tests.

She calls the district office to ask for help in summarizing the information, and together they find a correlation of .55 between homework scores and quiz averages, and a correlation of .44 between homework and test averages.

"I don't get that," Tyra says to Kim and Bill in another conversation. "I can see why the correlation between the homework and tests might be lower than the one between homework and quizzes, but why aren't both higher?"

"Well," Kim responds. "You're only giving the kids a 2, 1, or 0 on the homework, you're not actually grading it. So I suspect that some of the kids are simply doing it to finish it, and they aren't really thinking carefully about the work."

"On the other hand," Bill acknowledges, "homework and quizzes and tests are positively correlated, so maybe I'd better rethink my stand on no homework. . . . Maybe I'll change what I do next grading period."

"Well, I'm going to keep on giving homework," Tyra nods, "but I think I need to change what I'm doing too. . . . It's going to be a ton of work, but I'm going to repeat my study next grading period to see if I get similar results, and then, starting in the fall, I'm going to redesign my homework so it's easier to grade. I'll grade every assignment, and we'll see if the correlations go up."

"Good idea," Kim nods." If the kids see that it's important for learning, maybe they'll take it more seriously, and some of the not-doing-it problem will also get better. . . . I'm going to look at that in the fall."

Now let's look at Tyra's efforts to apply the principles suggested for conducting action research projects. She applied the first when she identified a problem that was important to her—the problem with homework. Addressing problems that are personally meaningful makes action research motivating for teachers (Mills, 2002; Quiocho & Ulanoff, 2002).

She applied the second principle by systematically designing and conducting her study, and its efficiency was an important feature. Unfortunately, school systems rarely provide extra time and resources for action research, so conducting projects that don't take inordinate amounts of teacher time is important (Bransford et al., 2000).

Tyra and her colleagues implemented the results of her project immediately, which is the third principle. Bill, for example, planned to give homework during the next grading period. Tyra applied the fourth when her project prompted further studies. Tyra planned another study to see if scoring the homework more carefully would increase the correlations between homework and quizzes and tests, and Kim planned to investigate whether more careful scoring would lead to students' more conscientiously doing their homework. (We discuss existing research examining the effectiveness of homework in Chapter 13.)

Perhaps Tyra and her colleagues will reap an additional benefit. As mentioned earlier, engaging in research increases teachers' feelings of professionalism; contributing to a body of knowledge that guides practice helps teachers grow professionally. And the results of well-designed studies can often be presented at professional conferences and published in professional journals. This allows the knowledge gained to be made public and integrated with other research, two important characteristics in the development of a professional body of knowledge (J. Hiebert, Gallimore, & Stigler, 2002).

Research and the Development of Theory

As research accumulates, results are summarized and patterns emerge. After a great many observations, for instance, researchers have concluded that the thinking of young children tends to be dominated by their perceptions (Piaget, 1970, 1977; Wadsworth, 2004). For example, when first graders see an inverted cup of water with a card beneath it, as we see in the accompanying picture, they commonly explain that the card doesn't fall because the water somehow holds it against the cup. They focus on the most perceptually obvious aspect of the object—the water—and ignore atmospheric pressure, the actual reason the card stays on the cup.

The statement "The thinking of young children tends to be dominated by perception" is considered a principle because it summarizes results consistently supported by large numbers of research studies. Some additional examples of research-based principles include

- Behaviors rewarded some of the time, but not all of the time, persist longer than behaviors rewarded every time they occur.
- People tend to imitate behaviors they observe in others.
- People strive for a state of order, balance, and predictability in the world.

As additional research is conducted, related principles are formed, which in turn generate further studies. As knowledge accumulates, theories are gradually constructed. A **theory** is a set of related principles derived from observations that are used to explain additional observations and make predictions. In the everyday world, the term is used more loosely. For instance, one person will make a point in a conversation, and a second will respond, "I have a theory on that." In this case, the person is merely offering an explanation for the point. In science, theory has a more precise definition.

Theories help organize research findings and can provide valuable guidance for teachers (Gall et al., 2003). Let's look at a brief example. One research-based principle is that reinforced behaviors increase in frequency, and as mentioned earlier, a related principle indicates that intermittently reinforced behaviors persist longer than those that are continuously reinforced (Baldwin & Baldwin, 2001; Skinner, 1957). Further, too much reinforcement can actually decrease its effectiveness. A classroom application of these principles occurs in learning activities. If students are praised for their attempts to answer questions (reinforced), they are likely to increase their efforts, but they will persist longer if they are praised for some, but not all, of their attempts (intermittently reinforced). If they are praised excessively, they may actually reduce their efforts (Ryan and Deci, 1996).

FAMILY CIRCUS

"How do they fit so much water in that little spigot?"

These related principles are part of the theory of behaviorism, which studies the effects of experiences on behavior. Our illustration, of course, is only a tiny portion of the complete theory. (We examine behaviorism in depth in Chapter 6.) The key feature of any theory is that a comprehensive body of information integrates a number of research-based principles.

Theories are useful in at least two ways. First, they allow us to *explain* behaviors and events. For instance, look at the accompanying cartoon. Piaget's theory of cognitive development (1970, 1977), which includes the principle mentioned earlier ("The thinking of young children tends to be dominated by perception"), helps us explain why the child in the cartoon thinks the way he does. Using Piaget's theory, we can explain this behavior by saying that the child can see only the water and the faucet, and because his thinking is dominated by his perception—what he can see—he concludes that all the water is in the faucet. Similarly, using the theory of behaviorism, we can explain why casino patrons persist in playing slot machines, though coins seldom fall into the trays, by saying that they are being intermittently reinforced.

Theories' second value is that they allow us to *predict* behavior and events. For instance, attribution theory, a theory of motivation, allows us to predict that students who believe they control their own grades try harder than those who believe their grades are due primarily to luck or the whim of the teacher (Brophy, 2004; Pintrich & Schunk, 2002).

Theory. A set of related principles derived from observations that are used to explain additional observations and make predictions

In all three instances, theories—cognitive development theory, behaviorism, and attribution theory—help us understand learning and teaching by allowing us to explain and predict people's actions.

Knowledge Extensions

To deepen your understanding of the topics in this section of the chapter and integrate them with topics you've already studied, go to the *Knowledge Extensions* module for Chapter 1 at *www.prenhall.com/eggen*. Respond to questions 3–5.

Checking Your Understanding

3.1 Describe and explain the different types of research.

3.2 Teachers who are high in personal teaching efficacy—the belief that they have an important positive effect on students—have higher achieving students than teachers who are low in personal teaching efficacy (Bruning et al., 2004). Is this finding based on descriptive, correlational, or experimental research? Explain.

3.3 Suppose that Tyra and her colleagues concluded that doing homework caused an increase in student achievement. Would this be a valid conclusion? Explain why or why not.

To receive feedback for these questions, go to Appendix B.

THE USE OF CASE STUDIES IN EDUCATIONAL PSYCHOLOGY

The different kinds of knowledge that teachers need in order to become experts have important implications both for you, who are learning to teach, and for us, who write textbooks designed to help you in this process. Our knowledge of learners and learning reminds us that students of all ages need concrete and real-world representations of the topics they study if those topics are to be meaningful.

The use of case studies, such as the one at the beginning of this chapter, is one of the most effective ways to provide concrete illustrations of learning and teaching in the real world of classrooms—classrooms such as those in which you will work when you finish your teacher preparation program (Putnam & Borko, 2000). Long popular in other professional fields, such as law and medicine, cases are now being increasingly used in education (Sudzina, 1999).

Because of the value of case studies in illustrating the complex processes involved in teaching and learning, we introduce and end each chapter in this book with a case study. The introductory case and the chapter closing case serve two different purposes. The beginning case provides a real-world introduction to the content and illustrates the topics presented in the chapter. As topics are discussed, we frequently refer back to the case, in some instances taking dialogue directly from it, to make concepts more meaningful. We also present short vignettes throughout each chapter to further link content to real-world examples.

The closing cases, found in the "Developing as a Professional" feature, have an additional purpose. To encourage critical thinking, decision making, and reflection, we ask you to analyze each case and assess the extent to which the teacher effectively applied the chapter content in his or her classroom. In some cases, the teacher's work was quite effective; in others it may not have been. The cases present the richness and complexity of actual classroom problems and provide opportunities to apply chapter content using multiple perspectives (Siegel, 2002). The cases and the format for your responses parallel the Praxis PLT tests, which we briefly described in our discussion of reform and accountability earlier in the chapter.

The case studies that introduce Chapters 8, 9, 11, 13, and 15 are also on the DVDs accompanying this book. This allows you to see teaching and learning in unrehearsed, real-world settings. A number of teaching-learning segments exist on the DVDs, and references to those segments appear in the margins of the chapters, as you saw on page 12. Each is designed to enrich your study of educational psychology by illustrating and asking you to analyze real-world events that you are likely to encounter in your own teaching.

We hope this introduction has provided a framework for the rest of your study of this book. Its organization and goals are outlined in Table 1.2.

Checking Your Understanding

4.1 Explain how using case studies to place educational psychology in real-world contexts makes it more meaningful than it would be without the use of these case studies.

4.2 Identify the advantages that case studies on videotape or DVD have over those in written form.

To receive feedback for these questions, go to Appendix B.

Table 1.2 Organization of this book

Part and Chapter		Goal
Chapter 1:	Educational Psychology: Developing a Professional Knowledge Base	To understand the role of knowledge in developing professionalism
Part I:	The Learner	
Chapter 2:	The Development of Cognition and Language	To understand how learners' intellectual capacities and language abilities develop over time
Chapter 3:	Personal, Social, and Emotional Development	To understand how learners' personal characteristics, moral reasoning, and socialization develop over time
Chapter 4:	Group and Individual	To understand how intelligence, culture, socioeconomic status, and gender affect learning
Chapter 5:	Learners With Exceptionalities	To understand how learner exceptionalities affect learning
Part II:	Learning	
Chapter 6:	Behaviorism and Social Cognitive Theory	To understand learning from behaviorist and social cognitive perspectives
Chapter 7:	Cognitive Views of Learning	To understand learning from cognitive perspectives
Chapter 8:	Constructing Knowledge	To understand the processes involved in constructing understanding
Chapter 9:	Complex Cognitive Processes	To understand concept learning, problem solving, and the development of strategic learners
Part III:	Classroom Processes	
Chapter 10:	Theories of Motivation	To understand motivation from behaviorist, humanistic, and cognitive perspectives
Chapter 11:	Motivation in the Classroom	To understand how theories of motivation can be used in classrooms
Chapter 12:	Creating Productive Learning Environments: Classroom Management	To understand how to create orderly classrooms focused on learning
Chapter 13:	Creating Productive Learning Environments: Principles and Models of Instruction	To understand how to plan, implement, and assess learning activities
Chapter 14:	Learning and Instruction and Technology	To understand how technology can influence learning
Chapter 15:	Assessing Classroom Learning	To understand how standardized tests can be used to increase student learning
Chapter 16:	Assessment Through Standardized Testing	To understand processes for accessing student learning

Meeting Your Learning Objectives

1. **Describe the characteristics of professionalism, and identify examples of the characteristics in the teachers' actions.**

   - Professionals are committed to the people they serve, and their actions are guided by a professional code of ethics.
   - Professionals rely on a thorough understanding of their professional knowledge as a basis for their decision making.
   - Professionals reflect on their practice and are able to make decisions in complex and ill-defined contexts.

2. **Describe the different kinds of knowledge professional teachers possess, and identify examples of professional knowledge in teachers' actions.**

   - Professionals thoroughly understand the topics they teach and are able to illustrate those topics in ways that make sense to learners.
   - Professionals are able to organize learning environments and use basic instructional skills in ways that promote as much learning as possible for their students.
   - Professionals understand the ways people learn, the factors that influence learning, and ways to capitalize on that understanding to maximize learning for their students.

3. **Describe different types of research, and analyze applications of these types.**

   - Research is the mechanism professionals use to expand their body of knowledge.
   - Descriptive research uses interviews, observations, and surveys to describe events; correlational research looks for relationships between two variables; and experimental research manipulates variables in attempts to determine cause and effect.
   - Teachers and other school personnel sometimes conduct action research designed to answer school- or classroom-related questions.

4. **Explain how using case studies to place educational psychology in real-world contexts makes it more meaningful.**

   - Research indicates that topics embedded in authentic contexts is more meaningful than the same topics presented in the abstract.
   - Written and video case studies provide authentic contexts for representing the content of educational psychology.

Developing as a Professional

Developing as a Professional: Praxis™ Practice

To begin learning how to prepare short-answer responses similar to those you will encounter on the Praxis Principles of Learning and Teaching exam, read the case studies and answer the questions that follow.

The following episodes illustrate four teachers at different classroom levels working with their students. In the first, Rebecca Atkins, a kindergarten teacher, talks with her children about planting a garden. Richard Nelms, a middle school teacher,

illustrates the concept of *symmetry* for his seventh-grade life science students in the second episode. In the third, Didi Johnson, a chemistry teacher, presents Charles's law to her 10th graders. Finally, in the fourth episode, Bob Duchaine, an American history teacher, is discussing the Vietnam War with his 11th graders.

As you read the episodes, think about the different types of professional knowledge that each teacher demonstrates and the kinds of decisions that each make.

Rebecca has the children seated on the floor in a semicircle in front of her. She sits on a small chair in front of them and begins, "We had a story on gardening, remember? Who remembers the name of the story? . . . Shereta?"

"'Together'," Shereta softly responds.

"Yes, 'Together'," Rebecca repeats. "What happened in 'Together'? . . . Andrea?"

"They had a garden."

"They planted a garden together, didn't they?" Rebecca smiles. "The boy's father helped them plant the garden."

She continues by referring the children to previous science lessons during which they had talked about plants and soil. She then asks them about helping their parents plant a garden.

"I helped put the seeds in the ground and put the dirt on top of it," Robert offers.

"What kinds of vegetables did you plant? . . . Kim?"

"I planted lots of vegetables . . . tomatoes, carrots."

"Shereta?"

"I planted lettuce in my own garden."

"Travis?"

"I planted okra."

"Raphael?"

"I planted beans."

She continues, "Tell about the story 'Together.' What did they have to do to take care of the garden? . . . Carlita?"

"Water it."

"Bengemar?"

"Pull the weeds from it."

"Pull the weeds from it," Rebecca repeats enthusiastically. "What would happen if we left those weeds in there? . . . Latangela?"

"It would hurt the soil."

"What's another word for *soil?*"

"Dirt," several of the children say in unison.

"How many of you like to play in the dirt?"

Most of the children raise their hands.

"So, planting a garden would be fun because you get to play in the dirt," Rebecca says enthusiastically.

"I like to play in the mud," Travis adds.

"You like to play in the mud," Rebecca repeats, attempting to stifle a laugh.

Next is Richard's lesson on animal symmetry with his seventh graders.

Richard begins his discussion of symmetry by using a sponge as an example of an asymmetrical object; he demonstrates radial symmetry using a starfish; and he then turns to bilateral symmetry.

"We have one more type of symmetry," he says. "Jason, come up here. . . . Stand up here."

Jason comes to the front of the room and stands on a stool.

"Would you say," Richard begins, "that Jason is asymmetrical—that there is not uniformity in his shape?"

The students shake their heads.

He has Jason extend his arms out from his sides and then asks, "Would you consider this radial, because he has extensions that go out in all directions? . . . Jarrett?"

"No."

"Why not? Explain that for us."

"There's nothing there," Jarrett says, pointing to Jason's sides.

"There's nothing coming from here, is there?" Richard nods.

"So, we move into the third type of symmetry," he continues, as Jason continues to stand with his arms extended. "Does anyone know what that is called? . . . Rachel?"

"A type of symmetry," Rachel responds uncertainly.

"Yes, it's a type of symmetry. . . . It's called bilateral. . . . *Bilateral* means that the form or shape of the organism is divided into two halves, and the two halves are consistent. . . . If I took a tree saw and started at the top," he says, pointing at Jason's head as the class laughs, "the two halves would be essentially the same."

"Now, tomorrow," he continues, "we're going to see how symmetry influences the ways organisms function in their environments."

Now, let's turn to Didi Johnson's chemistry lesson.

Didi wants her students to understand Charles's law of gases, the law stating that an increase in the temperature of a gas causes an increase in its volume when the pressure on the gas remains the same.

To illustrate that heat causes gases to expand, Didi prepares a demonstration in which she places three identical balloons filled with the same amount of air into three beakers of water. She puts the first into a beaker of hot water, the second into a beaker of water at room temperature, and the third into a beaker of ice water, as shown.

"This water is near boiling," Didi explains as she places the first balloon in the beaker. "This is room temperature, and this has had ice in it, so it is near the freezing point," she continues as she puts the other two balloons into the beakers.

"Now, today," she says as she begins writing on the board, "we're going to discuss Charles's law, but before we put it on the board and discuss it, we're going to see what happened to the balloons. . . . Look up here. . . . How is the size of the balloon related to the temperature of the water we placed it in?"

"The balloon in the hot water looks bigger," Chris responds.

"Can you see any difference in these two?" Didi continues, pointing to the other two balloons.

"The one in the cold water looks smaller than the one in the room temperature water," Chris adds.

"So, from what we see, if you increase temperature, what happens to the volume of the gas?"

"It increases," several students volunteer.

Didi writes, "Increase in temperature increases volume" on the board, emphasizes again that the amount of air and the pressure in the balloons were kept essentially constant, and then asks, "Who can state Charles's law based on what we've seen here?"

"Increased temperature will increase volume if you have constant pressure and mass," Jeremy offers.

Didi briefly reviews Charles's law, writes an equation for it on the board, and has the students solve a series of problems using the law.

Finally, let's look at Bob Duchaine's discussion of the Vietnam War.

Bob begins by saying, "To understand the Vietnam War, we need to go back to the beginning. Vietnam had been set up as a French colony in the 1880s, but by the mid-1900s, the military situation had gotten so bad for the French that they only controlled the little city of Dien Bien Phu."

Bob explains that the French surrendered in the summer of 1954, and peace talks followed. The talks resulted in Vietnam's being split, and provisions for free elections were set up.

"These elections were never held," Bob continues. "Ngo Dinh Diem, in 1956, said there will be no free elections: 'I am in charge of the South. You can have elections in the north if you want, but there will be no elections in the south.'"

Bob continues by introducing the domino theory, which suggested that countries such as South Vietnam, Cambodia, Laos, Thailand, Burma, and even India would fall into communist hands much as dominos tip over and knock each other down. The way to prevent the loss of the countries, he explains, was to confront North Vietnam.

"And that's what we're going to be talking about throughout this unit," he says. "The war that we took over from the French to stop the fall of the dominos soon was eating up American lives at the rate of 12 to 15 thousand a year . . . This situation went from a little simple plan—to stop the dominos from falling—to a loss of over 53,000 American lives that we know of.

"We'll pick up with this topic day after tomorrow . . . Tomorrow you have a fun day in the library."

Short-Answer Questions

In answering these questions, use information from the chapter, and link your responses to specific information in the case.

1. What type or types of knowledge did Rebecca Atkins primarily demonstrate? Explain.
2. What type or types of knowledge did Richard Nelms demonstrate in his lesson? Explain.
3. What type or types of knowledge did Didi Johnson primarily demonstrate? Identify at least two decisions that Didi made in an attempt to help her lesson progress smoothly.
4. What type or types of knowledge did Bob Duchaine primarily demonstrate?

PRAXIS These exercises are designed to help you prepare for the Praxis™ Principles of Learning and Teaching" exam. To receive feedback for your short-answer questions, go to the Companion Website at *www.prenhall.com/eggen*, then to the *Practice for Praxis*™ module for Chapter 1.

To acquire experience in preparing for the multiple-choice items on the Praxis™ exam, go to the *Self-Assessment* module for Chapter 1 at *www.prenhall.com/eggen*, and click on "Practice Quiz."

For additional connections between this text and the Praxis™ exam, go to Appendix A.

ONLINE PORTFOLIO ACTIVITIES

To develop your professional portfolio, further apply your understanding of chapter content, and address the INTASC standards, go the Companion Website, then to this chapter's Online Portfolio Activities. Complete the suggested activities.

Also on the Companion Website at *www.prenhall.com/ eggen*, you can measure your understanding of chapter content with multiple-choice and essay questions, and broaden your knowledge base in *Exploring Further* and *Web Links* to other educational psychology websites.

IMPORTANT CONCEPTS

accountability (p. 14)
action research (p. 19)
correlation (p. 17)
correlational research (p. 17)
descriptive research (p. 16)
experimental research (p. 18)
general pedagogical knowledge (p. 11)

pedagogical content knowledge (p. 9)
random assignment (p. 18)
reflective practice (p. 6)
reforms (p. 13)
research (p. 16)
technician (p. 6)
theory (p. 21)

CHAPTER 2

The Development of Cognition and Language

Chapter Outline	Learning Objectives
	After you have completed your study of this chapter you should be able to
What Is development?	**1** Describe the principles of development, and identify examples of the principles in children's behaviors.
Principles of Development • The Human Brain and Cognitive Development	
Piaget's Theory of Intellectual Development	**2** Use concepts from Piaget's theory of intellectual development to explain both classroom and everyday events.
The Drive for Equilibrium • Organization and Adaptation: The Development of Schemes • Factors Influencing Development • Stages of Development • Applying Piaget's Work in Classrooms: Instructional Principles • Putting Piaget's Theory into Perspective	
A Sociocultural View of Development: The Work of Lev Vygotsky	**3** Use Vygotsky's sociocultural theory to explain how language, culture, and instructional support can influence learner development.
Social Interaction and Development • Language and Development • Culture and Development • The Relationship Between Learning and Development • Vygotsky's Work: Instructional Principles • Piaget's and Vygotsky's Views of Knowledge Construction	
Language Development	**4** Explain language development using different theories of language acquisition.
Theories of Language Acquisition • Stages of Language Acquisition • Promoting Language Development: Suggestions for Teachers	

When we teach, an important goal is to advance our students' cognitive development—the way they think and acquire knowledge. As you read the following case study, think about the different ways that the teacher attempts to meet this goal.

Karen Johnson, an urban eighth-grade science teacher, walks into the teachers' workroom with a clear plastic drinking cup filled with cotton balls.

"What are you up to?" Ken, one of her colleagues asks. "Drinking cotton these days?"

"I just had the greatest class," Karen replies. "You know how I told you the other day that my third-period students didn't understand *density*? They would memorize the formula and try to solve problems but didn't really get it. I also found out they were confused about basic concepts such as mass, weight, size, volume—everything. To them, mass and weight were the same. If something was bigger, they figured it had to be heavier. It also had to have more mass and also be more dense. It was a disaster."

"You know how these kids are," Ken responds.

"That's not really it," Karen says, shaking her head. "They've never really done anything other than memorize some definitions and formulas. So what do we expect? I kept thinking they could do better, so I decided to try something a little different, even if it seemed sort of elementary. See," she goes on, compressing the cotton in the cup. "Now the cotton is more dense. . . . And now it's less dense," she points out, releasing the cotton.

"Then yesterday I made some different-sized blocks out of the same wood. We speculated about their densities, and some of the kids believed the density of the big block was greater. But then we weighed the blocks, measured their volumes, and computed their densities. As we discussed the results, they gradually began to understand that size is only one factor influencing density.

"This morning," she continues with increasing animation, "I had them put equal volumes of water and vegetable oil in little bottles on our balances. When the balance tipped down on the water side, they saw that the mass of the water was greater, so water is more dense. I had asked them to predict which was more dense before we did the activity, and most of them said oil. We talked about that, and they concluded the reason they predicted oil is the fact that it's thicker.

"Here's the good part," she continues, "Calvin—he hates science—remembered that oil floats on water, so it made sense to him that oil is less dense. He actually got excited about what we were doing.

"So we formed a principle: Less dense materials float on more dense materials. Then, even better, Donelle wanted to know what would happen if the materials mixed together, you know, like water and alcohol. You could almost see the wheels turning. So we discussed that and thought about more examples where that might be the case. We even got into population density and compared a door screen with the wires close together to a door with the wires farther apart, and how that related to what we were studying. It was exciting. I really felt as if I was teaching and the students were really into learning for a change, instead of poking each other. A day like that now and then keeps you going."

As you begin your study of this chapter, think about three questions: (1) Why did Karen's students struggle with a concept as basic as *density*? (2) What, specifically, did Karen do in response to their struggles? (3) How can we explain the advances her students made in their thinking? We address these and other questions in this chapter.

WHAT IS DEVELOPMENT?

Mike began playing the trumpet as a sixth grader in his middle school band. Evenings were filled with odd sounds coming from his bedroom, and even Chews, his devoted dog, retreated to the relative sanctuary of the living room. As an eighth grader, however, practicing his part in the piece that he and two friends were playing for a concert, he produced very different sounds. Now, after listening to his son play his last concert as a high school senior, Mike's dad is convinced that Mike can play in a professional orchestra.

Three factors influenced Mike's success. First, he practiced and acquired a great deal of experience, and in the process, he also learned much about playing the trumpet. He also matured; he simply became stronger and more physically capable as a high schooler than he was earlier. This example illustrates the concept of **development,** the orderly, adaptive

Development. The orderly, adaptive changes in learners that result from a combination of experience, learning, and maturation changes in learners that result from a combination of experience, learning, and maturation (Figure 2.1).

We all develop in a variety of ways. We become more emotionally mature, our physical skills develop, and we often develop a talent, as Mike did with his music.

As adults, our development depends primarily on learning and experience; for young children, maturation is also important.

In this chapter, we focus on the ways that learners' thinking, reasoning, and intellectual abilities develop. This will also help us understand differences in the ways that young children typically think compared to the thinking of older students and adults.

Figure 2.1 Factors influencing human intellectual development

Principles of Development

Although development is complex, some general principles exist that apply to all people and all forms of development.

- *Learning contributes to development. Learning* refers to increased understanding or improved skills, and development occurs when the understanding or skills are incorporated into the context of a complex activity (Bredo, 1997). For instance, you will learn specific questioning skills in your teacher-training program, and when you're able to use them effectively in a variety of lessons, your teaching will have developed.
- *Experience enhances development.* Children whose parents have read and talked to them at home have advantages in school, for example. Children exposed to music, physical activities, and social experiences become more capable in these areas than those having less experience.
- *Social interaction promotes development.* Social interaction allows students to share and compare and refine knowledge, beliefs, and perspectives through interactions with others.
- *Development depends on language.* Language provides a medium for thought and a vehicle for sharing ideas and social experiences.
- *Development is continuous and relatively orderly.* As people mature, learn, and gather experiences, their development continuously advances. They don't suddenly "jump" from one set of abilities to another (Berk, 2004, 2006).
- *Individuals develop at different rates.* One middle school girl, for example, will be a young woman, towering head and shoulders over her slower-developing classmates. In another case, two fourth graders will vary significantly in their ability to benefit from a learning activity.
- *Development is influenced by* **maturation,** genetically controlled, age-related changes in individuals. A 10-year-old will run faster than she did when she was 5, for example, and a first grader won't be able to solve problems a seventh grader can solve. In extreme cases, such as malnutrition or severe sensory deprivation, the environment can retard maturation. In most cases, genes and the environment interact to produce normal growth.

With these principles in mind, we now focus on cognitive development. We begin by considering research on the role of the brain in development.

A variety of experiences contributes to learners' development.

The Human Brain and Cognitive Development

In the past approximately 10 to 15 years, neuroscience has developed new brain imaging techniques that allow the exploration of the brain and how it operates as we learn (Craig, 2003). Some educators are attempting to apply this to classrooms, calling it *brain-based learning* (e.g., E. Jensen, 1998; Sousa, 1995; Wolfe & Brandt, 1998).

Maturation. Genetically controlled, age-related changes in individuals

The Learning Physiology of the Brain

The human brain is incredibly complex. Estimates suggest that it is composed of between 100 and 200 billion nerve cells, called *neurons* (Berninger & Richards, 2002; Merzenrich, 2001). The **neuron** is the learning unit of the brain. It is composed of a cell body; **dendrites,** which are branchlike structures that extend from the cell body and receive messages from other neurons; and **axons,** which transmit outgoing messages (Craig, 2003).

Interestingly, neurons don't actually touch one another. Instead, the messages sent from one neuron to another are transmitted across tiny spaces called **synapses.** When an electrical impulse is sent down an axon, it stimulates a chemical that crosses the synapse and stimulates the dendrites of neighboring neurons. Frequent transmissions of information between particular neurons can establish a permanent physical relationship between them (P. Howard, 2000). These components are illustrated in Figure 2.2.

Cognitive development involves both creating and eliminating synaptic connections (Bruer & Greenough, 2001; Byrnes, 2001b). For example, children learn reading and other cognitive skills, but they also learn that hitting other children and behaving impolitely are unacceptable. Considerable evidence from animal studies indicates that learning experiences increase the number of synaptic connections per neuron (Berninger & Richards, 2002). The creation of these synaptic connections probably represents the creation of most forms of memory (Bransford et al., 2000). These results suggest that learn-

Figure 2.2   The learning physiology of the brain

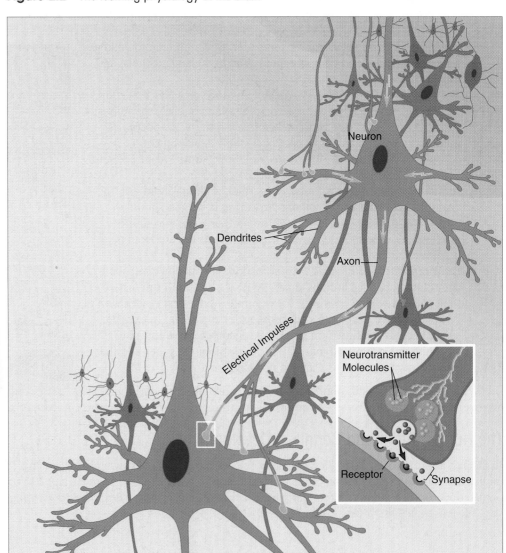

Neuron. Nerve cells composed of cell bodies, dendrites, and axons, which make up the learning capability of the brain

Dendrites. Branchlike structures within neurons, extending from the cell body and receiving messages from other neurons

Axons. Components of neurons that transmit outgoing messages to other neurons

Synapses. The tiny spaces across which messages are transmitted from one neuron to another

ing and experience are important for the creation of synaptic connections, and these results are consistent with the principles we outlined in the previous section.

Putting Brain Research Into Perspective

"Brain-based learning" is controversial, with proponents (e.g., Craig, 2003; Walsh & Bennett, 2004; Westwater & Wolfe, 2000; Wolfe & Brandt, 1998) lining up on one side and critics on the other (e.g., Bruer, 1999; Coles, 2004; A. Davis, 2004; Jorgenson, 2003; Lawton, 1999). For example, proponents of brain-based learning emphasize the existence of critical periods—time spans optimal for the development of certain capacities—and state that educators should capitalize on these periods. In addition, they emphasize the importance of deliberate practice and active learning strategies such as guided discovery, problem-solving, and hands-on learning.

Critics of brain-based learning, on the other hand, acknowledge that critical periods probably do occur in humans, but point out that our brains retain an enormous ability to benefit from environmental stimulation throughout our lives (Bransford et al., 2000; Bruer & Greenough, 2001; Craig, 2003). In addition, no evidence suggests the existence of critical periods in the development of traditional academic subjects, such as reading or math (Geary, 1998). Critics further argue that deliberate practice and the active learning strategies described by brain-based learning proponents have been widely accepted for years, and describing them as "brain based" adds nothing new. "The brain based learning advocates . . . have [merely] repackaged progressive educational principles favoring active learning and constructivist methods" (Jorgenson, 2003, p. 365). Indeed, deliberate practice and active learning are two of the most commonly stated suggestions for brain-based applications (Shaywitz & Shaywitz, 2004; Zull, 2004), and they have long been established principles of learning.

The critics' positions can be summarized in the following quotes:

> Neuroscience has only the broadest outline of principles to offer education at this time. And in a lot of cases, the principles suggest strategies that educators already know. (D'Arcangelo, 2000, p. 71)

> Educational applications of brain science may come eventually, but as of now neuroscience has little to offer teachers in terms of informing classroom practice. There is, however, a science of mind, cognitive science, that can serve as a basic science for the development of an applied science of learning and instruction. Practical, well-founded examples of putting cognitive science into practice already exist in numerous schools and classrooms. Teachers would be better off looking at these examples than at speculative applications of neuroscience. (Bruer, 1997, p. 4)

We discuss the cognitive science that Bruer refers to in detail throughout this text.

Exploring Further

To read more about the controversies involved in brain-based learning, go to "Brain-Based Education" in the *Exploring Further* module of Chapter 2 at *www.prenhall.com/eggen*.

Checking Your Understanding

1.1   Describe and explain the principles of cognitive development.

1.2   A first grader tries to shoot basketballs like her brother but has neither the strength nor the skill. She practices, receives tips from her brother about improving her technique, gets bigger and stronger, and by the fourth grade makes baskets consistently. This example contains evidence for five of the principles of development. Identify the principles, and explain how they are illustrated.

1.3   A second grader struggles with the problem $\begin{array}{r} 34 \\ -\ 16 \\ \hline \end{array}$

He gets 22 as an answer by subtracting the smaller from the larger numerals. With some teacher support, he learns the skills of regrouping, so he gets 18, the correct answer. With some additional practice, he can solve subtraction problems that require regrouping with ease. The example contains evidence for four of the principles of development. Identify the principles, and explain how they are illustrated.

To receive feedback for these questions, go to Appendix B.

PIAGET'S THEORY OF INTELLECTUAL DEVELOPMENT

Consider the following task: You have two identical containers of liquid. You then pour the contents of one glass into the third glass as shown here. Now, are the amounts of liquid in the first and third glasses the same or different?

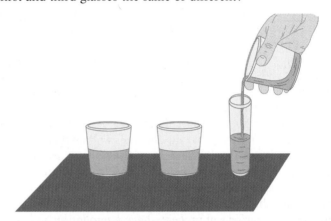

The question may seem ridiculous; the amounts are obviously the same, since you merely poured the contents of one container into the other. However, in the 1920s Jean Piaget (1896–1980), a Swiss biologist and psychologist, became interested in children's responses to problems such as this one. He found, for example, that young children (e.g., 4- and 5-year-olds) concluded that the third glass has more liquid, whereas older children noted that that the amounts are obviously the same. The differences in children's thinking proved fascinating to Piaget, and it caused a turn in his research and resulted in one of the most widely studied theories of cognitive development (Inhelder & Piaget, 1958; Piaget, 1952, 1959, 1980). We examine his theory in this section.

The Drive for Equilibrium

Think about some of your everyday experiences. Are you bothered when something doesn't make sense? Do you want the world to be predictable? Are you more comfortable in classes where the instructor specifies the requirements and outlines the grading practices? For most people, the answer to each of these questions is "Yes."

That people have an intrinsic need for understanding, order, and certainty is widely accepted by sources ranging from philosophy to the popular media (e.g., Marinoff, 2003; van Gelder, 2005). "We inquire about the past, present, and future. We investigate every conceivable subject. Human beings want and need to make sense of things that happen—or don't happen—in the short run as well as over the long haul" (Marinoff, p. 3).

Piaget (1952, 1959, 1980) described this need for understanding as the drive for **equilibrium,** a state of being able to explain new experiences by using existing schemes. When we can explain new experiences, we remain at equilibrium; when we can't, our equilibrium is disrupted and we are motivated to reestablish it. When our thinking advances as a result of regaining equilibrium, development occurs. These ideas are the foundation of Piaget's theory.

Organization and Adaptation: The Development of Schemes

To achieve and maintain equilibrium, people use two related processes: *organization* and *adaptation.* Let's look at them.

Achieving Equilibrium: The Process of Organization

To reach equilibrium, people create **schemes,** actions or mental operations that represent our constructed understanding of the world (Santrock, 2006). The process of forming and using schemes is called **organization.**

For instance, when you learned to drive a car, you had a series of experiences with attempting to start the engine, maneuver in traffic, and make routine driving decisions. As you organized and came to understand these experiences, they became your "driving" scheme.

As our example with the containers of liquid suggests, schemes vary with age. Infants develop psychomotor schemes such as reaching for and holding objects; school-age chil-

Exploring Further

Piaget's life and work are interesting. To read more about Piaget and his work, go to "Jean Piaget" in the *Exploring Further* module of Chapter 2 at *www.prenhall.com/eggen.*

Equilibrium. A state of being able to explain new experiences by using existing schemes

Schemes. Actions or mental operations that represent our constructed understanding of the world

Organization. The process of forming and using schemes

dren develop more abstract schemes such as classification and proportional reasoning. Piaget used the idea of schemes to refer to a narrow range of operations, such as infants' *object permanence scheme* (the idea that an object still exists even when we can't see it) or children's conservation-of-volume scheme (the idea that the amount of liquid doesn't change if it is poured into a different-shaped container, as you saw in our example) (Piaget, 1952). However, teachers and some researchers (e.g., Santrock, 2006; Wadsworth, 2004) find it useful to extend Piaget's idea to include content-related schemes, such as an *adding-fractions-with-unlike-denominators* scheme, a *creating-a-persuasive-essay* scheme, or a *reptiles* scheme. As with our driving scheme, each represents our understanding of a piece of the world. We use this expanded view in our description of Piaget's work.

Maintaining Equilibrium: The Process of Adaptation

As we acquire additional experiences, our existing schemes may become inadequate; that is, they can't explain the new experience, and our equilibrium is disrupted. To reestablish it, we adapt. **Adaptation** is the process of adjusting schemes and experiences to each other to maintain equilibrium. For example, if you learn to drive a car with an automatic transmission and then later buy one with a stick shift, you must adapt your "driving" scheme.

Adaptation consists of two reciprocal processes: *accommodation* and *assimilation* (J. P. Byrnes, 2001a). **Accommodation** is a form of adaptation in which an existing scheme is modified and a new one is created in response to experience. As you learn to drive with the stick shift, you modify your original *driving* scheme and create a *driving-with-a-stick-shift* scheme; you have accommodated your original *driving* scheme. Accommodation functions with its counterpart process, **assimilation,** which is a form of adaptation in which an experience in the environment is incorporated into an existing scheme. For instance, once you've learned to drive a car with a stick shift, you likely will also be able to drive a pickup truck with a stick shift. You will have assimilated the experience with the pickup truck into your *driving-with-a-stick-shift* scheme. The relationship between assimilation and accommodation is illustrated in Figure 2.3.

Figure 2.3 Maintaining equilibrium through the process of adaptation.

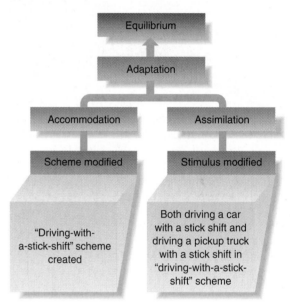

Factors Influencing Development

Accommodation is the primary mechanism influencing development, because it is through accommodation that schemes are modified and thinking is advanced. So, what is necessary for accommodation to occur? We consider this question in the next section.

Experience with the Physical World

Piaget's answer to this question is *experience;* direct, active experience is necessary for accommodation to occur. Because of your experience—attempting to drive vehicles with stick shifts—your driving ability developed. For young children, maturation is also important, but for older students and adults, experience is the key. Without it, development doesn't occur. (Piaget, 1970, 1977, subsumed the role of learning under a more general description of experience.)

The necessity of experience for accommodation also illustrates two of the developmental principles we discussed in the first section of the chapter: *Learning contributes to development,* and *experience enhances development,* and it helps us answer the first two questions we asked at the beginning of the chapter: "Why did Karen's students struggle with a concept as basic as *density?*" and "What, specifically, did Karen do in response?" Her students struggled because they lacked direct, physical experiences with the concept. Many of us have used the formula Density = Mass/Volume, put in numbers, and got answers that meant little to us. In contrast, Karen responded to their struggles by providing her students with experiences—the cotton balls in the cup, water and oil, and other examples. Now, because of their experiences and increased understanding, they're better equipped to explain why people float more easily in the ocean than in lakes, in hot-air and in balloons, the phenomena involved in weather fronts, and many others. This helps us answer the third question we asked at the beginning of the chapter: We explain the improvements Karen's students made in their thinking by saying that their development with respect to the concept *density* has advanced.

Adaptation. The process of adjusting schemes and experiences to each other to maintain equilibrium

Accommodation. A form of adaptation in which an existing scheme is modified and a new one is created in response to experience

Assimilation. A form of adaptation in which an experience in the environment is incorporated into an existing scheme

Social interaction encourages learners to examine their own schemes and compare them to those of others.

Social Experience

Piaget also emphasized the role of **social experience** in development, the process of interacting with others (Becker & Varelas, 2001; Wadsworth, 2004). Social experience allows learners to test their schemes against those of others. When schemes are comparable, people remain at equilibrium; when they aren't, equilibrium is disrupted, learners are motivated to adapt their schemes, and development occurs.

Recognizing that social interaction is essential for development has strongly influenced education and child-rearing practice. For example, parents organize play groups for their young children, schools emphasize cooperative learning, and teachers encourage students to conduct experiments and solve problems in groups. The fact that these activities contribute to development illustrates the value of social interaction.

Stages of Development

Among the most widely known elements of Piaget's theory are his descriptions of stages of development. The stages describe general patterns of thinking for children at different ages and with different amounts of experience.

As you study the characteristics of each stage, keep the following ideas in mind:

- Movement from one stage to another represents a qualitative difference in thinking; that is, a difference in the way children think about their experiences, not the amount that they know (Meece, 2002; Vidal, 2000).
- Children develop steadily and gradually, and experiences in one stage form the foundation for movement to the next (P. Miller, 2002).
- Although approximate chronological ages are attached to the stages, children pass through them at different rates, and students at the same age may be at different stages (Meece, 2002; P. Miller, 2002).
- Although rates vary, all people pass through each stage before progressing into a later one. Older children and even adults will process information in ways that are characteristic of young children if they lack experience in an area (Keating, 2004).

Piaget's stages of development are summarized in Table 2.1 and described in the sections that follow.

Sensorimotor (0 to 2 Years)

In the sensorimotor stage, children use their senses and motor capacities to make sense of the world. The schemes they develop are based on their physical interactions with their environments, such as using eye–hand coordination to grab objects and bring them to their mouths.

Early in the sensorimotor stage, children do not mentally represent objects; for these children, objects are "out of sight, out of mind." Later in the stage, however, they acquire **object permanence,** the understanding that objects have a permanent existence separate from the self. Children in this stage also develop the ability to imitate, an important skill that allows them to learn by observing others.

Preoperations (2 to 7 Years)

In the preoperational stage, perception dominates children's thinking. The name of this stage comes from the idea of "operation," or mental activity. A child who can classify different animals as dogs, cats, and bears, for example, is performing a mental operation.

Many changes occur in children as they pass through this stage. For example, they make enormous progress in language development, reflecting growth in the ability to use symbols. They also learn huge numbers of concepts. For example, a child will point excitedly and say, "Truck," "Horse," and "Tree," delighting in exercising these newly formed

Social experience. The process of interacting with others

Object permanence. The understanding that objects have a permanent existence separate from the self

Table 2.1 Piaget's stages and characteristics

Stage	Characteristics	Example
Sensorimotor (0–2)	Goal-directed behavior	Makes jack-in-the-box pop up
	Object permanence (represents objects in memory)	Searches for object behind parent's back
Preoperational (2–7)	Rapid increase in language ability with overgeneralized language	"We goed to the store."
	Symbolic thought	Points out car window and says, "Truck!"
	Dominated by perception	Concludes that all the water in a sink came out of the faucet (the second cartoon in Chapter 1)
Concrete Operational (7–11)	Operates logically with concrete materials	Concludes that two objects on a "balanced" balance have the same mass even though one is larger than the other
	Classifies and serial orders	Orders containers according to decreasing volume
Formal Operational (11–Adult)	Solves abstract and hypothetical problems	Considers outcome of WWII if the Battle of Britain had been lost
	Thinks combinatorially	Systematically determines how many different sandwiches can be made from three different kinds of meat, cheese, and bread

ideas. These concepts are concrete, however; the truck, horse, and tree are present or associated with the current situation. Children in this stage have limited notions of abstract ideas such as *fairness, democracy,* and *energy.*

The powerful effect of perceptual dominance is also seen in another widely publicized idea from Piaget's theory: preoperational students' inability to *conserve.*

Conservation. The concept of **conservation** refers to the idea that the "amount" of some substance stays the same regardless of its shape or the number of pieces into which it is divided. The thinking of young children can be demonstrated with a number of conservation tasks. The example with the containers of liquid that we used to introduce our discussion of Piaget's work is one example. A number of others exist, and two are outlined in Figure 2.4.

In Figure 2.4 we see that preoperational children don't "conserve." That is, it makes sense to them that the amount of liquid (as we saw in the example at the beginning of our discussion of Piaget's work), the number of coins, or the amount of clay can somehow change without adding or subtracting anything from them. Let's see how this occurs using the example with the liquids. (You will be asked to explain how this occurs with the coins and clay in Checking Your Understanding question 2.2.)

Conservation. The idea that the "amount" of some substance stays the same regardless of its shape or the number of pieces into which it is divided

A nonconserver is influenced by appearances, believing that the flat pieces of clay have different amounts than the balls of clay even though they were initially the same.

Figure 2.4   Conservation tasks for number and mass

Conservation Task	Initial Presentation by Observer	Change in Presentation by Observer	Typical Answer From Preoperational Thinker
Number	The observer shows the child two identical rows of objects. The child agrees that the number in each row is the same.	The observer spreads the bottom row apart while the child watches. The observer then asks the child if the two rows have the same number of objects or if there are more in one row.	The preoperational child typically responds that the row that has been spread apart has more objects. The child centers on the length, ignoring the number.
Mass	The observer shows the child two balls of clay. The child agrees that the amount of clay is the same in each. (If the child doesn't agree that they have the same amount, the observer then asks the child to move some clay from one to the other until the amount is the same.)	The observer flattens and lengthens one of the balls while the child watches. The observer then asks the child if the two have the same amount of clay or if one has more.	The preoperational child typically responds that the longer, flattened piece has more clay. The child centers on the length.

First, the children tend to *center* on the height of the liquid in the container. **Centration (or centering)** is the tendency to focus on the most perceptually obvious aspect of an object or event, neglecting other important aspects. The height is the most perceptually obvious feature of the liquids, so the children conclude that the tall, narrow container has more liquid. Second, young children lack **transformation,** which is the ability to mentally record the process of moving from one state to another. They don't mentally record the process of pouring the liquid into the third container; they see it as new and different. Third, they lack **reversibility,** which is the ability to mentally trace the process of pouring the liquid from the third back to the second container. When lack of transformation and reversibility are combined with their tendency to center, we can see why they conclude that the tall, narrow container has more liquid in it, even though no liquid was added or removed.

Egocentrism. **Egocentrism,** people's tendency to believe that other people look at the world as they do, is another characteristic of preoperational children. Egocentric people cannot consider the world from others' perspectives. As an example, imagine that you're looking at a straight-backed chair from the front and you're asked to describe how it would look to a person seated on the opposite side. As with Piaget's conserva-

Centration (centering). The tendency to focus on the most perceptually obvious aspect of an object or event, neglecting other important aspects

Transformation. The ability to mentally record the process of moving from one state to another

Reversibility. The ability to mentally trace a process, such as lengthening a row, back to its original state

Egocentrism. The tendency to believe that other people look at the world as the individual does

tion tasks, the description is obvious to us. Piaget and Inhelder (1956), in another famous experiment, showed young children a model of three mountains and asked them to describe how the mountains would look to a doll seated on the opposite side. Preoperational children describe the doll's view as identical to their own.

Analyzing Classrooms Video
To further analyze children's thinking, go to Episode 2, "Examining Learning Thinking: Piaget's Conservation Tasks," on DVD 1, accompanying this text.

Concrete Operations (7 to 11 Years)

The concrete operational stage, which is characterized by the ability to think logically about concrete objects, marks another important advance in children's thinking (Flavell, Miller, & Miller, 2002). For instance, when facing the conservation of number task, concrete operational thinkers simply observe, "You just made the row longer" or "You just spread the coins apart," so the number must be the same. This represents logical thought.

Concrete thinkers also overcome some of the egocentrism of preoperations, becoming better able to understand the views of others and able to take on the roles and perspectives of storybook characters.

Classification and Seriation. Classification and seriation are two logical operations that develop during this stage (Piaget, 1977), and both are essential for understanding number concepts (Siegler, 1998). **Classification** is the process of grouping objects on the basis of common characteristics. Before age 5, children can form simple groups, such as separating a pile of cardboard circles into one group of white and another group of black. When a black square is added, however, they typically include it with the black circles, instead of forming subclasses of black circles and black squares. By age 7, they can form subclasses, but they still have problems with more complex classification systems.

Seriation is the ability to order objects according to increasing or decreasing length, weight, or volume. Piaget's research indicates that this ability gradually evolves until it is acquired at about age 7 or 8.

Once children have acquired this ability, they can master **transitivity,** the ability to infer a relationship between two objects based on knowledge of their relationship with a third object. The following is an example:

An experimenter has three sticks. He presents 1 and 2, as shown here:

1   2

Now he removes Stick 2 and displays 1 and 3, as you see here:

1   3

He then asks, "What do you know about the relationship between Sticks 2 and 3?"

A concrete operational thinker concludes that 2 is longer than 3, reasoning that, because 2 is longer than 1 and 1 is longer than 3, 2 must be longer than 3. This illustrates the skill of transitivity.

Though concrete thinkers have made dramatic progress compared to preoperational learners, their thinking is still limited. For instance, they interpret aphorisms, such as "Make hay while the sun shines," literally, with a conclusion such as "You should gather your crop before it gets dark."

Let's see how this compares to formal thinkers.

Classification. The process of grouping objects on the basis of a common characteristic

Seriation. The ability to order objects according to increasing or decreasing length, weight, or volume

Transitivity. The ability to infer a relationship between two objects based on knowledge of their relationship with a third object

Formal operational learners can think logically about abstract and hypothetical ideas.

Formal Operations (Age 11 to Adult)

Although concrete thinkers are capable of logic, their thinking is tied to the real and tangible. Formal thinkers, in contrast, can think logically about the hypothetical and even the impossible. During the formal operational stage, learners can examine abstract problems systematically and generalize about the results. These abilities open a range of possibilities for thinking about the world that were unavailable to learners at the earlier stages.

Characteristics of Formal Thought. Formal thinking has three characteristics (Meece, 2002; P. Miller, 2002):

- Thinking abstractly
- Thinking systematically
- Thinking hypothetically

As an example, formal thinkers would conclude that "Make hay while the sun shines" means something more abstract, such as "Seize an opportunity when it exists." Their ability to consider the abstract and hypothetical makes the study of courses such as algebra, in which letters and symbols stand for numbers, meaningful on a different level from the concrete thinker. To the concrete operational child, $x + 2x = 9$ is meaningful only if it is represented concretely, such as:

Dave ate a certain number of cookies. His sister ate twice as many. Together they ate 9. How many did each one eat?

Formal operational learners, in contrast, can think about the equation as a general idea, just as they would in the transitivity problem by saying, "If *A* is greater than *B,* and if *B* is greater than *C,* then *A* is greater than *C.*" Formal thinkers also think systematically and recognize the need to isolate and control variables in forming conclusions. For example, a girl hearing her father say, "I've got to stop drinking so much coffee. I've been sleeping terribly the last few nights," responds, "But Dad, you've also been bringing work home every night, and you didn't do that before." She recognizes that her father's sleeplessness may be caused by extra work, rather than by the coffee, and that they can't tell until they isolate each variable.

Formal operational learners can also think hypothetically. For instance, considering what might have happened if the British had won the Revolutionary War requires hypothetical thinking for American history students. Biology students are asked to consider the results of crossing different combinations of dominant and recessive genes, and art students must imagine multiple perspectives and light sources when they create drawings. Middle and high school classrooms are filled with content requiring formal operational thought.

The difficulty Karen Johnson's students had in understanding the concept *density* further illustrates the need for formal thinking. When students cannot think abstractly and solve abstract problems, they revert to memorizing what they can or, in frustration, give up altogether.

Adolescent Egocentrism. While egocentrism is considered to be characteristic of preoperational thinking, it exists in the other stages as well. "Egocentrism is a constant companion of cognitive development" (Wadsworth, 2004, p. 130). It is prominent in adolescence and can include a sense of personal uniqueness and a desire to be noticed, a belief that others are as interested in them as they themselves are, and for some, a sense of invulnerability, which can lead to reckless behavior, such as drug use or unprotected sex (Berk, 2006). Egocentrism is more common in middle than high school, and it helps us understand the sometimes bizarre and frustrating behaviors we see in middle school students.

Formal Operations: Research Results. Much of the middle, junior high, and particularly the high school curriculum is geared toward formal operational thinking. This creates a dilemma, however, because research indicates that the thinking of most middle, junior high, and high school students is still concrete operational (P. Alexander, 2006; Cole, Cole, & Lightfoot, 2005; Flavell, Miller, & Miller, 2002). Additional research indicates that almost half of all college students can't consistently reason formally, especially in areas outside their majors (De Lisi & Straudt, 1980; Wigfield, Eccles, & Pintrich, 1996). Many individuals, including adults, never reach the stage of formal operations (Niaz, 1997).

You are likely to find that even well-educated adults have difficulty with abstract thinking!. . . Why is it that so many college students, and adults in general, are not fully formal operational? The reason is that people are most likely to think abstractly in situations in which they have had extensive experience. (Berk, 2004, p. 365)

These findings have important implications for teachers, particularly those in middle schools, junior highs, and high schools (and even universities). Many students come to these settings without the concrete experiences needed to think at the level of abstraction often required. Wise teachers realize this and provide concrete experiences for them, as Karen did with her eighth graders. The many examples that we include in discussions of the topics presented in this book are our effort to provide concrete experiences as you attempt to understand educational psychology. Without concrete experiences, students will revert to whatever it takes for them to survive—in most cases, memorization without understanding.

The description of the stages provides a more complete answer to the third question we asked at the beginning of the chapter: "How can we explain the advances her students made in their thinking?" Though eighth graders, Karen Johnson's students' thinking was concrete operational. With her examples and instructional support, their thinking with respect to the concept *density* became more nearly formal operational.

Exploring Further

A number of exercises can be used to assess the thinking of students. To see some examples, go to "Assessing Students' Cognitive Development" in the *Exploring Further* module of Chapter 2 at *www.prenhall.com/eggen*.

 **Instructional Principles**

Applying Piaget's Work in Classrooms: Instructional Principles

Piaget's theory suggests that you keep the developmental needs of your students in mind as you design and implement instruction. The following principles can guide you in your efforts to apply Piaget's work in your teaching:

1. Provide concrete experiences that represent abstract concepts and principles.
2. Help students link the concrete representations to the abstract idea.
3. Use social interaction to help students verbalize their developing understanding.
4. Design learning experiences as developmental bridges to more advanced stages of development.

Let's see how the principles for addressing developmental needs guide Kristen Michler, a second-grade teacher, as she works with her students.

Kristen is teaching her students about place value. She groups her students in pairs and gives each pair craft sticks with 10 beans glued on each and a number of separate beans, as shown here.

"What do we have here?" she begins. ". . . Jason?"

"Sticks . . . with beans on them."

"And other beans," Tenesha adds.

"And how many beans on each stick? . . . Go ahead and count them."

"Ten," Trang says after a couple seconds.

"Yes, good Trang," Kristen smiles. "We have several groups of 10 beans on the sticks, and we also have some beans just sitting by themselves."

"Now, . . . everyone hold up one of your sticks," Kristen directs and then turns to the board and writes 10. "You have one group of 10 beans, and we write it as the 10 you see here."

"Now, show us this with your beans," she says as she writes "2" on the board.

She watches, offering brief suggestions to some who are uncertain, to be sure that all students pick up two beans from their desks and hold them in their hands.

"Good," she says when she sees that all the students have picked up two beans.

"Now, tell me what I have here," she continues, as she holds up two sticks and three additional beans. "Chin?"

"Two sticks . . . and three others."

"Yes. . . . And how many beans on each stick?"

"Ten," Andrea answers.

"Good. . . . So, now I want you to work with your partner for a minute and write the number that these represent," Kristen says, again referring to the two sticks and three separate beans.

She watches as the students talk and write numbers on their papers.

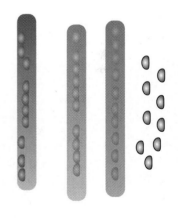

"Okay, what did you come up with? . . . Tiffany?"

"Ten and ten and three."

"Okay, what's this?"

"Ten," several students say.

"And this?" she continues with the other stick.

"Another 10."

"Good, so how do we write this?"

Seeing uncertainty on the students' faces, Kristen writes "20" on the board. "See this 2," she points. "This represents two groups of 10."

She then writes "23" on the board and asks, "What is this 3?"

"The three other beans," Clay volunteers.

"Very good thinking, Clay," Kristen smiles. "That's exactly right.

"Okay, now, I'm going to give you a challenge. I want you to work with your partners and show me this with your sticks and beans." She writes "32" on the board and watches as the students work together to demonstrate the number with their beans and sticks.

"Good," she smiles when everyone has finished. "Let's try one more," writing "22" on the board.

Again she watches as students demonstrate the number with their beans and sticks.

"Now, let's see what we have," she continues. "Everyone show me this 2," she says, pointing at the 2 in the tens place in 22.

She watches as the students hold up two sticks.

And what is this 2? . . . Bryan?"

" . . . Two . . . tens."

"Good. . . . Now show me this 2." She points to the 2 in the units place.

Again she watches as the students hold up two beans.

"And what is this 2?"

". . . Two . . . by itself," Brenda volunteers.

"Okay, excellent thinking, everyone."

Kristen has students practice several more examples. In some examples, the students demonstrate a number that she writes on the board, and in others, they write a number that she demonstrates with the materials.

Now, let's look at Kristen's attempts to apply the principles for addressing developmental needs in her teaching. She applied the first when she used her beans and sticks to represent the concept of place value. For instance, the idea that the 2 in the tens place represents two groups of 10 but the 2 in the units place represents two individual items is abstract for young children. The craft sticks and beans were concrete materials that helped Kristen's students understand this difference, because they could actually see the two groups of 10 as well as the two single items by themselves.

Kristen's lesson demonstrates the value of concrete experiences in math, but they are also important in other content areas. Working with concrete experiences helps students form mental images of abstract ideas, laying the foundation for more advanced thinking and development (Chao, Stigler, & Woodward, 2000; Fujimura, 2001). Examples of concrete experiences with other topics are shown in Table 2.2.

Kristen applied the second principle when she emphasized the link between the concrete materials (the beans and sticks) and the abstraction (the numbers written on the board). For example, she said, "Everyone show me this 2" (pointing at the 2 in the tens place in 22) and "Now show me this 2" (pointing to the 2 in the units place in 22). These conceptual links are essential for understanding. In fact, teachers sometimes mistakenly believe that if their students are using manipulatives, then learning is automatically taking place. This often is not the case (Ball, 1992). Unless teachers make specific connections between concrete materials and the abstractions they represent, students are left uncertain and may even view use of the concrete materials and the discussion of the concepts and symbols as two different lessons.

Concrete experiences provide opportunities for students to learn abstract concepts by modifying existing schemas.

Table 2.2 The use of concrete examples in teaching

Topic	Example
Geography: Longitude and latitude	A teacher draws longitude and latitude lines around a beach ball to illustrate that latitude lines are parallel and longitude lines intersect.
Elementary Science: Air takes up space	A first-grade teacher places an inverted cup into a fishbowl of water. To demonstrate that air keeps the water out of the cup, she tips it slightly to let some bubbles escape.
Chemistry: Charles's law (when pressure is constant, an increase in temperature causes an increase in the volume of a gas)	A teacher places one balloon into ice water; a second, equally inflated balloon, into room-temperature water; and a third into hot water. She asks the students to compare the final volumes of each.
History: Mercantilism	A teacher writes short case studies to illustrate England and France trading raw materials from their colonies for manufactured products, forbidding the colonies from trading with others, and requiring English and French ships for transport.

Kristen applied the third principle by using social interaction to help students assimilate and accommodate ideas into their existing schemes. For instance, when Bryan and Brenda described the difference between the 2 in the tens place and the 2 in the units place, students who didn't understand the difference had to accommodate an existing scheme. As students practice articulating their understanding, they have increased opportunities for assimilation and accommodation, and their development advances further. Kristen promoted social interaction with her questioning, which helped guide the students' thinking as they practiced. She also used group work to further encourage interaction.

Finally, Kristen designed her lesson to be slightly beyond her students' present level of development. We saw that students were initially uncertain about both representing numbers with the sticks and beans and writing numbers represented by the materials. Using the concrete materials and interacting socially, however, gradually brought the students to understanding. Such understanding can provide a developmental bridge to further advances in thinking, such as what the 4 in 436 means and what it means to "borrow" or "regroup" in a problem such as 45 − 27.

Also note that the principles Kristen applied in her lesson are applications of the principles of development outlined at the beginning of the chapter. She emphasized experience, social interaction, and language, principles in which all theories of cognitive development are grounded.

Putting Piaget's Theory into Perspective

As with all theories, Piaget's work has its critics. To put his work into perspective, we look at both criticisms and strengths of his theory in this section. The following are some common criticisms of Piaget's work:

- Piaget underestimated the abilities of young children. Abstract directions and requirements cause children to fail at tasks they can do under simpler, more realistic conditions (Chen & Siegler, 2000; Siegler, 1996). When 3-year-olds are given a simplified conservation-of-number task, for example, such as working with three instead of six or seven items, they succeed (Berk, 2006).
- Piaget overestimated the abilities of older learners. Teaching approaches that rely on his findings therefore can cause a problem for both learners and teachers. For

Analyzing Classrooms Video
To analyze a teacher's response to developmental differences in her students, go to Episode 3, "Developmental Differences: Studying Properties of Air in First Grade," on DVD 1 accompanying this text.

example, middle and junior high teachers often assume that their students can think logically in the abstract, but as you saw in our discussion of research examining formal thinking, often they cannot (Flavell et al., 2002).

■ Piaget's descriptions of broad developmental stages that affect all types of tasks aren't valid (Bjorklund, 2000; Gelman, 2000; Goswami, 2001). For example, learners' progressions to concrete operational thinking typically begins with conservation of mass, proceeds through a range of abilities, and ends with conservation of volume.

■ Children's logical abilities depend more strongly on knowledge and experience in a specific area than Piaget suggested (P. Alexander, 2006; Cole et al., 2005; Serpell, 2000). For example, if given adequate experiences, students can solve proportional reasoning problems, but without these experiences, they cannot (Fujimura, 2001).

■ Piaget's work fails to adequately consider the influence of culture on development (Berk, 2004, 2006; Cole et al., 2005). Cultures determine children's experiences, values, language, and their interactions with adults and each other (Rogoff, 2003). (We examine the role of culture in development in our discussion of Lev Vygotsky's work in the next section of the chapter.)

Despite these shortcomings, Piaget's work has been enormously influential. For instance, educators now see learning as an active process in which learners construct their own understanding of how the world works, instead of seeing it as a process in which students passively receive information or apply rules with little understanding. Piaget strongly contributed to this view.

Piaget's work has also influenced the curriculum (Meece, 2002; Parkay & Hass, 2000). Lessons are now organized with concrete experiences presented first, followed by more abstract and detailed ideas. This is how Kristen organized her lesson. Piaget's influence is evident in the emphasis on "hands-on" experiences in science, in children writing about their own experiences in language arts, and in children beginning social studies topics by studying their own neighborhoods, cities, states, cultures, and finally those of other nations.

In summary, some of the specifics of Piaget's theory are now criticized, but his emphasis on experience and his idea that learners actively create their own understanding are unquestioned. He continues to have an enormous influence on curriculum and instruction in this country.

Checking Your Understanding

2.1   The hands-on activities that we see in today's classrooms, such as Kristen's use of the craft sticks and beans to illustrate place value, are applications of Piaget's theory. Explain specifically how hands-on activities apply his theory.

2.2   Use the concepts *centration, transformation,* and *reversibility* to explain why preoperational children don't "conserve" number and mass in the coins and clay tasks.

2.3   Read the following vignette and explain in a paragraph how the concepts *accommodation, assimilation development, equilibrium, experience, organization,* and *scheme* are illustrated in it.

You have learned to drive a car with an automatic transmission, and you're comfortable driving a variety of cars with automatics.

Then, you are asked to help a friend move, and your friend asks you to drive her car to her new location as she drives a moving truck. However, the car has a stick shift, and you're very uncomfortable trying to drive it. Your friend helps you get started, and finally you can skillfully drive cars with both automatics and stick shifts.

Sometime later, you help another friend move, and he has a pickup truck with a stick shift. Now, you can comfortably drive the pickup truck.

To receive feedback for these questions, go to Appendix B.

Knowledge Extensions

To deepen your understanding of the topics in this section of the chapter and integrate them with topics you've already studied, go to the *Knowledge Extensions* module for Chapter 2 at *www.prenhall.com/eggen*. Respond to questions 1–6.

Classroom ⊞ Connections

Applying an Understanding of Piaget's Views of Development in Your Classroom.

1. Provide concrete and personalized examples, particularly when abstract concepts are first introduced.

   - *Elementary:* A kindergarten teacher begins her unit on animals by taking her students to the zoo. She plans for most of the time to be spent in the petting zoo.
   - *Middle School:* An English teacher encourages students to role-play different characters in a novel they are reading. The class then discusses the feelings and emotions of the characters.
   - *High School:* An American government teacher involves his students in a simulated trial to help them understand the American court system. After the activity, he has participants discuss the process from their different perspectives.

2. Use students' interactions to assess their present levels of development and expose them to the thought processes of more advanced students.

   - *Elementary:* After completing a demonstration on light refraction, a fifth-grade science teacher asks students to describe their understanding of what they saw. She encourages other students to ask questions of those offering the explanations.
   - *Middle School:* A science teacher gives his students a pretest at the beginning of the year on tasks that require controlling variables and proportional thinking. He uses this information to group students for cooperative learning projects, placing students with different levels of development in the same group. He models thinking aloud at the chalkboard and encourages students to do the same in their groups.
   - *High School:* A geometry teacher asks students to explain their reasoning as they demonstrate proofs at the chalkboard. She asks probing questions that require the students to clarify their explanations, and she encourages other students to do the same.

3. Provide your students with developmentally appropriate practice in reasoning.

   - *Elementary:* A kindergarten teacher gives pairs of children a variety of geometric shapes. He asks the students to group the shapes and then has different pairs explain their grouping while he organizes the shapes on a flannel board according to their explanations. He asks other students if the groupings make sense and if the shapes could be grouped differently. He repeats the process as the students offer other suggestions.
   - *Middle School:* An algebra teacher has her students factor this polynomial expression: $m^2 + 2m + 1$. She then asks, "If no 2 appeared in the middle term, would the polynomial still be factorable?"
   - *High School:* A history class concludes that people often emigrate for economic reasons. The teacher asks, "Consider a family named Fishwiera, who are upper-class Lebanese. What is the likelihood of them immigrating to the United States?" The class uses this and other hypothetical cases to test the generalizations it has formed.

A SOCIOCULTURAL VIEW OF DEVELOPMENT: THE WORK OF LEV VYGOTSKY

Piaget (1952) viewed developing children as busy and self-motivated individuals who, on their own, explore, form ideas, and test these ideas with their experiences. Lev Vygotsky (1896–1934), a Russian psychologist, provided an alternative view that emphasizes social and cultural influences on the child's developing mind.

As a boy, Vygotsky was instructed by private tutors who used Socratic dialogue, a question-and-answer process that challenges current ideas, to promote higher levels of understanding (Kozulin, 1990, 1998). These sessions, combined with his study of literature and experience as a teacher, convinced him of the importance of two factors in human development: social interaction and language (Vygotsky, 1978, 1986). This perspective, a **sociocultural theory of development,** emphasizes the crucial influence of social interactions and language, embedded within a cultural context, on cognitive development.

Let's look at two examples.

> Suzanne is reading *The Little Engine That Could* to her 5-year-old daughter, Perri, who sits on her lap. "I think I can, I think I can," she reads enthusiastically from the story.
>
> "Why do you think the little engine kept saying, 'I think I can, I think I can'?" she asks as they talk about the events in the story.
>
> ". . . We need to try . . . and . . . try and try," Perri finally says hesitantly and with some prompting.
>
> Sometime later, Perri is in school, working on a project with two of her classmates.
>
> "I don't get this," her friend Dana complains. "It's too hard."
>
> "No, we can do this if we hang in," Perri counters. "We need to try a little harder."

> Limok and his father look out and see a fresh blanket of snow on the ground.
>
> "Ahh, beautiful," his father observes. "Iblik, the best kind of snow for hunting, especially when it's sunny."

Sociocultural theory of development. A theory that emphasizes the influence of social interactions and language, embedded within a cultural context, on development

Figure 2.5   Learning and development in a cultural context

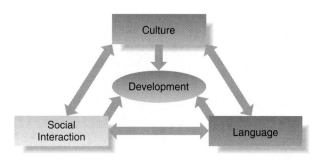

"What is iblik?" Limok wonders.

"It is the soft, new snow; . . . no crystals," his father responds, picking up a handful and demonstrating how it slides easily through his fingers.

"The seals like it," the father continues. "They come out and sun themselves in it. Then, we only need the spear. Our hunting will be good today."

Sometime later, as Limok and his friend Osool hike across the ice, Limok sees a fresh blanket of snow covering the landscape.

"Let's go back and get our spears," Limok says eagerly. "The seals will be out and easy to find today."

The relationships between social interaction, language, and culture are outlined in Figure 2.5 and discussed in the sections that follow.

Social Interaction and Development

In contrast with Piaget (1970, 1977), who saw social interaction primarily as a mechanism for promoting assimilation and accommodation in individuals, Vygotsky (1978, 1986) viewed learning and development as arising directly from social interactions. To see how, let's look again at the interactions in our two examples. First, in each, learning occurred directly within the context of a social situation. Perri learned about perseverance as her mother read and talked to her, and Limok learned about conditions conducive to hunting as he interacted with his father. According to Vygotsky, their thinking (cognition) developed as a direct result of interactions with other people.

Second, the interactions were between the children and a "more knowledgeable other," an adult in these cases, and third, through these interactions, the children developed an understanding that they wouldn't have been able to acquire on their own. Piaget proposed that children explore the world individually, but Vygotsky suggested that children need not, and should not, reinvent the knowledge of a culture on their own. This knowledge has accumulated over thousands of years and should be appropriated (internalized) through social interaction (Leont'ev, 1981).

Both adults—particularly parents, other caregivers, and teachers—and peers play an important role in the process of appropriation. Adults explain, give directions, provide feedback, and guide communication (Rogoff, 2003). Children use conversation to collaborate when solving problems, both in play and in classrooms. This interaction allows the exchange of information and provides feedback about the validity of existing ideas.

Finally, Perri and Limok didn't passively listen to the adults; they were active participants in the interactions. The concept of *activity* is essential in sociocultural theory. Vygotsky believed that children learn by doing, by becoming involved in meaningful activities with more knowledgeable people. Activity provides a framework in which dialogue can occur. Through dialogue driven by activity, ideas are exchanged and development occurs.

Social interaction provides opportunities for students to articulate their own ideas while comparing their developing understanding with that of others.

Language and Development

The role of language is central to Vygotsky's theory, and it plays three different roles in development. First, it gives learners access to knowledge others already have. Second, language provides learners with cognitive tools that allow them to think about the world and solve problems. For example, when Limok learned *iblik,* he didn't just learn the word and how to pronounce it; he also learned that it is snow that is soft, fresh, crystal free, and something that increases the likelihood of a successful hunt. Encouraging children to talk about their experiences promotes both learning and development (Pine & Messer, 2000).

Third, language gives us a means for regulating and reflecting on our own thinking (J. P. Byrnes, 2001a; Winsler & Naglieri, 2003). We all talk to ourselves. For example, we grumble when we're frustrated, and we talk ourselves through uncertain situations: "Oh no, a flat tire. Now what? The jack is in the trunk. Yeah. I'd better loosen the wheel nuts before I jack up the car."

Children also talk to themselves. Listen to them during free play, and you'll hear muttering that appears to have no specific audience. If you listen more closely, you'll hear them talking to themselves as they attempt tasks: "Hmm, which button goes where? . . . I better start at the bottom."

Vygotsky believed this free-floating external speech is the precursor of internalized, **private speech,** which is self-talk that guides thinking and action. Piaget (1926) observed it in young children and termed it "egocentric speech," believing it reflected the preoperational child's inability to consider the perspectives of others. Vygotsky (1986), in contrast, believed that it indicated the beginnings of self-regulation. Private speech forms the foundation for complex cognitive skills such as remembering ("If I repeat the number, I'll be able to remember it"), and problem solving ("Let's see, what kind of answer is the problem asking for?") (Winsler & Naglieri, 2003).

As development advances, private speech becomes silent but it remains important. Research indicates that children who use it extensively learn complex tasks more effectively than those who don't (Emerson & Miyake, 2003; B. Schneider, 2002).

Culture and Development

Culture is the third essential concept in Vygotsky's view of development, and it provides the context in which development occurs (Glassman, 2001). The language of a culture becomes a cognitive "tool kit" that children use to conduct their interactions and make sense of the world.

The role of culture was illustrated most concretely in the example with Limok and his father. As they interacted, they used the term *iblik,* which represents a concept unique to Limok's culture. It provided a mechanism for both communication and thinking.

The Relationship Between Learning and Development

In the list of principles at the beginning of the chapter, we said that "learning contributes to development," and we also saw that Piaget subsumed learning under the more general idea of experience. Vygotsky described it differently.

According to Vygotsky, learning occurs when people acquire specific understanding or develop distinct abilities, and development progresses when understanding or skills are incorporated into a larger, more complex context (Bredo, 1997). Both of the children in our examples, because of their experience with adults, learned something specific: Perri learned the value of perseverance, and Limok learned about the conditions for good hunting. Then, later, they incorporated their learning into a different and more complex context. Perri, for example, in her interaction with Dana—who wanted to give up—exhorted her to continue making an effort; Perri's behavior indicated an advanced level of development. Limok had a similar experience. He recognized the conditions for good hunting when he and Osool were merely hiking across the ice.

These descriptions illustrate that learning is necessary for development, development is stimulated by learning, and learning and development both occur in the context of a social situation mediated by language (Bredo, 1997).

Instructional ⌂ **Principles**   **Vygotsky's Work: Instructional Principles**

Now let's consider how you can apply Vygotsky's work to promote your students' learning and development. The following principles can help you in your efforts:

1. Embed learning activities in a context that is culturally authentic.
2. Create learning activities that involve students in social interactions.
3. Encourage students to use language to describe their developing understandings.
4. Create learning activities that are in learners' *zones of proximal development* (we discuss this concept later in this section).
5. Provide instructional assistance to promote learning and development.

Private speech. Self-talk that guides thinking and action

Let's see how these principles guide Jeff Malone, a seventh-grade teacher, as he works with his students.

Jeff begins his math class by passing out two newspaper ads for the same CD player. Techworld advertises, "The lowest prices in town"; Complete Computers offers a coupon that allows customers to "take an additional 15% off our already low prices." After allowing students time to read the two ads, Jeff asks, "So, where would you buy your CD player? Which store has the best buy? . . . Antonia?"

"I think it's Techworld, because they say they have the lowest prices in town. And their price is lower than Complete Computers by $5."

"Do you all agree? . . . Maria, what do you think?"

"I disagree, because Complete Computers says you can take an additional 15% off their price, so they would be the cheapest."

"How can we find out?" Jeff asks.

After additional discussion, the students decide they need to find the price with the 15% discount.

Jeff briefly reviews decimals and percentages and then places students into groups of three and gives each group three problems to solve. The following is the first one:

A store manager has 45 video games in his inventory. Twenty five of them are out of date, so he puts them on sale. What percent of the video games are on sale?

As he moves around the room, he sees that one group—Sandra, Javier, and Stewart—are having trouble. Sandra zips through the problems; Javier knows that a fraction is needed to find decimals and percentages, but he struggles to compute the decimal; and Stewart doesn't know how to begin.

"Let's talk about how we compute percentages in problems like this," Jeff says, kneeling in front of the group. "Sandra, explain how you did the first problem."

Sandra begins, "Okay, the problem asks what percent of the video games are on sale. Now, I thought, how can I make a fraction? . . . Then I made a decimal out of it and then a percent. . . . Yeah, that's what I did, . . . so here's what I do first," and she then demonstrates how she solved the problem.

"Okay, let's try this one," Jeff then says, turning to the second problem.

Joseph raised gerbils to sell to the pet store. He had 12 gerbils and sold 9 to the pet store. What percentage did he sell?

"The first thing," Jeff continues, "I need to find out is what fraction he sold. Now, why do I need to find a fraction? . . . Javier?"

"To . . . get a fraction, so we can make a decimal and then a percent."

"Good," Jeff smiles. "What fraction did he sell? . . . Stewart?"

". . . 9 . . . 12ths."

"Excellent, Stewart. Now, Javier, how might we make a decimal out of the fraction?"

". . . Divide the 12 into the 9," Javier responds hesitantly.

"Good," and he watches Javier get .75. Stewart also begins hesitantly, and then begins to grasp the idea.

After the groups have finished the review problems, Jeff calls the class back together and has some of the other students offer explanations. When they struggle to put their explanations into words, Jeff asks questions that guides both their thinking and their descriptions.

He then returns to the CD player problem and asks them to apply their knowledge of percentages to it.

Now let's look at Jeff's attempts to apply the principles based on Vygotsky's work. He applied the first when he began the lesson with a problem that was real for students. CDs and CD players are a part of our culture, and shopping is an activity familiar to middle school students. Jeff's problem was culturally authentic.

Second, his students were actively involved in interacting as they explained their thinking, and third, they used language to describe their understanding. For instance, when Jeff asked Javier why they needed a fraction, and provided encouragement, Javier said, "To . . . get a fraction, so we can make a decimal and then a percent." Javier initially struggled to put his understanding into words, but with additional practice, he will articulate his understanding more easily, and his development will advance. These efforts applied the second and third principles.

Jeff applied the fourth principle by conducting his learning activity within the students' zones of proximal development. Let's see what that means.

Zone of Proximal Development

When children can benefit from the experience of interacting with a more knowledgeable person, they are working in their **zone of proximal development,** a range of tasks that an individual cannot yet do alone but can accomplish when assisted by a more skilled partner (Glassman & Wang, 2004; Gredler & Shields, 2004). Vygotsky (1978) described it in this way, "It is the distance between the actual developmental level as determined by independent problem solving and the level of potential development as determined through problem solving under adult guidance or in collaboration with more capable peers" (p. 86). Learners have a zone of proximal development for each task they are expected to master, and they must be in the zone to benefit from assistance.

To illustrate this idea, let's look again at Jeff's work with Sandra, Javier, and Stewart, each of whom were at different developmental levels. Sandra's zone of proximal development was beyond the task Jeff presented; she was able to solve the problems without assistance. The task was within Javier's zone of proximal development, since he was able to solve the problems with Jeff's help, but Stewart's zone was below the task, so Jeff had to adapt his instruction to find the zone for Stewart. For instance, Stewart didn't initially know that the problem could be solved by first making a fraction, then a decimal, and finally a percentage. He was able to find the fraction of the gerbils that had be sold to the pet store, however. By asking Stewart to identify the fraction, Jeff adapted his instruction to find the zone for this task and, as a result, promoted Stewart's development. Had he not adapted, Stewart wouldn't have benefited from the interaction.

On the surface, Jeff's instruction seems quite simple, but was, in fact, very sophisticated. By observing and listening to students' responses to his questions, Jeff assessed their current understanding and then adapted the learning activities to the developmental level of each student. For instance, he asked Sandra to explain the problem, which required an advanced level of development. He also guided Javier's efforts to solve the problem, and he simplified the task for Stewart to ensure that it was within Stuart's zone.

Finally, in attempting to apply Vygotsky's work in his teaching, Jeff provided the instructional assistance necessary to promote learning and development. This assistance is a concept called *scaffolding.*

Scaffolding: Interactive Instructional Support

As small children learn to walk, their parents often walk behind them, holding onto their hands as they take their tentative steps. As they gain confidence, the parent will hold only one hand, and later will let the children walk on their own, but remain close to catch them before they fall. Eventually they walk comfortably on their own.

This example illustrates the concept of **scaffolding,** which is assistance that helps children complete tasks they cannot complete independently (Puntambekar & Hübscher, 2005; D. Wood, Bruner, & Ross, 1976). Jeff provided scaffolding for Javier and Stewart by asking questions that helped them understand the percentage problems. (Sandra's zone for

Teachers provide individualized scaffolding for students through their numerous personal interactions during the day.

Zone of proximal development. A range of tasks that an individual cannot yet do alone but can accomplish when assisted by a more skilled partner

Scaffolding. Assistance that helps children complete tasks they cannot complete independently

Figure 2.6 Scaffolding tasks in three zones of proximal development

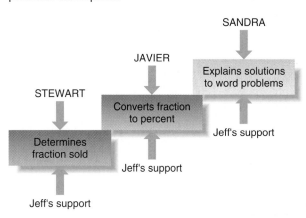

percentage problems was beyond the requirements of the task, so Jeff helped enhance her development by asking her to verbally model her thinking, a task appropriate for her zone.)

In providing support for Javier and Stewart, Jeff adjusted his questioning to keep the task within these learners' zones of proximal development and helped them through their zones. When they needed more help, he stepped in; when less was required, he stepped back to allow them to progress on their own. Effective scaffolding adjusts instructional requirements to learners' capabilities and levels of performance (Puntambekar & Hübscher, 2005). The relationship between the students' zones of proximal development and the scaffolding Jeff provided is illustrated in Figure 2.6.

Just as toddlers' development with respect to walking is advanced by their parents' support, learners' development is enhanced by their teachers' support (Rogoff, 2003). Without this support, development is impaired. It is important to note, however, that effective scaffolding provides only enough support to allow learners to progress on their own. Remember, Jeff provided the support, but the students solved the problems. Doing tasks for learners delays development.

Some different forms of instructional scaffolding are outlined in Table 2.3.

Piaget's and Vygotsky's Views of Knowledge Construction

As might be expected, Piaget's and Vygotsky's descriptions of development have both similarities and differences (Fowler, 1994). These comparisons are outlined in Table 2.4. For instance, both views attach importance to language and social interaction, but they differ in the role that each plays in development. Piaget more strongly emphasized individual learners' creations of

Table 2.3 Types of instructional scaffolding

Type of Scaffolding	Example
Modeling	An art teacher demonstrates drawing with two-point perspective before asking students to try a new drawing on their own.
Think aloud	A physics teacher verbalizes her thinking as she solves momentum problems at the chalkboard.
Questions	After modeling and thinking aloud, the same physics teacher "walks" students through several problems, asking them questions at critical junctures.
Adapting instructional materials	An elementary physical education teacher lowers the basket while teaching shooting techniques and then raises it as students become proficient.
Prompts and cues	Preschoolers are taught that "the bunny goes around the hole and then jumps into it" as they learn to tie their shoelaces.

Table 2.4 A comparison of Piaget's and Vygotsky's views of knowledge construction

	Piaget	Vygotsky
Basic question	How is new knowledge created in all cultures?	How are the tools of knowledge transmitted in a specific culture?
Role of language	Aids in developing symbolic thought. Does not qualitatively raise the level of intellectual functioning. (The level of functioning is raised by action.)	Is an essential mechanism for thinking, cultural transmission, and self-regulation. Qualitatively raises the level of intellectual functioning.
Social interaction	Provides a way to test and validate schemes.	Provides an avenue for acquiring language and the cultural exchange of ideas.
View of learners	Active in manipulating objects and ideas.	Active in social contexts and interactions.
Instructional implications	Design experiences to disrupt equilibrium.	Provide scaffolding. Guide interaction.

new knowledge, whereas Vygotsky focused on learners' appropriating the knowledge of a culture using language as a tool (Fowler, 1994; Rogoff, 2003). Regardless of differences, however, both views of development recommend that teachers move beyond lecturing and telling as teaching methods and toward instruction that emphasizes students' active involvement and use of language to describe their developing understanding. This view of teaching is grounded in the widely accepted idea that learners, instead of passively receiving knowledge from others, actively construct it for themselves. Piaget believed that learners construct knowledge essentially on their own, whereas Vygotsky believed that it is first socially constructed and then internalized by individuals. We examine the process of knowledge construction in detail in Chapter 8.

Checking Your Understanding

3.1 You're a math teacher. Explain what the discussion in the section "Language and Development" suggests that you should encourage with your students as they study math. How will your efforts impact learner development?

3.2 In mainstream American culture, the concept of *snow* is relatively simple. In contrast, the Inuit people have a great many terms for the concept. Use Vygotsky's theory to explain why this difference exists. How does this difference relate to learner development?

3.3 You are unsuccessfully trying to learn a new word processing program. A friend comes over. You do fine when she helps, but after she leaves, you again run into problems. Explain the difference between your zone of proximal development and your friend's zone. How does this difference relate to development?

To receive feedback for these questions, go to Appendix B.

Knowledge Extensions

To deepen your understanding of the topics in this section of the chapter and integrate them with topics you've already studied, go to the *Knowledge Extensions* module for Chapter 6 at *www.prenhall. com/eggen*. Respond to questions 7–9.

Classroom ┼ Connections

Applying Vygotsky's Theory of Development in Your Classroom

1. Use meaningful activities and authentic tasks as organizing themes for your instruction.
   - **Elementary:** A fourth-grade teacher teaches graphing by having students graph class attendance. Information is recorded for both boys and girls, figures are kept for several weeks, and patterns are discussed.
   - **Middle School:** A science teacher structures a unit on weather around a daily recording of the weather conditions at her school. Each day, students observe the temperature, cloud cover, and precipitation; record the data on a calendar; graph the data; and compare the actual weather to that forecasted in the newspaper.
   - **High School:** Before a national election, an American government teacher has his students poll their parents and students around the school. Students then have a class election and compare their findings with national results.
2. Use scaffolding to help students progress through their zones of proximal development.
   - **Elementary:** When her students are first learning to print, a kindergarten teacher initially gives them dotted outlines of letters and paper with half lines for gauging letter size. As students become more skilled, she removes these aids.

- **Middle School:** A science teacher helps her students learn to prepare lab reports by doing an experiment with the whole class and writing the report as a class activity. Later, she provides only an outline with the essential categories in it. Finally, she simply reminds them to follow the proper format.
- **High School:** An art teacher begins a unit on perspective by sharing his own work, showing slides, and displaying works from other students. As students work on their own projects, he provides individual feedback and asks the students to discuss how perspective contributes to each drawing.

3. Structure classroom tasks to encourage student interaction.
   - **Elementary:** After fifth-grade students complete a writing assignment, their teacher has them share their assignments with each other. To assist them in the process, she provides them with focusing questions that students use to discuss their work.
   - **Middle School:** An English teacher uses cooperative learning groups to discuss the literature the class is studying. The teacher asks each group to respond to a list of prepared questions. After students discuss the questions in groups, they share their perspectives with the whole class.
   - **High School:** Students in a high school biology class work in groups to prepare for exams. Before each test, the teacher provides an outline of the content covered, and each group is responsible for creating one question on each major topic.

Language development is facilitated by concrete experiences and opportunities to practice language.

LANGUAGE DEVELOPMENT

A miracle occurs in the time from birth to 5 years of age. Born with a limited ability to communicate, children enter school with an impressive command of the language spoken at home. Experts estimate that 6-year-olds know between 8,000 and 14,000 words, and by the sixth grade, children's vocabulary expands to 80,000 words (Biemiller, 2005). Just as important, school-age children can use these words to read and talk and write about the new ideas they are learning.

How does this language ability develop, and how does it contribute to the development of thinking? We answer these questions in this section.

Understanding language development is important for three reasons:

- As shown in our discussions of Piaget's and Vygotsky's work, language is a catalyst for development. As children interact with peers and adults, they construct increasingly complex ideas about the world.
- Language development facilitates learning in general (Berk, 2006), and it is closely tied to learning to read and write (Hiebert & Kamil, 2005). As students' language develops, their ability to learn abstract concepts also develops.
- The development of language provides a tool for social and personal development, as you'll see in Chapter 3.

Theories of Language Acquisition

Language experts differ in their views of how language is acquired. We discuss four theories in this section as we consider behaviorist, social cognitive, nativist, and sociocultural views of language acquisition.

Behaviorist Views

> A 2-year-old picks up a ball and says, "Baa."
> Mom smiles broadly and says, "Good boy! Ball."
> The little boy repeats, "Baa."
> Mom responds, "Very good."

Behaviorism explains language development by suggesting that children are reinforced for demonstrating sounds and words (B. Skinner, 1953, 1957). For example, Mom's "Good boy! Ball" and "Very good" reinforced the child's efforts, and over time, language develops. (We examine behaviorism in Chapter 6.)

Social Cognitive Perspectives

> "Give Daddy some cookie."
> "Cookie, Dad."
> "Good. Jacinta gives Daddy some cookie."

Social cognitive theory emphasizes the role of modeling, the child's imitation of adult speech, adult reinforcement, and corrective feedback (Bandura, 1986, 2001). In the example, the father modeled an expression, Jacinta attempted to imitate it, and he praised her for her efforts. (We also examine social cognitive theory in Chapter 6.)

Both behaviorism and social cognitive theory make intuitive sense. Children probably do learn certain aspects of language by observing and listening to others, trying it out themselves, and being reinforced (Owens, 2005). Scientists who study the development of languages in different cultures, however, believe something else is occurring.

Nativist Theory

> A parent listened one morning at breakfast while her 6- and her 3-year-old were discussing the relative dangers of forgetting to feed versus overfeeding goldfish:

six-year-old:	It's worse to forget to feed them.
three-year-old:	No, it's badder to feed them too much.
six-year-old:	You don't say badder, you say worser.

three-year-old:　But it's baddest to give them too much food.
six-year-old:　No it's not. It's worsest to forget to feed them.
　　　　　　　(Bee, 1989, p. 276)

Virtually all humans learn to speak, and all languages share basic structures, called *language universals,* such as a subject–verb sequence at the beginning of sentences (Lightfoot, 1999). In addition, children pass through basically the same age-related stages when learning these diverse languages.

Nativist theory asserts that all humans are genetically "wired" to learn language and that exposure to language triggers this development. Noam Chomsky (1972, 1976), the father of nativist theory, hypothesized that an innate language acquisition device predisposes children to learn language. According to Chomsky, the **language acquisition device (LAD)** is a genetic set of language-processing skills that enables children to understand and use the rules governing speech. When children are exposed to language, the LAD analyzes speech patterns for the rules of grammar—such as the subject after a verb when asking a question—that govern a language. The existence of a LAD would explain why children are so good at producing sentences they have never heard before. For example, our young fish caretakers said "badder," "baddest," "worser," and "worsest." Both behaviorists and social cognitive theorists have trouble explaining these original constructions (Lightfoot, 1999).

Chomsky's position also has its critics (Tomasello & Slobin, 2004). For instance, it cannot explain why some home environments are better than others for promoting language development and why people acquire certain dialects.

Most experts believe that language is learned through a combination of factors that include both an inborn disposition, as Chomsky proposed, and environmental factors that shape the specific form of the language (Hoff, 2001). In addition, researchers are placing increased emphasis on the child as an active participant in language learning (K. E. Nelson, Aksu-Koc, & Johnson, 2001; Stanovich, 2000). This sociocultural view emphasizes the importance of experience and interaction with others in a child's language development. Let's look at it.

Sociocultural Theory

As you saw in our discussion of Vygotsky's (1978, 1986) work, language is central to his theory of cognitive development. It provides a vehicle for social interaction, the transmission of culture, and the internal regulation of thinking. In addition, you saw that activity is also central in his view of development, and this is true for language as well. Vygotsky's theory provides insights into the process of language development itself. Let's see how.

Children learn language by practicing it in their day-to-day interactions, and language development appears effortless because it is embedded in everyday activities. In helping young children develop language, adults adjust their speech to operate within children's zones of proximal development (Tamis-LeMonda, Bornstein, & Baumwell, 2001). Baby talk and *motherese* use simple words, short sentences, and voice inflections to simplify and highlight important aspects of a message (Baringa, 1997). These alterations provide a form of linguistic scaffolding that facilitates communication and language development. As children's language skills develop, they use bigger words and more complex sentences, which keeps the process in the children's zones of proximal development. Practicing language and receiving feedback that helps extend and refine it is essential for language development (Hoff, 2001).

Stages of Language Acquisition

Children pass through a series of stages as they learn to talk. In the process, they make errors, and their speech is an imperfect version of adult language. They make huge strides, however, and understanding this progress helps teachers promote language growth through their interactions with learners.

Early Language: Building the Foundation

Learning to speak actually begins in the cradle when adults say "Ooh" and "Aah" and "Such a smart baby!" to encourage the infant's gurgling and cooing. These interactions

Nativist theory. A theory of language acquisition suggesting that all humans are "wired" to learn language and that exposure to language triggers this development

Language acquisition device (LAD). A genetic set of language-processing skills that enables children to understand and use the rules governing speech

lay the foundation for future language development by teaching the child that humans use language to communicate.

The first words, spoken between ages 1 and 2, are **holophrases,** one- and two-word utterances that carry as much meaning for the child as complete sentences. For example:

"Momma car."	That's Momma's car.
"Banana."	I want a banana.
"No go!"	Don't leave me alone with this scary babysitter!

During this stage, children also learn to use intonation to convey meaning. For example, the same word said differently has a very different message for the parent:

"Cookie."	That's a cookie.
"Cookie!"	I want a cookie.

Differences in intonation indicate that the child is beginning to use language as a functional tool.

Two patterns creep into speech at this stage and stay with the child through other stages. **Overgeneralization** occurs when a child uses a word to refer to a broader class of objects than is appropriate, such as using the word *car* to also refer to buses, trucks, and trains (Berk, 2006). **Undergeneralization,** which is harder to detect, occurs when a child uses a word too narrowly, such as using *kitty* for a specific cat but not for cats in general. Both are normal aspects of language development and in most instances are corrected through ordinary listening and talking. A parent or other adult may intervene, saying something like, "No, that's a truck. See, it has more wheels and a big box on it."

Children's language development closely parallels their development of schemes. Overgeneralization occurs when children inappropriately assimilate new information into an existing scheme; undergeneralization occurs when they overaccommodate. Concrete experiences and interactions with others help young children fine-tune their language.

Fine-Tuning Language

During the "twos," children expand and fine-tune their initial speech (Berk, 2004, 2006). Children elaborate on the present tense to include verb forms such as

Present progressive:	I eating.
Past regular:	He looked.
Past irregular:	Jimmy went.
Third-person irregular:	She does it.

One problem that surfaces in this stage is overgeneralization of grammar rules, as "badder," "worsest," and "He goed home." Piaget's (1970, 1977) work helps explain these utterances. "He goed home" uses an existing scheme (add *-ed* to make past tense), which allows the child to remain at equilibrium, whereas "He went home" requires accommodation–modification of the existing scheme and creation of a new scheme.

Increasing Language Complexity

At about age 3, a child learns to use sentences more strategically. Children begin to reverse subjects and verbs to form questions, and they modify positive statements to form negative statements (Bloome, Carter, Christian, Otto, & Shuart-Faris, 2005). For instance, the child can say not only "He hit him" but also "He didn't hit him" and "Did he hit him?" The idea that the form of language is determined by its function begins to develop more fully in this stage.

The introduction of more complex sentence forms happens at around age 6 and parallels other aspects of cognitive development. For instance, "Jackie paid the bill" and "She had asked him out" become "Jackie paid the bill because she had asked him out." The ability to form and use more complex sentences reflects the child's developing understanding of cause-and-effect relationships.

Holophrases. One- and two-word utterances that carry as much meaning for the child as complete sentences

Overgeneralization. A speech pattern that occurs when a child uses a word to refer to a broader class of objects than is appropriate

Undergeneralization. A speech pattern that occurs when a child uses a word too narrowly

The typical child brings to school a healthy and confident grasp of the powers of language and how it can be used to communicate with others and think about the world. The importance of this foundation for reading and writing instruction, as well as learning in general, is difficult to overstate (Berk, 2004, 2006; Tompkins, 2003).

Promoting Language Development: Suggestions for Teachers

So, what does this discussion say to teachers as they attempt to promote their students' language development? We have three suggestions:

First, encourage students to use language to describe their understanding of the topics they study (Gauvain, 2001). Students literally cannot get too much practice in their use of language. This is particularly true in math and science, where students tend to talk less about ideas than in other content areas. It is also an application of Vygotsky's (1978, 1986) work.

Second, remind students that struggling to put understanding into words is a normal part of learning and development. We've all said at some point in our lives, "I know what I'm trying to say, I just can't put it into words." The better students are able to articulate their understanding, the deeper that understanding will be. An emotional climate that makes students feel safe as they struggle with language is essential for motivation (Kuhn & Dean, 2004). Teacher patience and support are essential in this process.

Third, provide students with scaffolding as they practice language. For example, providing students with technical terms, articulating parts of definitions, and embellishing students' descriptions are all forms of scaffolding that help them develop in their ability to put their understanding into words. Then, encourage them to articulate the complete definition or description, including any new technical terms. Articulating their understanding for the first time marks an advance in development and sets the stage for further learning. Further, acquiring the ability to describe understanding is satisfying and further increases motivation to learn.

As with all forms of thinking, promoting language development is one of the most important contributions that we as teachers can make to our students' total growth.

Online Case Book

To analyze another lesson to assess the extent to which the teacher applied Piaget's and Vygotsky's theories of cognitive development together with effective strategies for promoting language development, go to the *Online Case Book* for Chapter 2 at *www.prenhall.com/eggen*.

Checking Your Understanding

4.1 A child is talking with his friend and says, "Mine is gooder." Which theory of language acquisition best explains the use of "gooder"?

4.2 Is the use of "gooder" an example of under- or overgeneralization? Explain.

4.3 Explain how each of the theories of language acquisition would recommend correcting grammatical overgeneralizations.

To receive feedback for these questions, go to Appendix B.

Knowledge Extensions

To deepen your understanding of the topics in this section of the chapter and integrate them with topics you've already studied, go to the *Knowledge Extensions* module for Chapter 2 at *www.prenhall.com/eggen*. Respond to questions 10–12.

Classroom ⊞ Connections

Promoting Language Development in Your Classroom

1. Provide students with opportunities to practice language.

- **Elementary:** A fifth-grade teacher says to a student who has solved a problem involving the addition of fractions with unlike denominators, "Okay, explain to us exactly what you did. Be sure to include each of the terms in your description."
- **Middle School:** An eighth-grade history teacher, in a study of the American Revolution, says to one of his students, "Now, go ahead and put into words the parallels we've discussed between the American, French, and Russian revolutions."

- **High School:** A physics teacher in a discussion of force and acceleration says, "Describe what we mean by the 'net force' operating on this object."

2. Create an emotional climate that makes students feel safe as they practice language.

- **Elementary:** When a fifth grader struggles to explain how he solved the problem, his teacher says, "That's okay. We all struggle to express ourselves. The more you practice, the better you'll get at it."

- **Middle School:** In response to snickers as a student struggles to describe the parallels in the three revolutions, the teacher states sternly, "We will all sit politely when one of our classmates is trying to explain his or her thoughts. We're here to help each other, and we will not laugh at each other."
- **High School:** In response to a student who says, "I know what 'net force' is, but I can't quite say it," the physics teacher in our above example smiles and says, "That's okay. We all struggle. Say as much as you can, and we'll take it from there."

3. Provide scaffolding when students struggle with language.
- **Elementary:** When the fifth grader says, "I tried to find for these numbers and,. . ." as he struggles to explain how he found a lowest common denominator, his teacher offers, "You attempted to find the lowest common denominator?"
- **Middle School:** As the student stammers in his attempts, the history teacher says, "First describe one thing the three revolutions had in common."
- **High School:** In response to the student's struggles, the physics teacher says, "Go ahead and identify two forces that are acting on the block."

Meeting Your Learning Objectives

1. **Describe the principles of development, and identify examples of the principles in children's behavior.**

   - Development describes the orderly, durable changes that occur over a lifetime and occur as a result of maturation, learning, and experience.
   - Principles of development suggest that learning, experience, social interaction, maturation, and the use of language contribute to development.
   - Principles of development also suggest that development is continuous and relatively orderly, and that learners develop at different rates.
   - Brain research suggests that development involves both creating and eliminating synaptic connections.

2. **Use concepts from Piaget's theory of intellectual development to explain both classrooms and everyday events.**

   - According to Piaget, people organize their experience into schemes that help them understand their world and achieve equilibrium. Compatible experiences are assimilated into existing schemes; incongruent experiences require an accommodation of these schemes to reestablish equilibrium.
   - Maturation and the quality of experiences in the physical and social world combine to influence development. As children develop, they progress through stages that describe general patterns of thinking. Progress through the stages represents qualitative differences in the ways learners process information and think about their experiences; it does not describe simple accrual of knowledge.

3. **Use Vygotsky's sociocultural theory to explain how language, culture, and instructional support can influence learner development.**

   - Vygotsky describes cognitive development as the interaction between social interaction, language, and culture.
   - Social interaction provides a mechanism to help children develop an understanding that they wouldn't be able to acquire on their own.
   - Language is a tool people use for cultural transmission, communication, and reflection on their own thinking.
   - Social interaction and language are embedded in a cultural context that uses the language of the culture as the mechanism for promoting development.

4. **Explain language development using different theories of language acquisition.**

   - Behaviorism describes language development by suggesting that children are reinforced for demonstrating sounds and words, and social cognitive theory focuses on the imitation of language that is modeled. Nativist theory suggests that children are genetically predisposed to language. Sociocultural theory suggests that language is developed through scaffolded practice that exists within children's zones of proximal development.
   - Children progress from an early foundation of one- and two-word utterances, to fine-tuning language that includes overgeneralizing and undergeneralizing, and finally to producing elaborate language use that involves complex sentence structures.

Developing as a Professional

Developing as a Professional Praxis™ Practice

At the beginning of the chapter, you saw how Karen Johnson used her understanding of student development to help her students learn about the concept *density*. Let's look now at Jenny Newhall, a first-grade teacher who is working with her children in a lesson on the properties of air. Read the case study, and answer the questions that follow.

Jenny gathers her first graders around her on the rug in front of a small table to begin her science lesson. After they're settled, she turns to a fishbowl filled with water and an empty glass and asks students to makes several observations of them. She then says, "I'm going to put this glass upside down in the water. What's going to happen? What do you think?. . . Michelle?"

". . . Water will go in the glass."

"No, it'll stay dry," Samantha counters.

Jenny then says, "Raise your hand if you think it will get water in it. . . . Okay,. . . raise your hand if you think it'll remain dry. . . . How many aren't sure?. . . Well, let's see if we can find out.

"First, we have to be sure it's dry. Terry, because you're not sure, I want you to help me by feeling the inside of the glass. How does it feel? Is it dry?"

"Yeah," Terry replies after putting his hand into the glass.

Then Jenny asks students to watch carefully as she pushes the inverted glass under the water, as shown here:

"Is the glass all the way under?" she asks.

The class agrees that it is.

Terry then offers, "There's water inside it. I can see the water inside."

"Then what will it feel like when I pull it out?"

"Wet," Terry responds.

Jenny pulls the glass carefully out of the water and asks Terry to check the inside.

"How does it feel?"

"Wet."

Jenny is momentarily taken aback. For students to begin to understand that air takes up space, the inside of the glass has to be dry. After a brief pause, she says, "Samantha, come up here and tell us what you feel."

Samantha touches the glass. "It's wet on the outside but dry on the inside."

"It's wet!" Terry asserts.

With a look of concern, Jenny says, "Uh, oh! We have two differing opinions. We've got to find out how to solve this problem."

She continues, "Let's dry this glass off and start again. Only this time, we're going to put a paper towel in the glass." She wads up a paper towel and pushes it to the bottom of the glass. "Now if water goes in the glass, what is the paper towel going to look like?"

The class agrees it will be wet and soggy.

She holds up the glass. "Okay, it's dry now. The paper towel is up in there. We're going to put it in the water again and see what happens."

The class watches as Jenny pushes the glass into the water again and, after a few seconds, pulls it back out.

"Okay, Marisse, come up here and check the paper towel and tell us whether it's wet or dry."

Marisse feels the towel, thinks for a moment, and says, "Dry."

"Why did it stay dry?. . . Raise your hand if you can tell us why it stayed dry. What do you think, Jessica?"

"'Cause it's inside and the water is outside?"

"But why didn't the water go into the glass? What kept the water out? . . . Anthony?"

"A water seal."

"A water seal," Jenny repeats, forcing herself not to smile. Hmm. . . . There's all that water on the outside. How come it didn't go inside? . . . How can the towel stay dry?"

A quiet voice volunteers, "Because there's air in there."

"Air. . . . Is that what kept the water out?" Jenny asks.

"Well, earlier Samantha said that when she was swimming in a pool and put a glass under the water, it stayed dry, but when she tipped it, it got wet inside. Now what do you think will happen if I put the glass under the water and tip it? . . . Devon?"

"It'll get wet."

Jenny removes the paper towel and returns the glass to the fishbowl.

"Let's see. Now watch very carefully. What is happening?" Jenny asks as she slowly tips the inverted glass, allowing some of the bubbles to escape. "Andrea?"

"There are bubbles."

"Andrea, what were those bubbles made of?"

"They're air bubbles."

"Now look at the glass. What do you see?" Jenny asked, pointing to the half-empty glass upside down in the water. "In the bottom half is water. What's in the top half?"

"It's dry."

"What's up in there?"

"Air."

"Air is up there. Well, how can I get that air out?"

"Tip it over some more," several students respond.

Jenny tips the glass, and additional bubbles float to the surface.

"Samantha, how does that work? When I tip the glass over, what's pushing the air out?"

". . . The water," Samantha offers.

"So, when I tip it this way"(tipping it until more bubbles came out),"what's pushing the air out?"

"Water," several students answer in unison.

Jenny then divides the class for small-group work. In groups of four or five, students use tubs of water, glasses, and paper towels to experiment on their own. After each student has a chance to try the activities, Jenny again calls the children together, and they review and summarize what they have found.

Short-Answer Questions

In answering these questions, use information from the chapter and link your responses to specific information in the case.

1. At what level of cognitive development were Jenny's students likely to be? Was her instruction effective for that level? Explain.
2. Why was the medium of water important for Jenny's lesson? How does this relate to Piaget's levels of development?
3. When Samantha and Terry disagreed about the condition of the inside of the glass, how did Jenny respond? What other alternatives might she have pursued? What are the advantages and disadvantages of these alternatives?
4. Did Jenny conduct the lesson in the students' zones of proximal development? Explain why you do or do not think so. What forms of scaffolding did Jenny provide? How effective was the scaffolding?

ONLINE PORTFOLIO ACTIVITIES

To develop your professional portfolio, further apply your understanding of chapter content, and address the INTASC standards, go the Companion Website, then to the *Online Portfolio Activities* for Chapter 2. Complete the suggested activities.

IMPORTANT CONCEPTS

accommodation (p. 35)
adaptation (p. 35)
assimilation (p. 35)
axon (p. 32)
centration (p. 38)
classification (p. 39)
conservation (p. 37)
dendrites (p. 32)
development (p. 30)
egocentrism (p. 38)
equilibrium (p. 34)
holophrases (p. 54)
language acquisition device
   (LAD) (p. 53)
maturation (p. 31)
nativist theory (p. 53)
neuron (p. 32)

object permanence (p. 36)
organization (p. 34)
overgeneralization (p. 54)
private speech (p. 47)
reversibility (p. 38)
scaffolding (p. 49)
schemes (p. 34)
seriation (p. 39)
social experience (p. 36)
sociocultural theory
   of development (p. 45)
synapses (p. 32)
transformation (p. 38)
transitivity (p. 39)
undergeneralization (p. 54)
zone of proximal development (p. 49)

CHAPTER 3

Personal, Social, and Emotional Development

Chapter Outline

Personal Development
Heredity • Parents and Other Adults • Peers

Social Development
Perspective Taking: Understanding Others' Thoughts and Feelings • Social Problem Solving • Violence and Aggression in Schools • Promoting Social Development: Instructional Principles

The Development of Identity and Self-Concept
Erikson's Theory of Psychosocial Development • The Development of Identity • The Development of Self-Concept • Promoting Psychosocial, Identity, and Self-Concept Development: Instructional Principles • Ethnic Pride: Promoting Positive Self-Esteem and Ethnic Identity

Development of Morality, Social Responsibility, and Self-Control
Increased Interest in Moral Education and Development • Piaget's Description of Moral Development • Kohlberg's Theory of Moral Development • Emotional Factors in Moral Development • Promoting Moral Development: Instructional Principles • Learning Contexts: Promoting Personal, Social, and Moral Development in Urban Environments

Learning Objectives

After you have completed your study of this chapter, you should be able to

1 Describe the factors influencing personal development, and explain how differences in parenting and peer interactions can influence this development.

2 Describe characteristics that indicate advancing social development, and explain how social development relates to school violence and aggression.

3 Use descriptions of psychosocial, identity, and self-concept development to explain learners' behaviors.

4 Use descriptions of moral reasoning to explain differences in people's responses to ethical issues.

In Chapter 2 you studied theories that describe cognitive development, and there you found that younger students think in ways that are qualitatively different from older learners. We now examine the personal, social, and moral development of our students. As you read the following case study, think about these forms of development and their influence on student learning.

"Ahh," Anne Dillard, an eighth-grade English teacher, sighs as she slumps into a chair in the faculty lounge.

"Tough day?" her friend Beth asks.

"Yes, it's Sean again," Anne nods. "I just can't seem to get through to him. He won't do his work, and he has a bad attitude about school in general. I talked with his mother, and she said he's been a handful since birth. He doesn't get along with the other students, and when I talk with him about it, he says they're picking on him for no reason. I don't know what's going to become of him. The funny thing is, I get the feeling that he knows he's out of line, but he just can't seem to change."

"I know what you mean," Beth responds. "I had him for English last year. He was a tough one, very distant. He lost his dad in a messy divorce; his mother got custody of him, and his father just split. Every once in a while, he'd open up to me, but then the wall would go up again. . . . And his younger brother seems so different. He's eager and cooperative, and he seems to get along with everyone. . . . Same home, same situation."

"Sean's a bright boy, too," Anne continues, "but he seems to prefer avoiding work to doing it. I know that I can help him . . . if I can just figure out how."

As you begin your study of this chapter, think about three questions. (1) How might we explain why Sean and his younger brother are so different? (2) What factors influence people's personal and social development? (3) How do personal and social development relate to academic achievement and satisfaction with school? We address these and other questions in this chapter.

PERSONAL DEVELOPMENT

When we use the term **personal development,** we are describing the growth of enduring personality traits that influence the way individuals interact with their physical and social environments. The primary causes of this development are heredity and the environmental influences of parents, other adults, and peers. These factors are outlined in Figure 3.1 and discussed in the sections that follow.

Figure 3.1 Influences on personal development

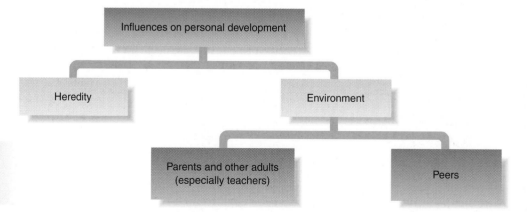

Personal development. The growth of enduring personality traits that influence the way individuals interact with their physical and social environments

Heredity

People differ in **temperament,** the relatively stable inherited characteristics that influence the way we respond to social and physical stimuli. For example, individuals vary in traits such as adventurousness, happiness, irritability, and confidence, and these differences persist over time (Berk, 2006). Siblings raised in the same environments often develop very different personalities. This helps us answer our first question. It is likely that heredity largely explains why Sean has been "a handful since birth," whereas his brother is "eager and cooperative."

Parents and Other Adults

Parents also exert an important influence on children's personal development (Grolnick, Kurowski, & Gurland, 1999). This isn't surprising, given the amount of time children, and especially young children, spend with their parents. Experts estimate that children up to age 18 spend 87 percent of their waking hours outside of school under the guidance of their parents (Kamil & Walberg, 2005).

Interaction with teachers and other adults provides opportunities for students' personal development.

Research indicates that certain parenting styles promote more healthy personal development than others (Baumrind, 1991), and the effects of these styles can last into the college years, influencing grades, motivation, and relationships with teachers (Collins, Maccoby, Steinberg, Hetherington, & Bornstein, 2000).

Researchers have found two important differences among parents in the ways they relate to their children: their *expectations* and their *responsiveness*. Some set high expectations and insist that these expectations are met; others expect little of their children and rarely try to influence them. Responsive parents accept their children and frequently interact with them; unresponsive parents tend to be rejecting, negative, or indifferent. Using expectations and responsiveness as a framework, researchers have identified four parenting styles and the patterns of personal development associated with them. They are summarized in Table 3.1.

As we see in Table 3.1, an authoritative parenting style, one that combines high expectations and responsiveness, is most effective for promoting healthy personal development. Children need challenge, structure, and support in their lives, and authoritative parents provide them.

Temperament. The relatively stable inherited characteristics that influence the way we respond to social and physical stimuli

Table 3.1 Parenting styles and patterns of personal development

Interaction Style	Parental Characteristics	Child Characteristics
Authoritative	Are firm but caring. Explain reasons for rules, and are consistent. Have high expectations.	High self-esteem. Confident and secure. Willing to take risks, and are successful in school.
Authoritarian	Stress conformity. Are detached, don't explain rules, and do not encourage verbal give-and-take.	Withdrawn. Worry more about pleasing parent than solving problems. Defiant, and lack social skills.
Permissive	Give children total freedom. Have limited expectations, and make few demands on children.	Immature, and lack self-control. Impulsive. Unmotivated.
Uninvolved	Have little interest in their child's life. Hold few expectations.	Lack self-control and long-term goals. Easily frustrated and disobedient.

The other styles are less effective. Authoritarian parents, for example, are rigid and unresponsive; at the extreme, they produce children with low self-esteem and aggressive coping behaviors (Maughan & Cicchetti, 2002). Further, if they set high expectations but are not responsive, children may view the expectations as unfair, and rebel. Permissive parents are emotionally responsive but fail to set and maintain high expectations. Uninvolved parents are laissez-faire, providing neither expectations nor responsiveness.

Healthy parent–child relationships promote personal development by helping children acquire a sense of autonomy, competence, and belonging (Christenson & Havsy, 2004; Grolnick et al., 1999; Wentzel, 1999a). Such relationships also support the development of personal responsibility, the ability to control one's own actions based on developing values and goals.

Other adults, most commonly teachers, also contribute to students' personal development. The interaction styles of effective teachers are similar to those of effective parents, and the description of authoritative parenting strongly parallels recommended classroom management practices for teachers (Gill, Achton, & Algina, 2003).

As you'll see in Chapter 12, effective teachers are clear about classroom rules and procedures, take the time to explain why they are necessary, and involve students in forming them. They have high expectations for their students, but they're simultaneously supportive. When disruptions occur, they quickly intervene, eliminate problems, and return just as quickly to learning activities. Like authoritative parents, they are firm but caring, establish rules and limits, and expect students to develop and use self-control. Research indicates that this kind of teacher support leads to increased student motivation, enhanced self-concept, and the development of self-regulation (Branson, 2000; Elias, 2004). Although they spend less time with children than parents, teachers strongly influence learners' personal development (K. Brown, Anfara, & Roney, 2004).

Peers

Peers also influence personal development in two important ways: by communicating attitudes and values and by offering, or not offering, friendship (Betts, Zau, & Rice, 2003; A. M. Ryan, 2000). Peers most commonly communicate their attitudes in day-to-day interactions. Many occur in organized clubs or teams, whereas others happen in informal cliques and neighborhood groups (A. M. Ryan, 2001; Trawick-Smith, 1997).

Peer influences can be both positive and negative (Farmer et al., 2002). Researchers have found that a student's choice of friends predicts grades, disruptive behaviors, and teachers' ratings of involvement in school (Berk, 2006). When students select academically oriented friends, their grades improve; when they choose disruptive friends, their grades decline and behavior problems increase.

In some instances, ethnicity plays a role (Horvat & Lewis, 2003; Steinberg, Brown, & Dornbusch, 1996). For example, as a general pattern, Asian students are more likely than American students to have friends who emphasize academic achievement. They are also more likely to say that their friends think it is important to do well in school and to say that they work hard to keep up with their friends (Steinberg et al., 1996). This helps explain the generally high academic success of Asian and Asian-American students.

The opposite is also sometimes true. In pockets of some minority groups, academic success is viewed as "selling out." Media messages sometimes portray successful minority youth as being hip, tough, or cool, but not academically oriented. To combat these messages, these youth need role models who can demonstrate that being a member of a minority group and being academically successful are compatible (Berndt, 1999).

Offering or not offering friendship is the second way that peers influence personal development. Students who are socially accepted and offered friendships are more motivated, achieve higher, have healthier self-concepts, and are generally more satisfied with life than those receiving less support (Gauvain, 2001; Wentzel, 1999a). At the other extreme, rejection by peers can hamper personal development and can lead to loneliness and isolation, poor academic work, and dropping out of school (Bierman, 2004).

Checking Your Understanding

1.1   Describe and explain the factors influencing personal development.

1.2   In the opening case study, Sean's mother commented, ". . . he's been a handful since birth." Which of the three factors influencing personal development does this suggest? What concept summarizes this influence?

1.3   A parent, discussing a behavioral problem with the teacher, throws his hands up in exasperation, and says, "I can't do anything with him. I don't think he'll ever amount to much. He has been a load of trouble since day one." What two elements of parental influence are suggested in these comments?

1.4   Explain how differences in peer interactions can influence individuals' personal development.

To receive feedback for these questions, go to Appendix B.

Knowledge Extensions

To deepen your understanding of the topics in this section of the chapter and integrate them with topics you've already studied, go to the *Knowledge Extensions* module for Chapter 3 at *www.prenhall.com/eggen*. Respond to questions 1 and 2.

SOCIAL DEVELOPMENT

Social development describes the advances people make in their ability to interact and get along with others, and it affects both learning and satisfaction with learning experiences (Coolahan et al., 2000). Understanding social development helps us contribute to this important process.

In a comprehensive review of research in this area, experts concluded, "there is a growing body of scientifically based research supporting the strong impact that enhanced social and emotional behaviors can have on success in school and ultimately in life" (Zins, Bloodworth, Weissberg, Wang, & Walberg, 2004, p. 19). These researchers linked healthy social development to a number of important outcomes including school success and reduced dropout and substance abuse rates. This helps us answer our third question, "How do personal and social development relate to academic achievement and satisfaction with school?" Students who are well developed personally and socially achieve higher and enjoy school more than their less well-developed peers.

In the following sections, we examine perspective taking and social problem solving, two important dimensions of social development.

Perspective taking and problem solving are important components in learners' social development.

Perspective Taking: Understanding Others' Thoughts and Feelings

To begin this section, let's look at four fifth graders working together on a project.

Octavio, Mindy, Sarah, and Bill are studying American westward expansion in social studies. They'd been working as a group for 3 days and are preparing a report to be delivered to the class. There is some disagreement about who should present which topics.

"So what should we do?" Mindy asks, looking at the others. "Octavio, Sarah, and Bill all want to report on the Pony Express."

"I thought of it first," Octavio argues.

"But everyone knows I like horses," Sarah counters

"Why don't we compromise?" Mindy asks "Octavio, didn't you say that you were kind of interested in railroads because your grandfather worked on them? Couldn't you talk to

Social development. The advances people make in their ability to interact and get along with others

him and get some information for the report? And Sarah, I know you like horses. Couldn't you report on horses and the Plains Indians? . . . And Bill, what about you?"

"I don't care . . . whatever," Bill replies, folding his arms and peering belligerently at the group.

Perspective taking is the ability to understand the thoughts and feelings of others. When Mindy suggested that Octavio and Sarah switch assignments because of their interest in different topics, for example, she demonstrated this ability.

Research indicates that perspective taking develops slowly and is related to Piaget's stages of cognitive development (Flavell, 2000). To measure perspective-taking abilities, researchers show children scenarios similar to the preceding one and ask them to explain different people's thinking. Children up to about age 8 typically don't understand Bill's angry response or why Octavio might be happy reporting on railroads. As they develop, their ability to see the world from other people's perspectives grows.

People skilled in perspective taking handle difficult social situations well, display empathy and compassion (Schult, 2002), and are well liked by their peers (Berk, 2006). Those less effective tend to interpret the intentions of others as hostile, which can lead to arguing, fighting, and other antisocial acts. They also tend to feel no guilt or remorse when they hurt other people's feelings (Crick, Grotpeter, & Bigbee, 2002; Dodge et al., 2003).

Social Problem Solving

Social problem solving, the ability to resolve conflicts in ways that are beneficial to all involved, is closely related to perspective taking. Mindy displayed social problem-solving skills when she suggested a compromise that would satisfy everyone.

Research suggests that social problem solving is similar to problem solving in general (we examine problem solving in Chapter 9) and involves processes that can be described in four sequential steps (Berk, 2006):

1. Observe and interpret social cues. ("Bill seems upset, probably because he isn't getting his first choice.")
2. Identify social goals. ("If we are going to finish this project, everyone must contribute.")
3. Generate strategies. ("Can we find different topics that will satisfy everyone?")
4. Implement and evaluate the strategies. ("This will work if everyone agrees to shift their topic slightly.")

Social problem solving is a valuable tool. Students who are good at it have more friends, fight less, and work more efficiently in groups than those who are less skilled (D. W. Johnson & Johnson, 2004; H. Patrick, Anderman, & Ryan, 2002).

Research indicates that, like perspective taking, social problem solving develops gradually and with practice (Berk, 2006). Young children, for example, are not adept at reading social cues, and they tend to create simplistic solutions that satisfy themselves but not others. Older children realize that persuasion and compromise can benefit everyone, and they're better at adapting when initial efforts aren't successful.

Violence and Aggression in Schools

Unfortunately, school violence and aggression are a persistent problem, and experts link this trend to problems with personal and social development (D. W. Johnson & Johnson, 2004; Lopes & Salovey, 2004). The widely publicized Columbine massacre in 1999, in which two students killed a teacher and 12 of their peers, and the more recent Red Lake, Minnesota, tragedy in 2005 in which a student killed 5 of his peers, a teacher, and an unarmed security guard, together with other shooting incidents in schools around the nation, dramatically underscore this problem.

National statistics are also disconcerting. Averages of 14 children die each day from gunfire in the United States (Children's Defense Fund, 1999). This country continues to have the highest rates of youth suicides, homicides, and firearms-related deaths of any of the world's 26 wealthiest nations (Aspy et al., 2004). Bullying, a more subtle form of school violence, is an ongoing problem, with up to one third of students saying they experience it frequently (D. Cooper & Snell, 2003; Viadero, 2003).

Perspective taking. The ability to understand the thoughts and feelings of others

Social problem solving. The ability to resolve conflicts in ways that are beneficial to all involved

Proactive aggression, aggression that involves overt hostile acts toward someone else, is the most troublesome pattern. Proactively aggressive students have difficulty maintaining friendships and are at increased risk for engaging in delinquent activities. Aggressive tendencies cause problems both in school and in life after the school years (Dodge et al., 2003).

The causes of aggressive behavior, like development in general, are complex. Genetics plays a role, and beginning in the preschool years, boys are more physically aggressive than girls (Lippa, 2002). Experts estimate that boys bully more than girls by a ratio of 3:1, although this ratio may be due to a greater tendency to report physical rather than verbal bullying and girls bullying tends to be more verbal (Ma, 2001). In addition, adolescent males are 10 times more likely than girls to be involved in antisocial behavior and violent crime (U.S. Department of Justice, 1999).

Aggression is also learned, with modeling and reinforcement playing major roles (N. E. Goldstein, Arnold, Rosenberg, Stowe, & Ortiz, 2001; Guerra, Huesman, & Spendler, 2003). For example, bullies typically come from homes where parents are authoritarian, hostile, and rejecting. Their parents frequently have poor problem-solving skills and often advocate fighting as the solution to conflicts (Ma, 2001). In addition, aggression may be linked to deficits in perspective taking, empathy, moral development, and emotional self-regulation (Crick et al., 2002).

Attempts to prevent aggression and violence in schools focus on peer mediation and programs designed to develop social problem-solving skills. Peer-mediation programs attempt to teach students conflict-resolution abilities. In one of the best known, designed by David and Roger Johnson (2004), a mediator guides peers through five conflict-resolution steps in which students jointly define the conflict, exchange positions and perspectives, reverse those perspectives, and invent solutions to the problem that are mutually beneficial and agreed upon. The students involved in the conflict not only resolve their own problems but also learn how to mediate others' disputes. Schools in which students were trained in conflict resolution and peer mediation had fewer management problems, both within classrooms and on school grounds (D. Johnson & Johnson, 2004). In addition, students continued to use these conflict-resolution strategies both at school and at home.

Programs designed to teach social problem-solving skills focus on substituting peaceful alternatives for force (Zirpoli & Melloy, 2001). With young children, teachers may use puppet skits to present social dilemmas, which children discuss and try to solve. In programs for older children, teachers often ask students to read and respond to scenarios like the one involving Octavio, Mindy, Sarah, and Bill. Research indicates that students in these programs improve in both their social problem-solving abilities and their classroom behavior (Berk, 2006; McDevitt & Ormrod, 2004).

These strategies attack the problem of violence and aggression at the individual level. Equally important is a school climate that discourages violence and aggression and openly communicates that they won't be tolerated (Ma, 2001). Parental involvement is important, and students need to know that teachers and administrators are committed to safe schools (Christenson & Havsy, 2004; Kerr, 2000).

Instructional [] Principles

Promoting Social Development: Instructional Principles

As with other aspects of learning, social development can be advanced through understanding, practice, and feedback. You can make important contributions to social development by modeling social skills and by organizing and maintaining your classroom in ways that contribute to this process (Elias, 2004). The following strategies can guide you in your efforts:

1. Model and explicitly teach the kinds of social skills that you expect in your students.
2. Establish rules governing acceptable classroom behavior.
3. Help students understand the reasons for rules by providing examples and guiding discussions.
4. Have students practice social skills, and give them feedback.

Proactive aggression. Aggression that involves overt hostile acts toward someone else

Teachers can promote learners' social development by acting as role models and creating classroom environments in which students can practice social skills.

Let's see how these principles guide Teresa Manteras, a first-year teacher, as she works with her sixth graders.

"How are you doing, Teresa?" Carla Ambergi, a colleague and veteran of 5 years, asks as Teresa slumps into a chair in the teachers' lounge. "Everything okay?"

"A little discouraged," Teresa sighs. "I learned about all those cooperative learning activities in my university classes, but when I try them out with my kids, all they want to do is fight and snip at each other. Maybe I should just lecture."

"Hang in there," Carla smiles. "They're just not used to working in groups, and they haven't yet learned how to cooperate with each other. Like everything else in life, the more they practice the better they get at it."

"Yes, I know that, . . . but I don't even know where to start. As I turn to help one group, two other groups start arguing."

"Would you like me to come in during my planning period? Maybe I can offer a few suggestions."

"That would be great!" Teresa replies with a big sense of relief.

Carla comes in the next day, and she and Teresa sit down together after school. "First," Carla smiles, "I think you do an excellent job of modeling social skills. You consider where the kids are coming from, you treat disagreements as an opportunity to solve problems, and you are courteous and supportive. . . . However, your modeling goes right over their heads. They don't notice what you're doing. So, I suggest that you tell the kids what you're modeling, and point out examples in your own behavior, or in the behavior of one of the kids, that illustrate the kinds of social skills you're trying to develop. It will take some time, but it will make a difference."

"Good point," Teresa nods. "I hadn't quite thought about it that way before."

Carla then helps Teresa develop some rules that specifically address student behavior in groups:

1. Listen politely until other people are finished before speaking.
2. Treat other people's ideas with courtesy and respect.
3. Paraphrase other people's ideas in your own words before disagreeing.
4. Encourage everyone in the group to participate.

The next day, armed with Carla's encouragement and her new rules, Teresa confronts the issue head on. Before breaking the students into groups for project work, she tells them that she is going to model social skills for them and that she wants them to do the same for each other. She gives several examples, and she presents the new rules and explains why they're necessary. For each, she asks volunteers to role-play an example in front of the others. She guides a discussion of each example to help the students understand what it is intended to illustrate.

Students then begin their group work. Teresa carefully monitors each group and intervenes when they have difficulties. In one case, several groups have the same problem, so she reconvenes the class, discusses the problem, and asks students to practice the new skill in their groups. The students are far from perfect, but they are improving.

Now let's look at Teresa's attempts to apply the principles for promoting social development in her classroom. She applied the first by modeling and explicitly teaching her students the social skills she wanted them to develop. Just as learning to write, for example, involves understanding grammar and punctuation together with a great deal of practice, developing social skills involves both understanding and practice in interactions with others (Elias, 2004; Osterman, 2000).

Teresa applied the second principle by creating a set of rules intended to guide students as they worked together. This is important because rules provide specific guidelines to assist students during social interaction. She presented only four rules, in part because they supplemented her general classroom rules, but also because too many rules increases the likelihood that students will forget one or more of them.

Third, Teresa provided concrete examples of the rules by having students role-play social situations and then, through discussion, helping them understand what the role-playing illustrated. Her modeling provided additional examples of desirable social skills and behaviors.

Finally, Teresa provided opportunities for students to practice their social skills during group work, and she gave them feedback during the activities. Students won't become socially skilled in one or two activities, but with time, practice, and explicit instruction, such as Teresa provided, they can become more skilled at working with each other in groups (Gillies, 2003; D W. Johnson & Johnson, 2004, 2006).

Checking Your Understanding

2.1 Describe and explain two characteristics that indicate advancing social development.

2.2 Two kindergarteners are arguing about who gets to play at the water table next. Their teacher approaches them and says, "Hmm. It looks like you both want to play at the water table at the same time. What could we do to make both of you happy?" What dimension of social development is this teacher trying to promote?

2.3 Explain how school violence and aggression relate to social development. Describe the causes of violent and aggressive behaviors in children.

To receive feedback for these questions, go to Appendix B.

Exploring Further

To read more about different instructional strategies to teach social problem solving skills, go to "Teaching Social Problem Solving Skills" in the *Exploring Further* module of Chapter 3 at *www.prenhall.com/eggen*.

Knowledge Extensions

To deepen your understanding of the topics in this section of the chapter and integrate them with topics you've already studied, go to the *Knowledge Extensions* module for Chapter 3 at *www.prenhall.com/eggen*. Respond to questions 3–5.

Classroom Connections

Applying an Understanding of Personal and Social Development in Your Classroom

Personal Development

1. Discuss peer relationships and personal responsibility with students.

- **Elementary:** At the end of each day, a third-grade teacher calls a "meeting" in which they discuss classroom problems that arose that day, the ways in which classmates should treat one another, and other issues related to personal responsibility.
- **Middle School:** An eighth-grade homeroom teacher spends time each week discussing topics such as friendship, the need to be personally responsible, and the effort everyone should make to influence friends in positive ways.
- **High School:** A health teacher encourages his students to think about the influence of peers when they discuss topics such as drugs, diet, and dating. He tries to help them understand how peers can have both a positive and negative influence on their personal development.

Social Development

2. Encourage students to consider the perspectives of others.

- **Elementary:** A fourth-grade teacher has her students analyze different characters' motives and feelings when they discuss a story they've read. She asks, "How does the character feel? Why does the character feel that way? How would you feel if you were that person?"
- **Middle School:** A middle school science teacher stays after school to provide opportunities for students to ask questions about their work in his class. The conversations often drift to interpersonal problems the students are having with parents or friends. The teacher listens patiently but also encourages students to think about the motives and feelings of the other people involved.
- **High School:** A history teacher encourages her students to consider point of view when they read reports of historical events. For example, when her students study the Civil War, she reminds them that both sides thought they were morally right, and she asks questions such as these: "Why was the topic of states' rights so controversial? How did the opponents interpret the Emancipation Proclamation?"

3. Involve students in social problem solving.

- **Elementary:** A third-grade teacher periodically has groups of four students check each others' math homework. He passes out two answer sheets to each group and asks students to decide how to proceed. When the students don't accept equal responsibilities, or conflicts arise, he encourages students to work out the problems themselves and intervenes only if they cannot resolve the problems.
- **Middle School:** An eighth-grade English teacher sometimes purposefully leaves decisions about individual assignments up to the groups in cooperative learning activities. When disagreements occur, she offers only enough assistance to get the group back on track. If the problem is widespread, she calls a whole-class meeting to discuss the problem.
- **High School:** When art students argue about space and access to materials and supplies, their teacher requires them to discuss the problem and suggest solutions acceptable to everyone.

THE DEVELOPMENT OF IDENTITY AND SELF-CONCEPT

People's **identity**—their sense of self, who they are, what their existence means, and what they want in life—combines with their **self-concept**—a cognitive assessment of their physical, social, and academic competence—to influence the way they respond to learning activities and their environments in general. In this section, we consider these factors and their implications for us as teachers.

Erikson's Theory of Psychosocial Development

The work of Erik Erikson (1902–1994) was strongly influenced by his search for his own identity, and he believed, as he described it, that he experienced a "crisis of identity" (Cross, 2001). He also believed that a primary motivation for human behavior was social and reflected a desire to affiliate with other people (Santrock, 2006). Because he integrated identity and social factors in his theory of development, it is described as a *psychosocial* theory (Erikson, 1968, 1980). His theory is also unique in the sense that he believed developmental changes occur throughout the lifespan.

Erikson believed that all people have the same basic needs. Personal development occurs in response to these needs and depends on the quality of the care and support provided by the social environment, particularly caregivers. Development proceeds in stages, each characterized by a **crisis,** a psychosocial challenge that presents opportunities for development (Santrock, 2006). Although no crisis is permanently resolved, a positive resolution of one psychosocial challenge increases the likelihood of a positive resolution at the next stage. The stages are summarized in Table 3.2.

Table 3.2 Erikson's eight life-span stages

Trust vs. Mistrust (Birth to 1 year)	Trust develops when infants receive consistently loving care. Mistrust results from unpredictable or harsh care.
Autonomy vs. Shame (1–3 years)	Autonomy develops when children use their newly formed mental and psychomotor skills to explore their worlds. Parents support autonomy by encouraging exploration and accepting the inevitable mistakes.
Initiative vs. Guilt (3–6 years)	Initiative, a sense of ambition and responsibility, develops from encouragement of children's efforts to explore and take on new challenges. Overcontrol or criticism can result in guilt.
Industry vs. Inferiority (6–12 years)	School and home provide opportunities for students to develop a sense of competence through success on challenging tasks. A pattern of failure can lead to feelings of inferiority.
Identify vs. Confusion (12–18 years)	Adolescents experiment with various roles in an atmosphere of freedom with clearly established limits. Confusion results when the home environment fails to provide either the necessary structure or when it is overly controlling, failing to provide opportunities for individual exploration with different identity roles.
Intimacy vs. Isolation (Young adulthood)	Intimacy occurs when individuals establish close ties with others. Emotional isolation may result from earlier disappointments or a lack of developing identity.
Generativity vs. Stagnation (Adulthood)	Generativity occurs when adults give to the next generation through child rearing, productive work, and contributions to society or other people. Apathy or self-absorption can result from an inability to think about or contribute to the welfare of others.
Integrity vs. Despair (Old age)	Integrity occurs when people believe they've lived as well as possible and accept the inevitability of death. Remorse over things done or left undone leads to despair.

Identity. Individuals' sense of self, who they are, what their existence means, and what they want in life

Self-concept. Individuals' cognitive assessment of their physical, social, and academic competence

Crisis. A psychosocial challenge that presents opportunities for development

While positive resolution of the crisis at one stage better prepares people for resolution at the next, Erikson didn't believe that a completely positive resolution is always ideal. For instance, while learning to trust people is a positive resolution of his first stage, we cannot trust all people under all circumstances. However, in a healthy solution to the challenge at each stage, the positive resolution predominates.

Putting Erikson's Work into Perspective

Erikson's work was popular and influential in the 1960s and 1970s, but since then, developmental theorists have taken issue with it on at least three points. First, some researchers argue that Erikson failed to adequately address the important role of culture in personal, emotional, and social development. For instance, some cultures discourage autonomy and initiative in young children, perhaps as a way of protecting them from dangers in their environments (Dennis, Cole, Zahn-Waxler, & Mizuta, 2002).

Second, Erikson's description of intimacy following the development of identity has been criticized. For many adolescents, especially female, establishing a sense of intimacy may occur with, or even precede, a focus on identity (Kroger, 2000).

Third, as we'll see in our discussion of identity development later in the chapter, many people don't achieve a sense of identity as early as Erikson suggested.

Erikson's work is intuitively sensible, however, and it helps explain behaviors we see in others. For example, we might explain Sean's contention that the other students are "picking on him for no reason," by saying that he didn't positively resolve the trust–distrust crisis. This left him less able to develop a sense of autonomy, initiative, or industry, which helps us understand why he "won't do his work." We've all met people we admire because of their positive outlook, openness, and commitment to making the world a better place. We've also encountered those who believe that others are trying to take advantage of them or are somehow inherently evil. We see good minds sliding into lethargy because of a lack of initiative or even substance abuse. We become frustrated by people's apathy and lack of a zest for living. Erikson's work helps us understand these issues.

Supporting Psychosocial Development

Erikson's work also reminds us that teachers are essential in creating social environments that contribute to students' growth, and it offers sensible suggestions for working with students during the early childhood, elementary, and adolescent years. Let's look at some of these suggestions.

Early Childhood. As children enter preschool and kindergarten, they are taking on more tasks and searching eagerly for experiences. "Let me help!" and "I want to do it" are signs of this initiative. As children go through these changes, teachers can do much to help them develop into happy and healthy individuals.

> Olivia Hernandez is watching her kindergarteners work on an art activity.
> "Good, Felipe. I see you've used a lot of colors to draw your bird. That's a very pretty bird," she comments as she moves around the room.
> "Nice, Taeko. Those are really bright colors. They make me feel happy.
> "Look what Raymond did. He cut out his picture when he was done. That's a nice job of cutting."

Felipe and Taeko made their own decisions about coloring, and Raymond decided on his own to cut out the picture when he finished. Olivia's encouragement and reinforcement supported that initiative. In contrast, criticism or overly restrictive directions detract from the sense of independence and, in extreme cases, lead to feelings of guilt and dependency. Simple, self-chosen tasks form the concrete challenges that children use to express their growing initiative. Healthy psychosocial development depends less on children's performance than on adults' responses to them. Adult affirmation in the form of support and encouragement is essential.

The Elementary Years.

> "I believe that Atlanta will have a warmer climate than Bogota," Enrique, one of Tim Duncan's fifth graders, comments during a geography lesson.

Early childhood and elementary classrooms should provide opportunities for students to develop personal independence and initiative.

Conversations with caring adults provide opportunities for adolescents to think about and refine their developing personal identities.

"That's an interesting idea," Tim responds. "Why do you think so, considering Bogota is much nearer the equator?"

"Bogota is high up . . . and Atlanta isn't. It isn't always just being farther south that makes it warm."

"That's very insightful," Tim smiles. "That's the kind of thinking we want to be doing in here. Excellent, Enrique."

During the elementary years, students are attempting to acquire a belief in their competence. Teachers support these efforts when they provide challenging learning experiences and help learners succeed in them. This isn't easy. Activities that are so challenging that students frequently fail can leave them with a sense of inferiority and a lack of confidence in their capabilities. On the other hand, success on trivial tasks does little to make students feel competent (Brophy, 2004). Tim's professional expertise helped him find the right mix in his geography lesson.

Erikson's concept of industry incorporates several elements of healthy development: a positive self-concept, pride in accomplishment, and responsibility for our actions (Berk, 2005). These same characteristics are found in students who are motivated to learn (Brophy, 2004).

Adolescence. Adolescence is a unique time when students experience physical, emotional, and intellectual changes. They go through growth spurts, and their coordination doesn't keep up with their bodies. The magnitude of physical change in early adolescence is surpassed only during infancy. Adolescents are frequently confused about how to respond to new sexual feelings. They are concerned with what others think of them and are preoccupied with their looks. They are caught in the awkward position of wanting to assert their independence, yet longing for the stability of structure and discipline. They want to rebel, but they want something solid to rebel against.

These changes and struggles don't necessarily doom teenagers to a period of distress and uncertainty, however. Most negotiate adolescence successfully and maintain positive relationships with their parents and other adults (Rudolph, Lambert, Clark, & Kurlakowsky, 2001). Contemporary theorists suggest that this is a time of *exploration* for them, because it reflects day-to-day experimentation with different roles and people (Berk, 2005, 2006).

Understanding emotionally developing adolescents helps teachers better respond to their sometimes capricious behavior. Fads and bizarre clothing and hairstyles, for example, reflect teenagers' urges to identify with groups while simultaneously searching for their individuality. If their behaviors don't interfere with learning or the rights of others, they shouldn't be major issues. You can help by taking the time to simply talk openly with students about their concerns. This is the best advice we can give teachers struggling to reach adolescents.

You saw that Anne and Beth, Sean's teachers, both tried to get Sean to "open up" to them. Perhaps more significant is the sensitivity they demonstrated in their efforts to reach him. Students, particularly at the middle and junior high levels, need firm, caring teachers, teachers who empathize with them while providing the security of clear limits for acceptable behavior (Rudolph et al., 2001).

The Development of Identity

At the beginning of this section, we said that identity is people's sense of self, who they are, what their existence means, and what they want in life. Social experiences, including informal cliques, organized clubs and teams, and neighborhoods and communities, all contribute to students' developing identities (Trawick-Smith, 2003). And for students who are members of cultural minorities, ethnic identity is also important (M. Jones, 1999). (We discuss the development of ethnic identity later in the chapter.)

During the process of identity development, adolescents often identify with a peer group, rigidly adhering to a style of dress or way of wearing their hair. Girls' skimpy, bare-stomach tops and boys' baggy pants, common in middle schools, are displays of these "temporary identities." In time they're replaced with a more individual sense of self and an awareness of lifelong goals.

Patterns in Identity Development

Four seniors are talking about what they plan to do after high school:

"I'm going into nursing," Taylor comments. "I've been working part-time at the hospital, and it feels really good. I thought I wanted to be a doctor at one time, but I don't think I can handle all the pressure. I've talked with the counselors, and I think I can do the chemistry and other science courses."

"I'm not sure what I want to do," Sandy comments. "I've thought about veterinary medicine, and also about teaching. I've been working at the vet clinic, and I like it, but I'm not sure about doing it forever. Some of my parents' friends are teachers, so I hear what they say about it. I don't know."

"I wish I could do that," Ramon replies. "But I'm off to the university in the fall. I'm going to be a lawyer. At least that's what my parents think. It's not a bad job, and lawyers make good money."

"How can you just do that?" Nancy wonders. "You've said that you don't want to be a lawyer. . . . I'm not willing to decide yet. I'm only 18. I'm going to think about it for a while."

The process of identity formation isn't smooth and uniform; it takes different paths, like a railroad train. Sometimes it's sitting on a holding spur beside the main track; at other times it's chugging full speed ahead.

To study the development of identity, researchers interviewed adolescents about their occupational, religious, and political choices and found that young people's decisions can be generally classified into one of four states. They're outlined in Table 3.3 (Marcia, 1980, 1987, 1999).

The different states vary in their ability to produce healthy outcomes. Identity moratorium, for instance, is a positive state that may eventually lead to identity achievement, which is also positive. In contrast, identity diffusion, common in younger adolescents, reflects haphazard consideration of different career choices. If it persists over time, it can result in apathy and confusion (Berzonsky & Kuk, 2000). Identity foreclosure, another less productive path, occurs when adolescents adopt the goals and values of others, usually their parents, without thoroughly examining the implications of those choices for their future. Many adolescents experience both identity moratorium and diffusion before arriving at identity achievement. Teachers and other adults can assist in this search by openly discussing the issues with students.

Research indicates that, in contrast with the predictions of Erikson's theory, identity achievement more often occurs after, than during, high school (Berzonsky & Kuk, 2000; Marcia, 1980, 1988). This delay is especially true for college students, who have more time to consider what they want to do with their lives.

Table 3.3 States in identity development

State	Description
Identity diffusion	Occurs when individuals fail to make clear choices. Characterized by haphazard experimentation with different career options. Choices may be difficult, or individuals aren't developmentally ready to make choices.
Identity foreclosure	Occurs when individuals prematurely adopt the positions of others, such as parents. This is an undesirable position because it is based on the identities of others.
Identity moratorium	Occurs when individuals pause and remain in a holding pattern. Long-range commitment is delayed.
Identity achievement	Occurs after individuals experience a period of crises and decision making. Identity achievement reflects a commitment to a goal or direction.

This research suggests that the uncertainty high school adolescents experience is related more to the demands of increased independence than to identity issues. Conflict with parents, teachers, and other adults peaks in early adolescence and then declines, as teenagers accept responsibility and adults learn how to deal with the new relationships (Arnett, 2002). The challenges of early adolescence help explain why teaching middle and junior high students can be particularly challenging.

Sexual Identity

Sexual identity, students' self-constructed definition of who they are with respect to gender orientation, is another important element of identity formation. Sexual identity influences students' choices, ranging from clothes and friends to the occupations they consider and ultimately pursue (Berk, 2004, 2006). **Sexual orientation,** the gender to which an individual is romantically and sexually attracted, is an important dimension of sexual identity (McDevitt & Ormrod, 2004).

For most students, sexual orientation is not a major issue, but for a portion of the student population (estimates range between 3 and 10 percent), sexual orientation is confusing and stressful (Berk, 2004, 2006; McDevitt & Ormrod, 2004). Attempts to describe the causes of homosexuality are both controversial and complex, with some believing that it is genetic and others attributing it to learning and choice (Gollnick & Chinn, 2004). Research suggests that there is a definite genetic component; if one member of identical twins is homosexual, for example, the other member is much more likely to also be homosexual than is the case with fraternal twins (Berk, 2004, 2006).

Research also suggests that homosexuals go through a three-phase sequence in their attempts to understand who they are sexually. The first is feeling different, a slowly developing awareness that they aren't like other children. One gay student described his experience:

> As long as I can remember, I always felt a little different when it came to having crushes on other people. When I was in elementary school I never had crushes on girls, and when I look back on that time now, I was probably most attracted to my male friends. I participated in some of the typical "boy" activities, like trading baseball cards and playing video games, but I was never very interested in rough sports. (McDevitt & Ormrod, 2004, p. 403)

The second phase is a feeling of confusion, which occurs during adolescence. In this phase, homosexuals attempt to understand their developing sexuality, looking for both social support and role models. The same gay male describes his feelings during this phase:

> To my dismay, middle school and the onset of puberty only brought more attention to my lack of interest in girls. The first time I thought about being gay was when I was in the 6th grade, so I was probably 11 or 12 years old at the time. But in my mind, being gay was not an option and I began to expend an incredible amount of energy repressing my developing homosexual urges. (McDevitt & Ormrod, 2004, p. 403)

Finally, in the third phase, the majority of gay and lesbian teenagers reach a point where they accept their homosexuality and share it with those who are close to them.

Why is this information important to teachers? First, you may be one of those people with whom students share this information, and your reaction to this disclosure can have a profound effect on students' acceptance of themselves. Second, research indicates that homosexual students are at greater risk for a number of troubling problems ranging from depression and substance abuse to suicide (Hershberger, Pilkington, & D'Augelli, 1997). Peer harassment in classes and hallways is a major contributor to these problems. Teachers play an essential role in setting the moral tone of their classrooms, ensuring that they are safe places for all students to learn and develop.

The Development of Self-Concept

At the beginning of this section, we also defined self-concept, saying it is a cognitive appraisal of one's own physical, social, and academic competence (Pintrich & Schunk, 2002). We can describe a girl who believes that she is a good athlete, for example, as having a positive physical self-concept, or a boy who believes he is good at getting along with people as having a positive social self-concept. People who believe they are intellectually competent are said to have high academic self-concepts. Researchers believe that the formation of a healthy self-concept is central to both social and emotional development (Davis-Kean & Sandler, 2001)

Sexual identity. Students' self-constructed definition of who they are with respect to gender orientation

Sexual orientation. The gender to which an individual is romantically and sexually attracted

Self-Concept and Self-Esteem

The terms *self-concept* and *self-esteem* are often used interchangeably, but in fact they are quite distinct. In contrast with self-concept, which is cognitive, **self-esteem,** or **self-worth,** is an emotional reaction to, or an evaluation of, the self (Pintrich & Schunk, 2002). People who have high self-esteem believe that they are inherently worthy people.

Young children tend to have both high self-esteem and positive self-concepts—sometimes unrealistically so—probably because they lack social comparisons and receive much support from parents (Stipek, 2002). Self-esteem tends to drop during the transition from elementary to middle school (D. A. Cole et al., 2001; Twenge & Campbell, 2001). This decline, present in both males and females, is probably due to several factors, including the impersonal nature of middle schools and the physical changes brought on by puberty. Self-esteem then rises during the high school years, to a greater extent for boys than for girls (Twenge & Campbell, 2001).

Self-concepts become more realistic as interactions with others give students a more accurate measure of their performance compared to their peers (Hay et al., 1999). As students move into adolescence, self-concept and a developing sense of identity interact, with each influencing the other and both influencing self-esteem.

Children form their academic self-concepts on the basis of the concrete experiences and feedback they receive in school.

Self-Concept and Achievement

The relationship between overall self-concept and achievement is positive but weak (Pintrich & Schunk, 2002). In attempting to understand why, researchers have found that social and physical self-concepts are virtually unrelated to academic achievement (Byrne & Gavin, 1996). This makes sense; we've all known socially withdrawn students who are happy as academic isolates as well as popular students content to earn average grades in school.

The relationship between achievement and academic self-concept is much more robust (Choi, 2005). Academic self-concept is important to teachers because it and achievement are interdependent; high achievement leads to high academic self-concept, and high academic self-concept can increase achievement (Chapman, Tunmer, & Prochnow, 2000). The opposite is also true. As we saw earlier, children commonly enter school expecting to learn and do well, but performance over time causes them to alter this expectation (Stipek, 2002). When learning experiences are positive, self-concept is enhanced; when they're negative, it suffers.

An even stronger relationship exists between specific subject matter self-concepts and achievement in those areas (Choi, 2005; Yeung et al., 2000). For example, people with positive self-concepts in math perform better on math tests (and vice versa). Researchers have also found that concepts of competence in different subjects, such as math and English, become more distinct over time (Marsh, 1992; Yeung et al., 2000). We've all heard people make statements such as "I'm okay in English, but I'm no good in math." Some evidence suggests that comments like these may not reflect actual competence; instead, people for whom societal expectations are low underestimate their abilities (American Association of University Women, 1992; C. Jackson, 2003).

The relationships between the components of self-concept and achievement are illustrated in Figure 3.2.

Instructional ⌂ **Principles**   **Promoting Psychosocial, Identity, and Self-Concept Development: Instructional Principles**

As a teacher you play an important role in promoting all forms of learner development, and you are the most significant influence on students' developing academic self-concepts. You design the learning activities and assessments and provide the feedback

Self-esteem, or self-worth. An emotional reaction to, or an evaluation of, the self

Figure 3.2 The relationships among the dimensions of self-concept and achievement

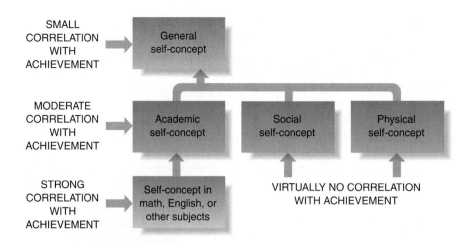

that students use to appraise their academic competence. The following principles can guide you in your efforts to promote psychosocial and self-concept development:

1. Communicate a learning-focused classroom and genuine interest in all students.
2. Maintain an authoritative interaction style.
3. Reward autonomy and initiative in your students.
4. Establish appropriately high expectations for all learners, and provide evidence of increasing competence.
5. Design grading systems that emphasize learning progress and avoid competition.

Let's see how these principles guide John Adler, an eighth-grade English teacher, as he works with his students.

> "Here are your papers," John announces on Friday as he hands back a set of quizzes that he had given the day before. "I'm very proud of you. You're all improving so much, particularly on your writing. . . . I know I expect a lot from you, but you've always risen to the task.
>
> "Be sure to put your scores in your logs. . . . And look at your improvement points on your papers and to add them to your logs."
>
> "Who improved the most, Mr. Adler?" Jeremy asks.
>
> "We don't care who improves the most," John replies, gently admonishing Jeremy. "Remember, as I've been saying, we're all in this together. I help you as much as I can, you take responsibility for your learning, and we all try to improve as much as possible. . . . That's why I put your scores on the last page of the quizzes. They're your business, and no one else's. You should be concerned about increasing your understanding, not with whether you're doing better than the person next to you."
>
> John then goes over some of the quiz items that had given students trouble, provides some additional examples, and closes the discussion by saying, "I know that these were challenging, but if you look back to the beginning of the year, you can see that you're getting better and better on them. That's what this is all about—improving.
>
> "Now, I want to take some time to have a classroom meeting," he says, changing the direction of the discussion. "One of you came to me after school last Friday, concerned about the way some kids are treating each other. . . . She didn't tattle or name any names; she simply expressed a concern, and I like it when someone takes the initiative to make our classroom environment better.
>
> "And, I agree. . . . For instance, I saw one of you get tripped when you walked down the aisle, and another had water splashed on him at the water fountain. . . . I'm also seeing more litter on the floor.
>
> "Frankly, I'm disappointed in some of your behaviors. We want a safe classroom in which we all can learn, and we're here to help one another. . . . So, I want to hear some ideas. What are we going to do about it?"
>
> The students offer comments, with suggestions ranging from kicking perpetrators out of class, to talking to them, to adding some more rules. The students agree that John has been attempting to enforce the rules fairly but that he has perhaps been a little too lenient in some cases. He acknowledges that possibility, saying that because he feels so strongly about students' accepting responsibility, he perhaps went too far.
>
> At the meeting's end, the students agree to redouble their efforts to be responsible, and John agrees to renew his efforts to enforce the rules equally and consistently.

Now, let's look at John's attempts to apply the principles for promoting psychosocial and self-concept development. He applied the first by attempting to create an orderly, learning-focused classroom environment and demonstrating genuine interest in his students. Like most people, they respond positively to such attitudes; when asked about their favorite teachers, students unsurprisingly mention such qualities as "caring about them as individuals and seeking to help them succeed as learners. . . . However, students also say that they want teachers to articulate and enforce clear standards of behavior. They view this not just as part of the teacher's job but as evidence that the teacher cares about them" (Brophy, 2004, pp. 29–30).

Second, by being caring but firm about standards for behavior, and by soliciting the students' input into rules and procedures, John displayed the authoritative interaction style discussed earlier in the chapter. Authoritative management, with its opportunity for practicing independence within limits, is particularly valuable in middle school classrooms where students are beginning the process of identity development.

Third, John realized that no psychosocial challenge is ever permanently resolved. So, although his students were eighth graders, he applied the third principle by rewarding behaviors associated with earlier stages, such as autonomy and initiative. This was the reason he praised one of his students for taking the initiative to raise the issue of student behavior.

John's comments "I'm very proud of you," "You're all improving so much," and "I realize that I expect a lot from you, but you've always risen to the task," communicated his expectations, his emphasis on increasing competence, and his attempts to apply the fourth principle. These efforts also promote a sense of industry and positive academic self concept.

Finally, he deemphasized competition, applying the fifth principle when he said, "We don't care who improves the most" and "We all try to improve as much as possible," in response to Jeremy's question. Also, by awarding points for improvement, he used his grading system to further emphasize increasing competence.

Research supports John's approach to developing his students' academic self-concepts. An alternate approach attempts to improve self-concept and self-esteem directly, using strategies such as having minority students study multicultural learning materials, sending children to summer camps, and implementing support groups and sensitivity training. Research consistently supports the achievement-oriented approach and largely discredits the alternate (Baumeister, Campbell, Krueger, & Voks, 2003). These results are intuitively sensible; without evidence of accomplishment, learners are unlikely to conclude that their competence is increasing (Hay et al., 1999; Marsh, Kong, & Hau, 2001).

Helping students resolve the psychosocial challenges described by Erikson's theory and develop positive identities and self-concepts isn't easy, and efforts such as John's won't work with all students or even with any student all the time. However, with time and continued effort, teachers make an important difference in these important areas of development.

Ethnic Pride: Promoting Positive Self-Esteem and Ethnic Identity

Maria Robles squeezes her mother's hand as they enter her new school. Her mother can tell she is nervous as she anxiously eyes the bigger boys and girls walking down the hallway.

As they enter a kindergarten classroom, Carmen Avilla, her teacher, comes to greet them.

"Hola. ¿Cómo te llamas, niña?" (Hello. What is your name, little one?)

Maria is still uneasy, but she feels some relief.

"Dile tu nombre" (Tell her your name), her mother prompts, squeezing her hand and smiling.

". . . Maria," she offers hesitantly.

Her mother adds quickly, "Maria Robles. Yo soy su madre." (I am her mother.)

Carmen looks on her list, finds Maria's name, and checks it off. Then she invites them, in Spanish, to come into the room and meet the other boys and girls. Music is playing in the background. Maria recognizes some of her friends who are playing with toys in one corner of the room.

"Maria, ven aquí y juega con nosotros." (Maria, come here and play with us.)

Maria hesitates for a moment and looks up at her mother to see whether it is all right. When her mother nods, Maria runs over to join her friends.

Ethnicity and Self-Esteem

We all wonder about our self-worth. Will others like us? Are we worthy of their love? Are we perceived by others as smart? beautiful? handsome? As we saw at the beginning of this

Teachers can help students develop ethnic pride and positive self-esteem by actively acknowledging and valuing the ethnic and cultural strengths different students bring to school.

chapter, our interactions with others help shape our beliefs, and schools provide a social environment in which students develop both positive self-concepts and high self-esteem.

Culture also influences the development of self-esteem, especially for minority youth. Researchers have found that the self-esteem of people from cultural minority groups often includes both a personal and a collective component (Wright & Taylor, 1995).

Collective self-esteem refers to individuals' perceptions of the relative worth of the groups to which they belong. Families, peers, and the ethnic groups that individuals identify with contribute to their sense of self-worth. When these groups are valued and perceived as having status, personal identities and self-esteem are enhanced. The opposite is also true.

Children as young as Maria know they are part of an ethnic minority, and research dating back to the 1930s indicates that minority children such as African-Americans (K. Clark & Clark, 1939), Mexican-Americans (Weiland & Coughlin, 1979), and Chinese-Americans (Aboud & Skerry, 1984) evaluate their ethnic reference groups as being inherently less worthy than the White majority. As ethnic minority children develop, they become increasingly aware of problems with inequality and discrimination.

More recent research suggests that African-American children actually possess higher levels of self-esteem than their Caucasian-American counterparts (Eccles, Wigfield, & Schiefele, 1998; Gray-Little & Hafdahl, 2000). This occurs when cultural minorities develop in warm, nurturant environments, both at home and school (C. Carlson, Uppal, & Prosser, 2000). Unfortunately, some cultural minorities experience developmental hardships that are often linked to poverty, crime, and drugs (Dwyer & Osher, 2000). In addition, schools that are unresponsive to the needs of minority children can damage their developing self-concepts (Ferguson, 2003; Noguera, 2003a). These findings suggest that being part of a cultural minority group can present unique challenges for schools' ethnic minority students.

Ethnic Pride and Identity Formation

Membership in an ethnic group also affects identity (M. Jones, 1999). Sometimes the messages children receive about their ethnic identities are mixed or even negative (Lopez del Bosque, 2003; Trawick-Smith, 2003). However, research also indicates that students who are encouraged and helped to explore their ethnic identities and who have adopted positive values from both the dominant culture and their own tend to have a clearer sense of self (Nieto, 1999). Students with a strong, positive ethnic identity also achieve higher, like school more, have higher self-esteem, and have a more positive view of their ability to cope with their environments (Chavous et al., 2003; Spencer, Noll, Stoltzfus, & Harpalani, 2001).

The research reveals consistent patterns. Minority students need to know that their cultures are valued and that the languages they bring to school are assets instead of liabilities (Marshall, 2001).

How can teachers do this? We can make every effort to communicate to students that their ethnic heritage and language are both recognized and valued. In a test of this idea, researchers taught native Canadian children in either their native (heritage) language or in a second language, such as French (Wright & Taylor, 1995). Children educated in their heritage language showed a substantial increase in their personal self-esteem, whereas children educated in the second language did not. The researchers concluded that "early heritage language education can have a positive impact on the personal and collective self-esteem of minority language students" (p. 251).

Students who hear their home language used in the classroom learn that the language and the culture in which it is embedded are valued. Like Maria, many students come to school wondering if they will be welcome and questioning whether the knowledge they bring with them will be valued (L. Jackson, 1999). The way a teacher reacts to these students influences their developing sense of self-worth.

Collective self-esteem. Individuals' perceptions of the relative worth of the groups to which they belong

Checking Your Understanding

3.1 You are teaching a ninth-grade student whom you can't "get going." He will do what is required of him and no more. He does a good job on his required work, however, and seems to be quite happy. Explain his behavior using Erikson's theory as a basis. What might a teacher do in response to his pattern of behavior?

3.2 Look again at the students' conversation at the beginning of the discussion of identity development. Use their statements to explain the state of identity development for each of the students.

3.3 "I know I can get this down the way I want to say it," a student says to his friend. "I've always been a decent writer. I'm not sure why I'm having a problem." Use the idea of self-concept and/or the idea of self-esteem to explain the student's behavior. Describe the relationships between self-concept, self-esteem, and academic achievement.

To receive feedback for these questions, go to Appendix B.

Knowledge Extensions

To deepen your understanding of the topics in this section of the chapter and integrate them with topics you've already studied, go to the *Knowledge Extensions* module for Chapter 3 at *www.prenhall.com/eggen*. Respond to questions 6–11.

Classroom ⊞ Connections

Applying Erikson's Work in Your Classroom

1. Try to understand the emotional needs of young people, and use that knowledge as an umbrella under which you conduct your interactions with them.
   - **Elementary:** A kindergarten student responsible for watering the classroom plants knocks one over on the floor. The teacher says evenly, "It looks like we have a problem. What needs to be done?" She pauses and continues, "Sweep up the dirt, and wipe up the water with some paper towels." When the student is done, the teacher gives her a hug and comments, "Everyone makes mistakes. The important thing is what we do about them."
   - **Middle School:** A math teacher designs her instruction so that all students can achieve success and develop a growing sense of industry. She spends extra time with students after school, and she lets students redo some of the assignments if they make an honest effort the first time. She frequently comments, "Math is for everyone—if you try!"
   - **High School:** A biology teacher pays little attention to the attire and slang of his students as long as offensive language isn't used, the rights of others are recognized, and learning occurs.

2. Help students understand that effort leads to success and competence.
   - **Elementary:** A second-grade teacher carefully teaches each topic and provides precise directions before making seat-work assignments. She conducts "monitored practice" with the first few items to be sure all students get started correctly. When students encounter difficulties, she meets with them separately or in small groups so they don't fall behind.
   - **Middle School:** A sixth-grade teacher develops a grading system based partially on improvement so that each student can succeed by improving his or her performance. He meets with students periodically during each grading period to help them monitor their learning progress.
   - **High School:** An art teacher uses portfolios and individual conferences to help her students set goals and see their growth over the year. During conferences, she emphasizes individual growth and tries to help students understand how their effort and accomplishments are linked.

Developing Positive Self-Concepts in Your Classroom

3. Make students feel wanted and valued in your class. Provide learning experiences that promote success.
   - **Elementary:** A fourth-grade teacher starts the school year by having students write autobiographical sketches and bring in pictures of themselves taken when they were preschoolers. They list their strengths, interests, and hobbies, and describe what they want to be when they grow up.
   - **Middle School:** A homeroom teacher for entering middle schoolers tries to make his classroom a place where students feel safe and secure. He begins the school year with classroom meetings where students get to know one another and form homeroom rules. As the year progresses, he uses these meetings to discuss issues and problems important to students.
   - **High School:** A ninth-grade English teacher begins each school year by announcing that everyone is important in her classes and that she expects everyone to learn. She structures her classrooms around success, minimizing competition. She also stays in her room after school and invites students who are having problems to come by for help.

Capitalizing on Diversity in Your Classroom

4. Build on students' cultures and ethnic backgrounds to develop positive self-esteem.

- **Elementary:** A first-grade teacher learns that three distinct native languages are spoken in the different homes of his students. With the help of other teachers and parent volunteers, he constructs a chart of common nouns and phrases (e.g., *chair, table, mother, hello*) in the different languages. He uses the chart to explain to his students differences in the languages and to establish commonalities between them.
- **Middle School:** A social studies teacher in an ethnically diverse school encourages her students to research the countries from which their ancestors came. Students display the information they discover on a poster and bring in things from home, such as clothes and food, to illustrate the cultures of the ancestral countries.
- **High School:** A tenth-grade English teacher makes a special effort to present literature written by authors from various minority groups. When the class reads the selections, he provides biographical information to help students understand who the authors are and how their experiences as youths shaped their writing.

5. Use ethnic role models as a foundation for the development of students' personal identities.

- **Elementary:** A third-grade teacher in an inner-city school encourages parents and family members of students to volunteer in the classroom. As the teacher gets to know the volunteers, she encourages them to talk about their occupations and backgrounds with students.
- **Middle School:** A language arts teacher in a career exploration unit makes a special effort to invite members of minority groups who have different occupations and professions. He encourages them to talk openly about the challenges and satisfactions they encountered in pursuing their careers.
- **High School:** A history teacher makes a special effort to educate students about the contributions of women and members of ethnic minorities to American society. As contemporary newspapers and magazines report the accomplishments of individuals who are ethnic minorities, she brings in the articles to share with her students.

DEVELOPMENT OF MORALITY, SOCIAL RESPONSIBILITY, AND SELF-CONTROL

"Listen, everyone. . . . I need to go to the office for a moment," Amanda Kellinger announces as her students work on their seat-work assignment. "You all have work to do, so work quietly until I get back."

The quiet shuffling of pencils and papers can be heard for a few moments, and then Gary whispers, "Psst, what math problems are we supposed to do?"

"Shh! No talking," Talitha says, pointing to the rules posted on the bulletin board.

"But he needs to know so he can do his work," Krystal replies. "It's the evens on page 79."

"Who cares?" Dwain growls. "She's not here. She won't catch us."

What influences our students' interpretation of classroom rules? More importantly, as they move through life, how do they think about the laws and conventions that govern our society? The concept of morality deals with matters of right and wrong, and we now examine **moral development,** the development of prosocial behaviors and traits such as honesty, fairness, and respect for others.

Increased Interest in Moral Education and Development

Interest in moral education and how it should be used to promote moral development is increasing, partially due to disturbing trends in the behavior patterns of our young people. For example, some surveys indicate that 75 percent of high school students have admitted to cheating on tests (Bracey, 2005), and cheating appears to be on the rise from elementary school through college (Goodman, 2005; Selingo, 2004). Substantial numbers of students express concerns about bullying and their safety in schools (Schlozman, 2002). Outside of schools, the corporate scandals that led to the collapse of businesses such as Enron and WorldCom, and questionable accounting practices in other companies, have sent shock waves through the financial community and American society in general. Rampant greed and a sense that "if you can get away with it, it's okay," seem to be the "moral" principles of the day. The American public is increasingly looking to education for solutions to problems such as these (L. Rose & Gallup, 2000).

Moral issues are also embedded in the school curriculum. History is not a mere chronology of events; it also includes study of humans' responses to moral issues, such as poverty and human suffering, peace, justice, and whether or not decisions to go to war are justified.

Ethical issues are also found in literature written for young people. For instance in E. B. White's (1974) children's classic *Charlotte's Web,* moral issues are involved when Charlotte,

Moral development. The development of prosocial behaviors and traits such as honesty, fairness, and respect for others

the spider, devises an ingenious plan to save Wilbur the pig. And teachers commonly choose books such as *The Yearling* (Rawlings, 1938), *The Scarlet Letter* (Hawthorne, 1850), and *A Tale of Two Cities* (Dickens, 1859), not only because they are good literature but also because they examine moral issues.

Moral development is an integral part of development in general. Students' beliefs about right and wrong influence their behavior. Incidents of cheating and vandalism, for example, decrease if students believe they are morally unacceptable. Socially and emotionally healthy learners have a moral compass that guides their behavior. Research also indicates that the moral atmosphere of a school (e.g., democratic and prosocial versus authoritarian) can influence motivation and the value students place on their learning experiences (Christenson & Havsy, 2004; Murdock, Miller, & Kohlhardt, 2004). Understanding moral development can help us better guide our students in this vital area.

Cheating is a persistent problem in classrooms. How students think about this problem and how teachers respond to it depend on students' levels of moral development.

Piaget's Description of Moral Development

Although we usually think of Piaget in the context of cognitive development, he examined the development of ethics and morals as well. He studied cognitive and moral development in much the same way; he presented children with problems and tasks and asked questions to gain insights into their thinking.

Piaget (1965) found that children's responses to moral problems could be divided into two broad stages, which he labeled *external morality* and *autonomous morality*.

In the first stage, **external morality,** children view rules as fixed and permanent and enforced by authority figures. When Talitha said, "Shh! No talking," and pointed to the rules, she was demonstrating thinking at this stage. It didn't matter that Gary was only asking about the assignment; rules are rules. In responding "Who cares? She's not here. She won't catch us," Dwain demonstrated similar thinking; he was focusing on the fact that no authority figure was there to enforce the rule. External morality typically lasts to about age 10. Piaget believed that parents and teachers who stress unquestioning adherence to adult authority retard moral development, inadvertently encouraging students to remain at this level.

In the second stage, **autonomous morality,** children develop rational ideas of fairness and see justice as a reciprocal process of treating others as they would want to be treated. Children at this stage begin to rely on themselves instead of others to regulate moral behavior. Krystal's comment, "But he needs to know so he can do his work," demonstrates this kind of thinking; she viewed Gary's whispering as an honest request for assistance rather than a rule infraction.

Kohlberg's Theory of Moral Development

To begin this section, read the follow vignette, and think about the moral issue involved in it.

> Steve, a high school senior, works at a night job to help support his mother, a single parent of three. Steve is conscientious and works hard in his classes, but he doesn't have enough time to study.
>
> History isn't Steve's favorite course, and because of his night work, he has a marginal D average. If he fails the final exam, he will fail the course and won't graduate. He arranges to miss work the night before the exam so that he can study extra hard, but early in the evening his boss calls, desperate to have Steve come in and replace another employee who called in sick at the last moment. His boss pressures him, so Steve goes to work at 8:00 p.m. and comes home exhausted at 2:00 a.m. He tries to study but falls asleep on the couch, with his book in his lap. His mother wakes him for school at 6:30 a.m.
>
> Steve goes to history, looks at the test, and goes blank. Everything seems like a jumble. Clarice, one of the best students in the class, happens to have her answer sheet positioned so that he can clearly see every answer by barely moving his eyes.
>
> Is he justified in cheating?

External morality. A stage of moral development in which individuals view rules as fixed and permanent and enforced by authority figures

Autonomous morality. A stage of moral development characterized by the belief that fairness and justice is the reciprocal process of treating others as they would want to be treated

Analyzing Classrooms Video
To analyze the responses to a moral dilemma of students at different ages, go to Episode 4, "Moral Reasoning: Examining a Moral Dilemma," on DVD 1, accompanying this text.

This vignette presents a **moral dilemma,** an ambiguous situation that requires a person to make a moral decision. It's a dilemma, because Steve has no clear course of action; any decision has both positive and negative consequences. If he cheats, he is likely to pass, but cheating is morally wrong. On the other hand, if he doesn't cheat, he behaves in a moral way, but he is likely to fail. Students' responses to moral dilemmas provide insight into their moral development (Rest, Narvaez, Bebeau, & Thoma, 1999).

Influenced by Piaget (1965) and John Dewey (1938), the famous American educational philosopher, Lawrence Kohlberg (1929–1987), a Harvard educator and psychologist, used responses to moral dilemmas, such as the one you just read, to develop a theory of moral development that extended Piaget's earlier work (Kohlberg, 1963, 1969, 1981, 1984). Like Piaget, he concluded that morality develops in stages, and all people pass through all the stages in the same order but at different rates. In addition, and on the basis of research conducted in cities and villages in Great Britain, Malaysia, Mexico, Taiwan, and Turkey, Kohlberg concluded that the development of moral reasoning is similar across cultures.

Kohlberg originally described moral development as occurring at three levels consisting of two stages each. These levels represent the perspectives people take as they wrestle with moral issues. The levels and stages are outlined in Table 3.4. As you read the descriptions of these stages, remember that the specific response to a moral dilemma isn't the primary issue; the level and stage of moral development are determined by the *reasons* a person gives for making the decision.

Level I: Preconventional Ethics

The preconventional level is an egocentric orientation focusing on moral consequences for the self. As you might predict, young children tend to reason at this level. Level I consists of two stages: punishment–obedience and market exchange. Some research indicates that 15 to 20 percent of the U.S. teenage population still reasons at this level (Turiel, 1973).

Stage 1: Punishment–Obedience. In the **punishment–obedience** stage, people make moral decisions based on their chances of getting caught and being punished. They reason

Moral dilemma. An ambiguous situation that requires a person to make a moral decision

Punishment–obedience. A stage of moral reasoning in which conclusions are based on the chances of getting caught and being punished

Table 3.4 Kohlberg's stages of moral reasoning

Level I Preconventional Ethics	The ethics of egocentrism. Typical of children up to about age 10. Called preconventional because children typically don't fully understand rules set down by others.
Stage 1: Punishment-Obedience	Consequences of acts determine whether they're good or bad. Individuals make moral decisions without considering the needs or feelings of others.
Stage 2: Market Exchange	The ethics of "What's in it for me?" Obeying rules and exchanging favors are judged in terms of the benefit to the individual.
Level II Conventional Ethics	The ethics of others. Typical of 10- to 20-year-olds. The name comes from conformity to the rules and conventions of society.
Stage 3: Interpersonal Harmony	Ethical decisions are based on concern for or the opinions of others. What pleases, helps, or is approved of by others characterizes this stage.
Stage 4: Law and Order	The ethics of laws, rules, and societal order. Rules and laws are inflexible and are obeyed for their own sake.
Level III Postconventional Ethics	The ethics of principle. Rarely reached before age 20 and only by a small portion of the population. The focus is on the principles underlying society's rules.
Stage 5: Social Contract	Rules and laws represent agreements among people about behavior that benefits society. Rules can be changed when they no longer meet society's needs.
Stage 6: Universal Principles	Rarely encountered in life. Ethics are determined by abstract and general principles that transcend societal rules.

Teachers' interactions with students provide opportunities to promote learner moral development.

that right or wrong is determined by the consequences of an action. For example, if a child is caught and punished, the act is morally wrong; if not, the act is right. A person who argues that Steve is justified in cheating because he can easily see every answer on Clarice's paper, and he is unlikely to get caught, is reasoning at this stage.

Stage 2: Market Exchange. Students reasoning at Stage 2 begin to include others in their moral decision making, but they continue to focus on what is best for them. In the **market exchange** stage, people feel that an act is morally justified if it results in an act of reciprocity on someone else's part. Positions such as "You do something for me, and I'll do something for you" and "Don't bite the hand that feeds you" reflect morality at this stage.

A person reasoning at Stage 2 might argue that Steve should go ahead and cheat because if he doesn't, he'll fail the course and won't graduate. The focus remains on the self, and "The right thing to do is what makes me the happiest." Political patronage, the tendency of successful office seekers to give their supporters desirable jobs regardless of qualifications, is a common example of Stage 2 ethics.

Level II: Conventional Ethics

As development progresses and egocentrism declines, students become better able to see the world from others' points of view. Moral reasoning no longer depends on the consequences for the individual but instead becomes linked to the perspectives of, and concerns for, others. Values such as loyalty, family expectations, obeying the law, and social order become prominent. A few older elementary school students, some middle and junior high students, and many high school students display conventional morality (McDevitt & Ormrod, 2004). Much of the adult population reasons at this level.

Stage 3: Interpersonal Harmony. Individuals reasoning at Stage 3 do not manipulate people to reach their goals, as they might at Stage 2. Rather, in the **interpersonal harmony** stage, people make decisions based on loyalty, living up to the expectations of others, and social conventions. Sometimes called the "nice girl/good boy" stage, a person is oriented toward maintaining the affection and approval of friends and relatives by being a "good" person. For example, a teenager on a date who meets a curfew because she doesn't want to worry her parents is reasoning at this stage.

A person reasoning at Stage 3 might offer two different perspectives on Steve's dilemma. One could argue that he needs to work to help his family and therefore is justified in cheating. A contrasting view, but still at this stage, would suggest that he should not cheat because people would think badly of him if they found out.

Market exchange. A stage of moral reasoning in which conclusions are based on an act of reciprocity on someone else's part

Interpersonal harmony. A stage of moral reasoning in which conclusions are based on loyalty, living up to the expectations of others, and social conventions

People reasoning at Stage 3 run the danger of being caught up in the majority opinion. For example, some people accept that cheating on income taxes is okay because "everybody cheats." We might call Stage 3 the "ethics of adolescence" because of the influence peers have on young people's thinking at this age.

Stage 4: Law and Order.   A person reasoning at Stage 4 would argue that Steve should not cheat because "It's against the rules to cheat." In the **law and order** stage, people follow laws and rules for their own sake. They don't make moral decisions to please other people, as in Stage 3; rather, they believe that laws and rules exist to guide behavior, and they should be followed uniformly.

Concern for the orderliness of society is also characteristic of this stage; for example, a person might argue that Steve should not cheat because "What would our country be like if everybody cheated?" Concern for others is still the focus, but rules and order are key criteria. People reasoning at Stage 4 don't care whether the rest of the world cheats on their income taxes; they pay theirs because the law says they should.

Level III: Postconventional Ethics

A person reasoning at Level III has transcended both the individual and societal levels and makes moral decisions based on principles. People operating at this level, also called *principled morality,* follow rules but also see that at times rules need to be changed or ignored. Only a small portion of the population attains this level, and most don't reach it until their middle to late 20s.

Some of the great figures in history have sacrificed their lives in the name of principle. Sir Thomas More, who knew that he was, in effect, ending his own life by refusing to acknowledge King Henry VIII as the head of the Church of England, nevertheless stood on a principle. Mohandas K. Gandhi chose jail rather than adhere to England's laws as he applied the principle of nonviolent noncooperation; his work, as well, ultimately led to his death.

Stage 5: Social Contract.   In the **social contract stage,** people make moral decisions based on socially agreed-upon rules. Stage 5 is the official ethic of the United States. The constitutional Bill of Rights is an example of a cultural social contract; for example, Americans agree in principle that people have the right to free speech (the First Amendment to the Constitution), and the legal profession is conceptually committed to interpreting the laws in this light. In addition, the American legal system has provisions for changing or amending laws when new values or conditions warrant it. A person reasoning at Stage 5 would say that Steve's cheating is wrong because teachers and learners agree in principle that grades should reflect achievement, and cheating violates the agreement.

Stage 6: Universal Principles.   At the **universal principles** stage, the individual's moral reasoning is based on abstract and general principles that are independent of society's laws. People at this stage define right and wrong in terms of internalized universal standards. "The Golden Rule" is a commonly cited example. Because very few people operate at this stage, and questions have been raised about the existence of "universal" principles, Kohlberg deemphasized this stage in his later writings (Kohlberg, 1984).

Putting Kohlberg's Theory Into Perspective

As with most theories, Kohlberg's has both proponents and critics. Kohlberg's work has been widely researched, and this research has led to the following conclusions (Berk, 2006; McDevitt & Ormrod, 2004):

- Every person's moral reasoning passes through the same stages in the same order.
- People pass through the stages at different rates.
- Development is gradual and continuous, rather than sudden and discrete.
- Once a stage is attained, a person tends to reason at that stage instead of regressing to a lower stage.
- Intervention usually advances a person only to the next higher stage of moral reasoning.

These results are generally consistent with what Kohlberg's theory would predict.

Law and order. A stage of moral reasoning in which conclusions are based on following laws and rules for their own sake

Social contract. A stage of moral reasoning in which conclusions are based on socially agreed-upon principles

Universal principles. A stage of moral reasoning in which conclusions are based on abstract and general principles that are independent of society's laws and rules

Criticisms have been directed at Kohlberg's work, however. First, people's thinking, while tending to be at a certain stage, often shows evidence of reasoning at other stages. Also, although Stages 1–4 appear in most cultural groups, postconventional reasoning isn't seen in all cultures, suggesting that Kohlberg's theory more strongly focuses on Western thinking (Snary, 1995).

People's moral reasoning also depends on context (Rest et al., 1999; Turiel, 1998). For example, people are more likely to believe that breaking a traffic law isn't immoral if it causes no one harm. They may consider driving faster than the speed limit on an interstate to be okay but object to passing a parked school bus whose stop sign is out.

Researchers have also found that young children's moral thinking is more advanced than Kohlberg predicted. For instance, 6-year-olds commonly believe, without being told by authority figures, that behaviors that are harmful or unfair to others are inherently wrong (Laupa & Turiel, 1995; Tisak, 1993). In addition, children as young as 3 can differentiate between **social conventions,** the rules and expectations of a particular group, and true moral issues (Turiel, 1998). For instance, it's rude to interrupt while someone else is talking, but it isn't morally wrong. It is, in fact, perfectly acceptable in some societies (Au, 1992). Kohlberg's work doesn't differentiate between social conventions and moral issues until the higher stages of moral reasoning (L. Walker & Pitts, 1998).

Although Kohlberg attempted to make his stages content free, research indicates that thinking about moral dilemmas, like problem solving in general, is influenced by domain-specific knowledge (Bebeau, Rest, & Narvaez, 1999). For example, a medical doctor asked to deliberate about an educational dilemma or a teacher asked to resolve a medical issue may be hampered by their lack of knowledge of the factors involved.

Kohlberg's data-gathering methods, interviews in which study participants describe their thinking, have also been questioned, with researchers arguing that self-reported explanations of thought processes have limitations (Carpendale, 2000). One researcher noted: "Using interview data assumes that participants can verbally explain the workings of their minds. In recent years, this assumption has been questioned, more and more" (Rest et al., 1999, p. 295).

Finally, Kohlberg's work has been criticized for focusing on moral *reasoning* instead of moral *behavior*. People may reason at one stage and behave at another. However, in support of a moral reasoning–moral behavior connection, Kohlberg (1975) found that only 15 percent of students reasoning at the postconventional level cheated when given the opportunity to do so, as opposed to 55 percent of conventional thinkers and 70 percent of preconventional thinkers. In addition, adolescents reasoning at the lower stages are likely to be less honest and to engage in more antisocial behavior, such as delinquency and drug use (Comunian & Gielan, 2000). In contrast, reasoning at the higher stages is associated with altruistic behaviors, such as defending free speech, victims of injustice, and the rights of minorities (Berk, 2006; Kuther & Higgins-D'Alessandra, 1997). Moral reasoning does influence behavior.

Gender Differences: The Morality of Caring. Some critics of Kohlberg's work also argue that it fails to adequately consider ways in which gender influences morality. Early research examining Kohlberg's theory identified differences in the ways men and women responded to moral dilemmas (Gilligan, 1982, 1998; Gilligan & Attanucci, 1988). Men were more likely to base their judgments on abstract concepts, such as justice, rules, and individual rights. Women were more likely to base their moral decisions on interpersonal connections and attention to human needs.

According to Kohlberg, these differences suggest a lower stage of moral development in women responding to moral dilemmas. Gilligan (1982) argued that the findings, instead, indicate an "ethic of care" in women that is not inferior; rather, Kohlberg's descriptions don't adequately represent the complexity of female thinking. In addition, when asked to identify moral dilemmas, females are more likely to choose real-world interpersonal problems than distant and abstract issues (Skoe & Dressner, 1994).

Gilligan (1977, 1982) suggests that a morality of caring proceeds through three stages. In the first, children are concerned primarily with their own needs. In the second, they show

Social conventions. The rules and expectations of a particular group or society

concern for others who are unable to care for themselves, such as infants and the elderly. And in the third, they recognize the interdependent nature of personal relationships and extend compassion to all of humanity. To encourage this development, Gilligan recommends an engaging curriculum with opportunities for students to think and talk about moral issues involving caring (Goldberg, 2000).

Nell Noddings (1992, 2002) has also emphasized the importance of caring. The need for caring teachers is widely accepted, and Noddings argues that students should be taught the importance of caring through a curriculum that emphasizes caring for self, family and friends, and even strangers and the world.

Though Gilligan makes an important point about gender differences, additional research is mixed, with some studies finding gender differences and others not (Leon, Lynn, McLean, & Perri, 1997; Turiel 1998). Like cross-cultural studies, Gilligan's research reminds us of the complexity of the issues involved in moral development.

Finally, Kohlberg focused exclusively on the cognitive aspects of moral development—how people reason about moral issues. There is more to moral development, however, as we will see now.

Emotional Factors in Moral Development

"Are you okay?" her mother asks as Melissa walks in the house after school.

"I feel really bad, Mom," Melissa answers softly. "We were working in a group, and Jessica said something sort of odd, and I said, 'That's dumb. Where did that come from?' . . . She didn't say anything for the rest of our group time. She doesn't get really good grades, and I know saying something about her being dumb really hurt her feelings. I didn't intend to do it. It just sort of came out."

"I know you didn't intend to hurt her feelings, Sweetheart. Did you tell her you were sorry?"

"No, when I realized it, I just sat there like a lump. I know how I'd feel if someone said I was dumb."

"Tell you what," her mom suggests. "Tomorrow, you go directly to her, tell her you're very sorry, and that it won't happen again."

"Thanks, Mom. I'll do it as soon as I see her. . . . I feel a lot better."

This exchange is about morality, but it doesn't involve reasoning; instead, it deals with emotions. Piaget and Kohlberg focused on cognitive aspects of moral development, but this example also includes an emotional dimension. Emotions are affective reactions to events and reflect how we feel about changes in our environment (Saarni, 2002). For instance, Melissa felt both **shame,** the painful emotion aroused when people recognize that they have failed to act or think in ways they believe are good, and **guilt,** the uncomfortable feeling people get when they know they've caused distress for someone else. Although unpleasant, experiencing shame and guilt indicates that moral development is advancing and future behaviors will improve.

When Melissa said, "I know how I'd feel if someone said I was dumb," she was also describing feelings of **empathy,** the ability to experience the same emotion someone else is feeling. Empathy promotes moral and prosocial behavior even in the absence of wrongdoing (Eisenberg, Losoya, & Guthrie, 1997).

Shame, guilt, and empathy are all components of **emotional intelligence,** the ability to understand emotions in ourselves and others. The term *emotional intelligence* was popularized by Daniel Goleman (2006), who claimed that success in life is largely due to people's ability to understand the role of emotions in our lives. The development of emotional intelligence is important because it is related to positive self-esteem and being able to get along with others. In addition, aggression appears related to low emotional intelligence (Lopes & Salovey, 2004; J. D. Mayer, Salovey, & Caruso, 2000).

As we see from this discussion, moral development is complex, with both cognitive and emotional components. Kohlberg's work doesn't provide a complete picture, but combined with other information about personal, social, and emotional development, it helps us understand people's thoughts and feelings about moral issues. It also reminds us that moral reasoning and development aren't handed down from others. Rather, they result from a constructive process in which learners use experiences to make sense of their worlds.

Exploring Further

To read more about emotional development, go to "Developing Emotional Awareness" in the *Exploring Further* module of Chapter 3 at *www.prenhall.com/eggen*.

Shame. The painful emotion aroused when people recognize that they have failed to act or think in ways they believe are good

Guilt. The uncomfortable feeling people get when they know they've caused distress for someone else

Empathy. The ability to experience the same emotion someone else is feeling

Emotional intelligence. The ability to understand emotions in ourselves and others

---

Instructional		**Principles**	**Promoting Moral Development:**
			Instructional Principles

Teachers have many opportunities to promote moral development, emotional intelligence, and prosocial behaviors such as cooperating, sharing, and comforting classmates who have been hurt (Elias, 2004; Saarni, 2002).

Teachers promote this development primarily through the kinds of classroom environments they create, their interactions with students, and how they guide students' interactions with one another. As you work to promote your students' moral development, the following principles can guide your efforts:

1. Model ethical thinking, behavior, and empathy in your interactions with students.
2. Use classroom management as a vehicle for promoting moral development.
3. Encourage students to understand and respect the perspectives of others.
4. Use moral dilemmas as concrete reference points for discussions of moral issues.
5. Encourage students to articulate and justify their moral positions in discussions.

Let's see how the principles guide Rod Leist, a fifth-grade teacher, as he works with his students:

> Rod begins language arts by saying, "We've been reading an interesting story, and now I'd like to focus on a particular part of it. Let's talk about Chris, the boy who found the wallet. He was essentially broke, so would it be wrong for him to keep it, and the money in it? . . . Okay, I see a lot of heads nodding. . . . Why? . . . Jolene?"
>
> "Because it didn't belong to him."
>
> "Ray?"
>
> "Why not keep it? It wasn't his fault."
>
> "That's terrible," Helena interrupts. "How would you like it if you lost your wallet?"
>
> "Helena," Rod admonishes, "remember, we agreed that in discussions we would let everyone finish their point before we speak. We have a right to disagree, but we're also responsible for our own behavior, . . . in this case listening to a different point of view and waiting until the person is finished."
>
> "I'm sorry for interrupting. . . . Please finish your point, Ray," Rod adds.
>
> "I was saying it wasn't his fault that the person lost it. He didn't do anything. . . . The person shouldn't have dropped it in the first place, and he was broke."
>
> "Okay, Helena, go ahead," Rod says encouragingly.
>
> "Just . . . how would you feel if you lost something and somebody else kept it? Pretty bad, I think. . . . That's why I think he should give it back."
>
> "That's an interesting point, Helena. When we think about literature, and life for that matter, it's good for us to try to put ourselves in someone else's shoes. . . . Of course, we would all feel badly if we lost something and it wasn't returned.
>
> "Go ahead, . . . Juan?"
>
> "I agree. It was a lot of money, and Chris's parents would probably make him give it back anyway."
>
> "And what if the person who lost the money really needed it?" Kristina adds.
>
> They continue the discussion for several more minutes, and then Rod says, "These are all good points. . . . Okay, here's what we're going to do. I want each of you to write a short paragraph telling whether or not you would keep the wallet. If you say yes, explain why you feel it would be right or fair to keep it, and if you say no, explain why you feel it would be wrong. . . . Then, we'll discuss your reasons some more tomorrow."

Now, let's look at Rod's attempts to apply the principles for promoting moral development in his classroom. He applied the first by modeling ethical thinking, behavior, and empathy in his interactions with his students. His simple and brief apology for interrupting the discussion communicated that he obeyed the same rules he expected his students to follow. Also, in saying, "That's an interesting point,

Discussing moral dilemmas provides students opportunities to analyze and evaluate their own moral views.

Helena. When we think about literature, and life for that matter, it's good for us to try to put ourselves in someone else's shoes," he reinforced Helena for being empathic and modeled his own empathy and prosocial behavior.

Efforts to be fair, responsible, and democratic in dealings with students speak volumes about teachers' values and views of morality (Kohn, 2004). Rod's management system and his response to Helena applied the second and third principles. When he stopped Helena to remind her of the class agreement about interrupting, he was attempting to help his students understand fairness, open-mindedness, cooperation, and tolerance for differing opinions. Acquiring this understanding is an important part of self-regulation, which can be developed only if students understand rules, understand why they are important, and agree to follow them (Brantlinger, Morton, & Washburn, 1999).

This kind of learning environment promotes *autonomous morality* (Berk, 2006). In contrast, in an environment where punishment or the threat of punishment is emphasized, a form of *external morality,* students obey rules but won't improve their self-regulation (Murdock et al., 2004).

Rod attempted to apply the fourth principle by using the story of the lost wallet as a reference point for discussion. Effective teachers frequently use moral dilemmas in literature to promote moral development but are careful to scaffold instruction so that the messages are meaningful (Goodman & Balamore, 2003; Koc & Buzzelli, 2004). And finally, during the discussion and in the writing exercise, Rod encouraged students to articulate and justify their moral positions on the issue.

Research supports this approach. Moral development is enhanced through classroom discussions that encourage students to examine their own moral thinking and compare it to others' (Kuther & Higgins-D'Alessandra, 1997; Thoma & Rest, 1996). Interaction encourages active listening and analysis of different ways of reasoning about moral issues. And being exposed to more sophisticated thinking can disrupt a person's equilibrium and promote development (Pyryt & Mendaglio, 2001).

Exploring Further

To read more about moral education and instruction, go to "Different Instructional Approaches to Moral Education" in the *Exploring Further* module of Chapter 3 at *www.prenhall.com/eggen*.

Learning Contexts: Promoting Personal, Social, and Moral Development in Urban Environments

Urban schools present unique challenges to teachers wanting to promote healthy social and moral development in their students. As you saw in Chapter 1, compared to their rural and suburban counterparts, urban schools tend to be large and impersonal (Kincheloe, 2004; Schutz, 2004). Urban high schools can be "tough, confusing places where students can easily get lost" (Ilg & Massucci, 2003, p. 69).

The problem of establishing meaningful interpersonal relationships, so essential for personal and social development, is compounded by diverse urban neighborhoods and the distances students must travel over public transportation (Kincheloe, 2004). Extracurricular activities, which can serve as a meeting point for students, are often inaccessible (R. Brown & Evans, 2002).

Establishing meaningful teacher–student relationships can also be a problem. Urban teachers typically don't come from the same neighborhoods as do the students, making it more difficult for teachers to empathize with students' lives outside of school (Charner-Laird, Watson, Szczesuil, Kirkpatrick, & Gordon, 2004). Cultural divides also make it difficult for teachers to establish meaningful relationships with students. As a result, the bond of mutual caring, an essential element in teacher–student relationships, is often missing. One study found that only 20 percent of urban African-American males and 28 percent of African-American female students felt that their teachers supported them and cared about their success (Noguera, 2003b). It is difficult for

Effective urban teachers create learning communities within their classrooms that foster both social and cognitive development.

teachers to influence their students' personal, social, and moral development when the essential bonds of mutual trust and caring are absent.

The challenge is to create contexts in which urban students can interact in meaningful ways with both teachers and other students. One proposed solution is to create smaller schools, or schools within a school, that allow for the creation of more personal learning communities. Students in smaller schools "behave better, are more likely to be involved in extracurricular activities, . . . fight less, feel safe, and feel more attached to their schools" (Ilg & Massucci, 2003, p. 69).

While teachers, alone, can't create smaller schools, they can attempt to create a "small-school" feeling in their classrooms by emphasizing that they and the students are all there to learn as much as possible and to support each other both emotionally and academically. They make a special effort to get to know students as people, and they're willing to spend extra time with them not only to listen but also to help with classroom-related tasks (B. L. Wilson & Corbett, 2001). They model courtesy and respect for the students and expect similar courtesy in return. And clear standards for behavior require that students treat each other the same way. This creates the sense of safety and attachment that we discussed in the previous paragraph.

In addition, teachers make personal, perspective-taking, and inviting statements to their students (Manouchehri, 2004). For instance, a comment such as "This has been hard for me too. I often try to do it this way," is a personal statement; "I know this is hard, and I can feel that you're frustrated," communicates that the teacher understands students' experiences and feelings; and statements such as "*We're* going to be working on fractions this week," is more inviting than "*You're* going to be working on. . . . " These seemingly minor differences help meet students' socioemotional needs and create the feeling that "we're all in this together" (Honora, 2003).

In addition, effective urban teachers scaffold their instruction to increase the likelihood of student success. One high school literature teacher commented:

> Sometimes for these stories, . . . they don't have the background knowledge to understand. They've never heard anything about Greek mythology. They're like "Polyphemus, Odysseus, what is that?" If they don't have the background knowledge, then it becomes harder for them to understand. So what I do is try to present information about Greek mythology in language they know. I use analogies or metaphors to help them make connections. (T. Howard, 2001, p. 192)

Urban teachers concerned about helping students develop positive academic self-concepts know that the process begins with academic achievement and that success comes from connecting with students' prior knowledge. This is only possible when teachers know their students and the world in which they live.

Online Case Book

To analyze additional examples of students' personal, social, and moral development, go to the *Online Case Book* for Chapter 3 at *www.prenhall.com/eggen*.

Checking Your Understanding

4.1 Heavy traffic is moving on an interstate highway at a speed limit of 65. A sign appears that says "Speed Limit 55." The flow of traffic continues as before. How might a driver at Stage 3 and a driver at Stage 4 react? Explain each driver's reasoning.

4.2 According to Gilligan, how might a woman respond to the problem of Gary not knowing the homework assignment (in the vignette on page 80)? How might her response differ from that of a man?

4.3 To which of Kohlberg's stages are empathy and prosocial behaviors most closely related? Explain.

To receive feedback for these questions, go to Appendix B.

Knowledge Extensions

To deepen your understanding of the topics in this section of the chapter and integrate them with topics you've already studied, go to the *Knowledge Extensions* module for Chapter 3 at *www.prenhall.com/eggen*. Respond to questions 12–16.

Classroom Connections

Promoting Moral Development in Your Classroom

1. Openly discuss ethical dilemmas when they arise.

   - **Elementary:** The day before a new student with an exceptionality joins the class, a second-grade teacher invites students to discuss how they would feel if they were new, how new students should be treated, and how they should treat one another in general.

   - **Middle School:** A seventh-grade math teacher has a classroom rule that students may not laugh, snicker, or make remarks of any kind when a classmate is trying to answer a question. In introducing the rule, she has the students discuss the reasons for it and the importance of the rule from other students' perspectives.

   - **High School:** A high school teacher's students view cheating as a game, seeing what they can get away with. The teacher addresses the issue by saying, "Because you feel this way about cheating, I'm going to decide who gets what grade without a test. I'll grade you on how smart I think you are."

This provocative statement precipitates a classroom discussion on fairness and cheating.

2. Model moral and ethical behavior for your students.

   - **Elementary:** One election November, fifth-grade students jokingly ask if the teacher votes. The teacher uses this as an opportunity to discuss the importance of voting and each person's responsibilities in a democracy such as ours.

   - **Middle School:** A science teacher makes a commitment to students to have all their tests and quizzes graded by the following day. One day he is asked if he has the tests ready. "Of course," he responds. "I made an agreement at the beginning of the year, and people can't go back on their agreements."

   - **High School:** A group of tenth-grade business education students finishes a field trip sooner than expected. "If we just hang around a little longer, we don't have to go back to school," one student suggests. "Yes, but that would be a lie, wouldn't it?" the teacher counters. "We said we'd be back as soon as we finished, and we need to keep our word."

Meeting Your Learning Objectives

1. **Describe the factors influencing personal development, and explain how differences in parenting and peer interactions can influence this development.**

   - Personal development is influenced by heredity, parents and other adults, and peers.
   - Parents can contribute to personal development by providing a structured environment that is both demanding and responsive to children's individual needs.
   - Peers affect personal development through the attitudes and values they communicate and by offering or not offering friendship.

2. **Describe characteristics that indicate advancing social development, and explain how social development relates to school violence and aggression.**

   - Perspective taking allows students to consider problems and issues from others' points of view.
   - Social problem solving includes the ability to read social cues, generate strategies, and implement and evaluate these strategies.
   - Social development influences children's ability to make and interact with friends and their ability to learn cooperatively in school.
   - Students who commit violent and aggressive acts typically have underdeveloped social skills.

3. **Use descriptions of psychosocial, identity, and self-concept to explain learners' behaviors.**

   - Erikson's psychosocial theory, an effort to integrate personal and social development, is based on the assumption that development of self is a response to needs. Development occurs in stages, each marked by a psychosocial challenge called a *crisis*. As people develop, the challenges change.
   - Positive resolution of the crisis in each stage results in an inclination to be trusting, autonomous, willing to take initiative, and industrious, from the period of birth through approximately the elementary school years. Continued resolution of crises leaves people with a firm identity, the ability to achieve intimacy, desire for generativity, and finally, a sense of integrity as life's end nears.
   - The development of identity usually occurs during high school and beyond. Identity moratorium and identity achievement are healthy states; identity diffusion and identity foreclosure are less healthy.
   - Self-concept, developed largely through personal experiences, describes people's cognitive assessments of their physical, social, and academic competence. Academic self-concept, particularly in specific content areas, is strongly correlated with achievement, but achievement, physical, and social self-concepts are essentially unrelated.

- Attempts to improve students' self-concepts by direct intervention are largely unsuccessful. In contrast, attempts to improve self-concept as an outcome of increased success and achievement have been quite successful.

4. **Use descriptions of moral reasoning to explain differences in people's responses to ethical issues.**

- Piaget suggested that individuals progress from the stage of external morality, where rules are enforced by authority figures, to the stage of autonomous morality, where individuals see morality as rational and reciprocal.
- Kohlberg's theory of moral development is based upon people's responses to moral dilemmas. He developed a classification system for describing moral reasoning that had three levels.

- At the preconventional level, people make egocentric moral decisions; at the conventional level, moral reasoning focuses on the consequences for others; and at the postconventional level, moral reasoning is based on principle.
- The experience of the unpleasant emotions of shame and guilt and the development of empathy mark advances in the emotional component of moral development.
- Teachers can promote moral development in their classrooms by emphasizing personal responsibility and the functional nature of rules that protect the rights of others. Students should be encouraged to think about topics such as honesty, respect for others, and basic principles of human conduct.

Developing as a *Professional*

Developing as a Professional: Praxis™ Practice

As you've studied this chapter, you've seen how personal and social development occur as well as factors that influence the formation of identity and self-concepts.

Let's look now at a teacher working with a group of middle school students and see to what extent she contributes to these important aspects of development. Read the case study, and answer the questions that follow:

"This is sure frustrating," Helen Sharman, a seventh-grade teacher, mumbles as she scores a set of quizzes in the teachers' workroom after school.

"What's up?" her friend Natasha asks.

"Look," Helen directs, pointing to item 6 on the quiz, in which a student had edited a sentence like this:

Their's were the first items to be loaded.

"These students just won't think," Helen continues. "Three quarters of them put an apostrophe between the *r* and the *s* in *theirs*. The quiz was on using apostrophes in possessives. I warned them I was going to put some questions on the quiz that would make them think and that some of them would have trouble if they weren't on their toes. I should have saved my breath. . . . Not only that, but I gave them practice problems that were just like those on the quiz. We had one almost exactly like item 6, and they still missed it. . . . And I explained it so carefully," she sighs, shaking her head and returning to scoring her papers.

A little later, Natasha asks, "Getting any better?"

"No. . . . Maybe worse."

"What are you going to do?"

"What's really discouraging is that some of the students won't even try. Look at this one. Half of the quiz is blank. This isn't the first time Karl has done this, either. When I confronted him about it last time, he said, 'But I'm no good at English.' I replied, 'But you're doing fine in science and math.' He thought about that for a while and said, 'But that's different.' I wish I knew how to motivate him. You should see him on the basketball floor—poetry in motion—but when he gets in here, nothing."

"That can be discouraging. I've got a few like that myself," Natasha nods.

"What's worse, I'm almost sure some of the kids cheated. I left the room to go to the office, and when I returned, several of them were whispering and had guilt written all over their faces."

"Why do you suppose they did it?" Natasha replies.

"I'm not sure; part of it might be grade pressure, but how else am I going to motivate them? Some just don't see any problem with cheating. If they don't get caught, fine. I really am discouraged."

"Well," Natasha shrugs, "hang in there."

The next morning, Helen returns the quizzes.

"We need to review the rules again," she comments as she finished. "You did so poorly on the quiz, and I explained everything so carefully. You must not have studied very hard."

"Let's take another look," she continues. "What's the rule for singular possessives?"

"Apostrophe *s*," Felice volunteers.

"That's right, Felice. Good. Now, how about plurals?"

"*S* apostrophe," Scott answers.

"All right. But what if the plural form of the noun doesn't end in *s*? . . . Russell?"

"Then it's like singular. . . . It's apostrophe *s*."

"Good. And how about pronouns?"

"You don't do anything," Connie adds.

"Yes, that's all correct," Helen nods. "Why didn't you do that on the quiz?"

" . . . "

"Okay, look at number 3 on the quiz."

It appears as follows:

The books belonging to the lady were lost.

"It should be written like this," Helen explains, writing, "*The lady's books were lost*" on the chalkboard.

"Ms. Sharman," Nathan calls from the back of the room. "Why is it apostrophe *s*?"

"Nathan," Helen says evenly. "Remember my first rule?"

"Yes, Ma'am," Nathan says quietly.

"Good. If you want to ask a question, what else can you do other than shout it out?"

"Raise my hand."

"Good. Now, to answer your question, it's singular. So that's why it's apostrophe *s*.

"Now look at number 6." Helen waits a few seconds and then continues, "You were supposed to correctly punctuate it. But it's correct already because *theirs* is already possessive. Now that one was a little tricky, but you know I'm going to put a few on each quiz to make you think. You'd have gotten it if you were on your toes."

Helen identifies a few more items that were commonly missed and then hands out a review sheet.

"Now, these are just like the quiz," she says. "Practice hard on them, and we'll have another quiz on Thursday. Let's all do better. Please don't let me down again.

"And one more thing. I believe there was some cheating on this test. If I catch anyone cheating on Thursday, I'll tear up your quiz and give you a failing grade. Now go to work."

PRAXIS These exercises are designed to help you prepare for the Praxis™ Principles of Learning and Teaching exam. To receive feedback on your short-answer questions, go to the Companion Website at *www.prenhall.com/eggen*, then to the *Practice for Praxis™* module for Chapter 3.

To acquire experience in preparing for the multiple-choice items on the Praxis™ exam, go to the *Self-Assessment* module for Chapter 3 at *www.prenhall.com/eggen*, and click on "Practice Quiz."

For additional connections between this text and the Praxis™ exam, go to Appendix A.

Short-Answer Questions

In answering these questions, use information from the chapter and link your responses to specific information in the case.

1. How might Erikson explain Karl's behavior in Helen's class?
2. Using findings from the research on self-concept, explain Karl's behavior.
3. Using concepts from Kohlberg's theory, analyze Helen's cheating problem. From Kohlberg's perspective, how well did she handle this problem?
4. If you think Helen's teaching could have been improved on the basis of the information in Chapter 3, what suggestions would you make? Again, be specific.

ONLINE PORTFOLIO ACTIVITIES

Also on the companion Website at *www.prenhall.com/eggen*, you can measure your understanding of chapter content with multiple-choice and essay questions, and broaden your knowledge base in *Exploring Further* and *Web Links* to other education psychology websites.

To develop your professional portfolio, further apply your understanding of chapter content, and address the INTASC standards, go the Companion Website, then to the *Online Portfolio Activities* for Chapter 3. Complete the suggested activities.

IMPORTANT CONCEPTS

autonomous morality (p. 81)
collective self-esteem (p. 78)
crisis (p. 70)
emotional intelligence (p. 86)
empathy (p. 86)
external morality (p. 81)
guilt (p. 86)
identity (p. 70)
interpersonal harmony (p. 83)
law and order (p. 84)
market exchange (p. 83)
moral development (p. 80)
moral dilemma (p. 82)
personal development (p. 62)
perspective taking (p. 66)

proactive aggression (p. 67)
punishment–obedience (p. 82)
self-concept (p. 70)
self-esteem (p. 75)
self-worth (p. 75)
sexual identity (p. 74)
sexual orientation (p. 74)
shame (p. 86)
social conventions (p. 85)
social contract (p. 84)
social development (p. 65)
social problem solving (p. 66)
temperament (p. 63)
universal principles (p. 84)

CHAPTER 4

Group and Individual Differences

Learning Objectives

After you have completed your study of this chapter, you should be able to

1 Describe differences in the way intelligence is viewed, and explain how ability grouping can influence learning.

2 Define socioeconomic status, and explain how it can affect school performance.

3 Describe cultural, ethnic, and language diversity, and explain how they can influence learning.

4 Explain gender-role identity, and describe steps for eliminating gender bias in classrooms.

5 Describe characteristics of schools and qualities of teachers that promote student resilience.

The learners we teach are different in several important ways. As you read the following case study, think about some of these differences and the influence they might have on learning.

Tim Wilkinson is a fifth-grade teacher in a large urban elementary school. He has 29 students: 16 girls and 13 boys. His class includes 10 African Americans, 3 students of Hispanic descent, and 2 Asian Americans. Most of his students come from low-income families.

Tim smiles as he watches his students busy at their seats. Walking among them, he glances at Selena's work. As usual, it is nearly perfect. Everything is easy for her, and she seems to be a happy, well-adjusted child.

He smiles again as he walks by Helen's desk. She is his "special project," and she has begun to blossom in response to his attention and effort. The quality of her work has improved dramatically since the beginning of the year.

As he steps past Juan, his glow turns to concern. Juan has been quiet from the first day of school, and he is easily offended by perceived slights from his classmates. Because his parents are migrant workers, the family moves constantly, and he repeated the first grade. His parents are separated, and his mother has settled in this area so the children can stay in the same school.

Juan struggles to keep up with the rest of the class. Spanish is his first language, and Tim isn't sure how much of his instruction Juan understands. What seems certain, however, is that Juan is falling further and further behind, and Tim doesn't know what to do. Not knowing where else to turn, he consults Jeanne Morton, the school psychologist.

After talking with Tim and meeting with Juan, Jeanne contacts Juan's mother and suggests some testing. On the basis of an individually administered intelligence test, Jeanne concludes that aptitude is not the source of Juan's problem. "Juan is definitely capable of doing better work," she comments to Tim. They agree to meet again to consider other alternatives.

Figure 4.1   Sources of learner individuality

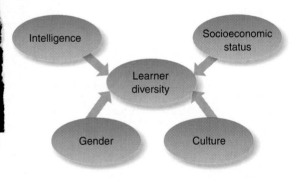

As you think about the title of this chapter and the case study you just read, look at Figure 4.1, which outlines four of the most common group differences that we see in our students. Then, consider these two questions: (1) How might these differences influence our students' learning? and (2) How should teachers respond to cultural differences in students? We try to answer these and other questions in this chapter. We begin by examining the concept of intelligence.

INTELLIGENCE

While all of us have an intuitive notion of **intelligence,** experts generally agree that it is composed of three components: (1) the ability to acquire knowledge, (2) the capacity to think and reason in the abstract, and (3) the ability to solve novel problems (Louis, Subotnik, Breland, & Lewis, 2000; Sattler, 2001).

From another perspective, intelligence is simply defined as the attributes that intelligence tests measure. Items like the following are commonly found on these tests, and people's intelligence is inferred from their responses.

1. Cave:Hole::Bag: _____ (Cave is to hole as bag is to _____?)
   a. paper
   b. container
   c. box
   d. brown
2. Sharon had x amount of money, and this could buy 8 apples. How much money would it take to buy 4 apples?
   a. $8x$
   b. $2x$
   c. $x/2$
   d. $x2$
3. Inspect the following list of numbers for 5 seconds:
   9 7 4 6 2 1 8 3 9
   Now cover them and name the digits in order from memory.

Intelligence. The ability to acquire knowledge, the capacity to think and reason in the abstract, and the ability to solve novel problems

As these items suggest, experience is an important factor in test performance (Halpern & LaMay, 2000; Perkins, 1995). Practice with vocabulary and analogies, for example, would improve the score on the first item. The second requires background in math, and even the third, a seemingly simple memory task, can be improved with training (A. Brown, Bransford, Ferrara, & Campione, 1983).

These results corroborate Piaget's work. In Chapter 2, we saw that experience is an important factor in cognitive development, and children who have the advantage of rich experiences consistently perform better than their less-fortunate peers. Clearly, intelligence tests measure more than innate ability.

Research suggests that a moderate positive correlation exists between intelligence and school achievement (Sattler, 2001). However, experts caution that other factors such as motivation and personality traits like persistence also contribute to both intelligent behavior and school performance (Ackerman, 2003).

Intelligence: One Trait or Many?

Because scores on different measures of intelligence, such as verbal ability and abstract reasoning, were highly correlated, early researchers believed intelligence to be a single trait. For example, Charles Spearman (1927) described it as "g," or general intelligence. Since then theorists have expanded the concept, and some now believe that intelligence is composed of several dimensions. We look at two of them in the next sections.

Gardner's Theory of Multiple Intelligences

Howard Gardner (1983, 1999b) analyzed people's performance in different domains and concluded that intelligence is composed of eight relatively independent dimensions. He is also considering a ninth, called *existential intelligence,* which is evident in a person's ability to think about life's fundamental questions, such as "Who are we?" and "Where do we come from?" (Gardner, 1999c). Table 4.1 outlines the eight dimensions currently in his theory.

The concept of multiple intelligences makes intuitive sense. We all know people who don't seem particularly "sharp" analytically but who excel in getting along with others, for example. This ability serves them well, and in some instances, they're more successful in life than their "brighter" counterparts. Others are extraordinary athletes or accomplished musicians. Gardner describes these people as high in interpersonal, bodily-kinesthetic, and musical intelligence, respectively.

Table 4.1 Gardner's theory of multiple intelligences

Dimension	Example
Linguistic Intelligence Sensitivity to the meaning and order of words and the varied uses of language	Poet, journalist
Logical-Mathematical Intelligence The ability to handle long chains of reasoning and to recognize patterns and order in the world	Scientist, mathematician
Musical Intelligence Sensitivity to pitch, melody, and tone	Composer, violinist
Spatial Intelligence The ability to perceive the visual world accurately and to re-create, transform, or modify aspects of the world on the basis of one's perceptions	Sculptor, navigator
Bodily-Kinesthetic Intelligence A fine-tuned ability to use the body and to handle objects	Dancer, athlete
Interpersonal Intelligence The ability to notice and make distinctions among others	Therapist, salesperson
Intrapersonal Intelligence Access to one's own "feeling life"	Self-aware individual
Naturalist Intelligence The ability to recognize similarities and differences in the physical world	Naturalist, biologist, anthropologist

Source: Adapted from Gardner and Hatch (1989) and Chekley (1997).

Spatial intelligence includes the ability to perceive and re-create physical relations in the world.

Bodily-kinesthetic intelligence allows dancers and athletes to use their bodies in effective and creative ways.

Applications of Gardner's Theory. Gardner (1999a) recommends that teachers adapt instruction to address the different intelligences. Teachers should present content in ways that capitalize on as many different intelligences as possible, and efforts should also focus on helping students understand their strengths and weaknesses in each (Denig, 2003; Krechevsky & Seidel, 2001; Shearer, 2002). Table 4.2 outlines different ways to differentiate instruction. Gardner warns, however, that not all ideas or subjects can be adapted for each intelligence: "There is no point in assuming that every topic can be effectively approached in [multiple] ways, and it is a waste of effort and time to attempt to do this" (Gardner, 1995, p. 206).

Criticisms of Gardner's Theory. While popular with educators, Gardner's theory also has its critics. Some caution that the theory and its applications have not been validated by research (Corno et al., 2002), and whether or not it even qualifies as a theory has been questioned (Chen, 2004). Others disagree with the assertion that abilities in specific domains, such as naturalist or musical, qualify as separate forms of intelligence (McMahon, Rose, & Parks, 2004; Sattler, 2001).

Failure to account for the role that a centralized working memory system plays in intelligent behavior is one of the strongest criticisms of Gardner's work (D. Lohman, 2001).

Table 4.2 Instructional applications of Gardner's multiple intelligences

Dimension	Application
Linguistic	How can I get students to talk or write about the idea?
Logical-Mathematical	How can I bring in number, logic, and classification to encourage students to quantify or clarify the idea?
Spatial	What can I do to help students visualize, draw, or conceptualize the idea spatially?
Musical	How can I help students use environmental sounds, or set ideas into rhythm or melody?
Bodily-Kinesthetic	What can I do to help students involve the whole body or to use hands-on experience?
Interpersonal	How can I use peer, cross-age, or cooperative learning to help students develop their interactive skills?
Intrapersonal	How can I get students to think about their capacities and feelings to make them more aware of themselves as persons and learners?
Naturalist	How can I provide experiences that require students to classify different types of objects and analyze their classification schemes?

(We examine working memory in detail in Chapter 7.) For example, when students solve word problems in math, they must keep the problems' specifics in mind as they search their memory for similar problems, select strategies, and use specific values to solve the problems. This cognitive juggling act occurs in all types of intelligent behavior. Because it views intelligence as consisting of separate dimensions, Gardner's theory ignores the fact that all knowledge is processed in working memory (D. Lohman, 2001).

Widely respected educational historian Larry Cuban (2004) puts Gardner's work into perspective in concluding that it has had an important influence on teachers' beliefs, moderate influence on curriculum and instructional materials, but limited impact on mainstream teaching and assessment practices.

Sternberg's Triarchic Theory of Intelligence

Robert Sternberg (Sternberg, 2000, 2003a, 2003b; Sternberg & Grigorenko, 2000), another multitrait theorist, describes three categories or types of intelligence:

- An *analytical,* or componential, dimension. This aspect of intelligence is used in thinking and problem solving and is similar to traditional definitions of intelligence (Sternberg, 1988, 2003).
- A *creative,* or experiential, dimension. This dimension involves the ability to deal effectively with novel situations and the ability to solve familiar problems efficiently. Sternberg believes that intelligent individuals quickly move from conscious learning in unfamiliar situations to performing tasks automatically as they become more familiar (Sternberg, 1998a, 1998b).
- A *practical,* or contextual, dimension. This feature of intelligence is the ability to deal effectively with everyday tasks. Intelligent behavior involves adapting to the environment, changing the environment if adaptation isn't effective, or selecting a better environment if necessary (Grigorenko & Sternberg, 2001). This reminds us of the importance of context in intelligent behavior (Barab & Plucker, 2002).

Sternberg's emphasis on the creative and practical aspects of intellect is what sets his theory apart from other views of intelligence. He sees functioning effectively in the real world as intelligent behavior, and because of this emphasis, he believes that individuals considered intelligent in one setting or culture may be viewed as unintelligent in another.

Improving Intelligence. Influenced by Piaget's emphasis on experience as essential for development, Sternberg believes that providing students with experiences in which they're expected to think analytically, creatively, and practically can increase intelligence. Some examples of applying Sternberg's theory are outlined in Table 4.3. With some awareness and thought, teachers can make suggestions such as these part of their routines.

Table 4.3 Applying analytic, creative, and practical thinking in different content areas

Content Area	Analytic	Creative	Practical
Math	Express the number 44 in base 2.	Write a test question that measures understanding of three different number bases.	How is the base 2 used in our everyday lives?
Language Arts	Why is *Romeo and Juliet* considered a tragedy?	Write an alternative ending to *Romeo and Juliet* to make it a comedy.	Write a TV ad for the school's production of *Romeo and Juliet.*
Social Studies	In what ways were the American and the French revolutions similar and different?	What would our lives be like today if the American revolution had not succeeded?	What lessons can countries take away from the study of revolutions?
Science	If a balloon is filled with 1 liter of air at room temperature, and it is then placed in a freezer, what will happen to the balloon?	How would the balloon filled with air behave on the moon?	Describe two common examples where heating or cooling affects solids, liquids, or gasses.
Art	Compare and contrast the artistic styles of Van Gogh and Picasso.	What would the Statue of Liberty look like if it were created by Picasso?	Create a poster for the student art show using the style of one of the artists we studied.

Intelligence can be enhanced by learning activities that emphasize abstract reasoning and problem solving.

Intelligence: Nature Versus Nurture

No aspect of intelligence has been more hotly debated than the influence of heredity versus environment. The extreme **nature view** of intelligence asserts that intelligence is essentially determined by genetics; the **nurture view** of intelligence emphasizes the influence of the environment. Most experts take a position somewhere in the middle, believing that a person's intelligence is influenced by both (Coll, Bearer, & Learner, 2004; Petrill & Wilkerson, 2000; Shepard, 2001). This view holds that a person's genes provide the potential for intelligence, and stimulating environments make the most of the raw material.

Evidence indicates that learning environments can have a significant effect on intelligence, which supports Sternberg's view that intelligence can be increased with experience (Sternberg 2000, 2002). For example, children exposed to enriched preschool learning experiences show increased scores on both intelligence and achievement tests (F. A. Campbell et al., 2001; Ramey, Ramey, & Lanzi, 2001). And, additional evidence suggests that school experiences also produce consistent gains in intelligence test scores (Ceci & Williams, 1997; Christian, Bachnan, & Morrison, 2001).

Ability Grouping

Although other adaptations exist (we discuss them in Chapter 5), schools most commonly respond to differences in learner ability by **ability grouping,** the process of placing students of similar abilities into groups, and attempting to match instruction to the needs of these groups (Lou, Abrami, & Spence, 2000). Though controversial, most elementary teachers endorse it, particularly in reading and math.

Ability grouping in elementary schools typically exists In three forms, described and illustrated in Table 4.4. In middle, junior high, and high schools, ability grouping goes further, with high-ability students studying advanced and college preparatory courses and lower ability students receiving vocational or work-related instruction (Oakes & Wells, 2002). In some cases, students are grouped only in certain content areas, such as English or math; in others, ability grouping occurs across all content areas. The latter practice, called **tracking,** places students in different classes or curricula on the basis of achievement. Some form of tracking exists in most middle, junior high, and high schools.

Ability Grouping: Research Results

Why is ability grouping so pervasive? Advocates argue that it allows teachers to adjust the instructional pace, methods, and materials to better meet learners' needs. And, because instruction is similar for a particular group, ability grouping is also easier for the teacher.

Critics counter by citing several problems:

- Within-class grouping creates logistical problems because different lessons and assignments are required, so monitoring students is difficult (Good & Brophy, 2003; Oakes, 1992).

Nature view of intelligence. The assertion that intelligence is essentially determined by genetics

Nurture view of intelligence. The assertion that emphasizes the influence of the environment on intelligence

Ability grouping. The process of placing students of similar abilities together and attempting to match instruction to the needs of these groups

Tracking. Placing students in different classes or curricula on the basis of achievement

---

Table 4.4 Types of ability grouping in elementary schools

Type	Description	Example
Between-class grouping	Divides students at a certain grade into levels, such as high, average, and low	A school with 75 third graders divides them into one class of high achievers, one of average achievers, and one of low achievers.
Within-class grouping	Divides students in a class into subgroups based on reading or math scores	A fourth-grade teacher has three reading groups based on reading ability.
Joplin plan	Regroups across grade levels	Teachers from different grade levels place students in the same reading class.

- Improper placements occur, which tend to become permanent. Members of cultural minorities are underrepresented in high-ability classes and overrepresented in low ones (Davenport et al., 1998; Mickelson & Heath, 1999; Oakes, 1992).
- Members of low groups are stigmatized by being labeled as low achievers (Oakes & Wells, 2002).
- Homogeneously grouped low-ability students achieve less than heterogeneously grouped students of similar ability (Good & Brophy, 2003).

The research on ability grouping reminds teachers of the need for positive expectations for all students.

The negative effects of grouping are related, in large part, to the quality of instruction. Research indicates that presentations to low groups tend to be more fragmented and vague, and they focus on low-level, memorization tasks to a greater extent than those to high groups. Students in low-ability classes are often taught by teachers who lack enthusiasm and stress conformity instead of autonomy and the development of self-regulation (Good & Brophy, 2003; S. Ross, Smith, Loks, & McNelie, 1994). As a result, self-esteem and motivation to learn decrease, and absentee rates increase. Tracking can also result in racial or cultural segregation of students, which negatively influences social development and opportunities to form friendships across cultural groups (Oakes & Wells, 2002).

Ability Grouping: Implications for Teachers

Suggestions for dealing with the issues involved in ability grouping vary (Loveless, 1999). At one extreme, critics argue that its effects are so negative that the practice should be abolished completely. A more moderate position suggests that grouping may be appropriate in some areas, such as reading and math (Good & Brophy, 2003), but that every effort should be made to de-emphasize groups in other content areas. Researchers have found that the **Joplin plan,** which uses homogeneous grouping in reading, but heterogeneous grouping in other areas, can increase reading achievement without negative side effects (Slavin, 1987). At the junior and senior high levels, between-class grouping should be limited to the basic academic areas.

When grouping is necessary, specific measures to reduce its negative effects should be taken. Some suggestions are outlined in Figure 4.2. These suggestions are demanding. Teachers must make careful decisions about group placements and closely monitor their students' progress. The need to maintain high expectations and instructional flexibility in this process is important.

Learning Styles

Historically, psychologists have used intelligence tests to measure mental abilities and have used concepts such as *introvert* and *extrovert* to describe different personality types. Researchers who study the interface between the two are exploring **learning styles**—students' personal approaches to processing information and problem solving (Denig, 2003). Researchers sometimes use the terms *learning style* and *cognitive style* interchangeably.

Figure 4.2   Suggestions for reducing the negative effects of ability grouping

- Keep group composition flexible, and reassign students to other groups when their rate of learning warrants it.
- Make every effort to ensure that the quality of instruction is as high for low-ability students as it is for high-ability students.
- Treat student characteristics as dynamic rather than static; teach low-ability students appropriate learning strategies and behaviors.
- Avoid assigning negative labels to lower groups.
- Constantly be aware of the possible negative consequences of ability grouping.

Joplin plan. Homogeneous grouping in reading, combined with heterogeneous grouping in other areas

Learning styles. Students' personal approaches to learning, problem solving, and processing information

One of the most common descriptions of learning style distinguishes between deep and surface approaches to processing information (C. J. Evans, Kirby, & Fabrigar, 2003). For instance, as you studied the concept of *centration* in Chapter 2, did you note that it is part of Piaget's theory (Piaget, 1970) and relate it to other concepts, such as egocentricity, conservation, and preoperational thinking? Did you also relate it to the fact that adults often center? If so, you were using a deep-processing approach. On the other hand, if you memorized the definition and identified one or two examples of centering, you were using a surface approach.

As you might expect, deep-processing approaches result in higher achievement if tests focus on understanding and application, but surface approaches can be successful if tests emphasize fact learning and memorization. Students who use deep-processing approaches also tend to be more intrinsically motivated and self-regulated, whereas those who use surface approaches tend to more motivated by high grades and their performance compared to others (Pintrich & Schunk, 2002). (We examine motivation in detail in Chapters 10 and 11.)

Learning Preferences: Research Results

The concept *learning style* is popular in education, and many consultants use this label when they conduct in-service workshops for teachers. However, these workshops typically focus on students' *preferences* for different learning environments. For example, workshops examine lighting and noise level, and consultants encourage teachers to match classroom environments to students' preferences.

Research on these practices is controversial. Advocates claim the match results in increased achievement and improved attitudes (Carbo, 1997; Farkas, 2003). Critics counter by questioning the validity of the tests used to measure learning styles (preferences) (S. A. Stahl, 1999), and they also cite research indicating that attempts to match learning environments to learning preferences have resulted in no increases and, in some cases, even decreases in learning (Klein, 2003; S. A. Stahl, 1999).

Learning Styles: Implications for Teachers

The concept of *learning style* has at least three implications for teachers. First, it reminds us of the need to vary instruction, since no instructional strategy will be preferred by all students (Brophy, 2004). Second, it suggests that we should help students understand how they learn most effectively. (We examine *metacognition,* the concept that describes learners' awareness of and control over their thinking and learning, in Chapter 7.) Third, awareness of learning style can increase our sensitivity to differences in our students, making it more likely that we will respond to our students as individuals.

Students' learning preferences unquestionably vary. However, it is not wise to categorize learners and prescribe methods on the basis of tests with questionable technical qualities. The idea of learning style is appealing, but a critical examination of this approach should cause educators to be skeptical. "Like most other reviewers who pay close attention to the research literature, I do not see much validity in the claims made by those who urge teachers to assess their students with learning style inventories and follow with differentiated curriculum and instruction" (Brophy, 2004, pp. 343–344).

Checking Your Understanding

1.1 Describe at least two different ways that intelligence is defined, as presented in this section.

1.2 Explain differences between historical views of intelligence compared to Gardner's and Sternberg's views.

1.3 Describe ability grouping. What does research indicate about its potential impact on learning?

To receive feedback for these questions, go to Appendix B.

Knowledge Extensions

To deepen your understanding of the topics in this section of Chapter 4 and to integrate them with topics you've already studied, go to the *Knowledge Extensions* module for Chapter 4 at *www.prenhall.com/eggen*. Respond to questions 1–6.

Classroom Connections

Applying an Understanding of Ability Differences in Your Classroom

1. Use intelligence test scores cautiously when making educational decisions, keeping in mind that they are only one indicator of ability.
   - **Elementary:** An urban third-grade teacher consults with a school counselor in interpreting intelligence test scores, and she remembers that language and experience influence test performance.
   - **Middle School:** When making placement decisions, a middle school team relies on past classroom performance and grades in addition to standardized test scores.
   - **High School:** An English teacher uses grades, assessments of motivation, and work samples in addition to aptitude test scores in making placement recommendations.

2. Use instructional strategies that maximize student interest and different abilities.
   - **Elementary:** In a unit on the Revolutionary War, a fifth-grade teacher assesses all students on basic information, but bases 25 percent of the unit grade on special projects, such as researching the music and art of the times.

   - **Middle School:** An eighth-grade English teacher has both required and optional assignments. Seventy percent of the assignments are required for everyone; the other 30 percent provide students with choices.
   - **High School:** A geometry teacher allows students to drop their two lowest quiz scores each marking period. He also provides help sessions two nights a week after school.

3. Use ability grouping only when essential, view group composition as flexible, and reassign students when warranted by their performance. Attempt to provide the same quality of instruction for all group levels.
   - **Elementary:** A fourth-grade teacher uses ability groups only for reading. She uses whole-class instruction for other language arts topics such as poetry and American folktales.
   - **Middle School:** A seventh-grade team meets regularly to assess group placements and to reassign students to different groups based on their academic progress.
   - **High School:** A history teacher videotapes lessons to compare his teaching behaviors in high-ability compared to standard-ability groups. He reminds his standard classes that he will maintain high expectations for their performance.

SOCIOECONOMIC STATUS

Students' **socioeconomic status (SES)**—the combination of parents' income, occupation, and level of education that describes relative standing in society—is one of the most powerful factors influencing student achievement (see Figure 4.3). Sociologists often divide families into four classes: upper, middle, working, and lower. Table 4.5 outlines some of the characteristics of these classes.

Socioeconomic status consistently predicts intelligence and achievement test scores, grades, truancy, and dropout and suspension rates (J. P. Byrnes, 2003; Macionis, 2006). It has its most powerful influence at the lower income levels. For example, low-SES fourth-graders are more than twice as likely as their higher SES peers to fall below basic levels of reading, they are only about one third as likely to achieve at a level described as proficient, and dropout rates for students from the poorest families exceed 50 percent (Allington & McGill-Franzen, 2003). Students from families in the highest income quartile are 2½ times more likely to enroll in college and 8 times more likely to graduate than

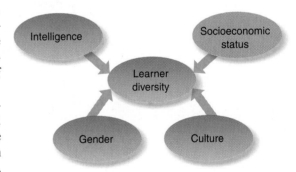

Figure 4.3 Sources of learner individuality: Socioeconomic status

Socioeconomic status (SES). The combination of income, occupation, and level of education that describes the relative standing in society of a family or individual

Table 4.5 Characteristics of Different Socioeconomic Levels

	Upper Class	Middle Class	Working Class	Lower Class
Income	$160,000+	$80,000–$160,000 (½) $40,000–$80,000 (½)	$25,000–$40,000	Below $25,000
Occupation	Corporate or professional (e.g., doctor, lawyer)	White collar, skilled blue collar	Blue collar	Minimum wage unskilled labor
Education	Attended college & professional schools & expect children to do the same	Attended high school, college or professional schools Strive to help their children do the same or higher.	Attended high school; may or may not encourage college	Attended high school or less; cost a major factor in education
Housing	Own home in prestigious neighborhood	Usually own home	About half own a home	Rent

Source: Macionis, 2006; U.S. Bureau of the Census, 2001.

Parents promote both cognitive and language development by discussing ideas and experiences with their children.

their low-SES peers (Levine & Nediffer, 1996; B. Young & Smith, 1999).

Some disconcerting trends exist in our country with respect to SES. The incidence of children living in poverty is increasing, with minorities and single-parent families over-represented. The rate of childhood poverty has risen every year since 2000, and the percentage of U.S. families below the poverty level in 2002 (defined as an income of $18,100 for a family of four in 2002) was five times greater than in other industrialized countries (Biddle, 2001; Education Vital Signs, 2005; U.S. Department of Health and Human Services, 2002). Biddle (2001) summarizes the impact of these data on education:

> What this means is that at least one-fifth of all children who come through the schoolhouse door in America today are likely to be experiencing poverty-associated problems such as substandard housing, an inadequate diet, threadbare or hand-me-down clothes, lack of health insurance, chronic dental or health problems, deprivation and violence in their communities, little or no funds for school supplies, and whose overburdened parents subsist on welfare or work long hours at miserably paid jobs. These facts pose enormous problems for America's schools. (Biddle, 2001, p. 5.)

Influence of SES on Learning

Researchers believe SES influences learning in at least three ways: (1) basic needs and experiences, (2) parental involvement, and (3) attitudes and values. Let's look at them.

Basic Needs and Experiences

Many low-SES children lack medical and dental care and live in substandard housing on inadequate diets (Duncan & Brooks-Gunn, 2000; Rothstein, 2004a, 2004b). Poor nutrition can affect attention and memory and lead to lower IQ scores (Berk, 2004). Homelessness is also a problem; the number of homeless children is higher than at any time since the Great Depression (Homes for the Homeless, 1999; Urban Institute, 2000).

Economic problems can also lead to family and marital conflicts, which result in less stable and nurturant homes (Rainwater & Smeedings, 2003). Children of poverty may come to school without the personal sense of security that equips them to tackle school-related tasks. Research indicates that students from poor families have a greater incidence of depression and other emotional problems than do their more advantaged peers (G. W. Evans & English, 2002).

Children of poverty also relocate frequently. In some low-income schools, mobility rates are above 100 percent (Rothstein, 2004a). Researchers have found that 30 percent of the poorest students attend at least three different schools by third grade compared to only 10 percent for middle class students. These frequent moves are a source of stress for students and a challenge for teachers attempting to develop caring relationships with them (P. Barton, 2004; Nakagawa, 1999).

SES also influences children's experiences (Duncan & Brooks-Gunn, 2000; Orr, 2003; Wenner, 2003). High-SES parents are more likely to provide their children with educational activities, such as travel and visits to art galleries and science museums. They also have more computers, reference books, and other learning materials in the home, and they provide more formal training outside of school, like music and dance lessons. These activities complement classroom learning (Lareau, 2003; V. E. Lee & Burkam, 2002).

Parental Involvement

Higher-SES parents also tend to be more involved in their children's schooling and other activities (K. Brown et al., 2004; Diamond & Gomez, 2004). One mother commented, "When she sees me at her games, when she sees me going to open house, when I attend her Interscholastic League contests, she knows I am interested in her activities. Plus, we have more to talk about" (M. Young & Scribner, 1997, p. 12). Time spent working, often at two jobs or more, is a major obstacle to school involvement for low-SES parents (H. Weiss et al., 2003).

In general, high-SES parents talk to their children more and differently than do those who are low SES. They ask more questions, explain the causes of events and provide reasons for rules. Their language is more elaborate, their directions are clearer, and they are more likely to encourage problem solving (Berk, 2006; McDevitt & Ormrod, 2004). Children expect the same in school and are more likely to pay attention and follow directions (Stright, Neitzel, Sears, & Hoke-Sinex, 2001). Sometimes called "the curriculum of the home," these rich interaction patterns, together with the background experiences already described, provide a strong foundation for future learning (Holloway, 2004; Lareau, 2003).

Attitudes and Values

The impact of SES is also transmitted through parental attitudes and values. For example, many high-SES parents encourage autonomy, individual responsibility, and self-control; low-SES parents are more likely to emphasis conformity and obedience (Macionis, 2006).

Values are also communicated by example. For instance, children who see their parents reading and studying learn that reading is valuable and are more likely to read themselves (Neuman & Celano, 2001). And, as we would expect, students who read at home show higher reading achievement than those who don't (Hiebert & Rafael, 1996).

High-SES parents also have positive expectations for their children and encourage them to graduate from high school and attend college (K. Brown et al., 2004; McGrath, Swisher, Elder, & Conger, 2001). They also know how to play the "schooling game," steering their sons and daughters into advanced high school courses and contacting schools for information about their children's learning progress (Lareau, 2003). Low-SES parents, in contrast, tend to have lower aspirations, allow their children to "drift" into classes, and rely on the decisions of others. Students often get lost in the shuffle, ending up in inappropriate or less challenging classes.

These descriptions help us begin to answer the first question we asked at the beginning of the chapter: "How might these difference influence students' learning?" Coming from disadvantaged homes can make learning and high achievement a challenge for students. However, as teachers we must be cautious about classifying students before we see how they perform.

SES: Some Cautions and Implications for Teachers

It's important to remember that the research findings we report here describe group differences, and individuals within the groups will vary widely. For example, many low-SES parents read and talk to their children, encourage their involvement in extracurricular activities, and attend school events. Both of your authors come from low-SES families, and we were given all the enriching experiences we've discussed in reference to high-SES parents. Conversely, belonging to a high-SES family does not guarantee a child enriching experiences and caring, involved parents.

When you work with your students, be careful to avoid stereotypes; remember that your students are individuals, and treat them as such. Keep your expectations appropriately high for all students.

Checking Your Understanding

2.1   Define socioeconomic status (SES), and explain each of its characteristics.

2.2   Describe three ways in which SES can influence learning.

2.3   As you work with your students, what important factor should you keep in mind when considering SES?

To receive feedback for these questions, go to Appendix B.

Knowledge Extensions

To deepen your understanding of the topics in this section of Chapter 4 and to integrate them with topics you've already studied, go to the *Knowledge Extensions* module for Chapter 4 at *www.prenhall.com/eggen*. Respond to questions 7–9.

CULTURE

Think about the clothes you wear, the music you like, and the activities you share with your friends. These and other factors, such as family structure, are all part of your **culture,** which refers to the knowledge, attitudes, values, and customs that characterize a social group (Chun, Organista, & Marin, 2002; Matsumoto, 2004). Its enormous impact on even the most basic aspects of our lives is illustrated in the following quote:

Figure 4.4   Sources of learner individuality: Culture

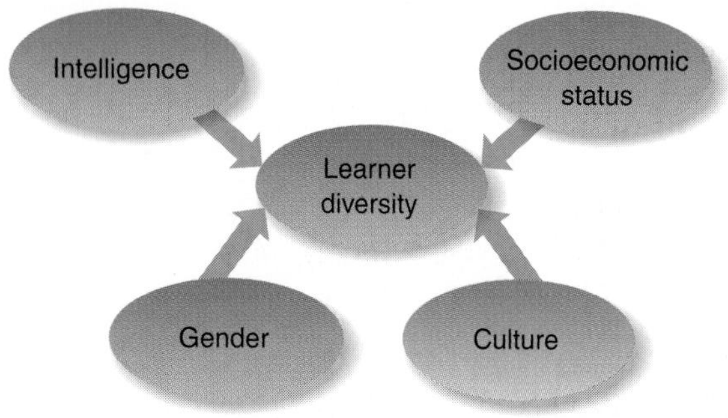

> Culture not only helps to determine what foods we eat, but it also influences when we eat (for example, one, three, or five meals and at what time of the day); with whom we eat (that is, only with the same sex, with children or with the extended family); how we eat (for example, at a table or on the floor; with chopsticks, silverware, or the fingers); and the ritual of eating (for example, in which hand the fork is held, asking for or being offered seconds, and belching to show appreciation of a good meal). These eating patterns are habits of the culture. (Gollnick & Chinn, 1986, pp. 6–7)

Like SES, culture can also influence school success (see Figure 4.4).

Ethnicity

Ethnicity, a person's ancestry and the way individuals identify with the nation from which they or their ancestors came, is an important part of culture (deMarrais & LeCompte, 1999). Members of an ethnic group have a common history, language (although sometimes not actively used), value system, and set of customs.

More than 7 million people immigrated to the United States in the 1970s and 1980s. The results of this and later immigration, together with differences in birth rate for various groups, can be seen in a comparison of U.S. population figures from 1980 to 2000 (see Table 4.6).

Experts estimate that by the year 2020 two thirds of the school population will be African American, Asian, Hispanic, or Native American (Meece & Kurtz-Costes, 2001; U.S. Department of Education, 2000). Each of these groups brings a distinct set of values and traditions that influences learning.

Culture and Schooling

A second-grade class in Albuquerque, New Mexico, is reading *The Boxcar Children* and is about to start a new chapter. The teacher says, "Look at the illustration at the beginning of the chapter and tell me what you think is going to happen." A few students raise their hands. The teacher calls on a boy in the back row.

He says, "I think the boy is going to meet his grandfather."

The teacher asks, "Based on what you know, how does the boy feel about meeting his grandfather?"

Table 4.6 U.S. Census ethnicity comparisons

Population Group	Percent of Total		
	1980	1990	2000
Non-Hispanic White	79.8	75.6	69.1
Black	11.5	11.7	12.1
Hispanic	6.4	9.0	12.5
Asian	1.6	2.8	3.7
American Indian	0.6	0.7	0.7
Some other race	0.1	0.1	0.2
Two or more races	NA	NA	1.6

Source: Kent, M., Pollard, K., Haaga, J., & Mather, M., 2001.

Culture. The knowledge, attitudes, values, and customs that characterize a social group

Ethnicity. A person's ancestry and the way individuals identify with the nation from which they or their ancestors came

Trying to involve the whole class, the teacher calls on another student—one of four Native Americans in the group—even though she has not raised her hand. When she doesn't answer, the teacher tries rephrasing the question, but again the student sits in silence.

Feeling exasperated, the teacher wonders if there is something in the way the lesson is being conducted that makes it difficult for the student to respond. She senses that the student she has called on understood the story and was enjoying it. Why, then, won't she answer what appears to be a simple question?

The teacher recalls that this is not the first time this has happened, and that, in fact, the other Native American students in the class rarely answer questions in class discussions. She wants to involve them, wants them to participate in class, but can not think of ways to get them to talk. (Villegas, 1991, p. 3)

Why do students respond differently to our instruction, and how does culture influence these differences? We try to answer these questions in this section as we examine cultural attitudes and values, patterns of adult–child interactions in different cultures, and how classroom organization can support or clash with these patterns.

Minority role models help minority youth understand how they can succeed without losing their ethnic or cultural heritage.

The Cultural Base of Attitudes and Values

When we defined *culture,* we said that it included the attitudes and values that characterize a social group. These aspects of culture sometimes complement school learning, and at other times they can detract from it. Research helps us understand how. For example, Asian Americans typically score higher on achievement tests and have higher rates of college attendance and completion than other groups, including Whites (National Center for Educational Statistics, 2005). Asian-American parents typically have high expectations for their children, encouraging them not only to attend college but also to attain graduate or professional degrees (Okagaki & Frensch, 1998).

Asian-American parents also translate these aspirations into academic work at home. One study found that Chinese-American parents were ten times more likely to provide school-related practice activities at home for their preschoolers and kindergarten children than were Caucasian-American parents (Huntsinger, Jose, & Larsen, 1998). A cross-cultural study found that more than 95 percent of native Chinese and Japanese fifth graders had desks and quiet study areas at home; only 63 percent of the American sample did. Also, more than half of the Chinese and Japanese parents supplemented their fifth graders' schoolwork with additional math and science work at home, whereas only about a fourth of American parents provided supplemental math work at home, and less then 1 percent of American parents provided additional science work at home (Stevenson, Lee, & Stigler, 1986). When families immigrate to the United States, they bring their cultural values with them.

Additional research has examined the remarkable successes of Vietnamese and Laotian refugee children in American classrooms. In spite of being in the United States less than 4 years, with vast language and cultural differences, these students earned better than B averages in school and earned high scores on standardized achievement tests (Caplan, Choy, & Whitmore, 1992). In attempting to explain these successes, researchers found that the students' families strongly emphasized hard work, autonomy, perseverance, and pride. These values were reinforced with a nightly ritual of family homework in which both parents and older siblings helped younger members of the family. For example, Indo-Chinese high schoolers spent twice as much time on homework as did mainstream American high school students (Caplan et al., 1992).

In contrast, some minorities, because of a long history of separatism and low status, sometimes defend themselves through **cultural inversion,** the tendency of members of cultural minorities to reject certain attitudes, values, and forms of behavior because they conflict with their own cultural values (Ogbu, 1992, 1999b, 2003).

Cultural inversion. The tendency of members of cultural minorities to reject certain attitudes, values, and forms of behavior because they conflict with their own cultural values

Attitudes about language and school success are examples of this inversion. Students from some cultural minorities retain nonstandard English dialects, because using "school English" might alienate their peers and distance their families (Ogbu, 1999a). These students may also interpret school success as rejecting their cultural values, so they either don't support learning or directly oppose it; they form what are called "resistance cultures" (Ogbu & Simons, 1998), and academic disidentification occurs (Ogbu, 2002). Low grades, management and motivation problems, truancy, and high dropout rates are symptoms of this cultural conflict (Faiman-Silva, 2002). To become a high achiever is to "become White," and students who study, want to succeed, and become actively involved in school risk losing the respect and friendship of their peers.

Ogbu (2002) encourages teachers to help members of cultural minorities adapt to the dominant culture (including schools) without losing their cultural identity, a process he calls "accommodation without assimilation." Other terms include *alternation,* the ability to comfortably function in both cultures (Hamm & Coleman, 1997), and *code switching,* the ability to use nonstandard dialects in social situations but standard English in school (DeMeulenaere, 2001). The challenge for teachers is to help students understand the "culture of schooling—the norms, procedures, and expectations necessary for success"—while honoring the value and integrity of students' home cultures.

Minority role models are especially important in this process (Quiocho & Rios, 2000; Stanton-Salazar & Spina, 2003).

> It all started in the second grade. One . . . Career day at Jensen Scholastic Academy in my teacher, Mrs. F.'s room, an M.D. came to speak to the class about his career as a doctor. . . . I can't remember his name but from that day forward I knew I was destined to be a doctor. From that point on I began to take my work seriously, because I knew to become a doctor grades were very important. Throughout my elementary career I received honors. In the seventh grade I really became fascinated with science, which I owe all to my teacher Mr. H. He made learning fun and interesting. I started to read science books even when it wasn't necessary, or I found myself watching the different specials on Channel 11 about operations they showed doctors performing. (Smokowski, 1997, p. 13)

Minority role models provide learners with evidence that they can both succeed and retain their cultural identity.

Cultural Differences in Adult–Child Interactions

Culture also influences the way children learn to interact with adults, which can affect school learning and communication (Weigel, Martin & Bennett, 2005). A study of differences in language patterns illustrates this possibility (Heath, 1989). For example, when teachers said, "Let's put the scissors away now," White students, accustomed to this indirect way of speaking, interpreted it as a command; African-American students did not. Failure to obey was then viewed as a management problem, which resulted from a mismatch between home and school cultures.

Similar disparities can cause problems during instruction. For example, research indicates that White children tend to respond comfortably to questions requiring specific answers, such as "What's this story about?" because of their home experiences. African-American children, accustomed to questions that are more "open-ended, story-starter" types, were sometimes confused by the specific questions because they weren't viewed as information-givers in their interactions with adults (Rogoff, 2003). One parent reported, "Miss Davis, she complain 'bout Ned not answerin' back. He says she asks dumb questions she already know about" (Heath, 1982, p. 107).

Made aware of these differences, teachers incorporated more open-ended questions in their lessons, and worded commands more directly, such as "Put your scissors away now." They also had all students practice answering factual questions and liberally praised their efforts to do so. In this way, teachers built bridges between the students' natural learning styles and the schools.

Cultural mismatches can also occur in interpretations of time and adult-sanctioned activities. One principal's experience working with Pacific Island students is an example (Winitzky, 1994). The principal had been invited to a community awards ceremony at a local church to honor students from her school. She readily accepted, arrived a few minutes early, and was ushered to a seat of honor on the stage. After an uncomfortable (to her) wait of over an hour, the ceremony began, and the students proudly filed to the stage to receive their awards. Each was acknowledged, given an award, and applauded. The children returned to their seats, which led to an eye-opening experience:

> Well, the kids were fine for a while, but as you might imagine, they got bored fast and started to fidget. Fidgeting and whispering turned into poking, prodding, and open chatting. I became a little anxious at the disruption, but none of the other adults appeared to even notice, so I ignored it, too. Pretty soon several of the children were up and out of their seats, strolling about the back and sides of the auditorium. All adult faces continued looking serenely up at the speaker on the stage. Then the kids started playing tag, running circles around the seating area and yelling gleefully. No adult response—I was amazed, and struggled to resist the urge to quiet the children. Then some of the kids got up onto the stage, running around the speaker, flicking the lights on and off, and opening and closing the curtain! Still nothing from the Islander parents! It was not my place, and I shouldn't have done it, but I was so beyond my comfort zone that with eye contact and a pantomimed shush, I got the kids to settle down.
>
> I suddenly realized then that when these children . . . come to school late, it doesn't mean that they or their parents don't care about learning. . . . that's just how all the adults in their world operate. When they squirm under desks and run around the classroom, they aren't trying to be disrespectful or defiant, they're just doing what they do everywhere else. (Winitzky, 1994, pp. 147–148)

Students from different cultures bring with them ways of acting and interacting with adults that may differ from the traditional teacher-as-authority-figure role (Trawick-Smith, 2003). The experience with Pacific Island culture gave the principal insights into the ways and reasons her students often acted as they did. (We discuss the difficult question of what to do about these differences later in the chapter.)

Classroom Organization and Culture

In most classrooms, teachers emphasize individual performance, which they reinforce by test scores and grades. This can lead to competition, which requires successes and failures; and the success of one student may be tied to the failure of another. This often detracts from the motivation of those who are not succeeding (Brophy, 2004).

Contrast this orientation with the cultural learning styles of the Hmong, a mountain tribe from Laos who immigrated to the United States after the Vietnam War. The Hmong culture emphasizes cooperation, and Hmong students constantly monitor the learning progress of their peers, offering help and assistance (Vang, 2003). The Hmong culture also de-emphasizes individual achievement in favor of group success. One teacher working with the Hmong described her classroom in this way:

> When Mee Hang has difficulty with an alphabetization lesson, Pang Lor explains, in Hmong, how to proceed. Chia Ying listens in to Pang's explanation and nods her head. Pang goes back to work on her own paper, keeping an eye on Mee Hang. When she sees Mee looking confused, Pang leaves her seat and leans over Mee's shoulder. She writes the first letter of each word on the line, indicating to Mee that these letters are in alphabetical order and that Mee should fill in the rest of each word. This gives Mee the help she needs and she is able to finish on her own. Mee, in turn, writes the first letter of each word on the line for Chia Ying, passing on Pang Lor's explanation.
>
> Classroom achievement is never personal but always considered to be the result of cooperative effort. Not only is there no competition in the classroom, there is constant denial of individual ability. When individuals are praised by the teacher, they generally shake their heads and appear hesitant to be singled out as being more able than their peers.
>
> (Hvitfeldt, 1986, p. 70)

Consider how well these students would learn if instruction were competitive, with few opportunities for student help and collaboration.

Native Americans and students from other cultures, including Mexican-American, Southeast Asian, and Pacific Island students, experience similar difficulties in competitive classrooms (Aronson, Wilson, & Akert, 2005; McDevitt & Ormrod, 2004). Their cultures teach them that cooperation is important; they view competition as silly, if not distasteful. When they come to school and are asked to compete, they experience cultural conflict. Raising hands and jousting for the right to give the correct answer isn't congruent with the ways they interact at home. This helps us answer the question we asked after the example with the story about the *Box Car Children* in the New Mexico classroom. The Native American children sat quietly because doing so was consistent with their culture.

This discussion also helps us answer the first question we asked at the beginning of the chapter: "How might these differences influence the students' learning?" When patterns of communication, for example, conflict with the patterns typical for classrooms, learning can be adversely affected. Sensitivity to these factors is essential for teachers.

Culture and Schooling: Some Cautions

As we emphasized in our study of SES, it is important to again remember that our discussion of culture describes group differences, and individuals within the groups will vary. For example, our discussion of resistance cultures centered on Ogbu's work, which focuses on African-American students. It is essential that we keep in mind the fact that many African-American students very much want to succeed in school and do so. To conclude that all African-American students are members of resistance cultures would be a major error.

Similarly, whereas Asian-American students as a group are hard workers and high achievers, it does not mean that all Asian-American students are members of a "model minority," a stereotypic term that some Asian Americans reject (Asian-Nation, 2005; Fong, 1998). Many encounter difficulties in school, and language and poverty are obstacles for them (Lei, 2003; Lew, 2004). Stereotyping, which often results in lowered expectations for members of cultural minorities, can also work in the opposite direction, blinding us to problems that our students encounter (Steele, Spencer & Aronson, 2002). We need to remember that exclusive focus on group differences can result in inappropriate expectations for and unjust treatment of individuals.

Language Diversity

As we saw earlier, members of ethnic groups have, among other characteristics, a common language, and, as with culture, language can exert a powerful influence on learning. Increasingly, our students bring different native languages to school, and their facility with English varies widely (Abedi, Hofstetter, & Lord, 2004). Let's look at this diversity and its implications for teaching.

English Dialects: Research Findings

Anyone who travels in the United States will notice that our country has many regional and ethnic dialects. Experts estimate that there are at least 11 distinct regional dialects in the United States (Owens, 2005). A **dialect** is a variation of standard English that is distinct in vocabulary, grammar, or pronunciation. Everyone speaks a dialect; people merely react to those different from their own (Wolfram, Adger, & Christian, 1999). Some are accepted more than others, however, and language is at the heart of what Delpit (1995) calls "codes of power," the cultural and linguistic conventions that control access to opportunity in our society.

Research indicates that when students use nonstandard English, teachers have lower expectations for their performance and make lower assessments of their work and of the students themselves (Hollie, 2001). Teachers often confuse nonstandard English with mistakes during oral reading (Wolfram et al., 1999), and some critics argue that dialects, such as Black English, are substandard. Linguists, however, argue that these variations are just as rich and semantically complex as standard English (Labov, 1972; Wheeler, 1999).

Dialects in the Classroom: Implications for Teachers

Teachers who respond effectively to cultural diversity accept and value learner differences, and these responses are particularly important when working with students who speak nonstandard dialects (Hollie, 2001; Ogbu, 1999a). Dialects are integral to the culture of students' homes and neighborhoods, and requiring the elimination of dialects communicates that differences are neither accepted nor valued.

Standard English, however, allows access to educational and economic opportunities, which is the primary reason for teaching it. Students realize this when they interview for a first job or when they plan for post-high school education. So, what should teachers do when a student says, "I ain't got no pencil," or brings some other nonstandard dialect into the classroom? Opinions vary from "rejection and correction" to complete acceptance.

Dialect. A variation of standard English that is distinct in vocabulary, grammar, or pronunciation

The approach most consistent with culturally responsive teaching is to first accept the dialect and then build on it. For example, when the student says, "I ain't got no pencil," the teacher might say, "Oh, you don't have a pencil. What should you do, then?" Although results won't occur immediately, the long-range benefits, both for language development and attitudes toward learning, are worthwhile.

Language differences don't have to form barriers between home and school. **Bidialecticism,** the ability to switch back and forth between a dialect and standard English, allows access to both (Gollnick & Chinn, 2004). For example, one teacher read a series of poems by Langston Hughes and focused on how Hughes used Black English to create vivid images. The class discussed contrasts with standard English and ways in which differences between the two dialects could be used to accomplish different goals (Shields & Shaver, 1990).

English Language Learners

Ellie Barton, a language arts teacher at Northeast Middle School, is the school's English Language Learner (ELL) Coordinator. She teaches ELL classes, and she is also in charge of the school's testing and placement program.

Her job is challenging, as her students vary considerably in their knowledge of English. For instance, one group of Somali-Bantu children just arrived from a refugee camp in Kenya. They cannot read or write, because there is no written language for their native tongue, Mai-Mai. Language isn't their only challenge; many had never been in a building with more than one floor, and others found urinals and other aspects of indoor plumbing a mystery. At the other end of the continuum is a young girl from India who can read and write in four languages: Hindi, the national language of India; Urdu, the language of her Persian ancestors; Telegu, a regional language in India; and Arabic.

To sort out this language diversity, the district uses a placement test that categorizes students into three levels: newcomer classrooms for students who have little or no expertise with English; self-contained ELL, classrooms where a primary emphasis is on learning to read and write English; and sheltered English, where students receive structured help in learning academic subjects such as science and social studies. The placement process is not foolproof, however, since English skills are sometimes nonexistent, and parents don't know the exact ages of their children. Ellie's principal deals with this information void in creative ways; he recently asked a dentist friend to look at a child's teeth to estimate one student's age.

(Adapted from Romboy & Kinkead, 2005)

More immigrants arrived in the United States during the 1990s than in any other decade on record. As a result of this increase in immigration a great many students with limited backgrounds in English are entering American classrooms (Gray & Fleischman, 2005). In the last three decades, the number of non-English-speaking students and those with limited English increased dramatically. In the 2003–2004 school year, U.S. public schools had 5.5 million English language learners (ELLs), up nearly 100 percent from a decade earlier (D. Short & Echevarria, 2005). The 1.6 million who reside in California make up 25 percent of that state's student population (Bielenberg & Fillmore, 2005). Nationwide, projections indicate that by 2015 more than half of all K–12 students will not speak English as their first language (Gray & Fleischman, 2005). The diversity is staggering. More than 450 languages are spoken in our schools (Kindler, 2002), with Spanish being the most common (Abedi et al., 2004).

Being an ELL creates obstacles for students; they are typically behind in achievement, more likely to be labeled as needing special education services, and much more likely to drop out of school (Bielenberg & Fillmore, 2005; Schmid, 2001; D. Short & Echevarria, 2005). This language diversity also challenges teachers because most of our instruction is verbal. How should schools respond to this linguistic challenge? Considerable controversy surrounds this question.

Types of ELL Programs

The primary goal of ELL programs is to teach English, but the way they attempt to do this varies considerably (see Table 4.7). Let's look at them.

Maintenance ELL Programs. **Maintenance ELL programs** build on students' native language by teaching in both it and English (Peregoy & Boyle, 2005). These programs are found primarily at the elementary level, with the goal of developing students who can

Bidialecticism. The ability to switch back and forth between a dialect and standard English

Maintenance ELL programs. Programs for English language learner (ELL) students that build on students' native language by teaching in both their language and English

Table 4.7 ELL Programs

Type of Program	Description	Advantages	Disadvantages
Maintenance	Students maintain first language through reading and writing activities in first language while teachers introduce English.	Students become literate in two languages.	Requires teachers trained in first language. Acquisition of English may not be as fast.
Transitional	Students learn to read in first language, and teachers give supplementary instruction in English as a Second Language. After mastering English, students enroll in regular classrooms and discontinue learning in first language.	Maintains first language. Transition to English is eased by gradual approach.	Requires teachers trained in first language. Literacy skills in first language not maintained and may be lost.
ELL Pullout Programs	Pullout programs in which students are provided with supplementary English instruction along with regular instruction in content classes.	Easier to administer when dealing with diverse language backgrounds because it requires only the pullout teachers to have ELL expertise.	Students may not be ready to benefit from content instruction in English. Pullout programs segregate students.
Sheltered English	Teachers adapt content instruction to meet the learning needs of ELL students.	Easier for students to learn content.	Requires an intermediate level of English proficiency. Also requires teachers with ELL expertise.

Effective ELL programs teach English while building on and enriching students' native language.

speak, read, and write in two languages. They have the advantage of retaining and building on students' heritage, language, and culture, but they are difficult to implement because they require groups of students with the same native language and bilingual teachers or teacher teams that have a member who speaks the heritage language.

Transitional ELL Programs. **Transitional ELL programs** attempt to use the native language as an instructional aid until English becomes proficient. Transitional programs begin by teaching reading and writing in the first language and gradually develop learners' English skills. Often, the transition period is too short, leaving students inadequately prepared for learning in English (Gersten & Woodward, 1995). In addition, loss of the first language and lack of emphasis on the home culture can result in communication gaps between children who no longer speak the first language and parents who don't speak English.

ELL Pullout Programs. In **ELL pullout programs,** students receive most of their instruction in regular classrooms but are also pulled out for extra help (Peregoy & Boyle, 2005). Instruction in these pullout programs focuses on both English language development and

Transitional ELL programs. English language learner (ELL) programs that attempt to use students' native language as an instructional aid until students become proficient in English

ELL pullout programs. Programs for English language learner (ELL) students who receive most of their instruction in regular classrooms but are also pulled out for extra help in both English language development and classroom content

the content being taught in the regular classroom. The programs require students who have enough English expertise to benefit from regular classroom instruction. When this isn't the case, sheltered English classes are more effective.

Sheltered English. Sheltered English classrooms modify instruction to assist students in learning content. Also called *Specially Designed Academic Instruction in English,* these classes require students with intermediate levels of English proficiency as well as instructors who know both their content and ELL strategies.

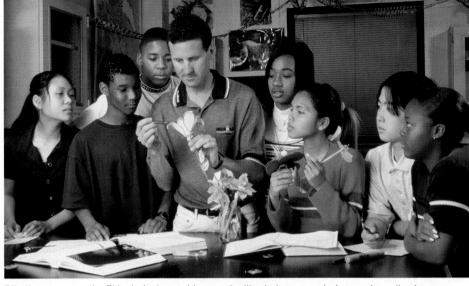

Effective programs for ELL students provide opportunities to learn vocabulary and practice language.

When working with ELL students, teachers should carefully avoid overestimating their students' English proficiency (Echevarria, Vogt, & Short, 2004). After about 2 years in a language-rich environment, students develop **basic interpersonal communication skills,** a level that allows students to interact conversationally with their peers (Cummins, 2000). Students may need an additional 5 to 7 years to develop **cognitive academic language proficiency,** a level that allows students to handle demanding learning tasks with abstract concepts.

Evaluating ELL Programs

Maintenance and transitional ELL programs are controversial. Critics contend that these programs are

- Divisive, encouraging groups of non-native English speakers to remain separate from mainstream American culture
- Ineffective, slowing the process of acquiring English for ELL students
- Inefficient, requiring expenditures for the training of bilingual teachers and materials that could better be spent on quality English programs (U.S. English, 2005)

Culturally responsive teachers build on the strengths that different students bring to school.

Proponents counter that maintenance programs make sense because, by building on the student's first language, they provide a smooth and humane transition to English. In addition, they argue that being able to speak two languages has both practical and learning benefits (Gutiérrez et al., 2002; Krashen, 1999).

Critics' views are prevailing. In a 1998 referendum, California voters passed Proposition 227, a ballot initiative that sharply reduced bilingual education, replacing it with **immersion,** an approach that requires all instruction and communication to be in English. Twenty-six other states have English-as-the-official-language laws on the books, indicating a general stance in favor of the exclusive use of English (U.S. English, 2005).

The federal government has also weighed in on the controversy. Recently, the English-acquisition component of the No Child Left Behind Act of 2001 mandated that a primary objective of U.S. schools should be the teaching of English. Accordingly, the Office of Bilingual Education was renamed the Office of English Acquisition.

What does research say about the relative benefits of ELL versus immersion programs? The results are mixed, with claims and counterclaims from both sides. Some research suggests that students in maintenance programs achieve higher in math and reading, have more positive attitudes toward school and themselves, and that the knowledge and skills acquired in a native language are transferable to the second language (Krashen, 1999, 2005; Slavin & Cheung, 2004). However, other research suggests that

Sheltered English. An approach to teaching ELL students in academic classrooms that modifies instruction to assist learners in acquiring content

Basic interpersonal communication skills. A level of proficiency in English that allows students to interact conversationally with their peers

Cognitive academic language proficiency. A level of proficiency in English that allows students to handle demanding learning tasks with abstract concepts

Immersion. A language-instruction approach that requires all instruction and communication to be in that language

students in immersion programs learn English faster and achieve higher in other academic areas (Barone, 2000; K. Hays & Salazar, 2001). The debate is likely to continue, as the issues are both complex and emotional (Hawkins, 2004).

Instructional Principles

Teaching Culturally and Linguistically Diverse Students: Instructional Principles

It is a virtual certainty that you will teach students who are members of cultural minorities, and it is highly likely that English will not be the first language for some of them. The following principles can help guide your efforts as you work with these students. They also begin to answer the second question at the beginning of the chapter: "How should teachers respond to cultural differences in students?"

1. Communicate that you respect all cultures and value the contributions that cultural differences make to learning.
2. Involve all students in learning activities.
3. Use concrete experiences as reference points for language development.
4. Target important vocabulary terms.
5. Provide opportunities for all students to practice language.

Let's see how the principles guide Gary Nolan, a third-grade teacher, as he works with his students.

Gary's class is diverse. Of his 28 students, 6 are African American, 8 are Hispanic, 4 are of Asian descent, 2 are from Morocco, and 3 recently immigrated from Russia. Eight are not native English speakers.

"It's time for the rest of the class to come in. . . . You're improving all the time," Gary comments to his group whose native language isn't English. Gary spends a half hour with them every morning working on both their English language skills and their assignments to help them keep up with the other students.

"Good morning, Tu. . . . New hat, Damon? . . . Nice haircut, Shah. . . . How's your new baby sister, Jack?" Gary greets students as they come in the door.

"Who's up today?" he asks as the students quickly settle down.

"Me," Anna says, raising her hand.

"Go ahead, Anna."

Anna moves to the front of the room, and takes out two posters showing the islands of Mallorca and Minorca. "I was born in Mexico, but my father is from Mallorca, and my mother is from Minorca," Anna explains.

"Show everyone on our map," Gary directs, and Anna points to the islands on a world map. Every Thursday morning, Gary has one of the students make a presentation about his or her background. The students bring foods, native costumes, pieces of art, and other artifacts that illustrate their culture, and they place a push pin with their name on it on the map.

Gary frequently comments about how lucky they are to have classmates from so many parts of the world and how much they learn from each other. "Remember when Shah told us about Omar Khayyam?" Gary had once asked. "He solved some math problems that people in Europe didn't solve until hundreds of years later. If Shah weren't in our class, we probably would never have learned that. . . . Aren't we lucky?"

Gary also keeps a chart on the wall with common words and phrases ("Hello," "Goodbye," "How are you?") in Spanish, Vietnamese, Arabic, Russian, and English. He has also labeled objects around the room, like the windows, chairs, tables, bookshelves, and others in both the students' native languages and English. And, he displays a large calendar that identifies important holidays in different cultures. Students from those cultures make special presentations on the holidays, and all the students' parents are invited to attend.

"Okay, story time," Gary says when Anna is finished. He now reads a story from a book that is liberally illustrated with pictures depicting events in the story. As he reads, he holds up the pictures and has the students identify the object or event being illustrated. One picture shows a cave in the woods that the boy and girl in the story decide to explore.

"Everyone say 'cave'," Gary directs, pointing at the picture of the cave, and the students say "cave" in unison. He does the same pointing at other objects in the picture, such as *tree, rock, path,* and *stream.*

After finishing the story, he begins a discussion.

"Tell us something you remember about the story. . . . Carmela?"

". . . A boy and a girl . . . lost . . . cave," Carmela responds slowly in her halting English.

"Yes, good. . . . The story is about a boy and a girl who got lost in a cave," Gary says slowly and clearly, pointing again to each of the objects in the picture.

"Have any of you ever been in a cave? . . . Have you ever dug a big, deep hole in the ground? . . . How is a hole different from a cave? Take a minute, and talk about differences with your partner, and then we'll discuss it."

The students turn to each other, talk briefly, and Gary then has them share their experiences with digging holes and going into caves. When they struggle with a term, Gary provides it, has the class repeat it in unison, and then he repeats the process with another student.

"Good everyone," Gary smiles, after they've practiced for several minutes. "Okay, let's get ready for math."

Now, let's look at Gary's efforts to apply the principles with his students. He implemented the first in several ways: by having students make presentations about their cultural heritage, having them identify where they were from on a map, emphasizing how lucky they were to have classmates from different parts of the world, and commenting on how much they learn from each other. His specific emphasis on the contributions of Omar Khayyam, who was little known to most of the students, and comments like, "If Shah weren't in our class, we probably would never have learned that," communicates to students that their cultures are respected and valued, which can promote personal pride and motivation (Gollnick & Chinn, 2004; Xu, 2002). He also spent personal time before school helping his non-native English speakers. Nothing communicates that a teacher values and cares for students better than the willingness to spend personal time helping them with their work. His greeting further communicated that he cared for his students. These gestures are subtle, but important, particularly with members of cultural minorities (Gollnick & Chin, 2004).

Gary applied the second principle by involving all of them in his learning activities. Every time he called on a student, he signaled that he wanted and expected the student to participate, and when they struggled, he provided prompts and cues to help them succeed.

Some teachers believe that students don't *want* to answer questions or participate in class. However, if students (including those from cultural minorities) believe they will be *able* to answer, they want to be called on (Eggen & Kauchak, 2002). Teachers should emphasize that learning is the goal of every discussion and should help students understand that wrong answers are an integral and important part of learning progress. (We examine strategies for involving all students in learning activities in Chapter 13.)

Gary further implemented the second principle by combining whole-class and small-group instruction in an attempt to accommodate possible differences in cultural learning styles. For example, through observing students, he had learned that many were more comfortable in small groups than in whole-class instruction. These adaptations can increase students' motivation to learn (Holliday, 2002).

By using concrete experiences to facilitate language development, Gary implemented the third principle. For example, he repeatedly referred back to pictures in the book, which provided concrete frames of reference for vocabulary learning, a practice supported by research (Echevarria & Graves, 2003). He also encouraged students to share their own personal experiences with the concepts, and he linked language to concrete experiences.

Gary applied the fourth principle by specifically targeting key vocabulary terms. Vocabulary, especially the technical vocabulary found in many content areas, poses specific challenges to ELL students (Carlo et al., 2004). Context cues together with specific strategies to differentiate words from closely related ones, such as Gary did with *cave* and *hole,* are particularly important. In addition, he further applied both the third and fourth principles by labeling objects around the room in both English and students' native languages, he spoke slowly and clearly in rephrasing students' responses, and he had the students repeat terms in unison. Each is an effective strategy with ELL students (Peregoy & Boyle, 2005; Verna, Wintergerst & DeCapua, 2001).

Finally, Gary had all of his students actively practice language. In large part, language is a skill, and students learn English by using it in their day-to-day lives. Students in general, and ELL students in particular, need to spend as much time as possible literally "practicing the language" (Boyd & Rubin, 2001). Open-ended questions that allow students to respond without the pressure of giving specific answers are particularly effective for eliciting student responses (Echevarria & Graves, 2003). Instruction where the teacher does most of the talking while students listen passively is ineffective (Peregoy & Boyle, 2005).

Analyzing Classrooms Video
To see a teacher describe responses to cultural diversity, go to Episode 5, "Culturally Responsive Teaching," DVD 1, accompanying this text.

Exploring Further
To see some additional suggestions for working with culturally and linguistically diverse students, go to "Culturally Responsive Teaching" in the *Exploring Further* module of Chapter 4 at *www.prenhall.com/eggen*.

As you saw in Gary's efforts, working with students whose first language is not English is challenging and demanding. However, these students respond very positively to displays of caring and genuine attempts to help them adapt to both school and mainstream American culture. The responses you get from them will be among the most rewarding you will have as a teacher.

Checking Your Understanding

3.1 Describe *culture* and *ethnicity,* and identify the relationship between the two concepts.

3.2 Describe English dialects, and explain why understanding them is important for teachers.

3.3 Describe the major approaches to helping ELL students, and explain how they are similar and different.

3.4 Describe four aspects of effectively working with students having culturally and linguistically diverse backgrounds.

To receive feedback for these questions, go to Appendix B.

Knowledge Extensions

To deepen your understanding of the topics in this section of Chapter 4 and to integrate them with topics you've already studied, go to the *Knowledge Extensions* module for Chapter 4 at *www.prenhall.com/eggen*. Respond to questions 10–15.

Classroom ⊞ Connections

Working Effectively with Culturally and Linguistically Diverse Students in Your Classroom

1. Communicate that you respect and value all cultures, and emphasize the contributions that cultural differences make to learning.

- **Elementary:** A third-grade teacher designs classroom "festivals" that focus on different cultures and invites parents and other caregivers to help celebrate and contribute to enriching them. He also emphasizes values, such as courtesy and respect, which are common to all cultures. He has students discuss the ways these values are displayed in different societies.

- **Middle School:** An art teacher decorates the room with pictures of Native American art and discusses how it contributes to art in general and how it communicates Native American values, such as a sense of harmony with nature and complex religious beliefs.

- **High School:** An urban English teacher has students read works written by African Americans and Middle Eastern, South Asian, and far Eastern authors. They compare both the writing approach and the different emphases that the authors represent.

2. Begin language development and concept learning activities with concrete experiences.

- **Elementary:** A fifth-grade teacher, in a unit on fractions, has students fold pieces of paper into halves, thirds, fourths, and eighths. At each point she has them state in words what the example represents, and she writes important terms on the board.

- **Middle School:** A science teacher begins a unit on the skeletal and muscular systems by having students feel their own legs, arms, ribs, and heads. As they touch parts of their bodies, such as their Achilles tendon, she has them repeat the term *tendon* and has them state in words that tendons attach bones to muscles.

- **High School:** An English teacher stops whenever an unfamiliar word occurs in a reading passage or discussion and asks for an example of it. He keeps a list of these words on a bulletin board and encourages students to use them in class and in their writing.

3. Provide students with opportunities to practice language.

- **Elementary:** The fifth-grade teacher who had the students fold the papers has them describe each step they take when they add fractions with both like and unlike denominators. When they struggle to put their understanding into words, she prompts them, in some cases providing essential words and phrases for them.

- **Middle School:** A social studies teacher has students prepare oral reports in groups of four. Each student must make a 2-minute presentation to the other three members of the group. After students practice their reports with each other in groups, each person presents a part of a group report to the whole class.

- **High School:** A history teacher calls on a variety of students to provide part of a summary of the previous day's work. As she conducts lecture discussions, she frequently stops and has other students describe what has been discussed to that point and how it relates to topics discussed earlier.

GENDER

What Marti Banes saw on the first day of her advanced-placement chemistry class was both surprising and disturbing. Of her 26 students, only 5 were girls, and they sat quietly, responding only when she asked them direct questions. One reason she had chosen teaching as a career was to share her interest in science with girls, but this situation gave her little opportunity to do so.

The fact that some of our students are boys and others are girls is so obvious that we may not even think about it. When we're reminded, we notice that they often act and think differently. Many differences are natural and positive, but problems can occur if societal or school influences limit the academic performance of either girls or boys. We examine these differences and their implications for teaching in this section (Figure 4.5).

Males and females *are* different. In general, females score higher on tests of verbal ability; boys score higher on those that measure visual imagery (Gurian & Stevens, 2005; Halpern & LaMay, 2000). Girls tend to be more extroverted and anxious, and they're more trusting, less assertive, and have slightly lower self-esteem than males of the same age and background (Halpern & LaMay, 2000). Girls develop faster, and they acquire verbal and motor skills at an earlier age. In play, girls gravitate toward activities with a social component, such as verbally interactive play with others. Boys are more oriented toward activities that are visual and active, such as rough-house play and playing with blocks, cars, or dinosaurs. Both prefer to play with members of the same gender. These tendencies, together with societal expectations, result in **gender-role identity differences,** beliefs about appropriate characteristics and behaviors of the two sexes.

Why do these gender-based differences exist? Like the nature–nurture question in reference to intelligence, most experts believe they result from an interaction between genetics and the environment (S. Jones & Dindia, 2004; Lippa, 2002). Genes control physical differences such as size and growth rate and probably differences in temperament, aggressiveness, and early verbal and exploratory behaviors (Berk, 2006). On the other hand, girls and boys are treated differently by parents, peers, and teachers, and this treatment influences how children view gender roles and what they ultimately become (C. Martin, Ruble, & Szkrybalo, 2002; Rogoff, 2003).

Schools also subtly impact gender role identities through the learning activities they offer and the ways that teachers interact with boys compared to girls (Garrahy, 2001; Lopez, 2003). Reading is an example. Male characters are typically presented as strong and adventurous, but seldom as warm and sensitive (L. Evans & Davies, 2000). Video games and computer software programs are heavily oriented toward boys with male heroes as the main characters (Meece, 2002). These messages influence the ways boys and girls view themselves.

How should teachers respond? Again, the suggestions are controversial, with some people believing that most differences between boys and girls are natural and little intervention is necessary, whereas others argue that every attempt should be made to minimize gender differences.

Gender differences are real and result in achievement differences between girls and boys. Some of these differences suggest that schools are not meeting girls' needs:

- In the early grades, girls score as high or higher than boys on almost every standardized measure of achievement and psychological well-being. By the time they graduate from high school or college, they have fallen behind boys.
- In high school, girls score lower on the Scholastic Aptitude Test (SAT) and American College Test (ACT), important tests for college admission. The greatest gender gaps are in science and math.
- Women score lower on all sections of the Graduate Record Exam, the Medical College Admissions Test, and admissions tests for law, dental, and optometry schools.
- Women still lag far behind men in traditionally male college majors, such as mathematics, physics, engineering, and computer science (Alperstein, 2005; Coley, 2001).

Figure 4.5   Sources of learner individuality: Gender

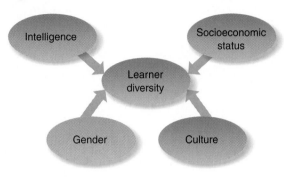

Gender-role identity differences.
Beliefs about appropriate characteristics and behaviors of the two sexes

Other research suggests that schools also fail to meet the learning needs of boys:

- Boys outnumber girls in remedial English and math classes, are held back in grade more often, and are more than twice as likely to be placed in special education classes.
- Boys receive the majority of failing grades, drop out of school four times more often than girls, and are cited for disciplinary infractions as much as 10 times more often than girls are.
- Girls hold more positions in student government and are more often class valedictorians.
- Boys score lower than girls on both direct and indirect measures of reading and writing ability, and with the addition of the writing component on the SAT, girls' and boys' performance has become essentially even.
- The proportion of both bachelor's and master's degrees earned favors women by a ratio of 53 to 47 (Gurian & Stevens, 2005; National Assessment of Educational Progress, 2001).
- Boys' struggles are receiving so much attention that *Newsweek* made the topic its cover story in the January 30, 2006 issue.

Some researchers explain these differences by suggesting that boys' and girls' brains are wired differently for learning. Components of the brain that build word centers and fine-motor skills are a year ahead in girls, which gives them an advantage in reading, use of pencils, cursive writing, and other small-motor tasks. Emotive centers in the brain are also advanced for girls, making them calmer and more able to sit still for the long periods that school often requires. These researchers argue that school systems as a whole are more compatible with girls' innate characteristics (Gurian & Stevens, 2005).

Differences in the Classroom Behavior of Boys and Girls

Given these genetic and societally influenced differences, it is not surprising that boys and girls behave differently in classrooms. Boys participate in learning activities to a greater extent than girls do (Brophy, 2004), and they are more likely to ask questions and make comments. Teachers call on them more often (S. Jones & Dindia, 2004), probably because boys are more verbally aggressive (Altermatt, Jovanovic, & Perry, 1998).

Gender-related differences are particularly pronounced in science and math (L. O'Brien & Crandall, 2003; Tiedemann, 2000). Boys are more likely to lead in setting up science experiments, relegating girls to passive roles such as recording data (Sanders & Nelson, 2004). These experiences are important because they influence girls' attitudes and perceptions of their ability to do science (Acherman et al., 2001). Differences become greater as students move through school, with a significant decrease in girls' participation during the middle school years. In addition, girls are more likely to attribute success in science to luck, and failures to lack of ability (L. Hoffman, 2002; Nosek, Banaji, & Greenwald, 2002).

Boys also display behaviors that detract from learning. They skip class more often than girls do, hold more part-time jobs out of school, read less for pleasure, do less homework, and are less likely to take college preparatory classes. In college they party and watch TV more than girls do (Riordan, 1996).

Although the areas of concern are different, evidence suggests that schools aren't effectively serving the needs of either boys or girls.

Gender Stereotypes and Perceptions

Society and parents communicate, both directly and unconsciously, different expectations for their sons and daughters (Tenenbaum & Leaper, 2003; Tiedemann, 2000). For example, researchers found that mothers' gender-stereotyped attitudes toward math and science adversely influenced their adolescent daughters entering these fields after high school (Bleeker & Jacobs, 2004). One woman recalled:

It was OK, even feminine, not to be good in math. It was even cute. And so I locked myself out of a very important part of what it is to be a human being, and that is to know all of oneself. I just locked that part out because I didn't think that was an appropriate thing for me to do. . . . [But] it was not OK for the men to not do well in math. It was *not* OK for them to not take calculus. It was not manly. (Weissglass, 1998, p. 160)

Science activities that actively involve female students in designing and carrying out science experiments help combat gender stereotypes that the sciences are a male domain.

The perception that certain areas, such as math, science, and computer science, are male domains has a powerful effect on career choices (J. D. Lee, 2002). Girls are less likely to take courses in calculus, physics, and computer science (College Entrance Examination Board, 2003), and as we saw earlier, girls are much less likely than boys to major in math, physics, engineering, and computer science in college (Alperstein, 2005; American Association of University Women, 1998). The problem of gender-stereotypic views of math- and science-related careers seems to be especially acute for low SES and minority females (Bleeker & Jacobs, 2004; V. O'Brien, Kopola, & Martinez-Pons, 1999). One study found that only 2 percent of new math faculty at U.S. colleges and universities were minority women (Herzig, 2004). These trends are troubling because the perception of these fields as male domains limits career options for females as well as the pool for future scientists and mathematicians (VanLeuvan, 2004).

What does this information suggest to you as a teacher? We attempt to answer this question in the next section.

 **Instructional Principles**

Responding to Gender Differences: Instructional Principles

You can do a great deal to make students aware of gender bias and stereotyping (Ginsberg, Shapiro, & Brown, 2004). The following principles can guide you in your efforts:

1. Communicate openly with students about gender issues and concerns.
2. Eliminate gender bias in instructional activities.
3. Present students with nonstereotypical role models.

Let's return to Marti's work with her students to see how she attempts to apply the principles.

Marti decides to take steps to deal with the gender issue in her chemistry class. First, she initiates an open discussion. "I almost didn't major in chemistry," she begins. "Some of my girlfriends scoffed, and others were nearly appalled. 'You'll be in there with a bunch of geeks,' some of them said. 'Girls don't major in chemistry. There will be 45 guys and two girls,' others added. They all thought science and math were only for guys."

"It *is* mostly for guys," Amy shrugs. "Look at us."

"It isn't our fault," Shane responds, a bit defensively. "The guys didn't try to keep you out of the class."

Several other students make comments.

"Listen, everyone. I'm not blaming either you guys, or the girls. . . . It's a problem for all of us, and I'm not saying that just because I'm a woman. I'd be just as concerned if I were a man, because we're losing a lot of talented people who could be majoring in science."

As the discussion continues, she encourages both the boys and the girls to keep their career options open. "There's no rule that says that girls can't be computer scientists or boys can't be nurses," she emphasizes. "In fact, there's an enormous shortage of both."

She has similar discussions in her other classes. During learning activities, she makes a special effort to be sure that girls and boys participate as equally as possible, and she tells the students why she is doing so. In lab activities, she organizes groups to include equal numbers of boys and girls and monitors the groups to be sure that the girls take an active role in designing and conducting the experiments.

For Career Week, Marti invites a female chemistry professor from a nearby university to come into her classes to talk about career opportunities for women in chemistry, and she invites a male nurse from one of the local hospitals to talk about his experiences in a female-dominated profession.

Marti also talks with other science teachers and counselors about gender stereotyping, and they work on a plan to encourage both boys and girls to consider career options in nonstereotypical fields.

Let's look now at Marti's attempts to apply the principles in her work. She implemented the first by openly discussing the issue of low participation by girls with her students. The discussions increased their awareness of stereotyping subjects and career choices. And the discussions with her colleagues helped increase their sensitivity to gender issues in the school.

Second, knowing that teachers sometimes unconsciously treat boys and girls differently, Marti made a special effort to ensure equal treatment of both, and again she openly communicated why she was making the effort. She called on the girls and boys as equally as possible, and she monitored lab activities to be sure that girls didn't slide into passive roles. In short, she expected the same academic behaviors from both girls and boys.

Notice the term *academic behaviors.* No one suggests that boys and girls are the same in every way, and they shouldn't be expected to behave in the same ways. Academically, however, boys and girls should be given the same opportunities and encouragement, just as students from different cultures and socioeconomic backgrounds should be. In this way, Marti applied the second principle.

Marti applied the third principle by inviting a female chemistry professor and a male nurse into her classes to discuss careers in those fields. Seeing that both men and women can succeed and be happy in nonstereotypical fields can broaden the horizon for both girls and boys thinking about career choices (Sanders & Nelson, 2004).

Exploring Further

To read more about different instructional strategies to address gender bias, go to "Eliminating Gender Bias" in the *Exploring Further* module of Chapter 4 at *www.prenhall.com/eggen.*

Knowledge Extensions

To deepen your understanding of the topics in this section of Chapter 4 and to integrate them with topics you've already studied, go to the *Knowledge Extensions* module for Chapter 4 at *www.prenhall.com/eggen.* Respond to questions 16 and 17.

Checking Your Understanding

4.1 Explain gender-role identity and why understanding it is important for teachers.

4.2 Describe an important first step in eliminating gender bias in classrooms.

4.3 You're working with your students in a learning activity. What important factor that can help reduce gender bias should you attempt to apply as you conduct these activities? Hint: Think about the way Marti interacted with her students.

To receive feedback for these questions, go to Appendix B.

Classroom ⊞ Connections

Eliminating Gender Bias in Your Classroom

1. Actively attack gender bias in your teaching.
   - *Elementary:* A first-grade teacher consciously de-emphasizes sex roles and differences in his classroom. He has boys and girls share equally in chores, and he eliminates gender-related activities, such as competitions between boys and girls and forming lines by gender.
   - *Middle School:* A middle school language arts teacher selects stories and clippings from newspapers and magazines that

   portray men and women in nontraditional roles. She matter-of-factly talks about nontraditional careers during class discussions about becoming an adult.
   - *High School:* At the beginning of the school year, a social studies teacher explains how gender bias hurts both sexes, and he forbids sexist comments in his classes. He calls on boys and girls equally, and emphasizes equal participation in discussions.

STUDENTS PLACED AT RISK

Laurie Ramirez looks over the papers she has been grading and shakes her head. "Fourth grade, and some of these kids don't know what zero means or how place value affects a number. Some can't add, others can't subtract, and most don't understand multiplication. How am I supposed to teach problem solving when they don't understand basic math facts?"

"Reading isn't much better," she thinks. "I have a few who can actually read at a fourth-grade level, but others are still sounding out words like *dog* and *cat.* How can I teach them to read when they are struggling with ideas this basic?"

Students placed at risk. Learners in danger of failing to complete their education with the skills necessary to survive in a modern technological society

Failing students can be found in any school. Many reasons exist, but some students share characteristics that decrease their chances for success. **Students placed at risk** are learners in danger of failing to complete their education with the skills necessary to succeed in today's society. Educators used to call these students *underachievers*, but the term *at risk* more clearly reflects the long-term consequences of school failure. Research consistently indicates that high school dropouts earn less than their more educated peers and also have an increased incidence of crime, alcoholism, and drug abuse (Hardre & Reeve, 2003; Macionis, 2006). Many jobs requiring few specialized skills no longer exist, and others are becoming rare in a world driven by technology.

Characteristics of students placed at risk include the following:

- *Poverty and Low SES.* As we saw earlier, poverty creates a number of stress factors that detract from learning (P. Barton, 2004; Biddle, 2001; V. E. Lee & Burkam, 2002, 2003).
- *Member of a Cultural Minority.* Being a member of a cultural minority can pose problems when schools are not responsive to cultural differences (Borman & Overman, 2004; Noguera, 2003a, 2003b).
- *Non-native English Speaker.* Learning is demanding for all students; struggling with both language and content can be overwhelming (Bielenberg & Fillmore, 2005; Zwiers, 2005).
- *Mobility.* High rates of mobility detract from learning continuity, which decreases achievement (Garza, Reyes, & Trueba, 2004; Ream, 2003).

These characteristics can result in a history of low achievement, which makes new learning even more challenging because students lack the knowledge and skills on which this learning depends (Barr & Parrett, 2001). A history of low achievement is often compounded by motivation and self-esteem problems (Dubois, 2001), disengagement from schools (R. Brown & Evans, 2002), and misbehavior (Barr & Parrett, 2001). The problem is often exacerbated by the fact that students who need quality education the most are often provided with substandard buildings and equipment as well as underqualified teachers (Crosnoe, 2005; Perkins-Gough, 2004; Thirunarayanan, 2004).

How do teachers react to these problems? Some are clearly overwhelmed:

I just don't know what I'm going to do. Every year, my first grade class has more and more of these kids. They don't seem to care about right or wrong, they don't care about adult approval, they are disruptive, they can't read and they arrive at school absolutely unprepared to learn. Who are these kids? Where do they come from? Why are there more and more of them? I used to think that I was a good teacher. I really prided myself on doing an outstanding job. But I find I'm working harder and harder, and being less and less effective. A good teacher? Today I really don't know. I do know that my classroom is being overwhelmed by society's problems and I don't understand it. What's happening to our schools? What's happening to society? I don't understand all of this and I sure don't know what we're going to do about it.

ELEMENTARY TEACHER, ATLANTA, GEORGIA
(Barr & Parrett, 2001, p. 1)

Other teachers respond differently,

While visiting a small elementary school, I was walking down the halls with two teachers on our way to lunch. While passing an open classroom door, one of my friends stopped and called out to a fellow teacher, "Come and join us for lunch." The teacher left a small group of students sitting around her desk and walked over to the door and replied, "I really can't. I've got a group of kids here who are having real problems with their reading, and I've been working with them over part of their lunch period all year." Knowing the type of students who generally attended this school I responded, "Isn't it sad how tragic so many of these poor kids' lives are?" The teacher turned and gave me a surprised look and said, "You know, I don't care who these kids are or where they're from or what their problems are. Before they leave my classroom I'm going to teach them to read. I can't do much about their home lives, but I can definitely teach them to read."

TEACHER, SUNRISE ELEMENTARY SCHOOL, ALBANY, OREGON.
(Barr & Parrett, 2001, p. 9)

Our goal in this section is to help you understand the nature of the problems and how you can increase students' resilience in responding to the environmental conditions your students encounter.

Resilience

Research on students placed at risk has increasingly focused on the concept of **resilience,** a learner characteristic that, despite adversity, raises the likelihood of success in school and later life (Borman & Overman, 2004; Downey, 2003; Knapp, 2001). This research has studied young people who have survived and even prospered despite obstacles such as poverty, poor health care, and fragmented support services. Resilient children have well-developed self-systems, including high self-esteem, optimism, and feelings that they are in control of their destinies. They set personal goals, expect to succeed, and believe they are responsible for their success (Downey, 2003). They are motivated to learn and satisfied with school (Borman & Overman, 2004).

How do these success skills develop? Resilient children come from nurturant environments, and one characteristic is striking. In virtually all cases, these children have one or more adults who have taken a special interest in them and hold them to high moral and academic standards; they essentially refuse to let the young person fail (Jew, Green, Millard, & Poscillico, 1999; Reis, Colbert & Hébert, 2005). These adults are often parents, but they could also be older siblings or other adults such as teachers who take a young person under their wing (Flores, Cicchetti, & Rogosch, 2005).

Schools also make important contributions to resilience. Let's see how.

Schools That Promote Resilience

Research has identified four school practices that promote resilience:

- *High and uncompromising academic standards.* Teachers emphasize mastery of content and do not accept passive attendance and mere completion of assignments (Jesse & Pokorny, 2001).
- *Strong personal bonds between teachers and students.* Teachers become the adults who refuse to let students fail, and students feel connected to the schools (Parish, Parish, & Batt, 2001).
- *Order and high structure.* The school and classes are orderly and highly structured. Teachers emphasize reasons for rules and consistently enforce rules and procedures (Ilg & Massucci, 2003; Pressley, Raphael, & Gallagher, 2004).
- *Participation in after-school activities.* Activities such as clubs and athletics give students additional chances to interact with caring adults and receive reinforcement for achievement (B. Davidson, Dell, & Walker, 2001).

Effective schools are both demanding and supportive; in many instances, they serve as homes away from home. The emphasis placed on school-sponsored activities reduces alienation and increases academic engagement and achievement (B. Davidson, et al., 2001; Jordan, 2001). School-sponsored activities also give teachers the chance to know students in contexts outside the classroom.

Teachers Who Promote Resilience

Schools are no more effective than the teachers who work in them. You saw earlier that teachers who promote resilience form strong personal bonds with students, and they become the adults who refuse to let students fail. This sometimes means spending extra time before or after school helping students succeed. Admittedly, spending out-of-class time with a student is demanding, but this kind of commitment is the essence of promoting resilience.

What else do we know about teachers who promote resilience? Research indicates that they talk frequently with students, learn about their families, and share their own lives (Doll, Zucker, & Brehm, 2004). They maintain high expectations, use interactive teaching strategies, and emphasize success and mastery of content (Tucker et al., 2002). They motivate students through personal contacts, instructional support, and attempts to link school to students' experiences (B. L. Wilson & Corbett, 2001).

Let's see what students say about these teachers. One middle school student commented,

> "Sometimes a teacher don't understand what people go through. They need to have compassion. A teacher who can relate to students will know when something's going on with them. If like the student don't do work or don't understand, the teacher will spend a lot of time with them." (B. L. Wilson & Corbett, 2001, p. 5)

Resilience. A learner characteristic that, despite adversity, raises the likelihood of success in school and later life

These teachers go the extra mile to ensure student success.

Teachers less effective in promoting resilience are more authoritarian and less accessible. They distance themselves from students and place primary responsibility for learning on them. They view instructional support as "babying students" or "holding students' hands." Lecture is a common teaching strategy, and motivation is the students' responsibility. Students perceive these teachers as adversaries, to be avoided if possible, tolerated if not. They also resent the teachers' lack of commitment:

> There's this teacher [over at the regular school] . . . you can put anything down and he'll give you a check mark for it. He doesn't check it. He just gives you a mark and says, 'OK, you did your work.' How you gonna learn from that? You ain't gonna learn nothing.
>
> Student, JFY Academy
> Boston, Massachusetts
>
> (Dynarski & Gleason, 1999, p. 13)

As with culturally responsive teaching, much of promoting resilience lies in teachers' attitudes and commitment to students. Effective teachers care about students as people and accept nothing less than consistent effort and quality work (Freese, 1999; Gschwend & Dembo, 2001). Caring teachers are important for all students; for students placed at risk, they're essential.

Instructional ⊞ Principles   **Teaching Students Placed at Risk:
Instructional Principles**

In addition to providing the human element we just discussed, what else can you do to ensure that students placed at risk will learn as much as possible? Research suggests that the same basic elements that work for all students also work for at-risk students (Borman & Overman, 2004; Knapp, 2001). In short, you don't need to teach in fundamentally different ways; you need to do what works with all students, but you need to do it better. The following principles can guide you in your efforts:

1. Create and maintain a productive learning environment with predictable routines.
2. Combine high expectations with frequent feedback about learning progress.
3. Use teaching strategies that actively involve all students and promote high levels of success.
4. Use high-quality examples that provide the background knowledge students need to learn new content.
5. Stress self-regulation and the acquisition of learning strategies.

Let's see how the principles guide Diane Smith, a fourth-grade teacher, as she works with her students.

> Diane has had her class working on adjectives in language arts, and she now wants them to be able to write using comparative and superlative forms of adjectives.
>
> Students file into the room from their lunch break, immediately go to their desks, and begin working on a set of exercises that has them identify all the adjectives and the nouns they modify in a paragraph displayed on the overhead.
>
> At 12:35, all students are seated and busy. As they work, Diane surveys the room and, on a small notepad, identifies students who have pencils of different lengths and those whose hair color varies.
>
> She begins the class by going over the passage, asking the students to explain how they know a word is an adjective and what noun it modifies. When students encounter difficulties, she explains the correct answer carefully.
>
> As they finish, Diane announces, "Okay, very good, everyone. Put your pencils down for now, and look up here."
>
> "Calesha and Daniel, hold your pencils up so everyone can see. What do you notice? . . . Naitia?"
>
> ". . . Calesha's is red, and Daniel's is blue."
>
> "Okay. What else?" Diane smiles, ". . . Sheila?"

"You write with them."

"Kevin?"

"Calesha's is longer."

"Does everyone see that? Hold them up again."

Calesha and Daniel hold their pencils up again, and Diane goes to the board and writes:

Calesha has a long pencil.
Calesha has a longer pencil than Daniel does.

"Now, let's look at Matt and Leroy," she continues. "What do you notice about their hair? . . . Judy?"

"Leroy's is black, and Matt's is brown," Judy responds.

"Okay. Good, Judy. So who's is darker?"

"LEROY!" several in the class blurt out, as Diane smiles at their eagerness.

"Good!" Diane again goes to the board and writes three more sentences:

Calesha has a long pencil.	*Leroy has black hair.*
Calesha has a longer pencil than Daniel does.	*Matt has brown hair.*
	Leroy has darker hair than Matt does.

"Now, how do the adjectives in the sentences compare? . . . Heather?" Diane asks, pointing to the bottom sentences on each list.

". . . The ones . . . at the bottom have an *-er* on the end of them," Heather responds hesitantly.

"Yes, good. . . . And, what are we doing in each of the sentences? . . . Jason?"

"We're comparing two things."

"Good thinking, Jason," Diane smiles.

She then repeats the process with the superlative form of adjectives by having the students compare three pencils and three different hair colors, leading them to conclude that superlative adjectives have an *-est* on the end of them.

"Very good, everyone. In describing nouns, if we're comparing two, we use the comparative form of the adjective, which has an *-er* on the end, and if we have three or more, we have an *-est* on the end of the adjective.

"Now, I have a little challenge for you." Diane reaches back and takes a softball, a tennis ball, and a golf ball from her desk. "Write two sentences each that use the comparative and superlative forms of adjectives and tell about the sizes of the balls."

As the students work, Diane walks up and down the rows, periodically making brief comments.

"Now let's look at your sentences," Diane begins after a few minutes. "Someone volunteer, and I'll write it on the chalkboard. . . . Okay, Rashad?"

"The tennis ball is bigger than the golf ball."

"Very good, Rashad. And why did you write *bigger* in your sentence?"

"We're comparing the size of two balls."

"And another one? . . . Bharat?"

"The softball is the biggest one."

After asking Bharat to explain his sentence, she continues, "That's excellent. . . . Now, I want you to write a paragraph with at least two sentences that use the comparative form of adjectives and at least two other sentences that use the superlative form of the adjectives. Underline the adjectives in each case."

"And what do we always do after we write something?"

"We read it to be sure it makes sense!" several of the students say simultaneously.

"Very good," Diane smiles. "That's how we become good writers."

The students go to work, and Diane circulates among them, periodically stopping for a few seconds to comment on a student's work and to offer brief suggestions. After the students finish, they share their paragraphs with a partner, who makes comments, and students then revise the paragraphs based on the feedback.

Now, let's look at Diane's attempts to apply the principles in her teaching. She applied the first by creating a productive learning environment with well-established routines. For example, when students came in from their break, they immediately went to work on exercises on the overhead without being told to do so, suggesting that this was a routine. Predictable routines not only maximize the time available for learning, they also provide a feeling of structure and order in the classroom, making them comfortable places to learn.

(We discuss specific strategies for creating productive learning environments in Chapters 12 and 13.)

Second, by calling on individual students—Naita, Sheila, and Kevin at the beginning of the lesson and several others as it developed—Diane communicated that she expected all students to participate. She also required that they explain their answers, communicating that understanding, and not mere participation, was the goal.

Establishing and maintaining high expectations is a simple idea but hard to put into practice, and, in spite of being encouraged to challenge students, teachers often fail to do so (Haycock, 2001). Effort and persistence are essential. Most students initially have trouble putting their understanding into words; for students placed at risk, it's an even greater challenge. Many teachers give up, concluding, "They can't do it." They can't because they haven't had enough practice. It isn't easy, but it can be done.

Also, Diane went over each of the beginning-of-class exercises to provide feedback to any students who were uncertain about the concepts, and students' explanations provided additional feedback. She also gave students feedback about their sentences at the end of the lesson before she had them work on their paragraphs on their own. This type of instructional scaffolding promotes success, minimizes mistakes, and increases motivation (Brophy, 2004). All of these teacher actions applied the second principle.

Diane applied the third principle with questioning that involved all students in the lesson. Open-ended questions such as "What do you notice?" and "How do the adjectives in the sentences compare?" virtually assured students of being able to answer successfully, a critical factor in both learning and motivation (Brophy, 2004).

Interactive teaching methods are effective for all students and essential for students placed at risk (Barr & Parrett, 2001; B. L. Wilson & Corbett, 2001). In a comparison of more- and less-effective urban elementary teachers, researchers found that the less-effective teachers interacted with students only about 45 percent of their time available for instruction, compared to nearly 75 percent for their more-effective counterparts (Waxman, Huang, Anderson, & Weinstein, 1997). Cooperative learning strategies, such as having students respond to each other's paragraphs, can also be effective for promoting involvement (Holliday, 2002).

Diane applied the fourth principle by developing her lesson around real-world examples. Teachers who promote resilience attempt to link school to students' lives, and using students' pencils and hair color to illustrate comparative and superlative adjectives was a simple application of this idea.

Finally, Diane emphasized self-regulation (principle 5) when she asked, "And what do we always do after we write something?" The fact that the students so quickly replied, "We read it to be sure it makes sense!" suggests that she placed a great deal of emphasis on student responsibility for their own learning.

The challenge for teachers who work with students placed at risk is how to help them be successful while still presenting a challenging intellectual menu. It isn't easy. It requires a caring environment and a great deal of effort. However, seeing students who were previously unsuccessful and apathetic succeed and meet challenges is enormously rewarding.

Online Case Book

To analyze another case study to assess a teacher's effectiveness in responding to group and individual differences, go to the *Online Case Book* for Chapter 4 at *www.prenhall.com/eggen.*

Exploring Further

To read more about different instructional strategies for teaching students placed at risk, go to "Effective Instruction for Students Placed at Risk" in the *Exploring Further* module of Chapter 4 at *www.prenhall.com/eggen.*

Checking Your Understanding

5.1   Describe characteristics of schools that promote resilience in students placed at risk.

5.2   Describe the qualities of teachers who are effective in promoting student resilience.

5.3   What instructional strategies are effective for developing resilience in students placed at risk?

To receive feedback for these questions, go to Appendix B.

Knowledge Extensions

To deepen your understanding of the topics in this section of Chapter 4 and to integrate them with topics you've already studied, go to the *Knowledge Extensions* module for Chapter 4 at *www.prenhall.com/eggen.* Respond to questions 18–21.

Classroom Connections

Using Effective Teaching Practices for Students Placed at Risk in Your Classroom

1. Communicate positive expectations to both students and their parents.

   - **Elementary:** A fourth-grade teacher spends the first 2 weeks of school teaching students her classroom procedures and explaining how they promote learning and create a learning community. She makes short assignments, carefully monitors students to be certain the assignments are turned in, and immediately calls parents if an assignment is missing.

   - **Middle School:** A math teacher carefully explains his course procedures. He emphasizes the importance of attendance and effort and communicates that he expects all to do well. He also makes himself available before and after school for help sessions.

   - **High School:** An English teacher sends home an upbeat letter at the beginning of the year describing her work requirements and grading practices. She has students help translate the letter for parents whose first language is not English and asks parents to sign the letter, indicating they have read it. She also invites questions and comments from parents or other caregivers.

2. Use teaching strategies that elicit high levels of student involvement and success.

   - **Elementary:** A fifth-grade teacher arranges the seating in his classroom so that minority and nonminority students are mixed. He combines small-group and whole-class instruction, and when he uses group work, he arranges the groups so they include high and low achievers, minorities and nonminorities, and boys and girls.

   - **Middle School:** An earth science teacher gives students a short quiz of one or two questions every day. It is discussed at the beginning of the following day, and students calculate their averages each day during the grading period. The teacher closely monitors these scores and spends time before school to work with students who are falling behind.

   - **High School:** An English teacher builds her teaching around questioning and examples. She comments, "My goal is to call on each student in the class at least twice during each lesson. I also use a lot of repetition and reinforcement as we cover the examples."

 *Meeting Your Learning Objectives*

1. **Describe differences in the way intelligence is viewed, and explain how ability grouping can influence learning.**

   - Intelligence is often defined as the ability to think and reason abstractly, to solve problems, and to acquire new knowledge. Some theories suggest that intelligence is a single entity; others describe intelligence as existing in several forms.

   - Some experts believe that intelligence is largely genetically determined; others believe it is strongly influenced by experiences. Most suggest that it is determined by a combination of the two.

   - Schools respond to differences in ability by grouping students. Within- and between-class ability grouping is common in elementary schools; tracking is prevalent in middle and secondary schools.

   - Learning styles are students' personal approaches to learning, problem solving, and processing information. Research generally does not support efforts to match instruction with learning preferences; rather, it suggests that teachers should help students develop awareness of their own learning strengths.

2. **Define socioeconomic status (SES), and explain how it can affect school performance.**

   - Socioeconomic status includes parents' income, occupation, and level of education. SES can strongly influence student attitudes, values, background experiences, and school success.

   - In using SES to think about instruction, experts recommend that we treat all students as individuals and exercise caution in generalizing from SES groups to individual students.

3. **Describe cultural, ethnic, and language diversity, and explain how they can influence learning.**

   - *Culture* refers to the attitudes, values, customs, and behavior patterns that characterize a social group. The match between a child's culture and the school has a powerful influence on school success. Culturally responsive teaching creates links between a student's culture and classroom instruction. It reminds us to continually keep cultural influences in mind as we interact with learners from different cultures.

- The United States has numerous local and regional dialects. Teachers often misinterpret dialects as substandard English. Teachers should accept and build on student dialects and develop bidialecticism in their students.
- English language learners are increasing in numbers in the United States due to increased immigration. Approaches to helping ELL students learn English vary in their emphasis on maintaining students' native language and the amount of support they provide in content-related instruction.
- Instructional strategies to assist ELL students emphasize that teachers should become familiar with their students' language backgrounds and capabilities and activate students' background knowledge. In addition, effective teachers use concrete experiences, target important vocabulary terms, and provide opportunities to practice language.

4. Explain gender-role identity, and describe steps for eliminating gender bias in classrooms.

- Gender-role identity describes beliefs about appropriate characteristics and behaviors of the two sexes.
- Teachers can minimize achievement differences by treating boys and girls equally and by actively combating gender stereotypes in their teaching.

5. Describe characteristics of schools and qualities of teachers that promote student resilience.

- Students placed at risk are those in danger of leaving school without the skills needed to function effectively in our modern world. Factors that increase the probability of being at-risk include poverty, transience, and not speaking English as a first language.
- Resilient learners can succeed in school despite environmental adversities.
- Schools that promote resilience stress high expectations, an academic focus, continuous monitoring of progress, and strong parent involvement.
- Teachers who promote resilience hold high expectations for academic success, use a variety of interactive instructional and motivational strategies, and demonstrate caring through sincere interest in students' lives. They provide greater structure and support, more active teaching, greater student engagement, challenge, and more feedback with higher success rates.

Developing as a Professional

Developing as a Professional: Praxis Practice

In this chapter, we've seen how intelligence, SES, culture, and gender can influence learning and how certain combinations of these factors can place students at risk.

Let's look now at a teacher working with students whose backgrounds are diverse. Read the case study, and answer the questions that follow.

Teri Hall is an eighth-grade American history teacher in an inner-city middle school. Most of her students are from low-income families, many of them are from diverse cultures, and some speak English as a second language.

Today, her class is studying the colonization of North America. Teri takes roll as students enter the room, and she finishes entering the information into the computer on her desk just as the bell rings.

"What were we discussing yesterday?" Teri begins immediately after the bell stops ringing. "Ditan?"

". . . The beginning of the American colonies."

"Good. . . . Go up to the map, point out where we live, and show us the first British, French, and Spanish colonies. . . . Kaldya?"

Kaldya walks to the front of the room and points to four different locations on a large map of North America.

Teri reviews for a few more minutes and then displays the following on the overhead:

In the mid-1600s, the American colonists were encouraged to grow tobacco, since it wasn't grown in England. The colonists wanted to sell it to France and other countries, but were told no. In return for sending the tobacco to England, the colonists were allowed to buy textiles from England. They were forbidden, however, from making their own textiles. All the materials were carried on British ships.

Early French colonists in the New World were avid fur trappers and traders. They got in trouble with the French monarchy, however, when they attempted to make fur garments and sell them to Spain, England, and others. They were told that they had to buy the manufactured garments from dealers in Paris instead. The monarchy also told them that traps and weapons would be made in France and sent to them as well. One of the colonists, Jean Forjea, complied with the monarchy's wishes but was fined when he hired a Dutch ship to carry some of the furs back to Nice.

"Now let's take a look," she begins. "Take a few seconds to read the paragraphs you see on the screen. Then, with your partner, write down as many similarities as you can about the subjects of the two paragraphs. You have 5 minutes."

Teri does a considerable amount of group work in her class. She sometimes has the students work in pairs, and at other times in groups of four. The students are seated together, so they can move into and out of the groups quickly. Students initially protested the seating assignments, because they weren't sitting near their friends, but Teri emphasized that *learning* and getting to know and respect people different from themselves were important goals for the class. Teri persisted, and the groups became quite effective.

Teri watches as students work, and at the end of the 5-minute period, she says, "Okay, you've done a good job . . . . Turn back up here, and let's think about this."

The class quickly turns their attention to the front of the room, and Teri asks, "Serena, what did you and David come up with?"

". . . Both of the paragraphs deal with a colony."

"Okay, Eric, how about you and Kyo?"

". . . The colonies both produced something their countries, England and France, wanted—like tobacco or furs."

"Excellent observation, you two," Teri smiles. "Go on Gustavo. How about you and Pam?"

". . . They sent the stuff to their country," Gustavo responds after looking at his notes.

"And they couldn't send it anywhere else!" Tito adds, warming up to the idea.

"That's very good, all of you. Where do you suppose Tito got that idea? . . . Connie?"

"It says it right in the paragraphs," Connie responds.

"Excellent, everyone! Connie, good use of information to support your ideas."

Teri continues to guide the students as they analyze the paragraphs. She guides the class to conclude that, in each instance, the colonies sent raw materials to the mother country, bought back finished products, and were required to use the mother country's ships to transport all materials.

She then tells them that this policy, called *mercantilism*, was a strategy countries used to make money from their colonies. "Mercantilism helps us understand why Europe was so interested in imperialism and colonization," she adds. "It doesn't explain everything, but it was a major factor in the history of this period.

"Let's look at another paragraph. Does this one illustrate mercantilism? Be ready to explain why or why not when you've made your decision," she directs, displaying the following on the screen:

> Canada is a member of the British commonwealth. Canada is a large grain producer and exporter and derives considerable income from selling this grain to Great Britain, France, Russia, and other countries. This trade has also enhanced the shipping business for Greece, Norway, and Liberia, who carry most of the products. Canada, however, doesn't rely on grain alone. It is now a major producer of clothing, high-tech equipment, and heavy industrial equipment.

The class discusses the paragraph and, using evidence from the text, concludes that it does not illustrate mercantilism.

PRAXIS These exercises are designed to help you prepare for the Praxis™ Principles of Learning and Teaching exam. To receive feedback on your short-answer responses, go to the Companion Website at *www.prenhall.com/eggen*, then to the Practice for Praxis™ module for Chapter 4.

To acquire experience in preparing for the multiple-choice items on the Praxis™ exam, go to the *Self-Assessment* module for Chapter 4 at *www.prenhall.com/eggen*, and click on "Practice Quiz."

For additional connections between this text and the Praxis™ exam, go to Appendix A.

Short-Answer Questions

In answering these questions, use information from the chapter and link your responses to specific information in the case.

1. What strategies did Teri use to eliminate gender bias in her classroom? What else might she have done?
2. One of the principles of effective teaching for students placed at risk recommends the use of high-quality examples that supplement students' background knowledge. How well did Teri apply this principle?
3. Success and challenge are essential for effective instruction for students placed at risk. Evaluate Teri's attempts to provide these components.
4. What strategies did Teri use to actively involve her students?

ONLINE PORTFOLIO ACTIVITIES

Also on the Companion Website at *www.prenhall.com/eggen*, you can measure your understanding of chapter content with multiple-choice and essay questions, and broaden your knowledge base in *Exploring Further* and *Web Links* to other educational psychology websites.

To develop your professional portfolio, further apply your understanding of chapter content, and address the INTASC standards, go to the Companion Website, then to the *Online Portfolio Activities* for Chapter 4. Complete the suggested activities.

IMPORTANT CONCEPTS

ability grouping (p. 100)
basic interpersonal communication
    skills (p. 113)
bidialecticism (p. 111)
cognitive academic language
    proficiency (p. 113)
cultural inversion (p. 107)

culture (p. 106)
dialect (p. 110)
ELL pullout programs (p. 112)
ethnicity (p. 106)
gender-role identity differences (p. 117)
immersion (p. 113)
intelligence (p. 96)

Joplin plan (p. 101)
learning styles (p. 101)
maintenance ELL programs (p. 111)
nature view of intelligence (p. 100)
nurture view of intelligence (p. 100)
resilience (p. 122)

sheltered English (p. 113)
socioeconomic status (SES) (p. 103)
students placed at risk (p. 120)
tracking (p. 100)
transitional ELL programs (p. 112)

CHAPTER 5

Learners with Exceptionalties

Chapter Outline	Learning Objectives
	After you have completed your study of this chapter, you should be able to
Changes in the Way Teachers Help Students with Exceptionalities	**1** Describe the provisions of, and amendments to, the Individuals with Disabilities Education Act (IDEA).
Individuals with Disabilities Education Act (IDEA) • Amendments to the Individuals with Disabilities Education Act	
Students with Learning Problems	**2** Describe the most common learning problems that classroom teachers are likely to encounter.
The Labeling Controversy • Mental Retardation • Learning Disabilities • Attention-Deficit/Hyperactivity Disorder • Behavior Disorders • Communication Disorders • Visual Disabilities • Hearing Disabilities • Assessment and Learning: Assessment Trends in Special Education	
Students Who Are Gifted and Talented	**3** Identify characteristics of learners who are gifted and talented, and describe methods for identifying and teaching these students.
Creativity • Identifying Students Who Are Gifted and Talented • Teaching Students Who Are Gifted and Talented: Instructional Principles	
The Teacher's Role in Inclusive Classrooms	**4** Explain the roles of classroom teachers and teaching strategies that are effective for working with students having exceptionalities.
Identifying Students with Exceptionalities • Teaching Students with Exceptionalities: Instructional Principles • Social Integration and Growth	

Virtually every classroom in our country includes students who have learning exceptionalities. As you read the following case study, think about some of the exceptionalities that students display and what teachers can do to accommodate learners who have them.

Celina Curtis, a beginning first-grade teacher in a large urban elementary school, has survived her hectic first weeks. She is beginning to feel comfortable, but at the same time, some things are bothering her.

"It's kind of frustrating," she admits, as she shares her half-hour lunch break with Clarisse, a "veteran" of 3 years who has become her friend and confidante. "I think I'm teaching, but some of the kids just don't seem to get it."

"Maybe you're being too hard on yourself," Clarisse responds. "Students *are* different. Remember some of the stuff you studied in college? One thing the professors emphasized was that we should be trying our best to treat students as individuals."

"Well, . . . yes, I understand that, but that seems too simple. I still have this feeling. For instance, there's Rodney. You've seen him on the playground. He's cute, but his engine is stuck on fast. I can barely get him to sit in his seat, much less work.

"When he sits down to do an assignment, he's all over his desk, squirming and wiggling. The smallest distraction sets him off. He can usually do the work if I can get him to stick to it, but it's a challenge. I've talked to his mother, and he's the same way at home.

"Then there's Amelia; she's so sweet, but she simply doesn't get it. I've tried everything under the sun with her. I explain it, and the next time, it's as if it's all brand new. I feel sorry for her, because I know she gets frustrated when she can't keep up with the other kids. When I work with her one-on-one, it seems to help, but I don't have enough time to spend with her. She's falling further and further behind."

"Maybe it's not your fault. You're supposed to be bright and energetic and do your best, but you're going to burn yourself out if you keep this up," Clarisse cautions. "Check with the Teacher Assistance Team. Maybe these students need some extra help."

As we begin our study of this chapter, we want to consider three questions. (1) What does the law say about working with students having exceptionalities? (2) Though we can't be certain from the brief descriptions, Rodney and Amelia may have problems that prevent them from taking full advantage of their education. If so, what kinds of exceptionalities do they display, and how common are they? (3) How can teachers accommodate students with exceptionalities in their classrooms?

Learners with exceptionalities are students who need special help and resources to reach their full potential (Kauffman, McGee, & Brigham, 2004). This category includes students with **disabilities**—functional limitations or an inability to perform a certain act, such as to hear or walk—as well as students with **gifts and talents**—abilities at the upper end of the continuum that require support beyond regular classroom instruction to reach full potential. Some students have both disabilities and gifts and talents at the same time. It is a virtual certainty that you will have some of these students in your classroom. **Special education** refers to instruction designed to meet the unique needs of these students.

CHANGES IN THE WAY TEACHERS HELP STUDENTS WITH EXCEPTIONALITIES

In the past, schools separated students with disabilities from their nondisabled peers and placed them in special classrooms or schools. Instruction in these placements was often inferior, achievement was no better than in regular classrooms, and students didn't learn the social and life skills needed to live in the real world (Karten, 2005; T. Smith, Polloway, Patton, & Dowdy, 2004). A series of federal laws redefined the way teachers assist these students. In this section, we attempt to answer the first question we asked at the beginning of this chapter, "What does the law say about working with students having exceptionalities?"

Individuals with Disabilities Education Act (IDEA)

In 1975 Congress passed Public Law 94-142, which made available a free and public education for all students with disabilities in the United States. This law, renamed the Individuals with Disabilities Education Act (IDEA), requires that educators working with students having exceptionalities do the following:

Learners with exceptionalities. Students who need special help and resources to reach their full potential

Disabilities. Functional limitations or an inability to perform a certain act

Gifts and talents. Abilities at the upper end of the continuum that require support beyond regular classroom instruction to reach full potential

Special education. Instruction designed to meet the unique needs of students with exceptionalities

- Provide a free and appropriate public education (FAPE).
- Educate children in the least restrictive environment (LRE).
- Protect against discrimination in testing.
- Involve parents in developing each child's educational program.
- Develop an individualized education program (IEP) of study for each student.

IDEA has affected every school in the United States and has changed the roles of regular and special educators. Let's look at its major provisions.

The least restrictive environment provides students with opportunities to develop to their fullest potential.

A Free and Appropriate Public Education

IDEA asserts that every student can learn and is entitled to a free and appropriate public education. Provisions related to FAPE are based on the 14th Amendment to the Constitution, which guarantees equal protection of all citizens under the law. The Supreme Court in 1982 defined an *appropriate education* as one specially and individually designed to provide educational benefits to a particular student (Hardman, Drew, & Egan, 2005).

Least Restrictive Environment: The Evolution Toward Inclusion

Educators attempting to provide a free and appropriate public education for all students realized that segregated classes and services were not meeting the needs of students with exceptionalities. **Mainstreaming,** the practice of moving students with exceptionalities from segregated settings into regular classrooms—often for selected activities only—was one of the first alternatives considered. Popular in the 1970s, it began the move away from segregated services and promoted interaction between students with and without exceptionalities. However, students with exceptionalities were often placed in classrooms without adequate support (Hardman et al., 2005).

As educators struggled with these problems, they developed the concept of the **least restrictive environment (LRE),** one that places students in as typical an educational setting as possible while still meeting the students' special needs. Broader than the concept of *mainstreaming,* the LRE can consist of a continuum of services, ranging from full-time placement in the regular classroom to placement in a separate facility. Full-time placement in the regular classroom occurs only if parents and educators decide it best meets the child's needs.

The LRE provision ensures that you will have learners with exceptionalities in your classroom, and you will be asked to work with special educators to design and implement programs for these students. The LRE means that students with exceptionalities should participate as much as possible in the regular school agenda, ranging from academics to extracurricular activities. The form of these programs varies with the capabilities of the students. Figure 5.1 presents a continuum of services for implementing the LRE, starting with the least confining at the top and moving to the most restrictive at the bottom. If students don't succeed at one level, they are moved to the next.

The concept of **adaptive fit** is central to the LRE. It describes the degree to which a school environment accommodates the student's needs and the degree to which a student can meet the requirements of a particular school setting (Hardman et al., 2005). Adaptive fit requires an individualized approach to working with students having exceptionalities; it can be determined only after an analysis of the student's needs. As educators examined mainstreaming, LRE, and adaptive fit, they gradually developed the concept of *inclusion.*

Inclusion is a comprehensive approach to educating students with exceptionalities that advocates a total, systematic, and coordinated web of services (J. M. Peterson & Hittie, 2003; Sailor & Roger, 2005). It has three provisions:

1. Students with special needs will be placed on a regular school campus.
2. Students with special needs will be placed in age- and grade-appropriate classrooms.
3. General and special education services will be coordinated.

Mainstreaming. The practice of moving students with exceptionalities from segregated settings into regular classrooms

Least restrictive environment (LRE). A policy that places students in as typical an educational setting as possible while still meeting their special needs

Adaptive fit. The degree to which a school environment accommodates the student's needs and the degree to which a student can meet the requirements of a particular school setting

Inclusion. A comprehensive approach to educating students with exceptionalities that advocates a total, systematic, and coordinated web of services

Figure 5.1   Educational service options for implementing the LRE

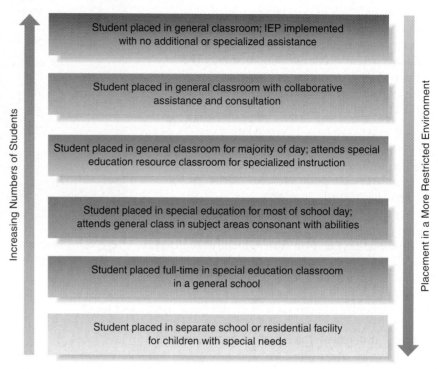

Source: U.S. Department of Education, 2002.

Collaborative Consultation: Help for the Classroom Teacher. Initially, inclusion was viewed as additive; students with exceptionalities received additional services to help them function in regular school settings (Turnbull, Turnbull, Shank, Smith, & Leal, 2004). Gradually, the concept of *coordination* replaced addition; today, the intent is for special and regular educators to collaborate in an attempt to ensure that experiences for students with exceptionalities are integrated.

Collaboration is essential if inclusion is to be effective (Karten, 2005; T. Smith et al., 2004). In working with the regular education teacher, the special educator

- Assists in collecting assessment information
- Maintains students' records
- Develops special curriculum materials
- Coordinates the efforts of team members in implementing individualized education programs
- Works with parents
- Assists in adapting instruction

Helping the regular education teacher adapt instruction is perhaps most important because it most directly influences academic success. (We discuss adaptations later in the chapter.)

When properly designed and implemented, collaborative consultation teaching can be effective. It allows efficient use of special education resources, reduces the stigma of pullout programs, and creates productive learning environments for students (Turnbull et al., 2004).

Putting Inclusion into Perspective. The practice of inclusion, while increasing, is controversial, with criticisms coming from regular classroom teachers, parents, and special educators themselves (M. Byrnes, 2002; Turnbull et al., 2004). Where inclusion works, regular education and special education teachers collaborate extensively (Vaughn, Bos, Candaces & Schumm, 2006; Rea, McLaughlin, & Walther-Thomas, 2002). Without this collaboration, however, full inclusion isn't effective, and regular classroom teachers resent being expected to individualize instruction without adequate support (Kavale & Forness, 2000). Some parents of students with disabilities, concerned that their children might get

Inclusion creates a web of services to integrate students with exceptionalities into the educational system.

lost in the shuffle, also question the effectiveness of inclusion, and often favor special classrooms (J. Johnson & Duffett, 2002). Other parents, seeing benefits, view inclusion as a valuable alternative (Buchan, 2000).

In the special education community, advocates of inclusion contend that placement in a regular classroom is the only way to eliminate the negative effects of segregation (Kluth, Villa, & Thousand, 2002; Stainback & Stainback, 1992). Opponents counter that inclusion is not for everyone and that some students are better served in special classes, at least for parts of the day (Holloway, 2001).

Protection Against Discrimination in Testing

In the past, students with disabilities were often placed in special education programs based on inadequate or invalid assessment information. IDEA requires that any testing used for placement be conducted in a student's native language by qualified personnel, and no single instrument, such as an intelligence test, can be used as the basis for placement. Recently, students' classroom performance and general adaptive behavior have been increasingly emphasized (Heward, 2006).

Due Process and Parents' Rights

Due process guarantees parents' right to be involved in identifying and placing their children in special programs, to access school records, and to obtain an independent evaluation if they're not satisfied with the one conducted by the school. Parents commonly complain that they aren't being told about available services (J. Johnson, 2002). Legal safeguards are also in place if parents don't speak English; they have the right to an interpreter, and their rights must be read to them in their native language.

Individualized Education Program

To ensure that inclusion works and learners with exceptionalities don't get lost in the regular classroom, an individualized education program is prepared if a student is found eligible for special education. An **individualized education program (IEP)** is an individually prescribed instructional plan devised by special education and general education teachers, resource professionals, and parents (and sometimes the student). It specifies the following:

- An assessment of the student's current level of performance
- Long- and short-term objectives
- Services or strategies to be used
- Schedules for implementing the plan
- Criteria to be used in evaluating the plan's success

Analyzing Classrooms Video
To see teachers reviewing a child's IEP with a parent, go to Episode 6, "Reviewing an IEP," on DVD 1, accompanying this text.

Due process. The guarantee of parents' right to be involved in identifying and placing their children in special programs, to access school records, and to obtain an independent evaluation if they're not satisfied with the one conducted by the school

Individualized education program (IEP). An individually prescribed instructional plan devised by special education and general education teachers, resource professionals, and parents (and sometimes the student)

Teachers and other professionals meet with parents to design an IEP that meets a student's individual learning needs.

A sample IEP is illustrated in Figure 5.2. It has three important features. First, the initials of all participants indicate that its development was a cooperative effort. Second, the information in sections 3–7 is specific enough to guide the classroom teacher and special education personnel as they implement the program. Third, the mother's signature indicates that a parent was involved in developing the program and agrees with its provisions. Computer software is now available to help teachers create effective IEPs by easing access to student records through current databases (Trotter, 2005).

The IEP performs four functions. First, it provides support for the classroom teacher, who may be uncertain about the specific instructional adaptations to be made. Second, it creates a link between the regular classroom and the resource team. Third, it helps parents monitor their child's educational progress. Fourth, and most important, it provides a program to meet the individual needs of the student.

IEPs sometimes provide for work in settings outside the regular classroom, such as a resource room; at other times, they focus exclusively on adaptations in the regular classroom. They are most effective when the two are coordinated, such as when a classroom teacher working on word problems in math asks the resource teacher to focus on the same type of problems.

Amendments to the Individuals with Disabilities Education Act

Since 1975, Congress has amended IDEA three times (PL 98-199, PL 99-457, PL 101-476) in attempts to ensure that all children with disabilities are protected and provided with a free and appropriate public education (Huefner, 1999; R. Lewis & Doorlag, 1999). For example, amendments in 1986 extended the rights and protections of IDEA to children aged 3 through 5 and held states accountable for locating young children who need special education. That service is sometimes called *Child Find.*

Amendment 1997, known as IDEA 97, attempted to clarify and extend the quality of services to students with disabilities. This amendment created the features that you saw in the previous sections, such as protection against discrimination in testing, the right to due process, and the requirement of the IEP.

This amendment also ensures confidentiality. Districts must keep confidential records of each child, protect their confidentiality, and share them with parents on request.

Recently, Congress enacted another change called IDEA 2004 (Council for Exceptional Children, 2005). It has the following elements:

- Reduce the special education paperwork burden by deleting short-term objectives and benchmarks from IEPs (except for students who take alternative assessments).
- Initiate a 15-state paperwork demonstration project to pilot 3-year IEPs.
- Create discipline provisions, which allow districts to remove students who "inflict serious bodily injury" from the classroom to an alternative setting during the appeals process.
- Establish methods to reduce the number of students from culturally and linguistically diverse backgrounds who are inappropriately placed in special education.
- Provide districts with more flexibility in meeting the highly qualified teacher requirements of the No Child Left Behind legislation of 2002. Special education teachers who teach more than one subject may prove their qualifications through HOUSSE (high, objective, uniform state standard of evaluation), which allows veteran teachers to demonstrate their qualifications by means other than a test.
- Provide professional development for special educators.
- Include students with disabilities in accountability systems.

The impact of these legislative changes on teaching will unfold in the next few years.

Exploring Further

To read more about inclusion, go to "Inclusion" in the *Exploring Further* module of Chapter 5 at *www.prenhall.com/eggen*.

Figure 5.2 Individualized education program (IEP)

INDIVIDUAL EDUCATION PROGRAM

Date _____3-1-06_____

(1) Student

Name: Joe S.
School: Adams
Grade: 5
Current Placement: Regular Class/Resource Room

Date of Birth: 10-1-94   Age: 11-5

(2) Committee

		Initial
Mrs. Wrens	Principal	D.a.W.
Mrs. Snow	Regular Teacher	AS
Mr. LaJoie	Counselor	dlJ
Mr. Thomas	Resource Teacher	M.T.
Mr. Ryan	School Psychologist	H.R.R.
Mrs. S.	Parent	J.d.
Joe S.	Student	Joe L.

·EP from __3-15-06__ to __3-15-07__

(3) Present Level of Educational Functioning	(4) Annual Goal Statements	(5) Instructional Objectives	(6) Objective Criteria and Evaluation
MATH Strengths 1. Can successfully compute addition and subtraction problems to two places with regrouping and zeros. 2. Knows 100 basic multiplication facts. Weaknesses 1. Frequently makes computational errors on problems with which he has had experience. 2. Does not complete seatwork. Key Math total score of 2.1 Grade Equivalent.	Joe will apply knowledge of regrouping in addition and renaming in subtraction to four-digit numbers.	1. When presented with 20 addition problems of 3-digit numbers requiring two renamings, the student will compute answers at a rate of one problem per minute and an accuracy of 90%. 2. When presented with 20 subtraction problems of 3-digit numbers requiring two renamings, the student will compute answers at the rate of one problem per minute with 90% accuracy. 3. When presented with 20 addition problems of 4-digit numbers requiring three renamings, the student will compute answers at a rate of one problem per minute and an accuracy of 90%. 4. When presented with 20 subtraction problems of 4-digit numbers requiring three renamings, the student will compute answers at a rate of one problem per minute with 90% accuracy.	Teacher-made tests (weekly) Teacher-made tests (weekly) Teacher-made tests (weekly)

(7) Educational Services to be provided

Services Required	Date initiated	Duration of Service	Individual Responsible for the Service
Regular reading-adapted	3-15-06	3-15-07	Reading Improvement Specialist and Special Education Teacher
Resource room	3-15-06	3-15-07	Special Education Teacher
Counselor consultant	3-15-06	3-15-07	Counselor
Monitoring diet and general health	3-15-06	3-15-07	School Health Nurse

Extent of time in the regular education program: 60% increasing to 80%
Justification of the educational placement:
It is felt that the structure of the resource room can best meet the goals stated for Joe, especially when coordinated with the regular classroom.
It is also felt that Joe could profit enormously from talking with a counselor. He needs someone with whom to talk and with whom he can share his feelings.

(8) I have had the opportunity to participate in the development of the Individual Education Program.
    I agree with Individual Education Program   (✓)
    I disagree with the Individual Education Program   ( )

Parent's Signature ____Mrs S.____

Source: Adapted from *Developing and Implementing Individualized Education Programs* (3rd ed., pp. 308, 316) by B. B. Strickland and A. P. Turnbull, 1990, Upper Saddle River, NJ: Merrill/Prentice Hall.

Knowledge Extensions

To deepen your understanding of the topics in this section of Chapter 5 and to integrate them with topics you've already studied, go to the *Knowledge Extensions* module for Chapter 5 at *www.prenhall.com/eggen*. Respond to questions 1 and 2.

Checking Your Understanding

1.1 Describe the major provisions of the Individuals with Disabilities Education Act (IDEA).

1.2 Explain how mainstreaming and inclusion relate to the FAPE (free and appropriate public education) provision of IDEA.

1.3 Describe recent amendments to the IDEA.

To receive feedback for these questions, go to Appendix B.

STUDENTS WITH LEARNING PROBLEMS

Educators often create labels to address student differences (Hardman et al., 2005). *Disorder, disability,* and *handicap* are common terms used to describe physical or behavioral differences. **Disorder,** the broadest of the three, refers to a general malfunction of mental, physical, or psychological processes. As you saw at the beginning of the chapter, a disability is a functional limitation or an inability to perform a certain act. A **handicap** refers to a condition imposed on a person's functioning that restricts the individual's abilities, such as being unable to enter a building in a wheelchair. This condition could be imposed by society, the physical environment, or the person's own attitudes (V. Lewis, 2002). Some, but not all, disabilities lead to handicaps. For example, a student with a visual disability may be able to wear glasses or sit in the front of the classroom; if these measures allow the student to function effectively, the disability isn't a handicap.

About 6 million students with exceptionalities are enrolled in special programs, two thirds for relatively minor learning problems (Hardman et al., 2005). Approximately 8½ percent of students in a typical school receive special education services, and the kinds of disabilities they have range from mild learning problems to physical impairments such as being deaf or blind (U.S. Department of Education, 2004). Federal legislation has created categories to identify learning problems, and educators use these categories in developing programs to meet the needs of students in each.

The Labeling Controversy

The use of categories and the labeling resulting from them are controversial. Advocates argue that categories provide a common language for professionals and encourage specialized instruction that meets the needs of students (Heward, 2006). Opponents claim that categories are arbitrary, many differences exist within them, and categorizing encourages educators to treat students as labels instead of people (Cook, 2001; National Council on Disability, 2000). Despite the controversy, these labels and categories are widely used, so you need to be familiar with the terms and how they apply to the students with exceptionalities in your classroom.

The percentage of students in each of the categories commonly used is outlined in Figure 5.3. The figure shows that a large majority (more than 70 percent) of the population of students with disabilities fall into three categories: mental retardation, learning disabilities, and behavior disorders. In the following sections, we discuss these and others you will likely encounter.

Figure 5.3   Population of students with disabilities

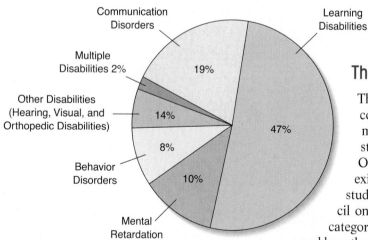

Source: U.S. Department of Education, 2004.

Mental Retardation

To begin this section, let's return to Celina's work with her students.

> She watches her children as they work on a reading assignment. Most of the class works quietly. Amelia, in contrast, is out of her seat for the third time, supposedly sharp-

Disorder. A general malfunction of mental, physical, or psychological processes

Handicap. A condition imposed on a person's functioning that restricts the individual's abilities

ening her pencil. Celina has reminded her once to sit down and this time goes over to see what the problem is.

"I can't do this! I don't get it!" Amelia responds in frustration when Celina asks her why she hasn't started her work.

After helping her calm down, Celina works with her for a few moments, but she can tell by Amelia's responses and her facial expression that she truly doesn't "get" the assignment. Celina makes a note as a reminder to talk to a special educator about Amelia.

Some students, like Amelia, learn less rapidly than others and become frustrated when they can't keep up with their peers. Unfortunately, this problem often isn't identified until students are several years into school. Many have mild mental retardation. (You may also encounter the terms *educationally* or *intellectually handicapped,* which some educators prefer.) Mental retardation is caused either by genetic factors or brain damage to the fetus during pregnancy (Nokelainen & Flint, 2002).

The American Association on Mental Retardation (AAMR) defines **mental retardation** as follows:

> Mental retardation is a disability characterized by significant limitations both in intellectual functioning and in adaptive behavior as expressed in conceptual, social, and practical adaptive skills. This disability originates before the age of 18. A complete and accurate understanding of mental retardation involves realizing that mental retardation refers to a particular state of functioning that begins in childhood, has many dimensions, and is affected positively by individualized supports. (AAMR Ad Hoc Committee on Terminology and Classification, 2002).

The AAMR definition emphasizes limitations in both intellectual functioning and adaptive skills, such as communication, self-care, and social skills (Luckasson et al., 2002; Turnbull et al., 2004). Functioning in both areas can improve when these students receive services designed to meet their needs.

Students with mental retardation are likely to display some or all of the following characteristics:

- Lack of general knowledge about the world
- Difficulty with abstract ideas
- Poor reading and language skills
- Poorly developed learning and memory strategies
- Difficulty transferring ideas to new situations
- Underdeveloped motor skills
- Immature interpersonal skills (Beirne-Smith, Ittenbach, & Patton, 2002)

Some of these characteristics affect learning directly; others, such as immature interpersonal skills, are less direct but still important.

Before the 1960s, definitions of mental retardation were based primarily on below-average scores on intelligence tests, but this approach had at least three problems. First, tests are imprecise, so misdiagnoses sometimes occurred. Second, disproportionate numbers of minorities and non-English-speaking students were identified as mentally retarded (Hallahan & Kauffman, 2006; Losen & Orfield, 2002). Third, educators found that individuals with the same intelligence test scores varied widely in their ability to cope with the real world (Heward, 2006). Because of these problems, **adaptive behavior,** the person's ability to perform the functions of everyday living, became more important in the definition. It is in this area that teachers' input is essential.

Levels of Mental Retardation

Educators describe mental retardation as existing at four levels that relate to the amount of support needed (Turnbull et al., 2004):

- *Intermittent:* Support on an as-needed basis
- *Limited:* Support consistently needed over time
- *Extensive:* Regular (e.g., daily) support required
- *Pervasive:* High-intensity, potentially life-sustaining support required

This classification system replaces an earlier one based on IQ scores alone. The older system categorized people as having mild (50 to 70 IQ), moderate (35 to 50 IQ), or severe

Mental retardation. A disability characterized by significant limitations both in intellectual functioning and in adaptive behavior

Adaptive behavior. A person's ability to manage the demands and perform the functions of everyday living

Although students with learning disabilities are found in almost every classroom, these students are often overlooked because they are often difficult to identify.

and profound (IQ below 35) mental retardation. The transition from the older, IQ-anchored system to the new one is not complete, so you may encounter both in your work.

Programs for Students with Mental Retardation

Programs for students who have intermittent (mild) mental retardation focus on creating support systems to augment existing instruction. These students are often placed in regular classrooms where teaching is adapted to meet their special needs, and attempts are made to help them develop socially and academically.

Research indicates that these students often fail to acquire basic learning strategies, such as maintaining attention, organizing new material, and studying for tests (Beirne-Smith et al., 2002; Heward, 2006). Amelia is an example of a student who needs additional help to function successfully in school. Celina recognized this need and attempted to provide additional support by working with her one-on-one.

Learning Disabilities

Tammy Fuller, a middle school social studies teacher, is surprised when she scores Adam's test. He seemed to be doing so well. He is rarely absent, pays attention, and participates in class activities. Why is his test score so low? Tammy makes a mental note to watch him more closely, because his behavior and test performance are inconsistent.

In her second unit, Tammy emphasizes both independent and cooperative work, so she prepares study guide questions and has students answer them in groups. As she moves around the room, she notices that Adam's sheet is empty; when she asks him about it, he mumbles something about not having time the night before. Because the success of the unit depends on students' coming to class prepared, Tammy asks Adam to come in after school to complete his work.

He arrives promptly and opens his book to the chapter. When Tammy stops to check on his progress, his page is blank; in another 10 minutes, it's still empty.

As she sits down to talk with him, he appears embarrassed and evasive. When they start to work on the questions together, she discovers that he can't read the text.

Some students, like Adam, have average or above-average intelligence but, despite their teachers' best efforts, struggle with learning. Students with **learning disabilities** (also called *specific learning disabilities*) encounter difficulties in acquiring and using reading, writing, reasoning, listening, or mathematical abilities (National Joint Committee on Learning Disabilities, 1994). Problems with reading, writing, and listening are most common (Shaywitz & Shaywitz, 2004), but math-related difficulties are also receiving attention (Hanich, Jordan, Kaplan, & Dick, 2001). Learning disabilities are believed to be due to central nervous system dysfunction and may exist along with, but are not caused by, other disabilities such as sensory impairments or attention problems. Experts stress that the term *learning disability* is broad and encompasses a range of learning problems (Hardman et al., 2005).

Students with learning disabilities are the largest group of learners with exceptionalities, making up 48 percent of the disabled student, and 4.4 percent of the total school-age population, in the 2002–2003 school year (U.S. Department of Education, 2004). The category first became widely used in the early 1960s, and the number of school-aged children diagnosed as having learning disabilities has continually increased (U.S. Department of Education, 2004).

Characteristics of Students with Learning Disabilities

Students with learning disabilities often share a number of problems, which are outlined in Table 5.1. However, each student is unique, and instructional adaptations should be individualized.

Some of the characteristics in Table 5.1 are typical of general learning problems or immaturity. Unlike developmental lags, however, problems associated with learning disabilities often increase over time. Achievement declines, management problems increase, and self-esteem decreases (Hardman et al., 2005; Heward, 2006). Lowered achievement and reduced self-esteem exacerbate each other and result in major learning problems (Wong & Donahue, 2002).

Learning disability. Difficulty in acquiring and using reading, writing, reasoning, listening, or mathematical abilities

Table 5.1 Characteristics of students with learning disabilities

General Patterns		
Attention deficits		
Disorganization and tendency toward distraction		
Lack of follow-through and completion of assignments		
Uneven performance (e.g., capable in one area, extremely weak in others)		
Lack of coordination and balance		
Academic Performance		
Reading	Lacks reading fluency	
	Reverses words (e.g., *saw* for *was*)	
	Frequently loses place	
Writing	Makes jerky and poorly formed letters	
	Has difficulty staying on line	
	Is slow in completing work	
	Has difficulty in copying from chalkboard	
Math	Has difficulty remembering math facts	
	Mixes columns (e.g., tens and ones) in computing	
	Has trouble with story problems	

Identifying and Working with Students Who Have Learning Disabilities

As with all exceptionalities, identification is the first step, and early identification is important to prevent damaging effects from accumulating (Pitoniak & Royer, 2001; Zambo, 2003). Early identification isn't simple, however; uneven rates of development can easily be mistaken for learning disabilities, and classroom management issues can complicate identification (Vaughn et al., 2006). Students with learning disabilities frequently display inappropriate classroom behavior, and students who misbehave are referred for testing at a much higher rate than those who don't (Hunt & Marshall, 2002). Students with learning disabilities who comply with rules and complete assignments on time are often passed over for referral. This is likely the reason Adam, in Tammy's class, got to middle school before his difficulties with reading were discovered. These patterns can be gender related; more boys than girls are identified because boys more commonly act out (Heward, 2006). Identification rates also vary from state to state and even within states. In Connecticut, for example, experts found identification rates varying from 7.2 percent in some districts to 23.8 percent in others (Sternberg & Grigorenko, 2001).

The Use of Classroom-Based Information for Identification. Teachers play a central role in identifying and working with students who have learning disabilities. Information from teacher-made assessments as well as teachers' direct observations are combined with standardized test scores. Often, a discrepancy model is then used to diagnose the problem (Hughes & McIntosh, 2002; M. Meyer, 2000). The model looks for differences between

1. Intelligence and achievement test performance
2. Intelligence test scores and classroom achievement
3. Subtests on either intelligence or achievement tests

Performance in one area, such as an intelligence test, should predict performance in others; when the two are inconsistent, a learning disability may be the cause. Some critics contend that the discrepancy model does not provide specific enough information about the nature of the learning problem and what should be done to correct it (Sternberg & Grigorenko, 2001; Stuebing et al., 2002). Other critics argue that discrepancy models identify a disability only after a problem surfaces, sometimes after several years of failure and frustration (M. Meyer, 2000). Instead, they argue, educators need to perform early screening measures, so that teachers can prevent failure before it occurs.

Earlier, we mentioned the problem of labeling. Critics contend that *learning disability* is a catchall term for students who have learning problems (Sternberg & Grigorenko, 2001). Part of this criticism results from the rapid growth of the category—nonexistent in the early 1960s—to the largest category of exceptionality at present. Before using the learning disability label, teachers should examine their own instruction to ensure it meets the needs of different students. In addition, teachers should be cautious in their work with English language learners to avoid confusing difficulties in students' learning a second language with a learning disability (Salend & Salinas, 2003).

Adaptive Instruction. Students with learning disabilities require modified instruction and teacher support. Because learning disabilities have different causes, teachers must tailor strategies to meet each student's needs. One study of college students with learning disabilities illustrates the range of modifications that can increase success (Ruzic, 2001). These students budgeted their time carefully, used other students as resources, and sought feedback from instructors to modify their study strategies. To compensate for reading deficits, they read in quiet environments, read aloud to themselves, and purchased previously highlighted books. In writing, they used a dictionary, frequently substituted an easier word if they had trouble spelling one, and asked other people to proofread their papers. They tape-recorded lectures to compensate for poor note taking and asked for extra time on tests. Students with learning disabilities can succeed if they acquire and use effective study strategies (Stanovich, 2000).

Attention-Deficit/Hyperactivity Disorder

Attention-deficit/hyperactivity disorder (ADHD) is a learning problem characterized by difficulties in maintaining attention. Hyperactivity and impulsive behaviors are often connected with ADHD. ADHD has long been associated with learning disabilities; in fact, experts estimate an overlap of between 25 and 70 percent in the two conditions (Hardman et al., 2005). ADHD is relatively new as a described exceptionality, and it is not listed as a distinct disability category in IDEA. Students with ADHD may qualify for special education under the "other health impairments" disability category in IDEA, however. Others seek educational accommodations and modifications under Section 504 of the Rehabilitation Act, which protects individuals from discrimination because of a disability.

The disorder has received a great deal of media attention, and teachers see many students who seem to fit the ADHD description. High activity levels and inability to focus attention are characteristics of developmental lags, especially in young boys, however, so teachers should be cautious about drawing conclusions on the basis of these characteristics alone.

Characteristics of ADHD include

- Hyperactivity
- Inattention, distractibility, difficulty in concentrating, and failure to finish tasks
- Impulsiveness (e.g., acting before thinking, frequent calling out in class, and difficulty awaiting turns)
- Forgetfulness and inordinate need for supervision

Students with ADHD have difficulty controlling the mental functions that monitor and regulate behavior (Casey, 2001; Jenkins, Bailey, & Fraser, 2004). It's easy to see why students with ADHD have difficulties adjusting to the "sit-down" pace of school life, where many activities are done alone and quietly (Schlozman & Schlozman, 2000).

ADHD usually appears early (at age 2 or 3) and, in at least 50 to 70 percent of the cases, persists into adolescence (Purdie, Hattie, & Carroll, 2002). The American Psychiatric Association (2000) estimates that three to four times as many boys as girls are identified, although other experts estimate this ratio higher (Purdie et al., 2002; Whalen, Jamner, Henker, Delfino, & Lozano, 2002). Treatments range from medication (e.g., the controversial medication, Ritalin) to reinforcement programs and structured teaching environments (described later in this chapter) (Swanson & Volkow, 2002). Diagnosis and treatment of ADHD are usually done in consultation with medical and psychological experts.

Rodney, in the case study at the beginning of the chapter, shows symptoms of ADHD. He's hyperactive, easily distracted, and has difficulties focusing his attention.

Attention-deficit/hyperactivity disorder (ADHD). A learning problem characterized by difficulties in maintaining attention

Celina is wise in seeking additional help for him. Before she does, however, she should examine her classroom environment to see if it meets Rodney's needs. For example, teachers often find that moving a student like Rodney to a quieter part of the room can eliminate distractions and help him focus on learning tasks (Tannock & Martinussen, 2001). Teachers have also had some success with behavioral interventions using principles of reinforcement and punishment for students with ADHD (Purdie et al., 2002). In addition, experts recommend teaching students how to break assignments into smaller components, requiring them to keep meticulously organized assignment books, and using flash cards and other drills to develop automaticity and confidence (Schlozman & Schlozman, 2000).

Behavior Disorders

Kyle comes in from recess sweaty and disheveled, crosses his arms, and looks at the teacher defiantly. The playground monitor has reported another scuffle. Kyle has a history of these disturbances and is a difficult student. He struggles with his studies but can handle them if provided with enough structure. When he becomes frustrated, he sometimes acts out, often ignoring the feelings and rights of others.

Ben, who sits next to Kyle, is so quiet that the teacher almost forgets he is there. He never causes problems; in fact, he seldom participates in class. He has few friends and walks around at recess by himself, appearing to consciously avoid other children.

Although their behaviors are very different, Kyle and Ben both display symptoms of a behavior disorder. This term is often used interchangeably with *emotional disturbance, emotional disability,* or *emotional handicap,* and you may encounter any of these terms in your work (Coleman & Webber, 2002). Reseachers prefer the term *behavior disorder* because it focuses on overt behaviors that can be targeted and changed (Turnbull et al., 2006).

Students with **behavior disorders** display serious and persistent age-inappropriate behaviors that result in social conflict, personal unhappiness, and often school failure. The terms *serious* and *persistent* are important. Many children occasionally fight with their peers, and all children go through periods when they want to be alone. When these patterns are chronic and interfere with normal development and school performance, however, a behavior disorder may exist.

Students with behavior disorders often have academic problems, some of which are connected with learning disabilities. The combination of these problems results in high absentee rates, low achievement, and a dropout rate of nearly 50 percent, the highest of any group of students with special needs (U.S. Department of Education, 2004).

Students with behavior disorders often have the following characteristics:

- Behaving impulsively and having difficulty interacting with others in socially acceptable ways
- Acting out and failing to follow school or classroom rules
- Diplaying poor self-concepts
- Lacking awareness of the severity of their problems
- Deteriorating academic performance and frequently missing school (Hardman et al., 2005; Turnbull et al., 2004)

Estimates of the frequency of behavior disorders vary (Hardman et al., 2005). For example, the U.S. Department of Education (2004) estimates that about 1 percent of the total school population and about 8 percent of the special education population were identified as having the problem during the 2002–2003 school year. Others suggest that the percentage was actually much higher because of identification problems (Hallahan & Kauffman, 2006; Hardman et al., 2005). Identification is difficult because the characteristics are elusive (Forness, Walker, & Kavale, 2005; Turnbull et al., 2004).

Kinds of Behavior Disorders

Behavior disorders can be *externalizing* or *internalizing* (Hallahan & Kauffman, 2006). Students like Kyle fall into the first category, displaying characteristics such as hyperactivity, defiance, hostility, and even cruelty. Boys are three times more likely to be labeled as having an externalizing behavior disorder than girls, and low-socioeconomic status and minority status also increase students' chances of being given this label.

Behavior disorders. Serious and persistent age-inappropriate behaviors that result in social conflict, personal unhappiness, and often school failure

Externalizing behavior disorders are characterized by hyperactivity and defiant behaviors, whereas internalizing disorders are characterized by behaviors related to social withdrawal and anxiety.

Internalizing behavior disorders are characterized by social withdrawal, guilt, depression, and anxiety, problems more directed at the self than others. Like Ben, these children lack self-confidence and are often shy, timid, and depressed, sometimes suicidal. They have few friends and are isolated and withdrawn (Coleman & Webber, 2002). Because they don't have the high profile of the acting-out student, many go unnoticed, so a teacher's sensitivity and awareness are crucial in identifying these students.

Teaching Students with Behavior Disorders

Students with behavior disorders require a classroom environment that invites participation and success while providing structure through clearly stated and consistently enforced rules (Hess & Brigham, 2001).

Behavior Management Strategies. Teachers commonly use behavior management strategies to reinforce positive behaviors and eliminate negative ones (Alberto & Troutman, 2006; Warner & Lynch, 2005). These strategies include the following:

- *Positive reinforcement:* Rewarding positive behaviors (e.g., praising a student for behaving courteously)
- *Replacement:* Teaching appropriate behaviors to substitute for inappropriate ones (e.g., teaching students to express personal feelings instead of fighting)
- *Ignoring:* Not recognizing disruptive behaviors in an attempt to avoid reinforcing them
- *Time-out:* Isolating a child for brief periods of time
- *Overcorrection:* Requiring restitution beyond the damaging effects of the immediate behavior (e.g., requiring a child to return one of his own cookies in addition to the one he took from another student)

We discuss the systematic use of these strategies, called *applied behavioral analysis,* in detail in Chapter 6. Teaching self-management skills can also be effective (Heward, 2006). For instance, students might be helped to identify behaviors they want to increase (e.g., making eye contact with the teacher) or decrease (e.g., finger snapping or playing with a pencil). Over a specified period of time, students record the incidents of a behavior and graph the results, so they have a concrete record of their progress. The teacher also meets with them, frequently at first, to reinforce their efforts and set new goals. Self-management strategies have been successful for both increasing desired behaviors, such as paying attention, and decreasing undesirable behaviors, such as talking out (Alberto & Troutman, 2006).

Teacher Sensitivity. Students with behavior disorders can be frustrating, and teachers sometimes forget that these students have unique needs (Avramidis, Bayliss, & Burden, 2000). An incident with a 4-year-old boy illustrates this point. He had been referred to a school psychologist for aggressive behaviors and acting "out of control." She found him friendly, polite, and cooperative, and the session went smoothly until he announced he was done. When she urged him to continue, he became hysterical and ran out of the room.

> I assumed the testing phase of the evaluation was over and started writing a few notes. . . . A few minutes later, however, the little boy returned . . . and said that he was ready to continue. After another 10 minutes or so . . . the child again said, "I'm done now," to which I replied, "That's fine." The child calmly got out of his chair, walked around the room for a minute, and then sat down to resume testing. This pattern was repeated. . . .
>
> It was easy to see in a one-to-one testing situation that this child recognized the limits of his concentration and coped with increasing frustration by briefly removing himself. . . . It is equally easy to see, however, how this behavior created problems in the classroom. By wandering around, he would be disrupting the learning of other children. When the teacher tried to make him sit back down, she was increasing his frustration by removing from him the one method he had developed for coping. (Griffith, 1992, p. 34)

But how do teachers manage behavior like this in the regular classroom? The psychologist suggested designating an area in the back of the room where the child could go when he became frustrated. With this safety valve in place, the teacher could then work with the boy on long-term coping strategies. By attempting to understand the child as an individual, the teacher was able to work smoothly with her other students while meeting his needs.

Communication Disorders

Communication disorders are exceptionalities that interfere with students' abilities to receive and understand information from others and express their own ideas. They exist in two forms (Bernstein & Tiegerman-Farber, 2002). **Speech disorders** (sometimes called *expressive disorders*) involve problems in forming and sequencing sounds. Stuttering and mispronouncing words, such as saying, "I taw it" for "I saw it," are examples. **Language disorders** (also called *receptive disorders*) include problems with understanding language or using language to express ideas. Language disorders are often connected to other problems, such as a hearing impairment, learning disability, or mental retardation (Turnbull et al., 2004).

As shown in Table 5.2, specialists have identified three kinds of speech disorders. If they are chronic, a therapist is usually required, but sensitive teachers can help students cope with the emotional and social problems that are often associated with them.

Because they affect learning, language disorders are more serious. The vast majority of students learn to communicate quite well by the time they start school, but a small percentage (less than 1 percent) continue to experience problems expressing themselves verbally (Hardman et al., 2005; Heward, 2006). Symptoms of a language disorder include

- Seldom speaking, even during play
- Using few words or very short sentences
- Overrelying on gestures to communicate

Table 5.2 Kinds of speech disorders

Disorder	Description	Example
Articulation disorders	Difficulty in producing certain sounds, including substituting, distorting, and omitting	"Wabbit" for *rabbit* "Thit" for *sit* "Only" for *lonely*
Fluency disorders	Repetition of the first sound of a word (stuttering) and other problems in producing "smooth" speech	"Y, Y, Y, Yes"
Voice disorders	Problems with the larynx or air passageways in the nose or throat	High-pitched or nasal voice

Communication disorders. Exceptionalities that interfere with students' abilities to receive and understand information from others and express their own ideas or questions

Speech disorders (or *expressive disorders*). Problems in forming and sequencing sounds

Language disorders (or *receptive disorders*). Problems with understanding language or using language to express ideas

Adaptive instructional materials—such as devices and books that use large print and Braille—allow students with visual disabilities to integrate into the regular classroom.

The causes of language disorders include hearing loss, brain damage, learning disabilities, mental retardation, severe emotional problems, and inadequate developmental experiences in a child's early years.

If teachers suspect a speech or language disorder, they should keep cultural diversity in mind. As you saw in Chapter 4, English is not the primary language for many students. The difficulties these students encounter in learning both content and a second language should not be confused with communication disorders. English language learners will respond to an enriched language environment and teacher patience and understanding. Students with communication disorders require the help of a speech and language specialist.

Helping Students with Communication Disorders

Primary tasks for teachers working with students who have communication disorders include identification, acceptance, and follow-through during classroom instruction. As with other exceptionalities, teachers play an important role in identification because they are in the best position to assess students' communication abilities in classroom settings.

It is not easy being a student who talks differently or who cannot communicate fluently. Modeling and encouraging acceptance are essential because teasing and social rejection can cause lasting emotional damage. In interacting with these students, a teacher should be patient and refrain from correcting their speech, which calls attention to the problem. Also, cooperative and small-group activities provide opportunities for students to practice language in informal and less-threatening settings.

Visual Disabilities

Approximately 20 percent of children and adults have some type of vision loss (Hardman et al., 2005). Fortunately, most problems can be corrected with glasses, surgery, or therapy. In some situations—approximately 1 child in 3,000—the impairment cannot be corrected (Batsashaw, 2003). People with this condition have a **visual disability**, an uncorrectable visual impairment that interferes with learning.

Nearly two thirds of serious visual disabilities exist at birth, and most children are screened for visual problems when they enter elementary school (Hardman et al., 2005; Hunt & Marshall, 2002). Some visual problems appear during the school years as a result of growth spurts, however, and teachers should remain alert to the possibility of an undetected impairment in students. Some symptoms of visual problems are outlined in Figure 5.4.

Figure 5.4   Symptoms of potential visual problems

- Holding the head in an awkward position when reading, or holding the book too close or too far away
- Squinting and frequently rubbing the eyes
- Tuning out when information is presented on the chalkboard
- Constantly asking about classroom procedures, especially when information is on the board
- Complaining of headaches, dizziness, or nausea
- Having redness, crusting, or swelling of the eyes
- Losing place on the line or page and confusing letters
- Using poor spacing in writing or having difficulty in staying on the line

Visual disability. An uncorrectable visual impairment that interferes with learning

Source: Hallahan and Kauffman, 2006; Hardman et al., 2002.

Checking Your Understanding

2.1 Describe the most common learning problems that classroom teachers are likely to encounter.

2.2 Identify at least one similarity and one difference between learning disabilities and mental retardation.

2.3 Describe the two major types of behavior disorders, and explain how they influence classroom behavior.

2.4 Describe communication disorders and how they affect classroom performance.

To receive feedback for these questions, go to Appendix B.

Knowledge Extensions

To deepen your understanding of the topics in this section of Chapter 5 and to integrate them with topics you've already studied, go to the *Knowledge Extensions* module for Chapter 5 at *www.prenhall.com/eggen*. Respond to questions 3–7.

STUDENTS WHO ARE GIFTED AND TALENTED

Although we don't typically think of students who are gifted and talented as having an exceptionality, they frequently cannot reach their full potential in the regular classroom. As you saw at the beginning of the chapter, these students are at the upper end of the ability continuum. At one time, *gifted* was the term used, but the category has been enlarged to include both students who do well on IQ tests (typically 130 and above) and those who demonstrate talents in a range of areas, such as math, creative writing, and music (G. Davis & Rimm, 2004; Winner, 2000a, 2000b).

Characteristics of students who are gifted and talented often include the following:

- Ability to learn more quickly and independently than their peers
- Advanced language, reading, and vocabulary skills
- More highly developed learning and metacognitive strategies
- Higher motivation on challenging tasks and less on easy ones
- High personal standards of achievement

The challenge for teachers is to provide learning experiences rich enough to help these children develop.

The history of gifted and talented education in the United States began with a longitudinal study conducted by Louis Terman and his colleagues (Holahan & Sears, 1995; Terman, Baldwin, & Bronson, 1925; Terman & Oden, 1947, 1959). Using teacher recommendations and IQ scores, Terman identified 1,500 gifted individuals to be tracked over a lifetime (the study is projected to run until 2010). The researchers found that, in addition to being high academic achievers, these students were better adjusted as children and adults, had more hobbies, read more books, and were healthier than their peers. This study, combined with more current research, has done much to dispel the stereotype of gifted students as maladjusted and narrow "brains" (Steiner & Carr, 2003; Winner, 2000a, 2000b).

The current definition used by the federal government describes gifted and talented students as

> Children and youth with outstanding talent who perform or show the potential for performing at remarkably high levels of accomplishment when compared with others of their age, experience, or environment.
>
> These children and youth exhibit high performance capability in intellectual, creative, and/or artistic areas, possess an unusual leadership capacity, or excel in specific academic fields. They require services or activities not ordinarily provided by the schools.
>
> Outstanding talents are present in children and youth from all cultural groups, across all economic strata, and in all areas of human endeavor. (*National Excellence*, 1993, pp. 54–57)

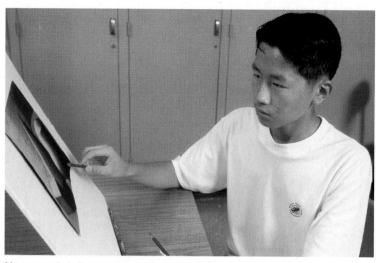

Many experts believe creativity is an essential component of giftedness.

One survey found that many state departments of education have incorporated components of the *National Excellence* definition into their definitions of giftedness and talent (Stephens & Karnes, 2000).

Another popular definition uses three criteria (Renzulli & Reis, 2003):

1. Above-average ability
2. High levels of motivation and task commitment
3. High levels of creativity

According to this definition, gifted people not only are "smart," but also use this ability in focused and creative ways.

More recent work in the area of gifted education has shifted away from the concept of giftedness as a general characteristic and toward talents in specific areas (Colangelo & Davis, 2003; G. Davis & Rimm, 2004). Teachers attempt to match instruction to the areas of students' talents.

Creativity

Creativity is the ability to produce or identify original and varied solutions to problems. It is related to but not identical to intelligence (G. Davis, 2003; Sternberg & Grigorenko, 2001); at least average intellectual ability is a necessary, but not sufficient, prerequisite for creativity. Like intelligence, it is probably influenced by both genetics and the environment (Simonton, 2000, 2001).

Divergent thinking, the ability to generate a variety of original answers to questions or problems, is an important component of creativity (G. Davis & Rimm, 2004; Sand, 2004; Sand & Burley, 2001). Divergent thinking has three dimensions:

- *Fluency:* the ability to produce many ideas relevant to a problem
- *Flexibility:* the ability to break from an established set to generate new perspectives
- *Originality:* the facility for generating new and different ideas

Howard Gardner, whose work you studied in Chapter 4, has defined the creative person as one "who regularly solves problems, fashions products, or defines new questions in a domain in a way that is initially considered novel but that ultimately becomes accepted" (1993, p. 35). Creativity is a recurring trait that typically occurs within a particular domain, such as art or music, but not both (von Károlyi, Ramos-Ford, & Gardner, 2003).

As with most aspects of learning, creativity requires prior knowledge (Lynch, 2001; Simonton, 2000), which prevents "reinventing the wheel," and allows a person to concentrate on new ideas. Creativity is usually measured by giving students a verbal or pictorial stimulus and asking them to generate as many responses as they can, such as listing as many uses as possible for a brick (e.g., doorstop, bookshelf, paperweight, weapon, building block) or suggesting ways to improve a common object such as a chair (G. Davis & Rimm, 2004). Pictorial tasks involve turning an ambiguous partial sketch into an interesting picture. Responses are then evaluated for fluency, flexibility, and originality. Methods of measuring creativity are controversial, with critics charging that existing tests are too narrow and fail to capture its varying aspects (Tannenbaum, 2003).

Identifying Students Who Are Gifted and Talented

Meeting the needs of students who are gifted and talented requires early identification and instructional modifications. Failure to do so can result in gifted underachievers with social and emotional problems linked to boredom and lack of motivation (G. Davis & Rimm, 2004; Louis, Subotnik, Breland, & Lewis, 2000). Current procedures often miss students who are

Creativity. The ability to produce or identify original and varied solutions to problems

gifted and talented because they rely heavily on standardized test scores and teacher nominations (Castellano & Diaz, 2002; J. Gallagher, 1998). Experts recommend, in addition to teacher recommendations, more flexible and less culturally dependent methods, such as creativity measures, tests of spatial ability, and peer and parent nominations (G. Davis & Rimm, 2004; Shea, Lubinski, & Benbow, 2001). Most states now have laws requiring that schools identify students who are gifted and talented, but by 2002 only 26 states had laws requiring that schools provide services for them (ERIC Clearinghouse, 2002).

Females and students from cultural minorities are typically underrepresented in programs for the gifted, and the reasons include limited definitions of giftedness, lack of culturally and gender-sensitive means of assessing potential, and overreliance on standardized tests (Kritt, 2004; T. Perry, Steele, & Hilliard, 2003). For example, tests usually require students to respond in English, either orally or in writing. Although test makers produce versions of the tests in other languages, those versions are not widely available. As a result, non-native English speakers who take the English version may earn scores that don't accurately measure their true potential. Also, students from cultural minorities may not understand the "classroom game" as well as other students, which teachers interpret as lack of potential. In addition, female students and those from cultural minorities often lack gifted role models, or mentors, who have succeeded in school or in work (Castellano & Diaz, 2002).

Teachers play an essential role in identifying learners who are gifted and talented because they work with these students every day and can identify strengths that tests may miss. However, research indicates that teachers often confuse conformity, neatness, and good behavior with being gifted and talented (Colangelo & Davis, 2003; G. Davis & Rimm, 2004).

Working with these students is challenging; their giftedness places unique demands on teachers, and teachers' flexibility is an important factor in the quality of their school experience.

Enrichment activities provide opportunities for gifted students to explore alternative areas of the curriculum.

Instructional Principles

Teaching Students Who Are Gifted and Talented: Instructional Principles

Programs for students who are gifted and talented are usually based on either **acceleration,** which keeps the curriculum the same but allows students to move through it more quickly, or **enrichment,** which provides alternate instruction (Schiever & Maker, 2003). Educators disagree over which approach better serves students' needs. Critics of enrichment charge that it often involves busywork and point to research suggesting that students benefit from acceleration (Feldhusen, 1998a, 1998b). Critics of acceleration counter that comparisons are unfair because the outcomes of enrichment, such as creativity and problem solving, are not easily measured. They further argue that the regular curriculum is narrow, and social development can be impaired when younger students who want accelerated content must take classes with older students. The question remains unanswered, and the debate is likely to continue.

Programs for students who are gifted and talented are typically organized in either self-contained classes or pullout programs that occupy a portion of the school day. Self-contained classes usually include both acceleration and enrichment; pullout programs focus primarily on enrichment. Table 5.3 provides examples of both enrichment and acceleration.

If you have students who are gifted and talented in your classes, and they're pulled out for part of the day, you'll be expected to provide enrichment activities during the time they're with you. The following principles can guide you as you attempt to adapt instruction to meet these students' needs:

1. Assess frequently to identify areas where students have already mastered essential content.
2. Provide alternative activities to challenge students' abilities and interests.
3. Utilize technology to provide challenge.

Acceleration. Instruction in which the curriculum is the same but allows students to move through it more quickly

Enrichment. Varied and alternate instruction for students who are gifted and talented

Table 5.3 Options in enrichment and acceleration programs

Enrichment Options	Acceleration Options
• Independent study and independent projects • Learning centers • Field trips • Saturday programs • Summer programs • Mentors and mentorships • Simulations and games • Small-group investigations • Academic competitions	• Early admission to kindergarten and first grade • Grade skipping • Subject skipping • Credit by exam • College courses in high school • Correspondence courses • Early admission to college

Let's see how the principles guide Jared Taylor, a sixth-grade teacher, as he works with his students.

Jared has three students—Darren, Sylvia, and Gabriella—who have been identified as gifted and talented. They meet with a teacher of the gifted twice a week in a pullout program. Jared's task is to provide a motivating menu for them while they are in his class.

To accomplish the task, Jared pretests his students before beginning a new unit, and he also closely monitors Darren's, Sylvia's, and Gabriella's homework. When he sees that they have mastered the content, he provides enrichment in the following ways:

First, he offers alternative learning activities. For instance, in a unit on plants in science, Jared arranges with the librarian to provide resources for a project, and he meets with the students to help them design its goals and scope.

Second, Jared creates a series of learning centers that are available to all the students. The centers focus on weather, geometry, music, and art, and students can go to them when they have free time. Each center has reading materials and projects that can be completed. When Darren, Sylvia, and Gabriella demonstrate that they have mastered the content the other students are studying, he substitutes projects from the centers for them.

Third, Jared supplements his curriculum with technology. He works with the district's media coordinator to locate software programs and Websites that provide enrichment and acceleration.

Jared attempted to apply the principles by first gathering as much information as he could to assess the students' understanding of the topics he was teaching. When he found they had mastered a topic, he substituted enrichment activities (principle 2). Acceleration may have many benefits, but it is difficult to implement in the regular curriculum. Jared's approach was manageable; it didn't require an inordinate amount of extra work, and it also provided enriching experiences for the students. Finally, he applied the third principle, providing challenge through technology, by working with the district's media coordinator to supply his students with relevant materials.

Exploring Further

To read more about students who are gifted and talented, go to "Teaching Students Who Are Gifted and Talented" in the *Exploring Further* module of Chapter 5 at *www.prenhall.com/eggen*.

Knowledge Extensions

To deepen your understanding of the topics in this section of Chapter 5 and to integrate them with topics you've already studied, go to the *Knowledge Extensions* module for Chapter 5 at *www.prenhall.com/eggen*. Respond to questions 8 and 9.

Checking Your Understanding

3.1 Describe the characteristics of students who are gifted and talented, and explain how the definition of students who are gifted and talented has changed over time. What implications does this changed definition have for teachers?

3.2 How are gifted and talented students commonly identified? What are some advantages and disadvantages of these methods?

3.3 Describe the two most common methods for teaching students who are gifted and talented. Explain the relative advantages and disadvantages of these methods.

To receive feedback for these questions, go to Appendix B.

THE TEACHER'S ROLE IN INCLUSIVE CLASSROOMS

Regular education teachers have three important responsibilities in working with students who have exceptionalities. First, they help identify students who may need additional help. Second, they must modify instruction to best meet individuals' needs, and third, they should encourage acceptance of all students in their classes.

Identifying Students with Exceptionalities

Current approaches to identification are team based, and because regular classroom teachers continually work with students, they are key members of the team. When teachers identify learning problems that they can't solve by modifying their instruction, they request the help of other educators who, together with the regular classroom teacher, then gather additional data, standardized test scores, performance measures, and interviews with parents and other teachers.

Teachers use assessment to gather essential information to identify students with exceptionalities.

If the data suggest that additional help is needed, a *pre-referral team,* usually consisting of a school psychologist, a special educator, and the classroom teacher, is formed. The team further evaluates the problem, consults with parents, and suggests additional instructional modifications to create a better adaptive fit.

Before a student is referred for a special education evaluation, teachers are expected to document the problem and strategies they've used in attempting to solve it (Hallahan & Kauffman, 2006). They should describe the following:

- The nature of the problem
- How it affects classroom performance
- Dates, places, and times problems have occurred
- Strategies they have tried
- Assessment of the strategies' effectiveness

Teachers should also check the student's records for any previous evaluations, physical problems, or participation in other special programs (Hallahan & Kauffman, 2006).

Parents play an integral role in the process. IDEA requires parents' involvement, they can provide valuable information about the student's educational and medical history, and notifying them is a professional courtesy, even if it weren't required by law.

When considering a referral, the teacher should check with school administrators or the school psychologist to learn about the school's specific policies. A referral initiates the evaluation process. If the evaluation results in a recommendation for special services, an IEP is then prepared.

 **Instructional** **Principles**   **Teaching Students with Exceptionalities: Instructional Principles**

Almost certainly, some of the students in your classroom will have exceptionalities, and you will be expected to help them reach their full potential. The following principles can guide you in your efforts:

1. Use effective teaching practices that promote learning for all students.
2. Provide additional instructional support.
3. Adapt seat work and homework activities to match the capabilities of students with exceptionalities.
4. Supplement reading materials to meet the learning needs of students.
5. Actively teach learning strategies.

To begin examining the principles, let's look back to Diane Smith's lesson on comparative and superlative adjectives in Chapter 4 (page 123). There we emphasized that a caring and supportive environment was important for all students and essential for learners with diverse backgrounds or those placed at risk. In addition, we saw that Diane created an orderly learning environment with predictable routines, combined high expectations with frequent feedback about learning progress, used high-quality examples and teaching strategies that involved all students and promoted success, and stressed student self-regulation and the acquisition of learning strategies. Diane's approach utilized the "effective teaching practices that promote learning for all students" that we see in our first principle here.

These practices apply as much to learners with exceptionalities as they do to other students (Mastropieri & Scruggs, 2004; Vaughn et al., 2006).

> Research on regular versus special classroom placement suggests that the achievement progress of special education students depends not so much on what kind of classroom they are assigned to as on the quality of the instruction they receive there. In general, the classroom management and instruction approaches that are effective with students with special needs tend to be the same ones that are effective with other students. (Good & Brophy, 2003, p. 268)

Although instruction that is effective for all students is also effective with learners having exceptionalities, teachers do need to incorporate some modifications when instructing these learners.

Provide Additional Instructional Support

To help students overcome a history of failure and frustration and to convince them that renewed effort will work, you likely will have to provide additional instructional support, which applies the second principle. For instance, while the majority of the class is completing a seat-work assignment, you can work with an individual student or small group. (You will find an example in Mike Sheppard's work with his students in the closing case study for this chapter.)

Peer tutoring has been used effectively, providing benefit to both the tutor and the person receiving the tutoring (Bos & Vaughn, 2006; Vaughn et al., 2006), and home-based tutoring programs that involve parents can also be successful. Effective programs also suggest soliciting parental cooperation and explaining specifically what parents can do to help their child succeed. Some additional adaptations include the following (Turnbull et al., 2004):

- Utilizing available technology. (We discuss ways of using technology to support instruction in Chapter 14.)
- Carefully modeling solutions to problems and other assignments.
- Calling on students with exceptionalities as equally as possible compared to other students in your classes.
- Providing outlines, hierarchies, charts, and other forms of organization for the content you're teaching.
- Increasing the amount of time available for tests and quizzes.

As we said earlier, these adaptations are effective for all students, but for learners with exceptionalities they are essential.

Adapt Seat Work and Homework

To help students succeed, and to apply the third principle, adapt seat-work and homework assignments to match student capabilities (Vaughn et al., 2006). Students with learning problems need to be taught in small steps that include sufficient scaffolding and detailed feedback.

Homework should be an extension of seat work successfully completed in class. Again, parents' assistance can be helpful; they can orally administer a quiz each night on material being studied, for example, and they can confirm with a signature that the homework and quiz have been completed. These adaptations are demanding, but when students begin making progress, the efforts can be highly rewarding.

Supplement Reading Materials

Reading poses particular problems because students needing special help often cannot read the required texts. You can adapt, applying the fourth principle, with some or all of the following in one-on-one sessions with students:

- Set goals at the beginning of assignments.
- Provide advance organizers that summarize passages.
- Introduce key concepts and terms before students read the text.
- Create study guide questions that focus attention on important information.
- Ask students to summarize information in the text. (Vaughn et al., 2006)

These strategies increase reading comprehension in general (Barr, 2001; E. Hiebert & Raphael, 1996), and using them with students having exceptionalities provides an additional level of support.

Creative teachers design learning activities that allow students of differing abilities to interact and learn about one another.

Teach Learning Strategies

Strategy training, the fifth principle, is one of the most promising approaches to helping students with learning problems (Swanson & Hoskyn, 1998). A *learning strategy* is a plan that students use to accomplish a learning objective. For example, in applying a strategy to learn a list of 10 spelling words, a student might say to himself,

> "Okay, . . . 10 words for the quiz on Friday. I have 2 days to learn them.
> "Let's see. These are all about airports. Which of these do I already know—*airplane, taxi, apron,* and *jet*? Hmmm, . . . some of these aren't so easy, like *causeway* and *tarmac.* I don't even know what a 'tarmac' is. I'll look it up. . . . Oh, that makes sense. It's the runway. I'd better spend more time on these words. I'll cover them up and try to write them down and then check them. Tonight, I can get Mom to give me a quiz, and then I'll know which ones to study extra tomorrow."

This student was strategic in at least three ways. First, separating the words he already knew from those he didn't, spending extra time on the difficult ones, and looking up *tarmac* in the dictionary indicated that he had clear objectives. Second, he took a deliberate approach to the task, allocating more time to the words he didn't know and skipping the ones he did. Third, he monitored his progress through quiz-like exercises.

Students with learning difficulties often approach tasks passively or use the same strategy for all objectives (Swanson, 2001). In studying the spelling words, for instance, they may just read the words, instead of trying to actually spell them, or they may spend as much time on the words they already know as on those they don't. Students with learning problems can use strategies, but they need to be taught the strategies explicitly (Gersten & Baker, 2001). Teacher modeling and explanation, together with opportunities for practice and feedback, are essential.

Social Integration and Growth

An important task in working with students having exceptionalities is to promote their social integration and growth. Students with disabilities often are labeled as different, often fall behind in their academic work, often misbehave in class, and sometimes lack social skills (Hallahan & Kauffman, 2006). As a result, other students develop negative attitudes toward them, and the impact of these attitudes on their confidence and self-esteem are among the most difficult obstacles they face. Teachers should make special efforts to promote the acceptance of students with exceptionalities in regular classrooms. These efforts include developing classmates' understanding and acceptance of them, helping them learn acceptable behaviors, and using strategies to promote social interaction among the students (Plata, Trusty, & Glasgow, 2005). Teachers' attitudes are central to the success of these efforts (Cook, 2004; Kliewer, et al., 2004).

Developing Classmates' Understanding and Acceptance

Students' negative attitudes toward students with exceptionalities often result from a lack of understanding. Open discussion and information about disabilities can help change these

Analyzing Classrooms Video
To analyze the effectiveness of a peer tutoring process, go to Episode 7, "Using Peer Tutoring with Students Having Exceptionalities," on DVD 1, accompanying this text.

Exploring Further
To read more about different instructional strategies to teach social problem solving skills, go to "The Teacher's Role in Inclusive Classrooms" in the *Exploring Further* module of Chapter 5 at *www.prenhall.com/eggen*.

attitudes (Heward, 2006). Emphasizing that people with disabilities want to have friends and be liked, want to succeed, and want to be happy, just as everyone else does, can do much to change attitudes. These discussions can reduce stereotypes about learners with exceptionalities and break down the barriers between them and other students. Literature and videos that explore the struggles and triumphs of people with disabilities, and guests that have overcome disabilities, are also valuable sources of information.

Helping Students Learn Acceptable Behaviors

Students with exceptionalities can help themselves by learning what constitutes acceptable behavior. Counseling and applied behavioral analysis are two strategies that can help students improve their behavior (Elbaum & Vaughn, 2001). The case study at the end of the chapter, page 158, includes an example of applied behavioral analysis.

Modeling and coaching can be particularly helpful for teaching students social skills. Students with disabilities often lack the skills needed to make friends (Turnbull et al., 2004); they may avoid other students or alienate them unknowingly. To teach a student how to initiate play, for example, a teacher might say, "Barnell's over there on the playground. I think I'll say, 'Hi, Barnell! Want to play ball with me?' Now you try it, and I'll watch."

Teachers can also model social problem solving; for instance, a teacher might comment, "Mary has a toy that I want to play with. What could I do to make her want to share that toy?" These direct approaches have been successful in teaching social skills such as empathy, perspective taking, negotiation, and assertiveness (Vaughn et al., 2006).

Strategies for Promoting Interaction and Cooperation

One of the most effective ways to promote acceptance of students with exceptionalities is to include them in learning activities by calling on them as often as possible. This sends a powerful message; it communicates that all students are valued and are expected to participate and succeed.

Cooperative learning and peer tutoring can also be used to promote interaction among students. (We discuss cooperative learning strategies in Chapter 13.) Peer tutoring typically places students in pairs and provides them with learning activities, practice, and feedback. For example, after introducing a new concept in math, the teacher assigns pairs to work on practice exercises and students take turns tutoring and being tutored.

Cross-age tutoring, in which older students with exceptionalities tutor younger ones, is especially promising. The older students' academic self-concepts increase, which makes intuitive sense; providing help for a younger student increases tutors' feelings of competence, which motivation theories describe as a basic need in all people (R. Ryan & Deci, 2000).

Unquestionably, having learners with exceptionalities in your classroom will increase your workload. On the other hand, helping a student with a disability adapt and even thrive can be one of the most rewarding experiences you will have as a teacher.

Online Case Book

To analyze another case study to assess a teacher's effectiveness in working with students having exceptionalities, go to the *Online Case Book* for Chapter 5 at *www.prenhall.com/eggen*.

Knowledge Extensions

To deepen your understanding of the topics in this section of Chapter 5 and to integrate them with topics you've already studied, go to the *Knowledge Extensions* module for Chapter 5 at *www.prenhall. com/eggen*. Respond to questions 10–12.

Checking Your Understanding

4.1 Explain the roles that classroom teachers are expected to fulfill in working with students with exceptionalities.

4.2 What does research indicate about teaching strategies that are effective for learners with exceptionalities? What implications do these strategies have for you as a classroom teacher?

4.3 Describe at least three ways that you can promote the social integration and growth of students with exceptionalities in your classroom.

To receive feedback for these questions, go to Appendix B.

Classroom ⊞ Connections

Teaching Students with Exceptionalities in the Regular Classroom

1. Discuss the subject of exceptionalities in an open and positive manner.
   - **Elementary:** A second-grade teacher uses role playing and modeling to illustrate problems such as teasing and taunting others. She emphasizes treating students who look or act differently with the same respect that other students receive.
   - **Middle School:** An English teacher uses literature, such as *Summer of the Swans,* by Betsy Byars (2005), as a springboard for talking about individual differences. He encourages students to reflect on their own individuality and how important this is to them.
   - **High School:** An English teacher leads a discussion of students' favorite foods, activities, movies, and music, and also discusses topics and issues that concern them. He uses the discussions as a springboard for helping create a sense of community in the classroom.

2. Adapt instruction to meet the needs of students with exceptionalities.
   - **Elementary:** A third-grade teacher carefully monitors students during seat work. She often gathers students with exceptionalities in a small group to provide additional assistance with assignments.
   - **Middle School:** A sixth-grade math teacher organizes his students in groups of four for seat-work assignments. Each student does a problem and confers with a partner. When two students disagree, they confer with the other pair in their group. The teacher carefully monitors the groups to be sure that all four are participating as equally as possible.
   - **High School:** A science teacher assesses frequently and provides detailed feedback on all assessment items. She spends time in one-on-one conferences with any students having difficulty.

3. Teach students with exceptionalities learning strategies.
   - **Elementary:** A fourth-grade math teacher emphasizes questions such as the following in checking answers to word problems: Does the solution answer the problem? Does it make sense? Are the units correct? He reinforces this process throughout the school year.
   - **Middle School:** A math teacher teaches problem-solving strategies by thinking aloud at the chalkboard while she's working through a problem. She breaks word problems into the following steps: (a) Read: What is the question? (b) Reread: What information do I need? (c) Stop and think: What do I need to do—add, subtract, multiply, or divide? (d) Compute: Put the correct numbers in and solve. (e) Label and check: What answer did I get? Does it make sense?
   - **High School:** An English teacher teaches and models step-by-step strategies. A unit on writing one-paragraph essays teaches students to use four steps: (a) Write a topic sentence, (b) write three sentences that support the topic sentence, (c) write a summary sentence, and (d) reread and edit the paragraph. The teacher models the strategy and provides positive and negative examples before asking the students to write their own.

Teaching Students Who Are Gifted and Talented in Your Classroom

4. Provide supplementary activities that challenge students who are gifted and talented.
   - **Elementary:** A fifth-grade teacher allows his students who are gifted and talented to substitute projects of their choice for homework assignments once they have demonstrated that they have mastered the regular curriculum.
   - **Middle School:** A pre-algebra teacher pretests students at the beginning of each unit. Whenever a student has mastered the concepts and skills, he or she receives an honor pass to work on an alternative activity in the school media center. The activities may be extensions or applications of the concepts taught in the unit, or they may involve learning about mathematical principles or math history not usually taught in the regular curriculum.
   - **High School:** A social studies teacher caps off every unit with a hypothetical problem, such as "What would the United States be like today if Great Britain had won the Revolutionary War?" Students work in groups to address the question, and the teacher gives extra credit to those who want to pursue the topic further in a paper or project.

Meeting Your Learning Objectives

1. Describe the provisions of, and amendments to, the Individuals with Disabilities Education Act (IDEA).

- Federal laws and regulations require that students with exceptionalities be taught in the least restrictive environment, guarantee the right to parental involvement through due process, protect against discrimination in testing, and provide learners with IEPs.
- Recent amendments to IDEA make states responsible for locating children who need special services and have strengthened requirements for nondiscriminatory assessment, due process, parental involvement in IEPs, and the confidentiality of student records.

2. Describe the most common learning problems that classroom teachers are likely to encounter.

- Students with learning disabilities (also called *specific learning disabilities*) encounter difficulties in acquiring and using reading, writing, reasoning, listening, or mathematical abilities.
- Students with behavior disorders display serious and persistent age-inappropriate behaviors that result in social conflict, personal unhappiness, and often school failure.
- Communication disorders are exceptionalities that interfere with students' abilities to receive and understand information from others and express their own ideas or questions.
- A visual disability is an uncorrectable visual impairment that interferes with learning.
- Hearing disabilities include students with partial hearing impairments—an impairment that allows a student to use a hearing aid and to hear well enough to be taught through auditory channels—and students who are deaf—hearing impaired enough so that students use other senses, usually sight, to communicate.

3. Identify characteristics of learners who are gifted and talented, and describe methods for identifying and teaching these students.

- Students who are gifted and talented display unique abilities in specific domains. Recent trends in identification deemphasize intelligence testing and include teacher, parent, and peer reports of unique talents and abilities.
- Acceleration moves these students through the regular curriculum at a faster rate; enrichment provides alternative instruction to encourage student exploration.

4. Explain the roles of classroom teachers and teaching strategies that are effective for working with students having exceptionalities

- Teachers' responsibilities in inclusive classrooms include identifying learners with exceptionalities, adapting instruction for them, and promoting their social integration and growth.
- In the process of identification, teachers should describe and document learning problems and strategies they've tried.
- Effective instruction for students with disabilities uses characteristics of instruction effective with all students. Providing additional scaffolding, modifying homework assignments and reading materials, and helping students acquire learning strategies are also helpful.
- Social acceptance for students with disabilities is developed through direct instruction, modeling, practice, and feedback. Attitudes of other students can be improved by discussions that focus on understanding and by strategies such as peer tutoring and cooperative learning.

Developing as a Professional: Praxis™ Practice

You've examined characteristics of students with exceptionalities, and you've learned that all students can learn if instruction is adapted to meet their needs.

Let's look now at a junior high math teacher and his efforts to work with students who have exceptionalities. Read the case study, and answer the questions that follow.

Mike Sheppard teaches math at Landrom Junior High School. He has introduced his pre-algebra class to a procedure for solving word problems, and he has assigned five problems for homework.

Mike has 28 students in his second-period class, including five with exceptionalities: Herchel, Marcus, and Gwenn, who have learning problems, and Todd and Horace, who have problems monitoring their own behavior. Herchel, Marcus, and Gwenn each have problems with decoding words, reading comprehension, and writing. Other teachers describe Todd as verbally abusive, aggressive, and

lacking in self-discipline. He is extremely active and has a difficult time sitting through a class period. Horace is just the opposite: a very shy, withdrawn boy.

At 10:07, Herchel, Marcus, and Gwenn are among the first of Mike's students to file into class. As the students enter, they look at the screen in the front of the room. Mike always displays one or two problems on the overhead for students to complete while he takes roll and finishes other beginning-of-class routines.

Mike watches as Herchel, Marcus, and Gwenn take their seats, and then he slowly reads the displayed problem:

On Saturday the Trebek family drove 17 miles from Henderson to Newton, stopped for 10 minutes to get gas, and then drove 22.5 miles from Newton through Council Rock to Gildford. The trip took 1 hour and 5 minutes, including the stop. On the way back, they took the same route but stopped in Council Rock for lunch. Council Rock is 9.5 miles from Gildford. How much farther will they have to drive to get back to Henderson?

As Mike reads, he points to each displayed word. "Okay," he smiles after he finishes reading. "Do you know what the problem is asking you?"

"Could you read the last part again, Mr. Sheppard?" Gwenn asks.

"Sure," Mike nods and repeats the part of the problem that describes the return trip, again pointing to the words as he reads.

"All right, jump on it. Be ready because I'm calling on one of you first today," he again smiles.

The students are in their seats, and most are studying the screen as the bell rings at 10:10. Mike quickly takes roll and then walks to Todd's desk.

"Let's take a look at your chart," he says. "You've improved a lot, haven't you?"

"Yeah, look," Todd responds, proudly displaying the following chart.

	2/9–2/13	2/16–2/20	2/23–2/27
Talking out	⊬⊬ ⊬⊬ ⊬⊬ ⊬⊬	⊬⊬ ⅠⅠⅠⅠ ⊬⊬	⊬⊬ ⅠⅠ
Swearing	⊬⊬ ⊬⊬	⊬⊬ ⅠⅠ	ⅠⅠⅠⅠ
Hitting/ touching	⊬⊬ ⅠⅠⅠ	⊬⊬ ⅠⅠⅠⅠ	ⅠⅠⅠ
Out of seat	⊬⊬ ⊬⊬ ⊬⊬ ⅠⅠⅠ	⊬⊬ ⊬⊬ ⊬⊬ ⅠⅠⅠⅠ	⊬⊬ ⊬⊬ ⊬⊬ ⅠⅠⅠ
Being friendly	ⅠⅠ	ⅠⅠⅠⅠ	⊬⊬ ⅠⅠ

"That's terrific," Mike whispers as he leans over the boy's desk. "You're doing much better. We need some more work on 'out-of-seat,' don't we? I don't like getting after you about it, and I know you don't like it either. . . . Stop by at the end of class. I have an idea that I think will help. Don't forget to stop. . . . Okay. Get to work on the problem." Mike gives Todd a light thump on the back and returns to the front of the room.

"Okay, everyone. How did you do on the problem?"

Amid a mix of "Okay," "Terrible," "Fine," "Too hard," some nods, and a few nonresponses, Mike begins, "Let's review for a minute. . . . What's the first thing we do whenever we have a word problem like this?"

He looks knowingly at Marcus, remembering the pledge to call on one of the five students first today. "Marcus?"

"Read it over at least twice," Marcus replies.

"Good. . . . That's what our problem-solving plan says," Mike continues, pointing to the following chart hanging on the chalkboard:

PLAN FOR SOLVING WORD PROBLEMS
1. Read the problem at least twice.
2. Ask the following questions:
What is asked for?
What facts are given?
What information is needed that we don't have?
Are unnecessary facts given? What are they?
3. Make a drawing.
4. Solve the problem.
5. Check to see whether the answer makes sense.

"Then what do we do? . . . Melissa?"

"See what the problem asks for."

"Good. What is the problem asking for? . . . Rachel?"

". . . How much farther they'll have to drive?"

"Excellent. Now, think about this. Suppose I solved the problem and decided that they had 39½ miles left to drive. Would that make sense? Why or why not? Everybody think about it for a moment."

"Okay. What do you think? . . . Herchel?" Mike asks after a moment.

". . . I . . . I . . . don't know."

"Let's look," Mike encourages. "How far from Henderson to Gildford altogether?"

"Thir—," Rico begins until Mike puts his hand up, stopping him in midword. He then waits a few seconds as Herchel studies a sketch he has made on his paper:

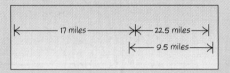

". . . 39½ miles," Herchel says uncertainly. "Oh! . . . The whole trip was only that far, so they couldn't still have that far to go."

"Excellent thinking, Herchel. See, you could figure it out.

"Now go ahead, Rico. How far do they still have to go?"

"Thirty miles," Rico, one of the higher achievers in the class, responds quickly.

"Okay. Not too bad for the first time through," he continues cheerfully. "Let's take a look at your homework."

Mike reviews each homework problem just as he did the first one, asking students to relate the parts to the steps in the problem-solving plan, drawing a sketch on the chalkboard, and calling on a variety of students to supply specific answers and describe their thinking.

With 20 minutes left in the period, he assigns five more problems for homework, and the students begin working. Once the class is working quietly, Mike gestures to Herchel, Marcus, and Gwenn to join him at a table at the back of the room.

"How'd you do on the homework?" Mike asks. "Do you think you get it?"

"Sort of," Gwenn responds, and the other two nod.

"Good," Mike smiles. "Now, let's see what we've got.

When about 5 minutes are left in the period, Mike tells the three students, "Run back to your desks now, and see whether you can get one or two problems done before the bell rings."

The bell rings, and the students begin filing out of the room. Mike catches Todd's eye, Todd stops, and Mike leads him to a small area in the back of the room where a partition has been set up. The area is partially enclosed but facing the class.

"Here's what we'll do," Mike directs. "When you have the urge to get out of your seat, quietly get up and move back here for a few minutes. Stay as long as you want, but be sure you pay attention to what we're doing. When you think you're ready to move back to your seat, go ahead. All I'm asking is that you move back and forth quietly and not bother the class. . . . What do you think?"

Todd nods, and Mike puts a hand on his shoulder. "You're doing so well on everything else; this will help, I think. You're a good student. You hang in there. . . . Now, get out of here," Mike smiles. "Here's a pass into Mrs. Miller's class."

Short-Answer Questions

In answering these questions, use information from the chapter and link your responses to specific information in the case.

1. Describe specifically what Mike did to create a supportive academic climate for his students.
2. How did Mike attempt to ensure success in his teaching?
3. What did Mike do to alter instruction for his students with learning disabilities? How effective were these modifications?
4. What did Mike do to meet the needs of his students with behavior disorders? How effective were these interventions?

ONLINE PORTFOLIO ACTIVITIES

To develop your professional portfolio, further apply your understanding of chapter content, and address the INTASC standards, go to the Companion Website, then to the *Online Portfolio Activities* for Chapter 5. Complete the suggested activities.

IMPORTANT CONCEPTS

acceleration (p. 151)
adaptive behavior (p. 139)
adaptive fit (p. 133)
attention-deficit/hyperactivity disorder (ADHD) (p. 142)
behavior disorders (p. 143)
communication disorders (p. 145)
creativity (p. 150)
curriculum-based assessment (p. 148)
deaf (p. 147)
disorder (p. 138)
disabilities (p. 132)
due process (p. 135)
enrichment (p. 151)
gifts and talents (p. 132)

handicap (p. 138)
inclusion (p. 133)
individualized education program (IEP) (p. 135)
language or receptive disorders (p. 145)
learners with exceptionalities (p. 132)
learning disabilities (p. 140)
least restrictive environment (LRE) (p. 133)
mainstreaming (p. 133)
mental retardation (p. 139)
partial hearing impairment (p. 147)
special education (p. 132)
speech, or expressive, disorders (p. 145)
visual disability (p. 146)

CHAPTER 6

Behaviorism and Social Cognitive Theory

Chapter Outline	**Learning Objectives**
	After you have completed your study of this chapter, you should be able to
Behaviorist Views of Learning What Is Behaviorism? • Classical Conditioning • Operant Conditioning • Behaviorism in the Classroom: Applied Behavior Analysis • Putting Behaviorism into Perspective	**1** Identify examples of classical conditioning concepts in events in and outside of classrooms.
	2 Identify examples of operant conditioning concepts in classroom activities.
Social Cognitive Theory Comparing Behaviorism and Social Cognitive Theory • Modeling • Vicarious Learning • Nonoccurrence of Expected Consequences • Functions of Modeling • Processes Involved in Learning from Models • Effectiveness of Models • Self-Regulation • Social Cognitive Theory in the Classroom: Instructional Principles • Putting Social Cognitive Theory into Perspective	**3** Use social cognitive theory concepts, such as the nonoccurrence of expected consequences, reciprocal causation, and vicarious learning, to explain examples of people's behaviors.
	4 Identify examples of social cognitive theory concepts, such as types of modeling, modeling outcomes, effectiveness of models, and self-regulation, in people's behaviors.
Addressing Diversity: Behaviorism and Social Cognitive Theory Classical Conditioning: Learning to Like and Dislike School • Motivating Hesitant Learners • Capitalizing on Minority Role Models	**5** Identify examples of behaviorist and social cognitive theory concepts in teachers' work with students from diverse backgrounds.

Our experiences and our observations of others strongly influence our behavior and emotions. As you read the following case study, consider how his experiences, together with observations of his friend's behavior, influence Tim Spencer, a tenth grader.

Tim had been doing fairly well in Algebra II—getting mostly Bs with a few Cs on the weekly quizzes. In fact, he was fairly confident until the last quiz, when something inexplicably went wrong. He became confused, got solutions mixed up, panicked, and failed the quiz. He was devastated.

On the next quiz, he was so nervous that when he started, the first few answers he circled had wiggly lines around them from his shaking hand. This happened during the following quiz, too.

"I'm not sure I can do this," he now concludes. "Maybe I should drop algebra."

His hand also starts to shake when he takes chemistry tests, even though he hasn't done poorly on any of them. Fortunately, he is still doing fine in his English and world history classes, and he isn't nervous in them.

Tim mentions his algebra troubles to his friend Susan, who always does well on the quizzes.

"I think they're tough," she comments, "so I really study for them. How about if we get together?"

Tim is a bit skeptical but he agrees, and on Thursday, the night before the next quiz, he goes to Susan's home to study with her. He sees how she selects problems from the book and solves them completely in writing, rather than just reading over the sample problems and explanations. As she begins working on her third problem, he asks her why she is doing another one.

"I try to do as many different kinds as I can, to be sure I don't get fooled on the quiz," she explains. "That way, I'm more confident when I go into it. . . . See, this one is different. . . . The first thing I look for is how it's different. Then I try it.

"I even make a little chart. I try to do at least three problems of each type we study, and then I check them off as I do them. It's sort of fun—I can see I'm making some progress. If I get all of them right, I treat myself with a dish of ice cream."

"Good idea," Tim nods. "I usually do a couple and if I'm okay on them, I quit."

Tim sets a new goal to do three of each type, selecting the odd problems so that he can check the correct answers in the back of the book. Also, when Mrs. Lovisolo uses a term in class that he doesn't understand, he writes it down, and looks up the definition, and then studies it so that he immediately understands what she means when she uses it in her explanations.

He does much better on the next quiz. "What a relief," he says to himself.

He's much less anxious for the following week's quiz, and his effort is paying off. He does well; in fact, his score is the highest so far.

"Maybe I can do this after all," he says to himself.

To begin our discussion, let's consider three questions. (1) How can we explain Tim's nervousness on the quiz following his bad experience? (2) Why did his nervousness later decrease? (3) Why did he change his study habits and sustain his efforts? We answer these and other questions in this chapter.

BEHAVIORIST VIEWS OF LEARNING

Learning is at the core of any study of educational psychology, and our goal as teachers is to promote as much learning as possible for all students. This chapter is the first of four devoted to theoretical descriptions of learning.

We begin by examining behaviorism, a view of learning that, in spite of controversy, continues to be widely applied in schools, especially in the area of classroom management (Kazden, 2001; G. Martin & Pear, 2002).

What Is Behaviorism?

In Chapter 1 you saw that theories are used to explain observations and events. **Behaviorism** is a theory that explains learning in terms of observable behaviors based on the influence of environmental stimuli. It defines **learning** as a relatively enduring change in observable behavior that occurs as a result of experience (Schunk, 2004; B. Skinner, 1953). Notice that the behaviorist definition of learning doesn't include thought processes (e.g., expec-

Behaviorism. A theory that explains learning in terms of observable behaviors based on the influence of environmental stimuli

Learning (behaviorist). According to behaviorism, a relatively enduring change in observable behavior that occurs as a result of experience

tations, beliefs, insights, or goals); temporary changes in behavior that result from illness, injury, or emotional distress; or permanent changes in behavior that occur as a result of maturation. (Later, when we study cognitive theories, we will see a different definition of learning.)

Tim experienced what we commonly call *test anxiety,* and we can explain it using behaviorism. Because of his experience—failing the quiz—he now makes wiggly lines around his problems. This behavior is observable, and it is relatively enduring; he *learned* to be nervous when he took math quizzes. Intuitively, we think of *learning* as involving some knowledge (e.g., knowing the causes of the War of 1812) or skill (e.g., being able to find 42 percent of 65), but emotions can also be learned. Let's see how by examining Tim's experience in more detail.

Behaviorism is a theory that examines the influence of experiences on people's behavior.

Classical Conditioning

We just said that Tim learned to be nervous in math quizzes. We can explain his nervousness (answering our first question at the beginning of the chapter) using **classical conditioning,** which occurs when an individual learns to produce an involuntary emotional or physiological response similar to an instinctive or reflexive response. Tim's anxiety in response to subsequent quizzes was emotional, and it was involuntary, that is, he couldn't control the way he felt.

Classical conditioning was originally described by Ivan Pavlov, a Russian physiologist who won a Nobel Prize in 1904 for his work on digestion. As a part of his research, he had his assistants feed dogs meat powder so their rates of salivation could be measured. As the research progressed, however, the dogs began to salivate at the sight of the assistants, even when they weren't carrying meat powder (Pavlov, 1928). This startling phenomenon caused a turn in Pavlov's work and opened the field of classical conditioning.

To understand how classical conditioning works, we focus on four concepts together with the process of association (Baldwin & Baldwin, 2001):

- An **unconditioned stimulus (UCS).** An object or event that causes an instinctive or reflexive (unlearned) physiological or emotional response. In Pavlov's experiment, the UCS was the meat powder, and in Tim's case it was his failure.
- An **unconditioned response (UCR).** The instinctive or reflexive (unlearned) physiological or emotional response caused by the unconditioned stimulus—the dogs' salivation resulting from the meat powder and Tim's initial devastation as a result of his failure.
- A **conditioned stimulus (CS).** An object or event that becomes associated with the unconditioned stimulus. The lab assistants became associated with the meat powder and tests became associated with failure for Tim.
- A **conditioned response (CR).** A *learned* physiological or emotional response that is similar to the unconditioned response. The dogs' salivation in the absence of the meat powder and Tim's anxiety in response to quizzes were conditioned responses.

An association is the key to learning in classical conditioning. Pavlov's dogs associated the lab assistants with the meat powder and Tim associated quizzes with failure. For the association to occur, the unconditioned and conditioned stimuli must be *contiguous,* that is, they must occur or be present at essentially the same time. Without this contiguity, an association couldn't be formed, and learning through classical conditioning couldn't take place.

Both real-world and classroom examples of classical conditioning are common (Pintrich & Schunk, 2002). If we are bitten by a dog, we can develop a fear of dogs. We are likely to react warmly when we smell Thanksgiving turkey and are often uneasy when we enter a dentist's office. Most of us have experienced test anxiety to some degree, and some children

Classical conditioning. A type of learning that occurs when an individual learns to produce an involuntary emotional or physiological response similar to an instinctive or reflexive response

Unconditioned stimulus (UCS). An object or event that causes an instinctive or reflexive (unlearned) physiological or emotional response

Unconditioned response (UCR). The instinctive or reflexive (unlearned) physiological or emotional response caused by the unconditioned stimulus

Conditioned stimulus (CS). An object or event that becomes associated with the unconditioned stimulus

Conditioned response (CR). A *learned* physiological or emotional response that is similar to the unconditioned response

An understanding of classical conditioning helps teachers see how supportive classroom environments and warm and caring teachers result in positive feelings toward schools and learning.

become physically ill in anticipation of school. In each of these examples, the individual learned an emotional response through classical conditioning.

Classical Conditioning in the Classroom

Sharon Van Horn greets Damon (and each of her other first graders) in a friendly, courteous manner every day when he comes into her classroom, and her greeting makes him feel good. Now, Damon experiences a comfortable feeling when entering Mrs. Van Horn's room, even when she isn't there.

While Tim's experience was unfortunate, Damon's was positive, and we can also explain it with classical conditioning. He associated Mrs. Van Horn's classroom with her inviting manner, so he *learned* to be comfortable when he entered her classroom. This experience can help sensitize teachers to the importance of students' emotional reactions toward learning experiences and school in general. In fact, some researchers suggest that students' emotional reactions resulting from their experiences in schools are among the most important outcomes of schooling (Gentile, 1996). For example, if students experience anxiety as they approach math, their math achievement will be impeded. On the other hand, while students are often uneasy about a new school or class, if their teachers treat them with respect and encouragement, as Damon was with Sharon, they will begin to associate school with the teacher's manner. Eventually, the class will elicit comfortable and safe feelings in students as it did with Damon. This is an important goal, and one that can be achieved with classical conditioning.

The mechanisms involved in Tim's and Damon's experiences are outlined in Table 6.1.

Generalization and Discrimination

Let's look once more at Tim's experience. He also became anxious in chemistry tests, even though he hadn't done poorly on any of them. His anxiety had generalized to chemistry. **Generalization** occurs when stimuli similar, but not identical, to a conditioned stimulus elicit the conditioned response by themselves (N. Jones, Kemenes, & Benjamin, 2001). Tim's chemistry tests were stimuli similar to his algebra quizzes, and they elicited the conditioned response—anxiety—by themselves.

The process can also work in a positive way. Students who associate a classroom with the warmth and respect demonstrated by one teacher may, through generalization, have similar reactions to other classes, club activities, and the school in general.

The opposite of generalization is **discrimination,** which is the ability to give different responses to related but not identical stimuli (W. F. Hill, 2002). For example, Tim was nervous during chemistry tests but not during those in English and history. He discriminated between English and algebra, and between history and algebra.

Generalization. The process that occurs when stimuli similar, but not identical, to a conditioned stimulus elicit the conditioned response by themselves

Discrimination. The process that occurs when a person gives different responses to similar but not identical stimuli

Table 6.1 Classical conditioning examples

Example	Stimuli and Responses		
Tim	UCS *Failure*	→	UCR *Devastation and anxiety* (unlearned and involuntary)
	CS *Quizzes*	→	CR *Anxiety* (learned and involuntary)
	Quizzes associated with failure		Anxiety similar to original anxiety
Damon	UCS *Mrs. Van Horn's manner*	→	UCR *Good feeling* (unlearned and involuntary)
	CS *The classroom*	→	CR *Comfort* (learned and involuntary)
	Classroom associated with Mrs. Van Horn's manner		Comfort similar to original good feeling

Abbreviations: CR, conditioned response; CS, conditioned stimulus; UCR, unconditioned response; UCS, unconditioned stimulus.

Extinction

After working with Susan and changing his study habits, Tim started to feel less nervous. In time, if he continued to succeed, his nervousness would disappear; that is, the conditioned response would become extinct. **Extinction (classical conditioning)** results when the conditioned stimulus occurs often enough in the absence of the unconditioned stimulus so that it no longer elicits the conditioned response (Schunk, 2004). This answers our second question at the beginning of the chapter: "Why did Tim's nervousness later decrease?" As he took additional quizzes (conditioned stimuli) without failing (the unconditioned stimulus), his anxiety (the conditioned response) gradually disappeared. Similarly, if you encounter a number of dogs and aren't again bitten, your fear of dogs also becomes extinct.

Checking Your Understanding

1.1 In our discussion of *classical conditioning*, we said that the "class will elicit comfortable and safe feelings in students." What concept from classical conditioning is illustrated by the class, and what concept is illustrated by the safe feelings? Explain.

1.2 Think about the example of learning to fear dogs as a result of being bitten by a dog. Identify the unconditioned and conditioned stimuli and the unconditioned and conditioned responses, and describe the association involved in the example.

1.3 Suppose the dog that bites us is big and black. Later we are exposed to a number of smaller, friendlier dogs, and we become quite comfortable with the little white poodle next door. However, we're still nervous around big, dark-colored dogs. What concepts are illustrated by our fear of big dogs but not of little friendly dogs?

To receive feedback for these questions, go to Appendix B.

Knowledge Extensions

To deepen your understanding of the topics in this section of Chapter 6 and to integrate them with topics you've already studied, go to the *Knowledge Extensions* module for Chapter 6 at *www.prenhall.com/eggen*. Respond to questions 1–3.

Extinction (classical conditioning). The disappearance of a conditioned response as the result of the conditioned stimulus occurring repeatedly in the absence of the unconditioned stimulus

---

Classroom Connections

Applying Classical Conditioning in Your Classroom

1. Provide a safe and orderly environment so that your classroom will elicit positive emotions.
   - **Elementary:** A first-grade teacher greets each of her students with a smile when they come into the room in the morning. She makes an attempt to periodically ask each of them about their family, a pet, or some other personal part of their lives.
   - **Middle School:** A seventh-grade teacher makes a point of establishing and enforcing rules that forbid students from ridiculing each other in any way, particularly when they're involved in class discussions or responding to teacher questions. He makes respect for one another a high priority in his classroom.
   - **High School:** A geometry teacher attempts to reduce anxiety by specifying precisely the information that students are accountable for on tests. She provides sample problems for practice and offers additional help sessions twice a week.

2. When questioning students, make them feel safe and take steps to ensure a positive outcome.
   - **Elementary:** An urban fourth-grade teacher encourages participation from all his students by asking reluctant responders or low-achieving students open-ended questions such as "What do you notice about the problem?" and "How would you compare the two examples?"
   - **Middle School:** When her seventh graders are unable or unwilling to respond, a seventh-grade math teacher prompts them until they give an acceptable answer. (We discuss effective prompting techniques in Chapter 13.)
   - **High School:** A world history teacher calls on all students in his class, so that students associate being in his class with responding and making an effort.

Applying principles of operant conditioning can help teachers create effective learning environments.

Operant Conditioning

We used classical conditioning to help explain how people learn involuntary emotional and physiological reactions to classroom activities and other events. However, classical conditioning can't explain why people often initiate behaviors instead of simply responding to stimuli. In other words, people often "operate" on their environments, changing them in certain ways. This is the source of the term *operant conditioning.*

This leads us to the work of B. F. Skinner (1904–1990), a behavioral psychologist whose influence was so great that heads of psychology departments in the late 1960s identified him as the most influential psychologist of the 20th century (Myers, 1970). Skinner argued that learners' actions are controlled more by **consequences,** outcomes (stimuli) that occur after behaviors, than by events preceding them. For example, being stopped by a highway patrol for speeding is a consequence. In classrooms, teachers' praise after student answers are also consequences, as are high test scores, recognition for outstanding work, and reprimands for inappropriate behavior. **Operant conditioning,** then, is a form of learning in which an observable response changes in frequency or duration as the result of a consequence.

Operant and classical conditioning are often confused. To help clarify the differences, we present a comparison of the two in Table 6.2. As the table shows, learning occurs as a result of experience for both operant and classical conditioning, but the type of behavior differs, and the behavior and stimulus occur in the opposite order for the two.

Earlier we said that behaviorism, although controversial, is widely used as a tool for managing student behavior in classrooms (Kazden, 2001; G. Martin & Pear, 2002). Operant conditioning, in particular, is used as a management tool. Teachers use reinforcers and punishers to shape student behaviors and help students learn acceptable boundaries for their actions. (We consider classroom management in depth in Chapter 12.)

Let's turn now to a discussion of operant conditioning and the different consequences of behavior as they are presented in Figure 6.1.

Reinforcement

Imagine that during a class discussion you make a comment, and your instructor responds, "That was a very insightful idea. Good thinking." The likelihood that you'll try to make another comment in the future increases. The instructor's comment is a **reinforcer,** a conse-

Consequences. Outcomes (stimuli) that occur after behaviors and influence the probability of the behavior recurring

Operant conditioning. A form of learning in which an observable response changes in frequency or duration as a result of a consequence

Reinforcer. A consequence (stimulus) that increases the likelihood of a behavior recurring

Table 6.2 A comparison of operant and classical conditioning

	Classical Conditioning	Operant Conditioning
Behavior	Involuntary (person does not have control of behavior)	Voluntary (person has control of behavior)
	Emotional	
	Physiological	
Order	Behavior follows stimulus.	Behavior precedes stimulus (consequence).
How learning occurs	Neutral stimuli become associated with unconditioned stimuli.	Consequences of behaviors influence subsequent behaviors.
Example	Learners associate classrooms (initially neutral) with the warmth of teachers, so classrooms elicit positive emotions.	Learners attempt to answer questions and are praised, so their attempts to answer increase.
Key researcher	Pavlov	Skinner

Figure 6.1   Consequences of behavior

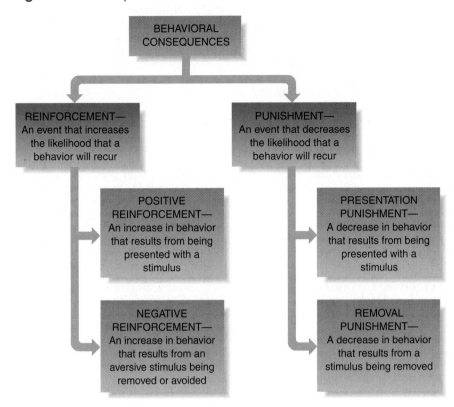

quence that increases the likelihood of a behavior recurring. **Reinforcement,** the process of applying reinforcers to increase behavior, exists in two forms: positive and negative.

Positive Reinforcement. **Positive reinforcement** is the process of increasing the frequency or duration of a behavior as the result of *presenting* a reinforcer. In classrooms we typically think of a positive reinforcer as something desired or valued, such as your instructor's praise. However, any increase in behavior as a result of being presented with a consequence is positive reinforcement, and teachers sometimes unintentionally reinforce undesirable behavior. For instance, if a student is acting out, the teacher reprimands him, and his misbehavior actually increases, the reprimand is a positive reinforcer because it was presented and the student's behavior increased.

Examples of positive reinforcers in classrooms include praise in all its forms—high test scores, "happy faces" for young children, tokens that can be cashed in for privileges, and stars on the bulletin board—with praise probably being the most common.

Teachers also use positive reinforcement when they take advantage of the **Premack principle** (named after David Premack, who originally described it in 1965), which states that a more desired activity serves as a positive reinforcer for a less desired activity. For example, when a geography teacher says, "As soon as you've finished your summaries, you can start working on your maps," he knows that the students prefer doing map work, so the promise of the map work serves as a positive reinforcer for completing the summaries.

Operant conditioning can also influence teachers' behaviors. For example, a student who raises her hand in an attempt to answer a question is reinforcing for the teacher and increases the likelihood of the teacher calling on her. Likewise, attentive looks from students, high student test scores, and compliments from students or their parents can also be positive reinforcers for teachers.

Negative Reinforcement. **Negative reinforcement** is the process of increasing behavior by avoiding or removing an aversive stimulus (Baldwin & Baldwin, 2001; B. Skinner, 1953). For example, suppose a mother says to her teenager, "If you straighten up your room, you don't have to rake the leaves in the yard," or if a teacher says, "If you're all sitting quietly when the bell rings, we'll go to lunch. If not, we'll miss 5 minutes of our lunch period." In

Reinforcement. The process of applying reinforcers to increase behavior

Positive reinforcement. The process of increasing the frequency or duration of a behavior as the result of *presenting* a reinforcer

Premack principle. The principle stating that a more-desired activity serves as a positive reinforcer for a less-desired activity

Negative reinforcement. The process of increasing behavior by avoiding or removing an aversive stimulus

both cases, *avoiding* the aversive stimulus—raking the leaves or missing lunch—acts as a negative reinforcer for the desired behavior—straightening the room or sitting quietly.

Let's look at another example.

> Kathy Long is discussing the skeletal system with her science students.
> "Why do you suppose the rib cage is shaped the way it is? . . . Jim?" she asks.
> He sits silently for several seconds and finally says, "I don't know."
> "Can someone help Jim out?" Kathy continues.
> "It protects our heart and other internal organs," Athenia volunteers.
> "Good, Athenia," Kathy smiles.
> Later, Kathy calls on Jim again. He hesitates briefly and says, "I don't know."
> "Go ahead, Edwin," Kathy says, seeing Edwin's raised hand.

In this example, Kathy unwittingly negatively reinforced Jim for saying, "I don't know," by *removing* the question after his response. We know he is being reinforced because he said, "I don't know," more quickly after being called on the second time. If students can't answer teachers' questions, being called on can be aversive, and they're likely to try to "get off the hook" as Jim did, or even avoid being called on by not making eye contact with the teacher.

This example has important implications for teachers. We want to reinforce students *for* answering, as Kathy did with Athenia, instead of for *not answering*, as she did with Jim. Instead of turning the question to another student, Kathy should have prompted him, so he could have provided an acceptable answer, which she could then have reinforced (Good & Brophy, 2003). (We discuss prompting in detail in Chapter 13.)

When thinking about reinforcement, think of positive and negative numbers rather than positive or negative emotions. Positive reinforcement means *adding* a stimulus, and negative reinforcement means *subtracting* a stimulus. In our examples above, Kathy "added" the praise when she responded to Athenia and "subtracted" the question when Jim said, "I don't know."

Shaping. You have a student who is shy and reluctant to interact with his peers. You know that acquiring social skills is an important part of students' overall development, so you encourage him to be more outgoing and plan to reinforce him for doing so. But he is so shy, you don't know where to begin.

In this case, you can use **shaping** to reinforce successive approximations of the desired behavior. For instance, you watch him carefully and first reinforce him for any interaction with others, such as a simple smile or sharing a pencil. Later, you reinforce him for greeting other students when they come into the classroom in the morning. Finally, you reinforce him only for more prolonged interactions.

Shaping can also be used to develop complex behaviors in learning activities. When students are initially struggling with difficult ideas, you can reinforce their efforts and partially correct responses. Let's look at an example.

> "I start out praising every answer even if it's only partially right," Maria Brugera comments. "I also praise them for trying even if they can't give me an answer. Then as they improve, I praise them only for better, more complete answers, until finally they have to give well thought-out explanations before I'll say anything."
> "I don't," Greg Jordan responds. "I like to use praise, but I think praising every answer takes too much time. I also think if you do it too much, you lose your credibility, so I start right off praising them only when they give me a really good answer."

Although Maria was obviously after the correct answer, she considered student effort a beginning step and a partially correct response an approximation of the desired behavior. Through shaping, she hoped to eventually get complete and thoughtful answers from her students.

Reinforcement Schedules. Maria's and Greg's conversation also illustrates an important principle of operant conditioning: *The timing and spacing of reinforcers can have different effects on learners' behaviors.* These effects are illustrated in **reinforcement schedules,** descriptions of the patterns in the frequency and predictability of reinforcers (Baldwin & Baldwin, 2001).

For example, Maria initially praised every answer, but Greg praised only some of his students' answers. Her reinforcement schedule was **continuous**—every desired behavior

Analyzing Classrooms Video
To analyze a teacher's attempts to use reinforcement with her first graders, go to Episode 8, "Using Reinforcement in Classrooms," on DVD 1, accompanying this text.

Exploring Further
The concept of negative reinforcement is difficult for many people. To read more about the topic and see some additional examples, go to "Negative Reinforcement" in the *Exploring Further* module of Chapter 6 at *www.prenhall.com/eggen*.

Shaping. The process of reinforcing successive approximations of a desired behavior

Reinforcement schedules. Descriptions of the patterns in the frequency and predictability of reinforcers

Continuous reinforcement schedule. A reinforcement schedule in which every behavior is reinforced

is reinforced—whereas Greg's was **intermittent**—some, but not all, of the desired behaviors are reinforced.

Two types of intermittent schedules exist. **Ratio schedules** depend on the number of individual behaviors, and **interval schedules** depend on time. Both can be either fixed—receiving the reinforcers is predictable, or variable—they're unpredictable. For instance, most of us know how slot machines work. You insert a coin, pull the handle or push a button, and periodically a few coins drop into the tray. Receiving coins (reinforcers) depends on the number of times you pull the handle, not on how long you play, and you can't predict when you'll receive coins, so it is a *variable-ratio* schedule.

Reinforcers can also be given on the basis of time, and when this is predictable, we call it a *fixed-interval* schedule. For example, suppose you're in a class that meets Mondays, Wednesdays, and Fridays; you have a quiz each Friday, and your instructor returns the quiz each Monday. You study on Sunday, Tuesday, and particularly, on Thursday evenings, but you aren't reinforced for studying until the following Monday when you receive your score. Reinforcement occurs at a predictable interval: every Monday.

The relationships among the different types of reinforcement schedules are illustrated in Figure 6.2, and additional classroom examples are outlined in Table 6.3.

Reinforcement schedules affect behavior differently, and each has advantages and disadvantages. For instance, a continuous schedule yields the fastest rates of initial learning, so it is effective when students are acquiring new skills such as solving simultaneous equations

Figure 6.2   Schedules of reinforcement

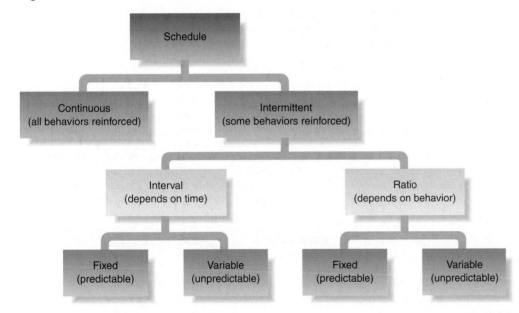

Table 6.3 Reinforcement schedules and examples

Schedule	Example
Continuous	A teacher "walks students through" the steps for solving simultaneous equations. Students are liberally praised at each step as they first learn the solution.
Fixed-ratio	The algebra teacher announces, "As soon as you've done two problems in a row correctly, you may start on your homework assignment so that you'll be able to finish by the end of class."
Variable-ratio	Students volunteer to answer questions by raising their hands and are called on at random.
Fixed-interval	Students are given a quiz every Friday.
Variable-interval	Students are given unannounced quizzes.

Intermittent reinforcement schedule. A reinforcement schedule in which some but not all behaviors are reinforced

Ratio schedules. An intermittent reinforcement schedule in which specific behaviors are reinforced, either predictably (fixed) or unpredictably (variable)

Interval schedules. An intermittent reinforcement schedule in which behaviors are reinforced after a certain predictable interval (fixed) or unpredictable interval (variable) of time has elapsed

in algebra. However, if teachers eliminate reinforcers, the frequency of continually reinforced behaviors decreases more quickly than behaviors reinforced using intermittent schedules.

Intermittent schedules also have disadvantages. With fixed schedules, behavior increases rapidly just before the reinforcer is given and then decreases rapidly and remains low until just before the next reinforcer is given. We saw this in the example of weekly quizzes on Friday; students often study carefully just before the quiz and then don't study again until just before the next quiz. On the other hand, intermittently reinforced behaviors are more enduring than those continually reinforced.

Extinction. In the last section, we said that a continuous reinforcement schedule results in behaviors that quickly disappear when the reinforcers are removed. When this happens, we say that **extinction,** or the disappearance of a behavior as a result of nonreinforcement, has occurred. Extinction occurs in operant conditioning just as it does in classical conditioning. Let's look at an example.

> Renita, a tenth-grader, enjoys school and likes to respond in her classes. She is attentive and raises her hand, eager to answer questions.
> When Mr. Frank, her world history teacher, asks a question, Renita raises her hand, but someone usually blurts out the answer before she can respond. This happens several times.
> Now Renita rarely raises her hand and often catches herself daydreaming in world history.

For Renita, being called on reinforced both her attempts to respond and her attention. Since she wasn't called on, she wasn't reinforced, so her behaviors (raising her hand) were becoming extinct, and her attention was waning.

This example has important implications for teaching. Student involvement and learning are closely related (Bruning et al., 2004; Good & Brophy, 2003), and Renita's experience helps us understand why. When students are involved, their interest and attention increase, and more learning results. When they aren't, their attention wanes, and learning decreases.

Satiation. Behaviors decrease when they are inadequately reinforced, but they can also decrease when they are reinforced too often. If teachers give too much praise, for instance, they may inadvertently decrease the likelihood that students will display desired behaviors. They might also over-reinforce on purpose to decrease unwanted behaviors:

> Isabelle Ortega is having a problem with Janice, Tyra, and Kasana passing notes in her seventh-grade English class, so she develops a plan. She requires each girl to write a personal note to the other two and to do so near the end of class while the other students begin their homework. The note cannot be related to classwork, nor can it be copied, and it must be a full page. She doesn't read the notes but glances at them to be certain they are of proper length.
> At the end of the second day, the girls ask if they can stop writing notes and work on their homework, and at the end of the third day, Isabelle stops the process. She is having no more problems with the girls writing notes in her class.

Extinction (operant conditioning). The disappearance of a behavior that results from lack of reinforcement

Satiation. The process of using a reinforcer so frequently that it loses its potency—its ability to strengthen behaviors

Punishers. Consequences that weaken behaviors or decrease the likelihood of them recurring

Punishment. The process of using punishers to decrease behavior

Presentation punishment. A decrease in behavior that occurs when a stimulus (punisher) is presented

Writing notes was reinforcing for Janice, Tyra, and Kasana, so Isabelle applied the concept of **satiation,** which is using a reinforcer so frequently that it loses its ability to strengthen behaviors.

Isabelle's actions also illustrate the importance of teacher sensitivity and professional judgment. For instance, she made a point of not reading any of the notes, so she didn't embarrass the students or violate their privacy, and she required that the topic be a personal note so that note writing, and not class work, became the aversive behavior. She demonstrated that she both cared about her students and expected them to learn. Had these factors not existed, her application of satiation might not have succeeded.

Punishment

Positive and negative reinforcers are consequences that increase behavior. Other consequences, called **punishers,** weaken behaviors or decrease the likelihood of them recurring (Mazur, 2006). The process of using punishers to decrease behavior is called **punishment.**

Two kinds of punishment exist. As you saw in Figure 6.1, **presentation punishment** occurs when a learner's behavior decreases as a result of being presented with a punisher. It occurs, for example, when a teacher puts her fingers to her lips, signaling "Shh," and students stop whispering. The students are presented with the teacher's signal, and their behavior—whispering—decreases.

Removal punishment occurs when a behavior decreases as a result of removing a stimulus, or the inability to get positive reinforcement. For example, if students are noisy before lunch and the teacher keeps them in the room for 5 minutes of their lunch period, she is using removal punishment. Under normal conditions, they go to lunch at the scheduled time, and the teacher takes away some of that free time in an attempt to eliminate the misbehavior.

Using Punishment Effectively. Some critics suggest that punishment should never be used (e.g., Kohn, 1996b), and systems focusing on positive behaviors are superior to those emphasizing a decrease in inappropriate behaviors (Alberto & Troutman, 2006; Miltenberger, 2004). However, completely eliminating punishment is probably unrealistic because it can be necessary in some cases; when all punishers are removed, some students actually become more disruptive (Pfiffner, Rosen, & O'Leary, 1985; Rosen, O'Leary, Joyce, Conway, & Pfiffner, 1984). A more practical approach is to use punishment judiciously, with liberal amounts of positive reinforcement for good behavior (Maag, 2001). If not used excessively, both presentation and removal punishment can be effective management techniques.

Some types of punishers research has found effective include the following:

- *Desists.* **Desists** are verbal or nonverbal communications teachers use to stop a behavior (Kounin, 1970). A simple form of presentation punishment, such as a teacher putting her fingers to her lips, signaling "Shh," as we saw earlier, is an example. When administered immediately, briefly, and unemotionally, they can be effective (Emmer et al., 2003; Evertson et al., 2003).
- *Timeout.* **Timeout** involves removing a student from the class and physically isolating him or her in an area away from classmates. Typically used with young children, the isolation eliminates the student's opportunities for positive reinforcement, so it is a form of removal punishment. It is effective for a variety of disruptive behaviors (Pfiffner & Barkley, 1998).
- *Detention.* Similar to timeout, and typically used with older students, detention involves taking away some of the students' free time (typically a half hour or more) by keeping students in school either before or after school hours. It is somewhat controversial (L. Johnson, 2004), but it is widely used and is generally considered to be effective (Gootman, 1998). While it may seem like a waste of time, detention is most effective when students are required to sit quietly and do nothing, because the possibility of positive reinforcement is eliminated (imagine sitting doing absolutely nothing for a half hour).
- *Response cost.* **Response cost** involves the removal of reinforcers already given (Zhou, Goff, & Iwata, 2000). For example, some teachers design systems where students receive tokens or other reinforcers for desirable behavior, which they can then use to purchase items from a school store, or redeem for free time and other privileges. Then, taking away some of them for inappropriate behavior is a form of response cost.

Ineffective Forms of Punishment. While judicious use of punishment can be effective, some forms are unacceptable and should never be used. They include the following:

- *Physical punishment.* Physical punishment, such as receiving "swats" or even a slap with a ruler can result in the undesirable side effects of individuals later demonstrating similar behaviors (Bandura, 1986), becoming even more defiant after receiving the punishers (Nilsson & Archer, 1989), or learning more sophisticated ways to avoid getting caught. Students avoid teachers who use punishment frequently, and a number of states forbid physical punishment (Zirpoli & Melloy, 2001).
- *Embarrassment and humiliation.* Embarrassment and humiliation can lead to some of the same side effects as physical punishment (J. E. Walker, Bauer, & Shea, 2004).

Removal punishment. A decrease in behavior that occurs when a stimulus is removed, or when a person cannot receive positive reinforcers

Desists. Verbal or nonverbal communications teachers use to stop a behavior

Timeout. The process of isolating a student from his or her classmates

Response cost. The process of taking away reinforcers already given

Teacher questions act as effective cues to elicit responses from a number of students.

■ *Classwork.* Using classwork as a form of punishment can teach students that it is aversive and may, through classical conditioning, cause negative emotional reactions to it (Baldwin & Baldwin, 2001). Learners may generalize their aversion to their assignments, other teachers, and the school as well.

As with the use of reinforcers, the use of punishers requires sensitivity and sound professional judgment. For example, if the attention a student receives when a teacher uses a desist is reinforcing, the desist is obviously ineffective. Similarly, if being in a class is aversive, timeout may also be ineffective. If undesirable behaviors don't decrease, teachers must use a different strategy. We examine these issues in detail in Chapter 12 when we discuss classroom management.

The Influence of Antecedents on Behavior

To this point, we have discussed the influence of consequences—reinforcers and punishers—on behavior. But behavior is also influenced by **antecedents,** stimuli that precede and signal or induce behaviors. Antecedents of behaviors that were reinforced in the past increase the likelihood of eliciting the behavior in the future, and antecedents of behaviors that were punished in the past decrease the likelihood of eliciting the behavior (Baldwin & Baldwin, 2001).

Common forms of antecedents include

■ Environmental conditions
■ Prompts and cues
■ Past reinforcers (which lead to generalization and discrimination)

Environmental Conditions. When we walk into a dark room, our first inclination is to turn on the lights. The darkness is an environmental antecedent that causes us to turn them on, for which we're reinforced because we're now able to see. We've been reinforced for turning on the lights in the past, so we repeat the behavior. On the other hand, a traffic light turning red is an antecedent that causes us to stop, because running the light increases the likelihood of being punished by either getting a ticket or getting hit by another car.

At school, if students are reinforced for interacting and playing cooperatively on the playground, that environment can become an antecedent that increases the likelihood of students behaving appropriately. In a similar way, some teachers dim the lights when students come in from recess. The dim light acts as an environmental antecedent, reminding students that they are inside and need to use inside voices and behaviors.

These examples remind us that we can use classroom environments as antecedents for positive and prosocial behaviors, which we can then reinforce.

Prompts and Cues. Prompts and cues are specific antecedent stimuli intended to produce behaviors teachers want to reinforce (B. A. Taylor & Levin, 1998). For example:

Alicia Wendt wants her students to understand the concept adverb. She writes this sentence on the chalkboard:

John quickly jerked his head when he heard his name called.

She then asks, "What is the adverb in the sentence? . . . Wendy?"
" . . . "
"Look at the sentence. What did John do?"
" . . . He . . . jerked his head."
"How did he jerk it?"
" . . . Quickly."

Antecedents. Stimuli that precede and signal or induce behaviors

"So what is the adverb?"

". . . is quickly."

"Yes . . . well done, Wendy," Alicia smiles.

Alicia's questions were prompts that helped Wendy make the desired response (behavior), which Alicia then reinforced.

Cues come in other forms as well. When a teacher moves to the front of the class or walks among the students as they do seat work, she is cuing them to turn their attention toward her or to remain on task. In each case, the teacher can then reinforce desired behaviors.

Figure 6.3 Squares and rectangles

Generalization and Discrimination. Past reinforcers also serve as antecedents for responses to similar, but not identical, stimuli. For instance, if a child has been reinforced for identifying object number 1 in Figure 6.3 as a square, that reinforcer can be an antecedent for her identifying 2, 3, and 4 as squares. However, if she labels 5 a square and is told, "No, it's a rectangle because two of the sides are longer," she is less likely to identify 6 as a square.

Identifying 2, 3, and 4 as squares illustrates generalization, which is the process of giving the same response to similar, but not identical, stimuli. No longer identifying 6 as a square illustrates discrimination, which is the process of giving different responses to slightly different stimuli (Hergenhahn & Olson, 2001; W. F. Hill, 2002).

Similarly, after dissecting a shark or frog, biology students recognize the heart in each case. A shark's heart is two-chambered, whereas a frog's is three-chambered, but when students conclude that they are both hearts, they are generalizing. When they learn to tell them apart, they are discriminating. They also learn to discriminate when they can distinguish between the animals' hearts and other body organs.

Exploring Further

While not widely used as a basis for instructional design, behaviorism serves as a framework for some specific instructional strategies. To read more about these strategies, go to "Mastery Learning and Programmed Instruction" in the *Exploring Further* module of Chapter 6 at *www.prenhall.com/eggen*.

Behaviorism in the Classroom: Applied Behavior Analysis

Behaviorism is widely used as a framework for two important tasks: creating productive learning environments and utilizing applied behavioral analysis. We examine the process of creating productive learning environments in detail in Chapter 12. Here we look at applied behavioral analysis.

Applied behavior analysis (ABA) is the process of systematically applying the principles of behaviorism to change student behavior (Baldwin & Baldwin, 2001). (It is also called *behavior modification,* but this term has a negative connotation for some people, so experts prefer the term we use here.) It has been used successfully in helping people increase their physical fitness, overcome fears and panic attacks, learn social skills, and stop smoking. It is widely used in working with students who have exceptionalities (Heward, 2006).

Steps in Applied Behavior Analysis

The application of behaviorist principles in ABA typically involves the following steps:

1. Identify target behaviors.
2. Establish a baseline for the target behaviors.
3. Choose reinforcers and punishers (if necessary).
4. Measure changes in the target behaviors.
5. Gradually reduce the frequency of reinforcers as behavior improves.

To see how these steps can be implemented, let's look back at Mike Sheppard's work with his seventh-grade pre-algebra class that appeared in the closing case study in Chapter 5. Todd, one of Mike's 28 students, was described by other teachers as verbally abusive, aggressive, and lacking in self-discipline. Mike saw that Todd was very active and had a difficult time sitting through a class period. After working with Todd to help him learn to control his behavior, Mike

Applied behavior analysis provides teachers with the tools they need to help students change their own behavior.

Applied behavior analysis (ABA). The process of systematically applying the principles of behaviorism to change student behavior

saw many positive changes. Four of five target behaviors had improved over a 3-week period:

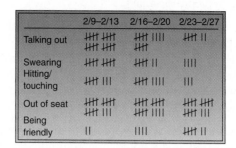

	2/9–2/13	2/16–2/20	2/23–2/27
Talking out	HHT HHT HHT HHT HHT HHT	HHT IIII HHT	HHT II
Swearing	HHT HHT	HHT II	IIII
Hitting/ touching	HHT III	HHT IIII	III
Out of seat	HHT HHT HHT III	HHT HHT HHT IIII	HHT HHT HHT III
Being friendly	II	IIII	HHT II

Now, let's see how Mike implemented each of the steps.

Identify Target Behaviors. The first step in ABA is to identify specific behaviors that you want to change. Mike identified five target behaviors: *talking out, swearing, hitting/touching other students, being out-of-seat,* and *being friendly.* Some experts might argue that Mike included too many target behaviors and might further suggest that "being friendly" isn't specific enough. As with most teaching–learning applications, these decisions are a matter of professional judgment.

Establish a Baseline. Establishing a baseline for the target behaviors simply means measuring their frequency to establish a reference point for later comparison. For instance, during the baseline period (the week of 2/9 to 2/13), Todd talked out in class 20 times, swore 10 times, hit or touched another student 8 times, was out of his seat 18 times, and was friendly to other students only twice. (You, or an objective third party, typically makes observations to determine the baseline. Mike created the behavior tally for the first week.) This baseline allowed both Mike and Todd to see what changes occurred in each of the target behaviors.

Choose Reinforcers and Punishers. Before attempting to change behavior, you need to identify the reinforcers and punishers that are likely to work for an individual student. Ideally, an ABA system is based on reinforcers instead of punishers, and this is what Mike used with Todd. If punishers are necessary, they should also be established in advance.

Mike used personal attention and praise as his primary reinforcers, and their effectiveness is indicated by the changes in Todd's behavior. If the undesirable target behaviors had not decreased, Mike would have needed to modify his system by identifying and then trying some additional reinforcers and perhaps some punishers as well.

Mike also used another reinforcer to increase the effectiveness of his system by involving Todd in the process. After the baseline was established, Todd could see evidence of his improvement, because he was responsible for monitoring his own behavior. This improvement, in itself, was reinforcing.

Measure Changes in Behavior. After establishing a baseline and determining possible reinforcers and punishers, measure the target behaviors for specified periods to see if changes occur. For example, Todd talked out six fewer times in the second week than in the first. Except for "out of seat," improvement occurred for each of the other behaviors during the 3-week period.

The first intervention produced no change in Todd's out-of seat behavior, so Mike designed an additional one. To help Todd satisfy his need for activity yet not disturb the class, Mike prepared a place where Todd could go when the urge to get out of his seat became overwhelming.

Reduce Frequency of Reinforcers. As Todd's behavior improved, Mike gradually reduced the frequency of reinforcers. Initially, a teacher might use a continuous, or nearly continuous, schedule; later, the schedule would become more intermittent. Reducing the frequency of reinforcers helps maintain the desired behaviors and increases the likelihood they will generalize to other classrooms and to behaviors out of school.

Functional Analysis

The preceding sections focused on measuring changes in behavior based on the use of reinforcers, and punishers when necessary. However, some researchers expand their focus to identify antecedents that trigger the inappropriate behaviors (Miltenberger, 2004). For example, Mike found that Todd's abusive behavior occurred most often during class discussions, and he believed that the attention Todd received was reinforcing. Similarly, Todd most commonly was out of his seat during seat work, so being out of his seat allowed him to avoid the seat work with which he struggled. Seat work was an antecedent for leaving his seat. The strategy used to identify antecedents and consequences that control a behavior is called a **functional analysis** (Miltenberger, 2004). In Todd's case, for example, class discussions served the *function* of triggering abusive behavior, and attention served the function of reinforcing the behavior. Similarly, leaving his seat was reinforcing for Todd, since it allowed him to avoid the seat work. These relationships in Todd's case are outlined in Figure 6.4.

Figure 6.4 A functional analysis of Todd's behavior

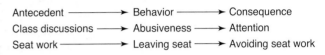

Functional analyses are useful for creating effective interventions, and the goal of reducing undesirable behaviors is usually coupled with reinforcing more appropriate and prosocial behaviors (Kahng & Iwata, 1999; Lalli & Kates, 1998). For example, Mike's positively reinforcing Todd for "being friendly" was a form of attention, so it served the same purpose that being abusive had served for Todd.

Mike also created a classroom environment that supported learning and appropriate behavior in at least three ways. First, he had well-established routines that made the classroom safe and predictable. Second, he spent extra time one-on-one with Todd to increase Todd's success on his seat work, making seat work a less likely antecedent for Todd's being out of his seat. And third, he adapted the environment for Todd by providing a place he could go for a few minutes when he simply could not remain in his seat. Teacher supports, such as these, contribute to improved behavior (Ruef, Higgins, Glaeser, & Patnode, 1998).

Like all interventions, ABA won't work magic, and its application can be labor intensive. In most cases, for example, you can't assume that a student will accurately measure the target behaviors, so you have to monitor those behaviors. This makes managing an already busy classroom even more complex.

Also, personal attention and praise were effective reinforcers for Todd, but if they hadn't been, Mike would have needed others. Finding a reinforcer that is simple to administer and that fits in easily with school procedures can be challenging.

These problems notwithstanding, ABA gives you an additional tool that you can use when conventional methods, such as a basic system of rules and procedures, don't work. As with all strategies, its effectiveness depends on your skill and professional judgment.

Putting Behaviorism into Perspective

Like any theory, behaviorism has both proponents and critics. In this section, we examine some of the arguments on both sides. Criticisms typically focus on the following areas:

- The ineffectiveness of behaviorism as a guide for instruction
- The inability of behaviorism to explain higher order functions
- The impact of reinforcers on intrinsic motivation
- Philosophical positions on learning and teaching

Let's look at them.

First, instruction based on behaviorism suggests that information should be broken down into specific items, which allows learners to display observable behaviors that can then be reinforced. For instance, most of us have completed exercises such as:

Juanita and (I, me) went to the football game.

If we identified "I" as the correct choice, we were reinforced. If we selected "me," we were given corrective feedback, so we learned to appropriately generalize and discriminate. Most of what is taught in schools cannot be effectively acquired through reinforcement of specific, decontextualized items of information, however. For example, we learn to write effectively by practicing writing in meaningful contexts, not by responding to exercises like the one above.

Also, while behaviorism focuses on learners' responses to environmental stimuli—reinforcers and punishers—learners commonly demonstrate misconceptions and sometimes "off-the-wall" ideas for which they haven't been reinforced. These ideas are better

Online Case Book
To analyze a case study to assess the extent to which it applies behaviorist principles, go to the *Online Case Book* for Chapter 6 at *www.prenhall.com/eggen*.

Functional analysis. The strategy used to identify the antecedents and consequences that control a behavior

explained by theories of learning that focus on learners' thought processes. (We examine these theories in detail in Chapters 7–9.)

Second, behaviorism cannot adequately explain higher-order functions, such as language. For instance, Chomsky and Miller (1958) demonstrated that even people with small vocabularies would have to learn sentences at a rate faster than one per second throughout their lifetimes if their learning was based on specific behaviors and reinforcers.

Third, research suggests that offering reinforcers for engaging in intrinsically motivating activities, activities that are interesting for their own sake, such as playing a video game, can decrease interest in those activities (R. Ryan & Deci, 1996).

Finally, some critics hold the philosophical position that schools should attempt to promote learning for its own sake rather than learning to gain rewards (Anderman & Maehr, 1994). Other critics argue that behaviorism is essentially a means of controlling people, rather than a way to help students learn to control their own behavior (Kohn, 1993b).

On the other hand, we all know that experience influences the ways we behave, an idea at the core of behaviorism. For example, teachers understand that a timely, genuine compliment can increase both learner motivation and the way students feel about themselves. Further, supporters of behaviorism ask if we would continue working if we stopped receiving paychecks, and do we lose interest in our work merely because we get paid for it (Gentile, 1996)?

Further, research indicates that reinforcing appropriate classroom behaviors, such as paying attention and treating classmates well, decreases misbehavior, and behaviorist classroom management techniques are often effective when others are not (Alberto & Troutman, 2006; Miltenberger, 2004).

Finally, proponents argue, if reinforcers enhance skills, such as learning a mathematical operation, the ability doesn't disappear merely because praise or some other reinforcer has been removed (J. Cameron & Pierce, 1996; Chance, 1993).

Behaviorism isn't a complete explanation for learning, but neither are other theories. As with most of what we know about teaching and learning, effective applications of all learning theories require the careful judgment of knowledgeable teachers.

Checking Your Understanding

2.1 Judy is off task in your class, and you admonish her. In about 10 minutes, she's off task again, and again you admonish her. About 5 minutes later, she's off task a third time. What concept from operant conditioning does Judy's behavior illustrate? Explain.

2.2 "This test was too long," Rick's students complain as he finishes a discussion of a test he just handed back. Rick reduces the length of his next test, but halfway through the discussion, the students again grumble, "Not again." Rick reduces the length of his third test even more, and as he is turning the test back, his students begin, "What's going on, Mr. Kane? Is writing long tests the only thing you do?" Identify the operant conditioning concept best illustrated by Rick's reducing the length of the test, and identify the concept best illustrated by the students' complaining.

2.3 To encourage on-task behaviors, Mrs. Emerick uses a beeper. If students are on task when the beeper goes off, the class earns points toward a classroom party. What reinforcement schedule is Mrs. Emerick using? Explain.

2.4 As part of her routine, Anita Mendez has a warmup exercise displayed on the overhead each day when the students walk in her room. They immediately begin working on the exercise as she takes roll. She frequently compliments them on their conscientiousness and good behavior as they work. Identify the antecedent, the behavior, and the reinforcers in this example.

To receive feedback for these questions, go to Appendix B.

Knowledge Extensions

To deepen your understanding of the topics in this section of Chapter 6 and to integrate them with topics you've already studied, go to the *Knowledge Extensions* module for Chapter 6 at *www.prenhall.com/eggen*. Respond to questions 4–10.

Classroom Connections

Applying Operant Conditioning in Your Classroom

Reinforcers and Punishers

1. Use reinforcement rather than punishment if possible. When punishment is necessary, use removal instead of presentation punishment.

- **Elementary:** After giving an assignment, a first-grade teacher moves around the room and gives tickets to students who are working quietly. The students may exchange the tickets for opportunities to play games and work at learning centers.
- **Middle School:** A seventh-grade teacher gives students "behavior points" at the beginning of the week. If students break a rule, they lose a point. At the end of the week, the students may trade their remaining points for tickets that they can use to purchase special privileges.
- **High School:** A math teacher increases the effectiveness of grades as reinforcers by awarding bonus points for improvement. Students receive incentive points for scoring higher than their averages.

Generalization and Discrimination

2. Promote generalization and discrimination by encouraging students to make comparisons among examples and other information.

- **Elementary:** A teacher praises a third grader who, on her own, notices that frogs and toads are not the same and that frogs climb trees but toads don't.
- **Middle School:** A life science teacher, in a unit on deciduous and coniferous plants, asks students to compare a pine and an oak tree. With questioning, he helps them identify the essential differences between the two.
- **High School:** An English teacher gives students examples of similes, metaphors, alliterations, and personifications in poems. She has the students identify the specific characteristics of each.

Reinforcement Schedules

3. Use appropriate schedules of reinforcement.

- **Elementary:** At the beginning of the school year, a first-grade teacher plans activities that all students can do. He praises

liberally and rewards frequently. As students' capabilities increase, he requires more effort.
- **Middle School:** A sixth-grade teacher periodically compliments students for consistent work and effort. She knows that students who do steady, average to above-average work and are not disruptive tend to be taken for granted and are often "lost in the shuffle."
- **High School:** A geometry teacher gives frequent announced quizzes to prevent the decline in effort that can occur after reinforcement with a fixed-interval schedule.

Shaping

4. Shape desired behaviors.

- **Elementary:** A second-grade teacher openly praises a student whose behavior is improving. As improvement continues, the teacher requires longer periods of acceptable behavior before he praises the student.
- **Middle School:** A language arts teacher begins a unit on writing paragraphs by having students write a five-sentence paragraph. As she scores this assignment, she is generous with positive comments, but as the students' work improves, she is more critical.
- **High School:** An Algebra II teacher reinforces students as they make the initial steps in solving sets of equations. As their skills improve, he reduces the amount of reinforcement.

Antecedents

5. Provide cues to elicit appropriate behaviors.

- **Elementary:** Before students line up for lunch, a first-grade teacher reminds them to stand quietly while waiting to be dismissed. When they do so, she compliments them on their good behavior and sends them to lunch.
- **Middle School:** After completing a lesson and assigning seat work, a seventh-grade English teacher circulates around the room, reminding students to begin working.
- **High School:** When a chemistry teacher's students can't respond correctly, he prompts them with additional questions that help them respond acceptably.

SOCIAL COGNITIVE THEORY

"What are you doing?" Jason asks Kelly as he comes around the corner and catches her swinging her arms back and forth.

"I'm trying to swing at a ball like the pros do, but I haven't been able to quite do it," Kelly responds, slightly embarrassed. "I was watching a game on TV last night, and the way those guys swing looks so easy, but they hit it so hard. I think I can do that if I work at it."

Three-year-old Jimmy crawls up on his dad's lap with a book. "I read too, Dad," he says as his father puts down his own book to help Jimmy up.

You're driving 65 miles an hour on the interstate, and you're passed by a sports car that appears to be going at least 75. The posted speed limit is 55. A moment later, you see the sports car that passed you pulled over by a highway patrol. You immediately slow down.

What do these incidents have in common? First, each involved learning by observing the behavior of others; Kelly tried to imitate the swing of professional baseball players she had observed on TV, and Jimmy observed his dad reading and wanted to imitate him. You observed the consequences for the other driver and modified your own behavior as a result.

Second, behaviorism can't explain them. It focuses on changes in behavior that have direct causes existing outside the learner. For instance, in our opening case study, taking algebra quizzes directly caused Tim's hand to shake. And, if the driver of the sports car drives 55 after being fined, we conclude that being fined directly caused him to drive slower. Nothing directly happened to Kelly, Jimmy, or you; you changed your behavior simply by observing others.

Research that looks at how people learn from observing others was pioneered by Albert Bandura (1925–). **Social cognitive theory,** a theory of learning that focuses on changes in behavior that result from observing others, emerged from his work (Bandura, 1986, 1997, 2001). Since behaviorism and social cognitive theory both examine changes in behavior, let's examine the relationships between the two.

Comparing Behaviorism and Social Cognitive Theory

You might be asking yourself, "If behaviorists focus on observable behavior (as opposed to thinking and other processes 'in learners' heads'), and the term *cognitive* implies memory and thinking, why is a cognitive learning theory included in the same chapter with behaviorism?"

Here's why: Social cognitive theory has its historical roots in behaviorism, but as the name implies, it has evolved over the years into a more cognitive perspective (Ormrod, 2004; Schunk, 2004). Even today, many authors continue to include aspects of social cognitive theory in books focusing on behavioral principles (e.g., Baldwin & Baldwin, 2001). In addition, the two theories are similar in at least three ways:

- They agree that experience is an important cause of learning (as do other cognitive descriptions, such as those found in Piaget's and Vygotsky's work [see Chapter 2]).
- They include the concepts of reinforcement and punishment in their explanations of behavior.
- They agree that feedback is important in promoting learning.

However, behaviorism and social cognitive theory differ in three important ways. First, they define learning differently. Second, they emphasize the role that expectations play in learning, and third, they believe that the environment, personal factors such as expectations, and behavior are interdependent, a concept called *reciprocal causation.* Let's look at these differences.

Definition of Learning
Behaviorists define learning as a change in observable behavior, whereas social cognitive theorists view **learning** as a change in mental processes that creates the capacity to demonstrate different behaviors (W. F. Hill, 2002). So, learning may or may not result in immediate behavioral change. The role of mental activity (cognition) in this internal process is illustrated in our examples. Kelly, for example, didn't try to imitate the baseball swing until the next day, so her observations of the players on television had to be stored in her memory or she wouldn't have been able to reproduce the behaviors. Nothing directly happened to either Jimmy or you, so you both were responding to mental processes and not directly to the environment.

The Role of Expectations
Expectations are cognitive processes that strongly influence our behavior, and they influence social cognitive theorists' interpretations of reinforcement and punishment. Instead of viewing reinforcers and punishers as direct causes of behavioral change, as is the behaviorist interpretation, they believe, instead, that reinforcers and punishers create expectations that in turn influence behavior. For example, students may study for a major exam for several days, but they aren't reinforced until they receive their score. They sustain their efforts because they *expect* to be reinforced for studying. You slowed down when you saw the other car stopped because you expected to be punished—pulled over—if you contin-

Exploring Further

Bandura's work that provided the foundation for social cognitive theory is fascinating. To read about this research, go to "Bandura's Original Research" in the *Exploring Further* module of Chapter 6 at *www.prenhall.com/eggen.*

Social cognitive theory. A theory of learning that focuses on changes in behavior that result from observing others

Learning (cognitive). A change in mental processes that creates the capacity to demonstrate different behaviors, which may or may not result in immediate behavioral change

ued speeding. Behaviorists don't consider the role of expectations in learning, but they are central to social cognitive theory.

The fact that people respond to their expectations means they are aware of which behaviors will be reinforced or punished. This is important because, according to social cognitive theory, reinforcement changes behavior only when learners know what behaviors are being reinforced (Bandura, 1986). Tim expected his changed study habits to improve his math scores, so he maintained those habits. If he had expected some other strategy to be effective, he would have used it. He wasn't merely responding to reinforcers; he was actively assessing the effectiveness of his strategy.

The importance of student cognitions has two implications for you as a teacher. First, you should clearly specify the behaviors you will reinforce, so students can adapt their behavior accordingly, and second, you should provide students with clear feedback so they know what behaviors have been reinforced. For instance, if a student gets full credit for an essay item on a test but doesn't know why the credit was given, she may not know how to respond correctly the next time.

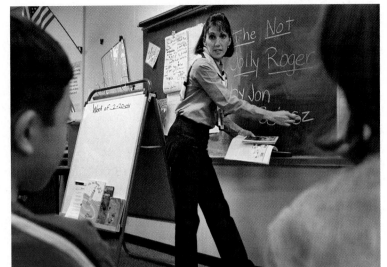

Students can learn a wide range of complex behaviors through modeling.

Reciprocal Causation

Behaviorism suggests a "one-way" relationship between the environment and behavior; the environment influences behavior, but the opposite doesn't occur. Social cognitive theory's explanation is more complex, suggesting that behavior, the environment, and personal factors, such as expectations, are interdependent, meaning each influences the other two. **Reciprocal causation** is the term used to describe the interdependence of the environment, behavior, and personal factors in learning.

For instance, Tim's low score on his algebra quiz (an environmental factor) influenced his expectations (a personal factor) about future success on algebra quizzes. His expectations, in turn, influenced his behavior (he adapted his study habits), and his behavior influenced the environment (he went to Susan's home to study).

Reciprocal causation was also involved in your experience with the other driver. Seeing the other driver pulled over (an environmental factor) influenced your expectations (a personal factor), which influenced your behavior (you slowed down). Your behavior then influenced the environment; you changed the way you drove, allowing you to pass other highway patrols without incident.

We turn now to essential concepts of social cognitive theory.

Modeling

Modeling is "a general term that refers to behavioral, cognitive, and affective changes deriving from observing one or more models" (Schunk, 2004, p. 88). It is the central concept of social cognitive theory. Tim, for example, observed that Susan was successful in her approach to studying for exams. As a result, he imitated her behavior; direct imitation of behavior is one form of modeling.

The importance of modeling in our everyday lives is difficult to overstate. For instance, in both Chapters 2 and 4, we emphasized that culture exerts a powerful influence on learning. To promote language development, educators urge parents to use correct grammar and pronunciation in talking to their infants. Studies of disadvantaged youth indicate that a lack of effective adult role models is one reason they have difficulty handling the problems they encounter (Ogbu, 1987, 1999b). Modeling helps explain each of these factors.

Modeling is equally powerful in schools. Teachers demonstrate a variety of skills, such as solutions to math problems, effective writing techniques, study strategies, and critical thinking (Braaksma et al., 2004). Equally important, teachers also display courtesy and respect for others, tolerance for dissenting opinions, motivation to learn, and other attitudes and values. Athletic coaches demonstrate techniques for correctly shooting a jump shot in basketball, making a corner kick in soccer, a kill in volleyball, and other skills, together with teamwork,

Exploring Further

To examine a brief excerpt that further illustrates the importance of modeling in working with students, go to "Practicing What We Preach" in the *Exploring Further* module of Chapter 6 at *www.prenhall.com.eggen.*

Reciprocal causation. The description of the interdependence of the environment, behavior, and personal factors in learning

Modeling. Behavioral, cognitive, and affective changes deriving from observing one or more models

a sense of fair play, humility in victory, and graciousness in defeat. Aspiring tennis players and golfers often watch videotapes of experts and themselves to assess their developing skills.

When teachers or coaches display intellectual or physical skills, they are direct models. Videotaped examples, as well as characters in movies, television, books, and plays are symbolic models, and combining different portions of observed acts represents synthesized modeling (Bandura, 1986). Table 6.4 describes and illustrates these different forms of modeling.

Cognitive Modeling

Teachers and other experts can also be cognitive models. **Cognitive modeling** is the process of incorporating demonstrations together with verbalization of the model's thoughts and reasons for performing the given actions (Schunk, 2004). Let's look at an example.

Television can have both positive and negative effects on learners through the role models it provides.

"Wait a minute," Jeanna Edwards said as she saw Joanne struggling with the microscope. "Let me show you once more. . . . Now, watch closely as I adjust it. This is important because these slides crack easily. The first thing I think about is getting the slide in place. Otherwise, I might not be able to find what I'm looking for in the microscope. Then, I want to be sure I don't crack the slide while I lower the lens, so I watch from the side. Finally, I slowly raise the lens until I have the object in focus. You were trying to focus as you lowered it. It's easier and safer if you try to focus as you raise it. Now go ahead and try it."

Cognitive modeling allows learners to benefit from the thinking of experts. As Jeanna showed Joanne how to use the microscope, she also described her thoughts, such as, "The first thing I think about is. . . ." When teachers put their thinking into words, or when they encourage other students to explain their thinking, they provide learners with specific, concrete examples of how to think about and solve problems (Braaksma et al., 2004).

Vicarious Learning

In addition to modeling, people also learn by observing the consequences of other's actions and adjusting their own behavior accordingly, a process called **vicarious learning** (Schunk, 2004). For example, Tim saw how well Susan did on quizzes with her approach to studying, so he was vicariously reinforced through her success. When students hear a teacher say, "I really like the way Kevin is working so quietly," they are also being vicariously reinforced, and when a student is reprimanded for leaving his seat without permission, other students in the class are vicariously punished. You were vicariously punished by observing the other driver pulled over.

Cognitive modeling. The process of incorporating modeled demonstrations together with verbalization of the model's thoughts and reasons for performing the given actions

Vicarious learning. The process of people observing the consequences of other's actions and adjusting their own behavior accordingly

Table 6.4 Different forms of modeling

Type	Description	Example
Direct modeling	Simply attempting to imitate the model's behavior	Tim imitates Susan in studying for exams. A first grader forms letters in the same way a teacher forms them.
Symbolic modeling	Imitating behaviors displayed by characters in books, plays, movies, or television	Teenagers begin to dress like characters on a popular television show oriented toward teens.
Synthesized modeling	Developing behaviors by combining portions of observed acts	A child uses a chair to get up and open the cupboard door after seeing her brother use a chair to get a book from a shelf and seeing her mother open the cupboard door.

The concept of expectations helps us understand vicarious learning. Tim *expected* to be reinforced for imitating Susan's behavior, and the other students *expect* to be reinforced for imitating Kevin's behavior. As we said earlier, you *expected* to be punished if you continued speeding, so you slowed down. These examples help us see why expectations are so important in social cognitive theory.

Nonoccurrence of Expected Consequences

Expectations are additionally important because they influence behavior when they aren't met. For example, your instructor gives you a homework assignment, you work hard on it, but she doesn't collect it. The nonoccurrence of the expected reinforcer (credit for the assignment) can act as a punisher; you are less likely to work hard for the next assignment.

Just as the nonoccurrence of an expected reinforcer can act as a punisher, the nonoccurrence of an expected punisher can act as a reinforcer (Bandura, 1986). A student who breaks a classroom rule, for example, and isn't reprimanded (punished) is more likely to break the rule in the future. Students expect to be punished for breaking rules. When the expected punisher doesn't occur, the fact that it doesn't acts as a reinforcer.

The nonoccurrence of expected consequences is common out in the real world. For example, if teachers are asked to provide input into school policy, but the input isn't used, they're less likely to offer advice in the future. Having the input used would be reinforcing, but when it isn't, the nonoccurrence of the expected reinforcer acts as a punisher and decreases the likelihood of teachers doing it again. Sports fans buy season tickets to see their local team play, but if the team consistently loses, they're less likely to buy tickets in the future. Seeing the team win would be reinforcing, and its nonoccurrence decreases fans' behavior—buying season tickets.

Checking Your Understanding

3.1 Teachers who do cooperative learning activities sometimes give all the students in the group the same grade. Research indicates that this practice is ineffective (Slavin, 1995). Explain why the practice is ineffective, using the information in this section.

3.2 Mike was taking chemistry from an instructor who only lectured and then assigned problems for practice. He found he often "drifted off" during class. Because he felt he wasn't learning, he managed (with the help of his parents) to get switched to Mr. Adams class. "If he sees you aren't paying attention, he calls on you," Mike comments. "So, I don't sleep in his class, and I'm getting to where I really understand the stuff now." Explain how reciprocal causation is illustrated in this example.

3.3 Coach Jeffreys emphasizes hard but fair play with his soccer team. Seeing one of his players cut an opposing team member's legs out from under him, Coach Jeffreys benches the player, explaining to him (and the rest of the team) why he did so. He doesn't see another incident of this type of foul for the rest of the year. Explain why this occurred. Include the role of expectations in your explanation.

To receive feedback for these questions, go to Appendix B.

Knowledge Extensions

To deepen your understanding of the topics in this section of Chapter 6 and to integrate them with topics you've already studied, go to the *Knowledge Extensions* module for Chapter 6 at *www.prenhall.com/eggen*. Respond to questions 11–13.

Having introduced modeling, vicarious learning, and the nonoccurrence of expected consequences, we now turn to a more detailed look at these concepts as we examine

- The functions of modeling
- The processes involved in learning from models
- The effectiveness of models
- Self-regulation

Functions of Modeling

Modeling is more complex than simple imitation of a behavior, and when we think of functions of modeling, we are answering questions such as, "What can result from observing models?" or "How do models influence behavior?"

Modeling serves four functions:

- Learning new behaviors
- Facilitating existing behaviors
- Changing inhibitions
- Arousing emotions

Learning New Behaviors

Through imitation, people can acquire abilities they couldn't display before observing the model. Solving an algebra problem after seeing the teacher show a solution, running a smooth bead with a welder after seeing it demonstrated, or learning to write a clear paragraph after seeing an exemplary one are all examples. Kelly's comment, "I was trying to swing at a ball like the pros do, but I haven't been able to quite do it," indicates that she was attempting to learn a new behavior when she watched the ball players on television.

Facilitating Existing Behaviors

You are attending a concert, and at the end of one of the numbers, someone stands and begins to applaud. Others notice and join in to create a standing ovation. Obviously, people already know how to stand and clap, so new behaviors weren't learned. Instead, the person "facilitated" your and others' behaviors.

This process was also demonstrated in Tim's behavior. He practiced solving problems before quizzes, but he admitted, "I usually do a couple, and if I'm okay on them, I quit." After observing Susan, he changed the way he studied. Her approach to preparing for quizzes facilitated Tim's studying behavior.

Changing Inhibitions

An **inhibition** is a self-imposed restriction on one's behavior, and observing a model and the consequences of the model's behavior can either strengthen or weaken it. Unlike actions that facilitate existing behaviors, changing inhibitions involves socially unacceptable behaviors, such as breaking classroom rules (Pintrich & Schunk, 2002).

For example, students are less likely to break a rule if one of their peers is reprimanded; their inhibition about breaking the rule has been strengthened. Jacob Kounin (1970), one of the pioneer researchers in the area of classroom management, called this phenomenon the *ripple effect.* On the other hand, if a student speaks without permission and isn't reprimanded, other students are more likely to do the same. The inhibition is weakened. *Vicarious learning* and *the nonoccurrence of expected consequences* help explain changed inhibitions. For instance, if students see a peer reprimanded for breaking a rule, they are vicariously punished; they *expect* the same result if they break the rule, and their inhibitions about breaking the rule are strengthened. However, if the student is not reprimanded, the nonoccurrence of the expected punisher acts as a reinforcer, and both the student and the rest of the class are more likely to break the rule. Their inhibition about breaking the rule has been weakened.

Arousing Emotions

Finally, a person's own emotional reactions can be changed by observing a model's display of emotions. For example, observing the uneasiness of a diver on a high board may cause an observer to become more fearful of the board as well. In a similar way, observing the pride of accomplishment in solving a difficult math problem could cause the observer to attempt similar problems in the future. The emotional arousal effect of modeling can also be used by teachers to motivate students. Observing teachers genuinely enjoying themselves as they discuss a topic can help generate similar enthusiasm in students (Brophy, 2004).

These examples help us better understand the definition of modeling that we presented earlier: behavioral, cognitive, and affective changes deriving from observing one or more models. We see behavioral changes when behaviors are learned or facilitated, cognitive changes in strengthening or weakening inhibitions, and affective changes when emotions are aroused.

Analyzing Classrooms Video
To analyze the effectiveness of a teacher's attempts to capitalize on the functions of modeling, go to Episode 9, "Demonstrating Problem Solving in High School Chemistry" on DVD 1, accompanying this text.

Inhibition. A self-imposed restriction on one's behavior

Processes Involved in Learning from Models

We saw that modeling can involve learning and facilitating behaviors, changing inhibitions, and arousing emotions, but how does this take place? Four processes are involved: *attention, retention, reproduction,* and *motivation* (Bandura, 1986). They're illustrated in Figure 6.5 and summarized as follows:

- *Attention:* A learner's attention is drawn to the critical aspects of the modeled behavior. For example, Tim paid attention to Susan's study strategies.
- *Retention:* The modeled behaviors are transferred to memory by mentally verbalizing or visually representing them. Tim mentally recorded Susan's behaviors.
- *Reproduction:* Learners reproduce the behaviors that have been stored in memory. Tim imitated Susan's study habits.
- *Motivation:* Learners are motivated by the expectation of reinforcement for reproducing the modeled behaviors. Tim was motivated to imitate Susan's behaviors because he expected to be reinforced for doing so.

Figure 6.5 Processes involved in learning from models

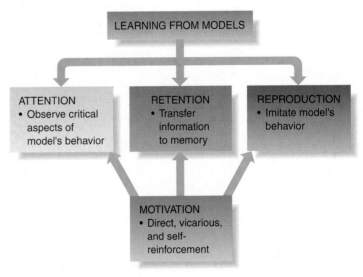

Three aspects of these processes are important for teachers. First, to learn from models, the learner's attention must be drawn to the essential aspects of the modeled behavior (Bandura, 1986). For example, preservice teachers often go into schools and observe veterans in action, but if they don't know what they're looking for, the observations don't significantly influence their learning. As teachers, we need to call attention to the important aspects of the skill we're demonstrating.

Second, attending to the modeled behaviors and recording them in memory don't necessarily ensure that learners will be able to reproduce them. Additional scaffolding and practice with feedback are often required. (We examine this issue in detail when we discuss instruction principles later in the chapter.)

Third, although motivation appears as a separate component in Figure 6.5, it is integral to each of the others. Motivated learners are more likely to attend to a model's behavior, to record the behavior in memory, and to reproduce it. Learners who make a conscious effort to do these things will be more successful than those who remain passive.

Effectiveness of Models

The "effectiveness" of a model describes the likelihood that the behavioral, cognitive, or affective changes deriving from observing one or more models will occur; that is, the change is more likely if the model is effective than if he or she is ineffective. A model's effectiveness depends on three factors:

- Perceived similarity
- Perceived competence
- Perceived status

For example, when we observe a model's behavior, we are more likely to imitate him or her if we perceive the model as similar to us. This helps us understand why presenting nontraditional career models and teaching students about the contributions of women and people from minority groups are important. Either gender can effectively demonstrate that engineering presents career opportunities, but girls are more likely to believe that it is a viable career choice for them if they observe the work of a female rather than a male engineer. Similarly, a Hispanic student is more likely to believe he can accomplish challenging goals if he sees the accomplishments of a successful Hispanic adult than if the adult is a member of a nonminority. In addition, several models are more effective than a single model, because the likelihood of finding a model perceived as similar increases as the number of models increases.

Perception of a model's competence, the second factor that increases a model's effectiveness, interacts with perceptions of similarity. People are more likely to imitate models perceived as competent than those perceived as less competent, regardless of similarity. Although Tim and Susan were similar in that they were classmates, Tim would have been unlikely to change his behavior in response to observing her if she had not been a successful student.

Status, the third factor, is acquired when individuals distinguish themselves from others in their fields. People tend to imitate high-status individuals, such as professional athletes, popular rock stars, and world leaders, more often than others. At the school level, athletes, cheerleaders, and in some cases even gang leaders have high status for some students.

Teachers are also influential models. Despite concerns expressed by educational reformers and teachers themselves, they remain and continue to be high-status models for students.

High-status models also enjoy an additional benefit. They are often tacitly credited for competence outside their own areas of expertise. This is the reason you see professional basketball players (instead of nutritionists) endorsing breakfast cereal, and actors (instead of engineers) endorsing automobiles and motor oil.

Self-Regulation

Earlier, we saw that learners' expectations can influence both behavior and the environment. This is accomplished through **self-regulation,** the process of taking responsibility for one's own learning (Zimmerman & Schunk, 2001). Self-regulated learners use their own thoughts and actions to identify goals, develop strategies for reaching them, and monitor their progress. Tim, for example, went to Susan's home to study, and he modified and monitored his study strategies as a result of his experience. Behaviorists can't explain Tim's change in behavior, since he wasn't reinforced for doing so until his efforts paid off sometime later. To behave as he did, Tim had to be self-regulated (Bandura, 1986).

Self-regulation includes the following components:

- Setting goals
- Monitoring progress toward the goals
- Assessing the extent to which goals are met
- Administering self-rewards (Meichenbaum, 2000; Paris & Paris, 2001; Winne, 2001)

Setting Goals

Goals provide direction for a person's actions and ways for measuring progress. Susan set the goal of working at least three of each type of algebra problem, and Tim imitated her behavior by setting goals of his own.

Goals set by students themselves, especially goals that are challenging but realistic, are more effective than those imposed by others (Pintrich & Schunk, 2002; Stipek, 2002). Helping students create effective goals is important, but difficult, because the tendency is for students to set lenient or low-level goals for themselves.

Monitoring Progress

Once they have established their goals, self-regulated learners monitor their progress. Susan, for example, said, "I sometimes even make a little chart. I try to do at least three problems of each type we study, and then I check them off as I do them." The chart allowed Susan to monitor her own learning progress.

Students can be taught to monitor a variety of behaviors. For example, they can keep a chart and make a check every time they catch themselves "drifting off" during an hour of study, every time they blurt out an answer in class, or every time they use a desired social skill. Research indicates that self-observation combined with appropriate goals can improve concentration, study habits, social skills, and a variety of others (Alberto & Troutman, 2006).

Self-Assessment

In schools, a person's performance is typically judged by someone else. Although teachers provide valuable feedback, they don't have to be the sole judges of student performance; students can learn to assess their own work (Stiggins, 2005). For example, students can assess the quality of their solutions to word problems by comparing their answers with estimates and asking themselves if their answers make sense. Tim's checking his answers against those in the back of the book is a form of self-assessment.

Self-regulation. The process of accepting responsibility for and taking control of one's own learning

Developing self-assessment skills takes time, and initially, students won't be good at it. The best way to help students develop these skills is to be sure their goals are specific and measurable, as were Susan's and Tim's. Helping students make valid self-assessments based on accurate self-observations is one of the most important tasks teachers face in promoting self-regulation.

Self-Reinforcement

We all feel good when we accomplish a goal, and we often feel guilty when we don't, vowing to do better in the future (Bandura, 1989). As learners become self-regulated, they learn to reinforce or punish themselves for meeting or failing to meet their goals.

Teachers act as powerful role models in the classroom, influencing both cognitive and affective outcomes.

The good feeling we have when we meet a goal is a potent form of self-reinforcement, and guilt can be an equally influential self-punisher. Other self-reinforcers can be something more tangible, such as the dish of ice cream Susan allowed herself when she got all of her problems right. A self-punisher might simply be the denial of this tangible treat.

Self-reinforcement is somewhat controversial. Some researchers argue that it is unnecessary; in other words, goals, self-observation, and self-assessment should be sufficient (S. Hayes et al., 1985). Others argue that self-reinforcement is effective, particularly for low achievers. In one study, low-achieving students were taught to award themselves points, which they could use to buy privileges, when they did well on their assignments. Within a few weeks, the low achievers were achieving as well as their classmates (Stevenson & Fantuzzo, 1986).

Developing self-regulation in students is powerful but difficult. As we said earlier, students often set lenient goals for themselves; teachers need to assist students in setting challenging but realistic goals (Yell, Robinson, & Drasgow, 2001). However, if it can be achieved, self-regulation is a capability that extends to everything in life.

Cognitive Behavior Modification

Self-regulation can be enhanced through **cognitive behavior modification,** a procedure that combines both behavioral and cognitive learning principles to help learners change their behavior through self-talk and self-instruction (Meichenbaum, 2000; Schunk, 2004). Teachers use cognitive modeling to help students develop self-monitoring and assessment abilities and develop other skills that are part of self-regulation, such as listening, organization, and time management. After observing the modeled abilities, students practice them under the guidance of the teacher, and then use self-talk to guide themselves as they perform the skills without supervision. Cognitive behavior modification strategies are particularly effective with students having exceptionalities (T. R. Robinson, Smith, Miller, & Brownell, 1999).

We examine specific strategies for developing learner self-regulation in Chapter 11.

Instructional Principles

**Social Cognitive Theory in the Classroom:
Instructional Principles**

Social cognitive theory has a wide range of applications, both in classrooms and in the world at large. In classrooms, the following principles help guide you as you attempt to capitalize on the characteristics of social cognitive theory:

1. Act in ways you want students to imitate.
2. Enforce classroom rules and procedures fairly and consistently.
3. Capitalize on modeling effects and processes to promote learning.
4. Place students in modeling roles.
5. Capitalize on guest role models when possible.

Cognitive behavior modification. A procedure that combines behavioral and cognitive learning principles to help learners change their behavior through self-talk and self-instruction

Let's see how the principles guide Sally Campese, an eighth-grade algebra teacher, as she works with her students.

"Good morning, everyone," Sally greets her students, as she moves to the front of the classroom. "I have something new that we're going to incorporate into our work. I recently subscribed to a 'word-of-the-day' online service, and I'm going to share the word with you." On the board, she writes

Recidivism—a tendency to lapse into a previous condition

"We don't want any recidivism with respect to our work habits," she smiles.

"This is an algebra class," Todd muses. "Why are we thinking about words in here?"

"This is, first, a class about learning," Sally replies. "I want to keep on learning, and I want you all to feel the same way. . . . No recidivism," she smiles again.

"You're gung ho about everything, aren't you, Mrs. Campese?" Jeff grins.

Sally smiles again and then turns to Jamie, who is coming through the door, "I'm sorry, but you're late."

In Sally's classroom, students are warned the first time they're tardy for the week and are given a half hour of detention for a second tardy.

"I know," Jamie nods wryly, realizing she had been warned.

"Just a reminder before we start. I've invited a man named Javier Sanchez in to speak on Friday. You remember that I told you Mr. Sanchez is an engineer in one of the big firms in town, and he's going to tell you about engineering and why math is so important for all of us.

"Okay, look up here," Sally says, turning to the day's topic. "We're having a little difficulty with some of these problems, so let's go over a few more examples.

"Try this one," she says, writing on the chalkboard:

$$4a + 6b = 24$$
$$5a - 6b = 3$$

Sally watches as the students try the problem, and seeing that Gabriel has solved it successfully, says, "Gabriel, go ahead and describe your thinking for us as you solved the problem."

". . . I saw that there's a $6b$ in the first equation and a negative $6b$ in the second. . . . So, I added the two together, . . . and that's how I did it."

"Okay, good, Gabriela. . . . And what do we get when we add the equations? . . . Hue?"

". . . Nine a plus zero b equals 27."

Sally writes on the board:

$$9a + 0b = 27$$

"Okay," she continues. "What is the value of a? . . . Chris?"

". . . Three."

"And how did you get that?"

"Zero b is zero, and then I divided both sides by 9, so I have $1a$ equals 3."

"Good! . . . Now let's find the value of b. What should we do first? . . . Mitchell?"

Let's look now at Sally's attempts to apply the principles in her lesson. First, by initiating the "word-of-the-day" activity, she attempted to model a desire to learn. The fact that this was an algebra class may have made her efforts even more significant. Her modeling communicated that learning in all its forms is valuable and that being in algebra class didn't mean students should learn only about algebra. Efforts like Sally's won't make all students enthusiastic learners, but they contribute, as Jeff's comment, "You're gung ho about everything, aren't you, Mrs. Campese?" indicates. Modeled teacher enthusiasm has a positive effect on both student motivation and learning.

Sally applied the second principle by consistently enforcing her classroom rules. Jamie's tardiness may have been minor, but her public interactions with Jamie demonstrated that classroom rules are important and are being enforced. If Sally hadn't warned Jamie, the other students' inhibitions about being tardy would have been weakened, increasing the chance that they, too, would come to class late.

Sally capitalized on basic modeling processes—*attention, retention, reproduction,* and *motivation*—and applied the third principle by guiding the students with questions rather than simply explaining the solution. This process increased the likelihood that they would attend to the demonstrated behavior, retain it, and reproduce it (Good & Brophy, 2003; Lambert & McCombs, 1998).

Sally applied the fourth principle, placing a student in a modeling role, when she said, "Gabriel, go ahead and describe your thinking for us as you solved the problem." In this way, she used Gabriel as a cognitive model for the rest of the students, and because of perceived similarity, peers can be effective models (Schunk, 2004).

Finally, Sally applied the last principle, capitalizing on a guest role model, by inviting a successful professional engineer to speak to her classes. Because Javier Sanchez was Hispanic, he would, through perceived similarity, be an effective role model for students who were members of cultural minorities. Teachers cannot routinely invite guests into their classrooms, but having a guest speak even twice a year can do much to capitalize on the influence of minority role models.

Putting Social Cognitive Theory into Perspective

Like all descriptions of learning, social cognitive theory has strengths and weaknesses. Modeling is one of the most powerful factors that exist in learning, and it overcomes some of the limitations of behaviorism by helping us understand the importance of learner cognitions, and particularly expectations, on their actions (Pintrich & Schunk, 2002).

Like any theory, however, social cognitive theory has limitations. For example:

- It cannot explain why learners attend to and imitate some modeled behaviors but not others.
- It doesn't account for the learning of complex tasks, such as learning to write (beyond mere mechanics).
- It cannot explain the role of context and social interaction in complex learning environments. For example, research indicates that student interaction in small groups facilitates learning (Greeno et al., 1996; Shuell, 1996). The processes involved in these settings extend beyond simple modeling and imitation.

We identify these limitations as a reminder that every theory of learning is incomplete—explaining some aspects of learning but not others. This is why it's important for teachers to thoroughly understand different theories of learning, so they can apply different aspects of a particular theory that are most appropriate for meeting their learning objectives.

Checking Your Understanding

4.1   With the goal of promoting idealism in her students, a teacher shows a videotape of Martin Luther King's famous speech in which he said, "I have a dream that my four little children will one day live in a nation where they will not be judged by the color of their skin but by the content of their character." What type of modeling is being illustrated, how effective is the modeling likely to be, and what is the most likely modeling outcome? Explain.

4.2   You're in a large city waiting to cross the street. No cars are coming from either direction, so another person who is standing there crosses against the red light. You and the rest of the people there then cross. Explain why you cross the street. Include all relevant concepts in your explanation.

4.3   To develop a deep understanding of the topics you're studying in this text, you decide that you're going to answer and understand each of the "Checking Your Understanding" questions in writing. You therefore make a chart with the question number on it, and you make a check mark on the chart when you've answered the question. Then, you go to the Website to compare your answers to those on the Web. If you get them all correct, you allow yourself some free time to read a novel or to watch your favorite show on TV. Identify each of the components of self-regulation in your behavior.

To receive feedback for these questions, go to Appendix B.

Knowledge Extensions

To deepen your understanding of the topics in this section of the chapter and to integrate them with topics you've already studied, go to the *Knowledge Extensions* module for Chapter 6 at *www.prenhall.com/eggen*. Respond to questions 14–16.

Classroom ⊞ **Connections**

Applying Social Cognitive Theory in Your Classroom

1. Use cognitive modeling in your instruction. Act as a role model for your students.

   - **Elementary:** A kindergarten teacher uses cognitive modeling to help her children form letters by saying, "I start with my pencil here and make a straight line down," as she begins to form a b.

   - **Middle School:** A seventh-grade teacher has a large poster at the front of his room that says, "I will always treat you with courtesy and respect, you will treat me with courtesy and respect, and you will treat each other with courtesy and respect." She models, reinforces, and calls attention to this rule throughout the school year.

   - **High School:** A physics teacher solving acceleration problems involving friction writes F = ma on the chalkboard and says, "Hmm . . . I know I want to find the net force on the object. So, then I think about what the problem tells me. . . . Someone, go ahead and tell us one thing we know about the problem."

2. As students learn to reproduce skills, provide group practice by walking them through examples before having them practice on their own.

   - **Elementary:** A fifth-grade class is adding fractions with unlike denominators. The teacher displays the problem 1/4 + 2/3 = ? and then begins, "What do we need to do first? . . . Karen?" She continues asking questions as the class works through the problem and then does a second example the same way.

   - **Middle School:** After showing students how to find exact locations using longitude and latitude, a seventh-grade geography teacher says to his students, "We want to find the city closest to 85° west and 37° north. . . . First, what do these numbers tell us? . . . Leslie?" He continues to guide students through the example until they locate Chicago as the closest city.

   - **High School:** After demonstrating several proofs, a geometry teacher wants her students to prove that angle 1 is greater than angle 2 in the accompanying drawing. She begins by asking, "What are we given in the problem?" After the students identify the given information, she asks, "What can we conclude about segments BE and BD?" She continues to guide students with questions as they complete the proof as a group.

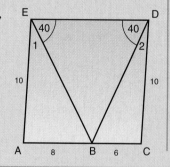

3. Use vicarious reinforcement to increase the effectiveness of modeling.

   - **Elementary:** As students in one reading group move back to their desks, a first-grade teacher comments loudly enough for the class to hear, "I like the way this group is quietly returning to their desks. Karen, Vicki, Ali, and David each get a star because they have gone so quickly and quietly."

   - **Middle School:** An eighth-grade English teacher displays several examples of well-written paragraphs on the overhead. He comments, "Each of these are well written. They have excellent paragraph structure, and each shows some imagination. Let's look at them more closely."

   - **High School:** An art teacher hands back students' pottery projects. She displays several well-done pieces and comments, "Look at these, everyone. These are excellent. Let's see why. . . . "

     The English and art teachers accomplished three things. First, the students whose paragraphs or pottery were displayed were directly reinforced, but they weren't put on the spot because the teachers didn't identify them. Second, the rest of the students in the classes were vicariously reinforced. Third, the teachers gave the classes feedback and provided models for future imitation.

4. Promote self-regulation in your students.

   - **Elementary:** A third-grade teacher helps his students design a checklist with which they can assess their own behavior. The first behavior they monitor is leaving their seats without permission. Initially, the teacher reminds them to make a check when they are out of their seats, and later he discretely monitors the students to see if they've given themselves a check. The students record a plus sign on the list for each day with no checks.

   - **Middle School:** A pre-algebra teacher helps her students create a rating scale to assess their progress on homework. For each assignment, they circle a 3 on the scale if they complete the assignment and believe they understand it, a 2 if they complete it but are uncertain about their understanding, and a 1 if they do not complete it.

   - **High School:** An English teacher helps his students set individual goals by asking each to write a study plan. He returns to the plan at the end of the unit and has each student assess his or her progress.

ADDRESSING DIVERSITY: BEHAVIORISM AND SOCIAL COGNITIVE THEORY

As Carlos enters his second-grade classroom early Tuesday morning, he hears salsa music in the background. The walls are decorated with colorful prints from Mexico and Central America, and vocabulary cards in both Spanish and English are hung around the room.

"Buenos días, Carlos. How are you today?" Donna Evans, his teacher, asks. "You're here very early."

"Buenos días. . . . I'm fine," Carlos responds, smiling as he goes to his desk to take out his homework from the night before.

Donna watches Carlos for a few moments as he works in the empty room. "What are we working on today, Carlos?"

"I can't do it! I do not understand," Carlos replies in his halting English, frustration in his voice.

Donna looks over his shoulder at the 12 math problems she had assigned for homework. He has done the first two correctly but has forgotten to borrow on the next three, and the last seven are undone.

"Carlos, look," she says, kneeling down so that she was at eye level with him. "You did the first two just fine. Look here. . . . How is this problem different from this one?" she asks, pointing to these problems:

$$36 \qquad 45$$
$$-14 \qquad -19$$

". . . The numbers . . . are different."

"Okay," she smiles. "What else?"

". . . This one is bigger," he says, pointing to the 45 and then to the 36.

"How about the 9 and the 5? . . . Which is bigger?"

". . . This," he says, pointing at the 9.

"Good, and how about the 6 and the 4?"

". . . Here," he answered and referred to the 6.

"And where is the bigger one in each case?"

". . . There," Carlos says, pointing to the 6 in the first problem, ". . . and there," pointing to the 9 in the second.

"Very good, Carlos. It is very important to know where the bigger number is," she continues. "Now let's work this one together. Watch what I do."

Donna works with Carlos to solve the next two problems, carefully describing her thinking as they go along and comparing problems that require regrouping to those that do not.

"Now try the next four on your own," she says, "and I'll be back in a few minutes to see how you're doing. . . . Remember what Juanita's father said about becoming a scientist when he came and visited our class. You have to study hard and do your math. I know you can do it, especially because you already did it on the first two. . . . Now go ahead."

Carlos nods and then bends over his work. A short while later, he is finishing the last of the four problems as the other students enter the classroom. Donna walks over to him, checks his work, and comments, "Very good, Carlos. You got three of them right. Now check this one. You have just enough time before we start."

In another elementary school in the same city, Roberto shuffles into class and hides behind the big girl in front of him. If he is lucky, his teacher won't discover that he hasn't done his homework—12 problems! How can he ever do that many? Besides, he isn't good at math.

Roberto hates school. It seems so strange and foreign. His teacher sometimes frowns when he speaks because his English isn't as good as most of the other students'. Sometimes when the teacher talks, he can't understand what she is saying.

Even lunch isn't much fun. If his friend Raul isn't there, he eats alone. One time when he sat with some other students, they started laughing at the way he talked, and they asked what he was eating. He had tortillas that day. He can't wait to go home.

As we saw in Chapter 4, for students from different cultures, schools sometimes seem strange and cold, and classrooms threatening. School tasks are difficult, and failure is common. Behaviorism and social cognitive theory can help teachers understand why schools aren't friendlier places for these students and what can be done about it.

Classical Conditioning: Learning to Like and Dislike School

At the beginning of the chapter, you saw how Sharon Van Horn greeted her students each morning in an attempt to capitalize on classical conditioning to make her classroom inviting. Donna did the same thing. Carlos had an instinctively positive emotional reaction to Donna's warmth and caring, and in time, her classroom became associated with her manner. We can all create warm and supportive learning environments for our students by the way we interact with them and with the consistent and supportive rules and procedures we establish.

Unfortunately, the opposite can also be true, as it was in Roberto's case. School was not associated with positive feelings for him, and he didn't feel wanted, safe, or comfortable.

Motivating Hesitant Learners

When students are struggling, how can appropriate use of reinforcers combined with modeling enhance their efforts? The answer to this question influences both initial learning and lifelong views of competence.

Let's look again at Donna's work with Carlos:

- She reinforced him for the problems he had done correctly.
- She provided corrective feedback to help him understand where he had made mistakes.
- She reduced the task to four problems to ensure that the reinforcement schedule would be motivating.
- She used both direct and cognitive modeling to show him the correct procedures for solving the problems.
- She helped Carlos increase his sense of accomplishment by encouraging him and by providing only enough assistance so that he could do the problems on his own.

Roberto's experience was very different. To him, the classroom was a strange and unfriendly place. His teacher didn't greet him, and nothing in the classroom made him feel welcome. When the problems seemed impossible, no one came to help. He had already "learned" that he wasn't "good" at math.

Capitalizing on Minority Role Models

Earlier, we saw that Sally Campese brought Javier Sanchez, an engineer, into her class to discuss the importance of math. Perhaps more important, Mr. Sanchez's presence provided clear evidence that a person of Hispanic background can succeed in a demanding academic field. Donna did the same thing when she invited Juanita's father into her class. Using role models in this way sends a powerful message to minority youth.

The problem of minority role models is especially acute in the teaching profession. While nearly a third of school-age children in the United States are members of cultural minorities, only 10 percent of the teaching force is minority (National Education Association, 2003). This lack of minority teachers is a problem for minority youth. First, they don't see members of minorities enjoying learning and dealing with ideas in the classroom, and second, they don't see teaching as a viable career option.

In their efforts to provide role models for minority youth, teachers often overlook the opportunity to use prominent figures from the popular press. For example, editorial columnists, such as Walter Williams and Clarence Page—both African American—are nationally syndicated, and they frequently express opinions about prosocial values, such as the need to accept responsibility for personal behavior and success. These columnists' pictures always appear with their columns, so teachers merely need to watch the newspapers and clip columns that are relevant to their goals. This strategy requires minimal effort, and again, minority youth receive a powerful message.

In Chapter 4, we examined the ways students from different backgrounds and cultures respond to schooling. In this chapter, behaviorism and social cognitive theory help us understand how teachers can use caring, reinforcement, modeling, and feedback to help all students learn successfully.

Checking Your Understanding

5.1 Using the concepts *unconditioned stimulus, unconditioned response, conditioned stimulus,* and *conditioned response,* explain how Donna Evans's room made Carlos feel good about being there.

5.2 Carlos was on which reinforcement schedule in Donna's class? Explain.

5.3 Identify specifically in the case study where Donna used direct modeling and where she used cognitive modeling in her work with Carlos.

5.4 On what type of modeling is a teacher attempting to capitalize by using clippings of syndicated columnists, such as William Raspberry? What modeling outcome is she attempting to achieve when she shows a clipping that emphasizes accepting personal responsibility? Explain.

To receive feedback for these questions, go to Appendix B.

Classroom ‖ Connections

Capitalizing on Diversity in Your Classroom

1. Make your classroom a place that welcomes all students.
   - **Elementary:** An elementary teacher invites students to bring in posters and pictures to decorate their room. On Friday afternoons during earned free time, he allows them to bring in and play music.
   - **Middle School:** An urban social studies teacher displays pictures of historical minority figures around her room. Throughout the year, she refers to these people and emphasizes that American history is the story of all people.
   - **High School:** An English teacher has his students study poetry written by people of Asian, Middle Eastern, European, African, and Native American descent. He emphasizes that people from all parts of the world have expressed themselves in poetry and that we can learn something from each of them.

2. Provide instructional support to ensure student success.
   - **Elementary:** A fifth-grade teacher uses student graders to provide immediate feedback on math assignments. Two students are chosen each week and receive answers for each day's assignment. After students have completed their work, they have it checked immediately; if their scores are below 80 percent, they see the teacher for help.
   - **Middle School:** A sixth-grade math teacher carefully discusses each day's homework. Students have the chance to repeat homework assignments to ensure that they understand the concepts and skills involved.
   - **High School:** An English teacher assigns a research paper at the beginning of the term. She breaks the assignment into parts, such as doing a literature search, making an outline, and writing a first draft. She meets with students each week to check their progress and give them feedback.

Meeting Your Learning Objectives

1. **Identify examples of classical conditioning concepts in events in and outside of classrooms.**

   - Classical conditioning occurs when a formerly neutral stimulus becomes associated with a naturally occurring (unconditioned) stimulus to produce a response similar to an instinctive or reflexive response. Classical conditioning can explain school-related events such as test anxiety, as well as outside-of-school events such as how people learn to fear riding horses if they've been thrown from a horse. It also helps us understand how these fears can be eliminated.

2. **Identify examples of operant conditioning concepts in classroom activities.**

   - Operant conditioning focuses on voluntary responses that are influenced by consequences. Consequences that increase behavior are called *reinforcers,* whereas consequences that decrease behavior are called *punishers.* The schedule of reinforcers influences both the rate of initial learning and the persistence of the behavior.
   - Antecedents precede and trigger or induce behaviors that are then usually reinforced. They exist in the form of environmental stimuli, prompts and cues, and past experiences.

3. **Use social cognitive theory concepts, such as the nonoccurrence of expected consequences, reciprocal causation, and vicarious learning, to explain examples of people's behaviors.**

   - Social cognitive theory extends behaviorism and focuses on the influence that observing others has on behavior. It considers, in addition to behavior and the environment, learners' beliefs and expectations. According to social cognitive theory, each can influence the other in a process described as reciprocal causation.
   - The nonoccurrence of expected reinforcers can act as punishers, and the nonoccurrence of expected punishers can act as reinforcers.

   - Modeling lies at the core of social cognitive theory, and vicarious learning occurs when people observe the consequences for others' actions and adjust their own behavior accordingly.

4. **Identify examples of social cognitive theory concepts, such as types of modeling, modeling outcomes, effectiveness of models, and self-regulation, in people's behaviors.**

   - Modeling can be direct (from live models), symbolic (from books, movies, and television), or synthesized (combining the acts of different models).
   - The effectiveness of models describes the likelihood of an observer's imitating a model's behavior and depends on perceived similarity, perceived status, and perceived competence.
   - Social cognitive theory also helps explain events such as why teachers' describing their thought processes as they demonstrate skills is effective, and why students who set goals, monitor progress toward the goals, and assess the extent to which the goals are met achieve higher than peers who don't.

5. **Identify examples of behaviorist and social cognitive theory concepts in teachers' work with students from diverse backgrounds.**

   - Behaviorism helps us understand why teachers who treat their students with courtesy and respect create classroom environments that are inviting for all students regardless of their racial, cultural, or ethnic backgrounds.
   - Social cognitive theory helps us understand why minority role models, both direct and symbolic, can be effective for promoting desirable personal characteristics, such as accepting personal responsibility and displaying prosocial behaviors.

Praxis™ Practice   *Developing*  *as a* **Professional**

You've seen how we can use classical and operant conditioning, modeling, vicarious learning, and self-regulation to explain the behavior of students. Let's look now at a teacher attempting to apply some of these concepts as he works with his middle school students. Read the case study, and answer the questions that follow.

Warren Rose, a seventh-grade math teacher, has his students involved in a unit on decimals and percentages. He begins class on Thursday by saying, "All right, let's review what we did yesterday."

Hearing some mumbles, he notes wryly, "I realize that percentages and decimals aren't your favorite topic, and I'm not wild about them either, but we have no choice, so we might as well buckle down and learn them."

"Let's start by looking at a few examples," he continues, displaying the following problem on the overhead:

You are at the mall, shopping for a jacket. You see one that looks great, originally priced at $84, marked 25% off. You recently got a check for $65 from the fast-food restaurant where you work. Can you afford the jacket?

"Now, . . . the first thing I think about when I see a problem like this one is, 'What does the jacket cost now?' I have to figure out the price, and to do that I will take 25% of the $84. . . . That means I first convert the 25% to a decimal. I know when I see 25% that the decimal is understood to be just to the right of the 5, so I move it two places to the left. Then I can multiply 0.25 times 84."

Warren demonstrates the process as he speaks, working the problem through to completion. He has his students work several examples at their desks and discusses their solutions.

He then continues, "Okay, for homework, do the odd problems on page 113."

"Do we have to do all six of them?" Robbie asks.

"Why not?" Warren responds.

"Aww, gee, Mr. Rose," Will puts in, "they're so hard."

"Yes," Ginny adds. "And they take so long."

Several other students chime in, arguing that six word problems were too many.

"Wait, people, please," Warren holds up his hands. "All right. You only have to do 1, 3, 5, 7, and 9."

"Yeah!" the class shouts.

"Yikes, Friday," Helen comments to Jenny as they walk into Warren's room Friday morning. "I, like, blanked out last week, and I felt like an idiot. Now, I get so nervous when he makes us go up to the board, and everybody's staring at us. If he calls me up today, I'll die."

Warren discusses the day's homework and then says, "Okay, let's look at this problem."

A bicycle selling for $145 is marked down 15%. What is the new selling price?

"First, let's estimate, so that we can see whether our answer makes sense. About what should the new selling price be? . . . Pamela?"

". . . I'm not sure," Pamela says.

"Callie, what do you think?"

"I think it would be about $120."

"Good thinking. Describe for everyone how you arrived at that."

"Well, 10% would be $14.50, . . . so 15% would be about another $7. That would be about $21, and $21 off would be a little over $120."

"Good," Warren nods. "Now, let's go ahead and solve it. What do we do first? . . . David?"

". . . We make the 15% into a decimal."

"Good, David. Now, what next? . . . Leslie?"

"Take the 0.15 times the 145."

"Okay. Do that everybody. . . . What did you get?"

". . . $200.17," Cris volunteers. "Whoops, that can't be right. That's more than the bicycle cost to start with. . . . Wait. . . . $21.75."

"Good," Warren smiles. "That's what we're trying to do. We are all going to make mistakes, but if we catch ourselves, we're making progress. Keep it up. You can do these problems. Now what do we do?" he continues.

"Subtract," Matt volunteers.

"All right, go ahead," Warren directs.

Warren finishes guiding students through the problem, has them do two additional problems, and then begins to assign 5 problems for homework. Just as he starts, several students chime in, "How about just four problems tonight, Mr. Rose. We always have so much math to do."

"Okay," Warren shrugs, "numbers 2, 6, 7, and 8 on page 114."

Warren continues monitoring the students until 2 minutes are left in the period. "All right, everyone, the bell will ring in 2 minutes. Get everything cleaned up around your desks, and get ready to go."

Short-Answer Questions

In answering these questions, use information from Chapter 6, and link your responses to specific information in the case.

1. Describe where classical conditioning occurred in the case study. Identify the classical conditioning concepts in your description.
2. Warren allowed himself to be punished in two different places in the case study. Explain where they occurred, and describe their likely impact on learning.
3. Warren inadvertently negatively reinforced the students at two points in the lesson. Identify and explain both points.
4. Warren's modeling had both effective and ineffective features. Identify and explain one effective and one ineffective feature.
5. Warren capitalized on the effects of perceived similarity and vicarious learning in the case study. Explain where and how this occurred.

PRAXIS These exercises are designed to help you prepare for the Praxis™ Principles of Learning and Teaching exam. To receive feedback on your short-answer questions, go to the Companion Website at *www.prenhall. com/eggen*, then to the *Practice for Praxis™* module for Chapter 6.

To acquire experience in preparing for the multiple-choice items on the Praxis™ exam, go to the *Self-Assessment* module for Chapter 6 at *www.prenhall.com/eggen* and click on "Practice Quiz."

For additional connections between this text and the Praxis™ exam, go to Appendix A.

ONLINE PORTFOLIO ACTIVITIES

To develop your professional portfolio, further apply your understanding of chapter content, and address the INTASC standards, go to the Companion Website, then to the *Online Portfolio Activities* for Chapter 6. Complete the suggested activities.

Also on the Companion Website at *www.prenhall.com/ eggen*, you can measure your understanding of chapter content with multiple-choice and essay questions, and broaden your knowledge base in *Exploring Further* and *Web Links* to other educational psychology websites.

IMPORTANT CONCEPTS

antecedents (p. 174)
applied behavior analysis (ABA) (p. 175)
behaviorism (p. 164)
classical conditioning (p. 165)
cognitive behavior modification (p. 187)
cognitive modeling (p. 182)
conditioned response (p. 165)
conditioned stimulus (p. 165)
consequences (p. 168)
continuous reinforcement schedule (p. 170)
desists (p. 173)
discrimination (p. 166)
extinction (classical conditioning) (p. 167)
extinction (operant conditioning) (p. 172)
functional analysis (p. 177)
generalization (p. 166)
inhibition (p. 184)
intermittent reinforcement schedule
　(p. 171)
interval schedules (p. 171)
learning (behaviorist) (p. 164)
learning (cognitive) (p. 180)
modeling (p. 181)

negative reinforcement (p. 169)
operant conditioning (p. 168)
positive reinforcement (p. 169)
Premack principle (p. 169)
presentation punishment (p. 172)
punishers (p. 172)
punishment (p. 172)
ratio schedules (p. 171)
reciprocal causation (p. 181)
reinforcement (p. 169)
reinforcement schedules (p. 170)
reinforcer (p. 168)
removal punishment (p. 173)
response cost (p. 173)
satiation (p. 172)
self-regulation (p. 186)
shaping (p. 170)
social cognitive theory (p. 180)
timeout (p. 173)
unconditioned response (p. 165)
unconditioned stimulus (p. 165)
vicarious learning (p. 182)

CHAPTER 7

Cognitive Views of Learning

Chapter Outline	Learning Objectives
	After you have completed your study of this chapter, you should be able to
Cognitive Perspectives on Learning Principles of Cognitive Learning Theory • A Definition of Learning	**1** Describe the principles on which cognitive learning theories are based, and identify illustrations of the principles.
Memory Stores in Our Information Processing System Sensory Memory • Working Memory • Long-Term Memory	**2** Use the characteristics of the memory stores in our information processing system to explain events in and out of the classroom.
Cognitive Processes in Our Information Processing System Attention: The Beginning of Information Processing • Perception: Finding Meaning in Stimuli • Rehearsal: Retaining Information Through Repetition • Meaningful Encoding: Making Connections in Long-Term Memory • Forgetting	**3** Describe the cognitive processes in our information processing system, and identify examples of the processes in classroom events.
Metacognition: Knowledge and Control of Cognitive Processes The Development of Metacognition	**4** Define metacognition and identify examples of metacognition in classroom events.
Information Processing in the Classroom: Instructional Principles The Impact of Diversity on Information Processing • Putting Information Processing Into Perspective	**5** Describe the principles for applying information processing theory in classrooms, and identify examples of the principles in learning activities.

Cognitive learning theory helps us understand the thought processes involved as people respond to stimuli from the environment, make sense of it, and store it in memory. As you read the following case study, keep the students' thinking in mind and consider how the teacher supported that thinking.

David Shelton has his ninth-grade earth science class working in a unit on the solar system. He has prepared a transparency showing the sun throwing globs of gases into space, another representing a model of the solar system that illustrates the planets in their orbital planes, and a large matrix taped to the back wall of the room.

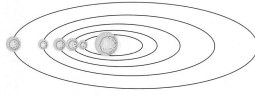

David introduces the unit on Monday by displaying and explaining the transparencies, emphasizing that the first relates to one theory of the formation of the solar system. He then assigns groups to gather information for the chart, using the Internet and books available in the classroom. With David's guidance, the students spend the rest of Monday and all period Tuesday collecting and putting information into the chart. (The completed chart appears on p. 215.)

On Wednesday David begins by saying, "I'm going to do a little demonstration, and I want you to think about how it relates to what you've been doing." He ties a pair of athletic socks to a 3-foot piece of string, another pair to a 5-foot string, tells the students to think of the socks as planets, and whirls the two around his head simultaneously to demonstrate that the planets revolve around the sun on the same plane and in the same direction.

After the class makes observations, he continues, "Now our jobs get a bit more challenging. Today I want each group to identify a piece of information from the chart that can be explained with information from a different part of the chart, like why Mercury is so hot on one side and so cold on another. Write the item of information, and then write your explanation immediately below it."

He reminds them to keep his demonstration and the information from the transparencies in mind, and the groups go to work. As they work, David moves from group to group, answering questions and making suggestions.

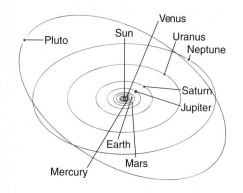

One Theory of How the Solar System Was Formed

Transparency model of the solar system

"Pluto wasn't part of the solar system to begin with," Juan comments to Randy and Tanya in one group.

"What do you mean?" Randy wonders.

"I was watching 'Nova' with my mom, and the person talking said that scientists think Pluto was an asteroid, or some other body floating around, and the sun kind of grabbed it. . . . See, when Mr. Shelton did that thing with the socks, they stayed sort of level," he continues, moving his hand back and forth to demonstrate a plane.

"What's that got to do with it?" Randy asks, still uncertain.

"Well, look," Juan says, pointing to the model on the second transparency, which David has left displayed at the front of the room.

"Gee, I didn't even notice that," Randy shrugs.

"Oh, I get it, now! . . . Pluto isn't level with the rest of them," Tanya jumps in. "I got kinda lost when Mr. Shelton was explaining all that Monday, but now it makes sense. . . . And look there," she says, pointing to the chart. "See how small Pluto is? It's the littlest, so it would be easy to capture."

"And it's the last one," Randy adds, beginning to warm to the task. "I better write some of this stuff down, or I'll never remember it."

To begin our discussion, let's consider three questions: (1) Why was Juan able to make connections between the different items of information they were studying that Randy and Tanya were initially unable to make? (2) Why did Tanya get "kinda lost when Mr. Shelton was explaining all that on Monday?" (3) What impact will Randy's decision to "write some of this stuff down" have on his future learning? We answer these and other questions in this chapter.

COGNITIVE PERSPECTIVES ON LEARNING

To begin this section, read the following passage:

Aoccdring to rscheearch at Cmabrigde Uinervtisy, it deosn't mttaer in waht oredr the ltteers in a word are, the olny iprmoetnt tihng is that the frist and lsat ltteer be at the rghit pclae. The rset can be a total mses and you can still raed it wouthit porbelm.

The fact that we can read this note—widely circulated on the Internet—with little difficulty demonstrates that learning and memory are more complex than responses to the environment, as behaviorism would require, or than actions based on observing the behavior of others, as suggested by social cognitive theory. Also, neither theory adequately explains Juan's ability to make connections in the information he was studying that neither Tanya nor Randy were able to make.

In addition to examples such as these, research conducted during World War II examining the development of complex skills, the inability of behaviorism to adequately explain how people learn language (Chomsky, 1959), and the development of computers all led to a search for alternative explanations for people's behaviors (Schunk, 2004). The result was the "cognitive revolution," which marked a shift away from behaviorism and toward cognitive theories of learning. It occurred some time between the mid-1950s and early 1970s (Bruning et al., 2004), and its influence on education has steadily increased since that time (Greeno et al., 1996; R. Mayer, 1996).

Principles of Cognitive Learning Theory

Cognitive learning theories explain learning by focusing on changes in mental processes and constructs that occur as a result of people's efforts to make sense of the world. These theories help us explain tasks as simple as remembering a phone number and as complex as solving ill-defined problems.

Most researchers agree that cognitive learning theories are grounded in the following principles:

- People are mentally active in their attempts to understand how the world works.
- Learning and development depend on learners' experiences.
- Learners construct—they do not record—knowledge in an attempt to make sense of those experiences.
- Knowledge that is constructed depends on knowledge that learners already possess.
- Learning is enhanced in a social environment.
- Learning requires practice and feedback.

Learners Are Mentally Active

Cognitive learning theories are grounded in the belief that learners are active in their attempts to understand how the world works, and as we saw in Chapter 2, this belief is consistent with both Piaget's (1952, 1959) and Vygotsky's (1978, 1986) views of cognitive development. Learners do much more than simply respond to reinforcers and punishers: They search for information that helps them answer questions, they modify their understanding based on new knowledge, and they change their behavior in response to their increased understanding. Cognitive learning theorists view humans as "goal-directed agents who actively seek information" (Bransford et al., 2000, p. 10).

This tendency was illustrated in the students' interaction and particularly in Tanya's comment, "Oh, I get it, now! . . . Pluto isn't level with the rest of them. . . . I got kinda lost when Mr. Shelton was explaining all that on Monday, but now it makes sense." She was active in her attempt to understand the ideas they were studying.

Learning and Development Depend on Learners' Experiences

The principle that learning and development depend on learners' experiences is self-evident, and we saw it illustrated in the students' discussion. The information they were gathering, together with David's transparencies and demonstration, all provided them with experience. Acquiring an understanding of the solar system without these experiences would literally be impossible. We also saw the influence of experience in Juan's and Randy's comments during the group work. Because Juan had experiences (watching *Nova*) that Randy lacked, he was able to make connections beyond those Randy made.

Learners Construct Knowledge

Learners don't behave like tape recorders, recording in their memories—in the form in which it is presented—everything someone, such as a teacher, tells them or everything they

Cognitive learning theories.
Explanations for learning that focus on changes in mental processes and constructs that occur as a result of people's efforts to make sense of the world

read. Instead, in an instinctive attempt to understand how the world works, people construct knowledge and understanding that makes sense to them (Greeno et al., 1996; R. Mayer, 1998b, 2002). We examine the process of knowledge construction in detail in Chapter 8.

Knowledge That Is Constructed Depends on Learners' Prior Knowledge

People don't construct knowledge in a vacuum; it depends on what they already know. For instance, some children continue to believe that the earth is flat even after teachers explain that it is a sphere. The children picture a pancake-like flat surface inside or on top of a sphere (Vosniadou & Brewer, 1989). They reason that people can't walk on a ball, and visualizing a flat surface—an idea children know and understand—helps them explain how people can stand or walk on the earth's surface. This example also helps us see why explaining, by itself, is often ineffective for changing learners' understanding.

The principle of knowledge constructs' depending on prior knowledge also helps answer our first question at the beginning of this chapter about Juan's ability to make connections that the other students could not. As a result of his experiences, such as watching *Nova* with his mother, Juan was able to find relationships (construct knowledge) that Tanya and Randy were initially unable to find.

Learning Is Enhanced in a Social Environment

Many researchers now believe that social interaction is an essential element in learning (Bruning et al., 2004; Meter & Stevens, 2000). Again we see this principle illustrated in the students' interactions. Tanya and Randy both heard David explain the information on the transparencies, and they all saw the same demonstration. Yet they didn't find the connections in the information until they discussed it.

Learning Requires Practice and Feedback

People learn to do well only what they practice doing (Ashcraft, 2001; Craig, 2003; Schunk, 2004). This principle is also self-evident and is supported by neurological studies (Craig, 2003). To shoot baskets accurately, we practice shooting; to become skilled writers, we practice writing; to solve problems effectively, we solve many problems. The same is true for all learning. Discussing ideas is a form of practice, and the more David's students discussed and worked with the information they were studying, the deeper their understanding became.

Feedback is information about existing understanding used to increase future understanding. As learners construct understanding, they use additional information to determine the extent to which their understanding is valid. For instance, if a child's understanding of dogs is based on experience with his family's gentle, lovable pooch, he is likely to conclude that all dogs are friendly. When he encounters one that growls and nips his hand, he will revise his understanding and conclude that some dogs are friendly but others aren't. The growl and nip are feedback the child uses to revise his understanding.

As with practice, this is true for all learning. One of teachers' most important roles is to provide students with feedback that can help them arrive at more sophisticated understanding. In this regard, feedback is additional experience that learners use to enhance their learning.

A Definition of Learning

In contrast with a focus on observable behaviors, as we saw in our discussion of behaviorism in Chapter 6, cognitive theorists define **learning** as a change in a person's mental structures that creates the capacity to demonstrate different behaviors. The phrase "creates the capacity" reminds us that learning can occur without any immediate change in behavior; evidence of the change in mental structures may occur sometime later.

The *mental structures* that change include beliefs, goals, expectations, and other components "in the learner's head." In David's lesson, for example, Randy consciously thought about his need to take notes; and Tanya, Randy, and Juan all connected information from the chart, transparencies, and demonstration into mental relationships. Neither behaviorism nor social cognitive theory can adequately explain these efforts.

How is information "in the learner's head" acquired, and how is it stored? Information processing, one of the first and most thoroughly researched cognitive descriptions of learning, helps answer the question (J. R. Anderson, 2005; Sternberg, 2003a).

Feedback. Information about existing understanding that is used to enhance future understanding

Learning. A change in people's mental structures that creates the capacity to demonstrate different behaviors

Figure 7.1 An information processing model

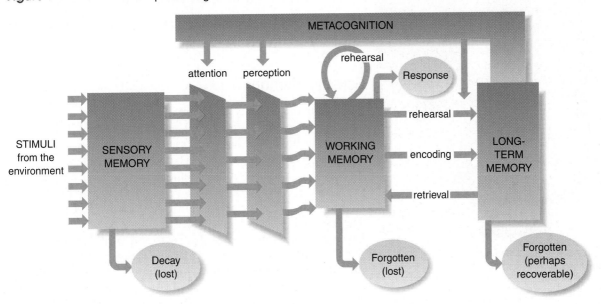

Information processing is a theory of learning that explains how stimuli that enter our memory systems are selected and organized for storage and are retrieved from memory. The most prominent cognitive learning theory of the 20th century, it has important implications for teaching today (R. Mayer, 1998b, 1999). The model in Figure 7.1 represents a current view of how cognitive psychologists think the mind processes information (R. Atkinson & Shiffrin, 1968; Leahey & Harris, 2001; Schunk, 2004).

The information processing model has three major components:

- Memory stores
- Cognitive processes
- Metacognition

Some researchers describe the combination of these components as our "cognitive architecture" (Paas, Renkl, & Sweller, 2004; Sweller, van Merrienboer, & Pass, 1998). Just as the architecture of a building is the structure in which its activities occur, our information processing system is the framework within which information is acquired, moved, and stored. We examine these components in the following sections.

Exploring Further

We described Figure 7.1 as a model. To see a more detailed discussion of models, go to "Different Types of Models" in the *Exploring Further* module of Chapter 7 at *www.prenhall.com/eggen*.

Information processing. A theory of learning that explains how stimuli that enter our memory systems are selected and organized for storage and are retrieved from memory

Checking Your Understanding

1.1 Describe and explain the six principles of cognitive learning theories.

1.2 You and a friend are trying to install a sound card in your computer, but you're a little uncertain about how to do it. You open the cabinet, look inside, and as you talk about how to proceed, she suggests looking to see where the speakers are attached. "Good idea," you say, and you easily install the card. Which principle of learning is best illustrated by this example?

1.3 Research indicates that properly designed homework increases learning (H. Cooper, Lindsay, Nye, & Greathouse, 1998; Stein & Carnine, 1999). To which principle of learning is this research most closely related?

To receive feedback for these questions, go to Appendix B.

Knowledge Extensions

To deepen your understanding of the topics in this section of the chapter and integrate them with topics you've already studied, go to the *Knowledge Extensions* module for Chapter 7 at *www.prenhall.com/eggen*. Respond to questions 1–3.

Working memory is the "workbench" where students think about and solve problems.

MEMORY STORES IN OUR INFORMATION PROCESSING SYSTEM

Memory stores are repositories that hold information in our information processing system. They are *sensory memory, working memory,* and *long-term memory.*

Sensory Memory

Hold your finger in front of you, and rapidly wiggle it. You'll see a faint "shadow" that trails behind your finger as it moves. This shadow is the image of your finger that has been briefly stored in your visual sensory memory. Likewise, when someone says, "That's an oxymoron," you retain "Ox see moron" in your auditory sensory memory, even if it has no meaning for you.

The first part, **sensory memory,** is the store that briefly holds incoming stimuli from the environment until they can be processed (Neisser, 1967). The material in sensory memory is "thought to be completely unorganized, basically a perceptual copy of objects and events in the world" (Leahey & Harris, 2001, p. 139). Sensory memory is nearly unlimited in capacity, but if processing doesn't begin almost immediately, the memory trace quickly fades away. Sensory memory is estimated to retain information for about 1 second for vision and 2 to 4 seconds for hearing (Leahey & Harris, 2001; Pashler & Carrier, 1996).

Sensory memory is the beginning point for further processing. In reading, for example, it would be impossible to get meaning from a sentence if the words at the beginning were lost from your visual sensory memory before you got to the end. The same is true for spoken language. Sensory memory holds information until you attach meaning to it and transfer it to working memory, the next store.

Working Memory

Working memory is the store that holds information as a person processes it (Baddeley, 2001). Working memory is the conscious part of our information processing system; deliberate thinking occurs in our working memory (Paas et al., 2004). We aren't aware of the contents of either sensory memory or long-term memory until they're pulled into working memory for processing.

Limitations of Working Memory

The most striking feature of working memory is its limitations (Ashcraft, 2001). It can hold only about seven items of information at a time (G. Miller, 1956), and it holds the information for a relatively short period (about 10 to 20 seconds for adults), particularly when new information is being received. Selecting and organizing information also take up working memory space, so usually we "are probably only able to deal with two or three items of information simultaneously when required to process rather than merely hold information" (Sweller et al., 1998, p. 252).

These limitations are important because working memory is where we make conscious decisions about how to link new information from the environment to our existing knowledge (R. C. Clark & Mayer, 2003; E. Smith, 1999). For example, in attempting to solve the problem "What is the area of a triangle whose base is 3 feet and height is 2 feet?" we must (a) retrieve the formula for finding the area of a triangle ($A = \frac{1}{2}bh$; 1/2 the length of the base times the height) from long-term memory; (b) put the appropriate values into the formula; and (c) calculate the answer. This all occurs in working memory. This is a simple problem; imagine the load on working memory when problems are ill-defined and complex.

The characteristics of working memory are summarized in Figure 7.2.

The limited capacity of working memory has important implications for teaching and learning. Consider the following research results:

■ Students' writing often improves more rapidly if they are initially allowed to ignore grammar, punctuation, and spelling (Graham, Berninger, Weintraub, & Schafer, 1998; McCutchen, 2000).

Memory stores. Repositories that hold information in our information processing system

Sensory memory. The memory store that briefly holds stimuli from the environment until they can be processed

Working memory. The conscious part of our information processing system; the memory store that holds information as people process it

Figure 7.2   Characteristics of working memory

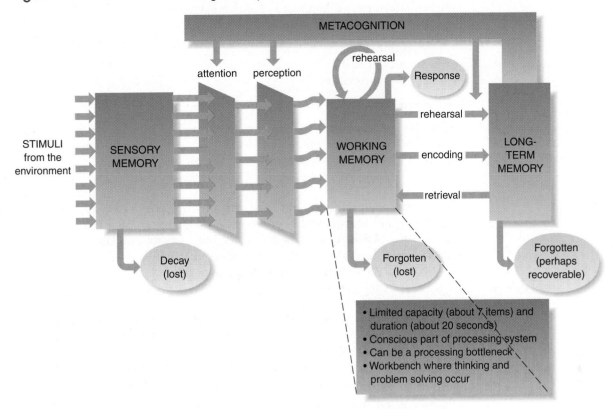

- Students write better essays using word processors if their word processing skills are well developed. If not, handwritten essays are superior (Roblyer, 2006).
- In spite of research about its ineffectiveness and enormous staff-development efforts to promote more sophisticated forms of instruction, lecturing persists as the most common teaching strategy (Cuban, 1993).

How is working memory related to these situations? The answer exists in the concept of **cognitive load,** which refers to the amount of mental activity imposed on working memory. One factor that contributes to cognitive load is the number of elements that must be attended to (Paas et al., 2004). For instance, remembering the sequence of digits 7 9 5 3 has a cognitive load of 4 and remembering the sequence 3 9 2 4 6 7 1 5 has a cognitive load of 8. The rapid pace of instruction in many classrooms often overextends our working memories, which can only accommodate a cognitive load of approximately 7 elements.

A second factor influencing cognitive load is the extent to which the elements are related to and interact with one another (Paas et al., 2004). For instance, attempting to incorporate new vocabulary in writing, while at the same time using correct grammar, punctuation, and spelling, imposes a heavy cognitive load on the writer. This is one reason why learning to write is so difficult. Beginning writers are attempting to juggle too many cognitive balls in working memory. Similarly, using sophisticated teaching strategies imposes a heavy cognitive load on teachers. If the load becomes too great, working memory cannot accommodate it, and teachers simplify by lecturing, a less cognitively demanding, but also less effective, instructional strategy.

Reducing the cognitive load by allowing students to ignore spelling, grammar, and punctuation, as we saw in the first example, or reverting to lecture as we saw in the third, is one way to accommodate the limitations of working memory. These compromises are often undesirable, however, because students must ultimately learn to spell and use correct grammar and punctuation in their writing and because teachers are encouraged to use techniques other than lecture. We examine some accommodation strategies in the next section.

Cognitive load. The amount of mental activity imposed on working memory

Reducing Cognitive Load: Overcoming the Limitations of Working Memory

Accommodating the limitations of working memory by reducing cognitive load can be accomplished in three primary ways:

- Chunking
- Automaticity
- Dual processing

Let's look at them.

Chunking. Chunking is the process of mentally combining separate items into larger, more meaningful units (G. Miller, 1956). As an illustration, try this simple exercise. Look at the following row of letters for 5 seconds:

A E E E G G I I I I L N N N N R R S S T T

Now cover the row, and try to write down the 21 letters. How did you do? Even though the letters are in alphabetical order, all but two are repeated and grouped together, and people are told there are 21 letters in all, most cannot remember the entire list, because the cognitive load exceeds working memory's capacity.

Now look at the same letters presented as follows:

LEARNING IS INTERESTING

The letters now are simple to remember because they have been "chunked" into three meaningful words (three units) and into a meaningful sentence (one unit), so the cognitive load has been significantly reduced.

Table 7.1 presents other examples of chunking. In each case, remembering the chunk lowers the cognitive load to the point where it doesn't exceed the capacity of working memory.

Automaticity. A second way of reducing cognitive load is to make the processes involved in a task automatic. **Automaticity** is the performance of mental operations with little awareness or conscious effort (Bruning et al., 2004; W. Schneider & Shiffrin, 1977). Computer keyboarding skill is an example of its power and efficiency. Once our word processing capabilities become automatic, we can devote our working memory space to the composition of our writing. Until then, we must devote working memory to placing our hands on the keys, and the cognitive load becomes too great to compose quality products. This explains why students compose better essays on word processors but only if they are skilled with word processing.

Earlier in our discussion, we said that students' writing often improves more rapidly if they are initially allowed to ignore grammar, spelling, and punctuation, and we also said that lecture continues to be the most common teaching strategy. Automaticity helps resolve these issues. In the first case, if grammar, spelling, and punctuation skills are developed to automaticity, cognitive load is reduced, and students can devote their working memory space to the content of their writing. For classroom instruction, developing essential teaching skills, such as questioning, to automaticity, also reduces cognitive load, which allows teachers to use more sophisticated strategies such as guided discovery and classroom discussions in their instruction.

Automaticity has important implications for your growth as a teacher. Expert teachers create well-practiced routines and practice essential skills, such as questioning, until they become automatic.

Dual Processing. Some researchers suggest that working memory is composed of a visual component that holds and processes visual information and a second component that does

Chunking. The process of mentally combining separate items into larger, more meaningful units

Automaticity. Performing mental operations with little awareness or conscious effort

Table 7.1 Saving working memory space through chunking

Information Unchunked	Information Chunked
u, n, r	run
2492520	24 9 25 20
I, v, o, I, o, u, e, y	I love you.
seeletsthiswhyworks	Let's see why this works.

the same with verbal information (Baddeley, 2001; R. C. Clark & Mayer, 2003). Though limited in capacity, each part works independently and additively (R. Mayer, 1997, 1998a; Sweller et al., 1998). This suggests that students learn more if verbal explanations are supplemented with visual representations (R. C. Clark & Mayer, 2003; Moreno & Duran, 2004). The visual processor supplements the verbal processor and vice versa. "[I]nformation processing is easier when to-be-learned information is distributed in working memory" (Bruning et al., 2004, p. 34).

Unfortunately, teachers often use words, alone, to present information, wasting some of working memory's processing capability and often imposing a cognitive load greater than working memory's capacity. As a result, learning is reduced.

To understand how dual processing helps students remember, think back to David's lesson. He used visuals—color transparencies and a matrix—while he discussed them with his students. "The integration of words and pictures is made easier by lessons that present the verbal and visual information together rather than separated" (R. C. Clark & Mayer, 2003, p. 38). A simultaneous presentation of visual and verbal information provides two routes to representing information in memory (R. Mayer, 1997).

Long-Term Memory

Our ultimate goal in teaching is to have students encode information in long-term memory. (We discuss encoding later in the chapter.) **Long-term memory** is our permanent information store. It's like a library with millions of entries and a network that allows them to be retrieved for reference and use (Schacter, 2001). It differs from working memory in both capacity and duration. Whereas working memory is limited to approximately seven items of information for a matter of seconds, long-term memory's capacity is vast and durable. Some experts suggest that information in it remains for a lifetime (Schunk, 2004).

One of the most widely accepted descriptions of long-term memory differentiates between **declarative knowledge**—knowledge of facts, definitions, procedures, and rules—and **procedural knowledge**—knowledge of how to perform tasks (J. R. Anderson, 2005; Hergenhahn & Olson, 2001). For example, a learner who says, "To add fractions, you must first have like denominators," knows the rule for adding fractions but might not be able to actually do the computation. Knowing the rule is a form of declarative knowledge; adding the fractions requires procedural knowledge. Declarative knowledge can be determined directly from a person's comments, whereas procedural knowledge is inferred from the person's performance. To develop procedural knowledge, students must practice skills, such as adding fractions or writing essays, and must receive feedback about their performance. Talking about or explaining the skills isn't sufficient.

Representing Declarative Knowledge in Memory: Schemas

Declarative knowledge is stored in long-term memory in the form of **schemas** (also called *schemata*), cognitive constructs that organize information into meaningful systems (J. R. Anderson, 2005; Schunk, 2004; D. T. Willingham, 2004).

As an example, look at Figure 7.3, which helps us visualize Randy's and Juan's schemas for the solar system. Note that schemas are actually structures "in people's heads" that have been constructed, hence the term *construct*. Figure 7.3 merely helps us visualize these structures. Both Randy's and Juan's schemas organize information into a system that makes sense to them. However, important differences exist in the two. For instance, both contain 10 individual elements, but Randy's has only 6 "links" in it, compared to 12 in Juan's. Juan's system is more **meaningful,** which describes the extent to which individual elements of a schema are interconnected (Gagne et al., 1997).

Meaningfulness: Reducing Cognitive Load on Working Memory. We are discussing schemas, and we know that schemas are stored in long-term memory. So, why are we again discussing working memory and cognitive load? Here is why: If the schemas stored in long-term memory are meaningful, they reduce cognitive load when they are retrieved back into working memory for further processing. "Although the number of elements is limited, the size, complexity, and sophistication of elements [are] not" (Sweller et al., 1998, p. 256). This is illustrated in Juan's and Randy's schemas as we saw earlier. Because all the items in Juan's are interconnected, it behaves as one chunk (Bransford et al., 2000), so it takes up only one slot when he retrieves it back into working memory. Because Randy's is less

Long-term memory. The permanent information store in our information processing system

Declarative knowledge. Knowledge of facts, definitions, procedures, and rules

Procedural knowledge. Knowledge of how to perform tasks

Schemas. Cognitive constructs that organize information into a meaningful system

Meaningfulness. The extent to which individual elements of a schema are interconnected

Figure 7.3   Schemas illustrating Randy's (on the left) and Juan's understanding

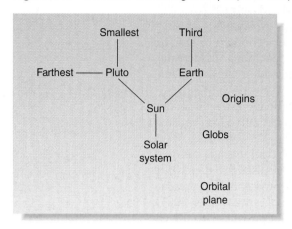

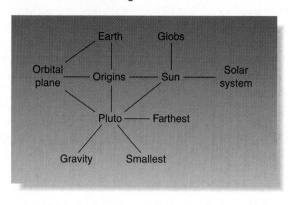

connected, it takes up four: one for the seven interconnected items and one each for *origins, globs,* and *orbital plane.* When Randy thought about the origins of our solar system, the cognitive load on his working memory was greater than the load on Juan's, making additional processing more difficult for him. This is illustrated in their dialogue.

Juan: Pluto wasn't part of the solar system to begin with.
Randy: What do you mean?
Juan: I was watching *Nova* with my mom, and the person talking said that scientists think Pluto was an asteroid, or some other body floating around, and the sun kind of grabbed it. . . . See, when Mr. Shelton did that thing with the socks, they stayed sorta level.
Randy: What's that got to do with it?
Juan: Well, look. (pointing to the model on the transparency)
Randy: Gee, I didn't even notice that.

Randy didn't "notice," because the cognitive load on his working memory was greater, leaving little room for thinking and making his learning inefficient.

Meaningfulness and Cognitive Load: Implications for Teaching and Learning. Understanding why Juan's and Randy's thinking was different has important implications for us as teachers: *We shouldn't teach individual items of information in isolation; rather, items should be taught as interconnected ideas.* Isolated information imposes a heavy load on students' working memories, which helps explain why they seem to retain so little of what they're taught. In contrast, connecting ideas to each other reduces the load, makes the information more meaningful, and increases learning by providing more places to connect new information. We saw this illustrated in Juan's thinking. He had prior knowledge that Randy didn't possess, which made understanding the new ideas easier for him. Earlier in the chapter, we saw that the way people construct new knowledge depends on their existing knowledge, and the better organized this knowledge is, the easier it is to build upon (Nuthall, 1999b, 2000).

Meaningfulness also has implications for us as learners. When we study, we should look for relationships in the material we're studying instead of learning ideas in isolation. This explains why memorizing definitions and other individual items of information is an ineffective study strategy.

Schemas as Scripts. In addition to organizing information into meaningful systems, schemas can also guide our actions. For example, when students first enter a college class, they may ask questions such as

- What are the instructor's expectations?
- What are the course requirements?
- How should I prepare for quizzes and other assessments?
- How will I interact with my peers?

Answers to these questions come from scripts, developed over years of experience. **Scripts,** which are "schema representations for *events*" (Bruning et al., 2004, p. 53), provide plans for action in particular situations. For example, you have a script that guides your behavior as you prepare for, attend, and participate in your classes. In this regard, scripts also contain procedural knowledge, which we consider next.

Representing Procedural Knowledge in Memory: Conditions and Actions

Earlier, we said that procedural knowledge involves knowing how to perform tasks. In using procedural knowledge, learners must adapt their actions to different task demands or conditions (J. R. Anderson, 2005; Star, 2004). For example, when adding fractions, if the denominators are the same, we merely add the numerators. If they differ, we must find a common denominator and then add the numerators. The conditions for adding fractions with like—compared to unlike—denominators differ, so being able to add them correctly depends on recognizing these conditions and acting appropriately.

The effectiveness of procedural knowledge depends on declarative knowledge; for example, students must first understand fractions and the rules for adding them before they can adapt to the different conditions. As another example, you will practice both classroom management and questioning skills as you move through your teacher preparation program, but you must understand the principles of sound management and the characteristics of effective questioning, or you won't know how to practice most efficiently. This is why you study theories of learning in this class; they help you understand when and why different strategies are effective.

Learners develop effective procedural knowledge by actively applying content in different contexts.

Developing Procedural Knowledge. Procedural knowledge is developed in three stages: declarative, associative, and automatic (J. R. Anderson, 2005; Gagne et al., 1997).

In the *declarative stage,* students simply acquire declarative knowledge about the procedure. For example, in word processing they learn where to place the fingers on a keyboard, or in the case of fractions, they learn the rules for adding, subtracting, multiplying, and dividing them. Some researchers call this stage *planning knowledge,* emphasizing an understanding of the steps to be followed (Star, 2002). Though this stage is essential for subsequent actions, learners cannot perform the procedure in the declarative stage.

During the *associative stage,* learners can perform the procedure but must think about what they are doing, and their thoughts place a heavy cognitive load on their working memories (J. R. Anderson, 2005). As we saw earlier, novice typists composing essays focus most of their working memory on correctly using the keyboard during this stage, making high-quality written products difficult.

With additional practice, learners finally move to the *automatic stage,* where they can perform the process with little conscious thought. Because of automaticity, cognitive load is reduced, allowing most of the typists' working memory, for example, to focus on what they're composing.

Developing Procedural Knowledge: Implications for Learning and Teaching. The stages involved in developing procedural knowledge have two important implications for learning and teaching. First, reaching the automatic stage requires a great deal of time and effort (Bruning et al., 2004), so students must be provided with ample opportunities to practice. Research indicates that complex procedural knowledge, such as the ability to speak and write a foreign language, continues to improve even after thousands of hours of practice (Bruning et al., 2004). This helps us understand the principle "Learning requires practice and feedback," which we discussed earlier in the chapter.

Second, the way procedural knowledge is developed helps us understand why context is so important (Star, 2004). For example, when learning to use grammar and punctuation rules in writing, learners should practice in the context of their own writing, instead of isolated sentences. Having students complete decontextualized exercises, such as commonly occur in worksheets, doesn't give them practice identifying different conditions and applying the appropriate actions.

Scripts. Schema representations for events, providing plans for action in particular situations

Figure 7.4   Characteristics of long-term memory

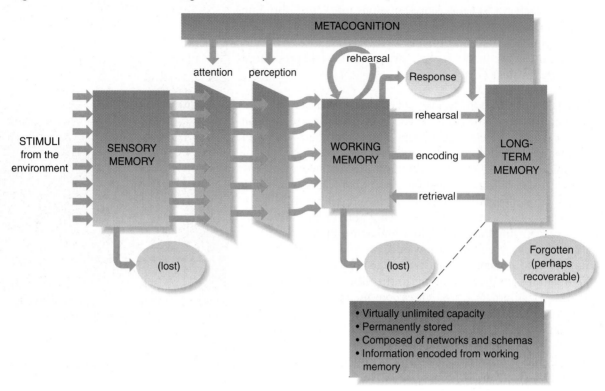

As another example, when learning how to solve math problems, students should practice in a variety of realistic settings. Many students identify the current condition based on the section in the textbook they're studying; for example, they use subtraction because they're on the subtraction section of a chapter (Bransford et al., 2000). These findings have implications for instruction. For example, when students are working on problems that require subtraction, teachers should also give them problems that require addition, multiplication, and division, so students learn to identify different conditions and apply the appropriate actions.

As a review, examine Figure 7.4, which summarizes the characteristics of long-term memory.

Knowledge Extensions

To deepen your understanding of the topics in this section of the chapter and integrate them with topics you've already studied, go to the *Knowledge Extensions* module for Chapter 7 at *www.prenhall.com/eggen*. Respond to questions 4–7.

Checking Your Understanding

2.1   Using the characteristics of the memory stores as a basis, explain why Tanya, from the opening case, might have become "kinda lost when Mr. Shelton was explaining all that yesterday." What implications does this have for our teaching?

2.2   Use the characteristics of the memory stores to explain why a health club would prefer to advertise its telephone number as 2HEALTH rather than 243–2584.

2.3   Procedural knowledge exists in which of our memory stores? Identify an example in the opening case study that illustrates students being required to demonstrate procedural knowledge. Explain.

To receive feedback for these questions, go to Appendix B.

Applying an Understanding of Memory Stores in Your Classroom

Sensory Memory

1. To keep students from losing a sensory memory trace, give them a chance to attend to one stimulus before presenting a second one.
   - **Elementary:** A second-grade teacher asks one question at a time and gets an answer before asking a second question.
   - **Middle School:** A pre-algebra teacher displays two problems on the overhead and waits until students have copied them before she starts talking.
   - **High School:** In a geography lesson, a teacher places a map on the overhead and says, "I'll give you a minute to examine the geography of the countries on this map in the front of the room. Then we'll go on."

Working Memory

2. To avoid overloading students' working memories, conduct lessons with questioning.
   - **Elementary:** A first-grade teacher gives students directions for seat work by presenting them slowly and one at a time. He asks different students to repeat the directions before he has them begin.
   - **Middle School:** A teacher in a woodworking class begins by saying, "The hardness and density of wood from the same kind of tree vary, depending on the amount of rainfall the tree has received and how fast it grows." Then, she waits a moment, holds up two pieces of wood, and says, "Look at these wood pieces. What do you notice about the rings on them?"
   - **High School:** An Algebra II teacher "walks" students through the solution to problems by having a different student describe each succeeding step to the solution.

3. Provide frequent practice to develop automaticity, and present information in both verbal and visual forms.
   - **Elementary:** A first-grade teacher has his students practice their writing by composing two sentences each day about an event of the previous evening.
   - **Middle School:** To capitalize on the dual-processing capability of working memory, an eighth-grade history teacher prepares a flowchart of the events that led up to the Revolutionary War. As she questions the students about the topic, she refers to the flowchart for each important point and encourages students to use the chart to organize their note taking.
   - **High School:** As a physics teacher discusses the relationship between force and acceleration, he demonstrates by pulling a cart along the desktop with a constant force so the students can see that the cart accelerates.

Long-Term Memory

4. To develop schemas, encourage students to explore relationships between ideas, and between new ideas and prior understanding.
   - **Elementary:** During story time, a second-grade teacher asks students to explain how the events in a story contribute to the conclusion.
   - **Middle School:** In developing the rules for solving equations by substitution, an algebra teacher asks, "How does this process compare to what we did when we solved equations by addition? What do we do differently? Why?"
   - **High School:** To help his students understand cause–effect relationships in their study of ancient Greece, a world history teacher asks questions such as "Why was shipping so important in ancient Greece?" "Why was Troy's location so important, and how does its location relate to the location of today's big cities?" and "Why did Greek city-states exist (instead of larger nation-states)?"

COGNITIVE PROCESSES IN OUR INFORMATION PROCESSING SYSTEM

How does information move from sensory to working to long-term memory? To answer this question, let's look again at the information processing model, focusing now on the processes—*attention, perception, rehearsal, encoding,* and *retrieval*—that move information from one store to another. They're highlighted in Figure 7.5 and discussed in the sections that follow.

Attention: The Beginning of Information Processing

Consider the room you're in right now. You are probably unaware of many of the environmental stimuli—pictures, furniture, other people moving and talking. Other stimuli, however, attract your **attention,** which is the process of consciously focusing on a stimulus. In Figure 7.5 *attention* appears next to *sensory memory,* and it is where information processing begins. All additional processing depends on the extent to which learners pay attention to appropriate stimuli and ignore distractions.

Attention. The process of consciously focusing on a stimulus

Figure 7.5 Cognitive processes in the information processing model

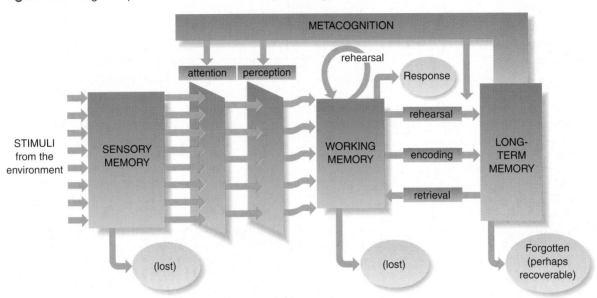

Attracting and Maintaining Attention

Because attention is where learning begins, attracting and maintaining student attention are essential (Mangels, Piction, & Craik, 2001; Valenzeno, Alibali, & Klatzky, 2003). Effective teachers plan their lessons so students attend to what is being taught and ignore irrelevant stimuli. If a teacher pulls a live, wriggling crab out of a cooler to begin a lesson on crustaceans, for example, even the most disinterested student is likely to pay attention. Similarly, if students are actively involved in learning activities, they're much more attentive than if they're passively listening to a lecture (Dolezal, Welsh, Pressley, & Vincent, 2003; B. Taylor, Pearson, Peterson, & Rodriguez, 2003).

David used four attention-getters in his lesson. His demonstration with the strings and socks was probably most significant, but his two transparencies and matrix also helped attract and maintain students' attention.

Some additional examples of ways to attract student attention are outlined in Table 7.2. Because of its importance, one deserves increased emphasis: *calling on students by name.* The use of students' names is one of the most powerful attention-getters, and effective teachers quickly learn their students' names and call on individual students instead of directing questions to the class as a whole. When this becomes a pattern, attention and achievement increase (Eggen & Kauchak 2006; McDougall & Granby, 1996).

Effective teachers use a variety of visual aids to attract and maintain students' attention.

Perception: Finding Meaning in Stimuli

Look at the picture in the margin. Do you see a young, glamorous woman, or do you see an old, wrinkled one? This classic example illustrates the nature of **perception,** the process people use to find meaning in stimuli. For those of you who "saw" an old woman, this is the meaning you attached to the picture; the same is true for those of you who "saw" a young woman. Technically, we were asking, "Do you 'perceive' a young or an old woman?" Neither behaviorism nor social cognitive theory can explain why people perceive stimuli differently, and this is one reason we examine cognitive theories of learning.

It is essential that students accurately perceive the information they study. Their perceptions of what they see or hear enter working memory, and if these perceptions are not accurate, the information that is ultimately encoded in long-term memory will also be inaccurate.

Perception. The process people use to find meaning in stimuli

Table 7.2 Strategies for attracting attention

Type	Example
Demonstrations	A science teacher pulls a student in a chair across the room to demonstrate the concepts *force* and *work*.
Discrepant events	A world history teacher who usually dresses conservatively comes to class in a sheet, makeshift sandals, and a crown to begin a discussion of ancient Greece.
Charts	A health teacher displays a chart showing the high fat content of some popular foods.
Pictures	An English teacher shows a picture of a bearded Ernest Hemingway as she introduces 20th-century American novels.
Problems	A math teacher says, "We want to go to the rock concert on Saturday night, but we're broke. The tickets are $45, and we need about $20 for gas and something to eat. We make $5.50 an hour in our part-time jobs. How many hours do we have to work to be able to afford the concert?"
Thought-provoking questions	A history teacher begins a discussion of World War II with the question, "Suppose Germany had won the war. How might the world be different now?"
Emphasis	A teacher says, "Pay careful attention now. The next two items are very important."
Student names	In his question-and-answer sessions, a teacher asks his question, pauses briefly, and then calls on a student by name to answer.

Earlier in the chapter, we stressed the importance of prior knowledge, both in constructing understanding and in making information meaningful, and prior knowledge influences perceptions as well. For instance, Randy didn't "notice" that Pluto's plane differed from those of the other planets, because his perception of the information on the transparency and demonstration was affected by his lack of prior knowledge.

An effective way of checking students' perceptions is to review by asking open-ended questions (Eggen & Kauchak, 2006). For example, a chemistry teacher writes the following equation on the board and then asks, "What do you notice about the equation?"

$$CaCO_3 + CO_2 + H_2O \rightarrow Ca + 2HCO_3$$

If students don't "notice" essential information, such as the elements involved, the numbers of each in the compounds, and the meaning of the arrow, the teacher knows that their prior knowledge is inaccurate or incomplete and can then adjust her review to clarify these features.

Rehearsal: Retaining Information Through Repetition

You want to make a phone call, so you look up the number and repeat it to yourself a few times until you dial it. You have rehearsed the number to keep it in working memory until you're finished with it. **Rehearsal** is the process of repeating information over and over, either aloud or silently, without altering its form (R. Atkinson & Shiffrin, 1968). It is analogous to rehearsing a piece of music. When rehearsing, people play the music as written; they don't alter it or change its form.

Although rehearsal can be used to hold information in working memory until used, if rehearsed enough, it can be transferred to long-term memory, as typically happens with your home or cell phone number. Rehearsal is a simple, but inefficient, method of transferring information from working to long-term memory. Not surprisingly, it's one of the first memory strategies that develops in young children (Berk, 2006).

Meaningful Encoding: Making Connections in Long-Term Memory

Encoding is the process of representing information in long-term memory (Bruning et al., 2004). This information can be represented either visually, such as Juan's forming an image of Pluto with a different orbital plane than the other planets, or verbally, when students

Analyzing Classrooms Video
To analyze the effectiveness of a teacher's attempts to attract students' attention, go to Episode 10, "Applying Information Processing: Attracting Students' Attention," on DVD 1, accompanying this text.

Rehearsal. The process of repeating information over and over, either aloud or mentally, without altering its form

Encoding. The process of representing information in long-term memory

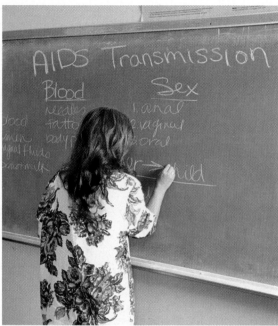

Organizational aids help learners construct organized and integrated schemas.

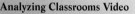

Analyzing Classrooms Video
To analyze the effectiveness of a teacher's attempts to organize information to make it meaningful to students, go to Episode 11, "Applying Information Processing: Organizing Information," on DVD 1, accompanying this text.

Organization. The process of clustering items of content into categories that illustrate relationships

construct schemas that relate ideas to each other. Juan's and Randy's schemas in Figure 7.3 illustrate the ways they had encoded the information about the solar system.

Our goal in encoding should be to make information as meaningful as possible, and as we saw earlier, meaningfulness describes the extent to which the elements in a schema are interconnected. Because Juan's schema had more connections than Randy's, for example, Juan's was more meaningful.

Teachers can encourage meaningful encoding by promoting four processes:

- Organization
- Imagery
- Elaboration
- Activity

These processes are outlined in Figure 7.6 and discussed in the sections that follow.

Organization: Representing Relationships in Content

Organization is the process of clustering related items of content into categories that illustrate relationships. Because well-organized content illustrates connections among its elements, learners more easily make it meaningful, cognitive load is decreased, and encoding (and subsequent retrieval) is more effective. Research in reading, memory, and classroom instruction confirm the value of organization in promoting learning (R. Mayer, 1997; Nuthall, 1999b). In addition, research indicates that experts learn more efficiently than do novices because their knowledge is better organized (Bransford et al., 2000; Simon, 2001).

Information can be organized in several ways:

- *Charts and matrices:* Useful for organizing large amounts of information into categories. David used a matrix in his lesson to help his students organize their information about the planets. The completed matrix is shown in Table 7.3.
- *Hierarchies:* Effective when new information can be subsumed under existing ideas. We made frequent use of hierarchies in our discussion of behaviorism in Chapter 6 (e.g., in Figure 6.1, "Consequences of Behavior"). Figure 7.7 contains an additional example from an English lesson.
- *Models:* Helpful for representing relationships that cannot be observed directly. The model of the solar system on David's transparency and the information processing models in this chapter are examples.
- *Outlines:* Useful for representing the organizational structure in a body of written material. For instance, a detailed outline for each of the chapters appears in the Student Study Guide that accompanies this book.

Other types of organization include graphs, tables, flowcharts, and maps (Merkley & Jefferies, 2001). Learners can also use these organizers as personal study aids in their attempts to make the information they're studying meaningful.

Figure 7.6   Making information meaningful

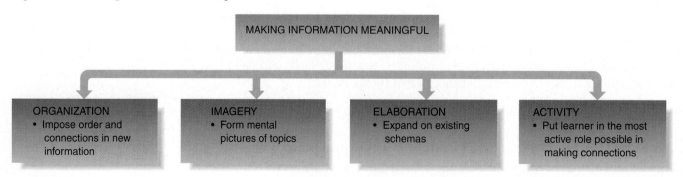

Table 7.3 David's completed planet matrix

	Diameter (miles)	Distance from Sun (millions of miles)	Length of Year (orbit)	Length of Day (rotation)	Gravity (compared to Earth's)	Average Surface Temperature (°F)	Characteristics
Mercury	3,030	35.9	88 E.D.[a]	59 E.D. counterclockwise	.38	300 below to 800 above zero	No atmosphere; no water; many craters
Venus	7,500	67.2	225 E.D.	243 E.D. clockwise	.88	900	Thick cloud cover; high winds; no water
Earth	7,900	98.0	365½ E.D.	24 hours counterclockwise	1	57	Atmos. of 78% nitrogen, 21% oxygen; 70% water on surface
Mars	4,200	141.5	687 E.D.	24½ hours counterclockwise	.38	67 below zero	Thin carbon dioxide atmos.; white caps at poles; red rocky surface
Jupiter	88,700	483.4	12 E.Y.[b]	10 hours counterclockwise	2.34	162 below zero	No water; great red spot; atmos. of hydrogen, helium, ammonia
Saturn	75,000	914.0	30 E.Y.	11 hours counterclockwise	.92	208 below zero	Atmos. of hydrogen, helium; no water; mostly gaseous; prominent rings
Uranus	31,566	1,782.4	84 E.Y.	24 hours counterclockwise	.79	355 below zero	Atmos. of hydrogen, helium; no water
Neptune	30,200	2,792.9	165 E.Y.	17 hours counterclockwise	1.12	266 below zero	Atmos. of hydrogen, helium; no water
Pluto	1,423	3,665.0	248 E.Y.	6½ days counterclockwise	.43	458 below zero	No atmos.; periodically orbits closer to sun than Neptune

[a] Earth days.
[b] Earth years.

Because learners construct knowledge that makes sense to them, if the organizational structure we offer *does not* make sense to learners, they will (mentally) reorganize it in a way that does, whether or not it is correct. When content organization is unclear, learners often memorize snippets of it, or they will reject or ignore it altogether.

Interaction is essential to making the organization of new material meaningful to learners. David, for example, not only organized his content by using a demonstration, transparencies, and matrix, he also guided his students' developing understanding through questioning and discussion.

Imagery: Applying Dual-Coding Theory

Dual-coding theory suggests that long-term memory contains two distinct memory systems: one for verbal information and one that stores images (Paivio 1991; Sadoski & Paivio, 2001). According to dual-coding theory, concepts that can be represented both visually and verbally, such as *ball, house,* or *dog,*

Figure 7.7 Organizational hierarchy in English

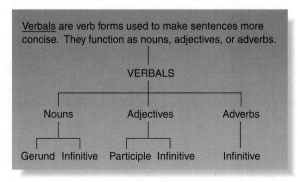

Verbals are verb forms used to make sentences more concise. They function as nouns, adjectives, or adverbs.

VERBALS
- Nouns — Gerund, Infinitive
- Adjectives — Participle, Infinitive
- Adverbs — Infinitive

Active learning encourages students to encode information in meaningful ways.

are much easier to remember than concepts that are more difficult to visualize, such as *value, truth,* and *ability* (Paivio, 1986).

Earlier in the chapter, we discussed research indicating that presenting verbal and visual information together can help capitalize the distributed processing capability of working memory. **Dual-coding theory** corroborates this research, suggesting that presenting topics both visually and verbally can capitalize on **imagery,** the process of forming mental pictures (N. Schwartz, Ellsworth, Graham, & Knight, 1998). For instance, as we study information processing, we can visualize the model (see Figure 7.1). The fact that we can both read about and create an image of the model helps us capitalize on the dual-coding capacity of long-term memory. The model is more meaningfully encoded than it would be if we had only described it verbally (J. Clark & Paivio, 1991; Willoughby, Porter, Belsito, & Yearsley, 1999). Dual-coding theory again reminds us of the importance of supplementing verbal information with visual representations (Igo, Kiewra, & Bruning, 2004). This not only addresses the limitations of working memory but also capitalizes on the beneficial effects of imagery.

Teachers can take advantage of imagery in several ways (Edens & Potter, 2001; van Meter, 2001). For instance, they can use pictures and diagrams, such as David's transparencies of the globs of gases and the solar system, they can ask students to form mental pictures of processes or events, and they can ask students to draw their own illustrations or diagrams about ideas they are learning.

Diagrams and illustrations are particularly helpful in problem solving (Kozhevnikov, Hegarty, & Mayer, 1999). For example, if students are attempting to find the areas of irregularly shaped polygons, having them impose a grid over the figures helps them think in area dimensions and also helps them filter out irrelevant information such as the figures' colors or physical orientations.

Elaboration: Extending Understanding

You're at a noisy party. When you miss some of a conversation, you fill in details, trying to make sense of an incomplete message. You do the same when you read or listen to a lecture. You expand on (and sometimes distort) information to make it fit your expectations and current understanding. In each case, you are elaborating on either the message or what you already know.

Elaboration is the process of increasing the meaningfulness of information by creating additional links in existing knowledge or by adding new information (O'Reilly, Symons, & MacLatchy-Gaudet, 1998; Terry, 2006). For example, when Tanya said, "Oh, I get it! Pluto isn't level with the rest of them," she formed an additional link in her schema without adding any new information.

David also promoted elaboration with his review and demonstration. His review helped the students reactivate their prior knowledge (pull existing schemas from long-term memory back into working memory), and his demonstration added new information to their existing understanding.

Three strategies are effective in promoting elaboration:

- *Provide examples:* Present specific cases that illustrate ideas.
- *Form analogies:* Make comparisons in which similarities are created between otherwise dissimilar ideas (Bulgren et al., 2000; R. Mayer & Wittrock, 1996).
- *Use mnemonic devices:* Use strategies that link items or ideas by forming associations that don't exist naturally in the content (Terry, 2006).

Working with examples—constructing, finding, or analyzing them—is perhaps the most powerful of the elaboration strategies (Cassady, 1999). Whenever learners can create or identify a new example of an idea, they elaborate on their understanding of that idea. Our extensive use of examples throughout this book demonstrates our belief in this strategy, and we encourage you to focus on the examples to increase your understanding of the topics you're studying. You can do the same with the concepts you teach.

Dual-coding theory. A theory suggesting that long-term memory contains two distinct memory systems: one for verbal information and one that stores images

Imagery. The process of forming mental pictures

Elaboration. The process of increasing the meaningfulness of information by creating additional links in existing knowledge or by adding new information

Table 7.4 Types and examples of mnemonic devices

Mnemonic	Description	Example
Method of loci	Learner combines imagery with specific locations in a familiar environment, such as the chair, sofa, lamp, and end table in a living room.	Student wanting to remember the first seven elements in order visualizes hydrogen at the chair, helium at the sofa, lithium at the lamp, and so on.
Peg-word method	Learner memorizes a series of "pegs"—such as a simple rhyme like "one is bun" and "two is shoe"—on which to-be-remembered information is hung.	A learner wanting to remember to get pickles and carrots at the grocery visualizes a pickle in a bun and carrot stuck in a shoe.
Link method	Learner visually links items to be remembered.	A learner visualizes *homework* stuck in a *notebook* which is bound to her *textbook, pencil,* and *pen* with a rubber band to remember to take the (italicized) items to class.
Key-word method	Learner uses imagery and rhyming words to remember unfamiliar words.	A learner remembers that *trigo* (which rhymes with tree) is the Spanish word for "wheat" by visualizing a sheaf of wheat sticking out of a tree.
First-letter method	Learner creates a word from the first letter of items to be remembered.	A student creates the word *Waimma* to remember the first six presidents in order: Washington, Adams, Jefferson, Madison, Monroe, and Adams.

When examples aren't available, using **analogies,** descriptions of relationships that are similar in some but not all respects, can be an effective elaboration strategy (Bulgren et al., 2000). As an example, consider the following analogy from science:

> Our circulatory system is like a pumping system that carries the blood around our bodies. The veins and arteries are the pipes, and the heart is the pump.

The veins and arteries are similar, but not identical, to pipes, and the heart is a type of pump. The analogy is an effective form of elaboration because it links new information to something learners already understand: the workings of a pumping system.

Mnemonic devices link knowledge to be learned to familiar information (Bruning et al., 2004). Acronyms, such as HOMES (Huron, Ontario, Michigan, Erie, and Superior) and SCUBA (self-contained underwater breathing apparatus) are examples, as are phrases such as "Every good boy does fine," for E, G, B, D, and F (the names of the notes in the treble clef), and rhymes such as the spelling aid "*i* before *e* except after *c.*" When learners think of the mnemonic, they link it to the information it represents, which aids the recall of information through elaboration. Mnemonics are used to help remember vocabulary, names, rules, lists, and other kinds of factual knowledge; Table 7.4 lists additional examples.

Teacher questioning is an effective way to facilitate the use of each of these strategies. It encourages students to elaborate on information through active cognitive processing. This leads us to the idea of activity.

Activity: Capitalizing on a Learning Principle

You and a friend are studying this book. You read and attempt to write an answer to each of the Checking Your Understanding questions in the chapters. Then you look at the feedback in Appendix B. Your friend simply reads each question and then reads the answer.

Your approach is more effective because *you've placed yourself in a more cognitively active role than has your friend.* Thinking about (and writing) an answer is active; it encourages you to search long-term memory for connections that allow you to elaborate on the new information. Merely reading the feedback is passive, resulting in fewer connections and less learning. Similarly, asking students to provide an additional example places them in an active cognitive role; your providing the example doesn't encourage as much active processing.

At the beginning of the chapter, we saw that "learners are mentally active in their attempts to understand how the world works" is one of the principles of cognitive learning theory, and encouraging students to be in the most active role possible in their study is consistent with that principle. For example, we've included the Checking Your Understanding questions in each section to encourage you to actively process the information you're studying. This increase in cognitive activity improves learning because it encourages elaboration

Analogies. Descriptions of relationships that are similar in some but not all respects

Mnemonic devices. Elaboration strategies that link knowledge to be learned to familiar information and meaningfulness (Bransford et al., 2000). Additional ways of putting students in active roles include the following:

- Develop lessons around examples, applications, and problems to be analyzed instead of definitions and other content to be memorized.
- Implement lessons with questioning instead of relying on lectures and explanations.
- Ask questions that require students to apply their understanding rather than simply recall information.
- Require students to provide evidence for conclusions instead of letting them stop with the conclusions themselves.
- Create tests, quizzes, and homework that require application rather than rote memory.
- Use hands-on activities and group work judiciously.

We emphasize *judiciously* in the last suggestion. Because science instruction encourages hands-on activities, for instance, teachers sometimes assume that learning automatically takes place if students are working with batteries and bulbs, or any other physical objects. This isn't necessarily true. If the learning objective isn't clear, or if the teacher doesn't encourage students to describe connections between what they're doing and their prior knowledge, learning may not occur. "Hands-on" activities don't ensure "minds-on" activities (R. Mayer, 1999).

The same is true with manipulatives in math (Ball, 1992), cooperative learning, and other strategies intended to promote active learner participation. The fact that students are physically active, or are talking, doesn't ensure that mearningful learning is occurring.

Activity can also be deceiving at an individual level, as we saw in our example of the study habits of educational psychology students. Continually asking yourself if you are as active as possible in your study will pay off in increased understanding.

Forgetting

Forgetting is the loss of, or inability to retrieve, information from memory, and it is both a very real part of people's everyday lives and an important factor in learning.

Look again at the model first presented in Figure 7.1. There we see that information lost from both sensory memory and working memory is unrecoverable. On the other hand, information in long-term memory has been encoded. Why can't we find it?

Forgetting as Interference

One explanation of forgetting uses the concept of **interference**, the loss of information because something learned either before or after detracts from understanding (M. Anderson & Neely, 1996; Schunk, 2004). For example, students learn that possessives are formed by adding an apostrophe *s* to singular nouns. Then they study plural possessives and contractions and find that the apostrophe is used differently. Students' understanding of plural possessives and contractions can interfere with their understanding of singular possessives and vice versa.

Interference increases when breadth of content coverage is emphasized over in-depth understanding, a common problem in today's schools (R. Dempster & Corkill, 1999). Textbooks that include too many topics create problems for students attempting to integrate ideas.

Teachers can reduce interference by emphasizing the relationships between topics using review and comparison. After a new topic is introduced, teachers should compare it with closely related information that students have already studied, identifying easily confused similarities. Doing so elaborates on the original schema, which reduces interference.

Another way to reduce interference is to teach closely related ideas together, such as adjectives and adverbs, longitude and latitude, and adding fractions with similar and different denominators (R. Hamilton, 1997). In doing so, teachers help students recognize similarities and differences, and identify areas that are easily confused.

Forgetting as Retrieval Failure

A second explanation of forgetting ties it to individuals' inability to **retrieve** information, to pull it from long-term memory into working memory for further processing. Many re-

Forgetting. The loss of, or inability to retrieve, information from memory

Interference. The loss of information because something learned either before or after detracts from understanding

Retrieval. The process of pulling information from long-term memory into working memory for further processing

searchers believe that learners don't literally *lose* information when they forget; instead, they can't retrieve it (C. Williams & Zacks, 2001). We've all had the experience of realizing that we know a name, fact, or some other information, but we simply can't pull it up; it's there but we can't find it.

As with acquiring procedural knowledge, retrieval strongly depends on context and the way information is encoded (C. Williams & Zacks, 2001). For instance, you know a person at work or school, but you can't remember his name when you see him at a party; his name was encoded in the work or school context, and you're trying to retrieve it in the context of the party. David accommodated the need for context when he presented his information about Pluto in different ways. He didn't merely say that the first eight planets had one origin and that Pluto had another. Instead, he presented the information in the context of the planets' orbital planes, their direction of revolution, and the origin of the solar system. Presenting information in a variety of ways encourages elaboration, which provides different pathways for retrieval.

Meaningfulness is the key to retrieval. The more detailed and interconnected knowledge is in long-term memory, the easier it is to retrieve (Nuthall, 1999a). By encouraging his students to learn and connect the new information in a variety of ways, David increased the likelihood that it would be meaningful and increased the chance of later retrieval (J. Martin, 1993).

Practice to the point of automaticity also facilitates retrieval (Chaffen & Imreh, 2002). When students know their math facts to the point of automaticity, for example, they can easily retrieve them for use in problem solving, leaving more working memory space to focus on solutions. In a similar way, when young readers' decoding skills are automatic, they can focus more of their cognitive energies on comprehension (Bruning et al., 2004).

Checking Your Understanding

3.1   Describe the cognitive processes in our information processing system.

3.2   A language arts teacher wants to involve her students in a discussion of moral dilemmas. She begins by asking, "What do we mean by a moral dilemma?" To which of the cognitive processes does the teacher's question most closely relate? Explain.

3.3   A second-grade teacher uses flash cards to help her students acquire math facts, such as $6 \times 8 = 48$ and $7 \times 9 = 63$, and she also has her students practice solving problems. Which cognitive process is primarily involved in acquiring the math facts, and which is primarily involved in solving the problems? Explain the important difference between the two.

To receive feedback for these questions, go to Appendix B.

Knowledge Extensions

To deepen your understanding of the topics in this section of the chapter and integrate them with topics you've already studied, go to the *Knowledge Extensions* module for Chapter 7 at *www.prenhall.com/eggen*. Respond to questions 8–13.

Classroom Connections

Applying an Understanding of Cognitive Processes in Your Classroom

Attention

1. Begin and conduct lessons to attract and maintain attention.
   - **Elementary:** A third-grade teacher calls on all his students, whether or not they have their hands up. He periodically asks, "Who have I not called on lately?" to be sure all students are attending to the lesson.
   - **Middle School:** A science teacher introducing the concept *pressure* has students stand by their desks, first on both feet and then on one foot. They then discuss the force and pressure on the floor in each case.
   - **High School:** To be sure that her students attend to important points, a world history teacher emphasizes, "Everyone, listen carefully now, because we're going to look at three important reasons that World War I broke out in Europe."

Perception

2. Check frequently to be certain that students are perceiving your examples and other representations accurately.

- **Elementary:** A kindergarten teacher wants his students to understand living things. He displays a large plant and then asks, "What do you notice about the plant?" He calls on several children for their reactions.
- **Middle School:** A geography teacher shows her class a series of colored slides of landforms. After displaying each slide, she asks students to describe the landform.
- **High School:** An English teacher and his students are reading an essay and come across the line, "I wouldn't impose this regimen on myself out of masochism." He stops and asks, "What does the author mean by 'masochism'?"

Meaningful Encoding

3. Carefully organize the information you present to students, and place them in active learning roles.

- **Elementary:** A fourth-grade teacher illustrates that heat causes expansion by placing a balloon-covered soft drink bottle in a pot of hot water and by presenting a drawing that shows the spacing and motion of the air molecules. She then uses questioning to guide students to the relationship between heat and expansion.
- **Middle School:** A math teacher presents a flowchart with a series of questions students are encouraged to ask themselves as they solve word problems. As students work on the problems, he asks them to describe their thinking and tell where they are on the flowchart.
- **High School:** A history teacher presents a matrix comparing four different immigrant groups, their reasons for relocating to the United States, the difficulties they encountered, and their rates of assimilation. The students then work in pairs to find patterns in the information in the chart.

4. Encourage students to elaborate on their understanding and to use imagery in their study.

- **Elementary:** A second-grade teacher says, "Let's see what we've found now about chemical and physical changes.

Picture the differences between the two, give me two new examples of each, and explain why they're chemical or physical changes."

- **Middle School:** A geography teacher encourages her students to visualize flat parallel lines on the globe as they think about latitude, and vertical lines coming together at the North and South Poles as they think about longitude. She then asks her students to describe the similarities and differences between them.
- **High School:** An English teacher asks students to imagine the appearance of the characters in the novels they read by pretending they are casting them for the movie version of the novel. He asks them to suggest a current actor or actress to play the role in the process, describing the characters in detail, including their facial features, hair, clothes, and behavior.

Retrieval

5. To prevent interference and aid retrieval, teach closely related ideas together and emphasize their differences.

- **Elementary:** A fifth-grade teacher, knowing that her students confuse area and perimeter, has them lay squares side by side to illustrate area, and she has them measure the distance around the filled area to illustrate perimeter. She then moves to irregular plane figures and repeats the process.
- **Middle School:** An English teacher presenting a unit on verbals displays a passage on the overhead that includes both gerunds and participles. He then asks the students to compare the way the words are used in the passage to demonstrate that gerunds are nouns and participles are adjectives.
- **High School:** A biology teacher begins a unit on arteries and veins by saying, "We've all heard of hardening of the arteries, but we haven't heard of 'hardening of the veins.' Why not? Are we using the term artery to mean both, or is there a difference? Why is hardening of the arteries bad for people? I'll write these questions down so that we keep them in mind as we study arteries, veins, and capillaries."

METACOGNITION: KNOWLEDGE AND CONTROL OF COGNITIVE PROCESSES

Have you ever said to yourself, "I'm going to sit near the front of the class so I won't fall asleep," or "I'm beat today. I'd better drink a cup of coffee before I go to class"? If you have, you were being *metacognitive.* As we saw at the beginning of the chapter, **metacognition** is our awareness of and control over our cognitive processes.

Attention is one type of metacognition. Knowing that you might be drowsy, you demonstrated an awareness of how this might affect your ability to attend. If you chose to sit in the front of the class or drink coffee, you exercised control over it. You demonstrated **meta-attention,** the knowledge of and control over your ability to pay attention, which is one kind of metacognition.

Students who are aware of the way they study and learn achieve more than those who are less aware (Bruning et al., 2004; Kuhn & Dean, 2004). In other words, students who are metacognitive learn more than those who aren't.

Let's see why. First, students who are aware of the importance of attention are more likely to create effective learning environments for themselves. The adaptation can be

Metacognition. The awareness of and control over one's own cognitive processes

Meta-attention. Knowledge of and control over our ability to pay attention

as simple as moving to the front of the class or turning off a distracting radio while studying.

Second, metacognition can also enhance perception. Learners who know they might misperceive something attempt to find corroborating information or might simply ask if their understanding is accurate. By doing so, they demonstrate awareness of and control over perception.

Third, metacognition can also help regulate the flow of information through working memory. Randy, in David's lesson, demonstrated metamemory when he said, "I better write some of this stuff down, or I'll never remember it." As another example, we all find ourselves in situations where we have to remember a phone number. If we must dial the number immediately, we simply rehearse; if we want to call later, we probably write the number down. Randy's and our decisions are examples of **metamemory,** which is knowledge of and control over our memory strategies (Schraw & Moshman, 1995; Son, 2004). The ability to monitor the processing of information in working memory is essential because of its limited capacity (K. Wilson & Swanson, 1999).

Finally, metacognition influences the meaningfulness of encoding. For example, learners who know that encoding is more effective if different items of information are linked, rather than stored in isolation, consciously look for relationships in the topics they study. This influences their study strategies, and ultimately how much they learn.

The metacognitive components of information processing are illustrated in Figure 7.8.

The Development of Metacognition

Young learners' metacognitive abilities are limited; they don't realize that they can influence how much they learn. As they mature, however, these abilities gradually develop (Berk, 2006). This development relates to, but doesn't totally depend on, intellectual ability. In addition, metacognitive skills tend to be general for older students, whereas the limited metacognitive abilities in young learners tend to be domain-specific (M. V. Veenman & Spaans, 2005). For example, older children are generally more aware of the importance of attention than their younger counterparts, are better at directing it toward important information in a learning task, and are more able to ignore distracting stimuli (Berk, 2006). Young children, in contrast, are likely to be aware of the need to pay attention only when repeatedly reminded of its importance by their teacher.

The process is similar for metamemory (Gaskill & Murphy, 2004; E. Short, Schatschneider, & Friebert, 1993). For example, when given a list of items to remember, kindergarteners don't use memory techniques, such as categorizing or forming images of the items, whereas fourth graders can and do both (Berk, 2006).

Exploring Further

Some experts believe that metacognition can be a tool to help students increase their emotional awareness. To read more about this approach, go to "Metacognition and Emotional Development" in the *Exploring Further* module of Chapter 7 at *www.prenhall.com/eggen.*

Metamemory. Knowledge of and control over our memory strategies

Figure 7.8 Metacognition in the information processing model

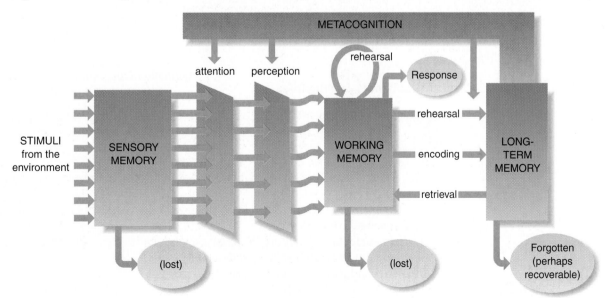

Older learners are also more aware of their memory limitations (Everson & Tobias, 1998; Sternberg, 1998b). For example, when asked to predict how many objects they could remember from a list, nursery school students predicted 7 but remembered fewer than 4 (Flavell et al., 1970). Adults given the same task predicted an average of 5.9 and actually remembered 5.5 (Yussen & Levy, 1975).

Although young children, older learners, and even some college students are not as metacognitive about their learning as is desirable (Peverly, Brobst, & Graham, 2003), learners can develop these skills with teacher guidance and practice. We discuss these processes in depth in Chapter 9.

Checking Your Understanding

Knowledge Extensions

To deepen your understanding of the topics in this section of the chapter and integrate them with topics you've already studied, go to the *Knowledge Extensions* module for Chapter 7 at *www.prenhall.com/eggen*. Respond to questions 14–16.

4.1   Define metacognition as a part of our information processing system.

4.2   As you read this book, you stop and go back to the top of a page and reread one of the sections. Is this an example of metacognition? Explain.

4.3   Note taking is a study strategy. You have a classmate, who, in an attempt to be sure that he doesn't miss anything, writes down virtually everything the instructor says. You write down only the points that you believe are most important. Which of you is more metacognitive in your approach to note taking? Explain.

To receive feedback for these questions, go to Appendix B.

Classroom Connections

Applying an Understanding of Metacognition in Your Classroom

1. Systematically integrate metacognition into your instruction, and model metacognitive strategies.
   - **Elementary:** A fourth-grade teacher plays an attention game with his students. During a lesson, he holds up a card with the sentence "If you're paying attention, raise your hand." He then acknowledges those who are and encourages them to share their strategies for maintaining attention during class.

   - **Middle School:** A social studies teacher tries to teach metamemory by saying, "Suppose you're reading, and the book states that there are three important differences between capitalism and socialism. What should you do?"

   - **High School:** An economics teacher frequently models metacognitive strategies by making statements such as, "Whenever I read something new, I always ask myself, 'How does this relate to what I've been studying?' For example, how is the liberal economic agenda different from the conservative agenda?"

Instructional Principles

Information Processing in the Classroom: Instructional Principles

Information processing theory has important implications for instruction. As you attempt to apply the theory in your teaching, the following principles can help guide your efforts:

1. Begin lessons with an activity that attracts attention.
2. Conduct frequent reviews to activate students' prior knowledge and check their perceptions.
3. Proceed in short steps, and represent content both visually and verbally to reduce cognitive load.
4. Help students make information meaningful, and aid encoding through organization, imagery, elaboration, and activity.
5. Model and encourage metacognition.

Let's see how Lisa Johnson, a fifth-grade teacher in an urban elementary school in the Midwest, attempts to implement these instruction principles with her students.

In social studies Lisa has recently begun a unit on the northern and southern states before the Civil War. She displays a large U.S. map and a chart summarizing the lesson's content. She begins today's class by saying, "Okay, everyone, look at the map, and let's see if we can locate where we live."

	People	Land and Climate	Economy
Northern States	Small towns Religious Valued education Cooperative	Timber covered Glacial remains Poor soil Short growing season Cold winters	Small farms Syrup Rum Lumber Shipbuilding Fishing
Southern States	Aristocratic Isolated Social class distinction	Fertile soil Hot weather Long growing season	Large farms Tobacco Cotton Unskilled workers Servants and slaves

Students peer intently at the map and then identify the location of their city.

"Now, you see that we're in the Midwest. . . . We began talking about the northern and southern states yesterday," she continues. "Let's see what we remember. . . . Where are they compared to where we live? . . . Lorenda?"

". . . They're over there," Lorenda answers, motioning to the right with her hand.

"Yes, they're east of us," Lisa adds, as she identifies the general location of the states on the map with a wave of her hand.

"Now, this is 2007, and we're talking about the 1840s, let's say 1847, so how long ago is that?"

"A hundred and sixty years," Greg says after a few seconds.

"Yes," Lisa smiles. So, that would be like when our great-great-great-grandfathers and -grandmothers might have lived.

"We also talked about some important ideas, like economy. . . . What do we mean by economy? . . . Carol?"

"It's . . . like the way they make their money, like when we said that the economy here is based on manufacturing, like making cars and parts for cars and stuff," Carol responds uncertainly.

"Good," Lisa smiles, pointing to the 'Economy' column on the chart. She also has the students describe what other terms, such as *aristocratic* and *isolated,* mean to them, and she then turns back to the chart. "We see that the economy for the two groups of states is quite different. Today we want to see what some of these specific differences are and why they exist."

She then continues, "What are some of the differences we see in the economies for the two regions? . . . Ann Marie?"

"The farms were bigger in the south than they were in the north," Ann Marie responds after studying the chart for several seconds.

"Okay, good observation. . . . Now why might that have been the case? . . . Jacinta?"

". . ."

"Look over at our map. . . . What does this represent?" Lisa prompts, pointing at the southern coastal plain represented by the green portion of the map.

"It's . . . plains," Jacinta responds hesitantly.

"Yes, good. . . . So, if these are plains, what might we expect? . . . Deanna?"

"Big farms."

Lisa continues guiding students' analysis of the information on the chart, in the process finding relationships between the geography, climate, and economy. When students are unable to answer, she rephrases her questions and provides cues to help them along. She then has them consider why the economy of their city might be the way it is.

"You have done very well, everyone," she smiles, waving her finger for emphasis. "Now, get with your partner, take 3 minutes, and write two or three summary statements about what we've learned here today. . . . Think carefully about your conclusions. For example, when I make a conclusion, I always ask myself, 'What do I see on the chart or map that helps me?' For example, I say that there is shipbuilding in the north because they had a lot of timber to build ships with. . . . Okay, go ahead."

The students start working, pointing at the chart, and one of the two in each pair begins writing. In some cases they stop, crumple their papers, and begin again. As they work, Lisa walks among them, offering encouragement and suggestions.

At the end of 4 minutes, Lisa announces, "One more minute, and we're going to look at what you wrote," and after another minute she begins, "Okay, let's see what you've got. What did you and Ling say, Josh?"

"We said that the weather and the land are what had to do with the way they made their money."

"Good conclusion. . . . Now, give us your reason for saying this? . . . Go ahead, Ling."

"They," Ling begins hesitantly, "had a lot of land in the south, and it's hot, so they could grow stuff like cotton, . . . but in the north they had more mountains, so they had small farms. . . . So, they needed to make money some other way."

"Excellent explanation," Lisa responds as she writes the conclusion on the board. . . . Danielle, how about you and Antonio?"

Lisa has several other pairs offer their summary statements, prompting them when necessary as they attempt to put their conclusions into words. The class then adds to the statements as a whole-group activity, and then Lisa collects the papers and ends the lesson.

Now let's look at Lisa's attempts to apply the information processing instruction principles in her teaching. She applied the first (begin lessons with an activity that attracts attention) by having students locate their city on the map as an attention-getter. Her map and chart also gave the students something to focus on to help maintain their attention.

Lisa applied the second principle (conduct frequent reviews) by reviewing the content they had discussed the previous day. She also checked students' perceptions with questions such as "What do we mean by economy?" and having them describe terms such as *aristocratic*.

Lisa applied the third principle (proceed in short steps, using visual and verbal representations) by developing the lesson in short steps and by asking questions such as "What are some of the differences we see in the economies of the two regions?" and then having students explain the differences. This type of analysis helps reduce the cognitive load on students and aids encoding. Also, by representing her information in visual form while discussing it verbally, she capitalized on the dual-processing capabilities of the students' working memories.

Lisa attempted to apply the fourth principle (help make information meaningful through organization, imagery, elaboration, and activity) by organizing her information before presenting it to the students. Her map organized the physical features of the states, and her chart provided comparisons among the people, land and climate, and economy. Then, realizing that the way the students organize the information in their personal schemas is not necessarily the same as the way she organized it, she used questioning to continue checking their perceptions and putting them in active roles. She further capital-

Online Case Book
To analyze another case study to assess the extent to which the teacher effectively applies information processing theory, go to the *Online Case Book* for Chapter 7 at *www.prenhall.com/eggen*.

Analyzing Classrooms Video
To analyze the effectiveness of a teacher's attempts to apply information processing theory in her teaching, go to Episode 12, "Applying Information Processing: *The Scarlet Letter* in High School English," on DVD 1, accompanying this text.

ized on the importance of students' being active by having them work with their partners to summarize what they had done. As the pairs offered their ideas, she guided them in elaborating on the conclusions as a whole class.

Finally, she encouraged students to be metacognitive in making their conclusions, and she modeled metacognition (principle 5) in saying, "For example, when I make a conclusion, I always ask myself, 'What do I see on the chart or map that helps me?' For example, I say. . . . " This was her attempt to apply the last principle.

Applying information processing theory in classrooms need not take an enormous amount of extra effort. For instance, Lisa's attempt to attract the students' attention by having them locate their city on the map required no extra preparation; it only took some thought. The same was true for checking students' perceptions, and calling on her students by name was nearly automatic for her. And, although preparing her chart took some initial effort, she could use it repeatedly.

This is true for applying learning theory in general: Effective application is more a matter of clear teacher thinking than it is significantly increased effort.

The Impact of Diversity on Information Processing

As a warm-up activity for his world geography class, Mike Havland asks his students to look at a "modern" map of Europe displayed on the overhead.

As Carl looks at the map, he thinks it looks familiar. "Yeah," he thinks, "there's England, France, Germany, and Russia. Hey, there's Yugoslavia. That's where Goran's grandparents came from."

Next to him, Celeena, who has grown up in a military family that has traveled all over Europe, is also looking at the map, but with disbelief. "How old is this map?" she thinks. "Look at Yugoslavia. It doesn't exist anymore. It's been torn apart for years. Hmm, where's Athens? . . . Oh yeah. Down on the Greek peninsula. We saw it when we went to the Olympics there."

After a few minutes, Mike begins, "Okay, everyone. It's important to have some idea of the geography of Europe, because the geography reflects an important idea that we'll return to again and again." With that, he writes on the chalkboard:

The history of Europe reflects a tension between nationalism and intercountry cooperation such as the adoption of a common currency, the Euro.

He continues by saying, "As you've already noticed, the face of Europe is continually changing. The Europe of today is very different from what you see on this map, and the changes happened within the last decade."

As he is talking, he notices a few nods but more blank looks. Celeena sits knowingly, while Carl thinks, "What's he talking about? Nationalism? The Euro? What is this?"

Teachers know that prior knowledge strongly influences perception and encoding. Students come to classes with widely varying experiences, and addressing this diversity is one of the biggest challenges teachers face (S. Veenman, 1984).

Diversity and Perception

As you saw in Mike's lesson, Carl perceived the map of Europe as an accurate representation, but to Celeena it was an antiquated document. Students' perception depends on their existing knowledge, and Celeena had prior knowledge Carl didn't possess. As another example, one person seeing a movie on the Vietnam conflict interprets the war as an effort to stop the spread of communism, whereas another perceives it as the imposition of American values on a distant country. The difference depends on what viewers already have learned about the conflict as well as their beliefs and values. The fact that learners' schemas influence the way they perceive new information has been confirmed in areas as varied as chess, reading, math, and physics (Bruning et al., 2004).

Teachers can use students' diverse experiential backgrounds to enrich the learning experiences of all students.

Diversity, Encoding, and Retrieval

Just as prior knowledge influences learners' perceptions, it also influences how effectively learners encode new information. For example, Celeena's rich experiences with travel made Mike's opening statements meaningful to her. They meant little to Carl; he had no information in long-term memory to which he could link ideas such as "nationalism" and "intercountry cooperation." We've all been in conversations, heard presentations, or read written passages that made no sense to us. In such cases, we may lack the prior knowledge to which new information can be linked, so meaningful encoding doesn't occur.

Instructional Adaptations for Background Diversity

What can teachers do when students can't encode the information presented in a lesson? Research suggests some strategies (M. Brenner et al., 1997; Nuthall, 1999b):

- Begin lessons by asking students what they know about the topic you plan to teach.
- Supplement students' prior experiences with rich examples and representations of the content.
- Use open-ended questions to assess student perceptions of your examples and representations.
- Use the experiences of students in the class to augment the backgrounds of those lacking the experiences.

For instance, Mike might say, "Celeena, you lived in Europe. What do people there say about the conflict in the former Yugoslavia?" Also, because nationalism was an organizing idea for much of what would follow, Mike could ask, "What does *nationalism* mean? Give an example of strong nationalism today." If students can't respond, he could then change his plans and focus on illustrating and discussing the concept, which would provide information students could use in later encoding activities. For example, he could use the school as context for his discussion of nationalism by describing school spirit, pride in the school, and the school's traditions as analogies for the feelings of nationalism in European countries. The analogy would make the concept of nationalism meaningful for students, and encoding would improve (Zook, 1991). The ability to adapt lessons in this way is one characteristic of teaching expertise.

Checking Your Understanding

5.1 Describe the principles for applying information processing theory in classrooms.

5.2 As we saw in the case study at the beginning of the chapter, David Shelton, "prepared a transparency showing the sun throwing globs of gases into space, another representing a model of the solar system that illustrates the planets in their orbital planes, and a large matrix, taped to the back wall of the room." Identify two of the principles that this planning helped illustrate, and explain how the principles are illustrated.

5.3 We also saw in the case study at the beginning of the chapter that David began his Wednesday class by saying, "I'm going to do a little demonstration, and I want you to think about how it relates to what you've been doing," and he then did the demonstration with the socks and strings. Which of the principles is best illustrated in this case? Explain.

5.4 In a poetry unit, a language arts teacher has introduced her students to the characteristics of Haiku, and she now wants them to write their own Haiku. She begins her day's lesson by saying, "Yesterday, we talked about the characteristics of Haiku. What are those characteristics?" Which instructional principle is best illustrated by her question? Explain.

To receive feedback for these questions, go to Appendix B.

Knowledge Extensions

To deepen your understanding of the topics in this section of the chapter and integrate them with topics you've already studied, go to the *Knowledge Extensions* module for Chapter 7 at *www.prenhall.com/eggen*. Respond to questions 17–19.

Classroom Connections

Capitalizing on Diversity in Your Classroom

1. Assess students' prior knowledge and perceptions throughout lessons.

   - **Elementary:** Because he has several recent-immigrant children in his class, a fourth-grade teacher begins a unit on communities by saying, "Tell us about the communities where you lived before coming to this country." He has students whose English skills are more fully developed work as interpreters for other students. He then uses the information as a framework for the study of their community.

   - **Middle School:** To supplement her students' prior knowledge, a science teacher introduces the study of refraction by having students put coins in opaque dishes and backing up until they can't see the coins. She then has partners pour water into the dishes until the coins become visible. Finally, she shows a model illustrating how the light rays are bent when they enter and leave the water.

   - **High School:** An art teacher begins a unit on perspective by asking students to sketch a three-dimensional scene. He has students put their names on the back of the sketches and then discusses the sketches during the following class period.

Putting Information Processing into Perspective

Information processing was the most influential cognitive learning theory in the 20th century (R. Mayer, 1998b). It has, however, been criticized for failing to adequately consider the social context in which learning occurs (Greeno et al., 1996) and personal factors in learning, such as students' emotions (Derry, 1992; R. Mayer, 1996). Critics also argue that information processing doesn't adequately emphasize the extent to which learners construct their own understanding, one of the principles of cognitive learning theory stated at the beginning of the chapter (Derry, 1992). (We examine the process of knowledge construction in detail in Chapter 8.)

Virtually all cognitive descriptions of learning, however, including those endorsing the principle that learners construct understanding, accept the architecture of information processing, including a limited-capacity working memory, an organized long-term memory, cognitive processes that move the information from one store to another, and the regulatory mechanisms of metacognition (Bruning et al., 2004; Mayer, 1998b; Schunk, 2004; Sweller et al., 1998). These components of our cognitive architecture help us explain learning events that neither behaviorism nor social cognitive theory can explain. Further, they help provide a framework for the process of constructing understanding, which you will study in the next chapter.

Meeting Your Learning Objectives

1. **Describe the principles on which cognitive learning theories are based, and identify illustrations of the principles.**

   - The principles of cognitive learning theory suggest (a) people are active, (b) learning and development depend on learners' experiences, (c) learners construct understanding, (d) prior knowledge influences knowledge construction, and (e) learning requires a social environment, practice, and feedback.

2. **Use the characteristics of the memory stores in our information processing system to explain events in and out of the classroom.**

   - Sensory memory is the store that briefly holds stimuli from the environment until they can be processed. Its capacity is essentially unlimited.

- Working memory is the store that holds information while it is being processed. It is the conscious part of our information processing system, and its most significant feature is its limited capacity.
- Long-term memory is our permanent information store. Information in it is organized in the form of schemas that include both declarative and procedural knowledge.

3. **Describe the cognitive processes in our information processing system, and identify examples of the processes in classroom events.**

- Attention and perception move information from sensory memory to working memory. Attention is the process of consciously focusing on a stimulus, and perception is the meaning we attach to the stimulus.
- Learners use rehearsal to retain information in working memory, and intensive rehearsal can move information into long-term memory.
- Encoding represents information in long-term memory. Learners encode information more effectively if it is represented both visually and verbally than if it is represented in only one way.
- Retrieval is the process of pulling information from long-term memory back into working memory for problem solving or further processing.

4. **Define metacognition and identify examples of metacognition in classroom events.**

- Metacognition increases the effectiveness of information processing by making learners aware of the way they study and learn. Learners who are aware create better learning environments for themselves, check to see if they perceive information accurately, and attempt to link items of information to each other to reduce the load on their working memories.
- Metacognition is developmental, with young children being less aware of their study strategies than their older counterparts.

5. **Describe the principles for applying information processing theory in classrooms, and identify examples of the principles in learning activities.**

- Learning activities that apply information processing theory begin with an event that attracts and maintains students' attention, followed by attempts to activate students' prior knowledge and check their perceptions.
- To reduce cognitive load, learning activities should proceed in short steps and emphasize relationships among ideas to promote chunking.
- Representing information in both verbal and visual forms helps capitalize on the dual-processing capability of working memory and the dual-coding capability of long-term memory.
- Providing rich examples and representations of content can help accommodate background diversity in students.

Developing as a Professional: Praxis™ Practice

Developing as a **Professional**

In the opening case study, David Shelton planned and conducted his lesson to make the solar system meaningful for his students. In the following case, a teacher helps a group of high school students understand different characters in the novel *The Scarlet Letter*. Read the case study, and then answer the questions that follow.

Sue Southam, an English teacher, decides to use Nathaniel Hawthorne's *The Scarlet Letter* as the vehicle to help her examine timeless issues, such as moral dilemmas involving personal responsibility and emotions like guilt, anger, loyalty, and revenge. The novel, set in Boston in the 1600s, describes a tragic love affair between the heroine (Hester Prynne) and a minister (Arthur Dimmesdale). The novel's title refers to the letter *A*, meaning "adulterer," which the Puritan community makes Hester wear as punishment for her adultery. The class has been discussing the book for several days, and they are now examining Reverend Dimmesdale's character.

To begin, Sue reads a passage from the text describing Dimmesdale and then says, "In your logs, jot down some of the important characteristics in that description. If you were going to draw a portrait of him, what would he look like? Try to be as specific as possible."

She gives the students a few minutes to write in their logs, asking them to describe what they think he looks like and who they might cast in the role of a movie adaptation of the novel.

Then she says, "Let's see if we can find out more about the Dimmesdale character through his actions. Listen carefully while I read the speech he gives in which he confronts Hester in front of the congregation and exhorts her to identify her secret lover and partner in sin."

She reads Dimmesdale's speech, then divides the class into "Dimmesdales" and "Hesters" around the room, and says, "Dimmesdales, in your logs I want you to tell me what Dimmesdale is really thinking during this speech. . . . Hesters, I want you to tell me what Hester is thinking while she listens. Write in your logs in your own words the private thoughts of your character."

After giving the students a few minutes to write in their logs, she organizes them into groups of four, with each group composed of two Hesters and two Dimmesdales. Once students are settled, she says, "In each group, I want you to start off by having Dimmesdale tell what he is thinking during the first line of the speech. Then I'd like a Hester to respond. Then continue with Dimmesdale's next line, and then Hester's reaction. Go ahead and share your thoughts in your groups."

She gives the students 5 minutes to share their perspectives, then calls the class back together: "Okay, let's hear it. A Dimmesdale first. Just what was he thinking during his speech? . . . Mike?"

"The only thing I could think of was, 'Oh God, help me. I hope she doesn't say anything. If they find out it's me, I'll be ruined.' And then here comes Hester with her powerful speech," Mike concludes, turning to his partner in the group, Nicole.

"I wrote, 'Good man, huh. So why don't you confess then? You know you're guilty. I've admitted my love, but you haven't. Why don't you just come out and say it?'" Nicole comments.

"Interesting. . . . What else? How about another Hester? . . . Sarah?"

"I just put, 'No, I'll never tell. I still love you, and I'll keep your secret forever,'" Sarah offers.

Sue pauses for a moment, looks around the room, and comments, "Notice how different the two views of Hester are. Nicole paints her as very angry, whereas Sarah views her as still loving him." Sue again pauses to look for reactions. Karen raises her hand, and Sue nods to her.

"I think the reason Hester doesn't say anything is that people won't believe her, because he's a minister," Karen suggests. "She's getting her revenge just by being there reminding him of his guilt."

"But if she accuses him, won't people expect him to deny it?" Brad adds.

"Maybe he knows she won't accuse him because she still loves him," Julie offers.

"Wait a minute," Jeff counters. "I don't think he's such a bad guy. I think he feels guilty about it all, but he just doesn't have the courage to admit it in front of all of those people."

"I think he's really admitting it in his speech but is asking her secretly not to tell," Caroline adds. "Maybe he's really talking to Hester and doesn't want the rest of the people to know."

The class continues, with students debating the meaning in the speech and trying to decide whether Reverend Dimmesdale is really a villain or a tragic figure.

"Interesting ideas," Sue says as the end of the class nears. "Keep them in mind, and for tomorrow, I'd like you to read Chapter 4, in which we meet Hester's husband," and she then closes the lesson.

Short-Answer Questions

In answering these questions, use information from the chapter, and link your responses to specific information in the case.

1. Assess the extent to which Sue applied the principles of cognitive learning theory in her lesson. Include both strengths and weaknesses in your assessment.
2. Assess the extent to which Sue applied information processing theory in her lesson. Include both strengths and weaknesses in your assessment.
3. Which cognitive process from information processing theory was most prominent in Sue's lesson? Explain.
4. Identify at least one instance in Sue's lesson in which she focused on declarative knowledge. Identify another in which she focused on procedural knowledge. Was the primary focus of Sue's lesson the acquisition of declarative knowledge or procedural knowledge?

PRAXIS These exercises are designed to help you prepare for the Praxis™ Principles of Learning and Teaching exam. To receive feedback on your short-answer questions, go to the Companion Website at *www.prenhall.com/eggen*, then to the *Practice for Praxis*™ module for Chapter 7.

To acquire experience in preparing for the multiple-choice items on the Praxis™ exam, go to the *Self-Assessment* module for Chapter 7 at *www.prenhall.com/eggen* and click on "Practice Quiz."

For additional connections between this text and the Praxis™ exam, go to Appendix A.

ONLINE PORTFOLIO ACTIVITIES

To develop your professional portfolio, further apply your understanding of chapter content, and address the INTASC standards, go to the Companion Website, then to *Online Portfolio Activities* for Chapter 7. Complete the suggested activities.

Also on the Companion Website at *www.prenhall.com/eggen*, you can measure your understanding of chapter content with multiple-choice and essay questions, and broaden your knowledge base in *Exploring Further* and *Web Links* to other educational psychology websites.

IMPORTANT CONCEPTS

analogies (p. 217)

attention (p. 211)

automaticity (p. 206)

chunking (p. 206)

cognitive learning theories (p. 201)

cognitive load (p. 205)

declarative knowledge (p. 207)

dual-coding theory (p. 216)

elaboration (p. 216)

encoding (p. 213)

feedback (p. 202)

forgetting (p. 218)

imagery (p. 216)

information processing (p. 203)

interference (p. 218)

learning (p. 202)

long-term memory (p. 207)

meaningfulness (p. 207)

memory stores (p. 204)

meta-attention (p. 220)

metacognition (p. 220)

metamemory (p. 221)

mnemonic devices (p. 217)

organization (p. 214)

perception (p. 212)

procedural knowledge (p. 207)

rehearsal (p. 213)

retrieval (p. 218)

schemas (p. 207)

scripts (p. 209)

sensory memory (p. 204)

working memory (p. 204)

CHAPTER 8

Constructing Knowledge

Chapter Outline	**Learning Objectives**

After you have completed your study of this chapter, you should be able to

What Is Constructivism?

Cognitive Constructivism • Social Constructivism

1 Describe the primary difference between cognitive and social constructivism, and identify examples of each in descriptions of learning activities.

Characteristics of Constructivism

Learners Construct Knowledge That Makes Sense to Them • New Learning Depends on Current Understanding • Social Interaction Facilitates Learning • Meaningful Learning Occurs Within Real-World Tasks

2 Identify characteristics and applications of constructivism in events in and outside of classrooms.

Outcomes of Knowledge Construction

Concepts • Schemas • Misconceptions and Conceptual Change

3 Analyze applications of concept learning, including teaching for conceptual change.

Implications of Constructivism for Teaching

The Teacher's Role in Constructivist Classrooms • Suggestions for Classroom Practice • Assessment and Learning: The Role of Assessment in Constructivist Classrooms • Putting Constructivism into Perspective

4 Identify suggestions for classroom practice in descriptions of learning activities.

Constructivism in Classrooms: Instructional Principles

Learning Contexts: Constructing Knowledge in Urban Environments

5 Analyze applications of constructivist learning theory in classroom activities.

As you saw in Chapter 7, students construct their own knowledge of the topics they study. Because of this, individuals' thinking about those topics may vary widely. Keep this idea in mind as you examine the thinking of the students in the following case.

Jenny Newhall, a fourth-grade teacher, wants her students to understand the principle behind beam balances: that they balance when the weight times the distance on one side of the fulcrum equals the weight times the distance on the other. She begins the lesson by dividing her students into groups of four, giving each group a balance with a numerical scale and presenting the following problem:

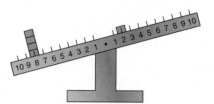

Jenny tells students that they are to figure out how to balance the beam, but before adding tiles to the actual balances, they need to write down possible solutions on paper and explain to their groupmates why they think their solutions will work.

Jenny circulates around the room as the class begins to work and then joins one of the groups—Molly, Suzanne, Tad, and Drexel—as the students attempt to solve the problem.

Suzanne begins by offering, "There are 4 on the 8 and 1 on the 2. I want to put 3 on the 10 so there will be 4 on each side."

Here's the solution she proposes to her group:

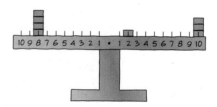

Molly agrees with Suzanne's arrangement of tiles but offers different reasoning for the arrangement: "I think we should put 3 on 10, because 4 on the 8 is 32 on one side. And since we only have 2 on the other side, we need to make them equal. So 3 on 10 would equal 30, plus 2, and we'd have 32 on both sides."

We return to the lesson later in the chapter, but for now, let's consider two questions. (1) Because it is highly unlikely that Jenny or another teacher suggested that the beam would balance if the number of tiles on each side was the same, where did Suzanne come up with this idea? (2) How might we explain the difference in the two girls' thinking? We examine these and other questions in this chapter.

WHAT IS CONSTRUCTIVISM?

Constructivism is a broad term used in different ways by philosophers, educational psychologists, and teachers (Palincsar, 1998; Phillips, 2000). Philosophers debate questions about reality, the validity of understanding, and whether or not misconceptions exist.

Educational psychologists study constructivism as a theory of learning and consider the implications of this theory for teaching. For teachers, it raises questions about the appropriateness of different learning objectives, approaches to instruction, and the role of assessment in learning. In this chapter, we focus primarily on constructivism as examined by educational psychologists and teachers.

Despite differences, all who study constructivism generally agree with the principle: "Learners construct, rather than record, knowledge," which you first saw in Chapter 7. Expanding on this principle, **constructivism** can be described as a view of learning suggesting that learners create their own knowledge of the topics they study rather than having that knowledge transmitted to them by some other source (e.g., another person or something they read) (Bransford et al., 2000; Bruning et al., 2004)

This definition helps us answer our first question from this chapter's introduction: "Where did Suzanne come up with this idea?" Suzanne didn't get her ideas about beam balances from Jenny, another teacher, or something she read; she "constructed" them on her own because they made sense to her. (For her it made sense that a beam would balance if the number of tiles on each side of the fulcrum was the same).

Constructivism adds to our understanding of learning, because no other theory, alone, can explain Suzanne's reasoning. It is unlikely that she had been reinforced for this thinking, as a behaviorist explanation would require, and it's equally unlikely that it had been modeled for her, so social cognitive theory can't provide an explanation either. And information processing doesn't address the issue of learners' unique constructions and misconceptions. Suzanne's thinking illustrates the principle that learners construct, rather than record, understanding.

Views of knowledge construction vary, influenced primarily by the works of Piaget (1952, 1959, 1970) and Vygotsky (1978, 1986), but also by other sources including Dewey (1938), Bruner (1966, 1973), and Gestalt psychology (Bruning et al., 2004; Schunk, 2004). In the following sections, we examine two perspectives: cognitive constructivism and social constructivism.

Constructivism suggests that learners construct their own knowledge rather than having it transmitted by some other source.

Cognitive Constructivism

Cognitive constructivism, which is based largely on Piaget's work, focuses on individual, internal constructions of knowledge (Greeno et al., 1996; Meter & Stevens, 2000; Nuthall, 1999a). It stresses individuals' search for meaning as they interact with the environment and test and modify existing schemas (Packer & Goicoechea, 2000). Social interaction influences the process, but primarily as a catalyst for individual cognitive conflict (Palincsar, 1998). When one child suggests an idea that causes disequilibrium in another, for example, the second child resolves the disequilibrium by individually reconstructing his or her understanding.

To illustrate this idea, consider the following exchange:

Devon: (Holding a beetle between his fingers and pointing at a spider) Look at the bugs.
Gino: Yech. . . . Put that thing down (gesturing to the spider). Besides, that's not a bug. It's a spider.
Devon: What do you mean? A bug is a bug.
Gino: Nope. Bugs have six legs. See (touching the legs of the beetle). This one has eight legs. . . . Look (pointing to the spider).
Devon: So, . . . bugs have . . . six legs, and spiders have eight? . . . Hmm?

Cognitive constructivists interpret this episode by saying that Devon's equilibrium was disrupted as a result of the discussion, and—individually—he resolved the problem by reconstructing his thinking to accommodate the new evidence Gino offered.

What does cognitive constructivism say to teachers? A literal interpretation of this position emphasizes learning activities that are experience based and discovery oriented. According to this view of learning, for example, children learn math most effectively if they discover ideas while manipulating concrete objects such as blocks and sticks, rather than having them presented by a teacher or other expert.

This interpretation posed a dilemma for educators because it "fundamentally distrusted all attempts to instruct directly" (Resnick & Klopfer, 1989, p. 3). The interpretation suggests that teacher–student interaction is important but that teachers need to guard against imposing their thoughts and values on developing learners (DeVries, 1997). So, other than providing materials and a supportive learning environment, what is the

Constructivism. A view of learning suggesting that learners create their own knowledge of the topics they study rather than having that knowledge transmitted to them by some other source

Cognitive constructivism. A form of constructivism that focuses on individual, internal constructions of knowledge

teacher's role? This question hasn't been satisfactorily answered (Airasian & Walsh, 1997; Greeno et al., 1996).

Social Constructivism

Most of us have had the experience of talking about an idea with another person, neither of whom understand it completely, but as the discussion continues, both of our understandings gradually increase. This experience illustrates the basic premise of **social constructivism,** which, strongly influenced by Vygotsky's (1978) work, suggests that learners first construct knowledge in a social context and then appropriate and internalize it (Bruning et al., 2004; Horn, 2003). Social constructivism has become the view that is most influential in guiding the thinking of educational leaders and teachers.

According to social constructivists, the process of sharing individual perspectives results in learners' constructing understanding together that wouldn't be possible alone (Gauvain, 2001; Greeno et al., 1996).

To see how this position differs from cognitive constructivism, let's think again about the exchange between Devon and Gino. Social constructivists would argue that Devon's understanding was increased as a direct result of the exchange. They would also assert that the dialogue, itself, played an essential role in helping Devon arrive at a clearer understanding of insects and spiders.

A social constructivist interpretation helps resolve the dilemma about teachers' roles. This perspective "does not suggest that educators get out of the way so children can do their natural work, as Piagetian theory often seemed to imply" (Resnick & Klopfer, 1989, p. 4). Social constructivism emphasizes teachers' roles and suggests that they consider all the traditional questions of teaching: how to organize and implement learning activities, motivate students, and assess learning. The answers, however, focus on facilitating students' constructions of understanding through social interaction (Fleming & Alexander, 2001; Shuell, 1996). From a social constructivist perspective, creating situations in which learners can exchange ideas and collaborate in solving problems is an essential teacher role (R. Anderson et al., 2001; Meter & Stevens, 2000).

Sociocultural Learning Theory

Just as constructivism, in general, is interpreted differently, theorists emphasize different dimensions of social constructivism. **Sociocultural theory,** while still emphasizing the social dimensions of learning, places greater emphasis on the larger cultural contexts in which learning occurs (Kozulin, 1998; Palincsar, 1998). Sociocultural theories remind us that our students' homes and communities strongly influence learning (Rogoff, 2003; Rogoff, Turkanis, & Bartlett, 2001). For example, the linguistic patterns of participation found in the home determine how students view their roles in the classroom (Cazden, 2002; Heath, 1989). In some homes, children are not viewed as legitimate partners in conversation, while in others, children speak frequently and openly with adults on a number of topics (Au, 1992; Tharp & Gallimore, 1991). When these different groups of children come to our classrooms, they bring different views on how they should act. As you saw in Chapter 4, differences also exist in the cultural experiences, attitudes, and values that students bring to school, and they all influence learning.

The Classroom as a Community of Learners

The sociocultural perspective also reminds us that our actions as teachers create microcultures in our classrooms. The rules and procedures that we follow and the way we interact with students can make classrooms either inviting places where students support each other's learning or environments where students compete for grades and honors. A **community of learners** is a learning environment in which the teacher and all the students work together to help everyone achieve (A. Brown & Campione, 1994; Palincsar, 1998).

The following are some characteristics of a learning community (A. Brown & Campione, 1994; Palincsar, 1998):

- All students actively participate in learning activities.
- Teachers and students work together to help one another learn; promoting learning isn't the teacher's responsibility alone.

Social constructivism. A form of constructivism suggesting that learners first construct knowledge in a social context and then appropriate and internalize it

Sociocultural theory. A social constructivist theory that emphasizes the larger cultural context in learning

Community of learners. A classroom in which the teacher and all the students work together to help everyone learn

Exploring Further

To read an analysis of some of the issues involved in attempting to apply constructivist views of learning in classrooms, go to "Assessing Constructivism in Classrooms" in the *Exploring Further* module of Chapter 8 at *www.prenhall.com/eggen*.

- Interaction isn't exclusively teacher–student; student–student interaction is an important part of the learning process.
- Teachers and students respect the diversity of student interests, thinking, and progress.
- The thinking involved in learning activities, such as problem solving, is as important as the outcome (the solution to the problem).

Each of these characteristics is grounded in the assumption that knowledge is first socially constructed before it is appropriated and internalized by individuals.

Cognitive Apprenticeship

Historically, apprenticeships helped novices, as they worked closely with experts, acquire skills they couldn't learn on their own. These skills were often found in trades such as furniture construction, weaving, or cooking, but apprenticeships were also common in areas such as learning to play musical instruments or creating pieces of art.

The concept of *cognitive apprenticeship* is another outcome of the influence of social constructivism on education. **Cognitive apprenticeship** occurs when a less-skilled learner works at the side of an expert in developing complex cognitive skills, such as reading comprehension, writing, or problem solving (Englert, Berry, & Dunsmoore, 2001; Palincsar, 1998). Apprenticeships in the classroom are similar to those of any apprenticeship, except the focus is on the development of cognitive abilities. Cognitive apprenticeships commonly include the following components:

- *Modeling:* Teachers demonstrate skills, such as solutions to problem, and simultaneously model their thought processes by describing their thinking out loud.
- *Scaffolding:* As students perform tasks, teachers ask questions and provide cues and other forms of support to ensure that students are making progress. As students' proficiency increases, teachers decrease scaffolding.
- *Verbalization:* Students put their understanding into words, which allows teachers to assess both the students' skills and their thinking.
- *Increasing complexity:* As students' proficiency increases, teachers present more complex and challenging problems or other tasks to complete.
- *Exploration:* Teachers ask students to identify new applications of what they've learned.

Research indicates that teachers who view their relationships with students in terms of cognitive apprenticeships increase student learning more than their peers who have a more didactic view of the teacher–student relationship (Englert et al., 2001).

Situated Cognition

An additional outcome of the influence of social constructivism is the idea of **situated cognition** (or *situated learning*), which is a view suggesting that learning is inherently social in nature and depends on, and cannot be separated from, the context in which it occurs (Gauvain, 2001; King, 2000; Putnam & Borko, 2000; Rogoff, 1990). According to this view, a student who learns to solve subtraction and division problems while determining a car's gas mileage on a trip, for example, has a different kind of understanding than one who solves subtraction and division problems in exercises in school.

Situated cognition is somewhat controversial. At the extreme, it suggests that transfer—the ability to take understanding acquired in one context and apply it in a different context—is virtually impossible because all learning is bound to the situation in which it occurs. For instance, if we learn to drive in a rural area or small town, we may have difficulty making the transition to big-city driving with its high speeds, multiple lanes, and quickly merging traffic. Our driving expertise is situated in a different setting. Evidence for transfer exists, however, both in the classroom and in everyday life (J. Anderson, Reder, & Simon, 1996; R. C. Clark & Mayer, 2003). For example, many people are comfortable driving in both rural areas and large cities. They develop this expertise by practicing driving in a variety of situations.

Similar accommodations can be made in the school curriculum. To encourage transfer, experts suggest that we present a variety of examples and problems during learning

Cognitive apprenticeship. The process of having a less-skilled learner work at the side of an expert in developing complex cognitive skills

Situated cognition. A view suggesting that learning is social in nature, depends on, and cannot be separated from the context in which it is learned

activities and that we purposefully design our instruction to match our learning objectives (R. C. Clark & Mayer, 2003). Examples are math students practicing with a variety of realistic problems, science students applying concepts to a variety of real-world settings, and language arts students writing in all of their content areas.

Checking Your Understanding

1.1 Describe the primary difference between cognitive and social constructivism.

1.2 Is Suzanne's thinking (in the case study at the beginning of the chapter) a better example of cognitive or of social constructivism? Explain why you think so.

1.3 Identify at least three characteristics of a community of learners that were illustrated in Jenny's lesson. Is a learning community more nearly grounded in cognitive constructivisim or social constructivisim? Explain.

To receive feedback for these questions, go to Appendix B.

Knowledge Extensions

To deepen your understanding of the topics in this section of the chapter and to integrate it with topics you've already studied, go to the *Knowledge Extensions* module for Chapter 8 at *www.prenhall.com/eggen*. Respond to questions 1–3.

CHARACTERISTICS OF CONSTRUCTIVISM

Though interpretations vary, most constructivists agree on four major characteristics that influence learning (Bruning et al., 2004; R. Mayer, 1996). They're outlined in Figure 8.1 and discussed in the sections that follow.

Figure 8.1   Characteristics of constructivism

- Learners construct knowledge that makes sense to them.
- New learning depends on current understanding.
- Social interaction facilitates learning.
- The most meaningful learning occurs within real-world tasks.

Learners Construct Knowledge That Makes Sense to Them

As we first saw in Chapter 7, learners' constructing knowledge is an accepted principle of all cognitive learning theories. Among theorists, "the view of the learner has changed from that of a recipient of knowledge to that of a constructor of knowledge" (R. Mayer, 1998b, p. 359).

We saw this process in Suzanne's thinking. She had a clear (to her) schema that guided her problem solving. For her, it made sense to think that having an equal number of tiles on each side of the fulcrum would cause the beam to balance. She didn't receive this understanding from anyone else; she constructed this intuitively sensible, but incorrect, conclusion on her own.

New Learning Depends on Current Understanding

We described the role of current understanding (prior knowledge) when we discussed the importance of making information meaningful in Chapter 7. Constructivists go further, emphasizing that the ideas that learners construct directly depend on the knowledge they currently possess (Bae, 2003; Shapiro, 2004). For instance, learners commonly conclude that summer is warmer than winter (in the Northern Hemisphere) because the Earth is closer to the Sun in summer. This makes sense. The closer to a candle or a hot burner we hold our hands, the warmer they feel, so, based on this experience, our conclusion that we're closer to the Sun makes more sense than the actual explanation involving the tilt of Earth's axis. An understanding of the seasons is constructed in the context of previous experiences with candles and stoves.

The influence of prior knowledge helps answer the second question we asked at the beginning of the chapter: "How might we explain the difference in the two girls' thinking?" The answer is simple. Molly had prior knowledge that Suzanne lacked. *Why* she had more prior knowledge could depend on a number of factors, such as more experiences provided by parents, other caregivers or teachers, greater motivation, or higher ability. Examples of differences in prior knowledge are common, and constructivism helps us understand why these differences influence learning in our classrooms.

Social Interaction Facilitates Learning

To examine this characteristic, let's return again to Jenny's lesson.

After the groups discuss their solutions, Jenny tells the students to test their ideas on the actual balances. Afterwards, she reassembles the class and calls for a student with a successful solution to come to the board and explain it. Jenny provides a sketch of the beam balance on the chalkboard to aid their explanation.

Mavrin volunteers, explains his solution, and writes his ideas under the sketch, which appears as follows:

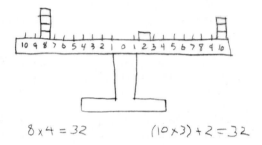

$$8 \times 4 = 32 \qquad (10 \times 3) + 2 = 32$$

As Jenny reviews Mavrin's solution, she emphasizes the logic of his thinking, "Over on this side he wrote 8 times 4 equals 32, because he had 4 tiles on the 8. Then, when he started out with the 2 over here, he needed something that added up to 30, so he came over here and put 3 on the 10. Ten times 3 equals 30, plus 2 more equals 32. . . . He has an excellent number sentence here."

An interviewer from a nearby university is observing the class, and following the lesson he talks with Suzanne, Molly, Tad, and Drexel about what they took from the lesson. He gives them the following problem:

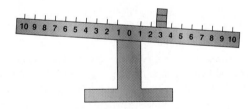

After giving students time to consider the problem, the interviewer says, "Suzanne, go ahead and offer a way to balance the beam."

"What I did was 2 plus 3 equals 5" she responds, pointing to the right side of the beam (and indicating that she had added 2 more tiles to the right side of the fulcrum), "and 2 plus 1 plus 2 equals 5 (indicating that she had put 5 tiles on the left side of the fulcrum)." She points to the left side.

Her proposed solution looks like this:

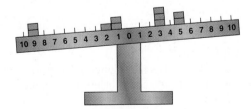

This segment raises an important question. Suzanne heard three correct explanations for the problem—Molly's, which we saw at the end of the first segment of our case study, Mavrin's at the board, and Jenny's—yet her thinking didn't change; she still believed that the number of tiles was the only factor determining whether or not the beam would balance. How might we explain her thinking?

In Chapter 7 we saw that putting learners in cognitively active roles is essential for making information meaningful. In spite of the fact that Suzanne had access to Molly's,

Mavrin's, and Jenny's thinking, she remained cognitively passive. Her ideas hadn't been *directly* confronted, which is essential for conceptual change (Dole & Sinatra, 1998). (We examine this issue in more detail in our discussion of misconceptions and conceptual change later in the chapter.)

To illustrate the powerful role that social interaction can play in promoting learning in general and conceptual change in particular, let's return once more to the interview.

> After Suzanne offers her solution, the interviewer asks, "Molly, what do you think of that solution?"
>
> "It won't work. . . . It doesn't matter how many blocks there are," Molly answers, shaking her head. "It's where they're put."
>
> "Okay, what do you think, Drexel?"
>
> Drexel shakes his head, indicating Suzanne's explanation won't work.
>
> "Why don't you think so?"
>
> "Because of Molly's reasoning," Drexel answers, motioning toward Molly. "It doesn't matter how many blocks you have; it's where you put them."
>
> "Tad, how about you? . . . What do you think?"
>
> "Same as them, I guess," Tad responds hesitantly (uncertain about the explanations). The students try Suzanne's solution, and the beam tips to the left.
>
> "If you take 1 off the 9, it might work," Suzanne suggests.
>
> "Why do you think that'll work?"
>
> "Because that's the farthest to the end, and sometimes the farthest to the end brings it down more." (Suzanne is starting to change her thinking as a result of the seeing the example and interacting with the others.)
>
> The interviewer nods but doesn't affirm any explanation, instead giving the students the following additional problem and asking for solutions:

> Molly offers, "Put 1 on the 8 and 4 on the 1."
>
> "That's what Molly thinks," the interviewer says. "What do you think? . . . Tad?"
>
> "Yeah," Tad answers slowly.
>
> "So, you *do* think it'll work. . . . Now give us a nice, clear explanation for why it'll work," the interviewer probes with a reassuring smile.
>
> "Okay," Tad begins, peering intently at the beam for several seconds. "Oh, okay," he begins slowly, "3 times 4 is 12, . . . and 4 times 1 is 4, . . . and 8 times 1 is 8, and 8 plus 4 is 12."
>
> "And so it should work, you think. . . . Suzanne, what do you think?"
>
> ". . . I think it'll work."
>
> "You *also* think it'll work," the interviewer repeats. "Okay, who has another solution?"
>
> "One on the 2 and 1 on the 10," Drexel says quickly.
>
> "Okay, I want you to tell us whether or not that'll work, Suzanne."
>
> ". . . I think it will."
>
> "Okay, explain why you think it will."
>
> "Because . . . 10 times 1 equals 10," Suzanne begins hesitantly, "and 2 times 1 equals 2, and 10 plus 2 equals 12. . . . So it'll be even."
>
> "Okay, Tad what do you think?"
>
> Tad nods affirmatively, and explains the solution in his own words.
>
> They try this solution on the beam, and it balances. The interviewer asks, "What do you think, Tad?"
>
> "Perfect," Tad grins.
>
> "Perfect," the interviewer laughs, finishing the interview.

Social interaction, interpreted from either a cognitive or social constructivist perspective, is widely accepted as important for learning, and the interview we just saw illustrates its powerful influence on constructing knowledge. Suzanne, for example, had a clear schema that guided her thinking, and she retained this understanding in spite of hearing correct explanations offered by Molly, Mavrin, and Jenny during the lesson. But when she was more involved and her views were more directly challenged, as occurred in the inter-

Analyzing Classrooms Video
To further analyze the discussion that took place in this section, go to Episode 13, "Constructing Knowledge of Beam Balances," on DVD 1, accompanying this text.

view, the interaction helped change her thinking. Tad's experience was similar. He too remained passive during the lesson, so most of his understanding developed during the interview when he was more actively involved in the discussion. We discuss the importance of interaction in greater detail when we examine the implications of constructivism for teachers.

Meaningful Learning Occurs Within Real-World Tasks

Earlier in the chapter, we discussed the concept of *situated cognition,* which suggests that "much of what is learned is specific to the situation in which it is learned" (J. Anderson et al., 1996, p. 5). This suggests that real-world situations are likely to be more meaningful for students, especially when our goal is application and transfer to the real world.

Jenny's lesson illustrates this characteristic. She used concrete materials to help her students advance their current understanding of beams that balance, and the knowledge they gained could later increase their understanding of teeter-totters and force and resistance in many everyday tools that use levers, such as pliers and scissors. Her lesson used a **real-world task** (often called an *authentic* task), a learning activity in which students practice thinking similar to that required in the real world (Van Merriënboer, Kirschner, & Kester, 2003). *Thinking* is the key: "Authentic activities foster the kinds of thinking and problem-solving skills that are important in out-of-school settings, whether or not the activities themselves mirror what practitioners do" (Putnam & Borko, 2000, pp. 4–5). So when students use their math skills to balance a checkbook, or apply their writing skills to a job application, they are involved in authentic learning activities.

Exploring Further

To rexamine real-world or "authentic" instruction in more depth, go to "Analyzing Authentic Instruction" in the *Exploring Further* module of Chapter 8 at *www.prenhall.com/eggen.*

Checking Your Understanding

2.1 Of the four characteristics of constructivism, which is best illustrated by Suzanne's initial conclusion that the beam would balance if the number of tiles on each side of the fulcrum was the same? Explain.

2.2 For centuries people believed that the Earth was the center not only of our solar system but also of the universe. Which of the four characteristics of constructivism is best illustrated by this historical fact? Explain.

2.3 You want your students to use grammatical rules correctly in their writing. Describe a real-world context that would be most effective for helping them reach the objective.

To receive feedback for these questions, go to Appendix B.

Knowledge Extensions

To deepen your understanding of the topic in this section of the chapter and to integrate it with topics you've already studied, go to the *Knowledge Extensions* module for Chapter 8 at *www.prenhall.com/eggen.* Respond to questions 4–7.

OUTCOMES OF KNOWLEDGE CONSTRUCTION

In Chapter 2, we described the idea that people instinctively organize their experiences in an attempt to understand the world (Marinoff, 2003), and they begin to do so as infants (Quinn, 2002). This is the foundation of the learning principle, *learners construct knowledge that makes sense to them,* which you first saw in Chapter 7 and again earlier in this chapter. One way of making sense of experiences is to categorize them into classes or sets. This leads us to concept learning, and it also helps us understand what we mean when we say *outcomes of knowledge construction.* One of the outcomes—what is it that people actually construct—is concepts. This is the topic of our next section.

Concepts

"A **concept** is a mental construct or representation of a category that allows one to identify examples and nonexamples of the category" (Schunk, 2004, p. 196). Concepts are constructed from our experiences and are fundamental building blocks of our thinking (Ferrari & Elik, 2003). A number of concepts have guided your thinking as you've studied this book. For example, you learned about *equilibrium, centration,* and *zone of proximal development*

Real-world (authentic) task. A learning activity that develops understanding similar to understanding that would be used outside the classroom

Concepts. Mental constructs that categorize sets of objects, events, or ideas

in Chapter 2, *initiative* and *self-concept* in Chapter 3, and *intelligence* and *socioeconomic status* in Chapter 4. Each is a concept. To aid you in constructing and organizing your knowledge of educational psychology, we define important concepts in the margins and list them at the end of each chapter. (We ask you to identify concepts from Chapters 5–7 as a *Knowledge Extensions* activity.)

Concepts help us simplify the world. For example, learners would identify each of the polygons in Figure 8.2 as a triangle, even though the shapes vary in size, configuration, and orientation. *Triangle* is a mental construct into which all examples of three-sided, closed-plane figures can be placed. The concept *triangle* allows us to think and talk about examples in Figure 8.2 as a group, instead of as specific objects. Having to remember each separately would make learning impossibly complex and unwieldy.

Figure 8.2 Triangles

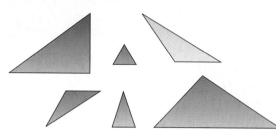

Concepts represent a major portion of the school curriculum (Brophy & Alleman, 2003; McCleery, Twyman & Tindal, 2003). Students study, for example, *major scale* and *tempo* in music, *perspective* and *balance* in art, and *aerobic exercise* and *isotonic exercise* in physical education. In addition, many other concepts, such as *honesty, bias, love,* and *internal conflict* are found in different areas of the curriculum. Additional examples of concepts in language arts, social studies, math, and science are listed in Table 8.1. This is only a brief list, and many more exist.

Theories of Concept Learning

Theorists offer different explanations for how people construct concepts. In this section, we consider three theories that focus on characteristics, prototypes, and exemplars, respectively.

Some concepts, such as *square, longitude* or *adverb,* have well-defined **characteristics** (sometimes called *attributes* or *features*), which are the concept's defining elements (Medin, Proffitt, & Schwartz, 2000). For instance, *closed, equal sides* and *equal angles* are the characteristics of the concept *square.* Learners can identify examples of squares based on a rule stating that squares must have these attributes. Other characteristics—such as size, color, or spatial orientation—aren't essential, so learners don't have to consider them in making their classifications. This *rule-driven theory* of concept learning was investigated by early researchers (e.g., Bruner, Goodenow, & Austin, 1956), who found that people differentiate concepts on the basis of the rules, or defining characteristics, of each (Bourne, 1982).

Many concepts don't have well-defined characteristics, however, so creating clear rules to help differentiate them is difficult. For instance, what are the characteristics of the concepts *Democrat* or *Republican?* Despite frequently hearing the terms in our popular news, most people can't define them with any precision. Even common concepts, such as *car,* can have "fuzzy boundaries" (Terry, 2006). For instance, some people describe pickup trucks as cars, but others don't. How about minivans? And railroad "cars" also exist.

A second theory of concept learning suggests that for concepts such as *Democrat, Republican,* and even *car,* people construct a **prototype,** the best representation of the category or class (Hampton, 1995; Medin et al., 2000). For example, George W. Bush or Justice Clarence Thomas might be prototypes for the concept *Republican,* and similar choices also exist for *Democrat.* Similarly, a common passenger car, like a Ford Taurus or Toyota Camry, might be a prototype for *car.*

Characteristics. A concept's defining elements

Prototype. The best representative of a category or class

Table 8.1 Concepts in different content areas

Language Arts	Social Studies	Science	Math
Adjective	Culture	Acid	Prime number
Verb	Longitude	Conifer	Equivalent fraction
Plot	Federalist	Element	Set
Simile	Democracy	Force	Addition
Infinitive	Immigrant	Inertia	Parabola

Prototypes aren't necessarily physical examples. Rather, they may be a mental composite, constructed from examples that individuals experience (Reisberg, 2006; B. Ross & Spalding, 1994). For instance, a person who has encountered a number of different dogs might construct a prototype that doesn't look exactly like any particular breed.

A third theory of concept learning holds that learners don't necessarily construct a single prototype from the examples they encounter; rather they store **exemplars,** the most highly typical examples of a concept (Medin et al., 2000). For instance, instead of constructing a prototype, the child trying to construct a concept of dogs may store images of a golden retriever, cocker spaniel, collie, dachshund, and German shepherd in memory as exemplars.

Each theory can explain different aspects of concept learning. For instance, concepts such as *square* or *odd number* are likely constructed based on their characteristics. Others—such as *car*—are probably represented as prototypes, and still others—such as *dog* or *bird*—may be constructed based on exemplars.

Examples: The Key to Learning and Teaching Concepts

Why do virtually all people, including small children, understand concepts like *square* and *triangle,* whereas few have a clear understanding of *democracy, justice,* or *bias?* And what can teachers do to increase learners' understanding of concepts?

When a concept has a small number of concrete characteristics, learning is simplified (Tennyson & Cocchiarella, 1986). For example, *plane, closed,* and *three straight lines* are the characteristics of the concept *triangle.* It has only three essential characteristics, and they're observable. We know that the concept is easy to learn, because most kindergarteners can identify triangles. However, concepts like *democracy, justice,* and *bias* don't have well-defined characteristics, and people's prototypes and sets of exemplars for them vary markedly. These concepts are much harder to learn, and consequently they're much harder to teach.

Regardless of a concept's complexity, the key to teaching a concept is giving students experience with a carefully selected set of examples and nonexamples combined with a definition that highlights essential characteristics (Schunk, 2004; Tennyson & Cocchiarella, 1986). An ideal example *contains all the information learners need to construct a valid concept.* If the examples are constructed on the basis of a well-defined rule, such as the rules for *square, adjective,* or *force,* they will illustrate all of the essential characteristics. If not, the examples will help learners construct a valid prototype or set of exemplars.

Nonexamples are important when the concept can be confused with a closely related concept. For instance, *frog* would be an important nonexample for the concept *reptile,* because many people believe frogs are reptiles, and *simile* would be an important nonexample for the concept *metaphor,* because the two are easily confused.

Analogies can also be used to make new concepts meaningful (Bulgren et al., 2000). For example, comparing the temperature control systems of mammals (new concept) to the analogous system in a house helps students make connections to experiences stored in long-term memory. Graphic organizers that highlight similarities and differences in two concepts can also be effective instructional aids (R. C. Clark & Mayer, 2003).

In teaching concepts, teachers may present the definition and then illustrate it with examples, or they may choose to present a sequence of examples and guide students' constructions of the concept. Both can be effective, and both should be used to add variety to instruction.

Concept Mapping: A Learning Strategy

Concepts don't exist in isolation. Rather, they're related to each other in complex schemas. **Concept mapping** is a learning strategy in which learners construct visual relationships among concepts (Liu, 2004; R. Mayer, 2002). Concept mapping capitalizes on the effects of organization, imagery, and the dual-processing capabilities of working memory—ideas we discussed in Chapter 7—to make relationships between concepts meaningful (D. Robinson, Katayama, Dubois, & Devaney, 1998).

Concept mapping benefits both students and teachers (Hall, Hall, & Saling, 1999). Creating concept maps puts students in active roles by encouraging them to visually represent relationships among concepts, and teachers can use the maps to assess students' understanding of these relationships. For example, the student who created the concept map in Figure 8.3 for *closed-plane figures* didn't include those with more than four sides or curved shapes other

Analyzing Classrooms Video
To assess the effectiveness of teachers' examples, go to Episode 14, "Constructing Concepts: Using Concrete Examples," on DVD 1, accompanying this text.

Exemplars. The most highly typical examples of a concept

Concept mapping. A learning strategy in which learners construct visual relationships among concepts

Figure 8.3   Concept map for closed plane figures

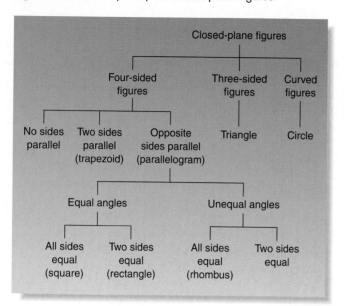

than circles. Seeing that the learner's understanding is incomplete, the teacher can provide examples of other figures with straight lines, such as pentagons and hexagons, as well as other curved figures, such as ellipses.

The concepts in Figure 8.3 are organized hierarchically, but not all relationships among concepts exist this way, so other types of concept maps may be more appropriate (D. Wallace, West, Ware, & Dansereau, 1998). Figures 8.4 and 8.5 illustrate two students' understanding of the concept *novel* represented in a **network,** a concept map illustrating nonhierarchical relationships.

The first student's network is simplistic; it includes only basic components—*plot, setting, and characters.* The second student's is more complex and sophisticated; it also includes factors that influence the quality of a novel. As with the example of closed-plane figures, teachers can use information from networks to assess students' understanding and help them further develop the concept.

The type of concept maps students use should be those that best illustrate relationships among the concepts (D. Wallace et al., 1998). Hierarchies often work best in math and science; in other areas, such as reading or social studies, a network may be more effective.

Schemas

Schemas are another outcome of our knowledge construction. In Chapter 7, you saw that schemas are cognitive structures that organize information into meaningful systems. Concepts and their attributes can be viewed as rudimentary schemas (Schunk, 2004). The concept maps in Figures 8.4 and 8.5 are more complex, just as were Juan's and Randy's schemas in Figure 7.3 of Chapter 7. Each represents the way knowledge has been constructed and organized in memory.

As with concept learning, schemas are constructed, and since they are, the process sometimes results in misconceptions. This leads us to our next section.

Misconceptions and Conceptual Change

As with all knowledge construction, learners' prior knowledge, expectations, beliefs, and emotions influence their thinking, which sometimes leads to invalid conceptions (Dole & Sinatra, 1998; Willard-Holt, 2003). We saw this illustrated in Suzanne's thinking earlier in the chapter. She initially believed that the number of tiles was the only factor that influenced whether or not the beam would balance. In spite of hearing correct solutions offered by Molly and Mavrin, and seeing and hearing Jenny's explanation, she retained this belief at the beginning of the interview, as indicated by her statement, "What I did was 2 plus 3 equals 5" (pointing to the right side of the beam and indicating that she had added

Network. A concept map illustrating nonhierarchical relationships

Figure 8.4   First learner's network for the concept *novel*

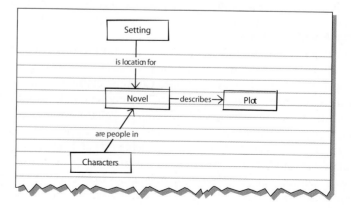

Figure 8.5   Second learner's network for the concept *novel*

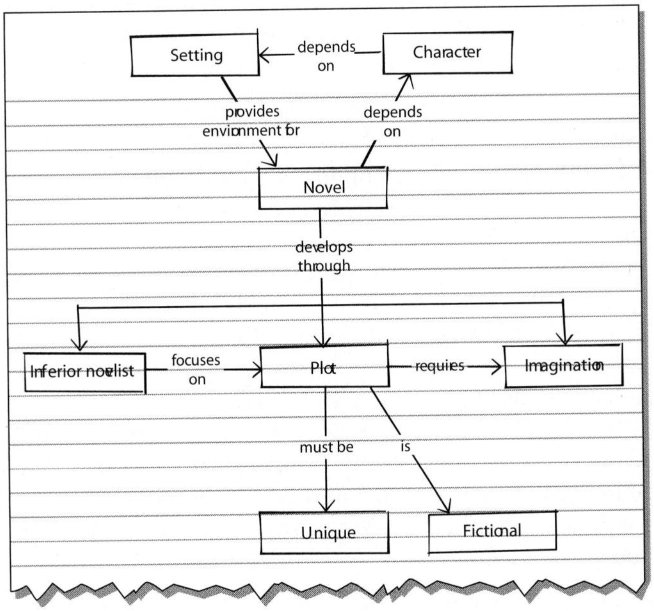

2 more tiles there), "and 2 plus 1 plus 2 equals 5 (indicating that she had put 5 tiles on the left side of the fulcrum)." She had constructed a schema for balance beam problems, and hearing explanations for the correct solutions didn't change her thinking.

A variety of factors can contribute to misconceptions. One is learners' basic attempts to make sense of their idiosyncratic experiences, which we discussed earlier (Vosniadou, 2003). Another is the tendency to infer cause–effect relationships between two objects or events because they occur at the same time (Kuhn, 2001), and a third is the inclination to draw conclusions based on the way things *appear* to be (Reiner, Slotta, Chi, & Resnick, 2000). We saw these factors operating in Suzanne's thinking. She inferred that it was the number of tiles that *caused* the beam to balance, because having the same number on each side and the beam's balancing occurred together in this case. As a result, having the same number of tiles on each side of the fulcrum *appeared* to be a correct solution.

Society can also contribute to misconceptions. For instance, many people in the United States think of Africa as a *country,* composed primarily of desert, and describe the peoples of Africa as if they share a common culture. (It is, of course, a vast continent, with a great deal of geographic and cultural diversity.)

Language is also a factor. For instance, we describe the Sun and Moon as "rising" and "setting," which can lead children to believe that they revolve around the earth; we refer to gold as a "heavy" metal, which can lead to misconceptions about the concept *density;* and we hear expressions like, "He is on a meteoric rise in his career," and "Our company is light years ahead of the competition," which can cause misconceptions about meteors and light years.

We even encounter misconceptions in educational psychology. The concept *negative reinforcement* is an example. We have emphasized that it is a process that *increases* behavior, yet most likely because of the intuitive reaction to the term *negative,* many students continue to view negative reinforcement as a process that *decreases* behavior, inappropriately equating it with punishment. Also, some people, including teachers, continue to believe that middle and high school students should be taught in the abstract, since their chronological age suggests that they are formal operational in their thinking. This is a common misconception about the application of Piaget's (1970, 1977) theory for instruction.

Misconceptions' Resistance to Change

Teachers also hold a common misconception. Realizing that their students come to their learning experiences with a number of misconceptions, they believe the solution is to provide information that contradicts the misconceptions, which will then eliminate them (Alparsian, Tekkaya, & Geban, 2004; Shuell, 1996; Yip, 2004). This rarely works, as we saw with Suzanne's thinking about the balance beam.

Why are misconceptions so resistant to change? Theory and research offer some answers.

- *Changing a misconception results in disequilibrium.* The misconception makes sense to the learner and is often embedded in a complex schema (Sinatra & Pintrich, 2003). Changing it would require an entire reconstruction of an existing schema, and as a result, it would be disequilibrating.
- *Misconceptions can be consistent with everyday experiences.* Learners' prior knowledge and experiences determine how new knowledge will be constructed. As we saw earlier, for example, the closer we move toward an open fire, the warmer we feel; it therefore makes sense to conclude that the earth is closer to the sun in the summer than it is in the winter.
- *Students don't identify inconsistencies between new information and their existing beliefs.* Since many students tend to learn ideas by rote and in isolation, they often fail to realize that new information contradicts their existing beliefs, so they continue to use their misconceptions to interpret the new information (Hynd, 2003; Luque, 2003).

Knowing that students often bring misconceptions to learning experiences and realizing that these misconceptions are resistant to change, what can we as teachers do in response? This leads us to the idea of teaching for conceptual change.

Teaching for Conceptual Change

Teaching for conceptual change attempts to directly address the fact that students often bring misconceptions to the classroom (Brophy & Alleman, 2003; Crockett, 2004; Hynd, 2003). Conceptual change is similar to Piaget's notions of disequilibrium, accommodation, and assimilation (Alparsian et al., 2004). From a conceptual change perspective, at least three conditions are required for students to change their thinking:

- The existing conception must become dissatisfying; that is, it must cause disequilibrium.
- An alternative conception must be understandable. The learner must be able to accommodate his or her thinking so that the alternative conception makes sense.
- The new conception must be useful in the real world. It must reestablish equilibrium, and the learner must be able to assimilate new experiences into it.

A growing body of research has demonstrated conceptual change instruction to be effective for learners ranging from preschool children (Havu-Nuutinen, 2005; Opfer & Siegler, 2004) to adults (Abed-El-Khalick & Akerson, 2004). As an example, let's look at Suzanne's thinking again. According to her original conception (schema), an equal number of tiles on each side of the fulcrum caused the beam to balance. The instruction in the lesson (prior to the interview) didn't result in conceptual change; she retained her original conception in spite of hearing correct solutions from Molly, Mavrin, and Jenny.

So, what led to conceptual change? First, she modified her schema only after it became dissatisfying. The group tried her solution during the interview, and she could see it didn't work (the beam didn't balance). This is the most important factor in promoting conceptual change. When learners encounter convincing evidence indicating that their existing conception is invalid, changing it becomes more likely.

Second, an alternative conception was understandable, as indicated by her ability to later explain a solution that involved both the number of tiles and the distance from the fulcrum. And third, the alternative conception was fruitful; she could explain additional examples, and it could be applied to real-world cases such as teeter-totters.

Even with these conditions in place, the process of conceptual change is not easy, as anyone who has attempted to convince someone to change their thinking about a topic will attest. Research suggests that considerable cognitive inertia exists, requiring teachers to take an active role in the conceptual change process (Southerland et al., 2002).

Questioning combined with additional concrete and real-world examples (when possible) is the most useful tool teachers have for promoting conceptual change (Crockett, 2004). Researchers have identified three types of conceptual change questions (Yip, 2004):

■ *Questions that reveal existing conceptions:* These questions ask students to describe their existing understanding. For example, when Suzanne was asked to explain what would make the beam balance, her misconception was revealed.

■ *Questions that challenge existing conceptions:* These questions ask students to explain an existing or new event, such as explaining why the beam wouldn't balance when the group tried Suzanne's solution during the interview. Conceptual change was beginning to take place when Suzanne said, "If you take 1 off the 9, it might work," and then "Because that's the farthest to the end, and sometimes the farthest to the end brings it down more," in response to the interviewer's question "Why do you think that'll work?"

■ *Questions that ask students to apply revised thinking to new situations:* These questions ask students to apply reconstructed understanding to new events. For instance, when Suzanne accurately explained why a solution worked, conceptual change had occurred.

As with constructing knowledge in general, conceptual change is grounded in the characteristics of constructivism. Suzanne went through the process of conceptual change because the new conception made sense to her. And, it made sense because the examples provided the needed experience, the task was authentic, and a great deal of social interaction occurred in the interview. These factors lead us to a discussion of the implications of constructivism for teaching.

Checking Your Understanding

3.1 Of the concepts *noun* and *culture,* which should be easier to learn? Which theory of concept learning best explains how each concept is constructed? Explain, basing your answer on the information in this section.

3.2 You're teaching the concept *reptile,* and you've shown common examples, such as a lizard, alligator, snake, and turtle. Identify at least one important additional example and one important nonexample that you should provide, and explain why they are important.

3.3 A fifth-grade teacher realizes that her students have misconceptions about parts of speech. They believe that adjectives precede the nouns they modify, words that end in *ing* are verbs, and adverbs are words that end in *ly.* In an attempt to promote conceptual change with respect to adjectives and adverbs, she shows them the following vignette:

> *John and Karen drove together in his old car to the football game. They soon met their very best friends, Latoya and Michael, at the large gate near the entrance. The game was incredibly exciting, and because the team's running game was in high gear, the home team won by a bare margin.*

Identify the examples in the vignette that are most important for promoting conceptual change. Explain in each case.

To receive feedback for these questions, go to Appendix B.

Knowledge Extensions

To deepen your understanding of the topics in this section of the chapter and to integrate them with topics you've already studied, go to the *Knowledge Extensions* module for Chapter 8 at *www.prenhall.com/eggen.* Respond to questions 8–10.

Classroom ⊞ Connections

Promoting Conceptual Change in Your Classroom

1. Ask questions that reveal and challenge students' existing understanding.

   - **Elementary:** When one of his second graders solves the first problem below, and gets 45, subtracting the smaller from the larger number in each case, an elementary teacher presents the second problem. When the student also gets 45 for this problem, he asks, "We have two very different problems. How can we get the same answer when the numbers are different?"

$$54 \qquad 59$$
$$\underline{-19} \qquad \underline{-14}$$

   - **Middle School:** When one of her eighth graders explains that transparent objects are objects that we can see through, and opaque objects are those we can't see through, a physical science teacher asks, "If we can see through a transparent object, why can't we see through it at night?

   - **High School:** When one of his students describes Native Americans as nomadic hunter gatherers, a history teacher shows pictures of pueblos and other permanent living structures and asks, "If they are nomadic, why would they build dwellings like these?"

2. Ask students questions and give students tasks that require them to apply reconstructed understanding to new situations.

   - **Elementary:** The second-grade teacher in suggestion 1 asks his students to solve a series of problems that require regrouping.

   - **Middle School:** The eighth-grade teacher in suggestion 1 asks her students to explain why they can't see a person they hear walking down the hall outside their classroom. She guides them to conclude that the light rays that are reflected from the person won't pass through the opaque wall of the classroom.

   - **High School:** The social studies teacher in suggestion 1 has the students describe the cultural and economic characteristics of different Native American groups, such as plains Indians and those who lived in the Northwest and Northeast.

IMPLICATIONS OF CONSTRUCTIVISM FOR TEACHING

Because learners construct knowledge that makes sense to them, individuals' conceptions of the topics they study vary, sometimes dramatically. We also saw in the last section that the process of knowledge construction can result in misconceptions. We examined instruction intended to produce conceptual change in that section, and we now consider instruction based on constructivist views of learning in more detail.

The Teacher's Role in Constructivist Classrooms

Many of teachers' roles—such as specifying learning objectives, preparing learning activities, and designing assessments—are the same when instruction is grounded in constructivist views of learning as they are in traditional classrooms. The primary change is a shift in emphasis away from the teacher's merely providing information and toward the teacher's promoting the interaction that makes students' thinking open and visible (Bransford et al., 2000; Donovan & Bransford, 2005). This shift results in several specific suggestions for classroom practice. Let's look at them.

Suggestions for Classroom Practice

Because students are the ones constructing knowledge, and, as we saw in the last section, misconceptions are possible, what should teachers do to ensure as much as possible that learners' constructions are valid? Some suggestions are outlined in Figure 8.6 and discussed in the sections that follow.

Provide a Variety of Examples and Representations of Content
We emphasized the powerful role that prior knowledge plays in both Chapter 7 and in this chapter. So, what can teachers do when students lack sufficient prior knowledge?

Teachers play a crucial role in guiding learners' knowledge construction.

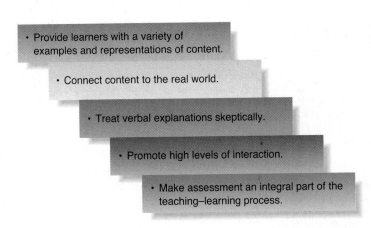

Figure 8.6 Suggestions for classroom practice

The answer is simple (but not necessarily easy): *Effective teachers supplement existing knowledge with examples and other representations of the content being taught.* These examples and representations become the experiences learners use to construct their knowledge (Eggen, 2001; J. Freeman, McPhail, & Berndt, 2002), and they apply the learning principle that you first saw in Chapter 7: Learning and development depend on learners' experiences. Examples (and nonexamples) are at the core of concept learning, and they provide the basis for conceptual change when it is necessary. Also, as you saw earlier in the chapter, this is one of the ways teachers address the restrictions of situated cognition.

Other than "How can I make my learning objectives clear?" the most basic planning question teachers can ask is, "What can I show students or have them do that will help them construct their knowledge?" In Jenny's lesson, for example, the actual beam balances and the problems she posed were essential if students were to construct a valid understanding of the principle. The importance of examples and concrete learning activities applies to all topics at all grade levels and are especially important for limited-English-proficiency learners because their prior experiences may not match those of other students (Bae, 2003; Echevarria & Graves, 2003). Table 8.2 includes additional examples of different ways teachers that you've studied in this text have represented their topics.

The process of presenting and discussing examples is especially important for learners first encountering a new idea (Kalyuga, Ayres, Chandler, & Sweller, 2003). Learners may not know what to look for or how to effectively analyze examples for their essential characteristics. Interactive, teacher-led dialogue provides both instructional scaffolding as well as opportunities to continually assess learning progress.

Table 8.2 Teachers' representations of content

Teacher and Chapter	Goal	Representations
Jan Davis, Chapter 1	Students will understand decimals.	12-ounce soft drink can 16-ounce bottle 6-pack of soft drinks
Karen Johnson, Chapter 2	Students will understand *density*.	Cotton balls in drink cup Wooden cubes Water and vegetable oil Population density Screen door screen
Jenny Newhall, Chapter 2	Students will understand that air takes up space.	Demonstration with drinking glass and paper towel Releasing air bubbles Hands-on experiences
Diane Smith, Chapter 4	Students will understand comparative and superlative adjectives.	Three pencils of different lengths combined with sentences written on the board Three hair colors combined with sentences on the board
David Shelton, Chapter 7	Students will understand characteristics of the solar system.	Transparencies of a solar system model and of "globs" thrown off by the sun Matrix with characteristics of the planets

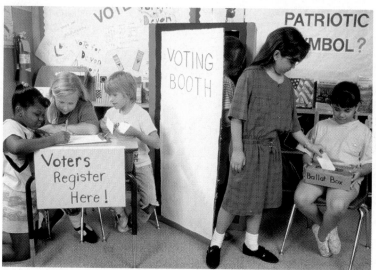

Social interaction embedded within authentic learning tasks provides opportunities for learners to share ideas and refine their own thinking.

Connect Content to the Real World

Authentic tasks provide tangible links to the real world, facilitating initial learning as well as transfer (van Merriënboer et al., 2003). Jenny created a real-world problem with the beam balance, and other teachers you've studied in this book have done the same. For example, Jan Davis (Chapter 1) used soft drink containers to illustrate the use of decimals to determine the best buys in supermarkets, Karen Johnson (Chapter 2) used population density and screen door screens to illustrate the concept *density;* and Mike Sheppard (Chapter 5) used a problem with distances from the children's school to teach number operations. Other examples of real-world (authentic) tasks include geography students' identifying the longitude and latitude of their school, language arts students' writing persuasive essays for a class newsletter, and science students' explaining the need for seatbelts in cars.

Treat Verbal Explanations Skeptically

To begin this section, think again about Jenny's lesson. We saw that Suzanne and Tad both heard three clear and accurate explanations for the beam balance problem—Molly's, Mavrin's, and Jenny's—yet at the beginning of the interview, Suzanne still believed that the number of tiles was the only factor determining whether or not the beam would balance. And after these same explanations, Tad still hadn't formed a clear schema for the principle. These explanations didn't work, and this is true for much of the talk that occurs in classrooms. In spite of this fact, many teachers continue to believe that the best way to get students to learn something is to lecture to them (Alparsian et al., 2004; Borko & Putnam, 1996; Yip, 2004).

We are not implying that teachers shouldn't explain topics to students, and we're not saying that learners will not or cannot construct understanding from explanations: "Constructivists assume that all knowledge is constructed from previous knowledge, irrespective of how one is taught ... even listening to a lecture involves active attempts to construct new knowledge" (Bransford et al., 2000, p. 11).

What we are saying instead is: *Don't conclude that your students understand an idea because you explained it to them.* Explanations need to be combined with examples and thorough discussions of how the examples illustrate ideas. As we said earlier, concrete examples are especially important for limited English-proficiency students because they provide reference points for their developing language (Bae, 2003; Echevarria & Graves, 2003). This brings us to the essential role of social interaction in learning.

Promote High Levels of Quality Interactions

Although essential, high-quality examples won't—by themselves—necessarily produce learning (Moreno & Duran, 2004). This was vividly illustrated in Jenny's lesson. Putting 3 tiles on the 10 point resulted in a clear example (the numbers times the distances on each side of the fulcrum were equal). All the information the students needed to understand the principle was illustrated in it. In spite of seeing a clear example and hearing the explanations, Suzanne retained her original idea, and Tad didn't form a clear schema until the discussion that occurred in the interview. Social interaction is essential to the success of virtually all learning activities.

Social interaction provides at least three learning benefits for students:

- Sharing ideas
- Appropriating understanding
- Articulating thinking

To see each of these benefits illustrated, let's look again at some dialogue from the interview.

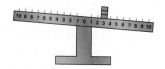

Interviewer:	Suzanne, go ahead and offer a solution, a way to balance the beam.
Suzanne:	What I did was 2 plus 3 equals 5 (pointing to the right side of the beam), and 2 plus 1 plus 2 equals 5 (pointing to the left side).
Interviewer:	Molly, what do you think of that solution?
Molly:	It won't work. . . . It doesn't matter how many blocks there are. It's where they're put.
Interviewer:	Okay, what do you think, Drexel?
Drexel:	(Shakes his head no)
Interviewer:	Why don't you think so?
Drexel:	Because of Molly's reasoning. It doesn't matter how many blocks you have; it's where you put them.
Interviewer:	Tad, how about you? . . . What do you think?
Tad:	(Hesitantly) Same as them, I guess.

The students try Suzanne's solution, and the beam tips to the left.

Suzanne:	If you took 1 off the 9, it might work.
Interviewer:	Why do you think that'll work?
Suzanne:	Because that's the farthest to the end, and sometimes the farthest to the end brings it down more.

The opportunity for students to *share ideas* is perhaps the most powerful outcome of social interaction. Suzanne offered her solution (based on her original schema), Molly and Drexel explained why it wouldn't work, and her understanding of how to balance the beam gradually evolved, as indicated by her suggestion to take one of the tiles off the end.

In this socially based process of knowledge construction, sharing ideas allows learners to think collaboratively, building on each others' understanding and negotiating meanings when ideas differ (D. Brenner, 2001). After understanding is developed in a social context, individuals can then internalize the knowledge by changing their mental structures (Meter & Stevens, 2000).

Sharing ideas also helps students learn to build on and utilize each others' ideas (Applebee, Langer, Nystrand, & Gamoran, 2003). For example, in one study students were discussing reintroducing wolves into northern forests, and some students spontaneously asked, "Yeah, but what if you were a rancher? Wouldn't you be upset if a wolf came and ate your cattle?" These students modeled perspective taking, and other students gradually learned to use this way of thinking in solving problems (R. Anderson et al., 2001).

Tad's responses in the dialogue illustrate the process of *appropriating understanding*—developing new meaning as a direct result of interaction (Leont'ev, 1981). His first comment, "Same as them, I guess," indicated that he didn't have a clear schema for what made the beam balance. He gradually acquired and internalized understanding based on the interactions with Suzanne, Molly, and Drexel.

After appropriating understanding, Tad solidified it by putting it into words, which illustrates the process of *articulating thinking*. In Chapter 2 we saw that Vygotsky emphasized the importance of language in the process of social construction. Putting ideas into words is a cognitively demanding activity (as anyone who has tried to write something can attest) that is especially powerful for promoting learning (Bransford et al., 2000; Mason & Boscolo, 2000). Let's see how this process helped Tad solidify his thinking:

Questioning helps teachers assess students' learning progress.

Molly:	Put 1 on the 8 and 4 on the 1.
Interviewer:	That's what Molly thinks. What do you think? Tad?"

Tad:	(Slowly) Yeah.
Interviewer:	You *do* think it'll work. . . . Now give us a nice, clear explanation for why it'll work.
Tad:	Okay. (peering intently at the balance for several seconds) Oh, okay, you put it on a times table. . . . Three times 4 is 12, . . . and 4 times 1 is 4, . . . and 8 times 1 is 8, and 8 plus 4 is 12.

In the videotape from which this dialogue was taken, we could almost see "the wheels turning" in Tad's head as he hesitantly describes his understanding. As he struggled with articulating his thinking, his understanding also increased.

Teachers play an essential role in ensuring that student interaction results in learning (Webb, Farivar, & Mastergeorge, 2002). They guide the interaction in whole-group lessons, and they monitor small-group activities to be sure students focus on understanding instead of simply getting the right answer. And, they design assessments that evaluate understanding and hold students accountable for their learning. Let's examine assessment further to see how it facilitates learning in constructivist classrooms.

Assessment and Learning: The Role of Assessment in Constructivist Classrooms

If teachers are to assist students in the process of knowledge construction, they must understand their students' developing thinking. In her lesson, for example, Jenny knew that Mavrin understood the principle, because she heard him explain it at the board. As teachers listen to students describe their understanding, they can assess the extent to which students' constructions are valid. This is a form of **informal assessment,** which is the process of using students' comments and answers in learning activities to assess their understanding.

Informal assessments are valuable, but incomplete and potentially misleading. For instance, hearing Mavrin explain the principle, combined with the fact that she explained it herself, could lead Jenny to conclude that all her students understood it. In fact, her informal assessments provided little information about the rest of her students' understanding (As we saw earlier, Suzanne and Tad did not understand the principle after the lesson.)

This leads us to the need for **formal assessment,** which is the process of systematically gathering information about understanding from all learners.

> Effectively designed learning environments must also be assessment centered. . . . They should provide opportunities for feedback and revision and that what is assessed must be congruent with one's learning goals. (Bransford et al., 2000, pp. 139–140)

Accessing students' thinking is an essential feature of effective classroom assessment. Jenny, realizing that she didn't have insights into students' thinking, assessed her students' understanding with two problems that she gave the class the day after the lesson.

The assessment, with Tad's responses, is shown in Figure 8.7.

From the information in Figure 8.7, we see that Tad's schema for the principle was still "a work in progress." He was able to determine that the beam would balance in the first problem, but he was unable to draw or write a solution to the second. His experience was not unique; Jenny's assessment revealed that several additional students in the class were also still uncertain about solving problems with beam balances.

When done well, formal assessment allows teachers to look into students' heads and provides students with feedback and practice with additional problems.

Putting Constructivism into Perspective

Constructivism makes an enormous contribution to our understanding of learning and classroom practice. It is powerful because it helps us understand why prior knowledge and interaction are so important for developing deep understanding, and it also helps us understand why monitoring student thinking is essential. Because we know that students

Figure 8.7 Beam balance problems for assessment

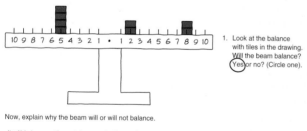

1. Look at the balance with tiles in the drawing. Will the beam balance? Yes or no? (Circle one).

Now, explain why the beam will or will not balance.

It will balance. 2 times 8 is 16, and 2 times 2 is 4 so that's 20. 4 times 5 is 20, so they are the same.

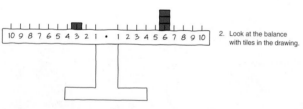

2. Look at the balance with tiles in the drawing.

Draw more tiles on the drawing so that the beam will be balanced. Then, explain why you placed the tiles where you did.

I want to place more tiles on so that it will balance.

Informal assessment. The process of using students' comments and answers in learning activities to measure their understanding

Formal assessment. The process of systematically gathering information about understanding from all learners

construct their own knowledge, we better understand why they don't grasp an idea that's been discussed several times, why they seem to ignore a point that's been emphasized, and why they retain misconceptions that we've attempted to help them change. With this understanding, our frustration can be reduced and our patience increased. Constructivism also helps us understand why explaining, alone, is often ineffective, and why relying on worksheets fails to produce deep understanding.

Constructivism is, however, often misunderstood and misinterpreted:

> A common misconception regarding "constructivist" theories of knowledge ... is that teachers should never tell students anything directly but, instead, should always allow them to construct knowledge for themselves. This perspective confuses a theory of pedagogy (teaching) with a theory of knowing. (Bransford et al., 2000, p. 11)

This distinction between a theory of learning and a theory of instruction is important. Theories of learning focus on students and help explain how they develop understanding. For example, constructivism helps us understand the changes in Suzanne's thinking in Jenny's lesson and the interview that followed.

In comparison, theories of instruction focus on teachers and what they can do to promote learning. Although commonly used, the terms "constructivist teacher" and "constructivist instruction" are misconceptions. As Bransford and colleagues (2000) point out, *constructivism is a theory of learning;* it is not a theory of instruction.

The relationship between constructivism and teaching method is also frequently confused. For example, "Social interaction facilitates learning" is sometimes interpreted to mean that a teacher who uses cooperative learning is "constructivist," whereas one who relies on large-group activities is not. In fact, both teachers may be basing their instruction on constructivist views of learning, or neither teacher may be. Large-group instruction, effectively done, may promote construction of knowledge, and cooperative learning, improperly done, may not. Confusing learning and instruction can lead to misconceptions about appropriate method and oversimplified suggestions for classroom practice.

For example, a potential problem when using social interaction in instructional strategies is the assumption that group processes and products equate with individual learning. In other words, if the group accomplishes a task, does that ensure that individual members can also do it? Research suggests not (B. Barron, 2000; Southerland et al., 2002). Students may be able to do things in groups that they are unable to do alone. This finding underscores the essential role that assessment plays in instruction grounded in constructivist views of learning.

Also, as with any theory, constructivism doesn't provide a complete picture of learning and its implications for teaching. For instance, research suggests that many skills must be practiced to automaticity (Bruning et al., 2004; Péladeau, Forget, & Gagné, 2003). This research is better explained by information processing than by constructivism, and in fact, discussions of constructivism tend to ignore learners' cognitive architectures (Eggen, 2001). Students will construct valid understandings of the topics they study, for instance, only to the extent to which they pay attention, correctly perceive the information, and avoid having their working memories overloaded. Further, students who are metacognitive about their learning are more successful than their peers who are less aware (Azevedo & Cromley, 2004; Eilam & Aharon, 2003). Attention, perception, working memory, and metacognition are all powerful concepts from information processing theory, and ignoring them leaves important parts of the learning puzzle unattended.

In addition, constructivism fails to address modeling, a concept from social cognitive theory, and one of the most powerful tools teachers have for promoting learning. Ignoring social cognitive theory not only provides an incomplete picture of learning but also robs teachers of an important tool in their repertoires.

Fortunately, many of the controversies that historically have been associated with constructivism seem to have been resolved. For instance, researchers now reject the philosophical position suggesting that all students' unique constructions of understanding are equally valid (Derry, 1992; Moshman, 1997; D. Phillips, 1997, 2000).

In addition, the teacher's role in classroom applications of constructivism has been clarified. These applications don't suggest that the teacher has a diminished role in promoting learning; in fact, they provide for an increased and more sophisticated one. As we said earlier, traditional teaching roles, such as establishing clear objectives and designing learning activities, are as important for applications of constructivism as they are for applications of any other theory (Airasian & Walsh, 1997; Bransford et al., 2000; Howe & Berv, 2000; Osborne, 1996; D. Phillips, 1995, 2000). However, instead of merely presenting information (commonly described as a transmission view of instruction), teachers must carefully listen to students as they describe their developing understanding and, when necessary, intervene to help students construct complete and valid schemas. The ability to monitor students' thinking, assist in the knowledge-construction process, and intervene soon enough to prevent misconceptions, but not so soon that students' ownership for learning is diminished, is very sophisticated and demanding instruction.

Checking Your Understanding

4.1 Which suggestion for classroom practice was best illustrated by the beam balances and tiles that Jenny used in her lesson and the interviewer used in his work with the students? Explain.

4.2 A language arts teacher wants his students to understand the rules for forming possessive nouns and writes a passage about the school in which he illustrates the rules. Which of the suggestions for classroom practice is best illustrated by this practice?

4.3 Assessments grounded in constructivist views of learning have an essential characteristic. What is this characteristic? Explain.

To receive feedback for these questions, go to Appendix B.

Knowledge Extensions

To deepen your understanding of the topics in this section of the chapter and to integrate it with topics you've already studied, go to the *Knowledge Extensions* module for Chapter 8 at *www.prenhall.com/eggen*. Respond to questions 11–14.

Online Case Book

To analyze a case study to assess the extent to which it applies constructivist principles, go to the *Online Case Book* for Chapter 8 at *www.prenhall.com/eggen*.

Instructional Principles

Constructivism in Classrooms: Instructional Principles

The suggestions for classroom practice that you first saw in Figure 8.6 provide the principles that can guide you as you attempt to use constructivism as a basis for your instruction. These suggestions are

1. Provide learners with a variety of examples and representations of content.
2. Connect content to the real world.
3. Treat verbal explanations skeptically.
4. Promote high levels of interaction.
5. Make assessment an integral part of the teaching–learning process.

Let's see how these principles guide Judy Nelson, an urban sixth-grade teacher as she works with her students.

Judy is beginning a study of longitude and latitude in social studies. In preparation, she buys a beach ball, finds an old tennis ball, and checks her wall maps and globes.

She begins by having students identify a popular meeting place and then says, "You want to meet some friends from another part of town, but the street signs are down for repair, so you can't give your friends an address. . . . It looks like we have a problem. We want to be able to tell our friends exactly where we should meet, but we don't have a way of doing it. Let's see if we can figure this out."

She then holds up the beach ball and globe and asks her students to compare them. They identify north, south, east, and west on the ball, and she draws a circle around its center, which they identify as the equator. They do the same with the tennis ball, and she then cuts it in half, so they see the two hemispheres.

Judy continues by drawing other horizontal lines on the beach ball and saying, "Now, compare the lines with each other."

". . . They're all even," Kathy volunteers.

"What do you mean by even?" Judy encourages.

". . . They don't cross each other," Kathy explains, motioning with her hands.

"Okay, good," Judy nods.

Judy asks for and gets additional comparisons, such as, "The lines all run east and west," and, "They get shorter as they move away from the equator." Judy writes them on the chalkboard. After the class finishes making comparisons, Judy introduces the term *latitude* to refer to the lines they've been discussing.

She continues by drawing vertical lines of longitude on the beach ball and identifies them as shown below:

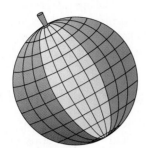

Discussion then follows:

Judy:	How do these lines compare with the lines of latitude?
Tenisha:	. . . They go all around the ball.
Judy:	Good. And what else?
LeBron:	. . . Length, . . . they're all as long, long as each other, same length.
Thomas:	Lengths of what?
LeBron:	The up-and-down lines and the cross ones.
Judy:	What did we call the cross ones?
LeBron:	. . . Latitude.
Jaime:	We said that they got shorter. . . . So how can they be the same length?
Tabatha:	I think those are longer (pointing to the longitude lines).
Judy:	How might we check to see about the lengths?
Jaime:	. . . Measure them, with a tape or string or something.
Judy:	What do you think of Jaime's idea?

The students agree that it seems to be a good idea, so Judy helps hold pieces of string in place while Jaime wraps them around the ball at different points, and the class compares the lengths.

Chris:	They're the same (holding up two "longitude" strings).
Nicole:	Not these (holding two "latitude" strings).

After comparing the strings, Judy asks students to work in pairs to summarize what they've found. They make several conclusions, which Judy helps them rephrase. Then she writes the following conclusions on the board:

Longitude lines are farthest apart at the equator; latitude lines are the same distance apart everywhere.

Lines of longitude are the same length; latitude lines get shorter north and south of the equator.

Lines of longitude intersect each other at the poles; lines of latitude and longitude intersect each other all over the globe.

Judy continues, asking, "Now, how does this help us solve our problem of identifying an exact location?" With some guidance, the class concludes that location can be pinpointed by where the lines cross. She notes that this is what they'll focus on the next day. (From Eggen, Paul, & Kauchak, Don, *Strategies and Models for Teachers: Teaching Content and Thinking Skills,* 5/e. Published by Allyn and Bacon, Boston, MA. Copyright © 2006 by Pearson Education. Adapted by permission of the publisher.)

Now, let's look at Judy's attempts to apply the principles. First, because her students lacked prior knowledge, she used the beach and tennis balls, the strings, the globe, and maps to illustrate longitude and latitude. The information students needed to construct the concepts was observable in the examples. This applied the first principle.

Exploring Further

Classroom discussion is another strategy based on constructivist views of learning. To see an example, go to "Classroom Discussions" in the *Exploring Further* module of Chapter 8 at *www.prenhall.com/eggen.*

She applied the second (connect content to the real world) by beginning her lesson with a real world problem—having students find the exact location of their meeting place. As applications of the third (treat verbal explanations skeptically) and fourth (promote high levels of interaction) principles, she developed the lesson through social interaction instead of explaining the content, making students' thinking visible throughout. And finally, assessment was an integral part of the lesson. As students' responded to her questions, Judy informally assessed their understanding, and she made adjustments, such as using the strings to measure the lengths of the lines, based on the responses.

As we said earlier in the chapter, basing instruction on constructivist views of learning does not imply that teachers' learning objectives aren't clear, or that students are left on their own to "construct" knowledge. Rather, it recognizes that students will use their existing knowledge to construct new knowledge that makes sense to them. These factors were apparent in Judy's lesson.

Learning Contexts: Constructing Knowledge in Urban Environments

Our discussion of situated cognition in this chapter emphasizes a factor affecting all learning: The context in which it occurs strongly influences the learning that takes place. As with the cognitive and social development of students, urban contexts influence the knowledge construction process. At least three factors exist in these environments. First, as you've seen in our discussions of urban environments in other chapters, these students typically come from diverse backgrounds, so they bring with them widely varying degrees of school-related prior knowledge (Serafino & Cicchelli, 2003; Weiner, 2000). Second, because of the environments they grow up in, the real world of urban students can be quite different from their suburban and rural peers. Textbooks are typically written for an idealized "average" student, making connections to the background experiences of urban students more difficult (Manzo, 2000). Third, the patterns of interaction typical for urban students are sometimes different from the patterns found in suburban or rural schools. Urban students may have difficulty with the fast-paced question-and-answer patterns typical of suburban classrooms, and they may interpret direct questions as threatening rather than as attempts by teachers to promote learning (Heath, 1989; T. Howard, 2001).

So, how should teachers in urban environments respond in their efforts to help their students construct usable knowledge? Some suggestions are outlined in the following sections.

Need for Examples

The need for high-quality examples is important for all learners, regardless of context (Cassady, 1999). However, because of the diversity of urban students' prior experiences, high-quality examples are critical when teaching in urban schools. Karen Johnson's illustrations of the concept *density,* which you first saw in the case study that introduced Chapter 2, and Judy's lesson are examples. Both teach in urban environments, so they used examples that contained all the information needed to understand the concept. In essence, their examples became the students' prior knowledge, and they provided students with the experiences needed to make the concepts meaningful.

Real-World Connections

Effective teachers in all environments attempt to connect their examples to situations with which their students can identify (Charner-Laird et al., 2004). This is why Judy began her lesson on longitude and latitude with the problem of finding the exact location of a popular student meeting place.

As another example, a sixth-grade world history teacher in an urban middle school was discussing the rise of nationalism as an important factor in the events leading up to World War I. The students' textbooks defined nationalism as a feeling of loyalty and devotion to one's country, lan-

Effective urban teachers connect the content they are teaching to students' lives and experiences.

guage, and culture. This definition is both abstract and distant from the world in which these students lived. In an attempt to personalize the concept, the teacher created a series of vignettes, which contain the name of the students' own school, Matthew Gilbert, as well as the name of a rival school in the same city, Mandarin Middle School. The following are two of the vignettes:

> The students at Matthew Gilbert love their school. "We don't want someone coming in here and changing our school," they say. "We understand each other when we talk. The rest of them are different than we are. They play funny music, and they don't do the things we do after school or on the weekends."
>
> "We're Gilbertites," they say. "We don't want to be anybody else, and we don't want anybody telling us what to do.".
>
> Students at Mandarin Middle School have some similar thoughts. "I don't like the way they talk at Gilbert," some of them have been overheard saying. "They want to hang around with each other after school, and we want to go to the Mall. I don't want anybody from there to tell us how to think.
>
> We're Mandariners, and we want to stay that way." (Eggen, 1998)

Connecting content to their day-to-day experiences is essential for the motivation of urban students, who sometimes question the importance of what they study for their daily lives. Similar adaptations can be made for suburban and rural students and different content areas.

Interactions

Interaction is essential for learning in all contexts, but it can be especially challenging in urban environments because of overcrowded classrooms and urban students' patterns of social interaction (Griffith, Hayes, & Pascarella, 2004). In addition, problems with lecturing and verbal explanations are even more acute in urban contexts, because of the wide variation in learners' prior experiences.

Open-ended questions that allow a variety of acceptable answers are effective for promoting interaction at the beginning of lessons and developing students' confidence in their ability to respond (Eggen, 1998). They are particularly useful in urban environments because they reduce the perceived threat that urban students associate with being questioned. Regardless of perceptions, questioning is essential, not only for involving students in knowledge construction but also in monitoring their progress. Aspects of questioning, such as prompting and adequate wait time, are crucial when working with urban students, and particularly those in middle and high schools, who may be sensitive about having their thinking and understanding revealed to peers.

As you see from this discussion, instruction in urban environments does not differ qualitatively from instruction in general. Instead, the factors that promote knowledge construction in general, such as high-quality examples, connections to the real world, and social interaction, are more important and more challenging in these environments.

Exploring Further

To see the rest of the teacher's examples and hear a description of the students' reactions to them, go to "Personalizing Content in an Urban Environment" in the *Exploring Further* module of Chapter 8 at *www.prenhall.com/eggen*.

Checking Your Understanding

5.1   In the section titled "Outcomes of Knowledge Construction," we discussed *concepts, schemas,* and *conceptual change*. Which of the three did Judy teach in her lesson? Explain.

5.2   A conceptual change issue came up in Judy's lesson with Jaime's question, "We said that they got shorter" (in reference to the lines of latitude). "So how can they be the same length?" (in reference to the lines of longitude.) Explain how Judy's response effectively taught for conceptual change.

5.3   Assess the extent to which Jenny Newhall applied the principles that guide instruction when applying constructivist views of learning in classrooms in her lesson (not including the interview).

To receive feedback for these questions, go to Appendix B.

Knowledge Extensions

To deepen your understanding of the topics in this section of the chapter and to integrate them with topics you've already studied, go to the *Knowledge Extensions* module for Chapter 8 at *www.prenhall.com/eggen*. Respond to questions 15–17.

Classroom ⊞ Connections

Applying Constructivist Views of Learning in Your Classroom

1. To accommodate differences in prior knowledge, provide a variety of examples and other representations of the content you want students to understand.

   - **Elementary:** A third-grade teacher in a unit on chemical and physical change has students melt ice, crumple paper, dissolve sugar, break toothpicks, and make Kool Aid to illustrate physical change. She then has them burn paper, pour vinegar into baking soda, burn sugar, and chew soda crackers to illustrate chemical change.

   - **Middle School:** An English teacher working with his students on the concept *internal conflict* presents excerpts such as these:

     Kelly didn't know what to do. She was looking forward to the class trip, but if she went, she wouldn't be able to take the scholarship qualifying test.

     Calvin was caught in a dilemma. He saw Jason take Olonzo's calculator but knew that if he told Mrs. Stevens what he saw, Jason would realize that it was he who reported the theft.

   - **High School:** While teaching about the Great Depression, a social studies teacher has students read excerpts from *The Grapes of Wrath,* presents a video of people standing in bread lines, shares statistics on the rash of suicides after the stock market crash, and passes out descriptions of Franklin D. Roosevelt's back-to-work programs.

2. Develop learning activities around real-world problems.

   - **Elementary:** In a lesson relating geography and lifestyle, a third-grade teacher has students describe the way they dress for their favorite forms of recreation. She also asks students who have moved from other parts of the country to do the same for their previous locations. She then guides them as they construct an understanding of the effect of geography on lifestyle.

   - **Middle School:** In a unit on percent increase and decrease, a math teacher has students look for examples of marked-down clothes while shopping. He also brings in newspaper ads. The class discusses the examples and calculates the amount saved in each case.

   - **High School:** To help her students understand the importance of persuasive writing, an English teacher brings in three examples of "Letters to the Editor." The students discuss the letters, determine which is most effective, and with the teacher's guidance, identify the characteristics of effective persuasive writing.

3. Promote high levels of quality interaction, and avoid relying on explanations.

   - **Elementary:** A fifth-grade teacher wants his students to understand the concept of *scale* on a map. After placing them in groups, he has them create a map of their desk tops. Then he has them draw a map of their room, and finally, they go outside and draw a map of their playground. When finished, he guides a class discussion to help them understand how the maps are similar and different.

   - **Middle School:** A sixth-grade science teacher has his students take 8 identical wooden cubes and make one stack of 5 and another stack of 3. He has them discuss the mass, volume, and densities of the two stacks. Then, with questioning, he guides them to conclude that the mass and volume of the stack of 5 are greater than the mass and volume of the stack of 3 but that the densities of the two stacks are equal.

   - **High School:** An algebra teacher "walks" students through the solutions to problems by calling on individuals to provide specific information about each step and explain why the step is necessary. When students have difficulty, the teacher asks additional questions to help them understand the step.

Meeting Your Learning Objectives

1. **Describe the primary difference between cognitive and social constructivism, and identify examples of each in descriptions of learning activities.**

   - Constructivism is a theory of learning suggesting that learners construct their own knowledge of the topics they study rather than having that understanding delivered to them in already organized form.

   - Cognitive constructivism focuses on individual construction of understanding. When an experience disrupts an individual's equilibrium, cognitive constructivists believe that the individual reconstructs understanding that reestablishes equilibrium. Social constructivism emphasizes that knowledge is first constructed in a social environment and is then appropriated by individuals. According to social constructivists, knowledge grows directly out of the interaction.

- Emphasis on sociocultural theory, communities of learners, cognitive apprenticeships, and situated cognition are all outcomes of the influence of social constructivism on instruction.

2. **Identify characteristics and applications of constructivism in events in and outside of classrooms.**

   - That learners construct, rather than record, knowledge is the basic principle of constructivism.
   - Constructivists also emphasize the importance of prior knowledge, the role of social interaction, and the value of real-world tasks in the process of constructing understanding.

3. **Analyze applications of concept learning, including teaching for conceptual change.**

   - Some concepts are constructed on the basis of a rule that specifies a number of well-defined characteristics.
   - When concepts don't have well-defined characteristics, a prototype—the best representative of the category or class—is often constructed.
   - Instead of being stored as a single prototype, some concepts are stored as sets of exemplars, the most highly typical examples of a concept.
   - Schemas—cognitive constructs that organize information into a meaningful system—represent the way constructed knowledge is stored in memory. Schemas include facts, concepts, and the relationships among them.

- In their efforts to make sense of the world, and because of prior experiences, ambiguous language, and societal factors, learners often develop misconceptions. Once formed and embedded in schemas, misconceptions are resistant to change.

4. **Identify suggestions for classroom practice in descriptions of learning activities.**

   - Instruction based on constructivism emphasizes high quality examples and representations of content, student interaction, and content connected to the real world.
   - Teachers who ground their instruction in constructivism realize that lecturing and explaining often fail to promote deep understanding in learners.
   - Basing instruction on constructivist learning theory requires teachers to use ongoing assessment as an integral part of the teaching–learning process.

5. **Analyze applications of constructivist learning theory in classroom activities.**

   - Instruction that applies constructivism in classrooms emphasizes both students' answers and how students arrived at those answers. Effective instruction makes students' thinking open and visible.
   - The suggestions from constructivism for teaching are the principles that guide teachers as they attempt to base their instruction on constructivist views of learning.

Developing as a Professional

Developing as a Professional: Praxis™ Practice

At the beginning of the chapter, you saw how Jenny Newhall designed and conducted a lesson to help her students construct an understanding of how balance beams work.

In the following case, a middle school science teacher has his students examine the factors that influence the frequency of a simple pendulum. Read the case study, and answer the questions that follow.

Scott Sowell, a middle school science teacher, is wondering why his seventh graders continue to have trouble controlling variables. "Funny, we did the plant experiment as a whole class, and they seemed to get it. . . . I explained it so carefully," he thinks to himself. He decides to give them additional experiences with controlling variables by working with simple pendulums in small groups.

The next day, Scott begins by demonstrating a simple pendulum. He asks students what factors they think will influence its frequency, explaining that *frequency* means the number of swings in a certain time period. After some discussion, they suggest length, weight, and angle of release as possible hypotheses. (In reality, only the length of the pendulum determines its frequency.)

"Okay, your job as a group is to design your own experiment," Scott continues. "Think of a way to test how each one of these affects the frequency. Use the equipment at your desk to design and carry out the experiment. . . . Go to it."

One group of four—Marina, Paige, Wensley, and Jonathan—tie a string to a ring stand and measure its length, as shown:

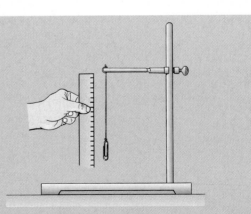

"Forty-nine centimeters," Wensley notes, measuring the length of the string.

"The frequency is the seconds . . . and the what?" Marina asks Scott as he comes by the group.

"The frequency is the number of swings in some time period. What time period are you using?" Scott responds.

The group agrees to use 15 seconds and then do their first test with the 49-centimeter length and one paper clip as weight. Marina counts 21 swings.

A few minutes later, Scott again walks by the group, examines their results, and says, "So you've done one test so far. . . . What are you going to do next? . . . I'm going to come back after your next test and look at it." He then moves to another group.

The group conducts their second test by shortening the string *and* adding a second paper clip. (Which violates the principle of only varying one variable at a time.)

"Mr. Sowell, we found out that the shorter it is and the heavier it is, the faster it goes," Marina reports to Scott when he returns to the group.

Scott then asks which of the two variables was responsible for the change in the frequency.

Wensley and Jonathan say simultaneously, "They both changed."

"Think about that. You need to come up with a conclusion about length, about weight, and about angle—how each of them influences the frequency of your pendulum," Scott reminds them as he moves from group to group.

(As the group investigates the three variables—length, weight, and angle of release—they continue to change two of these at the same time, confounding their results.)

"What did you find out?" Scott asks as he again returns to check on their progress.

Marina begins, "Okay, Mr. Sowell, we figured out that the shorter it is, the faster the frequency is, . . . and the heavier it is . . . the faster the frequency is."

Scott asks the students to explain their findings about the height.

"In the first one, the height (angle of release) was 56 and the weight was 3, and it came out to 21, and in the second one, the height was higher and the weight was lower, so it was still 21," Marina says, again concluding that the change in weight explains why the frequency was the same even though the angle of release was different.

"Let's do it out loud before you write it. . . . Talk to me about length," Scott directs.

"The longer the string is, the slower the frequency is," Wensley says.

"What about weight?" Scott probes.

"The heavier it is, the faster it goes," Marina adds.

"I want to look at these again. . . . Write those down for me."

Scott gives the students a few minutes to write their conclusions, and he then walks to the front of the room and rings a bell to call the class together.

"When I call your group, I want the speaker for your group to report your findings to the class," he continues to the class as a whole.

One by one, the spokesperson for each group goes to the front of the room to report their findings. In general, the groups conclude (erroneously) that each variable—length, weight, and angle—affect the frequency.

In response to this misconception, Scott decides to try a whole-class demonstration.

"Let's take a look at something here," Scott says, placing a ring stand onto his demonstration table. He attaches a paper clip to the pendulum, puts it in motion, and asks a student to count the swings. He adds a second paper clip and again has the students count, to demonstrate that weight doesn't affect the frequency. He has a student state this conclusion, and he writes it on the board. Then he does a second demonstration to show that angle also has no effect on the frequency and again asks a student to make a conclusion so Scott can write it on the board.

After the demonstrations, he says, "Now I want someone to make a conclusion about what we learned about designing experiments and how we use our variables when we design experiments. . . . Who wants to talk about that? . . . Wensley? Tell me what we learned about how to set up an experiment. What did we learn from this?"

"Each time, you do a different part of the experiment, only change one of the variables," Wensley explains.

"Why is that?"

"You're only checking one thing at a time. If you do two, there might be an error in the experiment."

"Okay, . . . if you change more than one thing at one time, why would it be difficult?"

"Because . . . if you change two . . . different things . . . you can't tell which one caused the change," Wensley continues.

"Good thinking, Wensley. So, for example, if you were testing weight and length, your group had to finally decide that we can't change weight at the same time as we change length, because when we test it . . . "

"You couldn't compare them," Marina responds.

"Right, you couldn't compare them. You couldn't tell which one was causing it, could you? . . . It might go faster, but all of a sudden you'd say, well, is it the weight or is it the length?"

Running out of time, Scott then asks if there are any questions, and hearing none, he dismisses the class.

PRAXIS These exercises are designed to help you prepare for the Praxis™ Principles of Learning and Teaching exam. To receive feedback on your short-answer questions, go to the Companion Website at *www.prenhall. com/eggen*, then to the *Practice for Praxis™* module for Chapter 8.

To acquire experience in preparing for the multiple-choice items on the Praxis™ exam, go to the *Self-Assessment* module for Chapter 8 at *www.prenhall.com/eggen* and click on "Practice Quiz."

For additional connections between Chapter 8 and the Praxis™ exam, go to Appendix A.

Short-Answer Questions

In answering these questions, use information from Chapter 8 and link your responses to specific information in the case.

1. Describe the extent to which Scott's lesson demonstrated the characteristics of constructivism.
2. Scott's students held some misconceptions about controlling variables, failing to keep length constant, for example, as they changed the weight. How effectively did Scott teach for conceptual change in responding to this misconception? Explain.
3. Assess how effectively Scott implemented the "Suggestions for Classroom Practice" (see Figure 8.6).
4. Assess the effectiveness of Scott's lesson for learners with diverse backgrounds.

ONLINE PORTFOLIO ACTIVITIES

To develop your professional portfolio, further apply your understanding of chapter content, and address the INTASC standards, go to the Companion Website, then to the *Online Portfolio Activities* for Chapter 8. Complete the suggested activities.

Also on the Companion Website at *www.prenhall.com/ eggen,* you can measure your understanding of chapter content with multiple-choice and essay questions, and broaden your knowledge base in *Exploring Further* and *Web Links* to other educational psychology websites.

IMPORTANT CONCEPTS

characteristics (p. 242)
cognitive apprenticeship (p. 237)
cognitive constructivism (p. 235)
community of learners (p. 236)
concept (p. 241)
concept mapping (p. 243)
constructivism (p. 235)
exemplars (p. 243)

formal assessment (p. 252)
informal assessment (p. 252)
network (p. 244)
prototype (p. 242)
real-world task (p. 241)
situated cognition (p. 237)
social constructivism (p. 236)
sociocultural theory (p. 236)

CHAPTER 9

Complex Cognitive Processes

Chapter Outline	Learning Objectives

After you have completed your study of this chapter, you should be able to

Problem Solving

Well-Defined and Ill-Defined Problems • A Problem-Solving Model • Expert–Novice Differences in Problem-Solving Ability • Helping Learners Become Better Problem Solvers: Instructional Principles • Problem-Based Learning

1 Identify examples of ill-defined and well-defined problems, and describe the role of deliberate practice in solving them.

The Strategic Learner

Metacognition: The Foundation of Strategic Learning • Study Strategies • Developing Strategic Learning in Students: Instructional Principles

2 Explain differences between effective and ineffective strategies in studying behaviors.

Critical Thinking

The Challenge of Critical Thinking • Elements of Critical Thinking • Developing Critical Thinking: Instructional Principles

3 Define critical thinking, and identify its characteristics in classroom activities.

Transfer of Learning

General and Specific Transfer • Factors Affecting the Transfer of Learning

4 Identify factors that influence transfer in classroom learning activities.

Developing students' complex cognitive abilities such as problem solving, study strategies, and critical thinking are important classroom goals. As you read the following case study, think about the teacher's approach to helping her students become better problem solvers and the extent to which the approach is effective.

Laura Hunter, a fifth-grade math teacher, is concerned about her students' tendency to memorize procedures for finding answers in math instead of understanding what they are doing or why. After reflecting on the issue, she decides, "I'm going to use a real problem about finding the areas of irregularly shaped figures instead of the ones in the book—something they can relate to."

She decides to have students find the area of the carpeted portion of their classroom; the floor under the computers and the sink is covered with linoleum, and the carpeted portion has an irregular shape.

She begins the lesson on Monday by reviewing the concepts of *area* and *perimeter,* and then to introduce the problem for the day, she displays the following on the overhead:

"When we try to solve a problem, we first need to be clear about what the problem is," Laura begins. "Here is our problem. We're going to get carpeting for this room, but Mr. Garcia (the school's principal) doesn't know how much to order. Your job is to figure that out."

Laura breaks the students into groups, and each group works for several minutes to decide how they will represent the problem. They come back together, discuss their ideas, and decide that they first need to know how big their room is. Laura then has the groups measure the room and different parts in it. Using the information they gather, Laura constructs a diagram of the room, gives each group a copy, and tells students that the "L" on the drawing stands for *linoleum.*

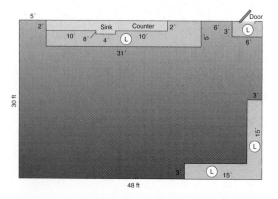

"Okay, look back up here at our overhead," Laura instructs. "This diagram represents our problem. . . . What's your next job?"

After a few seconds, Nephi volunteers, "We didn't actually measure the area; we just measured the perimeter. We need to figure out the area from our measurements."

"Okay, you guys understand what Nephi's saying?" Laura asks.

"Yeah," several students respond.

"Okay," Laura nods. "That's the part you're going to be working on with your team . . . . You need to select a strategy; decide how you're going to find the area of this part (pointing to the carpeted area in the diagram). We only want to know the area of the carpeted part . . . . Go ahead and get started."

Students return to their groups, and as they work on the problem, different groups identify two basic strategies. One is to find the area of the whole room and subtract the area of the linoleum; the other is to find the area of an interior rectangle and then add the extra areas of carpeting.

"Okay, let's look back up here at our diagram," Laura directs, after reassembling the class. "I saw different strategies as I was walking around. Raise your hand, and tell me what one of the strategies was. . . . Yashoda?"

"We found the whole area. And then we subtracted the places where the linoleum was."

"Okay, what did you find for the whole area?"

"1,440."

"Okay, and what was your next step?"

"Then we subtracted where the linoleum was."

Laura asks who used that strategy, several of the groups raise their hands, and she then says, "Matt, explain what your team did," seeing that Matt's group didn't raise their hands.

". . . First, we squared it off, like covering up this," he begins, referring to a carpeted rectangle inside all the areas that have linoleum. "We got that area, and then we added the other pieces . . . to it."

After all the groups describe their strategies, Laura has them report their results.

"1,173," one group reports.

"Okay," she says, and then nods to another group.

"1,378."

"1,347," a third group reports.

"1,440," a fourth group adds.

"1,169," another group offers.

"1,600," the last group puts in.

"Well, are you guys comfortable with that?"

Several of the students say no.

"If you were the person purchasing the carpet, would you be comfortable with that?" Laura continues.

Most of the students again shake their heads no.

"So, what might we do to try to be more accurate? Talk to your team for a minute."

The students talk to their teammates and offer some suggestions, such as measuring the room again, checking to see if the strategy makes sense, and even asking the janitor about the dimensions of the room.

Chuckling at the last suggestion, Laura says, "That's a strategy that we might call, 'Ask an expert,'" and she then has students get ready for recess, planning to address the problem again the next day.

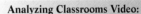

Analyzing Classrooms Video:
To analyze this lesson from an additional perspective, go to Episode 15, "Using a Problem-Solving Model: Finding Area in Elementary Math," on DVD 1, accompanying this text.

As you begin your study of this chapter, think about three questions: (1) Why did the groups get such varying answers to the same problem? (2) Because no group got the correct answer, was the time spent on the activity used wisely? (3) What must Laura now do to help her students improve their problem-solving abilities? We address these and other questions in this chapter.

PROBLEM SOLVING

As the title states, this chapter is about complex cognitive processes. Each is grounded in the cognitive learning theories you studied in Chapters 7 and 8. Keep these theories in mind as you study the following sections. We begin our study with problem solving.

Consider the following:

- You want to write a greeting card to a friend who has moved to New York, but you don't know her home address.
- You're a teacher, and your seventh graders resist thinking on their own. They expect to find the answer to every question specifically stated in the textbook.
- Laura asked her students to find the area of the carpeted portion of their classroom.

Concrete and hands-on experiences provide effective points for problem solving.

Although they look different, each describes a **problem,** which "occurs when a problem solver has a goal but lacks an obvious way of achieving the goal" (R. Mayer & Wittrock, 1996, p. 47). In our examples, the goals are finding the address, having students think on their own, and finding the carpeted area of the classroom. A broad definition of *problem* is beneficial because it recognizes the pervasiveness of problem solving in our everyday lives. Thinking of problems in this way allows people to apply general strategies to solve different kinds of problems (Bruning et al., 2004).

We saw that Laura's students struggled to accurately determine the carpeted area of their classroom. Solving the problem depended on their declarative knowledge about the concepts *area* and *perimeter* and on their procedural knowledge about finding the area, accurately measuring different parts of the room, devising strategies for finding the carpeted portions, and calculating the areas. This helps us understand why problem solving is one of the "complex cognitive processes" that you saw in the chapter title and we alluded to earlier. The notion that problem solving is complex is reinforced by the fact that the groups' answers varied by more than 400 square feet, and no group got the correct answer. This also helps us begin to answer the first question we asked in our introduction. The complexity of the task likely placed a cognitive load on students that was unmanageable. (We discuss ways of decreasing this load later in the chapter.)

Well-Defined and Ill-Defined Problems

Experts on problem solving find it useful to distinguish between well-defined and ill-defined problems (Bruning et al., 2004; J. Davidson & Sternberg, 2003). A **well-defined problem** has only one correct solution and a certain method for finding it, whereas an **ill-defined problem** has more than one acceptable solution, an ambiguous goal, and no generally agreed-upon strategy for reaching a solution (R. Mayer & Wittrock, 1996). Our first example is well defined; your friend has only one home address, and a straightforward strategy for finding it exists. Many problems in math, physics, and chemistry are well defined.

In contrast, the seventh-grade students' not wanting to think for themselves is an ill-defined problem. The goal state isn't clear—teachers are often not even sure what "thinking" means—and a readily agreed-on strategy for getting students to "think" doesn't exist. The problem can be solved with several strategies, and several "right" answers can be found.

As teachers, we have an ill-defined problem of our own. Research indicates that our students are not very good at solving problems (R. Mayer, 2002; R. Mayer & Wittrock, 1996), and our goal is obviously for them to become better at it. In attempting to get a handle on this problem, we can identify at least two subproblems. First, most of learners' experiences in schools focus on well-defined problems, but the majority of those we encounter in life are ill defined. For instance, you're encountering an ill-defined problem as you study this book. Your goal is to understand the content and do well in the class, but "understanding" is ambiguous, and many paths to understanding exist. Taking careful notes, studying with classmates, highlighting appropriate parts of the text, and completing the exercises in the Student Study Guide are all possibilities.

Our second subproblem is the fact that problem solving is personal and contextual (R. Mayer & Wittrock, 1996). A well-defined problem for one person is ill defined for another, and some evidence indicates that solving well-defined and ill-defined problems requires different abilities (N. Hong & Jonassen, 1999). Laura's lesson is an example. Finding the amount of carpeting necessary for the room is well defined for experienced problem solvers; they simply determine the total area of the floor and subtract the areas covered by linoleum. Only one answer exists, and the solution, while somewhat complex, is straightforward. For Laura's students, however, the problem was ill defined. Their understanding of the goal wasn't clear, some of them were uncertain about the difference between *area*

Problem. A state that occurs when a problem solver has a goal but lacks an obvious way of achieving the goal

Well-defined problem. A problem that has only one correct solution and a certain method for finding the solution

Ill-defined problem. A problem that has more than one acceptable solution, an ambiguous goal, and no generally agreed-upon strategy for reaching a solution

and *perimeter*—as an interview after the lesson revealed—and they used different strategies to reach the goal. Evidence of their uncertainty is indicated in their answers, which ranged from 1,169 square feet to 1,600 square feet (more than the total area of the room), and no group got 1,186 square feet, the actual amount of carpeting required.

Since our students are not very good at solving problems, helping them become better problem solvers is one of the biggest challenges teachers face. In an attempt to solve our problem, we offer three strategies:

- Help students understand a problem-solving model that can be applied in a variety of domains.
- Describe the characteristics of expert problem solvers to use as models for novices.
- Teach a specific set of strategies to help students improve their problem-solving abilities.

A Problem-Solving Model

By breaking down problem solving into specific steps, teachers can help students develop problem-solving strategies to use in many situations.

Since the 1950s, computer scientists and cognitive psychologists have attempted to develop a general problem-solving model that can be applied in a variety of domains (Bruning et al., 2004). For example, problem-solving approaches have been applied in domains ranging as widely as traditional math and science to school leadership (Canter, 2004), counseling in response to classroom management issues (Dwairy, 2005), and curbing excessive drinking on college campuses (Biscaro, Broer, & Taylor, 2004).

A number of models have been developed (e.g., Bransford & Stein, 1984, J. R. Hayes, 1988), but most are similar and can be summarized in the five-stage sequence that appears in Figure 9.1. We discuss the stages in the sections that follow.

Identifying the Problem

Question: There are 26 sheep and 10 goats on a ship. How old is the captain?

Amazingly, in one study, 75 percent of the second graders who were asked this question answered 36 (cited in Prawat, 1989)! Obviously, they didn't understand the problem.

At first glance, it appears that identifying a problem is straightforward, but in fact, it is one of the most difficult aspects of problem solving. It requires patience and a willingness to avoid committing to a solution too soon (Schunk, 2004). Obstacles to identifying problems effectively include the following:

- *Lack of domain-specific knowledge.* As in all areas of learning, prior knowledge is essential for problem solving (R. Mayer, 1998a; Tuovinen & Sweller, 1999). Laura's students, for example, confused area and perimeter.
- *Lack of experience in defining problems.* Most problem solving in schools involves well-defined problems in math in elementary schools and in math, chemistry, and physics in middle and high schools (Bruning et al., 2004).
- *The tendency to rush toward a solution before the problem has been clearly defined.* Novice problem solvers tend to "jump" into a solution before they've

Figure 9.1 A general problem-solving model

clearly identified the problem (Lan, Repman, & Chyung, 1998), as did the second graders who added the sheep and goats to get the age of the captain.

■ *The tendency to think convergently.* Novice problem solvers tend to focus on one approach to solving problems and often persist with this approach even when it isn't working (P. Alexander, 2006). Learning to think divergently results from experiences that require divergent thinking.

Representing the Problem

Representing the problem is important because it encourages the learner to conceptualize the problem in familiar terms. A problem can be represented in at least three ways (R. Mayer, 2002): (1) restated in different words that are more meaningful, (2) related to a previous problem, or (3) represented in visual form (e.g., the diagram that Laura's students used). Each of these strategies places the problem in a larger context and connects it to learners' prior knowledge (Mevarech, 1999). Research suggests that successful problem solvers use visual representations as scaffolds when encountering particularly difficult problems (Lowrie & Kay, 2001). Many problems are complex enough to overload learners' working memories, and putting problems on paper reduces this load. (As we said earlier, cognitive load is one likely reason Laura's students didn't succeed in solving their problem.)

Selecting a Strategy

After we identify and represent the problem, we must select a strategy for solving it. Algorithms and heuristics are two powerful problem-solving strategies.

Algorithms. To understand how algorithms facilitate problem solving, let's look at another problem:

A coat costing $90 is marked 25% off. What is the sale price of the coat?

For most of us, this is well-defined. We simply take 25% of 90, subtract the result from $90, and get $67.50 as the sale price. We used an **algorithm,** a specific set of steps for solving a problem. Algorithms vary widely in their complexity. For instance, when we subtract whole numbers with regrouping, add fractions with unlike denominators, or solve algebraic equations, we use simple algorithms. In contrast, computer experts use complex algorithms to solve sophisticated programming problems.

Heuristics. Many problems can't be solved with algorithms, because they don't exist for ill-defined problems and for many that are well-defined. In those cases, problem solvers use **heuristics,** general, widely applicable problem-solving strategies (P. Alexander, 2006; Chronicle, MacGregor, & Ormerod, 2004). The more complex and unfamiliar the task, the greater the need is for a heuristic approach to solving the problem (J. Lee & Reigeluth, 2003; Schunk, 2004). Our problem-solving model is a form of heuristic; it is a generally, widely applicable strategy.

Trial and error is another heuristic. It's inefficient, but problem solvers often try it first when faced with unfamiliar problems, and it provides learners with experience, which is important for acquiring expertise (J. Davidson & Sternberg, 2003).

Means–ends analysis, a strategy that breaks the problem into subgoals and works successively on each, is another heuristic that is effective for solving ill-defined problems. Returning to the case of the seventh graders who don't want to "think," for example, we might operationally define "thinking" as an inclination to search for relationships in the topics they study and to make conclusions based on evidence. With this as our goal, we can then design learning activities that give the students practice in these areas.

Drawing analogies, a strategy that is used to solve unfamiliar problems by comparing them with those already solved, is a third problem-solving heuristic (R. Mayer, 2002). It can be difficult to implement, however, because learners often can't find problems in their memories analogous to the one they want to solve, or they may make inappropriate connections between the two problems.

Some evidence indicates that specifically teaching heuristics can improve problem-solving ability even in early elementary students (Hohn & Frey, 2002), but ultimately, experience with problem solving and prior knowledge in the problem-solving domain are

Algorithm. A specific set of steps for solving a problem

Heuristics. General, widely applicable problem-solving strategies

Means–ends analysis. A strategy that breaks the problem into subgoals and works successively on each

Drawing analogies. A strategy used to solve unfamiliar problems by comparing them with those already solved

essential for successfully selecting a strategy, and no heuristic can replace them (Pittman & Beth-Halachmy, 1997).

Implementing the Strategy

Clearly defining and representing the problem and selecting an appropriate algorithm or heuristic are keys to successfully implementing a strategy. If these processes have been effective, implementation is routine. If learners cannot implement a strategy, they should rethink the original problem or the strategy they've selected. Laura's students, for example, had an uncertain understanding of the concepts *area* and *perimeter,* and they lacked experience in defining problems, which made selecting an effective strategy hard for them. Their difficulties occurred well before they attempted to implement their strategies.

Evaluating the Results

Evaluating results is the final step in our problem-solving model, and it is often a challenge for students. For example:

> One boy, quite a good student, was working on the problem "If you have six jugs, and you want to put two thirds of a pint of lemonade into each jug, how much lemonade will you need?" His answer was 18 pints. I [Holt] said, "How much in each jug?" "Two thirds of a pint." I said, "Is that more or less than a pint?" "Less." I said, "How many jugs are there?" "Six." I said, "But that doesn't make any sense." He shrugged his shoulders and said, "Well, that's the way the system worked out." (Holt, 1964, p. 18)

Situations like this are common in classrooms. Once students get an answer, they're satisfied, regardless of whether or not it makes sense (Schunk, 1994). This also occurred in Laura's class, where several of her students were satisfied with widely discrepant answers.

Teachers can help students who fail to evaluate their results by emphasizing the thinking involved in problem solving instead of focusing on the answer (R. Mayer, 2002). Each step should make sense, and teachers should constantly require students to justify their thinking. In addition, requiring estimates beforehand is important. Estimates require understanding, and answers and estimates that are far apart raise questions. The inclination to estimate is an important disposition that teachers should encourage at the beginning of problem solving.

Expert–Novice Differences in Problem-Solving Ability

Research has identified four important differences between experts and novices in problem-solving ability (Bruning et al., 2004; Hatano & Oura, 2003). **Experts** are individuals who are highly skilled or knowledgeable in a given domain. The expression "given domain" is important; experts tend to excel only in their own domain. An expert in math, for example, may be a novice in history or writing. These four differences are outlined in Table 9.1 and discussed in the paragraphs that follow.

Experts. Individuals who are highly skilled or knowledgeable in a given domain

Table 9.1 Expert–novice differences in problem-solving ability

Area	Experts	Novices
Representing problems	Search for context and relationships in problems.	See problems in isolated pieces.
Problem-solving efficiency	Solve problems rapidly and possess much knowledge that is automatic.	Solve problems slowly, and focus on mechanics.
Planning for problem solving	Plan carefully before attempting solutions to unfamiliar problems.	Plan briefly when attempting solutions to unfamiliar problems; quickly adopt and try solutions.
Monitoring problem solving	Demonstrate well-developed metacognitive abilities; abandon inefficient strategies.	Demonstrate limited metacognition; persevere with unproductive strategies.

The pattern we see in Table 9.1 is that experts are better at overcoming the limitations of working memory than are novices. Experts represent problems more effectively because their complex schemas allow them to "chunk" large amounts of information into single units that reduce the cognitive load on working memory. Much of their procedural knowledge is automatic, which further reduces cognitive load and leaves more of its space available to focus on representing the problem and selecting a strategy (Bruer, 1993). In addition, they are metacognitive in their approach to solving unfamiliar problems. They plan carefully, try new strategies when existing ones are unproductive, and carefully monitor results.

How do experts acquire these characteristics? The answer is simple. They possess a great deal of both domain-specific and general knowledge, which are acquired through experience. Because of their experience, they can use heuristics, like drawing analogies, effectively. Experts' experiences are stored in memory as "cases" that are indexed and searched, and can be applied analogically to new problems that occur (Bransford, 1993; Schunk, 2004).

For example, expert teachers possess a wide range of general knowledge, and they have a broad and deep understanding of learning, student characteristics, and the content they teach (Bruning et al., 2004). The same is true for experts in physics, computer science, history, music, and any other area. Unfortunately, no simple path to expertise exists, and some researchers estimate that it takes up to 10,000 hours to develop true expertise in a domain, such as teaching or computer science (Ericsson, 1996).

How can an understanding of expertise help us in our efforts to teach learners to become better problem solvers? Let's take a look.

Developing Expertise: Role of Deliberate Practice

Research on the development of expertise clearly suggests that it requires a great deal of experience in and knowledge about the area being studied. If students are to develop their problem-solving skills in math, for example, they must solve a great many problems, including those that are ill defined. Drill-and-practice that requires the application of memorized algorithms won't do it.

Recognizing this need, researchers have become interested in the concept of deliberate practice and its role in the acquisition of expertise (Ericsson, 1996; Ericsson, Krampe, & Tesch-Romer, 1993). Deliberate practice is consistent with the principle "learning requires practice and feedback," which you first saw in Chapter 7, and it has four essential characteristics:

- Learners are motivated to think about the task and must exert effort.
- Instruction takes learners' background knowledge into account.
- Feedback informs learners about errors and how to improve performance.
- Practice provides opportunities for learners to repeatedly perform similar (but not identical) tasks.

This framework is significant, because it goes beyond simple study time. Evidence indicates that increasing the amount of time spent studying doesn't necessarily increase achievement or expertise, whereas using the deliberate-practice framework can increase both (Plant, Ericsson, & Hill, 2005).

Deliberate practice can also overcome differences in native ability; researchers have found that extensive, deliberate practice provides opportunities for all students to improve their problem-solving abilities.

These findings don't imply that native ability is irrelevant; acquiring expertise will be easier for some than for others. It does mean, however, that if we're willing to work hard enough and long enough, we can acquire expertise and so can our students. In the vast majority of cases, talent doesn't block our road to competence. This is an encouraging finding.

We've now discussed a general problem-solving model, described the characteristics of expert performance, and shown that practice is essential for acquiring expertise in problem solving. We turn now to specific strategies for improving students' skills.

Instructional Principles

Helping Learners Become Better Problem Solvers: Instructional Principles

How can we help our students develop problem-solving expertise? Information processing and constructivist learning theory, combined with problem-solving research, help us answer this question. The following principles can guide you as you attempt to apply this research in your work with your students:

1. Present problems in real-world contexts, and take students' prior knowledge into account.
2. Capitalize on social interaction.
3. Provide scaffolding for novice problem solvers.
4. Teach general problem-solving strategies.

Let's return to Laura's work with her students to see how she attempts to implement these principles.

Laura begins Tuesday's math lesson by saying, "Yesterday, many of you said you weren't comfortable with the fact that we didn't agree about the amount of carpet we need for our classroom, so we'd better do some more work on it. . . . Let's take a look at our diagram again." She displays the diagram on the overhead.

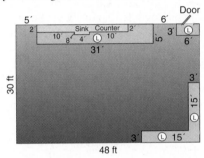

The class agrees that they're going to try implementing their strategies again and decide to try the first one (finding the area of the room and subtracting the parts with linoleum). Realizing that students have some misconceptions about area and perimeter, she reviews the concepts and then has the students calculate the area of the room.

They get 1,440 square feet, and Laura then asks, "So, what do we do next?"

"Subtract those parts," Elise offers, pointing to the parts on the diagram marked "L."

"How do we know that we must subtract?"

"There isn't any carpet there, . . . and it's part of the whole room," Adam volunteers.

"Okay, let's do that," Laura smiles. "Let's try this first," pointing to the top part of the diagram. "How long is this part? . . . Fred?"

"Thirty-one feet."

"Good, . . . so, how about our width; how wide is this section? Is it 2 feet or 5 feet? . . . Paige?"

"Five feet."

"Why is it 5?"

"The 2 is just that . . . the sink counter. . . . The linoleum goes under the whole 5 feet."

"Good thinking, Paige. . . . Okay, everyone calculate the area of that part, figure out the area by the door, and then we'll try the part here," Laura directs pointing to the linoleum at the lower right.

Most of the students get the first two areas, but many were uncertain about the third.

Laura then goes to the chalkboard and writes the following:

15 × 3 = 45 square feet
12 × 3 = 36 square feet
45 + 36 = 81 square feet

"Now, let's see where this came from. . . . Look carefully at it, also look at the diagram, and I'm going to ask you to explain these numbers."

Laura waits for several seconds and then says, "Someone explain where these numbers came from."

"The 15 is the length of that part," Nephi offers pointing to the bottom of the diagram. "And the 3 is how wide it is . . . so, the area is 45."

"Forty-five what?" Laura probes.

"Square feet," Nephi adds quickly.

"Now, let's be good thinkers. . . . Can someone explain the 12 times 3?"

"I've got it!" Anya nearly shouts after a few seconds. "It's because you already have that much," waving her hand back and forth.

"Come up and show us."

Anya goes to the overhead and alters the diagram, as shown here:

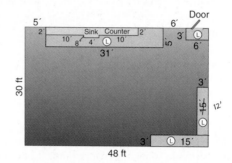

"I was thinking, . . . see, we already have this," she says, pointing to the lower right corner of the drawing. "So, this length is 12, not 15. . . . So, it's 12 times 3."

"What do the rest of you think? . . . Thank you, Anya," Laura smiles.

They agree that Anya's thinking makes sense, and Laura then asks, "Now what do we do?"

"Add up those amounts," Jared suggests.

The class adds the areas of the linoleum sections and gets a total of 254 square feet.

"So, how much carpet do we need?" Laura says finally. "How are we going to figure that out?"

"Subtract," Sam offers.

"Subtract what?"

"The 254 from . . . 1,440."

"And what is the 1,440?"

"The whole area, the area of the whole room."

The class agrees that Sam's thinking is valid, so Laura continues, "All right, . . . tomorrow we're going to look at the other strategy, where you take the inside area and add the other parts. . . . For your homework, I want you to figure out what the inside length and width are . . . . Now, what do we always ask ourselves when we try a strategy?"

"Does it make sense?" Shayna answers after thinking for several seconds.

"Yes, exactly," Laura smiles. Then, you'll be ready to explain how you got your answers when we start. . . . We'll look for that tomorrow. Now, go ahead."

The students begin, and as they work, Laura monitors them carefully and offers suggestions when they have questions or appear uncertain.

Let's look now at Laura's Tuesday lesson, its relationship with Monday's, and her attempts to apply the principles.

Present Problems in Real-World Contexts, and Take Students' Prior Knowledge into Account

By building her lessons around the carpeted area of her classroom, Laura presented a real-world problem, which applied the first principle. It is also one of the principles from constructivist learning theory, which you first saw in Chapter 8. In addition, she took her students' prior knowledge into account by reviewing *perimeter* and *area* and intervening when she realized that her students had misconceptions about differences between the two concepts.

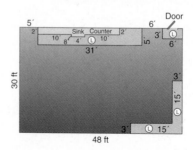

Capitalize on Social Interaction

Laura applied the second principle by developing both lessons using a great deal of social interaction. As you also saw in Chapter 8, it is one of the characteristics of constructivist learning theory, and, in addition, problem-solving research indicates that encouraging students to discuss and analyze problems increases their understanding and promotes transfer (B. Barron, 2000; Leinhardt & Steele, 2005).

Laura's emphasis in the lesson was on students' thinking, rather than correct answers, which is essential if students are to develop problem-solving expertise (R. Mayer, 2002). (This doesn't imply that correct answers are not important. Rather, it suggests that the thinking involved in arriving at the correct answer is also important.)

We also see that much of Monday's lesson was conducted in small groups, whereas, on Tuesday Laura led most of the lesson with the whole group. Although the format of the two lessons differed, the interaction was as important in one as in the other.

Social interaction in small groups provides opportunities for students to learn new problem-solving strategies from others.

Provide Scaffolding for Novice Problem Solvers

Seeing that her students struggled with some parts of the problem-solving process, and particularly with effectively implementing their strategies, Laura provided much more scaffolding in Tuesday's lesson than she did in Monday's. This applied the third principle.

The diagram she used to provide a visual representation of the problem was a form of scaffolding, and another was using Anya as a model in a form of cognitive apprenticeship, which you first saw discussed in Chapter 8.

Questioning, however, was her primary form of scaffolding. She asked a great many questions during Tuesday's lesson; in fact, she developed it almost entirely through questioning. To illustrate, let's look again at some of the dialogue.

Laura: So, what do we do next? (After the class determined that the total area of the room was 1,440 square feet.)

Elise: Subtract those parts. (Pointing to the parts on the diagram marked "L.")

Laura: How do we know that we must subtract?

Adam: There isn't any carpet there, . . . and it's part of the whole room.

Laura: Okay, let's do it. . . . Let's try this first (pointing to the top part of the diagram). How long is this part? . . . Fred?

Fred: Thirty-one feet.

Laura: Good, . . . so, how about our width; how wide is this section? Is it 2 feet or 5 feet? . . . Paige?

Paige: Five feet.

Laura: Why is it 5?

Paige: The 2 is just that . . . the sink counter. . . . The linoleum goes under the whole 5 feet.

Laura: Good thinking, Paige. . . . Okay, everyone calculate the area of that part.

"Walking" the students through the solution with questions such as, "How do we know that we must subtract?" and "Why is it 5?" helped ensure that students' thinking was visible throughout the process. Providing this scaffolding was the most important feature of Tuesday's lesson, and it was the primary difference between the way she conducted Tuesday's compared to Monday's.

Teachers can help students acquire general problem-solving skills through coaching in the form of instructional dialogues (Leinhardt & Steele, 2005; R. Mayer, 1998a). For example, prompts and questions, such as, "Explain specifically what you're doing," and "Why are you doing this?" have been shown to increase problem-solving ability (R. K. Atkinson et al., 2003). The practice students get in putting their understanding into words is important, and students rarely get as much practice as they need in this process.

Laura also presented students with worked examples, an effective form of scaffolding that teachers can capitalize on more frequently than they typically do. Let's look at this process.

Analyzing Worked Examples. In traditional instruction, teachers typically model solutions to problems that students then try to imitate, often with little understanding (R. Mayer, 2002). In comparison, **worked examples** are problems with completed solutions that provide students with one way of solving the problems. An expanding body of research confirms that worked examples make the process of problem solving more meaningful than traditional instruction (van Gog, Paas, & van Merriënboer, 2004). These results have been found with learners ranging from lower elementary to university students (R. Atkinson, Derry, Renkl, & Wortham, 2000).

Laura used simple worked examples in her lesson when she wrote the following on the board:

$15 \times 3 = 45$ square feet
$12 \times 3 = 36$ square feet
$45 + 36 = 81$ square feet

Then, she used some additional questioning to help clarify them. Let's look again at some dialogue as an illustration.

Laura: Someone explain where these numbers came from.
Nephi: The 15 is the length of that part (pointing to the bottom of the diagram), and the 3 is how wide it is . . . so, the area is 45.
Laura: Forty-five what?
Nephi: Square feet.
Laura: Now, let's be good thinkers. . . . Can someone explain the 12 times 3?
Anya: I've got it! . . . It's because you already have that much (pointing to the diagram).
Laura: Come up and show us.

Anya then went to the overhead and altered the diagram, as shown here:

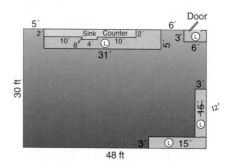

Anya: I was thinking, . . . see, we already have this (pointing to the lower right corner of the drawing). So, this length is 12, not 15. . . . So, it's 12 times 3.

Online Case Book

To assess another teacher's effectiveness in helping students develop problem-solving abilities, go to the *Online Case Book* for Chapter 9 at *www.prenhall. com/eggen*.

Combining the worked examples with discussion is essential; without the discussion, learners often miss important aspects of the process and are likely to try to memorize the steps in it instead of developing genuine understanding (Leinhardt & Steele, 2005; van Gog et al., 2004). And, it was in this discussion that she used Anya as a model in the form of cognitive apprenticeship that we referred to earlier.

Worked examples are especially helpful when students are first learning a procedure. As students acquire experience, teachers should place increased emphasis on applying the procedure in different contexts (R. K. Atkinson et al., 2003; Kalyuga, Chandler, Tuovinen, & Sweller, 2001; Renkl & Atkinson, 2003).

Research also indicates that learners prefer worked examples to traditional instruction (Renkl, Stark, Gruber, & Mandl, 1998). This is particularly important as teachers try to promote the extensive deliberate practice necessary to develop expertise.

This section helps answer the third question we asked at the beginning of the chapter, which was, "What must Laura now do to help her students improve their problem-solving abilities?" She responded to student confusion by taking a direct approach, and she pro-

Worked examples. Problems with complete solutions that provide students with one way of solving the problems

vided a great deal of scaffolding as the students attempted to solve the problem and get consistent answers.

Teach General Problem-Solving Strategies

Although general strategies in the absence of domain-specific knowledge have limited value, within specific domains, such as mathematics, they can increase problem-solving abilities (Higgins, 1997; Kramarski & Mevarech, 2003; R. Mayer, 2002). Emphasizing general strategies is effective because it helps students become more metacognitive about their problem solving (P. Alexander, 2006; R. Mayer, 2002).

Laura attempted to teach general strategies by using the problem-solving model as a framework for her lessons. She emphasized each step in Monday's lesson, and she began Tuesday's lesson by referring again to the model.

In addition, she modeled the attitudes necessary to promote thinking and the development of expertise. She had an accepting attitude, and her students knew that taking risks and making mistakes is a normal part of learning. She also carefully planned the explicit use of strategies; she had the class focus on one strategy on Tuesday, and she planned to consider a second the next day.

Problem-Based Learning

Think again about Scott Sowell's lesson at the end of Chapter 8 and Laura's lessons in this chapter. They illustrate **problem-based learning,** a teaching strategy that uses problems as the focus for developing content, skills, and self-direction (Hmelo-Silver, 2004; Serafino & Cicchelli, 2005). Problem-based learning activities typically have the following characteristics (Gijbels et al., 2005; Hmelo-Silver, 2004):

- Lessons begin with a problem, and solving it is the lesson focus.
- Students are responsible for investigating the problem, designing strategies, and finding solutions. Groups need to be small enough (typically 3 to 5) so that all students can actively participate in the process.
- The teacher guides students' efforts with questioning and other forms of scaffolding.

Problem-based learning provides opportunities for students to use learning strategies and develop their metacognitive abilities.

As we saw in Laura's lessons, the third characteristic is essential. She needed to judiciously intervene, because her students experienced difficulties in solving the problems. In spite of considerable guidance, Laura's students got widely varying answers to the area problem. In response, Laura used a direct approach and provided extensive scaffolding in her Tuesday lesson. Some would argue that she should have intervened sooner and more specifically, whereas others would suggest that the experience the students gained, in spite of the fact that they struggled, was a worthwhile goal in itself.

Some evidence indicates that content learned in problem-based lessons is retained longer and transfers better than content learned when other strategies are used (Barak & Dori, 2005). Most of the research, however, has been conducted with older or advanced students, and more research is needed to examine its implementation with learners whose skills are less developed (Hmelo-Silver, 2004).

This research addresses the second question we asked at the beginning of the chapter ("Was the time spent on the activity [Monday's lesson] used wisely?") Unfortunately, the answer is unclear. Laura's students acquired considerable experience with designing and implementing strategies and working cooperatively, all of which are valuable for promoting self-regulation. On the other hand, they could not solve the problem, and Laura had to spend an extra day together with a great deal of guidance in helping them reach the correct answer. The answer to the question ultimately is a matter of professional judgment.

Analyzing Classrooms Video
To analyze the effectiveness of another teacher's attempts to develop her students' problem-solving abilities, go to Episode 16, "Guiding Students' Problem Solving: Graphing in Second Grade," on DVD 2, accompanying this text.

Problem-based learning. A teaching strategy that uses problems as the focus for developing content, skills, and self-direction

When you use problem-based activities in your classes, the following guidelines may be helpful:

■ Begin with a clear problem. Laura's problem was clear and precise.
■ Organize the activity carefully. Be sure groups are small, roles are clear, and materials are readily accessible (M. Lohman & Finkelstein, 2000).
■ Carefully monitor students as they work. Intervene if students are proceeding based on a misconception.
■ Conduct a whole-class discussion to summarize the groups' work and provide feedback about the overall process.

As with most teaching strategies, problem-based learning can be effective, but it won't work automatically. It must be designed and implemented by knowledgeable and skilled teachers who carefully monitor the process.

Exploring Further

Some educators strongly advocate problem-based learning. To read more about the method, go to "Problem-Based Learning" in the *Exploring Further* module of Chapter 9 at *www.prenhall.com/eggen*.

Knowledge Extensions

To deepen your understanding of the topics in this section of the chapter and to integrate them with topics you've already studied, go to the *Knowledge Extensions* module for Chapter 9 at *www.prenhall.com/eggen*. Respond to questions 1–4.

Checking Your Understanding

1.1 You're involved in a relationship, but it isn't as satisfying as you would hope. Is this a well-defined or an ill-defined problem? Explain. Describe a means–ends analysis that might be used to solve the problem.

1.2 Which heuristic—*trial and error, means–ends analysis,* or *drawing analogies*—is deliberate practice most likely to help students use effectively? Explain.

1.3 Identify at least three ways in which Laura's assignment—trying the strategy of finding the inside area and adding the additional parts with linoleum—illustrates deliberate practice. Was her problem ill-defined or well-defined for students? Explain.

To receive feedback for these questions, go to Appendix B.

Classroom **Connections**

Developing Your Students' Problem-Solving Abilities

1. Use real-world problems, and promote high levels of interaction.
   - **Elementary:** A fourth-grade teacher emphasizes the first step in problem solving by having her students put problems into their own words. She asks them to discuss the problem with a partner before beginning to work on it and discusses the problem as a whole group before having them solve it in their group.
   - **Middle School:** A middle school teacher has a "problem of the week." Each student is required to bring in at least one "-real-world" problem each week. The teacher selects from among them, and the class works on them in groups. He is careful to ensure that each student has a problem selected during the year.
   - **High School:** An Algebra II teacher requires her students to explain each step as they "walk" through the solutions to

problems. She emphasizes that understanding the reasons is as important as getting the right answers.

2. Provide students with practice and scaffolding as they develop their problem-solving skills.
   - **Elementary:** A second-grade teacher begins a lesson on graphing by asking students how they might determine classmates' favorite jelly bean flavor. She guides them as they identify the problem and how they might represent and solve it.
   - **Middle School:** A seventh-grade pre-algebra teacher uses categories such as "We Know" and "We Need to Know" as scaffolds for analyzing word problems. They then solve at least one word problem each day.
   - **High School:** In a unit on statistics and probability, a teacher requires her students to make estimates before solving problems. They then compare the solutions to the estimates.

THE STRATEGIC LEARNER

Do you take notes in your classes? Do you first skim a chapter to help you understand its organization before you read it? Do you summarize important passages in an attempt to help you remember the essential ideas in them? If you do, you're using **strategies,** techniques to enhance performance on a learning task (P. Alexander & Jetton, 2000, 2003). Note taking is a strategy, for example, because it is a technique for increasing the amount you remember from a lecture or written passage.

A wide variety of general learning strategies exists, including note taking, highlighting and underlining, summarizing, self-questioning, and even creating a study environment free of distractions (Alexander, 2006). Each is a technique that can enhance learning.

Regardless of the strategy, students' ability to use it effectively depends on their metacognitive skills. Let's look at this idea more closely.

Metacognition: The Foundation of Strategic Learning

In Chapter 7 you saw that **metacognition** is the awareness of and control over one's cognitive processes. Although metacognitive skills are related to intelligence, they outweigh intelligence in predicting student achievement (Veenman & Spaans, 2005). In other words, if students can be taught to be aware of the way they study and learn and to take steps to improve both, they can compensate for lack of native ability. This is a powerful and encouraging result.

Metacognition is the mechanism used to match a strategy to a goal (Hennessey, 2003). When expert learners use note taking as a strategy, for example, they ask questions such as

- Am I writing down important ideas or trivial details?
- Am I taking enough notes, or am I taking too many?
- Am I simply reading my notes when I study, or do I attempt to elaborate on them with examples?

These questions demonstrate metacognition, and without this kind of monitoring, strategies can be essentially worthless.

Although most strategy research has focused on reading (Bruning et al., 2004), other studies have examined strategy use in areas such as problem solving in math and science, writing, and study skills (Conner & Gunstone, 2004; Georghiades, 2004). This research indicates that effective strategy users, in addition to being metacognitive about their learning, have two other characteristics: (1) extensive prior knowledge and (2) a repertoire of strategies.

Prior Knowledge

We've seen how important prior knowledge is for cognitive learning in general, and it is no less important for strategy use (Alao & Guthrie, 1999; Peverly, Brobst, & Graham, 2003). Trying to encode information and represent it in memory without a strong knowledge base makes strategy use extremely difficult (P. Alexander, Graham, & Harris, 1998). In contrast, students with extensive prior knowledge can use deep processing strategies to generate questions, create images, and use analogical thinking.

Metacognitive skills also depend on prior knowledge. It allows learners to make better decisions about what is important to study, so they are more capable of efficiently allocating their mental resources to a task (Verkoeijen, Rikers, & Schmidt, 2005).

A Repertoire of Strategies

Just as expert problem solvers draw on a wealth of experiences, effective strategy users have a variety from which to choose (P. Alexander, 2006; P. Alexander & Jetton, 2000). For instance, they take notes, skim, use outlines, generate diagrams and figures, take advantage of bold and italicized print, and capitalize on examples (Hacker, Dunlosky, & Graesser, 1998). They also use heuristics, such as means–ends analysis, to break ill-defined problems into manageable parts. Without a repertoire, learners cannot match strategies to different goals and task demands.

Strategies. Techniques to enhance performance on a learning task

Metacognition. The awareness of and control over one's own cognitive processes

Taking notes helps learners capture important information.

Becoming a strategic learner takes time and effort. Research indicates that, in spite of being aware of more sophisticated strategies, most students use primitive ones, such as simple rehearsal, regardless of the difficulty of the material. And, this is true even for college students (Peverly et al., 2003). Unfortunately, learners rarely receive strategy instruction before high school (E. Wood, Motz, & Willoughby, 1998).

Study Strategies

Study strategies are specific techniques students use to increase their understanding of written materials and teacher presentations. A variety of study strategies exist, and we examine five of them in this section:

- Note taking
- Using text signals
- Summarizing
- Elaborative questioning
- SQ3R

Note Taking

Note taking is probably the most common study strategy, and it has been studied extensively. In spite of its popularity, research indicates that many students, including those in college, are poor note takers (Austin, Lee, & Carr, 2004; Peverly et al., 2003). In fact, students often record less than 40 percent of pertinent information from lectures (Titsworth, 2004).

However, even though students often are not skilled at taking notes, the process is associated with increased achievement, especially if it encourages students to actively process information (Igo, Bruning, & McCrudden, 2005). Effective notes include both the main ideas presented in lectures and texts and details that support the main ideas (Peverly et al., 2003).

We can explain the positive effects of note taking with both information processing and constructivist learning theory. First, taking notes puts students in active roles and helps maintain attention, and second, the notes provide a form of external storage (Igo et al., 2005). As we saw in Chapters 7 and 8, memory is unreliable. We may fail to encode the information, or we may reconstruct our understanding in a way that makes more sense to us. The notes provide an external source of information against which we can check our understanding.

We can help our students improve their note-taking skills with **guided notes,** teacher-prepared handouts that "guide" students with cues and space available for writing key ideas and relationships. Using guided notes has been found to increase achievement in students ranging from those with learning disabilities (S. L. Hamilton, Seibert, Gardner, & Talbert-Johnson, 2000) to college students (Austin et al., 2004). Figure 9.2 illustrates a guided notes form used by a seventh-grade geography teacher in a discussion of different climate regions of the United States. (Remember, this is merely an example. You should use a form that will best help you reach your learning objectives.)

Guided notes have an additional benefit. Guided notes model the organization and key points of the topic, and, as students acquire experience with these notes, they gradually develop organizational skills that they can apply on their own. These skills, combined with metacognitive awareness, can significantly increase students' strategic learning abilities.

Using Text Signals

While note taking has been found to be a more effective strategy for learning from lectures and teacher explanations than from written materials (R. L. Williams & Eggert, 2002), using **text signals,** a strategy designed to capitalize on the organization of written materials, can also increase learning (Bruning et al., 2004; Lorch & Lorch, 1995).

Common text signals include the following:

- *Headings.* For example, in this chapter *note taking* and *using text signals* are each subheadings under the heading *study strategies,* so this organization

Study strategies. Specific techniques students use to increase their understanding of written materials and teacher presentations

Guided notes. Teacher-prepared handouts that "guide" students with cues and space available for writing key ideas and relationships

Text signals. A strategy designed to capitalize on the organization of written materials

Figure 9.2   Guided note taking in U.S geography

1. Give an example of how each of the following influences climate:

Latitude _____

Wind direction _____

Ocean currents _____

Land forms _____

2. Describe each climate, and identify at least one state that has this climate. Then identify one type of plant that lives in this climate and two different animals that are typically found in the climate.

The Mediterranean Climate _____

_____ State _____

Plant _____ Animals _____

The Marine West Coast Climate _____

_____ State _____

Plant _____ Animals _____

The Humid Subtropical Climate _____

_____ State _____

Plant _____ Animals _____

The Humid Continental Climate _____

_____ State _____

Plant _____ Animals _____

The Tropical Savannah Climate _____

_____ State _____

Plant _____ Animals _____

The Desert Climate _____

_____ State _____

Plant _____ Animals _____

The Subarctic Climate _____

_____ State _____

Plant _____ Animals _____

signals that each is a technique used to increase understanding of teacher presentations and written materials.

- *Numbered and bulleted lists.* For instance, the bulleted list you're reading right now provides you with a succinct overview of different text signals.
- *Underlined, bold, or italicized text.* For example, each of the important concepts throughout this text is emphasized by putting it in bold print. This is a signal that you should understand the definition and be able to identify examples of it.
- *Preview and recall sentences.* For instance, we introduced our discussion of metacognition by saying, "In Chapter 7 you saw that metacognition is. . . ." This statement links the concept to a discussion in an earlier chapter. This signal suggests that you recall or reread the section in the earlier chapter if you are uncertain about the topic.

Strategic learners use text signals to develop a framework for the topic they're studying. As teachers, we should encourage the use of this strategy by discussing the organization of a topic and reminding students of other text signals that can help make the information they're studying more meaningful (Bruning et al., 2004).

Summarizing

Summarizing is the process of preparing a concise description of verbal or written passages. It is one way to **monitor comprehension,** checking to see if we understand what we have read or heard. If we can prepare a summary of a topic, it is one indicator that we understand it.

Summarizing. The process of preparing a concise description of verbal or written passages

Comprehension monitoring. The process of checking to see if we understand what we have read or heard

Learning to summarize takes time and effort, but students can become skilled at it with training (P. Alexander, 2003, 2006). Training usually involves walking students through a passage and helping them construct general descriptions of lists of items, generate statements that relate ideas to each other, and identify unimportant information (J. P. Byrnes, 2001a).

For instance, we might summarize the problem-solving section of this chapter as follows:

To solve problems, we must identify and represent the problem, select and implement a strategy to solve it, and check to see if the solution makes sense. We can help our students become better problem solvers by examining the thinking of experts, using real-world problems, discussing problems and solutions, and using questioning and worked examples to scaffold novice problem solvers.

Research supports the effectiveness of summarizing as a comprehension-monitoring strategy. In one study, students who created summaries not only developed a greater understanding of the topics they studied but also improved their metacognitive skills to a greater extent than a control group (Thiede & Anderson, 2003). In a modification of traditional summaries, a second study had students generate five key words that captured the essence of a text passage. As with standard summaries, students who generated key words developed a greater understanding than did a control group (Thiede, Anderson, & Therriault, 2003).

Elaborative Questioning

Elaborative questioning is the process of drawing inferences, identifying examples, and forming relationships in the material being studied. It is perhaps the most effective comprehension-monitoring strategy because it encourages learners to create connections in the material being studied (E. Wood et al., 1999). Three elaborative questions are especially effective:

- What is another example of this idea?
- How is this topic similar to or different from the one in the previous section?
- How does this idea relate to other big ideas I have been learning?

To illustrate these strategies, consider your own study of this chapter. As you were studying the section on problem solving, you could have asked yourself questions, such as

What is another example of a well-defined problem in this class?
What is another example of an ill-defined problem?
What makes the first well defined and the second ill defined?
How are problem-solving and learning strategies similar?
How are they different?

Questions like these create links between new information and knowledge in long-term memory, which increases learning by making the new information more meaningful.

SQ3R

SQ3R is a complex study strategy that teaches students to use a series of sequential steps to monitor comprehension while reading. Its origins go back to the 1940s, and it has earned the title "the grandfather of study strategies" (Lipson & Wixson, 2003). The steps in SQ3R are

1. *Survey:* Students survey the text they're about to read.
2. *Question:* Based on their prereading, students create elaborative questions that they expect to be answered as they read.
3. *Read:* Students read the material.
4. *Recite:* Students reflect on what they've read, try to answer their elaborative questions, and find relationships between the passage and earlier passages. (As you see here, students are doing much more than literally "reciting" in this step.)
5. *Review:* Learners summarize what they've read, reread parts of the passage about which they're uncertain, and take notes if necessary.

Elaborative questioning. The process of drawing inferences, identifying examples, and forming relationships in the material being studied

The effectiveness of SQ3R as a comprehensive study strategy is uncertain. Some authors support its use (e.g., R. L. Potter, 1999; Topping & McManus, 2002), but their endorsement appears to be based primarily on the strategy's long-term reputation (Spor & Schneider, 1999). Evidence indicating that SQ3R is effective is largely lacking (Huber, 2004).

On the other hand, SQ3R incorporates effective strategies, such as *using text signals* in the first step, *elaborative questioning* in the second, and *summarizing* in the final step. Both elaborative questioning and summarizing are proven comprehension monitoring strategies (Thiede & Anderson, 2003; E. Wood et al., 1999). Whether or not they are more effective when incorporated into a comprehensive strategy like SQ3R than they would be alone is uncertain.

Research indicates that most strategies can be learned successfully, and strategy instruction is especially important for younger students and low achievers, because they have a smaller repertoire of strategies, which leaves more room for improvement (Bruning et al., 2004; Gaskill & Murphy, 2004). The effectiveness of the strategies depends on the extent to which students are metacognitive in their approach, make the effort to use the strategy actively, and can activate relevant prior knowledge and link it to the material being read (Huber, 2004). If one or more of these factors is missing, no strategy will work.

 **Instructional Principles** | **Developing Strategic Learning in Students: Instructional Principles**

You can help your students improve their strategy use by using effective instructional scaffolding while teaching strategies, having students practice them, and providing feedback throughout the process. The following principles can guide you in your efforts to help your students become more strategic in their study:

1. Describe the strategy, and explain why it is useful.
2. Explicitly teach the strategy by modeling both its use and metacognitive awareness.
3. Provide opportunities for students to practice the strategy in a variety of contexts.
4. Provide feedback as students practice (Carpenter, Levi, Fennema, Ansell, & Franke, 1995; Rickards, Fajen, Sullivan, & Gillespie, 1997).

Let's see how the principles guide Donna Evans, an urban middle school geography teacher, as she works with her students.

Donna begins her geography class by giving each of her middle schoolers a blank transparency and a nonpermanent marking pen.

"We need to read the section of our text that describes the low-latitude, middle-latitude, and high-latitude climates," she says. "Let's talk for a few minutes about how we can help ourselves remember and understand what we've read.

"One way to become more effective readers is to summarize the information we read in a few short statements that capture its meaning. This is useful because it makes the information easier to remember, and in our situation, it'll help us compare one climate region with another. You can do the same thing when you study different classes of animals in biology or parts of the court system in your government class . . . . Now go ahead and read the passage, and see if you can decide what makes a low-latitude climate a low-latitude climate."

After giving the class a few minutes to read the section, Donna continues, "As I was reading, I kept asking myself what makes the low-latitude climates what they are . . . . Here's how I thought about it. I read the section, and I saw that the low latitudes could be either hot and wet or hot and dry. Close to the equator, the humid tropical climate is hot and wet all year. A little farther away, it has wet summers and dry winters. For the dry tropical climate, high-pressure zones cause deserts, like the Sahara."

Donna displays a transparency that includes the information and says, "Now, let's all give it a try with the section on the middle-latitude climates. Go ahead and read the section, and try to summarize it the way I did . . . . Write your summaries on your individual transparencies, and we'll share what you've written."

The class reads the passage, and after they finish, Donna begins, "Okay. Who can give me a summary? . . . Go ahead, Dana."

Dana displays her summary on the overhead, and Donna and other students add information and comments to what Dana says. Donna then has Omar, Taeko, and Jesse display their summaries, and the class practices again with the section on the high-latitude climates.

Throughout the school year, Donna continues to have the students practice summarizing a day or two each week.

Now let's look at Donna's efforts to develop strategic learners. She began by describing the skill and its use, which applied the first principle. For instance, Donna said, "One way to become more effective readers is to summarize the information we read in a few short statements that capture its meaning. This is useful because. . . ."

She then applied the second principle by modeling both the skill and metacognition when she commented, "As I was reading, I kept asking myself what makes the low-latitude climates what they are. . . . Here's how I thought about it." Research indicates that young children's metacognitive awareness can be increased with explicit instruction such as this (J. Alexander, Johnson, & Leibham, 2005; Jacobs, 2004).

Donna then had students practice by having them read the passage and prepare a summary. This applied the third principle, and she applied the fourth by providing her students with feedback. Donna had students display their summaries on the overhead, so the process of giving and receiving feedback was clear to all. And, she continued the process throughout the school year.

Continued practice is essential. Students won't become strategic learners in one or even a few lessons. As with all forms of complex learning, it requires a great deal of experience and deliberate practice.

Checking Your Understanding

2.1   Three students are discussing the use of highlighting as a study strategy.

"I highlight the first sentence of nearly every paragraph, because that's supposed to be the topic sentence," Alexie comments. Sometimes I highlight other sentences if they seem to be the topic sentence.

"I highlight passages that I think are important," Ruiz adds. "I look for key terms and lists and examples.

"I highlight practically whole chapters," Will offers. "I read along with it as I'm highlighting.

Which student is likely to be using the most effective strategy? Whose strategy is least effective? Explain.

2.2   You read this chapter carefully in an effort to understand the content. Does your effort illustrate strategic learning? Explain why or why not.

2.3   We described *summarizing* and *elaborative questioning* as *comprehension-monitoring* strategies, but we didn't refer to *note taking* and *using text signals* in the same way. Explain why we would describe summarizing and elaborative questioning as different from the other two.

To receive feedback for these questions, go to Appendix B.

Knowledge Extensions

To deepen your understanding of the topics in this section of the chapter and to integrate them with topics you've already studied, go to the *Knowledge Extensions* module for Chapter 9 at *www.prenhall.com/eggen*. Respond to questions 5–7.

Critical thinking. An individual's ability and inclination to make and assess conclusions based on evidence

CRITICAL THINKING

Critical thinking is becoming more important in today's world because of the large amounts of information we need to sift through on a daily basis. **Critical thinking** has been defined in various ways, but most definitions converge on the idea that it is an individual's ability and inclination to make and assess conclusions based on evidence (Glassner, Weinstock, & Neuman, 2005; van Gelder, 2005). For example, an advertisement says, "Doctors recommend . . . more often," touting a health product. A person thinking critically is wary because the advertisement provides no evidence for its claims. Similarly, a critical thinker listens to another person's argument with skepticism because people often have unconscious biases.

The development of critical thinking is at the core of cognitive approaches to teaching (Kuhn & Dean, 2004). As with the development of problem-solving and learning strategies, it requires a great deal of practice. A classroom climate that values different perspectives and high levels of discussion is essential, and as we've said repeatedly, reasons for answers are as important as the answers themselves (Leinhardt & Steele, 2005).

Although critical thinking is related to strategic learning, the two differ in scope. Strategic learning involves specific techniques designed to enhance performance on a specific task. Critical thinking is broader; it is used to process information from a variety of sources (Beach, 1999; Bruning et al., 2004). For example, you might summarize a newspaper editorial to increase your comprehension of it. When looking for evidence of the author's position or identifying unstated assumptions in what the author says, you're going beyond comprehension; you are thinking critically.

Asking students to compare, contrast, analyze, and make predictions encourages them to use and develop higher-level cognitive processes.

The Challenge of Critical Thinking

While appearing straightforward, making and assessing conclusions based on evidence is difficult, and most people are not very good at it. Clearly, it involves "complex cognitive processes" as the title of this chapter states. For example, when asked to justify an opinion, "to provide some evidence to back it up—more than half the population flounder . . . . The problem is that they do not have a general grasp of the notion of evidence and what would properly count as providing evidence in support of their view" (van Gelder, 2005, p. 42).

Also, critical thinking, some experts assert, is not a natural disposition for humans. We want experiences to make sense, and we tend to be satisfied with the first account that seems valid, so we rarely pursue the matter further (Shermer, 2002). In addition, our minds also seem to have an intrinsic tendency toward illusion, distortion, and error (Piatelli-Palmarini, 1994).

An additional challenge to developing critical thinking is a concept called **belief preservation,** the tendency to make evidence subservient to belief, rather than the other way around (Douglas, 2000). When we strongly believe something (or desire it to be true), we tend to do the following (van Gelder, 2005):

- Seek evidence that supports what we believe and avoid or ignore evidence that disputes the belief.
- Rate evidence as good or bad depending on whether it supports or conflicts with our belief.
- Retain our beliefs in the face of overwhelming contrary evidence if we can find some minimal support for the belief.

As we saw in our discussion of misconceptions and their resistance to change in Chapter 8, we can explain these tendencies with constructivist views of learning and the concept of *equilibrium.* The basic principle of constructivist learning theory is that people construct understanding that makes sense to them. When experiences make sense, we are at equilibrium, so we have no need to pursue a matter further. This also explains the tendency toward illusion, distortion, and error, as well as belief preservation. If illusions exist or reality is distorted, but they make sense to us, equilibrium is preserved. The same is true for belief preservation. In fact, pursuing a matter further, or changing a belief is cognitively dangerous because equilibrium is disrupted, which then requires the energy to reestablish it. It is simpler and easier to retain the illusion or maintain the belief.

In addition, people sometimes have a personal investment in existing beliefs. They retain a belief because they feel that changing it would somehow negatively reflect on their intelligence or their resolve. The change then threatens their sense of self-worth (Linnenbrink &

Belief preservation. The tendency to make evidence subservient to belief, rather than the other way around

Figure 9.3 Elements of critical thinking

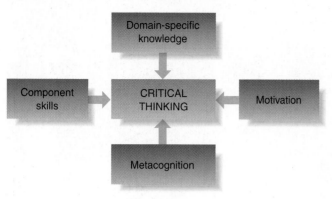

Source: Adapted from Nickerson, 1988.

Pintrich, 2003). Further, beliefs are sometimes integral to their culture or religion (Southerland & Sinatra, 2003).

Meeting these challenges is at the heart of instruction that promotes critical thinking, and over the years, educators have developed many programs to teach critical thinking outside of traditional content courses. However, transfer of the skills taught in these programs is limited (Bransford, Goldman, & Vye, 1991), and as a result, most critical thinking instruction now centers on integrating it into the regular curriculum (A. Brown, 1997; Kuhn, 1999).

Elements of Critical Thinking

Current approaches to instruction in critical thinking are generally organized around four elements (R. Mayer, 2002; Nickerson, 1988), illustrated in Figure 9.3 and described in the following sections.

Component Skills

Component skills are the "tools" of thinking; they are the cognitive processes learners use to make and assess their conclusions (Mayer, 2002). With some variation from one source to another (Halpern, 1998), most experts include the skills summarized in Table 9.2.

Research supports the idea of focusing on component skills, which should be specifically described, modeled, and practiced with feedback (R. Mayer, 2002; Sternberg, 1998b, 1998c). In addition, integrating these component skills into the regular school curriculum helps students develop a deeper understanding of the topics they study (Bransford et al., 1991).

Domain-Specific Knowledge

We have repeatedly emphasized the importance of prior knowledge for all aspects of cognitive learning, and it is no less important for critical thinking. As in other areas, prior knowledge is domain specific; the ability to think critically in history, for example, doesn't ensure that a person will also be able to think critically in chemistry. Nickerson (1988) summarized the importance of domain-specific knowledge as follows: "To think effectively in any domain one must know something about the domain and, in general, the more one knows the better" (p. 13).

Metacognition

Metacognition is important for all cognitive processing; it provides direction and purpose for our cognitive efforts (Donovan & Bransford, 2005). In the context of critical thinking,

Component skills. The cognitive processes learners use to make and assess their conclusions

Table 9.2 Component skills in thinking

Skill	Subskill
Observing	Recalling
	Recognizing
Finding patterns and generalizing	Comparing and contrasting
	Classifying
	Identifying relevant and irrelevant information
Forming conclusions based on patterns	Inferring
	Predicting
	Hypothesizing
	Applying
Assessing conclusions based on observation	Checking consistency
	Identifying bias, stereotypes, clichés, and propaganda
	Identifying unstated assumptions
	Recognizing overgeneralizations or undergeneralizations
	Confirming conclusions with facts

being metacognitive means that learners know when to use the component skills, how they relate to domain-specific knowledge, and why they're used. Effective thinkers not only find patterns and form conclusions based on evidence, for example, but they also are keenly aware of what they're doing and why.

Some researchers argue that metacognition is the essence of critical thinking, and its development is even more important than the component skills we identified earlier (Kuhn, 1999; Kuhn & Dean, 2004). Explicitly teaching about thinking as it occurs in the classroom is an effective way to develop these metacognitive abilities (Butler, 1998).

Motivation

Experts are becoming increasingly aware of the role motivation plays in thinking (Pintrich & Schunk, 2002). Learner motivation determines the attitudes and dispositions students bring to their learning experiences. Examples include

- The inclination to rely on evidence in making conclusions
- The willingness to respect opinions that differ from our own
- A sense of curiosity, inquisitiveness, and a desire to be informed
- A tendency to reflect before acting and consider whether or not conclusions make sense.
- The willingness to "let go" of previous ideas, beliefs, and assumptions (Bransford & Schwartz, 1999; van Gelder, 2005)

The willingness to let go of previous ideas is difficult, and much of teachers' efforts in developing thinking is directed toward helping learners acquire this and the other attitudes and dispositions. For example, ideally, we want our students to put extra effort into searching for evidence that contradicts their beliefs and a willingness to change their minds when evidence starts mounting against those beliefs.

We also want our students to ask themselves, "Where is the author coming from?" when they read a political commentary, knowing that political orientation will slant the author's opinion. In school we want learners to be skeptical about the truth of rumors, and in classroom settings, we want them to constantly wonder, "What does this relate to?" and, "How do we know?"

Attitudes and dispositions are difficult to teach directly. Students disposed to think critically have teachers who model these attitudes for them, seize opportunities to provide practice during learning activities, and establish an emotional climate that supports critical thinking.

Instructional △ **Principles**   **Developing Critical Thinking: Instructional Principles**

As we said at the beginning of this section, developing students' abilities to think critically is an essential part of cognitive approaches to teaching. And, learning to think critically requires a great deal of integrated practice. The following principles can guide you as you attempt to provide this practice for your students.

1. Integrate critical thinking into the context of the regular curriculum.
2. Require students to provide evidence for their conclusions with questions such as "How do we know?" and "Why?"
3. Promote students' awareness of their own thinking.
4. Capitalize on opportunities to develop thinking dispositions when they arise.

To illustrate, let's go back to Laura's Tuesday lesson and look again at some of the dialogue.

Laura: So, what do we do next? (After the students concluded that the total area of the room was 1,440 square feet.)
Elise: Subtract those parts. (Pointing to the parts on the diagram marked "L.")
Laura: How do we know that we must subtract?
Adam: There isn't any carpet there . . . and it's part of the whole room.

Laura: Okay, let's do it. Let's try this first. (Pointing to the top part of the diagram.) How long is this part? . . . Fred?

Fred: Thirty-one feet.

Laura: Good, . . . so, how about our width; how wide is this section? Is it 2 feet or 5 feet? . . . Paige?

Paige: Five feet.

Laura: Why is it 5?

Paige: The 2 is just that . . . the sink counter. . . . The linoleum goes under the whole 5 feet.

Later in the lesson, they continue:

Laura: Now, let's be good thinkers. . . . (She presents the worked example.) Can someone explain the 12 times 3?

Anya: I've got it! It's because you already have that much. (Referring to the 15-foot by 3-foot area.)

Laura: Come up and show us.

Anya then went to the overhead and altered the diagram to show that one area was 15 feet by 3 feet and another was 12 feet by 3 feet.

Anya: I was thinking, . . . see, we already have this. (Pointing to the 15-foot by 3-foot area.) So, this length is 12, not 15. . . . So, it's 12 times 3.

Now let's look at Laura's efforts in more detail. She applied the first principle by seamlessly integrating critical thinking with her regular instruction. In doing so, promoting thinking required little extra time and effort on her part.

Laura applied the second principle (require students to provide evidence) with questions, such as, "How do we know we must subtract?" "Why is it 5 [feet]?" and "Can someone explain the 12 times 3?" (in the worked example). Each question required students to provide evidence and justify their thinking, which is the essence of critical thinking. Opportunities to ask questions like these occur more often than we realize, and when teachers learn to recognize opportunities when they appear, critical thinking can become an integral part of instruction.

Laura applied the third principle (promote students' awareness of their own thinking) by asking Anya to model her thinking for the rest of the class. Teachers can also help students become aware of their thinking by reminding them of the need to think about what they're doing when the opportunity arises. For example, in Laura's Monday lesson, the class had determined that the total area of the room was 1,440 square feet, but one of the groups determined that the carpeted area was 1,600. This would have been an opportunity to remind students to examine their thinking. Questions such as the following could be used:

What is the total area of the room?
Will the carpeted portion be more, less, or the same as this amount? How do we know?
So, when we get an answer of 1,600, what should we do?

Encouraging students to ask themselves if their answers make sense is unlikely to be helpful without a concrete example to illustrate the flawed thinking. However, with practice, students' dispositions to ask themselves if their conclusions make sense will improve, and this also applies the fourth principle, capitalize on opportunities to develop critical thinking when they arise. Laura attempted to capitalize on this opportunity when, at the end of Tuesday's lesson she asked, "Now, what do we always ask ourselves when we try a strategy?" In response to Shayne's answer, "Does it make sense?" she emphasized, "Yes, exactly. . . . Then, you'll be ready to explain how you got your answers when we start. We'll look for that tomorrow." Teachers often miss opportunities such as this to teach critical thinking by overemphasizing content coverage at the expense of thinking (Torff, 2005). By reminding students of the importance of sense making in their strategies, Laura was developing metacognitive awareness, a critical component of both strategy use and critical thinking.

Checking Your Understanding

3.1   Define critical thinking, and describe its elements.

3.2   Look again at the dialogue between Laura and her students on page 285. What component skills are Adam, Paige, and Anya best illustrating with their comments in the dialogue? Explain.

3.3   Mrs. Solis's students are analyzing a table illustrating the average global temperature for the years 1960 to 2000. They conclude that the table shows a general increase. "What have we done here?" Mrs. Solis asks. "We've found a pattern in the data," Francisco responds.

Francisco's comment best illustrates which of the following: *Domain-specific knowledge, component skills, metacognition,* or *motivation?* Explain.

To receive feedback for these questions, go to Appendix B.

Classroom ⊞ Connections

Promoting Strategic Learning and Critical Thinking in Your Classroom

Study Strategies

1. Teach study strategies across the curriculum.

- **Elementary:** A second-grade teacher models elaborative questioning and encourages her children to ask themselves, after each lesson of the day, what the lesson was about and what they learned from it.

- **Middle School:** A sixth-grade teacher introduces note taking as a listening skill. He then provides note-taking practice in science and social studies by using skeletal outlines to organize his presentations and by having his students use them as a guide for their note taking.

- **High School:** A biology teacher closes each lesson by having her students provide summaries of the most important parts of the lesson. She adds material to summaries that are incomplete.

Critical Thinking

2. Plan and conduct lessons to promote thinking.

- **Elementary:** A fourth-grade teacher makes an effort to ask questions that promote thinking in his students. He has a list

he calls "The Big Five," which he places on a bulletin board and looks for opportunities to ask them whenever he can: (a) What do you see? observe? (b) How are these alike? How are they different? (c) Why are they alike? Why are they different? (d) What would happen if . . . ? (e) How do you know?

- **Middle School:** A seventh-grade world geography teacher develops the content in her units with charts, graphs, and tables. She begins units by asking her students to make comparisons among items of information in the charts and conclusions based on the comparisons. She requires students to provide evidence for each of the conclusions based on information they see in the charts.

- **High School:** An English teacher works to help his students analyze literature. As they talk about a work, he regularly asks, "How do you know that?" and, "What in the story supports your idea?"

TRANSFER OF LEARNING

Consider the following situation:

You get into your car, put the key into the ignition, and the seat belt buzzer goes off. You quickly buckle the belt. Or, anticipating the buzzer, you buckle the belt before you insert the key.

Think for a moment. What concept from behaviorism does your behavior—buckling the seat belt—best illustrate? Behaviorists would describe it as *negative reinforcement.* If you identified it as such, you have demonstrated **transfer,** "the effect of previous learning on new learning or problem solving" (R. Mayer, 2002, p. 4). When we can recognize or provide a new example of a concept, solve a unique problem, or apply a learning strategy to a new situation, we are demonstrating transfer. Transfer is essential because it allows learners to apply understanding—on their own—to new contexts.

> Schools are not able to teach students everything they will need to know, but rather must equip students with the ability to transfer—to use what they have learned to solve new problems successfully or to learn quickly in new situations. (R. Mayer & Wittrock, 1996, p. 49)

Recalling information doesn't involve transfer. If, for example, your instructor has previously discussed buckling the seat belt as an example of negative reinforcement, and if you later identify it as such, there is no transfer. You merely remembered the information. With respect to problem solving, transfer occurs when students can solve problems they haven't previously encountered, and in the case of learning strategies, transfer occurs, for example, when students use elaborative questioning in areas other than reading.

Transfer can be either positive or negative. Positive transfer occurs when learning in one context facilitates learning in another, whereas negative transfer occurs when learning in one situation hinders performance in another (R. Mayer & Wittrock, 1996). For instance, if students know that a mammal nurses its young and breathes through lungs and then conclude that a whale is a mammal, they are demonstrating positive transfer. If they believe that a fish is an animal that lives in the sea and then conclude that a whale is a fish, they are demonstrating negative transfer.

General and Specific Transfer

At one time, educators believed that taking courses such as Latin, Greek, and mathematics were valuable not only for learning Latin, Greek, and math but also to "discipline" the mind. The hope was that these courses would strengthen learners' general thinking ability. Such an occurrence would demonstrate **general transfer,** the ability to apply knowledge or skills learned in one context in a broad range of different contexts. If, for example, becoming an expert chess player would help a person learn math more easily because both require logic, general transfer would occur. **Specific transfer** is the ability to apply information in a context similar to the one in which it was originally learned. If understanding that the Greek prefix *photos* means "light" results in learners' better understanding words such as *photography* and *photosynthesis,* specific transfer has occurred.

Unfortunately, as researchers found more than 80 years ago and have since repeatedly confirmed, general transfer rarely occurs (Driscoll, 2005; Pugh, Bergin, & Rocks, 2003; E. Thorndike, 1924). Studying Latin, for example, results in learners' acquiring expertise in Latin and specific transfer to the Latin roots of English words; it does little to improve thinking in general.

Factors Affecting the Transfer of Learning

Several factors affect students' ability to transfer:

- Similarity between learning situations
- Depth of learners' original understanding
- Learning context
- Quality and variety of examples and other learning experiences
- Emphasis on metacognition

Similarity Between Learning Situations

As our discussion of general and specific transfer implies, the more closely two learning situations are related, the more likely transfer is to occur (L. S. Fuchs et al., 2003; Phye, 2001). For instance, when first graders are given this problem,

Angi has two pieces of candy. Kim gives her three more pieces of candy. How many pieces does Angi have now?

Transfer. The effect of previous learning on new learning or problem solving

General transfer. The ability to apply knowledge or skills learned in one context in a broad range of different contexts

Specific transfer. The ability to apply information in a context similar to the context in which it was originally learned

they do well on this one:

> *Bruce had three pencils. His friend Orlando gave him two more. How many pencils does Bruce have now?*

When they're given the problem about Angi and Kim followed by this problem,

> *Sophie has three cookies. Flavio has four cookies. How many do they have together?*

they perform less well (Riley, Greeno, & Heller, 1982). The first two problems are more closely related than the first and third. These results further demonstrate that transfer is very specific.

Depth of Original Understanding

Transfer requires a high level of original understanding (Bransford & Schwartz, 1999). This may seem obvious, but research indicates that students often fail to transfer because they don't understand the topic in the first place (DeCorte, 2003; Pugh et al., 2003).

The more practice and feedback learners are given with the topics they study, the deeper their understanding will be, and the more likely transfer will occur (Moreno & Mayer, 2005; Schunk, 2004). When planning instruction, teachers should identify the most important concepts and skills so that they can concentrate on the quality of understanding rather than on the quantity of information transmitted. In addition, the quality of the dialogue between teachers and students has a powerful effect on both learning and transfer (Engle, 2003; Leinhardt & Steele, 2005). This is another reason social interaction is so important.

So what do we do when students' original understanding lacks depth? This leads us to the notion of *context,* and the *quality* and *variety* of examples and other learning experiences, the next three factors. We place particular emphasis on them, because they are the ones we as teachers can control. We can, through our planning and instruction, provide a variety of high-quality examples, and we can embed them in meaningful contexts.

Learning Context

In Chapter 7, we saw that learners encode both the information they're studying and the context in which that information exists (J. Brown, Collins, & Duguid, 1989). This is important because contextualized information is more meaningful than information presented in the abstract.

To see why presenting examples in context is so important, let's look again at the paragraph a teacher used to promote conceptual change with respect to the concept *adjective,* which you first saw in Chapter 8, Checking Your Understanding, question 3.3.

> John and Karen drove together in his old car to the football game. They soon met their very best friends, Latoya and Michael, at the large gate near the entrance. The game was incredibly exciting, and because the team's running game was in high gear, the home team won by a bare margin.

As we see in the vignette, *football, running,* and *home* are all adjectives. If they were not presented in the context of the vignette, learners would likely conclude that *football* and *home* are nouns, and *running* is a verb. The context in which examples appear influences their meaning, and this illustrates why information presented in context is so important.

In general, context refers to real-world application. For instance, people don't read isolated words in the real world; they read books, newspapers, and other written materials. So, the preceding vignette is more nearly a real-world example than isolated words would be. Students would also be more likely to transfer learning about the area of irregular plane figures from Laura's carpeting problem than they would from area problems presented in the abstract.

Quality and Variety of Examples and Learning Experiences

Contextualizing examples can also have drawbacks; learners connect the content to a specific context, which inhibits transfer (Bransford & Schwartz, 1999). For knowledge and

Exploring Further

To examine the importance of context, experience, and application for promoting transfer in more depth, go to "Teaching in Context" in the *Exploring Further* module of Chapter 9 at *www.prenhall.com/eggen.*

Transfer is facilitated by quality learning experiences in a variety of contexts.

skills learned in one context to be applied in others, teachers should present high-quality examples, and, as we saw in the last section, they should be presented in a variety of contexts (Mayfield & Chase, 2002; Star, 2004).

In Chapter 8 we emphasized the importance of examples and other representations of content in helping learners acquire the information they need to construct knowledge. Table 8.2 also outlined the ways several teachers you've studied in this book represented their topics. You may want to reread this section beginning on page 248.

Quality of examples refers to the extent that examples and other content representations *include all the information that students need to understand the topic,* an idea that we emphasized in Chapter 8, and *quality learning experiences* require activities where the reasons for answers are as important as the answers themselves (Rittle-Johnson & Alibali, 1999).

For instance, Karen Johnson's compressed cotton (in the opening case of Chapter 2) is a high-quality example of the concept *density* because students can *see* that the cotton is more dense when compressed in the cup. They can see that the mass of cotton hasn't changed; no cotton balls were added, and none were removed. They can also see that the compressed cotton takes up less space. These kinds of experiences are important for all students, and they are particularly important for those who might lack school-related prior knowledge.

To illustrate the importance of variety of examples, let's look again at the vignette illustrating *adjectives.* There we saw that *old, football, best, large, exciting, running, high, home,* and *bare* are all examples of adjectives. In addition to *football, running,* and *home,* which we already discussed, *exciting* is a particularly important example, because it appears after the noun it modifies. Without it, learners may conclude that adjectives always precede the nouns they modify, which could then lead to a misconception.

The vignette illustrates the idea of "multiple knowledge representations" (M. Brenner et al., 1997; Spiro et al., 1992). As learners construct understanding that prepares them for transfer, each example adds connections and perspectives that other examples may miss. Also, the greater the variety, the greater the chance the example will connect to examples and contexts that exist in learners' prior knowledge, so they help capitalize on "similarity between the two learning situations" as a factor in promoting transfer.

In another case, a sea turtle would be an important example for a lesson on *reptiles.* This example would prevent learners from concluding that reptiles only live on land, and that only fish live in water. Inadequate variety results in students' undergeneralizing and forming an incomplete concept or developing a misconception.

As examples of high-quality experiences related to problem solving, think back to some of Laura's questions. When she asked, "How do we know that we must subtract?" "Why is it (the width of the sink) 5 (versus 2)?" and "Can someone explain the 12 times 3?" she was emphasizing the reasons for the answers. This emphasis helped link the concrete examples to students' developing understanding and increased the likelihood that their understanding will transfer (L. S. Fuchs et al., 2003; Mayfield & Chase, 2002).

Emphasis on Metacognition

An emphasis on metacognition, as with problem solving and strategic learning, also increases transfer (Donovan & Bransford, 2005; Langer, 2000). As metacognition improves, some evidence indicates that it transfers in a general sense (P. Alexander, 2006; Prawat, 1989). For example, remaining open-minded, reserving judgment, searching for facts to support conclusions, and taking personal responsibility for learning are general dispositions, all grounded in metacognition. Teachers can encourage transfer of these dispositions through modeling across disciplines and by communicating that learning is a meaningful activity that is facilitated by awareness of their own thinking.

Checking Your Understanding

4.1   You have shown your students pictures of a *dog, cat, horse,* and *deer* in an effort to help them understand the concept *mammal.* With respect to transfer, which of the following—*cow, mouse, bat,* or *squirrel*—are they *least likely* to identify as a mammal? Which factor influencing transfer is best illustrated in this case? Explain.

4.2   Using the factors that affect transfer as a basis, how effective were your efforts when you used the pictures of a dog, cat, horse, and deer in 4.1? Explain.

4.3   You want to teach your students the concept of *internal conflict.* Which of the following is the highest *quality* example? (a) a picture of a girl with a thoughtful look on her face, and a caption saying, "The girl is experiencing internal conflict; (b) the statement, "Shelly didn't know what to do. She was looking forward to the class trip, but if she went, she wouldn't be able to take the scholarship-qualifying test," displayed on the overhead; or (c) the statement, "Internal conflict represents a dilemma of a person caught between two unpleasant alternatives," displayed on the overhead. Explain.

To receive feedback for these questions, go to Appendix B.

Classroom Connections

Promoting Transfer in Your Classroom

1. Provide examples and applications of the content you teach in a variety of different contexts.
   - **Elementary:** A third-grade teacher selects samples of student writing to teach grammar and punctuation rules. She displays samples on overheads and uses the samples as the basis for her instruction.
   - **Middle School:** A science teacher begins a discussion of light refraction by asking students why they can see better with their glasses on than they can without them. He then illustrates refraction with a variety of demonstrations, such as immersing a pencil in a glass of water and looking at objects through magnifying lenses. The class discusses the demonstrations in detail.
   - **High School:** A geometry teacher illustrates applications of course content with examples from architecture. She also uses photographs from magazines and slides to illustrate how math concepts relate to the real world.

2. Plan examples and representations that provide all the information students need for understanding the topics they study.
   - **Elementary:** A fifth-grade teacher illustrates the concept volume by putting 1-cm cubes in a box 4 cm long, 3 cm wide, and 2 cm high. He has the students count the cubes as he puts them in the box, until it is filled with 24 cubes. He uses questioning to help students understand the idea that the box has a volume of 24 cubic centimeters.
   - **Middle School:** A history teacher writes short cases to illustrate concepts, such as *mercantilism,* that are hard to understand from text alone. She guides students' analyses of the cases, helping them identify the essential characteristics of the concepts.
   - **High School:** An English teacher prepares a matrix illustrating the characters, setting, and themes for several of Shakespeare's plays. Students use the information in summarizing and drawing conclusions about Shakespeare's works.

Meeting Your Learning Objectives

1. **Identify examples of ill-defined and well-defined problems, and describe the role of deliberate practice in solving them.**

   - A problem occurs when a problem solver has a goal but lacks an obvious way of achieving the goal.
   - A well-defined problem, such as "Student will find the solution for $3x + 4 = 13$," has only one correct solution and a certain method for finding it.
   - An ill-defined problem, such as "Students will accept more personal responsibility for their own learning," has more than one acceptable solution, an ambiguous goal, and no generally agreed-upon strategy for reaching a solution.
   - Deliberate practice involves learner motivation, instruction that takes learners' prior knowledge into account, feedback that provides learners with information about how to improve performance, and opportunities for learners to repeatedly perform similar, but not identical tasks.

2. **Explain differences between effective and ineffective strategies in studying behaviors.**

   - A strategy is a technique for enhancing performance on a learning task. Taking notes is a strategy, for example, because it is a technique used to help learners remember more of what they hear or read.
   - Learners who use strategies effectively are metacognitive about their approaches to studying. They also possess a repertoire of strategies and prior knowledge about the topics they're studying. Ineffective strategy users are less metacognitive in their approaches to studying, and they lack prior knowledge and possess fewer strategies.

3. **Define critical thinking, and identify its characteristics in classroom activities.**

   - Critical thinking is the process of making and assessing conclusions based on evidence.
   - Learners who think critically during classroom activities possess substantial domain-specific knowledge about the topics they study; they use component skills in their analyses of the topics; they are metacognitive in their approaches to study; and they are disposed to open-mindedness.

4. **Identify factors that influence transfer in classroom learning activities.**

   - Transfer occurs when learners can apply previously learned information in a new context. Specific transfer involves an application in a situation closely related to the original; general transfer occurs when two learning situations are quite different.
   - Factors that influence transfer include the depth of original understanding, the quality and variety of the representations learners study, and the context in which learning experiences are embedded.
   - Research indicates that transfer tends to be specific, but metacognitive and self-regulatory skills may transfer across domains.

Developing as a Professional: Praxis™ Practice_____

At the beginning of this chapter, you saw how Laura Hunter planned and conducted her lesson in an effort to promote thinking and problem solving in her students. Let's look now at a teacher with a group of second graders involved in a lesson on graphing. Read the case study, and answer the questions that follow.

Suzanne Brush has her second graders involved in a unit on graphing. She introduces the day's lesson by saying that she is planning a party for the class, but has a problem: She doesn't know the class's favorite flavor of jelly bean.

Several students offer suggestions for solving the problem, and they finally settle on having students taste a variety of jelly beans and indicate their favorite.

Anticipating the idea of tasting the jelly beans, Suzanne has prepared plastic bags with seven different-flavored jelly beans. She gives each student a bag, and after students taste each one, Suzanne says,

"Okay, I need your help . . . . How can we organize our information so that we can look at it as a whole group?

Jacinta suggests, "See how many people like the same one, and see how many people like other ones."

"Okay, can you add to that? . . . Josh?"

"You can write their names down and see how many . . . like each flavor," Josh answers hesitantly.

They discuss the ideas for a few more minutes, and Suzanne then says, "Here's what we're going to do. Stacey mentioned earlier that we could graph the information, and we have an empty graph up in the front of the room." She moves to the front of the room and displays the outline of a graph:

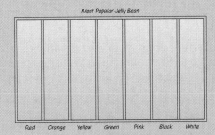

Most Popular Jelly Bean

Red Orange Yellow Green Pink Black White

She then has the students come to the front of the room and paste colored pieces that represent their favorite jelly beans on the graph.

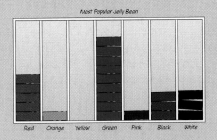

Most Popular Jelly Bean

Red Orange Yellow Green Pink Black White

"Now, look up here," she smiles. "We collected and organized the information, so now we want to analyze it. I need you to tell me what we know by looking at the graph. . . . Candice?"

"People like green," Candice answers.

"How many people like green?"

". . . Nine."

"Nine people like green . . . . And how did you find that out? Come up here and show us how you read the graph?"

Candice goes up to the graph and moves her hand up from the bottom, counting the nine green squares as she goes.

Suzanne continues having the students make observations, and then she changes the direction of the lesson by saying, "Okay, here we go. . . . How many more people liked green than red? . . . Look up at the graph, and set up the problem on your paper."

She watches as students look at the graph and set up the problem, and when they're finished, she says, "I'm looking for a volunteer to share an answer with us. . . . Dominique?"

"Nine plus 5 is 14," Dominique answers.

"Dominique says 9 plus 5 is 14. Let's test it out," Suzanne responds, asking Dominique to go up to the graph and show the class how she arrived at her answer.

As Dominique walks to the front of the room, Suzanne says, "We want to know the difference. . . . How many more people liked green than red, and you say 14 people, . . . 14 more people liked green. Does that work?"

Dominique looks at the graph for a moment and then said, "I mean 9 take away 5."

"She got up here and she changed her mind," Suzanne says with a smile to the rest of the class. "Tell them."

"Nine take away 5 is 4," Dominique says.

"Nine take away 5 is 4," Suzanne continued, "so how many more people liked green than red? . . . Carlos?"

"Four," Carlos responds.

"Four, good, four," she smiles at him warmly. "The key was, you had to find the difference between the two numbers."

Suzanne has students offer additional problems, they solve and explain them, and she then continues, "I have one more question, and then we'll switch gears. How many people took part in this voting?"

Suzanne watches as students consider the problem for a few minutes, and then said, "Matt? . . . How many people?"

"Twenty-four."

"Matt said 24. Did anyone get a different answer? So we'll compare. . . . Robert?"

"Twenty-two."

"How did you solve the problem?" she asks Robert.

"Nine plus 5 plus 3 plus 3 plus 1 plus 1 equals 22," he answers, adding up all the squares on the graph.

"Where'd you get all those numbers?"

"There," he says, pointing to the graph.

"He went from the highest to the lowest, added them, and the answer was 22." Suzanne then breaks the children into groups and has them work at centers where they gather and summarize information in bar graphs. They tally and graph the number of students who have birthdays each month, interview classmates about their favorite soft drinks, and call pizza delivery places to compare the cost of comparable pizzas.

As time for lunch nears, Suzanne calls the groups back together, and after they're settled, says, "Raise your hand if you can tell me what you learned this morning in math."

"How to bar graph," Jenny responds.

"So, a graph is a way of organizing information, so we can look at it and talk about it. Later we'll look at some additional ways of organizing information," and she ends the lesson.

Short-Answer Questions

In answering these questions, use information from the chapter and link your responses to specific information in the case.

1. How effectively did Suzanne teach problem solving in her lesson? To what extent did she apply the instructional strategies for helping students become better problem solvers?

2. To what extent did Suzanne encourage critical thinking in her lesson? What could she have done to give students more practice in developing critical-thinking abilities?

3. How effective would Suzanne's lesson have been for promoting transfer? What could Suzanne have done to increase the likelihood of transfer in her students?

PRAXIS™ These exercises are designed to help you prepare for the Praxis™ "Principles of Learning and Teaching" exam. To receive feedback on your short-answer questions, go to the Companion Website at www.prenhall.com/eggen, then to the Practice for Praxis™ module for Chapter 9.

To acquire experience in preparing for the multiple-choice items on the Praxis™ exam, go to the Self-Assessment module for Chapter 9 at www.prenhall.com/eggen and click on "Practice Quiz."

For additional connections between this text and the Praxis™ exam, go to Appendix A.

Also on the Companion Website at *www.prenhall.com/eggen,* you can measure your understanding of chapter content with multiple-choice and essay questions, and broaden your knowledge base in *Exploring Further* and *Web Links* to other educational psychology websites.

ONLINE PORTFOLIO ACTIVITIES

To develop your professional portfolio, further apply your understanding of chapter content, and address the INTASC standards, go to the Companion Website, then to the *Online Portfolio Activities* for Chapter 9. Complete the suggested activities.

IMPORTANT CONCEPTS

algorithm (p. 268)
belief preservation (p. 283)
component skills (p. 284)
comprehension monitoring (p. 279)
critical thinking (p. 282)
drawing analogies (p. 268)
elaborative questioning (p. 280)
experts (p. 269)
general transfer (p. 288)
guided notes (p. 278)
heuristics (p. 268)
ill-defined problem (p. 266)

means–ends analysis (p. 268)
metacognition (p. 277)
problem (p. 266)
problem-based learning (p. 275)
specific transfer (p. 288)
strategies (p. 277)
study strategies (p. 278)
summarizing (p. 279)
text signals (p. 278)
transfer (p. 288)
well-defined problem (p. 266)
worked examples (p. 274)

CHAPTER 10

Theories of Motivation

Chapter Outline	Learning Objectives

After you have completed your study of this chapter, you should be able to

What Is Motivation?

Extrinsic and Intrinsic Motivation • Motivation to Learn

1 Identify differences between extrinsic motivation, intrinsic motivation, and motivation to learn in classroom activities.

Behavioral Views of Motivation

Using Rewards in Classrooms • Criticisms of Behavioral Approaches to Motivation • Using Rewards in Classrooms: Instructional Principles

2 Describe criticisms of behavioral views of motivation, and explain how rewards can be used to increase motivation to learn.

Humanistic Views of Motivation

Development of the Whole Person • Humanistic Views of Motivation: Instructional Principles

3 Explain the basic premise of humanistic views of motivation, and identify applications of humanistic motivation theory in classrooms.

Cognitive Theories of Motivation

Expectancy × Value Theory • Self-Efficacy: Beliefs About Capability • Goals and Goal Orientation • Attribution Theory • Beliefs, Goals, and Attributions: Instructional Principles • Self-Determination Theory • Assessment and Learning: The Role of Assessment in Self-Determination • Developing Students' Self-Determination: Instructional Principles • Diversity in Motivation to Learn

4 Describe the basic assumption on which cognitive motivation theories are based, and analyze applications of these theories in events in and outside of classrooms.

5 Analyze applications of self-determination theory in classroom learning activities.

Affective Factors in Motivation

Self-Worth Theory • Arousal and Anxiety • Accommodating Affective Factors in Motivation: Instructional Principles

6 Use self-worth theory and studies of arousal and anxiety to explain learner behavior.

Students' motivation is one of the most important factors influencing how much they learn. As you read the following case study, which involves a world history teacher who has her class involved in a unit on the Crusades, consider what she does to influence her students' motivation.

"We'd better get moving," Susan urges Jim as they approach the door of Kathy Brewster's classroom. "The bell is gonna ring, and you know how Brewster is about this class. She thinks it's *so* important."

"Did you finish your homework?" Jim asks and then stops himself. "What am I talking about? You've done your homework in every class since I've known you."

"Sure, I don't mind it that much. . . . It bothers me when I don't get something, and sometimes it's even fun. My dad helps me. He says he wants to keep up with the world," Susan laughs.

"In some classes, I just do enough to get a decent grade, but not in here," Jim responds. "I used to hate history, but I sometimes even read ahead a little, because Brewster makes you think. It's kind of interesting the way she's always telling us about the way we are because of something that happened a zillion years ago—I never thought about this stuff in that way before."

"Gee, Mrs. Brewster, that assignment was impossible," Harvey grumbles as he enters the classroom.

"That's good for you," Kathy smiles. "I know it was a tough assignment, but you need to be challenged. It's hard for me, too, when I'm studying and trying to put together new ideas, but if I hang in, I always feel like I can get it."

"Aw, c'mon, Mrs. Brewster. I thought you knew everything."

"I wish. I have to study every night to keep up with you people, and the harder I study, the smarter I get. . . . And I feel good about it when I do."

"But you make us work so hard," Harvey continues in feigned complaint.

"Yes, but look how good you're getting at writing," Kathy smiles again, pointing her finger at him. "I think you hit a personal best on your last paper. You're becoming a very good writer."

"Yeah, yeah, I know," Harvey waves on his way to his desk, "and being good writers will help us in everything we do in life," echoing a rationale the students often hear from Kathy.

"Stop by and see me after class," Kathy quietly says to Jenny as she enters the room. "I'd like to talk to you for a minute."

We'll return to Kathy's lesson again later in the chapter, but for now we want to pose three questions: (1) How is Susan's general orientation toward school different from Jim's? (2) How is Jim's motivation in Kathy's class different from the way he responds to other classes? (3) How is Kathy influencing that orientation? We consider these and other questions in this chapter.

WHAT IS MOTIVATION?

Motivation is a force that energizes, sustains, and directs behavior toward a goal (Brophy, 2004; Pintrich & Schunk, 2002), and researchers have found a positive and robust correlation between motivation and achievement (McDermott, Mordell, & Stoltzfus, 2001; Wang, Haertel, & Walberg, 1993; R. Weinstein, 1998).

> Children's motivation to learn lies at the very core of achieving success in schooling. Given rapid technological advances, an ever-changing knowledge base, and shifting workplace needs, a continuing motivation to learn may well be the hallmark of individual accomplishment across the lifespan. (R. Weinstein, 1998, p. 81)

In general, motivated students

- Have more positive attitudes toward school and describe school as satisfying
- Persist on difficult tasks and cause fewer management problems
- Process information in depth and excel in classroom learning experiences (Stipek, 1996, 2002)

Motivation. A force that energizes, sustains, and directs behavior toward a goal

Not surprisingly, motivated students are a primary source of job satisfaction for teachers.

Extrinsic and Intrinsic Motivation

Motivation can be described in two broad categories. **Extrinsic motivation** is motivation to engage in an activity as a means to an end, whereas **intrinsic motivation** is motivation to be involved in an activity for its own sake (Pintrich & Schunk, 2002). Extrinsically motivated learners may study hard for a test because they believe studying will lead to high test scores, for example; intrinsically motivated learners study because they want to understand the content and they view learning as worthwhile in itself. This helps answer our first question (How is Susan's general orientation toward school different from Jim's?). Jim's comment, "In some classes, I just do enough to get a decent grade," reflects extrinsic motivation, whereas Susan's comment, "Sure, I don't mind it [homework] that much. . . . It bothers me when I don't get something, and sometimes it's even fun," suggests intrinsic motivation. These relationships are illustrated in Figure 10.1.

Although we think of extrinsic and intrinsic motivation as two ends of a continuum (meaning the higher the extrinsic motivation, the lower the intrinsic motivation and vice versa), they are actually on separate continua (Covington, 2000; Pintrich & Schunk, 2002). For example, students might study hard both because a topic is interesting and because they want good grades. Others might study only to receive the good grades. The first group is high in both extrinsic and intrinsic motivation; the second is high in extrinsic motivation but low in intrinsic motivation. Research indicates that intrinsic motivation is preferable because of its focus on learning and understanding (Brophy, 2004).

Extrinsic and intrinsic motivation are also contextual and can change over time (Wigfield et al., 2004). As the vignette showed, Jim was extrinsically motivated in other classes, but intrinsically motivated in Kathy's ("I used to hate history, but . . . Brewster really makes you think. It's actually interesting"). Kathy's class was different enough from other classes to influence his intrinsic motivation. This answers our second opening question (How is Jim's motivation in Kathy's class different?) and leads us to the third: How is Kathy influencing that orientation?

We can begin to answer the question by examining intrinsic motivation in more detail. Researchers have determined that learners are intrinsically motivated by activities or experiences that

- *Present a challenge.* Challenge occurs when goals are moderately difficult, and success isn't guaranteed. Meeting challenges is also emotionally satisfying (R. Ryan & Deci, 2000; Stipek, 2002).
- *Provide the learner with feelings of autonomy.* Learners are more motivated when they feel that they have command or influence over their own learning (N. Perry, 1998; Ryan & Deci, 2000).
- *Evoke curiosity.* Interesting, novel, surprising, or discrepant experiences create intrinsic motivation (Brophy, 2004).
- *Involve creativity and fantasy.* Experiences allow learners to personalize content by using their imaginations (Lepper & Hodell, 1989).

In addition, some researchers suggest that aesthetic experiences—those associated with beauty that evoke emotional reactions—may be intrinsically motivating as well (Ryan & Deci, 2000).

Jim's comments suggest that Kathy capitalized on two of these factors. "Brewster really makes you think," suggests he was reacting to the challenge in her class, and "It's actually interesting the way she's always telling us about the way we are because of something that happened a zillion years ago," suggests he was responding to the way she promoted curiosity in her teaching.

Motivation to Learn

Kathy capitalized on some aspects of intrinsically motivating activities, and teachers are sometimes (mistakenly) given the impression that their instruction should be so interesting and stimulating that students will be generally intrinsically motivated. This is a worthwhile

Figure 10.1 Extrinsic and intrinsic motivation

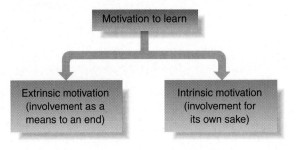

Extrinsic motivation. Motivation to engage in an activity as a means to an end

Intrinsic motivation. Motivation to be involved in an activity for its own sake

ideal, but it isn't realistic for all, or even most, learning activities. The following are some reasons (Brophy, 2004):

■ School attendance is compulsory, and curriculum content is selected on the basis of what society believes students should learn, not on what students would choose if given the opportunity to do so.
■ Teachers work with large numbers of students and cannot always meet individuals' needs.
■ Students' performances are evaluated and reported to parents and other caregivers, so students tend to focus on meeting parents' and caregivers' demands rather than on personal benefits they might derive from the experiences.

What is a reasonable alternative?

> If intrinsic motivation is ideal but unattainable as an all-day, everyday motivational state for teachers to seek to develop in their students, what might be a more feasible goal? I believe that it is realistic for you to seek to develop and sustain your students' **motivation to learn** from academic activities: their tendencies to find academic activities meaningful and worthwhile and to try to get the intended learning benefits from them. (Brophy, 2004, p. 15)

Students with a motivation-to-learn orientation make an effort to understand topics whether or not they find the topics intrinsically interesting or the process of studying them enjoyable. They maintain this effort because they believe that the understanding that results is valuable and worthwhile. This differs from a student who does assignments only to get by or for a grade, which is an emphasis on performance that detracts from motivation to learn.

The theories of learning presented in Chapters 6 through 9 help us understand motivation, and in fact, some researchers argue that learning and motivation are so interdependent that a person can't fully understand one without the other (Brophy, 2004; Pintrich & Schunk, 2002). In the following sections, we examine this interdependence as we study behavioral, humanistic, and cognitive theories of motivation. A framework for these theories is outlined in Figure 10.2.

Checking Your Understanding

1.1 On the basis of the information in the case study at the beginning of the chapter, is Susan high in both extrinsic and intrinsic motivation or high in one and low in the other? Explain.

1.2 Describe the primary difference between a teacher's attempt to stimulate students' motivation to learn compared to a teacher who focuses on extrinsic motivation.

1.3 Look again at Kathy's discussion with Harvey in the case study. Explain how this exchange illustrates Kathy's attempts to stimulate motivation to learn.

To receive feedback for these questions, go to Appendix B.

Knowledge Extensions

To deepen your understanding of the topic in this section and to integrate it with topics you've already studied, go to the *Knowledge Extensions* module for Chapter 10 at *www.prenhall.com/eggen*. Respond to questions 1–3.

Motivation to learn. Students' tendencies to find academic activities meaningful and worthwhile and to try to get the intended learning benefits from them

Figure 10.2 Theoretical views of motivation

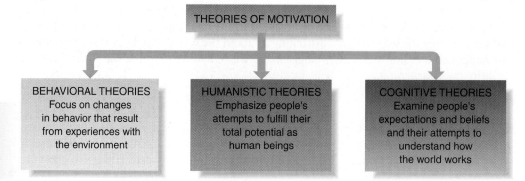

BEHAVIORAL VIEWS OF MOTIVATION

As you saw in Chapter 6, behaviorism views learning as a change in behavior that occurs as a result of experience. It treats motivation the same way. An increase in studying or learning behaviors is viewed as evidence of motivation (Pintrich & Schunk, 2002), so reinforcers, such as praise, comments on homework, high test scores, and good grades, are motivators.

Using Rewards in Classrooms

Although the use of rewards in classrooms is controversial (Kohn, 1992, 1993b, 1996b), it is still common (Eisenberger et al., 1999). Rewards commonly used in elementary classrooms include

- Approval, such as teacher praise or being selected as a class monitor
- Consumable items, such as candy or popcorn
- Entertainment, such as playing computer games
- Success in competition, such as being the first to finish a game or drill

In middle and secondary classrooms, common rewards are

- High test scores and good grades
- Teacher comments on papers
- Teacher compliments delivered quietly and individually
- Free time to talk to classmates

Effective teachers use reinforcers selectively to increase learning and motivation.

Criticisms of Behavioral Approaches to Motivation

The use of rewards as motivators is criticized on three grounds. One is philosophical; critics argue that schools should cultivate intrinsic motivation and believe that using rewards sends students the wrong message about learning (Anderman & Maehr, 1994; Kohn, 1993b, 1996a). A second is based on research indicating that the use of rewards decreases interest in intrinsically motivating tasks (Kohn, 1996b; R. Ryan & Deci, 1996; Sansone & Harackiewicz, 2000).

A third, and perhaps the most significant, is the fact that behaviorism provides an incomplete explanation for motivation. Behaviorism treats learning and motivation in the same way, and although they're closely related, they are not identical. Reinforcers can be extrinsic motivators, but their effects are not automatic; rather, they depend on learners' expectations, beliefs, and other thoughts. If students' reinforcement histories are inconsistent with their present beliefs, they are more likely to act based on their beliefs. For instance, if a student believes he can't complete a difficult assignment, he will be unlikely to work hard on it despite being reinforced in the past for completing assignments. Since behaviorism doesn't consider cognitive factors such as learner beliefs, the theory can't explain why the student isn't motivated to complete the assignment.

Instructional ⌂ Principles

Using Rewards in Classrooms: Instructional Principles

Although critics argue that rewards shouldn't be used in classrooms, eliminating them is neither realistic nor desirable (Brophy, 2004; Cameron, 2001). Used appropriately, rewards provide teachers with another tool to increase motivation to learn. The following principles can guide you in this process:

1. Use rewards for tasks that are not initially intrinsically interesting.
2. Base rewards on the quality of the work, not mere participation in an activity.
3. Use rewards to recognize increasing competence (Covington, 2000; Gehlbach & Roeser, 2002; Lepper & Henderlong, 2000).

Now let's look at two seventh-grade teachers' use of rewards and analyze the extent to which they apply the principles.

"Let's go over your homework," Amanda Shaw directs as she hands her seventh graders their papers. "I know that you weren't too crazy about word problems when we first started them, and I gave you a couple bonus points for your efforts, but you're all improving so much that you actually like them now. . . . Let's look at a couple of the problems. Take a look at number 3, where it says, 'A jacket at Coat Mart, originally priced at $65, was marked down to $40. What is the percent decrease in the cost of the jacket?' Explain how you did that one, . . . Omar?"

"I . . . first subtracted the 40 from the 65, so that was $25. . . . Then I took 65 into the 25 and got 0.38, so it was marked down 38%."

"Why did you divide the 25 by 65 instead of by 40?" Amanda probes.

"I needed to compare the marked-down price to the original price," Omar explains. "If I divided by 40, I would be comparing it to the new price, and that doesn't make sense."

"Excellent thinking, Omar," Amanda smiles. "You showed a good understanding of the difference between percent decrease and percent increase.

"Let's look at another one. Explain how you did number 5, . . . Cassy."

"Get busy on your homework everyone," Luanne Hawkins, the teacher in the room next to Amanda's, directs. "Problems just like these will be on your test on Friday, so if you don't understand them now, you'll have trouble with them on the test. . . . If you have difficulties, raise your hand, and I'll come around and help you."

The students busy themselves with their homework, and 15 minutes later, Luanne announces, "You're all doing your homework so conscientiously, I'm very proud of you. Not one of you has misbehaved or gone off task this whole time. . . . Since you've been so good, you can talk quietly among yourselves as soon as you're finished."

Now let's look at Amanda's attempts to apply the principles. She applied the first by giving her students bonus points to involve them in a task that wasn't intrinsically interesting. Then, her comment, "But you're all improving so much that you actually like them now," reinforced the students for the quality of their work, which applied the second. Finally, saying "Excellent thinking, Omar. You showed a good understanding of the difference between percent decrease and percent increase," communicated to him that his competence was increasing. This applied the third principle. Using rewards to communicate increased competence can increase intrinsic motivation, motivation to learn, and students' beliefs about their capabilities (Eisenberger et al., 1999). This is the primary reason that eliminating rewards completely is undesirable.

In comparison, when Luanne praised her students ("Since you've been so good, you can talk quietly among yourselves"), she was trying to control their behavior rather than provide information about quality of work or increased competence. Further, she offered students free time for simply doing the homework, not necessarily doing it thoroughly or accurately. Rewards that control behavior or that are given for merely participating in an activity decrease intrinsic motivation (Deci & Ryan, 2000; Eisenberger & Cameron, 1998).

From these examples, we see that rewards used appropriately can increase motivation to learn, but used inappropriately can detract from it. This again illustrates the need for teachers being knowledgeable professionals.

Knowledge Extensions

To deepen your understanding of the topics in this section of the chapter and to integrate them with topics you've already studied, go to the *Knowledge Extensions* module for Chapter 10 at *www.prenhall.com/eggen*. Respond to items 4–6.

Checking Your Understanding

2.1   Describe and explain the three most common criticisms of behavioral approaches to motivation.

2.2   Explain how teachers can use rewards to increase motivation to learn.

2.3   Identify at least two reasons why the complete elimination of rewards is neither realistic nor advisable.

To receive feedback for these questions, go to Appendix B.

HUMANISTIC VIEWS OF MOTIVATION

In the mid-1950s when the "cognitive revolution" in learning was emerging, a parallel movement called *humanistic psychology* also began. **Humanistic psychology** views motivation as people's attempts to fulfill their total potential as human beings (Pintrich & Schunk, 2002). This perspective remains popular both in schools and in the workplace.

Development of the Whole Person

In the first half of the 20th century, our understanding of motivation was dominated by two major forces: behaviorism and psychoanalysis. As we saw in the previous section, behaviorism focuses on reinforcement as an explanation for motivation. Psychoanalysis, influenced by the famous Sigmund Freud (1856–1939), described people as motivated by unconscious drives and directed by an *id, ego,* and *superego.* Humanistic psychology developed as a reaction against this "reductionist" thinking; instead, it emphasizes the total person—physical, social, emotional, and intellectual—and one's drive for "self-actualization," our inborn need to fulfill our potential (Maslow, 1968, 1970). During the 1950s, this orientation became known as a "third force" alongside behaviorism and psychoanalysis.

Exploring Further

Sigmund Freud remains a well-known name. To read more about him and his theories go to "Freud's Psychoanalytic Theories" in the *Exploring Further* module of Chapter 10 at *www.prenhall.com/eggen*.

Maslow's Hierarchy of Needs

Abraham Maslow (1968, 1970, 1987), one of the founders of the humanistic movement, developed a hierarchy reflecting the needs of the "whole person" (see Figure 10.3). For instance, we see the physical person in survival and safety needs; the social person in belonging needs; the emotional person in self-esteem needs; and intellectual, aesthetic, and self-actualized persons in growth needs. Let's look at these needs in more detail.

Deficiency and Growth Needs. Maslow (1968, 1970) described human needs as existing in two groups: deficiency needs and growth needs. **Deficiency needs** are those that, when unfulfilled, energize people to meet them; these needs occupy the bottom of the hierarchy in Figure 10.3. According to Maslow, people won't move to higher needs, such as intellectual achievement, unless the deficiency needs—*survival, safety, belonging,* and *self-esteem*—have all been met.

Once deficiency needs are met, an individual can focus on **growth needs,** needs that increase as people have experiences with them. In contrast with deficiency needs, growth needs are never "met." For instance, as people develop a greater understanding of literature, their interest in it actually increases rather than decreases. This can explain why some people seem to have an insatiable desire for learning or why an individual never tires of fine art or music.

Figure 10.3   Maslow's hierarchy of needs

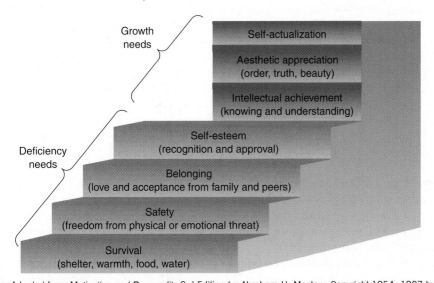

Humanistic psychology. A school of thought viewing motivation as people's attempts to fulfill their total potential as human beings

Deficiency needs. Needs that, when unfulfilled, energize people to meet them

Growth needs. Needs that expand and increase as people have experiences with them

Source: Adapted from *Motivation and Personality* 3rd Edition by Abraham H. Maslow. Copyright 1954, 1987 by Harper & Row, Publishers, Inc. Copyright © 1970 by Abraham H. Maslow. Reprinted by permission of Addison Wesley Educational Publishers Inc.

Humanistic theories of motivation remind us to treat students as developing human beings.

Maslow believed that all people strive for self-actualization, although less than 1 percent truly achieve it (Maslow, 1968). Those who do have the following characteristics:

- Clear perceptions of reality
- Autonomy, independence, and self-acceptance
- Problem-centeredness instead of self-centeredness
- Spontaneity in thought and action
- Sympathy to the conditions of other people

They also develop deep bonds with a few people rather than superficial relationships with many, and they have peak experiences marked by feelings of excitement, happiness, and insight. The concept *peak experience* originated with Maslow.

Putting Maslow's Work into Perspective. Maslow's work, while attractive, is controversial. The lack of research evidence to support his description of needs is one of the most commonly voiced criticisms (Pintrich & Schunk, 2002). A second is his hierarchy's inconsistency and lack of predictive ability. For instance, we've all heard of people with serious illnesses or disabling conditions—which suggests that their deficiency needs are not being met—who accomplish significant intellectual or aesthetic achievements and who seek order, truth, and beauty in their experiences. Maslow's work would predict that this could not happen.

On the other hand, think about some of your day-to-day experiences. For example, when you go to see your instructors, it's likely that your first reaction is to how "human" they are and how they treat you, not how intelligent or competent they seem to be. The same applies even with physicians, dentists, salespeople, and others. We react much more positively to people who are warm and inviting than to those who appear to be cold and distant. Warm, supportive people help us meet our needs for safety and belonging. Maslow's work reminds us that we're all initially social and emotional beings and that these factors influence our motivation.

Applications of Maslow's work in schools also seem to support its validity. Schools provide free or reduced cost breakfasts and lunches because it makes sense that motivation to learn will decrease if children are hungry. Schools also strive to make students feel safe—both physically and emotionally—because those who don't will also be less motivated to learn (Lambert & McCombs, 1998; McCombs, 2001). Ignoring the human side of teaching leaves out an essential domain.

The Need for Positive Regard: The Work of Carl Rogers

Carl Rogers, a humanistic psychologist who founded "person-centered" therapy, also emphasized people's attempts to become self-actualized (Rogers, 1963). According to Rogers, the actualizing tendency is oriented toward personal growth, autonomy, and freedom from control by external forces. The tendency is innate, but experiences with others can foster or hinder growth and the development of autonomy (Rogers, 1959; Rogers & Freiberg, 1994). Of those experiences, **unconditional positive regard,** or the belief that someone is innately worthy and acceptable regardless of their behavior, is one of the most essential.

Unconditional positive regard isn't as simple as it appears. Parents usually feel it for their small children, valuing them even if they don't accept all their behaviors. But as children get older, parents' regard often becomes *conditional*, dependent on certain actions, such as acceptable behavior or high grades (Kohn, 2005a). Outside of their families, people almost always experience conditional regard, because society does not distinguish between people and their actions. In schools, high achievers are regarded more positively than their lower-achieving peers, for example, as are students who excel in extracurricular activities like music and sports. According to Rogers (1959, 1963), this conditional regard hinders personal growth because it equates worth with actions or performance. Instead, he recommended treating all students as developing individuals with potential, and more recent work corroborates Rogers' views. "Students who felt

Unconditional positive regard. The belief that someone is innately worthy and acceptable regardless of their behavior

unconditionally accepted by their teachers were more likely to be interested in learning and to enjoy challenging academic tasks, instead of just doing schoolwork because they had to and preferring easier assignments at which they knew they would succeed" (Kohn, 2005b, p. 21).

Instructional ⊞ Principles

Humanistic Views of Motivation: Instructional Principles

According to humanistic psychologists, two elements of the teaching–learning process are essential for the development of motivation: (1) a strong student–teacher relationship and (2) a positive classroom climate (Hamachek, 1987). The following principles can guide you as you attempt to develop these elements:

1. Treat students as people first and learners second.
2. Provide students with unconditional positive regard by separating their behaviors from their intrinsic worth.
3. Create safe and orderly classrooms where students believe they can learn and where they are expected to do so.

Let's return to Kathy's work with her students to see how she attempts to put the principles into practice. We rejoin her after her class.

> As the students are leaving the room, Jenny stops at Kathy's desk. "You wanted to see me, Mrs. Brewster? . . . What's up?"
>
> "I've been watching you for a few days, and you don't seem to be yourself. . . . Is everything okay?"
>
> "I. . . yes, . . . no, not really," Jenny says, her eyes starting to fill with tears. "My mom and dad are having trouble, and I'm really scared. I'm afraid they're going to break up."
>
> "Do you want to talk?"
>
> ". . . No, . . . not right now."
>
> Kathy reaches over, touches Jenny on the shoulder, and says, "I realize that there isn't anything that I can do specifically, but I'm here if you want to talk about it, . . . or anything else . . . anytime."
>
> "Thanks," Jenny nods weakly as she turns to go.
>
> As Kathy is working after school, Harvey pokes his head into the room.
>
> "Come in," she smiles. "How's the writer?"
>
> "I just came by to say I hope I didn't offend you this morning, complaining so much about all the work."
>
> "Not at all. . . . I haven't given it a second thought."
>
> "I guess you already know how much you've done for me. . . . You believed in me when the rest of the world wrote me off. . . . My drug conviction is off my record now, and I've been clean for over a year. I couldn't have made it without you. You made me work and put in all kinds of extra time with me. You pushed me and wouldn't let me give up on myself. I was headed for trouble, and now . . . I'm headed for college."
>
> "We all need a nudge now and then," Kathy smiles. "That's what I'm here for. I appreciate it, but, I didn't do it; you did. . . . Now, scoot. I'm thinking up a rough assignment for you tomorrow."
>
> "Mrs. Brewster, you're relentless," Harvey waves as he heads out the door.

Now let's look at Kathy's attempts to apply the principles. We see the first illustrated in Kathy's interaction with Jenny and the second particularly in her talk with Harvey. She was concerned because Jenny wasn't herself, and she treated Harvey with unconditional positive regard, separating his drug conviction from his innate worth as a human being. She was concerned about both students first as people. In her earlier conversation with Harvey, we saw how she helped him believe that he could be successful academically, and this, combined with her high expectations, illustrates the third principle.

In the real world, unfortunately, you won't be able to "save" every troubled student; it isn't that easy. You can make a difference with many, however, and for those that you do, you will have made an immeasurable contribution to their lives.

Checking Your Understanding

3.1 Explain the basic premise of humanistic motivation theory.

3.2 Basing your conclusions on Maslow's work, decide if the following statements are true, false, or you don't have enough information to answer: (1) Learners who have a high need for aesthetic appreciation have high self-esteem. (2) Learners who have a high need for aesthetic appreciation have met their intellectual achievement needs. Provide a rationale for your conclusions.

3.3 Schools provide free or reduced-cost breakfasts and lunches because hungry children won't be motivated to learn, and the same is true for students who don't feel safe. Explain these statements using Maslow's work as a basis for your explanation.

3.4 A student is annoying you with her disruptions of your learning activity. Based on Rogers's work, how should you respond to her in general? How would Rogers say the disruption should be handled? How do you treat her the next day?

To receive feedback for these questions, go to Appendix B.

Knowledge Extensions

To deepen your understanding of the topics in this section of the chapter and to integrate them with topics you've already studied, go to the *Knowledge Extensions* module for Chapter 10 at *www.prenhall.com/eggen*. Respond to questions 7 and 8.

Classroom ⊞ Connections

Applying Behavioral Views of Motivation Effectively in Your Classroom

1. Reward students for genuine accomplishments and increasing competence, not for mere participation or to control behavior.

   - **Elementary:** Positive example: A second-grade teacher does a drill-and-practice activity on math facts each morning. All students who get all the facts correct or improve from the previous day have stars placed by their names on a chart. Negative example: A third-grade teacher says, "Every one of you turned in your math homework today, so each of you gets 2 bonus points."

   - **Middle School:** Positive example: An English teacher underlines well-written passages in her students' essays, comments positively about them, and explains why the sections warrant the comments. Negative example: A seventh-grade life science teacher says, "You worked so well together when we did our group activity, so we won't have any homework over the weekend."

   - **High School:** Positive example: A biology teacher comments to his class about an upcoming test, "Study hard for this test, everyone. The material we've been working on is very important, and your understanding will be a big help as we move on to the next topic." Negative example: Another biology teacher comments to his class about an upcoming test, "Study hard for this test. If you don't study, you might fail, and you could wind up back in this class again next year."

Applying Humanistic Views of Motivation Effectively in Your Classroom

2. Create a safe environment, and try to treat students with unconditional positive regard.

   - **Elementary:** A first-grade teacher encourages and accepts all students' comments and questions. She tells students that mistakes are a part of learning and treats them that way during learning activities.

   - **Middle School:** A seventh-grade teacher demands that all students treat each other with respect. The personal criticisms and sarcasm common in middle schools are strictly forbidden. He carefully models courtesy and respect for students and communicates that he expects them to respect him in return.

   - **High School:** A geometry teacher spends time before and after school helping students with problems and assignments. She also listens attentively when students talk about personal problems and uncertainties.

3. Help meet students' deficiency and growth needs.

   - **Elementary:** A fourth-grade teacher calls on each of his students to be certain they all feel that they're a part of the classroom community. He makes them feel safe by helping them respond correctly when they are unable to answer.

   - **Middle School:** A seventh-grade teacher asks two of the more popular girls in her class to introduce a new girl to some of the other students and to take her under their wings until she gets acquainted.

   - **High School:** An American government teacher brings in a newspaper columnist's political opinion piece, comments that it was interesting to her, and asks students for their opinions on the issue.

COGNITIVE THEORIES OF MOTIVATION

"C'mon, let's go," Melanie urges her friend Yelena as they're finishing an assignment.

"Just a sec," Yelena mutters. "I just can't seem to figure this out. I don't know why I missed this one. I thought I did the whole thing right, and it all made sense, but the answer turned out wrong."

"Let's work on it tonight. Everybody's leaving," Melanie urges.

"Go ahead, I'll catch up to you in a minute. I know that I can figure this out. . . . I just don't get it right now."

How might we explain Yelena's persistence in the face of her uncertainty? Behaviorist views of motivation don't give us much help. Although getting the right answer would be reinforcing, it doesn't account for her attempt to understand why the problem made sense but still came out wrong. Also, since behaviorism doesn't consider beliefs or expectations, it can't account for her statement, "I know that I can figure this out," which indicates that she believes she could resolve the discrepancy and expects to do so.

Humanistic theory tells us that Yelena's intellectual achievement need is greater than Melanie's, but it doesn't explain why. We need more helpful accounts. This leads us to cognitive motivation theory, which addresses aspects of motivated behavior that can't be explained by either behaviorism or humanistic views.

Cognitive theories of motivation focus on learners' beliefs, expectations, and needs for order, predictability, and understanding (Tollefson, 2000; Zimmerman & Schunk, 2001, 2004). The *need to understand* is at the heart of cognitive motivation theory: "Children are seen as naturally motivated to learn when their experience is inconsistent with their current understanding" (Greeno et al., 1996, p. 25). For example, why do young children so eagerly explore the environment? Why was Yelena unable to leave until she solved the problem? Cognitive theorists suggest that each is motivated by the need to understand and make sense of the world.

As you saw in Chapter 2, Piaget described the need for understanding in his concept of *equilibrium*. When people cannot explain experiences using their existing schemes, they are motivated to modify the schemes. Ultimately, the new understanding leads to advanced development.

Cognitive theories of motivation help explain a variety of human behaviors, such as

- Why people are intrigued by brain teasers and other problems with no practical application
- Why people are curious when something occurs unexpectedly
- Why students ask questions about incidental and unrelated aspects of lessons
- Why people persevere on challenging activities and then quit after they've mastered the tasks
- Why people want feedback about their performance

These behaviors all indicate an innate desire to understand the way the world works.

In the following sections, we examine five cognitive theories of motivation:

- Expectancy × value theory
- Self-efficacy theory
- Goal theory
- Attribution theory
- Self-determination theory

A note of clarification before we begin: Although some experts (e.g., Graham & Weiner, 1996; Pintrich & Schunk, 2002) distinguish between cognitive and social cognitive theories of motivation, the line is blurred, and we believe that for teachers in K–12 classrooms this distinction isn't essential. We discuss both cognitive theories and social cognitive approaches under the general framework of cognitive motivation theory.

Expectancy × Value Theory

Expectancy × value theory suggests that people are motivated to engage in an activity to the extent that they expect to succeed *times* the value they place on the success (Wigfield & Eccles, 1992, 2000). The × is important, because anything *times* zero is zero, so if either

Cognitive theories of motivation. Theoretical explanations for motivation that focus on learners' beliefs, expectations, and needs for order, predictability, and understanding

Expectancy × value theory. A cognitive theory of motivation suggesting that people are motivated to engage in an activity to the extent that they expect to succeed *times* the value they place on the success

Table 10.1 Student responses to activities as related to their success expectations and task values

	High Task Value	Low Task Value
High success expectation	Sustained effort. High motivation to learn.	Minimum effort. Low motivation to learn.
Low success expectation	Effort to project image of competence. Avoidance of task when possible. Low motivation to learn.	Rejection of activity. Refusal to participate. No motivation to learn.

Source: Based on work by Hansen (1989) and Brophy (2004).

the expectancy for success or the value placed on it is at or near zero, motivation will also be near zero (Tollefson, 2000). For example, as a young man, one of your authors toyed with the idea of a career in music. However, his lack of ability was obvious, resulting in low expectation for success. This resulted in low motivation for pursuing a career in music and a fortunate turn to a very rewarding one studying learning, motivation, and human behavior. The different combinations of expectancy and value are summarized in Table 10.1.

The information in Table 10.1 helps us understand why many students with a history of low achievement handicap themselves by not trying. Repeated failure results in success expectations that are so low that motivation is also very low. It also helps us understand why trivial tasks lead to minimum effort by students and low motivation to learn. Worse, it explains why it is so difficult to motivate students who neither value a learning task nor expect to be able to do it.

Let's look now at expectancy for success in more detail, and then we'll turn to a discussion of factors influencing task value.

Expectancy for Success

Expectancy for success describes students' beliefs about the probability that they can perform the task successfully (Schunk, 2004). It is influenced by two primary factors: (1) perception of task difficulty, and (2) self-schemas (Eccles, Wigfield, & Schiefele, 1998; Wigfield & Eccles, 2000). These relationships are outlined in Figure 10.4.

The influence of task difficulty on expectation for success is obvious. When people perceive a task as extremely difficult, they are less likely to expect success than when they perceive the task as easier.

The influence of self-schemas is more complex. In Chapter 7, you saw that schemas are organized networks of information stored in memory. **Self-schemas** are organized networks of information about ourselves. They include our self-concepts and sets of beliefs about the kind of person we believe ourselves to be (Pintrich & Schunk, 2002). For example, a person's self-schema might include the belief that she is a capable math student

Self-schemas. Organized networks of information about ourselves

Figure 10.4 Expectancy for success in expectancy × value theory

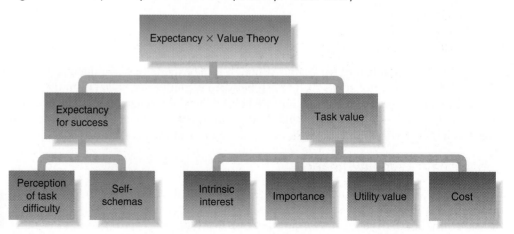

(math self-concept), outgoing, reasonably attractive, but not athletic. Because she has a positive self-concept of ability in math she will have a higher expectation for success than someone whose self-schema in this area is less positive.

Students with high success expectations persist longer on tasks, choose more challenging activities, and achieve higher than those whose expectations are lower (Eccles et al., 1998; Wigfield, 1994).

Factors Influencing Task Value

Task value answers the question, "Why should I do this task?" and is influenced by four factors, outlined in Figure 10.5 (Eccles et al., 1998).

Intrinsic Interest. **Intrinsic interest** addresses the characteristics of an activity that induce a person's willing involvement in it (Schraw & Lehman, 2001). "Because it's interesting" is an intuitively sensible answer to "Why should I do this task?" For example, Jim, in our opening case study commented, "I sometimes even read ahead a little, because Brewster makes you think. It's kind of interesting the way she's always telling us about the way we are because of something that happened a zillion years ago." He was motivated to learn by his developing interest.

Some topics, such as *death, danger, power, money, romance,* and *sex,* seem to be universally interesting (Hidi, 2001). This helps explain why so many movies and television programs focus on these topics. For younger students, scary stories, humor, and animals also seem to be intrinsically interesting (Worthy, Moorman, & Turner, 1999).

While we can't build a curriculum around danger, money, or romance, we can increase learner interest in a number of ways. Some include

- Authentic learning activities that match real-world tasks
- Personalized content linked to students' lives
- Student involvement
- Concrete examples
- Logical and coherent presentations

Students' interest is also increased when they're given choices, and, as with most factors in learning and motivation, the more prior knowledge students have about a topic, the more interest they have in it (Schraw, Flowerday, & Lehman, 2001; Schraw & Lehman, 2001). We examine strategies for increasing student interest in more detail in Chapter 11.

Importance. "Because it's important" also helps answer the question "Why should I do this task?" **Importance** is the extent to which an activity allows people to confirm or disconfirm important aspects of their self-schemas (Wigfield & Eccles, 1992). If a person believes she is a good athlete, for instance, doing well in an athletic event will be important

Learning tasks that involve students and connect to the real world, increase motivation to learn.

Figure 10.5 Task value in expectancy × value theory

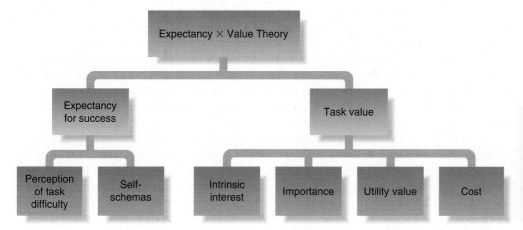

Intrinsic interest. The characteristics of an activity that induce a person's willing involvement in it

Importance. The extent to which an activity allows people to confirm or disconfirm important aspects of their self-schemas

to her, because it confirms her belief about her athletic ability. Similarly, doing well in math will be important to a student with a positive self-concept of math ability, because doing well is evidence that the self-concept is valid.

Utility Value.

> Javier has high motivation to learn in algebra. "I don't always get it completely, so I have to really study, and that can get a little old at times," he comments, "but I know that algebra is required for all the rest of the math courses I'll take, and I want a good math background for college."

For Javier, studying algebra has high **utility value,** the perception that a topic or activity is or will be useful for meeting future goals, including career goals (Wigfield & Eccles, 1992). He doesn't believe he is particularly good in algebra (self-schema), and he isn't intrinsically interested in it, but he believes that studying will be valuable to him in the future. At this point, Javier's motivation is primarily extrinsic, but as we saw in the last section, increased understanding leads to increased interest (Schraw & Lehman, 2001; Schraw et al., 2001). As his understanding of math improves, his intrinsic motivation is likely to increase as well. This example helps us see how extrinsic motivation influences motivation to learn, which in turn can increase intrinsic motivation.

Cost. **Cost** is the negative aspect of engaging in a task (Wigfield & Eccles, 1992). The amount of time Javier spends studying algebra, for instance, is a cost; it reduces the amount of time available for other activities. If the cost is too high, a person may avoid an activity. For instance, you may decide to not take a demanding course at this point in your program because you already have a heavy load.

Emotional costs also exist. If a person gets nervous speaking in front of people, for example, he may choose not to present at a meeting or conference because the emotional cost is too high. Emotional costs are influenced by **affective memories,** past emotional experiences related to an activity (Pintrich & Schunk, 2002). For instance, if the nervous young man had gone "blank" when about to make some past presentation, his affective memory would increase the emotional cost and decrease the likelihood that he would try to make another presentation.

Self-schemas are important in motivation because they influence both expectancy for success and task value according to expectancy × value theory. We turn now to self-efficacy theory, which explains how these beliefs about capability are formed and the impact they have on motivation.

Self-Efficacy: Beliefs About Capability

In your study of social cognitive theory in Chapter 6, you saw that an individual's beliefs can influence the likelihood that a person will imitate a model's behavior. One of the most important of these cognitions is **self-efficacy,** a belief about one's own capability to organize and complete a course of action required to accomplish a specific task (Bandura, 1986, 1997, 2004; Schunk, 2004).

Self-efficacy and *expectation for success* as described in expectancy × value theory are not the same concepts (Pajares & Schunk, 2002; Schunk, 2004). For example, a student may believe that if he answers a teacher's question successfully, the teacher will praise him; that is, he expects to be successful in receiving praise. However, if he doesn't believe that he is capable of answering correctly (low self-efficacy), it's unlikely that he will try to answer.

Self-efficacy and expectation for success are often—but not necessarily—connected. For instance, students who typically perform well (have success expectations met) also generally believe they can accomplish the tasks set out for them (have high self-efficacy). On the other hand, a student may believe he is capable (has high self-efficacy), but may expect a low grade (low success expectation) if he thinks the teacher doesn't like him.

Self-efficacy is also similar, but not identical to, self concept; self-efficacy is a more specific construct (Bong & Skaalvik, 2003). For example, a student may believe she's generally competent in math (positive self-concept of math ability), but when faced with a series of problems involving systems of equations, may not believe she is capable of solving them (low self-efficacy in this situation).

Utility value. The perception that a topic or activity is or will be useful for meeting future goals, including career goals

Cost. The negative aspect of engaging in a task

Affective memories. Past emotional experiences related to a topic or activity

Self-efficacy. A belief about one's own capability to organize and complete a course of action required to accomplish a specific task

Research also indicates that self-efficacy is domain specific (P. Smith & Fouad, 1999). For instance, a person might have high self-efficacy for writing quality essays, but have low self-efficacy for balancing chemical equations.

Factors Influencing Self-Efficacy

Four factors influence people's beliefs about their capability of succeeding on specific tasks (Bandura, 1986). They are outlined in Figure 10.6 and discussed in the paragraphs that follow.

Past performance on similar tasks is the most important factor influencing self-efficacy. A history of success in giving oral reports, for example, increases a person's self-efficacy for giving future reports. Observing the modeling of others, such as those delivering excellent reports, increases self-efficacy by raising expectations and providing information about how a skill should be performed (Bandura, 1986, 1997; Kitsantas, Zimmerman, & Cleary, 2000).

Although limited in its effectiveness, verbal persuasion, such as a teacher commenting, "I know you will give a fine report," can also increase self-efficacy. It probably does so indirectly by encouraging students to try challenging tasks; if students succeed, efficacy increases.

Finally, physiological factors, such as fatigue or hunger, can reduce efficacy even though they're unrelated to the task, and emotional states, such as anxiety, can reduce efficacy by filling working memory with thoughts of failure.

The Influence of Self-Efficacy on Motivation

Self-efficacy strongly influences motivation to learn. For instance, compared to low-efficacy students, high-efficacy learners accept more challenging tasks, exert more effort, persist longer, use more effective strategies, and generally perform better (Bandura, 1997; Eccles et al., 1998; Schunk & Ertmer, 2000). These characteristics are outlined in Table 10.2.

Developmental Differences in Self-Efficacy

Self-efficacy often changes as students move through school. For instance, young children generally have high self-efficacy, sometimes unrealistically so (Eccles et al., 1998). As they move through school, they become less confident, which may reflect more realistic beliefs. They also become more aware of, and are more concerned with, their performance compared to that of their peers (A. Elliot & McGregor, 2000).

Promoting high self-efficacy should be an important goal for teachers. How can this be accomplished? Experts suggest that "increases in self-efficacy perceptions, in task effort and persistence, and in ultimate performance levels can be achieved by . . . encouraging students to set specific and challenging, but attainable goals" (Brophy, 2004, p. 65). This suggestion leads us to goal theory.

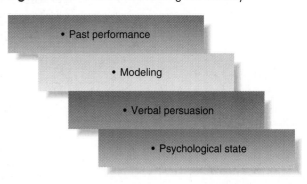

Figure 10.6 Factors influencing self-efficacy

- Past performance
- Modeling
- Verbal persuasion
- Psychological state

Table 10.2 The influence of self-efficacy on motivation

	High Self-Efficacy Learners	Low Self-Efficacy Learners
Task orientation	Accept challenging tasks	Avoid challenging tasks
Effort	Expend high effort when faced with challenging tasks	Expend low effort when faced with challenging tasks
Persistence	Persist when goals aren't initially reached	Give up when goals aren't initially reached
Beliefs	Believe they will succeed	Focus on feelings of incompetence
	Control stress and anxiety when goals aren't met	Experience anxiety and depression when goals aren't met
	Believe they're in control of their environment	Believe they're not in control of their environment
Strategy use	Discard unproductive strategies	Persist with unproductive strategies
Performance	Perform higher than low-efficacy students of equal ability	Perform lower than high-efficacy students of equal ability

Goals and Goal Orientation

Setting goals can also have a strong impact on motivation to learn (Thrash & Elliot, 2001). To see how, let's look at six students' reactions to a group project in Kathy's world history class.

Susan: This should be interesting. I don't know much about the Renaissance, and it began a whole new emphasis on learning all over the world. Mrs. Brewster has given us a lot of responsibility, so we need to come through. We need to make a presentation she'll like.

Damien: I'll get my Dad to help us. He's really up on history. Our presentation will be the best one of the bunch, and the class will be impressed.

Sylvia: Yikes! Everyone in my group is so smart. What can I do? They'll think I'm the dumbest one. I'm going to just stay quiet when we're working together.

Charlotte: This should be fun. We can get together to work on this at one of our houses. If we can get the project out of the way fairly quickly, I might have time to get to know Damien better.

Antonio: I don't know anything about this. I'd better do some studying before we start. I don't want the rest of my group to think I'm not pulling my weight.

Patrick: I like group activities. They're usually easy. Somebody is always gung ho and does most of the work.

Each of the students' thinking reflects a **goal,** an outcome an individual hopes to achieve. As we saw in the examples, students' goals vary. For instance, Susan's goal was to understand the Renaissance and please Mrs. Brewster, Charlotte wanted to socialize, and Patrick simply wanted to do as little work as possible. Let's see how each influences motivation and learning.

Learning and Performance Goals

Much of the research examining goals, motivation, and achievement has focused on differences between learning and performance goals (Pintrich & Schunk, 2002; Stipek, 2002). For example, consider the following:

- To understand each topic covered in this class
- To score in the top third of the class on the next quiz
- To run a 5K race in less time than my friend Melanie

The first is a *learning goal,* whereas the second and third are *performance goals.* A **learning goal** (sometimes called a *mastery goal*) focuses on mastery of a task, improvement, and increased understanding (Midgley, 2001; Pintrich, 2000). Susan's desire to understand the Renaissance is another example. In comparison, a **performance goal** focuses on competence or ability and how it compares to the competence of others (A. Elliot & McGregor, 2000; A. Elliot & Thrash, 2001; Midgley, 2001). Scoring in the top third of the class and running a race in less time than your friend involves comparing your performance to others.

There are two types of performance goals: **Performance-approach goals** emphasize looking competent and receiving favorable judgments from others. Damien's wanting to make the best presentation and impress the class is an example. In contrast, Sylvia's thinking to herself, "They'll think I'm the dumbest one. I'm going to just stay quiet when we're working together," reflects a **performance-avoidance goal,** an attempt to avoid looking incompetent and being judged unfavorably (Dai, 2000).

Some researchers use the labels *ego-involved* and *task-involved* (Nicholls, 1984), or *ability-focused* and *task-focused* (Maehr & Midgley, 1991), for performance and learning goals, respectively, but there is enough conceptual overlap that *performance* goal and *learning* goal are appropriate labels (Pintrich & Schunk, 2002).

Learning and performance goals are not mutually exclusive; students may simultaneously have two or three at the same time (Pintrich, 2000). For example, we could imagine a student in another group who wants to understand the Renaissance, make an impressive

Goal. An outcome an individual hopes to achieve

Learning goal. A goal that focuses on mastery of a task, improvement, and increased understanding

Performance goal. A goal that focuses on competence or ability and how it compares to the competence of others

Performance-approach goals. Goals that emphasize looking competent and receiving favorable judgments from others

Performance-avoidance goals. Goals that focus on avoiding looking incompetent and being judged unfavorably

presentation, and avoid looking like he doesn't know what he is doing (Covington & Müeller, 2001).

Adopting learning goals is the most effective approach. Students who do so have high efficacy; they persist in the face of difficulty; they attribute success to internal, controllable causes; they accept academic challenges; and they use effective strategies, such as self-questioning and summarizing (Kumar et al., 2002; Wolters, 2003). Learning goals lead to sustained interest and effort even after formal instruction is finished. Teachers can have a powerful positive influence on the development of a learning-goal orientation through instructional strategies that emphasize understanding and higher-order thinking (Morrone, Harkness, D'Ambrosio, & Caulfield, 2003).

The influence of performance goals on motivation to learn is more complex. To begin with, many students adopt both learning and performance goals; they want to both understand the topic and score near the top of their classes, for example (Covington & Müeller, 2001; Harackiewicz, Barron, Taurer, Carter, & Elliot, 2000). Also, students who want to demonstrate competence, a performance-approach orientation, tend to be confident and have high self-efficacy (Middleton & Midgley, 1997). Even so, performance-approach goals are less desirable than learning goals. To reach them, students may use superficial strategies, such as memorization; exert only enough effort to meet them; engage in self-handicapping behaviors, such as not trying when they're not sure they can meet the goals; or even cheat in order to reach them (Brophy, 2004; Midgley, Kaplan, & Middleton, 2001).

Students with learning goals focus on improvement and mastery of tasks.

In addition, learning goals have at least two other advantages over performance-approach goals. First, you are in control of your learning goals, but less so for performance goals. For instance, if your goal is to score in the top third of the class and you have trouble understanding the topics covered on your next quiz, you may not score in the top third even though you studied carefully.

The second advantage lies in responses to mistakes and failure. Failure on a learning goal can lead to increased effort or a change in strategies. Failure on a performance goal can lead to anxiety and a performance-avoidance orientation (Midgley et al., 2001).

Performance-avoidance goals are the most detrimental for motivation to learn and achievement (Midgley & Urdan, 2001). Students who adopt them tend to have low self-efficacy, lack self-confidence, and experience anxiety about tests and other tasks (Midgley et al., 2001). They often try to avoid the very tasks that will help them master new skills. As you saw earlier, Sylvia's only goal was to avoid looking "dumb" to the other students. As a result, her motivation to learn was low, and ultimately, her achievement will be hampered.

Unfortunately, as students progress through school, their performance orientation tends to increase while their learning orientation decreases (A. Elliot & McGregor, 2000). Teachers sometimes contribute to the problem by emphasizing that students need to get good grades if they want to go to college, by displaying grades, or by discussing differences in the way students are performing.

Goals and Theories About the Nature of Intelligence

Some researchers (e.g., Dweck, 1999; Dweck & Leggett, 1988) believe that the tendency to adopt learning or performance goals is related to personal theories about the nature of intelligence. Some people hold an **entity view of intelligence,** which is the belief that ability is stable and out of an individual's control; others hold an **incremental view of intelligence,** which is the belief that ability can be improved with effort. People with an entity view are likely to adopt performance goals, whereas those with an incremental view are more apt to adopt learning goals (Dweck, 1999; Quihuis et al., 2002).

Let's see why. Scoring in the top third of the class on a quiz, for example, could be interpreted as an indicator of high ability, and evidence of high ability is important if intelligence is viewed as fixed. This isn't a problem if individuals' confidence in their intelligence is high; they will seek challenging tasks and persist in the face of difficulty. However, if they aren't confident about their intelligence, they're likely to avoid challenge, because failure suggests low ability.

Entity view of intelligence. The belief that ability is stable and out of an individual's control

Incremental view of intelligence. The belief that ability can be improved with effort

In contrast, individuals with an incremental view are more likely to seek challenge and persist even if they aren't confident about their ability, because failure merely indicates that more work is required, and, as competence increases, so does intelligence.

An incremental view of intelligence can lead to increased motivation to learn and higher achievement (Dweck, 1999). This is the view that Kathy modeled when she said, "the harder I study, the smarter I get."

Social Goals

In addition to learning and performance goals, students also have social goals. To see how they affect learning, let's look again at our six students. Charlotte, for example, thought, "If we can get the project out of the way fairly quickly, I might have time to get to know Damien better," and Antonio decided, "I don't know anything about this. I'd better do some studying before we start. I don't want the rest of my group to think I'm not pulling my weight." Both had social goals; more specifically, Antonio had a *social responsibility goal.* Other social goals include

- Forming friendships
- Gaining teacher or peer approval
- Achieving status among peers
- Meeting social obligations
- Assisting and supporting others
- Underachieving to make others feel better (H. A. Davis, 2003; Dowson & McInerney, 2001; Wentzel, 1999b, 2000; P. White et al., 2002).

Social goals can either increase or decrease motivation to learn. For instance, Charlotte's wanting to "get the project out of the way fairly quickly," so she could get to know Damien detracted from her motivation to learn. As we might expect, low achievers report this orientation more often than do high achievers (Wentzel, 1999a; Wentzel & Wigfield, 1998). Social responsibility goals, by contrast, such as Antonio's, are associated with both high motivation to learn and achievement (Wentzel, 1996).

When social responsibility goals are combined with learning goals, motivation to learn and achievement can be even higher (Wentzel, 1999b, 2000). This is illustrated in Susan's thinking: "This should be interesting. I don't know much about the Renaissance" (a learning goal) and "Mrs. Brewster has given us a lot of responsibility, so we need to come through. We need to make a presentation she'll like" (a social responsibility goal).

Work-Avoidance Goals

Students like Patrick are a source of challenge and frustration for teachers; they simply want to avoid work. Students with work-avoidance goals feel successful when tasks are easy or can be completed with little effort (Dowson & McInerney, 2001; Gallini, 2000). They also tend to use ineffective learning strategies, make minimal contributions to group activities, ask for help even when they don't really need it, and complain about challenging activities. Most of the research on students with work-avoidance goals has been done at the middle school level, and more is needed to determine how those work-avoidance goals originate (Dowson & McInerney, 2001; Gallini, 2000).

Goals, Motivation, and Achievement

Table 10.3 summarizes the different types of goals and their influence on motivation and achievement.

Teachers obviously can't adapt to each student's goal orientation. However, by varying instruction, such as combining small-group work, which can help meet students' social goals, with whole-class instruction, which is often preferred by students with a performance-approach orientation, they can help a range of students meet their goals (Bong, 2001). Students who set learning goals flourish with any well-organized instruction. Although difficult, encouraging students with a performance-avoidance or work-avoidance orientation to set and monitor appropriately challenging goals can increase motivation to learn. Let's see how teachers can help students set effective goals.

Table 10.3 Goals, motivation, and achievement

Type of Goal	Example	Influence on Motivation and Achievement
Learning goals	To understand the influence of the Renaissance on American history	Leads to sustained effort, high self-efficacy, willingness to accept challenges, and high achievement.
Performance-approach goals	To produce one of the best essays on the Renaissance in the class	Can lead to sustained effort and high self-efficacy for confident learners. Can increase achievement. Can detract from willingness to accept challenging tasks, which decreases achievement.
Performance-avoidance goals	To avoid the appearance of low ability in front of peers and teachers	Detracts from motivation and achievement, particularly for learners lacking confidence.
Social goals	To be perceived as reliable and responsible	Enhances motivation and achievement, particularly when combined with learning goals.
	To make friends and socialize	Can detract from motivation and achievement if social goals compete for time with learning goals.
Work-avoidance goals	To complete assignments with as little effort as possible	Detracts from effort and self-efficacy. Strongly detracts from achievement.

Using Goals Effectively

Goal setting has been widely used to increase motivation and performance in the business world, and the importance of goals is being increasingly recognized in education (Murphy & Alexander, 2000). Goals increase self-efficacy because people set goals they believe they can meet and doing so increases their sense of competence.

Many learners, including university students, study without clear goals in mind, however (P. Alexander et al., 1998; Urdan, 2001). Students copy and reorganize their notes, for instance, but don't ask themselves if doing so contributes to their understanding. They seem to think that spending time equals learning.

Using goals effectively involves four processes that are outlined in Figure 10.7 and discussed in the paragraphs that follow.

Effective-Goal Setting. What is an effective goal; that is, which ones are we most likely to stick with and eventually attain? To begin answering this question, let's look at the following goals:

- To learn more in my classes
- To get into better shape
- To lose 20 pounds by the end of this year
- To answer and understand all the "Checking Your Understanding" questions for each chapter of this text

How effective is each one? The first two are general, and as a result, monitoring progress on them and identifying strategies to achieve them is difficult. What, specifically, will you do to learn more, or to get into better shape, for instance? The third goal is distant. Losing 20 pounds is likely a worthwhile goal, but the end of the year is too far into the future. Goals that are close at hand increase self-efficacy more than distant ones, because meeting them is more easily observed. The fourth goal is effective. It is specific, moderately challenging, and can be attacked immediately. It can also be readily monitored and it lends itself to strategy use.

To summarize, effective goals have three characteristics; they are

- Specific (versus broad and general)
- Immediate or close at hand (versus distant)
- Moderately challenging

The appropriate degree of challenge isn't easy to specify, but it's important. Goals that are too easily reached don't increase self-efficacy as much as those that are more challenging. On the other hand, goals that are too

Figure 10.7 Effective use of goals

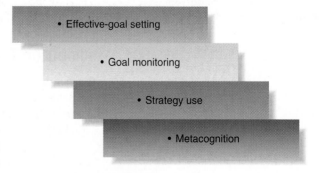

- Effective-goal setting
- Goal monitoring
- Strategy use
- Metacognition

challenging may reduce expectations for success so much that overall motivation is decreased.

For goals to work, people must be committed to them (Pintrich & Schunk, 2002). The best way to increase goal commitment in schools is to guide students in setting their own goals, rather than imposing goals on them (Ridley, McCombs, & Taylor, 1994). Students must be committed to goals, or the motivating influence of using them will be lost. Teachers and parents can play a powerful role in influencing the kinds of goals learners set (Church et al., 2001; McNeil & Alibali, 2000).

Goal Monitoring. Once people have committed to a set of goals, monitoring them leads to a sense of accomplishment, promotes self-efficacy, and can be a pleasant emotional experience. For instance, there are 20 "Checking Your Understanding" questions in this chapter, so suppose that on Monday you set the goal of answering all the questions by the following Sunday. If by Wednesday evening you've answered the first 10, and you believe you understand them, you feel good about your progress; you've answered half of them in 3 days. You have concrete evidence of your progress, and your self-efficacy increases. In addition, you've taken responsibility for your own learning, which further increases your sense of accomplishment.

Self-monitoring also has more general value (Schunk, 1997; Wolters, 1997). For example, suppose you are monitoring the amount of time devoted to "studying," and you find that you're actually spending a considerable amount getting up to check your computer for recent e-mail messages and the news, or reorganizing your notes without actually learning from them. This realization can result in your shutting the computer off and studying more efficiently, such as looking for relationships in the topics you're studying. If you believe your changed habits increase learning, your motivation will be sustained (Schunk, 1997).

Strategy Use. Use of appropriate strategies is the third process needed for effective goal use. For example, simply reading the "Checking Your Understanding" questions and then reading the answers on the Website is an ineffective strategy, because you are studying passively. Actually writing an answer to each question and then checking the feedback is more effective. Also, waiting until Saturday to start answering the questions doesn't work as well as answering three or four each day.

Effective strategy use requires a repertoire of strategies (Bruning et al., 2004). For instance, if you set a goal of writing two summary sentences for each section of the chapter, you must be skilled with summarizing in order to use the strategy.

Metacognition. Finally, the entire process of using goals is grounded in metacognition (Paris & Paris, 2001). For instance, think again about realizing that you're "studying" less than you previously thought. You first had to be aware enough of your study habits to begin monitoring your strategies, and you then had to exercise control over them by looking for relationships in the topics instead of studying each one in isolation.

Being metacognitive is essential. For instance, if you're writing definitions of concepts on note cards, but your instructor's tests measure application, you'll realize that you're using an ineffective strategy and you'll change it. You'll begin studying for application, such as completing the exercises in the Student Study Guide. Being metacognitive changed your strategy, and an increase in understanding is likely to result.

Teachers can help learners become more metacognitive by modeling their own metacognition and by explaining specific examples of effective and ineffective strategies (Paris & Paris, 2001). The message that teachers want to communicate is that learning is conscious, intentional, and requires effort.

Attribution Theory

Earlier, we said that students who adopt learning goals attribute success to internal, controllable causes. What does *attribute* mean, and why is it important for motivation? We examine these and other questions in this section.

Let's begin by looking at five students' responses to the results of a test.

"How'd you do, Bob?" Anne asks.

"Terrible," Bob answers sheepishly. "I just can't do this stuff. I'm no good at writing the kind of essays she wants. . . . I'll never get it."

Exploring Further

To read more about how goal theory can be applied in classrooms go to "Applying Goal Theory with At-Risk Students" in the *Exploring Further* module of Chapter 10 at *www.prenhall.com/eggen.*

"I didn't do so good either," Anne replies, "but I knew I wouldn't. I just didn't study hard enough. I won't let that happen again."

"Unbelievable!" Armondo adds. "I didn't know what the heck was going on, and I got a B. I don't think she read mine."

"I got a C," Billy shrugs. "Not bad, considering how much I studied. I could have done a lot better, but I couldn't get into it for this test."

"I just went blank," Ashley shakes her head. "I looked at the test, and all I could think of was, 'I've never seen this stuff before. Where did it come from?'"

At the beginning of our discussion of cognitive motivation theories we saw that they are grounded in the assumption that people are motivated by a need to understand and make sense of the world. We can explain Bob's, Anne's, and Armondo's reactions on this basis. (We consider Billy's and Ashley's reactions later in the chapter.) They all wanted to understand why they got the grades they did, so they created explanations (perceived causes) for their successes and failures. These explanations are called *attributions.* Bob explained his failure by saying that he wasn't good enough (he lacked ability), Anne used lack of effort as her explanation, and Armondo wrote the issue off to luck. In addition to ability, effort, and luck, learners also attribute successes and failures to other factors such as the difficulty of the task, effective or ineffective strategies, lack of help, interest, unfair teacher practices, or clarity of instruction. *Ability, effort, luck,* and *task difficulty* are the most common (B. Weiner, 1992, 2001).

Attribution theory attempts to systematically describe learners' explanations for their successes and failures and how these influence motivation and behavior. Attributions occur on three dimensions (B. Weiner, 1992, 2000, 2001). The first is called *locus,* or the location of the cause, which is either within or outside the learner. Ability and effort are within the learner, for example, whereas luck and task difficulty are outside. The second is *stability,* whether or not the cause can change. Effort and luck are unstable because they can change, whereas ability is considered stable in attribution theory. The third is *control,* the extent to which students accept responsibility for their successes or failures, or are in control of the learning situation. Learners control their effort, for example, but they cannot control luck or task difficulty. These relationships are outlined in Table 10.4.

Impact of Attributions on Learners

Attributions influence learners in four ways:

- Emotional reactions to success and failure
- Expectations for future success
- Future effort
- Achievement

To see how these influences work, let's look at Anne's and Bob's attributions again. Anne attributed her poor score to lack of effort. So, first, since she was responsible for her effort, guilt was her emotional reaction. Second, she can expect to be successful in the future because effort is unstable, and third, her comment "I won't let that happen again" suggests that she will increase her effort. Finally, improved achievement is likely (Weiner, 2000, 2001).

Bob attributed his failure to lack of ability. So, instead of guilt, his emotional reaction was shame and embarrassment, since he viewed ability as uncontrollable. Second, because he attributed his failure to lack of ability, he doesn't expect future success ("I'll never get it"). Third, because of his attributions, his effort is likely to decrease, with lower achievement the probable result (Weiner, 1994).

Attribution theory. A cognitive theory of motivation that attempts to systematically describe learners' explanations for their successes and failures and how these influence motivation and behavior

Table 10.4 Characteristics of attributions in relation to three dimensions of attributions

Attributions	Locus (location of cause)	Stability (of cause)	Control (of learning situation)
Ability	Inside the learner	Stable (cannot change)	Learner out of control
Effort	Inside the learner	Unstable (can change)	Learner in control
Luck	Outside the learner	Unstable (can change)	Learner out of control
Task difficulty	Outside the learner	Stable (cannot change)	Learner out of control

Motivation tends to increase when students attribute failure to lack of effort, as Anne did, because effort can be controlled. It tends to decrease when students attribute failure to uncontrollable causes (e.g., luck, or ability if it is viewed as stable), as Bob did (Weiner, 2000, 2001).

Research indicates that people tend to attribute success to internal causes, such as hard work or high ability, and failures to external causes, such as bad luck or the behaviors of others (Marsh, 1990). When students do poorly, for example, they commonly attribute their failure to poor teaching, boring topics, tricky tests, or some other external cause.

Attributions also influence teachers. For instance, if they believe students are succeeding because of their teaching, they're likely to continue making the effort (Shahid, 2001). If they believe, instead, that learners are doing poorly because of students' lack of prior knowledge, poor home lives, or some other cause beyond their control, their efforts decrease.

Learned Helplessness

In extreme circumstances, student attributions can lead to **learned helplessness,** the general belief, based on past experiences, that one is incapable of accomplishing tasks and has little control of the environment. Let's look at Bob's attributions again; attributing failure to lack of ability, which he viewed as uncontrollable, could lead to this debilitating state. This perspective results in overwhelming feelings of shame and self-doubt and giving up without trying.

Learned helplessness has both an affective and a cognitive component. Students with learned helplessness have low self-esteem and often suffer from anxiety and depression (Graham & Weiner, 1996). Cognitively, they expect to fail, attributing failure to lack of ability, so they exert little effort and use ineffective strategies, which results in less success and an even greater expectation for failure (Dweck, 2000). Students who have histories of failure are particularly susceptible to learned helplessness. Fortunately, efforts to intervene have been successful. Let's look at them.

Attribution Training

Learners can improve the effectiveness of their attributions through training (Robertson, 2000). In a pioneering study, Dweck (1975) provided students who demonstrated learned helplessness with both successful and unsuccessful experiences. When the students were unsuccessful, the experimenter specifically stated that the failure was caused by lack of effort or ineffective strategies. Comparable students were given similar experiences but no training. After 25 sessions, the learners who were counseled about their effort and strategies responded more appropriately to failure by persisting longer and adapting their strategies more effectively. Subsequent research has corroborated Dweck's findings (Pintrich & Schunk, 2002). Strategy instruction was most effective for students who believed that they were already trying hard. This research suggests that teachers can increase students' motivation to learn by teaching them learning strategies and encouraging them to attribute success to effort.

Instructional Principles

Beliefs, Goals, and Attributions: Instructional Principles

You can apply these cognitive theories of motivation in several ways. The following principles can guide you in your efforts:

1. Increase learner self-efficacy by providing students with evidence of accomplishment and modeling your own self-efficacy.
2. Encourage internal attributions for successes and controllable attributions for failures.
3. Emphasize the utility value of increased skills.
4. Promote student interest by modeling your own interest, personalizing content, providing concrete examples, involving students, and offering choices.
5. Emphasize learning and social responsibility goals, effective strategies, and metacognition.

Earlier in the chapter, we saw how Kathy applied humanistic views of motivation in her interactions with Jenny and Harvey. Let's return to her classroom and see how the prin-

Learned helplessness. The general belief, based on past experiences, that one is incapable of accomplishing tasks and has little control of the environment

ciples we've just listed guide her as she works with her whole class. She is in the second day of her unit on the Crusades.

She begins, "Let's review for a moment. We began our discussion of the Crusades yesterday. How did we start?"

"We imagined that we all left Lincoln High School and that it was taken over by people who believed that extracurricular activities should be eliminated," Carnisha volunteers.

"Good," Kathy smiles. "Then what?"

"We decided we'd talk to them . . . . We'd be on a 'crusade' to change their minds."

"Very good. . . . Now, what were the actual Crusades all about? . . . Selena?"

"The Christians wanted to get the Holy Land back from the Muslims."

"And why? . . . Becky?"

"The holy lands were important to the Christians."

The class then discusses reasons for the Crusades, such as religion, economics, the military threat posed by the Muslim world, and the amount of territory they held.

Student beliefs about their capabilities as learners can be enhanced by experiences in which challenging tasks are successfully accomplished.

"Excellent analysis. . . . In fact, we'll see that these factors also influenced Columbus's voyage to the New World. . . . Think about that. The Muslims and the Crusades nearly a 1,000 years ago have had an influence on us here today," she continues energetically.

"Now, for today's assignment, you were asked to write a paragraph answering the question, 'Were the Crusades a success or a failure?' and the quality depends on how you defended your position, not on the position itself. Remember, the ability to make and defend an argument is a skill that goes way beyond a specific topic.

"So, let's see how we did. Go ahead. . . . Nikki?"

"I said they were a failure. . . . The Europeans didn't get the Holy Land back for Christianity. There were several Crusades, and after only one did they get sort of a foothold, and it only lasted . . . like about 50 years, I think."

"How about you, Joe?"

"I said they were a success because the Europeans learned new military strategies like guerrilla fighting that they later used . . . like even here, when we were just colonies . . . . And, Europe took a lot from their culture . . . Like, some of the spices we eat today first came to Europe then."

"Also good, Joe," Kathy nods. "This is exactly what we're after. Nikki and Joe took opposite positions in their paragraphs, but they each provided several details in support. . . . See how interesting this is? Again, we see ourselves influenced by people who lived hundreds of years ago. . . . That's what history is all about."

"Brewster loves this stuff," David whispers to Kelly.

"Yeah," she replies. "History has never been my favorite subject, but some of this stuff is actually kind of neat."

Kathy has the class review another example, and then tells the students to revise their paragraphs based on what they recently discussed. "Remember, think about what you're doing as you make your revisions," she emphasizes. "Ask yourself, 'Do I actually have evidence here, or is it simply an opinion?' . . . The more aware you are when you write, the better your work will be. When you're done, switch with a partner and critique each other's paper. Remember, we made a commitment to ourselves at the beginning of the year to help each other as much as we can when we give each other feedback on our writing. . . . So, I know that you'll come through.

"One more reminder," Kathy says as the period is about to end, "group presentations on the Renaissance are on Thursday and Friday. You decide what groups will present on each day. For those who chose to write the paper on the Middle Ages, remember we agreed that they're due on Friday."

Now, let's look at Kathy's attempts to apply the principles we listed previously. Her interaction with Harvey in the case study at the beginning of the chapter illustrated three of the principles. She applied the first, attempting to increase self-efficacy, when she said, "Yes, but look how good you're getting at writing. I think you hit a personal best on your last paper." She also commented, "It's hard for me, too, when I'm studying and trying to put together new ideas, but if I hang in, I always feel like I can get it." Her first comment provided evidence of accomplishment, which is the most important factor influencing self-efficacy, and the second modeled her own developing self-efficacy.

She applied the second principle (encourage internal attributions for successes and controllable attributions for failures) when she responded to Harvey's comment, "But you make us work so hard," by saying, "Yes, but look how good you're getting at writing." Her response encouraged him to attribute his success to effort and increased ability, which are both internal causes. His comment, "Yeah, yeah, I know, and being good writers will help us in everything we do in life," reflected her emphasis on the utility value of what they were learning, an application of the third principle.

Kathy attempted to increase her students' interest in the topic by applying the fourth principle in several ways. First, she modeled her own interest, as indicated by her comments, "Think about that. The Muslims and the Crusades nearly a 1,000 years ago have had an influence on us here today," and "See how interesting this is? . . . Again, we see ourselves influenced by people who lived hundreds of years ago." Her statements' impact on students was reflected in David's reaction, "Brewster loves this stuff."

She also attempted to increase students' interest by personalizing the topic with the analogy of "crusading" to prevent the school from eliminating extracurricular activities, using the analogy as a concrete example of a *crusade*, and involving students throughout the activity. Kelly's response to David, "Yeah, history has never been my favorite subject, but some of this stuff is actually kind of neat," shows how these efforts can increase motivation to learn.

Kathy also attempted to increase interest by allowing students to choose either a presentation on the Renaissance or a paper on the Middle Ages, to decide which groups would present on certain days, and to negotiate the due date for the papers ("remember that we agreed that they're due on Friday").

Kathy attempted to apply the last principle by encouraging students to be metacognitive about their writing, "Remember, think about what you're doing. . . . Ask yourself, 'Do I actually have evidence here, or simply an opinion?'. . . The more aware you are when you write, the better your work will be," and she emphasized social responsibility goals when she said, "Remember, we made a commitment . . . to help each other as much as we could. . . . So, I know that you'll come through." As we saw earlier, the combination of social responsibility goals and learning goals increases motivation and achievement more than either alone.

At the beginning of the chapter, we said that with a positive approach to motivation teachers can influence the learning and motivation in their classrooms. This is what Kathy tried to do as she worked with her students.

Checking Your Understanding

4.1 Describe the basic assumption on which cognitive theories of motivation are based, and explain how the assumption is illustrated in the following incident: While reading his son a familiar story, a father sees that the child is getting sleepy and decides to skip a few pages by summarizing them. His son immediately corrects him and demands that he read all the pages.

4.2 Cite a specific example from Kathy Brewster's conversation with Harvey (p. 298) that illustrates emphasis on utility value in his learning. Utility value is a component of which theory of motivation? Explain.

4.3 In the discussion of goal theory, we identified the following goals and said they were not effective:

> To learn more in all of my classes
> To get into better shape
> To lose 20 pounds by the end of the year

Rewrite each to make them more effective.

4.4 Look again at the conversation among the five students at the beginning of our discussion of attribution theory. Explain Armondo's emotional reaction, expectations for future success, future effort, and achievement, based on attributing his success to luck.

To receive feedback for these questions, go to Appendix B.

Knowledge Extensions

To deepen your understanding of the topics in this section of the chapter and to integrate them with topics you've already studied, go to the *Knowledge Extensions* module for Chapter 10 at *www.prenhall.com/eggen*. Respond to questions 9–12.

Self-Determination Theory

Self-determination theory is one of the most comprehensive and thoroughly researched theories of motivation (Brophy, 2004; Pintrich & Schunk, 2002). It describes a continuum that proceeds through stages of extrinsic motivation and ends in intrinsic motivation (Deci & Ryan, 1985, 1991, 2000; R. Ryan & Deci, 2000). Although primarily a cognitive motivation theory, it also incorporates aspects of humanistic views of motivation.

Self-determination is the process of deciding how to act on one's environment (R. Ryan & Deci, 2000). According to self-determination theory, having choices and making decisions is intrinsically motivating, and people aren't content if all their needs are satisfied without opportunities to make decisions. Self-determination theory assumes that people have three innate psychological needs: competence, autonomy, and relatedness (Levesque et al., 2004; R. Ryan & Deci, 2000).

The Need for Competence

The need for **competence,** the ability to function effectively in the environment, can be described at several levels. At a basic, anthropological level, for instance, if an organism can't function effectively in its environment, it isn't likely to survive (Pintrich & Schunk, 2002). At another level, competent people succeed and grow in their careers, whereas those less competent languish and stagnate. In schools, competent students are successful learners, and they find school satisfying and rewarding. Competence and self-efficacy are sometimes equated (R. Ryan & Deci, 2000; Pintrich & Schunk, 2002).

At the beginning of the chapter, we saw that activities that present a challenge and those that evoke curiosity are intrinsically motivating, and the need for competence helps us understand why. Meeting challenges and resolving novel and discrepant experiences both provide evidence that competence is increasing. In contrast, completing trivial tasks, or solving predictable problems provides little evidence about competence, so they are rarely intrinsically motivating.

The need for competence is similar to the need for mastery of the environment described by R. White (1959) in a classic paper. He suggested that people acquire proficiency and skill "because it satisfies an intrinsic need to deal with the environment" (p. 318). The need for competence is also consistent with the need to understand the reasons for our successes and failures described by attribution theory (B. Weiner, 1986), and achievement needs in historical descriptions of achievement motivation theory (J. Atkinson, 1958).

As with self-efficacy, the most important factor influencing students' perception of competence is evidence that their understanding and skills are improving. As competence increases, so do perceptions of self-determination (Deci & Ryan, 2002).

Teachers also influence students' beliefs about their competence in subtle ways with:

- Attributional statements
- Praise and criticism
- Emotional displays
- Offers of help

Attributional Statements. **Attributional statements** are comments teachers make about the causes of students' performances. For instance, if a teacher says to a student struggling with a problem, "That's a very good effort. I know that these problems are hard for you," she is attributing the difficulty to lack of ability, which undermines beliefs about competence (Stipek, 1996). In contrast, the statement, "I believe if you tried a little harder, you'd be able to solve this problem," suggests that with increased effort competence can be achieved.

Attributional statements about success can also influence student beliefs about competence. For example, "Well done. I see that you've been working hard on this," doesn't suggest that competence is increasing, whereas a statement like, "You're getting very good at this" does.

Praise and Criticism. The use of praise and criticism also influences students' perceptions of their competence. Older students may perceive praise received for effort instead of accomplishment, or praise for performance on easy tasks, as an indication that the teacher believes they have low ability or are not competent (Larrivee, 2002; Stipek, 1996). By comparison, a critical statement such as, "Come on. You can do better work than this,"

Self-determination. The process of deciding how to act on one's environment

Competence. The ability to function effectively in the environment

Attributional statements. Comments teachers make about the causes of students' performances

Teachers can increase learner motivation by allowing students to choose some learning goals and activities.

communicates that the teacher believes the student can achieve competence. So, while we're not saying that teachers should make a habit of criticizing students, inappropriate praise can detract from motivation to learn, whereas timely criticism can actually increase it.

Emotional Displays. Teachers' emotional reactions to learners' successes and failures can also affect learners' beliefs about self-competence. For example, when teachers express annoyance in response to learner failure, students are likely to attribute it to lack of effort, which implies that with increased effort competence can be achieved. In comparison, students who receive sympathy from teachers tend to attribute their failure to lack of ability, which implies that they don't have the capacity to become competent (Stipek, 1996, 2002).

Offers of Help. Offering students unsolicited help can also be problematic. For instance, researchers have found that children as young as 6 rated a student offered unsolicited help lower in ability than another offered no help (Graham & Barker, 1990). Further, learners who are offered help may feel negative emotions, such as incompetence, anger, worry, or anxiety.

To put this section into perspective, we're not suggesting that teachers should avoid encouraging effort, praising students, expressing sympathy, or offering help. Rather, it reminds us that we must be aware of how our actions can be interpreted by learners. As always, the way we respond to students requires sensitivity and careful professional judgment.

The Need for Autonomy

The need for **autonomy**—independence and the ability to alter the environment when necessary—is the second innate need described by self-determination theory. As we saw earlier, autonomy is another source of intrinsic motivation (Lepper & Hodell, 1989). Conversely, lack of autonomy reduces intrinsic motivation and causes stress. For instance, it is widely believed that the stress of assembly line work comes from workers' having little control over their environments.

Autonomy as described in self-determination theory is similar to other historical discussions of the topic, such as *locus of control* (Rotter, 1966) and *personal causation* (deCharms, 1968, 1984). Also, autonomy and competence are strongly related. As learners' competence increases, so do their perceptions of autonomy (A. Black & Deci, 2000; Bruning et al., 2004).

What can teachers do to promote perceptions of autonomy in their students? The most obvious answer is to give them choices, as Kathy did by allowing her students to either make a presentation on the Renaissance or write a paper on the Middle Ages. However, since providing choices often isn't possible, perceptions of autonomy can be enhanced in other ways:

- Solicit student input in creating classroom rules and procedures and following them consistently.
- Encourage students to set and monitor their own learning goals.
- Create high levels of student participation in learning activities.
- Emphasize effort and strategy attributions while deemphasizing the role of ability in success.
- Use assessments that emphasize learning and provide feedback.

The Need for Relatedness

Relatedness, the feeling of being connected to others in one's social environment and feeling worthy of love and respect, is the third innate need described by self-determination theory. Relatedness is similar to Maslow's (1968, 1970) need for *belonging* as well as the need for *affiliation* as described by other early motivational researchers (e.g., Exline, 1962; Terhune, 1968).

Relatedness influences learning and motivation in three ways. First, students are more engaged—behaviorally, cognitively, and emotionally—in classroom activities when they believe their teachers like, understand, and empathize with them (Furrer & Skinner, 2003;

Autonomy. Independence and an individual's ability to alter the environment when necessary

Relatedness. The feeling of being connected to others in one's social environment and feeling worthy of love and respect

McCombs, 2001). Second, students who feel as though they belong and who receive personal support from their teachers report more interest in their class work and describe it as more important than students whose teachers are distant (Goodenow, 1993; Kohn, 2005b). Third, students who view their teachers as supportive are more likely to set desirable social goals, such as developing social responsibility (Wentzel, 1996).

Collectively, these findings suggest that a supportive classroom environment, where each student is valued regardless of academic ability or performance, contributes to relatedness and is important for both learning and motivation (Stipek, 1996, 2002).

Assessment and Learning: The Role of Assessment in Self-Determination

As we've emphasized throughout this book, assessment is an essential part of the learning–teaching process. This raises an issue, however, because some research suggests that evaluation detracts from self-determination and intrinsic motivation (Deci & Ryan, 1987).

As with most aspects of learning and teaching, the issue isn't simply a matter of do or do not emphasize assessment; it depends on how the process is handled. For instance, assessments that students view as punitive or controlling detract from intrinsic motivation, whereas those that provide information about increasing competence increase it (Deci & Ryan, 1987; Eggen, 1997). The following are some suggestions for using assessments effectively:

- Provide clear expectations for students, and align assessments with the expectations (Pintrich & Schunk, 2002). (We discuss instructional alignment in Chapter 13.)
- Assess frequently and thoroughly (Dochy & McDowell, 1997).
- Allow students to drop one or more of their lowest test or quiz scores for purposes of grading (Eggen, 1997).
- Provide detailed feedback about responses to assessments, and emphasize the reasons for answers as much as the answers themselves (Deci & Ryan, 1987; Pintrich & Schunk, 2002).
- Avoid social comparisons in communicating assessment results (H. Patrick, Anderman, Ryan, Edelin, & Midgley, 1999; Stipek, 1996, 2002).

Our goal in assessing student learning should be to establish a climate that gives students perceptions of autonomy and emphasizes learning and increased competence. Clear expectations and alignment make assessments predictable, which increases perceptions of autonomy, as does dropping one or more quiz scores for purposes of grading. Frequent assessment provides students with information about their increasing competence, which also promotes self-efficacy. Detailed feedback that includes reasons for answers emphasizes that increased competence is the purpose of assessment. It also contributes to students' perceptions of autonomy, because they learn where they need improvement and what strategies they might use to accomplish it. Finally, avoiding social comparisons promotes learning goals instead of performance goals. As a symbolic gesture, some teachers write students' scores on the back page of tests and quizzes and encourage students to avoid sharing their scores with each other. Although students will still probably share scores, the practice is a tangible symbol that assessments are private and their purpose is to increase learning, not see who is the "smartest."

Analyzing Classrooms Video
To analyze a teacher's application of cognitive motivation theories in her teaching, go to Episode 17, "Applying Cognitive Motivation Theory: Writing Paragraphs in Fifth Grade," on DVD 2, accompanying this text.

Exploring Further
Self-determination theory is more comprehensive than the discussion you've studied here. To read more about it, go to "Self-Determination Theory" in the *Exploring Further* module of Chapter 10 at *www.prenhall.com/eggen*.

Instructional ⌂ Principles	Developing Students' Self-Determination: Instructional Principles

Self-determination theory has a number of implications for you as a teacher. The following principles can guide you in your efforts to apply this theory in your teaching:

1. Use assessments that increase intrinsic motivation.
2. Reward increasing competence instead of compliance or mere participation in an activity.
3. Create classroom environments and learning activities that increase students' feelings of autonomy.
4. Design learning activities that challenge learners' existing understanding and skills.
5. Treat students with unconditional positive regard, and communicate that you are committed to their learning.

Let's see how the principles guide Elaine Goodman, a fifth-grade teacher, as she works with her students in a unit on fractions. We join her class as she is going over a weekly quiz designed to measure students' abilities to add fractions with unlike denominators.

"You did very well on the quiz," Elaine smiles. "But I knew that you would. We've been working hard, and you're understanding fractions better and better.

"Now, we want to look at a few of the problems," she says, turning the discussion to the quiz. "Let's look at number 3."

You're at a party at Jon's [a boy in the class] house, and you ate one slice of the first pizza and two slices of the second pizza. How much did you eat altogether?

"We know that the answer is five twelfths of a pizza, but how we got that is most important . . . . So, someone come up to the board and explain how you got five twelfths? . . . Go ahead, Ajma," she says, seeing Ajma's raised hand.

"Okay, . . . I knew I was adding 1/6 of the first pizza to 2/8 of the second one, but the size of the pieces weren't the same," Ajma explains after coming to the board. . . .

"So I found the lowest common multiple for 6 and 8, which is 24. . . . For 1/6 I multiplied the top and bottom by 4, and for 2/8 I multiplied the top and bottom by 3."

Ajma wrote her calculations on the board:

$$\frac{1\,(4)}{6\,(4)} = \frac{4}{24}$$

$$\frac{2\,(3)}{8\,(3)} = \frac{6}{24}$$

"And why did you multiply both the top and bottom?" Elaine probes.

". . . Well, 4 over 4 is the same as 1, and so is 3 over 3, so I'm really multiplying by 1, and that doesn't change the number."

"Excellent, Ajma. . . . Go on."

"Then I added and got 10/24, and that reduces to 5/12."

Elaine then has students explain other problems on the quiz, providing guidance when necessary. She completes the discussion by going over the last two problems. On each of her quizzes, Elaine gives the students the option of doing only one of the last two; if they do both, they can earn bonus points.

When they finish discussing the quiz, she again comments on how good they're getting at adding and subtracting fractions, and then says, "Now, remember, if any of you want a little extra help, I'm always here at 8:15, so we have 45 minutes before school to go over anything you need."

Then, changing the direction of the lesson, she asks, "Now, let's think about this," "When we multiply numbers, like 6 times 8, we get what?"

"Forty eight!" the students shout in unison.

"Yes, and 48 is a bigger number than either 6 or 8, isn't it? . . . How about when we divide, like 42 divided by 7?"

"Six. . . . A smaller number," Kiki responds.

"Exactly," Elaine nods. "But here's the kicker. When we multiply fractions, like 1/3 times 1/4, you know what we get? . . . One twelfth. . . . And what do you notice about 1/12 compared to 1/3 or 1/4?"

" . . . It's smaller," several of the students respond after thinking a few seconds.

"And when we divide fractions, it's just the opposite. One half divided by 1/4 is— you're not going to believe this—2. . . . Now, how can that be?

"That's going to be our challenge for the next few days. . . . We're going to understand why multiplying fractions gives us a smaller number and dividing fractions gives us a bigger number. What do you think? . . . Are you up to it?"

"Yeah!" the students shout.

"Of course you are," Elaine smiles. "You have been all year. . . . Let's get started."

Now, let's look at Elaine's attempts to apply the instruction principles for applying self-determination theory in classrooms. She attempted to apply the first (use assessment procedures that increase intrinsic motivation) through clear expectations and formal weekly assessment of her students, with a quiz aligned with her learning objectives. She discussed the problems carefully, so the students received detailed feedback about their learning progress, and she emphasized understanding as much as correct answers.

Elaine applied the second principle (reward increasing competence) through comments such as, "Your understanding is getting better and better," to emphasize that students' competence was increasing. As we saw earlier, comments that communicate increasing competence can increase intrinsic motivation (Deci & Ryan, 2000, 2002).

Knowing that giving students choices is difficult when teaching basic skills, such as operations with fractions, Elaine attempted to increase students' perceptions of autonomy (the third principle) by requiring that they only do one of the last two items on the quiz. Then, she gave them the opportunity to do the alternate problem as a bonus. She also attempted to increase their sense of autonomy by using meaningful and personalized examples (e.g., students' names in real-world problems), and she promoted high levels of participation in her discussion.

Elaine attempted to apply the fourth principle (design learning activities that challenge learners' existing understanding and skills) by challenging students to explain why, compared to whole numbers, multiplying fractions results in a smaller number, whereas dividing them results in a larger number. Accepting and meeting challenges increases students' perceptions of competence, self-efficacy, and beliefs about their ability to control their own learning. Each increases intrinsic motivation (Deci & Ryan, 2000, 2002).

Finally, by reminding students that they could come in for extra help any day before school, Elaine communicated that she cared about the students and was committed to their learning (principle 5). This kind of commitment helps meet students' needs for relatedness.

Cognitive motivation theories focus on learners' beliefs, expectations, and needs for order, predictability, and understanding. People's needs to understand their experiences lie at the core of each theory of motivation. The different theories are summarized in Table 10.5.

Table 10.5 Cognitive theories of motivation

Theory	Basic Premise	Can Explain Examples Such as The Following
Expectancy × Value Theory	People are motivated to work on a task if they expect to succeed and value success on the task.	• Why people are motivated to study an area even if they aren't intrinsically interested in it • Why people are motivated by involvement, and studying concrete and personalized examples • Why performance on a task, such as getting a high grade on a test, is important to one person, but not to another
Self-Efficacy Theory	People's beliefs about their capabilities influence their motivation.	• Why some students persevere on challenging tasks, whereas others quickly give up • Why students of equal ability perform differently
Goal Theory	Setting appropriate goals increases motivation.	• Why an individual goes to the gym and works out even if she is tired and doesn't want to exercise • Why this same individual enjoys making a chart to record the number of exercises she completed
Attribution Theory	People are intrinsically motivated to understand their successes and failures.	• Why students want feedback on their tests, negative as well as positive • Why teachers are irritated when they're observed and the observer says nothing to them afterward • Why some students increase their efforts after failure, whereas others don't
Self-Determination Theory	People have instinctive needs for competence, control, and relatedness in their lives.	• Why people are motivated by challenging experiences and praise that reflects genuine accomplishment • Why people strive to establish and maintain equilibrium • Why forced, routine tasks lead to stress • Why students work harder for teachers they perceive as committed to their learning • Why people devalue accomplishment of trivial tasks

Diversity in Motivation to Learn

The cognitive motivation theories discussed in this section describe general patterns of motivation. However, not all students or groups of students will fit these patterns (d'Ailly, 2003; Rogoff, 2003). For instance, some research indicates that both Asian-American and African-American students tend to focus on learning goals to a greater extent than European-American students, who tend to focus more on performance goals (R. Freeman, Gutman, & Midgley, 2002; Qian & Pan, 2002). Asian-American students are also more likely to attribute their successes to effort and their failures to lack of effort than are Caucasian students (Lillard, 1997; Steinberg, 1996). And, African-American students may have a greater tendency to develop learned helplessness than other groups, probably because of perceived prejudice (R. A. Goldstein, 2004; van Lar, 2000). Other research indicates that some Native American groups give their children more autonomy and control over decision making at a younger age than do parents in mainstream Western culture (Deyhle & LeCompte, 1999).

Gender differences in motivation also exist. For example, the stereotypical belief that some domains, such as English, are more nearly suited for girls, whereas others, such as math and science, are for boys, still exists (F. Pajares & Valiante, 1999), so motivation to learn in these domains can vary because of different perceptions of utility value in them (J. E. Jacobs et al., 2002). Further, boys' self-efficacy tends to remain higher than girls' in spite of the fact that girls get higher grades (Eccles et al., 1998; Middleton, 1999), and girls are more easily discouraged by failure than are boys (Dweck, 2000). Research suggests that these differences may be due to their attributions; boys tend to attribute success to high ability and failure to lack of effort, whereas girls show a reverse pattern (Vermeer, Boekaerts, & Seegers, 2000).

It is important to remember that individuals within these groups will also vary significantly. For instance, many European-American students set learning goals, and many Asian-American students set performance goals. Many girls have high efficacy, and the self-efficacy of many boys is low. As teachers, we want to avoid thinking that can result in stereotyping any group.

Knowledge Extensions

To deepen your understanding of the topic in this section and integrate it with topics you've already studied, go to the *Knowledge Extensions* module for Chapter 10 at *www.prenhall.com/eggen*. Respond to questions 13–15.

Checking Your Understanding

5.1   A student has just gotten a high score on one of your quizzes. Based on self-determination theory, which of the following is the better teacher comment?

"Well done. I see that your hard work is paying off."

"Well done. It looks like you really understand this stuff."
       Explain.

5.2   In addition to giving her students choices, identify at least two other ways in which Kathy Brewster helped increase her students' perceptions of autonomy.

5.3   In this section, we said that students who are offered help sometimes feel negative emotions, such as incompetence or anger. While supervising students doing seat work, one of them raises his hand and asks for help. Should you provide the help? Is the student asking for help more likely to be a high or a low achiever? Explain.

To receive feedback for these questions, go to Appendix B.

Classroom Connections

Applying Cognitive Theories of Motivation Effectively in Your Classroom

Expectancy × Value Theory

1. Develop expectations for success by giving students only as much help as they need to make progress on challenging tasks.
   - **Elementary:** After displaying a problem, a fourth-grade teacher asks students to suggest different ways of solving it. The class discusses each strategy, and the teacher points out areas in which the students' problem solving is improving.
   - **Middle School:** A seventh-grade English teacher has his students write paragraphs on transparencies. He displays and discusses students' products and makes suggestions for improvement. He emphasizes how much the quality of the paragraphs is increasing.
   - **High School:** An art teacher has students keep a portfolio of their work. She has them periodically review their products to demonstrate the progress they're making.

2. Promote task value by using concrete examples to increase interest, and emphasize the utility value of the topics students study.
   - **Elementary:** A third-grade teacher brings large shrimp and a lobster into his class. His students work in pairs to examine and describe the shrimp. The class discusses their findings, compares them to findings about the lobster, and they arrive at a description of crustaceans.
   - **Middle School:** A seventh-grade math teacher working on percentage problems brings in newspaper advertisements for marked-down products. The class determines the actual reduction in cost, and the teacher then emphasizes the value of understanding how much people save in promotions.
   - **High School:** An English teacher displays examples of well-written (and not so well-written) attempts to make and defend an argument. She uses the examples to emphasize the value of being able to clearly express oneself in writing.

Goal Theory

3. Promote learner responsibility with goal setting and self-monitoring. Emphasize learning goals.
   - **Elementary:** A fifth-grade teacher confers with students as they begin a writing project. He has them write down a schedule for completing the project, and he periodically meets with each to assess their progress.
   - **Middle School:** An eighth-grade history teacher promotes metacognition by saying to her students, "It's very important to think about and be aware of the way you study. If you have your stereo on, ask yourself, 'Am I really learning what I'm studying, or am I distracted by the stereo?'" She emphasizes that learning is always the goal and that being aware of the way they study will increase their understanding.
   - **High School:** An English teacher promotes strategy use by saying, "Let's read the next section in our books. After we've read it, we're going to stop and make a one-sentence summary of the passage. This is something each of you can do as you read on your own. If you do, your understanding of what you're reading will increase."

Attribution Theory

4. Model and encourage students to attribute success to increasing competence and failure to lack of effort or ineffective strategies.
   - **Elementary:** As they initially work on word problems, a second-grade teacher carefully monitors student effort during seat work. When he sees assignments that indicate effort, he makes comments to individual students, such as "Your work is improving all the time."
   - **Middle School:** A sixth-grade English teacher comments, "I wasn't good at grammar for a long time. But I kept trying, and I found that I can do it. I'm good at grammar and writing now. You can get good too, but you have to work at it."
   - **High School:** A chemistry teacher comments, "The way we're attacking balancing equations is working much better, isn't it? You tried to memorize the steps before, and now you're understanding what you're doing. And you're getting better and better at it."

Self-Determination Theory

5. Begin lessons with questions and activities that challenge students' understanding and arouse curiosity.
   - **Elementary:** A fifth-grade teacher drops an ice cube into a cup of clear alcohol (which the students initially think is water), and the ice cube drops to the bottom of the cup. "We know that ice floats on water," she says. "How can we explain what just happened?"
   - **Middle School:** A math teacher has a problem of the week that requires the students to bring in a challenging, everyday problem for the class to solve.
   - **High School:** A biology teacher beginning a unit on the skeletal system says, "Our skull is nearly solid and very hard. But when we were infants, it was flexible and there are even gaps in it. Why might this be the case?"

6. To provide evidence about increasing competence, give clear and prompt feedback on assignments and tests.
   - **Elementary:** A fourth-grade teacher has his students write their answers to word problems on transparencies. The class discusses the different solutions and analyzes how they are similar and different. The teacher praises solutions that are insightful.
   - **Middle School:** A pre-algebra teacher returns all tests and quizzes the following day and discusses frequently missed problems in detail. She comments that the students' skills are continually improving.
   - **High School:** A world history teacher has students identify specific archeological evidence for sites that represent Old Stone Age compared to New Stone Age civilizations. When warranted, he comments that the students' ability to link evidence to conclusions in their reports has improved significantly.

Teachers who emphasize learning over performance and use assessment as a tool for learning can reduce the negative effects of test anxiety.

AFFECTIVE FACTORS IN MOTIVATION

Earlier in the chapter, we presented a vignette in which five students describe their reasons for success or failure on a recent test (p. 316). Three made comments that could be explained by attribution theory, but two made comments attribution theory is unable to explain. Here's what they said:

> "I got a C," Billy shrugged. "Not bad, considering how much I studied. I could have done a lot better, but I couldn't get into it for this test."

> "I just went blank," Ashley said with a crestfallen look. "I looked at the test, and all I could think of was, 'I've never seen this stuff before. Where did it come from?'"

The factors behind Billy's and Ashley's comments are the topics of the next two sections.

Self-Worth Theory

As we saw in Chapter 3, **self-worth** (or self-esteem as it is more commonly called) is an emotional reaction to or an evaluation of the self (Pintrich & Schunk, 2002). Self-worth theory suggests that people have an innate need to protect their sense of self-worth and achieve self-acceptance (Covington, 1992). Self-worth theorists further suggest that our society so strongly values ability and competence that people will go to great lengths to protect perceptions of high ability (Covington, 1992; Graham & Weiner, 1996).

This helps us understand Billy's comment, "I could have done a lot better, but I couldn't get into it for this test." By emphasizing that he didn't study, he was attempting to preserve the perception of high ability, and with it, his self-worth.

Research reveals some interesting patterns in student behavior with respect to effort and ability. For instance, some students hide the fact that they've studied hard for a test, so if they do well, they can, at least in the eyes of their peers, attribute their success to high ability. Others engage in "self-handicapping" strategies to protect their self-worth, such as procrastinating ("I could have done a lot better, but I didn't start studying until after midnight"); making excuses, such as suggesting that the teacher was poor or the tests were tricky; anxiety ("I understand the stuff, but I get nervous in tests"), or making a point of not trying, as Billy did. In these cases, students believe that failure doesn't indicate low ability if they didn't try (Covington, 1992, 1998; A. Martin, Marsh, & Debus, 2001; Wolters, 2003). Self-handicapping behaviors are most common among low achievers, who often choose to not seek help when it's needed (Middleton & Midgley, 1997).

Perceptions of ability and self-worth change as children develop. For instance, when asked, most kindergarten-aged children say they're smart. And, young children assume that people who try hard are smart, and people who are smart try hard (Stipek, 2002). As students move through school, their views change. Their need to be perceived as having high ability increases, and they view expending effort as an indicator of low ability. Social comparisons, such as displaying scores on tests, and other competitive evaluations are the most significant factors in this process (Brophy, 2004). Children as young as second or third grade begin to judge their ability and competence based on their performance compared to others (Stipek, 2002).

Although teachers cannot eliminate all social comparisons, they can model effort and emphasize beliefs about the role of effort in increasing competence. For example, in Kathy's conversation with Harvey at the beginning of the chapter, she commented "It's hard for me, too, when I'm studying and trying to put together new ideas, but if I hang in, I always feel like I can get it." When Harvey responded, "Aw, c'mon, Mrs. Brewster. I thought you knew everything," she replied, "I wish. I have to study every night to keep up with you people, and the harder I study, the smarter I get." As you saw in Chapter 6, teachers can be powerful models, and modeling the belief that effort can increase ability is important. They can also emphasize learning instead of performance, and they can avoid social comparisons as much as possible. Each of these factors helps reduce students' emphasis on preserving perceptions of high ability.

Self-worth. An emotional reaction to or evaluation of the self

Arousal and Anxiety

At one time or another, virtually all of us have been nervous when anticipating a test or presentation to other people. Perhaps our heart rates increased, our mouths felt dry, we had "butterflies," or we worried about failing. Ashley undoubtedly had similar sensations when she took her test: "I just went blank. I looked at the test, and all I could think of was, 'I've never seen this stuff before. Where did it come from?'" Like us, Ashley experienced **anxiety,** a general uneasiness and feeling of tension.

The relationship between anxiety, motivation, and achievement is curvilinear; some is good, but too much can be damaging (Cassady & Johnson, 2002). For example, some anxiety makes us study hard and develop competence. Relatively high anxiety improves performance on tasks where our expertise is well developed (Covington & Omelich, 1987). Too much anxiety, however, can decrease motivation and achievement. Its main source is fear of failure and, with it, the loss of self-worth (K. Hill & Wigfield, 1984). Low achievers are particularly vulnerable.

Information processing theory helps us understand the debilitating effects of anxiety (Cassady & Johnson, 2002). First, anxious students have difficulty concentrating, so they don't pay attention as well as they should. Second, because they worry about—and even expect—failure, they often misperceive the information they see and hear. Third, test-anxious students often use superficial learning strategies (e.g., memorizing definitions), instead of productive strategies (e.g., summarizing and self-questioning), which can lead to meaningful schemas that reduce the load on working memory. Research suggests that the primary problem with highly test-anxious students is that they don't learn the content very well in the first place, which further increases their anxiety when they're required to perform on tests (Wolf, Smith, & Birnbaum, 1997; Zeidner, 1998). Finally, during assessments, test-anxious students often waste working memory space on thoughts such as "I'll never get this," leaving less available for thinking about the task.

Instructional strategies that promote understanding—such as clear expectations, high-quality examples and student involvement, specific feedback on assessments, modeling effective learning strategies, and providing outside help—can do more than anything else to help students cope with anxiety. When understanding increases, poor performance decreases. In time, fear of failure and the anxiety it produces will also decrease.

As we did in our discussion of diversity in motivation to learn, we want to again emphasize that the descriptions of self-worth theory and learner anxiety represent general patterns, and individuals will vary. For instance, some students are comfortable in stating that they work hard for what they achieve, and their self-worth isn't diminished by that fact. As another example, some high achievers continue to experience anxiety in spite of a long history of success. In all cases, we want to remember that we teach individuals and not groups, and we want to treat our students in the same way.

Online Case Book

To assess a teacher's application of the different views of motivation in her classroom, go to the *Online Case Book* for Chapter 10 at *www.prenhall.com/ eggen.*

Instructional ⌂ Principles	**Accommodating Affective Factors in Motivation: Instructional Principles**

Students will always have concerns about self-worth and at times will be anxious. However, in addition to using strategies that promote understanding, applying the following principles can help you reduce the negative effects of these affective factors:

- Model effort attributions and personal improvement, and deemphasize competition and ability.
- Emphasize incremental rather than entity views of intelligence.
- Give students the opportunity to practice exercises similar to those they'll encounter on assessments.
- Assess frequently, announce all assessments, and give students ample time to complete assessment activities.

We saw these principles applied in Kathy's and Elaine's work with their students. When Kathy commented that the harder she worked the smarter she got, she linked effort to her increasing competence and simultaneously modeled a worth ethic and an incremental view of ability. Emphasizing that ability can be improved with effort can reduce

Anxiety. A general uneasiness and feeling of tension

the risk involved in trying but failing, because failure implies only that more effort or improved strategies are needed to increase competence. As with many aspects of working with students, this type of modeling and emphasis won't work magic, but it can make a difference in students' beliefs about their ability and self-worth.

Both Kathy and Elaine emphasized deep understanding, which is the most important factor in reducing anxiety. They both gave students opportunities to practice the understanding and skills they expected students to demonstrate on their assessments: Kathy allowed her students to revise their essays, and Elaine gave her students the chance to practice problems similar to those on the test ("We've been working hard, and your understanding is getting deeper and deeper"). And, Elaine gave a quiz every week, so she assessed frequently.

We've now discussed different theories of motivation and related research. In Chapter 11, we synthesize this body of knowledge into a classroom model designed to help teachers increase student motivation at all levels.

Checking Your Understanding

6.1 Explain why emphasizing and modeling incremental views of ability are important applications of self-worth theory.

6.2 The night before the final exam, one of your friends says, "I feel like partying. Let's go out for awhile. We can study when we get back." Using self-worth theory as a basis, explain why he might behave this way.

6.3 You have a highly test-anxious student in your class. She reports that she has been practicing relaxation exercises before she takes your tests, but they don't seem to be helping. Based on the information in this section, what is the most likely explanation for the ineffectiveness of these exercises?

To receive feedback for these questions, go to Appendix B.

Knowledge Extensions

To deepen your understanding of the topic in this section and integrate it with topics you've already studied, go to the *Knowledge Extensions* module for Chapter 10 at *www.prenhall.com/eggen*. Respond to questions 16–18.

Classroom Connections

Accommodating Affective Motivational Factors in Your Classroom.

1. Emphasize that self-worth is an outcome of effort, and that ability is incremental.

   - **Elementary:** When her second graders are successful on word problems during their seat work, a teacher comments "You're really understanding what we're doing. Your hard work is paying off, isn't it?"

   - **Middle School:** A life-science teacher comments, "You're really seeing the connections between these animals' body structures and their ability to adapt to their environments. I'm feeling good about the progress we're making, and I'm sure you're feeling good about yourselves."

   - **High School:** As students' understanding of balancing equations increases, a chemistry teacher comments, "You

   people are getting smarter all the time. You've really gotten good at this stuff."

2. To reduce anxiety, emphasize focusing attention on the content of tests, provide practice, and give students ample time to finish assessments.

   - **Elementary:** A second-grade teacher monitors his students as they work on a quiz. When he sees their attention wander, he reminds them to concentrate on their work.

   - **Middle School:** An eighth-grade algebra teacher gives her students extensive practice with the types of problems they'll be expected to solve on their tests.

   - **High School:** At the beginning of a unit test, a physics teacher suggests, "Go immediately to the first problem you're sure you know how to solve. Force any thoughts not related to physics out of your heads, and don't let them back in."

Meeting Your Learning Objectives

1. **Identify differences between extrinsic motivation, intrinsic motivation, and motivation to learn in classroom activities.**

   - Motivation is a force that energizes, sustains, and directs behavior toward a goal.
   - Extrinsic motivation refers to motivation to engage in an activity as a means to an end; intrinsic motivation is motivation to be involved in an activity for its own sake. Challenge, control, curiosity, fantasy, and aesthetic value all promote intrinsic motivation.
   - Learners can be high in both extrinsic and intrinsic motivation, low in both, or high in one and low in the other. Learners' motivation also depends on context, and their motivations can change over time.
   - Motivation to learn describes learners' tendencies to find academic activities worthwhile and to try to get the intended learning benefits from them, regardless of whether or not they find the activities intrinsically motivating.

2. **Describe criticisms of behavioral views of motivation, and explain how rewards can be used to increase motivation to learn.**

   - Behaviorism is criticized on philosophical grounds, with critics suggesting that schools should cultivate intrinsic motivation, and using rewards sends students the wrong message about learning.
   - Critics also cite research indicating that the use of rewards decreases interest in intrinsically motivating tasks.
   - Critics also point out that, because behaviorism treats motivation and learning as identical, behaviorism provides an incomplete explanation for motivation.
   - Reinforcers can increase intrinsic motivation if they communicate that competence is increasing.

3. **Explain the basic premise of humanistic views of motivation, and identify applications of humanistic motivation theory in classrooms.**

   - Humanistic views of motivation are grounded in the premise that people want to fulfill their total potential as human beings.
   - Because people's personal, social, and emotional needs precede their intellectual needs, humanistic views of motivation suggest that teachers treat students as people first and learners second.
   - Humanistic views of motivation encourage teachers to treat students with unconditional positive regard by separating their behaviors from their intrinsic worth.
   - Humanistic views of motivation encourage teachers to create safe and orderly classrooms where students believe they can learn and where they are expected to do so.

4. **Describe the basic assumption on which cognitive motivation theories are based, and analyze applications of these theories in events in and outside of classrooms.**

   - Cognitive theories of motivation focus on learners' beliefs, expectations, and needs for order and understanding. People's innate need to understand their experiences is at the core of cognitive motivational theories.
   - Expectancy × value theory suggests that motivation results from students' beliefs about their abilities to learn as well as the value they place on the learning task.
   - Helping students set and monitor challenging but attainable goals can increase their beliefs about their capabilities of accomplishing specific tasks.
   - Frequent assessment together with detailed feedback helps learners meet their needs to understand their performances, as described by attribution theory.

5. **Analyze applications of self-determination theory in classroom learning activities.**

   - According to self-determination theory, people have three innate needs: the need for competence, the need for autonomy, and the need for relatedness.
   - Accomplishing challenging tasks helps students meet their need for competence, which helps explain the intrinsically motivating effects of challenge.
   - Involving students, giving them choices, using assessments that emphasize learning, and providing detailed feedback all increase perceptions of autonomy.
   - A genuine commitment to student learning and holding students to high standards increases feelings of relatedness.

6. **Use self-worth theory and studies of arousal and anxiety to explain learner behavior.**

   - Self-worth theory is based on the premise that all people have an intrinsic desire to preserve their sense of self-worth, and self-worth is strongly linked to perceptions of high ability in our society. Some learners will engage in self-handicapping behaviors, such as procrastinating, blaming others, or making a point of not studying to protect their perceptions of high ability.
   - Modeling effort and communicating incremental views of intelligence can help overcome students' tendency to perceive effort as an indicator of low ability.
   - Research indicates that the primary problem for test-anxious students is that they lack understanding of the content. Clear expectations, high-quality examples, modeling effective strategies, and providing outside help can increase understanding, and with it, a decrease in failure, which reduces anxiety.

Developing as a **Professional**

Developing as a Professional: Praxis™ Practice

We saw in this chapter how Kathy Brewster applied an understanding of theories of motivation in her teaching. We turn now to a case study involving another world history teacher who is also teaching the Crusades. Read the case study, and then answer the questions that follow. As you read, compare this teacher's approach to Kathy Brewster's.

Damon Marcus watches as his students take their seats, and then announces, "Listen, everyone, I have your tests here from last Friday. Liora, Ivan, Lynn, and Segundo, super job on the test. They were the only As in the class."

After handing back the tests, Damon writes the following on the chalkboard:

A - 4   D - 4
B - 7   F - 3
C - 11

"You people down here better get moving," Damon comments, pointing to the Ds and Fs on the chalkboard. "This wasn't that hard a test. Remember, we have another one in 2 weeks. We need some improvement. C'mon, now. I know you can do better. Let's give these sharp ones with the As a run for their money.

"Now let's get going. We have a lot to cover today. . . . As you'll recall from yesterday, the Crusades were an attempt by the Christian powers of Western Europe to wrest control of the traditional holy lands of Christianity away from the Muslims. Now, when was the First Crusade?"

"About 1500, I think," Clifton volunteers.

"No, no," Damon shakes his head. "Remember that Columbus sailed in 1492, which was before 1500, so that doesn't make sense. . . . Liora?"

"It was about 1100, I think."

"Excellent, Liora. Now, remember, everyone, you need to know these dates, or otherwise you'll get confused. I know that learning dates and places isn't the most pleasant stuff, but you might as well get used to it because that's what history is about. Plus, they'll be on the next test."

He continues, "The First Crusade was in 1095, and it was called the 'People's Crusade.' There were actually seven in all, starting in 1095 and continuing until enthusiasm for them had ended in 1300.

"They weren't just religiously motivated," he goes on. "The Muslim world was getting stronger and stronger, and it was posing a threat to Europe. For example, it had control of much of northern Africa, had expanded into southern Spain, and even was moving into other parts of southern Europe. So it was an economic and military threat as well."

Damon continues presenting information about the Crusades, and then, seeing that about 20 minutes were left in the period, he says, "Now, I want you to write a summary of the Crusades that outlines the major people and events and tells why they were important. You should be able to finish by the end of the period, but if you don't, turn your papers in at the beginning of class tomorrow. You may use your notes. Go ahead and get started."

As he monitors students, he sees that Jeremy has written only a few words on his paper. "Are you having trouble getting started?" Damon asks quietly.

"Yeah, . . . I don't quite know how to get started," Jeremy mumbles.

"I know you have a tough time with written assignments. Let me help you," Damon nods.

He takes a blank piece of paper and starts writing as Jeremy watches. He writes several sentences on the paper and then says, "See how easy that was? That's the kind of thing I want you to do. Go ahead—that's a start. Keep that so you can see what I'm looking for. Go back to your desk, and give it another try."

PRAXIS These exercises are designed to help you prepare for the Praxis™ "Principles of Learning and Teaching" exam.

To receive feedback on your short-answer questions, go to the Companion Website at *www.prenhall.com/eggen*, then to the Practice for Praxis™ module for Chapter 10.

To acquire experience in preparing for the multiple-choice items on the Praxis™ exam, go to the *Self-Assessment Module* for Chapter 10 at *www.prenhall.com/eggen* and click on "Practice Quiz."

For additional connections between this text and the Praxis™ exam, go to Appendix A.

Short-Answer Questions

In answering these questions, use information from the chapter and link your responses to specific information in the case.

1. With respect to humanistic views of motivation, assess the extent to which Damon helped students meet the deficiency needs and contribute to the growth needs in Maslow's hierarchy.
2. With respect to expectancy × value theory, how effectively did Damon promote intrinsic interest in the topic?
3. Assess Damon's effectiveness in applying self-determination theory with his students.
4. Assess Damon's effectiveness in accommodating students' needs to preserve feelings of self-worth.

ONLINE PORTFOLIO ACTIVITIES

To develop your professional portfolio, further apply your understanding of chapter content, and address the INTASC standards, go to the Companion Website, then to the *Online Portfolio Activities* for Chapter 10. Complete the suggested activities.

Also on the Companion Website at *www.prenhall. com/eggen*, you can measure your understanding of chapter content with multiple-choice and essay questions, and broaden your knowledge base in *Exploring Further* and *Web Links* to other educational psychology websites.

IMPORTANT CONCEPTS

affective memories (p. 310)
anxiety (p. 329)
attribution theory (p. 317)
attributional statements (p. 321)
autonomy (p. 322)
cognitive theories of motivation (p. 307)
competence (p. 321)
cost (p. 310)
deficiency needs (p. 303)
entity view of intelligence (p. 313)
expectancy × value theory (p. 307)
extrinsic motivation (p. 299)
goal (p. 312)
growth needs (p. 303)
humanistic psychology (p. 303)
importance (p. 309)
incremental view of intelligence (p. 313)

intrinsic interest (p. 309)
intrinsic motivation (p. 299)
learned helplessness (p. 318)
learning goal (p. 312)
motivation (p. 298)
motivation to learn (p. 300)
performance-approach goals (p. 312)
performance-avoidance goals (p. 312)
performance goal (p. 312)
relatedness (p. 322)
self-determination (p. 321)
self-efficacy (p. 310)
self-schemas (p. 308)
self-worth (p. 328)
unconditional positive regard (p. 304)
utility value (p. 310)

CHAPTER 11

Motivation in the Classroom

Chapter Outline	Learning Objectives
	After completing your study of this chapter, you should be able to
Class Structure: Creating a Learning-Focused Environment	**1** Explain the differences between a learning-focused and a performance-focused classroom.
Self-Regulated Learners: Developing Student Responsibility Developing Self-Regulation: Applying Self-Determination Theory • Helping Students Develop Self-Regulation: Instructional Principles	**2** Describe strategies that teachers can use to develop learner self-regulation, and explain different levels of student self-regulation.
Teacher Characteristics: Personal Qualities That Increase Student Motivation to Learn Personal Teaching Efficacy: Beliefs About Teaching and Learning • Modeling and Enthusiasm: Communicating Genuine Interest • Caring: Meeting the Need for Belonging and Relatedness • Teacher Expectations: Increasing Perceptions of Competence • Demonstrating Personal Qualities That Increase Motivation: Instructional Principles	**3** Identify the personal characteristics of teachers who increase students' motivation to learn, and analyze these characteristics in classroom activities.
Climate Variables: Creating a Motivating Environment Order and Safety: Classrooms as Secure Places to Learn • Success: Developing Learner Self-Efficacy • Challenge: Increasing Perceptions of Competence and Self-Determination • Task Comprehension: Increasing Perceptions of Autonomy and Value • The TARGET Program: Applying Goal Theory in Classrooms	**4** Analyze teachers' behaviors using the climate variables as a basis, and describe the relationships between the climate variables and the categories in the TARGET model.
Instructional Variables: Developing Interest in Learning Activities Introductory Focus: Attracting Students' Attention • Personalization: Links to Students' Lives • Involvement: Increasing Intrinsic Motivation • Feedback: Meeting the Need to Understand • Applying the Climate and Instructional Variables in Your Classroom: Instructional Principles • Assessment and Learning: Using Feedback to Increase Interest and Self-Efficacy • Learning Contexts: Motivation to Learn in the Urban Classroom	**5** Identify examples of teachers implementing the instructional variables in learning activities.

Teachers' personal characteristics, the kinds of classroom environments they create, and the way they teach can have important influences on their students' motivation to learn. Consider the extent to which these factors are applied in the following case study:

DeVonne Lampkin, a fifth-grade teacher, wants her students to understand the essential characteristics of *arthropods*. After briefly reviewing other animal groups that the class has previously studied, she turns to the day's lesson.

"Today we are going to learn about arthropods, an important group of animals, and I want you to figure out their essential characteristics," she begins. She then reaches into a cooler and takes out a live lobster as the students squeal and "ooh" and "aah" at the wriggling animal.

DeVonne asks Stephanie to carry the lobster around the room so everyone can look at it closely, and replies, "Yes, you can touch it," in response to students' queries.

"Observe carefully," she encourages, "because I'm going to ask you to tell me what you see."

After everyone has a chance to touch the lobster, tap its shell, and wiggle its legs, DeVonne walks to the front of the room and asks, "Okay, who can tell me one thing that you noticed?"

"Hard," Tu observes.

"Pink and green," Saleina adds.

"Wet," Kevin puts in.

The students make a number of additional observations, DeVonne lists them on the board, and prompts the students to conclude that the lobster has a hard outer covering, which she labels an exoskeleton, three body parts, and segmented legs. She then circles them as the essential characteristics of arthropods.

Reaching into her bag again, DeVonne pulls out a cockroach. Amid more squeals, she walks around the class holding it with tweezers.

"Everyone knows what this is, don't you? We all do, because we live in the South. Now, I want to know, . . . can this be an arthropod? . . . Remember the characteristics. . . . Look carefully and tell me."

The students decide that it has three body parts and segmented legs but disagree on whether or not it has an exoskeleton.

"What happens when we step on one?" DeVonne asks.

"It crunches," Anthony answers after thinking for a few seconds.

"So, does it have a hard shell?"

When the class concludes that it does, DeVonne next takes a clam out of her cooler to provide an additional example. "Is this an arthropod?" she asks.

Some students say that it is, because of its hard shell.

With additional prompting from DeVonne, the students realize that it doesn't have three body parts. A.J. comments, "It doesn't have any legs," and students finally decide that it isn't an arthropod.

"Now," DeVonne asks, "Do you think Mrs. Sapp (the school principal) is an arthropod? . . . Tell us why or why not."

Amid more giggles, some of the students conclude that she is, because she has segmented legs. Others disagree because she doesn't look like a lobster or a roach. After some discussion, Tu observes, "She doesn't have an exoskeleton," and the class finally agrees that she is not an arthropod.

DeVonne then has the students form pairs and passes out whole shrimp for examination. She calms the excited students and asks them to observe the shrimp carefully and decide whether or not they are arthropods.

During the whole-group discussion that follows, DeVonne discovers that some of the students are still uncertain about the idea of an exoskeleton, so she directs them to peel the shrimp and feel the head and hard, outer covering. After seeing the peeled covering, they conclude that the shrimp does, indeed, have an exoskeleton.

Finally, DeVonne introduces insects, arachnids, and crustaceans as subcategories of arthropods, and she has the students classify additional examples into each subcategory.

To begin our discussion of motivation in the classroom, we want to consider two questions: Students' reactions in the case study suggest that their intrinsic interest in the lesson was high. (1) What, specifically, did DeVonne do that stimulated students' high intrinsic interest? (2) What characteristics of DeVonne, herself; her classroom;

and her instruction increased students' motivation to learn? We address these questions in this chapter.

CLASS STRUCTURE: CREATING A LEARNING-FOCUSED ENVIRONMENT

We begin to answer our questions by considering two types of classroom environments. A **learning-focused environment** emphasizes effort, continuous improvement, and understanding. It is very different from a **performance-focused environment,** which makes high grades, public displays of ability, and performance compared to others priorities (Covington, 2000; D. M. Ryan & Patrick, 2001).

DeVonne attempted to create a learning-focused environment for her students in at least three ways. She involved them in a high-interest activity to teach the concept *arthropod,* she emphasized understanding, and she promoted cooperation versus competition as they studied the topic. The differences in the two types of environments are summarized in Table 11.1 (Covington, 2000; Pintrich, 2000; Urdan, 2001).

Within this learning-oriented framework, this chapter describes a model for promoting student motivation that synthesizes and applies the theory and research you studied in Chapter 10 (Eggen & Kauchak, 2002). It is outlined in Figure 11.1 and has four major components:

1. Self-regulated learners: Developing student responsibility
2. Teacher characteristics: Personal qualities that increase student motivation
3. Climate variables: Creating a motivating environment
4. Instructional variables: Developing interest in learning activities

The components of the model are interdependent; a single variable cannot be effectively applied if the others are missing. Keep this in mind as you study the following sections.

Four *variables* exist within each *component,* and the variables are interdependent; a single variable cannot be effectively applied if the others are missing. Keep this in mind as you study the following sections.

Checking Your Understanding

1.1 Explain the differences between a learning-focused and performance-focused classroom.

1.2 A teacher says, "Excellent job on the last test, everyone. More than half the class got an A or a B." Based on descriptions of learning-focused versus performance-focused classrooms, how appropriate is this comment? Explain.

Learning-focused environment. A classroom environment that focuses on effort, continuous improvement, and understanding

Performance-focused environment. A classroom environment that emphasizes high grades, public displays of ability, and performance compared to others

Table 11.1 Comparisons of learning-focused and performance-focused classrooms

	Learning-Focused	Performance-Focused
Success defined as . . .	Mastery, improvement	High grades, doing better than others
Value placed on . . .	Effort, improvement	High grades, demonstration of high ability
Reasons for satisfaction . . .	Meeting challenges, hard work	Doing better than others, success with minimum effort
Teacher oriented toward . . .	Student learning	Student performance
View of errors . . .	A normal part of learning	A basis for concern and anxiety
Reasons for effort . . .	Increased understanding	High grades, doing better than others
Ability viewed as . . .	Incremental, alterable	An entity, fixed
Reasons for assessment . . .	Measure progress toward preset criteria, provide feedback	Determine grades, compare students to one another

Figure 11.1   A model for promoting student motivation

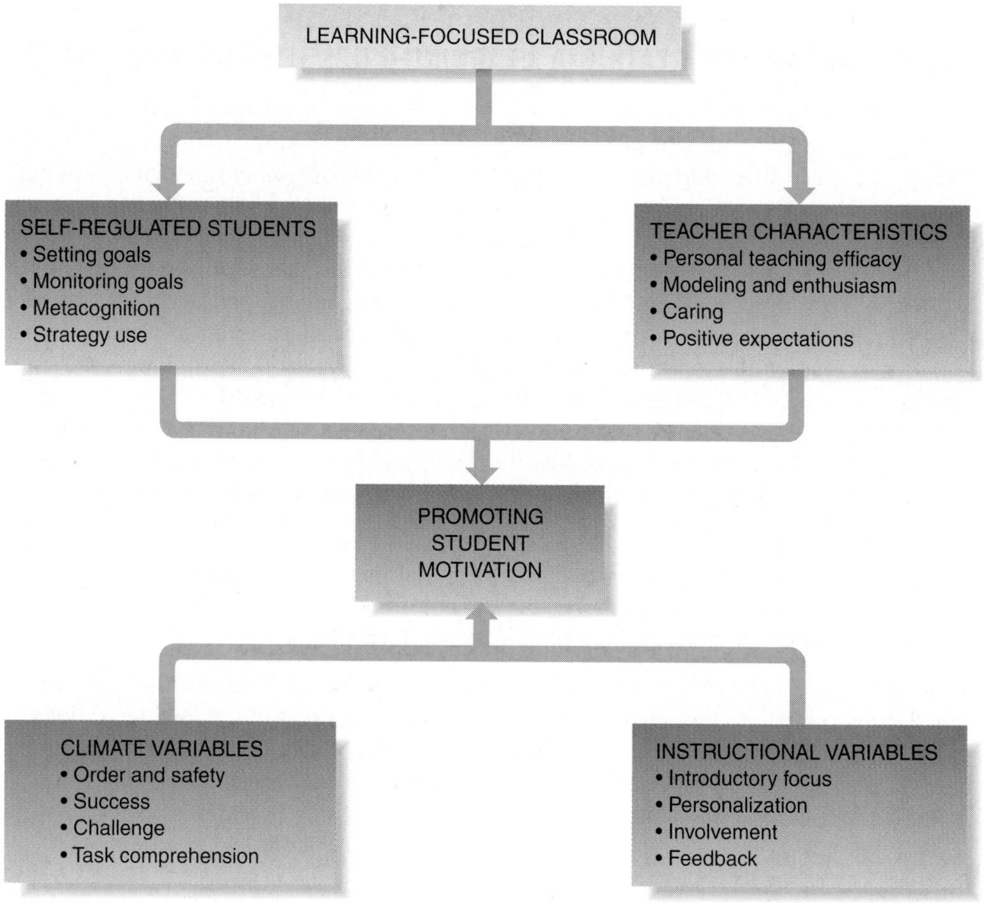

SELF-REGULATED LEARNERS: DEVELOPING STUDENT RESPONSIBILITY

Lack of student effort and responsibility is a common lament in many teachers' conversations (J. Cooper, Horn, Strahan, & Miller, 2003). All teachers want students to be responsible, and most emphasize it, but many are less successful than they would like to be:

> "My kids are so irresponsible," Kathy Hughes, a seventh-grade teacher grumbles in a conversation at lunch. "They don't bring their books, they forget their notebooks in their lockers, they come without pencils. . . . I can't get them to come to class prepared, let alone get them to read their assignments."
>
> "I know," Mercedes Blount, one of Kathy's colleagues, responds, smiling wryly. "Some of them are totally spacey, and others just don't seem to give a rip."

What can be done about this problem? While not easy to accomplish, the answer is the development of **self-regulation,** the process of setting personal goals, together with the thought processes and behaviors that lead to reaching the goals. As the definition suggests, self-regulation begins with students setting and monitoring goals (Schunk, 2005; Zimmerman, 2005). For goals to work, students must be committed to them, and they're most likely to be committed to goals they set themselves (Murphy & Alexander, 2000). This is an additional problem, because many students aren't inclined to set goals, and even if they are, they don't know what goals to set and how to set them. In the following sections, we look at ways to try to solve these problems.

Developing Self-Regulation: Applying Self-Determination Theory

How do we get students to set, commit to, and monitor goals? While the task is difficult, self-determination theory offers some suggestions. Though its focus is on intrinsic motivation, the theory acknowledges that initially not all behaviors are intrinsically motivated

Self-regulation. The process of setting personal goals, together with the thought processes and behaviors that lead to reaching the goals

(R. Ryan & Deci, 2000; Pintrich & Schunk, 2002). Learners pass through stages of extrinsic motivation as their self-determination increases. At the first stage, called *external regulation*, students attempt to meet goals to receive rewards and avoid punishers (R. Ryan & Deci, 2000). As their self-regulation develops, they gradually learn to become responsible for meeting their learning goals because, for example, they believe that meeting the goal is important for helping them get better grades. Although this behavior is still extrinsically motivated, it represents increasing self-regulation. As students develop further, they attempt to meet the goals because doing so is consistent with their developing self-schemas. For instance, if a student monitors goal achievement because she begins to view herself as a responsible person, she has made further progress toward self-determination.

Eventually (and ideally) learners set and monitor goals for their own sake, which is behavior that is intrinsically motivated and self-determined (Pintrich & Schunk, 2002). In the real world, many students never reach this point; however, for those who do, the probability of long-term achievement and success are greatly enhanced. As a teacher, you play a crucial role in helping self-determination develop.

 **Instructional Principles** | **Helping Students Develop Self-Regulation: Instructional Principles**

Because self-regulation is developmental, you need to initially scaffold students' efforts and then gradually turn more responsibility over to them (C. M. Bohn, Roehrig, & Pressley, 2004). The following principles can help guide you in this process:

1. Emphasize the relationship between accepting responsibility and learning.
2. Solicit student input in the process of establishing class procedures that include student responsibility.
3. Help students understand responsibility by treating it as a concept and by linking consequences to actions.
4. Model responsibility and a learning focus, and guide students as they initially set goals.
5. Provide concrete mechanisms to help students monitor and assess goal achievement.

Let's see how the principles for helping students develop self-regulation guide Sam Cook, a seventh-grade geography teacher, as he works with his students.

Sam begins the first day of school by saying, "Welcome to Carver Middle School. I'm looking forward to a very good year, and I'm sure you are, too." He has the students introduce themselves, and then he asks, "Now, why are we here, in this class and in school?"

The students sit silently for a few seconds, not sure where Sam is headed.

Finally, Dana responds hesitantly, "To learn . . . about geography."

"Exactly!" Sam responds. "That's why we go to school—to learn. The more we learn, the smarter we get, and the smarter we get, the better off we are. . . . And, to learn as much as possible, we need to work together. I need to help you, and you need to help yourselves.

For instance, I need to think about what we're trying to accomplish, and I need to bring the examples that will help you understand our topics. . . . That's my part.

"So, what is your part? . . . What do you need to be thinking about, and what do you need to bring to class every day to be sure you learn as much as possible?"

With some guidance from Sam, students conclude that they should bring their books, binders with paper, and pencils to class each day. They also agree that they need to be in their seats when the bell rings, and they need to conscientiously do their homework so they understand it instead of merely getting it done.

"Now, who is responsible for all this?" Sam asks.

"We are," several students respond simultaneously.

"Yes. . . . I'm responsible for my part, and you're responsible for your parts."

"Now, let's think about this," Sam continues. "Let's see what happens when people aren't responsible."

Teachers can help students develop self-regulation by involving them in setting classroom rules and by emphasizing individual responsibility.

He then displays the following on the overhead:

Josh always brings all his materials to school, and he carefully does his homework. He has a list that he checks off to be sure that he has each of the items and that he has done and understands his homework. If he's uncertain about any part, he asks the next day.

Josh is doing well in school. He likes his classes, says they're interesting, and he's learning a lot. His teachers respect his conscientiousness.

Andy is often in trouble with his teachers because he often forgets to bring his book, notebook, or pencil to class. He sometimes forgets his homework in his locker, so he doesn't get credit for the assignment. Andy's homeroom teacher called his mom to discuss his irresponsibility, and now Andy can't watch TV for a week.

Andy is struggling in his classes. He says he's bored and doesn't feel like he's learning very much.

"What are some differences you notice between Josh and Andy?" Sam asks after giving the students a minute to read the vignettes.

The students make several comments, and in the process Ronise concludes, "It's his own fault," in response to someone pointing out that Andy isn't learning as much as Josh.

"Those are all good comments, and yours is particularly important," Sam smiles, nodding to Ronise. "If we don't take responsibility for ourselves, and we don't study, whose fault is it if we don't learn?"

"Our own," several students respond.

"Yes," Sam emphasizes. "We're all responsible for ourselves."

Sam suggests that students set some goals that will help them take responsibility for their own learning. With his guidance, they offer some ideas, he writes them on the board, and the next day, he distributes a monitoring sheet (see Figure 11.2), which he has prepared based on the class discussion. He also suggests that they put the sheet in the front of their notebooks and check off the items the first thing each morning. As the sheets accumulate, the students have a "responsibility portfolio" that gives them a record of their progress.

Sam then asks students how they will determine whether or not they understand their homework, and after some discussion, they agree that they will either explain it in class or to their parents.

Finally, they agree that students who get 18 or more checks for the responsibility goals and 8 or more for the learning goals during the week will have free time on Fridays, during which they can bring snacks and play games. Those achieving fewer than 15 checks on the responsibility goals will spend "quiet time" alone during that period, and those who receive fewer than 8 checks for the learning goals will spend time with Sam working on areas that need improvement.

Now, let's examine Sam's efforts to apply the principles for helping his students develop self-regulation. First, he emphasized from the beginning of the year that they were there to learn and that accepting responsibility was necessary if they were to learn as

Figure 11.2   Monitoring sheet

Week of _____		Name_____			
Responsibility Goals	**Monday**	**Tuesday**	**Wednesday**	**Thursday**	**Friday**
Bring sharpened pencil	✓	✓			
Bring notebook					
Bring textbook					
In seat when bell rings					
Learning Goals	**Monday**	**Tuesday**	**Wednesday**	**Thursday**	**Friday**
Finish homework					
Understand homework					

much as possible. This applied the first principle (emphasize the relationship between accepting responsibility and learning) and began the process of establishing a learning-focused environment.

He applied the second principle by soliciting students' input into the class procedures. Being asked for input contributes to students' feelings of autonomy, a basic need according to self-determination theory (R. Ryan & Deci, 2000). It also increases the likelihood that students will commit to the goals they create.

Third, Sam treated responsibility as a concept and illustrated it with an example and a nonexample. Students sometimes fail to take responsibility because they don't clearly understand what responsibility is and the relationship between their actions and the consequences of those actions. By using examples to illustrate the consequences of behaving responsibly versus irresponsibly, Sam used an informational rather than a controlling strategy for promoting self-regulation. As you saw in Chapter 10, this strategy can contribute to intrinsic motivation (Charles & Senter, 2005; Emmer & Stough, 2001).

In saying, "I need to think about what we're trying to accomplish, and I need to bring the examples that will help you understand our topics. . . . That's my part," he personally modeled responsibility and a learning focus and applied the fourth principle. He further applied the principle by guiding students as they set goals, and by making the goals specific and immediate, and, for Sam's students, moderately challenging.

Finally, in applying the fifth principle, Sam prepared a concrete structure (the sheet) to help students monitor their goals. As his students accumulate checks on their monitoring sheets, they are likely to feel a sense of self-efficacy, even though the process is as basic as bringing required materials to class. Gradually, they may increasingly accept responsibility for following these procedures and also learn to make decisions that will increase their own learning. This marks progress on the path to self-regulation.

Sam's students were initially at the level of external regulation as described by self-determination theory; they wanted to meet goals to receive rewards—free time—and avoid punishers—quiet time alone during the free period. As self-regulation develops, his students hopefully will begin setting their own goals because they see that setting and monitoring goals increase learning (R. Ryan & Deci, 2000).

The preceding example focused on middle school students, but self-regulation can also be a goal for young children. To account for developmental level, the process must be adapted. The case study on page 379 of Chapter 12 describes how Martha Oakes taught her first graders to put away their worksheets. Martha incorporated several of the principles we saw Sam use. She taught the procedure as a concept, she modeled it, and she expected her students to accept responsibility for following it. And Martha believed that her first graders could make productive contributions in classroom meetings. These are all part of the development of self-regulation.

Checking Your Understanding

2.1 Describe strategies that teachers can use to increase learner self-regulation, and explain how Sam Cook implemented these strategies with his students.

2.2 Sam's students were at the *external regulation* stage with respect to the development of self-regulation. Explain why we would describe them as being externally regulated. Offer an example that would illustrate a move toward greater self-regulation (and ultimately self-determination).

2.3 We said in this section that, by using examples to illustrate behaving responsibly versus irresponsibly, Sam used an *informational* rather than a *controlling* strategy for promoting self-regulation. Explain how the two approaches are different using information from the case study.

To receive feedback for these questions go to Appendix B.

Knowledge Extensions

To deepen your understanding of the topics in this section of the chapter and to integrate them with topics you've already studied, go to the *Knowledge Extensions* module for Chapter 11 at *www.prenhall.com/eggen*. Respond to questions 1–3.

Classroom Connections

Promoting Self-Regulation in Your Classroom

Promote learner responsibility with goal setting, self-monitoring, and metacognition.

- **Elementary:** A fourth-grade teacher presents a "problem of the week" each Monday in math. The students set the goal of solving the problem, and when they've completed the solution, they put it in their math portfolios and put a check on the first page of the portfolio. When they've explained it to a parent, other adult, or sibling, they make a second check on the sheet. They then discuss solutions on Fridays.

- **Middle School:** A seventh-grade history teacher provides a study guide for her students. The students set the goal of answering and understanding all the study guide questions each week. They check off each question when they've answered and believe they understand it.

- **High School:** Physics students set the goal of creating one real-world application of each of the topics they study. When they believe they have a good application, they offer it to the class for analysis and discussion.

TEACHER CHARACTERISTICS: PERSONAL QUALITIES THAT INCREASE STUDENT MOTIVATION TO LEARN

That teachers make a difference in student learning is a theme of this text, and it is true for motivation as well. Teachers create learning environments, implement instruction, and establish learning-oriented or performance-oriented classrooms. None of the other components of the model are effective if the teacher characteristics are lacking. They are highlighted in Figure 11.3.

Figure 11.3   Teacher characteristics in the model for promoting student motivation

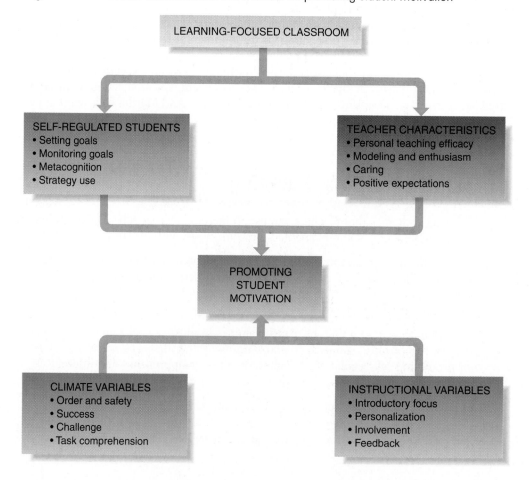

Personal Teaching Efficacy: Beliefs About Teaching and Learning

In Chapter 10, we saw that self-efficacy is individuals' beliefs about their capability of accomplishing specific tasks. **Personal teaching efficacy,** a teacher's belief that he or she can get all students to succeed and learn regardless of their prior knowledge or ability, is an extension of this concept (Bruning et al., 2004; Langer, 2000).

Teachers who are high in personal teaching efficacy take responsibility for the success or failure of their own instruction (V. Lee, 2000). They are fair but demanding. They maximize the time available for instruction, praise students for their increasing competence, avoid the use of rewards to control behavior, and persevere with low achievers (Roeser, Marachi, & Gehlbach, 2002). Low-efficacy teachers, in contrast, are more likely to blame low achievement on lack of intelligence, poor home environments, uncooperative administrators, or other external causes. They have lower expectations, spend less time on learning activities, "give up"

Enthusiastic teachers increase motivation by sharing their interest in the subjects they teach.

on low achievers, and are more critical when students fail (Brouwers & Tomic, 2001; Henson, Kogan, & Vacha-Haase, 2001). Low-efficacy teachers are also more controlling and value student autonomy less than do high-efficacy teachers (Henson et al., 2001).

Not surprisingly, students taught by high-efficacy teachers learn more and are more motivated than those taught by teachers with lower efficacy (Tschannen-Moran, Woolfolk-Hoy, & Hoy, 1998). In addition, low personal teaching efficacy contributes to negative teacher emotions, stress, and teacher burnout.

The entire student body benefits from a **high-collective-efficacy school,** one in which most of the teachers are high in personal teaching efficacy (Goddard, 2001; Goddard, Hoy & Woolfolk-Hoy, 2000). Such schools are particularly notable for the positive effects they have on the achievement levels of students from diverse backgrounds. From Chapter 4, you saw that the correlation between low socioeconomic status (SES) and low achievement is well documented (Macionis, 2006). In high-collective-efficacy schools, however, low-SES students have achievement gains nearly as high as those of high-SES students from low-collective-efficacy schools (V. Lee, 2000). Also, differences in achievement gains among low-, middle-, and high-SES students are smaller when collective school efficacy is high (V. Lee, 2000). In other words, such schools help reduce achievement differences between groups who typically benefit differently from schooling.

What can you do to promote collective efficacy? The best you can do is to remain positive when colleagues are cynical or pessimistic, and you can remind your fellow teachers of the research that confirms how important teachers are in promoting motivation to learn for all students.

Modeling and Enthusiasm: Communicating Genuine Interest

Teachers communicate their beliefs about teaching and learning in the ways that they act. Increasing student motivation to learn is virtually impossible if teachers model distaste or lack of interest in the topics they teach with statements such as, "I know this stuff is boring, but we have to learn it," "I know that proofs aren't all that much fun," or "This isn't my favorite topic, either."

In contrast, students will be more motivated to learn even routine and seemingly mundane topics if teachers model their own interest in them. For example, when a geography teacher says, "Geography has an enormous impact on our lives. For example, New York, Chicago, and San Francisco didn't become major cities for no reason. Their success is related to their geography," or, when an English teacher shows a well-written and an error-filled paragraph and comments, "Look how much better an impression this one makes on the reader," their genuine interest can increase students' motivation to learn. Unlike pep talks, theatrics, or efforts to entertain students, genuine interest can induce in students the

Personal teaching efficacy. A teacher's belief that he or she can get all students to succeed and learn regardless of their prior knowledge or ability

High-collective-efficacy school. A school where most of the teachers are high in personal teaching efficacy

Teachers demonstrate caring by their willingness to spend time interacting with their students.

feeling that the information is valuable and worth learning (Brophy, 2004; Good & Brophy, 2003). Research indicates that students with enthusiastic teachers achieve higher than those with less-enthusiastic teachers and have perceptions of greater autonomy and self-efficacy (B. C. Patrick, Hisley, & Kempler, 2000).

Teachers can also influence student motivation by modeling effort attributions and incremental views of intelligence. A teacher who says, "The harder I study, the smarter I get," communicates that effort is desirable and leads to higher ability. In doing so, he or she is increasing the likelihood that students will imitate these beliefs in their own thinking (Bruning et al., 2004).

Caring: Meeting the Need for Belonging and Relatedness

- A first-grade teacher greets each of her children every morning with a hug or a "high five."
- A fifth-grade teacher immediately calls or e-mails parents if one of his students fails to turn in a homework assignment or misses more than two days of school in a row.
- An algebra teacher learns the name of each student in all five of her classes by the end of the first week of school, and she stays in her room during her lunch hour to help students who are struggling.

Each of these teachers demonstrates **caring,** which refers to a teacher's empathy and investment in the protection and development of young people (Noddings, 2001). Caring teachers help meet a student's need for belonging, a need preceded only by safety in Maslow's hierarchy, and relatedness, which is innate according to self-determination theory (Maslow 1968, 1970). The importance of caring is captured in this comment by a fourth grader: "If a teacher doesn't care about you, it affects your mind. You feel like you're a nobody, and it makes you want to drop out of school" (Noblit, Rogers, & McCadden, 1995, p. 683).

Research supports this perception. In one study, researchers reported "lower intrinsic motivation in students who experienced their teachers as cold and uncaring" (R. Ryan & Deci, 2000, p. 71). Additional research indicates that students are more engaged in classroom activities when they perceive their teachers as liking them and being responsive to their needs (Osterman, 2000).

Communicating Caring

How do teachers communicate that they care about their students? Some ways include the following (Alder, 2002; Osterman, 2000; Wilder, 2000):

- Learn students' names quickly, and call on students by their first name.
- Greet them pleasantly, and get to know them as individuals.
- Make eye contact, smile, lean toward them when talking, and demonstrate relaxed body language.
- Use "we" and "our" in reference to class activities and assignments.
- Spend time with students.
- Demonstrate respect for students as individuals.

The last two items on the list deserve special emphasis. We all have 24 hours in our days—no more, no less—and the way we choose to allocate our time is the truest measure of our priorities. Choosing to allocate some of our time to an individual student communicates caring better than any other single factor. Helping students who have problems with an assignment or calling a parent after school hours communicates that teachers care about student learning. Spending personal time to ask a question about a baby brother or compliment a new hairstyle communicates caring about a student as a human being.

Showing respect is also essential. Teachers can show respect in a variety of ways, but maintaining standards is one of the most important:

> One of the best ways to show respect for students is to hold them to high standards—by not accepting sloppy, thoughtless, or incomplete work, by pressing them to clarify vague comments, by encouraging them not to give up, and by not praising work that does not reflect genuine effort. Ironically, reactions that are often intended to protect students' self-esteem—such as accepting low quality work—convey a lack of interest, patience, or caring. (Stipek, 2002, p. 157)

Caring. Teachers' ability to empathize with and invest in the protection and development of young people

This view is corroborated by research. When junior high students were asked, "How do you know when a teacher cares about you?" they responded that paying attention to them as human beings was important, but more striking was their belief that teachers who care are committed to their learning and hold them to high standards (B. L. Wilson & Corbett, 2001).

Respect, of course, is a two-way street. Teachers should model respect for students, and in turn they have the right to expect students to respect them and one another. "Treat everyone with respect" is a rule that should be universally enforced. An occasional minor incident of rudeness can be overlooked, but teachers should clearly communicate that chronic disrespect will not be tolerated.

Teacher Expectations: Increasing Perceptions of Competence

Positive expectations is the last of the four teacher characteristics in our model for promoting student motivation (Figure 11.3).

> Teacher expectations about students' learning can have profound implications for what students actually learn. Expectations affect the content and pace of the curriculum, the organization of instruction, evaluation, instructional interactions with individual students, and many subtle and not-so-subtle behaviors that affect students' own expectations for learning and thus their behavior. (Stipek, 2002, p. 210)

To increase student motivation to learn, teachers must strive to make all students feel competent, another innate need according to self-determination theory. Unfortunately, teachers' expectations for students can lead them—usually inadvertently—to say and do things that instead communicate a perception of incompetence (R. Weinstein, 2002).

In some cases, these actions are directed to the entire class. For example, compare the following two comments:

> "This is a new idea, and it will be challenging, but if you work hard I know you can get it. Start right in while the ideas are still fresh in your mind. I'll be coming around, so if you have any questions, just raise your hand."

> "This material is hard, but we've got to learn it. Some of you will probably have trouble with this, and I'll be around as soon as I can to straighten things out. No messing around until I get there."

The first teacher acknowledged that the assignment was difficult but communicated confidence in the students' competence by saying that she expected them to be successful. The second suggested that they were not competent: "Some of you will probably have trouble with this." These seemingly innocuous comments can strongly affect students' motivation to learn.

More often, teachers' expectations more directly affect individual students. Specifically, they treat students they perceive to be high achievers differently from those they perceive as low achievers (R. Weinstein, 2002). This differential treatment typically takes four different forms (Good, 1987a, 1987b; Good & Brophy, 2003):

- *Emotional support*: Teachers interact more with perceived high achievers; their interactions are more positive; they make more eye contact, stand closer, and orient their bodies more directly toward the students; and they seat these students closer to the front of the class.
- *Teacher effort and demands*: Teachers give perceived high achievers more thorough explanations, their instruction is more enthusiastic, they ask more follow-up questions, and they require more complete and accurate student answers.
- *Questioning:* Teachers call on perceived high achievers more often, they allow the students more time to answer, and they provide more encouragement and prompt perceived high achievers more often.
- *Feedback and evaluation:* Teachers praise perceived high achievers more and criticize them less. They offer perceived high achievers more complete and lengthier feedback and more conceptual evaluations.

Teachers communicate high learner expectations through interactive teaching strategies that involve all students.

Differential treatment influences learners' beliefs and expectations for success. In fact, teachers' expectations for a student—either high or low—can become a **self-fulfilling prophecy,** a phenomenon that occurs when a person's performance results from and confirms beliefs about his or her capabilities (R. Weinstein, 2002). We can explain this with self-efficacy theory. Communicating positive expectations suggests to students that they will be successful. When they are, their self-efficacy increases, and a positive relationship between motivation and achievement is created. The reverse can also occur. Communicating low expectations can lead children to confirm predictions about their abilities by exerting less effort and ultimately performing less well.

Children of all ages are aware of the different expectations teachers hold for students (Stipek, 2002). In one study, researchers concluded, "After ten seconds of seeing and/or hearing a teacher, even very young students could detect whether the teacher talked about or to an excellent or a weak student and could determine the extent to which that student was loved by the teacher" (Babad, Bernieri, & Rosenthal, 1991, p. 230).

One of our goals in writing this section is to make you aware of the influence of expectations on motivation and achievement. Expectations are usually unconscious, and teachers often don't realize that they have different expectations for their students. With awareness and effort, they are more likely to maintain appropriately high expectations for all students. The experience of Elaine Lawless, a first-grade teacher, is an example. When she began calling on her students as equally as possible, she saw immediate benefits: "Joseph made my day. He said to one of the other kids, 'Put your hand down. Mrs. Lawless calls on all of us. She thinks we're all smart'" (Elaine Lawless, personal communication, February 19, 2002).

Instructional Principles   **Demonstrating Personal Qualities That Increase Motivation: Instructional Principles**

Personal qualities that promote motivation to learn can be demonstrated in a number of ways. The following principles can guide you in your efforts:

1. Strive to believe in your capability to get all students to learn.
2. Maintain appropriately high expectations for all students.
3. Model responsibility, effort, and interest in the topics you're teaching.
4. Demonstrate caring and commitment to your students' learning by spending time outside of class with them.

Let's see how the principles for demonstrating personal qualities that increase motivation to learn guide DeVonne as she continues to work with her fifth graders.

"Wow, you're here early," Karla Utley, another teacher in the school, says to DeVonne at 7:15 one morning. "We don't have to be here for another 45 minutes."

"I've got some kids coming in," DeVonne replies. "I did a writing lesson yesterday, and we evaluated some of their paragraphs as a whole class." (DeVonne's writing lesson is the case study at the end of this chapter.) "Several of the kids, like Tu and Saleina, did really well . . . but some of the others are behind. So, Justin, Picey, and Rosa are coming in before school this morning, and we're going to practice some more. They aren't my highest achievers, but I know I can get more out of them than I am right now. They're good kids; they're just a little behind. . . . Particularly Rosa. She's only been in the States for a year, and she didn't speak a word of English when she came. She's already made tons of progress."

At 7:30 DeVonne is waiting as Justin, Picey, and Rosa come in the door. She smiles at them and says, "We're going to practice a little more on our writing. I know that you can all be good writers. It's the same thing for me. I've practiced and practiced and practiced, and now I'm good at it. You can do the same thing. . . . Let's look at your paragraphs again."

She displays Justin's paragraph on the overhead again (his was one of the papers evaluated in class the day before) and asks, "What did we suggest that you might do to improve this?"

Self-fulfilling prophecy. A phenomenon that occurs when a person's performance results from and confirms beliefs about his or her capabilities

"He needs to stay on either the boy or the house," Rosa offers.

"Good," DeVonne nods. "Staying focused on your topic sentence is important."

Together, the group looks at each of the students' original paragraphs and makes specific suggestions for improvement.

DeVonne then says, "Okay, now each of you rewrite your paragraphs based on our suggestions. When we're finished, we'll look at them again."

The three students rewrite their paragraphs, and the four of them again discuss their products.

"Much improvement," DeVonne says after they've finished. "If we keep at it, we're going to get there. . . . I'll see you again tomorrow at 7:30."

Now, let's look at DeVonne's efforts to apply the principles for demonstrating personal qualities that increase motivation. In saying to Karla, "I know I can get more out of them than I am right now," and "They're good kids," she applied the first principle (strive to believe in your capability to get all students to learn). Her comments indicate that she believes in herself and her capability of getting all her students to learn.

In commenting, "They aren't my highest achievers, but I know I can get more out of them than I am right now. They're good kids; they're just a little behind," she also communicated positive expectations and applied the second principle (maintain appropriately high expectations for all students). Her comment indicates that she expects all students to learn, not just high achievers like Tu, Saleina, and some of the others.

As she worked with the small group, she applied the third principle by modeling responsibility and effort, "I have practiced and practiced and practiced, and now I'm good at it. You can do the same thing. . . . Let's look at your paragraphs again."

Finally, and perhaps most significantly, DeVonne demonstrated caring and commitment by arriving at school 45 minutes early to devote her time to helping students who needed extra support. She kept the study session upbeat and encouraging and displayed the respect for the students that is essential for promoting motivation to learn.

We said at the beginning of the chapter that the elements of the model for promoting student motivation (Figure 11.3) are interdependent, and we see this interdependence in DeVonne's work with her students. For example, they tried to meet her expectations because they believed she cared about them and their learning, and she modeled her own interest in what they were doing. If students don't believe teachers are committed to their learning, having high expectations can actually be counterproductive because they perceive the expectations as unfair. Similarly, it is virtually impossible to hold students to high standards if teachers don't model interest in the topics they're teaching. One or two characteristics alone aren't enough. Teachers need to display all the personal characteristics to impact students' motivation to learn.

Checking Your Understanding

3.1 Identify the personal characteristics of teachers who increase students' motivation to learn.

3.2 Research indicates that high-efficacy teachers adopt new curriculum materials and change strategies more readily than do ones who are low-efficacy (Roeser et al., 2002). Using the characteristics of personal teaching efficacy as a basis, explain why this is likely to be the case.

3.3 Based on the information in this section, what is the most effective way to communicate your enthusiasm to students? Explain.

3.4 Explain why not being called on by a teacher communicates to students that the teacher has low expectations for them.

To receive feedback for these questions, go to Appendix B.

Knowledge Extensions

To deepen your understanding of the topics in this section of the chapter and to integrate them with topics you've already studied, go to the *Knowledge Extensions* module for Chapter 11 at *www.prenhall.com/eggen*. Respond to questions 4–8.

Classroom Connections

Demonstrating Personal Characteristics in the Model for Promoting Student Motivation in Your Classroom

Caring

1. Show students you care by showing respect and giving them your personal time.
   - **Elementary:** A first-grade teacher greets each of her students every day as they come into the classroom. She makes it a point to talk to each of the students about something personal several times a week.
   - **Middle School:** A geography teacher calls parents as soon as he sees a student having even minor academic or personal problems. He solicits parents' help in monitoring the student and offers his assistance in solving problems.
   - **High School:** An Algebra II teacher conducts help sessions after school three nights a week. Students are invited to attend to get help with homework or to discuss any other personal concerns about the class or school.

Modeling and Enthusiasm

2. Model interest in the topics you're teaching.
   - **Elementary:** During individual reading time, a fourth-grade teacher comments on a book she's interested in and also reads while the students are reading.

   - **Middle School:** A life science teacher brings science-related clippings from the local newspaper to class and asks students to do the same. He discusses them and pins them on a bulletin board for students to read.
   - **High School:** A world history teacher frequently describes connections between classroom topics and their impact on today's world.

Positive Expectations

3. Maintain appropriately high expectations for all students.
   - **Elementary:** A second-grade teacher makes a conscious attempt to call on all her students equally and asks high-level questions whenever possible.
   - **Middle School:** When his students complain about word problems, a seventh-grade pre-algebra teacher reminds them of how important the problems are and tells them that the only way to become good at solving the problems is to practice. Each day, he guides a detailed discussion of at least two challenging word problems.
   - **High School:** When her American history students turn in sloppily written essays, the teacher displays a well-written example on the overhead and then requires a second, higher quality product. She continues this process throughout the year.

CLIMATE VARIABLES: CREATING A MOTIVATING ENVIRONMENT

As students spend time in classrooms, they sense whether or not the classroom is a safe and nurturant place to learn. These feelings reflect the classroom climate. In a **positive classroom climate,** the teacher and students work together as a community of learners, to help everyone achieve as much as possible (Palincsar, 1998; Rogoff, 1998). The goal is to promote students' feelings of safety and security, together with a sense of success, challenge, and understanding (see Figure 11.4).

Let's see how teachers can create a positive classroom climate.

Order and Safety: Classrooms as Secure Places to Learn

Order and safety is a climate variable that creates a predictable learning environment and supports learner autonomy together with a sense of physical and emotional security. It is grounded in Piaget's (1970, 1977) work (see Chapter 2) and self-determination theory. A predictable environment helps meet students' needs for equilibrium, by making classrooms orderly and understandable.

Autonomy, an innate need according to self-determination theory (R. Ryan & Deci, 2000), is supported by sharing authority with students in making classroom decisions. Some examples of shared authority include soliciting student input into classroom rules and procedures and encouraging students to set and monitor their own learning goals. It can also include giving students choices in selecting the order and kinds of learning activities and establishing due dates for assignments when appropriate.

The need for a safe learning environment that promotes a sense of physical and emotional security can also be explained with humanistic views of motivation, additional aspects of self-determination theory, and information processing. For instance, safety is a deficiency need preceded only by survival in Maslow's (1970) hierarchy. Also, being in a safe classroom environment allows students to meet their needs for relatedness, a second innate need according to self-determination theory (Deci & Ryan, 2000). Finally, information processing theory suggests that fearful students' working memories can become

Positive classroom climate. A classroom environment where the teacher and students work together as a community of learners to help everyone achieve as much as possible

Order and safety. A climate variable intended to create a predictable learning environment that supports learner autonomy and a sense of physical and emotional security

Figure 11.4 Climate variables in the model for promoting student motivation

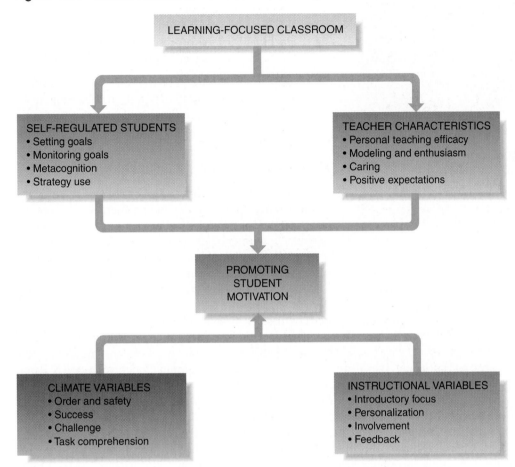

clogged with thoughts of being criticized or ridiculed, leaving less space to devote to academic tasks. The American Psychological Association Board of Educational Affairs (1995) believes emotional safety is so important that it is specifically addressed in its *Learner-Centered Psychological Principles.*

Teachers set the tone for this essential variable by modeling respect and courtesy and expecting students to treat each other and the teacher the same way in return (Barth, 2002; Blum, 2005).

Success: Developing Learner Self-Efficacy

Once the teacher has established a safe and orderly environment, student success becomes the most important climate variable. The need for success is fundamental according to expectancy × value theory (see Chapter 10) (Schunk, 2004; Wigfield & Eccles, 2000).

Success doesn't simply mean getting high scores on tests or other assignments, however. As we saw in our discussion of *learning-focused environments* at the beginning of the chapter, success means learning progress and mastery of tasks, not high grades and doing better than others. Praise and other rewards should communicate that personal competence is increasing. Mistakes don't mean that students aren't successful; rather, they're a normal part of the learning process.

Teachers can help promote success in several ways:

- Beginning lessons with open-ended questions that assess learners' current understanding and invite participation
- Using a variety of high-quality examples and representations that develop background knowledge and promote understanding
- Developing lessons with questioning together with prompting students when they have difficulty answering

Exploring Further

To read about the American Psychological Association's principles, go to the "APA's Learner-Centered Principles" in the *Exploring Further* module of Chapter 11 at *www.prenhall.com/eggen.*

Teachers promote self-efficacy through challenging activities that students can complete successfully.

- Providing scaffolded practice before putting students on their own
- Making assessment an integral part of the teaching–learning process, and providing detailed feedback about learning progress

However, success, even with continuous progress, won't increase motivation to learn if the learning tasks aren't challenging. Let's examine this idea.

Challenge: Increasing Perceptions of Competence and Self-Determination

Success, alone, doesn't increase perceptions of self-efficacy and competence; these also depend on characteristics of the learning task (Dolezal, Welsh, Pressley, & Vincent, 2003). For instance, with enough rehearsal, students can succeed in memorizing a list of meaningless facts. This success, however, does little to increase perceptions of competence. Only when learners succeed on tasks they perceive as challenging will perceptions of competence develop.

A long line of theory and research confirms the need for challenge. As you saw in Chapter 10, it is one characteristic of intrinsically motivating activities, and self-determination theory helps us understand why. Succeeding on challenging tasks helps meet students' needs for competence and autonomy, which are innate according to self-determination theory (Deci & Ryan, 2000). Feelings of competence and autonomy can then lead to increased effort and persistence. This helps us understand why, for example, children persevere in learning to ride a bicycle, even though they fall repeatedly, and why they lose interest in a skill after it has been mastered.

Teachers capitalize on the motivating features of challenge by encouraging students to identify relationships in the topics they study and the implications these relationships have for new learning (Brophy, 2004; B. Taylor, Pearson, Peterson, & Rodriguez, 2003). Limiting discussions to isolated, meaningless facts has the opposite effect. When students complain about the difficulty of their tasks, effective teachers don't decrease the challenge; they provide scaffolding to ensure that students can meet it.

Task Comprehension: Increasing Perceptions of Autonomy and Value

As with success, a challenging task won't increase motivation to learn if students don't perceive it as meaningful and worth understanding (Vavilis & Vavilis, 2004). For instance, an American Government teacher gives this reading assignment:

> Read Chapter 17 carefully, because . . . it will represent about 50% of the next unit test. In particular, the *Declaration of Independence* is a key document that you should know "cold." . . . Let's begin by considering the important facts. First, who was the most important person involved in drafting the *Declaration of Independence?* (Good & Brophy, 2003, p. 208)

In comparison, the teacher in a different class says,

> Before beginning our discussion of the *Declaration of Independence* . . . I want to raise four questions to provide some structure. . . . (1) What is a protest? (2) Under what circumstances is it appropriate? (3) Think about the rights and privileges that you have in school and the constraints that apply here. If you were to write a constitution for this school, what are three important points that you would include? (4) To what extent do you think that your view of a good government for this school is shared by other students? (Good & Brophy, 2003, pp. 208–209)

How is this message different from the one sent by the first teacher?

These differences lead to **task comprehension,** which is learners' awareness of what they are supposed to be learning and an understanding of why the task is important and worthwhile (Eggen & Kauchak, 2002). Task comprehension also includes decisions about time allocated to tasks, pace of instruction, and provisions for extra help if needed.

The first teacher above communicated that the reason we study the *Declaration of Independence* is to perform well on the unit test and that understanding depends on know-

Task comprehension. Learners' awareness of what they are supposed to be learning and an understanding of why the task is important and worthwhile

ing facts, such as who the most important person was in drafting it. In comparison, the second teacher suggested that we study the *Declaration of Independence* because it helps us understand protests in general, why they occur, and when they may be appropriate. He also implied that this would help students better understand their own rights and privileges in school. The task in the second example is more likely to increase task comprehension and motivation to learn.

The need for task comprehension can be explained with both expectancy × value theory and self-determination theory. First, it contributes to perceptions of utility value, the belief that understanding is useful for meeting future goals, which is a factor that increases task value according to expectancy × value theory (Wigfield & Eccles, 2000). Second, understanding what they're learning and why they're learning it increases students' feelings of autonomy, an innate need according to self-determination theory.

As with teacher characteristics, climate variables are interdependent. A challenging assignment can be motivating, for example, if students feel safe. If they're worried about the consequences of making mistakes, the motivating effects of challenge are lost. Similarly, if students don't understand the point in an activity or if expectations aren't clear, neither success nor challenge will increase motivation to learn. And each of the climate variables depends on the extent to which teachers care about students and hold them to high standards.

The TARGET Program: Applying Goal Theory in Classrooms

Carol Ames (1990, 1992) developed a program grounded in goal theory that is consistent with the climate variables in the model for promoting student motivation. TARGET is the program acronym, and it refers to *task, authority, recognition, grouping, evaluation,* and *time.* In Chapter 10 we saw that classroom environments in which learning goals are emphasized result in higher levels of motivation to learn than do other approaches, such as performance goals, some social goals, and work-avoidance goals. TARGET is grounded in research on family structures that influence students' motivation to learn in the home, and it has been expanded to applications in schools. Table 11.2, on page 352, outlines the TARGET categories and the related variables in the model for promoting student motivation.

Checking Your Understanding

4.1 "I try to keep my assignments basic," an urban seventh-grade life science teacher comments. "So, in one activity, I give them a drawing of a skeleton, and they can look up the names in their books. They need to succeed, and they do succeed on this activity." Analyze this teacher's approach for promoting her students' motivation to learn. Explain using the climate variables in the model for promoting student motivation as a basis for your explanation. Also, assess the approach based on the TARGET categories.

4.2 "I have an inviolable rule in my classroom management system," a middle school teacher comments. "They may make no sarcastic or demeaning comments of any kind when one of their classmates is trying to answer a question. I explained why this is so important, and they agreed. They slip now and then, but mostly they're quite good."

Which two climate variables in the model for promoting student motivation is this teacher attempting to address? Explain.

4.3 Look at Table 11.2. Describe specifically how each of the variables identified in the table relates to the corresponding TARGET category. For example, explain how *challenge* and *task comprehension* relate to the TARGET category *task.* Then, describe the relationship for each of the other TARGET categories and variables in the model for promoting student motivation.

To receive feedback for these questions, go to Appendix B.

Knowledge Extensions

To deepen your understanding of the topics in this section of the chapter and to integrate them with topics you've already studied, go to the *Knowledge Extensions* module for Chapter 11 at *www.prenhall.com/eggen.* Respond to questions 9–12.

Table 11.2 The TARGET Program for Motivation and related variables in the Model for Promoting Student Motivation

TARGET Category	Description	Related Variable(s) in the Model for Promoting Student Motivation
Task	Tasks are designed to be optimally challenging, so that students see their relevance and meaning.	Challenge Task comprehension
Authority	Authority is shared, and student autonomy is supported.	Order and safety
Recognition	Recognition is provided for all students who make learning progress.	Success
Grouping	Grouping is designed to foster a "community of learners."	Classroom climate variables
Evaluation	Evaluation is used to promote learning.	Success
Time	Time encompasses the workload, pace of instruction, and the amount allocated for completing work.	Task comprehension

---

Classroom Connections

Applying the Climate Variables

Order and Safety

1. Create a safe and orderly learning environment.
   - **Elementary:** A second-grade teacher establishes and practices daily routines until they're predictable and automatic for students.
   - **Middle School:** An eighth-grade American history teacher leads a discussion examining the kind of environment the students want to work in. They conclude that all "digs" and discourteous remarks should be forbidden. The teacher consistently enforces the agreement.
   - **High School:** An English teacher reminds her students that all relevant comments about a topic are welcome, and she models acceptance of every idea. She requires students to listen courteously when a classmate is talking.

Success and Challenge

2. Help students succeed on challenging tasks.
   - **Elementary:** A fifth-grade teacher comments, "We're really getting good at percentages. Now I have a problem that is going to make us all think. It will be tough, but I know that we'll be able to do it." After students attempt the solution, he guides a discussion of the problem and ways to solve it.
   - **Middle School:** A sixth-grade English teacher has the class practice three or four homework exercises as a whole group each day and discusses them before students begin to work independently.
   - **High School:** As she returns their homework, a physics teacher gives her students worked solutions to the most frequently missed problems. She has students put the homework and the worked examples in their portfolios to study for the biweekly quizzes.

Task Comprehension

3. Carefully describe rationales for your assignments.
   - **Elementary:** As he gives students their daily math homework, a third-grade teacher says, "We know that understanding math is really important, so that's why we practice word problems every day."
   - **Middle School:** A seventh-grade English teacher carefully describes her assignments and due dates and writes them on the board. Each time, she explains why the assignment is important.
   - **High School:** A biology teacher displays the following on an overhead: *We don't just study flatworms because we're interested in flatworms. As we look at how they've adapted to their environments, we'll get additional insights into ourselves.* He then says, "We'll repeatedly look at this idea to remind ourselves why we study each organism."

INSTRUCTIONAL VARIABLES: DEVELOPING INTEREST IN LEARNING ACTIVITIES

Teacher and climate variables form a general framework for motivation. Within this context, teachers can do much through their learning activities to enhance motivation to learn. From an instructional perspective, a motivated student is someone who is actively engaged in the learning process (Brophy, 2004; Stipek, 2002). To promote this engagement, we must initially capture—and then maintain—students' attention throughout a learning activity. Ways to help us meet this goal are outlined in Figure 11.5.

Figure 11.5 Instructional variables in the model for promoting student motivation

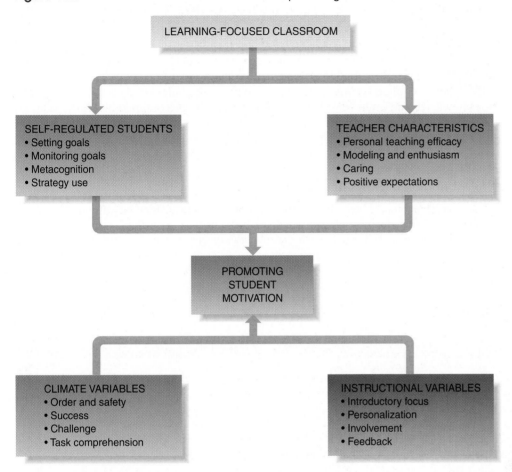

LEARNING-FOCUSED CLASSROOM

SELF-REGULATED STUDENTS
• Setting goals
• Monitoring goals
• Metacognition
• Strategy use

TEACHER CHARACTERISTICS
• Personal teaching efficacy
• Modeling and enthusiasm
• Caring
• Positive expectations

PROMOTING STUDENT MOTIVATION

CLIMATE VARIABLES
• Order and safety
• Success
• Challenge
• Task comprehension

INSTRUCTIONAL VARIABLES
• Introductory focus
• Personalization
• Involvement
• Feedback

Introductory focus. A lesson beginning that attracts attention and provides a conceptual framework for the lesson

Introductory Focus: Attracting Students' Attention

To begin this section, think about the way DeVonne began her lesson on arthropods: She brought out a whole lobster for students to see and touch. The squeals and "oohs" and "aahs" clearly indicated that she had attracted their attention. Let's look at a couple more examples.

> As an introduction to studying cities and their locations, Marissa Allen, a social studies teacher, hands out a map of a fictitious island. On it are physical features such as lakes, rivers, and mountains. Information about altitude, rainfall, and average seasonal temperature is also included. Marissa begins, "Our class has just been sent to this island to settle it. We have this information about its climate and physical features. Where should we make our first settlement?"
>
> Darrell Keen, a science teacher, passes a baseball and a golf ball around the room and has the students hold them. After the students confirm that the baseball feels heavier, he climbs onto his desk and holds the two balls in front of him. As he prepares to drop them, he says, "I'm going to drop these balls at the same time. What do you predict will happen?"

By beginning their lessons in these ways, these teachers were attempting to increase interest by creating **introductory focus,** a lesson beginning that attracts attention and provides a conceptual framework for the lesson (Marzano, 2003). Introductory focus attempts to capitalize on the effects of curiosity and novelty, which are characteristics of intrinsically motivating activities (Brophy, 2004).

Teachers can increase curiosity with unique problems, such as Marissa's fictitious island task; by asking paradoxical questions ("If Rome was such a powerful and advanced civilization, why did it fall apart?"); by using

Effective teachers use introductory focus to draw students into their lesson.

demonstrations with seemingly contradictory results (the two balls that Darrell planned to drop will hit the floor at the same time); or with eye-catching examples, such as De-Vonne's lobster.

Research indicates that teachers seldom use effective lesson introductions; when teachers do use introductions, they are usually short and fail to draw students into the lesson (Brophy, 2004). Providing for effective introductory focus need not be difficult, however. All that is required is conscious effort to connect the content of the lesson to students' prior knowledge and interests. Some additional examples are outlined in Table 11.3.

Once learners are attending and the teacher has provided a conceptual framework, the lesson has to maintain their attention and provide information about learning progress. *Personalization, involvement,* and *feedback* can help meet this goal.

Personalization: Links to Students' Lives

Sue Crompton, a second-grade math teacher, introduces the topic of graphing by measuring her students' height. She continues by giving them a length of construction paper that represents their height. Each student places their strip of paper on the appropriate spot on a graph that corresponds to their height. After discussing the results, she does a similar activity with hair color to reinforce the idea of graphing.

Table 11.3 Tools and techniques for providing introductory focus

Tool/Technique	Example
Problems and questions	• A literature teacher shows a picture of Ernest Hemingway and says, "Here we see 'Papa' in all his splendor. He seemed to have everything—fame, adventure, romance. Yet he took his own life. Why would this happen?" • A science teacher asks the students to explain why two pieces of paper come together at the bottom (rather than move apart) when students blow between them. • An educational psychology instructor introducing social cognitive theory displays the following vignette: *You're driving 75 mph on the interstate—with a posted speed limit of 65—when another car blazes past you. A minute later, you see the car stopped by the highway patrol. You immediately slow down. How would behaviorism explain your slowing down?*
Inductive sequences	• An English teacher displays the following: *I had a ton of homework last night! I was upset because I had a date with the most gorgeous girl in the world! I guess it was okay, because she had on the ugliest outfit ever!* The students find a pattern in the examples and develop the concept *hyperbole.* • An educational psychology instructor begins a discussion of development with these questions: Are you bothered when something doesn't make sense? Do you want the world to be predictable? Are you more comfortable in classes when the instructor specifies the requirements, schedules the classes, and outlines the grading practices? Does your life in general follow patterns more than random experiences? The class looks at the pattern and arrives at the concept of *equilibrium.*
Concrete examples	• An elementary teacher begins a unit on amphibians by bringing in a live frog. • A geography teacher draws lines on a beach ball to demonstrate that longitude lines intersect at the poles and latitude lines are parallel to each other. • An educational psychology instructor introduces the concept *negative reinforcement* by describing his inclination to take a pain killer to reduce his discomfort after a demanding workout.
Objectives and rationales	• A math teacher begins, "Today we want to learn about unit pricing. This will help us decide which product is a better buy. It will help us all save money and be better consumers." • A world history teacher says, "Today we're going to look at the concept of *mercantilism.* It will help us understand why, throughout history, Europe came to the New World and went into South Asia and Africa." • An educational psychology instructor says, "We know that learners construct, rather than record, understanding. Today we want to see what that principle suggests about the way we should teach most effectively."

As another example, Chris Emery, a science teacher, begins a unit on genetics by saying, "Reanne, what color are your eyes?"

"Blue," Reanne responds.

"And how about yours, Eddie?"

"Green."

"Interesting," Chris smiles. "When we're done with this unit, we'll be able to figure out why Reanne's are blue and Eddie's are green, and a whole bunch of other things related to the way we are."

Sue and Chris both attempted to increase their students' interest through **personalization** (Bruning et al., 2004), the process of using intellectually and/or emotionally relevant examples to illustrate a topic.

Personalization is a valuable motivation strategy for several reasons (Strong, Silver, Perini, & Tuculescu, 2003; Wortham, 2004). First, it is intuitively sensible and widely applicable. A survey of experienced teachers described it as one of the most important ways to promote student interest in learning activities (Zahorik, 1996), and additional research supports Zahorik's findings (Schraw & Lehman, 2001). Second, students feel a sense of autonomy when they study topics in which they're interested (Iyengar & Lepper, 1999), and third, as we saw in our examples, personalized content is meaningful because it encourages students to connect new information to structures already in long-term memory (Moreno & Mayer, 2000). Finally, according to expectancy × value theory, personalization is one way of increasing learners' intrinsic interest in a topic.

Personalization creates links between students' lives and the content they are learning.

Teachers in several of the case studies you've already studied in this book used personalization in an attempt to increase their students' motivation to learn. The teachers and the way they personalized their topics are outlined in Table 11.4.

Involvement: Increasing Intrinsic Motivation

Introductory focus and personalization pull students into lessons, but unless the topic is intriguing or timely, neither is likely to sustain interest. One key to maintaining motivation to learn is **involvement,** the extent to which students are actively participating in a learning activity.

Think about your experience at lunch with friends or a party. When you're talking and actively listening, you pay more attention to the conversation than you do when you're on its fringes. The same applies in classrooms. Deliberate teacher efforts to promote involvement result in increased interest and learning (Hidi, 2002; Schraw & Lehman, 2001).

As you saw in Chapter 7, being actively involved is essential for meaningful learning, and as students' understanding develops, their perceptions of competence and autonomy both increase (Bruning et al., 2004). Some educational leaders suggest that putting students in active roles is one way to personalize instruction (Schraw & Lehman, 2001).

Personalization. The process of using intellectually and/or emotionally relevant examples to illustrate a topic

Involvement. The extent to which students are actively participating in a learning activity

Table 11.4 Teachers' attempts to personalize topics

Teacher and Chapter	Attempt at Personalization
Karen Johnson (Chapter 2)	Used the population density of students' state and the density of window screens to illustrate the concept *density.*
Diane Smith (Chapter 4)	Used differences in the lengths of students' pencils and differences in students' hair color to illustrate comparative and superlative adjectives.
Mike Sheppard (Chapter 5)	Used distances from the students' hometown to neighboring towns as the basis for word problems in math.
Laura Hunter (Chapter 9)	Used finding the area of the classroom as a basis for developing skills in finding the areas of irregularly shaped figures.
Suzanne Brush (Chapter 9)	Used students' favorite flavor of jelly beans, their modes of transportation to school, and the cost of pizzas at local restaurants as a basis for a lesson on bar graphing.
Kathy Brewster (Chapter 10)	Used the class's "crusade" to prevent extracurricular activities from being eliminated at the school as an analogy for the Crusades in history.

Let's look at two specific strategies for increasing student involvement: open-ended questioning and hands-on activities.

Using Open-Ended Questioning to Promote Involvement

Questioning is the most generally applicable tool teachers have for maintaining involvement. Students' attention is high when they're being asked questions but drops during teacher monologues. Although we discuss questioning in detail in Chapter 13, we introduce open-ended questioning here because it is particularly effective for promoting involvement (Eggen & Kauchak, 2006). **Open-ended questions** are questions for which a variety of answers are acceptable.

One type of open-ended question asks students to make observations. For instance, DeVonne asked her students to examine the lobster:

> *DeVonne:* Okay, who can tell me one thing that you noticed?
> *Tu:* Hard.
> *Saleina:* Pink and green.
> *Kevin:* Wet.

Virtually any answer to her question would have been acceptable. As another example, a teacher in a lesson on Shakespeare's *Julius Caesar* might ask:

> "What has happened so far in the play?"
> "What are some of the major events?"
> "What is one thing you remember about the play?"

Like DeVonne's question, these are easy to answer, activate prior knowledge, and draw students into the lesson.

A second type of open-ended question asks for comparisons. For instance, a teacher in a lesson on amphibians and reptiles might ask the following questions:

> "How is a frog similar to a lizard?"
> "How are the frog and a toad similar to or different from each other?"
> In the lesson on Julius Caesar, the teacher might ask:
> "How are Brutus and Marc Antony similar? How are they different?"
> "How does the setting for Act I compare with that for Act II?"

Because many answers are acceptable, open-ended questions are safe and ensure success—two of the climate variables we discussed earlier. By combining safety and success, a teacher can encourage even the most reluctant student to respond without risk or fear of embarrassment. Also, because they can be asked and answered quickly, open-ended questions can help involve all the students in a class during a single lesson. A final advantage of open-ended questions is that they provide teachers with unique insights into students' thinking, allowing them to build on students' prior knowledge (Powell & Caseau, 2004).

Using Hands-On Activities to Promote Involvement

Hands-on activities are another way of promoting involvement and student interest (Zahorik, 1996). For example, when students are working with manipulatives in math, concrete materials in science, maps and globes in geography, or computers in language arts, their level of interest increases significantly. The level of involvement in DeVonne's lesson, for example, was at its highest when her groups worked with the shrimp. In addition, hands-on activities add variety to learning activities, which increases learner interest (Zahorik, 1996).

Additional strategies for promoting involvement and interest are outlined in Table 11.5.

Improvement drills add an element of gamelike novelty to otherwise routine activities, and personal improvement increases self-efficacy. Having students use chalkboards in individual work spaces is similar to having them solve problems on paper at their desks, but the chalkboards allow sharing and discussion, and students often will use them to attempt problems they wouldn't try on paper.

Group work, in which students work together toward common learning goals, can also increase involvement (D. W. Johnson & Johnson, 2006; Marzano, 2003). Group work provides opportunities for students to interact and compare their ideas with others. All the teachers in the cognitive learning chapters—David Shelton and Sue Southam in Chapter 7, Jenny Newhall and Scott Sowell in Chapter 8, and Laura Hunter and

Open-ended questions. Questions for which a variety of answers are acceptable

Table 11.5 Strategies for promoting involvement

Technique	Example
Improvement drills	Students are given a list of 10 multiplication facts on a sheet. Students are scored on speed and accuracy, and points are given for individual improvement.
Games	The class is divided equally according to ability, and the two groups respond in a game format to teacher questions.
Individual work spaces	Students are given their own chalkboards on which they solve math problems and identify examples of concepts. They hold the chalkboards up when they've solved the problem or when they think an example illustrates a concept. They also write or draw their own examples on the chalkboards.
Student group work	Student pairs observe a science demonstration and write down as many observations of it as they can.

Suzanne Brush in Chapter 9—used group work to promote involvement and interest. We also saw that DeVonne used group work when she had students examine the shrimp.

Feedback: Meeting the Need to Understand

As you saw in Chapter 7, the need for feedback is a principle of learning. Because learners construct their own understanding, they require feedback to determine the extent to which their constructions are valid.

The need for feedback is also supported by cognitive motivation theory. For instance, feedback indicating that competence is increasing contributes to self-efficacy and self-determination. In addition, feedback helps us meet our need to understand why we perform the way we do, which attribution theory considers a basic need.

Feedback also contributes to self-regulation. It gives us information about progress toward goals, and when they're met, our self-efficacy increases. If they're not met, we can then increase our effort or change strategies.

The type of feedback is important. When it provides information about learning progress, motivation increases. On the other hand, feedback that involves social comparisons or has a performance orientation can detract from motivation to learn (Brophy, 2004; Pintrich & Schunk, 2002). Performance-oriented feedback has a particularly detrimental effect on less-able students and detracts from intrinsic motivation for both low and high achievers.

Instructional ⌂ **Principles**

Applying the Climate and Instructional Variables in Your Classroom: Instructional Principles

Throughout the chapter, we've emphasized that the variables in our model for promoting student motivation are interdependent. This is particularly true for the climate and instructional variables. The following principles can help you capitalize on this interdependence as you attempt to apply the model in your classroom:

1. Establish rules and procedures that maintain a safe, orderly learning environment.
2. Attempt to link topics to students' personal lives.
3. Describe the reasons for studying particular topics, and provide evidence for increasing competence.
4. Establish and maintain high levels of student involvement in learning activities.
5. Provide specific and detailed feedback on student work.

Let's see how these principles guide David Crawford, a world history teacher at Baker County High School, as he works with his students.

As the bell rings to start the period, the students are in their seats and have their notebooks on their desks. David moves to the front of the room and begins, "Okay, everyone, let's think about some of the technology that we have in today's world. Go ahead. . . . Brenda?"

"Computers."

"Sure. . . . What else?"

"Cell phones," Mayte offers.

"Cars," Erin adds.

"Electricity," Darrell adds.

"All good examples," David nods. "Now, we tend to think of technology as something recent, but in fact it's existed throughout history, and we can tell a great deal about a people or civilization by looking at the technology artifacts from that civilization.

After clarifying the term *artifact,* he then says, "Today we're going to examine some artifacts to see what they might tell us about the people who left them behind. Being able to make these kinds of conclusions will give us the thinking tools to understand each of the civilizations we study as we look at the history of the world."

David reaches into a box, pulls out two animal skulls, a piece of coarsely woven fabric, and two stone spear points that are ground to fine edges, and puts them on the table at the front of the room. Then, he puts two other stone spear points that are also sharp but chipped, several pieces of charcoal, three small animal bones, and a fragment from an animal skin on the table next to the first group.

"We'll call this Civilization A, and this one Civilization B," David says, pointing to the first set of materials and then to the second set.

The class observes the artifacts and with David's guidance concludes that the two skulls are from a cow and a sheep and the bones are leg and rib bones from an antelope.

"Now," David continues energetically, "We're going to be sophisticated archeological teams, and we found these two sites," pointing to the materials on the table. "I want you to work with your partners and write down as many conclusions as you can about the people from each, and any comparisons between the two, such as which one you believe was more advanced. In each case, provide evidence for the conclusions you make. . . . You have 5 minutes."

The students begin, and David moves around the room as they work. He reads the students' conclusions and periodically asks "How do you know that?" or "What does that tell you?"

At the end of their allotted time, David says, "Okay, let's begin. . . . What did you come up with?"

"We think those are newer," Lori says, pointing at the chipped spear points.

"No way," Rodney interjects.

"Rod," David says firmly, "remember that we can disagree all we want, but we extend the courtesy of letting other people finish, and we always listen to what they have to say."

"Sorry."

"Go ahead, Lori."

"The points are sharp, and they're sort of like art."

"Okay, Rod, go ahead," David says after Lori finishes.

"Those look like they're ground," Rodney responds, pointing to the spear points with the fine edges. "And I think grinding would be a more advanced technology than chipping."

The class continues discussing the artifacts, and from the cow and sheep skulls and the coarse cloth, students conclude that Civilization A had domesticated animals and the ability to weave. And, they decide that the antelope bones and animal skin indicate that Civilization B probably consisted of hunter-gatherers who did not yet weave cloth.

After completing the discussion, David says, "Okay, for tonight, I want you to read about the Old, Middle, and New Stone Ages on pages 35 to 44 of your books and decide what ages these artifacts probably belonged to. . . . You did a great job today. You made some excellent conclusions and provided good evidence for them. . . . Turn in your papers, the period is nearly over."

Now, let's look at David's attempts to apply the principles for the climate and instructional variables in the model for promoting student motivation in his lesson. First, his classroom was orderly and safe. For instance, all the students were in their desks with their notebooks out when the bell rang, indicating a well-established routine. In addition, David's admonishing Rodney for interrupting Lori suggests that a student feeling safe enough to offer comments without fear of embarrassment was a high priority in his class. These were all applications of the first principle.

He attempted to *personalize* the activity and apply the second principle by beginning the lesson with examples of today's technology and by placing students in the role of archeologists.

Then, in displaying the artifacts and saying "Being able to make these kinds of conclusions will give us the thinking tools to better understand each of the civilizations we study, . . . " he provided a rationale for the activity and capitalized on *introductory focus* and *task comprehension*. Also, he challenged students to make conclusions and support them with evidence, which is the essence of critical thinking. Their increased ability to think critically contributed to their perceptions of competence, and his comment, "You did a great job today. You made some excellent conclusions and provided good evidence for them," provided further evidence of their increasing competence. Each of these factors helped apply the third principle.

Finally, David's students were highly involved in the lesson, and success was enhanced because the task—making conclusions—was open-ended and challenging. Any conclusion that the students could support was acceptable.

This brings us to the topic of assessment, feedback, and motivation to learn—the fifth principle.

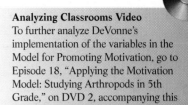

Analyzing Classrooms Video
To further analyze DeVonne's implementation of the variables in the Model for Promoting Motivation, go to Episode 18, "Applying the Motivation Model: Studying Arthropods in 5th Grade," on DVD 2, accompanying this text.

Assessment and Learning: Using Feedback to Increase Interest and Self-Efficacy

To examine the role of assessment and its influence on learning and motivation, let's look at David's work with his students the day after his lesson.

> The next day, David begins by saying, "One of our goals for yesterday and throughout the year is to be able to provide evidence for the conclusions we make. . . . You did a good job on this, but we need a little more practice in some cases. . . . I'm going to display the conclusions and evidence that some of you offered. . . . Now, remember the spirit we're doing this in. It's strictly for the sake of learning and improvement. It's not intended to criticize any of you.
>
> "I've put what you wrote on transparencies, so you all can remain anonymous. . . . Let's take a look at what three groups wrote," and he then displays the following:

Conclusion:	*The people had cloth.*
Evidence:	*There is cloth in Civilization A.*
Conclusion:	*The people in Civilization A made their own clothes, but those in B wore animal skins.*
Evidence:	*There is a piece of cloth in A and an animal skin in B.*
Conclusion:	*The people in Civilization A were more likely to survive.*
Evidence:	*They had cows and sheep, so they didn't have to find wild animals. The cloth piece suggests that they wove cloth, so they didn't have to use animal skins.*

> "What comments can you make about the three sets of conclusions?"
>
> "The first one isn't really a conclusion," Shantae offers. "You can see the cloth, so it really doesn't say anything."
>
> "Good observation, Shantae. . . . Yes, a conclusion is a statement based on a fact; it isn't the fact itself."
>
> The class then discusses the second and third examples and agrees that the conclusions are based on evidence.
>
> "This is the kind of thing we're looking for," David comments. "I know that you're all capable of this kind of thinking, so let's see it in your next writing sample."
>
> He then brings out a can of soup and asks students to make some conclusions about the civilization that might have produced such an artifact and to give evidence that supports each conclusion.
>
> The class, beginning to understand the process, makes a number of comments, and David writes the students' conclusions and evidence on the board.

Exploring Further
High-stakes testing has become a fact of teachers' lives. To examine researchers' assessments of its impact on motivation, go to "High-Stakes Testing and Student Motivation to Learn" in the *Exploring Further* module of Chapter 11 at *www.prenhall.com/eggen*.

Detailed feedback that results from assessment is essential for learning. Some of David's students had little experience in making and defending conclusions. Collecting and reading their papers was a form of assessment, and without the assessment combined with feedback, they were unlikely to understand the difference between good and poor conclusions. Likewise, language arts students won't construct an understanding of what makes a good essay without having their work assessed and being provided feedback on that work. And, math students won't learn to solve problems if their efforts aren't assessed and they don't receive feedback on their progress.

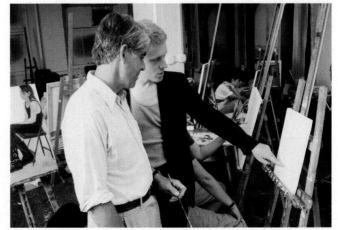

Assessment with feedback is an essential component of classroom motivation.

Feedback is also important for motivation to learn because it helps students improve the quality of their work. As they see that the quality actually is increasing, their perceptions of competence, self-determination, and intrinsic motivation also increase. None of this is possible without ongoing assessment and feedback based on that assessment.

Learning Contexts: Motivation to Learn in the Urban Classroom

One of the areas in which urban contexts play a particularly prominent role is in student motivation to learn. Motivation has been and continues to be one of the thorniest problems urban teachers face (Rubinson, 2004). While the causes are complex, three patterns emerge: (1) the impersonal nature of many urban schools, (2), the emphasis placed on control, and (3) the consistently low expectations teachers have for urban students.

Because urban schools tend to be large, teachers often have difficulty establishing the personal connections with students that helps meet students' needs for relatedness (Rubison, 2004), a basic component of intrinsic motivation according to self-determination theory (R. Ryan & Deci, 2000). The tendency of many urban teachers to view their jobs as primarily to deliver content instead of focusing on students' personal, social, and emotional needs, as well as intellectual needs, contributes to this problem (Charner-Laird et al., 2004).

The impersonal nature of urban environments is further exacerbated by teachers' tendencies to emphasize control and student discipline to a greater degree than in other learning environments (Rimm-Kaufman & Sawyer, 2004; L. Weiner, 2002). Though promoting acceptable student behavior is a basic component of safety and order, many urban teachers approach it from the perspective of external control rather than internal student self-regulation (Charner-Laird et al., 2004; L. Weiner, 2002).

And, perhaps most pernicious of the three, consistently low expectations for student achievement is prominent (Ferguson, 2003; Landsman, 2004). Academic focus tends to be on low-level, routine tasks (L. Weiner, 2002), and students spend a disproportionate amount of time completing worksheets and written exercises (Manouchehri, 2004). Over time, these factors can have a strong impact on students' beliefs. "Children treated with low regard come to believe it and often fulfill low expectations" (Rubinson, 2004, p. 59).

These factors, coupled with the personal and social challenges that urban students commonly face, result in disengagement from school (Honora, 2003; Rubinson, 2004). "African American students and students enrolled in urban school settings are particularly vulnerable to an emotional detachment from school" (Honora, 2003, p. 59).

While easy solutions to these problems don't exist, research provides some information.

The Impact of Teachers

While teachers influence motivation and learning for all students, their role is even more essential in urban environments. "When we pressed students to explain why they regarded a particular experience in a positive or negative light, they laid the praise or blame at teachers' feet. Being a hero or a scapegoat was an unavoidable part of being a teacher in these inner-city schools" (B. L. Wilson & Corbett, 2001, p. 32). This leads to the following question: *What factors that are under teachers' control can influence urban students' motivation to learn?* The following variables in the model for promoting student motivation are particularly prominent:

- Caring
- Order and safety
- Involvement
- Challenge

Caring. We emphasized the need for caring teachers in our discussion of urban environments in earlier chapters, and it is particularly important for promoting urban students' motivation to learn (T. Howard, 2001; Noddings, 2001). In an urban environment, caring is most strongly demonstrated in teachers' perseverance, helpfulness, and commitment to student learning (G. L. Gordon, 1999). Let's see what urban students, themselves, have to say.

I like the ones that don't allow excuses. . . . I need to have someone to tell me when I'm tired and don't feel like doing the work that I should do it anyway. If they don't

Teachers can create powerful links to school through their caring and supportive interactions with students.

keep after you, you'll slide and never do the work. You just won't learn anything if they don't stay on you. (Corbett & Wilson, 2002, p. 19).

Caring teachers go beyond "not allowing excuses" and "staying on you," however. They are also helpful. "If they help us with our work, help us understand, they care" (Alder, 2002, p. 257).

Order and Safety. Effective teachers in urban schools also create safe and orderly environments. Teachers who aren't able to maintain order create conditions that interfere with both learning and motivation. One student comments, "The kids don't do the work. The teacher is hollering and screaming, 'Do your work and sit down.' This makes the ones that want to learn go slower. . . . It just messes you up" (Corbett & Wilson, 2002, p. 19). Both student motivation to learn and achievement are reduced in chaotic learning environments.

Involvement. Involvement is essential for motivation to learn in all students. Ironically, urban students, for whom involvement is even more important, tend to be put in less active roles than their suburban or rural counterparts. Effective teachers of urban students ask more questions, distribute the questions more equitably, and respond more positively to student answers and student questions than do their less-effective counterparts (Manouchehri, 2004). Involving urban students in learning activities is particularly challenging because they often have a long history of being placed in passive roles. Developing their willingness to take academic risks and engage in learning activities takes time and effort, but when finally achieved, it can be very rewarding (Kincheloe, 2004).

Challenge. Urban students are commonly treated as though they're unintelligent and unable to do cognitively demanding work (Barr & Parrett, 2001). This is a double whammy. While they may lack the school-related prior knowledge that makes school success easy to attain, they are often "street smart" in ways that even their teachers don't understand. They fully understand the way they're being treated, which exacerbates their resentment and disengagement (R. A. Goldstein, 2004). Effective teachers provide background knowledge by using a variety of high-quality examples, and they don't simply "give" students answers and solutions to problems, instead providing the scaffolding needed to help students do their own thinking and arrive at their own understanding. The result is the development of self-efficacy and competence that, as we've seen repeatedly, is a basic need in self-determination theory (Manouchehri, 2004).

Unquestionably, the development of urban students' motivation to learn is one of the most daunting challenges that educators face. However, many rise to the challenge. "I am humbled, amazed, and inspired by gifted urban teachers who motivate and support resilient urban students in their efforts to avoid the pitfalls of growing up in urban poverty. They are some of the most heroic figures of our era, working their magic in the most difficult of circumstances" (Kincheloe, 2004, p. 269). This is the ideal that we strive for when teaching in urban environments.

Challenge is an essential ingredient for motivating urban learners.

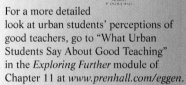

Exploring Further

For a more detailed look at urban students' perceptions of good teachers, go to "What Urban Students Say About Good Teaching" in the *Exploring Further* module of Chapter 11 at *www.prenhall.com/eggen*.

Online Case Book

To assess a teacher's application of the model for promoting student motivation in his instruction, go to the *Online Case Book* for Chapter 11 at *www.prenhall.com/eggen*.

Checking Your Understanding

5.1   Look back at Kathy Brewster's lesson in Chapter 10 on page 319. Describe how she applied *introductory focus* in her lesson.

5.2   Identify where DeVonne used *personalization* in her lesson.

5.3   Provide an example of "learning-oriented" and another example of "performance-oriented" feedback, using the topic of writing an effective paragraph. Explain the difference between the two.

To receive feedback for these questions, go to Appendix B.

Knowledge Extensions

To deepen your understanding of the topics in this section of the chapter and integrate them with topics you've already studied, go to the *Knowledge Extensions* module for Chapter 11 at *www.prenhall.com/eggen*. Respond to questions 13–18.

Classroom ⊞ **Connections**

Applying the Instructional Variables in the Model for Promoting Student Motivation in Your Classroom

Introductory Focus

1. Plan lesson introductions to attract students' attention and provide a conceptual umbrella for the lesson.
   - **Elementary:** A fourth-grade teacher introduces a lesson on measuring by bringing in a cake recipe and ingredients that have to be modified if everyone in the class is going to get a piece of cake. He says, "We want to make enough cake so we can all get a piece. This is what we're going to figure out today." He concludes the lesson by baking the cake in the school cafeteria and sharing it with his students.
   - **Middle School:** A physical science teacher begins her lessons with a simple demonstration, such as dropping an ice cube into a container of water and another into a container of alcohol to show that ice floats on water but sinks in alcohol. "Let's see what we need to figure this out," she says in beginning the lesson.
   - **High School:** An English teacher introduces *A Raisin in the Sun* (Hansberry, 1959) by saying, "Think about a Muslim family in Detroit. What do you think they talk about? What is important to them? How do you think they felt after the events of 9-11? Keep those questions in mind as we read *A Raisin in the Sun.*"

Personalization

2. Personalize content whenever possible.
   - **Elementary:** A fourth-grade teacher begins a lesson comparing animals with exoskeletons and those with endoskeletons by having students squeeze their legs to demonstrate that their bones are inside. He then passes out a number of crayfish and has the students compare the crayfish to themselves.
   - **Middle School:** A seventh-grade teacher begins a lesson on percentages by bringing in an ad for computer games and products from a local newspaper. The ad says "10% to 25% off marked prices." The class works problems to see how much they might save on popular computer games.

   - **High School:** In a unit on World War II, a history teacher has students interview someone who served in the military at the time. The class uses the results of the interviews to remind themselves of the "human" dimension of the war.

Involvement

3. Involve all students in learning activities.
   - **Elementary:** Each day a second-grade teacher passes out a sheet with 20 math facts on it. The students quickly write the answers and then score the sheets. Students who improve their scores from the previous day or get all 20 facts correct receive a bonus point on their math averages.
   - **Middle School:** A seventh-grade pre-algebra teacher has students work in pairs to complete seat-work assignments. They are required to work each problem individually, check with each other, and ask for help if they can't agree on the solution.
   - **High School:** An English teacher randomly calls on all students as equally as possible, whether or not they raise their hands. At the beginning of the year, he explains that this is his practice, that his intent is to encourage participation, and that students will soon get over any uneasiness about being "put on the spot." He prompts students who are unable to answer until they give an acceptable response.

Feedback

4. Provide prompt and informative feedback about learning progress.
   - **Elementary:** A fourth-grade teacher discusses the most frequently missed items on each of her quizzes, providing detailed information about each of the items.
   - **Middle School:** A seventh-grade teacher writes on a student paper, "You have some very good ideas. Now you need to rework your essay so that it is grammatically correct. Look at the notes I've made on your paper."
   - **High School:** A world history teacher displays an "ideal answer" on the overhead for each of the items on his homework assignments and essay items on his tests. Students compare their answers to the ideal and take notes with suggestions for improving their responses.

Meeting Your Learning Objectives

1. Explain the differences between a learning-focused and a performance-focused classroom.

- Learning-focused classrooms focus on learning goals, those that emphasize increased understanding and mastery of tasks. Performance-focused classrooms emphasize performance goals, those that focus on demonstrating high ability, and particularly ability compared to others.
- Learning-focused environments increase student motivation to learn, whereas performance-focused environments can detract from motivation to learn for all but the highest achievers.

2. Describe strategies that teachers can use to develop learner self-regulation, and explain different levels of student self-regulation.

- Learners' responsibility can be increased by emphasizing the relationships between accepting responsibility for their own learning and the increased achievement that can result.
- Soliciting student input in the process of establishing procedures that include student responsibility, treating responsibility as a concept by illustrating the consequences of taking and not taking responsibility, modeling responsibility, and providing concrete mechanisms that allow students to monitor and assess goal achievement are all strategies that can help students develop self-regulation.

3. Identify the personal characteristics of teachers who increase students' motivation to learn, and analyze these characteristics in classroom activities.

- *Personal teaching efficacy, modeling, caring,* and having *high expectations* are personal characteristics that can increase student motivation to learn.
- Teachers who are high in personal teaching efficacy believe they can help students learn, regardless of students' prior knowledge or other factors.
- Modeling courtesy and respect is essential for motivation, and demonstrating genuine interest in the topics they teach is the essence of teachers' enthusiasm.
- Teachers demonstrate that they care about their students by being willing to spend personal time with them and demonstrat-

ing respect for each individual. One of the most effective ways to demonstrate respect is to hold students to high standards. Holding students to high standards also communicates that teachers expect all students to succeed.

4. Analyze teachers' behaviors using the climate variables as a basis, and describe the relationships between the climate variables and the categories in the TARGET model.

- Motivating environments are safe, secure, and orderly places that focus on learning.
- Success on tasks students perceive as challenging increases motivation to learn. Meeting challenges provides evidence that competence is increasing, which also leads to feelings of autonomy. Both factors increase intrinsic motivation.
- In motivating environments, students understand what they're expected to learn and why they're expected to do so. Understanding what they're learning and why also increases perceptions of autonomy and contributes to task value.
- The climate variables in the model for promoting student motivation correspond to the categories in the TARGET program with relationships between "challenge" and "task comprehension" and the TARGET category *task;* "order and safety" and *authority;* "success" and *recognition;* each of the climate variables and *grouping;* "success" and *evaluation;* and "task comprehension" and *time.*

5. Identify examples of teachers implementing the instructional variables in learning activities.

- Teachers can increase motivation to learn by beginning lessons with examples, activities, or questions that attract students' attention and provide frameworks for information that follows.
- Students maintain their attention and interest when teachers make content personally relevant to them and keep them highly involved in learning activities.
- Teachers can increase student motivation to learn by providing feedback about learning progress. When feedback indicates that competence is increasing, self-efficacy and self-determination both improve, and intrinsic motivation increases.

Developing as a Professional

Praxis Practice

We saw at the beginning of the chapter how DeVonne taught the concept *arthropod.* Let's turn now to a language arts lesson on the construction of paragraphs that she taught later that same day. Read the case study, and answer the questions that follow.

DeVonne is working with her fifth graders on their writing skills. She plans to have them practice writing paragraphs and conduct self-assessments using criteria given in a 3-point rubric. She hands each student a blank transparency and pen, and then begins, "Today, we're going to practice some more on composing good paragraphs. . . . Now, we know the characteristics of a good paragraph, but let's review for a moment. . . . What do we look for in a well-composed paragraph?"

"Topic sentence," several students say immediately.

"Okay, what else?"

"Sentences that go with the topic," others add.

"Yes, 'go with the topic' means that the sentences support your topic sentence. You need to have at least four supporting sentences."

DeVonne reminds students that they also need to use correct grammar and spelling, and then displays the following paragraphs:

> Computers come in all shapes and sizes. One of the first computers, named UNIVAC, filled a room. Today, some large computers are as big as refrigerators. Others are as small as books. A few are even tiny enough to fit in a person's pocket.

> Ann's family bought a new color television. It had a 54-inch screen. There were controls for color and brightness. Ann likes police stories. There were also controls for sound and tone.

After some discussion, the class concludes that the first example met the criteria for an acceptable paragraph, but the second one did not, because the topic sentence didn't have four supporting sentences and the information "Ann likes police stories" didn't pertain to the topic.

She then says, "Now, you're going to write a paragraph on any topic on the transparencies I gave you at the beginning of class, and then the class is going to grade your paper." DeVonne smiles as she hears several calls of "Woo, woo" from the students.

The students go to work, and when they've finished, DeVonne says, "Okay, now we're going to grade the paragraphs." She reviews the criteria from the 3-point rubric, pointing out that a score of 3 means that all criteria for a good paragraph are met; 2 means that the paragraph has a topic sentence, it has fewer than four supporting sentences, some information doesn't pertain to the topic, and it contains a few grammatical errors; and a score of 1 means that a considerable amount of information does not pertain to the topic and many grammatical errors were present.

"Okay, who wants to go first?" DeVonne asks.

"Me!" several of the students shout.

"I should have known that," DeVonne smiles. "Okay, Tu, come on up."

Tu displays his paragraph and reads it aloud:

The class discusses his paragraph, agrees that it deserves a 3, and then several students call out, "I want to go next! I want to go next!"

DeVonne asks Justin to display his paragraph:

> There was a boy named Josh. He lives in a house with the roof falling in and the windows were broke. He had holes in the wall and the ceiling leaked when it rained. But then again it always rained and thunder over his house. No one ever goes to his gate because he was so weird. They say he is a vampire.

She has students raise their hands to vote on the score for this paragraph. About half give it a 2, and the remainder give it a 1.

"Samantha, why did you give it a 2?" DeVonne asks, beginning the discussion.

"He didn't stay on his topic. . . . He needs to stay on either the boy or the house," Samantha notes.

"Haajar? . . . You gave him a 1. . . . Go ahead."

"There was a boy named Josh, and then he started talking about the house. And then the weather and then the boy again," Haajar responds.

"Yes, that's similar to what Samantha said," DeVonne nods.

A few more students offered comments, and the class agrees that Justin's paragraph deserves a 1.5. Justin takes his seat.

"Me, me! I want to do mine!" several students exclaim with their hands raised.

DeVonne calls on Saleina to display her paragraph, the students agree that it deserves a 3, and DeVonne then says, "I am so impressed with you guys. . . . Your work is excellent."

"Okay, let's do one more," DeVonne continues. "Joshua."

"No! No!" the students protest, wanting to continue the activity and have theirs read.

"Okay, one more after Joshua," DeVonne relents with a smile.

The class assesses Joshua's paragraph and one more, and just before the end of the lesson, several students ask, "Are we going to get to do ours tomorrow?"

DeVonne smiles and assures them that they would get to look at the rest of the paragraphs the next day.

Short-Answer Questions

In answering these questions, use information from Chapter 11 and link your responses to specific information in the case.

1. Feelings of safety are essential for student motivation to learn. Assess the extent to which DeVonne's students felt safe in her classroom.
2. Assess DeVonne's application of the instructional variables in her classroom.
3. In spite of the fact that they were having their paragraphs publicly evaluated, De-Vonne's students were enthusiastic about displaying their work. Offer an explanation for their enthusiasm.
4. DeVonne's students' backgrounds are very diverse, and she teaches in an urban school. Assess her classroom environment for learners from urban contexts.

PRAXIS These exercises are designed to help you prepare for the Praxis™ "Principles of Learning and Teaching" exam.

To receive feedback on your short-answer questions, go to the Companion Website at *www.prenhall.com/eggen*, then to the Practice for Praxis™ module for Chapter 11.

To acquire experience in preparing for the multiple-choice items on the Praxis™ exam, go to the *Self-Assessment* module for Chapter 11 at *www.prenhall.com/eggen* and click on "Practice Quiz."

For additional connections between this text and the Praxis™ exam, go to Appendix A.

ONLINE PORTFOLIO ACTIVITIES

To develop your professional portfolio, further apply your understanding of chapter content, and address the INTASC standards, go to the Companion Website, then to the *Online Portfolio Activities* for Chapter 11. Complete the suggested activities.

Also on the Companion Website at *www.prenhall. com/eggen*, you can measure your understanding of chapter content with multiple-choice and essay questions, and broaden your knowledge base in *Exploring Further* and *Web Links* to other educational psychology websites.

IMPORTANT CONCEPTS

caring (p. 344)
high-collective-efficacy school (p. 343)
introductory focus (p. 353)
involvement (p. 355)
learning-focused environment (p. 337)
open-ended questions (p. 356)
order and safety (p. 348)

performance-focused environment (p. 337)
personal teaching efficacy (p. 343)
personalization (p. 355)
positive classroom climate (p. 348)
self-fulfilling prophecy (p. 346)
self-regulation (p. 338)
task comprehension (p. 350)

CHAPTER 12

Creating Productive Learning Environments:
Classroom Management

Chapter Outline	Learning Objectives
	After you have completed your study of this chapter, you should be able to
The Importance of Well-Managed Classrooms Public and Professional Concerns • The Complexities of Classrooms • Influence on Motivation and Learning • Goals of Classroom Management	**1** Describe the relationships between classroom management, the complexities of classrooms, and motivation and learning.
Planning for Productive Classroom Environments Accommodating Student Characteristics • Arranging the Physical Environment • Organizing for Instruction • Creating and Teaching Rules: Instructional Principles • Learning Contexts: Classroom Management in Urban Environments	**2** Analyze the planning components for creating productive learning environments in examples of classroom activities.
Communication with Parents Benefits of Communication • Involving Parents: Instructional Principles • Communication with Parents: Accommodating Learner Diversity	**3** Explain how effective communication with parents helps meet classroom management goals and why communication with parents who are members of cultural minorities is particularly important.
Intervening When Misbehavior Occurs Guidelines for Successful Interventions • Cognitive Interventions • Behavioral Interventions • An Intervention Continuum	**4** Describe effective interventions in cases of learner misbehavior.
Serious Management Problems: Violence and Aggression School Violence and Aggression • Long-Term Solutions to Violence and Aggression	**5** Describe teachers' legal responsibilities and the steps involved in responding to acts of violence and aggression.

Classroom management is an essential aspect of effective teaching. As you read the following case study, think how the teacher deals with management issues.

Judy Harris's seventh-grade geography class is involved in a cultural unit on the Middle East.

As Ginger enters the room, she sees a large map projected high on the screen at the front of the room. She quickly slides into her seat just as the bell stops ringing. Most students have already begun studying the map and the accompanying directions on the chalkboard:

Identify the longitude and latitude of Cairo and Damascus.

Judy's students begin each class by completing a review exercise while she takes roll and hands back papers. They also pass their homework forward as they work, each student putting his or her paper on top of the stack.

Judy waits a moment for students to finish, then pulls down another large map in the front of the classroom.

"We've been studying the Middle East, and you just identified Damascus here in Syria," she begins, pointing at the map. "Now, think for a moment and make a prediction about the climate in Damascus. . . . Bernice?" Judy asks as she walks down one of the rows.

"Damascus is about 34 North latitude, I think," Bernice replies.

As soon as Judy walks past him, Darren reaches across the aisle and taps Kendra on the shoulder with his pencil. The 32 students are squeezed into a room designed for 24, so the aisles are narrow. Darren watches Judy's back from the corner of his eye.

"Stop it, Darren," Kendra mutters, swiping at him with her hand.

Judy turns, comes back up the aisle, stands near Darren, and continues, "Good, Bernice. It's very close to 34."

"What would that suggest about its temperature at this time of the year? . . . Darren?" she asks looking directly at him.

"I'm not sure."

"Warmer or colder than here?"

"Warmer, I think."

"Okay. Good. And why might that be the case? . . . Jim?"

"Move up here," Judy says quietly to Rachel, who has been whispering and passing notes to Deborah across the aisle. Judy nods to a desk at the front of the room as she waits for Jim to answer.

"What did I do?" Rachel protests.

Judy leans over Rachel's desk and points to the classroom rule displayed on a poster and says, "When we talked about our rules at the beginning of the year, we agreed that it was important to listen when other people are talking.

> Listen when someone else is talking.
> Raise your hand for permission to speak.
> Leave your desk only when given permission.
> Bring all needed materials to class each day.
> Treat your classmates with courtesy and respect.

"We can't learn when people aren't paying attention, and I'm uncomfortable when my class isn't learning. Please move quickly now," Judy says evenly, looking Rachel in the eye.

"Damascus is south of us and also in a desert," Jim responds.

"Good, Jim. Now let's look at Cairo," she continues as she watches Rachel move to the new desk.

A **productive learning environment** is a classroom that is orderly and focused on learning. In it students feel physically and emotionally safe, and the daily routines, as well as the values, expectations, learning experiences, and standards for appropriate behavior are all designed to promote learning. This chapter focuses on using classroom management to help create productive learning environments.

To begin our discussion, we want to consider two questions: (1) What did Judy do to create a productive learning environment? (2) How can you establish and maintain a

Productive learning environment. A classroom that is orderly and focused on learning

similar environment in your own classroom? We address these and other questions in this chapter.

THE IMPORTANCE OF WELL-MANAGED CLASSROOMS

The ability to establish and maintain an orderly learning environment is one of the most important tasks teachers face, as indicated by at least three factors:

- Public and professional concerns about classroom management
- The complexities of classrooms
- The influence of orderly classrooms on learning and motivation

Public and Professional Concerns

From the 1960s until the present, national Gallup polls have consistently identified classroom management as one of teachers' most challenging problems. In the 2004 poll, it ranked second only behind lack of financial support as the most important problem schools face (L. Rose & Gallup, 2004). It has historically been the primary concern of beginning teachers, and disruptive students are an important source of stress for beginners and veterans alike (C. M. Bohn et al., 2004; Public Agenda, 2004). It is a major reason that teachers leave the profession during their first 3 years; it's a primary cause of teachers leaving urban classrooms (L. Weiner, 2002); and colleges of education are being asked to address the issue more carefully (J. Johnson, 2005).

The Complexities of Classrooms

The complexities of classrooms are a second reason classroom management is so important. Let's look at one teacher's experience.

> Ken, an elementary teacher in a third/fourth grade split classroom, shared this incident in his teaching journal:
>
> *March 3: My class is sitting in a circle. I look up and notice one of the girls, Sylvia, is crying. Joey, she claims, has called her a fat jerk. The rest of the students all look at me to watch my response. I consider the alternatives: send Joey to hallway and talk to him in a few minutes; have Joey sit next to me; ask Joey to apologize; direct Sylvia to get a thick skin; ask Sylvia, "How can you solve this problem?"; send Joey to principal; have Joey write an apology letter; ask Joey, "Why did you do this?"; ignore the situation completely; keep Sylvia and Joey in for recess for dialogue; put Joey's name on board; yell at Joey; send Sylvia and Joey in hallway to work out problem; tell them to return to their seats and write in journals about problem.*
>
> *It took me about 10 seconds to run through these alternatives, and after each one I thought of reasons why it wasn't a good idea. By the time I look up at Sylvia after this brief introspection, she had stopped crying and was chattering away with a friend about something else. On the surface, the problem had gone away. (Winograd, 1998, p. 296)*

Ken's experience illustrates the sometimes bewildering world of the classroom, as well as the constant and continual need for making wise professional decisions that are a part of every teacher's day.

Researchers, attempting to sort out these issues, have identified several characteristics of classrooms that make them complex and demanding (Doyle, 1986). Classrooms are

- *Multidimensional and simultaneous:* Large numbers of events and tasks occur at the same time.
- *Immediate:* The events occur rapidly.
- *Unpredictable:* Classroom events often take unexpected turns.
- *Public:* Teacher's decisions are visible to all and constantly scrutinized.

Let's look at them.

Classrooms Are Multidimensional and Simultaneous. Judy's experience illustrates these characteristics. She had to deal with two management issues—Darren's horseplay and

Classroom management is made more complex by the multidimensional, simultaneous, immediate, unpredictable, and public aspects of classroom events.

Rachel's and Deborah's whispering—while simultaneously keeping her lesson moving smoothly to avoid losing the attention of the rest of the class.

You will have similar demands on you as a teacher. You will be expected to keep students attentive and involved in a learning activity, while simultaneously maintaining order and dealing with minor disruptions, such as responding to the intercom or a student request for a bathroom break. At other times, you may work with a small group while simultaneously monitoring the rest of the students. At the same time, you will need to keep track of those who are being pulled out of class for varying reasons.

Classrooms Events Are Immediate. Because classrooms are complex, teachers make a great many decisions every day, and the decisions must be made right now (Emmer et al., 2003; Evertson et al., 2003). For example, to avoid having events escalate, Judy needed to react to Darren and Kendra, deciding immediately who was the victim and who was the perpetrator. In addition, she needed to decide whether to do anything about Rachel and Deborah, and once having decided to intervene, she had to make an immediate decision about which one to move. In a similar way, Ken needed to make an immediate decision about whether or not to intervene when he saw Sylvia crying. The need to make nearly split-second decisions can be overwhelming, particularly for beginning teachers.

Classroom Events Are Unpredictable. Diana Miller, a first-grade teacher, wants to involve her students in a lesson based on a story they had read about shoes, so she brings a shoe into class. Pulling it out of a bag, she begins, "What can you tell me about this shoe?"

> "It's red," Mike responds.
> The shoe was black; there was no sign of red anywhere!

Effective teachers carefully plan, and they try to anticipate as many contingencies as they can. However, it would have been impossible for Diana to anticipate Mike's response, just as Ken couldn't predict that Joey would make a comment that made Sylvia cry. Expert teachers remain alert and learn to expect the unexpected.

Classroom Events Are Public. We teach in front of people, and in a sense, we're continually on stage. Our triumphs and mistakes occur in the public arena for all to see, and mistakes are inevitable. For example, if Ken chose to ignore Joey's calling Sylvia a fat jerk, it might communicate to the class that verbally abusing one another was acceptable. On the other hand, if Ken reprimanded Joey and later learned that Sylvia was mistaken about what he said, the reprimand could communicate that a simple accusation can get someone into trouble.

Judy's experience was similar. Had she reprimanded Kendra instead of responding to Darren—the original perpetrator of the incident—it might communicate that she didn't know what was going on in her class. The public nature of teaching also increases its complexity.

Influence on Motivation and Learning

Perhaps the most important reason classroom management is so important is that students both learn more and are more motivated to learn in orderly environments. With respect to motivation, you saw in Chapter 11 that order and safety are foundations for motivating classrooms; it is difficult to excite students about a topic when they are worried about their own safety and security (Wessler, 2003). A long line of research indicates that safety and order are essential elements of productive learning environments (Barth, 2002; S. Purkey & Smith, 1983).

The relationship between classroom management and learning is also well documented (Good & Brophy, 2003). Effective classroom management increases student engagement, decreases disruptive behaviors, and increases instructional time, all of which are related to improved student achievement (Emmer et al., 2003; Evertson et al., 2003).

Goals of Classroom Management

Some of the earliest research on classroom management was done by Jacob Kounin (1970), who concluded that the key to orderly classrooms is the teacher's ability to prevent problems from occurring in the first place, rather than handling misbehavior once it happens. Kounin's findings have been consistently corroborated over the years (Emmer & Stough, 2001; Freiberg, 1999a; Good & Brophy, 2003). Experts estimate that anticipation and prevention are 80 percent of an effective management system (Freiberg, 1999b).

Kounin's research was also important because it helped teachers understand the difference between **classroom management,** teachers' strategies that create and maintain an orderly learning environment, and **discipline,** teachers' responses to student misbehavior. Expert teachers place primary emphasis on management, which reduces their need for discipline.

A second line of research revealed a historically overlooked relationship: the interdependence of classroom management and effective instruction (Emmer & Stough, 2001). It is virtually impossible to maintain an orderly classroom in the absence of good teaching, and vice versa (Good & Brophy, 2003; Rimm-Kaufman, La Paro, Downer, & Pianta, 2005). (We examine principles of effective instruction in Chapter 13). This interdependence is what led experts to the concept *productive learning environment.*

Based on this background, effective managers have three primary goals:

- Developing learner responsibility
- Creating a positive classroom climate
- Maximizing opportunity for learning

Let's look at them in more detail.

Developing Learner Responsibility

As conceptions of classroom management have moved away from discipline and toward prevention, increased emphasis has been placed on making students responsible for their role in creating productive learning environments. Developing student responsibility requires a **cognitive approach to management,** an approach that emphasizes the creation of orderly classrooms through the development of student understanding (Emmer & Stough, 2001; S. Jones, 2005). The goal is for students to understand the need for an orderly learning environment and accept responsibility for their part in creating one. Students obey rules because they view themselves as responsible persons and because it makes sense to do so, as opposed to obeying rules simply because they exist or because of the threat of punishment for breaking one. Teachers promote this orientation by explicitly teaching responsibility and emphasizing the reasons for rules and procedures. Students understand the need for rules in promoting order and why order is important for learning.

Cognitive approaches to management are grounded in both information processing and constructivist views of learning. With respect to information processing, management contributes to metacognition and is a vehicle for developing student self-control. Also, in effectively managed classrooms, learners construct understanding of what responsibility means, just as they construct understanding of any other topic. They know why rules and procedures are necessary and accept their role in contributing to productive learning environments. This understanding evolves from experience with everyday examples of appropriate and inappropriate behavior and from discussing the reasons for rules and procedures.

Developing student responsibility is both sensible and practical. Learners are more likely to obey rules when they understand the reasons for them, one of which is to protect their rights and the rights of others (Good & Brophy, 2003). This responsibility orientation can also contribute to ethical thinking and character development (Berk, 2006). For instance, in time, Joey may choose to not call a classmate a fat jerk, because name calling not only is unacceptable but also hurts other people's feelings. By promoting student responsibility and understanding, the teacher not only has helped Joey's personal development but also has reduced the management demands on the teacher. Such development takes time, but with effort, it usually can be accomplished.

Exploring Further

To examine this research in more detail, go to "Jacob Kounin's Research" in the *Exploring Further* module of Chapter 12 at *www.prenhall.com/eggen.*

Classroom management. Teachers' strategies that create and maintain an orderly learning environment

Discipline. Teachers' responses to student misbehavior

Cognitive approach to management. An approach to classroom management that emphasizes the creation of an orderly classroom through the development of student understanding and responsibility

Creating a Positive Classroom Environment

A positive classroom climate is an essential component of a productive learning environment (D. Brown, 2004; Emmer & Stough, 2001). When the climate is positive, both teacher and students demonstrate mutual respect and courtesy, and everyone feels safe to express thoughts and opinions without fear of embarrassment or ridicule.

An essential element of a positive classroom environment is a caring teacher who communicates respect and concern for others (Certo, Cauley, & Chafen, 2002; H. A. Davis, 2003). Positive teacher–student relationships affect classroom management and students' motivation, emotional well-being, and achievement. When students feel they belong and are valued, they are much more likely to follow classroom rules (Anderman, 2002).

Student responsibility, which we also discussed earlier, is another essential component of a positive classroom climate (Brand et al., 2003). When students accept responsibility for their own behavior, they let a classmate finish a thought before expressing their own, for example, so teachers don't have to rigidly enforce a rule requiring recognition by the teacher before speaking. Teachers create a positive climate by modeling courtesy and respect for students, expecting the same in return, and systematically teaching personal responsibility.

Maximizing Time and Opportunity for Learning

A third important classroom management goal is to maximize the amount of time students spend learning. To meet this goal, some reform efforts have suggested lengthening the school year, school day, and even the amount of time devoted to certain subjects. Improving learning by increasing study time isn't as simple as it appears on the surface, however (C. S. Weinstein & Mignano, 2003). As suggested in Table 12.1, different types of classroom time influence learning in different ways.

As one moves from allocated time to academic learning time, the correlation with learning becomes stronger (Nystrand & Gamoran, 1989). In classrooms where students are engaged and successful, achievement is high, learners feel a sense of competence and self-efficacy, and interest in the topics is increased (Bransford et al., 2000; Wigfield & Eccles, 2000).

The ideal, and an essential goal of classroom management, is to increase instructional, engaged, and academic learning time to maximize the use of allocated time. Expert teachers do this much more effectively than do novices (C. M. Bohn et al., 2004). For example, Judy gave her students a review exercise to complete while she took roll and handed back a set of papers. The exercise activated students' prior knowledge, focused students' attention on the topic at hand, and eliminated noninstructional time, when disruptions can occur. This begins to answer the first question in the beginning of the chapter, What did Judy do to create a productive learning environment? She simultaneously focused on learning and promoted order.

Less-effective teachers don't use their time as efficiently, wasting opportunities for learning and creating vacuums where management problems can occur. Further, some teachers seem unaware of the importance of time, viewing it as something to be filled—or

Table 12.1 Types of classroom time

Type	Description
Allocated time	The amount of time a teacher or school designates for a content area or topic
Instructional time	The amount left for teaching after routine management and administrative tasks are complete
Engaged time	The amount of time students are actively involved in learning activities
Academic learning time	The amount of time students are actively involved in learning activities during which they're successful

even "killed"—rather than a valuable resource that increases learning (Eggen, 1998; D. Wiley & Harnischfeger, 1974).

Maximizing time and opportunities for learning also helped Judy reach our management goals. Because she had taught students the importance of entering the class and getting right to work, she didn't have to spend time explaining what the students were supposed to do and reminding them to get started; they took responsibility for doing it on their own. And, because students behaved responsibly, more time was available for learning, and a positive classroom climate was created.

The general approach to meeting these goals should be an authoritative management style that parallels the authoritative parenting style you studied in Chapter 3 (Baumrind, 1991). Authoritative teachers have high expectations for their students, they're firm but caring, they provide reasons for rules, and they enforce the rules consistently. They contribute to both students' intellectual growth and their emotional well-being (D. Brown, 2004).

Now, we turn to our second question: How can you create a productive learning environment in your own classroom? The first step is careful planning, which we discuss in the next section.

Exploring Further

To examine the process of maximizing time available for learning in more depth, go to "Time Management" in the *Exploring Further* module of Chapter 12 at *www.prenhall.com/eggen*.

Checking Your Understanding

1.1 Describe the relationships between classroom management, the complexities of classrooms, and motivation and learning.

1.2 Which characteristic of classroom complexity did Judy most directly address by having an exercise waiting for the students when they entered the room?

1.3 A teacher tries to call on all students in her classes as equally as possible. To which component of time—*allocated time, instructional time, engaged time,* or *academic learning time*—is this suggestion most closely related? Explain.

To receive feedback for these questions, go to Appendix B.

Knowledge Extensions

To deepen your understanding of the topics in this section of the chapter and to integrate them with topics you've already studied, go to the *Knowledge Extensions* module for Chapter 12 at *www.prenhall.com/eggen*. Respond to questions 1–4.

PLANNING FOR PRODUCTIVE CLASSROOM ENVIRONMENTS

Some classes are obviously tougher to manage than others, and not all students accept as much responsibility for their behavior as we would like. However, we're still farther ahead by trying to create a classroom environment in which the emotional climate is positive and responsibility is taught. In addition, it is more productive to try to prevent problems instead of dealing with them after they occur.

Creating a productive learning environment begins with planning, and beginning teachers often underestimate the amount of time and energy it takes. The cornerstone of effective classroom management is a clearly understood and consistently monitored set of rules and procedures, which accommodate both the characteristics of students and the physical environment of the classroom (Emmer et al., 2003; Evertson et al., 2003).

The relationship among these factors is illustrated in Figure 12.1.

Accommodating Student Characteristics

Sam Cramer has completed his first semester's clinical work in a high school, and it's been a terrific experience. Except for a few rough spots, his

Figure 12.1 Planning for orderly classrooms

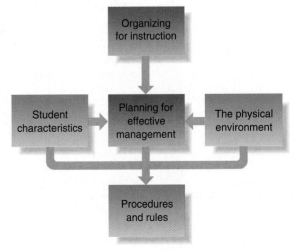

lessons went well, the students were interested and responsive, and classroom management wasn't an issue.

For his second semester, Sam moves to a middle school. He feels like he's on a different planet. Students are bubbling with energy; giggling, whispering, and note passing are constant distractions. His reminders to be quiet and pay attention appear to fall on deaf ears. His first lesson is a disaster.

You know from your study of Chapters 2 and 3 that students think, act, and feel differently at different stages of development. As Sam learned the hard way, students at different grade levels vary in the ways they interpret and respond to rules and procedures, and teachers need to anticipate these differences as they plan (Charles & Senter, 2005; McCarthy & Benally, 2003). Descriptions of developmental differences that influence management and their implications for preparing rules are outlined in Table 12.2.

These are general characteristics, and individual's behaviors will vary. As a pattern, however, we see increasing independence and self-regulation as learners develop. Their overt affection for teachers decreases, and they are more likely to question authority. This trend peaks in early adolescence, making classroom management at this age challenging (Freiberg, 1999a). During high school, students begin to behave like young adults and respond well to being treated as such. Students of all ages, however, need the emotional security of knowing that their teachers are genuinely interested in them and sincerely care about their learning.

Arranging the Physical Environment

"I can't see the board."

"Fred tripped me."

"What? I can't hear."

Few teaching situations are ideal. Classes are too large, storage space is limited, and maps or overhead projector screens cover the chalkboard. Arranging desks and furnishings can be a compromise between what teachers would like and what is possible. Regardless of their situation, however, teachers' planning should include the physical environment.

Table 12.2 Learner characteristics influencing classroom management

Stage	Student Characteristics	Implications for Preparing Rules and Procedures
Stage 1: Kindergarten through Second grade	• Compliant, eager to please teachers. • Short attention spans, tire easily. • Require close supervision. • Break rules because they forget.	Rules and procedures need to be explicitly taught, practiced, and reinforced.
Stage 2: Grades 3 through 6	• Increasingly independent but still like attention and affection from teachers. • Respond well to concrete incentives, such as stickers and free time, as well as praise and recognition. • Understand need for rules and enjoy participating in the rule-making process. • Know how far they can "push."	Rules need to be explicitly taught, and regularly reviewed.
Stage 3: Grades 7 through 9	• Attempt to test growing independence; can be rebellious and capricious. • Need firm foundation of stability. • Explicit boundaries and predictable outcomes are essential.	Rules need to be clearly stated and consistently and impartially enforced.
Stage 4: Grades 10 through 12	• Behave more stably. • Communicate effectively in an adult role. • Respond well to rationales.	Rules need to be created with student input, and clear rationales for rules are essential.

Source: Learning From Teaching: A Developmental Perspective, by J. Brophy and C. Evertson, 1976, Boston: Allyn & Bacon, Copyright 1976 by Allyn & Bacon. Adapted with permission.

Experts offer the following suggestions for arranging the classroom (Evertson et al., 2003):

- Be sure all students can see the chalkboard, overhead projector, or other displays. If students have to move to see this information, disruptions are more likely.
- Ensure that you can see all students. Monitoring students is essential, not only for learning but also for management.
- Make commonly used materials readily accessible. Students need to be able to easily access these materials without disrupting others.
- Keep high-traffic areas free of congestion. Avoid obstructions in areas through which students frequently move.

Classrooms need to be designed to address issues of visibility, accessibility, and distractibility.

Arranging Desks

When arranging desks, you should consider the types of learning activities students will be involved in (e.g., cooperative learning groups, whole-class instruction, individual assignments) (Crane, 2001; Fickes, 2001). For instance, many teachers combine group work with whole-class presentations, so students need to be able to make the transition from small- to large-group activities quickly and easily. Figure 12.2 illustrates a room arrangement that can be effective for these learning activities.

In Figure 12.2, we see that the students are seated with their group mates so they don't have to move to get into their groups. Then, when the learning activity moves from small to whole group, students merely have to turn their heads to see the teacher and board or overhead.

A more traditional arrangement is shown in Figure 12.3. It can be effective if most of the instruction is conducted in a whole group. Teachers tend to interact more with students near the front and in the middle of this arrangement (Eggen, 1998), so if you organize your

Figure 12.2   Sample seating arrangement for group work

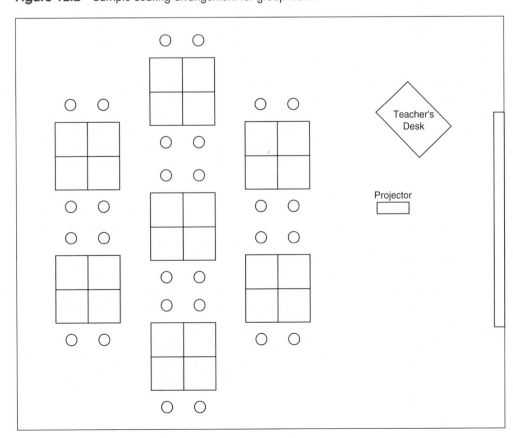

Figure 12.3 Sample seating arrangement for whole class instruction

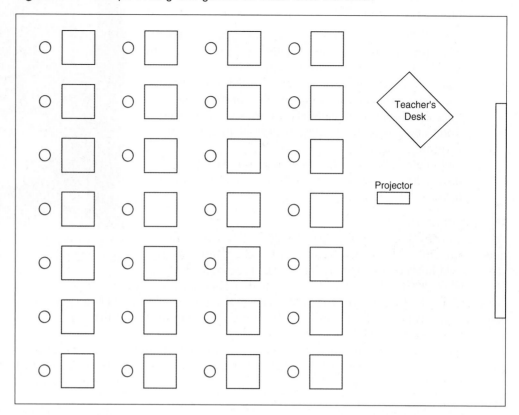

desks this way, make a conscious effort to move around the room, make eye contact with as many students as possible, and call on students toward the sides and back of the room.

Research indicates that no single room arrangement works for all situations. For example, one study found that behavior improved when learners were seated in rows (N. Bennett & Blundel, 1983), but another found that a semicircle was most effective (Rosenfield, Lambert, & Black, 1985). You should keep the suggestions above in mind, experiment, and use the arrangement that works best for you.

Personalizing Your Classroom

In Chapter 11 you saw that personalization increases student motivation to learn. We discussed personalization in the context of learning activities, but it applies to the physical environment as well. Many classrooms are pleasant but quite impersonal, and they reveal little about the people who spend time in them (C. S. Weinstein & Mignano, 2003). This is particularly true of secondary classrooms, where five or more classes may use the space in a single day.

The classroom can be made more inviting by posting personal items such as individual or class pictures, artwork, poetry, and other products prepared by students on bulletin boards or posters. A section of a bulletin board can be used for names of students who improved from one test to another or some other form of recognition where all students have an equal chance of being recognized.

You can also personalize the physical environment by involving students in decisions about its arrangement. If students know that the goal in all decisions is promoting learning, and if responsibility is stressed, their input can be positive and worthwhile.

Organizing for Instruction

We said earlier that classroom management and effective instruction are interdependent; you can't have one without the other. So, any effective management system must consider instruction as well. We present principles of effective instruction in detail in Chapter 13, but we want to discuss one aspect here because it is particularly important for creating a productive learning environment. It is **organization,** an essential teaching skill that includes

- Starting on time
- Preparing materials in advance
- Establishing routines and procedures
- Other actions that increase instructional time

Classroom rules and procedures establish standards for behaviors that allow learning to take place.

As an example, we saw earlier that Judy had an exercise waiting for students as they entered the room, so instruction began the instant the bell rang. When classes begin immediately, "dead" time, when disruptions can occur, is eliminated.

Having materials prepared in advance and ready for immediate use serves a similar function. When teachers have their materials ready and waiting, it both eliminates time when disruptions can occur, and it communicates that learning is the primary focus of the class.

This leads to the role that procedures play in productive learning environments. **Procedures** are guidelines for accomplishing recurring tasks, such as how students turn in papers, sharpen pencils, and make transitions from one activity to another (Good & Brophy, 2003).

As an example, let's look again at Judy's class. When students came into the room, they immediately began the review exercise. They also passed their papers forward, each putting his or hers on the top of the stack, and they did both without a word from Judy. These were well-practiced procedures that increased instructional time and involved little teacher effort.

Research indicates that experts in every field convert as many of their procedures as possible to automatic routines (Bransford et al., 2000; Bruning et al., 2004). Routines help establish the order and predictability that contributes to a sense of equilibrium for both students and the teacher. They also reduce the demands on teachers' working memories. Earlier in the chapter, you saw that teaching is complex, and well-established routines help reduce this complexity.

Instructional 🪟 Principles

Creating and Teaching Rules: Instructional Principles

We said earlier that the cornerstone of a productive learning environment is a clearly understood and consistently monitored set of rules and procedures. We outlined the importance of procedures in the last section, and now we turn to **rules,** which are descriptions of standards for acceptable behavior, such as "Listen when someone else is talking." Research confirms their value; evidence indicates that clear, reasonable rules, fairly and consistently enforced, not only reduce behavior problems that interfere with learning but also promote feelings of pride and responsibility in the school (Good & Brophy, 2003; Marzano & Marzano, 2003). Perhaps surprisingly, students also see setting clear standards of behavior as evidence that the teacher cares about them (Brophy, 2004).

A cognitive approach to management requires that learners understand the reasons behind rules so they can accept responsibility for their own behavior. The following principles can guide you in your efforts to promote this understanding:

1. State rules positively.
2. Minimize the number of rules.
3. Solicit student input.
4. Emphasize rationales for rules.
5. Use concrete examples to illustrate rules and procedures.
6. Monitor rules throughout the school year.

(We focus on rules in this section, but the principles apply equally well to procedures.)

Organization. An essential teaching skill that includes starting on time, preparing materials in advance, and establishing routines and procedures

Procedures. Guidelines for accomplishing recurring tasks

Rules. Descriptions of standards for acceptable classroom behavior

Let's see how these principles for creating and teaching rules guide Deanna McDonald, an eighth-grade English teacher as she works with her students.

> About 20 minutes are left in the period, so Deanna's students know it's time for the class meeting, as she does during all of her classes on Fridays.
>
> "I want to review our rules for a few minutes today," she begins. "We've been doing a good job, but when we begin our study of *To Kill a Mockingbird* next week, we'll be involved in a lot of discussions, so I'd like to talk about what we need to do to learn as much as possible from them. . . . What are some ideas about how we could do this?"
>
> " . . . We should listen," Jonique offers after pausing for a few seconds.
>
> "Sure, that makes sense. . . . What else?"
>
> " . . . Not interrupt. . . . Wait until they finish?" James adds after a few more seconds.
>
> "That also makes sense. . . . So, suppose we say, 'Listen attentively until a person is finished.' How does that sound?"
>
> The students nod, so Deanna writes *Listen attentively until a person is finished* on the board.
>
> "That adds one more rule to our original five," she comments, referring to the class rules posted on the bulletin board.
>
> "And," she continues, "Listening attentively is a part of treating everyone with respect and dignity, so we're actually refining our last rule.
>
> "Now why is this rule so important? . . . Barry?"
>
> " . . . It's . . . rude if we don't listen to each other or if we interrupt when someone is talking."
>
> "Of course," Deanna smiles. "What's the very most important reason?"
>
> "To learn stuff," Antonio responds, remembering one of Deanna's most common comments.
>
> "Absolutely, that's what school's all about. You learn, I learn, we all learn, and we learn less if we don't listen.
>
> "Plus," she adds, "it's important to me that you all participate. Each of you has important ideas to bring to the discussions, and I want you all to have a chance to share them. And ultimately, what happens when you leave here?"
>
> "We're responsible for ourselves," Yolanda responds knowing that Deanna repeatedly reminds them that they are the ones who ultimately control what they do.
>
> "That's right, Yolanda," Deanna smiles. "And that, together with being here to learn, is why we're in school. Out in the world, it's up to us. That's why I'm not going to hold a stick over your head. I want you to listen and be polite because you believe it's important for learning and treating each other well, not because I'll punish you if you aren't.
>
> "But," she continues, "what should you do if you really disagree with something someone says? . . . Kyle?"
>
> "Raise our hand and then tell them?" Kyle answers with a question in his voice.
>
> "Exactly. Disagreeing is perfectly okay. One of the reasons we have discussions is to share different perspectives. But we have to listen to the other person before we can disagree.
>
> "Keep this idea in mind, and we'll practice it when we start *To Kill a Mockingbird* on Monday. . . . I'll remind you if you happen to slip a little."

RULES

Be in your seat and ready to work when the bell rings.

Bring all materials to class each day.

Leave your seat only when given permission.

Raise your hand for permission to speak.

Treat everyone with respect and dignity.

Let's look now at Deanna's attempts to apply the principles for creating and teaching rules. The first two principles are illustrated in the rules themselves; they were stated positively, and only six were created. Positively stated rules specify desired behavior; those stated negatively identify only what students are not to do. To behave responsibly, students must be aware of the rules, and the more they have to remember, the more difficult this is. One of the most common reasons students break rules is that they simply forget them!

Table 12.3 contains additional examples of rules at the elementary, middle, and secondary levels. These are merely examples; you will need to create rules that work best for you.

The third principle (solicit student input) was illustrated when Deanna said, "I'd like to talk about what we should be doing to learn as much as possible from our discussions . . . . what are some ideas about how we could do this?" This comment asked students for input into their sixth rule. Being asked for input promotes students' feelings of ownership, which increases the likelihood that they will obey the rules (R. Lewis, 2001). In addition, providing input can increase students' feelings of autonomy, which contributes to motivation to learn (Brophy, 2004; R. Ryan & Deci, 2000).

Applying the fourth—and perhaps most important—principle, Deanna provided a rationale for the rules by emphasizing that they exist to promote learning. Students are more likely to accept a rule, even when they disagree with it, if they understand why it's impor-

Table 12.3 Examples of teachers' rules

First-Grade Teacher	Seventh-Grade Teacher	Tenth-Grade Teacher
• We raise our hands before speaking. • We leave our seats only when given permission by the teacher. • We stand politely in line at all times. • We keep our hands to ourselves. • We listen when someone else is talking.	• Be in your seat and quiet when the bell rings. • Follow directions the first time they're given. • Bring covered textbooks, notebook, pen, pencils, and planner to class every day. • Raise your hand for permission to speak or to leave your seat. • Keep hands, feet, and objects to yourself. • Leave class only when dismissed by the teacher.	• Do all grooming outside of class. • Be in your seat before the bell rings. • Stay in your seat at all times. • Bring all materials daily. This includes your book, notebook, pen/pencil, and paper. • Give your full attention to others in discussions, and wait your turn to speak. • Leave when I dismiss you, not when the bell rings.

tant. Providing reasons for rules also contributes to students' feelings that the world is a sensible place. Humanistic reasons, emphasizing the effect of our behaviors on others, can be particularly effective (Eisenberg & Fabes, 1998).

We see that Deanna used a classroom meeting as a forum for discussing rules and soliciting student input, a process also endorsed by management experts (Glasser, 1985; J. Nelson, Lott, & Glenn, 1997). These meetings can be used to first establish and then monitor (principle 6) and improve classroom rules. (We examine the application of the fifth principle in the next section.) They help create a sense of ownership in students, and they contribute to the development of responsibility and self-regulation.

Does involving students in forming classroom rules work? One middle school teacher reported the following:

> I began with my first-period class. We started slowly, with my asking them about what it would take for the class to work for them. I then told them what it would take for the class to work for me. I was amazed at the overlap. They wanted to know up front what I expected in terms of tests, quantity and quality of work, late assignments, talking in class, and amount and how often they would have homework, where they could sit, grading, and whether classroom participation counted. We talked about the best classes and the worst classes. We talked about respect and the need to respect ideas and each other, to listen to and be willing to be an active participant without [verbally] running over other people in the class or being run over. . . . Well, this was five months ago and I was amazed at the level of cooperation. I am well ahead of last year in the curriculum; we have class meetings once a week to see how things are going and adjust as needed. We created a classroom constitution and had a constitutional convention when we felt it needed to be changed. I didn't believe it would make a difference; the students really surprised me with their level of maturity and responsibility and I surprised myself with my own willingness to change. This has been a great year and I am sorry to see it end. (Freiberg, 1999c, p. 169)

Although involving students in management decisions won't solve all problems, it is an important first step in gaining students' cooperation.

Teaching Rules and Procedures

The fifth principle for creating and teaching rules, "Use concrete examples to illustrate rules and procedures," reminds us of the importance of students' understanding our management guidelines. Let's see how Martha Oakes, a first-grade teacher, attempts to get her students to understand how to put away worksheets.

> "I put each of their names, as well as my own, on cubby holes on the wall of my room. To demonstrate the process, I did a short worksheet myself and literally walked it over and put it in my storage spot, talking aloud as I went: 'I'm finished with my worksheet. . . . What do I do now? . . . I need to put it in my cubby hole. If I don't put it there, my teacher can't check it, so it's very important. . . . Now, I start on the next assignment.'
> "Then I gave my students the worksheet, directing them to take it to their cubbies, quietly and individually, as soon as they were finished. After they had done that, we spent a

few minutes discussing the reasons for taking the finished work to the cubbies immediately, not touching or talking to anyone as they move to the cubbies and back to their desks, and starting right back to work. Then I gave them another worksheet, asked them what they were going to do and why, and had them do it. We then spent a few more minutes talking about what might happen if we didn't put papers where they belong. I asked them whether they had ever lost anything and how this was similar.

"Now we have a class meeting nearly every day just before we leave for the day. We discuss classroom life and offer suggestions for improvement. Some people might be skeptical about whether or not first graders can handle meetings like this, but they can. This is also one way I help them keep our procedures fresh in their minds."

Martha's approach illustrates principles of effective teaching. She both demonstrated the behaviors she wanted to see in her students and she verbalized her thinking at the same time. Then, she had the students actually practice taking their worksheets to their cubby holes. Each of these actions provided the concrete examples they needed to construct their understanding of the process, just as they would use examples to construct their understanding of any concept. Being specific and concrete was essential for Martha's students because they were first graders; simply explaining how they were to deposit their papers wouldn't have been effective.

To understand abstract ideas, learners of all ages need examples. Even Deanna's students, who were eighth graders, needed examples of "Treating everyone with respect and dignity," for instance, to understand what the rule meant. The more thoroughly students understand rules and the reasons they exist, the more likely they are to obey them.

Beginning the School Year

Research consistently confirms that patterns of behavior for the entire year are established in the first few days of school (Charles & Senter, 2005; V. F. Jones & Jones, 2004). Effective teachers realize this and are ready to go immediately (C. M. Bohn et al., 2004). Let's see how two teachers handle the first day.

Donnell Alexander is waiting at the door for her eighth graders with prepared handouts as students come in the room. She distributes them and says, "Take your seats quickly, please. You'll find your name on the desk. The bell is going to ring in less than a minute, and everyone needs to be at his or her desk and quiet when it does. Please read the handout while you're waiting." She is standing at the front of the room, surveying the class as the bell rings. When it stops, she begins, "Good morning, everyone."

Vicki Williams, who also teaches eighth graders across the hall from Donnell, is organizing her handouts as the students come in the room. Some take their seats while others mill around, talking in small groups. As the bell rings, she looks up and says over the hum of the students, "Everyone take your seats, please. We'll begin in a couple minutes," and she turns back to finish organizing her materials.

In these first few minutes, students learned an important idea. Donnell's learned that they were expected to be in their seats and ready to start at the beginning of class; Vicki's learned just the opposite. Students quickly understand these differences, and unless Vicki changes this pattern, she will soon have problems, perhaps not dramatic, but chronic and low grade, like nagging sniffles that won't go away. Problems like these cause more teacher stress and fatigue than any other (L. Weiner, 2002).

Guidelines for beginning the first few days of school are summarized in Table 12.4.

Monitoring Rules

Finally, the sixth principle, "Monitor rules throughout the school year," reminds us that maintaining a productive learning environment is ongoing, regardless of how well rules are initially taught (Emmer et al., 2003; Evertson et al., 2003). Effective teachers continually monitor rules, react to misbehavior immediately, refer students to the rule that was broken, and explain why it is important. As an example, let's look again at Judy's class.

During the first few days of the school year, teachers establish both relationships with students as well as expectations for behavior.

Table 12.4 Guidelines for beginning the school year

Guideline	Examples
Establish expectations	• Explain requirements and grading systems, particularly with older students. • Emphasize that learning and classroom order are interdependent.
Plan structured instruction	• Plan with extra care during this period. • Conduct eye-catching and motivating activities. • Use the first few days to assess learners' skills and background knowledge. • Use large- rather than small-group instruction. • Minimize transitions from one activity to another.
Teach rules and procedures	• Begin teaching rules and procedures the first day. • Frequently discuss and practice rules and procedures during the first few days. • Intervene and discuss every infraction of rules.
Begin communication with parents	• Send a letter to parents that states positive expectations for the year. • Call parents after the first or second day to nip potential problems in the bud.

Judy: Move up here (in response to Rachel's whispering and note passing)

Rachel: What did I do?

Judy: When we talked about our rules at the beginning of the year, we agreed that it was important to listen when other people are talking. . . . We can't learn when people aren't paying attention, and I'm uncomfortable when my class isn't learning. Please move quickly now (pointing to the rule).

This was effective monitoring because Judy called Rachel's attention to the rule and reminded her that the class had agreed it was important. She treated the rule as a social contract, and in doing so, she demonstrated moral reasoning at Kohlberg's Stage 5 (see Chapter 3). Other students will obey rules simply because they know the teacher monitors them. The combination of student understanding and teacher monitoring will prevent or quickly eliminate most disruptive behaviors.

Learning Contexts: Classroom Management in Urban Environments

In our discussions of teaching in urban contexts in earlier chapters, three themes emerged. First, students in urban environments come from very diverse backgrounds. As an example, let's look at Mary Gregg, a first-grade teacher in an urban school in the San Francisco Bay Area.

> Mary's room, a small portable with a low ceiling and very loud air fans, has one teacher table and six rectangular student tables with six chairs at each. Mary has thirty-two first graders (fourteen girls and 18 boys). Twenty-five of the children are children of color; a majority are recent immigrants from Southeast Asia, with some African Americans and Latinos, and seven European Americans. (LePage et al., 2005, p. 328)

As a result of this diversity, students' prior knowledge and experiences vary, and what they view as acceptable patterns of behavior also varies, sometimes dramatically. Second, urban schools are large; Mary had 32 first graders in a room built for 25. Third, and perhaps most pernicious, negative stereotypes about urban environments create the perception that working in these contexts is difficult if not impossible. With respect to classroom management, two of the most common stereotypes are, "Students can't control themselves," and "Students don't know how to behave because the parents don't care" (R. A. Goldstein, 2004, p. 43). In response to this stereotype, urban teachers often "teach defensively" (McNeil, 2000), "choosing methods of presentation and evaluation that simplify content and reduce demands on students in return for classroom order and minimal student compliance on assignments" (LePage et al., 2005, p. 331). (We discuss instruction in urban classrooms in Chapter 13.)

The result is the lowered expectations and decreased student motivation that we discussed in Chapter 11. Students who are not motivated to learn are then more likely to be disruptive because they don't see the point in what they're being asked to do, a downward spiral of motivation and learning occurs, and management issues become increasingly troublesome.

It doesn't have to be this way. In spite of the diversity and large number of students in a small classroom, Mary Gregg created an active and orderly learning environment. Let's look at her classroom management during a lesson on buoyancy.

> Once into the science activity, management appears to be invisible. There is, of course, some splashing and throwing things into the water, but as the lesson progresses, the teacher engages in on-the-spot logistical management decisions. For instance, everyone is supposed to get a chance to go to the table to choose objects to be placed in cups. After choosing the first one to go, Mary sets them to the task. Very quickly, it is the second person's turn and the students do not know how to choose who should get the next turn. At first she says "you choose," then foresees an "It's my turn. No it's my turn" problem and redirects them with a counterclockwise motion to go around the table. (LePage et al., 2005, pp. 328–329)

This example demonstrates that, while very challenging, classroom management in an urban environment doesn't have to be overly restrictive, harsh, or punitive. How is this accomplished? Research provides some information. It suggests that at least four factors are important:

- Caring and supportive teachers
- Clear standards for acceptable behavior
- High structure
- Effective instruction

Caring and Supportive Teachers

We have emphasized the need for caring and supportive teachers in all our discussions of teaching in urban contexts. Teachers who care are important in all schools but are critical in urban environments. When students perceive their teachers as uncaring, the disengagement from school that we discussed in Chapter 11 often occurs, and disengaged students are much more likely to display disruptive behaviors than are their more-engaged peers (Charles & Senter, 2005; V. F. Jones & Jones, 2004).

Clear Standards for Acceptable Behavior

Because their prior knowledge and experiences are diverse, urban students' views of acceptable behaviors often vary. As a result, being clear about what behaviors are and are not acceptable is essential in urban contexts (D. Brown, 2004). Interestingly, a strong relationship exists between standards for behavior and the perception that teachers care. As we saw earlier in the chapter, students see setting clear standards of behavior as evidence that the teacher cares about them (Brophy, 1999). Let's see what one urban student has to say.

> She's probably the strictest teacher I've ever had because she doesn't let you slide by if you've made a mistake. She going to let you know. If you've made a mistake, she's going to let you know it. And, if you're getting bad marks, she's going to let you know it. She's one of my strictest teachers, and that's what makes me think she cares about us the most. (Alder, 2002, pp. 251–252)

The line between clear standards for behavior and an overemphasis on control is not cut and dried. Alder (2002) describes the difference as order being created through "the ethical use of power" (p. 245). Effective teachers are demanding but also helpful; they model and emphasize personal responsibility, respect, and cooperation; and they are willing to take the time to ensure that students understand the reasons for rules (C. S. Weinstein & Mignano, 2003). Further, in responding to the inevitable incidents of students' failing to bring needed materials to class, talking, or otherwise being disruptive, effective teachers in urban schools enforce rules but provide rationales for them and remind students that completing assigned tasks is essential because it helps develop the skills needed for more advanced work (D. Brown, 2004). In contrast, less-effective teachers tend to focus on negative consequences, such as, "If you don't finish this work, you won't pass the class" (Manouchehri, 2004).

High Structure

As you saw in Chapter 2, the need for equilibrium is one of the most basic in people, and students in urban schools sometimes come from environments that lack the stability that creates a sense of equilibrium. This makes order, structure, and predictability even more important in urban environments than in other kinds of classrooms. Procedures that lead to well-established routines are important, and predictable consequences for behaviors are essential. A predictable environment leads to an atmosphere of safety, which is crucial for developing the sense of attachment to school that is essential for learning and motivation. And, as we saw earlier, if students aren't learning, and they feel disengaged from their classroom and school, management problems are almost inevitable.

Effective Instruction

As you saw at the beginning of the chapter, classroom management and instruction are interdependent, and, unfortunately, students in urban classrooms are often involved in low-level activities and put in passive roles. This type of instruction contributes to low motivation and feelings of disengagement, which further increases the likelihood of management problems. We discuss instructional strategies that avoid disengagement in Chapter 13.

Checking Your Understanding

2.1 To which aspect of planning for effective classroom management— *accommodating student characteristics, arranging the physical environment, organizing for instruction,* or *planning and teaching rules*—does the example with Donnell Alexander and Vicki Williams, on page 380, most closely relate? Explain.

2.2 We see the rule "We keep our hands to ourselves" in the first-grade list in Table 12.3, and we see a similar rule in the seventh-grade list, but not in the tenth-grade list. How would you explain this difference?

2.3 Based on the information in the case study, was the engaged time in Judy's class greater than, equal to, or less than her instructional time? Explain.

To receive feedback for these questions, go to Appendix B.

Knowledge Extensions

To deepen your understanding of the topics in this section of the chapter and to integrate them with topics you've already studied, go to the *Knowledge Extensions* module for Chapter 12 at *www.prenhall.com/eggen*. Respond to questions 5–9.

Classroom Connections

Planning for Effective Classroom Management

1. Carefully plan and communicate your classroom procedures and rules at the beginning of the school year.
   - **Elementary:** A third-grade teacher gives his students and their parents a handout that describes homework procedures, how grades are determined, and how work is made up when a student is absent.
   - **Middle School:** A pre-algebra teacher prepares a short written list of rules before she starts class on the first day. She then asks students to suggest additional rules that will increase everyone's opportunity to learn.
   - **High School:** An English teacher explains at the beginning of the year how he will handle writing drafts, and how his class will use peer comments to improve essays. He displays the

procedure for peer reviews on the overhead and refers to it each time the class completes writing assignments.

2. Consider the developmental level of your students and your physical environment in preparing and teaching rules and procedures.
   - **Elementary:** At the beginning of the school year, a first-grade teacher takes a few minutes each day to review her procedure for turning in materials. She continues until students can follow it without directions.
   - **Middle School:** To prevent distractions, a sixth-grade teacher arranges students' desks so that they are facing away from the classroom window, which looks out on the PE field.
   - **High School:** A geometry teacher has the custodian move his projection screen into the corner of the room so that it

doesn't cover the chalkboard, which he uses to have students present proofs to the class.

Making Rules and Procedures Work

3. Be prepared for the first day of class. Explain and have students practice your classroom procedures.

- **Elementary:** A kindergarten teacher greets children as they come in her room. She takes each student by the hand and walks to a seat at a table with the student's name on it. Crayons and other materials are waiting, which students use until everyone arrives.

- **Middle School:** An eighth-grade history teacher is standing at the door as students file into the room. "Move to your seats quickly please," he says, "and begin reading the paper that's on your desk. We'll discuss it as soon as the bell rings."

- **High School:** A chemistry teacher takes a full class period to teach safe lab procedures. She models correct procedures, explains the reasons for them, and gives students a handout describing them. She monitors students as they work in the lab, reminding them about the importance of safety.

COMMUNICATION WITH PARENTS

Learning is a cooperative venture, and teachers, students, and parents are in it together. Because of the importance of the home environment, teachers should develop strategies to increase parental involvement in their children's academic life. They should go beyond traditional once-a-year parent–teacher conferences and continually work with parents, encouraging them to help with homework, monitor television viewing, and read to their young children (Wang et al., 1993). Communication with parents or other caregivers is an integral part of all aspects of teaching and learning, including classroom management.

Benefits of Communication

Students benefit from home–school cooperation in several ways. Some include

- Greater willingness to do homework
- Higher long-term achievement
- More positive attitudes and behaviors
- Better attendance and graduation rates
- Greater enrollment in postsecondary education (D. Garcia, 2004; Hong & Ho, 2005)

These outcomes likely result from parents' increased participation in school activities, higher expectations for their children's achievement, and teachers' increased understanding of learners' home environments. Deciding how to respond to a student's disruptive behavior is easier, for example, when his teachers know that his mother or father has lost a job, his parents are going through a divorce, or there's an illness in the family.

Parents can also help reinforce classroom management plans. One teacher reported:

I had this boy in my class who was extremely disruptive. He wouldn't work, kept "forgetting" his homework, distracted other children, wandered about the room. You name it; he did it. The three of us—the mother, the boy and I—talked about what we could do, and we decided to try a system of home rewards. We agreed that I would send a note home each day, reporting on the boy's behavior. For every week with at least three good notes, the mother let him rent a video game. In this way, the child's access to video games was directly dependent on his behavior. This system really made a difference. (C. S. Weinstein & Mignano, 2003, p. 117)

Parent–teacher collaboration can have long-term benefits for teachers. For example, teachers who encourage parental involvement report more positive feelings about teaching and their school. They also have higher expectations for parents and rate them higher in helpfulness and follow-through (Epstein, 2001).

Home–school partnerships facilitate classroom management as well as promote higher achievement and motivation.

Involving Parents: Instructional Principles

Instructional ⊞ Principles

Virtually all schools have formal communication channels, such as open houses (usually occurring within the first 2 weeks of the year, when teachers introduce themselves and describe general guidelines); interim progress reports, which tell parents about their youngsters' achievements at the midpoint of each grading period; parent–teacher conferences; and, of course, report cards. Although these processes are schoolwide and necessary, you can enhance existing communication processes. The following principles can guide your actions:

1. Begin early communication with an initial letter to parents or other caregivers.
2. Be proactive in maintaining communication links with the home.
3. Emphasize accomplishments.

Let's see how the principles for involving parents guide Joan Williams, a middle school English teacher, as she begins her second year of teaching.

Although her first year went fairly well, Joan vows to increase her home–school communication this year. She prepares a draft of a letter to parents, which outlines her expectations and solicits their support. She shares it with her students the first day of class, discusses it, and explains why having their parents involved is so important. She also asks for their suggestions on rules and procedures to include in the letter. She then takes the letter home, revises it, and brings a final copy to school the next day (see Figure 12.4). She checks to be sure that all letters are signed and returned, and she follows up on those that aren't with e-mails and phone calls.

Every 3 weeks throughout the year, Joan sends assignments and graded homework home to be read and signed. She encourages parents to contact her if they have any questions about the packets.

During the evening, Joan periodically calls parents to let them know about their children's progress. If students miss more than one assignment, she calls immediately, emphasizing her personal concern as well as the student's past accomplishments. She also makes a point of e-mailing parents to report positive news, such as a student's exceeding requirements, overcoming an obstacle, or showing uncommon kindness.

Her second year isn't perfect, but she can feel a tangible difference from her first.

Let's look now to see how Joan attempted to apply the principles for involving parents. Sending a letter home the second day of school applied the first (begin early communication with an initial letter). The letter began the communication process and was effective for several reasons:

- It expressed positive expectations and reminded parents that they are essential for their child's learning.
- It asked parents to sign a contract committing to the support of their child's education.
- It specified class rules (described as "guidelines") and outlined procedures for homework, absences, and extra credit.
- It asked students to sign a contract committing them to following the guidelines.
- It used correct grammar, punctuation, and spelling.

Signatures aren't guarantees, but they symbolize a commitment and increase the likelihood that the parents and students will attempt to honor it (Katz, 1999). Also, because students had input into the content of the letter, they felt ownership of the process and were more likely to ask parents for help on their homework.

The last item on the list bears special mention. The need for correct spelling, grammar, and punctuation should go without saying, but teachers sometimes send home communications with errors in them. Don't do it. First impressions are important and lasting. Your first letter creates a perception of your competence, and errors detract from your credibility, which is important for your effectiveness (Raths, 2001).

Joan applied the second principle (be proactive in maintaining communication) by continuing home–school communication, which maintains the momentum created by

Figure 12.4 Letter to parents

August 22, 2006

Dear Parents,

I am looking forward to a productive and exciting year, and I am writing this letter to encourage your involvement and support. You always have been and still are the most important people in your youngster's education. We cannot do the job without you.

For us to work together most effectively, some guidelines are necessary. With the students' help, we prepared the ones listed here. Please read this information carefully, and sign where indicated. If you have any questions, please call me at Southside Middle School (441-5935) or at home (221-8403) in the evenings.

Sincerely,

Joan Williams

AS A PARENT, I WILL TRY MY BEST TO DO THE FOLLOWING:

1. I will ask my youngsters about school every day. (Evening meal is a good time.) I will ask them about what they're studying and try to learn about it.

2. I will provide a quiet time and place each evening for homework. I will set an example by also working at that time or reading while my youngsters are working.

3. Instead of asking if their homework is finished, I will ask to see it. I will have them explain some of the information to see if they understand it.

    Parent's Signature _____

STUDENT SURVIVAL GUIDELINES:

1. I will be in class and seated when the bell rings.
2. I will follow directions the first time they are given.
3. I will bring covered textbook, notebook, paper, and two sharpened pencils to class each day.
4. I will raise my hand for permission to speak or leave my seat.
5. I will keep my hands, feet, and objects to myself.

HOMEWORK GUIDELINES:

1. Our motto is I WILL ALWAYS TRY. I WILL NEVER GIVE UP.
2. I will complete all assignments. If an assignment is not finished or ready when called for, I understand that I get no credit for it.
3. If I miss work because of an absence, it is my responsibility to come in before school (8:15–8:45) to make it up.
4. I know that I get one day to make up a test or turn in my work for each day I'm absent.
5. I understand that extra credit work is not given. If I do all the required work, extra credit isn't necessary.

    Student's Signature _____

the initial letter. For example, she regularly sent packets of students' work home and asked parents to sign and return them. In addition to creating a concrete link between home and school, this practice gives parents an ongoing record of their child's progress.

One of the most effective ways to maintain communication is to call parents. When you allocate some of your personal time to call, you communicate caring better than any other way. Also, talking to a parent allows you to be specific in describing a student's needs and gives you a chance to again solicit support. If a student is missing assignments, for example, you can ask for an explanation and can encourage the parents to more closely monitor their child's study habits.

When we talk to parents, we need to establish a positive, cooperative tone that lays the foundation for joint efforts. Consider the following:

"Hello, Mrs. Hansen? This is Connie Lichter, Jared's math teacher."

"Oh, uh, is something wrong?"

"Not really. I just wanted to call to share with you some information about your son. He's a bright, energetic boy, and I enjoy seeing him in class every day. But he's been having some problems handing in his homework assignments in my class."

"I didn't know he had math homework. He never brings any home"

"That might be part of the problem. He just might forget that he has any to do. I have a suggestion. Why don't we set up a system that will help him remember. I'll ask the class to write down their math homework in their folders every day. Please ask Jared to share that with you every night, and make sure that it's done. When it's done, why don't you initial it so I know you and he talked? I think that will help a lot. How does that sound?"

"Sure. I'll try that."

"Good. We don't want him to fall behind. If he has problems with the homework, have him come to my room before or after school, and I'll help him. Is there anything else I can do? . . . If not, I look forward to meeting you soon."

This phone conversation was positive and created a partnership between home and school. In addition, it created a specific plan of action.

Decisions about calling parents regarding a management issue is a matter of professional judgment. The question "To what extent does this issue influence learning?" is a good guideline. For instance, a middle school student swearing in class is probably best handled by the teacher. On the other hand, if the student's swearing or other behaviors are disrupting learning activities, a call to parents is appropriate.

The last principle—emphasize accomplishments—refers to all types of communication with parents. When you call parents about a problem, you should first try to describe accomplishments and progress if possible. You can also initiate communication for the sole purpose of reporting good news, as Joan did in her e-mails to parents. All parents want reasons to feel proud of their children, and sharing accomplishments can further improve the home–school partnership.

As it continues to expand, technology provides an additional channel for improving communication. For example, as they become more accessible, both voice mail and e-mail are useful to connect with busy parents. In many schools, newsletters and other communications are offered in electronic, as well as paper, form.

Communication with Parents: Accommodating Learner Diversity

Classrooms with large numbers of students having diverse backgrounds present unique communication challenges. Lower parent participation in school activities is often associated with families that are members of cultural minorities, lower-socioeconomic status (SES), and having a child enrolled in either special education or English-as-a-second-language programs (Hong & Ho, 2005). Each makes communication between home and school more challenging, both for parents and teachers.

Economic, Cultural, and Language Barriers

Economics, culture, and language can all create barriers that limit the involvement of minority and low-SES parents in school activities (A. C. Barton et al., 2004; Gollnick & Chinn, 2004). Jobs often prevent parents from helping their children with homework. In addition, high rates of family mobility can create obstacles to effective parent–school communication

(Nakagawa et al., 2002). Low-SES parents frequently lack resources, such as child care, transportation, Internet connections, and even telephones, that allow them to participate in school activities.

Parents who have had negative experiences with school as a child may remember them and be less likely to participate in school-related activities. These parents require a great deal of encouragement and support to become involved (D. Kaplan, Liu, & Kaplan, 2001).

Because of their respect for teachers, many Asian and Latino parents hesitate to become involved in matters they believe are best handled by the school (Harry, 1992), but this deference to authority is sometimes misinterpreted as apathy by teachers.

Management style can also be a source of cultural conflict. Some cultural minorities expect strong teacher input and misinterpret indirect approaches as not caring (Gollnick & Chinn, 2004; Irvine & Armenta, 2001). These parents want teachers to be "warm demanders" who show their caring through high expectations and a management style that is warm and direct.

Language can be another barrier. Parents of bilingual students may not speak English, which leaves the child responsible for interpreting communications sent home by teachers. Homework poses a special problem because parents cannot interpret assignments or provide help, and schools sometimes compound the difficulty by using educational jargon when they send letters home.

One solution to language barriers is a telephone network (Peña, 2000). Teachers ask bilingual parents to phone other parents, who can then assist in disseminating the message.

Involving Minority Parents

Teachers can narrow the home–school gap by offering parents specific strategies for working with their children (Epstein, 2001). Let's see how one teacher does this.

> Nancy Collins, a middle school English teacher, has students who speak five different native languages in her class. During the first 2 days of school, she prepares a letter to parents, and with the help of her students, translates it into their native languages. The letter begins by describing how pleased she was to have students from varying backgrounds in her class, saying that they enrich all her students' educations.
>
> She continues with a short list of procedures and encourages the parents to support their children's efforts by the following:
>
> 1. Ask their children about school each night.
> 2. Provide a quiet place to study for at least 90 minutes a day.
> 3. Limit television until homework is finished.
> 4. Ask to see samples of their children's work and grades they've received.
>
> She tells them that the school is having an open house and the class with the highest attendance will win a contest. She concludes the letter by reemphasizing that she is pleased to have so much diversity in her class. She asks parents to sign and return the letter.
>
> The day before the open house, Nancy has each of her students compose a handwritten letter to their parents in their native languages, asking them to attend. Nancy writes "Hoping to see you there" at the bottom of each note and signs it.

Nancy's letter was positive in at least three ways. First, writing it in the students' native languages communicated sensitivity and caring. Second, the letter included specific suggestions; these are important because they provide parents with concrete suggestions for helping their children (Smally & Reyes-Blanes, 2001). Even parents who cannot read a homework assignment are more involved if they ask their children to explain their schoolwork. The suggestions also let parents know they are needed. Third, by encouraging parents to attend the school's open house, Nancy increased the likelihood that they would do so. If they did, and the experience was positive, their involvement would likely increase.

The process of involving parents begins with awareness. As we more fully realize that parents from cultural minorities and low-SES backgrounds and those whose children have exceptionalities are often reluctant to become involved in school activities, we can redouble our efforts. We can also try to be as clear and specific as possible in our suggestions for parents as they work with their youngsters.

Finally, if parents speak English, phone calls are as effective with them as they are with nonminority parents. Experts suggest calling parents at work, where they are easier to reach,

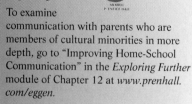

Exploring Further

To examine communication with parents who are members of cultural minorities in more depth, go to "Improving Home-School Communication" in the *Exploring Further* module of Chapter 12 at *www.prenhall. com/eggen*.

and scheduling conferences around their work schedules (Lindeman, 2001). Some teachers even conduct home visits (Bullough, 2001). Although home visits are demanding and time-consuming, nothing communicates a stronger commitment to a young person's education.

Checking Your Understanding

3.1 Explain how Joan's letter home helped to meet the classroom management goals discussed earlier in the chapter.

3.2 In this section, we said that calling parents communicates caring better than any other way. Explain how calling parents communicates caring. (Hint: Think about your study of time earlier in the chapter.)

3.3 Explain why communication with parents who are members of cultural minorities can be even more important than communication with parents in general.

To receive feedback for these questions, go to Appendix B.

Knowledge Extensions

To deepen your understanding of the topics in this section of the chapter and to integrate them with topics you've already studied, go to the *Knowledge Extensions* module for Chapter 12 at *www.prenhall.com/eggen*. Respond to questions 10–12.

Classroom ⊞ Connections

Communicating Effectively with Parents

1. Begin communication during the first few days of school, and maintain it throughout the year.
   - **Elementary:** A kindergarten teacher calls each of her students' parents during the first week of school, tells them how happy she is to have their children in her class, and encourages them to contact her at any time.
   - **Middle School:** Each month, a sixth-grade social studies teacher sends home a "class communicator" describing the topics the students will be studying and giving suggestions parents might follow in helping their children. Students write notes to their parents on the communicator, describing their efforts and progress.
   - **High School:** A geometry teacher sends a letter home at the beginning of the school year describing his homework and assessment policy. He calls parents when more than one homework assignment is missing.

2. Communicate in nontechnical language, and make specific suggestions to parents for working with their children.
   - **Elementary:** A third-grade teacher asks all her parents to sign a contract agreeing that they will (a) designate at least 1 hour an evening when the television is shut off and children do homework, (b) ask their children to show them their homework assignments each day, (c) attend the school's open house, and (d) look at, ask their children

about, and sign the packet of papers that is sent home every other week.
   - **Middle School:** A sixth-grade teacher discusses a letter to parents with his students. He has them explain what each part of the letter says and then asks the students to read and explain the letter to their parents.
   - **High School:** A ninth-grade basic math teacher makes a special effort at the beginning of the school year to explain to parents of students with exceptionalities how she'll modify her class to meet their children's needs. She strongly encourages parents to monitor homework and assist if they can.

3. Take extra steps to communicate with the parents of minority children.
   - **Elementary:** A second-grade teacher in an urban school enlists the aid of several teachers skilled in various languages. When he sends messages home, he asks these teachers' help in translating the notes for parents.
   - **Middle School:** At the beginning of each grading period, a sixth-grade teacher sends a letter home, in each student's native language, describing the topics that will be covered, the tests and the approximate times they will be given, and any special projects that are required.
   - **High School:** A biology teacher, who has many students with parents who speak little English, holds student-led conferences in which the students report on their progress. She participates in each conference and has students serve as translators.

INTERVENING WHEN MISBEHAVIOR OCCURS

Our focus to this point has been on preventing management problems. We emphasized the interdependence of instruction and classroom management, the importance of planning, and the role of carefully taught and monitored rules and procedures. Despite

Successful management interventions stop the unwanted behavior while maintaining the flow of the lesson.

teachers' best efforts, however, they must intervene in cases of disruptive behavior or chronic inattention. In the following sections, we discuss interventions as we consider

- General guidelines for successful intervention
- Cognitive approaches to intervention
- Behavioral approaches to intervention

Guidelines for Successful Interventions

Intervening when problems occur is never easy. If it were, management wouldn't remain an ongoing difficulty for teachers. As you work with your students, we recommend a cognitive management system, but a behavioral approach may be necessary in some cases.

Regardless of the theoretical orientation, several general guidelines increase the likelihood that your interventions will succeed:

- Demonstrate withitness.
- Preserve student dignity.
- Be consistent.
- Follow through.
- Keep interventions brief.
- Avoid arguments.

Demonstrate Withitness. An essential component of successful interventions is known as **withitness,** a teacher's awareness of what is going on in all parts of the classroom at all times and the communication of this awareness to students (Kounin, 1970). Expert teachers describe withitness as "having eyes in the back of your head." Let's look at two teachers.

> Ron Ziers is explaining the process for finding percentages to his seventh graders. While Ron illustrates the procedure, Kareem, in the second desk from the front of the room, is periodically poking Katilyna, who sits across from him. She retaliates by kicking him in the leg. Bill, sitting behind Katilyna, pokes her in the arm with his pencil. Ron doesn't respond to the students' actions. After a second poke, Katilyna swings her arm back and catches Bill on the shoulder. "Katilyna!" Ron says sternly. "We keep our hands to ourselves! . . . Now, where were we?"
>
> Karl Wickes has the same group of students in life science. He puts a transparency displaying a flowering plant on the overhead. As the class discusses the information, he notices Barry whispering something to Julie, and he sees Kareem poke Katilyna, who kicks him and loudly whispers, "Stop it." As Karl asks, "What is the part of the plant that produces fruit?" he moves to Kareem's desk, leans over, and says quietly but firmly, "We keep our hands to ourselves in here." He then moves to the front of the room, watches Kareem out of the corner of his eye, and says, "Barry, what other plant part do you see in the diagram?"

Karl, in contrast with Ron, demonstrated withitness in at least three ways:

- He identified the misbehavior immediately, and quickly responded by moving near Kareem. Ron did nothing until the mischief had spread to other students.
- He correctly identified Kareem as the original cause of the incident. In contrast, Ron reprimanded Katilyna, leaving students with a sense that he didn't know what was going on.
- He responded to the more serious infraction first. Kareem's poking was more disruptive than Barry's whispering, so Karl first responded to Kareem and then simply called on Barry, which drew him back into the activity, making further intervention unnecessary.

Withitness. A teacher's awareness of what is going on in all parts of the classroom at all times and the communication of this awareness to students, both verbally and nonverbally

Withitness involves more than dealing with misbehavior after it happens (Hogan et al., 2003). Teachers who are withit also watch for evidence of inattention or confusion; they approach, or call on, inattentive students to bring them back into lessons; and they respond to signs of confusion with questions such as "Some of you look puzzled. Do you want me to rephrase that question?" They are sensitive to students and make adjustments to ensure that they are as attentive and successful as possible.

Preserve Student Dignity. Preserving a student's dignity is a basic principle of any intervention. As we saw in Chapters 10 and 11, safety is essential for motivation, and the emotional tone of your interactions with students influences both the likelihood of their compliance and their attitudes toward you and the class. Loud public reprimands, criticism, and sarcasm reduce students' sense of safety, create resentment, and detract from classroom climate. When students break rules, simply reminding them of why the rule is important, as Judy did with Rachel, and requiring compliance is as far as a minor incident should go.

Be Consistent. "Be consistent" is recommended so often that it has become a cliché. The need for consistency is obvious, but achieving complete consistency in the real world is difficult, if not impossible. In fact, experts recommend that our interventions be contextualized and individual, appropriate for the situation and student (Doyle, 1986). For example, most classrooms have a rule about speaking only when recognized by the teacher, and as you're monitoring seat work, someone asks another student a brief question about the assignment and then goes back to work. Failing to remind the student that talking is not allowed during seat work is technically inconsistent, but you don't intervene, and you shouldn't. On the other hand, a student who repeatedly turns around and whispers becomes a disruption, and intervention is necessary.

Follow Through. Following through means doing what you've said you'll do. Without follow-through, a management system breaks down because students learn that teachers aren't fully committed to maintaining an orderly environment. This is confusing and leaves them with a sense of uncertainty. Once again, the first few days of the school year are important. If you follow through consistently during this period, management will be much easier during the rest of the year.

Keep Interventions Brief. Keep all interventions as brief as possible. A negative relationship exists between time spent on discipline and student achievement; extended interventions break the flow of a lesson and take time away from instruction (Good & Brophy, 2003).

Judy applied this principle in her work with her seventh graders in the opening case study. She communicated her withitness and resolve by moving near him and calling on him. She spoke briefly to Rachel, and her interventions didn't disrupt the flow of her lesson.

Avoid Arguments. Finally, avoid arguing with students. Teachers never "win" arguments. They can exert their authority, but resentment is often a side effect, and the encounter may expand into a major incident.

Consider the following example that occurred after a teacher directed a chronically misbehaving student to move:

> *Student:* I wasn't doing anything.
> *Teacher:* You were whispering, and the rule says listen when someone else is talking.
> *Student:* It doesn't say no whispering.
> *Teacher:* You know what the rule means. We've been over it again and again.
> *Student:* Well, it's not fair. You don't make other students move when they whisper.
> *Teacher:* You weren't listening when someone else was talking, so move.

The student knew what the rule meant and was simply playing a game with the teacher, who allowed herself to be drawn into an argument. Let's look at another example.

> *Teacher:* Please move up here (pointing to an empty desk in the first row).
> *Student:* I wasn't doing anything.
> *Teacher:* One of our rules says that we listen when someone else is talking. If you would like to discuss this, come in and see me after school. Please move now (turning back to the lesson as soon as the student moves).

This teacher maintained an even demeanor and didn't allow herself to be pulled into an argument or even a brief discussion. She handled the event quickly, offered to discuss it with the student, and immediately turned back to the lesson.

Having considered these general guidelines, we turn now to cognitive interventions.

Cognitive approaches to management emphasize learner understanding.

Cognitive Interventions

As we emphasized earlier in the chapter, understanding is at the core of cognitive approaches to management because learner understanding is essential for accepting rules and interventions. In the last section, for example, you saw that achieving complete consistency is virtually impossible. A cognitive approach assumes that students can accommodate minor inconsistencies because they understand the differences in incidents.

In this section, we examine three factors, each intended to promote learner understanding:

- Verbal–nonverbal congruence
- I-messages
- Logical consequences

Verbal–Nonverbal Congruence

To become responsible for their actions, students must understand teachers' communications, and to be understandable, verbal and nonverbal communication must be congruent. Let's look at two examples.

Karen Wilson's eighth graders are working on their homework as she circulates among them. She is helping Jasmine when Jeff and Mike begin whispering loudly behind her.

"Jeff. Mike. Stop talking, and get started on your homework," she says, glancing over her shoulder.

The two slow their whispering, and Karen turns back to Jasmine. Soon, the boys are whispering as loudly as ever.

"I thought I told you to stop talking," Karen says over her shoulder again, this time with irritation in her voice.

The boys glance at her and quickly resume whispering.

Isabel Rodriguez is in a similar situation with her pre-algebra students. As she is helping Vicki, Ken and Lance begin horseplay at the back of the room.

Isabel excuses herself, turns, and walks directly to the boys. Looking Lance in the eye, she says evenly and firmly, "Lance, we have plenty to do before lunch, and noise disrupts others' work. Begin your homework now." Then, looking directly at Ken, she continues, "Ken, you, too. Quickly now. We have only so much time, and we don't want to waste it." She waits briefly until they are working quietly and then returns to Vicki.

The teachers had similar intents, but their impact on the students was very different. When Karen glanced over her shoulder to tell the boys to stop whispering and then failed to follow through, her communication was confusing; her words said one thing, but her body language said another. When messages are inconsistent, people attribute more credibility to tone of voice and body language than to the spoken words (Aronson et al., 2005).

In contrast, Isabel's communication was clear and consistent. She responded immediately, faced her students directly, emphasized the relationship between order and learning, and made sure her students were on-task before she went back to Vicki. Her verbal and nonverbal behaviors were consistent, so her message made sense. Characteristics of effective nonverbal communication are outlined in Table 12.5.

I-Messages

Successful cognitive interventions should both focus on the inappropriate behavior and help students understand the effects of their actions on others. To illustrate, let's look again at Judy's encounter with Rachel.

Judy:	Move up here (Quietly in response to Rachel's whispering and note passing).
Rachel:	What did I do?
Judy:	When we talked about our rules at the beginning of the year, we agreed that it was important to listen when other people are

Effective interventions require both clear verbal and congruent nonverbal communication.

Table 12.5 Characteristics of nonverbal communication

Nonverbal Behavior	Example
Proximity	A teacher moves close to an inattentive student.
Eye contact	A teacher looks an off-task student directly in the eye when issuing a directive.
Body orientation	A teacher directs himself squarely to the learner, rather than over the shoulder or sideways.
Facial expression	A teacher frowns slightly at a disruption, brightens her face at a humorous incident, and smiles approvingly at a student's effort to help a classmate.
Gestures	A teacher puts her palm out (Stop!) to a student who interjects as another student is talking.
Vocal variation	A teacher varies the tone, pitch, and loudness of his voice for emphasis and displays energy and enthusiasm.

talking. . . . We can't learn when people aren't paying attention, and I'm uncomfortable when my class isn't learning.

In this encounter, Judy sent an **I-message,** a nonaccusatory communication that addresses a behavior, describes the effects on the sender, and the feelings it generates in the sender (T. Gordon, 1974, 1981).

In using an I-message, Judy addressed Rachel's behavior rather than her character or personality. When teachers say, "You're driving me up the wall," for example, they're implying weaknesses in students' characters. Focusing on the incident communicates that a student is valued but the behavior is unacceptable. Judy also described the behavior's effect on the sender—herself—and the feelings it generated: "We can't learn when people aren't paying attention, and I'm uncomfortable when my class isn't learning." The intent of an I-message is to promote understanding, as it always is in cognitive interventions. Judy wanted Rachel to understand the effects of her actions on others, and if successful, this became a step toward responsible behavior.

Logical Consequences
Logical consequences are outcomes that are conceptually related to the misbehavior; they help learners see a link between their actions and the consequences that follow. For example:

Allen, a rambunctious sixth grader, is running down the hall toward the lunchroom. As he rounds the corner, he bumps Alyssia, causing her to drop her books.

"Oops," he replies, continuing his race to the lunchroom.

"Hold it, Allen," Doug Ramsay, who is monitoring the hall, says. "Go back and help her pick up her books and apologize."

"Aww."

"Go on," Doug says firmly.

Allen walks back to Alyssia, helps her pick up her books, mumbles an apology, and then returns. As he approaches, Doug again stops him.

"Now, why did I make you do that?" Doug asks.

"'Cuz we're not supposed to run."

"Sure," Doug says pleasantly, "but more important, if people run in the halls, they might crash into someone, somebody might get hurt, and we don't want that to happen. . . . Remember that you're responsible for your actions. Think about not wanting to hurt yourself or anybody else, and the next time, you'll walk whether a teacher is here or not. . . . Now, go on to lunch."

In this incident, Doug helped Allen understand that having to pick up Alyssia's books was the logical outcome of running in the hall and the problems it caused (bumping into Alyssia and causing her to drop her books). Applying logical consequences is a "cognitive" intervention because the goal is learner understanding. Children who understand the effects of their actions on others become more altruistic and are more likely to take actions to make up for their misbehavior (Berk, 2006).

I-message. A nonaccusatory communication that addresses a behavior, describes the effects on the sender, and the feelings it generates in the sender

Logical consequences. Outcomes that are conceptually related to the misbehavior

Behavioral approaches to management stress positive reinforcement for desired behaviors.

Behavioral Interventions

We have emphasized cognitive approaches to management in this chapter, so a discussion of behavioral interventions may appear inconsistent with the chapter's message. In the real world, however, students sometimes seem either unable or unwilling to accept responsibility for their behavior, and time or safety concerns require more direct approaches. In situations such as these, behavioral interventions can be effective. Experts recommend using behavioral interventions as short-term solutions to specific problems (Freiberg, 1999a), with development of responsibility remaining the long-term goal (Gottfredson, 2001).

Let's see how Cindy Daines, a first-grade teacher, uses a behavioral intervention with her students.

Cindy has a problem during transitions. Although she tries alerting the groups and having the whole class make transitions at the same time, every one takes several minutes.

In an attempt to improve the situation, she makes "tickets" from construction paper, buys an assortment of small prizes, and displays the items in a fishbowl on her desk. She then explains, "We're going to play a little game to see how quiet we can be when we change lessons. . . . Whenever we change, such as from language arts to math, I'm going to give you 2 minutes, and then I'm going to ring this bell." She rings the bell to demonstrate. "Students who have their books out and are waiting quietly when I ring the bell will get one of these tickets. On Friday afternoon, you can turn them in for prizes you see in this fishbowl. The more tickets you have, the better the prize will be."

During the next few days, Cindy moves around the room, handing out tickets and making comments such as "I really like the way Merry is ready to work," "Ted already has his books out and is quiet," and "Thank you for moving to math so quickly."

She realizes her strategy is starting to work when she hears "Shh" and "Be quiet!" from the students, so she moves away from awarding prizes and instead allows the students to "buy" free time with their tickets. Soon she is giving students Friday afternoon parties as group rewards when the class has accumulated enough tickets. She gradually is able to space out the group rewards as the students' become more responsible.

Cindy used concepts from both behaviorism and social cognitive theory in her system. Her tickets, free time, and Friday afternoon parties were all positive reinforcers for making quick and quiet transitions. In addition, her comments, such as, "I really like the way Merry is ready to work" and "Ted already has his books out and is quiet" were vicarious reinforcers for the other children.

As you saw in Chapter 6, reinforcement is more effective than punishment for changing behavior, and this principle applies when using behavioral interventions (Alberto & Troutman, 2006). However, as you also found, punishment may be necessary in some cases. *Desists, timeout, detention,* and *response cost* can be effective forms of punishment, whereas *physical punishment, embarrassment and humiliation,* and *class work* are ineffective. Guidelines for using punishment as management alternatives are outlined in Figure 12.5.

Designing and Maintaining a Behavioral Management System

The foundation of a behavioral management system comprises clear rules and expectations followed by consistent consequences. Designing a management system based on behaviorism involves the following steps:

- Prepare a list of specific rules, such as "Leave your desk only when given permission."
- Specify reinforcements for obeying each rule and punishments for breaking the rules, such as the consequences in Table 12.6.
- Display the rules, and explain the consequences.
- Consistently apply consequences.

A behavioral system doesn't preclude providing rationales or creating the rules with learner input. The primary focus, however, is on clearly speci-

Figure 12.5 Guidelines for using punishment in classrooms

- Use punishment as infrequently as possible.
- Apply punishment immediately and directly to the behavior.
- Apply punishment only severe enough to eliminate the behavior.
- Apply punishment dispassionately instead of angrily.
- Explain and model alternative positive behaviors.

Table 12.6   Sample consequences for following or breaking rules

Consequences for Breaking Rules	
First infraction	Name on list
Second infraction	Check by name
Third infraction	Second check by name
Fourth infraction	Half-hour detention
Fifth infraction	Call to parents
Consequences for Following Rules	
A check is removed for each day that no infractions occur. If only a name remains, and no infractions occur, the name is removed.	
All students without names on the list are given 45 minutes of free time Friday afternoon to do as they choose. The only restrictions are that they must stay in the classroom, and they must not disrupt the students who didn't earn the free time.	

fying behavioral guidelines and applying consequences, in contrast with a cognitive approach, which emphasizes learner understanding and responsibility.

In designing a comprehensive management system, teachers usually combine elements of both cognitive and behavioral approaches. Behavioral systems have the advantage of being immediately applicable; they're effective for initiating desired behaviors, particularly with young students; and they're useful for reducing chronic misbehavior. Cognitive systems take longer to produce results, but they are more likely to develop learner responsibility.

Despite the most thorough planning and effective implementation, the need for periodic teacher intervention is inevitable. Keeping both cognitive and behavioral approaches in mind, we next consider a series of intervention options.

An Intervention Continuum

Disruptions can vary from isolated incidents, like a student briefly whispering to a neighbor, to chronic infractions, such as someone repeatedly poking and kicking other students, or even fighting. Because infractions vary, teachers' reactions should also vary. To maximize instructional time, interventions should be as unobtrusive as possible. A continuum of interventions is shown in Figure 12.6 and described in the following sections.

Praising Desired Behavior

Because promoting desired behaviors is an important goal, praising students for displaying them is a sensible first intervention. Praise occurs less often than might be expected, so efforts to "catch 'em being good" are worthwhile, especially as a method of prevention. Elementary teachers can praise openly and freely, and middle and secondary teachers can make private comments such as "I'm extremely pleased with your work this week—keep it up." Making an effort to acknowledge desired behavior and good work significantly contributes to a positive classroom climate.

Exploring Further

Assertive discipline is a behavioral classroom management system that has received a great deal of attention over the years. To read more about it, including a critical analysis, go to "Assertive Discipline" in the *Exploring Further* module of Chapter 12 at *www.prenhall.com/eggen*.

Online Case Book

To analyze a case study involving a comprehensive classroom management system, go to the *Online Case Book* for Chapter 12 at *www.prenhall.com/eggen*.

Figure 12.6   An intervention continuum

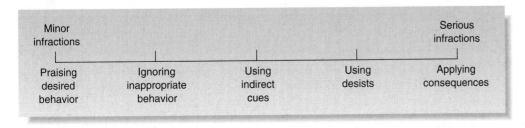

Reinforcing behaviors that are incompatible with misbehavior is an extension of this idea (Kellam, Ling, Meriaca, Brown, & Ialongo, 1998; Zanolli, Daggett, Ortiz, & Mullins, 1999). For instance, participating in a learning activity is incompatible with daydreaming, so calling on a student, and reinforcing any attempt to respond, is more effective than reprimanding a student for not paying attention.

Ignoring Inappropriate Behavior

In Chapter 6, you saw that behaviors that aren't reinforced become extinct. The attention students receive when they're admonished for minor misbehaviors is often reinforcing, so ignoring the behavior can eliminate the reinforcers teachers might be inadvertently providing (Alberto & Troutman, 2006; Baldwin & Baldwin, 2001). This is effective, for example, when two students are whispering, but soon stop. A combination of praising desired behaviors, reinforcing incompatible behaviors, and ignoring misbehavior can be effective with minor disruptions.

Using Indirect Cues

Effective teachers use indirect cues—such as proximity, methods of redirecting attention, and vicarious reinforcers—when students are displaying behaviors that can't be ignored but can be stopped or diverted without addressing them directly (Babad, Avni-Babad, & Rosenthal, 2003; V. F. Jones & Jones, 2004). For example, Judy moved near Darren and called on him after she heard Kendra mutter. Her proximity stopped his misbehavior, and calling on him directed his attention back to the lesson.

Vicarious reinforcement can also be effective. Teachers, especially in the lower grades, can use other students as models and vicariously reinforce the rest of the students for imitating their behaviors with statements such as, "I really like the way Row 1 is working quietly."

Using Desists

As you saw in Chapter 6, a desist is a verbal or nonverbal communication a teacher uses to stop a behavior (Kounin, 1970). "Glenys, we leave our seats only when given permission," "Glenys!" and a finger to the lips, or a stern facial expression are all desists. They are the most common teacher reactions to misbehavior.

Clarity and tone are important for the effectiveness of desists. For example, "Randy, what is the rule about touching other students?" or "Randy, how do you think that makes Willy feel?" are more effective than "Randy, stop that," because they link the behavior to a rule or to the behavior's effects. Students react to these subtle differences, preferring rule and consequence reminders to teacher commands (Nucci, 1987).

The tone of desists should be firm but not angry. Kounin (1970) found that kindergarten students handled with rough desists actually became more disruptive, and older students are uncomfortable in classes where harsh desists are used. In contrast, firm but pleasant reprimands, the suggestion of alternative behaviors, and questioning that maintains student involvement in learning activities can reduce off-task time in most classrooms.

Clear communication (including congruence between verbal and nonverbal behavior), an awareness of what is happening in the classroom (withitness), and effective instruction are essential in using desists. However, even when these elements exist, desists sometimes aren't enough.

Applying Consequences

Careful planning and effective instruction often eliminate most misbehavior before it starts. Some minor incidents can be ignored, and simple desists will stop others. When these strategies don't work, however, teachers must apply consequences. Logical consequences are preferable because they treat misbehaviors as problems and create a conceptual link between behaviors and outcomes. However, because classrooms are complex and busy, it isn't always possible to solve problems with logical consequences. In these instances, behavioral consequences—those solely intended to change a behavior quickly and efficiently—offer an acceptable alternative. Let's look at an example.

Jason is an intelligent and active fifth grader. He loves to talk and seems to know just how far he can go before Mrs. Aguilar becomes exasperated with him. He understands the rules and the reasons for them, but his interest in talking seems to take precedence. Ignoring him isn't working. A call to his parents helped for a while, but soon he's back to his usual behavior—never quite enough to require a drastic response, but always a thorn in Mrs. Aguilar's side.

Finally, she decides to give him only one warning. At a second disruption, he's placed in time-out from regular instructional activities. She meets with him and explains the rules. The next day, he begins to misbehave almost immediately.

"Jason," she warns, "you can't work while you're talking, and you're keeping others from finishing their work. Please get busy."

He stops, but a few minutes later, he's at it again.

"Jason," Mrs. Aguilar says quietly as she moves back to his desk, "Please go back to the time-out area."

Now, a week later, Jason is working quietly with the rest of the class.

Behavior like Jason's is common, particularly in elementary and middle schools, and it causes teacher stress more often than does highly publicized threats of violence and bodily harm (V. F. Jones & Jones, 2004). The behavior is disruptive, so it can't be ignored; praise for good work helps to a certain extent, but students get much of their reinforcement from friends; desists work briefly, but teachers tire of constant monitoring. Mrs. Aguilar had little choice but to apply behavioral consequences with him.

Consistency is the key to promoting change in students like Jason. He understood what he was doing, and he was capable of controlling himself. When he could, with certainty, predict the consequences of his behavior, he quit. He knew that his second infraction would result in a time-out, and when it did, he quickly changed his behavior. There was no argument, little time was used, and the class wasn't disrupted.

Checking Your Understanding

4.1 One of your students is talking without permission. Describe an I-message that would be appropriate as a response.

4.2 A teacher sees a seventh-grader spit on the door to the classroom. According to the information in this section, which is the more appropriate response: putting the student in after-school detention (which is part of the school's management policy) or having the student wash the door? Explain.

4.3 Using the information in this section of the chapter, explain why *verbal–nonverbal congruence, I-messages,* and *logical consequences* are "cognitive" interventions.

To receive feedback for these questions, go to Appendix B.

Knowledge Extensions

To deepen your understanding of the topics in this section of the chapter and to integrate them with topics you've already studied, go to the *Knowledge Extensions* module for Chapter 12 at *www.prenhall.com/eggen*. Respond to questions 13–19.

Classroom ⊞ Connections

Using Interventions Successfully in Your Classroom

1. Use problem-solving strategies and logical consequences to help students develop responsibility. Hold discussions regarding fairness or equity after class and in private.

- **Elementary:** During weekly classroom chores, two first graders begin a tug-of-war over a cleaning rag and knock over a potted plant. The teacher talks to the students, they agree to clean up the mess, and they write a note to their parents explaining that they will be working in the classroom before school the next week to pay for a new pot.

- **Middle School:** A social studies teacher tries to make her interventions learning experiences, identifying rules that were broken and explaining why the rules exist. In cases of uncertainty, she talks privately to students to clear up misunderstanding.

- **High School:** After having been asked to stop whispering for the second time in 10 minutes, a ninth grader protests that he was asking about the assigned seat work. The teacher reminds him of the incidents, points out that his behavior is disruptive, and applies a consequence without further discussion. After class, the teacher talks to him, explaining why rules exist, and reminding him that he is expected to accept responsibility for his behavior.

2. Use positive reinforcers to initiate and teach desirable behaviors.

- **Elementary:** A first-grade teacher, knowing that the times after recess and lunch are difficult for many students, institutes a system in which the class has 1 minute after a timer rings to settle down and get out their materials. When the class meets the requirement, they earn points toward free time.

- **Middle School:** To encourage students to clean up quickly after labs, a science teacher offers 5 minutes of free time to talk in their seats if the lab is cleaned up in time. Students who don't clean up in time are required to finish in silence.
- **High School:** A ninth-grade basic math teacher is encountering problems getting his students to work quietly in small groups. He discusses the problem with the class and then closely monitors the groups, circulating and offering praise and reinforcement when they are working smoothly.

3. Follow through consistently in cases of disruptive behavior.

- **Elementary:** A second-grade teacher finds that transitions to and from recess, lunch, and bathroom breaks are noisy and disruptive. She talks with the class about the problem, initiates a "no-talking" rule during these transitions, and carefully enforces the rule.

- **Middle School:** A teacher separates two seventh graders who disrupt lessons with their talking, telling them the new seat assignments are theirs until further notice. The next day, they sit in their old seats as the bell is about to ring. "Do you know why I moved you two yesterday?" the teacher says immediately. After a momentary pause, both students nod. "Then move quickly now, and be certain you're in your new seats tomorrow. You can come and talk with me when you believe you're ready to accept responsibility for your talking."
- **High School:** An eleventh-grade history teacher reminds students about being seated when the bell rings. As it rings the next day, two girls remain standing and talking. The teacher turns to them and says, "I'm sorry, but you must not have understood me yesterday. To be counted on time, you need to be in your seats when the bell rings. Please go to the office and get a late-admit pass."

SERIOUS MANAGEMENT PROBLEMS: VIOLENCE AND AGGRESSION

As you work with a small group of your fourth graders, a fight suddenly breaks out between Trey and Neil, who are supposed to be working on a group project together. You look up to the sounds of shouting and see Trey flailing at Neil, who is essentially attempting to fend off Trey's blows. Trey is often verbally aggressive and sometimes threatens other students.

What do you do?

Matt, one of your seventh graders, is shy and a bit small for his age. As he comes into your class this morning, he appears disheveled and depressed. Concerned, you take him aside and ask if anything is wrong. With some prodding he tells you that he repeatedly gets shoved around on the school grounds before school, and two boys have been taunting him and calling him gay. "I hate school," he comments.

How do you respond?

Tyrone, one of your students, has difficulty maintaining his attention and staying on task. He frequently makes loud and inappropriate comments in class and disrupts learning activities. You warn him, reminding him that being disruptive is unacceptable, and blurting out another comment will result in time-out.

Within a minute, Tyrone blurts out again. "Please go to the time-out area," you say evenly.

"I'm not going and you can't make me," he says defiantly. He remains seated at his desk.

How do you react?

We discuss situations such as these in this section.

School Violence and Aggression

As you saw in Chapter 3, school violence is a problem in the United States. Since 1993, this country has had the highest rates of childhood homicides, suicides, and firearm-related deaths of any of the world's 26 wealthiest nations (Aspy et al., 2004).

Youth violence has declined in the past decade, but rates remain high, with more than a third of students reporting being involved in a physical fight, and 9.3 percent of youth having carried a weapon to school in the past 12 months (Kodjo, Auinger, & Ryan, 2003). You may have to respond to students' fighting or some other act of violence at some point in your teaching career.

Serious management problems require both short- and long-term strategies.

Responding to Aggression Against Peers

Aggressive students must not be allowed to hurt peers or damage property. In the situation between Trey and Neil, you are required by law to intervene. If you don't, you and the school can be sued for **negligence,** the failure to exercise sufficient care in protecting students from injury. However, the law doesn't say that you're required to physically break up the fight; immediately reporting it to administrators is an acceptable response.

An effective response to violence involves three steps: (1) Stop the incident (if possible), (2) protect the victim, and (3) get help. For instance, in the case of the classroom scuffle, a loud noise, such as shouting, clapping, or slamming a chair against the floor, will often surprise the students enough so they'll stop (Evertson et al., 2003). At that point, you can begin to talk to them, check to see if the victim is all right, and then take the students to the main office, where you can get help. If your interventions don't stop the fight, you should immediately send an uninvolved student for help. Unless you're sure that you can separate the students without danger to yourself, or them, attempting to do so is unwise. As a guideline, teachers' responsibilities in situations such as these is first to the safety of the other students and their own safety, second to the involved students, and then to property (Good & Brophy, 2003).

Responding to Bullying

As you also saw in Chapter 3, bullying, a more subtle form of school violence, is receiving increased attention. Educators now recognize its damaging effects on students, as well as possible links to suicide and other forms of school violence (Nansel et al., 2001). In most cases of school shooting incidents, the perpetrators had been victims of bullying (Aspy et al., 2004).

Teachers should respond to bullying in the same way as they react to other aggressive acts (Pellegrini, 2002). Those committing the acts should be stopped, and victims should be protected. Attempts can then be made to help the bullies understand the consequences of their actions, both for the victims and for themselves. (We examine long-term efforts later in this section.)

Responding to Defiant Students

Most teachers find the possibility of dealing with a student like Tyrone frightening. What do you do when he says, "I'm not going, and you can't make me?" Experts offer two suggestions (Henricsson & Rydell, 2004). First, remain calm to avoid a power struggle. A teacher's natural tendency is to become angry and display a show of force to demonstrate to students that they "can't get away with it." Remaining calm gives you time to get your temper under control, and the student's mood when facing a calm teacher is likely to change from anger and bravado to fear and contrition (Good & Brophy, 2003).

Second, if possible, give the rest of the class an assignment, and then tell the student calmly but decisively to please step outside the classroom so you can talk. Communicate a serious and concerned, but not threatening tone.

Defiance is often the result of a negative student–teacher relationship (Gregory & Weinstein, 2004). These negative relationships occur most often with students who display externalizing behavior problems, such as aggressive behavior toward others, temper tantrums, or impulsive and hyperactive behavior (Henricsson & Rydell, 2004). When a problem occurs with such a student, it is important to let the student say everything that is on his or her mind in a private conference before responding. Finally, arrange to meet with the student before or after school, treat the defiance as a problem, and attempt to generate solutions that are acceptable to both of you.

In the case of a student who refuses to step outside the classroom, or one who becomes physically threatening, immediately send someone to the front office for help. Defiance at this level likely requires help from a mental health professional.

Long-Term Solutions to Violence and Aggression

Long-term, students must be helped to understand that aggression will not be permitted and that they're accountable for their behavior (Burstyn & Stevens, 2001). Trey, for

Negligence. The failure to exercise sufficient care in protecting students from injury

example, must understand that his aggressive actions are unacceptable and that they won't be tolerated. Then, teaching students broadly applicable personal and social competencies such as self-control, perspective taking, and constructive assertiveness can reduce aggressive behaviors and improve social adjustment (Weissberg & Greenberg, 1998). For example, one program taught students to express anger verbally instead of physically and to solve conflicts through communication and negotiation instead of fighting (J. Lee et al., 1998). Learning to make and defend a position—to argue effectively—is one approach. Students taught to make effective arguments, and who learn that arguing and verbal aggression are very different, become less combative when encountering others with whom they disagree (Burstyn & Stevens, 1999). Learning to argue also has incidental benefits: Those skilled in this area are seen by their peers as intelligent and credible.

To decrease aggressive incidents, experts also recommend the involvement of parents and other school personnel (Burstyn & Stevens, 2001). Not surprisingly, research indicates that students who communicate openly with their families are less likely to be involved in aggressive acts or behave as bullies (Aspy et al., 2004). In addition, school counselors and psychologists, social workers, and principals have all been trained to deal with these problems and can provide advice and assistance (Greenberg et al., 2003). Experienced teachers can also provide a wealth of information about how they've handled similar problems. No teacher should face serious problems of violence or aggression alone.

In conclusion, we want to put violence and aggression into perspective. Although they are possibilities, and you should understand options for dealing with them, the majority of your management problems will involve issues of cooperation and motivation. Many problems can be prevented, others can be dealt with quickly, and some require individual attention. We have all heard about students carrying guns to school and incidents of assault on teachers. Statistically, however, considering the huge numbers of students who pass through schools each day, these incidents remain very infrequent.

Exploring Further

A number of conflict resolution programs have been developed to help aggressive students learn to behave in socially acceptable ways. To read more about these programs, go to "Conflict Resolution" in the *Exploring Further* module of Chapter 12 at *www.prenhall.com/eggen*.

Knowledge Extensions

To deepen your understanding of the topics in this section of the chapter and to integrate them with topics you've already studied, go to the *Knowledge Extensions* module for Chapter 12 at *www.prenhall.com/eggen*. Respond to questions 20–22.

Checking Your Understanding

5.1   Describe your legal responsibilities in the event of a fight or other aggressive act in your classroom.

5.2   If you encounter two students fighting, or you see a smaller student being bullied by one or more other students, what is the first step you should take?

5.3   Describe the focus of a long-term cognitive approach to bullying and other acts of aggression.

To receive feedback for these questions, go to Appendix B.

Meeting Your Learning Objectives

1. Describe the relationships between classroom management, the complexities of classrooms, and motivation and learning.

- Orderly classrooms help reduce teachers' concerns about classroom management, typically viewed as one of the most important problems teachers face. Management is the primary concern of beginning teachers and an ongoing issue for veterans.

- Classroom management helps teachers cope with the multidimensional, immediate, unpredictable, and public nature of teaching.
- Students in well-managed classrooms are more motivated to learn and achieve higher than those in environments that are less orderly.

2. **Analyze the planning components for creating productive learning environments in examples of classroom activities.**

   - Effective planning for classroom management considers developmental differences in students.
   - The physical arrangement of the classroom affects teachers' efforts to create an orderly classroom.
   - Organizing instruction to maximize instructional time is an essential element of management planning.
   - The cornerstone of an effective management system is a well-planned system of rules and procedures.

3. **Explain how effective communication with parents helps meet classroom management goals and why communication with parents who are members of cultural minorities is particularly important.**

   - Effective communication with parents includes early communication and maintains communication throughout the school year.
   - Effective communication with parents helps meet classroom management goals because home–school cooperation increases students' willingness to do homework, improves attitudes and behaviors, and increases attendance and graduation rates.
   - Effective communication with parents who are members of cultural minorities includes making special efforts to involve them in school activities, as well as attempting to communicate with them in their native languages.
   - Communication with parents who are members of cultural minorities is particularly important because economic, cultural, and language barriers can all limit the involvement of these parents.

4. **Describe effective interventions in cases of learner misbehavior.**

   - Effective interventions should be brief and consistent. Arguments should be avoided and student dignity preserved.
   - Effective characteristics of cognitive interventions include verbal–nonverbal congruence, I-messages, active listening, and logical consequences.
   - Behavioral interventions center around a list of clearly stated rules and specific consequences for obeying or breaking the rules.
   - Interventions should intrude on learning activities no more than necessary and proceed from the least intrusive, such as praise for desired behavior, to those more intrusive, such as application of behavioral consequences.

5. **Describe teachers' legal responsibilities and the steps involved in responding to acts of violence and aggression.**

   - Teachers are required by law to intervene in cases of violence or aggression.
   - The first steps involved in responding to fighting or bullying are to stop the incident, protect the victim, and seek assistance.
   - Long-term responses to violence and aggression include attempts to help aggressive students understand the impact of their behavior on others and the development of skills that include the ability to behave in socially acceptable ways.

Developing as a Professional

Developing as a Professional: Praxis™ Practice

In the opening case study, you saw how instruction and classroom management converged in Judy Harris's classroom. In the following case study, Janelle Powers, another seventh-grade geography teacher, also has her students working on a lesson about the Middle East. As you read, compare the two teachers' approaches to classroom management, and answer the questions that follow.

Janelle teaches geography in a large, urban middle school. With 29 students, her classroom is crowded.

This morning, in homeroom, Shiana comes through the classroom doorway just as the tardy bell rings.

"Take your seat quickly, Shiana," Janelle directs. "You're just about late. All right. Listen up, everyone," she continues. "Ali?"

"Here."

"Gaelen?"

"Here."

"Chu?"

"Here."

Janelle finishes taking the roll and then walks around the room, handing back a set of papers.

"You did quite well on the assignment," she comments. "Let's keep up the good work. . . . Howard and Manny, please stop talking while I'm returning papers. Can't you just sit quietly for 1 minute?"

The boys, who were whispering, turn back to the front of the room.

"Now," Janelle continues, returning to the front of the room, "we've been studying the Middle East, so let's review for a moment. . . . Look at the map and identify the longitude and latitude of Cairo. Take a minute, and figure it out right now."

The students begin as Janelle goes to her file cabinet to get out some transparencies.

"Stop it, Damon," she hears Leila blurt out behind her.

"Leila," Janelle responds sternly, "we don't talk out like that in class."

"He's poking me, Mrs. Powers."

"Are you poking her, Damon?"

". . ."

"Well?"

"Not really."

"You did, too," Leila complains.

"Both of you stop it," Janelle warns. "Another outburst like that, Leila, and your name goes on the board."

As the students are finishing the problem, Janelle looks up from the materials on her desk to check an example on the overhead. She hears Howard and Manny talking and laughing at the back of the room.

"Are you boys finished?"

"Yes," Manny answers.

"Well, be quiet then until everyone is done," Janelle directs and goes back to rearranging her materials.

"Quiet, everyone," she again directs, looking up in response to a hum of voices around the room. "Is everyone finished? . . . Good. Pass your papers forward. . . . Remember, put your paper on the top of the stack. . . . Roberto, wait until the papers come from behind you before you pass yours forward."

Janelle collects the papers, puts them on her desk, and then begins, "We've talked about the geography of the Middle East, and now we want to look at the climate a bit more. It varies somewhat. For example, Syria is extremely hot in the summer but is actually quite cool in the winter. In fact, it snows in some parts.

"Now, what did we find for the latitude of Cairo?"

"Thirty," Miguel volunteers.

"North or south, Miguel? . . . Wait a minute. Howard? . . . Manny? . . . This is the third time this period that I've had to say something to you about your talking, and the period isn't even 20 minutes old yet. Get out your rules and read me the rule about talking without permission. . . . Howard?"

" . . . "

"It's supposed to be in the front of your notebook."

" . . . "

"Manny?"

"'No speaking without permission of the teacher,'" Manny reads from the front page of his notebook.

"Howard, where are your rules?"

"I don't know."

"Move up here," Janelle directs, pointing to an empty desk at the front of the room. "You've been bothering me all week. If you can't learn to be quiet, you will be up here for the rest of the year."

Howard gets up and slowly moves to the desk Janelle has pointed out. After Howard is seated, Janelle begins again, "Where were we before we were rudely interrupted? . . . Oh yes. What did you get for the latitude of Cairo?"

"Thirty North," Miguel responds.

"Okay, good. . . . Now, Egypt also has a hot climate in the summer—in fact, very hot. The summer temperatures often go over 100 Fahrenheit. Egypt is also mostly desert, so the people have trouble making a living. Their primary source of subsistence is the Nile River, which floods frequently. Most of the agriculture of the country is near the river."

Janelle continues presenting information to the students for the next several minutes.

"Andrew, are you listening to this?" Janelle interjects when she sees Andrew poke Jacinta with a ruler.

"Yes," he responds, turning to the front.

"I get frustrated when I see people not paying attention. When you don't pay attention, you can't learn, and that frustrates me because I'm here to help you learn." Janelle continues with her presentation.

Short-Answer Questions

In answering these questions, use information from the chapter and link your responses to specific information in the case.

1. Analyze Janelle's planning for classroom management.
2. Evaluate the effectiveness of Janelle's management interventions.
3. The chapter stressed the interdependence of management and instruction. Analyze the relationship between management and instruction in Janelle's class. Include both strengths and weaknesses in the relationship.

ONLINE PORTFOLIO ACTIVITIES

To develop your professional portfolio, further apply your understanding of chapter content, and address the INTASC standards, go to the Companion Website, then to this chapter's Online Portfolio Activities. Complete the suggested activities.

IMPORTANT CONCEPTS

classroom management (p. 371)
cognitive approach to management (p. 371)
discipline (p. 371)
I-message (p. 393)
logical consequences (p. 393)
negligence (p. 399)

organization (p. 377)
procedures (p. 377)
productive learning environment (p. 368)
rules (p. 377)
withitness (p. 390)

CHAPTER 13

Creating Productive Learning Environments:
Principles and Models of Instruction

Chapter Outline	Learning Objectives
	After completing your study of this chapter, you should be able to
Planning for Instruction Selecting Topics • Preparing Learning Objectives • Preparing and Organizing Learning Activities • Planning for Assessment • Instructional Alignment • Planning in a Standards-Based Environment	**1** Describe the steps involved in planning for instruction, and identify an additional step when planning in a standards-based environment.
Implementing Instruction: Essential Teaching Skills Attitudes • Organization • Communication • Focus: Attracting and Maintaining Attention • Feedback • Questioning • Review and Closure • Learning Contexts: Instruction in Urban Classrooms	**2** Identify examples of essential teaching skills in learning experiences, and analyze the role of feedback in promoting learning.
Models of Instruction Direct Instruction • Lecture and Lecture-Discussion • Guided Discovery • Cooperative Learning • Cooperative Learning: A Tool for Capitalizing on Diversity	**3** Explain the relationships between essential teaching skills and models of instruction, and analyze the components of different models.
Assessment and Learning: Using Assessment as a Learning Tool	**4** Identify the characteristics of effective assessments, and explain the relationships between effective assessments and essential teaching skills.

A
s with basic skills in reading, writing, and mathematics that all people must possess to function in our society, essential professional knowledge and skills exist that all teachers must possess if they are to promote as much learning as possible in their students. As you read the following case study, and the content of this chapter, think about the knowledge and skills that Scott Sowell, a middle school science teacher in an urban school in the southeast, demonstrates as he plans and conducts lessons on force and the movement of air.

As Scott is working on a Saturday afternoon to plan his next week he looks at his textbook and his state's standards for middle school science. One standards says:

"The student knows that if more than one force acts on an object, then the forces can reinforce or cancel each other, depending on their direction and magnitude" (Florida Department of Education, 2003, p. 12 [italics added]).

He also thinks about his past experience with the topic and decides that he will incorporate the standard into lessons on Bernoulli's principle, the law that helps explain how different forces enable airplanes to fly. "The kids like it," he remembers, "because it's both interesting and has a lot of real-world applications. These applications are important, and I'll build my lesson around them."

He first decides that he wants his students to understand that a force is a push or a pull, and he thinks about the examples of *force* he will use, such as pulling a student's chair across the floor, pushing on the chalk board, and having students lift their books above their desks. Then, he thinks, "I'll demonstrate that objects move in the direction of the greater force, which will get them to the idea in the standard that 'forces can reinforce or cancel each other, depending on their direction and magnitude.' I'll do a little tug of war with one of the kids," he smiles to himself, "and I'll let him pull me to show that since his force is greater, we'll move that way."

He then decides to teach Bernoulli's principle on Tuesday and Wednesday with a review Thursday and a quiz on Friday.

We will return to Scott's lesson later in the chapter, but before we do, we want to begin with two questions. (1), What specific planning decisions did Scott make to create a productive learning environment? (2) How did professional knowledge influence his decision making as he planned? We examine these questions in the next section of the chapter.

PLANNING FOR INSTRUCTION

As we said in Chapter 12, when teachers create productive learning environments (environments that are orderly and focused on learning), classroom management and instruction are interdependent. In Chapter 12 we discussed classroom management in detail, and now we turn to instruction.

We introduced our study of educational psychology in Chapter 1 with a discussion of the different types of professional knowledge that expert teachers possess: knowledge of content, pedagogical content knowledge, general pedagogical knowledge, and knowledge of learners and learning. Nowhere is the need for this knowledge more prominent than in planning and implementing instruction. Scott drew on each of the four kinds of knowledge as he made decisions about the following:

- Select topics that are important for students to study.
- Specify learning objectives related to the topics.
- Prepare and organize learning activities to help students reach the objectives.
- Design assessments to measure the amount students have learned.
- Ensure that instruction and assessments are aligned with the learning objectives. (L. Anderson & Krathwohl, 2001)

We examine these decisions in the sections that follow, and our discussion will help us answer the first question we asked at the beginning of this section: "What specific planning decisions did Scott make to create a productive learning environment?"

Selecting Topics

"What is important to study?" is one of the most fundamental questions that teachers face as they plan (L. Anderson & Krathwohl, 2001). Textbooks, curriculum guides, and standards, such as the one Scott considered in his planning, are sources teachers commonly use to help answer the question (Reys, Reys, & Chavez, 2004). Their personal philosophies, students' interests in the topic, and real-world applications are other sources. Scott, for example, believed that Bernoulli's principle was important, because it was related to *force*, a key idea in science, and because it helps students understand a number of real-world phenomena such as how airplanes can fly.

Some teachers tacitly avoid making decisions about what is important to study by simply teaching the topics as they appear in their textbooks or curriculum guides (Zahorik, 1991). This can be a problem, however, because more content appears in textbooks than can be effectively learned in depth. Teachers' knowledge of content is particularly important in helping decide if a topic is important enough to allocate time to teaching it.

Preparing Learning Objectives

Although deciding what is important to study is an essential first step, teachers must answer the question: What do I want the students to know or be able to do with respect to the topic? The answer to this question is a **learning objective.** Clear learning objectives are essential because they guide the rest of the decisions teachers make when they plan. Without clear objectives, teachers don't know how to design their learning activities, and they can't create accurate assessments. Learning objectives also guide teachers as they implement their learning activities. Unsuccessful learning activities are often the result of teachers' not being clear about their learning objectives.

Having "clear" learning objectives doesn't imply that they must be written. It means that teachers are clear in their thinking about the objectives. For example, Scott didn't have his objectives for the lesson explicitly written. He was very clear about what he wanted his students to understand, however, as we'll see when he implemented his lesson.

Objectives in the Cognitive Domain

Scott wanted his students to understand the concept of *force,* the relationships among forces, and how to apply Bernoulli's principle to real-world examples. These describe learning objectives in the **cognitive domain,** the area of learning that focuses on memory and higher processes such as applying and analyzing. Let's take a brief historical look at objectives in this domain.

In his classic work *Basic Principles of Curriculum and Instruction,* Ralph Tyler (1950) suggested that the most useful form for stating objectives is "to express them in terms which identify both the kind of behavior to be developed in the student and the content or area of life in which this behavior is to operate" (p. 46). Applications of his ideas, such as management-by-objectives in the business world, became popular in the 1950s and 1960s. Some approaches, such as Robert Mager's in his highly readable book *Preparing Instructional Objectives* (1962), expanded Tyler's original conception to include the conditions under which learners would demonstrate the behavior and the criteria for acceptable performance. Mager's work also strongly influenced teaching and remains popular today (Mager, 1998). Examples of objectives using Mager's approach are outlined in Table 13.1.

A popular alternative to Mager's approach was offered by Norman Gronlund (2004), who suggested that teachers state a general objective, such as *know, understand,* or *apply,* followed by specific learning outcomes that operationally define these terms. Table 13.2 includes examples of objectives written according to Gronlund's suggestions.

Each of these approaches to preparing objectives was influenced by behaviorism. Ralph Tyler used *behavior* and *content* in his description of objectives, Mager also used the term *behavior* in his, and Gronlund emphasized that each specific learning outcome, "starts with an action verb that indicates observable student responses; that is, responses that can be seen by an outside observer" (Gronlund, 2004, p. 23).

More recent thinking about objectives reflects the influence of cognitive learning theory on teaching and avoids the use of both behavior and content (L. Anderson & Krathwohl, 2001). Educational leaders today recommend stating objectives in terms of students'

Learning objective. Statement that specifies what students should know or be able to do with respect to a topic or course of study

Cognitive domain. The area of learning that focuses on memory and higher processes such as applying and analyzing

Table 13.1 Objectives using Mager's approach

Objective	Condition	Performance	Criteria
Given 3 examples of *force* in a real-world problem, students will identify each.	Given 3 examples of force in a real-world problem.	Identify	Each
Given 10 problems involving subtraction with regrouping, students will correctly solve 7.	Given 10 problems involving subtraction with regrouping	Solve	7 of 10
Using a topic of their choice, students will write a paragraph that includes at least two examples each of metaphors, similes, and personification.	Using a topic of their choice	Write	A paragraph including 2 examples each of metaphors, similes, and personification

Table 13.2 Objectives using Gronlund's approach

General Objective	Specific Learning Outcome
Understands *force*	1. Identifies examples of force in problems 2. Gives examples of forces
Understands fractions with grouping	1. Recognizes need for regrouping 2. Performs operations 3. Solves problems
Uses figurative language in writing	1. Gives written examples 2. Puts examples into written context

cognitive processes instead of *behaviors*. In addition, they replace the inert concept of content with knowledge to reflect what students should know or acquire (L. Anderson & Krathwohl, 2001). For example, "Students will understand the concept *force*" was one of Scott's objectives. *Force* is the knowledge, and *understand* is the cognitive process; it specifies what the students will do with that knowledge.

A Taxonomy for Cognitive Objectives

One of Scott's objectives was for his students to "understand that force is a push or a pull." Other objectives involving the same knowledge exist, however. For example, possibilities include

- Students will state the definition of force in their own words.
- Students will solve a problem requiring them to determine the net effect of two forces on the same object.

Although all three objectives involve the same topic—the concept *force*—they reflect different ways of demonstrating that knowledge: understanding the concept, knowing a definition, and determining the net force. Each requires different cognitive processes. In response to these differences, researchers developed a system to classify different objectives (L. Anderson & Krathwohl, 2001). A revision of the famous "Bloom's taxonomy" first published in 1956 (Bloom, Englehart, Furst, Hill, & Krathwohl, 1956), the system is a matrix with 24 cells that represent the intersection of four types of knowledge with six cognitive processes. The revision reflects the dramatic increase in understanding of learning and teaching since the middle of the 20th century, when the original taxonomy was created, and it now more nearly reflects the influence of cognitive learning theory on education (L. Anderson & Krathwohl, 2001). The revised taxonomy appears in Figure 13.1.

To understand this matrix, let's analyze the three objectives we stated earlier. *Force* is a concept, so Scott's objective would be placed in the cell where *understand* intersects with *conceptual knowledge*. The second objective, being able to state a definition of *force*, would be classified into the cell where *remember* intersects with *conceptual knowledge*.

Exploring Further

The original taxonomy developed by Bloom et al. (1956) still interests many people. To read more about it, go to "Bloom's Taxonomy" in the *Exploring Further* module of Chapter 13 at *www.prenhall.com/eggen*.

Figure 13.1 A taxonomy for learning, teaching, and assessing

The Knowledge Dimension	The Cognitive Process Dimension					
	1. Remember	2. Understand	3. Apply	4. Analyze	5. Evaluate	6. Create
A. Factual knowledge						
B. Conceptual knowledge						
C. Procedural knowledge						
D. Metacognitive knowledge						

Source: From Lorin W. Anderson & David R. Krathwohl, *A Taxonomy for Learning, Teaching, and Assessing: A Revision* of Bloom's Objectives, © 2001. Published by Allyn and Bacon, Boston, MA. Copyright © 2001 by Pearson Education. Reprinted by permission of the publisher.

The third objective, solving a problem, would be placed in the cell where *apply* intersects with *procedural knowledge,* since solving a problem requires the application of procedural knowledge.

The taxonomy reminds us that learning is complex, with many possible outcomes. It also reminds us that we want our students to do more than remember factual knowledge. Unfortunately, a great deal of schooling focuses as much on this most basic type of objective as it does on the other 23 combined. Focusing on the other forms of knowledge and more advanced cognitive processes is even more important now in the 21st century, as student thinking, decision making, and problem solving are increasingly emphasized.

Preparing and Organizing Learning Activities

Once Scott had specified his learning objectives, he then prepared and organized his learning activities. This process involves four steps:

1. Identify the components of the topic—the concepts, principles, and relationships among them that students should understand.
2. Sequence the components of the topic.
3. Prepare examples that students can use to construct their knowledge of each component.
4. Order the examples with the most concrete and obvious presented first.

Scott used a task analysis to accomplish these steps. Let's examine this planning tool.

Task Analysis: A Planning Tool

Task analysis is the process of breaking content down into component parts and making decisions about sequencing the parts. Task analysis can take three different forms: behavioral, information processing, or subject matter analysis (Alberto & Troutman, 2006; Jonassen, Hannum, & Tessmer, 1989).

In a behavioral analysis, the teacher identifies and sequences the behaviors students must demonstrate to complete the learning activity (the task). For instance, when learning to do word processing, the student must be able to turn on the computer; access the desired program; input text; save, move, and delete files; and change formatting. Each is necessary before learning more sophisticated skills, such as creating and inserting tables, artwork, and graphics.

In an information processing analysis, the teacher identifies and sequences the cognitive processes required for the learning activity. For instance, to solve word problems in math, students must correctly recognize the type of problem, retrieve the necessary math facts, apply the appropriate operations, and use metacognitive skills to assess their answers.

Exploring Further

While most of the focus in schools is on cognitive outcomes, *attitudes and values* and *motor skills* are also important. To read more about objectives in these areas, go to "Objectives in the Affective and Psychomotor Domains" in the *Exploring Further* module of Chapter 13 at *www.prenhall.com/eggen.*

Task analysis. The process of breaking content down into component parts and making decisions about sequencing the parts

Planning for assessment is an integral part of the total planning process.

In a subject matter analysis, the teacher first breaks down the topic into specific concepts and principles, then sequences them in a way that will be most understandable to students, and finally prepares examples for each.

This is what Scott did. He knew that his students needed to understand the concept *force* and the principle relating forces and movement in order to understand Bernoulli's principle. He then sequenced these topics and prepared examples of each. Finally, he planned to teach *force* and movement on Monday and Bernoulli's principle on Tuesday and Wednesday. Scott's task analysis is outlined in Table 13.3.

The preceding discussion helps us answer the second question we asked at the beginning of the chapter: "How did professional knowledge influence Scott's decision making as he planned?" Scott's planning in general, and his task analysis in particular, was grounded in his professional knowledge. For example, his knowledge of content helped him decide what topics were important to study, and his decisions about what examples to use reflected his pedagogical content knowledge. Deciding to first illustrate force by pulling a student across the floor because it was an attention getter was based on his knowledge of learners and learning. Each was essential in helping him promote as much learning as possible. (His general pedagogical knowledge will be demonstrated in the way he conducted the lesson, which you will see later in the chapter.)

Planning for Assessment

Formal assessments are given after students complete learning activities, so we might assume that thinking about assessment also occurs after learning activities are conducted. This isn't true; effective teachers think about assessment while preparing objectives and learning activities. Effective assessments not only answer the question: "How can I determine if my students have reached the learning objectives?" but also "How can I use assessment to facilitate learning?" Assessment decisions are essential during planning because they help teachers align their instruction, the topic of the next section.

Instructional Alignment

Thinking about assessment during planning served an additional function for Scott. It helped him answer the question, "How do I know that my instruction and assessments are logically connected to my objectives?"

Instructional alignment is the match between learning objectives, learning activities, and assessments, and it is essential for promoting learning (Bransford et al., 2000; L. Anderson & Krathwohl, 2001).

Instructional alignment. The match between learning objectives, learning activities, and assessments

Table 13.3 A task analysis for teaching force and Bernoulli's principle

Task Analysis Step	Example
1. Identify components of the topic.	Scott identified the concept *force*, the principle *objects move in the direction of the greater force* and *Bernoulli's principle* as different components of the topic.
2. Sequence the components.	Scott planned to first teach the concept *force;* second, the principle stating that *objects move in the direction of the greater force;* and third, *Bernoulli's principle.*
3. Prepare examples of each.	Scott prepared examples of each, such as pulling a student in a chair, pushing on the chalkboard, and having students lift their books.
4. Order the examples.	Scott first planned to pull a student in his chair because it was the best attention getter, then push on the chalkboard, and finally have the students lift their books.

Without this alignment, it is difficult to know what is being learned. Students may be learning valuable information, but one cannot tell unless there is alignment between what they are learning and the assessment of that learning. Similarly, students may be learning things that others don't value unless curricula and assessments are aligned with . . . learning goals. (Bransford et al., 2000, pp. 151–152)

Instructional alignment helps students understand what is important to learn and helps teachers match instructional strategies and assessments to learning objectives (Morrison, Ross, & Kemp, 2004). Scott's instruction was aligned. His objectives were for students to understand the concept *force* and the principle relating force and movement; his learning activity focused on those objectives, and his assessment measured the extent to which students understood these ideas.

Maintaining alignment isn't as easy as it appears. For instance, if a teacher's objective is for students to be able to write effectively, yet learning activities focus on isolated grammar skills, the instruction is out of alignment. It is similarly out of alignment if the objective is for students to apply math concepts to real-world problems, but learning activities have students practicing computation problems. Instructional alignment encourages teachers to ask, "What does my objective (e.g., "apply math concepts") actually mean, and do my learning and assessment activities actually lead to the objective?"

Planning in a Standards-Based Environment

A great deal has been written about Americans and American students lacking knowledge about their history and their world. Research suggests, for example, that 60% of adult Americans don't know the name of the president who ordered the dropping of the atomic bomb, 42% of college seniors can't place the Civil War in the correct half century, and most Americans can't find the Persian Gulf on a map (Bertman, 2000). These examples are in social studies, and similar concerns have been raised about math and science, where international comparisons indicate that American students lag behind many of their counterparts in other countries (Gonzales et al., 2004; Lemke et al., 2004). The result has been a move toward establishing **standards,** statements that describe what students should know or be able to do at the end of a prescribed period of study (Darling-Hammond, 2001). Some standards are stated specifically, whereas others are quite general. Those stated in general terms are often followed by more specific statements called, for example, *benchmarks, expectations,* or *indicators.*

Although the standards movement is highly controversial, with critics (e.g., Amrein & Berliner, 2002; Berliner, 2005; Paris, 1998) and proponents (e.g., Bishop, 1998; Hirsch, 2000) lining up on opposite sides, virtually every professional organization in education has prepared lists of standards. They exist in most academic areas ranging from core subjects, such as math, science, and English, to the arts, foreign language, and physical education. Even support organizations such as the National Parent Teacher Association (2000) have created standards. In addition, every state as well as the District of Columbia and Puerto Rico have set academic standards for students.

It is virtually certain that your planning decisions will be influenced by standards. Your school will be held accountable for helping students meet the standards, so you must be able to design learning activities to reach this goal.

Standards are essentially statements of objectives. Since they're prescribed, you might think that this would reduce the number of decisions you must make, but this often isn't true. For example, you will probably have to interpret the meaning of the standard, which can be more demanding than establishing your own objectives. Then, once you've made this decision, planning is similar to what it would be under any other circumstance.

Scott did this as he planned. He decided that the principle *objects move in the direction of the greater force* would be an appropriate interpretation of the standard you saw in the case study; then he identified examples; and finally, he prepared assessment items to measure the amount his students learned. His planning ensured both that he helped his students meet the standard and that his objectives, learning activities, and assessments were aligned.

One way that Scott used standards to frame his decisions was through a process called **backward design,** an approach to planning that first identifies desired learning objectives, then specifies ways to assess whether or not these objectives are met, and finally, establishes learning experiences to reach the objectives (Wiggins & McTighe, 2005). It really is

Analyzing Classrooms Video
To analyze the extent to which a teacher's instruction is aligned, go to Episode 20, "Analyzing Instructional Alignment," on DVD 2, accompanying this text.

Exploring Further
Professional organizations have Websites that publish standards in those areas. To read about them in your area of interest, go to "Organizations' Standards" in the *Exploring Further* module of Chapter 13 at *www.prenhall.com/eggen.*

Standards. Statements that describe what students should know or be able to do at the end of a prescribed period of study

Backward design. A planning approach that begins with learning objectives, then specifies assessments and learning activities to ensure that all are aligned

nothing more than good instructional planning that ensures that objectives, learning activities, and assessments are aligned.

In some cases, professional organizations assist the process of backward design by offering sample assessments linked to their standards. For example, the National Council of Teachers of Mathematics (2000) created the following standard for middle school math:

Number and Operations Standard for Grades 6–8

Instructional programs from prekindergarten through grade 12 should enable all students to compute fluently and make reasonable estimates:
In grades 6–8 all students should:

- work flexibly with fractions, decimals, and percents to solve problems;
- compare and order fractions, decimals, and percents efficiently and find their approximate locations on a number line;
- develop meaning for percents greater than 100 and less than 1. (p. 214)

NCTM (2000) then suggests the following to assess students' ability to "work flexibly with fractions":

a. If ▮▮▮▮▮▮ is 3/4, draw the fraction strip for 1/2, for 2/3, for 4/3, and for 3/2. Be prepared to justify your answers.

b. ◄———┼——┼———► Using the points you are given on the number line
        1 1½ above, locate 1/2, 2 1/2, and 1/4. Be prepared to justify your answer. (p. 214)

Sample assessments are helpful because they make interpreting standards easier. You then need to prepare learning activities aligned with the standard and the assessment. This is the essence of *backward design*.

As you see, the thinking involved in planning for standards-based instruction is similar to the thinking involved in any planning. The standard begins the decision making process by presenting an objective in a form with varying degrees of specificity. You then are responsible for making decisions about learning activities and assessments.

Checking Your Understanding

1.1 Describe the four essential steps involved in planning for instruction.

1.2 Planning in a standards-based environment involves one additional step beyond the planning steps described in this section of the chapter. Identify this additional step.

1.3 Classify the following learning objective into one of the cells of the taxonomy table (Figure 13.1, on page 409), and explain your classification: *Students will learn to search for relevant and irrelevant information in applications of all the topics they study.*

To receive feedback for these questions, go to Appendix B.

Knowledge Extensions

To deepen your understanding of the topic in this section and to integrate it with topics you've already studied, go to the *Knowledge Extensions* module for Chapter 13 at *www.prenhall.com/eggen*. Respond to questions 1–6.

Classroom Connections

Applying an Understanding of Expert Planning in Your Classroom

1. Consider the level of your instruction, and prepare objectives that require students to do more than remember factual knowledge.

- **Elementary:** A fourth-grade teacher wants her students to understand the different functions of the human skeleton, such as why the skull is solid, the ribs are curved, and the femur is the largest bone in the body. "This is better than simply having them label the different bones," she thinks.

- **Middle School:** A seventh-grade geography teacher wants his students to understand how climate is influenced by the interaction of a number of variables. To reach his objective, he gives students a map of a fictitious island, together with longitude, latitude, topography, and wind direction. He then has students make and defend conclusions about the climate of the island.
- **High School:** A biology teacher wants her students to understand the relationships between an organism's body structure and its adaptation to its environment. She has her students identify the characteristics of parasitic and nonparasitic worms and the differences between them. The students then link the differences to the organisms' abilities to adapt to their environments.

2. Ensure that your objectives, learning activities, and assessments are aligned. Prepare assessments during planning, and keep the need for alignment in mind as you plan.

- **Elementary:** The fourth-grade teacher in her unit on the skeletal system prepares the following as an assessment: "Suppose we humans walked on all fours, as chimpanzees and gorillas do. Describe how our skeletons would be different from our skeletons now."
- **Middle School:** To assess his students' developing knowledge, the geography teacher gives them another map of a fictitious island with different mountain ranges, wind directions, ocean currents, and latitude and longitude. He then asks them to identify and explain where the largest city on the island would most likely be.
- **High School:** The biology teacher describes two organisms, one with radial symmetry and the other with bilateral symmetry. She asks her students to identify the one that is most advanced with respect to evolution and to explain their choices.

IMPLEMENTING INSTRUCTION: ESSENTIAL TEACHING SKILLS

To introduce this section, let's return to Scott's work with his students. He taught the concept of *force* and the principle stating that objects move in the direction of the greater force on Monday. We join him as he begins class Tuesday.

"Let's go over what we did yesterday," he begins just as the bell stops ringing. "What is a force? . . . Shantae?"

". . . A push or a pull," she responds after thinking for a second.

"Good. . . . Yes, a force is a push or a pull."

He then pushes on the board and blows on an object sitting on his desk, asks the students if they're forces, and hearing "Yes," has them explain why.

He continues by having Damien tug on one end of a stapler while he holds the other end to illustrate the principle relating force and movement, first tugging hard enough to move the stapler toward himself, stating that he is exerting the greater force and then allowing Damien to exert the greater force to move the stapler in the opposite direction.

"Keep those ideas in mind," Scott says as he moves around the room quickly placing two pieces of 8 1/2 × 11 paper in front of each student.

He tells students to pick up one of the papers and demonstrates how to blow over the surface as shown here.

"What did you notice when we blew over the top? . . . David?"

"The paper moved."

"How did the paper move?" Scott continues. "Do it again."

David again blows over the surface of the paper, and Scott repeats, "What did the paper do?"

". . . It came up."

"Yes," Scott waves energetically. "When you blow over it, it comes up."

He then has the students pick up both pieces of paper and demonstrates how to blow between them, as shown here.

"What did you notice here? . . . Sharon?" Scott asks after they've all completed the demonstration.

". . . The papers came together."

"Okay, good," Scott smiles. "Now, Let's look at one more. . . . I have a funnel and a ping-pong ball. . . . Watch what happens. I'm going to shoot Tristan in the head when I blow," he jokes, pointing to one of the students.

He places the ball into the mouth of the funnel, blows through the funnel's stem, and takes his hand away from the mouth. To the students' surprise, the ball stays in the funnel.

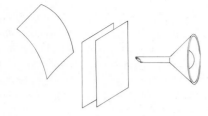

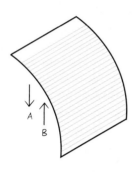

Figure 13.2 Essential teaching skills

Scott has several of the students repeat the demonstration, has the students make observations, and then draws sketches of the three examples on the board and says, "Let's look at these."

Referring to the first sketch, Scott asks, "Was I blowing on the top or the bottom? . . . Rachel?"

"The top."

"And what happened there? . . . Heather?"

"The paper rose up."

Referring to the second sketch he asks, "What did we do here . . . Shantae?"

"We blew in between them."

"And what happened there . . . Ricky?"

"They came together."

"So we saw this paper rise up," he says, pointing at the first sketch, "and we saw these papers come together," he continues.

Scott does a similar analysis of the funnel and then says, "Let's think about the forces here," as he turns back to the first sketch . . . . What forces are acting on the paper? . . . Colin?"

"Gravity."

"And which direction is gravity pulling?"

"Down."

Scott draws an arrow pointing downward indicating the force of gravity.

"What other force is acting on the paper? . . . William?" he continues.

"Air," William says, pointing up.

"How do you know it's pushing up?"

"The paper moved up."

"Exactly. You know there's a force pushing up, because the paper moved up. . . . And objects move in the direction of the greater force."

Scott guides the students through a similar analysis of the second and third examples, leading them to conclude that the forces pushing the two papers together were greater than the forces pushing them apart, since they moved together, and, the force pushing the ball into the funnel was greater than the force pushing the ball out, since the ball stayed in the funnel.

"Now let's look again at the forces and where we blew," Scott continues, as he moves back to the first sketch. "Study the drawings carefully, and see what kind of relationship exists between the two."

After several seconds Heather concludes, "It seems like wherever you blew, the force was stronger on the opposite side."

"So every place you blew, where was the force greater?"

"In the opposite direction."

Seeing that the bell is going to ring in a minute, Scott continues, "So, a person named Bernoulli first discovered this principle. . . . He said that every time you increase the speed of the air over a surface, the force goes down. . . . So, when I speed up the wind on the top of the paper by blowing over it (holding up the single sheet of paper), the force goes down and this force takes over (motioning underneath the paper to illustrate a force pushing up).

He summarizes the other two examples in the same way, finishing just as the bell ending the period begins to ring.

In the previous section, we looked at Scott's thinking as he planned his unit. Now let's examine the skills he demonstrated as he implemented it. He displayed several **essential teaching skills,** basic abilities that all teachers, including those in their first year of teaching, should have to promote order and as much student learning as possible. We expect to see teachers demonstrating essential teaching skills regardless of the content area, grade level, or specific teaching strategy being used.

Derived from a long line of research (Good & Brophy, 2003; Shuell, 1996), the essential teaching skills are outlined in Figure 13.2 and discussed in the sections that follow. We describe them separately for the sake of clarity, but they are interdependent; none is as effective alone as it is in combination with the others. Let's look at them.

Attitudes

Admittedly, *attitudes* are not skills, but positive teacher attitudes are fundamental to effective teaching. As we saw in Chapter 11, teacher characteristics such as *personal teaching efficacy, modeling and enthusiasm, caring,* and *high expectations* promote learner motivation. They also lead to increased student achievement, which isn't surprising, because motivation and learning are so strongly linked (Brophy, 2004; Bruning et al., 2004).

Scott displayed several positive attitudes during his instruction. He was energetic and enthusiastic, he demonstrated respect for students that is one indicator of caring, and his questioning suggested that he expected all of his students to participate and learn. These are the attitudes we hope to see in all teachers.

Organization

Organization demonstrates the interdependence of classroom management and effective teaching. In Chapter 12 you saw that classroom organization included *starting instruction on time, having materials ready,* and *developing automatic routines.* These components help prevent management problems before they start, and they also maximize instructional time. And, the more time available for learning, the more students learn.

Scott was well organized. He began his lesson as soon as the bell finished ringing, he had the sheets of paper, balls, and funnels ready to be handed out, and he made the transition from his review to the learning activity quickly and smoothly. This effective organization was the result of clear thinking and decision making as he planned his lesson.

Effective organization allows teachers to make the best use of instructional time.

Communication

The link between effective communication, student achievement, and student satisfaction with instruction is well documented (Good & Brophy, 2003; I. Weiss & Pasley, 2004). Four aspects of effective communication are especially important for learning and motivation:

- Precise language
- Connected discourse
- Transition signals
- Emphasis

Precise language omits vague terms (e.g., *perhaps, maybe, might, and so on,* and *usually*) from explanations and responses to students' questions. For example, if you ask, "What do high-efficacy teachers do that promotes learning?" and your instructor responds, "Usually, they use their time somewhat better and so on," you're left with a sense of uncertainty about the idea. In contrast if the instructor responds, "They believe they can increase learning, and one of their characteristics is the effective use of time," you're given a clear picture, and this clarity leads to increased achievement.

Connected discourse refers to instruction that is thematic and leads to a point. If the point of the lesson isn't clear, if it is sequenced inappropriately, or if incidental information is interjected without indicating how it relates to the topic, classroom discourse becomes *disconnected* or *scrambled.* Effective teachers keep their lessons on track, minimizing time on matters unrelated to the topic (Burbules & Bruce, 2001; Leinhardt, 2001).

Transition signals are verbal statements indicating that one idea is ending and another is beginning. For example, an American government teacher might signal a transition by saying, "We've been talking about the Senate, which is one house of Congress. Now we'll turn to the House of Representatives." Because not all students are cognitively at the same place, a transition signal alerts them that the lesson is making a conceptual shift—moving to a new topic—and allows them to prepare for it.

Emphasis, a fourth aspect of effective communication, consists of verbal and vocal cues that alert students to important information in a lesson (Jetton & Alexander, 1997).

For example, Scott raised his voice—a form of vocal emphasis—in saying, "Keep those ideas in mind," as he moved from his review to the lesson itself. When teachers say, "Now remember everyone, this is very important" or "Listen carefully now," they're using verbal emphasis.

Precise language. Teacher talk that omits vague terms from explanations and responses to students' questions

Connected discourse. Instruction that is thematic and leads to a point

Transition signals. Verbal statements indicating that one idea is ending and another is beginning

Emphasis. Verbal and vocal cues that alert students to important information in a lesson

Sensory focus helps maintain students' attention throughout a lesson.

Redundancy, or repeating a point, is also an effective form of emphasis. Asking students, "What did we say earlier that these problems have in common?" stresses an important feature in the problems and helps students link new to past information. Redundancy is particularly important when reviewing abstract rules, principles, and concepts (Brophy & Good, 1986; Shuell, 1996).

Knowledge of Content: Its Role in Clear Communication

At the beginning of the chapter, we said that expert teachers' knowledge of content is deep and thorough. This knowledge is important for clear communication, because teachers who clearly understand the topics they teach use clearer language, and their lessons are more thematic (their discourse is more connected) than those whose background is weaker (Carlsen, 1987; Cruickshank, 1985).

If you are uncertain about a topic, you should spend extra time studying to help develop your own understanding, which will then be reflected in clearer language.

You should also be metacognitive. In other words, carefully monitor your speech to be sure that you're using language that is as clear as possible. Videotaping and watching a lesson is a good tool for helping meet this goal. Taping a lesson takes little extra time, and watching the tape on a weekend can be both enlightening and entertaining.

Focus: Attracting and Maintaining Attention

We saw in Chapter 11 that introductory focus *attracts students' attention and provides a framework for a lesson.* Scott provided introductory focus for his students by beginning his lesson with his demonstrations. They attracted students' attention and also provided a context for the rest of the lesson.

Scott's demonstrations and drawings also acted as a form of **sensory focus,** concrete objects, pictures, models, materials displayed on the overhead, or even information written on the chalkboard that teachers use to maintain attention during learning activities.

The following are some examples of forms of sensory focus that teachers in case studies in earlier chapters used:

- Jenny Newhall's demonstration with the cup and water in Chapter 2
- David Shelton's matrix and transparencies in Chapter 7
- Jenny's balances in Chapter 8
- Laura Hunter's classroom diagram and Suzanne Brush's graph in Chapter 9
- DeVonne Lampkin's paragraphs on the overhead in Chapter 11

Examples and other representations of content, which we've strongly emphasized throughout this text, are an effective way to provide sensory focus. Building lessons around high-quality examples both provides the information students need to construct their understanding and also helps maintain attention.

Feedback

The importance of **feedback**—information learners receive about the accuracy or appropriateness of their verbal responses and written work—in promoting learning is so important that it was one of the principles of learning we first stated in Chapter 7 (Bransford et al., 2000; Marzano, 2003). Feedback allows learners to assess the accuracy of their prior knowledge, gives them information about the validity of their knowledge constructions, and helps them elaborate on existing understanding. And, as you saw in Chapters 10 and 11, it is also important for motivation because it provides students with information about their increasing competence and helps satisfy their intrinsic need to understand how they're progressing (Brophy, 2004).

Effective feedback has four essential characteristics:

Sensory focus. Stimuli that teachers use to maintain attention during learning activities

Feedback. Information learners receive about the accuracy or appropriateness of their verbal responses and written work

- It is immediate or given soon after a learner response.
- It is specific.
- It provides corrective information for the learner.
- It has a positive emotional tone (Brophy & Good, 1986; Moreno, 2004).

To illustrate these characteristics, let's look at three examples.

Mr. Dole:	What kind of figure is shown on the overhead, Jo?
Jo:	A square.
Mr. Dole:	Not quite. Help her out, . . . Steve?
Ms. West:	What kind of figure is shown on the overhead, Jo?
Jo:	A square.
Ms. West:	No, it's a rectangle. What is the next figure, . . . Albert?
Ms. Baker:	What kind of figure is shown on the overhead, Jo?
Jo:	A square.
Ms. Baker:	No, remember, we said that all sides have the same length in a square. What do you notice about the lengths of the sides in this figure?

In each case, the teacher gave immediate feedback. However, Mr. Dole gave Jo no information at all, and Ms. West merely identified the figure as a rectangle. Neither gave Jo any corrective information. Ms. Baker, in contrast, provided Jo with specific information that helped her understand the concept.

Although the examples don't illustrate the emotional tone of the teachers' responses, it is important. Harsh, critical, or sarcastic feedback detracts from students' feelings of safety and relatedness, which decreases both motivation and learning (Pintrich & Schunk, 2002).

Praise

Praise is probably the most common and adaptable form of teacher feedback. Research reveals some interesting patterns in its use:

- Praise is used less often than most teachers believe—less than five times per class.
- Praise for good behavior is quite rare; it occurs once every 2 or more hours in the elementary grades and even less as students get older.
- Praise tends to depend as much on the type of student—high achieving, well behaved, and attentive—as on the quality of the student's response.
- Teachers praise students based on the answers they expect to receive as much as on those they actually hear. (Brophy, 1981; Good & Brophy, 2003)

Praising effectively is more complex than it appears. For instance, young children tend to accept praise at face value even when overdone, whereas older students assess the validity of the praise and what they believe it communicates about their ability. Young children bask in praise given openly in front of a class, whereas adolescents often react better if it's given quietly and individually (Stipek, 2002). Experts suggest that praise delivered to older students should reflect genuine accomplishment and be delivered simply and directly using a natural voice (Good & Brophy, 2003). Highly anxious students and those from low-socioeconomic status backgrounds tend to react more positively to praise than students who are confident and those from more advantaged backgrounds (Brophy, 1981; Good & Brophy, 2003).

Finally, although research indicates that specific is more effective than general praise, if every desired answer is praised specifically, it sounds stilted and artificial and disrupts the flow of a lesson. You must judge the appropriate mix of specific and general praise. Experts suggest that praise for student answers that are correct but tentative should provide additional, affirming information, whereas praise for answers delivered with confidence should be simple and general (Rosenshine, 1987).

Written Feedback

Much of the feedback students receive is verbal, but teachers also provide valuable feedback through their notes and comments on student work. Because writing detailed comments is time-consuming, written feedback is often brief and sketchy, providing students little useful information.

Questioning allows teachers to guide student learning while also gauging learning progress.

Figure 13.3 Characteristics of effective questoning

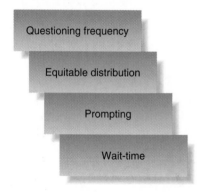

Questioning frequency

Equitable distribution

Prompting

Wait-time

Questioning frequency. The number of questions a teacher asks during a learning activity

Equitable distribution. A questioning strategy in which all students in a class are called on as equally as possible

One solution to this problem is to provide model responses to written assignments. For instance, to help students evaluate their answers to essay items, teachers can write ideal answers, display them on an overhead, and encourage students to compare their answers with the model. The model, combined with discussion and time available for individual help, provides informative feedback that is manageable for the teacher.

Questioning

As instruction becomes more learner centered in response to the cognitive revolution in general and constructivist views of learning in particular, teachers are increasingly being asked to guide learning rather than simply deliver information (Bransford et al., 2000; Leinhardt & Steele, 2005). Questioning is the most effective tool they have for helping students build understanding (J. Olson & Clough, 2004).

Skilled questioning is very sophisticated, but with practice, effort and experience, teachers can and do become expert at it (Kauchak & Eggen, 2003; I. Weiss & Pasley, 2004). To avoid overloading their own working memories, teachers need to practice questioning strategies to the point of automaticity, which leaves working memory space available to monitor students' thinking and assess learning progress.

The characteristics of effective questioning are outlined in Figure 13.3 and discussed in the sections that follow.

Questioning Frequency

Questioning frequency refers to the number of questions a teacher asks during a learning activity, and we saw this illustrated in Scott's work with his students. He developed his entire lesson around questioning.

Questioning increases student involvement, which raises achievement (J. Finn et al., 2003; Leinhardt & Steele, 2005), and greater involvement also increases a learner's sense of control and autonomy, which are essential for intrinsic motivation (R. Ryan & Deci, 2000). Effective teachers ask many more questions than do less effective teachers, and their questions remain focused on their learning objectives (Morine-Dershimer, 1987).

Equitable Distribution

Teachers not only should question frequently, they should also be strategic in who they call on. To illustrate this idea, let's look again at some dialogue from Scott's lesson:

Scott: (Referring to the sketch of the single piece of paper) Was I blowing on the top or the bottom? . . . Rachel?
Rachel: The top.
Scott: And what happened there? . . . Heather?
Heather: The paper rose up.
Scott: (Referring to sketch of the two pieces of paper) What did we do here . . . Shantae?
Shantae: We blew in between them.
Scott: And what happened there . . . Ricky?
Ricky: They came together.

In directing each of his questions to a different student and calling on each student by name, Scott demonstrated a concept called **equitable distribution,** a questioning strategy in which all students in a class are called on as equally as possible (Kerman, 1979). Research indicates that the highest-achieving and most assertive students typically answer most of teachers' questions, and less-assertive and lower-achieving students fall into a pattern of not responding (Good & Brophy, 2003; S. M. Jones & Dindia, 2004). This practice has negative effects on both learning and motivation:

A few reticent students who rarely participate in discussions may still get excellent grades, but most students benefit from opportunities to practice oral communication skills, and distributing response opportunities helps keep them attentive and accountable. Also, teachers who restrict their questions primarily to a small group of active (and usually high-achieving) students are likely to communicate undesirable expectations. (Good & Brophy, 2003, p. 384)

Calling on individual students as equally as possible communicates that the teacher expects all students to be involved and participating. When this becomes a pattern, achievement and motivation improve for both high and low achievers, and classroom management problems decrease (Good & Brophy, 2003; McDougall & Granby, 1996).

Equitable distribution is a simple idea but difficult to implement because it requires careful monitoring of students and a great deal of teacher energy. However, it increases both motivation and learning, and we strongly encourage you to persevere and pursue it rigorously.

Prompting

In attempting equitable distribution, teachers often ask: *What do you do when the student you call on doesn't answer or answers incorrectly?* One answer is **prompting,** an additional question or statement teachers use to elicit an appropriate student response after a student fails to answer correctly. Its value is well documented (Brophy & Good, 1986; Shuell, 1996).

To illustrate, let's look again at some dialogue from Scott's lesson.

Scott: What did you notice when we blew over the top? . . . David?
David: The paper moved.
Scott: How did the paper move? Do it again.

David again blew over the surface of the paper.

Scott: What did the paper do?
David: It came up.

David didn't initially give the answer necessary to help him understand the relationship between force and the movement of the paper, so having him repeat the demonstration was a form of prompting.

As another example, Ken Duran, a language arts teacher, has the following displayed on an overhead:

The girl was very athletic.

He begins a class discussion:

Ken: Identify an adjective in the sentence, . . . Chandra.
Chandra: . . .
Ken: What do we know about the girl?
Chandra: She was athletic.

Ken's prompt, which elicited an acceptable response from Chandra, kept her involved in the activity and provided a successful experience. She hadn't arrived at the answer Ken wanted, but the question kept the process in her zone of proximal development, so she continued to make learning progress.

Prompting isn't always appropriate. For instance, if the question calls for remembering specific factual knowledge, such as "What is 7 times 8?" or "What is the first Amendment to the Constitution?" and the student can't answer, prompting isn't useful; students either know the fact or they don't. It is effective, however, when studying conceptual, procedural, and metacognitive knowledge, and when using cognitive processes beyond remembering (L. Anderson & Krathwohl, 2001).

Wait-Time

After asking a question, teachers should wait a few seconds—alerting all students that they may be called on—before selecting an individual student to answer, and they should then wait a few more seconds to give the student time to think. This period of silence, both before and after calling on a student, is called **wait-time,** and in most classrooms, it is too short, often less than 1 second (Rowe, 1974, 1986; R. Stahl et al., 2005).

A more precise label for wait-time might be "think-time," because waiting gives all students—both the one called on and the rest of the students in the class—time to think. Increasing wait-time, ideally to about 3 to 5 seconds, communicates that all students are expected to answer, results in longer and better answers, and contributes to a positive classroom climate (Rowe 1974, 1986; R. Stahl et al., 2005).

Wait-time should be implemented strategically, however. For example, if students are practicing basic skills, such as multiplication facts, quick answers are desirable, and wait-times should be short (Rosenshine & Stevens, 1986). Also, if a student appears uneasy,

Prompting. An additional question or statement teachers use to elicit an appropriate student response after a student fails to answer correctly

Wait-time. The period of silence that occurs both before and after calling on a student

you may choose to intervene earlier. However, if you expect students to use demanding cognitive processes like *apply, analyze,* or *evaluate* (L. Anderson & Krathwohl, 2001), wait-times should be longer, sometimes exceeding the 3- to 5-second rule of thumb.

Cognitive Levels of Questions

The kinds of questions teachers ask also influence learning, and the relative merits of low- and high-level questions have been widely researched. The results are mixed, however. Both low-level questions (e.g., *remember* on the taxonomy in Figure 13.1) and high-level questions (e.g., *apply* or *analyze* on the taxonomy) correlate positively with achievement, depending on the teaching situation (Good & Brophy, 2003).

The appropriate cognitive level for a question depends on your learning objective, and you should think about asking sequences of questions instead of single questions in isolation. For example, if a teacher wants students to understand factors leading to the American Revolutionary War, she might begin with a series of lower-level questions asking students to remember specific events. She might then proceed to higher-level questions asking students to identify cause-and-effect relationships among those events (Eggen & Kauchak, 2006). We saw this type of sequence illustrated in Scott's lesson. After completing the demonstrations, Scott first asked the students to remember how the papers and the ball behaved. He followed this sequence with questions asking them to identify the relationship between the speed of the air and the forces it exerted on the objects.

You should focus on your learning objectives and not on the level of questions you choose to ask. When your objectives are clear, the levels of questions will take care of themselves.

Review and Closure

Review is a summary that helps students link what they have already learned to what will follow in the next learning activity. It can occur at any point in a lesson, although it is most common at the beginning and end.

Beginning reviews help students activate the prior knowledge needed to understand the content of the current lesson. Scott's beginning review on Tuesday was one of the most effective aspects of his lesson. For instance, he didn't just ask the students to recall the definition of force and the principle relating opposing forces and movement; he provided examples. Though it may seem redundant to use additional examples, because he had shown examples on Monday, it is often necessary. Providing students with concrete examples during the review increases its effectiveness by providing additional links in long-term memory.

Scott's review was also important because students had to understand force and the principle relating the direction of movement to the stronger force in order to understand Bernoulli's principle. His review was essential if the lesson was to be meaningful.

Closure is a form of review occurring at the end of a lesson. The purpose of closure is to help students organize what they've learned into a meaningful schema; it pulls the different aspects of the topic together and signals the end of a lesson. When students are involved in higher-level learning, an effective form of closure is to have them identify additional examples of a concept, or apply a principle, generalization, or rule to a new situation. When teaching problem solving, summarizing the thinking involved in solving the problem can be another effective form of closure.

Learning Contexts: Instruction in Urban Classrooms

In our discussions of urban contexts in earlier chapters, two themes have evolved: First, negative stereotypes of urban students are common, and second, their backgrounds are very diverse (Armour-Thomas, 2004; R. A Goldstein, 2004). In this chapter we want to consider what these themes suggest for the application of principles of instruction in urban environments. Let's look at them.

Essential teaching skills are the abilities that all teachers should possess regardless of teaching context, which means that they are as important for working with urban students as with any others. However, we want to emphasize three of them here and explain why they are even more important in urban environments. They are

- Attitudes
- Questioning
- Feedback

Online Case Book
To analyze an additional case study to assess the extent to which the teacher implements the essential teaching skills in her lesson, go to the *Online Case Book* for Chapter 13 at *www.prenhall.com/eggen.*

Review. A summary that helps students link what they have already learned to what will follow in the next learning activity

Closure. A form of review occurring at the end of a lesson

Attitudes

Teacher attitudes influence the way they treat students, and negative attitudes about the learning capabilities of urban students can be particularly damaging. "Such stereotypes are not only dehumanizing, they are also hard to fight against, because they have become the image that comes to people's minds the moment they think about all people, things, and places urban" (R. A. Goldstein, 2004, p. 45). The effects of stereotyping can be devastating, which is why teachers' attitudes, such as *personal teaching efficacy, modeling, caring,* and *positive expectations* are so critical.

Effective urban teachers use questioning to involve students in learning activities.

Some researchers suggest that a sense of belonging generated by caring teachers is the most important factor that exists in promoting resilience in urban students (Judson, 2004; Valenzuela, 1999). The need for belonging can be explained with self-determination theory (see Chapter 10), which suggests that relatedness (belonging) is one of people's basic needs. Nothing can destroy urban students' sense of relatedness more than being in a classroom with a teacher who holds negative stereotypes about their ability to learn.

Positive teacher attitudes don't mean that teachers are naively optimistic; urban contexts do present additional challenges. "Believing in students does not automatically mean that urban students will miraculously become 'A' students and score well on all standardized tests. That takes hard work and an intricate understanding of other aspects of students' lives" (R. A. Goldstein, 2004, p. 46). To succeed in urban classrooms, teachers need to care, and this caring has to be translated into teaching that encourages and even requires student success.

Questioning

When working in challenging environments, teachers have a tendency to revert to instructional strategies that afford them the most control. This often results in the use of an inordinate amount of passive learning activities such as lecture and seat work (Duke, 2000; Eggen, 1998). Exactly the opposite is needed. "A great deal of classroom research suggests that students need active instruction from their teachers, not solitary work with instructional materials, in order to make good achievement progress" (Brophy, 2004, p. 155). This quote, describing students in general, is even more important for urban students. As you saw in your study of Vygotsky's work in Chapter 2, language and experience are essential components of learning and development. The only way urban students develop the ability to put their understanding into words is to practice, and responding to questions is the most effective way for them to practice.

A common lament is, "I tried calling on students, but they either couldn't or wouldn't answer." This is why questioning skills, such as open-ended questions and prompting are so important. Initially, your students may encounter difficulties, because they may have limited experience with using school-related language. With scaffolding and encouragement, however, they will improve over time, and improved motivation and increased learning will result.

Finally, careful implementation of equitable distribution is crucial. Nothing better communicates that you expect all students to achieve and that you're holding them accountable for learning than developing your lessons with questioning, calling on all students, and prompting them when necessary to ensure their active participation and use of language. Making equitable distribution the prevailing pattern in your classroom can do more than anything else to communicate that you believe all students can learn and you expect them to do so.

Feedback

Both in Chapter 7 and earlier in the chapter, we said that feedback is a learning principle, and, as with attitudes and questioning, it is even more important when working with urban students. The knowledge constructions of urban students are likely to be highly varied because of the diversity of their background experiences and prior knowledge. This means that detailed discussions of seat work, homework, and quiz results are essential when working with urban students. Time spent providing feedback provides a tangible link between you and your students and assists them in the knowledge construction process.

Analyzing Classrooms Video
To further analyze the effectiveness of Scott's lesson for urban students, go to Episode 21, "Essential Teaching Skills in An Urban Classroom" on DVD 2, accompanying this text.

Knowledge Extensions

To deepen your understanding of the topics in this section of Chapter 13 and to integrate them with topics you've already studied, go to the *Knowledge Extensions* module for Chapter 13 at *www.prenhall.com/eggen*. Respond to questions 7–10.

Checking Your Understanding

2.1 We try to model with our writing the content that we're discussing in each chapter. What are we doing to provide introductory focus for each chapter's contents?

2.2 Identify at least two other essential teaching skills that we utilize in each of the chapters of this book.

2.3 From which do students learn more, feedback to a correct response or feedback to an incorrect one? Explain.

To receive feedback for these questions, go to Appendix B.

Classroom Connections

Demonstrating Essential Teaching Skills in Your Classroom

Attitudes

1. Demonstrate attitudes that increase student motivation and achievement.
   - **Elementary:** A third-grade teacher communicates her personal efficacy and caring by calling a student's parents and soliciting their help as soon as the student fails to turn in an assignment or receives an unsatisfactory grade on a quiz or test.
   - **Middle School:** A seventh-grade teacher commits himself to being a role model by displaying the statement, "I will always behave in the way I expect you to behave in this class," on the bulletin board. He uses the statement as a guiding principle in his class.
   - **High School:** A geometry teacher, knowing that her students initially have problems with proofs, conducts help sessions twice a week after school. "I would much rather help them than lower my expectations," she comments.

Organization and Communication

2. Carefully plan and organize materials and communicate clearly to maximize instructional time.
   - **Elementary:** A first-grade teacher has several boxes filled with frequently used science materials, such as soft drink bottles, balloons, matches, baking soda, vinegar, funnels, and a hot plate. The night before a science demonstration, he spends a few minutes selecting his materials from the boxes and sets them on a shelf near his desk so that he'll have everything ready at the beginning of the lesson.
   - **Middle School:** An eighth-grade American history teacher asks a member of her team to visit her class and check to see how many minutes she spends before actually beginning instruction. She also asks her colleague to check to see if she clearly emphasizes the important points in the lesson, sequences the presentation logically, and communicates changes in topics.
   - **High School:** A biology teacher begins each class with an outline of the day's topics and activities on the board. As she makes transitions from one activity to the other, she calls students' attention to the outline so students can understand where they've been and where they're going.

Focus and Feedback

3. Use problems, demonstrations, and displays to provide introductory and sensory focus during lessons. Provide feedback throughout all learning experiences.
   - **Elementary:** A fourth-grade teacher beginning a study of different groups of animals brings a live lobster, a spider, and a grasshopper to class and builds a lesson on arthropods around these animals. After making a list of arthropods' characteristics on the board, she asks students if a clam is an arthropod. When some say it is, she provides feedback by referring them to the list and asking them to identify each in the clam. After a short discussion, they conclude that the clam isn't an arthropod.
   - **Middle School:** A science teacher dealing with the concept of kindling temperature soaks a cloth in a water–alcohol mix, ignites it, and asks, "Why isn't the cloth burning?" He provides feedback during the class discussion by asking guiding questions to help students develop their understanding.
   - **High School:** A physical education teacher shows students a videotape of Justine Henin, a professional tennis player, executing a nearly perfect backhand. She then videotapes the students as they practice backhands, and they attempt to modify their swings to more nearly imitate Henin's.

Questioning and Review

4. Begin and end each class with a short review. Guide the review with questioning.
   - **Elementary:** A fifth-grade teacher whose class is studying different types of boundaries says, "We've looked at three kinds of boundaries between the states so far today. What are the three, and where do they occur?"
   - **Middle School:** An English teacher begins, "We studied pronoun–antecedent agreement yesterday. Give me an example that illustrates this idea, and explain why your example is correct."
   - **High School:** An art teacher says, "Today we've found that many artists use color to create different moods. Let's summarize some of the features that we've learned about. Go ahead, offer one, someone."

MODELS OF INSTRUCTION

As we said earlier in the chapter, essential teaching skills are abilities that teachers apply in all their learning activities. By comparison, **models of instruction** are prescriptive approaches to teaching designed to help students acquire a deep understanding of specific forms of knowledge. They are grounded in learning theory and supported by research, and they include sets of steps designed to help students reach specified learning objectives.

Essential teaching skills support all instructional models. For instance, just as students use reading in all their content areas, organization, clear communication, and the other essential teaching skills are important regardless of the model being used.

Research indicates that no single instructional model is most effective for all students or for helping students reach all learning objectives (Knight, 2002; Kroesbergen & van Luit, 2002; Marzano, 2003; Shuell, 1996), and further, teachers should vary the way they teach (Shuell, 1996; Wasley, Hample, & Clark, 1997). For these reasons, in this section we examine four models, the first two of which are explicit and teacher directed and the third and fourth less explicit and more learner directed:

Effective teachers use different models of instruction to help students reach their learning objectives.

- Direct instruction
- Lecture discussion
- Guided discovery
- Cooperative learning

Direct Instruction

Direct instruction is an instructional model designed to teach well-defined knowledge and skills that are needed for later learning (Eggen & Kauchak, 2006; Rosenshine & Stevens, 1986). Examples of these skills include young students' using basic operations to solve math problems, students' using specific writing strategies, chemistry students' balancing equations, and geography students' using longitude and latitude to pinpoint locations. Direct instruction is useful when skills can be broken down into specific steps and has been found to be particularly effective in working with low achievers and students with exceptionalities (Kroesbergen, van Luit, & Maas, 2004; Troia & Graham, 2002; Turnbull et al., 2004).

Direct instruction ranges from a highly structured, nearly scripted, and somewhat behaviorist approach (Carnine, Silbert, Kame'enui, Tarver, Jongjohann, 2006; Kozioff, LaNunziata, & Cowardin, 2000) to one that is more flexible and cognitive in its direction (Eggen & Kauchak, 2006; Rosenshine & Stevens, 1986). We discuss the latter here, which typically occurs in four phases:

- Introduction and review
- Developing understanding
- Guided practice
- Independent practice

The cognitive approach to direct instruction is grounded in information processing theory, together with modeling and Vygotsky's (1978) concept of scaffolding. Table 13.4 outlines the phases of this form of direct instruction and their relationships to learning.

Let's look at the phases in a second-grade math lesson where the teacher wants his students to understand the addition of two-digit numbers.

> Sam Barnett begins his lesson on the addition of two-digit numbers by saying, "Today we are going to go a step further with our work in addition so that we'll be able to solve problems like this," and displaying the following on the overhead:
>
> *Jana and Patti are friends. They were saving special soda cans to get a free CD. They can get the CD if they save 35 cans. Jana had 15 cans and Patti had 12. How many did they have together?*
>
> He gives students a few seconds to read the problem and then asks, "Now, what are we being asked?"

Table 13.4 The relationships between phases and learning components in cognitive-based direct instruction

Phase	Learning Component
Introduction and Review: Teachers begin with a form of introductory focus and review previous work.	• Attract attention. • Access prior knowledge from long-term memory.
Developing Understanding: Teachers describe and model the skill or explain and present examples of the concept. Teachers emphasize understanding.	• Acquire declarative knowledge about the skill or concept. • Encode declarative knowledge into long-term memory.
Guided Practice: Students practice the skill or identify additional examples of the concept, and the teacher provides scaffolding.	• Move through the associative stage of developing procedural knowledge.
Independent Practice: Students practice on their own.	• Develop automaticity with the skill or concept.

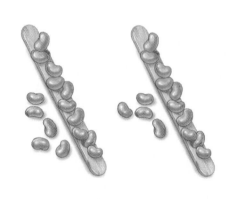

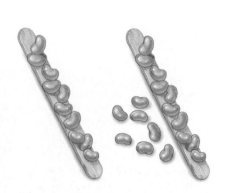

". . . How many cans Jana and Patti have together," Devon answers haltingly.

"Why is that important? . . . Flavia?"

"So they can see how close they are to getting their CD."

"Sure," Sam smiles. "If they know how many they have, they'll know how close they are. If they don't, they're stuck. That's why it's important."

All of Sam's students have boxes on their desks that contain craft sticks with 10 beans glued on each as well as a number of individual beans. Sam reviews single-digit addition by having the students demonstrate their answers to problems like 8 + 7 and 9 + 5, with their sticks and beans.

He then turns back to the problem, has the students demonstrate 15 and 12 with their beans, and writes the following on the board:

$$\begin{array}{r} 15 \\ +12 \\ \hline \end{array}$$

"Now, watch what I do here," he continues. "When I add 5 and 2, what do I get? Let me think about that. . . . 5 and 2 are 7. Let's put a 7 on the board," he says as he walks to the board and adds a 7.

"Now show me that with your beans." He watches as the students combine 5 beans and 2 beans on their desks.

"Now, we still have to add the tens. What do we get when we add two tens? . . . Let's see. One ten and one ten is two tens. Now, look where I've put the 2. It is under the tens column because the 2 means two tens." With that, he writes the following on the chalkboard:

$$\begin{array}{r} 15 \\ +12 \\ \hline 27 \end{array}$$

"So, how many cans did Jana and Patti have together? . . . Alesha?"

". . . 27?"

"Good. They have 27 altogether."

Sam has students demonstrate with their beans and explain what the 7 and the 2 in 27 means, and then asks, "Now, we saw that I added the 5 and the 2 before I added the two tens. Why do you suppose I did that? . . . Anyone?"

". . . You have to find out how many ones you have to see if we can make a 10," Callie offers.

"Good thinking, Callie. That's exactly right. We'll see why again tomorrow when we have some problems in which we'll have to regroup, but for now, let's remember what Callie said."

"So let's look again," he continues. "There's an important difference between this 2," he says, pointing to the 2 in 27, "and this 2," pointing to the 2 in the 12. "What is this difference? . . . Katrina?"

"That 2 . . . is two groups of 10, . . . and that one is just 2 by itself."

"Good, Katrina. Good work, everyone. . . . Show me this 2," Sam directs, pointing to the 2 in 27.

The students hold up two sticks with the beans glued on them.

"Good, and show me this 2." He points to the 2 in the 12, and the students hold up two beans.

"Great," Sam smiles. He has the students demonstrate their answers to three additional problems, and then says, "When we've had enough practice with our sticks and beans to be sure that we really understand these problems, we'll start practicing with the numbers by themselves. We're going to get so good at these problems that we'll be able to do them without even thinking about it."

He assigns 10 more problems and watches carefully as the students work at their desks.

Now, let's look at Sam's attempts to use direct instruction with his students. As you read the following sections, keep the information processing model that you first saw in Figure 7.1 in mind to see how each of the direct instruction phases relates to different aspects of information processing.

Introduction and Review. From your study of Chapter 7, recall that information processing begins with *attention,* and Sam used the attention-getting characteristics of a real-world problem to begin his lesson. He then checked students' *perceptions* by having them describe what the problem asked, and reviewed what they had already done to retrieve prior knowledge from long-term memory. The value of this process is well established by research (Gersten et al., 1999), and although its importance seems obvious, the majority of teacher lessons begin with little or no attempt to attract attention or activate relevant prior knowledge (Brophy, 2004).

Developing Understanding. An essential part of encoding procedural knowledge into long-term memory involves recognizing different conditions and applying procedures appropriate for those conditions. The second phase addresses this need when the teacher models the skill, and explains when and how it will be used. Sam modeled the skill when he said "Now, watch what I do here," and he modeled his thinking (cognitive modeling) when he said "When I add 5 and 2, what do I get? Let me think about that. . . . 5 and 2 are 7. Let's put a 7 on the board." His cognitive modeling was a particularly important part of developing students' understanding.

During this phase, students acquire the declarative knowledge that allows them to adapt when applying their procedural knowledge in different conditions. When they fail to connect procedural knowledge to declarative knowledge (organized in schemas), students apply procedures mechanically or use superficial strategies, such as subtracting when they see the words "how many more" in a math problem (R. Mayer, 1999; Novick, 1998).

To see how Sam emphasized understanding, let's look at some dialogue from his lesson:

> *Sam:*   So let's look again. There's an important difference between this 2 (pointing to the 2 in 27) and this 2 (pointing to the 2 in the 12). What is this difference? . . . Katrina?
>
> *Katrina:* That 2 . . . is two groups of 10, . . . and that one is just 2 by itself.
>
> *Sam:*   Good, Katrina. Good work, everyone. . . . Show me this 2 (pointing to the 2 in 27).

The students held up two sticks with the beans glued on them.

> *Sam:*   Good, and show me this 2 (pointing to the 2 in the 12).

The students then held up two beans.

Sam used questioning and concrete examples throughout this phase, both of which are essential. Questioning puts students in active roles, helps break up an explanation to reduce the cognitive load on students' working memories, and promotes encoding. Concrete examples also take advantage of working memories' distributed processing capabilities.

Teachers often fail to fully develop the understanding called for in this phase. They may emphasize memorization, fail to ask enough questions, or move too quickly to practice (Rittle-Johnson & Alibali, 1999). Or, they may involve learners in hands-on activities but then fail to establish the connection between the materials (e.g., sticks and beans) and the abstractions they represent (the numbers on the board) (Ball, 1992).

Guided Practice. Once students have developed an understanding of the procedure, they begin practicing with teacher assistance, which helps them through the *associative stage* of acquiring procedural knowledge. Initially, the teacher uses questioning to provide enough scaffolding to ensure success, but not so much that students' sense of challenge that can lead to perceptions of competence is reduced (Gersten et al., 1999; Rosenshine & Meister, 1992). Practice improves both long-term retention and motivation to learn in students; as they practice, they develop automaticity and become more confident with the new content (Péladeau, Forget, & Gagné, 2003). Sam had his students work a problem, and they discussed it carefully while he assessed their understanding. He continued with this process until he believed that all students were ready to work on their own.

Independent Practice. In this final phase, the teacher attempts to help students gradually make the transition from consciously thinking about the skill to performing it automatically. The teacher reduces scaffolding and shifts responsibility to the students. The goal is automaticity, so working memory space can be devoted to high-level applications (Sweller et al., 1998).

Teacher monitoring continues to be important. Effective teachers carefully monitor students to assess their developing understanding (Safer & Fleischman, 2005); less-effective teachers are more likely to merely check to see that students are on task (e.g., on the right page and following directions).

Homework. Homework is a type of independent practice, and when properly used, can help students achieve automaticity (H. Cooper, Lindsay, Nye, & Greathouse, 1998; Stein & Carnine, 1999). *Properly used* means that teachers assign homework that is an extension of what students have studied and practiced in class; that is, it is aligned with learning objectives and learning activities (Bransford et al., 2000). Although grading homework can be time-consuming, teachers should have some mechanism for giving students credit and providing feedback if they are to take it seriously and use it as a learning tool.

The effects of homework are especially strong at the middle and high school levels, and frequency is important (H. Cooper, Valentine, Nye, & Lindsay, 1999). For example, five problems every night are more effective than 25 once a week. Effective homework has four characteristics, which are outlined in Table 13.5.

Homework tends to be less effective with younger students, however, for at least two reasons (H. Cooper & Valentine, 2001). First, young children may have poorly developed study and attention skills, which limit the amount of time they productively spend on homework. Second, children who are struggling to learn an idea can have even more problems at home, where distractions and lack of help hamper learning efforts. Elementary teachers who assign homework should monitor students' progress closely to ensure that the homework is contributing to learning.

Teachers should view homework as an integral part of a comprehensive plan to teach students responsibility and self-regulation (H. Cooper et al., 1998; Corno & Xu, 1998). For example, homework requires that students accept the responsibility for taking materials home, finding a quiet place to work, completing the assignment, and attempting to understand the topics. Parents' support is essential in this effort (H. Cooper, Jackson, Nye, & Lindsay, 2001), and it is particularly important for younger and less motivated students. (Think about the strategies for involving parents that we presented in Chapter 12.)

Table 13.5 Characteristics of effective homework

Characteristic	Rationale
Extension of classwork	The teacher teaches; homework reinforces.
High success rates	Success is motivating. Success leads to automaticity. No one is available to provide help if students encounter problems.
Part of class routines	Becomes a part of student expectations, increases likelihood of students completing assignments.
Graded	Increases accountability and provides feedback.

Source: Based on work by Berliner (1984) and H. Cooper & Valentine (2001).

Lecture and Lecture-Discussion

Lecture-discussion is an instructional model designed to help students acquire organized bodies of knowledge and develop complex schemas (Eggen & Kauchak, 2006). **Organized bodies of knowledge** are topics that connect facts, concepts, principles, and make the relationships among them explicit (Rosenshine, 1987). For example, when students examine relationships among plot, character, and symbolism in a novel such as *Moby Dick* in literature, study landforms, climate, and economy in different regions of the world in geography, or compare parasitic and nonparasitic worms and how differences between them are reflected in their body structures in biology, they are acquiring organized bodies of knowledge.

As you saw in Chapters 7 and 8, *learners construct their own knowledge of the topics they study* is a learning principle. When students study an organized body of knowledge, the knowledge they construct exists in the form of schemas. It is important to remember that, because learners will construct knowledge that makes sense to them, the way they organize knowledge in memory is not necessarily the same as the way the teacher organizes and presents a body of knowledge. We examine this point in more detail later in this section.

Lecture-discussions are modifications of traditional lectures. Let's begin by looking at traditional lectures.

Lectures

The prevalence of the lecture as a teaching method is paradoxical. Although it is the most criticized of all teaching methods, it continues to be the most commonly used (Cuban, 1993). Its popularity is due in part to its ability to

- Help students acquire information not readily accessible in other ways; lectures can be effective if the goal is to provide students with information that would take them hours to find on their own (Ausubel, 1968).
- Assist students in integrating information from a variety of sources.
- Expose students to different points of view (Henson, 1996).

If the teacher is trying to accomplish one or more of these goals, lectures can be used periodically.

Lectures have at least three other advantages. First, because planning time is limited to organizing content, they're efficient. Second, they're flexible—they can be applied to virtually any content area—and third, they're simple. Cognitive load (for the teacher) is low, and all of teachers' working memory space can be devoted to organizing and presenting content. Even novice teachers can learn to deliver acceptable lectures.

Despite their ease, efficiency, and widespread use, lectures have several disadvantages:

- They are ineffective for attracting and maintaining attention. We have all sat through mind-numbing lectures with a goal of simply getting the time to pass more quickly.
- Lectures don't allow teachers to check students' perceptions and developing understanding. Teachers can't determine whether or not students are interpreting information accurately.
- While lowering the cognitive load for teachers, they impose a heavy cognitive load on learners, so information is often lost from working memory before it can be encoded.
- Lectures put learners in passive roles. This is inconsistent with cognitive views of learning and is arguably the primary disadvantage of the strategy.

Lectures are especially problematic for young students because of their short attention spans and limited vocabularies, and they're also ineffective if higher-order thinking is a goal. In seven studies comparing lecture to discussion, discussion was superior in all seven on measures of retention and higher-order thinking. In addition, discussion was superior in seven of nine studies on measures of student attitude and motivation (McKeachie & Kulik, 1975).

Overcoming the Weaknesses of Lectures: Lecture-Discussions

Lecture-discussions help overcome the weaknesses of lectures by interspersing short periods of presenting information with systematic teacher questioning.

Lecture-discussion. An instructional model designed to help students acquire organized bodies of knowledge and develop complex schemas

Organized bodies of knowledge. Topics that connect facts, concepts, generalizations, and principles, and make the relationships among them explicit

Lecture discussions help overcome the weaknesses of lectures.

Lecture-discussions consist of four phases:

- Introduction and review
- Presenting information
- Comprehension monitoring
- Integration

Lecture-discussion is grounded in both information processing theory and constructivism. Table 13.6 outlines the phases of lecture-discussion and their relationships to learning theory.

Let's see how a 10th-grade American history teacher attempts to implement these phases with her students.

Diane Anderson is discussing the events leading up to the American Revolutionary War. She begins with a review by saying, "About where are we now in our progress?" as she points to a timeline above the chalkboard.

"About there," Adam responds, pointing to the middle of the 1700s.

"Yes, good," Diane smiles. "We're almost to the Revolutionary War. However, I would like for us to understand what happened before that time, so we're going to back up a ways, actually, all the way to the early 1600s. When we're finished today, we'll see that the Revolutionary War didn't just happen; there were events that led up to it that made it almost inevitable. . . . That's the important part of history . . . to see how events that happen at one time affect events at other times, and all the way to today.

"For instance, the conflicts between the British and the French in America became so costly for the British that they began policies in the colonies that ultimately led to the Revolution. That's what we want to begin looking at today. . . . Here we go."

She then begins, "We know that the British established Jamestown in 1607, but we haven't really looked at French expansion into the New World. Let's look again at the map. "Here we see Jamestown, but at about the same time, a French explorer named Champlain came down the St. Lawrence River and formed Quebec City, here." She points again to the map. "Over the years, at least 35 of the 50 states were discovered or mapped by the French, and they founded several of our big cities, such as Detroit, St. Louis, New Orleans, and Des Moines," she continues pointing to a series of locations she had marked on the map.

"Now, what do you notice about the location of the two groups?"

After thinking a few seconds, Alfredo offers, "The French had a lot of Canada, . . . and it looks like this country too." He points to the north and west on the map.

"It looks like the east was . . . British, and the west was French," Troy adds.

"Yes, and remember, this was all happening at about the same time," Diane continues. "Also, the French were more friendly with the Native Americans than the British were. The French had what they called a seignorial system, where the settlers were given land if they would serve in the military. So, . . . what does this suggest about the military power of the French?"

"Probably powerful," Josh suggests. "The people got land if they went in the army."

Table 13.6 The relationships between phases and learning components in lecture-discussions

Phase	Learning Component
Introduction and Review: The teacher begins with a form of introductory focus and reviews previous work.	• Attract attention. • Access prior knowledge from long-term memory.
Presenting Information: The teacher presents information. The teacher keeps presentations short to prevent overloading learners' working memories.	• Acquire declarative knowledge about the topic.
Comprehension Monitoring: The teacher asks a series of questions to check learners' understanding.	• Check students' perceptions. • Put students in active roles. • Begin schema construction.
Integration: The teacher asks additional questions to help learners integrate new and prior knowledge.	• Construct integrated schemas that organize information and reduce cognitive load.

"And the Native Americans probably helped, because they were friendly with the French," Tenisha adds.

"Now, what else do you notice here?" Diane asks, moving her hand up and down the width of the map.

"Mountains?" Danielle answers uncertainly.

"Yes, exactly," Diane smiles. "Why are they important? What do mountains do?"

". . . The British were sort of fenced in, and the French could expand and do as they pleased."

"Good. And now the plot thickens. The British needed land and wanted to expand. So they headed west over the mountains and guess who they ran into? . . . Sarah?"

"The French?" Sarah responded.

"Right! And conflict broke out. Now, when the French and British were fighting, why do you suppose the French were initially more successful than the British? . . . Dan?"

"Well, they had that sig . . . seignorial system, so they were more eager to fight, because of the land and everything."

"Other thoughts? . . . Bette?"

"I think that the Native Americans were part of it. The French got along better with them, so they helped the French."

"Okay, good thinking everyone, now let's think about the British . . . . Let's look at some of their advantages."

Let's look now at Diane's efforts to help her students acquire an organized body of knowledge and promote schema production. She introduced the lesson with a review and attempted to capture students' *attention* by explaining how events in the past influence the way we live today. Then, she *presented information* about Jamestown, Quebec, and French settlements in the present-day United States. After this brief presentation, she used questioning to involve her students in the *comprehension-monitoring* phase. To illustrate, let's review a brief portion of the lesson.

> *Diane:*   Now, what do you notice about the location of the two groups?
> *Alfredo:*   The French had a lot of Canada, . . . and it looks like this country too (pointing to the north and west on the map).
> *Troy:*   It looks like the east was . . . British, and the west was French.

Diane's questions were intended to put students in *cognitively active roles,* check their *perceptions,* and begin the process of *schema* production. Satisfied that their perceptions were accurate, she returned to presenting information when she said, "Yes, and remember, this was all happening at about the same time." She continued by briefly describing the French seignorial system and pointing out the friendly relations between the French and the Native Americans.

Then she again turned back to the students.

> *Diane:*   So, . . . what does this suggest about the military power of the French?
> *Josh:*   Probably powerful. The people got land if they went in the army.
> *Tenisha:*   And the Native Americans probably helped, because they were friendly with the French.

The two segments appear similar, but there is an important distinction. In the first, Diane was *monitoring comprehension;* students' responses to the question, "Now, what do you notice about the location of the two groups?" helped her assess their perceptions of what she had presented in the first segment. In the second, she attempted to promote schema production by encouraging students to *integrate* the seignorial system, the relationship between the French and the American Indians, and French military power.

After completing this cycle of *presenting information, monitoring comprehension,* and *integration,* she would repeat the process, with the second integration being broader than the first. Diane's goal for the entire lesson was the development of complex schemas that would represent the students' understanding of the cause–effect relationships between the French and Indian Wars and the American Revolutionary War.

The effectiveness of lecture discussions depends on the quality of the discussions during the lesson. As we said earlier in this section, since students construct understanding that makes sense to them, the schemas they construct won't necessarily mirror the way the teacher has organized the body of knowledge. The discussions allow the teacher to assess the process of schema construction and helps students reconstruct their understanding when necessary. This is a primary reason lecture discussion is a more effective instructional model than is traditional lecture.

Exploring Further

David Ausubel, a prominent learning theorist in the 1960s and 1970s, was an advocate of instruction similar to lecture-discussion. To read more about his theory, go to "Ausubel's Theory of Meaningful Verbal Learning" in the *Exploring Further* module of Chapter 13 at *www.prenhall.com/eggen.*

Guided discovery can increase students' intrinsic interest in the topics being studied.

Guided Discovery

Guided discovery is an instructional model in which teachers guide students as the students construct knowledge of concepts and the relationships among them (Eggen & Kauchak, 2006; R. E. Mayer, 2004). When using the model, a teacher identifies learning objectives, arranges information so that patterns can be found, and guides students to the objectives (R. C. Clark & Mayer, 2003; Moreno, 2004). It is often contrasted with "pure" or unstructured discovery, where learners identify patterns and relationships without help from a teacher. Research indicates that unstructured discovery is less effective than guided approaches because time isn't used efficiently, and, without help, students often become lost and frustrated, and this confusion can lead to misconceptions (R. C. Clark & Mayer, 2003; R. Mayer, 2002, 2004). As a result, unstructured discovery is rarely seen in today's classrooms, except in student projects and investigations.

When done well, guided discovery's effectiveness is supported by research: "Guided discovery may take more or less time than expository instruction, depending on the task, but tends to result in better long-term retention and transfer than expository instruction" (R. Mayer, 2002, p. 68). When using guided discovery, teachers spend less time explaining and more time asking questions, so students have more opportunities to share thinking and articulate understanding (Bay, Staver, Bryan, & Hale, 1992; Moreno & Duran, 2004).

Guided discovery occurs in four phases:

- Introduction and review
- The open-ended phase
- The convergent phase
- Closure

Guided discovery is grounded in cognitive theories of learning, including information processing, and particularly social constructivism. Table 13.7 outlines the phases of guided discovery and their related learning components.

Scott's lesson on Bernoulli's principle at the beginning of our discussion of essential teaching skills was an application of guided discovery. You might want to read it again before studying the following sections. Let's look now at Scott's application of the phases.

Introduction and Review. Scott began his lesson by reviewing the concept of force and the principle, "Objects move in the direction of a greater force." The review activated stu-

Table 13.7 The relationships between phases and learning components in guided discovery

Phase	Learning Component
Introduction and Review: The teacher begins with a form of introductory focus and reviews previous work.	• Attract attention. • Activate prior knowledge.
The Open-Ended Phase: The teacher provides examples and asks for observations and comparisons.	• Provide experiences from which learners will construct knowledge. • Promote social interaction.
The Convergent Phase: The teacher guides students as they search for patterns in the examples.	• Begin schema production. • Promote social interaction.
Closure: With the teacher's guidance, students state a definition of the concept or a description of the relationship among concepts.	• Complete schema production.

Guided discovery. An instructional model in which teachers guide students as the students construct knowledge of concepts and the relationships among them

dents' prior knowledge, and the examples he used in his review, such as pushing on the board, and tugging on the stapler, attracted students' attention.

The Open-Ended Phase. Scott implemented the open-ended phase when he had students blow over the pieces of paper, between the papers, and through the necks of the funnels. Each was an example that illustrated Bernoulli's principle.

After the students worked with each example, Scott asked for observations, such as, "What did you notice when we blew over the top? . . . David?" and "What did you notice here? . . . Sharon?" The open-ended questions promoted active involvement and helped students begin the process of schema production.

The Convergent Phase. The convergent phase continues to capitalize on social interaction and advances schema construction. Scott began the transition to the convergent phase when he drew the sketches on the board and had students restate the essential observations and conclusions. Let's look again at some dialogue that illustrates this process.

Scott:	Was I blowing on the top or the bottom? . . . Rachel? (Referring to the first sketch)
Rachel:	The top.
Scott:	And what happened there? . . . Heather?
Heather:	The paper rose up.

Scott did a similar analysis with the second and third example and then guided the students as they formed conclusions.

Scott:	Let's think about the forces acting on these (turning back to the first sketch). What forces are acting on the paper? . . . Colin?
Colin:	Gravity.
Scott:	And which direction is gravity pulling?
Colin:	Down.
Scott:	What other force is acting on the paper? . . . William?
William:	Air (pointing up).
Scott:	How do you know it's pushing up?
William:	The paper moved up.

Scott then guided a similar analysis of the second and third example. The lesson then moved to closure. Teacher guidance in the form of questions and prompts is essential if students are to reach the desired learning objectives (Moreno, 2004; Moreno & Duran, 2004).

Closure. Closure completes the process of schema production by explicitly identifying the content objective. Scott moved toward closure when he said, "Now let's look at the forces and where we blew. Study the drawings carefully, and see what kind of relationship exists between the two." Students are then scaffolded as they attempt to put their understanding into words. As you saw in your study of Vygotsky's work in Chapter 2, language is a learning and development tool. Practice in articulating understanding during closure is an essential part of the process.

Closure is particularly important when using guided discovery because the instruction is less explicit and the direction the lesson is taking is less obvious than it is with either direct instruction or lecture discussion. Articulating the definition of a concept or stating the principle, as was the case in Scott's lesson, helps eliminate any uncertainty that may remain in students' thinking.

Several of the lessons you've already studied used guided discovery to varying degrees, such as Jenny Newhall's in Chapter 2, and Diane Smith's and Teri Hall's, both in Chapter 4. You may want to refer again to these case studies as additional examples of guided discovery.

Cooperative Learning

Cooperative learning is a set of instructional models in which students work in mixed-ability groups to reach specific learning and social interaction objectives. Cooperative learning is grounded in social constructivism, and as its name implies, it relies on cooperative social interaction to facilitate knowledge construction. Several of the teachers in cases you've already studied used it as part of their instruction—Jan Davis in Chapter 1, David Shelton and Sue Southam in Chapter 7, and Jenny Newhall and Scott Sowell in Chapter 8,

Analyzing Classrooms Video
To analyze another lesson in which the teacher is using guided discovery, go to Episode 22 "Guided Discovery in an Elementary Classroom" on DVD 2, accompanying this text.

Exploring Further
Inquiry is a teaching model in which learners gather real-world problems that they use to investigate real-world problems. To read more about it, go to "The Inquiry Model" in the *Exploring Further* module of Chapter 13 at *www.prenhall.com/eggen*.

Cooperative learning. A set of instructional strategies that help learners meet specific learning and social interaction objectives in structured groups

Cooperative learning activities encourage knowledge construction through social interaction.

for example. It has become one of the most popular instructional models in schools today; one study found that 93 percent of elementary teachers used some form of cooperative learning in their classrooms (Antil, Jenkins, Wayne, & Vadasy, 1998). However, many teachers equate any form of getting students into groups with cooperative learning, and they tend to ignore research about components that are essential if it is to promote learning (Cohen, 1994; D. W. Johnson & Johnson, 2006).

When implemented effectively, a cooperative learning activity involves all students, which can be difficult in large groups. In whole-class discussions, less-confident students may get few chances to participate, so they often drift off.

Cooperative learning can also be effective for teaching students to collaborate in their thinking (Keefer et al., 2000; Meter & Stevens, 2000). Advocates, grounding their positions in Vygotsky's work, argue that groups of learners co-construct more powerful understandings than individuals do alone (Lehman, Kauffman, White, Horn, & Bruning, 1999; Summers, Woodruff, Tomberlin, Williams, & Svinicki, 2001). This co-constructed knowledge can then be appropriated by individuals (D. Brenner, 2001).

Although a single view doesn't exist, most researchers agree that cooperative learning consists of students working together in groups small enough (typically two to five) so that everyone can participate in a clearly assigned task (Cohen, 1994; D. W. Johnson & Johnson, 2006; Slavin, 1995). They also agree that cooperative learning shares at least four other features:

- Learning objectives direct the groups' activities.
- Teachers emphasize social interaction.
- Teachers hold students individually accountable for their understanding.
- Learners depend on one another to reach objectives.

The last characteristic, called *positive interdependence* (D. W. Johnson & Johnson, 2006) or *reciprocal interdependence* (Cohen, 1994), is important because it emphasizes the crucial role that peer cooperation plays in learning. Accountability is also essential because it keeps students focused on the objectives and reminds them that learning is the purpose of the activity (Antil et al., 1998; Slavin, 1995).

Unlike the first three models we discussed, cooperative learning activities don't follow a specific set of steps or phases. However, successful implementation of cooperative learning activities requires careful thought and planning. We examine some of the factors influencing its success in the following sections.

Introducing Cooperative Learning

Introducing students to cooperative learning requires careful planning (Gillies, 2000; Terwel et al., 2001). Poorly organized activities can result in less learning than whole-group lessons.

Suggestions for initially planning and organizing cooperative learning activities include the following:

- Seat group members together, so they can move back and forth from group work to whole-class activities with little disruption.
- Have materials ready for easy distribution to each group.
- Introduce students to cooperative learning with short, simple tasks, and make objectives and directions clear.
- Specify the amount of time students have to accomplish the task (and keep it relatively short).
- Monitor groups while they work.
- Require that students produce a product as a result of the cooperative learning activity (e.g., written answers to specific questions).

Each of the teachers' lessons that we mentioned earlier illustrated these characteristics. In all cases, the teachers seated the groups together, the task was clear and specific, they required students to write conclusions, and they carefully monitored group progress.

Table 13.8 Cooperative learning models

Model	Description	Example
Reciprocal Questioning	Pairs work together to ask and answer questions about a lesson or text.	Teacher provides question stems, such as "Summarize . . ." or "Why was . . . important?" and students use the stems to create specific questions about the topic.
Scripted Cooperation	Pairs work together to elaborate on each other's thinking.	Math: First member of a pair offers a problem solution. The second member then elaborates, and the process is repeated. Reading: Pairs read a passage, and the first member offers a summary. The second elaborates, and the process continues.
Jigsaw II	Individuals become expert on subsections of a topic and teach it to others in their group.	One student studies the geography of a region, another the economy, a third the climate. Each attends "expert" meetings, and the "experts" then teach the content to others in their group.
Student Teams Achievement Divisions (STAD)	Social interaction helps students learn facts, concepts, and skills.	The independent practice phase of direct instruction is replaced with team study, during which team members check and compare their answers. Team study is followed by quizzes, and individual improvement points lead to team awards.

Cooperative Learning Strategies

Different models of cooperative learning are all grounded in social constructivism, but each accomplishes different objectives. Some examples are outlined in Table 13.8.

Other cooperative learning strategies exist, and although they differ in format, all incorporate the instructional principles described earlier. As with all instruction, none of the cooperative learning models can reach all learning objectives, and they should not be overused.

Cooperative Learning: A Tool for Capitalizing on Diversity

Although it's essential for constructing understanding, social interaction doesn't always occur naturally and comfortably; people tend to be wary of others from different cultures and backgrounds. Common in nonschool social settings, this tendency also occurs in classrooms. Students of specific ethnic groups tend to spend most of their time together, so they don't learn that all of us are much more alike than we are different (Webb, Baxter, & Thompson, 1997).

Teachers can't mandate tolerance, trust, and friendship among students with different backgrounds; they need additional tools, and cooperative learning can be one of them. Students working in cooperative groups improve their social skills, accept students with exceptionalities, and develop friendships and positive attitudes with others who differ in achievement, ethnicity, and gender (D. W. Johnson & Johnson, 2006; Vaughn & Bos, 2006).

The benefits of student cooperation likely stem from four factors:

- Students with different backgrounds working together
- Group members having equal status
- Students learning about each other as individuals
- The teacher emphasizing the value of cooperation among all students (Slavin, 1995)

As learners work together, they do indeed find that they are much more alike than different. Let's see how Maria Sanchez, a third-grade teacher, attempts to accomplish these goals in her classroom.

> As Maria watches her third graders work, she is both pleased and uneasy. They've improved a great deal in their math and reading, but there is little mixing among her minority and nonminority students—and among other groups as well. She worries about six children from Costa Rica who are struggling with English and four students with exceptionalities who leave her class every day for extra help.
>
> To promote a more cohesive atmosphere, Maria spends time over the weekend, organizing the students into groups of four, with equal numbers of high- and low-ability read-

ers in each group. She also mixes the students by ethnicity and gender, and she makes sure that no group has more than one student for whom English is a second language or more than one student with an exceptionality.

On Monday she explains how they are to work together. To introduce the process, she sits with one group and models cooperation and support for the others.

Then she sends the groups to different parts of the room. One student from each group reads a paragraph, and a second asks questions of the third and fourth members, using stems that Maria provides. At her signal, they change roles. As they work, she moves around the room, encouraging the involvement of all group members, and preventing individuals from dominating the groups.

Her first session is demanding but fairly successful. "Phew," she thinks to herself at the end of the day. "This isn't any easier, but it already seems better."

Let's look at Maria's efforts in more detail. First, because her objective was to promote interpersonal relationships, she organized the groups so that high- and low-ability students, boys and girls, members of minorities and nonminorities, and students with and without exceptionalities were represented as equally as possible. One of the most common mistakes that beginning teachers make is to let students form their own groups.

Second, knowing that effective interaction must be planned and taught, she modeled desired behaviors, such as being supportive, listening, asking questions, and staying on task. Teachers can also directly teach interaction strategies or use role-plays and videotapes of effective groups to help students learn cooperation skills (Fitch & Semb, 1992; King, 1999). These skills are especially important for students from minority groups, who are often hesitant about seeking and giving help (Webb & Farivar, 1994).

Third, using a form of reciprocal questioning, Maria began with a task that required cooperation and communication. By rotating students through these roles, she encouraged participation from all group members and helped prevent higher-status or more aggressive students from dominating the activity. Other tasks that teachers can use to encourage cooperation include presenting and checking math problems, practicing spelling and grammar exercises, and solving open-ended problems (Cohen, 1994; Quin, Johnson, & Johnson, 1995).

Finally, Maria monitored the students while they worked. Initial training, alone, won't ensure cooperation. Groups need constant monitoring and support, particularly with young children and when cooperative learning is first introduced (Hulse-Killachy, Killachy, & Donigan, 2001; Vaughn et al., 2006). If problems persist, teachers may need to reconvene the class for additional training.

Exploring Further

Social domination and social isolation can reduce the effectiveness of cooperative learning. To examine some ways to help solve this problem, go to "Making Cooperative Learning Equitable" in the *Exploring Further* module of Chapter 13 at *www.prenhall.com/eggen*.

Checking Your Understanding

3.1   Using the essential teaching skills as a basis, explain why the introduction phase is important in *direct instruction, lecture discussion,* and *guided discovery.*

3.2   Which phase of direct instruction is most important for ensuring successful independent practice? Explain.

3.3   We said, "When done well, guided discovery's effectiveness is supported by research." What is necessary in order for instruction to be "done well"? Explain.

3.4   A teacher places her third graders in groups of three, gives each group magnets and a packet including a dime, spoon, aluminum foil, rubber band, wooden pencil, paper clip, and nails. She tells the groups to experiment with the magnets and items for 10 minutes and write their observations on paper. As they work, she answers questions and makes comments. The class as a whole group discusses the results. How effectively did the teacher introduce cooperative learning to her students? Cite evidence from the example to support your conclusion.

To receive feedback for these questions, go to Appendix B.

Knowledge Extensions

To deepen your understanding of the topics in this section of the chapter and to integrate them with topics you've already studied, go to the *Knowledge Extensions* module for Chapter 13 at *www.prenhall.com/eggen*. Respond to questions 11–12.

Classroom Connections

Using Models of Instruction Effectively in Your Classroom.

Direct Instruction

1. Emphasize understanding, and provide practice to develop automaticity.

- **Elementary:** A fourth-grade teacher, in a lesson on possessives, first explains the difference between singular and plural possessives, and then asks students to punctuate the following sentences.

  The students books were lost when he forgot them on the bus.

  The students books were lost when they left them on the playground.

  Who can describe the boys adventure when he went to the zoo?

  Who can describe the boys adventure when they swam in the river?

  He then has the students write paragraphs that incorporate both singular and plural possessives.

- **Middle School:** In a unit on percentages and decimals, a math teacher comments that the star quarterback for the state university completed 14 of 21 passes in the last game. "What does that mean? Is that good or bad? Was it better than the 12 of 17 passes completed by the opposing quarterback?" she asks. She then explains how to calculate the percentages with the class and then has the students practice finding percentages in other real-world problems.

- **High School:** A ninth-grade geography teacher helps his students locate the longitude and latitude of their city by "walking them through" the process, using a map and a series of specific questions. He then has them practice finding the longitude and latitude of other cities, as well as finding the major city nearest sets of longitude and latitude locations.

Lecture Discussion

2. Design lessons to maintain students' attention and promote schema production.

- **Elementary:** A third-grade teacher wants her students to know similarities and differences between zoo animals and pets. To do this, she constructs a large chart with pictures of both. As they discuss the two groups of animals, she continually asks students to identify similarities and differences between the two groups.

- **Middle School:** An American history teacher discussing immigration in the 19th and early 20th centuries compares immigrant groups of the past with today's Cuban population in Miami, Florida, and Mexican immigrants in San Antonio, Texas. He asks students to summarize similarities and differences between the two groups with respect to the difficulties they encounter and the rates of assimilation into the American way of life.

- **High School:** A biology teacher is presenting information related to transport of liquids in and out of cells, identifying and illustrating several of the concepts in the process. After about 3 minutes, she stops presenting information and asks,

"Suppose a cell is in a hypotonic solution in one case and a hypertonic solution in another. What's the difference between the two? What would happen to the cell in each case?"

Guided Discovery

3. Provide examples that include all the information students need to understand the topic, and guide student interaction.

- **Elementary:** A fifth-grade teacher begins a unit on reptiles by bringing a snake and turtle to class. He includes colored pictures of lizards, alligators, and sea turtles. He has students describe the animals and pictures and then guides them to an understanding of the essential characteristics of reptiles.

- **Middle School:** A seventh-grade English teacher embeds examples of singular and plural possessive nouns in the context of a paragraph. She then guides the students' discussion as they develop explanations for why particular sentences are punctuated the way they are, for example, "The girls' and boys' accomplishments in the middle school were noteworthy, as were the children's efforts in the elementary school."

- **High School:** A world history teacher presents students with vignettes such as

  You're part of an archeological team, and at one site you've found some spear points. In spite of their ages, the points are still quite sharp, having been chipped precisely from hard stone. You also see several cattle and sheep skulls and some threads that appear to be the remains of coarsely woven fabric.

  He then guides the students to conclude that the artifacts best represent a New Stone Age society.

Cooperative Learning

4. Provide clear directions for groups, and carefully monitor students as they work.

- **Elementary:** A second-grade teacher begins the school year by having groups work together on short word problems in math. When students fail to cooperate, she stops the groups and immediately discusses the issues with the class.

- **Middle School:** A life-science teacher has students create and answer questions about the characteristics, organelles, and environments of one-celled animals. He periodically offers suggestions to the pairs to help them ask more meaningful questions.

- **High School:** A geometry teacher has pairs use scripted cooperation to solve proofs. When they struggle, she offers hints to help them continue to make progress.

5. Use cooperative learning groups to capitalize on the richness that learner diversity brings to classrooms, and design tasks that require group cooperation.

- **Elementary:** A second-grade teacher waits until the third week of the school year to form cooperative learning groups. During that time, she observes her students and gathers information about their interests, talents, and friendships. She then uses the information in making decisions about group membership.

- **Middle School:** A sixth-grade math teacher uses cooperative learning groups to practice word problems. He organizes the class into pairs, forming, whenever possible, pairs that are composed of a minority and nonminority student, a student with and a student without an exceptionality, and a boy and a girl.

- **High School:** An English teacher has students work in groups of four to provide feedback on one another's writing. The teacher organizes all groups so that they're composed of equal numbers of boys, girls, minorities and nonminorities, and students who do and do not have exceptionalities.

ASSESSMENT AND LEARNING: USING ASSESSMENT AS A LEARNING TOOL

We are now at the third point of the planning–implementing–assessing process. Earlier in the chapter, you saw that creating assessments during planning is important. Let's look now at how Scott's assessment contributed to learning for his students. Let's look at an item on his Friday quiz and the students' responses to it.

> Look at the drawing that represents the two pieces of paper that we used in the lesson. Explain what made the papers move together. Make a drawing that shows how the air flowed as you blew between the papers. Label the forces in the drawing as we did during the lesson.

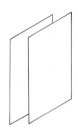

Shown here are two students' sketches of the flow of air between the papers:

The students' responses illustrate an essential characteristic of effective assessments: *Assessments must provide information about students' thinking.* For instance, the responses pictured here show that two students correctly concluded that the force (pressure) on the outside of the papers pushing in was greater than the force (pressure) on the inside of the papers pushing out. This doesn't provide a great deal of evidence about their understanding, however, because the lesson emphasized this conclusion.

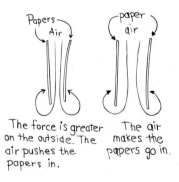

Effective teachers use a variety of assessments to gather information about whether learning goals have been achieved.

The students' drawings of the air flow together with their explanations are more revealing. They concluded that the moving air curled around the bottoms of the papers and pushed the papers together, which revealed a misconception. (The correct explanation is that the papers moved together because increasing the speed of the air over a surface [in this case over the surface of the papers] decreases the pressure the air exerts on the surface [the papers], and the still air on the outside of the papers pushes them together, as illustrated in the sketch here. This is an application of Bernoulli's principle.) If Scott's assessment hadn't asked for both an explanation and a drawing, he may not have learned that his students left the lesson with misconceptions.

Assessments such as these provide opportunities for teachers to directly address student misconceptions. For instance, a detailed discussion of these responses together with additional examples (demonstrating that air exerts pressure in all directions and that all objects, including air particles, move in a straight line unless a force acts on them) would greatly expand the students' understanding of some basic principles in science. In fact, teaching these principles after the assessment likely produces more learning than trying to teach them beforehand, because the students' responses to the assessment provide both motivation and context for learning. Ideally, all assessments provide similar opportunities to extend learning.

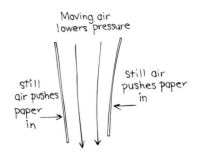

Checking Your Understanding

4.1 Identify two essential characteristics of effective assessments.

4.2 Identify the essential teaching skill that teachers must use in conjunction with assessments in order for the assessments to increase student learning.

4.3 An English teacher wants his students to use figurative language, such as similes, metaphors, and personification in their writing. He gives them several examples of each, and then he gives them a quiz on which they have to identify additional examples of figurative language. Evaluate his assessment with respect to its effectiveness.

To receive feedback for these questions, go to Appendix B.

Knowledge Extensions

To deepen your understanding of the topics in this section of the chapter and to integrate them with topics you've already studied, go to the *Knowledge Extensions* module for Chapter 13 at *www.prenhall.com/eggen*. Respond to questions 13–14.

Meeting Your Learning Objectives

1. **Describe the steps involved in planning for instruction, and identify an additional step when planning in a standards-based environment.**

   - Planning for instruction involves thinking about what topics are important for students to learn, specifying learning objectives, preparing and organizing learning activities, and designing assessments.
   - When planning for instruction based on specified standards, teachers first interpret the standard and then design learning activities to help students meet the standard and assessments to determine whether or not the standard has been met.

2. **Identify examples of essential teaching skills in learning experiences, and analyze the role of feedback in promoting learning.**

   - Essential teaching skills are the abilities and attitudes that all teachers must have. These abilities and attitudes include high personal teaching efficacy—the belief that they are responsible for student learning and can increase it. It also includes caring, modeling, enthusiasm, and high expectations for student achievement and behavior.
   - Essential abilities also include efficient organization, clear communication, and the ability to attract and maintain student attention, to provide informative feedback, and to deliver succinct reviews.

- Questioning is one of the most important essential teaching skills. Characteristics of effective questioning include high frequency and equitable distribution of questions, prompts when students can't answer, and enough time for students to think about their answers.

3. **Explain the relationships between essential teaching skills and models of instruction, and analyze the components of different models.**

- Essential teaching skills support and are incorporated in all models of instruction.
- Direct instruction is an instructional model designed to teach clearly structured knowledge and essential skills that students need for later learning. Teachers conduct direct instruction in four phases: Introduction and review, to attract students' attention and activate prior knowledge; developing understanding, to develop declarative knowledge about the skill; and guided and independent practice, to develop the skill to automaticity.
- Lecture-discussion is an instructional model designed to help students acquire organized bodies of knowledge. It consists of an introduction and review, to attract attention and activate prior knowledge; presenting information, to provide information; comprehension monitoring, to check students' perceptions; and integration, to promote schema production.
- Guided discovery is an instructional model that helps students learn concepts and the relationships among them. It begins

with an introduction and review, to attract students' attention and activate prior knowledge; an open-ended phase in which students make observations of examples; a convergent phase in which teachers identify patterns and begin schema production; and closure, when teachers complete schema production and clarify the learning objective.

- Cooperative learning is a set of instructional models that use group interaction to reach specified learning objectives. Teachers hold learners individually accountable for understanding, and learners must depend on each other to reach the objectives.

4. **Identify the characteristics of effective assessments, and explain the relationships between effective assessments and essential teaching skills.**

- Productive learning environments are assessment centered. This means that assessment is an integral part of the learning–teaching process, and that assessments are aligned with objectives and learning activities.
- Effective assessments provide teachers with information about students' thinking and aren't limited to determining whether or not students get answers correct.
- Effective assessments provide opportunities for increasing students' understanding through detailed feedback and discussion. Discussion following assessments often increases understanding as much or more than the learning activity itself.

Developing as a Professional: Praxis™ Practice

At the beginning of this chapter, you saw how Scott Sowell planned his lesson, demonstrated essential teaching skills, and assessed his students' learning. Let's look now at a teacher working with a class of ninth-grade geography students. As you read the case study, consider the extent to which the teacher applied the information you've studied in this chapter in her lesson. Read the case study, and answer the questions that follow.

Judy Holmquist, a ninth-grade geography teacher, has her students involved in a unit on climate regions of the United States. The class has worked in groups to gather information about the geography, economy, ethnic groups, and future issues in Florida, California, New York, and Alaska, and the students have entered the information on a matrix. The first two columns of the matrix are shown here.

In today's lesson, Judy wants the students to understand how the geography of each region influenced its economy.

As the bell signaling the beginning of the class period stops ringing, Judy refers students to the matrix, which she has hung at the front of the classroom. She reminds them they will be looking for similarities and differences in the information about the states, organizes the students into pairs, and begins by saying, "I want you to get with your partner and write down three differences and three similarities that you see in the geography portion of the chart."

The groups begin their work, and Judy moves around the classroom, answering questions and making brief suggestions.

A few minutes later, she calls the students back together. "You look like you're doing a good job. . . . Okay, I think we're ready."

"Okay, go ahead Jackie," Judy begins, pointing to the chart.

"Mmm, they all have mountains except for Florida."

"Okay, they all have mountains except for Florida," Judy repeats and writes the information under "Similarities" on the chalkboard.

"Something else. . . . Jeff?"

"They all touch the oceans in places."

"What else? . . . Missy?"

Geography	Economy
Geography	**Economy**
Coastal plain	Citrus industry
F Florida uplands	Tourism
L Hurricane season	Fishing
O Warm ocean currents	Forestry
R	Cattle

	Temp.	Moisture
I Dec.	69	1.8
D March	72	2.4
A June	81	9.3
Sept.	82	7.6

Geography	Economy
C Coastal ranges	Citrus industry
A Cascades	Wine/vineyards
L Sierra Nevadas	Fishing
I Central Valley	Lumber
F Desert	Television/Hollywood
O	Tourism
	Computers

	Temp.	Moisture
R Dec.	54	2.5
N March	57	2.8
I June	66	T
A Sept.	69	.3

Geography	Economy
N Atlantic Coastal Plain	Vegetables
E New England uplands	Fishing
W Appalachian Plateau	Apples
Adirondack Mts.	Forestry
Y	Light manufacturing
	Entertainment/TV

	Temp.	Moisture
O Dec.	37	3.9
R March	42	4.1
June	72	3.7
K Sept.	68	3.9

Geography	Economy
Rocky Mountains	Mining
Brooks Range	Fishing
A Panhandle area	Trapping
L Plateaus between mountains	Lumbering/forestry
A Islands/treeless	Oil/pipeline
S Warm ocean currents	Tourism
K	

	Temp.	Moisture
A Dec	−7	.9
March	11	.4
June	60	1.4
Sept.	46	1.0

"New York and Florida both have coastal plains."

The class continues identifying similarities for a few more minutes, and Judy then says, "How about some differences? . . . Chris?"

"The temperature ranges a lot."

"All right. . . . John?"

"Different climate zones."

"Alaska is the only one that has an average temperature below zero," Kiki puts in.

"Carnisha, do you have anything to add?"

"All except Alaska have less than 4 inches of moisture in the winter," Carnisha adds.

After the students offer several more differences, Judy asks, "Okay, have we exhausted your lists? Anyone else have anything more to add?"

Judy waits a couple seconds and then says, "Okay, now I want you to look at the economy, and I want you to do the same thing; write down three similarities and three differences in the economy column. You have 3 minutes."

The students again return to their groups, and Judy monitors them as she had earlier.

After they finish, she again calls for and receives a number of similarities and differences based on the information in the economy column.

She then shifts the direction of the lesson, saying, "Okay, great . . . . Now, let's see if we can link geography and economics. For example, why do they all have fishing?" she asks, waving her hand across the class as she walks toward the back of the room. "John?"

"They're all near the coast."

"And, why do they all have forestry? . . . Okay, Jeremy?"

"They all have lots of trees," Jeremy replies as the rest of the class smiles at this obvious conclusion.

"So, what does this tell you about their climate?"

"They all have the right temperature . . . and soil . . . and enough rain for trees."

"Good, Jeremy," Judy smiles, and then says, "Now, let's look again at our chart. We have the citrus industry in California and Florida. Why do they have the citrus industry there?"

". . . It's the climate," Jackie answers hesitantly.

"All right, what kind of climate allows the citrus industry? . . . Tim?"

". . . Humid subtropical."

"Humid subtropical means that we have what? . . . Go ahead."

". . . Long humid summers. . . . Short mild winters," he replies after thinking for a few seconds.

"Now let's look at tourism. Why does each area have tourism?" Judy continues. "Okay, Lance?"

"Because they're all spread out. They're each at four corners, and they have different seasons that they're popular in."

"Good, Lance," Judy nods, and then seeing that they are near the end of the period, Judy says, "Okay, I want you to describe in a short summary statement what effect climate has on the economy of those regions."

She gives the class a couple minutes to work again in their pairs, and then says, "Let's see what you've come up with. "Braden, go ahead."

"If you have mountains in the area, you can't have farmland," he responds.

"Okay, what else? . . . Becky?"

"The climate affects what's grown and what's done in that area."

"Okay, great. Climate affects what's grown, and what was the last part of that?"

With Judy's guidance, the class makes a summarizing statement indicating that the climate of a region is a major influence determining what the economy of the region will be, and she then dismisses the class.

Short-Answer Questions

In answering these questions, use information from the chapter and link your responses to specific information in the case.

1. Describe the types of teacher knowledge Judy displayed in the lesson. Provide evidence from the case study to support your conclusions.
2. Describe Judy's thinking as she planned the lesson. Identify at least three decisions that she made as she planned.
3. Analyze Judy's instructional alignment. Offer any suggestions that you might have that would have increased the alignment of the lesson.
4. Analyze Judy's application of the essential teaching skills in her lesson. Which did she demonstrate most effectively? Which did she demonstrate least effectively?

ONLINE PORTFOLIO ACTIVITIES

To develop your professional portfolio, further apply your understanding of chapter content, and address the INTASC standards, go to the Companion Website, then to the Online Portfolio Activities for Chapter 13. Complete the suggested activities.

IMPORTANT CONCEPTS

backward design (p. 411)
closure (p. 420)
cognitive domain (p. 407)
connected discourse (p. 415)
cooperative learning (p. 431)
direct instruction (p. 423)
emphasis (p. 415)
equitable distribution (p. 418)
essential teaching skills (p. 414)
feedback (p. 416)
guided discovery (p. 430)
instructional alignment (p. 410)
learning objective (p. 407)

lecture-discussion (p. 427)
models of instruction (p. 423)
organized bodies of knowledge (p. 427)
precise language (p. 415)
prompting (p. 419)
questioning frequency (p. 418)
review (p. 420)
sensory focus (p. 416)
standards (p. 411)
task analysis (p. 409)
transition signals (p. 415)
wait-time (p. 419)

CHAPTER 14

Learning and Instruction and Technology

Chapter Outline	Learning Objectives

After you have completed your study of this chapter, you should be able to

1 Identify different views of technology in descriptions of classroom support materials.

2 Explain how different theories of learning are applied to technology use in classrooms.

3 Describe the uses of different forms of technology to support instruction, and identify the learning theories that support these forms of technology.

4 Explain how word processing, the Internet, and assistive technology can increase learning.

5 Identify different ways that teachers can use technology to make their work more effective.

Technology has the potential to strongly influence teaching and learning. As you read the following case study, consider the different ways that the teachers are using technology and to what extent this use is impacting the amount students are learning.

Mary Banks, a principal at an urban middle school in the northeast, is walking through the halls of her school. "I enjoy this," she thinks to herself. "I like knowing what's happening in my classrooms."

As she passes Angela Travers's room, she sees Angela's science students working on a genetics project. The students have collected information from their families and put it in a database, which organized it and made it available for analysis. "The kids will be interested in that," Mary thinks with a smile, remembering the time she did a similar activity when she was teaching. One student with brown eyes reported that both of her parents had blue eyes, which seemed genetically impossible and promoted a lively discussion.

Next door, she passes Bill Logan's math class, which is working on a problem-based video simulation. Jasper, the main character, has bought a boat and now is faced with questions of when he should leave for home and whether or not he can make it without running out of gas. As the students watch the video, they are given information such as the time of day, the distance he has to reach home, how many miles per gallon the boat makes, the average speed of the boat, and the amount of money he has.

"They sure seem interested," Mary thinks.

She walks into Conchita Martinez's room. Conchita's students are working on a tutorial designed to improve their skills with adding and subtracting fractions. "How are they doing?" Mary asks, knowing that the students' basic math skills are weak.

"They're coming along," Conchita responds. "Some of these kids didn't know that ¼ was larger than ⅛ at the beginning of the year, and they've come a long ways. And, the fact that they can immediately see the progress they're making really helps. Plus, combining the computer time with class time adds enough variety so that motivation isn't as much a problem as it has been in the past."

"That's great," Mary smiles. "Keep up the good work."

"It will be interesting to see how we do on the state math tests next month," Mary reflects as she heads out the door.

Walking down the next hallway, Mary hears an animated discussion coming from Karl Iverson's history. "It couldn't be a temple. If it was a temple, why would we find spear points there?" one student asks. "Maybe they were using them as offerings to the gods," another counters. "Or maybe they came from a different time period. We don't know exactly where the spear points came from," a third puts in.

"Great," Mary thinks. "That's impressive thinking for these kids. . . . And, who would have thought that they would be interested in ancient civilizations like Greece and Rome?"

"It looks like the in-service time we invested in technology is working," Mary muses. "The teachers seem to be using it, and it looks like the kids are excited. But, with all the emphasis on accountability, test scores are the bottom line. . . . Will it pay off when test scores come back?"

To introduce the chapter, we want to consider three questions: (1) Did the use of technology increase the amount the students in each class learned, and if so, how? (2) How did using technology change the nature of the teachers' work and their interactions with students? And finally (3), Mary's question, "Will it pay off when test scores come back?" is important. We address these and other questions in this chapter.

WHAT IS TECHNOLOGY?

Before we attempt to answer the preceding questions, we need to see what we mean by *technology*. We tend to think of it as a recent innovation, and we commonly link it to computers. In fact, technology is much broader and has been used in teaching for as long as schools have existed. For example, children in our country's first schools used individual slate boards to practice their "letters and numbers." As the one-room school evolved into those organized by grade levels, the chalkboard became an essential tool for communicating with larger groups of students. These are rudimentary forms of technology.

The invention of electricity revolutionized instruction by allowing teachers to use television, film strips, films, and overhead projectors. Technology further evolved, and teachers now routinely use videotapes, CD-ROMs, and DVDs; most have at least one computer in their classrooms, and some regularly make PowerPoint presentations. These are all forms of technology.

Historically, experts have defined educational technology in two distinct ways. One view focuses on hardware and the other more strongly emphasizes process. Those holding a hardware view see technology as primarily "gadgets, instruments, machines, devices . . . [and] computers" (Muffoletto, 1994, p. 25).

Over time, views of technology became more comprehensive, and the emphasis on process became more prominent. Educators now view technology as an integral part of teaching and learning, instead of as a classroom accessory. For example, teachers can use technology to improve both the effectiveness of instructional strategies and student motivation, and students can use it directly as both a learning and communication tool. A process perspective asks teachers to think more broadly about technology and how they can systematically use it in classrooms. Most experts now integrate the two views and think that definitions of **educational technology** must "focus on the process of applying tools for educational purposes as well as the tools and materials used" (Roblyer, 2006, p. 6). Keep this definition in mind as you study the following sections.

Checking Your Understanding

1.1 As we look at technology in a historical sense, such as using the chalkboard, overhead, or filmstrip projector, which view of technology—hardware or process—was more prominent? Explain.

1.2 "This school is turning us into technology geeks," Jim Fisher, a teacher in an elementary school comments with delight. "We now have a lab with 30 computers in it. We can take our whole class down there, and all the students have their own computer." Which view of technology—hardware or process—does Jim primarily hold? Explain.

1.3 Explain how the following definition of educational technology was illustrated in Bill Logan's work with his students: "A combination of the processes and tools involved in addressing educational needs and problems."

To receive feedback for these questions, go to Appendix B.

Knowledge Extensions

To deepen your understanding of the topics in this section of the chapter and to integrate them with topics you've already studied, go to the *Knowledge Extensions* module for Chapter 14 at *www.prenhall.com/eggen*. Respond to questions 1–3.

TECHNOLOGY AND LEARNING

Regardless of teachers' perspectives on technology, the way they apply it in classrooms depends on their learning objectives and their views of learning. In this section, we review the learning theories you studied in Chapters 6 to 8 with specific emphasis on their implications for the use of technology.

Behaviorism and Technology

Behaviorism, and particularly operant conditioning, has strongly influenced the use of technology in classrooms. Experts estimate that 85 percent of the existing educational software emphasizes skill learning based on behaviorist principles (Jonassen, 2000).

As you saw in Chapter 6, behaviorists define learning as a change in behavior that results from experience. The behavioral change results from both antecedents—events that precede and elicit the behavior—and consequences—events that follow and either strengthen or weaken it—in a relationship that can be represented visually as follows (Schunk, 2004):

Antecedent → Behavior → Consequence

For example, an antecedent could be the question, "What is 7 times 8?" and if the student responds, "Fifty-six," a consequence, such as the comment, "Good!" reinforces the response. B. F. Skinner, in his book *The Technology of Teaching* (1968), argued that

Educational technology. The process of applying tools for educational purposes as well as the tools and materials used

Teachers can use technology to develop basic skills through practice and reinforcement.

classrooms are inefficient places for learning because large numbers of students, together with differences in their learning progress, make it difficult for teachers to effectively reinforce and shape behaviors. For example, if a teacher has students involved in a question-and-answer session, some may respond correctly, but others will answer incorrectly, and still others may give no response, making immediate reinforcement impossible. Assignments and homework present similar challenges.

As an alternative, Skinner advocated a system of individualized instruction that shapes behaviors through reinforcement that is immediate and consistent. But how can this be achieved in a classroom with 25 to 30 students? Advocates of technology claim they have the answer.

Originally, Skinner's ideas took shape in programmed instruction and teaching machines that were true to the principles of operant conditioning, but they were often bulky and inefficient. As the personal computer became more widely used, pages of printed text and teaching machines were replaced by software that allowed computers to immediately reinforce desired behaviors and provide corrective feedback.

Currently, an enormous amount of software exists that is designed to teach everything from typing skills to foreign language vocabulary. As we'll see in the next section, teaching software is divided into drill-and-practice programs intended to reinforce existing skills and tutorials that both present and reinforce new content. Most are based on behaviorist learning principles.

Technology and Cognitive Learning Theory

Just as behaviorism has influenced the design and use of technology, so too have cognitive perspectives on learning. We examine them in this section.

Information Processing

One approach to designing technology based on cognitive learning theory focuses on the characteristics of our information processing system, which you first studied in Chapter 7 (see Figure 14.1). There you saw that it begins with attention and perception, proceeds through organizing new information and prior knowledge in working memory, and con-

Figure 14.1   Learning from an information processing model

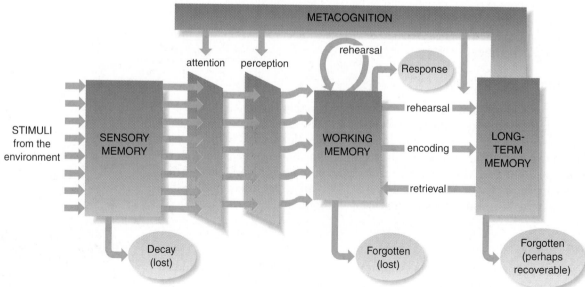

cludes with encoding of new meaning in long-term memory. Learners monitor and regulate all of these processes through metacognition.

Using our information processing system as a framework, software designers identify the following tasks as essential for learning from technology:

- Attract attention and create accurate perceptions.
- Manage the resources of working memory.
- Promote encoding into long-term memory.
- Manage processing with metacognitive skills.

These tasks are outlined in Table 14.1 and discussed in the sections that follow.

Attracting Attention and Creating Accurate Perceptions. As with all forms of learning, attention and perception are essential for learning from technology. Technology's capacity to provide rich learning environments in the form of diagrams, videos, and animation can make attending to appropriate information and perceiving it correctly challenging (de Vries, 2001; Triona & Klahr, 2003). Software designers attempt to address these challenges in several ways. Providing learning objectives is one. As with other learning formats, objectives at the beginning of technology lessons help focus students' attention on important aspects of the content (R. C. Clark & Mayer, 2003). In addition, software uses arrows pointing to important features in diagrams, contrasting colors, and motion to focus learners' attention. For example, a presentation on the workings of the heart uses color and motion to highlight the blood flowing sequentially through the atrium and ventricles, specifically calling students' attention to the direction and sequence of the flow. A simultaneous voice-over explaining how the right side flows to the lungs and the left to the rest of the body is an attempt to prevent students from misperceiving the information.

Managing the Resources of Working Memory. Working memory has two important characteristics, and software designers attempt to address both. The first is its limited capacity. Lessons involving technology can place a heavy cognitive load on working memory, just as lectures and even questioning sessions do. In an attempt to address this problem, software designers minimize irrelevant visuals, omit extraneous background music and environmental sounds, and use succinct text that remains focused on learning objectives (Mayer, Fennell, Farmer, & Campbell, 2004). Effective software also uses captions to clarify graphics. These efforts are all aimed at reducing the cognitive load on working memory.

Working memory's dual-processing capability is the second characteristic that software designers attempt to utilize. To take advantage of this capability, software presents verbal narrations with visual information (R. C. Clark & Mayer, 2003). In the case of blood flowing through the heart, for example, a verbal description explains the direction, flow,

Table 14.1 Software design and our information processing system

Information Processing Components	Tasks	Technology Design Strategy
Attention and perception	• Attract and maintain attention.	• Specify learning objectives. • Use pointing arrows, contrasting colors, and motion to focus attention.
	• Create valid perceptions.	• Use voice-overs to create valid perceptions.
Working memory	• Manage the limited capacity of working memory. • Capitalize on the dual-processing capability of working memory.	• Minimize irrelevant visuals, and omit extraneous background music and sounds to reduce cognitive load. • Simultaneously present visual and verbal information.
Long-term memory	• Encode new and prior knowledge into meaningful schemas.	• Provide practice exercises and worked examples that require the application of new knowledge and skills.
Metacognition	• Increase learner self-regulation.	• Insert structural scaffolds such as objectives, cues, and prompts to remind students of learning goals.

Teachers can provide instructional scaffolding as students use technology to construct knowledge.

and function of blood at the same time that the learner sees these processes presented visually.

As another example, Figure 14.2 provides a visual representation that demonstrates why $(X + Y)^2 = X^2 + 2XY + Y^2$. A simultaneous verbal narration directs learners to focus on the two squares, explaining that they are A^2 and B^2 and the two rectangles, noting that they are the identical products of $A \times B$.

Promoting Encoding Into Long-Term Memory. After simultaneous visual and auditory presentations, effective software then provides a variety of practice exercises, problems, and worked examples that promote the encoding of new understanding into meaningful schemas that learners will store in long-term memory.

Managing Processing with Metacognitive Skills. As you saw in Chapter 7, students who are aware of the way they study and learn achieve higher than those who are less aware (Bruning et al., 2004; Kuhn & Dean, 2004), and this is true for using technology as well (Eilam & Aharon, 2003; Guercin, 2001; Rouet, 2001). However, because technology-based activities can provide rich learning environments, navigating through them can be challenging for students (P. Alexander, 2006). They can lose sight of their learning objectives and the reason they're participating in the activity in the first place (Beitzel & Derry, 2004).

Strategies to prevent this confusion exist in two forms. One is to train students to be more metacognitive in their approach to technology use (R. Wallace, 2004). For example, one study taught students to create subgoals and consciously attempt to activate prior knowledge before beginning an activity, combined with teaching them to monitor their time and learning progress (Azevedo & Cromley, 2004). A second strategy embeds scaffolding in the software to encourage metacognitive monitoring (Clark & Mayer, 2003). Scaffolds are often prompts and cues that remind students of learning objectives, shifts in topics, and progress.

Constructivism and Technology

A second cognitive approach to designing technology is based on constructivist views of learning (Bransford et al., 2000; Bruning et al., 2004). This approach immerses students in realistic simulations in which they can experience, for example, what it was like to travel the Oregon Trail or go to a distant planet. Technology can also present complex and ill-defined problems that are similar to those we encounter in life outside the classroom. It can also facilitate data gathering and analysis, becoming "mind tools" that help refine and extend students' cognitive capabilities (Forcier & Descy, 2005; Jonassen, 2000). For example, students can use hand-held probes to measure the temperature, salinity, and pH of pond water, and then use databases and spreadsheets to look for patterns in the data they have gathered. And finally, technology allows students to readily access and share information with other researchers around the world.

Figure 14.2 Effective technology software integrates verbal and auditory messages and reduces the cognitive load on working memory

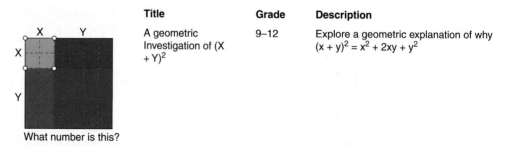

What number is this?

Source: Adapted from the National Council of Teachers of Mathematics. Retrieved January 2006 from *http://illuminations.nctm.org/tools/index.asp*

From a cognitive constructivist perspective, technology provides experiences that allow students to build on and modify their schemas. From a social constructivist view, the Internet, chatrooms, and bulletin boards provide access to different points of view, which helps expand the concept of learning communities that you first saw discussed in Chapter 8. Finally, from a situated learning perspective, technology can provide rich contexts that learners can use to anchor their developing ideas.

Social Cognitive Theory and Technology

Our concept of technology is so closely linked to computers that we tend to forget that it exists in other forms, such as videotape, digital video, and even television, and these forms of technology can capitalize on symbolic modeling to promote learning. For example, teachers can use videotape to demonstrate skills that move so rapidly that they are hard to analyze, such as jump shots in basketball, corner kicks in soccer, and tennis serves. Coaches can show videos repeatedly or in slow motion to demonstrate appropriate technique. Science teachers use videos and DVDs to make complex processes like dissecting a frog visible and reversible. Social studies teachers can share Martin Luther King, Jr.'s, "I Have a Dream" speech, allowing students to experience an important and emotional moment in U.S. history. Language arts teachers can use technology to project and analyze student essays, allowing them to learn from their peers. In each instance, technology grounded in social cognitive theory can increase learning.

Looking at these theories helps us begin to answer the first question we asked at the beginning of the chapter, "Did the use of technology increase the amount the students in each class learned?" Theoretical explanations would suggest "Yes." For instance, in each case, the use of technology placed students in cognitively active roles. For example, Angela's students organized information using a database, and, according to information processing, organization is one way of making information meaningful. Both Angela's and Bill's students were involved in real-world situations, and connecting content to the real world is one of the suggestions for classroom practice according to constructivist views of learning. Conchita gave her students the opportunity to practice and receive feedback, and the need for practice and feedback are principles of learning that you first studied in Chapter 7.

Using technology doesn't automatically produce learning, however. Teachers' learning objectives must be clear, and teachers must also think clearly about how technology can help learners reach the objectives (Roblyer, 2006). We examine these issues in the following sections as we consider different ways that technology utilizes the learning theories we discussed to increase students' achievement.

Exploring Further

The impact of television as a source of symbolic modeling has been widely researched. To read more about this topic, go to "The Influence of Television on Behavior" in the *Exploring Further* module of Chapter 14 at *www.prenhall.com/eggen*.

Checking Your Understanding

2.1 Which teacher in the case study at the beginning of the chapter most nearly used an application of technology based on behaviorism? Explain.

2.2 On what theory or theories of learning was Angela Travers's application of technology with her students most nearly based? Explain.

2.3 On what theory or theories of learning was Bill Logan's application of technology most nearly based? Explain.

To receive feedback for these questions, go to Appendix B.

Knowledge Extensions

To deepen your understanding of the topics in this section of the chapter and to integrate them with topics you've already studied, go to the *Knowledge Extensions* module for Chapter 14 at *www.prenhall.com/eggen*. Respond to questions 4–6.

TECHNOLOGY AND INSTRUCTION

In this section, we look at different instructional uses of technology. We begin with drill-and-practice software and tutorials, which are applications of technology based primarily on behaviorism.

Drill-and-practice and tutorial software still require teachers to closely monitor students' learning progress.

Figure 14.3 Technology can be used to teach difficult math concepts like place value

Cubes Stand for Numbers

Hundreds   Tens   Ones

Source: Adapted from EME corporation.

Drill-and-Practice Software

As a student, you may have used flash cards to help you memorize math facts like $6 \times 9 = 54$, foreign language vocabulary, important historical dates, or the definitions of new concepts in science. **Drill-and-practice programs** are forms of software that allow students to work problems or answer questions on their own and receive immediate feedback (Lever-Duffy, McDonald, & Mizell, 2003).

Being able to use the programs on their own doesn't substitute for a teacher's expertise, however, and developers assume that learners have had previous experience related to the topics. For example, before students use the programs to practice math facts, teachers should first help them understand the facts' conceptual foundation, such as 6×9 means 6 sets of 9 items or 9 sets of 6 items. Effective teachers illustrate these ideas with concrete examples and discuss them thoroughly.

Though primarily designed to provide students with the opportunity to practice and receive feedback, technology supporting drill-and-practice programs can also provide visual representations of hard-to-illustrate concepts such as place value and "carrying" (Roblyer, 2006) (see Figure 14.3). Then, learners can use the drill-and-practice software to help them practice the facts and skills to automaticity. Here we see that the programs, though grounded in behaviorism, also have cognitive applications. Their ability to help students develop skills to automaticity is one way of reducing the cognitive load on working memory.

Drill-and-practice software attempts to increase motivation to learn with both fantasy and challenge, which, as you saw in Chapter 10, can increase intrinsic motivation (Pintrich & Schunk, 2002). For example, rather than simply typing in the correct response to $6 \times 9 = $, some programs attempt to capitalize on fantasy by having students aim a laser blaster at an alien emblazoned with the correct answer. Then, as students become more proficient, the programs decrease the amount of time students are given to answer, which increases the challenge.

Research indicates that drill-and-practice programs can be effective. For instance, some studies suggest that, on average, students using these programs improve from the 50th to the 63rd percentile or gain roughly three months over their noncomputer group counterparts (Attewell, 2001; Cognition & Technology Group at Vanderbilt, 1996). Research also supports their effectiveness in increasing learner motivation. Compared to students using paper-and-pencil exercises, learners using drill-and-practice programs have more positive attitudes toward the subject being studied, the instruction, and the technology itself (Gee, 2005).

Researchers caution, however, that more time with technology doesn't necessarily equal more learning (Roblyer, 2006). To be used effectively, learning objectives must be clear and teachers must also think clearly about how technology can help them reach the objectives.

This discussion helps us answer the second question we asked at the beginning of the chapter: "How did using technology change the nature of the teachers' work and their interactions with students?" When teachers attempt to capitalize on drill-and-practice software, they teach concepts and skills in typical ways. Then, they use software to help the students reach automaticity. Practice with the software, in essence, replaces homework. This means that the drill-and-practice activities must be aligned with teachers' learning objectives and learning activities just as any homework would be. "Because it is available" is not a valid reason for using software if it isn't aligned with learning objectives.

Tutorials

In contrast with drill-and-practice software, which emphasizes the mastery of skills and concepts that have already been taught, **tutorials** offer an entire instructional sequence similar to a teacher's presentation of the topic (Lever-Duffy et al., 2003). Tutorials attempt to create learning systems that act like effective teachers by responding to student questions and errors with immediate scaffolding (P. Alexander, 2006). Tutorials include specific learning objectives, multiple pathways to reaching them, and assessments with feedback geared to the objectives. Conchita's students, for example, were using a tutorial to help them with fractions. As you saw in the case study, it began with ideas as basic as

Drill-and-practice programs. Forms of software that allow students to work problems or answer questions and receive immediate feedback

Tutorials. Instructional software that offers an entire integrated instructional sequence

understanding that ¼ is a larger quantity than ⅛ and continued until students developed skills with adding and subtracting fractions.

Carnegie Learning's *Cognitive Tutor* is another example (Carnegie Learning, 2005). A series of programs pretests students and then combines instruction with frequent assessment and feedback through math problems of increasing complexity. For example, when the student responds 2.8 to the problem, $-2.3 + .5 = ?$, the program responds, "Think about the sign of the numbers." Challenge is provided with a "Skillometer," a bar graph that increases with learning progress and decreases when students ask for hints.

One of the most popular applications of tutorials are programs that teach word processing skills including printing, saving, spell-checking, and formatting text with different fonts, sizes, and styles (Keller, 2004). The best include motivational features such as timed tests that provide challenge and lead to automaticity, as well as charts that illustrate the progression of skill mastery.

Tutorials can fulfill several needs, including initial instruction, additional support for students whose understanding isn't fully developed, advanced study for higher achievers, or alternatives to teacher-led instruction. Tutorials can be linear, but the best are branched, which adapt to learners' responses (Roblyer, 2006). For example, when a student responds incorrectly to a multiple-choice item, the program explains why that choice isn't correct and repeats instruction. Effective tutorials are carefully sequenced so that new concepts and skills are systematically developed and grounded in existing understanding.

As with all forms of instruction, the effectiveness of tutorials depends on the quality of interactions between the technology (teacher) and the learner, and the best require users to respond frequently. When students answer, the best tutorials accept all possible variations of correct answers, and they provide corrective feedback only when necessary. They also record and report individual students' performance to allow teachers to monitor learning progress and intervene when necessary.

Multimedia and Hypermedia

Tutorials can be simple software, like the one Conchita's students used, or they can use **multimedia,** combinations of media forms that include text, graphics, pictures, audio, and video. **Hypermedia,** a linked form of multimedia, allows learners to make connections to different points in the program based on their prior knowledge and learning progress. In current technologies, most multimedia products are also hypermedia systems (Roblyer, 2006).

For example, a multimedia presentation on the solar system might include written material, DVD, video, and graphics. Students view a computer screen that contains **icons,** pictures that act as symbols for some item or action. They click on a text icon, which then brings up written information about Saturn's rings, for instance. Then, they can click on a DVD icon (such as a small picture of a DVD), and they can view a clip that provides a telescopic image of the rings. They can also click on a video icon that will present a simulated flight to the planet, and a graphic illustrating the relative sizes of the planets in the solar system. Multimedia systems vary in complexity, but they all have some combination of the forms we have just described. They attempt to capitalize on the dual-processing capability of learners' working memories by presenting information in both verbal and visual form.

Strengths of Tutorials

Effective tutorials have at least three strengths. First, they're available anytime. Science students, for example, could work on the solar system tutorial whether or not a teacher is present. Second, they are individualized, with each student being given the right amount of practice needed to master the content. Conchita's students, for example, had varying amounts of prior knowledge related to fractions, and the tutorial adapted to each student's current understanding. Third, well-designed multimedia and hypermedia can increase motivation because working with different media is more intrinsically interesting than completing worksheets, and they provide immediate and informative feedback to users, which can increase motivation (Brophy, 2004).

Weaknesses of Tutorials

Critics argue that tutorials too strongly focus on memorized information at the expense of understanding (Newby, Stepich, Lehman, & Russell, 2000; Roblyer, 2006). While this

Multimedia. Combinations of media, including text, graphics, pictures, audio, and video that communicate information

Hypermedia. A linked form of multimedia that allows learners to make connections to different points in the program based on their background knowledge and learning progress

Icons. Pictures displayed on computer screens that act as symbols for some action or item

Simulations provide students with realistic problem solving environments.

isn't true in all cases, finding high-quality software can be a problem. In addition, one of the strengths of tutorials, the fact that they're self-contained, is also a weakness. Because students are on their own, it is hard for teachers to monitor learning progress. The best tutorials address this problem by providing daily printouts that allow teachers to quickly identify learning problems and intervene when necessary.

Our discussion of tutorials gives us another answer to the second question we asked at the beginning of the chapter. Tutorials change the nature of teachers' work and their interactions with students in a way that is different from the change that results from using drill-and-practice software. Because tutorials provide the entire sequence of instruction, teachers then face two questions: (1) Does the tutorial actually perform as advertised? and (2) How do I incorporate it into my curriculum? As with drill-and-practice software, having tutorials available doesn't justify using them if they don't fit into the curriculum or if they aren't aligned with teachers' learning objectives.

Simulations

Simulations are programs, either in software or web-based form, that model a system or process (Jonassen, 2000; Roblyer, 2006). Sometimes called *microworlds,* simulations are technological learning environments in which learners can navigate, manipulate, or create objects, and test their effects on one another. Grounded in constructivist views of learning, simulation software enables students to attempt to construct an understanding of the characteristics of the system represented in the simulation. As an example, let's return to Karl Iverson's history class, first introduced in our chapter opening case study.

> Karl is concluding a unit on ancient Greece in world history. Connecting his urban students with cultures that existed thousands of years ago is a constant challenge. In an attempt to increase the students' interest, he has them work on an archeological simulation. Teams of students are responsible for excavating different quadrants of the simulated archeological site. They "dig up" pottery shards, fragments of weapons, pieces of masonry, and bits of ancient texts. They try to identify each artifact and fit it into an emerging picture of the site as a whole. They also consult reference works on Greek history, art, and architecture. Some ambiguous evidence exists in the site, so some teams find data suggesting it was a temple, whereas others find artifacts indicating a home or battlefield. The teams present their findings to the class in weekly meetings, and a spirited debate follows as the amateur archeologists struggle to reconcile inconsistencies in the data. On this day, students take turns at computers, graphing their findings on large wall-charts, calling across the room to ask if anyone has a spearhead to compare with one just found, and arguing about whose final interpretation will best explain the bulk of the evidence. (Adapted from Brunner & Tally, 1999)

In this case, Karl's students constructed their knowledge about archeological research by actually doing this work in the simulation.

Simulations' ability to involve students in realistic learning tasks usually unavailable in classrooms is their primary value. For example, one biology program allows students to experiment with laws of genetics by pairing animals with different characteristics and showing the resulting offspring (Roblyer, 2006). As another example, *Oregon Trail* (and subsequent versions), one of the most popular social studies simulations, allows students to travel from Independence, Missouri, to Oregon's Willamette Valley, as did the original pioneers (Forcier & Descy, 2005). They shop for supplies with a budget before they start and make decisions along the way about the pace of travel, food supplies, and health problems. They also interact with Native Americans and other settlers. A new networked version allows a number of users to interact simultaneously during their journeys. In each of these simulations, students learn both content, such as information about genetics and the Oregon Trail, and skills, such as how to conduct genetics experiments or plan for a trip across the continent.

Teachers typically use simulations in two ways. One is to introduce topics with realistic experiences that provide a foundation for additional learning. For example, a social studies teacher might use *Sim City 2000®,* which introduces students to the

Simulations. Programs, either in software or web-based form, that model a system or process

problems and challenges of population growth in large cities by allowing them to build their own city.

A second way that teachers use simulations is to provide an opportunity for experimentation after introducing basic concepts. For example, a physics teacher might first introduce concepts such as voltage, current, and resistance and then have students experiment with them in simulated electrical experiments.

Benefits of Simulations

Simulations have at least three benefits (Alessi & Trollip, 2001; Triona & Klahr, 2003):

- Time alteration
- Safety
- Expense

Time Alteration. Simulations can either compress time or slow it down. For example, the genetics simulation compresses time; students can observe the results of genetic crosses that would take months or even years to occur in nature. As another example, *Sim City 2000®* allows students to see the effects of population growth on factors such as transportation, sanitation, education, and fire and police protection, processes that would also take years to observe in the real world.

Simulations can also model processes that are difficult to see because they happen so quickly. For example, they can allow physical education students to observe how changes in a tennis serve influence the direction and spin on the ball, or they can allow physics students to see the actual acceleration of a falling object.

Safety. Simulations also provide safety. One driver's education course, for example, has students use a driving simulator to experience a near accident, which is designed to help them learn to drive defensively (and avoid the wrath of their driving instructors) (Trotter, 2003). The simulator also presents students with risky situations such as driving in rain, in fog, or at night. The combination of safety with realism makes the simulation particularly valuable.

Expense. Many school districts are eliminating science labs because the cost of chemicals and materials is prohibitive. As an alternative, students can use computer software to simulate a frog dissection, for example, rather than cut up actual frogs (Roblyer, 2006). While the simulation has the disadvantage of not allowing students the experience of working with a real frog, it has at least three advantages: it is less expensive, since it can be used over and over; it is more flexible, because the frog can be "reassembled"; and the simulation avoids sacrificing a frog for science.

Simulations as Problem-Solving Tools

To introduce this section, let's return to Bill Logan's math class in the case study that introduced the chapter.

> *Bill begins his class by showing a DVD episode that presents the following problem:*
> *Jasper has just purchased a new boat and is planning to drive it home. The boat consumes 5 gallons of fuel per hour and travels at 8 mph. The gas tank holds 12 gallons of gas. The boat is currently located at mile marker 156. Jasper's home dock is at mile marker 132. There are two gas stations on the way home. One is at mile marker 140.3 and the other is at mile marker 133. They charge $1.109 and $1.25 per gallon, respectively. They don't take credit cards. Jasper started the day with $20. He bought 5 gallons of gas at $1.25 per gallon (not including a discount of 4 cents per gallon for paying cash) and paid $8.25 for repairs to his boat. It's 2:35. Sundown is at 7:52. Can Jasper make it home before sunset without running out of fuel? (S. Williams et al., 1996, p. 2)*

After students view the episode, Bill breaks them into groups of four and says,

"Okay everyone, I'd like each group to work on this problem for the rest of this class period and next. Let's see how far we get. But before we break into groups, I want to remind you. What's the first thing each group needs to do? . . . Javier?"

"Find out what the problem is asking."

"Good. . . . Did everyone hear what Javier said? . . . The first thing you need to do is decide what the problem is asking. Okay, go to it."

Students then move into their groups as Bill circulates around the room, answering questions.

As we see with Bill's class, teachers can also use simulations to teach problem solving (Jonassen et al., 2003). Creating ill-defined, real-world problems is a challenge for teachers in traditional classrooms, because problems presented in textbooks are usually well defined and routine. Typically, the information needed to solve the problem (and only that information) is included, and even the procedure for finding the solution, such as subtraction in a math problem, is suggested by where the problem is presented (e.g., in a chapter on subtraction) (Bransford et al., 2000).

Unlike those presented in textbooks, the problems people face in the real world are often ill-defined and don't have routine solutions. Here is where technology can be helpful. For example, the Jasper Woodbury problem that Bill gave his students is a condensed episode taken from a DVD-based, problem-solving series called *The Adventures of Jasper Woodbury* (Cognition and Technology Group at Vanderbilt, 1997). The series consists of 12 episodes, each beginning with a 15- to 20-minute video segment. The segment presents challenge to the characters in the episode. The problems are purposefully left ill-defined to give students practice in defining problems, and they include extraneous material, so students learn to separate relevant from irrelevant information. They also get experience in breaking problems down into subgoals, such as finding out how much money Jasper has left for the trip home. Students work on these problems in teams over several class periods (ranging from a few days to more than a week). They share their ideas, receive feedback to refine their thinking, and present their solutions to the class.

Software designers have developed problem-solving simulations in other areas, as well. In geometry, programs such as *The Geometric Supposer* and *The Geometer's Sketchpad* allow students to physically manipulate figures as they attempt to solve geometry problems. Another software program called *Interactive Physics* (*http://www.interactivephysics.com*) provides objectives and tools to allow students to solve problems using concepts like force, acceleration, and momentum.

Considering the use of problem-solving simulations raises three questions. The first is whether they are as effective as hands-on experience with concrete materials. In an attempt to answer this question, researchers compared the performance of two groups of fourth and fifth graders on their ability to design effective experiments (Triona & Klahr, 2003). One group was allowed to physically manipulate springs and weights to determine how variables like spring length and width would influence how far different weights would move them. The other group conducted similar tests with a computer simulation. The researchers found no differences with respect to learning, and they concluded that the two approaches were equally effective. While these results are promising, additional research is required to conclusively answer the question.

A second question relates to transfer and Mary's question, "Will it pay off when test scores come back?" which we first posed at the beginning of the chapter. Despite the realism offered by problem-solving software, experts remind us that the skills learned are likely to be domain specific. For example, students working with the Jasper series will probably improve their abilities to solve problems of this nature, but their ability to solve ill-defined problems in science or social studies are likely to be minimally improved (Greeno et al., 1996; Schunk, 2004).

The third question relates to one asked earlier, "How does using technology change the nature of teachers' work?" We first answered this question in our discussion of drill-and-practice software and tutorials, but simulations present a different challenge. For instance, students who are used to straightforward, well-defined problems will initially struggle and likely become frustrated in attempting to solve Jasper's problem. This makes teachers' roles very demanding. They must provide enough scaffolding to help students make progress toward a solution, but not so much that they rob students of experience with solving ill-defined problems. This is very sophisticated and demanding instruction.

Experts caution that simulations' biggest advantage—realism and complexity—may also be one of their biggest weaknesses. Simulations can present students with an overly rich learning environment, making it difficult for them to attend to essential elements of the simulation. As with all forms of learning, students' prior knowledge is important in determining how much they learn from the activity, so teachers must precede simulations with learning experiences that provide the knowledge and tools needed to make sense of their complexities (Beitzel & Derry, 2004). Many people, including school leaders and teachers themselves, believe technology makes teachers' jobs easier, but this often isn't true. It has the potential to increase learning, but using it effectively requires highly knowledgeable professionals who are clear about their learning objectives and how to use technology to reach them.

Exploring Further

To read more about this technology-based program, go to "The Jasper Series" in the *Exploring Further* module of Chapter 14 at *www.prenhall.com/eggen*.

Databases and Spreadsheets

To introduce this section, let's return to Angela Travers's lesson on genetics in our chapter opening case study.

To begin her unit on human genetics, Angela divides her students into teams of 4. She has the teams gather information about the physical characteristics of their families, such as eye color, hair color, gender, height, and weight. To help them find patterns and make conclusions about the genetic backgrounds of their group, they put the information into a database. A portion of this database appears in Figure 14.4.

Students usually need teacher assistance when they are first introduced to databases and spreadsheets.

Databases

If you have ever used a card catalog in the library (either the old index card or an electronic version), you have used a form of database. A telephone directory is another example. To use it effectively, you need to know how it is organized. For instance, white pages contain alphabetical listings of individuals and businesses together with their addresses and phone numbers. The yellow pages are organized by categories such as florists, plumbers, and auto rental companies.

The same applies to electronic **databases,** which are computer programs that allow users to store, organize, and manipulate information, including both text and numerical data (Forcier & Descy, 2005; Roblyer, 2006). The ability to organize vast amounts of information is the primary strength of databases. Users can then find specific information in the database and look for patterns.

Angela used a database to help her students organize information in their genetics investigation (see Figure 14.4). As they identified patterns, they also began to construct knowledge about genetics and its influence on different traits in humans. Commercial programs such as *AppleWorks* or *Microsoft Office* are available to assist teachers as they integrate databases into their instruction.

Analyzing Classrooms Video
To see students using laptop computers to create databases, go to Episode 23, "Laptops for Data in Fifth Grade," on DVD 2, accompanying this text.

Spreadsheets

Spreadsheets are computer programs that allow users to organize and manipulate numerical data. Spreadsheets are the much-advanced cousins of calculators. They were first used for accounting purposes but have evolved into sophisticated problem-solving tools. Spreadsheets produce a two-dimensional matrix of interrelated rows and columns.

To see how spreadsheets can support instruction, let's see how Brad Evers, a social studies teacher, used one to help his students understand research methods in history.

> Brad, who teaches in a small New England town, is struggling to help his students understand where the history they are studying came from and what historians do. He decides to focus his class on the history of a local cemetery to help them gain insights into the story of their own town. Students divide into groups and gather data from tombstones in different sections of the local cemetery. They discuss questions such as, "How long did people live in different time periods?" "How does this compare to today?" "Did women live longer than men?" and "Were there periods of unusually high mortality?"

Figure 14.4 Database structure for investigating genetics

Record	Field 1 Student Name	Field 2 Father's Hair Color	Field 3 Father's Eye Color	Field 4 Father's Height	Field 5 Father's Weight	Field 6 Mother's Hair Color
1	Alvarez, Maria					
2	Battle, Ken					
3	Chu, Karen					
Etc.						

Databases. Computer programs that allow users to store, organize, and manipulate information, including both text and numerical data

Spreadsheets. Computer programs that allow users to organize and manipulate numerical data

Figure 14.5   Spreadsheet to analyze historical trends

Time Period	Person	Gender	Date of Birth	Date of Death	Additional Information on Tombstone
1700–1800					
1800–1900					

After visiting the cemetery, individuals enter the data into a spreadsheet, organizing it by gender, age, and year of death. Brad uses the spreadsheet for a class discussion about what they have learned, both about local history and about the work of historians. (Adapted from Forcier & Descy, 2005)

Because of its ability to manipulate numerical information, a spreadsheet allowed Brad's students to calculate averages and make comparisons, such as the average lifespan of people in the 1700s and 1800s with lifespans today (see Figure 14.5). Learners can also use spreadsheets to create charts and graphs that correspond to data trends.

Teachers typically have two goals when they use databases and spreadsheets. One is to have students learn about the capabilities of these tools, and the other is to use them in their problem solving. The tools won't work on their own, however. Students must be given explicit instruction, both with respect to their capabilities, and in how they can be applied in problem-solving activities (Forcier & Descy, 2005). As we saw in our discussion of simulations, tools like databases and spreadsheets don't replace teachers, and in many cases increase rather than decrease the demands on them. These tools do, however, have the potential to increase students' learning.

Checking Your Understanding

3.1   Describe at least one way in which drill-and-practice software supports instruction and at least one additional way in which tutorial software supports instruction. On what learning theory or theories are drill-and-practice and tutorial software primarily based?

3.2   As tools for supporting instruction, describe the primary functions of simulations, databases, and spreadsheets.

3.3   Using simulations, databases, and spreadsheets has been described as an application of constructivist learning theory. Explain how these instructional tools are applications of constructivist views of instruction.

To receive feedback for these questions, go to Appendix B.

Knowledge Extensions

To deepen your understanding of the topics in this section of the chapter and integrate them with topics you've already studied, go to the *Knowledge Extensions* module for Chapter 14 at *www.prenhall. com/eggen*. Respond to questions 7–9.

Classroom ⊞ Connections

Using Technology Effectively in Your Classroom

1. To maximize student learning, align technology use with learning objectives.

   • **Elementary:** To help her second graders decode consonant blends such as *sh* and *ch,* the teacher selects a software program and sets up a learning station that students experiencing problems in this area can visit.

   • **Middle School:** A social studies teacher designs a unit in which students gather information about their grandparents' and great grandparents' immigration histories. They interview family members, and go to an Ellis Island Website. They enter the information in a database and search for patterns in the information.

- **High School:** A physics teacher finds a problem-based simulation that allows students to apply the laws of thermodynamics to real-world situations. The teacher then selects additional problems from their text to reinforce their developing understanding.

2. Carefully monitor students' learning during technology use.

- **Elementary:** A third-grade teacher uses drill-and-practice programs twice a week to help students develop automaticity with math facts. After each session, she studies a printout of the students' learning progress and uses this information to make decisions about instruction.

- **Middle School:** A seventh-grade science teacher has her students working in groups on science projects using simulations. She meets with each group for a few minutes each day to monitor their progress.

- **High School:** An economics teacher working on a unit involving factors that influence economic growth has students develop a database that includes several countries' populations and population densities, gross national products, defense budgets, literacy rates, and personal incomes. He conducts a class discussion each day to gather information about the students' understanding.

Word Processing: Using Technology to Teach Writing

Though grounded in different views of learning, drill-and-practice programs, tutorials, simulations, databases, and spreadsheets are all tools designed to help students acquire skills, concepts, and organized bodies of knowledge.

Word processing is different in that it is a skill that is used to support other forms of learning, and it has dramatically changed the way writing is taught in schools. Think back to your first letter-writing assignment.

> Your teacher emphasized that a draft copy was to be done in pencil, so you could erase your mistakes and write in corrections. When you were given approval to make a final copy, you took out a nice, clean sheet of white notebook paper and a new ballpoint pen. Using your best hand-writing to copy the letter, you had the date, address, greeting, and first paragraph looking great when Bobby "accidentally" bumped your arm. Your pen slashed across the letter, ruining it. After yelling at Bobby, you pulled out another clean sheet of notebook paper and began again. . . .
>
> [It] looked great! Then your teacher reminded you to proofread your letter before turning it in. You thought it was a waste of time, but you did it anyway. To your dismay, you realized that a complete sentence had been left out, so that the last paragraph did not make any sense. You reluctantly pulled out yet another clean sheet of notebook paper. All of the elation was gone. In fact, you were beginning to dislike writing. (Morrison, & Lowther, 2002, p. 179)

Many of us have memories similar to this example, but word processing can change this. It has the potential to improve student writing by

- Increasing the legibility of written materials
- Increasing the amount of text available for viewing at one time
- Making it easier to enter, revise, and edit text
- Allowing students to store and combine ideas
- Facilitating the development of communities of writers by using e-mail to provide feedback (Morrison & Lowther, 2002)

Research indicates that students who use word processing write more, revise their products more thoroughly, make fewer grammatical and punctuation errors, and have more positive attitudes toward writing (Roblyer, 2006). However, just as technology, alone, never replaces a skilled teacher, word processing, alone, can't teach writing. Teachers still play an essential role in setting learning objectives, guiding students, and providing feedback. Word processing is only a tool; it isn't a panacea.

Issues in the Use of Word Processing

Word processing, like other technologies, raises instructional issues. One is the age at which it should be introduced. For example, some experts suggest that early emphasis on word processing interferes with learning handwriting and the development of other fine motor skills (Roblyer, 2006). A second is the question of whether students should be allowed to hunt and peck when they begin, or if they should learn full-scale ten-finger keyboarding. Research indicates that students using hunt-and-peck word processing take twice as

Technology provides opportunities for students to collaborate and share ideas during writing assignments.

long to produce a product as those who handwrite their materials (Morrison & Lowther, 2002). On the other hand, is instructional time allocated to learning keyboarding well spent, given the importance of other essential skills like math and reading?

Another question is the extent to which technology can be used to teach effective writing. *Summary Street,* a software program, helps writers improve the quality of summaries by analyzing the summary content and providing feedback. The program uses specified topics and articles and compares the content of the students' summaries to key words and terms in the original article. In an experimental trial with sixth graders, students using the program wrote better summaries, with more balanced coverage of key ideas, than did a comparable control group (Wade-Steen & Kintsch, 2004).

A final issue involving word processing is the extent to which it promotes thinking. David Jonassen (2000) in his book, *Computers as Mindtools for Schools,* differentiates between technologies that encourage and amplify thinking and those that just make our work more efficient. He places word processing in the latter category, but other experts disagree (Quinlan, 2004). Research indicates that an obstacle to quality writing is undeveloped handwriting or processing skills that overload working memory (Quinlan, 2004). Students spend so much effort thinking about producing words on paper that they don't have enough working memory space left to create a quality product. If students develop word processing skills to automaticity, more working memory space is available for developing and organizing ideas.

Internet-Based Technologies

Individual computers provide a number of instructional options (and challenges), but students remain isolated. The **Internet,** a complex web of interconnections among computers, solves this problem by allowing students to communicate and share information worldwide.

The Internet was established in 1969 by the U.S. Department of Defense to facilitate communication among researchers in 30 different locations around the country (Roblyer, 2006). The **World Wide Web,** a system on the Internet, allows people to access, view, and maintain documents that include text, data, sound, and video. The advantages of the Internet became apparent, and its use has grown dramatically.

In today's world, anyone who isn't at least somewhat familiar with the Internet has been living in a cave; it has literally become a part of our daily lives. We use it to communicate with friends and colleagues, and to shop for items as wide ranging as clothes, music, and plane tickets.

In addition, it is a virtually inexhaustible source of information. Some people joke, "You can find literally anything on the Internet." Government agencies, businesses, schools, and many individuals have their own **Websites,** which are locations on the World Wide Web identified with a **Uniform Resource Locator (URL).** URLs are series of letters and/or symbols that act as an address for a site on the Internet.

The Internet can provide students with access to information and allow links to other teachers and learners. In this section, we examine the Internet as (1) a resource for problem-based learning and (2) a communication tool.

The Internet in Problem-Based Learning

As you saw in Chapter 9, problem-based learning is an instructional strategy that uses a problem as the focal point of a lesson; students then gather data in their attempts to solve it. The goals of problem-based learning typically include acquiring knowledge, improving research and writing skills, and developing self-direction.

The Internet has two important capabilities that support problem-based learning (Roblyer, 2006). First, it allows students to access large amounts of information through the more than a million Websites that currently exist. Search engines such as Google (*http://www.google.com*) and Yahoo (*http://www.yahoo.com*) help students find Websites on virtually any topic. Second, students can communicate with other research teams to share data and collaborate. For example, a social studies simulation asks high school students to act as diplomats and policymakers to grapple with solutions to real international problems (Rottier, 1995). Students from all over the world dialogue and negotiate about possible solutions to issues such as world health, human rights, and the spread of nuclear weapons.

Internet. A complex web of interconnections among computers

World Wide Web. A system on the Internet that allows people to access, view, and maintain documents that include text, data, sound, and video

Websites. Locations on the World Wide Web identified with a Uniform Resource Locator (URL)

Uniform Resource Locator (URL). A series of letters and/or symbols that act as an address for a site on the Internet

In addition to developing problem-solving abilities, students also learn how to use technology to gather and organize information, and develop their communication skills. Research generally supports the effectiveness of the Internet as a problem-based learning tool (Bernard et al., 2004).

However, the abundance of information on the Internet presents several challenges (R. Wallace, 2004). For example, it makes planning difficult because the information sources aren't structured like a textbook, where ideas are sequenced and linked conceptually. In addition, because students typically navigate through sites on their own, a mismatch between new information and students' prior knowledge can exist. Also, because students are often working on different sites, it is difficult to address learning problems and misconceptions. Assessment poses similar problems. Because students have accessed different information sources, some of which may exceed the teacher's knowledge of the topic, it may be difficult to determine how much students have actually learned.

Using the Internet also poses learning challenges for students. The sheer amount of information available is one problem. They often become distracted by seductive sites that may not be related to their learning objectives (Jonassen, 2000). Also, information may not match their learning needs or capabilities, making connections with their existing knowledge in long-term memory difficult.

Teachers can use different forms of scaffolding to remedy these problems. One is to limit the number of Internet options by providing a list of acceptable sites. A second is to provide specific directions about how to locate information in the sites. A third is to construct a question sheet that helps students identify key points. As students become proficient, these scaffolds can be faded out.

Experts caution that surfing the Internet does not equal thinking and learning (Jonassen, 2000). A cognitive orientation that helps students match learning objectives with Internet content is an important ingredient of web-based learning efforts, and the teacher is essential in guiding and monitoring students in this process.

The Internet as a Communication Tool

Computer-mediated communication (CMC), telecommunication between people via electronic mail (e-mail), has revolutionized the way we interact with others. We can quickly and efficiently communicate with people virtually anywhere in the world, for example, and we can also transmit pictures and other attachments, such as written text, databases, or spreadsheets.

Variations of e-mail exist that allow people to interact with other groups. **Chatrooms** are expanded versions that occur synchronously. For example, when one user in a chatroom types comments, everyone in the "room" sees what they type in real time. In this respect, they are like telephones or CB radios. They're considered the most interactive of all the written communication options. **Bulletin boards** are asynchronous communication devices that serve as electronic message centers for a given topic. In that they're a place where messages can be posted, they function as physical bulletin boards.

The Companion Website for this text provides access to both a chatroom and bulletin board. To access them, go to *www.prenhall.com/eggen*.

Advantages and Disadvantages of Internet Communication

Because the Internet efficiently connects people all over the world, students can inexpensively share their views with others. This kind of access is impossible in any other way. However, as with any educational tool, Internet communication has both advantages and disadvantages (Forcier & Descy, 2005; Morrison & Lowther, 2002; Winn, 2002). For example, Internet interactions are more equitable than face-to-face communication, because extraneous factors such as attractiveness, prestige, and material possessions are eliminated. Communicating on the Internet also gives students time to think, reflect, and connect ideas, so their thoughts and arguments are often more complete (Marttunen & Laurinen, 2001). In addition, learning to express ideas systematically and logically can develop writing skills (Bernard et al., 2004).

However, Internet communication uses only one channel—the written word—which doesn't help students learn to read nonverbal social cues, such as facial expressions and eye contact, or vocal signals such as emphasis and intonation. This is a problem for two reasons. First, research suggests that a large part (some estimate 70 percent or more) of a

Exploring Further

Plagiarism from the Internet has become a problem for teachers. To read more about this problem and what teachers can do to solve it, go to "Plagiarism" in the Exploring Further module of Chapter 14 at *www.prenhall.com/eggen*.

Computer-mediated communication (CMC). Telecommunication between people via electronic mail (e-mail)

Chatrooms. Expanded, collective versions of electronic mail (e-mail) that occur synchronously or at the same time

Bulletin boards. Asynchronous communication devices that serve as electronic message centers for a given topic

message's credibility is communicated through nonverbal channels (Aronson, Wilson, & Akert, 2005). It is difficult to fully understand others' messages in the absence of nonverbal cues. Second, this social isolation can result in a sense of anonymity in Internet communication, which can lead to insensitivity and treating others as objects instead of people.

Some experts caution that the amount of time students spend on the Internet can impair social development by limiting the number of face-to-face interactions they have (Kuh & Vesper, 1999). However, other research suggests that children who are active online are no less likely to spend time reading, playing outside, or interacting with their family (Trotter, 2000), and they are less likely to spend large amounts of time watching television (UCLA Center for Communication Policy, 2001).

Distance Education

When we think of instruction, we typically imagine a teacher working directly with a group of students. **Distance education,** a term used to describe instructional programs in which teachers and learners, though physically separated, are connected through technology, is changing that view (Bernard et al., 2004). Distance education can meet student learning needs in at least three ways. First, it provides courses for rural populations in specialized areas such as advanced physics or a foreign language like Japanese for which a local teacher is unavailable (Honowar, 2005). Second, it can provide instruction for nontraditional students such as adults who can't attend classes during the day or those who are homebound. Research indicates that 90 percent of current distance education users are adults, many of whom are individuals attempting to upgrade professional skills or become recertified (Picciano, 2001). Third, distance education can deliver classes to students over a broad geographic area where driving to a central location is not possible. Students enrolled in online courses appreciate the increased flexibility that allows them to combine learning with family time and busy careers (L. Cooper, 2001).

Currently, distance education includes a number of options:

- Web-based systems that allow learners to both watch instructional programs on television and access information for research. For example, in one program, students had access to Gettysburg battlefields complete with individual soldier profiles and Websites that provided additional information (Furlan, 2000).
- Video conferencing, which allows learners and teachers from various sites to ask and answer questions face-to-face over great distances.
- Computer conferencing that allows students and teachers to interact via the Internet. These distance learning systems can facilitate student–student interaction through bulletin boards and chatrooms that provide either synchronous or asynchronous interaction.

Synchronous interaction has the advantage of immediate reactions and feedback, but requires everyone to be there at the same time. Asynchronous interaction provides the freedom of individuals interacting at their convenience, but delays feedback. Research suggests that the structure of synchronous distance education may be more effective for younger students and those lacking self-regulatory skills (Bernard et al., 2004). High dropout rates, probably due to a lack of structure, is one of the biggest problems with distance education courses. Convenience is a double-edged sword.

Research suggests that the type of distance learning is not as important as the quality and organization of the course and the availability of the instructor for help and feedback (Dabbagh & Bannan-Ritland, 2005). Careful planning is essential; learning objectives, instructional activities, and assessment procedures need to be clearly outlined and explained.

When problems arise, they typically center around three issues:

- Technical problems, either in the system itself or with students' inability to use the technology
- Lack of clear directions and instruction
- Infrequent or inadequate interaction with the instructor, including failure to provide timely feedback

Research indicates that designing and implementing distance learning courses require more time and effort than traditional instruction because of the need to be precise and

Distance education. Instructional programs in which teachers and learners, though physically separated, are connected through technology

proactive in designing and communicating course components (Dabbagh & Bannan-Ritland, 2005; Picciano, 2001).

The greatest interest in distance education has been in secondary and post-secondary education; about 60 percent of American colleges and universities presently offer some type of distance learning program, and these numbers are growing (Roblyer, 2006). In the 2002–2003 school year, 328,000 public school students were enrolled in distance education, with the vast majority (76 percent) at the high school level (Honowar, 2005). The U.S. Army is planning to spend $453 million over a 5-year period to create an on-line university capable of teaching as many as 80,000 soldier-students at locations around the world (Trotter, 2001a).

Virtual K–12 school programs that provide Web-based learning activities as alternatives to standard attendance at school are also beginning to appear. Currently, 19 states have virtual schools, and 14 allow for the creation of cyber charter schools (Ansell & Park, 2003).

The use of this technology has its critics, with many arguing that the lack of face-to-face interaction reduces learning and slows social development (Maeroff, 2003). However, in several comparisons with traditional courses, researchers found no major differences in achievement, attitudes, or retention (Bernard et al., 2004). However, they did find considerable variability in these comparisons; with respect to achievement, some distance education courses were 50 percent better than traditional ones, whereas others were 50 percent poorer. This suggests that the medium per se is not the essential element; rather, it is the thought and effort that goes into the design and implementation of the course. Again, this parallels classroom teaching.

Technology can provide students with exceptionalities with opportunities for practice with frequent and specific feedback.

Exploring Diversity: Employing Technology to Support Learners with Disabilities

Julio is partially deaf, barely able to use a hearing aid to understand speech. Kerry Tanner, his seventh-grade science teacher, works closely with the special education instructor assigned to her classroom to help Julio. Seated near the front of the room to facilitate speechreading, Julio takes notes on a laptop computer during teacher presentations. Other students take turns sharing their notes with him so he can compare and fill in gaps. He especially likes to communicate with other students on the Internet, as this levels the communication playing field.

Jaleena is partially sighted, with a visual acuity of less than 20/80, even with corrective lenses. Despite this disability, she is doing well in her fourth-grade class. Tera Banks, her teacher, has placed her in the front of the room so that she can better see the chalkboard and overhead and has assigned students to work with her on her projects. Using a magnifying device, Jaleena can read most written material, but the computer is giving her special problems. The small letters and punctuation on Website addresses and other information make it difficult for her to use the computer as an information source. Tera works with the special education consultant in her district to get a monitor that magnifies the display. She knows it is working when she sees Jaleena quietly working alone at her computer on the report due next Friday.

As we've said repeatedly, technology is changing the ways we teach and the way students learn. **Assistive technology,** a set of adaptive tools that support students with disabilities in learning activities and daily life tasks, is having a particularly important impact on students with exceptionalities. These assistive tools are required by federal law under the Individuals With Disabilities Education Act (IDEA)(Heward, 2006). These tools include motorized chairs, remote control devices that turn machines on and off with the nod of the head or other muscle action, and machines that amplify sights and sounds.

Probably the most widespread contribution of assistive technology is in the area of computer adaptations. Let's look at them.

Adaptations to Computer Input Devices

To use computers, students must be able to input their words and ideas. This can be difficult for those with visual or other physical disabilities that don't allow standard keyboarding. Devices that enhance the keyboard, such as making it larger and easier to see, arranging the letters alphabetically to make them easier to find, or using pictures for

Assistive technology. A set of adaptive tools that support students with disabilities in learning activities and daily life tasks nonreaders are adaptations that accommodate these disabilities. *AlphaSmart,* one widely used program, helps developing writers by providing spell-check and word-prediction scaffolding (Fine, 2002). When a student hesitates to finish a word, the computer, based on the first few letters, then either completes the word or offers a menu of suggestions. Advocates claim it frees students to concentrate on ideas and text organization.

Additional adaptations completely bypass the keyboard. For example, speech/voice-recognition software can translate speech into text on the computer screen (Newby et al., 2000). These systems can be invaluable for students with physical disabilities that affect hand and finger movement. Other adaptations use switches activated by a body movement, such as a head nod, to interact with the computer. Touch screens also allow students to go directly to the monitor to indicate their responses.

Research also indicates that students with learning disabilities encounter difficulties translating ideas into written words (Quinlan, 2004). Speech-recognition technology eases the cognitive bottleneck in working memory by helping to produce initial drafts that are longer with fewer errors.

Adaptations to Output Devices

Adaptations to output devices also exist. For example, the size of the visual display is increased by using a special large screen monitor, such as the one Jaleena used, or by using a magnification device that increases the size of the print. For students who are blind, speech synthesizers can read words and translate them into sounds. In addition, special printers can convert words into Braille and Braille into words.

These technologies are important because they prevent disabilities from becoming obstacles to learning. Their importance to students with exceptionalities is likely to increase as technology becomes a more integral part of classroom instruction.

| Instructional Principles | Technology in the Classroom: Instructional Principles |

In earlier sections, we've shown how software designers and teachers apply different theories of learning in the design and use of technology. In addition, increases in technology development have produced a variety of instructional options for teachers. The following principles can provide guidance as you make decisions about how to most effectively use technology to increase your students' learning:

1. Begin planning by specifying learning objectives.
2. Use technology only when it helps students meet your learning objectives.
3. Ensure that your expertise with technology allows you to support students when they struggle.
4. Carefully monitor students as they use technology.

Let's see how these principles guide Jacinta Lopez, a first-year, seventh-grade science teacher, as she attempts to use technology in a unit on the different systems of the body.

"Wow! There's a lot of information here," Jacinta thinks to herself on a Thursday after school, as she looks over her planning materials, which include state standards, the district's curriculum guide, and her students' text.

I'll use PowerPoint," she thinks to herself, remembering that the materials that support her textbook include a PowerPoint presentation. (We discuss PowerPoint in the next section of the chapter.)

Friday morning, she enthusiastically introduces the topic, explaining how the information will help her students understand how their own bodies work. She then begins her PowerPoint presentation, urging students to take detailed notes as she proceeds. By the end of her fourth-period class, she knows that something isn't working.

"I don't get it!" she exclaims as she throws her lunch bag on the table in the teachers' lounge. "My book comes with this really neat PowerPoint presentation on the systems of the body, so I was excited to use it. . . . What did I get from them? . . . Blank stares and yawns. I thought they would be interested in the material. . . . It *is* about their own bodies, but evidently they don't want to learn about this stuff. . . . All I heard when I was in college was how great technology was and how all my kids were going to learn so much and be so motivated. . . . I give up."

"Well, before you do that, maybe you'd better start on your lunch so you don't starve in the process," Patty Springer, a fourth-year veteran replies. "I'll stop by after school if you would like, and we can talk about it."

"On a Friday?"

"Sure. . . . We can go out and celebrate the weekend afterward."

"That would be great," Jacinta says with relief.

After school, Patty sits with Jacinta and they talk about revising her plans. "First," Patty suggests after Jacinta reiterates the problem, "you need to be sure of exactly what you want to accomplish in the unit. *Then,* you decide whether or not the PowerPoint will help you meet your objectives. If not, don't use it simply because it's there. . . . Also, if you think about it, kids often sit somewhat passively during a PowerPoint presentation, much like they do when you lecture. So, it's not so surprising that you got blank stares.

"So, let's set the PowerPoint aside for now, and let's first think about your objectives, and then how you can reach them. If your PowerPoint, or some other type of technology can help you, fine. . . . Use it. . . . If not, don't."

Using the standards, her curriculum guide, and some probing from Patty to help clarify her thinking, Jacinta identifies a series of objectives for her unit. Then, she plans to have students work in groups to gather information about each of the body systems, enter the information in a database, and then have a class discussion to compare the structure and function of each system and how the systems work together to make our bodies perform smoothly. She also plans to have students conduct their own experiments on physical activity and its effect on respiration and heart rate, and put the information in a spreadsheet that allows them to make comparisons based on height and weight and boys compared to girls.

Over the weekend, she gathers materials the students will use to find the information for their database, and she searches several sites on the Internet for additional information.

Armed with her revised plans, she begins on Monday. The students initially struggle with organizing the information and entering it in the database, so Jacinta finds herself scurrying from group to group, but by the end of the day, they're beginning to improve.

With careful supervision, her students make progress each day. At the end of the week she is exhausted, but her students have come a long way both in their understanding and interest in their body systems and in their ability to use different forms of technology. "It'll be a lot easier next year," she says to herself. "I finally know what I'm doing."

Let's look now at Jacinta's attempts to apply the principles in her use of technology. She began her planning with the common assumption that technology would, by itself, increase her students' learning and motivation. As a result, she fell into the trap of using technology for its own sake. Because her PowerPoint presentation was available, she used it, even though it didn't help her meet her learning objectives. In a sense, her thinking was backward; she started her planning with her PowerPoint presentation and decided how she would use it rather than thinking about learning objectives and then how to best help students meet them.

Because she is a first-year teacher, Jacinta's thinking is understandable. The technology was available, so she felt she needed to use it. With her resource materials and Patty's help, she applied the first principle by developing a clear set of learning objectives before deciding to use technology.

Realizing that her PowerPoint presentation would not help her meet her learning objectives, she applied the second principle by setting it aside. If learning objectives are better met without the use of technology, it should not be used. In Jacinta's case, using a database and spreadsheet did support her students' learning, so they were used effectively.

Jacinta's students are typical. They struggled both with gathering information and the process of entering it in the database. If Jacinta had lacked expertise in working with databases and spreadsheets, her entire unit could have become a frustrating experience for both her and the students. Her expertise with the different forms of technology applied the third principle.

Finally, Jacinta applied the fourth principle by carefully monitoring students as they worked. In an unconscious effort to save energy, teachers sometimes have students work with different forms of technology without providing adequate supervision. As with all learning activities, teacher guidance and assistance are essential (R. Mayer, 2002).

Online Case Book

To analyze another teacher's application of technology in the classroom, go to the *Online Case Book* for Chapter 14 at *www.prenhall.com/eggen*.

Using Technology in Classrooms: Findings from Research

Having seen how Jacinta used technology, let's see what research has to say about its effectiveness. Reviews of a number of studies suggest that technology *can* increase learning, but the effects are generally quite small (Center for Applied Research in Educational Technology,

2004; Blok, Oostdam, Otter, & Overmaat, 2002). Advocates cite these results to argue that technology has enormous potential for increasing learning (Bransford et al., 2000; Jonassen, 2000). Critics use the same results to question the amount of money spent on technology (experts estimate the U.S. spent $40 billion on technology from 1993–2003) (Cuban, 2001; Culp, Honey, & Madinach, 2004).

Research strongly supports our first principle that we cited earlier: "Begin planning by specifying learning objectives." Without a link to learning objectives, technology can be counterproductive. A study of national achievement test data found that eighth graders whose teachers used computers in their math classes primarily for drill-and-practice versus problem solving and application actually scored lower on standardized tests (Wenglinsky, 1998).

Technology can also detract from learning if it isn't employed properly. For example, if students are spending an inordinate amount of time selecting fonts and colors for multimedia reports, they devote less to planning, conceptualizing, and revising their ideas, which are the reasons reports are assigned in the first place (Bransford et al, 2000). As with the use of manipulatives and other hands-on experiences, "hands on" with technology does not ensure "minds on." Similarly, experiences with simulations are effective only if the learning activities are carefully structured (Triona & Klahr, 2003). Just as thrusting students into lab experiences for which they're ill prepared is ineffective, simulation software can overwhelm them.

Collectively, research suggests that simply immersing students in technology does not ensure learning. This supports another of the principles we cited earlier: "Use technology only when it helps students meet your objectives." Properly used, it has the potential to increase learning and motivation; improperly used it can detract from both. As with all types of learning activities, teacher guidance and assistance are essential (R. Mayer, 2002).

Checking Your Understanding

Knowledge Extensions

To deepen your understanding of the topics in this section of the chapter and to integrate them with topics you've already studied, go to the *Knowledge Extensions* module for Chapter 14 at *www.prenhall.com/eggen*. Respond to questions 10–15.

4.1 Identify three advantages that word processing has over conventional methods of teaching writing.

4.2 Describe two ways that teachers can use the Internet to increase students' learning.

4.3 What is assistive technology, and what are its major uses in the classroom?

To receive feedback for these questions, go to Appendix B.

Classroom Connections

Using Technology to Maximize Student Learning

1. Match technology demands to student capabilities.

- **Elementary:** A first-grade teacher takes her students to the computer lab once a week and gradually introduces them to word processing. As they work, she supplements the software program with individual help.
- **Middle School:** A social studies teacher makes a whole-class presentation on databases, and then monitors his students as they gather and enter information in a database. He intervenes whenever he sees that their efforts are not productive.
- **High School:** An English teacher has her students enter information in weekly journals. They share their drafts via e-mail, use the feedback to revise their products, and then discuss the drafts face to face.

2. When using the Internet, specify learning objectives and monitor students carefully.

- **Elementary:** A fifth-grade teacher supplements a unit on flight with selected Websites. She identifies a half-dozen sites and provides a set of questions to guide students in their explorations.
- **Middle School:** An eighth-grade science teacher helps her students learn how to use the Internet to find Websites for their science projects. She prepares a list of sites, the class discusses them, and the teacher then asks students to submit three of their own together with an evaluation of the benefits to their project.
- **High School:** An American history teacher provides an overview of searching the Internet as an information source for the students' research papers. She discusses different ways to access and reference information as well as the ethical and legal problems with plagiarism.

TEACHER-SUPPORT APPLICATIONS OF TECHNOLOGY

So far we have emphasized the use of technology as a tool to support student learning. It can also make teachers' work simpler and more efficient. Technology can assist teachers in three major areas:

- Preparing instructional materials
- Assessing student learning and maintaining student records
- Communicating with parents

Preparing Instructional Materials

Increasingly, teachers need to help learners understand ideas that are complex and abstract. Technology provides one tool they can use to make these ideas accessible. For example, language arts teachers often use samples of student work to illustrate effective writing. Technology allows teachers to readily extract these examples and share them anonymously with the class. Revising learning materials is simple with the support of technology, but labor intensive without it.

Technology provides teachers with an effective planning tool.

Teachers can also create databases and spreadsheets that they can use in learning activities, such as the example involving factors that influence economic development that you saw earlier. In that case, students gathered the information to be included in the database, or teachers may choose to create the databases themselves and have students analyze them.

PowerPoint: Planning for Presentation Options

Presenting new information is an important instructional role that is sometimes de-emphasized with a focus on constructivist learning theory. All learning begins with prior knowledge, and teachers often face the problem of presenting information in clear and motivating formats. Microsoft's PowerPoint format provides one alternative.

Jokingly referred to as "an overhead on steroids" (Cuban, 2001), PowerPoint is actually a versatile presentation format. Once mastered, it can allow teachers to include the following in presentations:

- Clearly written text
- Photographs
- Samples of student work
- Charts and graphs
- Video clips
- Voice-overs

Students can also learn to use PowerPoint presentations, and these options can encourage them to think more deeply about the material they are presenting and the effect on their audience (Saltpeter, 2005).

As with lecture-discussions (see Chapter 13), using PowerPoint does not have to be a one-way presentation of information. As teachers make a presentation, they can—and should—check comprehension and encourage integration, just as they do in a lecture discussion. Teachers can also use PowerPoint to present quizzes that provide both teachers and students with feedback about learner progress (Finkelstein, 2005).

Analyzing Classroom Videos
To analyze the effectiveness of a teacher's use of PowerPoint to structure her presentation, go to Episode 24, "Using PowerPoint in the Classroom," on DVD 2, accompanying this text.

Classroom Assessment

Assessing student learning is one of the most important and demanding tasks teachers face, and research confirms that frequent and thorough assessments increase learning (Shepard, 2001). Technology can serve three important assessment functions. Table 14.2 summarizes these functions, and we discuss them in the sections that follow.

Planning and Constructing Tests

The word processing capabilities of computers provide teachers with an effective tool for writing, storing, and revising individual test items, and constructing tests. In addition, a number of commercially prepared software programs can assist in this process. These programs can

Table 14.2 Assessment functions supported by computers

Function	Examples
Plan and construct tests	Prepare objectives Write, edit, and store items Compile items into tests Print tests
Administer tests	Administer tests online Provide feedback Analyze results
Score and interpret tests	Score tests Summarize results Analyze items
Maintain student records	Record results Develop class summaries Report results to students Prepare grade reports

- Develop a test file or item bank of multiple-choice, true–false, matching, and short-answer items that teachers can store in the system. Within a file, teachers can organize items by topic, chapter, objective, or difficulty.
- Select items from the test file randomly, selectively, or by categories to generate multiple versions of a test.
- Modify items and integrate them into the total test.
- Produce student-ready copies and an answer key.

These software test generators have at least three advantages over basic word processing. First, they produce a standard layout; the teacher doesn't have to worry about spacing or format. Second, they automatically produce alternate forms, which can be helpful for creating makeup tests and preventing cheating. Third, they can be used to customize commercially prepared test banks that come with textbooks.

Administering Tests

Computer software now exists that allows teachers to construct and administer tests online (Roblyer, 2006). This is useful in dealing with students who are absent on the day of the test or in individualized programs where students progress at different rates. These programs can also give students immediate feedback about right and wrong answers and can provide the teacher with updated information about student performance.

Experts believe that online testing will play an increasing role in states' accountability programs in the future (Edwards, 2003). Currently, 12 states and the District of Columbia have either a computerized exam or pilot project under way to evaluate the effectiveness of computer-based testing. The almost immediate feedback provided to both teachers and students is a strength of these systems. Experts also predict that online technologies will become increasingly important in preparing students for high-stakes tests (Borja, 2003).

Personal response system technologies, a variation of online testing, allow teachers to gather assessment information during a presentation. Each student uses a handheld infrared transmitter that resembles a TV remote. The instructor asks a question in either multiple-choice or true–false format and then asks students to respond. The software records and analyzes answers, and instructors receive immediate feedback in the form of a histogram that shows the number of students who chose each alternative. This allows teachers to clear up misconceptions immediately. While most popular at the college level with large lecture classes, this innovation is also being considered for K–12 classrooms.

Technology provides teachers with tools that help them construct and analyze tests and maintain student records.

Scoring and Interpreting Tests

Technology can also assist in scoring tests and reporting results, saving time for the teacher and providing students with immediate feedback. For example, a high school teacher with 5 sections of 30 students on a 40-item exam faces the daunting task of grading 6,000 individual items! Scoring and analyzing test data, converting scores to grades, and recording the grades can be enormously time-consuming without the help of technology.

A number of software programs are available to machine-score tests (e.g., QuickSCORE). They can:

- Score objective tests and provide descriptive statistics such as mean, median, mode, range, and standard deviation.
- Generate a list of items showing difficulty level, the percent of students who selected each response, the percent of students who didn't respond to an item, and the correlation of each item with the total test.
- Sort student responses by score, grade/age, or gender.

Maintaining Student Records

Technology can also assist with record keeping, another time-consuming task. One teacher commented,

> I keep my grades in an electronic gradebook. By entering my grades into an electronic gradebook as I grade papers, I always know how my students are progressing and exactly where my students stand in relation to each other. It does take a little time to enter the grades, but it makes my job easier during reporting periods. All I have to do is open my disk and record my students' grades on the grade sheet. (Morrison & Lowther, 2002, p. 348)

In addition to saving teacher time and energy, these programs are accurate (assuming the original data are accurately entered) and immediate, which allows teachers to generate grades at the end of a marking period with a few keystrokes. In addition, records are available at any time, providing students with ongoing feedback. Some programs can even print student reports in other languages, such as Spanish (Forcier & Descy, 2005).

Schools are also using technology to maintain attendance records (M. Jennings, 2000). When students enter school, they slide their identification cards into a device similar to those used by credit card machines. In addition to keeping daily attendance, the machines are effective for helping schools identify unwelcome outside visitors and students who cut classes during the day.

Communicating with Parents

We saw in Chapter 12 that helping parents become involved in their children's education is an important instructional role. Communication is an essential step in that process, and technology can help make home–school links more effective.

Parents' and teachers' busy schedules are obstacles to home–school communication. Voice mail and e-mail can help overcome these obstacles by creating communication channels between parents who work and teachers who are busy with students all day.

A growing number of teachers use Websites that describe current class topics and assignments. In addition, students and parents now can monitor missing assignments, performance on tests, and current grades via e-mail. Schools also use electronic hotlines to keep parents informed about current events, schedule changes, lunch menus, and bus schedules. However, research indicates that many parents still prefer traditional information sources such as newsletters and open houses (Langdon, 1999). This may be because some households don't have e-mail, as well as the instinctive desire for the face-to-face contact that exists in open houses.

One innovation uses the Internet to provide parents with real-time images of their children (Kleiman, 2001). Increasing numbers of preschool and day-care programs are installing cameras and Internet systems that provide parents with secure-access Websites that can be used to monitor their children during the day.

Exploring Further

To read more about utilizing technology for your own professional work and development, go to "Teacher Support Applications of Technology" in the *Exploring Further* module of Chapter 14 at *www.prenhall.com/eggen*.

Checking Your Understanding

5.1 Identify at least two ways in which teachers can use technology in preparing learning materials.

5.2 Identify the major logistical challenges teachers face in assessment and how teachers can use technology to address these challenges.

5.3 How can technology assist teachers in their efforts to communicate with parents and other caregivers?

To receive feedback for these questions, go to Appendix B.

Classroom Connections

Using Technology to Increase Your Effectiveness

1. To increase efficiency, use technology tools to support instructional efforts.

   - **Elementary:** A third-grade teacher maintains electronic records for each of her reading groups and uses the records to move students from one group to another.
   - **Middle School:** A sixth-grade math teacher develops a simple computer program that allows him to list the learning objectives and quizzes as well as individual student's performances. He sends updates home every Friday, and asks parents to sign and return them on Monday.
   - **High School:** A chemistry teacher creates a program that allows students to monitor their progress by accessing quizzes, tests, and homework. The students merely enter a personal password, and their records are immediately available.

2. Capitalize on technology for assessing students and providing feedback to students and parents.

   - **Elementary:** A fourth-grade teacher creates an electronic record of his students' performance. He sends a midterm report that includes all the information to parents via e-mail at the middle and at the end of the marking period.
   - **Middle School:** An eighth-grade science teacher generates a file of test items that require critical thinking and stores them in word processing files. After students respond to tests made up of the items, she revises them to eliminate ambiguity, and reuses them on future tests.
   - **High School:** An English teacher whose students are learning to write persuasive essays has students submit them electronically. He then provides feedback in the same way.

 *Meeting Your Learning Objectives*

1. **Identify different views of technology in descriptions of classroom support materials.**

   - One definition of technology describes it as hardware—instruments, machines, and computers.
   - A second definition of technology describes it as a process, integrated into and an integral part of the teaching–learning process.
   - Most experts now describe technology as a combination of hardware and process.

2. **Explain how different theories of learning are applied to technology use in classrooms.**

   - Behaviorist applications of technology utilize software that provides students with immediate and informative reinforcement for correct responses.
   - Information processing applications of technology utilize the strengths and limitations of cognitive structures to maximize meaningful learning.

- Constructivist applications of technology emphasize the capabilities of technology to promote the knowledge construction process.
- Social cognitive theories of learning capitalize on the effects of symbolic modeling on promoting learning.

3. **Describe the uses of different forms of technology to support instruction, and identify the learning theories that support these forms of technology.**

- Drill-and-practice and tutorial software promote learning by providing practice with effective feedback.
- Simulations provide learners with realistic settings for problem solving. Databases and spreadsheets allow learners to organize and present information in coherent patterns.

4. **Explain how word processing, the Internet, and assistive technology can increase learning.**

- Word processing technologies can be used to increase writing skill, allowing students to focus their cognitive energies on the meaning and organization of text.

- The Internet provides a rich source of information for students and allows teachers and students to connect over wide distances.
- Assistive technology provides accommodations for the unique needs of students with exceptionalities.

5. **Identify different ways that teachers can use technology to make their work more effective.**

- Technology provides effective ways for teachers to present information and represent difficult-to-learn ideas.
- Technology assists teachers in assessing student learning by allowing them to plan, construct, and administer tests, score tests and interpret results, and integrate scores into a comprehensive record keeping system.
- Technology makes communication with parents more efficient. E-mails, Websites, and phone messages are all effective ways for teachers to communicate with caregivers.

Developing as a Professional

Developing as a Professional: Praxis™ Practice

At the beginning of the chapter, we saw how four different teachers used technology in an attempt to increase their students' learning. Let's look now at another teacher's attempts to capitalize on technology as a learning tool. Read the case study, and answer the questions that follow.

Callie DeSantis knows that many of her fourth graders have pets, and she wants to use the topic to teach problem solving, word processing, and other technology skills. She begins the unit by asking different students to describe their pets. After several students respond, she asks, "What would be an ideal pet?" As she anticipates, opinions vary, with many students talking about and even defending the pet they currently own. She uses this interest to encourage students to investigate the topic further.

She organizes the students into groups based on interest. Several choose traditional pets such as dogs, cats, birds, and fish, but others choose less common ones such as hamsters, gerbils, and lizards. Each group is responsible for gathering information about the pet they select, including different varieties, history of the pet's relationship with humans, initial cost, common diseases, and things you could do with the pet. Each group is responsible for preparing a report and display to share their findings with the class.

Initially, students spin their wheels, trying to locate relevant information on the Internet. To help the students focus, Callie narrows student options to four sites and provides information about where to go to access relevant information in each. She makes a presentation to the class, shares a handout with Website addresses and directions, and spends the next day helping students organize and write their presentations.

Her students' widely varying word processing skills presents another problem. She decides to allow the more proficient students to take the lead on preparing the reports but makes a note to help the struggling students develop their word processing capabilities.

Callie gives the students two more days to finish their work and then spends one day having them give their reports. In the course of the discussion, a disagreement develops about what is the most common pet in the United States. Fish lovers claim that there are 192 million fish in the United States versus only 78 million cats and 65 million dogs. Dog and cat lovers reply that 41 million households have cats, and 35 million have dogs, but only 14 million households have fish. Callie uses this as an opportunity to teach about different kinds of statistics and asks students to think about different kinds of graphs and charts that the class can use to display the different kinds of information they acquire.

Short-Answer Questions

In answering these questions, use information from the chapter and link your responses to specific information in the case.

1. How does Callie's experience with the Internet compare with other teachers'? What do experts suggest to remedy this problem?
2. How was Callie's experience with her students' word processing capabilities similar to other teachers'? What options does Callie have to remedy this problem?
3. Callie wanted to teach her students to learn to organize the different kinds of information they gathered about pets. What technology tool could Callie use to teach her students to do this, and how should she introduce this tool to students?

ONLINE PORTFOLIO ACTIVITIES

Companion Website

Also on the Companion Website at *www.prenhall.com/eggen*, you can measure your understanding of chapter content in *Practice Quiz* and *Essay* modules, apply concepts in *Online Cases*, and broaden your knowledge base with the *Additional Content* module and *Web Links* to other educational psychology Websites.

To develop your professional portfolio, further apply your understanding of chapter content, and address the INTASC standards, go to the Companion Website, then to this chapter's *Online Portfolio Activities*. Complete the suggested activities.

IMPORTANT CONCEPTS

assistive technology (p. 461)
bulletin boards (p. 459)
chatrooms (p. 459)
computer-mediated communication
     (CMC) (p. 459)
databases (p. 455)
distance education (p. 460)
drill-and-practice programs (p. 450)
educational technology (p. 445)
hypermedia (p. 451)

icons (p. 451)
Internet (p. 458)
multimedia (p. 451)
simulations (p. 452)
spreadsheets (p. 455)
tutorials (p. 450)
Uniform Resource Locator (URL)
     Websites (p. 458)
World Wide Web (p. 458)

CHAPTER 15

Assessing Classroom Learning

Chapter Outline	**Learning Objectives**
	After you have completed your study of this chapter, you should be able to
Classroom Assessment	**1** Identify examples of basic assessment concepts, such as formal and informal assessments, validity, and reliability in classroom activities.
Functions of Classroom Assessment • Validity: Making Appropriate Assessment Decisions • Reliability: Consistency in Assessment	
Traditional Assessment Strategies	**2** Analyze assessment items based on criteria used to create effective assessments, and explain how rubrics can increase the validity and reliability of essay items.
Teachers' Assessment Patterns • Constructing Valid Test Items: Instructional Principles • Commercially Prepared Test Items	
Alternative Assessment	**3** Describe applications of different forms of alternative assessments.
Performance Assessment • Designing Performance Assessments: Instructional Principles • Portfolio Assessment: Involving Students in Alternative Assessment • Putting Traditional and Alternative Assessments into Perspective	
Effective Assessment Practices: Instructional Principles	**4** Describe and explain applications of effective assessment practices.
Planning for Assessment • Preparing Students for Assessments • Administering Assessments • Analyzing Results	
Grading and Reporting: The Total Assessment System	**5** Describe the components and decisions involved in designing a total assessment system.
Designing a Grading System • Assigning Grades: Increasing Learning and Motivation • Learning Contexts: Assessment in Urban Environments	

Assessment is one of the essential elements of teaching. As you read the following case study, consider how DeVonne Lampkin, a fifth-grade teacher (and the teacher in the case studies in Chapter 11) uses assessment in her attempts to increase her students' learning.

DeVonne is beginning a unit on fractions. She knows that fractions were introduced in the fourth grade, but she isn't sure how much her students remember. She begins her unit by administering a pretest. When she scores it, she finds student responses such as the following:

Draw a figure that will illustrate each of the fractions.

¼   3/8   1/3

You need 3 pieces of ribbon for a project. The pieces
should measure 2 5/16, 4 2/16, and 1 3/16 inches.
How much ribbon do you need in all?

$7 \frac{10}{16}$

So, they seem to understand the concept *fraction,* and adding fractions with like denominators. But the following student responses suggest that they struggle with adding fractions when the denominators are different.

Latoya made a punch recipe for a party.

Punch Recipe
¾ gallon ginger ale   ½ gallon grapefruit juice
1 2/3 gallon orange juice   2/3 gallon pineapple juice

a. Will the punch she made fit into one 3-gallon
punch bowl? Explain why or why not.

No because
when added
correctly it
is more.

b. How much punch, if any, is left over?

None

On Saturday, Justin rode his bicycle 12 ½ miles.
On Sunday, he rode 8 3/5 miles.

a. How many miles did he ride altogether?

21

b. How many more miles did Justin ride on Saturd
than on Sunday?

4 miles more.

Based on these results, DeVonne plans her first lesson to focus on *equivalent fractions,* because her students must understand this concept to be able to add fractions with unlike denominators.

She starts the lesson by passing out chocolate candy bars divided into 12 equal pieces and with her guidance the students show how 3/12 is the same as 1/4, 6/12 is equal to 1/2, and 8/12 equals 2/3. In each case she has them explain what they are demonstrating.

DeVonne then goes to the board and demonstrates how to create equivalent fractions using numbers. At the end of the lesson, she gives a homework assignment that includes the following problems:

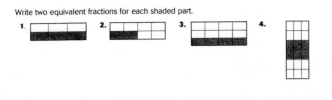

Write two equivalent fractions for each shaded part.

When she scores the homework, she discovers that some students are still having difficulties.

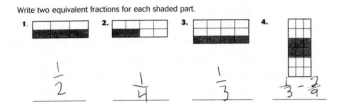

Write two equivalent fractions for each shaded part.

So she designs another activity for the next day to further illustrate the concept. She begins the activity by having the students construct a model fraction city with equivalent-length streets divided into different parts:

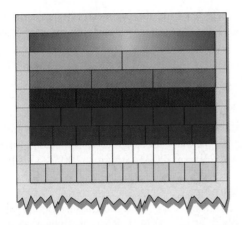

When the students are finished making their strips, she has them move cars along the different streets to illustrate equivalent fractions such as 1/2 = 3/6 and 1/3 = 3/9. Next she illustrates adding fractions with like denominators, using the cars and strips as concrete examples. Then, she uses the same cars and strips to illustrate adding fractions with unlike denominators.

Finally, DeVonne then moves to the board and shows how to perform the same operations using numbers.

Several days later, DeVonne gives a cumulative test on fractions. Her students' answers suggest that they seem to understand equivalent fractions and how to add fractions with unlike denominators:

Write the equivalent fraction.

$$\frac{2}{3} = \frac{8}{12} \qquad \frac{3}{8} = \frac{6}{16} \qquad \frac{4}{5} = \frac{16}{20} \qquad \frac{5}{6} = \frac{50}{60}$$

Write each fraction in simplest terms.

$$\frac{5}{10} = \frac{1}{2} \qquad \frac{8}{12} = \frac{2}{3} \qquad \frac{4}{20} = \frac{1}{5} \qquad \frac{9}{27} = \frac{1}{3}$$

$$\frac{24}{30} = \frac{4}{5} \qquad \frac{16}{18} = \frac{8}{9} \qquad \frac{35}{49} = \frac{5}{7} \qquad \frac{32}{40} = \frac{4}{5}$$

An alien from a far-off planet landed her spacecraft on Earth. She had left her planet with a full tank of super interplanetary fuel. She knew that she'd need at least 3/8 of that fuel to return home from Earth. She used half a tank of fuel to get here. How much fuel did she use all together?

$$\frac{3}{8} + \frac{1}{2} =$$

$$\frac{3}{8} + \frac{4}{8} = \frac{7}{8}$$

To begin our discussion, we want to consider three questions: (1) What is assessment? (2) What forms of assessment did DeVonne use in her teaching? (3) How did the assessment process contribute to her students' learning? We answer these and other questions in this chapter.

CLASSROOM ASSESSMENT

Classroom assessment includes all the processes involved in making decisions about students' learning progress (Nitko, 2004). It includes observations of students' written work, their answers to questions in class, and performance on teacher-made and standardized tests. It also includes performance assessments, such as watching first graders print or observing art students create a piece of pottery. In addition, it involves decisions such as reteaching a topic or assigning grades. In DeVonne's case, deciding to begin her unit with a lesson on equivalent fractions was part of the assessment process, as was the decision to teach a second lesson on the topic and deciding when to give the unit test. This helps us answer the first two questions we asked as we introduced the chapter.

As you can see, assessment is an integral part of teaching and learning. Despite its importance, and the amount of time it requires—experts estimate up to a third of teachers' professional time—teachers often feel ill-prepared to deal with its demands (Stiggins, 2004, 2005). Our goal in writing this chapter is to help you feel better prepared for this essential process.

Functions of Classroom Assessment

Increasing learning is the primary function of classroom assessment. For example, the students' performance on DeVonne's homework assignment suggested that they didn't fully understand equivalent fractions, so she designed a second lesson on the topic. As a result, their understanding increased, as indicated by their performance in her unit test. Without the information teachers gather through assessment, making decisions that increase learning is impossible.

Research indicates that students learn more in classes where assessment is an integral part of instruction than in those where it isn't, and brief assessments that provide frequent feedback about learning progress are more effective than long, infrequent ones, like once-a-term tests (McGlinchey & Hixson, 2004; Stiggins, 2005). This helps us answer the third question we asked at the beginning of the chapter: "How did the assessment process contribute to her students' learning?"

Research also indicates that a well-designed assessment system increases students' motivation to learn (P. Black et al., 2004; J. Ross, Rolheiser, & Hogaboam-Gray, 2002). Think about your own experiences. Almost certainly, you study the hardest and learn the most when you're thoroughly assessed and given informative feedback. As you saw in Chapter 10, motivation theory suggests that learners have an innate need to understand how they're performing and why they're performing that way. Assessment helps students meet this need (Nitko, 2004; Stiggins, 2005).

Formal and Informal Assessment

Teachers gather information through both informal and formal assessments. **Informal assessment** is the process of gathering incidental information about learning progress and making decisions based on that information. For example, if a teacher sees a student "drifting off," and she decides to call on him to bring him back into the lesson, she is involved in informal assessment. In contrast, **formal assessment** is the process of systematically gathering information and making decisions about learning progress. DeVonne, for example, was involved in formal assessment when she observed the students' responses on their homework and decided to teach another lesson on equivalent fractions. Teachers use tests and quizzes in formal assessment, and teachers also use observable performances, such as a physical education teacher's observing the number of sit-ups a student can do.

The Need for Formal Assessment

Informal assessment is essential in helping teachers make the many decisions required in their work (P. Black et al., 2004). For example, it helps them decide who to call on, how long

---

Analyzing Classrooms Video:
To further analyze DeVonne's attempts to use assessment to increase her students' learning, go to Episode 25, "Using Assessment in Decision Making," on DVD 2, accompanying this text.

Exploring Further
To read more about the connections between assessment and learning, go to "Assessment and Learning" in the *Exploring Further* module of Chapter 15 at *www.prenhall.com/eggen*.

Classroom assessment. All the processes involved in making decisions about students' learning progress

Informal assessment. The process of gathering incidental information about learning progress and making decisions based on that information

Formal assessment. The process of systematically gathering information about learning progress and making decisions based on that information

the student is given to answer, and how quickly to move through a lesson. Without it, making these decisions would be impossible (K. Rose, Williams, Gomez, & Gearon, 2002).

Informal assessments provide an incomplete picture of learning, however (Green & Mantz, 2002). For example, concluding that all students understand an idea on the basis of responses from only a few (who usually have their hands up) is a mistake that teachers often make. And, they sometimes make decisions as important as assigning grades on the basis of informal assessment. Students who readily respond, have engaging personalities, and are physically attractive are often awarded higher grades than their less fortunate peers (Ritts, Patterson, & Tubbs, 1992). Systematically gathering information with formal assessments is important in preventing these potential biases. As we saw earlier, DeVonne's homework was a formal assessment, as was her unit test. All students responded to the same items, so they gave her a comprehensive look at the students' understanding.

Gathering systematic information about each student and keeping current records about students' learning progress help ensure valid assessment.

Formal assessment is particularly important in the lower elementary grades, where teachers often use performance measures, such as handwriting samples or students' verbally identifying written numerals. These assessments are often subjective, influenced by factors other than the students' understanding. The question, "Could I document and defend this decision to a parent if necessary?" is a helpful guideline in this process.

Validity: Making Appropriate Assessment Decisions

Validity is the degree to which an assessment actually measures what it is supposed to measure (Linn & Miller, 2005). In classroom practice, an assessment is valid if it is aligned with learning objectives. For example, if a teacher's objective is for students to understand the causes of the Civil War, but a quiz asks them to recall names, dates, and places, it would be invalid. Based on the quiz results, the teacher might decide the students had met the objective, when in fact she had gathered little information about their understanding of the causes of the war.

Also, assessment decisions are invalid if they're based on personality, appearance, or other factors unrelated to learning objectives, such as giving lower scores on essay items because of messy handwriting (Lambating & Allen, 2002). These actions are usually unconscious; without realizing it, teachers base their assessments on appearance rather than substance.

Creating valid assessments, while challenging, is certainly not impossible, however. If you continually look for ways to improve your tests, quizzes, and other assessments; analyze trends and patterns in student responses; and conscientiously revise your assessments, validity will improve. Doing so is part of being a professional.

Reliability: Consistency in Assessment

Reliability is an intuitively sensible concept; it is a description of the extent to which assessments are consistent and free from errors of measurement (Linn & Miller, 2005). For instance, if your bathroom scale is reliable, and your weight doesn't change, the readings shouldn't vary from one day to the next. Hypothetically, if we could repeatedly give a student the same reliable test, and if no additional learning or forgetting occurred, the scores would all be the same. Unreliable assessments cannot be valid, even if they are aligned with teachers' learning objectives, because they give inconsistent information.

Ambiguous items on tests and quizzes and directions that aren't clear are two common factors that detract from reliability. And inconsistent scoring, which is common on essay items, is a third factor. Research indicates that different instructors with similar backgrounds, ostensibly using the same criteria, have awarded grades ranging from excellent to failure on the same essay (Gronlund, 2003). If scoring is inconsistent, lack of reliability makes the process invalid.

Information from informal assessments is also unreliable because the teacher doesn't systematically gather information from all students. For instance, a quick, confident answer

Validity. The degree to which an assessment actually measures what it is supposed to measure

Reliability. A description of the extent to which assessments are consistent and free from errors of measurement

Figure 15.1   The relationships between validity and reliability

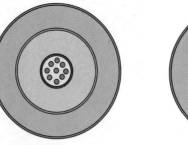 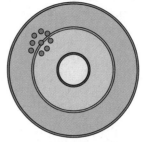 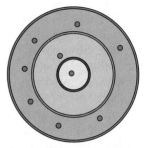

Valid and reliable
measurements

Reliable but not valid
measurements

Unreliable and invalid
measurements

Source: Adapted from MEASUREMENT AND ASSESSMENT IN TEACHING 8/E by Linn & Gronlund, © 2000. Reprinted by permission of Pearson Education, Inc., Upper Saddle River, NJ.

from one student doesn't mean the entire class understands the topic. The solution is to use formal, systematic measures, which gather information from all students.

The following are some suggestions for increasing reliability:

- Use a sufficient number of items or tasks in an instrument. For instance, a quiz of 15 items is likely to be more reliable than a quiz that has only 5 items.
- Clearly explain requirements for responding to the assessment items.
- Identify specific criteria in advance for scoring students' essay items. Score all students' responses to a particular item before moving to a second one.
- To avoid being influenced by your expectations of students, score assessments anonymously, particularly if you're scoring essay items or solutions to problems where partial credit is given. For example, have students put their names on the last page of the quiz, so you won't know whose quiz you're scoring until you're finished.

One way to think about the relationship between validity and reliability is to visualize a target and a person practicing shooting (Linn & Miller, 2005). A valid and reliable shooter consistently clusters shots in the target's bull's-eye. A reliable but invalid shooter clusters shots, but the cluster is not in the bull's-eye. And a shooter that scatters shots randomly over the target is analogous to an assessment instrument that is neither valid nor reliable. These relationships are illustrated in Figure 15.1.

Checking Your Understanding

1.1   Identify the formal and informal assessments that occur in the following: A middle school science teacher walks around the room while his students are working on a lab assignment. He listens to their comments and occasionally asks questions about what they are doing. The next day, he collects the lab reports, scores them that evening, and gives the students a quiz at the end of the week.

1.2   An eighth-grade history teacher reminds his students that correct grammar and punctuation are important parts of expression, and he gives his students two scores on their history essay items: one for responding to the history content and a second for grammar and punctuation. Is his assessment valid? Explain why or why not.

1.3   A high school science teacher wants her students to be able to design effective experiments. After discussing the process with them, she has them complete a lab assignment in which they are required to design an experiment. On Friday she gives a quiz that requires the students to list the steps, in order, for designing an experiment. Is her assessment valid? Explain why or why not. Is her quiz likely to be reliable? Explain why or why not.

To receive feedback for these questions, go to Appendix B.

Knowledge Extensions

To deepen your understanding of the topics in this section of the chapter and to integrate them with topics you've already studied, go to the *Knowledge Extensions* module for Chapter 15 at *www.prenhall.com/eggen*. Respond to questions 1–5.

TRADITIONAL ASSESSMENT STRATEGIES

Teachers have historically assessed learning using quizzes and tests, which likely will continue to be important assessment strategies. If well designed and constructed, they can be valid and reliable for assessing many aspects of student learning (Linn & Miller, 2005). In this section, we first examine teachers' assessment patterns and then turn to the process of creating effective test items.

Teachers' Assessment Patterns

To begin, let's look at one teacher's assessment practices.

> Laura Torrez's second graders are working on subtracting one-digit from two-digit numbers with regrouping. She puts a series of problems on the chalkboard, and as she moves around the room, her students work on them.
>
> "Check this one again, Kelly," Laura says, seeing that Kelly has written
>
> $$\begin{array}{r} 24 \\ -9 \\ \hline 25 \end{array}$$
>
> "I think I'll take a grade on this one," Laura says to herself. She collects the papers after the students finish, scores them, and writes *90* in her grade book for Kelly because she has missed one of the 10 problems from the chalkboard.

Laura's on-the-spot decision to use an in-class learning activity for grading purposes is typical of elementary teachers, particularly at the primary level. They use informal assessments more frequently than do teachers at the higher levels; they rely on commercially prepared items, such as those that come with a textbook series; and they also emphasize affective goals (Frey & Schmitt, 2005; Guskey, 2002). These patterns are summarized in Table 15.1.

Middle and high school teachers, in contrast, depend more on traditional tests and quizzes and more commonly prepare their own items instead of relying on those from publishers. Figure 15.2 summarizes characteristics of these teacher-made items (Bol, Stephenson, O'Connell, & Nunnery, 1998; Stiggins & Conklin, 1992).

Because teachers' jobs are so demanding, they attempt to simplify their work, and this helps explain the patterns in Figure 15.2. For instance, reusing an item is simpler than revising it. Essay items are easy to write but difficult and time-consuming to score, and multiple-choice items are just the opposite. The simplest alternatives are the completion and matching formats. Also, because of inadequate training, teachers have difficulty writing clear items at a level above knowledge and recall (Kahn, 2000), so they revert to those at a lower level, which are easier to score and defend. These characteristics indicate a need for better-quality assessments, particularly items that are unambiguous and require more of students than the simple recall of facts and other information. Helping you learn to develop these assessments is the goal of the next section.

Table 15.1   Elementary teachers' assessment patterns

Characteristic	Description
Performance measures	Primary teachers rely heavily on actual samples of student work (e.g., the ability to form letters or write numerals) to evaluate student learning (Marso & Pigge, 1992).
Informal measurements	Measurement is often informal, as was the case in Laura's class. She comments, "I take a grade a few times a week. I don't really have a regular schedule that I follow for grading." Further, teachers sometimes give social and background characteristics greater emphasis than ability (McMillan et al., 1999).
Commercially prepared tests	When they do test, elementary teachers depend heavily on commercially prepared and published tests. Teachers in the primary grades rarely prepare their own formal tests, instead using informal assessments or using exercises from texts or teachers' editions (McMillan et al., 1999).
Emphasis on affective goals	Primary teachers emphasize affective goals, such as "Gets along well with others." In one analysis of kindergarten progress reports sent home to parents, more than a third of the categories were devoted to intrapersonal or interpersonal factors (Freeman & Hatch, 1989).

Figure 15.2 Characteristics of teacher-made tests

1. Teachers commonly use test items containing many technical errors.

2. Teachers rarely use techniques such as item analysis and tables of specifications to improve the quality of their items. Once items are constructed, teachers tend to reuse them without revision.

3. Even though teachers state that higher order objectives are important, more than three fourths of all items are written at the knowledge/recall level, and most of those above the knowledge level are in math and science. In other areas, 90% to 100% of the items are written at the knowledge level.

4. About 1% of all teacher-made test items use the essay format. This figure is higher in English classes.

5. The short-answer format is used most frequently, such as:

   Which two countries border on Mexico? _____

   _____

   Why does a cactus have needles, whereas an oak tree has broad leaves?_____

   _____

6. Matching items are common; for example:

   _____ A quadrilateral with one pair of opposite equal sides
   _____ A three-sided plane figure with two sides equal in length
   _____ A quadrilateral with opposite sides equal in length

   a. Parallelogram
   b. Pentagon
   c. Rhombus
   d. Scalene triangle
   e. Square
   f. Isosceles triangle

Instructional ⌂ Principles

Constructing Valid Test Items: Instructional Principles

Test items are commonly classified as *selected-response formats,* such as multiple-choice, true–false, and matching, because they require learners to select the correct answer from a list of alternatives, or *supply formats,* such as completion or essay, because they require learners to supply their answers (Stiggins, 2005). Items can also be classified as *objective,* such as multiple-choice, where scorers don't have to make decisions about the quality of an answer, or *subjective,* such as essay, where scorer judgment is a factor (Linn & Miller, 2005).

Although each of these item types requires specific strategies, the following principles can help increase validity and reliability of the test items you construct, regardless of the format:

1. Write items with specific learning objectives in mind.
2. Match items to the learning objectives. Different item types assess different objectives.
3. Construct test items during planning. This increases the likelihood that you will align your assessments with learning objectives.
4. Continually keep validity and reliability in mind as you construct, administer, and revise assessment items.

Now, let's turn to a discussion of different formats.

Multiple-Choice

Multiple-choice. An assessment format that consists of a question or statement, called a stem, and a series of answer choices

Distracters. The incorrect alternatives in a multiple-choice assessment, which are designed to distract students who don't understand the content that the item is measuring

Multiple-choice is an assessment format that consists of a question or statement, called a stem, and a series of answer choices called **distracters** because they are designed to distract students who don't understand the content that the item is measuring.

Items may be written so that only one choice is correct, or they may be in a *best-answer* form, in which two or more choices are partially correct but one is clearly better than the others. The best-answer form is more demanding, promotes higher level thinking, and measures more complex achievement.

Figure 15.3   Guidelines for preparing multiple-choice items

1. Present one clear problem in the stem of the item.
2. Make all distracters plausible and attractive to the uninformed.
3. Vary the position of the correct choice randomly. Be careful to avoid overusing choice *c*.
4. Avoid similar wording in the stem and the correct choice.
5. Avoid phrasing the correct choice in more technical terms than distracters.
6. Keep the correct answer and the distracters similar in length. A longer or shorter answer should usually be used as an incorrect choice.
7. Avoid using absolute terms (e.g., *always, never*) in the incorrect choices.
8. Keep the stem and distracters grammatically consistent.
9. Avoid using two distracters with the same meaning.
10. Emphasize *negative wording* by underlining if it is used.
11. Use "none of the above" with care, and avoid "all of the above" as a choice.

Source: How to Construct Achievement Tests, 4th ed., by N. Gronlund, © 1988, Needham Heights, MA: Allyn & Bacon. Adapted by permission of Allyn & Bacon.

Figure 15.4   Multiple-choice items of differing quality

1. The circulatory system is the system that
    *a. transports blood throughout the body
    b. includes the lungs
    c. protects the vital organs of the body
    d. turns the food we eat into energy
2. Which of the following is a part and function of the circulatory system?
    *a. The blood vessels that carry food and oxygen to the body cells
    b. The blood veins that carry blood away from the heart
    c. The lungs that pump blood to all parts of the body
    d. The muscles that help move a person from one place to another
3. Which of the following describes the function of the circulatory system?
    *a. It moves blood from your heart to other parts of your body.
    b. It turns the sandwich you eat into energy you need to keep you going throughout the day.
    c. It removes solid and liquid waste materials from your body.
    d. It protects your heart, brain, and other body parts from being injured.

Multiple-choice is one of the most effective formats for preparing effective items at different levels of thinking; most standardized tests use it, and it is popular with teachers (Gronlund, 2003; Kahn, 2000). Guidelines for preparing multiple-choice items are summarized in Figure 15.3.

The Stem. The stem should pose one question or problem for students to consider. With this guideline in mind, analyze the items in Figure 15.4.

The first item in Figure 15.4 is essentially a series of true–false statements linked only by the fact that they fall under the same stem. The second item is misleading, because choice *b* includes both correct and incorrect information. Veins *are* part of the circulatory system, but they carry blood back to the heart rather than away from it. The third item presents a single, clearly stated problem, with the distracters providing plausible alternatives.

Distracters. Although carefully written stems are important, good distracters are also essential. Distracters should address students' likely misconceptions so that these mistaken views can be identified. One way to generate effective distracters is to first include the stem on a test as a short answer or fill-in-the-blank item. As students respond, you can use incorrect answers as distracters for future tests (Stiggins, 2005).

Many problems with faulty multiple-choice items involve clues in distracters that allow students to answer the question correctly without knowing the content. "Checking Your Understanding" item 2.1 at the end of this section asks you to identify features of test items that are inconsistent with the guidelines outlined in Figure 15.3.

Assessing Higher Level Learning. Although most of the examples presented to this point measure at the *factual knowledge–remember* level of the taxonomy table you studied in Chapter 13 (see Figure 13.1), the multiple-choice format can be effective for assessing higher-order thinking (Braun & Mislevy, 2005). In an "interpretive exercise," students encounter information covered in class in a different context, and the distracters represent different "interpretations" of it (Gronlund, 2003). The material may be a graph, chart, table, map, picture, or written vignette.

Most of the higher-level items that appear on the quizzes that you take for this class are interpretative exercises. Figure 15.5 is an example in science. In this case, the teacher's goal is for students to apply information about heat, expansion, mass, volume, and density to a unique situation. This type of exercise promotes transfer, helps develop critical thinking, and can increase learner motivation.

Matching Items

The multiple-choice format can be inefficient if all of the items require the same set of answer choices, as in the following (asterisk indicates correct answer):

1. The statement "Understanding is like a light bulb coming on in your head" is an example of
   *a. simile
   b. metaphor
   c. hyperbole
   d. personification

Figure 15.5   Interpretive exercise used with the multiple-choice format

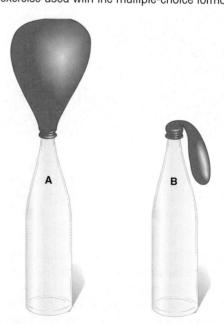

Look at the drawings above. They represent two identical soft drink bottles covered with identical balloons sitting side-by-side on a table. Bottle A was then heated. Which of the following is the most accurate statement?
  a. The density of the air in Bottle A is greater than the density of the air in Bottle B.
 *b. The density of the air in Bottle A is less than the density of the air in Bottle B.
  c. The density of the air in Bottle A is equal to the density of the air in Bottle B.
  d. We don't have enough information to compare the density of the air in Bottle A to the density of the air in Bottle B.

2. "That's the most brilliant comment ever made" is a statement of
   a. simile
   b. metaphor
*c. hyperbole
   d. personification

The problem can be solved by combining items into a single matching item. **Matching** is a format that requires learners to classify a series of examples using the same alternatives. The following is a case based on the multiple-choice items above.

Match the following statements with the figures of speech by writing the letter of the appropriate figure of speech in the blank next to each statement. You may use each figure of speech *once, more than once,* or *not at all.*

_____ 1. Understanding is like a light bulb
        coming on in your head.

_____ 2. That's the most brilliant comment ever made.

_____ 3. His oratory was a bellow from the bowels of his soul.

_____ 4. Appropriate attitudes are always advantageous.

_____ 5. Her eyes are limpid pools of longing.

_____ 6. He stood as straight as a rod.

_____ 7. I'll never get this stuff, no matter what I do.

_____ 8. The colors of his shirt described the world in which he lived.

a. alliteration
b. hyperbole
c. metaphor
d. personification
e. simile

The preceding example illustrates four characteristics of effective matching items. First, the content is homogeneous; all the statements are figures of speech, and only figures of speech appear as the alternatives. Homogeneity is necessary to make all alternatives plausible. Other topics appropriate for the matching format include people and their achievements, historical events and dates, terms and definitions, and authors and their works (Linn & Miller, 2005). Second, the item includes more statements than possible alternatives (to prevent getting the right answer by process of elimination). Third, the students may use the alternatives more than once or not at all, as specified in the directions. Finally, the entire item fits on a single page. If the matching item involves more than 10 statements, you should break the item down into two items to prevent overloading learners' working memories.

True–False Items

True–false is an assessment format that includes statements of varying complexity that learners judge as being correct or incorrect. Because true–false items usually measure lower-level outcomes, and because students have a 50–50 chance of guessing the correct answer, teachers should use this format sparingly (Linn & Miller, 2005). The following are some guidelines for improving the effectiveness of these items:

- Write more false than true items. Teachers tend to do the reverse, and students tend to mark items they're unsure of as "true."
- Make each item one clear statement.
- Avoid clues that may allow students to answer correctly without fully understanding the content. Examples of clues include the term *most,* which usually indicates a true statement, or *never,* typically suggesting a false statement.

"Checking Your Understanding" item 2.2 asks you to assess some true–false items using the guidelines.

Completion Items

Completion is an assessment format that includes a question or an incomplete statement that requires the learner to supply appropriate words, numbers, or symbols.
   The following are two examples.

1. What is an opinion? _____
2. _____ is the capital of Canada.

Matching. An assessment format that requires learners to classify a series of examples using the same alternatives

True-false. An assessment format that includes statements of varying complexity that learners judge as being correct or incorrect

Completion. An assessment format that includes a question or an incomplete statement that requires the learner to supply appropriate words, numbers, or symbols

Essay items provide opportunities for teachers to assess writing ability as well as other complex cognitive processes.

Items that consist of questions, such as the first example, are also called *short-answer items.* As you saw earlier, this format is popular with teachers, probably because the questions seem easy to construct. This is misleading, however, because completion items have two important disadvantages.

The first is that it is difficult to phrase a question so that only one possible answer is correct. A number of defensible responses could be given to item 1, for example. Overuse of completion items can put students in the position of trying to guess the answer the teacher wants instead of giving the one they think is correct. Second, unless the item requires solving a problem, completion items usually measure knowledge-level outcomes, as in item 2. Because of these weaknesses, teachers should use completion formats sparingly (Gronlund, 2003). Table 15.2 presents guidelines for preparing completion items.

Essay Items: Measuring Complex Outcomes

Essay is an assessment format that requires students to make extended written responses to questions or problems. Essay items are valuable for at least three reasons. First, they can assess dimensions of learning, such as creative and critical thinking, that can't be measured with other formats. Second, the ability to organize ideas, make and defend an argument, and describe understanding in writing is an essential goal throughout the curriculum, and the essay format is the primary way progress toward this goal is measured (Stiggins, 2005). Third, essay items can improve the way students study. If they know an essay format will be used, for example, they are more likely to look for relationships in what they study and to organize information in a meaningful way (Shepard, 2001).

Essay items also have disadvantages. Because essay tests require extensive writing time, it isn't possible to assess learning across as broad a spectrum, so coverage can be a problem. In addition, scoring them is time-consuming and, as we discussed earlier, sometimes unreliable. Scores on essay items are also influenced by writing skill, including grammar, spelling, and handwriting (Haladyna & Ryan, 2001; Nitko, 2004).

Essay items appear easy to write, but they can be ambiguous, leaving students uncertain about how to respond. As a result, students' ability to interpret the teacher's question is often the outcome measured. Figure 15.6 presents general guidelines for preparing and scoring essay items (Stiggins, 2005). In addition to these suggestions, *rubrics* can help improve the reliability of scoring essays. We look at them next.

Using Rubrics

A **rubric** is a scoring scale that describes criteria for grading (Stiggins, 2005). Originally created to help teachers with the complex task of scoring essays, rubrics are also useful for assessing performances (e.g., a student speech or presentation) or products other than essays (e.g., a science lab report).

Rubrics provide guidance for teachers during planning, they can be useful in learning activities, and they are essential for assessment. During planning, the process of constructing a rubric guides teachers' thinking by providing specific targets to focus on during instruction. Experts recommend the following steps (Huba & Freed, 2000):

- Establish criteria based on elements that must be present in students' work.
- Decide on the number of levels of achievement for each criterion.

Essay. An assessment format that requires students to make extended written responses to questions or problems

Rubric. A scoring scale that describes the criteria for grading

Table 15.2   Guidelines for preparing completion items

Guideline	Rationale
1. Use only one blank, and relate it to the main point of the statement.	Several blanks are confusing, and one answer may depend on another.
2. Use complete sentences followed by a question mark or period.	Complete sentences allow students to more nearly grasp the full meaning of the statement.
3. Keep blanks the same length. Use "a(an)" at the end of the statement or eliminate indefinite articles.	A long blank for a long word or a particular indefinite article commonly provides clues to the answer.
4. For numerical answers, indicate the degree of precision and the units desired.	Degree of precision and units clarify the task for students and prevent them from spending more time than necessary on an item.

Figure 15.6 Guidelines for preparing and scoring essay items

1. Elicit higher order thinking by using such terms as *explain* and *compare*. Have students defend their responses with facts.
2. Write a model answer for each item. You can use this both for scoring and for providing feedback.
3. Require all students to answer all items. Allowing students to select particular items prevents comparisons and detracts from reliability.
4. Prepare criteria for scoring in advance.
5. Score all students' answers to a single item before moving to the next item.
6. Score all responses to a single item in one sitting if possible. This increases reliability.
7. Score answers without knowing the identity of the student. This helps reduce the influence of past performance and expectations.
8. Develop a model answer complete with points, and compare a few students' responses to it, to see if any adjustments are needed in the scoring criteria.

Figure 15.7 Sample rubric for paragraph structure

| Criteria | Levels of Achievement | | |
	1	2	3
Topic Sentence	Not present; reader has no idea of what paragraph is about	Present but does not give the reader a clear idea of what the paragraph is about	Provides a clearly stated overview of the paragraph
Supporting Sentences	Rambling and unrelated to topic sentence	Provides additional information but not all focused on topic sentence	Provides supporting detail relating to the topic sentence
Summarizing Sentence	Nonexistent or unrelated to preceding sentences	Relates to topic sentence but doesn't summarize information in paragraph	Accurately summarizes information in paragraph and is related to topic sentence
Overall Score (9 Possible)			

- Develop clear descriptors for each level.
- Determine a rating scale for the entire rubric.

Figure 15.7 is a rubric used for assessing paragraph structure. In it, we see three elements the teacher believes must exist in an effective paragraph: *topic sentence, supporting sentences,* and *summarizing sentence.* These elements appear in a column along the left side of the matrix (Huba & Freed, 2000). Next, the rubric clearly describes levels of achievement for each element. Clear descriptors guide students as they write and also provide concrete reference points for teachers when they score the products. As the final step, teachers make decisions about grading. For example, they might decide that 9 points would be an A, 7–8 points a B, and 5–6 points would be a C. So, a student would be required to be at a level of achievement of 3 on all three criteria to earn an A, for example, and would have to be at level 2 on two of the three elements and at level 3 on the third to earn a B.

During learning activities, teachers can use rubrics to communicate objectives. For example, they might display the rubric in Figure 15.7, which could help focus students' attention on essential aspects of their writing (Arter & McTighe, 2001; Saddler & Andrade, 2004).

When assessing students' work, rubrics are essential for increasing reliability. As a teacher scores her student's paragraphs, for example, the descriptions of the dimensions and levels of achievement in Figure 15.7 can help her maintain consistency in evaluating each student's work. Without the rubric as a guide, the likelihood of inconsistent scoring is much higher.

Exploring Further

To read more about using rubrics to promote learning in the classroom, go to "Rubrics in the Classroom" in the *Exploring Further* module of Chapter 15 at *www.prenhall.com/eggen.*

Commercially Prepared Test Items

As we said earlier, many teachers depend on the tests included in textbooks, teachers' guides, and other commercially prepared materials. Although these materials save time, teachers should use them with caution for at least three reasons (Nitko, 2004):

1. *Compatibility of learning objectives:* The learning objectives of the curriculum developers may not be the same as yours. If items don't reflect the objectives in your course, they are invalid.
2. *Uneveness of quality:* Many commercially prepared tests are low in quality.
3. *Emphasis on lower-level items:* Commercially prepared items typically measure at a knowledge-recall level.

The time and labor saved using commercially prepared items are important advantages, however. The following guidelines can help you capitalize on these benefits:

- Select items that are consistent with your learning objectives, and put them in a file in your computer for editing.
- Using feedback from students and analysis of test results, revise ineffective items.
- Create additional items that help you accurately measure your students' understanding.

Remember, only you know what your objectives are, and you are the best judge of the extent to which commercially prepared items assess them.

Checking Your Understanding

2.1 Each of the following items has flaws in the distracters that might allow students to identify the correct answer without fully understanding the content. Identify the flaw in each case.

1. Which of the following is a function of the circulatory system?
   a. to support the vital organs of the body
   *b. to circulate the blood throughout the body
   c. to transfer nerve impulses from the brain to the muscles
   d. to provide for the movement of the body's large muscles

2. Of the following, the definition of *population density* is
   a. the number of people who live in your city or town
   b. the number of people who voted in the last presidential election
   *c. the number of people per square mile in a country
   d. the number of people in cities compared to small towns

3. Of the following, the most significant cause of World War II was
   a. American aid to Great Britain
   b. Italy's conquering of Ethiopia
   c. Japan's war on China
   *d. the devastation of the German economy as a result of the Treaty of Versailles

4. Which of the following is the best description of an insect?
   a. It always has one pair of antennae on its head.
   *b. It has three body parts.
   c. None lives in water.
   d. It breathes through lungs.

5. The one of the following that is not a reptile is a
   a. alligator
   b. lizard
   *c. frog
   d. turtle

6. Which of the following illustrates a verb form used as a participle?
   a. Running is good exercise.
   *b. I saw a jumping frog contest on TV yesterday.
   c. Thinking is hard for many of us.
   d. All of the above.

2.2   Assess each of the following items using the guidelines for preparing true–false items: Choose One

   T   F   1. Mammals are animals with four-chambered hearts that bear live young.
   T   F   2. Most protists have only one cell.
   T   F   3. Negative wording should never be used when writing multiple-choice items.
   T   F   4. All spiders have exoskeletons.

2.3   Explain how rubrics increase both validity and reliability in the scoring of essay items.

To receive feedback for these questions, go to Appendix B.

Knowledge Extensions

To deepen your understanding of the topics in this section of the chapter and to integrate them with topics you've already studied, go to the *Knowledge Extensions* module for Chapter 15 at *www.prenhall.com/eggen*. Respond to questions 6–12.

ALTERNATIVE ASSESSMENT

Critics have argued that traditional assessments, most commonly in the form of multiple-choice tests, lack validity (Corcoran et al., 2004; French, 2003). In response to these criticisms, the use of **alternative assessment,** or direct examinations of student performance on tasks that are relevant to life outside of school, is growing in importance, especially in the language arts (Frey & Schmitt, 2005; Popham, 2005). One national survey found that 37 states use some form of alternative assessment in their statewide evaluation systems (Jerald, 2000). Some examples include

- Designing menus for a week's worth of nutritionally balanced meals
- Identifying and fixing the problems with a lawn mower engine that won't start
- Writing a persuasive essay

In this section, we look at two forms of alternative assessment: performance assessments and portfolios.

Alternative assessment. Direct examination of student performance on tasks that are relevant to life outside of school

Performance Assessment

A middle school science teacher notices that her students have difficulty applying scientific principles to real-world events. In an attempt to improve this ability, she focuses on everyday problems, such as why an ice cube floats in one cup of clear liquid but sinks in another, which students have to solve in groups and discuss as a class. On Fridays, she presents additional problems. For example, on one Friday she puts two clear liquids of the same volume on a balance, and the students have to explain why the beam becomes unbalanced (a balance measures mass). As they work, she circulates among them, taking notes to use for assessment and feedback.

A health teacher reads in a professional journal that the biggest problem people have in applying first aid is not the mechanics per se, but knowing what to do and when. In an attempt to address this problem, the teacher periodically plans "catastrophe" days. Students entering the classroom encounter a catastrophe victim with an unspecified injury. In each case, they have to first diagnose the problem and then apply first aid. The teacher observes them as they work and uses the information she gathers in discussions and assessments.

Performance assessments measure students' ability to demonstrate skills similar to those required in real-world settings.

These teachers used **performance assessments,** forms of assessment in which students demonstrate their abilities by completing an activity or producing a product (Nitko, 2004). The term *performance assessment* originated in content areas such as science and the performing arts, where students were required to demonstrate an ability in a real-world situation (e.g., a laboratory demonstration or recital) rather than recognize correct answers on a teacher-made or standardized test.

Instructional Principles	Designing Performance Assessments: Instructional Principles

Experts (e.g., Linn & Miller, 2005) recommend that teachers follow four principles to design effective performance assessments:

1. Clearly specify the type of performance you are trying to assess.
2. Decide whether the assessment will focus on processes or products.
3. Structure the evaluation setting, balancing realism with pragmatic concerns.
4. Design evaluation procedures with clearly identified criteria.

Figure 15.8   Performance outcomes in speech

Oral Presentation

1. Stands naturally.
2. Maintains eye contact.
3. Uses gestures effectively.
4. Uses clear language.
5. Has adequate volume.
6. Speaks at an appropriate rate.
7. Topics are well organized.
8. Maintains interest of the group.

Source: Gronlund, 1993.

Performance assessment. A form of assessment in which students demonstrate their abilities by completing an activity or producing a product

Specifying the Performance

Specifying what you're attempting to measure is the first step in designing any assessment. A clear description of the performance helps students understand what is required and assists you in designing appropriate instruction. An example in the area of speech is outlined in Figure 15.8.

Selecting the Focus of Assessment

Having specified the expected performance, you next decide whether the assessment will focus on processes or products. Processes are often the initial focus, with a shift to products after procedures are mastered (Gronlund, 2003). Examples of processes and products as components of performance assessments are shown in Table 15.3.

Structuring the Evaluation Setting

Performance assessments are valuable because of their emphasis on real-world tasks. However, time, expense, or safety may prevent performance in the real world, so intermediate steps might be necessary. For example, in driver education, the goal is to produce safe drivers. However, putting beginning drivers in heavy traffic to assess how well they function behind the wheel is both unrealistic and dangerous. Figure 15.9 contains evaluation options ranging from low to high realism to assess driver education skills.

Simulations provide opportunities for teachers to measure performance in cases where high realism is not feasible, and a driving simulator is an example. As another example, a geography teacher wanting to measure students' understanding of the impact of climate and geography on the location of cities might display the information shown in Figure 15.10. The simulation asks students to identify the best location for a city on the is-

Table 15.3   Processes and products as components of performance

Content Area	Product	Process
Math	Correct answer	Problem-solving steps leading to the correct solution
Music	Performance of a work on an instrument	Correct fingering and breathing that produces the performance
English Composition	Essay, term paper, or composition	Preparation of drafts and thought processes that produce the product
Word Processing	Letter or copy of final draft	Proper stroking and techniques for presenting the paper
Science	Explanation for the outcomes of a demonstration	Thought processes involved in preparing the explanation

Figure 15.9 Continuum of realism on performance tasks

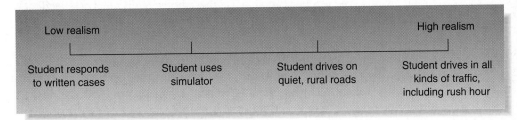

Low realism   High realism

Student responds   Student uses   Student drives on   Student drives in all
to written cases   simulator   quiet, rural roads   kinds of traffic,
                                                          including rush hour

Figure 15.10 Simulation in geography

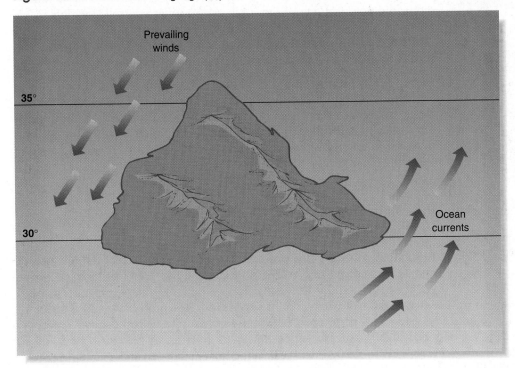

land and the criteria they use in determining the location. Their criteria provide the teacher with additional insights into students' thinking.

Designing Evaluation Procedures

Designing evaluation procedures is the final step in creating effective performance assessments. Reliability is a primary concern. Scoring rubrics, similar to those used with essay items, increase both reliability and validity (Mabry, 1999; Stiggins, 2005).

We turn now to three different strategies to evaluate learner performance: (a) systematic observation, (b) checklists, and (c) rating scales.

Systematic Observation. Teachers routinely observe students in classroom settings, but these observations usually are not systematic, and records are rarely kept. **Systematic observation,** the process of specifying criteria for acceptable performance in an activity and taking notes based on the criteria, is an attempt to solve these problems. For example, a science teacher attempting to assess her students' ability to use the scientific method might establish the following:

1. *States problem or question*
2. *States hypotheses*
3. *Specifies independent and dependent variables*
4. *Specifies controlled variables*
5. *Describes the way data will be gathered*
6. *Orders and displays data*
7. *Evaluates hypotheses based on the data*

Systematic observation. The process of specifying criteria for acceptable performance in an activity and taking notes during observation based on the criteria

Systematic observation incorporating checklists and rating scales allows teachers to assess accurately and to provide students with feedback about their performance.

The teacher's notes then refer directly to the criteria, making them consistent for all groups. The teacher can also use these notes to give learners feedback and obtain information for use in future planning.

Checklists. Checklists, written descriptions of dimensions that must be present in an acceptable performance of an activity, extend systematic observation by specifying important aspects of performance and by sharing them with students. During the assessment, teachers check off the desired dimensions rather than describing them in notes, as in systematic observation. For instance, the science teacher in the preceding example would check off each of the seven criteria if they appeared in the report.

Checklists are useful when a teacher can determine whether a student did or did not meet a criterion, such as "Specifies controlled variables." In other cases, however, such as "Evaluates hypotheses based on the data," the results aren't cut-and-dried; some evaluations will be more thorough and precise than others. Rating scales address this problem.

Rating Scales. Rating scales are written descriptions of the dimensions of an acceptable performance and scales of values on which each dimension is rated. Teachers can construct rating scales in numerical, graphic, or descriptive formats, such as illustrated in Figure 15.11. Rating scales allow teachers to gather more precise information than is possible with checklists, and the increased detail gives students more specific feedback.

Portfolio Assessment: Involving Students in Alternative Assessment

Portfolio assessment, the process of selecting collections of student work that both students and teachers evaluate using preset criteria (Popham, 2005; Stiggins, 2005), is another form of alternative assessment. The portfolio is the actual collection of works, such as essays, quizzes, projects, samples of poetry, lab reports, and videotaped performances. The use of portfolios is popular and appears in areas varying as widely as measuring readiness in children at risk for school failure (J. Smith, Brewer, & Heffner, 2003) and assessing biology students' understanding of complex life forms (Dickson, 2004). Table 15.4 shows some examples of portfolio assessments in different content areas.

Portfolio assessment has two unique features. First, it involves the collection of work samples, so it reflects learning progress. For example, writing samples can document improved skills that occur over a specified time period, which teachers can then use as discussion points in conferences with both parents and students.

Second, portfolio assessment involves students in design, collection, and evaluation of the materials to be included in the portfolio. Involving students in evaluating their own work encourages them to be more metacognitive about their approaches to studying and can increase their self-regulation (Juniewicz, 2003). Further, some evidence indicates that learners, both with and without learning disabilities, feel a greater sense of autonomy with portfolio assessment (Ezell & Klein, 2003).

Guidelines to make portfolios effective learning tools include the following:

- Integrate portfolios into your instruction, and refer to them frequently as you teach.
- Provide examples of portfolios when introducing them to students.
- Involve students in the selection and evaluation of their work.
- Require students to provide an overview of each portfolio, a rationale for the inclusion of individual works, criteria they used to evaluate individual pieces, and a summary of progress.
- Provide students with frequent and detailed feedback about their decisions.

Checklists. Written descriptions of dimensions that must be present in an acceptable performance of an activity

Rating scales. Written descriptions of the dimensions of an acceptable performance and scales of values on which each dimension is rated

Portfolio assessment. The process of selecting collections of student work that both students and teachers evaluate using preset criteria

Figure 15.11   Three rating scales for evaluating oral presentations

Numerical Rating Scale

Directions: Indicate how often the pupil performs each of these behaviors while giving an oral presentation. For each behavior circle **1** if the pupil **always** performs the behavior, **2** if the pupil **usually** performs the behavior, **3** if the pupil **seldom** performs the behavior, and **4** if the pupil **never** performs the behavior.

Physical Expression

A. Stands straight and faces audience.

    1   2   3   4

B. Changes facial expression with change in the tone of the presentation.

    1   2   3   4

Graphic Rating Scale

Directions: Place an **X** on the line that shows how often the pupil did each of the behaviors listed while giving an oral presentation.

Physical Expression

A. Stands straight and faces audience.

    always   usually   seldom   never

B. Changes facial expression with change in the tone of the presentation.

    always   usually   seldom   never

Descriptive Rating Scale

Directions: Place an **X** above the statement that best describes the pupil's performance on each behavior.

Physical Expression

A. Stands straight and faces audience.

| **stands straight, always looks at audience** | **weaves, fidgets, eyes roam from audience to ceiling** | **constant, distracting movements, no eye contact with audience** |

B. Changes facial expressions with change in tone of the presentation.

| **matches facial expressions to content and emphasis** | **facial expressions usually appropriate, occasional lack of expression** | **no match between tone and facial expression; expression distracts** |

Source: From P. Airasian, *Classroom Assessment*, p. 229. Copyright 1997 by McGraw-Hill Company. Reproduced with permission of the McGraw-Hill Company.

Table 15.4   Portfolio samples in different content areas

Content Area	Example
Elementary Math	Homework, quizzes, tests, and projects completed over time.
Writing	Drafts of narrative, descriptive, and persuasive essays in various stages of development. Samples of poetry.
Art	Projects over the course of the year collected to show growth in an area perspective or in a medium painting.
Science	Lab reports, projects, classroom notes, quizzes, and tests compiled to provide an overview of learning progress.

Collecting work in portfolios fosters self-regulation by providing students with opportunities to assess their own learning progress.

Student-led conferences can be an effective way to communicate with parents about portfolio achievements (Juniewicz, 2003). Researchers have found that these conferences increase students' sense of responsibility and pride and improve both home–school cooperation and student–parent relationships (Stiggins, 2005). Time constraints and logistics are obstacles to full-scale implementation of student-led conferences, but the educational benefits of learner involvement and initiative help balance these limitations.

Putting Traditional and Alternative Assessments into Perspective

The idea of alternative assessment is not new. Oral exams, art exhibits, performances in music, athletics, and business education, proficiency testing in language, and hands-on assessments in vocational areas have been used for years. Increased interest in alternative assessments is likely for at least three reasons.

First, traditional assessments have been increasingly criticized, with critics arguing that they focus on low-level knowledge and skills, fail to measure learners' ability to apply understanding in the real world, and measure only outcomes, so these assessments provide no insight into students' thinking (Bandalos, 2004; French, 2003; Popham, 2004c). Performance assessments and portfolios respond to these criticisms by attempting to tap higher-level thinking and problem-solving skills, emphasizing real-world applications, and focusing on the processes learners use to produce their products (Cizek, 1997; French, 2003; Paris & Paris, 2001).

Second, critics argue that traditional formats are grounded in behaviorism, whereas alternative assessments are more consistent with cognitive views of learning, which stress problem solving and self-regulation (Avery & Palmer, 2001).

Third, designers of alternative assessments hope to increase access to higher education for learners with diverse backgrounds, particularly low-income students (E. Hiebert & Raphael, 1996).

On the other hand, little evidence indicates that access to higher education has been improved as the result of the alternative assessment movement (Haertel, 1999; Madaus & O'Dwyer, 1999), and, because of the additional writing demands placed on learners, alternative assessments may result in some minority students scoring lower than they would have on traditional assessments (Worthen, 1993). Further, evidence doesn't support the claim that alternative assessments do a better job of measuring higher-order thinking than do traditional assessments (Terwilliger, 1997).

Implementation is another problem; without extensive staff development, teachers are unlikely to use alternative assessments effectively (Avery & Palmer, 2001), and the process is very time consuming, even with support (Ellsworth, 2001; Tzuriel, 2000). In addition, teachers faced with the demands of standards-based accountability feel pressured to prepare their students for the more traditional high-stakes tests they are required to take (Blocher et al., 2002), and some research suggests that teachers at higher grade levels prefer traditional to alternative assessment (Watt, 2005).

Finally, reliability remains an issue. Obtaining acceptable levels of reliability with alternative assessments is possible if care is taken (Nystrand et al., 1992; M. Wilson, Hoskens, & Draney, 2001), but in practice this has been a problem (Haertel, 1999; Shepard, 2001; Stecher & Herman, 1997).

At the classroom level, allowing students to determine portfolio content creates additional problems. For example, when students choose different items to place in their portfolios, cross-student comparisons are difficult, which decreases reliability. To address this issue, experts suggest supplementing portfolios with traditional measures to obtain the best of both processes (Reckase, 1997).

As with virtually all aspects of learning and teaching, assessment is complex, and it again illustrates the need for knowledgeable and skilled teachers. Only they can develop the combination of traditional and alternative assessments that will be most effective in promoting as much learning as possible.

Checking Your Understanding

3.1 Describe how you would create a rating scale that would allow you to assess someone's performance in creating high-quality multiple-choice test items. Provide an example.

3.2 Describe the primary difference between portfolio assessment and other alternative assessments. What does this difference suggest for teachers first using portfolio assessments in their classrooms?

3.3 Are essay items performance assessments? Defend your answer using the information from this section.

To receive feedback for these questions, go to Appendix B.

Knowledge Extensions

To deepen your understanding of the topics in this section of the chapter and to integrate them with topics you've already studied, go to the *Knowledge Extensions* module for Chapter 15 at *www.prenhall.com/eggen*. Respond to question 13.

Classroom Connections

Creating Valid and Reliable Assessments in Your Classroom

1. Increase validity through careful planning prior to assessment.
   - **Elementary:** A third-grade teacher compares items on her quizzes, tests, and graded homework to the objectives in the curriculum guide and her unit plan to be sure all the appropriate objectives are covered.
   - **Middle School:** A social studies teacher writes a draft of one test item at the end of each day to be certain the emphasis on his tests is consistent with his instruction. When he puts the test together, he checks to be sure that all content areas and difficulty levels are covered.
   - **High School:** After composing a test, a biology teacher rereads the items to eliminate wording that might be confusing or too advanced for her students.

2. Use alternative assessments to increase validity.
   - **Elementary:** A first-grade teacher uses a rating scale to assess his students' oral reading ability. While he listens to each student read, he uses additional notes to help him remember each student's strengths and weaknesses.
   - **Middle School:** A math teacher working on decimals and percentages assigns her students the task of going to three supermarkets and comparing prices on a list of five household items. Students must determine which store provided the best bargains and the percentage difference between the stores on each item.
   - **High School:** A teacher in business technology has students write letters in response to job notices in the newspaper. The class then critiques the letters in terms of format, grammar, punctuation, and clarity.

3. Use portfolios and performance assessments to develop learner self-regulation.
   - **Elementary:** A fourth-grade teacher uses portfolios as an organizing theme for his language arts curriculum. Students collect pieces of work during the year and evaluate and share them with other members of their writing teams.
   - **Middle School:** A math teacher asks each student to compile a portfolio of work and present it at parent–teacher conferences. Before the conference, the teacher meets with students and helps them identify their strengths and weaknesses.
   - **High School:** An auto mechanics teacher makes each student responsible for keeping track of the competencies and skills each has mastered. Each student is given a folder and must document the completion of different shop tasks.

Instructional Principles

Effective Assessment Practices: Instructional Principles

To this point, we have examined basic assessment concepts, such as validity and reliability, as well as traditional and alternative assessment. To maximize learning, however, teachers need to combine individual items into tests; plan alternative assessments; prepare students; and administer, score, analyze, and discuss assessments. The following principles can help guide you with these processes:

1. Plan systematically using tables of specifications or other organizational guides to ensure a match between learning objectives and assessments.

2. Prepare students so the assessments you use measure their understanding and skills rather than test-taking abilities.
3. Administer tests and quizzes under the best conditions possible to maximize student performance.
4. Analyze results to ensure that current and future assessments are valid and reliable.

Planning for Assessment

Teachers implement the first principle (plan systematically to align learning objectives and assessments) during planning. The task is to ensure that assessments are consistent with your learning objectives and instruction. This seems obvious, but because teachers usually prepare tests some time after completing instruction, it often doesn't occur. For example, a teacher might give little emphasis to a topic in class but supply several quiz items related to it; conversely, a teacher might give greater emphasis to a topic in class but cover it less thoroughly on the quiz. Or, a teacher might discuss a topic at the applied level, in class, but write the test items at a knowledge level. Finally, an objective may call for student performance of some skill, but the assessment consists of multiple-choice questions. Each of these situations reduces the validity of a test.

Tables of Specifications: Increasing Validity Through Planning

One way to ensure that learning objectives and assessments are consistent is to prepare a **table of specifications,** a matrix that helps teachers organize learning objectives by cognitive level or content area (C. Campbell & Evans, 2000; Notar, Zuelke, Wilson, & Yunker, 2004). For example, a geography teacher based her instruction in a unit on the Middle East on the following list of objectives:

> Understands location of cities
>   1. States location
>   2. Identifies historical factors in settlement
>
> Understands climate
>   1. Identifies major climate regions
>   2. Explains reasons for existing climates
>
> Understands influence of physical features
>   1. Describes topography
>   2. Relates physical features to climate
>   3. Explains impact of physical features on location of cities
>   4. Analyzes impact of physical features on economy
>
> Understands factors influencing economy
>   1. Describes economies of countries in the region
>   2. Identifies characteristics of each economy
>   3. Explains how economies relate to climate and physical features

Table of specifications. A matrix that helps teachers organize learning objectives by cognitive level or content area

Table 15.5 presents a table of specifications for a content-level matrix based on the objectives for the geography unit on the Middle East. The teacher had a mix of items, with greater emphasis on physical features than other topics. This emphasis reflects the

Table 15.5   Sample table of specifications

Content	Outcomes			
	Knowledge	Comprehension	Higher Order Thinking and Problem Solving	Total Items in Each Content Area
Cities	4	2	2	8
Climate	4	2	2	8
Economy	2	2	—	4
Physical features	4	9	7	20
Total items	14	15	11	—

teacher's objectives, which stressed the influence of physical features on the location of cities, the climate, and the economy of the region. It also reflects the time and effort spent on each area. Increasing validity of assessments by ensuring this match between objectives, instruction, and assessment is the primary function of a table of specifications.

For alternative assessments, establishing criteria serves a function similar to that of a table of specifications. The criteria identify performance, determine emphasis, and attempt to ensure congruence between learning objectives and assessments.

Preparing Students for Assessments

Preparing students for the assessment applies the second principle. To illustrate this process, let's return to DeVonne's work with her students, which you first saw in the case study at the beginning of the chapter.

"Get out your chalkboards and chalk," she directs the students, referring to small individual chalkboards she has made for each of them at the beginning of the year.

"Look up here," she begins, pointing to the chalkboard at the front of the room. "You know we're having a test tomorrow on finding equivalent fractions and adding fractions with unlike denominators, and we decided that the test will go in your math portfolios. On the test, you will have to add some fractions in which the denominators are the same and others in which they're different. There will also be word problems in which you will need to do the same thing. I'll give the test back Friday, and if we all do well, we won't have any homework over the weekend."

"YEAH!" the students shout in unison, as DeVonne smiles at their response.

She holds up her hand, they quiet down, and she continues. "I have some problems on the test that are going to make you think," she smiles. "But you've all been working hard, and you're getting so good at this, you'll be able to do it. You're my team, and I know you'll come through," she says energetically.

"To be sure we're okay, I have a few problems that are just like those on the test, so let's see how we do. Write these two on your chalkboards."

$$\frac{1}{3} + \frac{1}{4} = ? \qquad \frac{2}{7} + \frac{4}{7} = ?$$

DeVonne watches as the students work on the problems and then hold their chalkboards up when they finished. Seeing that three of the students miss the first problem, she reviews it with the class, and then displays the following three:

$$\frac{2}{3} + \frac{1}{6} = ? \qquad \frac{4}{9} + \frac{1}{6} = ? \qquad \frac{2}{9} + \frac{4}{9} = ?$$

Two students miss the second one, so again she reviews it carefully.

"Now, let's try one more," she continues, displaying the following problem on the overhead:

You are at a pizza party with 5 other people, and you order 2 pizzas. The 2 pizzas are the same size, but one is cut into 4 pieces and the other is cut into 8 pieces. You eat 1 piece from each pizza. How much pizza do you eat in all?

Again, she watches the students work and reviews the solution with them when they finish. In the process, she asks questions such as "What information in the problem is important, and how do we know?" "What do we see in the problem that's irrelevant?" and "What should we do first in solving it?"

After she displays two more word problems, she tells students, "The problems on the test are like the ones we practiced here today." Responding to additional questions from the students, she concludes her review by saying, "All right, when we take a test, what do we always do?"

"WE READ THE DIRECTIONS CAREFULLY!" the students shout in unison.

"Okay, good," DeVonne smiles. "Now, remember, what will you do if you get stuck on a problem?"

"Go on to the next one so we don't run out of time."

"And what will we be sure *not* to do?"

"We won't forget to go back to the one we skipped."

In preparing students for tests, you have both long- and short-term goals. Long term, you want your students to understand test-taking strategies and enter testing situations

Frequent assessment within the context of a supportive learning environment can help alleviate text anxiety.

with confidence and minimum of anxiety. Short term, you want them to understand the format and the content being tested. By preparing students, you help reach both.

Teaching Test-Taking Strategies

You can help students improve their test-taking skills by helping them understand the importance of strategies such as the following:

- Use time efficiently and pace themselves.
- Read directions carefully.
- Identify the important information in questions.
- Understand the demands of different testing formats.
- Determine how questions will be scored.

To be most effective, you should teach these strategies and illustrate them with concrete examples. Students also need practice with a variety of formats and testing situations. Research indicates that strategy instruction improves test-taking performance, and that young, low-ability, and minority students who have limited test-taking experience benefit the most (S. Walton & Taylor, 1996/97).

Reducing Test Anxiety

"Listen my children and you shall hear. . . . Listen my children and you shall hear. . . . Rats! I knew it this morning in front of Mom."

Like this student, many of us have experienced **test anxiety,** an unpleasant reaction to testing situations that can lower performance. Usually, it is momentary and minor, but for a portion of the school population (estimates run as high as 10 percent), it is a serious problem (J. Williams, 1992).

Research suggests that test anxiety consists of both an affective and a cognitive component (E. Hong, 1999; Pintrich & Schunk, 2002). Its *affective,* or *emotional, component* can include physiological symptoms, such as increased pulse rate, dry mouth, and headache, as well as feelings of dread and helplessness and sometimes "going blank." Its *cognitive,* or *worry, component* involves preoccupation with test difficulty, thoughts of failure and other concerns, such as parents being upset or embarrassment by a low score. These thoughts take working memory space, which leaves less to analyze specific items.

Test anxiety is triggered by testing situations that (a) involve pressure to succeed, (b) are perceived as difficult, (c) impose time limits, and (d) contain unfamiliar items or formats (Zohar, 1998). Unannounced tests are particularly significant in causing anxiety.

Teachers can do much to minimize test anxiety, and the most successful efforts focus on the worry component (Pintrich & Schunk, 2002). Suggestions include the following:

- Use criterion measures to minimize the competitive aspects of tests, and avoid social comparisons, such as public displays of test scores. (We discuss criterion referencing in the next section.)
- Give more, rather than fewer, quizzes and tests.
- Discuss test content and procedures before testing, and give clear directions for responding to test items.
- Teach test-taking skills, and give students ample time to take tests.
- Use a variety of assessments to measure students' understanding and skills.

Specific Test-Preparation Procedures

Before any test, teachers want to ensure that learners understand test content and procedures and expect to succeed on the exam. In preparing her students, DeVonne did three important things:

1. She specified precisely what would be on the test.
2. She gave students a chance to practice similar items under testlike conditions.
3. She established positive expectations and encouraged her students to link success and effort.

Clarifying test formats and content establishes structure for students, which reduces test anxiety. Knowing what will be on the test and how items will be formatted leads to higher achievement for all students, particularly those of low ability.

Test anxiety. An unpleasant reaction to testing situations that can lower performance

Merely specifying the content often isn't enough, however, particularly with young learners, so DeVonne actually gave students practice exercises and presented them in a format that paralleled their appearance on her test. In learning math skills, for instance, her students first practiced adding fractions with like denominators, then learned to find equivalent fractions, and finally added fractions with unlike denominators, each in separate lessons. On the test, however, the problems were mixed, and DeVonne gave students a chance to practice integrating these skills before the test.

Finally, DeVonne clearly communicated that she expected students to do well on the test. The motivational benefits of establishing positive expectations have been confirmed by decades of research (Pintrich & Schunk, 2002; Stipek, 2002). She also emphasized effort, and she modeled an incremental view of ability by saying, "But you've all been working hard, and you're getting so good at this, you'll be able to do it." As you recall from your study of motivation in Chapters 10 and 11, encouraging the belief that ability is incremental and can be improved through effort benefits both immediate performance and long-term motivation.

Online Case Book

To analyze another teacher's attempts to prepare her students for an assessment, go to the *Online Case Book* for Chapter 15 at *www.prenhall.com/eggen.*

Administering Assessments

When teachers administer assessments, they want to create conditions to ensure that results reflect what students know and can do. Let's return again to DeVonne's efforts.

> At 10:00 the next morning, DeVonne shuts a classroom window because of noise from delivery trucks outside. She considers rearranging the desks in the room but decides to wait until after the test.
>
> "Okay, everyone, let's get ready for our math test," she directs, and the students put their books under their desks.
>
> She waits a moment, sees that everyone's desk is clear, and says, "When you're finished, turn the test over, and I'll come and get it. Now look up at the board. After you're done, work on the assignment listed there until everyone is finished. Then we'll start reading." As she hands out the tests, she says, "If you get too warm, raise your hand, and I'll turn on the air conditioner. I shut the window because of the noise outside."
>
> "Work carefully," she says after everyone has a copy. "You've all been working hard, and I know you will do well. You have as much time as you need."
>
> The students begin working, and DeVonne stands at the side of the room, watching them.
>
> After several minutes, she notices Anthony doodling at the top of his paper and glancing around the room. She goes over and says, "It looks like you're doing fine on these problems," pointing to some near the top of the paper. "Now concentrate a little harder. I'll bet you can do most of the others." She smiles reassuringly and again moves to the side of the room.
>
> DeVonne goes over to Hajar in response to her raised hand. "The lead on my pencil broke, Mrs. Lampkin," she whispers.
>
> "Take this one," DeVonne responds, handing her another. "Come and get yours after the test."
>
> As students finish, DeVonne picks up their papers, and they begin the assignment on the board.

Now let's look at DeVonne's actions in administering the test. First, she arranged the environment to be comfortable, free from distractions, and similar to the way it was when students learned the content. Distractions can depress test performance, particularly in young or low-ability students.

Second, she gave precise directions for taking the test, turning in the papers, and spending time afterward. These directions helped maintain order and prevented distractions for late-finishing students.

Finally, she carefully monitored the students as they worked on the test. This not only allowed her to encourage those who became lost or distracted but also discouraged cheating. In the real world, unfortunately, some students will cheat if given the opportunity (Bracey, 2005). However, an emphasis on learning versus performance and efforts to create the feeling that students are part of a learning community decrease the likelihood of cheating (K. Finn & Frone, 2004; Murdock, Hale, & Weber, 2001). In addition, external factors, such as the teacher leaving the room, influence cheating more than whether students are inherently inclined to do so (Blackburn & Miller, 1999; Newstead, Franklyn-Stokes, & Armstead, 1996).

Monitoring student progress during assessment allows teachers to answer questions and clear up misunderstandings.

In DeVonne's case, monitoring was more a form of giving support than of being a watchdog. When she saw that Anthony was distracted, she quickly intervened, encouraged him, and urged him to increase his concentration. This encouragement is particularly important for underachieving and test-anxious students, who tend to become distracted (J. Elliott & Thurlow, 2000). DeVonne's efforts in all these areas applied the third principle that we described at the beginning of this section.

Analyzing Results

"Do you have our tests finished, Mrs. Lampkin?" the students ask Friday morning.

"Of course!" she smiles, returning their papers.

"Overall, you did well, and I'm proud of you. I knew all that hard work would pay off. . . . There are a few items I want to go over, though. We had a little trouble with number 13, and you all made nearly the same mistake, so let's take a look at it."

She waits a moment while the students read the problem and then asks, "Now, what are we given in the problem? . . . Saleina?"

"Mr. El had two dozen candy bars."

"Okay. Good. And how many is that? . . . Kevin?"

"Umm . . . two dozen is 24."

"Fine. And what else do we know? . . . Hajar?"

DeVonne continues the discussion of the problem and then goes over two others that were frequently missed. In the process, she makes notes at the top of her copy, identifying the problems that were difficult. She writes "Ambiguous" by one and underlines some of the wording in it. By another, she writes, "Teach them how to draw diagrams of the problem." She then puts her copy of the test in a folder, lays it on her desk to be filed, and turns back to the class.

DeVonne's efforts didn't end with administering the test. She scored and returned it the next day, discussed the results, and gave students feedback as quickly as possible. Feedback helps learners correct misconceptions, and knowledge of results promotes student motivation (Olina & Sullivan, 2002). Because student attention is high during discussions of missed items, many teachers believe that students learn more in these sessions than they do in original instruction (Haertel, 1986).

In addition, DeVonne made positive comments about the students' performance on the test. In a study examining this factor, students who were told they did well performed better on a subsequent measure than those who were told they did poorly, even though the two groups did equally well on the first test (Bridgeman, 1974). Research also supports the benefits of individual comments; students who see notes such as "Excellent! Keep it up!" and "Good work, keep at it!" do better on subsequent measures (Page, 1992).

Finally, DeVonne made notes on her copy of the test before filing it. Her notes reminded her that the wording on one of her problems was misleading, so she could revise it. This, plus other information taken from the test, will assist her in future planning for both instruction and assessment. These efforts applied the last principle that we presented at the beginning of this section.

Checking Your Understanding

4.1   Creating tables of specifications for assessments is considered to be an effective assessment practice. Explain the primary purpose of a table of specifications. When should it be created?

4.2   Effective assessment practices suggest that students be taught test-taking strategies. Explain at least three test-taking strategies that DeVonne emphasized with her students as she prepared them for their test.

4.3   To keep his students informed about the amount of time remaining during a test, a teacher reminds them every 10 minutes. Is this a good idea? How will it affect test anxiety? If at all possible, what should teachers do in scheduling the amount of time students have to take a test?

To receive feedback for these questions, go to Appendix B.

Knowledge Extensions

To deepen your understanding of the topics in this section of the chapter and to integrate them with topics you've already studied, go to the *Knowledge Extensions* module for Chapter 15 at *www.prenhall.com/eggen*. Respond to questions 14–17.

GRADING AND REPORTING: THE TOTAL ASSESSMENT SYSTEM

To this point, we have discussed the preparation of traditional and alternative assessments and the assessment process itself, which includes preparing students, administering assessments, and analyzing results. Designing a total system requires some additional decisions, such as

- How many tests and quizzes should I give?
- How will I use alternative assessments?
- How will I count homework?
- How will I assess and report affective dimensions, such as cooperation and effort?

A teacher's grading system can provide one way to communicate with students about learning progress.

These decisions will be your responsibility, a prospect that may seem daunting, since you have little experience to fall back on. Merely knowing that the decisions are yours, however, removes some of the uncertainty. We discuss these issues in this section.

Designing a Grading System

An effective grading system provides feedback to students, helps them develop self-regulation, and can increase motivation to learn. It also aids communication between teachers and parents (Guskey, 2002). The following are some guidelines that can help you in designing your system:

- Create a system that is clear, understandable, and consistent with school and district policies.
- Design your system to support learning and instruction by gathering frequent and systematic information from each student.
- Base grades on observable data.
- Assign grades consistently regardless of gender, class, race, or socioeconomic status.

You should be able to confidently defend the system to a parent or administrator if necessary (Linn & Miller, 2005; Loyd & Loyd, 1997).

With these guidelines in mind, let's look at elements of an effective system.

Formative and Summative Assessments

Although we often think that the purpose of giving tests and quizzes is to assign grades, its most important function is to provide information about learning progress. In some instances, teachers give, score, and discuss assessments but do not include them in a grading decision. In these cases they're part of **formative assessment,** the process of using ungraded assessments during instruction to provide students with feedback and aid teachers in diagnosis and planning. Pretests, work samples, and writing assignments that can be rewritten are common forms of formative assessment. Providing students with feedback, which is essential for increasing motivation and helping students learn to monitor their own progress, is its primary purpose (Frey & Schmitt, 2005; Olina & Sullivan, 2002). Unfortunately, despite its positive effects, research suggests that teachers rarely use formative assessment (Frey & Schmitt, 2005).

Summative assessment is the process of assessing after instruction and using the results for making grading decisions. Although used for grading, feedback on summative assessments is as essential as it is for any other. In public schools, most assessments are used for summative purposes; however, used properly, both formative and summative assessments can be useful for making instructional decisions and increasing student motivation to learn (Stipek, 1996).

Norm-Referenced and Criterion-Referenced Grading Systems

Assigning value to students' work is an integral part of assessment. Norm-referenced and criterion-referenced systems are two ways to assign value to student performance. In **norm-referenced grading,** teachers base assessment decisions about an individual's work on comparisons with the work of peers. This type of grading gets its name from

Formative assessment. The process of using ungraded assessments during instruction to provide students with feedback and aid the teacher in diagnosis and planning

Summative assessment. The process of assessing after instruction and using the results for making grading decisions

Norm-referenced grading. Assessment decisions about an individual student's work based on comparisons with the work of peers

the normal curve (see Figure 16.4 in Chapter 16), and teachers using it might establish a grading system such as the following:

A   Top 15% of students

B   Next 20% of students

C   Next 30% of students

D   Next 20% of students

F   Last 15% of students

In **criterion-referenced grading,** teachers make assessment decisions according to a predetermined standard, such as 90–100 for an A, 89–80 for a B, and so on. The specific standards will vary among school districts, and even schools. They are usually established by the school or district, but in some cases the decision will be yours.

Criterion-referenced systems have two important advantages over those that are norm referenced (Haladyna, 2002; Stiggins, 2005). First, because they reflect the extent to which learning objectives are met, they more nearly describe content mastery. Second, they de-emphasize competition. Competitive grading systems can discourage students from helping each other, threaten peer relationships, and decrease motivation to learn (Ames, 1992; P. Black & William, 1998a; Stipek, 1996). While norm-referencing is important for standardized testing, teachers rarely use it in their classroom assessment systems.

Traditional and Alternative Assessments

For teachers in upper elementary, middle, and high schools, traditional assessments in the form of tests and quizzes are the cornerstones of a grading system. Some add tests and quizzes together and count them as a certain percentage of the overall grade; others weigh them differently in assigning grades.

If you're using alternative assessments, you should include them in determining grades. To do otherwise communicates that they are less important than the traditional measures you're using. If you rate student performance on the basis of well-defined criteria, scoring will have acceptable reliability, and alternative assessments can then be an integral part of the total assessment system.

Homework

As you saw in Chapter 13, properly designed homework contributes to learning. To be most effective, teachers should collect, score, and include homework in the grading system (H. Cooper et al., 1998; Stein & Carnine, 1999). Beyond this point, however, research provides little guidance as to how teachers should manage homework. Accountability, feedback, and your own workload will all influence this decision. Table 15.6 outlines some options.

As you can see, each option has advantages and disadvantages. The best strategy is one that results in learners making the most consistent and conscientious effort on their homework without costing you an inordinate amount of time.

Assigning Grades: Increasing Learning and Motivation

Having made decisions about traditional and alternative assessments and homework, you are now ready to design your grading system. At this point, you must make two decisions: (1) what to include and (2) the weight to assign each component. In addition to tests, quizzes, alternative assessments, and homework, some teachers build in additional factors, such as effort, class participation, and attitude. Assessment experts discourage this practice, though it is common in classrooms (Linn & Miller, 2005; McMillan et al., 1999). Gathering systematic information about affective variables is difficult, and assessing them is highly subjective. In addition, a high grade based on effort suggests to both students and parents that important content was learned when it may not have been. Factors such as effort, cooperation, and class attendance should be reflected in a separate section of the report card.

Learners with exceptionalities pose special grading challenges. Research indicates that 60 to 70 percent of these students receive below-average grades in their general education classes (Munk & Bursuck, 1997/98). The effects of these low grades can be dev-

Criterion-referenced grading. Assessment decisions made according to a predetermined standard

Table 15.6 Homework assessment options

Option	Advantages	Disadvantages
Grade it yourself	Promotes learning. Allows diagnosis of students. Increases student effort.	Is very demanding for the teacher.
Grade samples	Reduces teacher work, compared with first option.	Doesn't give the teacher a total picture of student performance.
Collect at random intervals	Reduces teacher workload.	Reduces student effort unless homework is frequently collected.
Change papers, students grade	Provides feedback with minimal teacher effort.	Consumes class time. Doesn't give students feedback on their own work.
Students score own papers	Is the same as changing papers. Lets students see their own mistakes.	Is inaccurate for purposes of evaluation. Lets students not do the work and copy in class as it's being discussed.
Students get credit for completing assignment	Gives students feedback on their work when it's discussed in class.	Reduces effort of unmotivated students.
No graded homework, frequent short quizzes	Is effective with older and motivated students.	Reduces effort of unmotivated students.

astating to students who already experience frustration in attempting to learn and keep up with their peers.

To help solve this problem, teachers often adapt their grading systems by grading on improvement, assigning separate grades for process and for products, and basing a grade on meeting the objectives of an individualized education program (IEP) (Venn, 2000). The dilemma for teachers is how to increase motivation to learn while providing an accurate indicator of learning progress. Experts suggest that districts develop comprehensive grading policies in this area to guide teacher efforts (Munk & Bursuck, 1997/98).

Let's look now at two teachers' systems for assigning grades:

Kim Ngin (Middle school science)		**Lea DeLong (High school algebra)**	
Tests and quizzes	50%	Tests	45%
Homework	20%	Quizzes	45%
Performance assessment	20%	Homework	10%
Projects	10%		

We see that they are quite different. Kim, an eighth-grade physical science teacher, emphasizes both homework and alternative assessments, which include projects and performance assessments. Traditional tests and quizzes count only 50 percent in his system. Lea emphasizes tests and quizzes much more heavily; they count 90 percent in her system. The rationale in each case is simple. Kim indicates that homework is important to student learning, and he believes that unless it is emphasized, students won't do it. He also includes projects as an important part of his assessment system, believing they involve his students in the study of science. He uses performance assessments to chart students' progress as they work on experiments and other hands-on activities. Lea, a secondary Algebra II teacher, thinks that students fully understand the need to do their homework in order to succeed on tests and quizzes, so she de-emphasizes this component in her grading system. Instead, she gives a weekly quiz and three tests during a 9-week grading period.

To promote learning, your students must understand your assessment system (Loyd & Loyd, 1997; Thorkildsen, 1996). Even young students can understand the relationship between effort and grades if they are assessed frequently and if their homework is scored and returned promptly. Conversely, even high school students can have problems understanding a grading system if it is too complex (E. Evans & Engelberg, 1988).

Parents must also understand your assessment system if they are to become actively involved in their children's learning (Guskey, 2002). Parents view parent–teacher conferences and graded examples of their child's work together with report cards as valuable sources of information about their children's learning progress (Shepard & Bliem, 1995).

Points or Percentages?

In assigning scores to assessments, teachers have two options. In a percentage system, they convert each score to a percentage and then average the percentages as the marking period progresses. In the other system, teachers accumulate raw points and convert them to a percentage only at the end of the marking period.

To illustrate these options, let's return to Laura Torrez's work with her second graders, first presented in our discussion of teachers' assessment patterns. Kelly, one of her students, missed 1 of 10 problems on a seat-work assignment. As is typical of many teachers, Laura uses a percentage system, and because 9 correct of 10 is 90 percent, she wrote 90 for Kelly on this assignment. This is a straightforward and simple process.

Suppose now that Laura grades her students on another assignment; this time, it contains 5 items and Kelly gets 3 of the 5 correct. Her grade on this assignment would be 60. Teachers who use a percentage system typically average the percentages, so Kelly's average at this point would be 75 (the average of 90 and 60). As the example illustrates, this process is flawed. By finding the percentage for each assignment and averaging the two, the assignments are given equal weight. On the two assignments, Kelly has correctly responded to 12 of 15 problems. If Laura had computed Kelly's percentage based on her raw points, her average would be 80 (12/15), 5 points higher than the average based on a percentage system.

If averaging percentages is flawed, why is it so common? The primary reason is simplicity. It is both simpler for teachers to manage and easier to communicate to students and parents. Many teachers, particularly those in the elementary and middle schools, have attempted point systems and later returned to percentages because of pressure from students, who better understand percentage systems.

Research indicates that computer grade-keeping programs, now commonly used in schools, facilitate the use of point systems (Feldman, Kropkf, & Alibrandi, 1996). These researchers also found that systems that award students points for merely turning in assignments and projects can reduce both achievement and motivation by tacitly communicating that completing tasks (vs. learning) is the goal. To avoid communicating this message, teachers need to hold students accountable for the quality of their work.

As with most aspects of teaching, the choice of a grading system is a matter of professional judgment. A percentage system is fair if assignments are similar in length, tests are also similar in length, and tests receive more weight than quizzes and assignments. On the other hand, a point system can work if you have the students keep a running total of their points and tell them the number they must have for an A, a B, and so on at frequent points in the marking period.

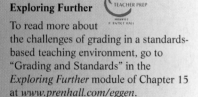

Exploring Further

To read more about the challenges of grading in a standards-based teaching environment, go to "Grading and Standards" in the *Exploring Further* module of Chapter 15 at *www.prenhall.com/eggen*.

Learning Contexts: Assessment in Urban Environments

As we've found in earlier chapters, urban contexts influence teaching and learning in a number of ways. The process of assessment is one of the most important, raising an ongoing issue in urban environments.

The current reform movement, with its emphasis on standards and academic excellence for all, has heightened interest in and awareness of the seemingly ubiquitous problem of educating children and youth from diverse backgrounds. The problem is particularly acute in the urban setting, where population diversity is the most pronounced. (Armour-Thomas, 2004, p. 109)

Because of the diversity of urban students, frequent assessment is essential to gauge learning progress.

Student diversity in urban environments influences the assessment process in three important ways. First, urban students may lack experience with general testing procedures, different test formats, and test-taking strategies. Second, they may not fully understand that assessments promote learning, and instead view them as punitive. Third, because most assessments are strongly language based, language may be an obstacle (E. Garcia, 2005).

The following recommendations respond to these issues (Heubert & Hausser, 1999; Popham, 2005):

- Attempt to create a learning-focused classroom environment, such as you saw in our discussion in Chapter 11. Emphasize that assessments promote learning, provide feedback, and measure learning progress.
- De-emphasize grades, and keep all assessment results private. Establish a rule that students may not share their scores and grades with each other. (You can't enforce this rule, but it is an attempt to take students who want to succeed, but face peer pressure not to, "off the hook.")
- Increase the number and frequency of assessments, and provide detailed and corrective feedback for all assessment items. Encourage students to ask questions about test items, and when they answer incorrectly, ask them to explain their answers. Emphasize that mistakes are part of learning, and present students with evidence of their learning progress.
- Drop one or two quizzes a marking period for purposes of grading. This practice reduces assessment anxiety and communicates to students that you are "on their side" and want them to succeed. It also contributes to a positive classroom climate.
- Make provisions for non-native English speakers by allowing extra time and providing extra help with language aspects of your assessments.

Of these suggestions, feedback and discussion are the most important. While important in all environments, they are critical for effective assessment in urban settings. First, students' explanations for their answers might reveal misconceptions, which you can then address. Second, feedback can help you identify content bias in your questions. Because of the diversity that exists in urban environments, content bias is always a possibility (Hanson, Hayes, Schriver, LeMahieu, & Brown, 1998; Popham, 2005). Learners from ethnic and cultural minority groups may encounter difficulties with items that contain information with which they are not familiar. For example, some urban students may have limited experiences with electric appliances such as an iron or vacuum cleaner, summertime activities such as camping and hiking, musical instruments such as a banjo, or transportation such as cable cars (Cheng, 1987). If assessment items include unfamiliar background information, you are measuring both the intended topic and students' general knowledge, which detracts from assessment validity. The only way you can identify these potential sources of bias is to discuss assessment items afterward. Then, you can revise and more carefully word your assessments to help eliminate bias.

The possibility of content bias is even more likely if you have non-native English speakers in your classes. Some suggestions for supporting these students include the following (Abedi, Hofstetter & Lord, 2004):

- Provide extra time to take tests.
- Allow a translation glossary or dictionary to be used during the test.
- Read directions aloud. (It is even better if you can read the students the directions in their native languages.)
- Allow them to take the test at a different time, and read it to them, clarifying misunderstandings where possible.

The primary function of assessment in general, and in urban environments in particular, is to provide evidence of increasing competence. And, evidence of learning progress can then be an important source of motivation to learn.

Knowledge Extensions

To deepen your understanding of the topics in this section of the chapter and to integrate them with topics you've already studied, go to the *Knowledge Extensions* module for Chapter 15 at *www.prenhall.com/eggen*. Respond to questions 18–20.

Checking Your Understanding

5.1 Describe the components and the decisions involved in designing a total assessment system.

5.2 Describe the differences between formative and summative assessment.

5.3 Describe the advantages and disadvantages of a percentage compared to a point system for grading.

To receive feedback for these questions, go to Appendix B.

Classroom ⊞ Connections

Using Assessment Effectively in Your Classroom

1. Try to ensure that students and their caregivers understand the importance of assessment.
   - **Elementary:** An urban third-grade teacher carefully explains that homework is essential for learning and that it is included in the grading system. He carefully monitors students and notifies parents immediately if work isn't being turned in.
   - **Middle School:** A math teacher in an urban magnet school displays his grading system on a wall chart. He explains the system and what it requires of students. He emphasizes that it is designed to promote learning and returns to the chart periodically to remind students of their learning progress.
   - **High School:** A history teacher in a school with high percentages of minority students takes extra time and effort during parent–teacher conferences to explain how she arrives at grades for her students. She saves students' work samples and shares them with the parents during conferences.

2. Use assessments to promote learning.
   - **Elementary:** A second-grade teacher continually emphasizes to her students that the work they are doing is designed to promote learning. When she assigns seat work and homework, she talks about the skills they are targeting. When she gives quizzes, she clearly explains what goals the quiz is assessing and why these goals are important.
   - **Middle School:** A geography teacher attempts to be explicit about what assessments will cover. In addition, he explains, "On Thursday's test, an essay question will ask you to explain how the physical characteristics of the northern, middle, and southern colonies affected the economy of each region." The test the next day closely follows this blueprint.
   - **High School:** A history teacher provides practice for her students under testlike conditions. As she prepares her class for an essay exam, she displays the following question on the overhead: "Before the Civil War the South was primarily agricultural rather than industrial. Explain how this might influence the outcome of the Civil War." She discusses the item and appropriate responses to it, reminding students that this is the type of question they will have on the actual test.

3. Use assessment results to provide feedback to students and inform future instructional decisions.
   - **Elementary:** A second-grade teacher discusses problems that several students missed on a math test and then asks them to rework the problems. If students are still having problems with the content, he reteaches it.
   - **Middle School:** After giving a test, a sixth-grade teacher surveys the distribution of student responses. She then revises items that are misleading or that have ineffective distracters. She stores the revisions in her computer for her next test.
   - **High School:** A tenth-grade English teacher provides extensive individual comments on students' papers. In addition, he identifies problem areas common to the whole class and uses anonymous selections from students' papers to provide feedback.

4. Adapt testing procedures to meet the needs of all students.
   - **Elementary:** A second-grade teacher arranges to give his non-native English-speaking students extra time, and he provides an older student to act as a translator for those whose command of English is still rudimentary.
   - **Middle School:** A social studies teacher encourages his students to ask him about any terms on the test that they don't understand. Unless their understanding of the term is part of what he is measuring, he defines and illustrates it for them.
   - **High School:** A physics teacher discusses all of the frequently missed items on her tests. She asks students why they responded as they did and what their thinking was. She writes notes during the discussion to revise items that may have been ambiguous or that required knowledge not all students should be expected to know.

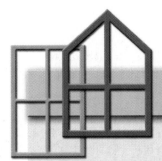

Meeting Your Learning Objectives

1. **Identify examples of basic assessment concepts, such as formal and informal assessments, validity, and reliability in classroom activities.**

   - Classroom assessment includes the information teachers gather through tests, quizzes, homework, and classroom observations, together with the decisions they make about student progress.
   - Teachers informally assess student understanding during classroom activities and discussions. Formal assessment attempts to systematically gather information for grading and reporting.
   - Validity involves the appropriateness of interpretations made from assessments. Reliability describes the extent to which assessments are consistently interpreted. Both concepts provide standards for effective assessment.

2. **Analyze assessment items based on criteria used to create effective assessments, and explain how rubrics can increase the validity and reliability of essay items.**

   - Teachers can improve the effectiveness of their assessments by keeping validity and reliability issues in mind when they construct items.
   - Teachers can improve multiple-choice, true–false, matching, and completion items by applying criteria for writing effective items using these formats. Teachers can then analyze the effectiveness of existing items using the same criteria.
   - Teachers tend to use weak formats, such as completion items, and their assessments overemphasize memory and low-level outcomes.
   - Rubrics can increase the validity and reliability of essay items by providing specific elements that must exist in a quality essay and by establishing criteria to determine the extent to which the elements exist.

3. **Describe applications of different forms of alternative assessments.**

   - Alternative assessments involve the direct examination of student performance on tasks relevant to life outside of school.
   - Performance assessments, including systematic observation, checklists, and rating scales, measure the extent to which students have demonstrated their understanding and skills by completing an activity or producing a product.
   - Portfolio assessment involves students in the construction of a collection of work samples that documents learning progress. Teachers can improve the reliability of alternative assessments through careful application of predetermined criteria.

4. **Describe and explain applications of effective assessment practices.**

   - Teachers use effective assessment practices when they design assessments that are congruent with learning objectives and instruction, communicate what will be covered on assessments, allow students to practice on items similar to those that will appear on tests, teach test-taking skills, and express positive expectations for student performance.
   - Effective assessment practices also include attempts to reduce test anxiety, such as increasing testing frequency, using criterion referencing, providing clear information about tests, and giving students ample time.

5. **Describe the components and decisions involved in designing a total assessment system.**

   - A total assessment system includes creating traditional and alternative assessments, preparing students, administering assessments, analyzing results, and assigning grades.
   - Some of the decisions involved in designing a total assessment system include the number of tests and quizzes; the uses of alternative assessments; the level at which the teacher will write the assessment items, such as knowledge, application, or analysis; the role of homework in assigning grades; and the assessment and reporting of affective dimensions, such as cooperation and effort.

Developing as a Professional

Developing as a Professional
Praxis™ Practice

At the beginning of the chapter, you saw how DeVonne Lampkin used her understanding of assessment to help increase her students' achievement and align her instruction with her students' learning needs.

Let's look now at Ron Hawkins, an urban middle school teacher, who is also involved in assessing his students' understanding. Read the case study, and answer the questions that follow.

Ron is beginning a unit on pronoun cases in his English classes. "All right, listen, everyone," he begins. "Today we're going to begin studying pronoun cases. Everybody turn to page 484 in your text. . . . This is important in our writing because we want to be able to write and use standard English correctly, and this is one of the places where people often get mixed up. So, when we're finished with our study here, you'll all be able to use pronouns correctly in your writing."

He then writes the following on the chalkboard:

> Pronouns use the nominative case when they're subjects and predicate nominatives. Pronouns use the objective case when they're direct objects, indirect objects, or objects of prepositions.

"Let's review briefly," Ron continues. He reviews direct and indirect objects, predicate nominatives and objects of prepositions.

"Now let's look at some additional examples up here on the overhead," he continues, as he displays the following four sentences:

1. *Did you get the card from Esteban and (I, me)?*
2. *Will Meg and (she, her) run the concession stand?*
3. *They treat (whoever, whomever) they hire very well.*
4. *I looked for someone (who, whom) could give me directions to the theater.*

"Okay, look at the first one. Which is correct? . . . Omar?"
"*Me.*"

"Good, Omar. How about the second one? . . . Lonnie?"
"*Her.*"

"Not quite, Lonnie. Listen to this. Suppose I turn the sentence around a little and say, 'Meg and her will run the concession stand.' See, that doesn't sound right, does it? 'Meg and she' is a compound subject, and when we have a subject, we use the nominative case. Are you okay on that, Lonnie?"

Lonnie nods and Ron continues, "Look at the third one, . . . Cheny."

"I don't know . . . *whoever,* I guess."

"This one is tricky all right," Ron nods. "When we use *whoever* and *whomever, whoever* is the nominative case and *whomever* is the objective case. In this sentence, *whomever* is a direct object, so it is the correct form."

After he finishes, Ron gives students another list of sentences in which they are to select the correct form of the pronoun.

On Tuesday, Ron reviews the exercises the students completed for homework and gives some additional examples that use *who, whom, whoever,* and *whomever.* He then discusses the rules for pronoun–antecedent agreement (pronouns must agree with their antecedents in gender and number). He again has students work examples as he did with pronoun cases.

He continues with pronouns and their antecedents on Wednesday and begins a discussion of indefinite pronouns as antecedents for personal pronouns—*anybody, either, each, one, someone*—and has students work examples as done before.

Near the end of class on Thursday, Ron announces, "Tomorrow, we're going to have a test on this material: pronoun cases, pronouns and their antecedents, and indefinite pronouns. You have your notes, so study hard. . . . Are there any questions? . . . Good. I expect you all to do well. I'll see you tomorrow."

On Friday morning as students file into class and the bell rings, Ron picks up a stack of tests from his desk. The test consists of 30 sentences, 10 of which deal with case, 10 with antecedents, and 10 with indefinite pronouns. The final part of the test directs students to write a paragraph. The following are some sample items from the test:

Part I. *For each of the items below, mark A on your answer sheet if the pronoun case is correct in the sentence, and mark B if it is incorrect. If it is incorrect, supply the correct pronoun.*

1. *Be careful who you tell.*
2. *Will Rennee and I be in the outfield?*
3. *My brother and me like water skiing.*

Part II. *Write the pronoun that correctly completes the sentence.*

1. *Arlene told us about _____ visit to the dentist to have braces put on.*
2. *The Wilsons planted a garden in _____ backyard.*
3. *Cal read the recipe and put _____ in the file.*
4. *Each of the girls on the team wore _____ school sweater to the game.*
5. *None of the brass has lost _____ shine yet.*
6. *Few of the boys on the team have taken _____ physicals yet.*

The directions for the final part of the test were as follows:

Part III. *Write a short paragraph that contains at least two examples of pronouns in the nominative case and two examples of pronouns in the objective case. (Circle and label these.) Include also at least two examples of pronouns that agree with their antecedents. Remember!! The paragraph must make sense. It cannot be just a series of sentences.*

Ron watches as his students work, and seeing that 15 minutes remain in the period and that some students are only starting on their paragraphs, he announces, "You only have 15 minutes left. Watch your time and work quickly. You need to be finished by the end of the period."

He then continues monitoring students, again reminding them to work quickly when 10 minutes are left and again when 5 minutes are left.

Luis, Simao, Moy, and Rudy are hastily finishing the last few words of their tests as the bell rings. Luis finally turns in his paper as Ron's fourth-period students are filing into the room.

"Here," Ron says. "This pass will get you into Mrs. Washington's class if you're late. . . . How did you do?"

"Okay, I think," Luis says over his shoulder as he scurries out of the room, "except for the last part. It was hard. I couldn't get started."

"I'll look at it," Ron says. "Scoot now."

On Monday, Ron returns the tests, saying, "Here are your papers. You did fine on the sentences, but your paragraphs need a lot of work. Why did you have so much trouble with them, when we had so much practice?"

"It was hard, Mr. Hawkins."

"Not enough time."

"I hate to write."

Ron listens patiently and then says, "Be sure you write your scores in your notebooks. . . . Okay, . . . you have them all written down? . . . Are there any questions?"

"Number 3," Enrique requests.

"Okay, let's look at 3. It says, 'My brother and me like water skiing.' There, the pronoun is part of the subject, so it should be *I* and not *me.*"

"Any others?"

A sprinkling of questions come from around the room, and Ron responds, "We don't have time to go over all of them. I'll discuss three more."

He responds to the three students who seem to be most urgent in waving their hands. He then collected the tests and begins a discussion of adjective and adverb clauses.

Short-Answer Questions

In answering these questions, use information from the chapter and link your responses to specific information in the case.

1. How well were Ron's curriculum and assessment aligned? Explain specifically. What could he have done to increase curricular alignment?
2. In the section on effective assessment practices, we discussed preparing students for assessments, administering them, and analyzing results. How effectively did Ron perform each task? Describe specifically what he might have done to be more effective in these areas.
3. Ron teaches in an urban environment, so his students likely had diverse backgrounds. How effective were his teaching and assessment for urban students?
4. What were the primary strengths of Ron's teaching and assessment? What were the primary weaknesses? If you think Ron's teaching and assessment could have been improved on the basis of information in this chapter, what suggestions would you make? Be specific.

PRAXIS These exercises are designed to help you prepare for the Praxis™ "Principles of Learning and Teaching" exam.

To receive feedback on your short-answer questions, go to the Companion Website at *www.prenhall.com/eggen*, then to the Practice for Praxis™ module for Chapter 15.

To acquire experience in preparing for the multiple-choice items on the Praxis™ exam, go to the *Self-Assessment* module for Chapter 15 at *www.prenhall.com/eggen* and click on "Practice Quiz."

For additional connections between this text and the Praxis™ exam, go to Appendix A.

ONLINE PORTFOLIO ACTIVITIES

To develop your professional portfolio, further apply your understanding of chapter content, and address the INTASC standards, go to the Companion Website, then to the *Online Portfolio Activities* for Chapter 15. Complete the suggested activities.

Also on the companion Website at *www.prenhall. com/eggen*, you can measure your understanding of chapter content with multiple-choice and essay questions, and broaden your knowledge base in Exploring Further and Web Links to other educational psychology websites.

IMPORTANT CONCEPTS

alternative assessment (p. 487)
checklists (p. 490)
classroom assessment (p. 476)
completion (p. 483)
criterion-referenced grading (p. 500)
distracters (p. 480)
essay (p. 484)
formal assessment (p. 476)
formative assessment (p. 499)
informal assessment (p. 476)
matching (p. 485)
multiple-choice (p. 480)

norm-referenced grading (p. 499)
performance assessment (p. 488)
portfolio assessment (p. 490)
rating scales (p. 490)
reliability (p. 477)
rubric (p. 484)
summative assessment (p. 499)
systematic observation (p. 489)
table of specifications (p. 494)
test anxiety (p. 496)
true–false items (p. 483)
validity (p. 477)

CHAPTER 16

Assessment Through
Standardized Testing

Chapter Outline	Learning Objectives
	After you have completed your study of this chapter, you should be able to

Standardized Tests

Functions of Standardized Tests • Types of Standardized Tests • Evaluating Standardized Tests: Validity Revisited • The Teacher's Role in Standardized Testing: Instructional Principles

1 Identify functions and types of standardized tests and the forms of validity associated with the tests.

Understanding and Interpreting Standardized Test Scores

Descriptive Statistics • Interpreting Standardized Test Results

2 Explain standardized test results using statistics and standard scores.

Accountability Issues in Standardized Testing

Standards-Based Education and Accountability • Testing Teachers

3 Describe the relationships between standards-based education, accountability, and high-stakes testing.

Diversity Issues in Standardized Testing

Student Diversity and Test Bias • Eliminating Bias in Standardized Testing: Instructional Principles • Issues in Standardized Testing: Implications for Teachers

4 Describe potential types of testing bias and strategies teachers can use to minimize bias in the use of standardized tests with their students.

With the present emphasis on standards and accountability, standardized testing is even more a part of teachers' lives than it has been in the past. As you read the following case study, think about standardized testing and teachers' roles in this process to increase student learning.

"Hello Mrs. Palmer. I'm glad you could come in," Mike Chavez, a fourth-grade teacher, says, offering his hand in greeting.

"Thank you," Doris Palmer responds. "I'm anxious to see how David's doing. His sister always did so well."

"Well, let's take a look," Mike says as he offers Mrs. Palmer a seat next to his desk.

"Here are the results from the Stanford Achievement Test David took earlier this spring, referring to a printout (see Figure 16.1). "Let me walk you through it."

After giving Mrs. Palmer a chance to look at the report, Mike begins by saying, "Let's take a look at reading first. . . . You see we have vocabulary, reading comprehension, and total reading. David is strong in reading comprehension . . . 80th percentile locally."

"What does this 5.6 mean?" Mrs. Palmer interjects, pointing to the "Grade Equiv." column. "Should he be in the fifth grade?"

"No," Mike smiles. "It says his score on this part of the test was about the same as that of the average fifth grader in the sixth month of school. It means that he did well in reading, but these tests don't tell us where kids should be placed.

Figure 16.1   David Palmer's achievement test report

TESTS	NO. OF ITEMS	RAW SCORE	NATL PR-S	LOCAL PR-S	GRADE EQUIV	NATIONAL GRADE PERCENTILE BANDS
Total Reading	94	70	65–6	75–6	5.6	
Vocabulary	40	27	54–5	59–5	5.0	
Reading Comp.	54	43	72–6	80–7	6.7	
Total Math	118	58	28–4	29–4	4.2	
Concepts of No.	34	14	20–3	21–3	3.6	
Computation	44	22	28–4	29–4	4.0	
Applications	40	22	37–4	38–4	4.3	
Total Language	60	47	64–6	60–6	5.8	
Lang. Mechanics	30	21	41–5	38–4	4.4	
Lang. Expression	30	26	80–7	75–6	9.7	
Spelling	40	22	37–4	37–4	4.2	
Study Skills	30	21	53–5	55–5	5.2	
Science	50	31	60–6	80–7	5.5	
Social Science	50	42	88–7	90–8	8.7	
Listening	45	25	34–4	35–4	3.9	
Using Information	70	35	24–4	25–4	3.5	
Thinking Skills	101	45	27–4	30–4	3.5	
Basic Battery	387	243	44–5	45–5	4.6	
Complete Battery	487	316	52–5	55–5	5.1	

Ψ THE PSYCHOLOGICAL CORPORATION
HARCOURT BRACE JOVANOVICH, INC.

Source: "Stanford Achievement Test Report" from the *Stanford Achievement Test: 8th Edition* (as provided). Reproduced by permission.

"You already know he's in our top reading group," Mike continues. "This test confirms that he's properly placed. . . . I have some other materials from his portfolio that give us some more information."

"So what's the point in the tests if we already know that he's good at reading? They seem to make him nervous."

"Good question. We actually use the tests for several reasons. They help us understand how our students are doing compared to others around the country. They give us an objective, outside measure. And, they can help us pinpoint some problem areas like in math. . . . For example, David isn't quite as strong there."

"He says he doesn't like math."

"That's what he says," Mike smiles, "but I'm not sure that's the whole picture. Look here. Notice how his lowest math score is on concepts of numbers. His percentile rank is 21 locally. . . . And look over here," he notes, pointing to the percentile bands column. "See how this band is lower than most of his others. This could suggest that he has difficulty understanding math concepts."

"You're telling me. He complains about all the problems you have him do. He says he knows the answer but you keep asking him 'why'?"

"That's interesting, because the test is telling us something that I can see in his work. It suggests that he may have relied on memorizing in his earlier math classes. Now that he's in fourth grade, I'm trying to help him understand *why* he's doing what he's doing. I really believe it will pay off if he sticks with it . . . and if you and I encourage him."

"Well," she responds uncertainly, "if you're sure, we'll hang in there."

"Overall, Mrs. Palmer, I'm pleased with David's performance," Mike interjects, sensing her uncertainty. "If he can keep his reading scores up and work to get those math scores up some by next year, he will be making excellent progress."

As we begin our discussion, we want to consider two questions: (1) What is the purpose of standardized testing? (2) How can teachers use standardized test results to increase their students' learning? We address these and other questions in this chapter.

STANDARDIZED TESTS

Standardized tests are assessment instruments given to large samples of students (in many cases nationwide) under uniform conditions and scored according to uniform procedures. We're all familiar with them. We took achievement tests as we moved through elementary school, and the Scholastic Aptitude Test (SAT) or American College Test (ACT) is a rite of passage from high school to college. And, with increased emphasis on holding schools and teachers accountable for student learning, standardized testing has become an even more prominent part of teachers' lives.

Standardized tests are designed to answer questions difficult to answer based on teacher-made assessments alone. Some include: How do the students in my class compare with others across the country? How well is our curriculum preparing students for college or future training? How does a particular student compare to those of similar ability? (Haladyna, 2002; Nitko, 2004).

To answer these questions, educators compare individuals' scores to the scores of a **norm group;** the representative sample whose scores are compiled for the purpose of national comparisons. The norm group includes students from different geographical regions, private and public schools, boys and girls, and different cultural and ethnic groups (Linn & Miller, 2005). **National norms** are scores on standardized tests earned by representative groups from around the nation. Educators then compare individuals' scores to the national norms.

The influence of standardized testing can hardly be overstated. The fact that students in other industrialized countries, such as Japan and Germany, score higher than American students on some of these tests has alarmed many in this country (D. Hoff, 2003). Reform movements that began in the early 1980s and continue today are largely due to concerns about low scores on standardized tests. The results of a morning's testing often influence decisions about the future of individual students (J. Hoffman, Assaf, & Paris, 2001).

Standardized testing is also controversial. In a given year, millions of students take state-mandated tests at a cost of more than a billion dollars annually. Many teachers and parents feel that standardized testing is overemphasized, arguing that these tests detract

Standardized tests. Assessment instruments given to large samples of students under uniform conditions and scored according to uniform procedures

Norm group. The representative group of individuals whose average standardized test scores are compiled for the purpose of national comparisons

National norms. Average scores on standardized tests earned by representative groups of students from around the nation to which an individual's score is compared

from a balanced curriculum (J. Hoffman et al., 2001; Wallace, 2000). In addition, research suggests that beginning teachers are inadequately prepared to deal with the new assessment roles required of them by the accountability movement (Lawson & Childs, 2001). To put these concerns into perspective, let's look at some of the ways that teachers and school districts use standardized tests.

Functions of Standardized Tests

Standardized tests serve at least three functions (Aiken, 2003; Stiggins, 2005). They include

- Assessment and diagnosis of learning
- Selection and placement
- Program evaluation and accountability

Assessment and Diagnosis of Learning

The most common function of standardized testing is to provide an external, objective picture of student progress. In Mike's class, for example, David consistently receives As in reading, but this doesn't tell his parents, teachers, or school administrators how he compares to other children at his grade level across the nation. Were his As due to high achievement or generous grading? Standardized tests help provide a complete picture of student progress (Brennan, Kim, Wenz-Gross & Siperstein, 2001).

Standardized tests also help diagnose student strengths and weaknesses (Popham, 2005). For example, after learning that David scored low in math, Mike might schedule a diagnostic test. Teachers usually administer these tests individually, with the goal of getting specific information about students' achievement in particular aspects of a content area.

Selection and Placement

Selecting and placing students in specialized or limited-size programs is another function of standardized tests. For instance, students entering a high school may come from "feeder" middle schools, private schools, and schools outside the district, many with different programs. Scores from the math section of a standardized test, for example, can help the math faculty place students in classes that will best match their backgrounds and capabilities.

Educators can also use standardized test results to make decisions about admission to college or placement in advanced programs, such as programs for the gifted. As we said earlier, the SAT or ACT is a rite of passage to college, and scores students make on these tests are important in determining whether they're accepted by the college of their choice. And standardized test scores are virtually always considered in recommending that students be placed in programs for the gifted.

Program Evaluation and Accountability

Standardized tests can also provide information about instructional programs. For example, suppose an elementary school moves from a reading program based on writing and children's literature to one that emphasizes phonics and basic skills. The faculty can use standardized test results to assess the effectiveness of this change.

As an extension of program evaluation, schools and teachers are increasingly being held accountable for student learning (Linn & Miller, 2005). Parents, school board members, state officials, and decision makers at the federal level are demanding evidence that tax dollars are being used efficiently. Standardized test scores provide one indicator of this effectiveness. (We examine accountability issues in more detail later in the chapter.)

Types of Standardized Tests

Educators commonly use four different kinds of standardized tests in educational settings:

- Achievement tests
- Diagnostic tests

Standardized tests provide information about learning progress, diagnose students strengths and weaknesses, and assist in placement decisions.

- Intelligence tests
- Aptitude tests

Let's look at them.

Achievement Tests

Achievement tests, the most widely used type of standardized test, assess how much students have learned in specific content areas, most commonly reading, language arts, and math, but also in areas such as science, social studies, computer literacy, and critical thinking. Achievement tests usually break down these subject areas into descriptions of more specific skills. For example, David's test results included, in addition to a total math score, a score for concepts of number, computation, and applications (see Figure 16.1). Popular achievement tests include the Iowa Test of Basic Skills, the California Achievement Test, the Stanford Achievement Test, the Comprehensive Test of Basic Skills, and the Metropolitan Achievement Test, as well as individual statewide assessments (Nitko, 2004; Stiggins, 2005).

Standardized achievement tests usually are batteries of specific tests that are administered over several days. They reflect a curriculum common to most schools, which means they will assess some, but not all, of the goals of a specific school. This is both a strength and a weakness. Because they are designed for a range of schools, they can be used in a variety of locations, but this "one-size-fits-all" approach may not accurately measure achievement for a specific curriculum. For example, one study found that less than half of the math content measured on commonly used standardized achievement batteries was the same as content covered in popular elementary math textbooks (Berliner, 1984).

Individual intelligence tests such as the Stanford-Binet and WISC-III provide valuable information about individual capabilities.

Diagnostic Tests

Whereas achievement tests measure students' progress in a variety of curriculum areas, **diagnostic tests** provide a detailed description of learners' strengths and weaknesses in specific skill areas. They are common in the primary grades, where teachers design instruction to match the developmental level of the child. Educators usually administer diagnostic tests individually, and compared to achievement tests, they include a larger number of items, use more subtests, and report scores in more specific areas (R. M. Thorndike, 2005). A diagnostic test in reading, for example, might measure letter recognition, word analysis skills, sight vocabulary, vocabulary in context, and reading comprehension. The Detroit Test of Learning Aptitude (AGS Publishing, 2006), the Durrell Analysis of Reading Difficulty (Durrell & Catterson, 1980), and the Stanford Diagnostic Reading Test (Karlsen & Gardner, 1995) are popular diagnostic tests.

Intelligence Tests

Intelligence tests are standardized tests that measure an individual's capacity to acquire knowledge, think and reason in the abstract, and solve novel problems. We included these capabilities in our definition of *intelligence* in Chapter 4. The two most widely used intelligence tests in existence are the Stanford-Binet and the Wechsler Scales (Kaufman & Lictenberger, 2002). Let's look at them.

The Stanford-Binet. The Stanford-Binet is an individually administered intelligence test composed of subtests. It comes in a kit that includes the testing materials, such as manipulatives and pictures, along with a test manual. Earlier versions heavily emphasized verbal tasks, but the most recent edition is more diverse, targeting five factors: *reasoning, knowledge, working memory, visual,* and *quantitative,* each of which contains a verbal and nonverbal subtest. Table 16.1 contains descriptions of some sample subtests in the latest revision.

The Stanford-Binet is a technically sound instrument that is second only to the Wechsler scales (described in the next section) in popularity (Roid & Barram, 2005). It has been revised and renormed a number of times over the years, most recently in 2003, using 4,800 schoolchildren, stratified by economic status, geographic region, and community size. The test developers used the 2000 U.S. Census to ensure proportional representation of each of White, African-American, Hispanic, Asian, and Asian/Pacific Islander subcultures (U.S. Bureau of the Census, 2001).

Exploring Further

To see how intelligence tests, and particularly the Stanford-Binet, came to exist, go to "A Brief History of Intelligence Tests" in the *Exploring Further* module of Chapter 16 at *www.prenhall.com/eggen*.

Achievement tests. Standardized tests designed to assess how much students have learned in specified content areas

Diagnostic tests. Standardized tests designed to provide a detailed description of learners' strengths and weaknesses in specific skill areas

Intelligence tests. Standardized tests designed to measure an individual's capacity to acquire knowledge, think and reason in the abstract, and solve novel problems

Table 16.1 Sample subtests from the revised (5th ed.) Stanford-Binet

Subtest	Example Description
Nonverbal Knowledge	Students are shown picture absurdities (e.g., a man in a bathing suit in the snow) and asked to explain.
Verbal Knowledge	Students are asked to explain the meaning of common vocabulary words.
Nonverbal Working Memory	Students are shown block patterns and asked to describe or reproduce after a brief delay.
Verbal Working Memory	Students are given sentences and asked to provide key words after a brief delay.

Source: Riverside Publishing, 2003.

The Wechsler Scales. Developed by David Wechsler over a period of 40 years, the Wechsler scales are the most popular intelligence tests in use today (Kaufman & Lictenberger, 2002; Salvia & Ysseldyke, 2004). The three Wechsler tests, aimed at preschool-primary, elementary, and adult populations, have two main parts: verbal and performance.

The Wechsler Intelligence Scale for Children—Fourth Edition (Wechsler, 2003) is an individually administered intelligence test with 13 subtests, of which 6 are verbal and 7 are performance. (Table 16.2 outlines some sample subtests.) The test developers added performance sections because of dissatisfaction with the strong verbal emphasis of earlier intelligence tests. Like the Stanford-Binet, the Wechsler scales are considered technically sound by testing experts (Kaufman & Lictenberger, 2002; Salvia & Ysseldyke, 2004).

The Wechsler's two scales, yielding separate verbal and performance scores, are an asset. For example, a substantially higher score on the performance compared with the verbal scale could indicate a language problem related to poor reading or language-based cultural differences (R. L. Taylor, 2006). Because performance subtests demand a minimum of verbal ability, these tasks are helpful in studying students who resist school-like tasks, learners with disabilities, and persons with limited education.

Aptitude Tests

Although *aptitude* and *intelligence* are often used synonymously, aptitude—the ability to acquire knowledge—is only one characteristic of intelligence. The concept of *aptitude* is intuitively sensible; for example, people will say, "I just don't have any aptitude for math," implying that their potential for learning math is limited.

Aptitude tests are standardized tests designed to predict the potential for future learning and measure general abilities developed over long periods of time. Aptitude tests are commonly used in selection and placement decisions, and they correlate highly with achievement tests (Linn & Miller, 2005; Popham, 2005).

The two most common aptitude tests at the high school level are the SAT and ACT. As we suggested earlier, educators use these tests to measure a student's potential for success in college. Experience is important, however; classroom-related knowledge, particularly in language and mathematics, is essential for success on the tests. But, because the tests are reliable, they eliminate teacher bias and differences in teachers' grading practices. In this regard, they add valuable information in predicting future college success.

The class of 2006 was the first to write a timed essay as part of the SAT, in addition to taking the traditional verbal and math sections, which were also revamped. The ACT also made an essay an optional part of its exam. Both changes occurred with tests taken in the spring of 2005. From that time, a perfect SAT score rose from 1600 to 2400, with the writing test worth up to 800 points.

The oldest college admission exam in the U.S., the SAT was revised in an attempt to more closely align it with today's high school curriculum, and address concerns among employers and university professors that the quality of student writing has severely declined.

Aptitude tests. Standardized tests designed to predict the potential for future learning and measure general abilities developed over long periods of time

Table 16.2 Sample items from the WISC-III

Verbal Section	
Subtest	**Description/Examples**
Information	This subtest taps general knowledge common to American culture: 1. How many wings does a bird have? 2. How many nickels make a dime? 3. What is steam made of? 4. Who wrote "Tom Sawyer"? 5. What is pepper?
Arithmetic	This subtest is a test of basic mathematical knowledge and skills, including counting and addition through division: 1. Sam had three pieces of candy and Joe gave him four more. How many pieces of candy did Sam have altogether? 2. Three women divided eighteen golf balls equally among themselves. How many golf balls did each person receive? 3. If two buttons cost 15¢, what will be the cost of a dozen buttons?
Similarities	This subtest is designed to measure abstract and logical thinking through use of analogies: 1. In what way are a lion and a tiger alike? 2. In what way are a saw and a hammer alike? 3. In what way are an hour and a week alike? 4. In what way are a circle and a triangle alike?

Performance Section	
Subtest	**Description/Examples**
Picture completion	Students are shown a picture with elements missing, which they are required to identify. This subtest measures general knowledge as well as visual comprehension.
Block design	This subtest focuses on a number of abstract figures. Designed to measure visual-motor coordination, it requires students to match patterns displayed by the examiner.

Picture Completion

Block Design

Source: Simulated items similar to those in the *Wechsler Intelligence Scale for Children: Third Edition (WISC-III).* Copyright © 1991 by the Psychological Corporation. Reproduced by permission. All rights reserved. "Wechsler intelligence Scale for Children" and "WISC-III" are registered trademarks of The Psychological Corporation.

Evaluating Standardized Tests: Validity Revisited

You first saw some of Mike Chavez's work related to standardized testing in our chapter opening case study. Let's look now at another role that he is playing.

Mike has been asked to serve on a district-wide committee to select a new standardized achievement test battery for the elementary grades. His job is to get feedback from the faculty at his school about two options, the Stanford Achievement Test and the California Achievement Test.

After giving a brief overview of the tests during a faculty meeting, Mike asks if people have questions.

"How much do the two tests cover problem solving?" a fifth-grade teacher asks.

"We're moving our language arts curriculum more in the direction of writing. What about it?" a first-grade teacher wonders.

As the discussion continues, a confused colleague asks, "Which is better? That's really what we're here for. How about a simple answer?"

Mike couldn't offer a simple answer, not because he was unprepared, but instead because he was asked to make judgments about validity.

In Chapter 15, you saw that validity is the degree to which an assessment actually measures what it is supposed to measure (Linn & Miller, 2005). When creating their own tests, teachers consider the design and the extent to which the tests are congruent with learning objectives in attempts to ensure validity. Standardized tests are already constructed, so teachers must judge only the suitability of a test for a specific purpose.* Validity involves the appropriate use of a test, not the design of the test itself.

Experts describe three kinds of validity—*content, predictive,* and *construct*—and each provides a different perspective on the issue of appropriate use.

Content Validity

Content validity refers to a test's ability to accurately sample the content taught and measure the extent to which learners understand it. It is determined by comparing test content with curriculum objectives, and it is a primary concern when considering standardized achievement tests (Aiken, 2003). The question Wendy was asked about which test was "better" addresses content validity. The "better" test is the one with the closer match between the school's learning objectives and the content of the test.

Predictive Validity

Predictive validity is the measure of a test's ability to gauge future performance (Aiken, 2003; Linn & Miller, 2005). It is central to the SAT and ACT, which are designed to measure a student's potential for doing college work, and it is also the focus of tests that gauge students' readiness for academic tasks in the early elementary grades.

Predictive validity is usually quantified by correlating two variables, such as a standardized test score and student grades. For example, a correlation of .42 exists between the SAT and college grades (Shepard, 1993). High school grades are the only predictor that is better (a correlation of .48).

Why isn't the correlation between standardized tests and college performance higher? The primary reason is that the SAT and ACT are designed to predict "general readiness"; other factors such as motivation, study habits, and prior knowledge affect performance.

Construct Validity

Construct validity describes the extent to which an assessment accurately measures a learning-related characteristic that is not directly observable (Anastasi & Urbina, 1997; Gronlund, 2003). For instance, *intelligence* is not directly observable, and it impacts the amount people learn. Testing experts generally believe that the Stanford-Binet and the Weschler scales do indeed measure intelligence, so the tests have construct validity. Similarly, experts believe the SAT has construct validity because it measures students' ability in abstract thinking about words and numbers, tasks that students will face in college.

Content validity. A test's ability to accurately sample the content taught and measure the extent to which learners understand it

Predictive validity. The measure of a test's ability to gauge future performance

Construct validity. A description of the extent to which an assessment accurately measures a characteristic that is not directly observable

---

*A complete review of more than 1,400 standardized tests of achievement, aptitude, diagnosis, and personality can be found in the *Mental Measurements Yearbook* (Plake, Impara, & Spies, 2003). Originally edited by Oscar Buros, the yearbook provides accurate and critical reviews of all major standardized tests and is an important source of information for selecting and using these tests.

	The Teacher's Role in Standardized Testing:
Instructional ⌂ **Principles**	**Instructional Principles**

You will play an important role in ensuring that standardized test scores reflect what your students have actually learned. In addition, you will communicate test results to students and their caregivers, and you will use the results to improve your instruction. The following principles can guide you as you perform these essential functions:

1. Carefully examine tests to ensure that learning objectives match test content.
2. Prepare students so that test results accurately reflect what they know and can do.
3. Administer tests in ways that maximize student performance.
4. Communicate results to students and their caregivers to help them make wise educational decisions.

Let's see how these principles operate in classrooms.

Matching Tests and Learning Objectives

As you saw earlier, the validity of standardized tests depends on the match between the test and the purpose for using it. For achievement tests, this means that learning objectives must be consistent with the content of the test, and teachers are the ones who will ensure that this match exists. In the past, educators emphasized selecting an appropriate test to match teachers' objectives; with the present emphasis on district, state, and even nationally mandated tests, emphasis has shifted to teachers' responsibilities for ensuring that students have learned the content covered on the tests (Linn & Miller, 2005; Popham, 2004a).

Preparing Students

Preparing students is another essential teacher role (McMillan, 2004). Ensuring as much as possible that students reach learning objectives is the first step, and this depends on the effectiveness of instruction.

The second is teaching general test-taking strategies. They are similar to the test-taking strategies we discussed in Chapter 15, and they focus specifically on preparing students for standardized tests. The strategies include the following:

- Read and follow all directions.
- Determine how questions will be scored. For example, is guessing penalized (e.g., subtracting the number of wrong from the number of right answers), and will points be taken off for spelling, grammar, and neatness in written responses?
- Eliminate options on multiple-choice items, and make informed guesses with remaining items (if guessing isn't penalized).
- Pace yourself so that you have enough time to answer all the questions.
- Go back and check your answers if time permits. (Nitko, 2004; Linn & Miller, 2005)

In addition to teaching test-taking strategies, teachers can provide students with practice using items similar to those that will appear on the test. For example, teachers commonly assess spelling by giving quizzes that ask students to correctly spell lists of words. However, in spelling assessment on most standardized tests, students encounter a list of four closely matched words and select the one spelled correctly. To do as well as possible on these items, students need practice with this format.

Administering Tests

For standardized tests to yield valid results, educators must administer them uniformly at different sites and with different populations. Most standardized test developers explain in detail how the test should be administered (Nitko, 2004; McMillan, 2004). Manuals specify the amount of time for each test and subtest (which should be written on

Teachers play a crucial role in selecting and administering standardized tests, preparing students, and interpreting results.

Teachers should understand standardized tests so they can interpret them for students and their caregivers.

the board for students) and provide scripts for introducing and describing the subtests. If scripts and time frames aren't followed precisely, the results can be invalidated.

Interpreting Results

Once test results are returned, teachers are responsible for using them to improve instruction and communicate performance to students and their caregivers. To identify areas of instruction that may need improvement, teachers commonly compare the scores of one year's class with those in earlier years to detect performance trends (Nichols & Singer, 2000).

Teachers' primary role in interpreting results is helping students and their parents understand what test scores mean. Standardized test scores should not be reported separately from other information about students, and teachers should emphasize that test scores are approximations rather than absolute indicators of student performance. And, to the extent possible, teachers should avoid technical language in discussing results.

To accurately interpret standardized test results, teachers must understand how these scores are calculated. We address this topic next.

Knowledge Extensions

To deepen your understanding of the topics in this section of the chapter and to integrate them with topics you've already studied, go to the *Knowledge Extensions* module for Chapter 16 at *www.prenhall.com/eggen*. Respond to items 1–13.

Checking Your Understanding

1.1   A school district is in the process of making decisions about a new standardized achievement test. Officials want to know how well their students are doing with a new math curriculum, and they also want to determine how effectively individual teachers are implementing the program. Which of the functions of standardized tests are the officials applying?

1.2   As the district examines different standardized math tests, they find that some provide broad coverage of math concepts and skills, whereas others provide more detailed information about individual student's strengths and weaknesses in math. What two types of standardized tests is the district considering?

1.3   In a committee meeting, teachers express different views about what they are looking for. One comments, "I want to make sure that the test matches the concepts and skills we're supposed to teach." A second replies "That's all fine, but it also needs to tell us if our students will succeed in college math." Which of the different forms of validity are the teachers addressing?

To receive feedback for these questions, go to Appendix B.

UNDERSTANDING AND INTERPRETING STANDARDIZED TEST SCORES

The fact that they're given to thousands of students, which allow comparisons with samples across the United States and around the world, is one of the advantages of standardized tests. But these large samples result in unwieldy data. To process the vast amount of information and to allow users to compare individuals' performances, test publishers use statistical methods to summarize test results.

Descriptive Statistics

As an introduction to the use of statistics in summarizing information, take a look at Table 16.3, which contains scores made by two classes of 31 students on a 50-item test. (As you examine this information, keep in mind that a standardized test would have a sample much larger than 31 students and would contain a larger number of items. We are using a class-size example here for the sake of illustration.)

The scores for each class are ranked from highest to lowest, and the mean, median, and mode are labeled. (We discuss these concepts in the sections that follow.) As you can see in the table, a simple array of scores can be cumbersome and not very informative, even when the scores are ranked. We need more efficient ways of summarizing the information.

Table 16.3   Scores of two classes on a 50-item test

Class #1	Class #2
50	48
49	47
49	46
48	46
47	45
47	45 ⎤
46	44
46	44
45	44 mode
45	44 ⎦
45 ⎤	44
44	43
44 mode	43
44 ⎦	43
44	43
43— median	42— median & mean
42— mean	42
41	42
41	42
40	41
40	41
39	41
39	40
38	40
37	39
37	39
36	38
35	38
34	37
34	36
33	35

Figure 16.2   Frequency distributions for two classes on a 50-item test

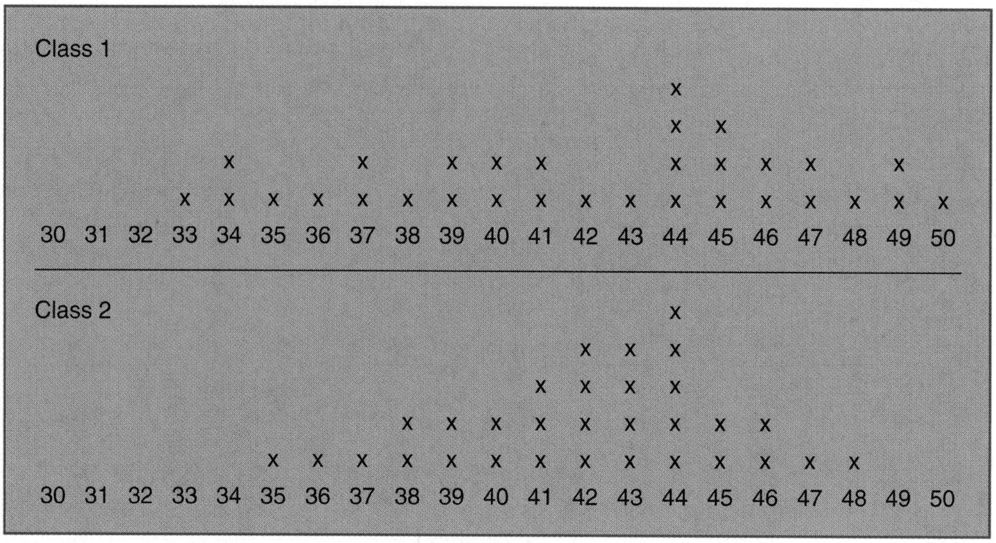

Frequency Distributions

A **frequency distribution** is a distribution of test scores that shows a simple count of the number of people who obtained each score. It can be represented in several ways, one of which is a graph with the possible scores on the horizontal (x) axis and the frequency, or the number of students who got each score, on the vertical (y) axis.

The frequency distributions for our two classes are shown in Figure 16.2. This information is still in rough form, but we already begin to see differences between the two classes. For instance, a wider range of scores exists in the first class than in the second, and the scores are more nearly grouped near the middle of the second distribution. Beyond this qualitative description, however, the distributions aren't particularly helpful. We need a better way to quantitatively summarize the information. Measures of central tendency do this.

Measures of Central Tendency

Measures of central tendency—the mean, median, and mode—are quantitative descriptions of how a group performed as a whole. In a distribution of scores, the **mean** is the average score, the **median** is the middle score in the distribution, and the **mode** is the most frequent score.

To obtain a mean, we simply add the scores and divide by the number of scores. As it turns out, both distributions have a mean of 42 (1,302/31). A mean of 42 is one indicator of how each group performed as a whole.

The median for the first distribution is 43, because half the scores (15) fall equal to or above 43 and the other half are equal to or below 43. Using the same process, we find that the median for the second distribution is 42.

The median is useful when extremely high or low scores skew the mean and give a false picture of the sample. For example, you commonly hear or read demographic statistics such as "The median income for families of four in this country went from . . . in 2000 to . . . in 2005." The *median* income is reported because a few multimillion-dollar incomes would make the mean quite high and would give an artificial picture of typical families' standards of living. The median, in contrast, is not affected by these extremes and provides a more realistic picture. The median serves the same function when used with test scores.

Looking once more at the two samples, you can see that the most frequent score for each is 44, which is the mode. Small samples, such as those here, often have more than one mode, resulting in "bimodal" or even "trimodal" distributions.

Using our measures of central tendency, you can see that the two groups of scores are much alike: They have the same mean, nearly the same median, and the same mode. As you saw from examining the frequency distribution, however, this doesn't give us a complete picture. We also need a measure of their variability, or "spread."

Frequency distribution. A distribution of test scores that shows a count of the number of people who obtained each score

Measures of central tendency. Quantitative descriptions of how a group performed as a whole

Mean. The average score in the distribution of a group of scores

Median. The middle score in the distribution of a group of scores

Mode. The most frequent score in the distribution of a group of scores

Measures of Variability

To get a more accurate picture of the samples, we need to see how they vary. One measure of variability is the **range,** the distance between the top and bottom score in a distribution. The range in the first class is 17, and in the second it's 13, confirming the spread of scores in the frequency distribution. Although easy to compute, the range is overly influenced by one or more extreme scores.

The **standard deviation,** a statistical measure of the spread of scores, reduces this problem. With the use of computers, teachers rarely have to calculate a standard deviation manually, but we'll briefly describe the procedure to help you understand the concept. To find the standard deviation:

1. Calculate the mean.
2. Subtract the mean from each of the individual scores.
3. Square each of these values. (This eliminates negative numbers.)
4. Add the squared values.
5. Divide by the total number of scores (31 in our samples).
6. Take the square root.

In our samples, the standard deviations are 4.8 and 3.1, respectively. We saw from merely observing the two distributions that the first was more spread out, and the standard deviation provides a quantitative measure of that spread.

The Normal Distribution

Standardized tests are administered to large (in the hundreds of thousands) samples of students, and the distribution of scores often approximates a *normal distribution.* To understand this concept, look again at our two distributions and then focus specifically on the second one. If we drew a line over the top of the frequency distribution, it would appear as shown in Figure 16.3.

Now imagine a very large sample of scores, such as we would find from a typical standardized test. The curve would approximate the one shown in Figure 16.4. This is a **normal distribution,** a distribution of scores in which the mean, median, and mode are equal and the scores distribute themselves symmetrically in a bell-shaped curve. Many large samples of human characteristics, such as height and weight, tend to distribute themselves this way, as do the large samples of most standardized tests.

The sample of scores in Figure 16.3 has both a mean and median of 42, but a mode of 44, so its measures of central tendency don't quite fit the normal curve. Also, as we see from Figure 16.4, 68 percent of all the scores fall within 1 standard deviation from the mean, but in our classroom sample distribution, about 71 percent of the scores are within 1 standard deviation above and below the mean. We can see from these illustrations that our samples aren't normal distributions, which is typical of the smaller samples found in most classrooms.

Interpreting Standardized Test Results

Using our two small samples, we have illustrated techniques that statisticians use to summarize standardized test scores. Again, keep in mind that data gathered from standardized tests come from hundreds of thousands of students instead of the small number in our illustrations. When educators use standardized tests, the goal is to compare students from different schools, districts, states, and even countries. To make these comparisons,

Figure 16.3 Frequency distribution for the second class

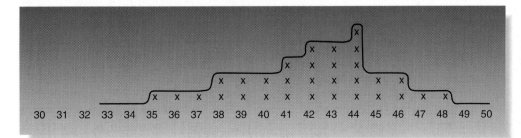

Range. The distance between the top and bottom score in a distribution of scores

Standard deviation. A statistical measure of the spread of scores

Normal distribution. A distribution of scores in which the mean, median, and mode are equal and the scores distribute themselves symmetrically in a bell-shaped curve

Figure 16.4   Normal distribution

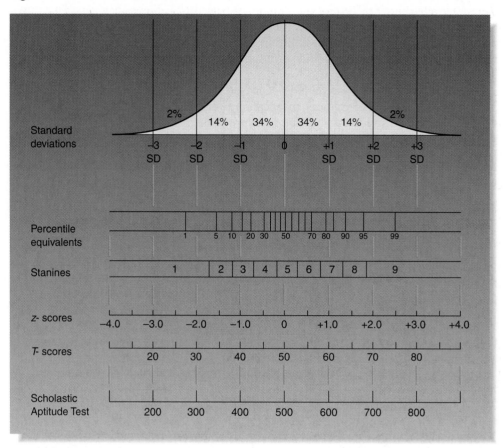

test makers use raw scores, percentiles, stanines, and grade equivalents. Some of these scores are illustrated in Figure 16.1 on David Palmer's report from the Stanford Achievement Test.

Raw Scores

All standardized tests begin with and are based on raw scores. The **raw score** is simply the number of items an individual answered correctly on a standardized test or subtest. For example, we can see in Figure 16.1 that David's raw score for reading comprehension was a 43; David answered 43 out of 54 items correctly. But what does this mean? Was the test easy or hard? How did he do compared to others taking the test? As you can see, this raw score doesn't tell us much until we compare it to others. Percentiles, stanines, grade equivalents, and standard scores help us do that.

Percentiles

The percentile is one of the most commonly reported scores on standardized tests. The **percentile, or percentile rank (PR),** is the proportion of scores in a distribution that a specific score is greater than or equal to. For instance, if you received a score of 95 on a math test and this score was greater than or equal to the scores of 88 percent of the students taking the test, then your percentile rank would be 88. You would be in the 88th percentile. As another example, David's raw score of 43 in reading comprehension placed him in the 72nd percentile nationally and the 80th percentile locally (Figure 16.1). That means his score was as high or higher than 72 percent of the scores of people who took the test across the nation and 80 percent of the scores of people who took the test in his district.

Parents and students often confuse percentiles with *percentages*. Percentages reflect the number of correct items compared to the total number possible. Percentile rank, in contrast, tells us how a student did in comparison to other students taking the test.

Percentiles are used because they are simple and straightforward. However, they have a major weakness; they're *rankings,* and the differences between the ranks are not equal (Linn

Raw score. The number of items an individual answered correctly on a standardized test or subtest

Percentile, or percentile rank (PR). The proportion of scores in a distribution that a specific score is greater than or equal to

& Miller, 2005). For instance, in our first distribution of 31 students, a score of 48 would be in the 90th percentile, 46 would be in the 80th, 44 would be in the 60th, and 43 would be the 50th percentile. In this sample, the difference between scores representing the 90th and 80th percentiles is twice as great (2 points) as the difference between scores representing the 60th and 50th percentiles (1 point). With large samples, this difference can be even more pronounced. Students who score at the extremes in the sample vary more from their counterparts than those who score near the middle of the distribution. This finding is confirmed in Figure 16.4, where we see that the range of scores from the 50th to the 60th percentile is much smaller than the range from the 90th to the 99th percentile.

Percentile bands are ranges of percentile scores on standardized tests. (Percentile bands are illustrated for David Palmer's results in the last column of Figure 16.1.) The advantage of a percentile band is that it takes into account the possibility of measurement error (McMillan, 2004). Instead of a single percentile, the band is a range of percentile scores within which an individual's test performance might fall. In this respect, percentile bands function somewhat like stanines.

Stanines

The stanine is another commonly used way to describe standardized test scores. For example, David's reading comprehension score placed him in stanine 6 nationally and stanine 7 locally (the stanines are given after the dashes in the "Natl PR-S" and "Local PR-S" columns in Figure 16.1). A **stanine (S),** or "standard nine," is a description of an individual's standardized test performance that uses a scale ranging from 1 to 9 points. Stanine 5 is in the center of the distribution and includes all the scores within 0.25 standard deviation on either side of the mean. Stanines 4, 3, and 2 are each a band of scores, 0.5 standard deviation in width, extending below stanine 5. Stanines 6, 7, and 8, also 0.5 standard deviation in width, extend above stanine 5. Stanines 1 and 9 cover the tails of the distribution. A student's score that falls 1 standard deviation above the mean will be in stanine 7; a student's score 2 standard deviations above the mean will be in stanine 9. Figure 16.4 shows how stanines correspond to other measures we've discussed.

Stanines are widely used because they're simple, and they encourage teachers and parents to interpret scores based on a range instead of fine distinctions that may be artificial (McMillan, 2004). For instance, a score in the 57th percentile may be the result of 1 or 2 extra points on a subtest compared to a score in the 52nd percentile, and the student may have guessed the answer correctly, so the difference between the two wouldn't be meaningful. Both scores fall in stanine 5, however. Because it describes performance as a range of possible scores, the stanine is probably a more realistic indicator of performance.

Reducing the scores to a simple 9-point band sacrifices information, however, so it is important to keep the advantages and disadvantages of stanines in mind as you help parents and students interpret standardized test scores.

Grade Equivalents

A third commonly reported score is the **grade equivalent,** a score that is determined by comparing an individual's score to the scores of students in a particular age group; the first digit represents grade and the second the month of the school year. For example, David's grade equivalent for total reading is 5.6. This means that he scored as well on the test as the average score for those students taking the test who are in the sixth month of the fifth grade.

As we saw when David's mother asked, "Should David be in the fifth grade?" grade equivalents can be misleading because they oversimplify results and suggest comparisons that aren't necessarily valid. A grade equivalent of 5.6 tells us that David is somewhat advanced in reading. Grade equivalents don't suggest that he should be promoted to fifth grade, nor do they necessarily suggest that he should be reading with fifth graders. Other factors such as social development, motivation, classroom behavior, and performance on teacher-made assessments must be considered in making decisions about students. Because of these limitations and the possibility of misinterpretation, some standardized tests no longer use grade equivalents. Teachers should use caution when using grade equivalents to communicate with students and parents, and teachers

Percentile bands. Ranges of percentile scores on standardized tests

Stanine (S). A description of an individual's standardized test performance that uses a scale ranging from 1 to 9 points

Grade equivalent. A score that is determined by comparing an individual's score on a standardized test to the scores of students in a particular age group

should never use them in isolation from other measures (Linn & Miller, 2005; Salvia & Ysseldyke, 2004).

Standard Scores

As you saw in our discussion of percentiles, differences in raw scores don't result in comparable differences in the percentile rank. For instance, you saw that it took only 1 raw score point difference—43 compared with 42—to move from the 50th to the 60th percentile, but it took a 2-point difference—48 compared with 46—to move from the 80th to the 90th percentile in our first distribution in Figure 16.2. To deal with this type of discrepancy, test developers use standard scores. A **standard score** is a description of performance on a standardized test that uses the standard deviation as the basic unit (Linn & Miller, 2005; McMillan, 2004). Standardized test makers use the mean and standard deviation to report standard scores.

One type of standard score is the z **score,** which is the number of standard deviation units from the mean. A z score of 2 is 2 standard deviations above the mean, for example, and a z score of -1 is 1 standard deviation below the mean. The T **score** is a standard score that defines the mean as 50 and the standard deviation as 10. A T score of 70 is 2 standard deviations above the mean and corresponds to a z score of 2.

Standard scores such as z scores and T scores are useful because they make comparisons convenient. Because they are based on equal units of measurement throughout the distribution, intergroup and intertest comparisons are possible.

Standard Error of Measurement

Although standardized tests are technically sophisticated, they contain measurement error; scores represent only an approximation of a student's "true" score. Hypothetically, if we could give a student the same test over and over, for example, and the student neither gained nor lost any knowledge, we would find that the scores would vary. If we averaged those scores, we would have an estimate of the student's "true" score. A **true score** is the hypothetical average of an individual's scores if repeated testing under ideal conditions were possible. An estimate of the true score is obtained using the **standard error of measurement,** the range of scores within which an individual's true score is likely to fall. This range is sometimes termed the *confidence interval, score band,* or *profile band.* For example, suppose Ben has a raw score of 46 and Kim has a raw score of 52 on a test with a standard error of 4. This means that Ben's true score is between 42 and 50, and Kim's is between 48 and 56. At first glance, Kim appears to have scored significantly higher than Ben, but considering the standard error, their scores may be equal, or Ben's true score may even be higher than Kim's. Understanding standard error is important when we make decisions based on standardized tests. For instance, it would be unwise to place Ben and Kim in different ability groups based solely on the results illustrated here.

Standard score. A description of performance on a standardized test that uses the standard deviation as the basic unit

z score. The number of standard deviation units from the mean

T score. A standard score that defines the mean as 50 and the standard deviation as 10

True score. The hypothetical average of an individual's scores if repeated testing under ideal conditions were possible

Standard error of measurement. The range of scores within which an individual's true score is likely to fall

Knowledge Extensions

To deepen your understanding of the topics in this section of the chapter and to integrate them with topics you've already studied, go to the *Knowledge Extensions* module for Chapter 16 at *www.prenhall.com/eggen.* Respond to questions 14–21.

Checking Your Understanding

2.1 A student named Carol is at the 96th percentile rank in number concepts; her friends Marsha and Lenore are at the 86th and 76th, respectively. Is the difference between Carol's and Marsha's scores greater than the difference between Marsha's and Lenore's, or vice versa? Explain.

2.2 A student in our first class (illustrated in Table 16.3 and Figure 16.2) scored 47 on the test. In what stanine is this score? In what stanine would a score of 47 be for the second class?

2.3 A fourth grader in your class has taken a standardized test, and the summary gives his grade equivalent as 6.7. Explain what this means. What implications does this have for your teaching?

To receive feedback for these questions, go to Appendix B.

Classroom Connections

Using Standardized Tests Effectively in Your Classroom

1. Carefully analyze results to increase instructional alignment.

   - **Elementary:** A fourth-grade team goes over the previous year's test scores to identify areas in the curriculum that need greater attention.
   - **Middle School:** The math teachers in a middle school go over standardized results item by item. Seeing that a large numbers of students missed a particular item, the teachers plan to place more emphasis on this topic in their instruction.
   - **High School:** English teachers in an urban high school use a scoring rubric to analyze student scores on a statewide writing assessment. They share the rubric with their students and use it to help them improve their writing skills.

2. Communicate test results clearly to both students and their caregivers.

   - **Elementary:** Third-grade teachers in an urban elementary school prepare a handout that explains standardized test scores including examples and answers to frequently asked questions. They use the handout in parent–teacher conferences.
   - **Middle School:** A middle school team integrates standardized test scores into a comprehensive packet of assessment materials. When they meet with students and these caregivers, they use the information to identify areas of strength and those that need improvement.
   - **High School:** During an orientation meeting with parents, members of an English Department first give an overview of tests that students will encounter in high school and describe how scores are reported. During individual meetings with parents, teachers provide specific information about individuals' scores.

ACCOUNTABILITY ISSUES IN STANDARDIZED TESTING

You saw at the beginning of the chapter that standardized testing is controversial. Two areas are prominent, as indicated by the amount of publicity they receive both in professional publications and in the popular media. These areas are (1) standards-based education and accountability, and (2) the testing of teachers. Let's examine them.

Standards-Based Education and Accountability

As you saw in Chapter 13, Americans perform poorly when polled about their world knowledge. Other studies lead to doubts about our science, reading, writing, and math knowledge as well. For example, results from the National Assessment of Educational Progress indicate that only 38 percent of U.S. eighth graders can calculate a 15 percent tip on a meal, even when given five choices to select from (Stigler & Hiebert, 2000). Social commentators have written much about these inadequacies, and educators have responded by promoting **standards-based education,** the process of focusing curricula and instruction on predetermined goals or standards. Standards specify what students at different ages and in particular content areas should know and be able to do. (As an example of standards in mathematics, look on page 412 of Chapter 13.)

Accountability is the process of requiring students to demonstrate that they have met specified standards and holding teachers responsible for students' performance. Calls for accountability have resulted from evidence that students are being promoted from one grade to the next without mastering essential content, and some students are graduating from high school barely able to read, write, or do basic mathematics.

No Child Left Behind

The accountability movement received a big boost from the passage of the No Child Left Behind Act (NCLB) of 2001, which one expert calls, "the most significant change in federal regulation of public schools in three decades" (Hardy, 2002, p. 201). Signed by President George W. Bush, NCLB was the reauthorization of the Elementary and Secondary Education Act, which began in 1965 and resulted in billions of dollars being spent on compensatory education programs for disadvantaged students. Standardized testing and accountability are two key provisions of the act.

NCLB calls for accountability at several levels. For example, states are required to create standards for what every child should know for all grades. States were to develop standards for math and reading immediately, and standards for science were due by the 2005–2006 school year. States must implement these standards and gather information about their attainment in order to receive continued federal funding. Individual schools are

Standards-based education. The process of focusing curricula and instruction on predetermined goals or standards

Accountability. The process of requiring students to demonstrate that they have met specified standards and of holding teachers responsible for students' performance

High-stakes tests and accountability place new pressures on both teachers and their students.

Exploring Further

To read more about the potential of standards-based education to improve teaching and learning, go to "Standards-Based Education" in the *Exploring Further* module of Chapter 16 at *www.prenhall.com/eggen*.

Exploring Further

To read additional criticisms of high-stakes testing, go to "High-Stakes Testing" in the *Exploring Further* module of Chapter 16 at *www.prenhall. com/eggen*.

held accountable for ensuring that every child in that school is making satisfactory progress. Schools, districts, and states must keep records of performance to document achievement of different groups of students by race, ethnicity, gender, and English proficiency.

If a school fails to make adequate yearly progress with any of these student subgroups for 2 consecutive years, students may transfer to another school. If a school's performance is sub-par for 3 years, students are entitled to outside tutoring at district expense. After 4 years the school will be placed on probation and corrective measures taken. States, districts, individual schools, and teachers within those schools are feeling the pressures of this accountability, virtually all of which depends on standardized test results (Christie, 2003).

High-Stakes Tests

High-stakes tests are standardized tests designed to measure the extent to which standards are being met (Linn & Miller, 2005; Popham, 2004b). High-stakes testing, also called *minimum competency testing,* has three components: (1) an established standard for acceptable performance; (2) a requirement that all students of designated grades (such as 5th, 8th, and 10th) take the tests; and (3) the use of test results for decisions about promotion and graduation. When students cannot move to the next grade level or graduate from high school because they fail a test, for example, the "stakes" are very high, thus the term "high-stakes tests."

As you would expect, high-stakes testing is controversial. Advocates claim the process helps clarify the goals of school systems, sends clear messages to students about what they should be learning, and provides the public with hard evidence about school effectiveness (Hirsch, 2000). While conceding that teacher preparation, materials, and the tests themselves need to be improved, advocates also argue that the tests are the fairest and most effective means of achieving the aim of democratic schooling—a quality education for all students. Further, they assert, educational systems that establish standards and use tests that thoroughly measure the extent to which the standards are met greatly improve achievement for all students, including those from disadvantaged backgrounds (Bishop, 1995, 1998). Hirsch (2000) summarized the testing advocates' position: "They [standards and tests that measure achievement of the standards] are the most promising educational development in half a century" (p. 64).

Critics counter that teachers spend too much class time helping students practice for the tests, the tests don't reflect the curriculum being taught, and they don't accurately assess student learning (Amrein & Berliner, 2002; Berliner, 2005; Behuniak, 2002; Meier, 2002). They also contend that the cutoff scores are arbitrary, and the instruments are too crude to be used in making crucial decisions about students, teachers, and schools (Popham, 2004b). In addition, the tests have had a disproportionately adverse impact on minority students, particularly those with limited proficiency in English (Hafner, 2001; Neill, 2003; Popham, 2003).

Pressure to do well on the tests is so great that some teachers and administrators feel compelled to cheat (Viadero, 2000). In Massachusetts, high-stakes testing became so controversial that the state's largest teacher union, in a highly unusual move, launched a $600,000 television campaign that sharply criticized the Massachusetts Comprehensive Assessment System exam, an exam students in the state had to pass to graduate (Gehring, 2000).

In spite of the criticisms, standards-based education and high-stakes testing are widespread. For example, because of NCLB:

- Every state has adopted standards in reading, math, and science.
- All states have testing programs designed to measure the extent to which students meet the standards.
- All states are required to issue overall ratings of their schools based on their students' performance on the tests.
- States must close or overhaul schools that are identified as failing (Hardy, 2002; J. Jennings, 2002; Linn, Baker, & Betebenner, 2002).

Testing Teachers

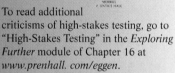

High-stakes tests. Standardized tests designed to measure the extent to which standards are being met

Increasingly, school districts are also asking teachers to pass competency tests that measure their background in academic areas, such as chemistry, history, or English; their understanding of learning and teaching; and their ability to perform basic skills. For example, a report prepared by a panel of educational leaders and released in 2005 by the National Academy of Education called for a national teacher test with results incorporated into state licensing requirements (Darling-Hammond & Baratz-Snowdon, 2005). Many states already require teachers to pass tests before they're licensed. At the present time

- Thirty-four states require prospective teachers to pass a basic skills test.
- Thirty states require high school teachers to pass a test of the subject matter knowledge they plan to teach.
- Twenty-seven states require school principals to evaluate new teachers (L. Olson, 2000; Wayne & Youngs, 2003).

The Praxis™ Series

The Praxis™ test series from the Educational Testing Service, which we introduced in Chapter 1, is the most commonly used teacher test; 80 percent of the states that test teachers use this series (Educational Testing Service, 2005). The Praxis series consists of three components (Educational Testing Service, 2005):

- Praxis I: Academic Skills Assessments. These tests are designed to measure basic or "enabling" skills in reading, writing, and math that all teachers need.
- Praxis II: Subject Assessments. These tests are designed to measure teachers' knowledge of the subjects they will teach. In addition to 70 content-specific tests, Praxis II also includes the Principles of Learning and Teaching (PLT) tests. (We discussed the PLT tests in Chapter 1, and our closing case studies in each chapter use the PLTs as a model.)
- Praxis III: Classroom Performance Assessments. These tests are designed to use classroom observations and work samples to assess teachers' ability to plan, instruct, manage, and understand professional responsibilities. In addition, Praxis III assesses the teacher's sensitivity to learners' developmental and cultural differences.

You are most likely to encounter Praxis I during your teacher preparation, Praxis II after its completion, and Praxis III during your first year of teaching.

Teacher testing has also sparked controversy in at least two areas. First, critics argue that teachers' classroom performance depends on factors other than teachers' knowledge (as measured on the tests), the most powerful being teachers' capacities to manage the complexities of classroom life and their ability to work with students (Kohn, 2000; Nagel & Peterson, 2001)). Second, of teacher candidates who fail the tests, a disproportionate number come from cultural minority groups (McIntosh & Norwood, 2004). Despite the controversies, the use of these tests, when properly developed and validated, has been upheld in courts (Fischer, Schimmel, & Kelly, 1999; Melnick & Pullin, 2000). The American Federation of Teachers, the second largest professional organization for educators in the United States, now proposes that prospective teachers pass tests that measure understanding of content, such as math and English, and knowledge of teaching principles (Blair, 2000). This proposal signals a change in policy from the past and suggests that teacher testing is not only here to stay but also likely to increase.

Checking Your Understanding

3.1   Describe the relationships between standards-based education, accountability, and high-stakes testing.

3.2   Describe at least two arguments for, and two arguments against high-stakes testing.

3.3   Identify the three main areas in which teachers are being tested, and explain how they relate to instruction.

To receive feedback for these questions, go to Appendix B.

Knowledge Extensions

To deepen your understanding of the topics in this section of the chapter and to integrate them with topics you've already studied, go to the *Knowledge Extensions* module for Chapter 16 at *www.prenhall.com/eggen*. Respond to questions 22 and 23.

Teachers should continually guard against bias in test content, procedures, and uses.

DIVERSITY ISSUES IN STANDARDIZED TESTING

One of the most volatile controversies in the use of standardized tests in high-stakes testing involves critics' claims that the tests are biased against members of cultural minorities (R. Brennan et al., 2001; Platt, 2004). This is particularly true for Hispanic and African-American students, who, on average, consistently score lower on standardized tests than do White and Asian-American students (Bowman, 2000; McIntosh & Norwood, 2004). Failing to earn a passing score on high-stakes tests can have serious consequences, such as grade retention or failure to graduate. An example of the controversy occurred in 1999 when the Mexican American Legal Defense and Educational Fund (MALDEF) filed a federal lawsuit seeking to end the practice of requiring students to pass a test to graduate from high school in Texas. MALDEF argued that the Texas Assessment of Academic Skills (TAAS) (since renamed the Texas Assessment of Knowledge and Skills—TAKS) is unfair to thousands of Hispanic and African American students (Wildavsky, 1999). Supporters of testing countered that critics were tacitly assuming that eliminating the tests would somehow increase achievement among lower-scoring groups, and this is not true, they asserted (Viadero & Johnston, 2000).

The MALDEF lawsuit, although not successful, was just one case in a continuing controversy over race and testing (J. Hoffman et al., 2001; Walpole, McDonough, & Bauer, 2005). All raise the same question: As standardized tests are increasingly used to measure and improve student performance, will historically lower-scoring African-American and Hispanic students be treated fairly? Advocates and critics of standardized testing, of course, disagree. Other educators suggest comprehensive strategies for narrowing the achievement gap between minority and nonminority students, and testing is an integral part of those strategies (C. J. Gallagher, 2003; Singham, 2003).

As least three issues related to high-stakes testing with minority students remain unresolved. One is whether the tests are valid enough to justify using results to make decisions about students' academic lives (Kohn, 2000). A second relates to technical problems involved in testing minorities in general (Land, 1997), and particularly students who speak English as a second language (Abedi, 1999). The question of whether test scores reflect differences in achievement or simply cultural or language differences remains controversial. Third, making decisions about promotion or graduation on the basis of one test score is being increasingly criticized by professional organizations including the American Educational Research Association, the American Psychological Association, and the National Council on Measurement in Education.

Student Diversity and Test Bias

Because of the controversies surrounding standardized testing, educators are focusing increased attention on efforts to ensure that test results accurately reflect student achievement. An important question to anyone testing students from diverse backgrounds is whether the instruments and procedures are fair for all students. Measurement experts have identified three types of testing bias that detract from validity (Anastasi & Urbina, 1997; Linn & Miller, 2005):

- Bias in content
- Bias in testing procedures
- Bias in test use

Bias in Content

Critics contend that the content of standardized tests is geared to White, middle-class American students, and anyone who does not fit this description faces a disadvantage. For example, the following item is drawn from a standardized science test to measure the knowledge of sixth graders:

Exploring Further
To read more about the potential problems involving standardized tests and minorities, go to "Minorities and Testing" in the Exploring Further module of Chapter 16 at *www.prenhall. com/eggen.*

If you wanted to find out if a distant planet had mountains or rivers on it, which of the following tools should you use?

a. binoculars
b. microscope
c. telescope
d. camera (Popham, 2004b, p. 48)

Performance on this item is likely to be linked to socioeconomic status and the students' exposure to high-cost items such as microscopes and telescopes (Popham, 2004b).

Bias can also occur in math word problems (Linn & Miller, 2005). For example, consider the following:

> *Alex Rodriguez is batting .310 after 100 trips to the plate. In his next three times at bat, he gets a single, double, and home run. What is his batting average now?*

Word problems using content that not all children can be expected to know (e.g., how are batting averages computed, and do doubles and home runs count more than singles?) can put students who lack the necessary prior knowledge at a disadvantage. Word problems can also be biased if students miss the problem because of limited reading skills.

Mismatches between test content and the cultural backgrounds of students can also result in test bias. For example, in one test of English proficiency, students are shown the picture of a smiling boy and asked to describe the picture. The expected response is that he is happy. However, to Vietnamese students, a smiling boy may be embarrassed, confused, or even angry (Cargill, 1987). Responding with any one of these answers would result in an incorrect response, not from lack of knowledge, but rather from cultural differences. As another example, students from a remote Eskimo community were asked the following question on a standardized vocabulary test, "Which of the following would most likely take you to the hospital if you got hurt?" The "correct" answer was ambulance, but most Eskimo students replied airplane because that is how people in their village receive emergency medical aid (Platt, 2004).

Bias in Testing Procedures

Bias can also occur in testing procedures. Students from different cultures respond to testing situations differently. They generally become more knowledgeable about testing as they move through the grades and gain experience, but if exposure to testing is limited or if the process isn't compatible with their cultures, performance can be reduced. For example, in one study, researchers found that Navajo students were unaware of the consequences of poor test performance, instead treating tests as gamelike events (Deyhle, 1987). Other research has found that some minority students *believe* tests will be biased, and as a result, they don't try as hard to do well on them (Morgan & Mehta, 2004; K. E. Ryan & Ryan, 2005).

Timed tests are another possible source of bias in testing procedures, particularly for students with limited English proficiency. Our study of information processing in Chapter 7 helps us understand why. Students with limited knowledge of English require extra time and working memory space to decode the words and comprehend questions. A time limit makes this process more difficult. Providing English language learners with more time is one of the most effective ways to ensure that test performance accurately captures what these students know and can do (Hafner, 2001).

Bias in Test Use

Bias can also occur in the use of test results. Experts are concerned about the adverse effects of testing on minority students' progress through public schools and entrance into college (Gollnick & Chinn, 2004). Evidence suggests that test results are sometimes used in ways that discriminate against minority students and those who do not speak English as a first language. For example, a historic study of 812 students classified as having mental retardation found 300 percent more Mexican-Americans and 50 percent more African-Americans than would be expected from their numbers in the general population, and, the study population had 40 percent fewer Anglo-Americans than would be expected. Further, people in lower income brackets were overrepresented, whereas people in the upper brackets were underrepresented (J. Mercer, 1973).

Instructional Principles	Eliminating Bias in Standardized Testing: Instructional Principles

You have strategies available that can reduce test bias and its negative effects. Some are short-term and can help students adjust to testing conditions, whereas others are long-term and aimed at modifying test content. The following principles can help you in your efforts:

1. Examine test content before administering tests, and analyze results after testing to help minimize content bias.
2. Adapt testing procedures to specific student needs, and teach students to adapt to testing procedures.
3. Use standardized test results as only one source of information in individual educational decisions.

Let's look at them in more detail.

Analyze Test Content

Before administering standardized tests, you should familiarize yourself with the test content. Then, if you encounter items or topics that you believe put a particular group at a disadvantage, bring the problem to the attention of test creators by alerting your school administrators. This is a long-term effort. Short term, you may be tempted to address the problem by teaching students the knowledge needed to perform well in the test. This is a difficult professional decision, because "teaching to the test" jeopardizes the validity of test results.

In addition to examining test content and aligning your instruction with it, you can also examine test results for potential content bias. The printouts that detail test performance include class means and individual students' scores, and they also describe student performance on specific item types. You can use this information to detect content bias and perhaps improve your instruction. For example, consider the following responses from 28 students on three multiple-choice items. For each item, B is the correct answer.

	A	B*	C	D
1.	1	24	1	2
2.	4	12	5	7
3.	1	4	3	20

Most of the students correctly answered item 1, and there was no major problem with alternatives. This indicates that students knew the content and suggests that instruction was aligned with the information in the item. Less than half the class correctly answered item 2, and the incorrect answers were spread somewhat evenly over the possible choices. This suggests that instruction may not have been effective. For item 3, the majority of students chose an incorrect response. This suggests either a problem with the item or a mismatch between it and instruction.

This simplified form of item analysis (Linn & Miller, 2005) can provide you with one analytical tool to identify potential content bias. If you find that significant numbers of students from a particular group respond in a pattern like that seen for item 3, you should consider the possibility of content bias.

Adapt Testing Procedures

A second way to minimize standardized test bias is to adapt testing procedures to the specific needs of students. This strategy poses professional dilemmas for teachers because the validity of standardized test results depends on uniform administration. The issue of adapting test procedures is becoming increasingly important because of the growing use of high-stakes tests, as well as pressures to include diverse populations, such as students with exceptionalities and students with limited English proficiency in the testing population (Pitoniak & Royer, 2001). The Individuals with Disabilities Act (IDEA) mandates that students with disabilities be included in testing programs, but with accommodations or modifications if needed (Spinelli, 2004).

In response to these pressures, teachers have made accommodations to meet the testing needs of students. The *Standards for Educational and Psychological Testing*, jointly published by the American Educational Research Association, American Psychological Association, and National Council on Measurement in Education (1999), suggest the following accommodation strategies:

- Modify the presentation format; for example, use Braille or large print booklets for examinees with visual impairments.
- Modify the response format; for example, provide a scribe to mark answers for students who have difficulty writing or typing.
- Alter time to provide either extended testing time or frequent breaks.
- Modify the test setting; for example, allow the test to be individually administered, or alter the dimensions of the physical setting (e.g., the lighting)

Teachers need to be well informed to make professional decisions about standardized tests.

In testing students with disabilities, the most common adaptations are presenting tests orally, paraphrasing directions or content, and allowing students who have writing problems to dictate their answers (Koretz & Hamilton, 2000). The legal foundations for these adaptations in specific settings are not clear, and you should consult with administrators before adapting standardized test procedures (Pitoniak & Royer, 2001).

Use Alternate Assessment Data Sources

Testing experts are clear on the following point: No single test should be used as the basis for educational decisions about individual students. At the school level, you can use alternate data sources such as grades, work samples, and classroom observations in making decisions about individual students. At the policy level, you can become an advocate for the use of comprehensive assessment data in making these decisions.

Issues in Standardized Testing: Implications for Teachers

What do the issues involved in standardized testing have to do with you as a teacher? At least three implications exist. First, although standardized testing is controversial, it is an integral part of schooling and almost certainly will remain so. As you saw earlier in the chapter, you will be expected to interpret standards, align your instruction with them, and prepare students for testing. In addition, you are likely to be held accountable for your students' performance on tests.

Second, you will be expected to know more. You will likely be required to take more courses in English, math, science, history, and geography than have been required of teachers in the past. You will also be expected to understand learners and learning and how content can be presented so it's understandable to students. It is likely that you will be required to pass a test of competence before you're licensed. Standardized testing is a fact of life for both teachers and students.

Third, and perhaps most important, you must be well informed about the strengths and limitations of standardized tests. Knowing that test bias may exist can help you avoid inappropriately lowering your expectations or stereotyping students based on the results of a single test. Other than students' caregivers, you are the person most important in determining the quality of students' education, and the better informed you are, the more capable you will be of making the best professional decisions possible.

Checking Your Understanding

Knowledge Extensions

To deepen your understanding of the topics in this section of the chapter and to integrate them with topics you've already studied, go to the *Knowledge Extensions* module for Chapter 15 at *www.prenhall.com/eggen*. Respond to questions 24–26.

4.1 Describe three potential types of testing bias, and explain how they detract from validity.

4.2 Describe two strategies teachers can use to minimize content bias in the use of standardized tests with their students.

To receive feedback for these questions, go to Appendix B.

Classroom ┼ **Connections**

Eliminating Test Bias in Your Classroom

1. Attempt to understand the potential effects that learner diversity can have on assessment performance.

   - **Elementary:** Before any of her non-native English-speaking students are referred for special education testing, a first-grade teacher talks with the testing expert and describes the child's background and language patterns.
   - **Middle School:** Before administering a statewide exam, an eighth-grade math teacher explains the purpose and format of the test and gives students practice with the content covered on the test. He reads the directions for taking the test slowly and clearly and writes the amount of time remaining on the board.
   - **High School:** A high school English teacher holds sessions after school to help her students with limited English proficiency prepare for a high-stakes test. She explains test purposes and formats and provides the students with timed practice.

2. Adapt testing procedures to meet the needs of all students.

   - **Elementary:** An urban third-grade teacher states positive expectations for all students as they prepare for a standardized test and carefully monitors them to be sure they stay on task during the test.
   - **Middle School:** Before standardized tests are given each year, a middle school language arts teacher takes time to teach test-taking strategies (Some examples are on page 517 of this chapter and on page 496 of Chapter 15.). She models the strategies, discusses them with her students, and provides opportunities to practice them under test-like conditions.
   - **High School:** An algebra teacher makes a special effort to ensure that students understand the vocabulary on the state standardized test. Before the test, he carefully reviews important concepts the class has learned during the school year.

Meeting Your Learning Objectives

1. **Identify functions and types of standardized tests forms of validity associated with the tests.**

   - Educators can use standardized tests to assess student academic progress, diagnose strengths and weaknesses, and place students in appropriate programs. These tests can also provide information for program evaluation and improvement.
   - Achievement tests provide information about student learning; diagnostic tests provide in-depth analysis of specific student strengths and weaknesses; intelligence tests measure students' ability to acquire knowledge, capacity to think and reason in the abstract, and ability to solve novel problems; and aptitude tests predict potential for future learning.

   - Validity measures the appropriateness of a test for a specific purpose and includes content, predictive, and construct validity.
   - Teachers play a central role in standardized testing. They are integral in test selection, student preparation, test administration, and interpreting and communicating results to students and their caregivers.

2. **Explain standardized test results using statistics and standard scores.**

   - Educators interpret standardized test scores by using descriptive statistics to compare an individual's performance to the performance of a norming group.

- The mean, median, and mode are measures of central tendency, and the range and standard deviation are measures of variability.
- Percentiles, stanines, grade equivalents, and standard scores all allow educators to compare a student's score with the scores of comparable students in a norming group.

3. **Describe the relationships between standards-based education, accountability, and high-stakes testing.**

- Standards-based education has made teachers more accountable for their students' learning. Standards establish learning goals that all students are expected to attain. Administrators use minimum competency tests to hold both students and teachers accountable for performance on these tests. Tests are called high-stakes if educators use test results in making decisions about promotion to the next grade level or graduation from high school.
- Advocates of accountability argue that standardized tests efficiently assess the educational achievements of large numbers of students. Critics counter that misuse of standardized tests discourages innovation, and encourages teaching to low-level skills.

- The accountability movement is also targeting teachers. Prospective teachers are now expected to demonstrate competency in basic skills, content area knowledge, and pedagogy.

4. **Describe potential types of testing bias and strategies teachers can use to minimize bias in the use of standardized tests with their students.**

- The accountability movement raises questions about validity with respect to testing members of cultural minorities. Content bias occurs when incidental information in items discriminates against certain cultural groups. Bias in testing procedures occurs when groups don't fully understand testing procedures and the implications of time limits. Bias in the use of test results occurs when educators use test results alone to make important decisions about students.
- Teachers play an essential role in ensuring that standardized test results are unbiased. They examine test content before and test results after testing to ensure that both accurately reflect what their students have learned. They also ensure uniform testing conditions.

Developing as a *Professional*

Developing as a Professional: Praxis™ Practice

At the beginning of the chapter, we saw how Mike Chavez interpreted standardized test scores for a parent. Let's look now at another situation in which using standardized tests can help answer questions about learning and teaching. Read the case study, and answer the questions that follow.

Peggy Barret looks up from the stack of algebra tests that she is grading as her colleague, Stan Witzel, walks into the teacher's lounge.

"How's it going?" Stan asks.

"Fine . . . I think. I'm scoring tests from my Algebra I class. That's the one where I'm trying to put more emphasis on problem solving. Quite a few kids are actually getting into the applications now, and they like the problem solving when they do small-group work. The trouble is, some of the others are really struggling. . . . So, I'm not so sure about it all."

"I wish I had your problems. It sounds like your kids are learning, and at least some of them like it," Stan replies.

"Yeah, I know," Peggy nods. "Getting these kids to like any kind of math is an accomplishment, but still I wonder. . . . It's just that I'm not sure if they're getting all that they should. I don't know whether this class is *really* doing better than last year's class, or even my other classes this year, for that matter. The tests I give are pretty different in the different classes. I think the kids are doing better on problem solving, but to be honest about it, I see quite a few of them struggling with mechanics. I work on the mechanics, but not as much as in other classes. I'm not sure if I've drawn the line in the right place as far as the emphasis I'm putting on each part of the class."

"Good point," Stan shrugs. "I always wonder when I make changes. Are they missing out on something?"

"As important," Peggy continues, "I wonder how they'll do when they go off to college. Quite a few of them in this class will be going. . . . Got any ideas?"

"Good questions, Peggy. I wish I knew, but . . . I guess that's part of teaching."

"Yeah," she replies with her voice trailing off, "it seems as if we should be able to get some better information. I can see that some of the kids just don't seem to get it. I would say their background is weak; they seem to be trying. On the other hand, I checked out some of their old standardized test results, and their math scores weren't that bad. Maybe it's not background. Maybe they just don't belong in my class."

"Tell me about the kids who are struggling," Stan suggests.

"Well, Jacinta tries really hard. Quan is a whiz at computation but struggles when I ask him to think. Carlos actually seems to do fairly well with mechanics but has a hard time with word problems. For example, I tried to motivate the class the other day with several word problems involving statistics from our basketball team. Most of the class liked them and got them right. Not these three."

"Maybe you ought to talk to Yolanda," Stan suggests. "She's been in this game for awhile and might know about some tests that are available that can help you answer some of your questions."

PRAXIS These exercises are designed to help you prepare for the Praxis™ "Principles of Learning and Teaching" exam.

To receive feedback on your short-answer questions, go to the Companion Website at *www.prenhall.com/eggen*, then to the Practice for Praxis™ module for Chapter 16.

To acquire experience in preparing for the multiple-choice items on the Praxis™ exam, go to the *Self Assessment* module for Chapter 16 at *www.prenhall.com/eggen* and click on "Practice Quiz."

For additional connections between this text and the Praxis™ exam, go to Appendix A.

Short-Answer Questions

In answering these questions, use information from the chapter and link your responses to specific information in the case.

1. What type of standardized test would help Peggy determine "whether this class is *really* doing better than last year, or even my other classes this year"?
2. What type of validity would be the primary concern with this test? Explain.
3. One of Peggy's concerns was the prior knowledge of her students. What type of standardized test might Peggy use to gather data related to this concern?
4. In investigating the problems that her students were having in math, Peggy checked out their overall test scores from past standardized tests. What else might she have done?

 Also on the Companion Website at *www.prenhall.com/eggen*, you can measure your understanding of chapter content with multiple-choice and essay questions, and broaden your knowledge base in *Exploring Further* and *Web Links* to other educational psychology websites.

Online Portfolio Activities

To develop your professional portfolio, further apply your understanding of chapter content, and address the INTASC standards, go to the Companion Website, then to the *Online Portfolio Activities* for Chapter 16. Complete the suggested activities.

Important Concepts

accountability (p. 525)
achievement tests (p. 513)
aptitude tests (p. 514)
construct validity (p. 516)
content validity (p. 516)
diagnostic tests (p. 513)
frequency distribution (p. 520)
grade equivalent (p. 523)
high-stakes tests (p. 526)
intelligence tests (p. 513)
mean (p. 520)
measures of central tendency (p. 520)
median (p. 520)
mode (p. 520)
national norms (p. 511)
normal distribution (p. 521)

norm group (p. 511)
percentile (percentile rank, PR) (p. 522)
percentile bands (p. 523)
predictive validity (p. 516)
range (p. 521)
raw score (p. 522)
standard deviation (p. 521)
standard error of measurement (p. 524)
standardized tests (p. 511)
standard score (p. 524)
standards-based education (p. 525)
stanine (S) (p. 523)
true score (p. 524)
T score (p. 524)
z score (p. 524)

APPENDIX A

Using This Text to Practice for the Praxis™ Principles of Learning and Teaching Exam

In the United States, approximately thirty-five states use Praxis™ exams as part of their teacher licensing requirement. Among the Praxis™ tests are three Principles of Learning and Teaching (PLT) tests, one each for teachers seeking licensure for grades K–6, 5–9, and 7–12. *Educational Psychology: Windows on Classrooms* addresses most of the topics covered in the PLT tests.

The Principles of Learning and Teaching exam has two parts (Educational Testing Service, 2001). One consists of multiple-choice questions similar to those in the Eggen and Kauchak test banks, Student Study Guide, and Companion Website interactive Practice Quizzes that accompany this text. The second part is based on cases, which you will be asked to read and analyze, similar to the ones at the beginning and end of each chapter in this text.

The case-based part of the Praxis™ Principles of Learning and Teaching exam has two types of items: constructed response and document based. In the first type, you read a case study and then analyze it, responding to short-answer Constructed Response Questions (Educational Testing Service, 2005). In the Document-Based Analysis Questions, you evaluate student- or teacher-prepared documents, such as student work, excerpts from student records, teachers' lesson plans, assignments, or assessments. We have designed this text to help you succeed on the Praxis™ Principles of Learning and Teaching exam by including both types of case-based formats at the end of each chapter and providing feedback to the end-of-chapter questions on the Companion Website at *www.prenhall.com/eggen*.

Praxis™ Topic	Chapter Content Aligned with Praxis™ Topic
I. Students as Learners (approximately 33% of total test)	
A. Student Development and the Learning Process	
1. Theoretical foundations about how learning occurs: how students construct knowledge, acquire skills, and develop habits of mind	**Chapter 2:** The Development of Cognition and Language • The human brain and cognitive development (pp. 31–33) • Piaget's theory of intellectual development (pp. 34–44) • A sociocultural view of development: The work of Lev Vygotsky (pp. 45–51) • The relationship between learning and development (pp. 47–50) **Chapter 6:** Behaviorism and Social Cognitive Theory (Entire chapter) **Chapter 7:** Cognitive Views of Learning (Entire chapter) **Chapter 8:** Constructing Knowledge (Entire chapter) **Chapter 9:** Complex Cognitive Processes (Entire chapter) **Chapter 10:** Theories of Motivation • Extrinsic and intrinsic motivation (p. 299)
2. Human development in the physical, social, emotional, moral, and cognitive domains	**Chapter 2:** The Development of Cognition and Language (Entire chapter) **Chapter 3:** Personal, Social, and Emotional Development (Entire chapter) **Chapter 6:** Behaviorism and Social Cognitive Theory • Self-regulation (pp. 186–189) **Chapter 7:** Cognitive Views of Learning • Metacognition: Knowledge and control of cognitive processes (pp. 220–227) **Chapter 9:** Complex Cognitive Processes • The strategic learner (pp. 277–282) **Chapter 11:** Motivation in the Classroom • Self-regulated learners: Developing student responsibility (pp. 338–342)
B. Students as Diverse Learners	
1. Differences in the ways students learn and perform	**Chapter 2:** The Development of Cognition and Language • Factors influencing development (pp. 35–36) • Social interaction and development (p. 46) • Language and development (pp. 52–55) • Culture and development (p. 47) **Chapter 4:** Group and Individual Differences • Intelligence: One trait or many? (pp. 97–100) • Learning styles (pp. 101–102) • Influence of SES on learning (pp. 104–105) • Culture and schooling (pp. 106–110) • Responding to gender differences: Instructional principles (pp. 119–120) • Students placed at risk (pp. 120–125)
2. Areas of exceptionality in students' learning	**Chapter 2:** The Development of Cognition and Language • Stages of language acquisition (pp. 53–55) **Chapter 5:** Learners with Exceptionalities • Mental retardation (pp. 138–140) • Learning disabilities (pp. 140–142) • Attention deficit/hyperactivity disorder (ADHD) (pp. 142–143) • Behavior disorders (pp. 143–145) • Communication disorders (pp. 145–146) • Visual disabilities (pp. 146–147) • Hearing disabilities (pp. 147–148) • Students who are gifted and talented (pp. 149–152)
3. Legislation and institutional responsibilities relating to exceptional students	**Chapter 5:** Learners with Exceptionalities • Individuals with Disabilities Education Act (pp. 132–136) • Amendments to the Individuals with Disabilities Education Act (pp. 136–137)
4. Process of second language acquisition and strategies to support the learning of students for whom English is not a first language	**Chapter 2:** The Development of Cognition and Language • Language and development (pp. 52–55) • Theories of language acquisition (pp. 52–53) • Stages of language acquisition (pp. 53–55)
5. Understanding of influences of individual experiences, talents, and prior learning, as well as language, culture, family, and community values on students' learning	**Chapter 2:** The Development of Cognition and Language (Entire chapter) **Chapter 3:** Personal, Social, and Emotional Development • Personal development: Peers (pp. 62–65) • Personal development: Parents and other adults (pp. 63–64) • Social development (pp. 65–69)

Praxis™ Topic	Chapter Content Aligned with Praxis™ Topic
B. Students as Diverse Learners—continued	**Chapter 3—continued** • Promoting psychosocial and self-concept development: Instructional principles (pp.75–76) • Ethnic pride: Promoting self-esteem and ethnic identity (pp. 77–79) • Development of morality, social responsibility, and self-control (pp. 80–89) **Chapter 4:** Group and Individual Differences • Language diversity (pp. 110–116) • Influence of SES on learning (pp. 104–105) • Culture and schooling (pp. 106–110) **Chapter 6:** Behaviorism and Social Cognitive Theory • Addressing diversity: Behaviorism and social cognitive theory (pp. 190–193) **Chapter 7:** Cognitive Views of Learning • The impact of diversity on information processing (pp. 225–226)
6. Approaches for accommodating various learning styles, intelligences, or exceptionalities	**Chapter 4:** Group and Individual Differences • Ability grouping (pp. 100–101) • Learning styles (pp. 101–102) • Teaching culturally and linguistically diverse students: Instructional principles (pp. 114–115) • Responding to gender differences: Instructional principles (pp. 119–120) • Teaching students placed at risk: Instructional principles (pp. 123–124) **Chapter 5:** Learners with Exceptionalities • Identifying students with exceptionalities (pp. 132–136) • Teaching students with exceptionalities: Instructional principles (pp. 136–137) **Chapter 6:** Behaviorism and Social Cognitive Theory • Addressing diversity: Behaviorism and social cognitive theory (pp. 190–193) • Capitalizing on minority role models (pp. 192–193) **Chapter 14:** Learning and Instruction and Technology • Exploring diversity: Employing technology to support learners with disabilities (pp. 461–462) **Chapter 15:** Assessing Classroom Learning • Learning contexts: Assessment in urban classrooms (pp. 502–503) **Chapter 16:** Assessment Through Standardized Testing • Eliminating bias in standardized testing: Instructional principles (pp. 530–531)
C. Student Motivation and the Learning Environment	
1. Theoretical foundations about human motivation behavior	**Chapter 3:** Personal, Social, and Emotional Development • Erikson's theory of psychosocial development (pp. 70–72) • The development of identity (pp. 72–74) • The development of self-concept (pp. 74–76) **Chapter 6:** Behaviorism and Social Cognitive Theory • Classical conditioning: Learning to like and dislike school (pp. 165–167) **Chapter 10:** Theories of Motivation • Behavioral views of motivation (pp. 301–302) • Humanistic views of motivation (pp. 303–305) • Cognitive theories of motivation (pp. 307–327)
2. How knowledge of human motivation and behavior should influence strategies for organizing and supporting individual and group work in the classroom	**Chapter 10:** Theories of Motivation • Using rewards in classrooms: Instructional principles (pp. 301–302) • Humanistic views of motivation: Instructional principles (p. 305) **Chapter 11:** Motivation in the Classroom • Class structure: Creating a learning-focused environment (p. 337) • Self-regulated learners: Developing student responsibility (pp. 338–342) • Climate variables: Creating a motivating environment (pp. 348–351) • Instructional variables: Developing interest in learning activities (pp. 352–362)
3. Factors and situations that are likely to promote or diminish students' motivation to learn; how to help students become self-motivated	**Chapter 3:** Personal, Social, and Emotional Development • Ethnic pride: Promoting self-esteem and ethnic identity (pp. 77–79) **Chapter 6:** Behaviorism and Social Cognitive Theory • Self-regulation (pp. 186–189) **Chapter 10:** Theories of Motivation • Developing students' self-determination: Instructional principles (pp. 323–325) • Accommodating affective factors in motivation: Instructional principles (pp. 329–330)

Praxis™ Topic	Chapter Content Aligned with Praxis™ Topic

C. Student Motivation and the Learning Environment—continued

Chapter 11: Motivation in the Classroom
- Self-regulated learners: Developing student responsibility (pp. 338–342)
- Helping students develop self-regulation: Instructional principles (pp. 339–341)
- Modeling and enthusiasm: Communicating genuine interest (pp. 343–344)
- Caring: Meeting the need for relatedness (pp. 344–345)
- Teacher expectations: Increasing perceptions of competence (pp. 345–346)
- Climate variables: Creating a motivating environment (pp. 348–351)
- Learning contexts: Motivation to learn in the urban classroom (pp. 360–362)

Chapter 13: Creating Productive Learning Environments: Principles and Models of Instruction
- Focus: Attracting and maintaining attention (p. 416)

4. Principles of effective classroom management and strategies to promote positive relationships, cooperation, and purposeful learning

Chapter 6: Behaviorism and Social Cognitive Theory
- Motivating hesitant learners (p. 192)

Chapter 11: Motivation in the Classroom
- Class structure: Creating a learning-focused environment (p. 337)
- Order and safety: Classrooms as secure places to learn (pp. 348–349)

Chapter 12: Creating Productive Learning Environments: Classroom Management (Entire chapter)

II. Instruction and Assessment (approximately 33% of total test)

A. Instructional Strategies

1. The major cognitive processes associated with student learning

Chapter 2: The Development of Cognition and Language
- Applying Piaget's work in the classroom: Instructional principles (pp. 41–42)
- Vygotsky's work: Instructional principles (pp. 47–48)

Chapter 6: Behaviorism and Social Cognitive Theory
- Social cognitive theory (pp. 179–190)

Chapter 7: Cognitive Views of Learning (Entire chapter)
Chapter 8: Constructing Knowledge (Entire chapter)
Chapter 9: Complex Cognitive Processes
- Problem solving (pp. 265–276)
- The strategic learner (pp. 277–282)
- Critical thinking (pp. 282–287)

2. Major categories, advantages, and appropriate uses of instructional strategies

Chapter 7: Cognitive Views of Learning
- Information processing in the classroom: Instructional principles (pp. 222–225)

Chapter 8: Constructing Knowledge
- Constructivism in classrooms: Instructional principles (pp. 254–256)

Chapter 9: Complex Cognitive Processes
- Helping learners become better problem solvers: Instructional principles (pp. 271–275)
- Developing strategic learning in students: Instructional principles (pp. 281–282)
- Developing critical thinking: Instructional principles (pp. 285–286)

Chapter 13: Creating Productive Learning Environments: Principles and Models of Instruction
- Implementing instruction: Essential teaching skills (pp. 413–422)

3. Methods for enhancing student learning through the use of a variety of resources and materials

Chapter 2: The Development of Cognition and Language
- Applying Piaget's work in classrooms: Instructional principles (pp. 41–42)
- Vygotsky's work: Instructional principles (pp. 47–48)

Chapter 7: Cognitive Views of Learning
- Information processing in the classroom: Instructional principles (pp. 222–225)

Chapter 8: Constructing Knowledge
- Constructivism in classrooms: Instructional principles (pp. 254–256)

Chapter 9: Complex Cognitive Processes
- Helping learners become better problem solvers: Instructional principles (pp. 271–275)
- Developing strategic learning in students: Instructional principles (pp. 281–282)
- Developing critical thinking: Instructional principles (pp. 285–286)

Chapter 13: Creating Productive Learning Environments: Principles and Models of Instruction
- Preparing and organizing learning activities (pp. 409–410)

Chapter 14: Learning and Instruction and Technology (Entire chapter)

Praxis™ Topic	Chapter Content Aligned with Praxis™ Topic
A. Instructional Strategies—continued 4. Principles, techniques, and methods associated with major instructional strategies, especially direct instruction and student-centered models	**Chapter 3:** Personal, Social, and Emotional Development • Promoting moral development: Instructional principles (p. 87) **Chapter 7:** Cognitive Views of Learning • Information processing in the classroom: Instructional principles (pp. 222–225) **Chapter 8:** Constructing Knowledge • Constructivism in classrooms: Instructional principles (pp. 254–256) **Chapter 9:** Complex Cognitive Processes • Helping learners become better problem solvers: Instructional principles (pp. 271–275) • Developing strategic learning in students: Instructional principles (pp. 281–285) • Developing critical thinking: Instructional principles (pp. 285–286) **Chapter 13:** Creating Productive Learning Environments: Principles and Models of Instruction • Implementing instruction: Essential teaching skills (pp. 413–422) • Direct instruction (pp. 423–426) • Lecture and lecture-discussion (pp. 427–429) • Guided discovery (pp. 430–431) • Cooperative learning (pp. 431–433)
B. Planning Instruction 1. Techniques for planning instruction to meet curriculum goals, including the incorporation of learning theory, subject matter, curriculum development, and student development	**Chapter 2:** The Development of Cognition and Language • Applying Piaget's work in classrooms: Instructional principles (pp. 41–42) • Vygotsky's work: Instructional principles (pp. 47–48) **Chapter 7:** Cognitive Views of Learning • Information processing in the classroom: Instructional principles (pp. 222–225) **Chapter 8:** Constructing Knowledge • Constructivism in classrooms: Instructional principles (pp. 254–256) **Chapter 9:** Complex Cognitive Processes • Helping learners become better problem solvers: Instructional principles (pp. 271–275) • Developing strategic learning in students: Instructional principles (pp. 281–282) • Developing critical thinking: Instructional principles (pp. 285–286) **Chapter 13:** Creating Productive Learning Environments: Principles and Models of Instruction • Selecting topics (p. 407) • Preparing learning objectives (pp. 407–409) • Preparing and organizing learning activities (pp. 409–410) • Planning for assessment (p. 410) • Instructional alignment (pp. 410–411) • Planning in a standards-based environment (pp. 411–412)
2. Techniques for creating effective bridges between curriculum goals and students' experiences	**Chapter 6:** Behaviorism and Social Cognitive Theory • Modeling (pp. 181–182) **Chapter 7:** Cognitive Views of Learning • Information processing in the classroom: Instructional principles (pp. 222–225) **Chapter 8:** Constructing Knowledge • Concepts (pp. 241–244) • Constructivism in classrooms: Instructional principles (pp. 254–256) **Chapter 9:** Complex Cognitive Processes • Helping learners become better problem solvers: Instructional principles (pp. 271–275) • Developing strategic learning in students: Instructional principles (pp. 281–282) • Developing critical thinking: Instructional principles (pp. 285–286)
C. Assessment Strategies 1. Types of assessments	**Chapter 8:** Constructing Knowledge • Assessment and learning: The role of assessment in constructivist classrooms (p. 252) **Chapter 10:** Theories of Motivation • Assessment and learning: The role of assessment in self-determination (pp. 323–325)

Praxis™ Topic	Chapter Content Aligned with Praxis™ Topic
C. Assessment Strategies—continued	
	Chapter 11: Motivation in the Classroom • Assessment and learning: Using feedback to increase interest and self-efficacy (pp. 359–360) **Chapter 13:** Creating Productive Learning Environments: Principles and Models of Instruction • Assessment and learning: Using assessment as a learning tool (pp. 436–437) **Chapter 15:** Assessing Classroom Learning • Constructing valid test items: Instructional principles (pp. 480–485) • Designing performance assessments: Instructional principles (pp. 488–490) • Portfolio assessment: Involving students in alternative assessment (pp. 490–492) **Chapter 16:** Assessment Through Standardized Testing • Types of standardized tests (pp. 512–515) • The teacher's role in standardized testing: Instructional principles (pp. 517–518)
2. Characteristics of assessments	**Chapter 15:** Assessing Classroom Learning • Validity: Making appropriate assessment decisions (p. 477) • Reliability: Consistency in assessment (pp. 477–478) • Constructing valid test items: Instructional principles (pp. 480–485) **Chapter 16:** Assessment Through Standardized Testing • Evaluating standardized tests: Validity revisited (pp. 515–518)
3. Scoring assessments	**Chapter 15:** Assessing Classroom Learning • Using rubrics (pp. 484–485) • Performance assessment (pp. 487–490) • Designing performance assessments: Instructional principles (pp. 488–490) • Portfolio assessment: Involving students in alternative assessment (pp. 490–492) • Analyzing results (p. 498) **Chapter 16:** Assessment Through Standardized Testing • Understanding and interpreting standardized test scores (pp. 518–524)
4. Uses of assessments	**Chapter 13:** Creating Productive Learning Environments: Principles and Models of Instruction • Planning for assessment (p. 410) **Chapter 15:** Assessing Classroom Learning • Performance assessment (pp. 487–490) • Designing a grading system (pp. 499–500) • Portfolio assessment: Involving students in alternative assessment (pp. 490–492)
5. Understanding of measurement theory and assessment-related issues	**Chapter 15:** Assessing Classroom Learning • Constructing valid test items: Instructional principles (pp. 480–485) • Commercially prepared test items (p. 486) • Planning for assessment (pp. 494–495) • Preparing students for assessments (pp. 495–497) • Administering assessments (pp. 497–498) • Designing a grading system (pp. 499–500) • Assigning grades: Increasing learning and motivation (pp. 500–502)
III. Communication Techniques (approximately 11% of total test)	
A. Basic, effective verbal and nonverbal communication techniques	
	Chapter 2: The Development of Cognition and Language • Language and development (pp. 52–55) • Promoting language development: Suggestions for teachers (p. 55) **Chapter 8:** Constructing Knowledge • Social interaction facilitates learning (pp. 239–241) **Chapter 12:** Creating Productive Learning Environments: Classroom Management • Benefits of communication (pp. 384–387) **Chapter 13:** Creating Productive Learning Environments: Principles and Models of Instruction • Attitudes (pp. 414–415) • Communication (pp. 415–416)

Praxis™ Topic	Chapter Content Aligned with Praxis™ Topic

B. Effect of cultural and gender differences on communications in the classroom

Chapter 4: Group and Individual Differences
- Language diversity (pp. 110–116)
- Teaching culturally and linguistically diverse students: Instruction principles (pp. 114–115)
- Gender stereotypes and perceptions (pp. 118–120)
- Responding to gender differences: Instructional principles (pp. 119–120)

Chapter 7: Cognitive Views of Learning
- The impact of diversity on information processing (pp. 225–226)

Chapter 8: Constructing Knowledge
- Learning contexts: Construction of knowledge in urban classrooms (pp. 256–257)

Chapter 11: Motivation in the Classroom
- Learning contexts: Motivation to learn in the urban classroom (pp. 360–362)

Chapter 13: Creating Productive Learning Environments: Principles and Models of Instruction
- Cooperative learning: A tool for capitalizing on diversity (pp. 433–434)

Chapter 15: Assessing Classroom Learning
- Learning contexts: Assessment in urban classrooms (pp. 502–503)

Chapter 16: Assessment Through Standardized Testing
- Diversity issues in standardized testing (pp. 528–532)

C. Types of questions that can stimulate discussion in different ways for particular purposes

Chapter 2: The Development of Cognition and Language
- Applying Piaget's work in classrooms: Instructional principles (pp. 41–42)
- Social interaction and development (p. 46)
- Language and development (pp. 52–55)
- Vygotsky's work: Instructional principles (pp. 47–48)

Chapter 7: Cognitive Views of Learning
- Information processing in the classroom: Instructional principles (pp. 222–225)

Chapter 8: Constructing Knowledge
- Constructivism in classrooms: Instructional principles (pp. 254–256)

Chapter 13: Creating Productive Learning Environments: Principles and Models of Instruction
- Questioning (pp. 418–420)
- Direct instruction (pp. 423–426)
- Lecture and lecture-discussion (pp. 427–429)
- Guided discovery (pp. 430–431)

IV. Teacher Professionalism (approximately 11% of total test)

A. The Reflective Practitioner

1. Types of resources available for professional development and learning

Chapter 1: Educational Psychology: Developing a Professional Knowledge Base
- Educational psychology and becoming a professional (pp. 5–7)
- Professional knowledge and learning to teach (pp. 7–15)

2. Ability to read and understand articles and books about current views, ideas, and debates regarding best teaching practices

Chapter 1: Educational Psychology: Developing a Professional Knowledge Base
- Educational psychology and becoming a professional (pp. 5–7)
- Professional knowledge and learning to teach (pp. 7–15)
- The role of research in acquiring knowledge (pp. 15–22)

3. Why personal reflection on teaching practices is critical, and approaches that can be used to do so

Chapter 1: Educational Psychology: Developing a Professional Knowledge Base
- Characteristics of professionalism (pp. 5–6)
- Professional knowledge and learning to teach (pp. 7–15)
- Conducting research in classrooms: Action research strategies (pp. 19–20)

B. The Larger Community

1. The role of the school as a resource to the larger community

Chapter 3: Personal, Social, and Emotional Development
- Personal development: Parents and other adults (pp. 63–64)

Chapter 12: Creating Productive Learning Environments: Classroom Management
- Involving parents: Instructional principles (pp. 385–387)

Praxis™ Topic	Chapter Content Aligned with Praxis™ Topic
B. The Larger Community—continued	
2. Factors in the students' environment outside of school (family circumstances, community environments, health and economic conditions) that may influence students' life and learning	**Chapter 4:** Group and Individual Differences • Influence of SES on learning (pp. 104–105) • Culture and schooling (pp. 108–110) • Gender stereotypes and perceptions (pp. 118–120) • Resilience (pp. 122–125) **Chapter 12:** Creating Productive Learning Environments: Classroom Management • Communication with parents: Accommodating learner diversity (pp. 387–389)
3. Basic strategies for involving parents/guardians and leaders in the community in the educational process	**Chapter 6:** Behaviorism and Social Cognitive Theory • Capitalizing on minority role models (pp. 192–193) **Chapter 12:** Creating Productive Learning Environments: Classroom Management • Benefits of communication (pp. 384–387) • Involving parents: Instructional principles (pp. 385–387) **Chapter 3:** Personal, Social, and Emotional Development • Violence and aggression in schools (pp. 66–69)
4. Major laws related to students' rights and teacher responsibilities	**Chapter 5:** Learners with Exceptionalities • Individuals with Disabilities Education Act (pp. 132–136) • Amendments to the Individuals with Disabilities Education Act (pp. 136–137) **Chapter 16:** Assessment Through Standardized Testing • Standards-based education and accountability (pp. 525–526) • Student diversity and test bias (pp. 528–531)

APPENDIX B

Feedback for "Checking Your Understanding" Questions

CHAPTER 1

1.1 The characteristics of professionalism follow:
- Commitment to learners. Professional educators are committed to helping their students grow, both as learners and as people. This commitment is also reflected in a code of ethics that guides their professional practice.
- Decision making. Teaching is a complex and, in many ways, an ill-defined practice. Professionals are able to make decisions that are designed to increase learning for all students in these ill-defined situations.
- Reflective practice. Professionals continually question their classroom performance and assess their practice with the goal of continual improvement.
- A body of specialized knowledge. Professionals base their decisions and self-assessments on a deep and thorough understanding of a professional body of specialized knowledge.

1.2 First, Keith was committed to his students and their learning, as indicated by both his concern about their dislike of word problems and Kelly's behavior. Second, he reflected on his work, as suggested by Jan's comment, "You look deep in thought," at the beginning of their conversation. Third, he made a series of decisions in his attempt to work with Kelly. This helps us answer the second question asked at the beginning of the chapter, "What characteristics did Jan and Keith demonstrate that suggested they are professionals?"

1.3 Jan demonstrated commitment to her students as indicated by her efforts to make her learning activities more meaningful for them. Second, she reflected on her work, as represented by her comment, "It changed my thinking," and her concerns about sometimes intervening too soon and sometimes letting her students stumble around too long. Third, she made a number of decisions that led to the way she designed and conducted her learning activity.

Finally, and most significantly, she based her decisions on a thorough understanding of professional knowledge. This understanding is the foundation of professionalism. This also helps answer the second question we asked at the beginning of the chapter, about the characteristics of professionals.

1.4 The primary difference between Keith's and Jan's level of professional behavior is in the depth of their professional knowledge. Because Jan was more knowledgeable, she made decisions that Keith's professional development didn't yet allow him to make.

2.1 Knowledge of content, pedagogical content knowledge, general pedagogical knowledge, and knowledge of learners and learning are the types of knowledge professional teachers possess. *Knowledge of content* describes knowledge of math, reading, geography, or whatever topic is being taught. *Pedagogical content knowledge* is the ability to represent the topic in ways that are understandable, such as the folded pieces of paper discussed in Chapter 1 as a way of representing the multiplication of fractions. *General pedagogical knowledge* refers to the abilities that exist in all teaching situations, such as questioning skills, or the ability to organize classrooms. *Knowledge of learners and learning* refers to factors such as an understanding of how students learn, students' motivation, and students' needs.

2.2 Keith's statement that best indicates that he lacks pedagogical content knowledge is, "I've tried explaining the stuff until I'm blue in the face." As Chapter 1 shows, when teachers lack pedagogical content knowledge, they commonly revert to abstract explanations that aren't meaningful to students. We're not implying that teachers shouldn't try to explain topics; rather we're suggesting that relying on explanations alone often fails to increase learners' understanding as much as a teacher might expect.

2.3 The teacher in this case is using the pieces of bubble wrap to help the students visualize the way that cells form tissues. The ability to create this representation is an indicator of the teacher's pedagogical content knowledge. (In this case, the bubble wrap is a model for the formation of tissue; it helps students visualize what they can't observe directly.)

3.1 The types of research discussed in the chapter follow:
- *Descriptive research.* Descriptive research uses interviews, observations, and surveys to describe events. Descriptive research does not imply relationships between variables, and it should not be used to predict future events.
- *Correlational research.* Correlational research describes a relationship between two or more

variables. Correlational research does not imply that changes in one variable cause changes in the other.

- *Experimental research.* Experimental research systematically manipulates variables in an attempt to identify cause-and-effect relationships. Comparability of groups, control of extraneous variables, the size of the sample groups, and clear descriptions of how the independent variable is being manipulated are all important when conducting experimental research.

- *Action research.* Action research is a form of applied research designed to answer specific school- or classroom-related questions. Action research can be descriptive, correlational, or experimental.

3.2 This finding is the result of correlational research. A relationship exists between the variables *personal teaching efficacy* and *student achievement.* However, the researchers didn't consciously manipulate one of the variables; that is, they didn't train some of the teachers to be high in efficacy. They merely observed the relationship between teaching efficacy and achievement.

3.3 Concluding that doing homework caused achievement to increase would not be valid. Correlational research does not imply that one variable causes the other.

4.1 Many of the ideas in educational psychology are quite abstract. Because they're abstract, they're difficult to apply to teaching. The use of case studies provides concrete reference points that make the abstract ideas of educational psychology more applicable to the real world that you will face when you begin your career.

4.2 Video case studies have the advantage of being more authentic and real than written case studies. They allow viewers to see, for example, differences between a confident and a hesitant student answer and why the difference might exist, or differences in room arrangements that might influence student behavior.

CHAPTER 2

1.1 The principles of development follow:

- *Learning contributes to development.* Learning refers to increased understanding and skills, and evidence of increasing development exists when this understanding or these skills are applied in a new context.

- *Experience enhances development.* People who have a range of experiences in a variety of areas are likely to become more fully developed than are those whose experiences are narrower.

- *Social interaction is essential for development.* Without connections and interactions with others, development is retarded.

- *Development depends on language.* Language provides a medium for thought and communication.

- *Development is continuous and relatively durable.* People don't suddenly jump from one set of abilities to another set, and, once having acquired a set of abilities, they rarely lose them. Learning to ride a bicycle can be used as a metaphor. Once having learned to ride, people don't forget how.

- *Individuals develop at different rates.* People's ability, level of maturation, and experiences all influence how quickly they develop.

- *Development is influenced by maturation.* Individuals' genetic makeup, general health, and nutrition also influence how quickly they develop.

1.2 The following principles are involved in the child's development:

- *Learning contributes to development.* The tips her brother gave her about her technique illustrate the role of learning in development.

- *Experience enhances development.* She acquired experience as she practiced.

- *Social interaction promotes development.* The child's brother and she interacted as he made suggestions to improve her technique.

- *Development depends on language.* She and her brother used language as they interacted.

- *Development is influenced by maturation.* In the vignette, she "gets bigger and stronger," which is evidence of maturation.

  The vignette does not contain evidence for the following principles: *Individuals develop at different rates,* and *development is continuous and relatively orderly.*

1.3 The following principles are illustrated in the example.

- *Learning contributes to development.* The second grader learned to solve problems that required regrouping.

- *Experience enhances development.* The child practiced with problems that required regrouping.

- *Social interaction promotes development.* He interacted with his teacher as she provided instructional support.

- *Development depends on language.* The child and his teacher used language as they interacted.

  The vignette does not contain evidence for the following principles: *Individuals develop at different rates, development is continuous and relatively orderly,* and *development is influenced by maturation.*

2.1 Hands-on activities provide the *direct experiences* Piaget so strongly believed are necessary for development. Experience also helps us understand the following statement made in this section, "Although approximate chronological ages are attached to the stages, children pass through them at different rates." (Differences in maturation, and the extent to which the culture emphasizes experience with respect to specific tasks, also influence the rates at which they pass through the stages.)

2.2 First, the children demonstrate centration as they tend to *center* on the length of the row in the case of the coins and the length of the clay in the case of the flattened piece of clay. The length of the row and the longer, flatter clay are more perceptually obvious than is the number of coins or the amount of clay, so the children conclude that there are more coins in the bottom row, and more clay in the flattened piece. Second, since young children lack *transformation,* they don't mentally record the process of spreading the coins apart, or flattening the clay, so they see each as new and different. Third, because they lack *reversibility,* they can't mentally trace the process of lengthening the row back to its original state, or mentally trace the process of reforming the flattened clay back into a ball. When lack of transformation and reversibility are combined with the students' tendency to center, we can see why they conclude that the bottom row has more coins, even though no coins were added or removed, and conclude that the amount of clay is different even though no clay is added or taken away.

2.3 You have had a variety of *experiences* with driving cars having automatic transmissions, and you have *organized* those experiences into a "driving" *scheme.* Your scheme has helped you to achieve *equilibrium.* However, when you encountered the car with a stick shift your equilibrium was disrupted, and you were forced to *accommodate* your scheme. You modified your original driving scheme and contructed a new "driving-with-a-stick-shift" scheme, and your equilibrium was re-established. You were then able to *assimilate* the experience with the pickup truck into your "driving-with-a-stick-shift" scheme. As a result of your added experience with driving vehicles having stick shifts, your driving ability is more fully *developed* than it was when you were only able to drive vehicles with automatic transmissions.

3.1 The discussion in the section "Language and Development" suggests that you should encourage your students to talk about their developing understanding of mathematics. Language is a cognitive tool that allows learners to think about the world and solve problems, and the more practice students get putting their understanding into words, the better their understanding will be, and the more their development will be advanced.

3.2 This section illustrates the idea that language in a culture is a cognitive "tool kit." In our culture, *snow* is a fairly simple idea. In the Eskimo culture, however, *snow* is a more complex concept, and they have more terms and more ways of describing it. Their language reflects the fact that snow is a more complex idea in their culture than it is in ours. Because of the cultural influence their concept of snow is more fully developed than is ours.

3.3 The zone of proximal development is the point in your development where you can benefit from instructional support. So, being able to perform word processing skills with support represents your zone of proximal development. Your friend's zone is somewhere beyond your zone, and it might involve sophisticated presentation skills beyond mere word processing. This would be the point where she would need support to advance her development. The differences suggest that her word processing skills are more fully developed than are yours.

4.1 Nativist theory, which asserts that children have a language acquisition device that allows them to produce sentences they haven't heard before, provides the best explanation.

Neither behaviorism nor social cognitive theory can adequately explain this particular misuse of language, because it is unlikely that anyone reinforced the child for using the adjective form, "gooder," and it is also unlikely that anyone has modeled it for the child.

Sociocultural theory, which stresses the learning of language in functional settings, also has difficulty explaining this adjective form, because it isn't viewed as culturally acceptable usage.

4.2 Overgeneralization is the language acquisition concept best illustrated by the use of "gooder," in this example. When children use a form, such as "gooder," they are overgeneralizing the rule, "To make a comparative adjective, add *er* to it."

4.3 Behaviorist theory would recommend using reinforcement to shape correct behaviors (e.g., "No, 'gooder' isn't correct; you should say 'better'"). Social cognitive theory would suggest using modeling to demonstrate correct usage (e.g., "Oh, you think yours is better, but I think mine is better, too"). Nativist theory doesn't offer a direct solution to this problem; it would suggest that the child's language acquisition device and frequent exposure to correct talk would solve the problem. Sociocultural theory views language as an integral part of the whole developmental process, and, rather than correcting this specific problem, would recommend immersing the child in language-rich activities.

CHAPTER 3

1.1 The three most prominent factors influencing personal development are heredity, parents and other adults, and peers. Heredity influences our temperament, the way we tend to respond to our social and physical environments. Through the expectations they establish and the way they respond to their children, parents also influence enduring personality traits. And, peers influence personal development by communicating attitudes and values and by offering, or not offering, friendship.

1.2 Sean's mother's comment illustrates the powerful influence that heredity plays in personal development.

1.3 Researchers have identified expectations and responsiveness as two parenting factors that influence children's personal development. When the father said, "I don't think he'll ever amount to much," he was expressing low expectations, and he demonstrated a lack of responsiveness when he said, "I can't do anything with him."

1.4 Differences in peers' interactions first influence personal development through the attitudes and values they communicate. For example, if peers communicate—directly or indirectly—that achievement is important, the impact will obviously be different than if they communicate negative values about schools and learning. Similarly, if peers offer friendship, children are more likely to develop confidence and social skills than if peers are rejecting in their interactions.

2.1 Perspective taking and social problem solving are two characteristics that indicate advancing social develpment. Perspective taking is the ability to understand the thoughts and feelings of others, and teachers can promote it by encouraging students to consider the way others might think or feel. Social problem solving is the ability to resolve conflicts in ways that are beneficial to all involved. Like perspective taking, developing this social skill takes time and practice.

2.2 The teacher in this case is trying to develop social problem solving. By asking, "What could we do to make both of you happy?" she was attempting to help the children learn to resolve a conflict in ways that would be beneficial to both.

2.3 School violence and aggression are closely related to underdeveloped social skills. For example, aggressive students rarely consider others' perspectives, and they have trouble maintaining friendships. They are also more likely to react to social problems with aggressive or hostile behaviors instead of using social problem-solving skills. The same three factors that influence personal development—genetics, parents, and peers—also influence the development of aggression in children.

3.1 Based on Erikson's theory, we would explain the student's behavior by saying that he hasn't positively resolved the initiative-guilt crisis. This doesn't imply that his industry-inferiority or identity-confusion crises cannot be resolved somewhat satisfactorily, however, as indicated by the fact that "he does a good job on his required work," and he "seems to be quite happy." Erikson's work would suggest that this student simply has a personality "glitch" with respect to initiative. It may never have a significant effect on his personal functioning unless he finds himself in a job in which initiative is needed and valued.

A teacher might respond by encouraging him to take initiative and then reinforcing any initiative that he takes. In addition, creating a classroom environment that deemphasizes competition can also encourage student initiative.

3.2 Based on their comments in the conversation, it appears that Taylor is in the state of identity achievement. He stated, "I'm going into nursing," and he appeared to have few doubts about his decision.

Sandy's comments suggest that she is at the state of identity diffusion. She has considered veterinary medicine, and she has also given some thought to teaching, but her thinking is somewhat haphazard.

Ramon is at the state of identity foreclosure. His parents want him to be a lawyer, and he has acquiesced to their wishes.

Nancy's comments, "I'm not willing to decide yet," and "I'm going to think about it a while," indicate that she is at the state of identity moratorium.

3.3 The student's comments reflect a description of his self-concept, which is a cognitive appraisal of one's physical, social, and academic competence. Self-esteem, by contrast, is our emotional evaluation of the self, and we see no evidence of either high or low self-esteem in the comments. Self-concept is more closely related to academic achievement than is self-esteem.

4.1 A driver reasoning at Stage 3 would be likely to say that everybody else is going 65, so it's okay for me to do the same. At Stage 4, a person would be more likely to say that the law says 55, so I'm slowing down. I don't care what everyone else is doing.

4.2 Gilligan's work would suggest that a woman would be more likely than a man to interpret this incident from an interpersonal perspective. For example, a woman might

reason that whispering is justified because we're helping Gary, whereas a man might be more likely to reason that the assignment was given, and Gary, as with everyone else, should know it. According to Gilligan, the major difference between women and men involves the relative emphasis placed on caring and social problem solving (for women) versus abstract justice (for men).

4.3 Empathy and prosocial behaviors are most closely related to Kohlberg's Stage 3. People reasoning at this stage make moral decisions based on their concern for others, which is similar to empathy.

CHAPTER 4

1.1 One definition of intelligence suggests that it is composed of three characteristics: (1) the ability to acquire knowledge, (2) the ability to think in the abstract, and (3) the ability to solve problems.

A second perspective simply suggests that intelligence is the characteristic or set of characteristics that intelligence tests measure.

1.2 Historical views of intelligence suggest that it is a single trait. Gardner and Sternberg, in contrast, argue that it is composed of several dimensions. In Gardner's view, the dimensions are relatively independent.

1.3 Ability grouping is the process of placing students with similar academic abilities in the same learning environments. Research indicates that, while well-intentioned, it has potential drawbacks that can decrease achievement, such as lowered teacher expectations and poorer instruction for those in lower-ability groups. Experts recommend that teachers minimize its use in classrooms and constantly be aware of potentials for adverse effects.

2.1 Socioeconomic status (SES) is defined as the relative standing in society resulting from a combination of family income, parents' occupations, and the level of education parents attain. High-income parents, and parents who are in fields such as medicine, law, education, or engineering and architecture, and level of education, such as earning college degrees, are considered to be high in SES.

2.2 First, SES influences learning by affecting the quality of the way in which students' basic needs are met and the quality of their experiences. Poverty can influence a family's ability to provide adequate housing, nutrition, and medical care. SES can also affect the quality of background experiences that adults offer to children. A second way that SES affects learning is by influencing the level of parental involvement; lower-SES parents tend to be less involved in their children's education. A third way that SES influences learning is through attitudes and values. For example, many high-SES parents encourage autonomy, individual responsibility, and self-control, whereas lower-SES parents tend to value obedience and conformity. High-SES parents also have positive expectations for their children and to encourage them to graduate from high school and attend college; low-SES parents tend to have lower aspirations for academic advancement.

2.3 When considering a student's SES, you should be careful about stereotyping students based on their SES. You should remember that the research describes group patterns, which may or may not apply to individuals. Many lower-SES families provide rich learning environments for their children and have positive attitudes and values that promote learning.

3.1 *Culture* refers to differences in the knowledge, attitudes, values, customs and ways of acting that characterize different social groups. *Ethnicity* is a part of cultural diversity, and refers to differences in people's ancestry, the way they identify themselves with the nation from which they or their ancestors come. *Culture* is the broader of the two terms, describing differences in the total sets of attitudes, values, and customs of different groups. *Ethnicity* is narrower, referring specifically to differences in people's ancestral heritage.

3.2 English dialects are variations of standard English that are distinct in vocabulary, grammar, or punctuation. Teachers sometimes misinterpret students' dialects as substandard English, which can lead to lowered evaluations of student work and lowered expectations for student achievement. Effective teachers accept and build on students' dialects and develop bidialecticism in their students.

3.3 The major approaches to helping English language learners (ELLs) are maintenance, transitional, ELL pullout, sheltered English, and immersion programs. They are similar in that they all have the goal of teaching English. They differ in the extent to which they emphasize maintaining and building on students' native languages, and the amount of structure and support they provide in learning academic content. For example, maintenance programs have the dual goals of maintaining and developing literacy in the native language and also teaching English literacy skills. Transition programs use the first language as an aid to learning English. Pullout and sheltered English programs adapt instruction in content areas by providing scaffolds that assist content acquisition. Immersion programs place ELLs in English-only classrooms.

3.4 First, communicating that you respect and value all cultures is essential. You can communicate this in a variety of ways, some examples of which Gary Nolan applied with his students. Second, teachers should involve all students—regardless of cultural background or language skills—in learning activities. Involving students communicates that you believe each student is important and that you expect all students to participate and learn. Third, represent the topics you teach as concretely as possible. Actual objects are most effective, and when they are unavailable, pictures are an acceptable alternative. Finally, give students as much practice as possible in using language, placing extra emphasis on important vocabulary. When students struggle with particular terms, or with putting their understanding into words, provide prompts and cues to scaffold their efforts.

4.1 Gender-role identity describes beliefs about appropriate characteristics and behaviors of the two sexes. It is important to teachers because a student's gender-role identity can influence how a student approaches different subjects. For example, when girls believe that math and science are male domains, or

when boys believe that nursing is a female domain, they are less likely to take related courses or attempt to excel in them.

4.2 Developing students' awareness of potential sources of gender bias is an important first step that teachers can take in eliminating it in classrooms. Communicating openly about gender issues and concerns, and about the problem of gender stereotypes, such as Marti Banes did with her students, is an effective beginning. Using nontraditional role models as she also did is a valuable additional step.

4.3 Treating boys and girls as equally as possible in learning activities is an important factor that you should attempt to apply as you conduct these activities. This means calling on boys and girls as equally as possible, keeping the level of questions similar for both, providing similar detail in feedback, and putting them in leadership and other roles on as equal a basis as possible.

5.1 Schools that promote resilience have high and uncompromising standards, promote strong personal bonds between teachers and students, have high order and structure, and encourage student participation in after-school activities.

5.2 Teachers who are effective in promoting resilience in students placed at risk form strong personal bonds with their students, interacting with them to get to know their families and lives. They maintain high expectations, use interactive teaching strategies, and emphasize success and mastery of content. They also motivate students through personal contacts and instructional support, and they attempt to link school to students' lives.

5.3 Effective teachers promote resilience in their students by creating and maintaining productive learning environments. They also combine high expectations with frequent feedback about learning progress. They use interactive teaching strategies that use high-quality examples; both of these help ensure student success. Finally, they stress student self-regulation and the acquisition of learning strategies.

CHAPTER 5

1.1 The Individuals with Disabilities Education Act (IDEA) was passed in 1975 to ensure a free and appropriate public education for all students with disabilities. Its provisions stipulate that these children be educated in a least restrictive environment (LRE) and be protected against discrimination in testing. The provisions further guarantee that parents are involved in the development of each child's individualized education program (IEP).

1.2 The FAPE provision of IDEA asserts that every student can learn and is entitled to a free and appropriate public education. Mainstreaming, the practice of moving students with exceptionalities from segregated settings into regular classrooms, was the first attempt to meet the requirements of FAPE. Over time, mainstreaming evolved into inclusion, a comprehensive approach to educating students with exceptionalities that advocates a total, systematic, and coordinated web of services.

1.3 Recent amendments to IDEA make states responsible for locating children who need special services and have strengthened requirements for nondiscriminatory assessment, due process, parents' involvement in IEPs, and the confidentiality of school records.

2.1 The most common learning problems that teachers in regular classrooms are likely to encounter include mild mental retardation, characterized by limitations in intellectual functioning and adaptive behavior; learning disabilities, which represent difficulties in specific areas, such as reading; attention-deficit/hyperactivity disorders, indicated by problems with maintaining attention; and behavior disorders, characterized by persistent, age-inappropriate behaviors. Communication disorders and visual and hearing disabilities also may exist.

2.2 Learning disabilities and mental retardation are similar in that both are disabilities that interfere with learning. In addition, both can result from a variety of causes, and they are related to some type of central nervous system dysfunction. They are different in that learning disabilities usually involve students with average intelligence or above and are often limited to a specific area such as math or reading, whereas intellectual handicaps involve a broad range of intellectual functioning.

2.3 Students with behavior disorders display serious and persistent age-inappropriate behaviors that result in social conflict, personal unhappiness, and often school failure. Externalizing behavior disorders are characterized by hyperactivity, defiance, hostility, and failure to respond to typical rules and consequences. Internalizing behavior disorders, by contrast, are characterized by social withdrawal, guilt, depression, and anxiety problems.

2.4 Communication disorders are exceptionalities that interfere with students' abilities to receive and to understand information from others and to express their own ideas or questions. Because much of the information and interaction in classrooms are verbal, communication disorders can disrupt the flow of communication and information.

3.1 Characteristics of students who are gifted and talented commonly include the ability to learn quickly and independently, advanced language and reading skills, effective learning and metacognitive strategies, and high motivation and achievement. Educators have broadened the definition of students who are gifted and talented to encompass not only students who score well on intelligence tests but also students who may have unique talents in specific areas such as art, music, or writing. The broadening of this definition means that teachers play a crucial role in helping to identify these students, whose talents may not show up on standardized tests.

3.2 Gifted and talented students are commonly identified through performance on standardized tests and nominations from teachers. However, because tests depend heavily on language, these scores are not always valid, particularly for cultural minorities. And teachers sometimes confuse conformity, neatness, and good behavior with being gifted and talented. Experts recommend the inclusion of—in addition to test scores and teacher recommendations—more flexible and less culturally dependent methods, such as creativity measures, tests of spatial ability, and peer and parent nominations when attempting to identify gifted and talented students.

3.3 Acceleration and enrichment are the two most common methods used for teaching gifted and talented students. Acceleration keeps the curriculum the same but allows students to move through it more quickly. Because it keeps curriculum the same, it is easier to implement, but it maintains a narrow focus on the regular curriculum and may cause developmental problems when younger students are mixed with older ones.

Enrichment, by contrast, alters curriculum and instruction by providing varied instruction. Though harder to implement, it provides students with more choice and flexibility.

4.1 Teachers are expected to fulfill the following roles when working with students having exceptionalities: First, they help identify students who may have exceptionalities. Experts now emphasize a shift away from the sole use of standardized tests toward the use of more ecologically valid measures, such as performance on classroom tasks and teacher observations. This makes teachers even more important in the process of identifying students with exceptionalities, because they are most familiar with students' classroom behavior and performance. Second, teachers adapt instruction to best meet individuals' needs. Third, teachers encourage acceptance of all students in their classes.

4.2 Research indicates that the teaching strategies that are effective for all students are also effective for learners with exceptionalities. This means that you teach in the same way that you teach all students, but you make an even greater effort with your students having exceptionalities. In addition, you should provide additional instructional scaffolding, such as working with these students one-on-one, to ensure their success. Homework, seat-work assignments, and reading may need to be adapted. You also should teach these students learning strategies, such as how to monitor their attention, take notes, summarize important points, and organize their time.

4.3 You can promote the social integration and growth of students with exceptionalities in the following ways: First, try to help all students understand and appreciate different forms of diversity, including exceptionalities. Second, help students with exceptionalities learn acceptable behaviors through direct instruction and modeling. Third, use interactive teaching strategies and peer interaction strategies such as peer tutoring and cooperative learning to promote social interaction.

Chapter 6

1.1 The class is a conditioned stimulus. It has become associated with the warmth and support of the teacher. The safe feeling is a conditioned response. It is a learned and involuntary response that is caused by the conditioned stimulus. These concepts were illustrated in the example with Damon and Mrs. Van Horn. Note also in this example that the conditioned response is similar to the unconditioned response.

1.2 In the example of learning to fear dogs as a result of being bitten, the unconditioned stimulus is *being bitten*. It is an event that causes pain and fear as the unconditioned response, which is unlearned (instinctive) and involuntary. Dogs have become associated with being bitten, so they are conditioned stimuli that cause fear as conditioned responses. The conditioned response is also involuntary, but learned.

Our fear is eliminated if we encounter a variety of dogs and are not again bitten. In this case, the conditioned stimuli (dogs) occur repeatedly in the absence of the unconditioned stimulus (being bitten), so that the conditioned response (fear) disappears (becomes extinct).

1.3 Our fear of big dogs illustrates the concept *generalization*. Big, dark-colored dogs are stimuli similar to the initial conditioned stimulus (the big black dog that bit us), so our fear has generalized to all large dogs. We discriminate, however, between large and small dogs, so we are not fearful of small dogs.

2.1 The concept being illustrated is positive reinforcement. You are presenting Judy with your admonishment, and her behavior is increasing (she goes off task sooner).

2.2 Rick's reducing the length of the assignment can be best explained with the concept of presentation punishment. His behavior is decreasing—he is decreasing the length of his tests—as a result of being presented with the students' complaints.

The students' complaining can best be explained with the concept of negative reinforcement. Their complaining is increasing—they complained sooner each time—as a result of Rick removing an aversive stimulus—some of the test material.

2.3 Because the beeper alarm depends on time, it is an interval schedule, and because it is unpredictable, it is a variable-interval schedule.

2.4 The displayed exercise is the antecedent; it induces the desired behavior. The students' conscientious work is the behavior, and Anita's compliments are the reinforcers.

3.1 The ineffectiveness of this practice can be explained by the concept of nonoccurrence of expected consequences. In cooperative learning groups, some students make a greater contribution than do others. Those who make the greater contribution expect to be reinforced by receiving a better grade than those who contributed less. When all members of the group receive the same grade, the expectation isn't met, so the nonoccurrence of the expected reinforcer can act as a punisher, making a similar contribution in the next cooperative learning activity less likely. The nonoccurrence of the expected reinforcer can also lead to resentment, a problem in some cooperative learning activities (Cohen, 1994).

3.2 Reciprocal causation describes the interdependence of the environment, personal factors (e.g., beliefs and expectations), and behavior. In Mike's case, the environment (the first instructor's class) influenced his behavior (he often drifted off), and his behavior influenced his expectations (he believed he wasn't learning). In turn, his behavior influenced the environment (he switched to Mr. Adams's class); the environment influenced a personal factor (he expected to be called on); and the personal factor influenced his behavior (he paid attention as a result of his expectation).

3.3 The benched player was punished, and being punished explains why that player didn't commit the foul again. The rest of the team was vicariously punished through the benching of the player who committed the foul. They expected to be benched for committing a similar foul, so they avoided doing so.

4.1 Because the speech was seen on videotape, it is a form of symbolic modeling. The modeling is likely to be effective because Martin Luther King, Jr., is a high-status model. For African-American students viewing the tape, the modeling would also be effective because of perceived similarity. Assuming that students knew how to be idealistic, the modeling outcome most likely would facilitate existing behaviors. If we assume that the students didn't know how to be idealistic, the outcome could involve learning new behaviors. While some emotional arousal is also possible, we don't have evidence for it in the vignette.

4.2 The person who first crossed the street is a direct model. You imitated the behavior of a live person instead of someone you saw on TV, in the movies, or in a book. The model's behavior weakened your inhibition about crossing the street against the red light. The modeling outcome is changing inhibitions instead of facilitating an existing behavior because crossing the street against a red light is socially unacceptable.

4.3 Your self-regulation began with a goal—to answer and understand each of the "Checking Your Understanding" questions in the chapter. You monitored your progress by checking off each question that you answered and understood. You completed a self-assessment by checking your answers against the feedback that appears on the Web, and you reinforced yourself with free time in an enjoyable activity when you met your goal.

5.1 Donna's manner with Carlos was the unconditioned stimulus, and the comfortable feeling her manner caused was the unconditioned response. Because she was consistently supportive with him, he gradually associated the classroom with her manner, so the classroom became the conditioned stimulus that resulted in similar comfortable feelings as conditioned responses.

5.2 Carlos was on a variable-ratio reinforcement schedule. He was reinforced after he had correctly completed two problems, so being reinforced depended on his behavior and not on time. He was praised again after he had done three more problems correctly, so he couldn't predict when he would be reinforced. These are the characteristics of a variable ratio schedule.

5.3 She used direct modeling when she demonstrated the solution to the problem after saying, "Watch what I do." She used cognitive modeling when she articulated her thinking as she demonstrated the solution.

5.4 A teacher who uses these clippings is attempting to capitalize on symbolic modeling, because the models appear in print form. If we assume that the students know how to accept personal responsibility, she is attempting to facilitate existing behaviors. If not, she is attempting to help the students learn new behaviors.

CHAPTER 7

1.1 The principles on which cognitive learning theories are based follow:

- *People are mentally active in their attempts to understand how the world works.* People instinctively strive to understand their experiences. They want the world to make sense, and as a result, they attempt to create understanding that makes sense to them.
- *Learning and development depend on learners' experiences.* This principle is evident in our everyday lives. Learning to drive is a simple example. If our only experience with driving involves vehicles with automatic transmissions, our ability to drive is less fully developed than it would be if we have experiences driving cars both with automatic transmissions and with stick shifts.
- *Learners construct—they do not record—knowledge in an attempt to make sense of those experiences.* Learners don't behave like tape recorders, keeping an exact copy of what they hear or read in their memories. Instead, they mentally modify the experiences so the experiences make sense. This is consistent with their instinctive drive to understand their world, which was explained in the description of the first principle.
- *Knowledge that is constructed depends on knowledge that learners already possess.* People construct understanding based on what they already know. For example, many people believe our summers (in the northern hemisphere) are warmer than our winters because we are closer to the Sun in the summer. (We, in fact, are slightly farther away, but the Sun's rays are more direct.) This idea is based on knowing that as we move closer to an open fire or a hot stove burner we get warmer.
- *Learning is enhanced in a social environment.* As people discuss ideas, they construct understanding that they wouldn't have acquired on their own. This is consistent with the old adage, "Two heads are better than one."
- *Learning requires practice and feedback.* People only learn to do well what they practice doing. And learning requires feedback that gives them information about the validity of their understanding.

1.2 This example illustrates the principle *Learning is enhanced in a social environment.* You have a problem, discuss it, and solve it during the course of the discussion.

1.3 Homework is a form of practice, so it best illustrates the principle *Learning requires practice and feedback.* "Properly designed" homework means that the homework is directly related to teachers' learning objectives and learning activities.

2.1 We can explain why Tanya might have become "kinda lost when Mr. Shelton was explaining all that yesterday," with the characteristics of working memory. It is likely that the cognitive load imposed by the information David presented exceeded Tanya's working memory capacity, so she was unable to process it, and as a result, she lost the information. The implication this has for teaching is that we should present only small amounts of information at a time and intersperse our presentations with questioning to encourage elaboration and reduce the cognitive load.

2.2 We can also use the characteristics of working memory to explain why a health club would prefer to advertise its telephone number as 2HEALTH rather than 243-2584. 2HEALTH has been chunked into two units, so 2HEALTH imposes a lighter load on working memory than do the numbers 243-2584. Because the load is lighter, the information is easier to encode and remember.

2.3 Procedural knowledge, as with declarative knowledge, is stored in long-term memory. An example in the opening case study that illustrates students being required to demonstrate procedural knowledge occurred when David said, "Today I want each group to identify a piece of information from the chart that can be explained with information from a different part of the chart, like why Mercury is so hot on one side and so cold on the other. Write the item of information, and then write your explanation immediately below it." Completing this writing assignment requires procedural knowledge. Developing procedural knowledge requires a great deal of practice and also strongly depends on declarative knowledge. In this case, declarative knowledge about the particular aspect of the solar system that they were examining was required.

3.1 The cognitive processes in our information processing system follow:

- *Attention.* Attention is the process of focusing on a particular stimulus or group of stimuli and ignoring the myriad of other stimuli that exist. The idea of "white noise" relates to the concept of attention. We are often not aware of "white noise," such as the whisper of an air conditioner, until we're made aware of its existence, that is, until we attend to it.
- *Perception.* Perception is the meaning we attach to stimuli. It is illustrated by the fact that we commonly see two people have the same experience but interpret it very differently.
- *Rehearsal.* Rehearsal is the process of repeating information over and over without altering its form, such as memorizing names, dates, and other facts, like $8 \times 7 = 56$.
- *Encoding.* Encoding is the process of representing information in long-term memory. While rehearsal focuses on memorized information, encoding attempts to make information meaningful by connecting it to other information already in long-term memory.
- *Retrieval.* Retrieval is the process of pulling information from long-term memory back into working memory for further processing. Retrieval is an essential process, because constructing new knowledge depends on the knowledge that already exists in long-term memory.

3.2 When a teacher asks, "What do we mean by a moral dilemma?" she is checking her students' perceptions because she is attempting to determine what the idea means to them. The most effective way of checking students' perceptions is to simply ask them—ask them what they see or notice, or ask them what the information in a picture, term, passage, map, graph, or whatever is displayed means to them.

3.3 Rehearsal is the cognitive process involved in acquiring the math facts, and encoding is the cognitive process involved in solving the problems. Rehearsal and encoding are similar in that they are both ways of getting information into long-term memory. (Rehearsal can also be used to retain information in working memory.) Rehearsal and encoding differ in that rehearsal involves repeating information in basically the same form (e. g., repeating $7 \times 9 = 63$ over and over), whereas encoding is the process of representing information in long-term memory in a meaningful way, which is required for solving problems.

4.1 Metacognition is our awareness of, and control over, our cognitive processes. Metacognition regulates the way we process information. For instance, if an individual is aware that she is not fully comprehending the information she is reading, and if she stops periodically to summarize what she has read, she is demonstrating metacognition. Because she is metacognitive, she will process the information she is reading more efficiently.

4.2 Yes, stopping and going back to the top of the page and rereading one of the sections is an example of metacognition. You realize that you haven't understood the section (which is knowledge [awareness] of your memory strategy), and you go back and reread (which is exercising control over your memory strategy).

4.3 You are more metacognitive about your note taking than is your friend. You are continually making decisions about what information is most important to write down, which demonstrates knowledge of, and control over, your thinking about note taking.

On the other hand, if your friend believes writing everything down works the best for him, he is also being metacognitive, because he is demonstrating an awareness of what works for him, and he is exercising control over the process. This illustrates how important it is to continually think about the study strategies you use, and this helps us understand why students who are metacognitive achieve higher than those who aren't.

5.1 The principles for applying information processing theory in classrooms follow:
- *Begin lessons with an activity that attracts attention.* Because information processing begins with attention, beginning lessons with an attention getter is a logical first step.
- *Conduct frequent reviews to activate students' prior knowledge and check perceptions.* Perception immediately follows attention in the information processing model, so checking perception is essential. Also, when students attempt to make new information meaningful, they connect it to their prior knowledge. Reviews help them retrieve their prior knowledge, which aids meaningful encoding.

- *Proceed in short steps, and represent content both visually and verbally to reduce cognitive load.* Proceeding in short steps gives students time to encode information, which reduces cognitive load. Representing information both verbally and visually helps capitalize on the dual-processing capability of working memory and the dual-coding characteristics of long-term memory.
- *Help students make information meaningful, and aid encoding through organization, imagery, elaboration, and activity.* Teachers can capitalize on organization with aids such as hierarchies, matrices, and outlines; imagery with pictures, models, and other visual aids; elaboration by presenting and asking students to supply examples; and activity by developing lessons with questioning, putting students into groups, and other learning activities that put students in active roles.
- *Model and encourage metacognition.* When teachers share their thinking with students, they are modeling their own metacognition, and encouraging students to stop and ask themselves questions also encourages metacognition.

5.2 David's transparencies and matrix most nearly help illustrate the third principle (proceed in short steps, and represent content both visually and verbally to reduce cognitive load) and fourth principle (help students make information meaningful, and aid encoding through organization, imagery, elaboration, and activity). His transparencies and matrix represent aspects of his content in visual form, which applies a feature of the third principle. The transparencies also capitalize on imagery, and his matrix is a form of organization, which capitalizes on features of the fourth principle.

5.3 The demonstration would be an effective attention getter, so it capitalizes on the first principle (begin lessons with an activity that attracts attention).

5.4 When the teacher says, "Yesterday, we talked about the characteristics of Haiku. What are those characteristics?" she is reviewing what the students have already learned, which applies the second principle (conduct frequent reviews to activate students' prior knowledge and check their perceptions).

CHAPTER 8

1.1 Cognitive constructivism is based on the view that knowledge construction is an internal, individual process, whereas social constructivism is grounded in the position that knowledge construction first occurs in the social environment and then is appropriated and internalized by individuals.

1.2 Suzanne's thinking better illustrates cognitive constructivism. She had a clear (to her) schema that guided her thinking (her belief that keeping the number of tiles equal on each side of the fulcrum would make the beam balance), and she brought this view to the learning activity. It didn't result from her interaction with her peers.

1.3 First, all the students were actively involved in the learning activity. Second, the students worked together to help each other learn, and third, the lesson involved high levels of student–student interaction. In addition, Jenny emphasized the process when she directed her students to explain to their peers why they thought their solutions would work.

We don't have evidence from the case study to determine whether or not diversity of thinking was respected.

The concept of a *community of learners* is more nearly grounded in social constructivism than in cognitive constructivism. It is based on the idea that knowledge is first constructed in a social environment and is then appropriated and internalized by individuals.

2.1 "Learners construct knowledge that makes sense to them" is the characteristic best illustrated by Suzanne's initial conclusion. We are virtually certain that she didn't get the conclusion from a teacher or something she read; she constructed it on her own. We don't have evidence about her prior knowledge, and we don't know about her prior social interaction or real-world experiences.

2.2 "New learning depends on current understanding" is the characteristic that is best illustrated. When people saw the Sun rise in the morning and move across the sky, they assumed they were stationary and the Sun was moving. This was similar to most of their experiences observing moving objects, so they used these experiences as the basis for their belief.

2.3 Analyzing written passages is one effective context for learning the rules of grammar. Written passages are more nearly real-world examples than are sentences or words in isolation. Having students actually use the rules of grammar in their own writing would be even more effective.

3.1 The concept *noun* should be easier to learn than the concept *culture,* because it obeys a well-defined rule; it is the name of a person, place, or thing. And the characteristics are more concrete than are the characteristics of the concept *culture.* The rule-driven theory best explains how people learn the concept *noun.* The concept *culture* most likely is constructed from a set of exemplars.

3.2 An additional example you would want to show for the concept *reptile* is a reptile such as a sea turtle or a water snake, so that students learn that some reptiles live in water. A frog would be an important nonexample, because, although it's an amphibian, students often think it's a reptile.

3.3 With respect to adjectives, *exciting* is probably the most important example, because it follows instead of precedes the noun. *Running, football,* and *home* are also important, because students think that words ending in *ing* are verbs, and *football* and *home* are commonly nouns.

With respect to adverbs, *soon* is probably the most important example, because it is an adverb but doesn't end in *ly.*

This example also illustrates the need for social interaction. The students would need to realize, through discussion, that *exciting, running, football,* and *home* are all adjectives, because they describe nouns, and that *soon* is an adverb because it describes how the friends met. Simply explaining this information to the students would not be likely to result in conceptual change.

4.1 "Provide a variety of examples and representations of content" is the suggestion best illustrated. Each correct solution on the beam balance contained all the information the students needed to construct an understanding of the principle.

4.2 "Connect content to the real world" is the suggestion best illustrated. Studying the rules in the context of a written passage is a more nearly real-world task than studying the rules in the context of isolated sentences. Having the students write their own essays using possessives would be even more authentic.

4.3 Effective assessments give teachers insights into students' thinking. This means that the reasoning students use to arrive at their answers is at least as important as the answers themselves.

5.1 Judy taught concepts. *Longitude* and *latitude* are concepts. Each is a category with well-defined characteristics.

5.2 Judy had her students measure both lines of latitude and lines of longitude at different places on the globe. The students could then see that the lines of latitude had different lengths, but the lines of longitude were the same length. Observable evidence is essential for preventing or changing misconceptions.

5.3 Jenny applied some of the principles quite effectively and others less effectively. For instance, the first principle says "Provide a variety of high-quality examples and other representations of content." Further, ideal examples contain all the information learners need to construct their knowledge. The example Jenny used didn't contain all the information the students needed to construct their knowledge of balance beams. Molly and Drexel were able to solve the problem because they possessed prior knowledge that Suzanne and Tad didn't have. As a result, Jenny's example wasn't effective. In addition, Jenny used only one example, the beam balance. Additional authentic examples, like a teeter-totter, would have broadened the schema that students were constructing.

Also, while social interaction occurred in the group, Suzanne and Tad remained passive, so the discussion didn't change their thinking. It wasn't until the interview, when they were more cognitively active, that they constructed their knowledge of the balance beam principle.

Jenny presented the students with a real-world problem, but she tended to rely on explanations to help students understand the principle. Her assessment, which she administered the next day, was an integral part of her lesson.

CHAPTER 9

1.1 This is an ill-defined problem. You are probably not completely clear as to what a "satisfying relationship" should be, and it's unlikely that you have a clear idea of how a satisfying relationship can be achieved, even if you did know what it meant.

A means–ends analysis would first define a "satisfying" relationship. Improved communication would likely be one aspect. Then, a strategy for improving communication could be devised, such as making it a point to always actively listen to what your partner is saying. Strategies for reaching goals when problems are ill-defined can vary greatly.

1.2 Deliberate practice is most likely to help students use drawing analogies effectively. As students gain experience, they acquire a large number of examples that they can use as analogies to solve new problems, and the more they practice, the more efficiently they'll be able to use the examples.

1.3 Laura's assignment illustrated deliberate practice in three ways. First, her assignment focused on a real problem—the strategy for finding the area of their classroom—which was likely to increase their motivation. Second, she gave her students the chance to perform a task similar to the one they worked on in class. Third, she monitored students and gave them feedback throughout the process.

Although this would be a well-defined problem for adults or students with problem-solving expertise, it was an ill-defined problem for Laura's students. Although the goal was clear, her students had misconceptions about differences between area and perimeter, and they were uncertain about how to reach the goal.

2.1 Ruiz's strategy is likely to be the most effective because he is demonstrating the highest level of metacognition in his approach. He is making conscious decisions about what information is most important to highlight. Will's strategy is likely to be least effective, because passive highlighting requires little cognitive effort and is the least metacognitive. (Even though he is physically "active" in highlighting whole chapters, he is cognitively passive, because he isn't thinking about the process.) While Alexie's strategy isn't particularly effective, at least she is thinking about which sentence in the paragraph best captures the topic. By highlighting most of the information, Will is avoiding decisions about what is important.

2.2 No, reading the chapter carefully in an effort to understand the content would not be described as effective strategic learning. In fact, it isn't strategic at all. Strategic learning is considered to be the application of techniques to enhance performance on a learning task. While you are attempting to read carefully and understand the content, you are not applying any specific technique that is designed to enhance your performance.

2.3 Comprehension monitoring is the process of checking to see if we understand what we have read or heard. When you summarize or ask yourself elaborative questions, you are involved in this process. In contrast, taking notes is primarily a mechanism to capture and store information you hear in a lecture; it doesn't involve checking to see if you understand the information. Using text signals is a mechanism to make information you study more meaningful by trying to understand the way it is organized. It also doesn't help you check to see if you understand the content.

3.1 Critical thinking can be defined as an individual's ability and inclination to make and assess conclusions based on evidence. Its elements include the following:
- *Domain-specific knowledge.* As with all areas of learning, domain-specific knowledge is essential.

- *Component skills.* Component skills are the cognitive processes individuals use to make and assess their conclusions.
- *Metacognition.* Effective critical thinkers are aware of their thought processes and why they're using these processes.
- *Motivation.* Motivation is the primary factor that influences individuals' inclination to think critically.

3.2 In responding to Laura's question, "How do we know we must subtract?" Adam responded, "There isn't any carpet there." His response provided evidence for the conclusion that they must subtract, so he was confirming conclusions with facts.

Paige, in concluding that the width was 5 feet, was identifying irrelevant information. She recognized that the 2-foot width of the sink counter was irrelevant.

Anya, in explaining the 12 times 3, recognized an unstated assumption. Laura gave the students the 12×3 in the worked example as a conclusion, so Anya didn't form any conclusion of her own. Rather, she explained where the conclusion came from by recognizing the unstated assumption.

3.3 Francisco's comment, "We found a pattern in the data," best illustrates metacognition. He recognized that they had previously found a pattern; his comment didn't describe the pattern itself.

4.1 With respect to transfer, the students are least likely to identify a bat as a mammal, because it is least similar to the other examples. Similarity between the two learning situations is the factor that is best illustrated in this case.

4.2 Based on the factors that affect transfer, your efforts were not effective. First, pictures of the mammals, while better than written words, are not as high quality as a live mammal, such as a student's hamster, would be. A combination of one or two live mammals, such as the hamster and the students themselves, combined with pictures, would be much higher quality. Second, the variety of examples is inadequate. Better variety would include a bat, so they see that some mammals fly; a dolphin or some other mammal that lives in water, so the students don't conclude that only fish live in water; and perhaps an egg-laying mammal, such as a duck-billed platypus. Finally, we have no evidence of whether or not the examples were presented in any realistic context.

4.3 Choice "b" is the most effective example. It is the only one that actually illustrates the concept. Choice "a" only illustrates a thoughtful look, and the words, "The girl is experiencing internal conflict," provide little critical information. It could even lead to the misconception that whenever a person looks thoughtful, they're experiencing internal conflict. Choice "c" is only a definition. Definitions are abstract, and many students can't do much more than memorize definitions. Definitions, alone, lead to superficial learning.

CHAPTER 10

1.1 Based on the information in the case study, it appears that Susan is high in intrinsic motivation (at least in Kathy Brewster's history class). Her comment, "It bothers me when I don't get something, and sometimes it's even fun," suggests that she does her homework because she feels that it's worthwhile for its own sake. Her comment about homework, "I don't mind it that much," doesn't give us a clear idea about whether she also is influenced by grades or approval (extrinsic motivation).

1.2 The primary difference between the two teachers' approaches is that the teacher who is attempting to stimulate students' motivation to learn will emphasize learning, whereas a person focusing on extrinsic motivation will focus on performance. The former will emphasize understanding of the content, and the latter will reward students for their performance on some activity related to the content, such as a quiz or an assignment.

1.3 In her exchange with Harvey, Kathy made two points that can increase motivation to learn. First, she emphasized that he was becoming a very good writer, and second, she reminded him that being a skilled writer "will help us in everything we do in life," which echoed the rationale the students often heard from her.

2.1 One criticism of behaviorist approaches to motivation is philosophical; critics contend that schools should promote intrinsic motivation and the use of rewards sends students the wrong message about learning.

A second criticism is based on research indicating that the use of rewards can decrease interest in intrinsically motivating activities.

The third is based on the fact that behaviorism provides an incomplete explanation for motivation. Behaviorism addresses only observable behaviors and ignores cognitions that have to do with expectations or beliefs. Research indicates that students' interpretations of rewards are more important than the rewards themselves.

2.2 Teachers can use rewards to increase motivation to learn if the rewards are based on genuine accomplishment. Research indicates that rewards reflecting accomplishment suggest to learners that their competence is increasing, and perceptions of increasing competence increase intrinsic motivation.

2.3 First, as you saw in exercise 2.2, rewards that communicate to students that their competence is increasing can increase student motivation to learn. Second, teachers can use rewards to involve students in important tasks for which they may not initially have an intrinsic interest. Then, once involved, and if they succeed, their motivation to learn is likely to increase.

3.1 Researchers developed humanistic motivation theory as a reaction to the "reductionist" aspects of both psychoanalysis, which "reduces" people to responses to unconscious drives, and behaviorism, which "reduces" people to responses to the environment. Humanistic views of motivation are based on the premise that people are motivated to fulfill their total potential as human beings. Humanistic views emphasize the "whole person"—physical, social, emotional, and intellectual—and one's drive for "self-actualization," or the fulfilling of one's full potential.

3.2 Based on Maslow's work, the first statement is true. We would conclude that people with high needs for aesthetic appreciation have high self-esteem. Aesthetic appreciation

is a growth need, and, according to Maslow, in order to be at the level of growth needs, all the deficiency needs must be met, so the need for self-esteem must have been met.

Based on Maslow's work, the second statement is false. According to him, the growth needs are never "met" in the same sense that deficiency needs are. In fact, growth needs expand as people have growth experiences.

3.3 If students are hungry, their survival needs are not being met, and survival is a deficiency need. According to Maslow, until deficiency needs are met, people will not move to growth needs, such as intellectual achievement, which is where motivation to do academic work lies.

Similarly, according to Maslow, safety is the second of the deficiency needs, and again, if it isn't met, people will not move to higher needs.

3.4 Rogers would recommend that you treat her with unconditional positive regard. This means her innate worth as a person hasn't changed. However, you clearly communicate that her disruptions are unacceptable and will not be tolerated, and you do what is necessary to stop the disruptions, including applying consequences if necessary. Research indicates that one of the most important indicators of caring is respect. And, one of the most effective ways to demonstrate that you respect students is to hold them to high standards, both for academics and acceptable behavior (Stipek, 2002).

In keeping with the idea of unconditional positive regard, the next day, you're back to "square one." It's as if the disruption the day before never happened.

4.1 Cognitive motivation theory is grounded in the assumption that people are motivated to establish a sense of order and predictability in their lives (Piaget's concept of equilibrium). The child is responding to this need. When the story sounds the same each time it is read, the child's need for order and predictability is maintained. If it sounds different, his equilibrium is disrupted, and he is motivated to reestablish it. Hearing the story as it has always been read is the easiest way to remain at equilibrium.

4.2 In their conversation, Kathy said, "Yes, but look how good you're getting at writing. I think you hit a personal best on your last paper. You're becoming a very good writer." Harvey then responded, "Yeh, yeh, I know, . . . and being good writers will help us in everything we do in life," suggesting that Kathy had emphasized the utility value of writing as an important skill in the world outside of school.

Utility value is one of the components that increases task value according to expectancy × value theory. This means that students are motivated to learn about a topic if they believe the topic will help them be successful in some future activity that is important to them.

4.3 A variety of possibilities exist for each of the goals. The essential features of effective goals are that they're specific, immediate (close at hand), and moderately challenging. Given these characteristics, a modification for the first goal might be, "To answer and understand all the items on all of the practice quizzes for each chapter (in this class, for instance)."

For getting in shape, a more effective goal would be, "To jog a minimum of 9 miles a week (e.g., jogging 3 miles, 3 times a week).

For losing weight, a better goal would be, "To limit calorie consumption to 1,500 calories a day."

4.4 Because Armondo attributed his success to luck, his emotional reaction is likely to be neutral. Because luck is external, he won't feel the pride that attributing his success to either ability or effort would cause. (Because he was successful, he also won't feel the shame that results from failure that is attributed to lack of ability, or guilt that people feel when they attribute failure to lack of effort.) Because his success resulted from luck, he won't expect similar results in the future, his future effort is likely to decrease, and, as a result, his achievement is also likely to decrease.

5.1 Based on self-determination theory, the second statement is better. It communicates that the student's competence is increasing. The first statement can be perceived as the teacher's believing that the student lacks competence, because he or she must work so hard to accomplish the task.

5.2 First, Kathy began her lesson with a concrete, personalized example (their "crusade" to have extracurricular activities reinstated in the school). Second, the students were highly involved in her lesson, and third, she modeled effort attributions when she said, "It's hard for me too, when I'm studying and trying to put together new ideas, but if I hang in, I always feel like I can get it." Each increases students' perceptions of autonomy. Increasing students' perceptions of autonomy is an application of self-determination theory.

5.3 Yes, by all means you should provide the help. The information in this section refers to unsolicited offers of help. You should provide only the amount of help required to ensure that the student makes progress essentially on his own, however, so he perceives himself as responsible for making progress. The student is more likely to have confidence about his or her ability, which suggests that he or she is a high achiever. Low achievers are sometimes reluctant to ask for help, because they perceive that doing so implies low ability or lack of competence. High achievers are less likely to perceive needing help as an indicator of low ability.

6.1 According to self-worth theory, people's sense of self-worth is linked to perceptions of high ability, because ability is so strongly valued in our society. By emphasizing and modeling incremental views of ability, teachers communicate that ability can be increased with effort. This increases the likelihood that students will value and expend effort in an effort to increase their ability and, with it, their self-worth.

6.2 Partying the night before an exam is a self-handicapping behavior. If he does poorly on the exam, he can attribute the performance to the fact that he partied, and he can suggest that he would have done well if he hadn't partied. This would be an attempt to preserve perceptions of high ability, so that his self-worth wouldn't be threatened.

6.3 The relaxation exercises do nothing to increase her understanding of the content. This is the most likely reason that she is unsuccessful, which leads to her anxiety. A more effective approach would be to adopt study strategies, such as summarizing and self-questioning, that would lead to a more thorough understanding of the topic. As her understanding increases, her success will also increase, and, in time; her anxiety will decrease.

CHAPTER 11

1.1 Learning-focused classrooms emphasize effort, mastery of content, continuous improvement, and meeting challenges. Teachers in learning-focused classrooms design activities to increase learning and view mistakes as a normal part of the learning process.

Performance-focused classrooms emphasize high grades and competition among students. Teachers in performance-focused classrooms design assessment for evaluation and as a basis for determining grades, and treat mistakes as a basis for concern and anxiety.

1.2 Based on the characteristics of a learning-focused classroom, the comment, "Excellent job on the last test, everyone. More than half the class got an A or a B," is not appropriate and would not be recommended. It promotes a performance focus rather than a learning focus by comparing learners' results to each other. It also defines success as getting high grades instead of mastery of the content or continuous improvement.

2.1 Strategies for promoting learning self-regulation typically involve setting and monitoring goals. Getting students to commit to the goals is an essential aspect of the process. Sam promoted commitment to goals by emphasizing the relationship between personal responsibility and learning, soliciting student input into class procedures, providing examples of responsible and irresponsible behavior, modeling responsibility, and providing a chart that allowed students to monitor progress toward their goals.

2.2 Sam recognized that his students would initially be externally regulated, which meant that they would behave responsibly to receive rewards for meeting their responsibility and learning goals and avoid being punished (e.g., spending "quiet time" alone) if they failed to meet their social responsibility goals.

His students would demonstrate an advance in self-regulation if, at a later point in the year, they decided to set and meet social responsibility and learning goals because they believed that meeting the goals would help them get better grades. This would still illustrate extrinsic motivation, but it would be an advance in self-regulation.

2.3 A controlling strategy for promoting self-regulation would involve the immediate use of punishers for failing to behave responsibly, such as being punished for failing to be in their seats when the bell rang. Instead, Sam gave examples of logical consequences that Josh and Andy, the students in his vignettes, experienced as a result of behaving responsibly compared to behaving irresponsibly.

3.1 Teachers who increase students' motivation to learn believe they can increase student learning regardless of their teaching conditions or students' backgrounds (*high personal teaching efficacy*). They *care* about their students as people, and they are committed to their students' learning. They *model* desirable characteristics, *demonstrate enthusiasm* by communicating their own genuine interest in the topics they teach, and *create positive expectations* for their students.

3.2 High-efficacy teachers believe that their efforts to help students learn make a difference, whereas low-efficacy teachers believe that their efforts are largely in vain. Because low-efficacy teachers don't believe that they make a difference anyway, trying something new—according to their beliefs—is not likely to matter. As a result, they are not inclined to try new curriculum materials or strategies.

3.3 The most effective way to communicate your enthusiasm to students is to model your own genuine interest in the topics you're teaching. Because people tend to imitate behaviors they observe in others, if students see that you are truly interested in the topics you're teaching, the likelihood that they also will be interested increases.

3.4 Teachers call on students who, they expect, will be able to answer their questions. If they don't believe that a student can answer, they are less likely to call on the student.

Two factors come into play. First, a student's answering the question is reinforcing for the teacher. Second, if a student can't answer, the teacher should provide prompts or cues that will help the student give an acceptable answer. Thinking of these prompts and cues during the course of a lesson presents a heavy cognitive load for the teacher.

4.1 Based on the discussion of the climate variables in the model for promoting student motivation, the teacher's approach would be unlikely to increase students' motivation to learn, even if they succeed. First, the task presents a minimal level of *challenge,* and no rationale for the task is evident. So, based on the *task* category in the TARGET model together with the *challenge* and *task comprehension* categories in the model for promoting student motivation, the teacher's approach is unlikely to increase students' motivation to learn.

4.2 The two variables in the model for promoting student motivation that the teacher is attempting to address are *order and safety* and *task comprehension*. Enforcing a rule that prevents students from making sarcastic or demeaning comments promotes a sense of emotional security, and providing a rationale is consistent with task comprehension.

4.3 The TARGET model describes ideal *tasks* as optimally challenging, so this relates directly to the *challenge* variable in the model for promoting student motivation. The TARGET model also describes tasks so that students see their relevance and meaning, and part of the definition of *task attraction* states that the students have "an understanding of why the task is important and worthwhile."

The TARGET model describes *authority* as shared, and the model supports autonomy. The model for promoting student motivation defines *order and safety* as "a climate variable intended to create a predictable learning environment that supports learner autonomy and a sense of physical and emotional security," so both models emphasize autonomy.

The TARGET model emphasizes *recognition* for all students who make learning progress, and in the model for promoting student motivation, "success means continuous learning progress. . . . Praise and other rewards should communicate that competence is increasing. Mistakes

don't mean that students aren't successful; rather, they're a normal part of the learning process."

In the TARGET model, *grouping* fosters a community of learners, and the introduction to the *classroom climate variables* defines a positive classroom climate as follows: "the teacher and students work together as a community of learners, a learning environment in which the teacher and all the students work together to help everyone achieve."

The TARGET model describes *evaluation* as a mechanism to promote learning, and suggestions for promoting success in the model for promoting student motivation include "making assessment an integral part of the teaching learning process, and providing detailed feedback about learning progress."

The TARGET model describes *time* as encompassing the workload, pace of instruction, and amount allocated for completing work. The description of *task comprehension* in the model for promoting student motivation includes the statement, "Task comprehension also includes decisions about time allocated to tasks, pace of instruction, and provision for extra help if it is needed."

5.1 Kathy applied introductory focus in her lesson on the Crusades by having the students imagine that they had left Lincoln High School and that it was taken over by people who believed that extracurricular activities should be eliminated. She then used the suggestion of them being on a "crusade" to change the school officials' minds as an analogy for the actual Crusades.

5.2 The best example of the way DeVonne personalized her lesson was by asking the students if Mrs. Sapp (the school principal) was an arthropod.

5.3 Learning-oriented feedback provides information about existing understanding or information that can be used to increase understanding. For instance, "Your paragraph needs to include at least two supporting details for your conclusion. Your second sentence is the only supporting detail in your paragraph" is an example of learning-oriented feedback about the quality of written paragraphs.

Performance-oriented feedback describes grades or comparisons among students. Examples include statements such as, "Well done. You got all the points on your essay," or "There were five As and four Bs on the last quiz."

CHAPTER 12

1.1 Classroom management, the complexities of classrooms, and learning and motivation are interrelated. First, classroom management and classroom complexity are related in that many unpredictable events occur at the same time, and teachers must respond to them immediately and in public view. Well-managed classrooms make accommodating the complexities of classrooms easier.

Classroom management and learning and motivation are related in that students are more motivated to learn and learn more in well-managed classrooms.

1.2 Although Judy addressed aspects of each of the characteristics with her beginning-of-class exercise, she addressed the multidimensional and simultaneous characteristics of classrooms most directly. Doing routine activities, such as taking roll and handing back papers, and conducting learning activities are two different classroom events, and Judy conducted them simultaneously. Being able to conduct them simultaneously reduced the opportunity for off-task behavior.

1.3 The suggestion to call on all students as equally as possible most closely relates to *engaged time.* Teachers call on students to involve them in learning activities, or in other words, to engage them. Being called on doesn't ensure that students will succeed, so academic learning time isn't as directly addressed.

2.1 *Organizing for instruction* is the aspect of planning for effective classroom management that is best illustrated in the example with Donnell Alexander and Vicki Williams. Having materials ready is one of the characteristics of effective organization, and it is important for classroom management because it eliminates "dead" time, when students can become disruptive.

2.2 As students mature, they're less likely to touch, poke, or grab at each other in the same way that is common with younger students. The differences in the rules reflect the teachers' abilities to take developmental differences into account in creating them.

2.3 Engaged time is the time students spend actively involved in learning activities. In a whole-class discussion, for example, this means that the students are paying attention. In the case of seat work, this means that the students are on task. Darren, Rachel, and Deborah were all off task during Judy's lesson, so her engaged time was less than her instructional time. Engaged time being equal to instructional time would mean that all students are paying attention all the time, which in the real world never occurs. Our goal as teachers is to have engaged time be as nearly equal to instructional time as possible.

3.1 First, the letter contributed to the creation of a positive classroom climate. Involving students in preparing a letter home, and asking students to write a letter to parents inviting them to the open house, contributed to their developing responsibility. Second, her efforts contributed to a positive classroom climate by making all students in her class feel welcome and important. Eventually, reaching the first two goals would contribute to reaching the third—maximizing time and opportunity for learning.

3.2 Time is a unique resource in that everyone has the same amount of it. So, the way people choose to allocate their time is a direct indicator of their priorities. When teachers choose to allocate some of their time to calling parents, it communicates to parents that the child is important.

3.3 Parents who are members of minorities sometimes feel a sense of alienation; they feel as if their children are not welcome or wanted in school. Communication with the parents can help dispel this perception.

4.1 An appropriate I-message that a teacher could use in responding to a student's talking might be as follows: "Talking interrupts my teaching, this makes me lose my train of thought, and I get annoyed when my train of thought is disrupted." It addressed the behavior (talking), describes the effect on the sender (makes me lose my train of thought), and describes the feelings generated in the sender (annoyance when my train of thought is disrupted).

4.2 Having the student wash the door is the preferred consequence. It is logical; if you spit on the door and make it dirty, you should wash it. Being put in detention is a punishment, but no logical link between the behavior and the consequence would exist.

4.3 Verbal–nonverbal congruence, I-messages, and logical consequences are "cognitive" interventions because they all emphasize understanding. Each attempts to help students understand what is important and why.

5.1 You are required to respond. If possible, you should break up the fight. If that isn't possible, you must immediately seek help. Your first obligation is to protect the victim and yourself.

5.2 The first step is to stop the fight, if possible. That's why we suggest yelling, slamming a chair on the floor, or some other act that startles the students. If the fight doesn't stop, immediately seek help.

5.3 The focus of a long-term cognitive approach to bullying and other acts of aggression is an attempt to help the aggressors understand the effects of their actions on others. Aggressive students often come from homes where aggression is modeled, or they may have peers who also model aggression. As a result, they don't understand that this behavior is inappropriate, and they don't understand how this behavior affects others.

CHAPTER 13

1.1 The four essential steps involved in planning for instruction consist of the following:

1. Select topics. Standards, curriculum guides, textbooks, and the teacher's professional knowledge are sources that help make this decision.

2. Prepare learning objectives. Though the format for preparing learning objectives varies, the important aspect of preparing learning objectives is being clear about what learning outcomes are desired.

3. Prepare and organize learning activities. A task analysis can be helpful in this process, which includes identifying the components of the topic, sequencing them, and preparing and ordering examples.

4. Prepare assessments. This means that assessments are created during planning instead of after learning activities have been completed.

1.2 When teachers' planning involves standards, interpreting the standard is an additional step, and it precedes the other steps. Descriptions of standards vary; some are very specific, whereas others are quite general. When working with a standard described in general terms, teachers must first make a decision about what the standard means, then follow the rest of the planning steps, that is, plan learning activities and assessments.

1.3 This objective would be best classified into the cell where metacognitive knowledge intersects with analyze. The tendency to look for relevant and irrelevant information in all the topics suggests metacognition, and determining what is relevant and irrelevant involves analysis.

2.1 The case studies that introduce each chapter are our attempts to provide introductory focus for the chapters. They are intended to attract your attention by beginning the chapter with a realistic look at classrooms. Then, the cases provide an umbrella under which the content of the chapter is developed.

2.2 The two essential teaching skills that are best illustrated in each chapter are feedback and review and closure. For example, here, in Appendix B, you receive feedback for all of the "Checking Your Understanding" questions. When you go to the book's Website, you receive feedback for all of the "Knowledge Extensions" questions and for the "Praxis Practice" questions that appear at the end of each chapter. In addition, you have access to feedback for the exercises in the Student Study Guide and the Practice Quizzes that appear on the Website.

In the "Meeting Your Learning Objectives" section of each chapter, you receive a review of the chapter's contents, which are aligned with the learning objectives.

We also attempt to model effective communication in our writing. We try to use clear language; to emphasize important points with figures, tables, bulleted lists, and margin definitions; and to develop the chapters in thematic ways that represent connected discourse.

2.3 Students learn more from feedback to an incorrect response because it helps correct misconceptions. To illustrate, your instructor asks you a question, you answer correctly, and you receive positive feedback in the form of an acknowledgment of the answer or praise. All you learned from the feedback was that your answer was correct.

On the other hand, if you answer a question, and the answer is incorrect, feedback that provides corrective information increases your understanding by correcting a misconception or providing additional information.

3.1 The introduction phase of *direct instruction, lecture discussion,* and *guided discovery* is important because it capitalizes on the essential teaching skill, introductory focus. Introductory focus attracts students' attention and provides a conceptual umbrella for the lesson.

We can also explain the need for the introduction phase using information processing theory. In thinking about information processing theory, we see that attention is where processing begins. If learners don't attend to the information, it is lost, so attracting and maintaining attention is essential. The introduction phase helps meet this need.

3.2 The presentation phase of direct instruction is most important to ensuring successful independent practice, and it is in this phase that we see the most difference between effective and ineffective teachers. If the presentation phase is ineffective, both guided practice and independent practice will be difficult and confusing. Remember, independent practice strengthens earlier understanding; it does not teach the skill. If teachers have to provide a great deal of explanation during independent practice, error rates increase and student achievement decreases.

3.3 If instruction is well done, the teacher's objectives are clear and the learning activity is aligned with the objectives. Also, the teacher carefully monitors students' thinking throughout and intervenes soon enough to prevent misconceptions, but not so soon that opportunities for constructing understanding are reduced.

3.4 She introduced cooperative learning quite effectively. Her task was short and simple, it was clear and specific (write observations on paper), the written observations provided a product, and she monitored the students' work. We have no evidence about them moving into and out of the groups, nor the amount of time they had to work.

4.1 First, effective assessments are aligned with a teacher's objectives and learning activity. Second, effective assessments give teachers information about students' thinking, as you saw with Scott's item that asked the students to explain what made the papers go together.

4.2 *Feedback* is the essential teaching skill that teachers must use in conjunction with assessments if the assessments are to increase student learning. This means that teachers should always thoroughly discuss assessment items after scoring and returning them to students, which allows students to revise and elaborate on their thinking.

4.3 The primary problem with the assessment (and the learning activity) is that it is not aligned with his learning objective. His objective was for them to use figurative language in their writing. But we saw no evidence that they practiced writing. Giving them examples, and having them identify examples is an effective first step, but if the assessment is aligned with the objective, his assessment must require them to write.

CHAPTER 14

1.1 In thinking of technology historically, the hardware view was more prominent. Educators viewed the chalkboard, overhead, and other aids primarily as tools that teachers used to increase learning.

1.2 Jim primarily holds a hardware view of technology. In focusing on the computers, he thinks of technology as a set of instruments or machines.

1.3 Bill's students were involved in a process as they attempted to determine what time Jasper should leave for home and whether or not he had enough fuel. The videodisc was a tool that they used as they attempted to solve the problem.

2.1 Conchita Martinez was the teacher who used an application of technology based on behaviorism. The students were involved in a tutorial designed to improve their skills with adding and subtracting fractions. When the students gave correct responses, the tutorial reinforced them. When they gave incorrect responses, the tutorial supplied them with immediate and corrective feedback.

2.2 Angela's application of technology was grounded in both information processing and constructivist views of learning. The database that the students created helped organize the information they gathered, and organization is one of the factors that makes information meaningful and aids encoding into long-term memory. In addition, the students were active as they created the database and analyzed the information in it, and activity is a second factor that helps make information meaningful.

As the students analyzed the data, they constructed their understanding of the information derived from their analyses, which resulted in the schemas that they encoded into long-term memory.

2.3 Although aspects of information processing applications were present, such as the students' being in active roles, Bill Logan's application of technology was based primarily on constructivist views of learning. In the discussion of constructivism, we said, "Technology can also present complex and ill-defined problems that are realistic and more like those we encounter in real life." Bill's students were attempting to solve a complex and ill-defined problem when they determined what time Jasper should leave for home and whether or not he had enough fuel to get there.

3.1 Drill-and-practice software supports instruction primarily by providing students with the opportunities to practice their skills and receive feedback. Teachers typically use it after some other form of initial instruction.

Tutorials support instruction by providing an entire instructional sequence for a particular topic, such as adding fractions.

Both drill-and-practice and tutorial software are grounded in behaviorist views of learning. However, because they are designed to increase understanding, they are also grounded in cognitive learning theory.

3.2 Simulations provide realistic contexts for complex learning; they are especially useful in teaching problem solving. As tools for promoting learning, the primary function of databases and spreadsheets is to assist learners in organizing and presenting data during problem-based learning.

3.3 In the application of simulations, databases, and spreadsheets, learners receive information (in the case of simulations), or gather and enter information into a database or spreadsheet. Students then attempt to construct understanding of the information. For instance, when Bill Logan had his students attempt to solve Jasper's problem, they received data, such as the fuel economy, average speed, capacity of the gas tank on the boat, and the distance Jasper was from home. They then had to separate relevant from irrelevant information and make a series of decisions and calculations.

Similarly, Angela Travers' students entered information about the physical characteristics of their families into a database, and they then looked for patterns and made conclusions about the information. In both cases, the students were constructing their understanding of the problem and the information. The same is true when students used spreadsheets.

4.1 Probably the most important advantage of word processing over conventional methods of teaching writing is that it enables writers to efficiently enter, revise, and edit text. Second, it allows writers to store and combine ideas from a variety of sources, and third, it facilitates communities of writers by allowing written products to be e-mailed to others for feedback.

4.2 One way of using the Internet to increase students' learning is by using it as an information source. It provides a vast array of resources to both teachers and students. The second is as a means of connecting teachers and students over vast distances, which increases communication and promotes a form of social interaction unavailable in any other way.

4.3 Assistive technology consists of an array of adaptive tools that support students with disabilities in learning activities and daily life tasks. Two major instructional adaptations focus on computer input and output devices.

5.1 First, teachers can use technology to store examples, such as examples of effective writing. Teachers can then easily access and display the examples for students. Second, teachers can also create databases and spreadsheets that they can use in learning activities.

5.2 The major logistical challenges teachers face in assessment are planning and constructing tests, administering and scoring them, and maintaining student records. Technology can assist in meeting all of these challenges by storing information in a systematic way, making subsequent retrieval and use easier.

5.3 Voice mail, Websites, and e-mail provide asynchronous means of sending and receiving messages. These allow both parents and teachers to communicate outside the strictures of time.

CHAPTER 15

1.1 The teacher uses informal assessment as he monitors his students during the lab activity and asks questions. He switches to formal assessment in collecting and scoring the lab reports and giving his quiz.

1.2 Assuming that the assessment is consistent with his learning objectives, it is valid. Specifying that grammar and punctuation are important and then giving the students a score for this component of the essay is a valid procedure.

1.3 Her assessment is not valid. Her learning objective is for students to be able to design experiments, but she assesses their recall of the steps involved. Her assessment isn't aligned with her learning objective, so it is invalid. It is likely that her assessment is reliable, because she will be able to score it consistently.

2.1 In item 1, forms of the term *circulate* appear in both the stem and the correct answer. In item 2, the correct choice is written in more technical terms than are the distracters. Teachers fall into this trap when they take the correct choice directly from the text and then make up the distracters. Their informal language appears in the distracters, whereas text language appears in the correct answer.

In item 3, the correct choice is significantly longer than the incorrect choices; the teacher gives a similar clue when the correct choice is shorter than the distracters. If one choice is significantly longer or shorter than others, it should be a distracter.

In item 4, choices *a* and *c* are stated in absolute terms, which alerts testwise students. Absolute terms, such as *all, always, none,* and *never,* are usually associated with incorrect answers. If used, they should be in the correct answer, such as "All algae contain chlorophyll."

The stem in item 5 is stated in negative terms without this fact being emphasized (the word *not* should be underlined). Also, choice *a* is grammatically inconsistent with the stem. One solution to the problem is to end the stem with "a(n)," so grammatical consistency is preserved.

In item 6, choices *a* and *c* are automatically eliminated, because both are gerunds and only one answer can be correct. Also, item 6 uses "all of the above" as a choice; it can't be correct if *a* and *c* are eliminated. That makes *b* the only possible choice. A student could get the item right and have no idea what a participle is.

Preparing valid multiple-choice items requires both thought and care. With effort and practice, however, you can become skilled at it, and when you do, you have a powerful learning and assessment tool.

2.2 Item 1 contains two ideas: (a) mammals have four-chambered hearts, and (b) they bear live young. The first is true, but the second is not true in all cases; some mammals, such as the duck-billed platypus, are egg layers. Therefore, the item is false and potentially confusing for students. If both ideas are important, they should be written as separate items.

Item 2 contains the qualifying word *most,* which is a clue that the statement is true, and item 3 uses the term *never,* which usually indicates a false statement. (As you saw in the discussion of multiple-choice items, negative wording should be used with caution in these items, but to say *never* is false.) In general, true–false items should be free of qualifying terms such as *may, most, usually, possible,* and *often,* and of absolutes such as *always, never, all,* and *none.* If a test question uses qualifiers, they're most appropriate in false statements, and absolutes are most effective in true statements.

Item 4 is effective. It uses the absolute *all,* but the statement is true.

2.3 Rubrics can increase validity by identifying the important points that the essay should include for the person doing the scoring. Rubrics can also increase scoring consistency by ensuring that evaluators score all essays the same way, using the same criteria, which increases reliability.

3.1 You would create a rating scale by first identifying the criteria for effective multiple-choice items. You would then describe each of these criteria in a single statement, which could be rated.

An example might appear as follows:

DIRECTIONS: Assess each of the test items using the following dimensions. For each dimension, circle a 5 for an excellent performance, 4 for a very good performance, 3 for good performance, 2 for fair, and 1 for poor.

5 4 3 2 1   States one clear problem in the stem.

5 4 3 2 1   Each distracter is plausible.

5 4 3 2 1   Wording in the stem and in the correct choice is dissimilar.

5 4 3 2 1   Phrasing in the correct choice and in the distracters is similar.

5 4 3 2 1   The correct choice and distracters are similar in length.

5 4 3 2 1   Negative wording is appropriately emphasized.

5 4 3 2 1   All distracters have different meanings.

3.2 The primary difference between portfolios and other alternative assessments is the central role that students play in structuring the portfolio. This suggests that teachers need to prepare students for this new responsibility, explaining the purpose and demonstrating ways that portfolios can enhance learning.

3.3 Essay items can be performance assessments to the extent that they tap higher-level thinking in real-life situations. For example, asking students to write an essay on a topic of their choice, using available resources, would be closer to the idea of a performance assessment than a closed-book, timed test, with the teacher specifying the topic.

4.1 The primary purpose of a table of specifications is to ensure that assessments are valid by aligning them with learning objectives. A table of specifications increases validity in two ways: First, by systematically identifying the important information, it helps guarantee content coverage. Second, by focusing on the level of the items, it helps ensure that the level of each item on the test matches the level of the objectives and instruction.

Tables of specifications should be created during the process of planning for instruction.

4.2 First, DeVonne emphasized reading the directions carefully. Second, she told them to skip a problem if they got stuck. Third, she reminded them not to forget to go back to any problem that they had skipped.

4.3 In general, these actions aren't effective. Continuous reminders are likely to increase test anxiety, particularly if students are having difficulty finishing in the allotted time. Teachers should schedule ample time for the students to complete tests. Then, one reminder, about 15 or 20 minutes before the time expires, would be appropriate.

5.1 The components of a total assessment system include preparing traditional and alternative assessments, preparing students, administering assessments, analyzing results, and assigning grades.

Some of the decisions involved in designing a total assessment system include the following:

- The number of tests and quizzes
- The uses of alternative assessments
- The level at which the teacher will write the assessment items, such as knowledge, application, or analysis
- The role of homework in assigning grades
- The assessment and reporting of affective dimensions, such as cooperation and effort

5.2 Formative assessment is an ongoing process that uses ungraded quizzes and tests to provide students with feedback and to allow teachers to diagnose learning problems. Summative assessment occurs after instruction, and teachers use it for grading purposes. Providing students with detailed feedback about their performance on the assessments is an essential component of both.

5.3 A grading system based on percentages is easier to manage and easier to communicate to students and parents. However, it can provide a distorted picture of learning progress, because percentages for different assignments are usually averaged, which attaches equal weight to assignments that differ in length. A point system may be harder to communicate to students and parents but provides a more accurate picture of learning progress.

CHAPTER 16

1.1 Testing to know how well students are learning from the new math program is an example of using standardized testing for the assessment of learning. Testing to know how effectively individual teachers and schools are implementing the new program is an example of using standardized testing for program evaluation and accountability.

1.2 The district is considering both achievement and diagnostic tests. Standardized achievement tests are designed to provide comprehensive coverage of different content areas. Diagnostic tests, in comparison, are designed to provide more specific, detailed information about an individual student's strengths and weaknesses.

1.3 The first teacher is addressing content validity, the match between a test's contents and the content of the math curriculum. The second is addressing predictive validity, the test's ability to gauge future performance in college. (Because the ability to succeed in college depends in part on a student's aptitude, the second teacher is also addressing construct validity to a certain extent; aptitude is a learning-related characteristic that isn't directly observable.)

2.1 A greater difference exists between the performances of Carol and Marsha than between Marsha and Lenore. Students' percentile ranks at the extremes of a distribution vary more from their counterparts than those who score near the middle of the distribution.

2.2 In the first class, with a standard deviation of 4.8, a score of 47 would be in stanine 7 (slightly more than 1 standard deviation above the mean). In the second distribution, with a standard deviation of 3.1, a score of 47 would be in stanine 8 (more than 1.5 standard deviations above the mean).

2.3 A grade equivalent of 6.7 means that he scored as well as the average sixth grader in the seventh month of the sixth grade. It means that the fourth grader is somewhat advanced. (It does not mean that the student should be in the sixth grade, nor does it mean that the student is generally capable of doing sixth-grade work.)

3.1 Accountability is the process of holding both teachers and students responsible for essential learning outcomes. Educators define these outcomes in terms of standards, or specific goals that students must attain. Educators verify the attainment of these goals through tests. When these tests have potentially serious consequences for students, such as not being promoted or not being allowed to graduate, the tests are called high stakes.

3.2 Arguments for high-stakes testing include the following: The process identifies important learning outcomes, communicates them to both students and the public, and provides evidence about whether or not students are acquiring essential knowledge. Advocates also claim that this process improves learning for all students.

Arguments against high-stakes testing suggest that it narrows the curriculum; in essence, what is tested becomes the curriculum. This encourages teachers to ignore areas that aren't tested, such as art and music. Critics also argue that minimum-competency testing stifles teacher creativity because they are essentially teaching to the test.

3.3 The areas in which teachers are being tested include basic skills such as reading, writing, and math; content area knowledge; and principles of learning and teaching. Proponents of teacher testing argue that teachers must be skilled and knowledgeable in these areas in order to teach effectively. For example, basic skills are required in order to communicate effectively; knowledge of content is essential, because teachers can't teach what they don't understand themselves, and they must understand both the instructional process and the characteristics of their students in order to teach effectively.

4.1 Three types of bias include bias in content, bias in testing procedures, and bias in test use. Content bias exists if performance on a test depends on knowledge that is not relevant to the concept or skill being tested. Bias in testing procedures exists if students are not familiar with the procedures or if procedural elements, such as time, place an unfair burden on certain students. Tests can also be biased with respect to use if educators make decisions about students based on the results of a single test.

4.2 One strategy teachers can use to minimize content bias in standardized tests is to carefully examine the test to familiarize themselves with test content. If they believe an unfair item is present, they should call this to the attention of their administrators. A second strategy is to analyze results on individual items to determine if students missed some items for reasons other than not understanding the content.

GLOSSARY

Ability grouping. The process of placing students of similar abilities together and attempting to match instruction to the needs of these groups.

Acceleration. Instruction in which the curriculum is the same but allows students to move through it more quickly.

Accommodation. A form of adaptation in which an existing scheme is modified and a new one is created in response to experience.

Accountability. The process of requiring learners to demonstrate that they possess specified knowledge and skills as demonstrated by standardized measures and making teachers responsible for student performance.

Achievement tests. Standardized tests designed to assess how much students have learned in specified content areas.

Action research. A form of applied research designed to answer a specific school- or classroom-related question.

Adaptation. The process of adjusting schemes and experiences to each other to maintain equilibrium.

Adaptive behavior. A person's ability to manage the demands and perform the functions of everyday living.

Adaptive fit. The degree to which a school environment accommodates the student's needs and the degree to which a student can meet the requirements of a particular school setting.

Affective memories. Past emotional experiences related to a topic or activity.

Algorithm. A specific set of steps for solving a problem.

Alternative assessment. Direct examination of student performance on tasks that are relevant to life outside of school.

Analogies. Descriptions of relationships that are similar in some but not all respects.

Antecedents. Stimuli that precede and signal or induce behaviors.

Anxiety. A general uneasiness and feeling of tension.

Applied behavior analysis (ABA). The process of systematically applying the principles of behaviorism to change student behavior.

Aptitude tests. Standardized tests designed to predict the potential for future learning and measure general abilities developed over long periods of time.

Assimilation. A form of adaptation in which an experience in the environment is incorporated into an existing scheme.

Assistive technology. A set of adaptive tools that support students with disabilities in learning activities and daily life tasks.

Attention. The process of consciously focusing on a stimulus.

Attention-deficit/hyperactivity disorder (ADHD). A learning problem characterized by difficulties in maintaining attention.

Attribution theory. A cognitive theory of motivation that attempts to systematically describe learners' explanations for their successes and failures and how these influence motivation and behavior.

Attributional statements. Comments teachers make about the causes of students' performances.

Automaticity. Performing mental operations with little awareness or conscious effort.

Autonomous morality. A stage of moral development characterized by the belief that fairness and justice is the reciprocal process of treating others as they would want to be treated.

Autonomy. Independence and an individual's ability to alter the environment when necessary.

Axons. Components of neurons that transmit outgoing messages to other neurons.

Backward design. A planning approach that begins with learning objectives, then specifies assessments and learning activities to ensure that all are aligned.

Basic interpersonal communication skills. A level of proficiency in English that allows students to interact conversationally with their peers.

Behavior disorders. Serious and persistent age-inappropriate behaviors that result in social conflict, personal unhappiness, and often school failure.

Behaviorism. A theory that explains learning in terms of observable behaviors based on the influence of environmental stimuli.

Belief preservation. The tendency to make evidence subservient to belief, rather than the other way around.

Bidialecticism. The ability to switch back and forth between a dialect and standard English.

Bulletin boards. Asynchronous communication devices that serve as electronic message centers for a given topic.

Caring. Teachers' ability to empathize with and invest in the protection and development of young people.

Centration (centering). The tendency to focus on the most perceptually obvious aspect of an object or event, neglecting other important aspects.

Characteristics. A concept's defining elements.

Chatrooms. Expanded, collective versions of electronic mail (e-mail) that occur synchronously or at the same time.

Checklists. Written descriptions of dimensions that must be present in an acceptable performance of an activity.

Chunking. The process of mentally combining separate items into larger, more meaningful units.

Classical conditioning. A type of learning that occurs when an individual learns to produce an involuntary emotional or physiological response similar to an instinctive or reflexive response.

Classification. The process of grouping objects on the basis of a common characteristic.

Classroom assessment. All the processes involved in making decisions about students' learning progress.

Classroom management. Teachers' strategies that create and maintain an orderly learning environment.

Closure. A form of review occurring at the end of a lesson.

Cognitive academic language proficiency. A level of proficiency in English that allows students to handle demanding learning tasks with abstract concepts.

Cognitive apprenticeship.   The process of having a less-skilled learner work at the side of an expert in developing complex cognitive skills.

Cognitive approach to management.   An approach to classroom management that emphasizes the creation of an orderly classroom through the development of student understanding and responsibility.

Cognitive behavior modification.   A procedure that combines behavioral and cognitive learning principles to help learners change their behavior through self-talk and self-instruction.

Cognitive constructivism.   A form of constructivism that focuses on individual, internal constructions of knowledge.

Cognitive domain.   The area of learning that focuses on memory and higher processes such as applying and analyzing.

Cognitive learning theories.   Explanations for learning that focus on changes in mental processes and constructs that occur as a result of people's efforts to make sense of the world.

Cognitive load.   The amount of mental activity imposed on working memory.

Cognitive modeling.   The process of incorporating modeled demonstrations together with verbalization of the model's thoughts and reasons for performing the given actions.

Cognitive theories of motivation.   Theoretical explanations for motivation that focus on learners' beliefs, expectations, and needs for order, predictability, and understanding.

Collective self-esteem.   Individuals' perceptions of the relative worth of the groups to which they belong.

Communication disorders.   Exceptionalities that interfere with students' abilities to receive and understand information from others and express their own ideas or questions.

Community of learners.   A classroom in which the teacher and all the students work together to help everyone learn.

Competence.   The ability to function effectively in the environment.

Completion.   An assessment format that includes a question or an incomplete statement that requires the learner to supply appropriate words, numbers, or symbols.

Component skills.   The cognitive processes learners use to make and assess their conclusions.

Comprehension monitoring.   The process of checking to see if we understand what we have read or heard.

Computer-mediated communication (CMC).   Telecommunication between people via electronic mail (e-mail).

Concept mapping.   A learning strategy in which learners construct visual relationships among concepts.

Concepts.   Mental constructs that categorize sets of objects, events, or ideas.

Conditioned response (CR).   A learned physiological or emotional response that is similar to the unconditioned response.

Conditioned stimulus (CS).   An object or event that becomes associated with the unconditioned stimulus.

Connected discourse.   Instruction that is thematic and leads to a point.

Consequences.   Outcomes (stimuli) that occur after behaviors and influence the probability of the behavior recurring.

Conservation.   The idea that the "amount" of some substance stays the same regardless of its shape or the number of pieces into which it is divided.

Construct validity.   A description of the extent to which an assessment accurately measures a characteristic that is not directly observable.

Constructivism.   A view of learning suggesting that learners create their own knowledge of the topics they study rather than having that knowledge transmitted to them by some other source.

Content validity.   A test's ability to accurately sample the content taught and measure the extent to which learners understand it.

Continuous reinforcement schedule.   A reinforcement schedule in which every behavior is reinforced.

Cooperative learning.   A set of instructional strategies that help learners meet specific learning and social interaction objectives in structured groups.

Correlation.   A relationship, either positive or negative, between two or more variables.

Correlational research.   The process of looking for relationships between two or more variables that enables researchers to predict changes in one variable on the basis of changes in another variable without implying a cause–effect relationship between the variables.

Cost.   The negative aspect of engaging in a task.

Creativity.   The ability to produce or identify original and varied solutions to problems.

Crisis.   A psychosocial challenge that presents opportunities for development.

Criterion-referenced grading.   Assessment decisions made according to a predetermined standard.

Critical thinking.   An individual's ability and inclination to make and assess conclusions based on evidence.

Cultural inversion.   The tendency of members of cultural minorities to reject certain attitudes, values, and forms of behavior because they conflict with their own cultural values.

Culture.   The knowledge, attitudes, values, and customs that characterize a social group.

Curriculum-based assessment.   Measurement of learners' performance in specific areas of the curriculum.

Databases.   Computer programs that allow users to store, organize, and manipulate information, including both text and numerical data.

Deaf.   A hearing impairment that requires the use of other senses, usually sight, to communicate.

Declarative knowledge.   Knowledge of facts, definitions, procedures, and rules.

Deficiency needs.   Needs that, when unfulfilled, energize people to meet them.

Dendrites.   Branchlike structures within neurons, extending from the cell body and receiving messages from other neurons.

Descriptive research.   Research that uses interviews, observations, and surveys to describe opinions, attitudes, and events.

Desists.   Verbal or nonverbal communications teachers use to stop a behavior.

Development.   The orderly, adaptive changes in learners that result from a combination of experience, learning, and maturation.

Diagnostic tests.   Standardized tests designed to provide a detailed description of learners' strengths and weaknesses in specific skill areas.

Dialect.   A variation of standard English that is distinct in vocabulary, grammar, or pronunciation.

Direct instruction.   An instructional model designed to teach well-defined knowledge and skills that are needed for later learning.

Disabilities.   Functional limitations or an inability to perform a certain act.

Discipline.   Teachers' responses to student misbehavior.

Discrimination.   The process that occurs when a person gives different responses to similar but not identical stimuli.

Disorder.   A general malfunction of mental, physical, or psychological processes.

Distance education. Instructional programs in which teachers and learners, though physically separated, are connected through technology.

Distracters. The incorrect alternatives in a multiple-choice assessment, which are designed to distract students who don't understand the content that the item is measuring.

Drawing analogies. A strategy used to solve unfamiliar problems by comparing them with those already solved.

Drill-and-practice programs. Forms of software that allow students to work problems or answer questions and receive immediate feedback.

Dual-coding theory. A theory suggesting that long-term memory contains two distinct memory systems: one for verbal information and one that stores images.

Due process. The guarantee of parents' right to be involved in identifying and placing their children in special programs, to access school records, and to obtain an independent evaluation if they're not satisfied with the one conducted by the school.

Educational technology. The process of applying tools for educational purposes as well as the tools and materials used.

Egocentrism. The tendency to believe that other people look at the world as the individual does.

Elaboration. The process of increasing the meaningfulness of information by creating additional links in existing knowledge or by adding new information.

Elaborative questioning. The process of drawing inferences, identifying examples, and forming relationships in the material being studied.

ELL pullout programs. Programs for English language learner (ELL) students who receive most of their instruction in regular classrooms but are also pulled out for extra help in both English language development and classroom content.

Emotional intelligence. The ability to understand emotions in ourselves and others.

Empathy. The ability to experience the same emotion someone else is feeling.

Emphasis. Verbal and vocal cues that alert students to important information in a lesson.

Encoding. The process of representing information in long-term memory.

Enrichment. Varied and alternate instruction for students who are gifted and talented.

Entity view of intelligence. The belief that ability is stable and out of an individual's control.

Equilibrium. A state of being able to explain new experiences by using existing schemes.

Equitable distribution. A questioning strategy in which all students in a class are called on as equally as possible.

Essay. An assessment format that requires students to make extended written responses to questions or problems.

Essential teaching skills. Abilities that all teachers, including those in their first year, should have to promote order and as much student learning as possible.

Ethnicity. A person's ancestry and the way individuals identify with the nation from which they or their ancestors came.

Exemplars. The most highly typical examples of a concept.

Expectancy × value theory. A cognitive theory of motivation suggesting that people are motivated to engage in an activity to the extent that they expect to succeed times the value they place on the success.

Experimental research. Research that systematically manipulates variables in attempts to determine cause and effect.

Experts. Individuals who are highly skilled or knowledgeable in a given domain.

External morality. A stage of moral development in which individuals view rules as fixed and permanent and enforced by authority figures.

Extinction (classical conditioning). The disappearance of a conditioned response as the result of the conditioned stimulus occurring repeatedly in the absence of the unconditioned stimulus.

Extinction (operant conditioning). The disappearance of a behavior that results from lack of reinforcement.

Extrinsic motivation. Motivation to engage in an activity as a means to an end.

Feedback. Information about existing understanding that is used to enhance future understanding.

Forgetting. The loss of, or inability to retrieve, information from memory.

Formal assessment. The process of systematically gathering information about learning progress and making decisions based on that information.

Formative assessment. The process of using ungraded assessments during instruction to provide students with feedback and aid the teacher in diagnosis and planning.

Frequency distribution. A distribution of test scores that shows a count of the number of people who obtained each score.

Functional analysis. The strategy used to identify the antecedents and consequences that control a behavior.

Gender-role identity differences. Beliefs about appropriate characteristics and behaviors of the two sexes.

General pedagogical knowledge. The type of professional knowledge that involves an understanding of general principles of instruction and classroom management that transcends individual topics or subject matter areas.

General transfer. The ability to apply knowledge or skills learned in one context in a broad range of different contexts.

Generalization. The process that occurs when stimuli similar, but not identical, to a conditioned stimulus elicit the conditioned response by themselves.

Gifts and talents. Abilities at the upper end of the continuum that require support beyond regular classroom instruction to reach full potential.

Goal. An outcome an individual hopes to achieve.

Grade equivalent. A score that is determined by comparing an individual's score on a standardized test to the scores of students in a particular age group.

Growth needs. Needs that expand and increase as people have experiences with them.

Guided discovery. An instructional model in which teachers guide students as the students construct knowledge of concepts and the relationships among them.

Guided notes. Teacher-prepared handouts that "guide" students with cues and space available for writing key ideas and relationships.

Guilt. The uncomfortable feeling people get when they know they've caused distress for someone else.

Handicap. A condition imposed on a person's functioning that restricts the individual's abilities.

Heuristics. General, widely applicable problem-solving strategies.

High-collective-efficacy school. A school where most of the teachers are high in personal teaching efficacy.

High-stakes tests.   Standardized tests designed to measure the extent to which standards are being met.

Holophrases.   One- and two-word utterances that carry as much meaning for the child as complete sentences.

Humanistic psychology.   A school of thought viewing motivation as people's attempts to fulfill their total potential as human beings.

Hypermedia.   A linked form of multimedia that allows learners to make connections to different points in the program based on their background knowledge and learning progress.

I-message.   A nonaccusatory communication that addresses a behavior, describes the effects on the sender, and the feelings it generates in the sender.

Icons.   Pictures displayed on computer screens that act as symbols for some action or item.

Identity.   Individuals' sense of self, who they are, what their existence means, and what they want in life.

Ill-defined problem.   A problem that has more than one acceptable solution, an ambiguous goal, and no generally agreed-upon strategy for reaching a solution.

Imagery.   The process of forming mental pictures.

Immersion.   A language-instruction approach that requires all instruction and communication to be in that language.

Importance.   The extent to which an activity allows people to confirm or disconfirm important aspects of their self-schemas.

Inclusion.   A comprehensive approach to educating students with exceptionalities that advocates a total, systematic, and coordinated web of services.

Incremental view of intelligence.   The belief that ability can be improved with effort.

Individualized education program (IEP).   An individually prescribed instructional plan devised by special education and general education teachers, resource professionals, and parents (and sometimes the student).

Informal assessment.   The process of gathering incidental information about learning progress and making decisions based on that information.

Information processing.   A theory of learning that explains how stimuli that enter our memory systems are selected and organized for storage and are retrieved from memory.

Inhibition.   A self-imposed restriction on one's behavior.

Instructional alignment.   The match between learning objectives, learning activities, and assessments.

Intelligence.   The ability to acquire knowledge, the capacity to think and reason in the abstract, and the ability to solve novel problems.

Intelligence tests.   Standardized tests designed to measure an individual's capacity to acquire knowledge, think and reason in the abstract, and solve novel problems.

Interference.   The loss of information because something learned either before or after detracts from understanding.

Intermittent reinforcement schedule.   A reinforcement schedule in which some but not all behaviors are reinforced.

Internet.   A complex web of interconnections among computers.

Interpersonal harmony.   A stage of moral reasoning in which conclusions are based on loyalty, living up to the expectations of others, and social conventions.

Interval schedules.   An intermittent reinforcement schedule in which behaviors are reinforced after a certain predictable interval (fixed) or unpredictable interval (variable) of time has elapsed.

Intrinsic interest.   The characteristics of an activity that induce a person's willing involvement in it.

Intrinsic motivation.   Motivation to be involved in an activity for its own sake.

Introductory focus.   A lesson beginning that attracts attention and provides a conceptual framework for the lesson.

Involvement.   The extent to which students are actively participating in a learning activity.

Joplin plan.   Homogeneous grouping in reading, combined with heterogeneous grouping in other areas.

Language acquisition device (LAD).   A genetic set of language-processing skills that enables children to understand and use the rules governing speech.

Language disorders (or receptive disorders).   Problems with understanding language or using language to express ideas.

Law and order.   A stage of moral reasoning in which conclusions are based on following laws and rules for their own sake.

Learned helplessness.   The general belief, based on past experiences, that one is incapable of accomplishing tasks and has little control of the environment.

Learners with exceptionalities.   Students who need special help and resources to reach their full potential.

Learning.   A change in people's mental structures that creates the capacity to demonstrate different behaviors.

Learning (behaviorist).   According to behaviorism, a relatively enduring change in observable behavior that occurs as a result of experience.

Learning (cognitive).   A change in mental processes that creates the capacity to demonstrate different behaviors, which may or may not result in immediate behavioral change.

Learning disability.   Difficulty in acquiring and using reading, writing, reasoning, listening, or mathematical abilities.

Learning-focused environment.   A classroom environment that focuses on effort, continuous improvement, and understanding.

Learning goal.   A goal that focuses on mastery of a task, improvement, and increased understanding.

Learning objective.   Statement that specifies what students should know or be able to do with respect to a topic or course of study.

Learning styles.   Students' personal approaches to learning, problem solving, and processing information.

Least restrictive environment (LRE).   A policy that places students in as typical an educational setting as possible while still meeting their special needs.

Lecture-discussion.   An instructional model designed to help students acquire organized bodies of knowledge and develop complex schemas.

Logical consequences.   Outcomes that are conceptually related to the misbehavior.

Long-term memory.   The permanent information store in our information processing system.

Mainstreaming.   The practice of moving students with exceptionalities from segregated settings into regular classrooms.

Maintenance ELL programs.   Programs for English language learner (ELL) students that build on students' native language by teaching in both their language and English.

Market exchange.   A stage of moral reasoning in which conclusions are based on an act of reciprocity on someone else's part.

Matching.   An assessment format that requires learners to classify a series of examples using the same alternatives.

Maturation.   Genetically controlled, age-related changes in individuals.

Mean.   The average score in the distribution of a group of scores.

Meaningfulness.   The extent to which individual elements of a schema are interconnected.

Means–ends analysis. A strategy that breaks the problem into subgoals and works successively on each.

Measures of central tendency. Quantitative descriptions of how a group performed as a whole.

Median. The middle score in the distribution of a group of scores.

Memory stores. Repositories that hold information in our information processing system.

Mental retardation. A disability characterized by significant limitations both in intellectual functioning and in adaptive behavior.

Meta-attention. Knowledge of and control over our ability to pay attention.

Metacognition. The awareness of and control over one's own cognitive processes.

Metamemory. Knowledge of and control over our memory strategies.

Mnemonic devices. Elaboration strategies that link knowledge to be learned to familiar information.

Mode. The most frequent score in the distribution of a group of scores.

Modeling. Behavioral, cognitive, and affective changes deriving from observing one or more models.

Models of instruction. Prescriptive approaches to teaching designed to help students acquire a deep understanding of specific forms of knowledge.

Moral development. The development of prosocial behaviors and traits such as honesty, fairness, and respect for others.

Moral dilemma. An ambiguous situation that requires a person to make a moral decision.

Motivation. A force that energizes, sustains, and directs behavior toward a goal.

Motivation to learn. Students' tendencies to find academic activities meaningful and worthwhile and to try to get the intended learning benefits from them.

Multimedia. Combinations of media, including text, graphics, pictures, audio, and video that communicate information.

Multiple-choice. An assessment format that consists of a question or statement, called a stem, and a series of answer choices.

National norms. Average scores on standardized tests earned by representative groups of students from around the nation to which an individual's score is compared.

Nativist theory. A theory of language acquisition suggesting that all humans are "wired" to learn language and that exposure to language triggers this development.

Nature view of intelligence. The assertion that intelligence is essentially determined by genetics.

Negative reinforcement. The process of increasing behavior by avoiding or removing an aversive stimulus.

Negligence. The failure to exercise sufficient care in protecting students from injury.

Network. A concept map illustrating nonhierarchical relationships.

Neuron. Nerve cells composed of cell bodies, dendrites, and axons, which make up the learning capability of the brain.

Norm group. The representative group of individuals whose average standardized test scores are compiled for the purpose of national comparisons.

Norm-referenced grading. Assessment decisions about an individual student's work based on comparisons with the work of peers.

Normal distribution. A distribution of scores in which the mean, median, and mode are equal and the scores distribute themselves symmetrically in a bell-shaped curve.

Nurture view of intelligence. The assertion that emphasizes the influence of the environment on intelligence.

Object permanence. The understanding that objects have a permanent existence separate from the self.

Open-ended questions. Questions for which a variety of answers are acceptable.

Operant conditioning. A form of learning in which an observable response changes in frequency or duration as a result of a consequence.

Order and safety. A climate variable intended to create a predictable learning environment that supports learner autonomy and a sense of physical and emotional security.

Organization. An essential teaching skill that includes starting on time, preparing materials in advance, and establishing routines and procedures. (Chapter 12)

Organization. The conceptual process of clustering items of content into categories that illustrate relationships. (Chapter 7)

Organization. The process of forming and using schemes.

Organized bodies of knowledge. Topics that connect facts, concepts, generalizations, and principles, and make the relationships among them explicit.

Overgeneralization. A speech pattern that occurs when a child uses a word to refer to a broader class of objects than is appropriate.

Partial hearing impairment. An impairment that allows a student to use a hearing aid and to hear well enough to be taught through auditory channels.

Pedagogical content knowledge. An understanding of effective teaching methods for a specific content area, as well as an understanding of what makes specific topics easy or hard to learn.

Percentile bands. Ranges of percentile scores on standardized tests.

Percentile, or percentile rank (PR). The proportion of scores in a distribution that a specific score is greater than or equal to.

Perception. The process people use to find meaning in stimuli.

Performance assessment. A form of assessment in which students demonstrate their abilities by completing an activity or producing a product.

Performance goal. A goal that focuses on competence or ability and how it compares to the competence of others.

Performance-approach goals. Goals that emphasize looking competent and receiving favorable judgments from others.

Performance-avoidance goals. Goals that focus on avoiding looking incompetent and being judged unfavorably.

Performance-focused environment. A classroom environment that emphasizes high grades, public displays of ability, and performance compared to others.

Personal development. The growth of enduring personality traits that influence the way individuals interact with their physical and social environments.

Personal teaching efficacy. A teacher's belief that he or she can get all students to succeed and learn regardless of their prior knowledge or ability.

Personalization. The process of using intellectually and/or emotionally relevant examples to illustrate a topic.

Perspective taking. The ability to understand the thoughts and feelings of others.

Portfolio assessment. The process of selecting collections of student work that both students and teachers evaluate using preset criteria.

Positive classroom climate. A classroom environment where the teacher and students work together as a community of learners to help everyone achieve as much as possible.

Positive reinforcement.   The process of increasing the frequency or duration of a behavior as the result of presenting a reinforcer.

Precise language.   Teacher talk that omits vague terms from explanations and responses to students' questions.

Predictive validity.   The measure of a test's ability to gauge future performance.

Premack principle.   The principle stating that a more-desired activity serves as a positive reinforcer for a less-desired activity.

Presentation punishment.   A decrease in behavior that occurs when a stimulus (punisher) is presented.

Private speech.   Self-talk that guides thinking and action.

Proactive aggression.   Aggression that involves overt hostile acts toward someone else.

Problem.   A state that occurs when a problem solver has a goal but lacks an obvious way of achieving the goal.

Problem-based learning.   A teaching strategy that uses problems as the focus for developing content, skills, and self-direction.

Procedural knowledge.   Knowledge of how to perform tasks.

Procedures.   Guidelines for accomplishing recurring tasks.

Productive learning environment.   A classroom that is orderly and focused on learning.

Prompting.   An additional question or statement teachers use to elicit an appropriate student response after a student fails to answer correctly.

Prototype.   The best representative of a category or class.

Punishers.   Consequences that weaken behaviors or decrease the likelihood of them recurring.

Punishment.   The process of using punishers to decrease behavior.

Punishment–obedience.   A stage of moral reasoning in which conclusions are based on the chances of getting caught and being punished.

Questioning frequency.   The number of questions a teacher asks during a learning activity.

Random assignment.   A process used to ensure that an individual has an equal likelihood of being assigned to any group within a study.

Range.   The distance between the top and bottom score in a distribution of scores.

Rating scales.   Written descriptions of the dimensions of an acceptable performance and scales of values on which each dimension is rated.

Ratio schedules.   An intermittent reinforcement schedule in which specific behaviors are reinforced, either predictably (fixed) or unpredictably (variable).

Raw score.   The number of items an individual answered correctly on a standardized test or subtest.

Real-world (authentic) task.   A learning activity that develops understanding similar to understanding that would be used outside the classroom.

Reciprocal causation.   The description of the interdependence of the environment, behavior, and personal factors in learning.

Reflective practice.   The process of conducting a critical self-examination of one's teaching.

Reforms.   Suggested changes in teaching and teacher preparation intended to increase the amount students learn.

Rehearsal.   The process of repeating information over and over, either aloud or mentally, without altering its form.

Reinforcement.   The process of applying reinforcers to increase behavior.

Reinforcement schedules.   Descriptions of the patterns in the frequency and predictability of reinforcers.

Reinforcer.   A consequence (stimulus) that increases the likelihood of a behavior recurring.

Relatedness.   The feeling of being connected to others in one's social environment and feeling worthy of love and respect.

Reliability.   A description of the extent to which assessments are consistent and free from errors of measurement.

Removal punishment.   A decrease in behavior that occurs when a stimulus is removed, or when a person cannot receive positive reinforcers.

Research.   The process of systematically gathering information in an attempt to answer questions.

Resilience.   A learner characteristic that, despite adversity, raises the likelihood of success in school and later life.

Response cost.   The process of taking away reinforcers already given.

Retrieval.   The process of pulling information from long-term memory into working memory for further processing.

Reversibility   The ability to mentally trace a process, such as lengthening a row, back to its original state.

Review.   A summary that helps students link what they have already learned to what will follow in the next learning activity.

Rubric.   A scoring scale that describes the criteria for grading.

Rules.   Descriptions of standards for acceptable classroom behavior.

Satiation.   The process of using a reinforcer so frequently that it loses its potency—its ability to strengthen behaviors.

Scaffolding.   Assistance that helps children complete tasks they cannot complete independently.

Schemas.   Cognitive constructs that organize information into a meaningful system.

Schemes.   Actions or mental operations that represent our constructed understanding of the world.

Scripts.   Schema representations for events, providing plans for action in particular situations.

Self-concept.   Individuals' cognitive assessment of their physical, social, and academic competence.

Self-determination.   The process of deciding how to act on one's environment.

Self-efficacy.   A belief about one's own capability to organize and complete a course of action required to accomplish a specific task.

Self-esteem, or self-worth.   An emotional reaction to, or an evaluation of, the self.

Self-fulfilling prophecy.   A phenomenon that occurs when a person's performance results from and confirms beliefs about his or her capabilities.

Self-regulation.   The process of accepting responsibility for and taking control of one's own learning.

Self-schemas.   Organized networks of information about ourselves.

Self-worth.   An emotional reaction to or evaluation of the self.

Sensory focus.   Stimuli that teachers use to maintain attention during learning activities.

Sensory memory.   The memory store that briefly holds stimuli from the environment until they can be processed.

Seriation.   The ability to order objects according to increasing or decreasing length, weight, or volume.

Sexual identity.   Students' self-constructed definition of who they are with respect to gender orientation.

Sexual orientation.   The gender to which an individual is romantically and sexually attracted.

Shame.   The painful emotion aroused when people recognize that they have failed to act or think in ways they believe are good.

Shaping. The process of reinforcing successive approximations of a desired behavior.

Sheltered English. An approach to teaching ELL students in academic classrooms that modifies instruction to assist learners in acquiring content.

Simulations. Programs, either in software or web-based form, that model a system or process.

Situated cognition. A view suggesting that learning is social in nature, depends on, and cannot be separated from the context in which it is learned.

Social cognitive theory. A theory of learning that focuses on changes in behavior that result from observing others.

Social constructivism. A form of constructivism suggesting that learners first construct knowledge in a social context and then appropriate and internalize it.

Social contract. A stage of moral reasoning in which conclusions are based on socially agreed-upon principles.

Social conventions. The rules and expectations of a particular group or society.

Social development. The advances people make in their ability to interact and get along with others.

Social experience. The process of interacting with others.

Social problem solving. The ability to resolve conflicts in ways that are beneficial to all involved.

Sociocultural theory. A social constructivist theory that emphasizes the larger cultural context in learning.

Sociocultural theory of development. A theory that emphasizes the influence of social interactions and language, embedded within a cultural context, on development.

Socioeconomic status (SES). The combination of income, occupation, and level of education that describes the relative standing in society of a family or individual.

Special education. Instruction designed to meet the unique needs of students with exceptionalities.

Specific transfer. The ability to apply information in a context similar to the context in which it was originally learned.

Speech disorders (or expressive disorders). Problems in forming and sequencing sounds.

Spreadsheets. Computer programs that allow users to organize and manipulate numerical data.

Standard deviation. A statistical measure of the spread of scores.

Standard error of measurement. The range of scores within which an individual's true score is likely to fall.

Standard score. A description of performance on a standardized test that uses the standard deviation as the basic unit.

Standardized tests. Assessment instruments given to large samples of students under uniform conditions and scored according to uniform procedures.

Standards. Statements that describe what students should know or be able to do at the end of a prescribed period of study.

Standards-based education. The process of focusing curricula and instruction on predetermined goals or standards.

Stanine (S). A description of an individual's standardized test performance that uses a scale ranging from 1 to 9 points.

Strategies. Techniques to enhance performance on a learning task.

Students placed at risk. Learners in danger of failing to complete their education with the skills necessary to survive in a modern technological society.

Study strategies. Specific techniques students use to increase their understanding of written materials and teacher presentations.

Summarizing. The process of preparing a concise description of verbal or written passages.

Summative assessment. The process of assessing after instruction and using the results for making grading decisions.

Synapses. The tiny spaces across which messages are transmitted from one neuron to another.

Systematic observation. The process of specifying criteria for acceptable performance in an activity and taking notes during observation based on the criteria.

T score. A standard score that defines the mean as 50 and the standard deviation as 10.

Table of specifications. A matrix that helps teachers organize learning objectives by cognitive level or content area.

Task analysis. The process of breaking content down into component parts and making decisions about sequencing the parts.

Task comprehension. Learners' awareness of what they are supposed to be learning and an understanding of why the task is important and worthwhile.

Technician. Someone who uses specific skills to complete a well-defined task.

Temperament. The relatively stable inherited characteristics that influence the way we respond to social and physical stimuli.

Test anxiety. An unpleasant reaction to testing situations that can lower performance.

Text signals. A strategy designed to capitalize on the organization of written materials.

Theory. A set of related principles derived from observations that are used to explain additional observations and make predictions.

Timeout. The process of isolating a student from his or her classmates.

Tracking. Placing students in different classes or curricula on the basis of achievement.

Transfer. The effect of previous learning on new learning or problem solving.

Transformation. The ability to mentally record the process of moving from one state to another.

Transition signals. Verbal statements indicating that one idea is ending and another is beginning.

Transitional ELL programs. English language learner (ELL) programs that attempt to use students' native language as an instructional aid until students become proficient in English.

Transitivity. The ability to infer a relationship between two objects based on knowledge of their relationship with a third object.

True-false. An assessment format that includes statements of varying complexity that learners judge as being correct or incorrect.

True score. The hypothetical average of an individual's scores if repeated testing under ideal conditions were possible.

Tutorials. Instructional software that offers an entire integrated instructional sequence.

Unconditional positive regard. The belief that someone is innately worthy and acceptable regardless of their behavior.

Unconditioned response (UCR). The instinctive or reflexive (unlearned) physiological or emotional response caused by the unconditioned stimulus.

Unconditioned stimulus (UCS). An object or event that causes an instinctive or reflexive (unlearned) physiological or emotional response.

Undergeneralization. A speech pattern that occurs when a child uses a word too narrowly.

Uniform Resource Locator (URL).   A series of letters and/or symbols that act as an address for a site on the Internet.

Universal principles.   A stage of moral reasoning in which conclusions are based on abstract and general principles that are independent of society's laws and rules.

Utility value.   The perception that a topic or activity is or will be useful for meeting future goals, including career goals.

Validity.   The degree to which an assessment actually measures what it is supposed to measure.

Vicarious learning.   The process of people observing the consequences of other's actions and adjusting their own behavior accordingly.

Visual disability.   An uncorrectable visual impairment that interferes with learning.

Wait-time.   The period of silence that occurs both before and after calling on a student.

Websites.   Locations on the World Wide Web identified with a Uniform Resource Locator (URL).

Well-defined problem.   A problem that has only one correct solution and a certain method for finding the solution.

Withitness.   A teacher's awareness of what is going on in all parts of the classroom at all times and the communication of this awareness to students, both verbally and nonverbally.

Worked examples.   Problems with complete solutions that provide students with one way of solving the problems.

Working memory.   The conscious part of our information processing system; the memory store that holds information as people process it.

World Wide Web.   A system on the Internet that allows people to access, view, and maintain documents that include text, data, sound, and video.

z score.   The number of standard deviation units from the mean.

Zone of proximal development.   A range of tasks that an individual cannot yet do alone but can accomplish when assisted by a more skilled partner.

REFERENCES

AAMR Ad Hoc Committee on Terminology and Classification. (2002). *Mental retardation: Definition, classification, and systems of support* (10th ed.). Washington, DC: American Association on Mental Retardation.

Abed-El-Khalick, F., & Akerson, V. L. (2004). Learning as conceptual change: Factors mediating the development of preservice elementary teachers' views of nature of science. *Science Education, 88,* 785–810.

Abedi, J. (1999, spring). CRESST report points to test accommodations for English Language Learning students. *The CRESST Line,* pp. 6–7.

Abedi, J., Hofstetter, C., & Lord, C. (2004). Assessment accommodations for English language learners: Implications for policy-based empirical research. *Review of Educational Research, 74*(1), 1–28.

Aboud, F., & Skerry, S. (1984). The development of ethnic identity: A critical review. *Journal of Cross-Cultural Psychology, 15,* 3–34.

Acherman, P. L., Bowen, K. R., Beier, M., & Kanfer, R. (2001). Determinants of individual differences and gender differences in knowledge. *Journal of Educational Psychology, 93,* 797–825.

Ackerman, P. (2003). Cognitive ability and non-ability trait determinants of expertise. *Educational Research, 32*(8), 15–20.

AGS Publishing. (2006). *Detroit tests of learning aptitude* (4th ed.). Circle Pines, MN: Author.

Aiken, L. R. (2003). *Psychological testing and assessment* (11th ed.). Boston: Allyn & Bacon.

Airasian, P., & Walsh, M. (1997). Constructivist cautions. *Phi Delta Kappan, 78*(6), 444–449.

Alao, S., & Guthrie, J. (1999). Predicting conceptual understanding with cognitive and motivational variables. *Journal of Educational Research, 92*(4), 243–254.

Alberto, P., & Troutman, A. (2006). *Applied behavior analysis for teachers* (7th ed.). Upper Saddle River, NJ: Merrill/Prentice Hall.

Alder, N. (2002). Interpretations of the meaning of care: Creating caring relationships in urban middle school classrooms. *Urban Education, 37*(2), 241–266.

Alessi, S., & Trollip, S. (2001). *Multimedia for learning: Methods and development.* Needham Heights, MA: Allyn & Bacon.

Alexander, J. M., Johnson, K. E., & Leibham, M. E. (2005). Constructing domain-specific knowledge in kindergarten: Relations among knowledge, intelligence, and strategic performance. *Learning and Individual Differences, 15,* 35–52.

Alexander, P. (2003). The development of expertise: The journey from acclimation to proficiency. *Educational Researcher, 32*(8), 10–14.

Alexander, P. (2006). *Psychology in learning and instruction.* Upper Saddle River, NJ: Merrill/Prentice Hall.

Alexander, P., Graham, S., & Harris, K. (1998). A perspective on strategy research: Progress and prospects. *Educational Psychology Review, 10*(2), 129–153.

Alexander, P., & Jetton, T. (2000). Learning from text: A multidimensional and developmental perspective. In M. Kamil, P. Mosenthal, P. D. Pearson, & R. Barr (Eds.), *Handbook of reading research* (Vol. 3, pp. 285–310). Mahwah, NJ: Erlbaum.

Alexander, P. A., & Jetton, T. L. (2003). Learning from traditional and alternative texts: New conceptualization for an information age. In A. Graesser, M. Gernsbacher, & S. Goldman (Eds.), *Handbook of discourse processes* (pp. 199–241). Mahwah, NJ: Erlbaum.

Allington, R. L., & McGill-Franzen, A. (2003). The impact of summer setback on the reading achievement gap. *Phi Delta Kappan, 85*(1), 68–71.

Alparsian, C., Tekkaya, C., & Geban, Ö. (2004). Using the conceptual change instruction to improve learning. *Journal of Biological Education, 37,* 133–137.

Alperstein, J. F. (2005). Commentary on girls, boys, test scores and more. *Teachers College Record,* May 16. ID Number: 11874. Retrieved June 21, 2005, from http://www.tcrecord.org

Altermatt, E., Jovanovic, J., & Perry, M. (1998). Bias or responsivity? Sex and achievement-level effects on teachers' classroom questioning practices. *Journal of Educational Psychology, 90*(3), 516–527.

American Association of University Women. (1992). *How schools shortchange girls.* Annapolis Junction, MD: Author.

American Association of University Women. (1998). *Gender gaps: Where schools still fail our children.* Annapolis Junction, MD: Author.

American Educational Research Association, American Psychological Association, & National Council on Measurement in Education. (1999). *Standards for educational and psychological testing* (2nd ed.). Washington, DC: Author.

American Psychological Association. (2000). *Diagnostic and statistical manual of mental disorders, text revision: DSMV-IV-TR* (4th ed.). Washington, DC: Author.

American Psychological Association Board of Educational Affairs. (1995). *Learner-centered psychological principles: A framework for school redesign and reform.* Retrieved October 1, 2002, from http://www.apa.org/ed/lcp.html

Ames, C. (1990). Motivation: What teachers need to know. *Teachers College Record, 91,* 409–421.

Ames, C. (1992). Classrooms: Goals, structures, and student motivation. *Journal of Educational Psychology, 84*(3), 261–271.

Amrein, A., & Berliner, D. (2002). High-stakes testing, uncertainty, and student learning. *Education Policy Analysis Archives, 10*(18). Retrieved October 1, 2002, from http://epaa.asu.edu/epaa/v10n18/

Anastasi, A., & Urbina, S. (1997). Psychological testing (7th ed.). Englewood Cliffs, NJ: Prentice Hall.

Anderman, E. M. (2002). School effects on psychological outcomes during adolescence. *Journal of Educational Psychology, 94,* 795–809.

Anderman, E., & Maehr, M. (1994). Motivation and schooling in the middle grades. *Review of Educational Research, 64,* 287–309.

Anderson, J., Reder, L., & Simon, H. (1996). Situated learning and education. *Educational Researcher, 25*(4), 5–10.

Anderson, J. R. (2005). *Cognitive psychology and its implications* (6th ed.). New York: Worth.

Anderson, L., Evertson, C., & Brophy, J. (1979). An experimental study of effective teaching in first-grade reading groups. *Elementary School Journal, 79,* 193–223.

Anderson, L., & Krathwohl, D. (Eds.). (2001). *A taxonomy for learning, teaching, and assessing: A revision of Bloom's taxonomy of educational objectives.* New York: Addison Wesley Longman.

Anderson, M., & Neely, J. (1996). Interference and inhibition in memory retrieval. In E. Bjork & R. Bjork (Eds.), *Memory* (pp. 237–313). San Diego, CA: Academic Press.

Anderson, R., Nguyen-Jahiel, K., McNurlen, B., Archodidou, A., Kim, S., Reznitskaya, A., Tillmanns, M., & Gilbert, L. (2001). The snowball phenomenon: Spread of ways of talking and ways of thinking across groups of children. *Cognition and Instruction, 19*(1), 1–46.

Ansell, S., & Park, J. (2003). Tracking tech trends. *Education Week, 22*(35), 43–49.

Antil, L., Jenkins, J., Wayne, S., & Vadasy, P. (1998). Cooperative learning: Prevalence, conceptualizations, and the relation between research and practice. *American Educational Research Journal, 35*(3), 419–454.

Applebee, A., Langer, J., Nystrand, M., & Gamoran, A. (2003). Discussion-based approaches to developing understanding: Classroom instruction and student performance in middle and high school English. *American Educational Research Journal, 40*(3), 685–730.

Armour-Thomas, E. (2004). What is the nature of evaluation and assessment in an urban context? In S. R. Steinberg & J. L. Kincheloe (Eds.), *19 Urban questions: Teaching in the city* (pp. 109–118). New York: Peter Lang.

Arnett, J. J. (2002). High hopes in a grim world: Emerging adults' views of their futures and of "Generation X." *Youth and Society, 31,* 267–286.

Aronson, E., Wilson, T., & Akert, R. (2005). *Social psychology* (5th ed.). Upper Saddle River, NJ: Pearson.

Arter, J., & McTighe, J. (2001). *Scoring rubrics in the classroom.* Thousand Oaks, CA: Corwin.

Ashcraft, M. (2001). *Human memory and cognition* (3rd ed.). Upper Saddle River, NJ: Merrill/Prentice Hall.

Asian-Nation. (2005). The model minority image. Retrieved February 17, 2005, from http://www.asian-nation.org/model-minority.shtml

Aspy, C. B., Oman, R. F., Vesely, S. K., McLeroy, K., Rodine, S., & Marshall, L. (2004). Adolescent violence: The protective effects of youth assets. *Journal of Counseling and Development, 82,* 268–276.

Atkinson, J. (1958). *Motives in fantasy, action, and society.* Princeton, NJ: Van Nostrand.

Atkinson, R., Derry, S., Renkl, A., & Wortham, D. (2000). Learning from examples: Instructional principles from the worked examples research. *Review of Educational Research, 70*(2), 181–214.

Atkinson, R., & Shiffrin, R. (1968). Human memory: A proposed system and its control processes. In K. Spence & J. Spence (Eds.), *The psychology of learning and motivation: Advances in research and theory* (Vol. 2). San Diego, CA: Academic Press.

Atkinson, R. K., Renkl, A., & Merril, M. M. (2003). Transitioning from studying examples to solving problems: Effects of self-explanation prompts and fading worked-out steps. *Journal of Educational Psychology, 95,* 774–783.

Attewell, P. (2001). The first and second digital divides. *Sociology of Education, 74(July),* 252–259.

Au, K. (1992, April). *"There's almost a lesson here": Teacher and students' purposes in constructing the theme of a story.* Paper presented at the annual meeting of the American Educational Research Association, San Francisco.

Austin, J. L., Lee, M., & Carr, J. P. (2004). The effects of guided notes on undergraduate students' recording of lecture content. *Journal of Instructional Psychology, 31,* 314–320.

Ausubel, D. (1968). *Educational psychology: A cognitive view.* New York: Holt, Rinehart & Winston.

Avery, P., & Palmer, E. (2001, April). *Developing authentic instruction and assessment to promote authentic student performance.* Paper presented at the annual meeting of the American Educational Research Association, Seattle.

Avramidis, E., Bayliss, P., & Burden, R. (2000). Student teachers' attitudes toward the inclusion of children with special education needs in the ordinary school. *Teaching and Teacher Education, 16,* 277–293.

Azevedo, R., & Cromley, J. (2004). Does training on self-regulated learning facilitate students' learning with hypermedia? *Journal of Educational Psychology, 96(3),* 523–535.

Babad, E., Avni-Bada, D., & Rosenthal, R. (2003). Teachers' brief nonverbal behaviors in defined instructional situations can predict students' evaluations. *Journal of Educational Psychology, 95,* 553–562.

Babad, E., Bernieri, F., & Rosenthal, R. (1991). Students as judges of teachers' verbal and nonverbal behavior. *American Educational Research Journal, 28(1),* 211–234.

Baddeley, A. (2001). Is working memory still working? *American Psychologist, 56,* 851–864.

Bae, G. (2003, April). *Rethinking constructivism in multicultural context: Does constructivism in education take the issue of diversity into consideration?* Paper presented at the annual meeting of the American Educational Research Association, Chicago.

Baldwin, J. D., & Baldwin, J. I. (2001). *Behavior principles in everyday life* (4th ed.). Upper Saddle River, NJ: Prentice Hall.

Ball, D. (1992, Summer). Magical hopes: Manipulatives and the reform of math education. *American Educator,* pp. 28–33.

Bandalos, D. L. (2004). Introduction to the special issue on Nebraska's alternative approach to statewide assessment. *Educational Measurement, 23(2),* 6–8.

Bandura, A. (1986). *Social foundations of thought and action: A social cognitive theory.* Upper Saddle River, NJ: Merrill/Prentice Hall.

Bandura, A. (1989). Social cognitive theory. In R. Vasta (Ed.), *Annals of child development* (Vol. 6, pp. 1–60). Greenwich, CT: JAI Press.

Bandura, A. (1997). *Self-efficacy: The exercise of control.* New York: Freeman.

Bandura, A. (2001). Social cognitive theory. In *Annual Review of Psychology.* Palo Alto, CA: Annual Review.

Bandura, A. (2004, May). *Toward a psychology of human agency.* Paper presented at the meeting of the American Psychological Society, Chicago.

Barab, S. A., & Plucker, J. A. (2002). Smart people or smart contexts? Cognition, ability, and talent development in an age of situated approaches to

knowing and learning. *Educational Psychologist, 37,* 165–182.

Barak, M., & Dori, Y. J. (2005). Enhancing undergraduate students' chemistry understanding through project-based learning in an IT environment. *Science Education, 89,* 117–139.

Baringa, M. (1997). New insights into how babies learn language. *Science, 277,* 641.

Barone, M. (2000). In plain English: Bilingual education flunks out of schools in California. *U.S. News and World Report, 128(21),* 37.

Barr, R. (2001). Research on the teaching of reading. In J. Richardson (Ed.), *Handbook of research on teaching* (4th ed., pp. 390–415). Washington, DC: American Educational Research Association.

Barr, R. D., & Parrett, W. H. (2001). *Hope fulfilled for at-risk and violent youth* (2nd ed.). Boston: Allyn & Bacon.

Barron, B. (2000). Problem solving in video-based microworlds: Collaborative and individual outcomes of high-achieving sixth-grade students. *Journal of Educational Psychology, 92(2),* 391–398.

Barth, R. (2002). The culture builder. *Educational Leadership, 59(8),* 6–12.

Barton, A. C., Drake, C., Perez, J. G., St. Louis, K., & George, M. (2004). Ecologies of parental engagement in urban education. *Educational Researcher, 33(4),* 3–12.

Barton, P. (2004). Why does the gap persist? *Educational Leadership, 62(3),* 9–13.

Batsashaw, M. L. (2003). *Children with disabilities* (5th ed.). Baltimore, MD: Paul H. Brookes.

Baumeister, R., Campbell, J., Krueger, J., & Voks, K. (2003). Does high self-esteem cause better performance, interpersonal success, happiness or healthier lifestyles? *Psychological Science in the Public Interest, 4,* 1–44.

Baumrind, D. (1991). The influence of parenting style on adolescent competence and substance use. *Journal of Early Adolecence, 11,* 56–95.

Bay, M., Staver, J., Bryan, T., & Hale, J. (1992). Science instruction for the mildly handicapped: Direct instruction versus discovery teaching. *Journal of Research in Science Teaching, 29,* 555–570.

Beach, K. (1999). Consequential transitions: A sociocultural expedition beyond transfer in education. In A. Iran-Nejad & P. Pearson (Eds.), *Review of research in education* (Vol. 24, pp. 101–140). Washington, DC: American Educational Research Association.

Bebeau, M., Rest, J., & Narvaez, D. (1999). Beyond the promise: A perspective on research in moral education. *Educational Researcher, 28(4),* 18–26.

Becker, J., & Varelas, M. (2001). Piaget's early theory of the role of language in intellectual development: A comment on DeVries' account of Piaget's social theory. *Educational Researcher, 30(6),* 22–23.

Bee, H. (1989). *The developing child* (5th ed.). New York: Harper & Row.

Behuniak, P. (2002). Consumer-referenced testing. *Phi Delta Kappan, 84,* 199–206.

Beirne-Smith, M., Ittenbach, R. F., & Patton, J. R. (2002). *Mental retardation* (6th ed.). Upper Saddle River, NJ: Merrill/Prentice Hall.

Beitzel, B., & Derry, S. (2004, April). *Designing contrasting video case activities to facilitate learning of complex subject matter.* Paper presented at the annual meeting of the American Educational Research Association, San Diego.

Bennett, N., & Blundel, D. (1983). Quantity and quality of work in rows of classroom groups. *Educational Psychology, 3,* 93–105.

Berk, L. (2004). *Development through the lifespan* (3rd ed.). Boston: Allyn & Bacon.

Berk, L. (2005). *Infants & children* (5th ed.). Boston: Allyn & Bacon.

Berk, L. E. (2006). *Child development* (7th ed.). Boston: Allyn & Bacon.

Berliner, D. (1984). *Making our schools more effective: Proceedings of three state conferences.* San Francisco: Far West Laboratory.

Berliner, D. (1994). Expertise: The wonder of exemplary performances. In J. Mangieri & C. Collins (Eds.), *Creating powerful thinking in teachers and students* (pp. 161–186). Fort Worth, TX: Harcourt Brace.

Berliner, D. (2000). A personal response to those who bash education. *Journal of Teacher Education, 51,* 358–371.

Berliner, D. C. (2005). Our impoverished view of educational reform. *Teachers College Record,* August 2. ID Number: 12106. Retrieved January 12, 2006, from http://www.tcrecord.org

Bernard, R., Abrami, P., Lou, Y., Borokhovski, E., Wade, A., Wozney, L., Wallet, P., Fiset, M., & Huang, B. (2004). *How does distance education compare with classroom instruction? A meta-analysis of the empirical literature. Review of Educational Research, 74(3),* 379–439.

Berndt, T. (1999). Friends' influence on students' adjustment to school. *Educational Psychologist, 34,* 15–28.

Berninger, V. W., & Richards, T. L. (2002). *Brain literacy for educators and psychologists.* San Diego, CA: Academic Press.

Bernstein, D. K., & Tiegerman-Farber, E. (2002). *Language and communication disorders in children* (5th ed.). Boston: Allyn & Bacon.

Bertman, S. (2000). *Cultural amnesia: America's future and the crisis of memory.* Westport, CT: Praeger.

Berzonsky, M. D., & Kuk, L. S. (2000). Identity status, identity processing style, and the transition to university. *Journal of Adolescent Research, 15,* 81–98.

Betts, J., Zau, A., & Rice, L. (2003). *Determinants of student achievement: New evidence from San Diego.* Retrieved June 1, 2005, from http://www.ppic.org

Biddle, B. J. (2001). Poverty, ethnicity, and achievement in American schools. In B. J. Biddle (Ed.), *Social class, poverty, and education* (pp. 1–30). New York: Routlege Falmer.

Bielenberg, B., & Fillmore, L. W. (2005). The English they need for the test. *Educational Leadership, 62(4),* 45–49.

Biemiller, A. (2005). Addressing developmental patterns in vocabulary. In E. H. Hiebert & M. L. Kamil (Eds.), *Teaching and learning vocabulary.* Mahwah, NJ: Erlbaum.

Bierman, K. (2004). *Peer rejection: Developmental processes and intervention strategies.* New York: Guilford.

Biklen, S., & Pollard, D. (2001). Feminist perspectives on gender in classrooms. In V. Richardson (Ed.), *Handbook of research on learning* (4th ed., pp. 695–722). Washington, DC: American Educational Research Association.

Biscaro, M., Broer, K., & Taylor, N. (2004). Self efficacy, alcohol expectancy and problem-solving appraisal as predictors of alcohol use in college students. *College Student Journal, 38,* 541–555.

Bishop, J. (1995). The power of external standards. *American Educator, 19,* 10–14, 17–18, 42–43.

Bishop, J. (1998). The effect of curriculum-based external exit systems on student achievement. *Journal of Economic Education, 29,* 171–182.

Bjorkland, D. F. (2000). *Children's thinking* (3rd ed.). Belmont, CA: Wadsworth.

Black, A., & Deci, E. (2000). The effects of instructors' autonomy support and students' autonomous motivation on learning organic chemistry: A self-determination theory perspective. *Science Education, 84,* 740–756.

Black, P., Harrison, C., Lee, C., Marshall, B., & Wiliam, D. (2004). Working inside the black box: Assessment for learning in the classroom. *Phi Delta Kappan, 86(1),* 9–21.

Black, P., & William, D. (1998a). Assessment and classroom learning. *Assessment in Education: Principles, Policy and Practice, 5*(1), 7–75.

Black, P., & William, D. (1998b). Inside the black box. *Phi Delta Kappan, 80*(2), 139–148.

Blackburn, M., & Miller, R. (1999, April). *Intrinsic motivation for cheating and optimal challenge: Some sources and some consequences.* Paper presented at the annual meeting of the American Educational Research Association, Montreal, Canada.

Blair, J. (2000). AFT urges new tests, expanded training for teachers. *Education Week, 19*(32), 11.

Bleeker, M. M., & Jacobs, J. E. (2004). Achievement in math and science: Do mothers' beliefs matter 12 years later? *Journal of Educational Psychology, 96*(1), 97–109.

Blocher, M., Echols, J., Tucker, G., de Montes, L., & Willis, E. (2002, April). *Re-thinking the validity of assessment: A classroom teacher's dilemma.* Paper presented at the annual meeting of the American Educational Research Association, New Orleans.

Blok, H., Oostdam, R., Otter, M., & Overmaat, M. (2002). Computer-assisted instruction in support of beginning reading instruction: A review. *Review of Educational Research, 72*(1), 101–130.

Bloom, B., Englehart, M., Furst, E., Hill, W., & Krathwohl, O. (1956). *Taxonomy of educational objectives: The classification of educational goals: Handbook 1. The cognitive domain.* White Plains, NY: Longman.

Bloome, D., Carter, S. P., Christian, B. M., Otto, S., & Shuart-Faris, N. (2005). *Discourse analysis and the study of classroom language and literacy events.* Mahwah, NJ: Erlbaum.

Blum, R. (2005). A case for school connectedness. *Educational Leadership, 62*(8), 16–19.

Bohn, A. P. (2003). Familiar voices: Using ebonics communication techniques in the primary classroom. *Urban Education, 38*(6), 688–707.

Bohn, C. M., Roehrig, A. D., & Pressley, M. (2004). The first days of school in the classrooms of two more effective and four less effective primary-grades teachers. *Elementary School Journal, 104*(4), 269–288.

Bol, L., Stephenson, P., O'Connell, A., & Nunnery, J. (1998). Influence of experience, grade level, and subject area on teachers' assessment practices. *Journal of Educational Research, 91*(8), 323–330.

Bong, M. (2001). Between- and within-domain relations of academic motivation among middle and high school students: Self-efficacy, task-value, and achievement goals. *Journal of Educational Psychology, 93*, 23–34.

Bong, M., & Skaalvik, E. (2003). Academic self-concept and self-efficacy: How different are they really? *Educational Psychology Review, 15*, 1–40.

Borja, R. (2003). Prepping for the big test. *Education Week, 22*(35), 23–26.

Borko, H., & Putnam, R. (1996). Learning to teach. In D. Berliner & R. Calfee (Eds.), *Handbook of educational psychology* (pp. 673–708). New York: Macmillan.

Borman, G. D., & Overman, L. R. (2004). Academic resilience in mathematics among poor and minority students. *Elementary School Journal, 104*(3), 177–196.

Bourne, L. (1982). Typicality effects in logically defined categories. *Memory & Cognition, 10*, 3–9.

Bowman, D. (2000). White House proposes goals for improving Hispanic education. *Education Week, 19*(41), 9.

Boyd, M., & Rubin, D. (2001, April). *Elaborated student talk in elementary ESL instruction.* Paper presented at the annual meeting of the American Educational Research Association, Seattle.

Braaksma, M., Rijlaarsdam, G., van den Bergh, H., & van Hout-Wolters, B. (2004). Observational learning and its effects on the orchestration of writing processes. *Cognition & Instruction, 22*(1), 1–36.

Bracey, G. (2005). A nation of cheats. *Phi Delta Kappan, 86*(5), 412–413.

Brand, S., Felner, R., Shim, M., Sertsinger, A., & Duman, T. (2003). Middle school improvement and reform: Development and validation of a school-level assessment of climate, cultural pluralism, and school safety. *Journal of Educational Psychology, 95*, 570–588.

Bransford, J. (1993). Who ya gonna call? Thoughts about teaching problem solving. In P. Hallinger, K. Leithwood, & J. Murphy (Eds.), *Cognitive perspectives on educational leadership* (pp. 2–30). New York: Teachers College Press.

Bransford, J., Brown, A., & Cocking, R. (Eds.). (2000). *How people learn: Brain, mind, experience, and school.* Washington, DC: National Academy Press.

Bransford, J., Darling-Hammond, L., & LePage, P. (2005). Introduction. In L. Darling-Hammond & J. Bransford (Eds.), *Preparing teachers for a changing world: What teachers should learn and be able to do* (pp. 1–39). San Francisco: Jossey-Bass/Wiley.

Bransford, J., Goldman, S., & Vye, N. (1991). Making a difference in people's abilities to think: Reflections on a decade of work and some hopes for the future. In L. Okagaki & R. Sternberg (Eds.), *Directors of development* (pp. 147–180). Hillsdale, NJ: Erlbaum.

Bransford, J., & Schwartz, D. (1999). Rethinking transfer: A simple proposal with multiple implications. In A. Iran-Nejad & P. Pearson (Eds.), *Review of research in education* (Vol. 24, pp. 61–100). Washington, DC: American Educational Research Association.

Bransford, J., & Stein, B. (1984). *The IDEAL problem solver.* New York: Freeman.

Branson, M. (2000). *Self-regulation in early childhood: Nature and nurture.* New York: Guilford.

Brantlinger, E., Morton, M., & Washburn, S. (1999). Teachers' moral authority in classrooms: (Re)Structuring social interactions and gendered power. *Elementary School Journal, 99*(5), 490–504.

Braun, H., & Mislevy, R. (2005). Intuitive test theory. *Phi Delta Kappan, 86*(7), 489–497.

Bredo, E. (1997). The social construction of learning. In G. Phye (Ed.), *Handbook of academic learning: Construction of knowledge* (pp. 3–45). San Diego, CA: Academic Press.

Brennan, R., Kim, J., Wenz-Gross, M., & Siperstein, G. (2001). The relative equitability of high stakes testing versus teacher-assigned grades: An analysis of the Massachusetts Comprehensive Assessment System. *Harvard Educational Review, 71*(2), 173–212.

Brenner, D. (2001, April). *Translating social constructivism into methodology for documenting learning.* Paper presented at the annual meeting of the American Educational Research Association, Seattle.

Brenner, M., Mayer, R., Moseley, B., Brar, T., Durán, R., Reed, B., & Webb, D. (1997). Learning by understanding: The role of multiple representations in learning algebra. *American Educational Research Journal, 34*(4), 663–689.

Bridgeman, B. (1974). Effects of test score feedback on immediately subsequent test performance. *Journal of Educational Psychology, 66*, 62–66.

Brophy, J. (1981). On praising effectively. *Elementary School Journal, 81*, 269–278.

Brophy, J. (1999). Perspectives of classroom management. In J. Freiberg (Ed.), *Beyond behaviorism: Changing the classroom management paradigm* (pp. 43–56). Boston: Allyn & Bacon.

Brophy, J. (2004). *Motivating students to learn* (2nd ed.). Boston: McGraw-Hill.

Brophy, J., & Alleman, J. (2003). Primary-grade students' knowledge and thinking about the supply of utilities (water, heat, and light) to modern homes. *Cognition & Instruction, 21*(1), 79–112.

Brophy, J., & Good, T. (1986). Teacher behavior and student achievement. In M. Wittrock (Ed.), *Handbook of research on teaching* (3rd ed., pp. 328–375). New York: Macmillan.

Brouwers, A., & Tomic, W. (2001). The factorial validity of the Teacher Interpersonal Self-Efficacy Scale. *Educational and Psychological Measurement, 61*, 433–445.

Brown, A. (1997). Transforming schools into communities of thinking and learning about serious matters. *American Psychologist, 52*, 399–413.

Brown, A., Bransford, J., Ferrara, R., & Campione, J. (1983). Learning, remembering, and understanding. In J. Flavell & E. Markman (Eds.), *Handbook of child psychology: Vol. 3. Cognitive development* (4th ed., pp. 77–166). New York: Wiley.

Brown, A., & Campione, J. (1994). Guided discovery in a community of learners. In K. McGilly (Ed.), *Classroom lessons: Integrating cognitive theory and classroom practice* (pp. 229–270). Cambridge, MA: MIT Press.

Brown, D. (2004). Urban teachers' professed classroom management strategies: Reflections of culturally responsive teaching. *Urban Education, 39*(3), 266–289.

Brown, J., Collins, A., & Duguid, P. (1989). Situated cognition and the culture of learning. *Educational Researcher, 18*, 32–42.

Brown, K., Anfara, V., & Roney, K. (2004). Student achievement in high performing, suburban middle schools and low performing, urban middle schools: Plausible explanations for the differences. *Education and Urban Society, 36*(4), 428–456.

Brown, R., & Evans, W. (2002). Extracurricular activity and ethnicity: Creating greater school connections among diverse student populations. *Urban Education, 37*(1), 41–58.

Bruer, J. (1993). *Schools for thought: A science of learning for the classroom.* Cambridge, MA: MIT Press.

Bruer, J. (1997). Education and the brain: A bridge too far. *Educational Researcher, 26*(8), 4–16.

Bruer, J. (1999). In search of brain-based education. *Phi Delta Kappan, 89*(9), 649–657.

Bruer, J. T., & Greenough, W. T. (2001). The subtle science of how experience affects the brain. In D. B. Bailey, Jr., J. T. Bruer, F. J. Symons, & J. W. Lichtman (Eds.), *Critical thinking about critical periods* (pp. 209–232). Baltimore: Brookes.

Bruner, J. (1973). *Beyond the information given: Studies in the psychology of knowing.* New York: Norton.

Bruner, J. (1996). *Toward a theory of instruction.* New York: Norton.

Bruner, J., Goodenow, J., & Austin, G. (1956). *A study of thinking.* New York: Wiley.

Bruning, R. H., Schraw, G. J., Norby, M. M., & Ronning, R. R. (2004). *Cognitive psychology and instruction* (4th ed.). Upper Saddle River, NJ: Merrill/Prentice Hall.

Brunner, C., & Tally, W. (1999). *The new media literacy handbook: An educator's guide to bringing new media into the classroom.* New York: Anchor Books.

Buchan, J. (2000). When different is the same. *Exceptional Parent, 30*(9), 71–73.

Bulgren, J., Deshler, D., Schumaker, J., & Lenz, B. K. (2000). The use and effectiveness of analogical instruction in diverse secondary content classrooms. *Journal of Educational Psychology, 92*(3), 426–441.

Bullough, R. (2001). *Uncertain lives: Children of promise, teachers of hope.* New York: Teachers College Press.

Burbules, N., & Bruce, B. (2001). Theory and research on teaching as dialogue. In V. Richardson (Ed.), *Handbook of research on teaching* (4th ed., pp. 1102–1121). Washington, DC: America Educational Research Association.

Burstyn, J., & Stevens, R. (1999, April). *Education in conflict resolution: Creating a whole school approach.* Paper presented at the annual meeting of the American Educational Research Association, Montreal, Canada.

Burstyn, J., & Stevens, R. (2001). Involving the whole school in violence prevention. In J. Burstyn, G. Bender, R. Casella, H. Gordon, D. Guerra, K. Luschen, R. Stevens, & K. Williams (Eds.), *Preventing violence in schools: A challenge to American democracy* (pp. 139–158). Mahwah, NJ: Erlbaum.

Butler, D. (1998). The strategic content learning approach to promoting self-regulated learning: A report of three studies. *Journal of Educational Psychology, 90*(4), 682–697.

Byars, B. C. (2005). *The summer of the swans.* New York: Penguin Young Readers Group.

Byrne, B., & Gavin, D. (1996). The Shavelson Model revisited: Testing for the structure of academic self-concept across pre, early, and late adolescents. *Journal of Educational Psychology, 88*(2), 215–228.

Byrnes, J. P. (2001a). *Cognitive development and learning in instructional contexts* (2nd ed.). Boston: Allyn & Bacon.

Byrnes, J. P. (2001b). *Minds, brains, and learning: Understanding the psychological and educational relevance of neuroscientific research.* New York: Guilford Press.

Byrnes, J. P. (2003). Factors predictive of mathematics achievement in White, Black, and Hispanic 12th graders. *Journal of Educational Psychology, 95*, 316–326.

Byrnes, M. (2002). *Taking sides: Clashing views on controversial issues in special education.* Guilford, CT: McGraw-Hill/Dushkin.

Cameron, J., & Pierce, D. (1996). The debate about rewards and intrinsic motivation: Protests and accusations do not alter the results. *Review of Educational Research, 66*, 39–51.

Cameron, J. R. (2001). Negative effects of reward on intrinsic motivation—A limited phenomenon. *Review of Educational Research, 71*, 29–42.

Campbell, C., & Evans, J. (2000). Investigation of preservice teachers' classroom assessment practices during student teaching. *Journal of Educational Research, 93*(6), 350–353.

Campbell, F. A., Pungello, E. P., Miller-Johnson, S., Burchinal, M., & Ramey, C. T. (2001). The development of cognitive and academic abilities: Growth curves from an early childhood educational experiment. *Developmental Psychology, 37*, 231–243.

Canter, A. (2004). A problem-solving model for improving student achievement. *Principal Leadership, 5*, 11–15.

Caplan, N., Choy, M., & Whitmore, J. (1992). Indochinese refugee families and academic achievement. *Scientific American, 266*(2), 36–42.

Carbo, M. (1997). Reading styles times twenty. *Educational Leadership, 54*, 38–42.

Cargill, C. (1987). Cultural bias in testing ESL. In C. Cargill (Ed.), *A TESOL professional anthology: Culture.* Lincolnwood, IL: National Textbook.

Carlo, M., August, D., McLaughlin, B., Snow, C., Dressler, C., Lippman, D., Lively, T., & White, C. (2004). Closing the gap: Addressing the vocabulary needs of English-language learners in bilingual and mainstream classroom. *Reading Research Quarterly, 59*(2), 188–215.

Carlsen, W. (1987, April). *Why do you ask? The effects of science teacher subject-matter knowledge on teacher questioning and classroom discourse.* Paper presented at the annual meeting of the American Educational Research Association, Washington, DC.

Carlson, C., Uppal, S., & Prosser, E. (2000). Ethnic differences in processes contributing to self-esteem of early adolescent girls. *Journal of Early Adolescence, 20*, 44–67.

Carlson, K. (2004). Test scores by race and ethnicity. *Phi Delta Kappan, 85*(5), 379–380.

Carnegie Learning. (2005). Retrieved March 16, 2005, from http://www.carnegielearning.com

Carnine, D., Silbert, J., Kameenui, E., Tarver, S., & Jongjohann, K. (2006). *Teaching struggling and at-risk readers: A direct instruction approach.* Upper Saddle River, NJ: Merrill/Prentice Hall.

Carpendale, J. (2000). Kohlberg and Piaget on stages and moral reasoning. *Developmental Review, 20*, 181–205.

Carpenter, T., Levi, L., Fennema, E., Ansell, E., & Franke, M. (1995, April). *Discussing alternative strategies as a context for developing understanding in primary grade mathematics classrooms.* Paper presented at the annual meeting of the American Educational Research Association, San Francisco.

Casey, B. J. (2001). Disruption of inhibitory control in developmental disorders: A mechanistic model of implicated frontostriatal circuitry. In J. L. McClelland & R. S. Sielger (Eds.), *Mechanisms of cognitive development: Behavioral and neural perspectives* (pp. 327–349). Mahwah, NJ: Erlbaum.

Cassady, J. (1999, April). *The effects of examples as elaboration in text on memory and learning.* Paper presented at the annual meeting of the American Educational Research Association, Montreal, Canada.

Cassady, J. C., & Johnson, R. E. (2002). Cognitive anxiety and academic performance. *Contemporary Educational Psychology, 27*, 270–295.

Castellano, J. A., & Diaz, E. (Eds.). (2002). *Reaching new horizons: Gifted and talented education for culturally and linguistically diverse students.* Boston: Allyn & Bacon.

Cazden, C. B. (2002). *Classroom discourse: The language of teaching and learning* (2nd ed.). Portsmouth, NH: Heinemann.

Ceci, S., & Williams, W. (1997). Schooling, intelligence, and income. *American Psychologist, 53*, 185–204.

Center for Applied Research in Educational Technology. (2004). *Topic: Student learning.* Eugene, OR: Author. Retrieved July 29, 2004, from http://caret.iste.org/index.cfm? fuseaction=topics

Certo, J., Cauley, K., & Chafen, C. (2002, April). *Students' perspectives on their high school experience.* Paper presented at the annual meeting of the American Educational Research Association, New Orleans.

Chaffen, R., & Imreh, G. (2002). Practicing perfection: Piano performance and expert memory. *Psychological Science, 13*, 342–349.

Chance, P. (1993). Sticking up for rewards. *Phi Delta Kappan, 74*, 787–790.

Chao, S., Stigler, J., & Woodward, J. A. (2000). The effects of physical materials on kindergartners' learning of number concepts. *Cognition and Instruction, 18*(3), 285–316.

Chapman, J. W., Tunmer, W. E., & Prochnow, J. E. (2000). Early reading-related skills and performance, reading self-concept, and the development of academic self-concept: A longitudinal study. *Journal of Educational Psychology, 92*, 703–708.

Charles, C. M., & Senter, G. W. (2005). *Building classroom discipline* (8th ed.). Boston: Allyn & Bacon.

Charner-Laird, M., Watson, D., Szczesuil, S., Kirkpatrick C., & Gordon, P. (2004, April). *Navigating the 'Culture Gap': New teachers experience the urban context.* Paper presented at the annual meeting of the American Educational Research Association, San Diego.

Chavous, T. M., Bernat, D. H., Schmeelk-Cone, K., Caldwell, C. H., Kohn-Wood, L., & Zimmerman, M. A. (2003). Racial identity and academic attainment among African American Adolescents. *Child Development, 74*, 1076–1090.

Chekley, K. (1997). The first seven . . . and the eighth. *Educational Leadership, 55*, 8–13.

Chen, Z., & Siegler, R. (2000). Intellectual development in childhood. In R. J. Sternberg (Ed.), *Handbook of intelligence* (pp. 92–116). New York: Cambridge University Press.

Cheng, L. R. (1987). *Assessing Asian language performance.* Rockville, MD: Aspen.

Children's Defense Fund. (1999). *The state of America's children yearbook, 1999.* Washington, DC: Author.

Choi, N. (2005). Self-efficacy and self-concept as predictors of college students' academic performance. *Psychology in the Schools, 42*(2), 197–205.

Chomsky, N. (1959). A review of Skinner's verbal behavior. *Language, 35*, 25–58.

Chomsky, N. (1972). *Language and mind* (2nd ed.). Orlando, FL: Harcourt Brace.

Chomsky, N. (1976). *Reflections on language.* London: Temple Smith.

Chomsky, N., & Miller, G. (1958). Finite-state languages. *Information and Control, 1*, 91–112.

Christenson, S., & Havsy, L. (2004). Family–school–peer relationships: Significance for social, emotional, and academic learning. In J. Zins, R. Weissberg, M. Wang, & H. Walberg (Eds.), *Building academic success on social and emotional learning* (pp. 59–75). New York: Teachers College Press.

Christian, K., Bachnan, H. J., & Morrison, F. J. (2001). Schooling and cognitive development. In R. J. Sternberg & E. L. Grigorenko (Eds.), *Environmental effects on cognitive abilities.* Mahwah, NJ: Erlbaum.

Christie, I. (2003). States ain't misbehavin' but the work is hard! *Phi Delta Kappan, 84*, 565–566.

Chronicle, E., MacGregor, J., & Ormerod, T. (2004). What makes an insight problem? The roles of heuristics, goal conception, and solution recoding in knowledge-lean problems. *Journal of Experimental Psychology: Learning, Memory, and Cognition, 30*(1), 14–217.

Chun, K. M., Organista, P. B., & Marin, G. (Eds.). (2002). *Acculturation.* Washington, DC: American Psychological Association.

Church, M., Elliott, A., & Gable, S. (2001). Perceptions of classroom environment, achievement goals, and achievement outcomes. *Journal of Educational Psychology, 93*, 43–54.

Cizek, G. (1997). Learning, achievement, and assessment: Constructs at a crossroads. In G. Phye (Ed.), *Handbook of classroom assessment* (pp. 1–31). San Diego, CA: Academic Press.

Clark, J., & Paivio, A. (1991). Dual coding theory and education. *Educational Psychology Review, 3*, 149–210.

Clark, K., & Clark, M. (1939). The development of consciousness of self and the emergence of racial identification in Negro preschool children. *Journal of Social Psychology, 10*, 591–599.

Clark, R. C., & Mayer, R. E. (2003). *e-learning and the science of instruction: Proven guidelines for consumers and designers of multimedia learning.* San Francisco: Pfeiffer/Wiley.

Cochran, K., & Jones, L. (1998). The subject matter knowledge of preservice science teachers. In B. Fraser & K. Tobin (Eds.), *International handbook of science education:* Part II. Dordrecht, Netherlands: Kluwer.

Cognition and Technology Group at Vanderbilt. (1992). The Jasper Series as an example of anchored instruction: Theory, program description, and assessment data. *Educational Psychologist, 27*, 291–315.

Cognition and Technology Group at Vanderbilt. (1996). Looking at technology in context: A framework for understanding technology and education research. In D. Berliner & R. Calfee

(Eds.), *Handbook of educational psychology* (pp. 807–840). New York: Macmillan.

Cohen, E. (1994). Restructuring the classroom: Conditions for productive small groups. *Review of Educational Research, 64*, 1–35.

Colangelo, N., & Davis, G. (Eds.). (2003). *Handbook of gifted education* (3rd ed.). Boston: Allyn & Bacon.

Cole, D. A., Maxwell, S. E., Martin, J. M., Peeke, L. G., Seroczynski, A. D., Tram, J. M., Hoffman, K. B., Ruiz, M. D., Jacquiz, F., & Maschman, T. (2001). The development of multiple domains of child and adolescent self-concept: A cohort sequential longitudinal design. *Child Development, 72*, 1723–1746.

Cole, M., Cole, S. R., & Lightfoot, C. (2005). *The development of children* (5th ed.). New York: W. H. Freeman.

Coleman, M. C., & Webber, J. (2002). *Emotional and behavioral disorders: Theory and practice* (4th ed.). Boston: Allyn & Bacon.

Coles, G. (2004). Danger in the classroom: 'Brain glitch' research and learning to read. *Phi Delta Kappan, 85*(5), 344–351.

Coley, R. (2001). *Differences in the gender gap: Comparisons across racial/ethnic groups in education and work.* Princeton: Educational Testing Service.

Coll, C., Bearer, E., & Lerner, R. (Eds.). (2004). *Nature and nurture: The complex interplay of genetic and environmental influences on human behavior and development.* Mahwah, NJ: Erlbaum.

College Entrance Examination Board. (2003). *School AP grade distributions, national totals.* Princeton, NJ: Author.

Collins, W. A., Maccoby, E. E., Steinberg, L., Hetherington, E. M., & Bornstein, M. H. (2000). Contemporary research on parenting: The case for nature and nurture. *American Psychologist, 55*, 218–232.

Comunian, A. L., & Gielan, U. P. (2000). Sociomoral reflection & prosocial & antisocial behavior: Two Italian studies. *Psychological Reports, 87*, 161–175.

Conner, L., & Gunstone, R. (2004). Conscious knowledge of learning: Accessing learning strategies in a final year high school biology class. *International Journal of Science Education, 26*, 1427–1443.

Cook, B. G. (2001). A comparison of teachers' attitudes toward their included students with mild and severe disabilities. *Journal of Special Education, 34*(4), 203–213.

Cook, B. G. (2004). Inclusive teachers' attitudes toward their students with disabilities: A replication and extension. *Elementary School Journal, 104*(4), 307–320.

Coolahan, K., Fantuzzo, J., Mendez, J., & McDermott, P. (2000). Preschool peer interactions and readiness to learn: Relationship between classroom peer play and learning behaviors and conduct. *Journal of Educational Psychology, 92*, 458–465.

Cooper, D., & Snell, J. (2003). Bullying—not just a kid thing. *Educational Leadership, 60*(6), 22–25.

Cooper, H. (1989). Synthesis of research on homework. *Educational Leadership, 47*(3), 85–91.

Cooper, H., Jackson, K., Nye, B., & Lindsay, J. (2001). A model of homework's influence on the performance evaluations of elementary school students. *Journal of Experimental Education, 69*(2), 181–199.

Cooper, H., Lindsay, J., Nye, B., & Greathouse, S. (1998). Relationships among attitudes about homework, amount of homework assigned and completed, and student achievement. *Journal of Educational Psychology, 90*(1), 70–83.

Cooper, H., & Valentine, J. (2001). Using research to answer practical questions about homework. *Educational Psychologist, 36*(3), 143–153.

Cooper, H., Valentine, J., Nye, B., & Lindsay, J. (1999). Relationships between five after-school activities and academic achievement. *Journal of Educational Psychology, 91*(2), 369–378.

Cooper, J., Horn, S., Strahan, D., & Miller, S. (2003, April). *"If only they would do their homework:" Promoting self-regulation in high school English classes.* Paper presented at the annual meeting of the American Educational Research Association, Chicago.

Cooper, L. (2001). A comparison of online and traditional computer applications classes. *T.H.E. Journal, 28*(8), 52–58.

Corbett, D., & Wilson, B. (2002). What urban students say about good teaching. *Educational Leadership, 60*(1), 18–22.

Corcoran, C. A., Dershimer, E. L., & Tichenor, M. S. (2004). A teacher's guide to alternative assessment: Taking the first steps. *The Clearing House, 77*(5), 213–216.

Corno, L., Cronbach, L. J., Kupermintz, H., Lohman, D. F., Mandinach, E. B., Porteu, A. W., & Talbert, J. E. (2002). *Remaking the concept of aptitude: Extending the legacy of Richard E. Snow.* Mahwah, NJ: Erlbaum.

Corno, L., & Xu, J. (1998, April). *Homework and personal responsibility.* Paper presented at the annual meeting of the American Educational Research Association, San Diego.

Council for Exceptional Children (2005). Retrieved May 17, 2005, from http://www.CEC.sped.org. IDEALaw&resources

Covington, M. (1992). *Making the grade: A self-worth perspective on motivation and school reform.* Cambridge, MA: Harvard University Press.

Covington, M. (1998). *The will to learn: A guide for motivating young people.* New York: Cambridge University Press.

Covington, M. (2000). Intrinsic versus extrinsic motivation in schools: A reconciliation. *Current Directions in Psychological Science, 9*, 22–25.

Covington, M., & Omelich, C. (1987). "I knew it cold before the exam": A test of the anxiety blockage hypothesis. *Journal of Educational Psychology, 79*, 393–400.

Covington, M. V., & Müeller, K. J. (2001). Intrinsic versus extrinsic motivation: An approach/avoidance reformulation. *Educational Psychology Review, 13*, 157–176.

Craig, D. (2003). Brain-compatible learning: Principles and applications in athletic training. *Journal of Athletic Training, 38*(4), 342–350.

Crane, C. (2001). General classroom space. *School Planning & Management, 40*, 54–55.

Crick, N. R., Grotpeter, J. K., & Bigbee, M. A. (2002). Relationally and physically aggressive children's intent attributions and feelings of distress for relational and instructional peer provocation. *Child Development, 73*, 1134–1142.

Crockett, C. (2004). What do kids know—and misunderstand—about science? *Educational Leadership, 61*(5), 34–37.

Crosnoe, R. (2005). Double disadvantage or signs of resilience? The elementary school contexts of children from Mexican immigrant families. *American Educational Research Journal, 42*(2), 269–303.

Cross, T. L., (2001). Gifted children and Erikson's theory of psychosocial development. *Gifted Child Today, 24*(1), 54–55, 61.

Cruickshank, D. (1985). Applying research on teacher clarity. *Journal of Teacher Education, 35*(2), 44–48.

Cuban, L. (1993). *How teachers taught: Constancy and change in American classrooms*: 1890–1990 (2nd ed.). New York: Teachers College Press.

Cuban, L. (2001). *Computers in the classroom: Oversold and underused.* Cambridge, MA: Harvard University Press.

Cuban, L. (2004). Assessing the 20-year impact of multiple intelligences on schooling. *Teachers College Record, 106*(1), 140–146.

Culp, K. M., Honey, M., & Mandinach, E. (2004, April). *A retrospective on twenty years of education technology policy.* Paper presented at the annual meeting of the American Educational Research Association, San Diego.

Cummins, J. (2000). *Language, power, and pedagogy: Bilingual children in the crossfire.* Clevedon, UK: Multilingual Matters.

Dabbagh, N., & Bannan-Ritland, B. (2005). *Online learning.* Upper Saddle River, NJ: Pearson.

Dai, D. (2000). To be or not to be (challenged), that is the question: Task and ego orientations among high-ability, high-achieving adolescents. *Journal of Experimental Education, 68*, 311–330.

d'Ailly, H. (2003). Children's autonomy and perceived control in learning: A model of motivation and achievement in Taiwan. *Journal of Educational Psychology, 95*, 84–96.

D'Arcangelo, M. (2000). How does the brain develop? *Educational Leadership, 58*(3), 68–71.

Darling-Hammond, L. (1996). *What matters most: Teaching for America's future.* Washington, DC: National Commission on Teaching and America's Future.

Darling-Hammond, L. (1997). *The right to learn.* San Francisco: Jossey-Bass.

Darling-Hammond, L. (2001). Standard setting in teaching: Changes in licensing, certification, and assessment. In V. Richardson (Ed.), *Handbook of research on teaching* (4th ed., pp. 751–776). Washington, DC: American Educational Research Association.

Darling-Hammond, L., & Baratz-Snowdon, J. (Eds.). (2005). *A good teacher in every classroom: Preparing the highly qualified teachers our children deserve.* San Francisco: Jossey-Bass/Wiley.

Davenport, E., Davison, M., Kuang, H., Ding, S., Kim, S., & Kwak, N. (1998). High school mathematics course-taking by gender and ethnicity. *American Educational Research Journal, 35*(3), 497–514.

Davidson, B., Dell, G., & Walker, H. (2001, April). *In-school clubs: Impacting teaching and learning for at-risk students.* Paper presented at the annual meeting of the American Educational Research Association, Seattle.

Davidson, J., & Sternberg, R. (Eds.). (2003). *The psychology of problem solving.* Cambridge: Cambridge University.

Davis, A. (2004). The credentials of brain-based learning. *Journal of Philosophy of Education, 38*(1), 21–35.

Davis, G. (2003). Identifying creative students, teaching for creative growth. In N. Colangelo & G. Davis (Eds.), *Handbook of gifted education* (3rd ed., pp. 311–324). Boston: Allyn & Bacon.

Davis, G., & Rimm, S. (2004). *Education of the gifted and talented* (5th ed.). Boston: Allyn & Bacon.

Davis, H. A. (2003). Conceptualizing the role and influence of student–teacher relationships on children's social and cognitive development. *Educational Psychologist, 38*, 207–234.

Davis-Kean, P. E., & Sandler, H. M. (2001). A meta-analysis of measures of self-esteem for young children: A framework for future measurers. *Child Development, 72*, 887–906.

De Lisi, R., & Straudt, J. (1980). Individual differences in college students' performance on formal operations tasks. *Journal of Applied Developmental Psychology, 1*, 201–208.

de Vries, E. (2001). Hypermedia for physics learning: The case of the energy concept. In J. Rouet, J. Levonen, & A. Biardeau (Eds.), *Multimedia learning: Cognitive and instruction issues* (pp. 141–154). New York: Pergamon.

deCharms, R. (1968). *Personal causation.* San Diego: Academic Press.

deCharms, R. (1984). Motivation enhancement in education settings. In R. Ames & C. Ames (Eds.), *Research on motivation in education* (Vol. 1, pp. 275–310). New York: Academic Press.

Deci, E., & Ryan, R. (1985). *Intrinsic motivation and self-determination in human behavior.* New York: Plenum Press.

Deci, E., & Ryan, R. (1987). The support of autonomy and the control of behavior. *Journal of Personality and Social Psychology, 53,* 1024–1037.

Deci, E., & Ryan, R. (1991). A motivational approach to self: Integration in personality. In R. Dienstbier (Ed.), *Nebraska Symposium on Motivation 1990* (Vol. 38, pp. 237–288). Lincoln: University of Nebraska Press.

Deci, E., & Ryan, R. (2000). The "what" and "why" of goal pursuits: Human needs and the self-determination of behavior. *Psychological Inquiry, 11,* 227–268.

Deci, E., & Ryan, R. (Eds.).(2002). *Handbook of self-determination research.* Rochester, NY: University of Rochester Press.

DeCorte, E. (2003). Transfer as the productive use of acquired knowledge, skills, and motivations. *Current Directions in Psychological Science, 12,* 142–146.

Delpit, L. (1995). *Other people's children: Cultural conflict in the classroom.* New York: The New Press.

deMarrais, K., & LeCompte, M. (1999). *The way schools work* (3rd ed.). New York: Longman.

DeMeulenaere, E. (2001, April). *Constructing reinventions: Black and Latino students negotiating the transformation of their academic identities and school performance.* Paper presented at the annual meeting of the American Educational Research Association, Seattle.

Dempster, R., & Corkill, A. (1999). Interference and inhibition in cognition and behavior: Unifying themes for educational psychology. *Educational Psychology Review, 11*(1), 1–88.

Denig, S. J. (2003, April). *A proposed relationship between multiple intelligences and learning styles.* Paper presented at the annual meeting of the American Educational Research Association, Chicago.

Dennis, T. A., Cole, P. M., Zahn-Waxler, C., & Mizuta, I. (2002). Self in context: Autonomy and relatedness in Japanese and U. S. mother–preschooler dyads. *Child Development, 73,* 1803–1817.

Derry, S. (1992). Beyond symbolic processing: Expanding horizons for educational psychology. *Journal of Educational Psychology, 84,* 413–419.

DeVries, R. (1997). Piaget's social theory. *Educational Researcher, 26*(2), 4–18.

Dewey, J. (1938). *Experience and education.* New York: Macmillan.

Deyhle, D. (1987). Learning failure: Tests as gatekeepers and the culturally different child. In H. Trueba (Ed.), *Success or failure?* (pp. 85–108). Cambridge, MA: Newbury House.

Deyhle, D., & LeCompte, M. (1999). Cultural differences in child development: Navajo adolescents in middle schools. In R. H. Sheets & E. R. Holins (Eds.), *Racial and ethnic identity in school practices: Aspects of human development* (pp. 123–139). Mahwah, NJ: Erlbaum.

Diamond, J., & Gomez, K. (2004). African American parents' educational orientations: The importance of social class and parents' perceptions of schools. *Education and Urban Society, 36*(4), 383–427.

Dickens, C. (1859). *A tale of two cities.* (Introduction by Gillen D'Arcy Woods, 2004). New York: Barnes & Noble Books.

Dickson, S. M. (2004). Tracking concept mastery using a biology portfolio. *The American Biology Teacher, 66*(9), 628–634.

Dochy, F., & McDowell, L. (1997). Introduction: Assessment as a tool for learning. *Studies in Educational Evaluation, 23*(4), 279–298.

Dodge, K. A., Lansford, J. E., Burks, V. S., Bates, J. E., Pettit, G. S., Fontaine, R., & Price, J. M. (2003). Peer rejection and social information-processing factors in the development of aggressive behavior problems in children. *Child Development, 74,* 374–393.

Dole, J., & Sinatra, G. (1998). Reconceptualizing change in the cognitive construction of knowledge. *Educational Psychologist, 33*(2/3), 109–128.

Dolezal, S., Welsh, L., Pressley, M., & Vincent, M. (2003). How nine third-grade teachers motivate student academic engagement. *Elementary School Journal, 103*(3), 239–268.

Doll, B., Zucker, S., & Brehm, K. (2004). *Resilient classrooms: Creating healthy environments for learning.* New York: Guilford Press.

Donovan, M. S., & Bransford, J. D. (2005). Introduction. In M. S. Donovan & J. D. Bransford (Eds.), *How students learn: History, mathematics, and science in the classroom* (pp. 1–26). Washington, DC: National Academies Press.

Douglas, N. L. (2000). Enemies of critical thinking: Lessons from social psychology research. *Reading Psychology, 21,* 129–144.

Downey, J. (2003, April). *Listening to students: Perspectives of educational resilience from children who face adversity.* Paper presented at the annual meeting of the American Educational Research Association, Chicago.

Dowson, M., & McInerney, D. (2001). Psychological parameters of students' social and work avoidance goals: A qualitative investigation. *Journal of Educational Psychology, 93,* 35–42.

Doyle, W. (1986). Classroom organization and management. In M. Wittrock (Ed.), *Handbook of research on teaching* (3rd ed., pp. 392–431). New York: Macmillan.

Driscoll, M. (2005). *Psychology of learning for instruction* (3rd ed.). Needham Heights, MA: Allyn & Bacon.

Dubois, D. L. (2001). Family disadvantage, the self, and academic achievement. In B. J. Biddle (Ed.), *Social class, poverty, and education* (pp. 133–174). New York: Routlege Falmer.

Duke, N. (2000). For the rich it's richer: Print experience and environments offered to children in very low- and very high-socioeconomic status first-grade classrooms. *American Educational Research Journal, 37,* 441–478.

Duncan, G. J., & Brooks-Gunn, J. (2000). Family poverty, welfare reform, and child development. *Child Development, 71,* 188–196.

Durrell, D., & Catterson, J. (1980). *Durrell analysis of reading difficulty* (3rd ed.). San Antonio, TX: Harcourt Brace Educational Measurement.

Dwairy, M. (2005). Using problem-solving conversation with children. *Intervention in School and Clinic, 40,* 144–150.

Dweck, C. (1975). The role of expectations and attributions in the alleviation of learned helplessness. *Journal of Personality and Social Psychology, 31,* 674–685.

Dweck, C. (1999). Self-theories and goals: Their role in motivation, personality, and development. In R. Dienstbier (Ed.), *Perspectives on motivation: Nebraska Symposium on Motivation 1990* (Vol. 38, pp. 199–325). Lincoln: University of Nebraska Press.

Dweck, C. (2000). *Self-theories: Their role in motivation, personality, and development.* Philadelphia: Psychology Press.

Dweck, C., & Leggett, E. (1988). A social-cognitive approach to motivation and personality. *Psychological Review, 95,* 256–273.

Dwyer, K., & Osher, D. (2000). *Safeguarding our children: An action guide.* Washington, DC: U.S. Department of Education and Justice, American Institutes for Research. Retrieved June 13, 2005, from http://www.ed.gov/pubs/edpubs.html

Dynarski, M., & Gleason, P. (1999, April). *How can we help? What we have learned from evaluations of federal dropout-prevention programs.* Paper presented at the annual meeting of the American Educational Research Association, Montreal, Canada.

Eccles, J. S., Wigfield, A., & Schiefele, U. (1998). Motivation to succeed. In W. Damon (Series Ed.) & N. Eisenberg (Vol. Ed.), *Handbook of child psychology: Vol. 3. Social, emotional, and personality development* (5th ed., pp. 1017–1095). New York: Wiley.

Echevarria, J., Vogt, M., & Short, D. (2004). *Making content comprehensible to English learners: The SIOP model.* Boston: Allyn & Bacon.

Echevarria, J. E., & Graves, A. W. (2003). *Sheltered content instruction: Teaching English-language learners with diverse abilities* (2nd ed.). Boston: Allyn & Bacon.

Edens, K. M., & Potter, E. F. (2001). Promoting conceptual understanding through pictorial representation. *Studies in Art Education, 42,* 214–233.

Education Vital Signs (2005). Poverty. *American School Board Journal, February,* 22–23.

Educational Testing Service. (2005). *The Praxis Series 2005–2006: Information and Registration Bulletin.* Retrieved from http://www.ets.org/praxis/prxtest.html

Edwards, V. (2003). Techs answer to testing. *Education Week, 22*(35), 8, 10.

Eggen, P. (1997, March). *The impact of frequent assessment on achievement, satifaction with instruction, and intrinsic motivation of undergraduate university students.* Paper presented at the annual meeting of the American Educational Research Association, Chicago.

Eggen, P. (1998, April). *A comparison of urban middle school teachers' classroom practices and their expressed beliefs about learning and effective instruction.* Paper presented at the annual meeting of the American Educational Research Association, San Diego.

Eggen, P. (2001, April). *Constructivism and the architecture of cognition: Implications for instruction.* Paper presented at the annual meeting of the American Educational Research Association, Seattle.

Eggen, P., & Kauchak, D. (2002, April). *Synthesizing the literature of motivation: Implications for instruction.* Paper presented at the annual meeting of the American Educational Research Association, New Orleans.

Eggen, P., & Kauchak, D. (2006). *Strategies and models for teachers: Teaching content and thinking skills* (5th ed.). Boston: Allyn & Bacon.

Eilam, B., & Aharon, I. (2003). Students' planning in the process of self-regulated learning. *Contemporary Educational Psychology, 28,* 304–334.

Eisenberg, N., & Fabes, R. A. (1998). Prosocial development. In N. Eisenberg (Ed.), *Handbook of child psychology: Vol. 3. Social, emotional, and personality development* (5th ed., pp. 701–778). New York: Wiley.

Eisenberg, N., Losoya, S., & Guthrie, I. (1997). Social cognition and prosocial development. In S. Hala (Ed.), *The development of social cognition: Studies in developmental psychology* (pp. 329–363). Hove, England: Psychology Press/Erlbaum.

Eisenberger, R., & Cameron, J. (1998). Reward, intrinsic interest, and creativity: New findings. *American Psychologist, 53,* 676–679.

Eisenberger, R., Pierce, W. D., & Cameron, J. (1999). Effects of reward on intrinsic motivation: Negative, neutral, and positive. *Psychological Bulletin, 125,* 677–691.

Elbaum, B., & Vaughn, S. (2001). School-based interventions to enhance the self-concept of students with learning disabilities: A meta-analysis. *Elementary School Journal, 101*(3), 303–330.

Elias, M. (2004). Strategies to infuse social and emotional learning into academics. In J. Zins, R. Weissberg, M. Wang, & H. Walberg (Eds.), *Building academic success on social and emotional learning* (pp. 113–134). New York: Teachers College Press.

Elliot, A., & McGregor, H. (2000, April). Approach and avoidance goals and autonomous-controlled regulation: Empirical and conceptual relations. In A. Assor (Chair), *Self-determination theory and achievement goal theory: Convergences, divergences, and educational implications.* Symposium conducted at the annual meeting of the American Educational Research Association, New Orleans.

Elliot, A., & Thrash, T. (2001). Achievement goals and the hierarchical model of achievement motivation. *Educational Psychology Review, 13,* 139–156.

Elliott, J., & Thurlow, M. (2000). *Improving test performance of students with disabilities.* Thousand Oaks, CA: Corwin Press.

Ellsworth, J. Z. (2001, April). *Effects of state standards and testing on teacher inquiry and reflective classroom practice: A case study.* Paper presented at the annual meeting of the American Educational Research Association, Seattle.

Emerson, M. J., & Miyake, A. (2003). The role of inner speech in task switching: A dual-task investigation. *Journal of Memory and Language, 48,* 148–168.

Emmer, E. (1988). Praise and the instructional process. *Journal of Classroom Interaction, 23,* 32–39.

Emmer, E., Evertson, C., & Worsham, M. (2003). *Classroom management for secondary teachers* (6th ed.). Boston: Allyn & Bacon.

Emmer, E. T., & Stough, L. M. (2001). Classroom management: A critical part of educational psychology with implications for teacher education. *Educational Psychologist, 36,* 103–112.

Engle, R. (2003, April). *Successful transfer from only one specific problem: The importance of how learning events are framed.* Paper presented at the annual meeting of the American Educational Research Association, Chicago.

Englert, C., Berry, R., & Dunsmoore, K. (2001). A case study of the apprenticeship process. *Journal of Learning Disabilities, 34,* 152–171.

Epstein, J. (2001, April). *School, family, and community partnerships: Preparing educators and improving schools.* Paper presented at the annual meeting of the American Educational Research Association, Seattle.

ERIC Clearinghouse on Disabilities and Gifted Education. (2002). *GT—legal issues.* Retrieved November 10, 2002, from http://ericed.org/faq/gt-legal.html

Ericsson, K. (1996). The acquisition of expert performance. In K. Ericsson (Ed.), *The road to excellence: The acquisition of expert performance in the arts, sciences, sports, and games* (pp. 1–50). Mahwah, NJ: Erlbaum.

Ericsson, K., Krampe, D., & Tesch-Romer, C. (1993). The role of deliberate practice in the acquisition of expert performance. *Psychological Review, 100,* 363–406.

Erikson, E. (1968). *Identity: Youth and crisis.* New York: Norton.

Erikson, E. (1980). *Identity and the life cycle* (2nd ed.). New York: Norton.

Evans, C. J., Kirby, J. R., Fabrigar, L. R. (2003). Approaches to learning, need for cognition, and strategic flexibility among university students. *The British Journal of Educational Psychology, 73,* 507–528.

Evans, E., & Engelberg, R. (1988). Student perceptions of school grading. *Journal of Research and Development in Education, 21*(2), 45–54.

Evans, G. W., & English, K. (2002). The environment of poverty: Multiple stressor exposure, psychophysiological stress, and socioemotional adjustment. *Child Development, 73,* 1238–1248.

Evans, L., & Davies, K. (2000). No sissy boys here: A content analysis of the representation of masculinity in elementary school reading texts. *Sex Roles, 42,* 255–270.

Everson, H., & Tobias, S. (1998). The ability to estimate knowledge and performance in college: A metacognitive analysis. *Instructional Science, 26*(1–2), 65–79.

Evertson, C., Emmer, E., & Worsham, M. (2003). *Classroom management for elementary teachers* (6th ed.). Boston: Allyn & Bacon.

Exline, R. (1962). Need affiliation and initial communication behavior in problem solving groups characterized by low interpersonal visibility. *Psychological Reports, 10,* 405–411.

Ezell, D., & Klein, C. (2003). Impact of portfolio assessment on locus of control of students with and without disabilities. *Education and Training in Developmental Disabilities, 38*(2), 220–228.

Faiman-Silva, S. (2002). Students and a "culture of resistance" in Provincetown's schools. *Anthropology & Education Quarterly, 33*(2), 189–212.

Farkas, R. (2003). Effects of traditional versus learning-styles instructional methods on middle school students. *Journal of Educational Research, 97*(1), 42–51.

Farmer, T. W., Leung, M. C., Pearl, R., Rodkin. P. C., Cadwallader, T. W., & Van Acker, R. (2002). Deviant or diverse peer groups? The peer affiliations of aggressive elementary students. *Journal of Educational Psychology, 94,* 611–620.

Feldhusen, J. (1998a). Programs and service at the elementary level. In J. VanTassel-Baska (Ed.), *Excellence in educating gifted and talented learners* (3rd ed., pp. 211–223). Denver: Love.

Feldhusen, J. (1998b). Programs and services at the secondary level. In J. VanTassel-Baska (Ed.), *Excellence in educating gifted and talented learners* (3rd ed., pp. 225–240). Denver: Love.

Feldman, A., Kropkf, A., & Alibrandi, M. (1996, April). *Making grades: How high school science teachers determine report card grades.* Paper presented at the annual meeting of the American Educational Research Association, New York.

Ferguson, R. (2003). Teachers' perceptions and expectations and the black-white test score gap. *Urban Education, 38*(4), 460–507.

Ferrari, M., & Elik, N. (2003). Influences on intentional conceptual change. In G. M. Sinatra & P. R. Pintrich (Eds.), *Intentional conceptual change* (pp. 21–54). Mahwah, NJ: Erlbaum.

Fickes, M. (2001). The furniture of science. *School Planning and Management, 50,* 71–73.

Fine, L. (2002). Writing takes a digital turn for special-needs students. *Education Week, 21*(20), 8.

Finkelstein, E. (2005). Making PowerPoint quizzes. *Presentations, 19*(1), 18–20.

Finn, J., Pannozzo, G., & Achilles, C. (2003). The "why's" of class size: Student behavior in small classes. *Review of Educational Research, 72*(3), 321–368.

Finn, K., & Frone, M. (2004). Academic performance and cheating: Moderating role of school identification and self-efficacy. *Journal of Educational Research, 97*(3), 115–122.

Fischer, L., Schimmel, D., & Kelly, C. (1999). *Teachers and the law.* New York: Longman.

Fitch, M., & Semb, M. (1992, April). *Peer teacher learning: A comparison of role playing and video evaluation for effects on peer teacher outcomes.* Paper presented at the annual meeting of the American Educational Research Association, San Francisco.

Flavell, J., Friedrichs, A., & Hoyt, J. (1970). Developmental changes in memorization processes. *Cognitive Psychology, 1,* 324–340.

Flavell, J. H. (2000). Development of children's knowledge about the mental world. *International Journal of Behavioral Development, 24*(1), 15–23.

Flavell, J. H., Miller, P. H., & Miller, S. A. (2002). *Cognitive development* (4th ed.). Upper Saddle River, NJ: Prentice Hall.

Fleming, V., & Alexander, J. (2001). The benefits of peer collaboration: A replication with a delayed posttest. *Contemporary Educational Psychology, 26,* 588–601.

Flores, E., Cicchetti, D., & Rogosch, F. A. (2005). Predictors of resilience in maltreated and nonmaltreated Latino children. *Developmental Psychology, 41*(2), 338, 351.

Florida Department of Education. (2003). *Grade level expectations for the Sunshine State Standards: Science Grades 6–8.* Retrieved from http://www.firn.edu/doe/curric/prek12/frame2.htm

Fong, T. (1998). *The contemporary Asian-American experience: Beyond the model minority.* Upper Saddle River, NJ: Merrill/Prentice Hall.

Forcier, R., & Descy, D. (2005). *The computer as an educational tool: Productivity and problem solving* (4th ed.). Upper Saddle River, NJ: Merrill/Prentice Hall.

Forness, S., Walker, H., & Kavale, K. (2005). Psychiatric disorders and treatments: A primer for teachers. In K. Freiberg (Ed.), *Educating exceptional children 05/06* (7th ed., pp. 107–115). Dubuque, IA: McGraw-Hill/Dushkin.

Fowler, R. (1994, April). *Piagetian versus Vygotskian perspectives on development and education.* Paper presented at the annual meeting of the American Educational Research Association, New Orleans.

Freeman, E., & Hatch, J. (1989). What schools expect young children to know: An analysis of kindergarten report cards. *Elementary School Journal, 89,* 595–605.

Freeman, J., McPhail, J., & Berndt, J. (2002). Sixth graders' views of activities that do and do not help them learn. *Elementary School Journal, 102*(4), 335–347.

Freeman, K. E., Gutman, L. M., & Midgley, C. (2002). Can achievement goal theory enhance our understanding of the motivation and performance of African American young adolescents? In C. Midgely (Ed.), *Goals, goal structures and patterns of adaptive learning* (pp. 175–204). Mahwah, NJ: Erlbaum.

Freese, S. (1999, April). *The relationship between teacher caring and student engagement in academic high school classes.* Paper presented at the annual meeting of the American Educational Research Association, Montreal, Canada.

Freiberg, J. (Ed.). (1999a). *Beyond behaviorism: Changing the classroom management paradigm.* Boston: Allyn & Bacon.

Freiberg, J. (1999b). Consistency management and cooperative discipline. In J. Freiberg (Ed.), *Beyond behaviorism: Changing the classroom management paradigm* (pp. 75–97). Boston: Allyn & Bacon.

Freiberg, J. (1999c). Sustaining the paradigm. In J. Freiberg (Ed.), *Beyond behaviorism: Changing the classroom management paradigm* (pp. 164–173). Boston: Allyn & Bacon.

French, D. (2003). A new vision of authentic assessment to overcome the flaws in high-stakes testing. *Middle School Journal, 35*(1), 14–23.

Frey, B., & Schmitt, V. (2005, April). *Teachers' classroom assessment practices.* Paper presented at the annual meeting of the American Educational Research Association, Montreal, Canada.

Fuchs, D., Fuchs, L., Mathes, P., & Simmons, D. (1997). Peer-assisted learning strategies: Making classrooms more responsive to diversity.

American Educational Research Journal, 34(1), 174–206.

Fuchs, L. S., Fuchs., D., Prentice, K., Burch, M., Hamlett, C. L., Owen, R., Hosp, M., & Jancek, D. (2003). Explicitly teaching for transfer: Effects on third-grade students' mathematical problem solving. *Journal of Educational Psychology, 95*, 295–305.

Fujimura, N. (2001). Facilitating children's proportional reasoning: A model of reasoning processes and effects of intervention on strategy change. *Journal of Educational Psychology, 93*, 589–603.

Furlan, C. (2000). Satellite broadcasts seek to enliven study of history. *Education Week, 19*(26), 8.

Furrer, C., & Skinner, E. (2003). Sense of relatedness as a factor in children's academic engagement and performance. *Journal of Educational Psychology, 95*, 148–162.

Gagne, E. D., Yekovich, F. R., & Yekovich, C. W. (1997). *The cognitive psychology of school learning* (2nd ed.). Boston: Allyn & Bacon.

Gall, M., Gall, J., & Borg, W. (2003). *Educational research: An introduction* (7th ed.). Boston: Allyn & Bacon.

Gallagher, C. J. (2003). Reconciling a tradition of testing with a new learning paradigm. *Educational Psychology Review, 15*(1), 83–99.

Gallagher, J. (1998). Accountability for gifted students. *Phi Delta Kappan, 79*(10), 739–742.

Gallini, J. (2000, April). *An investigation of self-regulation developments in early adolescence: A comparison between non at-risk and at-risk students.* Paper presented at the annual meeting of the American Educational Research Association, New Orleans.

Garcia, D. (2004). Exploring connections between the construct of teacher efficacy and family involvement practices: Implications for urban teacher preparation. *Urban Education, 39*(3), 290–315.

Garcia, E. (2005, April). *A test in English is a test of English: Assessment's new role in educational equity.* Paper presented at the annual meeting of the American Educational Research Association, Montreal, Canada.

Gardner, H. (1983). *Frames of mind: The theory of multiple intelligences.* New York: Basic Books.

Gardner, H. (1993). *Creating minds: An anatomy of creativity seen through the lives of Freud, Einstein, Picasso, Stravinsky, Elliot, Graham, and Gandhi.* New York: Basic Books.

Gardner, H. (1995). Reflections on multiple intelligences: Myths and messages. *Phi Delta Kappan, 77*, 200–209.

Gardner, H. (1999a). *The disciplined mind: What all students should understand.* New York: Simon & Schuster.

Gardner, H. (1999b). The understanding pathway. *Educational Leadership, 57*(3), 12–17.

Gardner, H. (1999c, April). *The well-disciplined mind: What all students should understand.* Paper presented at the annual meeting of the American Educational Research Association, Montreal, Canada.

Gardner, H., & Hatch, T. (1989). Multiple intelligences go to school. *Educational Researcher, 18*(8), 4–10.

Garrahy, D. (2001). Three third-grade teachers' gender-related beliefs and behavior. *Elementary School Journal, 102*, 81–94.

Garza, E., Reyes, P., & Trueba, E. T. (2004). *Resiliency and success: Migrant children in the United States.* Boulder, CO: Paradigm.

Gaskill, P. J., & Murphy, P. K. (2004). Effects of a memory strategy on second-graders' performance and self efficacy. *Contemporary Educational Psychology, 29*, 27–49.

Gauvain, M. (2001). *The social context of cognitive development.* New York: Guilford Press.

Geary, D. (1998). What is the function of mind and brain? *Educational Psychology Review, 10*, 377–387.

Gee, J. P. (2005). *Learning by Design: Games as learning machines.* Retrieved from http://labweb.education.wisc.edu/room130/papers.htm

Gehlbach, H., & Roeser, R. (2002). The middle way to motivating middle school students: Avoiding false dichotomies. *Middle School Journal, 33*, 39–46.

Gehring, J. (2000). Massachusetts teachers blast state tests in new TV ads. *Education Week, 20*(12), 1, 22.

Gelman, R. (2000). Domain specificity and variability in cognitive development. *Child Development, 71*, 854–856.

Gentile, J. (1996). Setbacks in the advancement of learning" *Educational Researcher, 25*, 37–39.

Georghiades, P. (2004). Making pupils' conceptions of electricity more durable by means of situated metacognition. *International Journal of Science Education, 26*, 85–99.

Gersten, R., & Baker, S. (2001). Teaching expressive writing to students with learning disabilities: A meta-analysis. *Elementary School Journal, 101*(3), 251–272.

Gersten, R., Taylor, R., & Graves, A. (1999). Direct instruction and diversity. In R. Stevens (Ed.), *Teaching in American schools* (pp. 81–106). Upper Saddle River, NJ: Merrill/Prentice Hall.

Gersten, R., & Woodward, J. (1995). A longitudinal study of transitional and immersion bilingual education programs in one district. *Elementary School Journal, 95*(3), 223–239.

Gijbels, D., Dochy, F., Van den Bossche, P., Segers, M. (2005). Effects of problem-based learning: A meta-analysis from the angle of assessment. *Review of Educational Research, 75*(1), 27–61.

Gill, M., Achton, P., & Algina, J. (2003). Authoritative schools: A test of a model to resolve the school effectiveness debate. *Contemporary Educational Psychology, 29*, 389–409.

Gillies, R. (2000). The maintenance of cooperative and helping behaviours in cooperative groups. *British Journal of Educational Psychology, 70*, 97–111.

Gillies, R. M. (2003). The behaviors, interactions, and perceptions of junior high school students during small-group learning. *Journal of Educational Psychology, 95*, 137–147.

Gilligan, C. (1977). In a different voice: Women's conceptions of the self and of morality. *Harvard Educational Review, 47*, 481–517.

Gilligan, C. (1982). *In a different voice: Psychological theory and women's development.* Cambridge, MA: Harvard University Press.

Gilligan, C. (1998). *Minding women: Reshaping the education realm.* Cambridge, MA: Harvard University Press.

Gilligan, C., & Attanucci, J. (1988). Two moral orientations: Gender differences and similarities. *Merrill-Palmer Quarterly, 34*, 223–237.

Ginsberg, A. E., Shapiro, J. P., & Brown, S. P. (2004). *Gender in urban education: Strategies for student achievement.* Portsmouth, NH: Heinemann.

Glasser, W. (1985). *Control theory in the classroom.* New York: Perennial Library.

Glassman, M. (2001). Dewey and Vygotsky: Society, experience, and inquiry in educational practice. *Educational Researcher, 30*(4), 3–14.

Glassman, M., & Wang, Y. (2004). On the interconnected nature of interpreting Vygotsky: Rejoinder to Gredler and Shields *Does no one read Vygotsky's words. Educational Researcher, 33*(6), 19–22.

Glassner, A., Weinstock, M., & Neuman, Y. (2005). Pupils' evaluation and generation of evidence and explanation in argumentation. *British Journal of Educational Psychology, 75*, 105–118.

Goddard, R. D. (2001). Collective efficacy: A neglected construct in the study of schools and student achievement. *Journal of Educational Psychology, 93*, 467–476.

Goddard, R. D., Hoy, W. K., & Woolfolk-Hoy, A. (2000). Collective teacher efficacy: Its meaning, measure, and impact on student achievement. *American Educational Research Journal, 37*, 479–507.

Goldberg, M. (2000). An interview with Carol Gilligan: Restoring lost voices. *Phi Delta Kappan, 81*(9), 701–704.

Goldstein, N. E., Arnold, D. H., Rosenberg, J. L., Stowe, R. M., & Ortiz, C. (2001). Contagion of aggression in day care classrooms as a function of peer and teacher responses. *Journal of Educational Psychology, 93*, 708–719.

Goldstein, R. A. (2004). Who are our urban students and what makes them so different? In S. R. Steinberg & J. L. Kincheloe (Eds.), *19 Urban questions: Teaching in the city* (pp. 41–51). New York: Peter Lang.

Goleman, D. (2006). *Emotional intelligence* (10th ed.). New York: Bantam.

Gollnick, D., & Chinn, P. (1986). *Multicultural education in a pluralistic society* (2nd ed.). Upper Saddle River, NJ: Merrill/Prentice Hall.

Gollnick, D., & Chinn, P. (2004). *Multicultural education in a pluralistic society* (6th ed.). Upper Saddle River, NJ: Merrill/Prentice Hall.

Gonzales, P., Guzmán, J. C., Partelow, L., Pahlke, E., Jocelyn, L., Kastberg, D., & Williams, T. (2004). *Highlights From the Trends in International Mathematics and Science Study (TIMSS) 2003 (NCES 2005–005).* U.S. Department of Education. Washington, DC: National Center for Educational Statistics.

Good, T. (1987a). Teacher expectations. In D. Berliner & B. Rosenshine (Eds.), *Talks to teachers* (pp. 159–200). New York: Random House.

Good, T. (1987b). Two decades of research on teacher expectations: Findings and future directions. *Journal of Teacher Education, 37*(4), 32–47.

Good, T., & Brophy, J. (1986). School effects. In M. Wittrock (Ed.), *Handbook of research on teaching* (3rd ed., pp. 570–604). New York: Macmillan.

Good, T., & Brophy, J. (2003). *Looking in classrooms* (9th ed.). Boston: Allyn and Bacon.

Goodenow, C. (1993). Classroom belonging among early adolescent students: Relationships to motivation and achievement. *Journal of Early Adolescence, 13*, 21–43.

Goodman, J. F. (2005). How bad is cheating? *Education Week, 24*(16), 32, 35.

Goodman, J. R., & Balamore, U. (2003). *Teaching goodness: Engaging the moral and academic promise of young children.* Boston: Allyn & Bacon.

Gootman, M. E. (1998). Effective in-house suspension. *Educational Leadership, 56*(1), 39–41.

Gordon, G. L. (1999). Teacher talent and urban schools. *Phi Delta Kappan, 81*, 304–307.

Gordon, T. (1974). *Teacher effectiveness training.* New York: Wyden.

Gordon, T. (1981). Crippling our children with disruption. *Journal of Education, 163*, 228–243.

Goswami, U. (2001). No stages please—we're British. *British Journal of Psychology, 92*, 257–277.

Gottfredson, P. (2001). *Schools and delinquency.* Cambridge, England: Cambridge University Press.

Graham, S., & Barker, G. (1990). The downside of help: An attributional–developmental analysis of helping behavior as a low ability cue. *Journal of Educational Psychology, 82*, 7–14.

Graham, S., Berninger, V., Weintraub, N., & Schafer, W. (1998). Development of handwriting speed and legibility in grades 1–9. *Journal of Educational Research, 92*(1), 42–49.

Graham, S., & Weiner, B. (1996). Theories and principles of motivation. In D. Berliner & R. Calfee (Eds.), *Handbook of educational psychology* (pp. 63–84). New York: Macmillan.

Gray, T., & Fleischman, S. (2005). Successful strategies for English language learners. *Educational Leadership, 62*(4), 84–85.

Gray-Little, B., & Hafdahl, A. R. (2000). Factors influencing racial comparisons of self-esteem: A quantitative review. *Psychological Bulletin, 126,* 26–54.

Gredler, M., & Shields, C. (2004). Does no one read Vygotsky's words? Commentary on Glassman. *Educational Researcher, 33*(2), 21–25.

Green, S., & Mantz, M. (2002, April). *Classroom assessment practices: Examining impact on student learning.* Paper presented at the annual meeting of the American Educational Research Association, New Orleans.

Greenberg, M., Weissberg, R., O'Brien, M., Zins, J., Fredericks, L., Resnik, H., & Elias, M. (2003). Enhancing school-based prevention and youth development through coordinated social, emotional, and academic learning. *American Psychologist, 58,* 466–474.

Greeno, J., Collins, A., & Resnick, L. (1996). Cognition and learning. In D. Berliner & R. Calfee (Eds.), *Handbook of educational psychology* (pp. 15–46). New York: Macmillan.

Gregory, A., & Weinstein, R. (2004, April). *Toward narrowing the discipline gap: Cooperation or defiance in the high school classroom.* Paper presented at the annual meeting of the American Educational Research Association, San Diego.

Griffith, D. (1992, April). Prenatal exposure to cocaine and other drugs: Developmental and educational prognoses. *Phi Delta Kappan, 74,* 30–34.

Griffith, D., Hayes, K., & Pascarella, J. (2004). Why teach in urban settings? In S. Steinberg & J. Kincheloe (Eds.), *19 Urban questions: Teaching in the city* (pp. 267–280). New York: Peter Lang.

Grigorenko, E. L., & Sternberg, R. J. (2001). Dynamic testing. *Psychological Bulletin, 124,* 75–111.

Grolnick, W., Kurowski, C., & Gurland, S. (1999). Family processes and the development of children's self-regulation. *Educational Psychologist, 34*(1), 3–14.

Gronlund, N. (1993). *How to make achievement tests and assessments.* Needham Heights, MA: Allyn & Bacon.

Gronlund, N. (2003). *Assessing student achievement* (7th ed.). Needham Heights, MA: Allyn & Bacon.

Gronlund, N. (2004). *Writing instructional objectives for teaching and assessment* (7th ed.). Upper Saddle River, NJ: Merrill/Prentice Hall.

Gschwend, L., & Dembo, M. (2001, April). *How do high-efficacy teachers persist in low-achieving, culturally diverse schools?* Paper presented at the annual meeting of the American Educational Research Association, Seattle.

Guercin, F. (2001). Can children process complex information from different media? In J. Rouet, J. Levonen, & A. Biardeau (Eds.), *Multimedia learning: Cognitive and instruction issues* (pp. 59–64). New York: Pergamon.

Guerra, N. G., Huesmann, L. R., & Spendler, A. (2003). Community violence exposure, social cognition, and aggression among urban elementary school children. *Child Development, 74,* 1561–1576.

Gurian, M., & Stevens, K. (2005). What is happening with boys in school? *Teachers College Record,* May 2. ID Number: 11854. Retrieved June 21, 2005, from http://www.tcrecord.org

Guskey, T. (2002, April). *Perspectives on grading and reporting: Differences among teachers, students, and parents.* Paper presented at the

annual meeting of the American Educational Research Association, New Orleans.

Gutiérrez, K., Asato, J., Pacheco, M., Moll, L., Olson, K., Horng, E., Ruiz, R., García, E., & McCarty, T. (2002). "Sounding American": The consequences of new reforms on English language learners. *Reading Research Quarterly, 37*(2), 328–343.

Hacker, D., Bol, L., Horgan, D., & Rakow, E. (2000). Test prediction and performance in a classroom context. *Journal of Education Psychology, 92,* 160–170.

Hacker, D., Dunlosky, J., & Graesser, A. (Eds.). (1998). *Metacognition in educational theory and practice.* Mahwah, NJ: Erlbaum.

Haertel, E. (1986, April). *Choosing and using classroom tests: Teachers' perspectives on assessment.* Paper presented at the annual meeting of the American Educational Research Association, San Francisco.

Haertel, E. (1999). Performance assessment and education reform. *Phi Delta Kappan, 80*(9), 662–666.

Hafner, A. (2001, April). *Evaluating the impact of test accommodations on test scores of LEP students and non-LEP students.* Paper presented at the annual meeting of the American Educational Research Association, Seattle.

Haladyna, T., & Ryan, J. (2001, April). *The influence of rater severity on whether a student passes or fails a performance assessment.* Paper presented at the annual meeting of the American Educational Research Association, Seattle.

Haladyna, T. H. (2002). *Essentials of standardized achievement testing: Validity and accountability.* Boston: Allyn & Bacon.

Hall, R., Hall, M., & Saling, C. (1999). The effects of graphical postorganization strategies on learning from knowledge maps. *Journal of Experimental Education, 67,* 101–112.

Hallahan, D., & Kauffman, J. (2006). *Exceptional children* (10th ed.). Needham Heights, MA: Allyn & Bacon.

Halpern, D. (1995). *Thought and knowledge: An introduction to critical thinking* (3rd ed.). Hillsdale, NJ: Erlbaum.

Halpern, D. (1998). Teaching critical thinking for transfer across domains. *American Psychologist, 53,* 449–455.

Halpern, D., & LaMay, M. (2000). The smarter sex: A critical review of sex differences in intelligence. *Educational Psychology Review, 12*(2), 229–245.

Halpern, D. F. (2000). *Sex differences in cognitive abilities.* Mahwah, NJ: Erlbaum.

Hamachek, D. (1987). Humanistic psychology: Theory, postulates, and implications for educational processes. In J. Glover & R. Ronning (Eds.), *Historical foundations of educational psychology* (pp. 159–182). New York: Plenum Press.

Hamilton, R. (1997). Effects of three types of elaboration on learning concepts from text. *Contemporary Education Psychology, 22,* 299–318.

Hamilton, S. L., Seibert, M. A., Gardner, III, R., & Talbert-Johnson, C. (2000). Using guided notes to improve the academic achievement of incarcerated adolescents with learning and behavior problems. *Remedial and Special Education, 21,* 133–140.

Hamm, J., & Coleman, H. (1997, March). *Adolescent strategies for coping with cultural diversity: Variability and youth outcomes.* Paper presented at the annual meeting of the American Educational Research Association, Chicago.

Hampton, J. (1995). Testing the prototype theory of concepts. *Journal of Memory and Language, 32,* 686–708.

Hanich, L., Jordan, N., Kaplan, D., & Dick, J. (2001). Performance across different areas of mathematical cognition in children with learning

difficulties. *Journal of Educational Psychology, 93*(3), 615–626.

Hansbury, L. (1959). *A raisin in the sun.* New York: Random House.

Hansen, D. (1989). Lesson evading and lesson dissembling: Ego strategies in the classroom. *American Journal of Education, 97,* 184–208.

Hanson, M., Hayes, J., Schriver, K., LeMahieu, P., & Brown, P. (1998). *A plain language approach to the revision of test items.* Paper presented at the annual meeting of the American Educational Research Association, San Diego.

Harackiewicz, J., Barron, K., Taurer, J., Carter, S., & Elliot, A. (2000). Short-term and long-term consequences of achievement goals: Predicting interest and performance over time. *Journal of Educational Psychology, 92,* 316–330.

Hardman, M., Drew, C., & Egan, W. (2005). *Human exceptionality* (8th ed.). Needham Heights, MA: Allyn & Bacon.

Hardre, P. L., & Reeve, J. (2003). A motivational model of rural students' intentions to persist in, versus drop out of, high school. *Journal of Education Psychology, 95,* 347–356.

Hardy, L. (2002). A new federal role. *American School Board Journal, 18*(9), 20–24.

Harry, B. (1992). An ethnographic study of cross-cultural communication with Puerto Rican American families in the special education system. *American Educational Research Journal, 29*(3), 471–488.

Hatano, G., & Oura, Y. (2003). Commentary: Reconceptualizing school learning using insight from expertise research. *Educational Researcher, 32*(8), 26–29.

Havu-Nuutinen, S. (2005). Examining young children's conceptual change process in floating and sinking from a social constructivist perspective. *International Journal of Science Education, 27,* 259–279.

Hawkins, M. (2004). Researching English language and literacy development in schools. *Educational Researcher, 33*(3), 14–25.

Hawthorne, N. (1850). *The scarlet letter.* (Introduction by N. Stade, 2003). New York: Barnes & Noble Books.

Hay, I., Ashman, A., van Kraayenoord, C., & Stewart, A. (1999). Identification of self-verification in the formation of children's academic self-concept. *Journal of Educational Psychology, 91*(2), 225–229.

Haycock, K. (2001). Closing the achievement gap. *Educational Leadership, 58*(6), 6–11.

Hayes, J. R. (1988). *The complete problem solver* (2nd ed.). Mahwah, NJ: Erlbaum.

Hayes, K., & Salazar, J. (2001, April). *Evaluation of the Structured English Immersion Program, final report: Year 1.* Paper presented at the annual meeting of the American Educational Research Association, Seattle.

Hayes, S., Rosenfarb, I., Wulfert, E., Munt, E., Korn, Z., & Zettle, R. (1985). Self-reinforcement effects: An artifact of social standard setting? *Journal of Applied Behavior Analysis, 18,* 201–214.

Heath, S. (1989). Oral and literate traditions among Black Americans living in poverty. *American Psychologist, 44,* 367–373.

Heath, S. B. (1982). Questioning at home and at school: A comparative study. In G. Spindler (Ed.), *The ethnography of schooling: Educational anthropology in action* (pp. 102–131). New York: Holt, Rinehart & Winston.

Hennessey, M. G. (2003). Metacognitive aspects of students' reflective discourse: Implications for intentional conceptual change teaching and learning. In G. M. Sinatra & P. R. Pintrich (Eds.), *Intentional conceptual change* (pp. 103–132). Mahwah, NJ: Erlbaum.

Henricsson, L., & Rydell, A. M. (2004). Elementary school children with behavior problems: Teacher–child relations and self-perception. A prospective study. *Merrill-Palmer Quarterly, 50,* 111–138.

Henson, K. (1996). *Methods and strategies for teaching in secondary and middle schools* (2nd ed.). White Plains, NY: Longman.

Henson, R. K., Kogan, L. R., & Vacha-Haase, T. (2001). A reliability generalization study of the Teacher Efficacy Scale and related instruments. *Educational and Psychological Measurement, 61,* 404–420.

Hergenhahn, B. R., & Olson, M. H. (2001). *An introduction to theories of learning* (6th ed.). Upper Saddle River, NJ: Merrill/Prentice Hall.

Hershberger, S., Pilkington, S., & D'Augelli, A. (1997). Predictors of suicide attempts among gay, lesbian, and bisexual youth. *Journal of Adolescent Research, 12,* 477–497.

Herzig, A. (2004). Becoming mathematicians: Women and students of color choosing and leaving doctoral mathematics. *Review of Educational Research, 74*(2), 171–214.

Hess, F., & Brigham, F. (2001). How federal special education policy affects schooling in Virginia. In C. Finn, Jr., A. Rotherham, & C. Hokanson, Jr., (Eds.), *Rethinking special education for a new century.* New York: Thomas B. Fordham Foundation.

Heubert, J., & Hauser, R. (Eds.). (1999). *High stakes testing for tracking, promotion, and graduation.* Washington, DC: National Academy Press.

Heward, W. (2006). *Exceptional children* (8th ed.). Upper Saddle River, NJ: Merrill/Prentice Hall.

Hidi, S. (2001). Interest, reading, and learning: Theoretical and practical considerations. *Educational Psychology Review, 13,* 191–209.

Hidi, S. (2002). An interest researcher's perspective: The effects of extrinsic and intrinsic factors on motivation. In C. Sansone & J. Harackiewicz (Eds.), *Intrinsic and extrinsic motivation: The search for optimal motivation and performance* (pp. 309–339). San Diego: Academic Press.

Hiebert, E., & Raphael, T. (1996). Psychological perspectives on literacy and extensions to educational practice. In D. Berliner & R. Calfee (Eds.), *Handbook of educational psychology* (pp. 550–602). New York: Macmillan.

Hiebert, E. H., & Kamil, M. L. (Eds.). (2005). *Teaching and learning vocabulary.* Mahwah, NJ: Erlbaum.

Hiebert, J., Gallimore, R., & Stigler, J. (2002). A knowledge base for the teaching profession: What would it look like and how can we get one? *Educational Researcher, 31*(5), 3–15.

Higgins, K. (1997). The effect of year-long instruction in mathematical problem-solving on middle-school students' attitudes, beliefs, and abilities. *Journal of Experimental Education, 66,* 5–28.

Hill, K., & Wigfield, A. (1984). Test anxiety: A major educational problem and what can be done about it. *Elementary School Journal, 85,* 105–126.

Hill, W. F. (2002). *Learning: A survey of psychological interpretations* (7th ed.). Boston: Allyn & Bacon.

Hirsch, E. (2000). The tests we need and why we don't quite have them. *Education Week, 19*(21), 40–41.

Hmelo-Silver, C. E. (2004). Problem-based learning: What and how do students learn? *Educational Psychology Review, 16,* 236–266.

Hoff, D. (2001). Missing pieces. *Education Week, 20*(17), 43–52.

Hoff, D. (2003). Adding it all up. *Education Week, 22*(23), 28–31.

Hoffman, J., Assaf, L., & Paris, S. (2001). High-stakes testing in reading: Today in Texas, tomorrow? *Reading Teacher, 54*(5), 482–491.

Hoffman, L. (2002). Promoting girls' interest and achievement in physics classes for beginners. *Learning and Instruction, 12,* 447–465.

Hoffman, L. (2003). *Overview of public elementary and secondary schools and districts: School year 2001–02* (NCES 2003–411). U.S. Department of Education, National Center for Education Statistics. Washington, DC: U.S. Government Printing Office.

Hogan, T., Rabinowitz, M., & Craven, J. (2003). Representation in teaching: Inference from research on expert and novice teachers. *Educational Psychologist, 38,* 235–247.

Hohn, R. L., & Frey, B. (2002). Heuristic training and performance in elementary mathematical problem solving. *The Journal of Educational Research, 95,* 374–390.

Holahan, C., & Sears, R. (1995). *The gifted group in later maturity.* Stanford, CA: Stanford University Press.

Holliday, D. (2002, April). *Using cooperative learning to improve the academic achievements of inner-city middle school students.* Paper presented at the annual meeting of the American Educational Research Association, New Orleans.

Hollie, S. (2001, April). *Acknowledging the language of African American students: Instructional strategies.* Paper presented at the annual meeting of the American Educational Research Association, Seattle.

Holloway, J. (2001). Inclusion and students with learning disabilities. *Educational Leadership, 58*(6), 86–88.

Holloway, J. (2004). Family literacy. *Education Leadership, 61*(6), 88–89.

Holt, J. (1964). *How children fail.* New York: Putnam.

Homes for the homeless. (1999). Retrieved from http://www.opendoor.com/hfh

Hong, E. (1999, April). *Effects of gender, math ability, trait test anxiety, statistics course anxiety, statistics achievement, and perceived test difficulty on state test anxiety.* Paper presented at the annual meeting of American Educational Research Association, Montreal, Canada.

Hong, N., & Jonassen, D. (1999, April). *Well-structured and ill-structured problem-solving in multimedia simulation.* Paper presented at the annual meeting of the American Educational Research Association, Montreal, Canada.

Hong, S., & Ho, H. (2005). Direct and indirect longitudinal effects of parental involvement on student achievement: Second-order latent growth modeling across ethnic groups. *Journal of Educational Psychology, 97*(1), 32–42.

Hong, Y., Morris, M. W., Chiu, C., & Benet-Martinez, V. (2000). Multicultural minds: A dynamic constructivist approach to culture and cognition. *American Psychologist, 55,* 709–720.

Honora, D. (2003). Urban African American adolescents and school identification. *Urban Education, 38*(1), 58–76.

Honowar, V. (2005). Education Department tracks growth in distance learning. *Education Week, 24*(26), 6.

Horn, R. (2003, April). *Utilizing Vygotsky to promote critical constructivism in the age of standardization.* Paper presented at the annual meeting of the American Educational Research Association, Chicago.

Horvat, E., & Lewis, K. (2003). Reassessing the "burden of 'acting white' ": The importance of peer groups in managing academic success. *Sociology of Education, 76*(October), 265–280.

Howard, P. (2000). *The owner's manual for the brain: Everyday applications from mind-brain research* (2nd ed.). Atlanta, GA: Bard Press.

Howard, T. (2001). Powerful pedagogy for African American students: A case of four teachers. *Urban Education, 36*(2), 179–202.

Howe, K., & Berv, J. (2000). Constructing constructivism, epistemological and pedagogical. In D. Phillips (Ed.), *Constructivism in education: Opinions and second opinions on controversial issues* (pp. 19–40). Chicago: National Society for the Study of Education.

Howell, K. W., & Nolet, V. (2000). *Curriculum-based evaluation.* Stamford, CT: Wadsworth.

Huba, M., & Freed, J. (2000). *Learner-centered assessment on college campuses.* Boston: Allyn & Bacon.

Huber, J. A. (2004). A closer look at SQ3R. *Reading Improvement, 41,* 108–112.

Huefner, D. (1999). *Selected changes in IDEA regulations compared to the proposed regulations.* Paper presented at the annual meeting of the American Educational Research Association, Montreal, Canada.

Hughes, T. L., & McIntosh, D. E. (2002). Differential ability scales: Profiles of preschoolers with cognitive delay. *Psychology in the Schools, 39,* 19–29.

Hulse-Killachy, D., Killachy, J., & Donigan, J. (2001). *Making task groups work in your classroom.* Upper Saddle River, NJ: Merrill/Prentice Hall.

Hunt, N., & Marshall, K. (2002). *Exceptional children and youth: An introduction to special education* (3rd ed.). Boston: Houghton Mifflin.

Huntsinger, C. S., Jose, P. E., & Larsen, S. L. (1998). Do parent practices to encourage academic competence influence the social adjustment of young European American and Chinese American children? *Developmental Psychology, 34,* 747–756.

Hvitfeldt, C. (1986). Traditional culture, perceptual style, and learning: The classroom behavior of Hmong adults. *Adult Education Quarterly, 36*(2), 65–77.

Hynd, C. (2003). Conceptual change in response to persuasive messages. In G. M. Sinatra & P. R. Pintrich (Eds.), *Intentional conceptual change* (pp. 291–315). Mahwah, NJ: Erlbaum.

Igo, L. B., Bruning, R., & McCrudden, M. (2005). Exploring differences in students' copy-and-paste decision making and processing: A mixed-methods study. *Journal of Educational Psychology, 97*(1), 103–116.

Igo, L. B., Kiewra, K., & Bruning, R. (2004). Removing the snare from the pair: Using pictures to learn confusing word pairs. *Journal of Experimental Education, 72*(3), 165–178.

Ilg, T., & Massucci, J. (2003). Comprehensive urban high schools: Are there better options for poor and minority children? *Education and Urban Society, 36*(1), 63–78.

Ingersoll, R. (2003). *Who controls teachers' work?* Cambridge, MA: Harvard University Press.

Inhelder, B., & Piaget, J. (1958). *The growth of logical thinking from childhood to adolescence* (A. Parsons & S. Milgram, Trans.). New York: Basic Books.

Interstate New Teacher Assessment and Support Consortium. (1993). Principles. In *Model standards for beginning teacher licensing and development: A resource for state dialogues.* Washington, DC: Council of Chief State School Officers.

Irvine, J., & Armenta, B. (2001). *Culturally responsive teaching: Lesson planning for elementary and middle grades.* New York: McGraw-Hill.

Iyengar, S., & Lepper, M. (1999). Rethinking the role of choice: A cultural perspective on intrinsic motivation. *Journal of Personality and Social Psychology, 76,* 349–366.

Jackson, C. (2003). Transitions into higher education: Gendered implications for academic self-concept. *Oxford Review of Education, 29*(3), 331–346.

Jackson, L. (1999). *"Doing" school: Examining the role of ethnic identity and school engagement in academic performance and goal attainment.* Paper presented at the annual meeting of the American Educational Research Association, Montreal, Canada.

Jackson, P. (1968). *Life in classrooms.* New York: Holt, Rinehart & Winston.

Jacobs, G. M. (2004). A classroom investigation of the growth of metacognitive awareness in kindergarten children through the writing process. *Early Childhood Journal, 32,* 17–23.

Jacobs, J. E., Lanza, S., Osgood, D. W., Eccles, J. S., & Wigfield, A. (2002). Changes in children's self-competence and values: Gender and domain differences across grades one through twelve. Child Development, 73, 509–527.

Jenkins, H., Bailey, J., & Fraser, B. (2004, April). *Predictors of mathematics skills in boys with and without attention deficit hyperactivity disorder (ADHD).* Paper presented at the annual meeting of the American Educational Research Association, San Diego.

Jennings, J. (2002). Knocking on your door. *American School Board Journal, 189*(9), 25–27.

Jennings, M. (2000). Attendance technology easing recordkeeping burden. *Education Week, 19*(35), 7.

Jensen, A. (1998). *The g factor: The science of mental ability.* Westport, CT: Prager/Greenwood.

Jensen, E. (1998). *Teaching with the brain in mind.* Alexandria, VA: Association for Supervision and Curriculum Development.

Jerald, C. D. (2000). The state of the states. *Quality Counts 2000, Education Week.* Retrieved October 1, 2002, from http://www.edweek.org/sreports/qc00

Jesse, D., & Pokorny, N. (2001, April). *Understanding high achieving middle schools for Latino students in poverty.* Paper presented at the annual meeting of the American Educational Research Association, Seattle.

Jetton, T., & Alexander, P. (1997). Instruction importance: What teachers value and what students learn. *Reading Research Quarterly, 32,* 290–308.

Jew, C., Green, K., Millard, J., & Posillico, M. (1999, April). *Resiliency: An examination of related factors in a sample of students from an urban high school and a residential child care facility.* Paper presented at the annual meeting of the American Educational Research Association, Montreal, Canada.

Johnson, A. P. (2005). *A short guide to action research* (2nd ed.). Boston: Pearson.

Johnson, B., & Christensen, L. (2000). *Educational research: Quantitative and qualitative approaches.* Boston: Allyn & Bacon.

Johnson, D. W., & Johnson, R. (2006). *Learning together and alone: Cooperation, competition, and individualization* (8th ed.). Needham Heights, MA: Allyn & Bacon.

Johnson, D. W., & Johnson, R. T. (2004). The three Cs of promoting social and emotional learning. In J. Zins, R. Weissberg, M. Wang, & H. Walberg (Eds.), *Building academic success on social and emotional learning* (pp. 40–58). New York: Teachers College Press.

Johnson, J. (2002). Will parents of special-needs children endorse reform in special ed? *Phi Delta Kappan, 84*(2), 160–163.

Johnson, J. (2005). Isn't it time for schools of education to take concerns about student discipline more seriously? *Teachers College Record.* ID Number: 11739. Retrieved March 22, 2005, from http://www.tcrecord.org

Johnson, J., & Duffett, A. (2002). *When it's your own child: A report on special education and the families who use it.* New York: The Public Agenda.

Johnson, L. (2004). Down with detention. *Education Week, 24*(14), 39–40.

Johnston, R. (2000). In a Texas district, test scores for minority students have soared. *Education Week, 19*(30), 14–15.

Jonassen, D. (2000). *Computers as mindtools for schools* (2nd ed.). Upper Saddle River, NJ: Merrill/Prentice Hall.

Jonassen, D., Hannum, W., & Tessmer, M. (1989). *Handbook of task analysis procedures.* New York: Praeger.

Jonassen, D., Howland, J., Moore, J., & Marra, R. (2003). *Learning to solve problems with technology* (2nd ed.). Upper Saddle River, NJ: Merrill/Prentice Hall.

Jones, M. (1999). *Identity as strategy: Rethinking how African American students negotiate desegregated schooling.* Paper presented at the annual meeting of the American Educational Research Association, Montreal, Canada.

Jones, N., Kemenes, G., & Benjamin, P. (2001). Selective expression of electrical correlates of differential appetitive classical conditioning in a feedback network. *Journal of Neurophysiology, 85,* 89–97.

Jones, S. (2005). More discipline? *Teachers College Record.* ID Number: 11746. Retrieved March 29, 2005, from http://www.tcrecord.org

Jones, S., & Dindia, K. (2004). A meta-analytic perspective on sex equity in the classroom. *Review of Educational Research, 74*(4), 443–471.

Jones, S. M., & Dindia, K. (2004). A meta-analytic perspective on sex equity in the classroom. *Review of Educational Research, 74*(4), 443–471.

Jones, V. F., & Jones, L. S. (2004). *Comprehensive classroom management: Creating communities of support and solving problems* (7th ed.). Boston: Allyn & Bacon.

Jordan, W. (2001). Black high school students' participation in school-sponsored sports activities: Effects on school engagement and achievement. *Journal of Negro Education, 68*(1), 54–71.

Jorgenson, O. (2003). Brain scam? Why educators should be careful about embracing 'brain research'. *The Educational Forum, 67,* 364–369.

Judson, M. (2004, April). *Smaller learning communities in urban high schools: Increasing communication among teachers and students.* Paper presented at the annual meeting of the American Educational Research Association, San Diego.

Juniewicz, K. (2003). Student portfolios with a purpose. *The Clearing House, 77*(2), 73–77.

Kahn, E. (2000). A case study of assessment in a grade 10 English course. *Journal of Educational Research, 93*(5), 276–286.

Kahng, S. W., & Iwata, B. A. (1999). Correspondence between outcomes of brief and extended functional analyses. *Journal of Applied Behavior Analysis, 32,* 149–159.

Kalyuga, S., Ayres, P., Chandler, P., & Sweller, J. (2003). The expertise reversal effect. *Educational Psychologist, 38*(1), 23–31.

Kalyuga, S., Chandler, P., Tuovinen, J., & Sweller, J. (2001). When problem solving is superior to studying worked examples. *Journal of Educational Psychology, 93*(3), 579–588.

Kamil, M., & Walberg, H. (2005). The scientific teaching of reading. *Education Week, 24*(20), 38, 40.

Kaplan, D., Liu, X., & Kaplan, H. (2001). Influence of parents' self-feelings and expectations on children's academic performance. *Journal of Educational Research, 94*(6), 360–365.

Karlsen, B., & Gardner, E. (1995). *Stanford diagnostic reading test* (4th ed.). San Antonio, TX: Psychological Corporation.

Karten, T. (2005). *Inclusion strategies that work: Research-based methods for the classroom.* Thousand Oaks, CA: Corwin Press.

Katz, A. (1999, April). *Keepin' it real: Personalizing school experiences for diverse learners to create harmony instead of conflict.* Paper presented at the annual meeting of the American Educational Research Association, Montreal, Canada.

Kauchak, D., & Eggen, P. (2003). *Learning and teaching: Research-based methods* (4th ed.). Needham Heights, MA: Allyn & Bacon.

Kauffman, J., McGee, K., & Brigham, M. (2004). Enabling or disabling?: Observations on changes in special education. *Phi Delta Kappan, 85*(8), 613–620.

Kaufman, A. S., & Lictenberger, E. O. (2002). *Assessing adolescent and adult intelligence* (2nd ed.). Boston: Allyn & Bacon.

Kavale, K. A., & Forness, S. R. (2000). History, rhetoric, and reality. *Remedial and Special Education, 21*(5), 279–296.

Kazden, A. (2001). *Behavior modification in applied settings* (6th ed.). Belmont, CA: Wadsworth.

Keating, D. P. (2004). Cognitive and brain development. In R. Lerner & L. Steinberg (Eds.), *Handbook of adolescent psychology* (2nd ed.). New York: Wiley.

Keefer, M., Zeitz, C., & Resnick, L. (2000). Judging the quality of peer-led student dialogues. *Cognition and Instruction, 18*(1), 53–81.

Kellam, S. G., Ling, X., Meriaca, R., Brown, C. H., & Ialongo, N. (1998). The effect of the level of aggression on the first grade classroom on the course and malleability of aggressive behavior into middle school. *Development & Psychology, 10,* 165–185.

Keller, J. (2004). Just their type. *Technology and Learning, 25*(2), 12–18.

Kerman, S. (1979). Teacher expectations and student achievement. *Phi Delta Kappan, 60,* 70–72.

Kerr, M. (2000). Bullying: The hidden threat to a safe school. *Utah Special Educator, 21*(3), 9–10.

Kincheloe, J. (2004). Why a book on urban education? In S. Steinberg and J. Kincheloe (Eds.), *19 Urban questions: Teaching in the city* (pp. 1–27). New York: Peter Lange.

Kindler, A. L. (2002). *Survey of the states' limited English proficient students and available educational programs and services, 2000–2001 Summary Report.* Washington, DC: National Clearinghouse for English Language Acquisition and Language Instruction Educational Programs.

King, A. (1999). Teaching effective discourse patterns for small-group learning. In R. Stevens (Ed.), *Teaching in American schools* (pp. 121–139). Upper Saddle River, NJ: Merrill/Prentice Hall.

King, A. (2000). Situated cognition. In A. Kazdin (Ed.), *Encyclopedia of psychology.* Washington, DC: American Psychological Association and Oxford University Press.

Kitsantas, A., Zimmerman, B., & Cleary, T. (2000). The role of observation and emulation in the development of athletic self-regulation. *Journal of Educational Psychology, 92*(4), 811–817.

Kleiman, C. (2001, October 30). Internet helps parents keep an eye on kids [Electronic version]. *Chicago Tribune.* Retrieved from http://www.chicagotribune.com

Klein, P. (2003). Rethinking the multiplicity of cognitive resources and curricular representations: Alternatives to "learning styles" and "multiple intelligences." *Journal of Curriculum Studies, 35,* 45–81.

Kliewer, C., Fitzgerald, L., Meyer-Mork, J., Hartman, P., English-Sand, P., & Raschke, D. (2004). Citizenship for all in the literate community: An ethnography of young children with significant disabilities in inclusive early childhood settings. *Harvard Educational Review, 74*(4), 373–403.

Kluth, P., Villa, R., & Thousand, J. (2002). "Our school doesn't offer inclusion" and other legal blunders. *Educational Leadership, 83*(4), 24–27.

Knapp, M. S. (2001). Policy, poverty, and capable teaching: Assumptions and issues in policy design. In B. J. Biddle (Ed.), *Social class, poverty, and education* (pp. 175–212). New York: Routlege Falmer.

Knight, J. (2002). Crossing the boundaries: What constructivists can teach intensive-explicit instructors and vice versa. *Focus on Exceptional Children, 35,* 1–14, 16.

Koc, K., & Buzzelli, C. A. (2004). The moral of the story is . . . Using children's literature in moral education. *Young Children, 59*(1), 92–97.

Kodjo, C. M., Auinger, P., & Ryan, S. (2003). Demographic, intrinsic, and extrinsic factors associated with weapon carrying at school. *Archives of Pediatrics & Adolescent Medicine, 157,* 96–103.

Kohlberg, L. (1963). The development of children's orientation toward moral order: Sequence in the development of human thought. *Vita Humana, 6,* 11–33.

Kohlberg, L. (1969). Stage and sequence: The cognitive-developmental approach to socialization. In D. Goslin (Ed.), *Handbook of socialization theory and research.* Chicago: Rand McNally.

Kohlberg, L. (1975). The cognitive development approach to moral education. *Phi Delta Kappan, 56,* 670–677.

Kohlberg, L. (1981). *Philosophy of moral development.* New York: Harper & Row.

Kohlberg, L. (1984). *Essays on moral development: Vol. 2. The psychology of moral development.* New York: Harper & Row.

Kohn, A. (1992). *No contest: The case against competition.* Boston: Houghton Mifflin.

Kohn, A. (1993a). Why incentive plans cannot work. *Harvard Business Review, 71,* 54–63.

Kohn, A. (1993b). *Punished by rewards: The trouble with gold stars, incentive plans, A's, praise, and other bribes.* Boston: Houghton Mifflin.

Kohn, A. (1996a). *Beyond discipline: From compliance to community.* Alexandria, VA: Association for Supervision and Curriculum Development.

Kohn, A. (1996b). By all available means: Cameron and Pierce's defense of extrinsic motivators. *Review of Educational Research, 66,* 1–4.

Kohn, A. (2000). Burnt at the high stakes. *Journal of Teacher Education, 51*(4), 315–327.

Kohn, A. (2004). Challenging students—and how to have more of them. *Phi Delta Kappan, 86*(3), 184–194.

Kohn, A. (2005a). *Unconditional parenting: Moving from rewards and punishments to love and reason.* New York: Atria Books.

Kohn, A. (2005b). Unconditional teaching. *Educational Leadership, 63*(1), 20–24.

Koretz, D., & Hamilton, L. (2000). Assessment of students with disabilities in Kentucky: Inclusion, student performance, and validity. *Educational Evaluation and Policy Analysis, 22*(3), 255–272.

Kounin, J. (1970). *Discipline and group management in classrooms.* New York: Holt, Rinehart & Winston.

Kozhevnikov, M., Hegarty, M., & Mayer, R. (1999, April). *Students' use of imagery in solving qualitative problems in kinematics.* Paper presented at the annual meeting of the American Educational Research Association, Montreal, Canada.

Kozioff, M. A., LaNunziata, L., & Cowardin, J. (2000). Direct instruction: Its contributions to high school achievement. *The High School Journal, 84,* 54–71.

Kozulin, A. (1990). *Vygotsky's psychology: A biography of ideas.* Cambridge, MA: Harvard University Press.

Kozulin, A. (1998). *Psychological tools: A sociocultural approach to education.* Cambridge: Harvard University Press.

Kramarski, B., & Mevarech, Z. R. (2003). Enhancing mathematical reasoning in the classroom: The effects of cooperative learning and metacognitive training. *American Educational Research Journal, 40,* 281–310.

Kramer, P. A. (2003). The ABC's of professionalism. *Kappa Delta Pi Record, 40*(1), 22–25.

Krashen, S. (1999). *Condemned without a trial: Bogus arguments against bilingual education.* Portsmouth, NH: Heineman.

Krashen, S. (2005). Skyrocketing scores: An urban legend. *Educational Leadership, 62*(4), 37–39.

Krechevsky, M., & Seidel, S. (2001). Minds at work: Applying multiple intelligences in the classroom. In J. Collins & D. Cook (Eds.), *Understanding learning: Influences and outcomes* (pp. 44–59). London, Paul Chapman.

Kritt, D. (2004). Strengths and weaknesses of bright urban children: A critique of standardized testing in kindergarten. *Education and Urban Society, 36*(4), 457–466.

Kroesbergen, E. H., & van Luit, E. H. (2002). Teaching multiplication to low math performers: Guided versus structured instruction. *Instructional Science, 30,* 361–378.

Kroesbergen, E. H., van Luit, E. H., & Maas, C. J. (2004). Effectiveness of explicit and constructivist mathematics instruction for low-achieving students in the Netherlands. *Elementary School Journal, 104,* 233–251.

Kroger, J. (2000). *Identity development: Adolescence through adulthood.* Thousand Oaks, CA: Sage.

Kuh, D., & Vesper, N. (1999, April). *Do computers enhance or detract from student learning?* Paper presented at the annual meeting of the American Educational Research Association, Montreal, Canada.

Kuhn, D. (1999). A developmental model of critical thinking. *Educational Researcher, 28*(2), 16–26, 46.

Kuhn, D. (2001). Why development does (and does not) occur: Evidence from the domain of inductive reasoning. In J. L. McClelland & R. S. Seigler (Eds.), *Mechanisms of cognitive development: Behavioral and neural perspectives* (pp. 221–249). Mahwah, NJ: Erlbaum.

Kuhn, D., & Dean, D., Jr. (2004). Metacognition: A bridge between cognitive psychology and educational practice. *Theory into Practice, 43*(4), 268–273.

Kumar, R., Gheen, M. H., & Kaplan, A. (2002). Goal structures in the learning environment and students' disaffection from learning and schooling. In C. Midgely (Ed.), *Goals, goal structures and patterns of adaptive learning* (pp. 143–173). Mahwah, NJ: Erlbaum.

Kuther, T., & Higgins-D'Alessandra, M. (1997, March). *Effects of a just community on moral development and adolescent engagement in risk.* Paper presented at the annual meeting of the American Educational Research Association, Chicago.

Labov, W. (1972). *Language in the inner city: Studies in the "Black" English vernacular.* Philadelphia: University of Pennsylvania Press.

Lalli, J. S., & Kates, K. (1998). The effects of reinforcer preference on functional analysis outcomes. *Journal of Applied Behavior Analysis, 31,* 79–90.

Lambating, J., & Allen, J. (2002, April). *How the multiple functions of grades influence their validity and value as measures of academic achievement.* Paper presented at the annual meeting of the American Educational Research Association, New Orleans.

Lambert, N., & McCombs, B. (1998). Introduction: Learner-centered schools and classrooms as a direction for school reform. In N. Lambert & B. McCombs (Eds.), *How students learn: Reforming schools through learner-centered education* (pp. 1–22). Washington, DC: American Psychological Association.

Lan, W., Repman, J., & Chyung, S. (1998). Effects of practicing self-monitoring of mathematical problem-solving heuristics on impulsive and reflective college students' heuristics knowledge and problem-solving ability. *Journal of Experimental Education, 67*(1), 32–52.

Land, R. (1997). Moving up to complex assessment systems: Proceedings from the 1996 CRESST Conference. *Evaluation Comment, 7*(1), 1–21.

Landsman, J. (2004). Confronting the racism of low expectations. *Educational Leadership, 62*(3), 28–32.

Langdon, C. (1999, April). The fifth Phi Delta Kappan poll of teachers' attitudes toward the public schools. *Phi Delta Kappan.* Retrieved February, 2004, from http://www.pdkintl.org/kappan/klan9904.htm

Langer, E. J. (2000). Excellence in English in middle and high school: How teachers' professional lives support student achievement. *American Educational Research Journal, 37,* 397–439.

Lareau, A. (2003). *Unequal childhoods: Class, race, and family life.* Berkeley: University of California Press.

Larrivee, B. (2002). The potential perils of praise in a democratic interactive classroom. *Action in Teacher Education, 23*(4), 77–88.

Laupa, M., & Turiel, E. (1995). Social domain theory. In W. Kurtines & J. Gewirtz (Eds.), *Moral development: An introduction.* Boston: Allyn & Bacon.

Lawson, A., & Childs, R. (2001, April). *Making sense of large-scale assessments: Communicating with teachers.* Paper presented at the annual meeting of the American Educational Research Association, Seattle.

Lawton, M. (1999). The brain-based ballyhoo. *Harvard Education Letter* (July/August), 5–7.

Leahy, T., & Harris, R. (2001). *Learning and cognition* (5th ed.). Upper Saddle River, NJ: Merrill/Prentice Hall.

Lee, J., Pulvino, C., & Perrone, P. (1998). *Restoring harmony: A guide for managing conflicts in schools.* Upper Saddle River, NJ: Merrill/Prentice Hall.

Lee, J., & Reigeluth, C. M. (2003). Formative research on the heuristic task analysis process. *Educational Technology Research and Development, 51,* 5–24.

Lee, J. D. (2002). More than ability: Gender and personal relationships influence science and technology involvement. *Sociology of Education, 75*(October), 349–373.

Lee, V. (2000). Using hierarchical linear modeling to study social contexts: The case of school effects. *Educational Psychologist, 35,* 125–141.

Lee, V. E., & Burkam, D. T. (2002). *Inequality at the starting gate: Social background differences in achievement as children begin school.* Washington, DC: Economic Policy Institute.

Lee, V. E., & Burkam, D. T. (2003). Dropping out of high school: The role of school organization and structure. *American Educational Research Journal, 40*(2), 353–393.

Lehman, S., Kauffman, D., White, M., Horn, C., & Bruning, R. (1999, April). *Teacher interaction: Motivating at-risk students in Web-based high school courses.* Paper presented at the annual meeting of the American Educational Research Association, Montreal, Canada.

Lei, J. L. (2003). (Un)necessary toughness?: Those "loud Black girls" and those "quiet Asian boys." *Anthropology & Education Quarterly, 34*(2), 158–181.

Leinhardt, G. (2001). Instructional explanations: A commonplace for teaching and location for contrast. In V. Richardson (Ed.), *Handbook of research on teaching* (4th ed., pp. 333–357). Washington, DC: American Educational Research Association.

Leinhardt, G., & Steele, M. (2005). Seeing the complexity of standing to the side: Instructional dialogues. *Cognition and Instruction, 23*(1), 87–163.

Lemke, M., Sen, A., Pahlke, E., Partelow, L., Miller, D., Williams, T., Kastberg, D., & Jocelyn, L. (2004). *International outcomes of learning in mathematics literacy and problem solving: PISA 2003 results from the U.S. perspective* (NCES 2005–003). U.S. Department of Education. Washington, DC: National Center for Education Statistics.

Leon, M., Lynn, T., McLean, P., & Perri, L. (1997, March). *Age and gender trends in adults' normative moral reasoning.* Paper presented at the annual meeting of the American Educational Research Association, Chicago.

Leont'ev, A. (1981). The problem of activity in psychology. In J. Wertsch (Ed.), *The concept of activity in Soviet psychology* (pp. 37–71). Armonk, NY: Sharpe.

LePage, P., Darling-Hammond, L., & Akar, H., with Gutierrez, C., Jenkins-Gunn, E., & Rosebrock, K. (2005). Classroom management. In L. Darling-Hammond & J. Bransford (Eds.), *Preparing teachers for a changing world: What teachers should learn and be able to do* (pp. 327–357). San Francisco: Jossey-Bass/Wiley.

Lepper, M., & Henderlong, J. (2000). Turning "play" into work and "work" into play. In C. Sansone & J. Harackiewicz (Eds.), *Intrinsic and extrinsic motivation: The search for optimal motivation and performance* (pp. 257–307). San Diego: Academic Press.

Lepper, M., & Hodell, M. (1989). Intrinsic motivation in the classroom. In C. Ames & R. Ames (Eds.), *Research on motivation in education* (Vol. 3, pp. 73–105). San Diego: Academic Press.

Lever-Duffy, J., McDonald, J., & Mizell, A. (2003). *Teaching and learning with technology.* Boston: Allyn & Bacon.

Levesque, C., Stanek, L., Zuehlke, A. N., & Ryan, R. (2004). Autonomy and competence in German and American university students: A comparative study based on self-determination theory. *Journal of Educational Psychology, 96*(1), 68–84.

Levine, A., & Nediffer, J. (1996). *Beating the odds: How the poor get to college.* San Francisco: Jossey-Bass.

Lew, J. (2004). The "other" story of model minorities: Korean American high school dropouts in an urban context. *Anthropology and Education Quarterly, 35*(3), 303–323.

Lewis, R. (2001). Classroom discipline & student responsibility: The students' view. *Teaching and Teacher Education, 17,* 307–319.

Lewis, R., & Doorlag, D. (1999). *Teaching special students in general education classrooms.* Upper Saddle River, NJ: Merrill/Prentice Hall.

Lewis, V. (2002). *Development and disability* (2nd ed.). Malden, MA: Blackwell.

Lightfoot, C. (1999). *The development of language: Acquisition, change, and evolution.* Malden, MA: Blackwell.

Lillard, A. S. (1997). Other folks' theories of mind and behavior. *Psychological Science, 8,* 268–274.

Lindeman, B. (2001). Reaching out to immigrant parents. *Educational Leadership, 58*(6), 62–66.

Linn, R. L., & Baker, E. L., & Betebenner, D. W. (2002). Accountability systems: Implications of the requirements of the No Child Left Behind Act of 2001. *Educational Researcher, 31*(6), 3–16.

Linn, R. L., & Miller, M. D. (2005). *Measurement and assessment in teaching* (9th ed.). Upper Saddle River, NJ: Pearson.

Linnenbrink, E. A., & Pintrich, P. R. (2003). Achievement goals and intentional conceptual change. In G. M. Sinatra & P. R. Pintrich (Eds.), *Intentional conceptual change* (pp. 347–374). Mahwah, NJ: Erlbaum.

Lippa, R. A. (2002). *Gender, nature, and nurture.* Mahwah, NJ: Erlbaum.

Lipson, M. Y., & Wixson, K. K. (2003). *Assessment and instruction of reading and writing disability* (3rd ed.). New York: Longman.

Liu, X. (2004). Using concept mapping for assessing and promoting relational conceptual change in science. *Science Education, 88,* 373–396.

Lohman, D. (2001, April). *Fluid intelligence, inductive reasoning, and working memory: Where the theory of multiple intelligences falls short.* Paper presented at the annual meeting of the American Educational Research Association, Seattle.

Lohman, M., & Finkelstein, M. (2000). Designing groups in problem-based learning to promote problem-solving skill and self-directedness. *Instructional Science, 28,* 291–307.

Lopes, P., & Salovey, P. (2004). Toward a broader education: Social, emotional, and practical skills. In J. Zins, R. Weissberg, M. Wang, & H. Walberg (Eds.), *Building academic success on social and emotional learning* (pp. 76–93). New York: Teachers College Press.

Lopez, N. (2003). *Hopeful girls, troubled boys: Race and gender disparity in urban education.* New York: Routledge.

Lorch, R. F., Jr., & Lorch, E. P. (1995). Effects of organizational signals on text-processing strategies. *Journal of Educational Psychology, 87,* 537–544.

Losen, D., & Orfield, G. (2002). *Racial inequality in special education.* Cambridge, MA: Harvard Education Press.

Lou, Y., Abrami, P., & Spence, J. (2000). Effects of within-class grouping on student achievement: An exploratory model. *Journal of Educational Research, 94*(2), 101–112.

Loughran, J., Mulhall, P., & Berry, A. (2004). In search of pedagogical content knowledge in science: Developing ways of articulating and documenting professional practice. *Journal of Research in Science Teaching, 41,* 370–391.

Louis, B., Subotnik, R. F., Breland, P. S., & Lewis, M. (2000). Establishing criteria for high ability versus selective admission to gifted programs: Implications for policy and practice. *Educational Psychology Review, 12,* 295–314.

Loveless, T. (1999). Will tracking reform promote social equity? *Educational Leadership, 56*(7), 28–32.

Lowrie, T., & Kay, R. (2001). Relationship between visual and nonvisual solution methods and difficulty in elementary mathematics. *Journal of Educational Research, 94*(4), 248–255.

Loyd, B., & Loyd, D. (1997). Kindergarten through grade 12 standards: A philosophy of grading. In G. Phye (Ed.), *Handbook of classroom assessment* (pp. 481–490). San Diego, CA: Academic Press.

Luckasson, R., Borthwick-Duffy, S., Buntinx, W. H. E., Coulter, D. L., Craig, E. M., Reeve, A., Schalock, R. L., Snell, M. E. Spitalnik, D. M., Spreat, S., & Tassé, M. J. (Eds.). (2002). *Mental retardation: Definition, classification, and systems of supports* (10th ed.). Washington, DC: American Association on Mental Retardation.

Luque, M. L. (2003). The role of domain-specific knowledge in intentional conceptual change. In G. M. Sinatra & P. R. Pintrich (Eds.), *Intentional conceptual change* (pp. 133–170). Mahwah, NJ: Erlbaum.

Lynch, M. (2001). *Fostering creativity in children, K–8: Theory and practice.* Boston: Allyn & Bacon.

Ma, X. (2001). Bullying and being bullied: To what extent are bullies also victims? *American Educational Research Journal, 38*(2), 351–370.

Maag, J. (2001). Rewarded by punishment: Reflections on the disuse of positive reinforcement in schools. *Exceptional Children, 67,* 173–186.

Mabry, L. (1999). Writing to the rubrics: Lingering effects of traditional standardized testing on direct writing assessment. *Phi Delta Kappan, 80,* 673–679.

Macionis, J. (2006). *Society: The basics* (8th ed.). Upper Saddle River, NJ: Merrill/Prentice Hall.

Madaus, G., & O'Dwyer, L. (1999). A short history of performance assessment. *Phi Delta Kappan, 80*(9), 688–695.

Maehr, M., & Midgley, C. (1991). Enhancing student motivation: A schoolwide approach. *Education Psychologist, 26,* 399–427.

Maeroff, G. (2003). The virtual schoolhouse. *Education Week, 22*(24), 40, 28.

Mager, R. (1962). *Preparing instructional objectives.* Palo Alto, CA: Featon.

Mager, R. (1998). *Preparing instructional objectives: A critical tool in the development of effective instruction* (3rd ed.). Atlanta, GA: Center for Effective Performance.

Mangels, J., Piction, T., & Craik, F. (2001). Attention and successful episodic encoding: An event-related potential study. *Brain Research, 11,* 77–95.

Manouchehri, A. (2004). Implementing mathematics reform in urban schools: A study of the effect of teachers' motivation style. *Urban Education, 38,* 472–508.

Manzo, K. (2000). Book binds. *Education Week, 19*(17), 29–33.

Marcia, J. (1980). Identity in adolescence. In J. Adelson (Ed.), *Handbook of adolescent psychology.* New York: Wiley.

Marcia, J. (1987). The identity status approach to the study of ego identity development. In T. Honess & K. Yardley (Eds.), *Self and identity: Perspectives across the life span.* London: Routledge & Kegan Paul.

Marcia, J. (1988). Common processes underlying ego identity, cognitive/moral development and individuation. In D. Lapsley & F. Power (Eds.), *Self, ego, and identity: Integrative approaches* (pp. 211–225). New York: Springer-Verlag.

Marcia, J. E. (1999). Representational thought in ego identity, psychotherapy, and psychosocial development. In I. E. Sigel (Ed.), *Development of mental representation: Theories and applications.* Mahwah, NJ: Erlbaum.

Marinoff, L. (2003). *The big questions: How philosophy can change your life.* New York: Bloomsbury.

Marsh, H. (1990). Causal ordering of academic self-concept and academic achievement: A multiwave, longitudinal panel analysis. *Journal of Educational Psychology, 82,* 646–656.

Marsh, H. (1992). Content specificity of relations between academic achievement and academic self-concept. *Journal of Educational Psychology, 84*(1), 34–52.

Marsh, H., Kong, C., & Hau, K. (2001). Extension of the internal/external frame of reference model of self-concept formation: Importance of native and non-native languages for Chinese students. *Journal of Educational Psychology, 93*(3), 543–553.

Marshal, H. (2001). Cultural differences on the development of self-concept; Updating our thinking. *Young Children, November,* 19–22.

Marso, R., & Pigge, F. (1992, April). *A summary of published research: Classroom teachers' knowledge and skills related to the development and use of teacher-made tests.* Paper presented at the annual meeting of the American Educational Research Association, San Francisco.

Martin, A., Marsh, H., & Debus, R. (2001). Self-handicapping and defensive pessimism: Exploring a model of predictors and outcomes from a self-protection perspective. *Journal of Educational Psychology, 93*(1), 87–102.

Martin, C., Ruble, D., & Szkrybalo, J. (2002). Cognitive theories of early gender development. *Psychological Bulletin, 128,* 903–933.

Martin, G., & Pear, J. (2002). *Behavior modification* (7th ed.). Upper Saddle River, NJ: Merrill/Prentice Hall.

Martin, J. (1993). Episodic memory: A neglected phenomenon in the psychology of education. *Educational Psychologist, 28*(2), 169–183.

Marttunen, M., & Laurinen, L. (2001). Learning of argumentation skills in networked and face-to-face environments. *Instructional Science, 29,* 127–153.

Marzano, R. (2003). *What works in schools.* Alexandria, VA: Association for Supervision and Curriculum Development.

Marzano, R., & Marzano, J. (2003). The key to classroom management. *Educational Leadership, 61*(1), 6–13.

Maslow, A. (1968). *Toward a psychology of being* (2nd ed.). New York: Van Nostrand.

Maslow, A. (1970). *Motivation and personality* (2nd ed.). New York: Harper & Row. (Original work published 1954)

Maslow, A. H. (1987). *Motivation and personality* (3rd ed.). New York: Harper & Row.

Mason, L., & Boscolo, P. (2000). Writing and conceptual change. What changes? *Instructional Science, 28,* 199–226.

Mastropieri, M. A., & Scruggs, T. E. (2004). *The inclusive classroom: Strategies for effective instruction.* (2nd ed.) Upper Saddle River, NJ: Merrill/Prentice Hall.

Matsumoto, D. (2004). *Culture and psychology* (3rd ed.). Belmont: CA: Wadsworth.

Maughan, A., & Ciccetti, D. (2002). Impact of child maltreatment and interadult violence on children's emotion regulation abilities and socioemotional adjustment. *Child Development, 73,* 1525–1542.

Mayer, J. D., Salovey, P., & Caruso, D. R. (2000). Selecting a measure of emotional intelligence: The case for ability scales. In R. Bar-On & J. D. A. Parker (Eds.), *Handbook of emotional intelligence* (pp. 320–342). San Francisco: Jossey-Bass.

Mayer, R. (1996). Learners as information processors: Legacies and limitations of educational psychology's second metaphor. *Educational Psychologist, 31*(4), 151–161.

Mayer, R. (1997). Multimedia learning: Are we asking the right questions? *Educational Psychologist, 32*(1), 1–19.

Mayer, R. (1998a). Cognitive, metacognitive, and motivational aspects of problem solving. *Instructional Science, 26,* 49–63.

Mayer, R. (1998b). Cognitive theory for education: What teachers need to know. In N. Lambert & B. McCombs (Eds.), *How students learn: Reforming schools through learner-centered instruction* (pp. 353–378). Washington, DC: American Psychological Association.

Mayer, R. (1999). *The promise of educational psychology: Learning in the content areas.* Upper Saddle River, NJ: Merrill/Prentice Hall.

Mayer, R. (2002). *The promise of educational psychology: Volume II. Teaching for meaningful learning.* Upper Saddle River, NJ: Merrilll/Prentice Hall.

Mayer, R., Fennell, S., Farmer, L., & Campbell, J. (2004). A personalization effect in multimedia learning: Students learn better when words are in conversational style rather than formal style. *Journal of Educational Psychology, 96*(2), 389–395.

Mayer, R., & Moreno, R. (1998). A split-attention effect in multimedia learning: Evidence for dual processing systems in working memory. *Journal of Educational Psychology, 90*(2), 312–320.

Mayer, R., & Wittrock, M. (1996). Problem-solving transfer. In D. Berliner & R. Calfee (Eds.), *Handbook of educational psychology* (pp. 47–62). New York: Macmillan.

Mayer, R. E. (2004). Should there be a three-strikes rule against pure discovery learning? *American Psychologist, 59,* 14–19.

Mayfield, K. H., & Chase, P. N. (2002). The effects of cumulative practice on mathematics problem solving. *Journal of Applied Behavior Analysis, 35,* 105–123.

Mazur, J. E. (2006). *Learning and behavior* (6th ed.). Upper Saddle River, NJ: Merrill/Prentice Hall.

McCarthy, J., & Benally, J. (2003, April). *Classroom management in a Navajo middle school.* Paper presented at the annual meeting of the American Educational Research Association, Chicago.

McCaughtry, N. (2004). The emotional dimensions of a teacher's pedagogical content knowledge: Influences on content, curriculum, and pedagogy. *Journal of Teaching in Physical Education, 23,* 30–47.

McCleery, J., Twyman, T., & Tindal, G. (2003, April). *Using concepts to frame history content with explicit instruction.* Paper presented at the annual meeting of the American Educational Research Association, Chicago.

McCombs, B. L. (2001, April). *What do we know about learners and learning? The learner-centered framework.* Paper presented at the annual meeting of the American Educational Research Association, Seattle.

McCutchen, D. (2000). Knowledge, processing, and working memory: Implications for a theory of writing. *Educational Psychologist, 35*(1), 13–23.

McDermott, P., Mordell, M., & Stoltzfus, J. (2001). The organization of student performance in American schools: Discipline, motivation, verbal learning, and nonverbal learning. *Journal of Educational Psychology, 93*(1), 65–76.

McDevitt, T., & Ormrod, J. (2004). *Child development: Educating and working with children and adolescents* (2nd ed.). Upper Saddle River, NJ: Merrill/Prentice Hall.

McDougall, D., & Granby, C. (1996). How expectation of questioning method affects undergraduates' preparation for class. *Journal of Experimental Education, 65,* 43–54.

McGlinchey, M., & Hixson, M. (2004). Using curriculum-based measurement to predict performance on state assessments in reading. *School Psychology Review, 33*(2), 193–203.

McGrath, D., Swisher, R., Elder, G., & Conger, R. (2001). Breaking new ground: Diverse routes to college in rural America. *Rural Sociology, 66*(2), 244–267.

McIntosh, S., & Norwood, P. (2004). The power of testing; Investigating minority teachers' responses to certification examination questions. *Urban Education, 39*(1), 33–51.

McKeachie, W., & Kulik, J. (1975). Effective college teaching. In F. Kerlinger (Ed.), *Review of research in education Vol. 3* (pp. 24–39). Washington, DC: American Educational Research Association.

McMahon, S., Rose, D., & Parks, M. (2004). Multiple intelligences and reading achievement: An examination of the Teele Inventory of Multiple Intelligences. *Journal of Experimental Education, 73*(1), 41–52.

McMillan, J. (2004). *Classroom assessment* (3rd ed.). Boston: Allyn & Bacon.

McMillan, J., Workman, D., & Myran, S. (1999). *Elementary teachers' classroom assessment and grading practices.* Paper presented at the annual meeting of the American Educational Research Association, Montreal, Canada.

McNeil, L. (2000). *Contradictions of school reform: Educational costs of standardized testing.* New York: Routledge.

McNeil, N., & Alibali, M. (2000). Learning mathematics from procedural instruction: Externally imposed goals influence what is learned. *Journal of Educational Psychology, 92*(4), 734–744.

Medin, D., Proffitt, J., & Schwartz. H. (2000). Concepts: An overview. In A. Kazdin (Ed.), *Encyclopedia of psychology* (Vol. 2, pp. 242–245). New York: Oxford University Press.

Meece, J. L. (2002). *Child and adolescent development for educators* (2nd ed.). New York: McGraw-Hill.

Meece, J. L., & Kurtz-Costes, B. (2001). Introduction: The schooling of ethnic minority children and youth. *Educational Psychologist, 36,* 1–7.

Meichenbaum, D. (1986). Cognitive behavior modification. In F. H. Kanfer & A. P. Goldstein (Eds.), *Helping people change: A textbook of methods* (3rd ed., pp. 346–380). New York: Pergamon.

Meichenbaum, D. (2000). *Cognitive behavior modification: An integrative approach.* Dordrecht, Netherlands: Kluwer Academic Publishers.

Meier, D. (2002). Standardization versus standards. *Phi Delta Kappan, 84,* 190–198.

Melnick, S., & Pullin, D. (2000). Can you take dictation? Prescribing teacher quality through testing. *Journal of Teacher Education, 51*(4), 262–275.

Mercer, J. (1973). *Labeling the mentally retarded.* Berkeley: University of California Press.

Merkley, D., & Jefferies, D. (2001). Guidelines for implementing a graphic organizer. *Reading Teacher, 54*(4), 350–357.

Merzenich, M. M. (2001). Cortical plasticity contributing to child development. In J. L. McClelland & R. S. Siegler (Eds.), *Mechanisms of cognitive development: Behavioral and neural perspectives* (pp. 67–95). Mahwah, NJ: Erlbaum.

Meter, P., & Stevens, R. (2000). The role of theory in the study of peer collaboration. *Journal of Experimental Education, 69*(1), 113–127.

Mevarech, Z. (1999). Effects of metacognitive training embedded in cooperative settings on mathematical problem solving. *Journal of Educational Research, 92*(4), 195–205.

Meyer, M. S. (2000). The ability–achievement discrepancy: Does it contribute to an understanding of learning disabilities? *Educational Psychology Review, 12,* 315–337.

Mickelson, R., & Heath, D. (1999, April). *The effects of segregation and tracking on African American high school seniors' academic achievement, occupational aspirations, and interracial social networks in Charlotte, North Carolina.* Paper presented at the annual meeting of the American Educational Research Association, Montreal, Canada.

Middleton, M., & Midgley, C. (1997). Avoiding the demonstration of lack of ability: An underexplored aspect of goal theory. *Journal of Educational Psychology, 89,* 710–718.

Middleton, M. J. (1999). *Classroom effects on the gender gap in middle school students' math self-efficacy.* Paper presented at the annual meeting of the American Educational Research Association, Montreal, Canada.

Midgley, C. (2001). A goal theory perspective on the current status of middle level schools. In T. Urdan & F. Pajares (Eds.), *Adolescence and education* (pp. 33–59). Volume I. Greenwich, CT: Information Age Publishing.

Midgley, C., Kaplan, A., & Middleton, M. (2001). Performance-approach goals. Good for what, for whom, under what circumstances, and at what cost? *Journal of Educational Psychology, 93,* 77–86.

Midgley, C., & Urdan, T. (2001). Academic self-handicapping and achievement goals: A further examination. *Contemporary Educational Psychology, 26,* 61–75.

Miller, G. (1956). The magical number seven, plus or minus two: Some limits on our capacity for processing information. *Psychological Review, 63,* 81–97.

Miller, P. (2002). *Theories of developmental psychology* (4th ed.). New York: Worth.

Mills, G. (2002, April). *Teaching and learning action research.* Paper presented at the annual meeting of the American Educational Research Association, New Orleans.

Miltenberger, R. (2004). *Behavior modification: Principles and procedures* (3rd ed.). Belmont, CA: Wadsworth.

Moreno, R. (2004). Decreasing cognitive load for novice students: Effects of explanatory versus corrective feedback in discovery-based multimedia. *Instructional Science, 32,* 99–113.

Moreno, R., & Duran, R. (2004). Do multiple representations need explanations: The role of verbal guidance and individual differences in multimedia mathematics learning. *Journal of Educational Psychology, 96,* 492–503.

Moreno, R., & Mayer, R. (2000). Engaging students in active learning: The case for personalized multimedia messages. *Journal of Educational Psychology, 92*(4), 724–733.

Moreno, R., & Mayer, R. (2005). Role of guidance, reflection, and interactivity in an agent-based multimedia game. *Journal of Educational Psychology, 97*(1), 117–128.

Morgan, S. L., & Mehta, J. D. (2004). Beyond the laboratory: Evaluating the survey evidence for the disidentification explanation of black–white differences in achievement. *Sociology of Education, 77*(1), 82–101.

Morine-Dershimer, G. (1987). Can we talk? In D. Berliner & B. Rosenshine (Eds.), *Talks to teachers* (pp. 37–53). New York: Random House.

Morrison, G., Ross, S., & Kemp, J. (2004). *Designing effective instruction* (4th ed.). Hoboken, NJ: John Wiley & Sons.

Morrison, G. R., & Lowther, D. L. (2002). *Integrating computer technology into the classroom* (2nd ed.). Upper Saddle River, NJ: Merrill/Prentice Hall.

Morrone, A., Harkness, S., D'Ambrosio, B., & Caulfield, R. (2003, April). *Patterns of instructional discourse that promote the perception of mastery goals in a social constructivist mathematics course.* Paper presented at the annual meeting of the American Educational Research Association, Chicago.

Moshman, D. (1997). Pluralist rational constructivism. *Issues in Education: Contributions From Education Psychology, 3,* 229–234.

Muffoletto, R. (1994). Technology and restructuring education: Constructing a context. *Educational Technology, 34*(2), 24–28.

Munby, H., Russel, T., & Martin, A. (2001). Teachers' knowledge and how it develops. In V. Richardson (Ed.), *Handbook of research on teaching* (4th ed., pp. 877–904). Washington, DC: American Educational Research Association.

Munk, D., & Bursuck, W. (1997/1998). Can grades be helpful and fair? *Educational Leadership, 55*(4), 44–47.

Murdock, T., Hale, N., & Weber, M. (2001). Predictors of cheating among early adolescents: Academic and social motivations. *Contemporary Educational Psychology, 26*(2), 96–115.

Murdock, T. B., Miller, A., & Kohlhardt, J. (2004). Effects of classroom context variables in high school students' judgments of the acceptability and likelihood of cheating. *Journal of Educational Psychology, 96*(4), 765–777.

Murphy, P. K., & Alexander, P. (2000). A motivated exploration of motivation terminology. *Contemporary Educational Psychology, 25,* 3–53.

Myers, C. (1970). Journal citations and scientific eminence in contemporary psychology. *American Psychologist, 25,* 1041–1048.

Nagel, G., & Peterson, P. (2001). Why competency tests miss the mark. *Educational Leadership, 58*(8), 46–48.

Nakagawa, K. (1999, April). *Portraits of the schools and communities experiencing student mobility.* Paper presented at the annual meeting of the American Educational Research Association, Montreal, Canada.

Nakagawa, K., Stafford, M., Fisher, T., & Matthews, L. (2002). The "city migrant" dilemma: Building community at high-mobility urban schools. *Urban Education, 37*(1), 96–125.

Nansel, T. R., Overpeck, M., Pilla, R. S., Ruan, W. J., Simmons-Morton, B., & Scheift, P. (2001). Bullying behaviors among U.S. young: Prevalence and association with psychosocial adjustment. *Journal of the American Medical Association, 285,* 2094–2100.

National Assessment of Educational Progress. (2001). *National report: 2000.* Washington, DC: National Center for Educational Statistics.

National Center for Educational Statistics. (2005). Retrieved February 17, 2005, from http://nces.ed.gov/programs

National Center for Research on Teacher Learning. (1993). *Findings on learning to teach.* East Lansing: Michigan State University.

National Council of Teachers of Mathematics. (2000). *Principles and standards for school mathematics.* Reston, VA: Author.

National Council on Disability (2000, January). *Achieving independence: The challenge for the 21st century.* Washington, DC: Author.

National Education Association. (2003). *Status of the American public school teacher, 2000–2001.* Washington, DC: Author. Retrieved February, 2004, from http://www.nea.org/edstats/

National excellence: A case for developing America's talent. (1993). Washington, DC: U.S. Department of Education, Office of Educational Research and Improvement.

National Joint Committee on Learning Disabilities. (1994). Learning disabilities: Issues on definition. A position paper of the National Joint Committee in Learning Disabilities. In *Collective perspectives on issues affecting learning disability: Position papers and statements.* Austin, TX: Pro-Ed.

National Parent Teacher Association. (2000). *Standards for parent/family involvement programs.* Retrieved October 1, 2002, from http://www.pta.org/programs/INVSTAND

Neill, M. (2003). High stakes, high risk. *American School Board Journal, 190*(2), 18–21.

Neisser, U. (1967). *Cognitive psychology.* New York: Appleton-Century-Crofts.

Nelson, J., Lott, L., & Glenn, S. (1997). *Positive discipline in the classroom* (2nd ed.). New York: Ballantine Books.

Nelson, K. E., Aksu-Koc, A., & Johnson, C. E. (Eds.). (2001). *Children's language* (Vol. 10). Mahwah, NJ: Erlbaum.

Neuman, S., & Celano, D. (2001). Access to print in low-income and middle-income communities: An ecological study of our neighborhoods. *Reading Research Quarterly, 36*(1), 8–26.

Newby, T., Stepich, D., Lehman, J., & Russell, J. (2000). *Instructional technology and teaching and learning* (2nd ed.). Upper Saddle River, NJ: Merrill/Prentice Hall.

Newstead, J., Franklyn-Stokes, A., & Armstead, P. (1996). Individual differences in student cheating. *Journal of Educational Psychology, 88*(2), 229–241.

Niaz, M. (1997). How early can children understand some form of "scientific reasoning"? *Perceptual and Motor Skills, 85,* 1272–1274.

Nicholls, J. (1984). Achievement motivation: Conceptions of ability, subjective experience, task choice, and performance. *Psychological Review, 91,* 328–346.

Nichols, B., & Singer, K. (2000). Developing data mentors. *Educational Leadership, 57*(5), 34–37.

Nickerson, R. (1988). On improving thinking through instruction. In E. Rothkopf (Ed.), *Review of research in education* (pp. 3–57). Washington, DC: American Educational Research Association.

Nieto, S. (1999). *Identity, personhood, and Puerto Rican students: Challenging paradigms of assimilation and authenticity.* Paper presented at the annual meeting of the American Educational Research Association, Montreal, Canada.

Nilsson, L., & Archer, T. (1989). Aversively motivated behavior: Which are the perspectives? In T. Archer & L. Nilsson (Eds.), *Aversion, avoidance and anxiety.* Hillsdale, NJ: Erlbaum.

Nitko, A. (2004). *Educational assessment of students* (4th ed.). Upper Saddle River, NJ: Pearson.

No Child Left Behind Act of 2001. *Public Law 107–110* (8 January 2002). Washington, DC: U.S. Government Printing Office.

Noblit, G., Rogers, D., & McCadden, B. (1995). In the meantime: The possibilities of caring. *Phi Delta Kappan, 76,* 680–685.

Noddings, N. (1992). *The challenge to care in schools: An alternative approach to education.* New York: Teachers College Press.

Noddings, N. (2001). The caring teacher. In V. Richardson (Ed.), *Handbook of research on teaching* (4th ed., pp. 99–105). Washington, DC: American Educational Research Association.

Noddings, N. (2002). *Educating moral people: A caring alternative approach to education.* New York: Teachers College Press.

Noguera, P. (2003a). *City schools and the American dream: Reclaiming the promise of public education.* New York: Teachers College Press.

Noguera, P. (2003b). The trouble with black boys: The role and influence of environmental and cultural factors on the academic performance of African American males. *Urban Education, 38*(4), 431–459.

Nokelainen, P., & Flint, J. (2002). Genetic effects on human cognition: Lessons from the study of mental retardation syndromes. *Journal of Neurology, Neurosurgery, and Psychiatry, 43,* 287–296.

Nosek, B., Banaji, M., & Greenwald, A. (2002). Math = male, me = female, therefore math [not equal to] me. *Journal of Personality and Social Psychology, 83,* 44–59.

Notar, C. E., Zuelke, D. C., Wilson, J. D., & Yunker, B. D. (2004). The table of specifications: Ensuring accountability in teacher made tests. *Journal of Instructional Psychology, 31*(2), 115–129.

Novick, L. (1998, April). *Highly skilled problem solvers use example-based reasoning to support their superior performance.* Paper presented at the annual meeting of the American Educational Research Association, San Diego.

Nucci, L. (1987). Synthesis of research on moral development. *Educational Leadership, 44*(5), 86–92.

Nuthall, G. (1999a). Learning how to learn: The evolution of students' minds through the social processes and culture of the classroom. *International Journal of Educational Research, 31*(3), 141–256.

Nuthall, G. (1999b). The way students learn: Acquiring knowledge from an integrated science and social studies unit. *Elementary School Journal, 99*(4), 303–342.

Nuthall, G. (2000). The anatomy of memory in the classroom: Understanding how students acquire memory processes from classroom activities in science and social studies units. *American Educational Research Journal, 37*(1), 247–304.

Nystrand, M., Cohen, A., & Dowling, N. (1992, April). *Reliability of portfolio assessment for measuring verbal outcomes.* Paper presented at the annual meeting of the American Educational Research Association, San Francisco.

Nystrand, M., & Gamoran, A. (1989, March). *Instructional discourse and student engagement.* Paper presented at the annual meeting of the American Educational Research Association, San Francisco.

Oakes, J. (1992). Can tracking research inform practice? *Educational Researcher, 21*(4), 12–21.

Oakes, J., & Wells, A. S. (2002). Detracking for high student achievement. In L. Abbeduto (Ed.), *Taking sides: Clashing views and controversial issues in educational psychology* (2nd ed., pp. 26–30). Guilford, CT: McGraw-Hill Duskin.

O'Brien, L., & Crandall, C. (2003). Stereotype threat and arousal: Effects on women's math performance. *Personality and Social Psychology Bulletin, 29,* 782–789.

O'Brien, V., Kopola, M., & Martinez-Pons, M. (1999). Mathematics self-efficacy, ethnic identity, gender, and career interests related to mathematics and science. *Journal of Educational Research, 92*(4), 231–235.

Ogbu, J. (1987). Variability in minority school performance: A problem in search of an explanation. *Anthropology and Education Quarterly, 18,* 312–334.

Ogbu, J. (1992). Understanding cultural diversity and learning. *Educational Researcher, 21*(8), 5–14.

Ogbu, J. (1999a). Beyond language: Ebonics, proper English, and identity in a Black-American speech community. *American Educational Research Journal, 36*(2), 147–184.

Ogbu, J. (1999b, April). *The significance of minority status.* Paper presented at the annual meeting of the American Educational Research Association, Montreal, Canada.

Ogbu, J. (2003). *Black American students in an affluent suburb: A study of academic disengagement.* Mahwah, NJ: Erlbaum.

Ogbu, J., & Simons, H. (1998). Voluntary and involuntary minorities: A cultural-ecological theory of school performance with some implications for education. *Anthropology & Education Quarterly, 29*(2), 155–188.

Okagaki, L., & Frensch, R. A. (1998). Parenting and children's achievement: A multiethnic perspective. *American Educational Research Journal, 35,* 123–144.

Olina, Z., & Sullivan, H. (2002, April). *Effects of teacher and self-assessment on student performance.* Paper presented at the annual meeting of the American Educational Research Association, New Orleans.

Olson, J., & Clough, M. (2004). *What questions do you have? In defense of general questions: A response to Croom.* ID=11366. Retrieved August 20, 2004, from http://www.tcrecord.org/content.asp?content

Olson, L. (2000). Finding and keeping competent teachers. *Education Week, 19*(18), 12–18.

Opfer, J., & Siegler, R. S. (2004). Revisiting preschoolers' living things concept: A microgenetic analysis of conceptual change in basic biology. *Cognitive Psychology, 49,* 301–332.

O'Reilly, T., Symons, S., & MacLatchy-Gaudet, H. (1998). A comparison of self-explanation and elaborative interrogation. *Contemporary Educational Psychology, 23,* 434–445.

Ormrod, J. E. (2004). *Human learning* (4th ed.). Upper Saddle River, NJ: Merrill/Prentice Hall.

Orr, A. (2003). Black–white differences in achievement: The importance of wealth. *Sociology of Education, 76*(October), 281–304.

Osborne, J. (1996). Beyond constructivism. *Science Education, 80,* 53–81.

Osterman, K. F. (2000). Students' need for belonging in the school community. *Review of Educational Research, 70,* 323–367.

Owens, R. E., Jr. (2005). *Language development* (6th ed.). Boston: Allyn & Bacon.

Paas, F., Renkl, A., & Sweller, J. (2004). Cognitive load theory: Instructional implications of the interaction between information structures and cognitive architecture. *Instructional Science, 32*(1), 1–8.

Packer, M., & Goicoechea, J. (2000). Sociocultural and constructivist theories of learning: Ontology, not just epistemology. *Educational Psychologist, 35*(4), 227–241.

Page, E. (1992). Is the world an orderly place? A review of teacher comments and student achievement. *Journal of Experimental Education, 60*(3), 161–181.

Paivio, A. (1986). *Mental representations: A dual-coding approach.* New York: Oxford University.

Paivio, A. (1991). Dual coding theory: Retrospect and current status. *Canadian Journal of Psychology, 45,* 255–287.

Pajares, F., & Valiante, G. (1999, April). *Writing self-efficacy of middle school students: Relation to motivation constructs, achievement, gender, and gender orientation.* Paper presented at the annual meeting of the American Educational Research Association, Montreal, Canada.

Pajares, R., & Schunk, D. H. (2002). Self and self-belief in psychology and education: A historical perspective. In J. Aronson & D. Cordova (Eds.), *Improving academic achievement: Impact of psychological factors on education* (pp. 3–21). New York: Academic Press.

Palincsar, A. (1998). Social constructivist perspectives on teaching and learning. *Annual Review of Psychology, 49,* 345–375.

Paris, S. (1998). Why learner-centered assessment is better than high-stakes testing. In N. Lambert & B. McCombs (Eds.), *How students learn: Reforming schools through learner-centered education* (pp. 189–209). Washington, DC: American Psychological Association.

Paris, S. G., & Paris, A. H. (2001). Classroom application of research on self-regulated learning. *Educational Psychologist, 36,* 89–101.

Parish, J., Parish, T., & Batt, S. (2001, April). *Academic achievement and school climate—interventions that work.* Paper presented at the annual meeting of the American Educational Research Association, Seattle.

Parkay, F., & Hass, G. (2000). *Curriculum planning: A contemporary approach* (7th ed.). Boston: Allyn & Bacon.

Pashler, H., & Carrier, M. (1996). Structures, processes, and the flow of information. In E. Bjork & R. Bjork (Eds.), *Memory* (pp. 3–29). San Diego, CA: Academic Press.

Patrick, B. C., Hisley, J., & Kempler, T. (2000). "What's everybody so excited about?": The effects of teacher enthusiasm on student intrinsic motivation and vitality. *The Journal of Experimental Education, 68,* 217–236.

Patrick, H., Anderman, L., Ryan, A., Edelin, K., & Midgley, C. (1999, April). *Messages teachers send: Communicating goal orientations in the classroom.* Paper presented at the annual meeting of the American Educational Research Association, Montreal, Canada.

Patrick, H., Anderman, L. H., & Ryan, A. M. (2002). Social motivation and the classroom social environment. In C. Midgley (Ed.), *Goals, goal structures, and patterns of adaptive learning* (pp. 85–108). Mahwah, NJ: Erlbaum.

Pavlov, I. (1928). *Lectures on conditioned reflexes* (W. Gantt, Trans.). New York: International Universities Press.

Péladeau, N., Forget, J., & Gagné, F. (2003). Effect of paced and unpaced practice on skill application and retention: How much is enough? *American Educational Research Journal, 40*(3), 769–801.

Pellegrini, A. D. (2002). Bullying, victimization, and sexual harassment during the transition to middle school. *Educational Psychologist, 37,* 151–163.

Peña, D. (2000). Parent involvement: Influencing factors and implications. *Journal of Educational Research, 94*(1), 42–54.

Peregoy, S., & Boyle, O. (2005). *Reading, writing, and learning in ESL: A resource book for teachers* (4th ed.). Boston: Allyn & Bacon.

Perkins, D. (1995). *Outsmarting IQ.* New York: Free Press.

Perkins-Gough, D. (2004). A two-tiered education system. *Educational Leadership, 62*(3), 87–88.

Perry, N. (1998). Young children's self-regulated learning and contexts that support it. *Journal of Educational Psychology, 90*(4), 715–729.

Perry, T., Steele, C., & Hilliard, A. (2003). *Young, gifted, and Black: Promoting high achievement among African American students.* Boston: Beacon Press.

Peterson, C. C. (2002). Drawing insight from pictures: The development of concepts of false drawing and false belief in children with deafness, normal hearing, and autism. *Child Development, 73,* 1442–1459.

Peterson, J. M., & Hittie, M. M. (2003). *Inclusive teaching: Creating effective schools for all learners.* Boston: Allyn & Bacon.

Petrill, S. A., & Wilkerson, B. (2000). Intelligence and achievement: A behavioral genetic perspective. *Educational Psychology Review, 12,* 185–199.

Peverly, S. P., Brobst, K. E., & Graham, M. (2003). College adults are not good at self-regulation: A study on the relationship of self-regulation, note taking, and test taking. *Journal of Educational Psychology, 95,* 335–346.

Pfiffner, L., Rosen, L., & O'Leary, S. (1985). The efficacy of an all-positive approach to classroom management. *Journal of Applied Behavior Analysis, 18,* 257–261.

Pfiffner, L. J., & Barkley, R. A. (1998). Treatment of ADHD in school settings. In R. A. Barkley (Ed.), *Attention-deficit hyperactivity disorder: A handbook for diagnosis and treatment* (2nd ed., pp. 458–490). New York: Guilford Press.

Phillips, D. (1995). The good, the bad and the ugly: The many faces of constructivism. *Educational Researcher, 24*(7), 5–12.

Phillips, D. (1997). How, why, what, when, and where: Perspectives on constructivism in psychology and education. *Issues in Education, 3,* 151–194.

Phillips, D. (2000). An opinionated account of the constructivist landscape. In D. Phillips (Ed.), *Constructivism in education: Opinions and second opinions on controversial issues* (pp. 1–16). Chicago: National Society for the Study of Education.

Phye, G. D. (2001). Problem-solving instruction and problem-solving transfer: The correspondence issue. *Journal of Educational Psychology, 93,* 571–578.

Piaget, J. (1926). *The language and thought of the child.* New York: Harcourt, Brace & World.

Piaget, J. (1952). *Origins of intelligence in children.* New York: International Universities Press.

Piaget, J. (1959). *Language and thought of the child* (M. Grabain, Trans.). New York: Humanities Press.

Piaget, J. (1965). The *moral judgment of the child.* New York: Free Press. (Original work published 1932)

Piaget, J. (1970). *The science of education and the psychology of the child.* New York: Orion Press.

Piaget, J. (1977). Problems in equilibration. In M. Appel & L. Goldberg (Eds.), *Topics in cognitive development: Vol. 1. Equilibration: Theory, research, and application* (pp. 3–13). New York: Plenum Press.

Piaget, J. (1980). *Adaptation and intelligence: Organic selection and phenocopy* (S. Eames, Trans.). Chicago: University of Chicago Press.

Piaget, J., & Inhelder, B. (1956). *The child's conception of space.* Boston: Routledge & Kegan-Paul.

Piatelli-Palmarini, M. (1994). *Inevitable illusions: How mistakes of reason rule our mind.* New York: Wiley.

Picciano, A. (2001). *Distance learning.* Upper Saddle River, NJ: Pearson.

Pierangelo, R., & Guiliani, G. (2006). *Assessment in special education* (2nd ed.). Boston: Allyn & Bacon.

Pine, K., & Messer, D. (2000). The effect of explaining another's actions on children's implicit theories of balance. *Cognition and Instruction, 18*(1), 35–51.

Pintrich, P. (2000). Multiple goals, multiple pathways: The role of goal orientation in learning and achievement. *Journal of Educational Psychology, 92,* 544–555.

Pintrich, P., & Schunk, D. (2002). *Motivation in education: Theory, research, and applications* (2nd ed.). Upper Saddle River, NJ: Merrill/Prentice Hall.

Pitoniak, M., & Royer, J. (2001). Testing accommodations for examinees with disabilities: A review of psychometric, legal, and social policy issues. *Review of Educational Research, 71*(1), 53–104.

Pittman, K., & Beth-Halachmy, S. (1997, March). *The role of prior knowledge in analogy use.* Paper presented at the annual meeting of the American Educational Research Association, Chicago.

Plant, E. A., Ericsson, K. A., & Hill, L. (2005). Why study time does not predict grade point average across college students: Implications of deliberate practice for academic performance. *Contemporary Educational Psychology, 30,* 96–116.

Plata, M., Trusty, J., & Glascow, D. (2005). Adolescents with learning disabilities: Are they allowed to participate in activities? *Journal of Educational Research, 98*(3), 136–143.

Platt, R. (2004). Standardized tests: Whose standards are we talking about? *Phi Delta Kappan, 85*(5), 381–382.

Popham, W. (2003). The seductive lure of data. *Educational Leadership, 60*(5), 48–51.

Popham, W. J. (2004a). A game without winners. *Educational Leadership, 62*(3), 46–50.

Popham, W. J. (2004b). *American's failing schools: How parents and teachers can cope with No Child Left Behind.* New York: Routledge Falmer.

Popham, W. J. (2004c). "Teaching to the test": An expression to eliminate. *Educational Leadership, 62*(3), 82–83.

Popham, W. J. (2005). *Classroom assessment: What teachers need to know* (4th ed.). Boston: Pearson.

Potter, R. L. (1999). Technical reading in the middle school. *Phi Delta Kappa Fastbacks, 456,* 7–56.

Powell, R., & Caseau, D. (2004). *Classroom communication and diversity.* Mahwah, NJ: Erlbaum.

Prawat, R. (1989). Promoting access to knowledge, strategy, and disposition in students: A research synthesis. *Review of Educational Research, 59,* 1–41.

Premack, D. (1965). Reinforcement theory. In D. Levine (Ed.), *Nebraska Symposium on Motivation* (Vol. 13, pp. 3–41). Lincoln: University of Nebraska Press.

Pressley, M., Raphael, L., & Gallagher, J. G. (2004). Prodience-St. Mel School: How a school that works for African American students works. *Journal of Educational Psychology, 96*(2), 216–235.

Public Agenda. (2004). *Teaching interrupted.* Retrieved June 12, 2004, from http://www.publicagenda.org

Pugh, K. J., Bergin, D. A., & Rocks, J. (2003, April). *Motivation and transfer: A critical review.* Paper presented at the annual meeting of the American Educational Association, Chicago.

Puntambekar, S., & Hübscher, R. (2005). Tools for scaffolding students in a complex learning environment: What have we gained and what have we missed? *Educational Psychologist, 40*(1), 1–12.

Purdie, N., Hattie, J., & Carroll, A. (2002). A review of the research on interventions for attention deficit hyperactivity disorder: What works best? *Review of Educational Research, 72*(1), 61–100.

Purkey, S., & Smith, M. (1983). Effective schools: A review. *Elementary School Journal, 83,* 427–452.

Putnam, R., & Borko, H. (2000). What do new views of knowledge and thinking have to say about research on teacher learning? *Educational Researcher, 29*(1), 4–15.

Putnam, R., Heaton, R., Prawat, R., & Remillard, J. (1992). Teaching mathematics for understanding: Discussing case studies of four fifth-grade teachers. *Elementary School Journal, 93,* 213–228.

Pyryt, M., & Mendaglio, S. (2001, April). *Intelligence and moral development: A meta-analytic review.* Paper presented at the annual meeting of the American Educational Research Association, Seattle.

Qian, G., & Pan, J. (2002). A comparison of epistemological beliefs and learning from science text between American and Chinese high school students. In B. K. Hofer & P. R. Pintrich (Eds.), *Personal epistemology: The psychology of beliefs about knowledge and knowing* (pp. 365–385). Mahwah, NJ: Erlbaum.

Quihuis, G., Bempechat, J., Jiminez, N., & Boulay, P. (2002). Implicit theories of intelligence across academic domains: A study of meaning making in adolescents of Mexican descent. In J. Bempechat, & J. Elliott (Eds.), *Learning in culture and context: Approaching the complexities of achievement motivation in student learning* (pp. 87–100). San Francisco: Jossey-Bass.

Quin, Z., Johnson, D., & Johnson, R. (1995). Cooperative versus competitive efforts and problem solving. *Review of Educational Research, 65*(2), 129–143.

Quinlan, T. (2004). Speech recognition technology and students with writing difficulties: Improving fluency. *Journal of Education Psychology, 96*(2), 337–346.

Quinn, P. C. (2002). Category representation in your infants. *Current Directions in Psychological Science, 11,* 66–70.

Quiocho, A., & Rios, F. (2000). The power of their presence: Minority group teachers and schooling. *Review of Educational Research, 70*(4), 485–528.

Quiocho, A., & Ulanoff, S. (2002, April). *Teacher research in preservice teacher education: Asking burning questions.* Paper presented at the annual meeting of the American Educational Research Association, New Orleans.

Rainwater, L., & Smeedings, T. (2003). *Poor kids in a rich country.* New York: Russell Sage Foundation.

Ramey, C. T., Ramey, S. L., & Lanzi, R. G. (2001). Intelligence and experience. In R. J. Sternberg & E. L. Grigorenko (Eds.), *Environmental effects on cognitive abilities.* Mahwah, NJ: Erlbaum.

Raths, J. (2001, April). *Indicators of subject matter knowledge in the classroom!* Paper presented at the annual meeting of the American Educational Research Association, Seattle.

Rawlings, M. K. (1938). *The yearling.* (Forward by Patricia Reilly Giff, 2001). New York: Aladdin/Simon & Schuster.

Rea, P. J., McLaughlin, V. L., & Walther-Thomas, C. (2002). Outcomes of students with learning disabilities in inclusive and pullout programs. *Exceptional Children, 68,* 203–222.

Ream, R. K. (2003). Counterfeit social capital and Mexican-American underachievement. *Educational Evaluation and Policy Analysis, 25*(3), 237–262.

Reckase, M. (1997, March). *Constructs assessed by portfolios: How do they differ from those assessed by other educational tests?* Paper presented at the annual meeting of the National Educational Research Association, Chicago.

Reiner, M., Slotta, J. D., Chi, M. T. H., & Resnick, L. B. (2000). Naïve physics reasoning: A commitment to substance-based conceptions. *Cognition and Instruction, 18,* 1–34.

Reis, S. M., Colbert, R. D., & Hébert, T. P. (2005). Understanding resilience in diverse, talented students in an urban high school. *Roeper Review, 27*(2), 110–120.

Reisberg, D. (2006). *Cognition: Exploring the science of the mind* (3rd ed.). New York: Norton.

Renkl, A., & Atkinson, R. K. (2003). Structuring the transition from example study to problem solving in cognitive skills acquisition: A cognitive load perspective. *Educational Psychologist, 38,* 15–22.

Renkl, A., Stark, R., Gruber, H., & Mandl, H. (1998). Learning from worked-out examples: The effects of example variability and elicited self-explanations. *Contemporary Educational Psychology, 23,* 90–108.

Renzulli, J., & Reis, S. (2003). The schoolwide enrichment model: Developing creative and productive giftedness. In N. Colangelo & G. Davis (Eds.), *Handbook of gifted education* (3rd ed., pp. 184–203). Boston: Allyn & Bacon.

Resnick, L., & Klopfer, L. (1989). Toward the thinking curriculum: An overview. In L. Resnick & L. Klopfer (Eds.), *Toward the thinking curriculum: Current cognitive research* (pp. 1–18). Alexandria, VA: Association for Supervision and Curriculum Development.

Rest, J., Narvaez, D., Bebeau, M., & Thoma, S. (1999). A neo-Kohlbergian approach: The DIT and schema theory. *Educational Psychology Review, 11,* 291–324.

Reys, B., Reys, R., & Chávez, O. (2004). Why mathematics textbooks matter. *Educational Leadership, 62*(5), 61–66.

Richardson, V., & Placier, P. (2001). Teacher change. In V. Richardson (Ed.), *Handbook of research on teaching* (4th ed., pp. 905–950). Washington, DC: American Educational Research Association.

Rickards, J., Fajen, B., Sullivan, J., & Gillespie, G. (1997). Signaling, notetaking, and field independence–dependence in text comprehension and recall. *Journal of Educational Psychology, 89*(3), 508–517.

Ridley, D., McCombs, B., & Taylor, K. (1994). Walking the talk: Fostering self-regulated learning in the classroom. *Middle School Journal, 26*(2), 52–57.

Riley, M., Greeno, J., & Heller, J. (1982). The development of children's problem-solving ability in arithmetic. In H. Ginsburg (Ed.), *Development of mathematical thinking.* San Diego, CA: Academic Press.

Rimm-Kaufman, S., La Paro, K., Downer, J., & Pianta, R. (2005). The contribution of classroom setting and quality of instruction to children's behavior in kindergarten classrooms. *Elementary School Journal, 105*(4), 377–394.

Rimm-Kaufman, S. E., & Sawyer, B. E. (2004). Primary-grade teachers' self-efficacy beliefs, attitudes toward teaching, and discipline and teaching practice priorities in relation to the Responsive Classroom approach. *Elementary School Journal, 104*(4), 321–341.

Riordan, C. (1996). *Equality and achievement: An introduction to the sociology of education.* New York: Longman.

Rittle-Johnson, B., & Alibali, M. (1999). Conceptual and procedural knowledge of mathematics: Does one lead to the other? *Journal of Educational Psychology, 91*(1), 175–189.

Ritts, V., Patterson, M., & Tubbs, M. (1992). Expectations, impressions, and judgments of physically attractive students: A review. *Review of Educational Research, 62,* 413–426.

Robertson, J. (2000). Is attribution training a worthwhile classroom intervention for K–12 students with learning difficulties? *Educational Psychology Review, 12*(1), 111–134.

Robinson, D., Katayama, A., Dubois, N., & Devaney, T. (1998). Interactive effects of graphic organizers and delayed review on concept application. *Journal of Experimental Education, 67*(1), 17–31.

Robinson, T. R., Smith, S. W., Miller, M. D., & Brownell, M. T. (1999). Cognitive behavior modification of hyperactivity-impulsivity and aggression: A meta-analysis of school-based studies. *Journal of Educational Psychology, 91,* 195–203.

Roblyer, M. (2006). *Integrating educational technology into teaching* (4th ed.). Upper Saddle River, NJ: Merrill/Prentice Hall.

Roeser, R. W., Mariachi, R., & Gehlbach, H. (2002). A goal theory perspective on teachers' professional identities and the contexts of teaching. In C. Midgley (Ed.), *Goals, goal structure, and patterns of adaptive learning* (pp. 205–241). Mahwah, NJ: Erlbaum.

Rogers, C. (1959). A theory of therapy, personality, and interpersonal relationships, as developed in the client-centered framework. In S. Koch (Ed.), *Psychology: A study of a science* (Vol. 3, pp. 184–256). New York: McGraw-Hill.

Rogers, C. (1963). Actualizing tendency in relation to motives and to consciousness. In M. Jones (Ed.), *Nebraska Symposium on Motivation* (Vol. 11, pp. 1–24). Lincoln: University of Nebraska Press.

Rogers, C., & Freiberg, H. J. (1994). *Freedom to learn* (3rd ed.). Upper Saddle River, NJ: Merrill/Prentice Hall.

Rogoff, B. (1990). *Apprenticeship in thinking: Cognitive development in social context*. New York: Oxford University Press.

Rogoff, B. (1998). Cognition as a collaborative process. In W. Damon (Series Ed.), D. Kuhn, & R. S. Siegler (Vol. Eds.), *Handbook of child psychology: Vol. 2* (5th ed., pp. 679–744). New York: Wiley.

Rogoff, B. (2003). *The cultural context of human development*. Oxford, England: Oxford University Press.

Rogoff, B., Turkanis, C., & Bartlett, L. (Eds.). (2001). *Learning together: Children and adults in a school community*. New York: Oxford University Press.

Roid, G. H., & Barram, R. A. (2005). *Essentials of Stanford-Binet intelligence scales (SB5) assessment*. New York: Wiley.

Romboy, D., & Kinkead, L. (2005). Surviving in America. *Deseret Morning News, 155*(303), April 14, 1, 11, 12.

Rose, K., Williams, K., Gomez, L., & Gearon, J. (2002, April). *Building a case for what our students know and can do: How trustworthy are our judgments?* Paper presented at the annual meeting of the American Educational Research Association, New Orleans.

Rose, L., & Gallup, A. (2000). The 32nd annual Phi Delta Kappa/Gallup Poll of the public's attitudes toward the public schools. *Phi Delta Kappan, 82,* 41–58.

Rose, L. C., & Gallup, A. M. (2004). *The 36th annual Phi Delta Kappa/Gallup poll of the public's attitude toward the public schools* [Electronic version]. Retrieved from http://www.pdkintl.org/kappan/k0409pol.htm

Rosen, L., O'Leary, S., Joyce, S., Conway, G., & Pfiffner, L. (1984). The importance of prudent negative consequences for maintaining the appropriate behavior of hyperactive students. *Journal of Abnormal Child Psychology, 12,* 581–604.

Rosenfield, P., Lambert, S., & Black, R. (1985). Desk arrangement effects on pupil classroom behavior. *Journal of Educational Psychology, 77,* 101–108.

Rosenshine, B. (1987). Explicit teaching. In D. Berliner & B. Rosenshine (Eds.), *Talks to teachers*. New York: Random House.

Rosenshine, B., & Meister, C. (1992, April). *The use of scaffolds for teaching less structured academic tasks*. Paper presented at the annual meeting of the American Educational Research Association, San Francisco.

Rosenshine, B., & Stevens, R. (1986). Teaching functions. In M. Wittrock (Ed.), *Handbook of research on teaching* (3rd ed., pp. 376–391). New York: Macmillan.

Ross, B., & Spalding, T. (1994). Concepts and categories. In R. Sternberg (Ed.), *Handbook of perception and cognition* (Vol. 12). New York: Academic Press.

Ross, J., Rolheiser, C., & Hogaboam-Gray, A. (2002, April). *Influences on student cognitions about evaluation*. Paper presented at the annual meeting of the American Educational Research Association, New Orleans.

Ross, S., Smith, L., Loks, L., & McNelie, M. (1994). Math and reading instruction in tracked first-

grade classes. *Elementary School Journal, 95*(2), 105–118.

Rothstein, R. (2004a). *Class and schools: Using social, economic, and educational reform to close the black-white achievement gap*. New York: Teachers College Press.

Rothstein, R. (2004b). The achievement gap. *Educational Leadership, 62*(3), 40–43.

Rotter, J. (1966). Generalized expectancies for internal versus external control of reinforcement. *Psychological Monographs, 80*(1, Whole No. 609).

Rottier, K. (1995, October). If kids ruled the world: Icons. *Educational Leadership, 53*(2), 51–53.

Rouet, J. (2001). Designing multimedia systems for learning: Some lessons and further issues. In J. Rouet, J. Levonen, & A. Biardeau (Eds.), *Multimedia learning: Cognitive and instruction issues* (pp. 155–166). New York: Pergamon.

Rowe, M. (1974). Wait-time and rewards as instructional variables, their influence on language, logic, and fate control: Part I. Wait time. *Journal of Research in Science Teaching, 11,* 81–94.

Rowe, M. (1986). Wait-time: Slowing down may be a way of speeding up. *Journal of Teacher Education, 37*(1), 43–50.

Rubinson, F. (2004). Urban dropouts: Why so many and what can be done? In S. R. Steinberg & J. L. Kincheloe (Eds.), *19 Urban questions: Teaching in the city* (pp. 53–67). New York: Peter Lang.

Rudolph, K. D., Lambert, S. F., Clark, A. G., & Kurlakowsky, K. D. (2001). Negotiating the transition to middle school: The role of self-regulatory processes. *Child Development, 72,* 926–946.

Ruef, M. B., Higgins, C., Glaeser, B., & Patnode, M. (1998). Positive behavioral support: Strategies for teachers. *Intervention in School and Clinic, 34,* 21–32.

Ruzic, R. (2001, April). *Lessons for everyone: How students with reading-related learning disabilities survive and excel in college courses with heavy reading requirements*. Paper presented at the annual meeting of the American Educational Research Association, Seattle.

Ryan, A. M. (2000). Peer groups as a context for the socialization of adolescents' motivation, engagement, and achievement in school. *Educational Psychologist, 35,* 101–111.

Ryan, A. M. (2001). The peer group as a context for the development of young adolescent motivation and achievement. *Child Development, 72,* 1135–1150.

Ryan, A. M., & Patrick, H. (2001). The classroom social environment and changes in adolescents' motivation and engagement during middle school. *American Educational Research Journal, 38,* 437–460.

Ryan, K. E., & Ryan, A. M. (2005). Psychological processes of stereotype threat and standardized math test performance. *Educational Psychologist, 40*(1), 53–63.

Ryan, R., & Deci, E. (1996). When paradigms clash: Comments on Cameron and Pierce's claim that rewards do not undermine intrinsic motivation. *Review of Educational Research, 66,* 33–38.

Ryan, R., & Deci, E. (2000). Intrinsic and extrinsic motivations: Classic definitions and new directions. *Contemporary Educational Psychology, 25,* 54–67.

Saarni, C. (2002). *The development of emotional competence*. New York: Guilford.

Saddler, B., & Andrade, H. (2004). The writing rubric. *Educational Leadership, 62*(2), 48–52.

Sadoski, M., & Paivio, A. (2001). *Imagery and text: A dual coding theory of reading and writing*. Mahwah, NJ: Erlbaum.

Safer, N., & Fleischman, S. (2005). How student progress monitoring improves instruction. *Educational Leadership, 62*(5), 81–83.

Sagor, R. (2000). *Guiding school improvement with action research*. Alexandria, VA: Association for Supervision and Curriculum Development.

Sailor, W., & Roger, B. (2005). Rethinking inclusion: Schoolwide applications. *Phi Delta Kappan, 86*(7), 503–509.

Salend, S., & Salinas, A. (2003). Language differences or learning difficulties. In K. Freiberg (Ed.), *Educating exceptional children 05/06* (7th ed., pp. 70–77). Dubuque, IA: McGraw-Hill/Dushkin.

Saltpeter, J. (2005). Telling tales about technology. *Technology and Learning, 25*(7), 18–24.

Salvia, J., & Ysseldyke, J. (2004). *Assessment in special and remedial education* (9th ed.). Boston: Houghton Mifflin.

Samuels, S. (1983). A cognitive approach to factors influencing reading comprehension. *Journal of Educational Research, 76*(5), 261–266.

Samuels, S. (1988). Decoding and automaticity: Helping poor readers become automatic at word recognition. *Reading Teacher, 41*(8), 756–760.

Sand, B. (2001, April). *Toward a definition of creativity; Construct validation and the cognitive components of creativity*. Paper presented at the annual meeting of the American Educational Research Association, Seattle.

Sand, B., & Burley, H. (2001, April). *Divergent and convergent thinking and selected independent variables: A meta-analysis*. Paper presented at the annual meeting of the American Educational Research Association, Seattle.

Sanders, J., & Nelson, S. C. (2004). Closing gender gaps in science. *Educational Leadership, 62*(3), 74–77.

Sansone, C., & Harackiewicz, J. (Eds.). (2000). *Intrinsic and extrinsic motivation: The search for optimal motivation and performance*. San Diego: Academic Press.

Santrock, J. W. (2006). *Life-span development* (10th ed.). Boston: McGraw-Hill.

Sattler, J. M. (2001). *Assessment of children: Cognitive applications* (4th ed.). San Diego: Jerome M. Sattler.

Schacter, D. (2001). *The seven deadly sins of memory*. Boston: Houghton Mifflin.

Schiever, S., & Maker, C. J. (2003). New directions in enrichment and acceleration. In N. Colangelo & G. Davis (Eds.), *Handbook of gifted education* (3rd ed., pp. 163–173). Boston: Allyn & Bacon.

Schlozman, S. (2002). The shrink in the classroom: Fighting school violence. *Educational Leadership, 60*(2), 89–90.

Schlozman, S., & Schlozman, V. (2000). Chaos in the classroom: Looking at ADHD. *Educational Leadership, 58*(3), 28–33.

Schmid, C. (2001). Educational achievement, language-minority students, and the new second generation. *Sociology of Education, Extra Issue,* 71–87.

Schneider, B. (2002). Social capital: A ubiquitous emerging conception. In D. L. Levinson, P. W. Cookson, Jr., & A. R. Sadovnik (Eds.), *Education and sociology: An encyclopedia* (pp. 545–550). New York: Routledge Falmer.

Schneider, W., & Shiffrin, R. (1977). Controlled and automatic human information processing: Detection, search, and attention. *Psychological Review, 84,* 1–66.

Schommer, M. (1994). An emerging conceptualization of epistemological beliefs and their role in learning. In R. Garner & P. Alexander (Eds.), *Beliefs about text and instruction with text*. Hillsdale, NJ: Erlbaum.

Schraw, G., Flowerday, T., & Lehman, S. (2001). Increasing situational interest in the classroom. *Educational Psychology Review, 13*(3), 211–224.

Schraw, G., & Lehman, S. (2001). Situational interest: A review of the literature and directions for future research. *Educational Psychology Review, 13*(1), 23–52.

Schraw, G., & Moshman, D. (1995). Metacognitive theories. *Educational Psychology Review, 7,* 351–371.

Schult, C. A. (2002). Children's understanding of the distinction between intentions and desires. *Child Development, 73,* 1737–1747.

Schunk, D. (1994, April). *Goal and self-evaluative influences during children's mathematical skill acquisition.* Paper presented at the annual meeting of the American Educational Research Association, New Orleans.

Schunk, D. (1997, March). *Self-monitoring as a motivator during instruction with elementary school students.* Paper presented at the annual meeting of the American Educational Research Association, Chicago.

Schunk, D. (2004). *Learning theories: An educational perspective* (4th ed.). Upper Saddle River, NJ: Merrill/Prentice Hall.

Schunk, D. (2005). Self-regulated learning: The educational legacy of Paul R. Pintrich. *Educational Psychologist, 40*(2), 85–94.

Schunk, D. & Ertmer, P. (2000). Self-regulation and academic learning: Self-efficacy enhancing interventions. In M. Boekaerts, P. Pintrich, & M. Zeidner (Eds.), *Handbook of self-regulation* (pp. 631–649). San Diego: Academic Press.

Schutz, A. (2004, April). *Home is a prison in the global city: A critical review of urban school–community relationships.* Paper presented at the annual meeting of the American Educational Research Association, San Diego.

Schwartz, N., Ellsworth, L., Graham, L., & Knight, B. (1998). Accessing prior knowledge to remember text: A comparison of advance organizers and maps. *Contemporary Educational Psychology, 23,* 65–89.

Sears, S., Kennedy, J., & Kaye, G. (1997). Myers-Briggs personality profiles of prospective educators. *The Journal of Education Research, 90,* 195–202.

Segall, A. (2004). Revising pedagogical content knowledge: The pedagogy of content/the content of pedagogy. *Teaching and Teacher Education, 20,* 489–504.

Seligman, D. (1975). *Helplessness.* San Francisco: Freeman.

Selingo, J. (2004). The cheating culture. *ASEE Prism, 14*(1), 24–30.

Serafino, K., & Cicchelli, T. (2003). Cognitive theories, prior knowledge, and anchored instruction on mathematical problem solving and transfer. *Education and Urban Society, 36*(1), 79–93.

Serafino, K., & Cicchelli, T. (2005, April). *Mathematical problem-based learning: Theories, models for problem solving and transfer.* Paper presented at the annual meeting of the American Educational Research Association, Montreal, Canada.

Serpell, R. (2000). Intelligence and culture. In R. J. Sternberg (Ed.), *Handbook of intelligence* (pp. 549–577). New York: Cambridge University Press.

Shahid, J. (2001, April). *Teacher efficacy: A research synthesis.* Paper presented at the annual meeting of the American Educational Research Association, Seattle.

Shapiro, A. (2004). How including prior knowledge as a subject variable may change outcomes of learning research. *American Educational Research Journal, 41*(1), 159–189.

Shaywitz, S. E., & Shaywitz, B. A. (2004). Reading disability and the brain. *Educational Leadership, 61*(6), 7–11.

Shea, D., Lubinski, D., & Benbow, C. (2001). Importance of assessing spatial ability in intellectually talented young adolescents: A 20-year longitudinal study. *Journal of Educational Psychology, 93*(3), 604–614.

Shearer, C. (2002, April). *Using a multiple intelligences assessment to facilitate teacher development.* Paper presented at the annual meeting of the American Educational Research Association, New Orleans.

Shepard, L. (1993). Evaluating test validity. In L. Darling-Hammond (Ed.), *Review of research in education* (Vol. 19, pp. 405–450). Washington, DC: American Educational Research Association.

Shepard, L. (2001). The role of classroom assessment in teaching and learning. In V. Richardson (Ed.), *Handbook of research on learning* (4th ed., pp. 1066–1101). Washington, DC: American Educational Research Association.

Shepard, L., & Bliem, C. (1995). Parents' thinking about standardized tests and performance assessments. *Educational Researcher, 24*(5), 25–32.

Shermer, M. (2002). *Why people believe weird things: Pseudoscience, superstition, and other confusions of our time.* New York: Freeman.

Shields, P., & Shaver, D. (1990, April). *The mismatch between the school and home cultures of academically at-risk students.* Paper presented at the annual meeting of the American Educational Research Association, Boston.

Short, D., & Echevarria, J. (2005). Teacher skills to support English language learners. *Educational Leadership, 62*(4), 8–13.

Short, E., Schatschneider, C., & Friebert, S. (1993). Relationship between memory and metamemory performance: A comparison of specific and general strategy knowledge. *Journal of Educational Psychology, 85*(3), 412–423.

Shuell, T. (1996). Teaching and learning in a classroom context. In D. Berliner & R. Calfee (Eds.), *Handbook of educational psychology* (pp. 726–764). New York: Macmillan.

Shulman, L. (1986). Those who understand: Knowledge growth in teaching. *Educational Researcher, 15*(2), 4–14.

Shulman, L. (1987). Knowledge and teaching: Foundations of the new reform. *Harvard Educational Review, 57,* 1–22.

Siegel, M. (2002, April). *Models of teacher learning: A study of case analyses by preservice teachers.* Paper presented at the annual meeting of the American Educational Research Association, New Orleans.

Siegler, R. S. (1996). *Emerging minds: The process of change in children's thinking.* New York: Oxford.

Siegler, R. S. (1998). *Children's thinking* (3rd ed.). Upper Saddle River, NJ: Prentice Hall.

Simon, H. (2001). Learning to research about learning. In S. M. Carver & D. Klake (Eds.), *Cognition and instruction.* Mahwah, NJ: Erlbaum.

Simonton, D. K. (2000). Creativity: Cognitive, personal, developmental, and social aspects. *American Psychologist, 55,* 151–158.

Simonton, D. K. (2001). Talent development as a multidimensional, multiplicative, and dynamic process. *Current Directions in Psychological Science, 10,* 39–42.

Sinatra, G. M., & Pintrich, P. R. (2003). The role of intentions in conceptual change learning. In G. M. Sinatra & P. R. Pintrich (Eds.), *Intentional conceptual change* (pp. 1–18). Mahwah, NJ: Erlbaum.

Singham, M. (2003). The achievement gap: Myths and reality. *Phi Delta Kappan, 84*(8), 586–591.

Skinner, B. F. (1953). *Science and human behavior.* New York: Macmillan.

Skinner, B. F. (1957). *Verbal behavior.* Upper Saddle River, NJ: Prentice Hall.

Skinner, B. F. (1968). *The technology of teaching.* New York: Appleton-Century-Crofts.

Skoe, E., & Dressner, R. (1994). Ethics of care, justice, identity, and gender: An extension and replication. *Merrill-Palmer Quarterly, 40*(2), 272–289.

Slavin, R. (1987). Ability grouping and student achievement in elementary schools: A best-evidence synthesis. *Review of Educational Research, 57,* 293–336.

Slavin, R. (1995). *Cooperative learning: Theory, research, and practice* (2nd ed.). Needham Heights, MA: Allyn & Bacon.

Slavin, R., & Cheung, A. (2004). *Effective reading programs for English language learners: A best-evidence synthesis.* Baltimore: Center for Research on the Education of Students Placed at Risk, Johns Hopkins University. Retrieved from www.csos.jhu.edu/crespar/techReports/Report66.pdf

Smally, S., & Reyes-Blanes, M. (2001). Reaching out to African American parents in an urban community: A community–university partnership. *Urban Education, 36*(4), 518–533.

Smith, E. (1999). Working memory. In R. A. Wilson & F. C. Keel (Eds.), *The MIT encyclopedia of the cognitive sciences* (pp. 888–890). Cambridge, MA: MIT Press.

Smith, J., Brewer, D. M., & Heffner, T. (2003). Using portfolio assessments with young children who are at risk for school failure. *Preventing School Failure, 48*(1), 38–40.

Smith, P., & Fouad, N. (1999). Subject-matter specificity of self-efficacy, outcome expectancies, interest, and goals: Implications for the social-cognitive model. *Journal of Counseling Psychology, 46,* 461–471.

Smith, T., Polloway, E., Patton, J., & Dowdy, C. (2004). *Teaching students with special needs in inclusive settings* (4th ed.). Boston: Allyn & Bacon.

Smokowski, P. (1997, April). *What personal essays tell us about resiliency and protective factors in adolescence.* Paper presented at the annual meeting of the American Educational Research Association, Chicago.

Snary, J. (1995). In a communitarian voice: The sociological expansion of Kohlbergian theory, research, and practice. In W. Kurtines & J. Gewirtz (Eds.), *Moral development: An introduction.* Boston: Allyn & Bacon.

Son, L. (2004). Spacing one's study: Evidence for a metacognitive control strategy. *Journal of Experimental Psychology: Learning, Memory, and Cognition, 3*(3), 601–604.

Sousa, D. A. (1995). *How the brain learns: A classroom teacher's guide.* Reston, VA: National Association of Secondary School Principals.

Southerland, S., Kittleson, J., & Settlage, J. (2002, April). *The intersection of personal and group knowledge construction: Red fog, cold cans, and seeping vapor or children talking and thinking about condensation in a third grade classroom.* Paper presented at the annual meeting of the National Association for Science Teaching, New Orleans.

Southerland, S. A., & Sinatra, G. M. (2003). Learning about biological evolution: A special case of intentional conceptual change. In G. M. Sinatra & P. R. Pintrich (Eds.), *Intentional conceptual change* (pp. 317–345). Mahwah, NJ: Erlbaum.

Spearman, C. (1927). *The abilities of man: Their nature and measurement.* New York: Macmillan.

Spencer, M. B., Noll, E., Stoltzfus, J., & Harpalani, V. (2001). Identity and school adjustment: Revisiting the "acting White" phenomenon. *Educational Psychologist, 36,* 21–30.

Spinelli, C. G. (2004). *Classroom assessment for students with special needs in inclusive classrooms.* Upper Saddle River, NJ: Merrill/Prentice Hall.

Spiro, R., Feltovich, P., Jacobson, M., & Coulson, R. (1992). Knowledge representation, content specification, and the development of skill in situation-specific knowledge assembly: Some constructivist issues as they relate to cognitive flexibility theory and hypertext. In T. Duffy & D. Jonassen (Eds.), *Constructivism and the technology of instruction: A conversation* (pp. 121–127). Hillsdale, NJ: Erlbaum.

Spor, M., & Schneider, B. (1999). Content reading strategies: What teachers know, use, and want to learn. *Reading Research and Instruction, 38,* 221–231.

Stahl, R., DeMasi, K., Gehrke, R., Guy, C., & Scown, J. (2005, April). *Perceptions, conceptions and misconceptions of wait time and wait time behaviors among pre-service and in-service teachers.* Paper presented at the annual meeting of the American Educational Research Association, Montreal, Canada.

Stahl, S. A. (1999). Why innovations come and go (and mostly go): The case of whole language. *Educational Researcher, 28*(8), 13–22.

Stainback, S., & Stainback, W. (Eds.). (1992). *Curriculum considerations in inclusive classrooms.* Baltimore: Brookes.

Stanovich, K. (2000). *Progress in understanding reading: Scientific foundations and new frontiers.* New York: Guilford Press.

Stanton-Salazar, R. D., & Spina, S. U. (2003). Informal mentors and role models in the lives of urban Mexican-origin adolescents. *Anthropology & Education Quarterly, 34*(3), 231–254.

Star, J. (2002, April). *Re-conceptualizing procedural knowledge in mathematics.* Paper presented at the annual meeting of the American Educational Research Association, New Orleans.

Star, J. (2004, April). *The development of flexible procedural knowledge in equation solving.* Paper presented at the annual meeting of the American Educational Research Association, San Diego.

Stecher, B., & Herman, J. (1997). Using portfolios for large-scale assessment. In G. Phye (Ed.), *Handbook of classroom assessment* (pp. 490–514). San Diego, CA: Academic Press.

Steele, C., Spencer, S., & Aronson, J. (2002). Contending with group image: The psychology of stereotype and social identity threat. In M. Zanna (Ed.), *Advances in experimental social psychology* (Vol. 34, pp. 379–440). San Diego: Academic Press.

Stein, M., & Carnine, D. (1999). Designing and delivering effective mathematics instruction. In R. Stevens (Ed.), *Teaching in American schools* (pp. 245–270). Upper Saddle River, NJ: Merrill/Prentice Hall.

Steinberg, L. (1996). *Beyond the classroom: Why school reform has failed and what parents need to do.* New York: Touchstone.

Steinberg, L., Brown, B., & Dornbusch, S. (1996). Ethnicity and adolescent achievement. *American Education, 20*(2), 28–35.

Steiner, H. H., & Carr, M. (2003). Cognitive development in gifted children: Toward a more precise understanding of emerging differences in intelligence. *Educational Psychology Review, 15,* 215–246.

Stephens, K., & Karnes, F. (2000). State definitions for the gifted and talented revisited. *Exceptional Children, 66*(2), 219–238.

Sternberg, R. (1988). *The triarchic mind.* New York: Viking.

Sternberg, R. (1998a). Applying the triarchic theory of human intelligence in the classroom. In R. Sternberg & W. Williams (Eds.), *Intelligence, instruction, and assessment* (pp. 1–16). Mahwah, NJ: Erlbaum.

Sternberg, R. (1998b). Metacognition, abilities, and developing expertise: What makes an expert student? *Instructional Science, 26*(1–2), 127–140.

Sternberg, R. (1998c). Principles of teaching for successful intelligence. *Educational Psychologist, 33*(2/3), 65–72.

Sternberg, R. (2000). Looking back and looking forward on intelligence: Toward a theory of successful intelligence. In M. Bennet (Ed.), *Developmental psychology.* Philadelphia: Psychology Press.

Sternberg, R. (2003a). *Cognitive psychology* (3rd ed.). Belmont, CA: Wadsworth.

Sternberg, R. (2003b). *Wisdom, intelligence, and creativity synthesized.* Cambridge: Cambridge University Press.

Sternberg, R., & Grigorenko, E. (2000). Theme-park psychology: A case study regarding human intelligence and its implications for education. *Educational Psychology Review, 12*(2), 247–268.

Sternberg, R., & Grigorenko, E. (2001). Learning disabilities, schooling, and society. *Phi Delta Kappan, 83*(4), 335–338.

Stevenson, H., & Fantuzzo, J. (1986). The generality and social validity of a competency-based self-control training intervention for underachieving students. *Journal of Applied Behavior Analysis, 19,* 269–276.

Stevenson, H., Lee, S., & Stigler, J. (1986). Mathematics achievement of Chinese, Japanese, and American children. *Science, 231,* 693–699.

Stiggins, R. (2004). New assessment beliefs for a new school mission. *Phi Delta Kappan, 86*(1), 22–27.

Stiggins, R. (2005). *Student-centered classroom assessment* (4th ed.). Upper Saddle River, NJ: Merrill/Prentice Hall.

Stiggins, R., & Conklin, N. (1992). *In teachers' hands.* Albany: State University of New York Press.

Stigler, J., & Hiebert, J. (2000). *The teaching gap.* New York: Free Press.

Stipek, D. (1996). Motivation and instruction. In D. Berliner & R. Calfee (Eds.), *Handbook of educational psychology* (pp. 85–113). New York: Macmillan.

Stipek, D. (2002). *Motivation to learn* (4th ed.). Boston: Allyn & Bacon.

Strickland, B. B., & Turnbull, A. P. (1990). *Developing and implementing individualized education programs* (3rd ed.). Upper Saddle River, NJ: Merrill/Prentice Hall.

Stright, A., Neitzel, C., Sears, K., & Hoke-Sinex, L. (2001). Instruction begins in the home: Relations between parental instruction and children's self-regulation in the classroom. *Journal of Educational Psychology, 93*(3), 456–466.

Strong, R., Silver, H., Perini, M., & Tuculescu, G. (2003). Boredom and its opposite. *Educational Leadership, 61*(1), 24–29.

Stuebing, K., Fletcher, J., LeDoux, J., Lyon, G., Shaywitz, S., & Shaywitz, B. (2002). Validity of IQ-discrepancy classifications of reading disabilities: A meta-analysis. *American Educational Research Journal, 39*(2), 469–518.

Sudzina, M. (Ed.). (1999). *Case study applications for teacher education.* Needham Heights, MA: Allyn & Bacon.

Swanson, H. (2001). Research on interventions for adolescents with learning disabilities: A meta-analysis of outcomes related to higher-order processing. *Elementary School Journal, 101*(3), 331–348.

Swanson, H., & Hoskyn, M. (1998). Experimental intervention research on students with learning disabilities: A meta-analysis of treatment outcomes. *Review of Educational Research, 68*(3), 277–321.

Swanson, J. M., & Volkow, N. D. (2002). Pharmacokinetic and pharmacodynamic properties of stimulants: Implications of the design of new treatments for ADHD. *Behavior and Brain Research, 130,* 73–80.

Sweller, J., van Merrienboer, J., & Paas, F. (1998). Cognitive architecture and instructional design. *Educational Psychology Review, 10,* 251–296.

Tamis-LeMonda, C. S., Bornstein, M. H., & Baumwell, L. (2001). Maternal responsiveness and children's achievement of language milestones. *Child Development, 72,* 748–767.

Tannenbaum, A. (2003). Nature and nurture of giftedness. In N. Colangelo & G. Davis (Eds.),

Handbook of gifted education (3rd ed., pp. 45–59). Boston: Allyn & Bacon.

Tannock, R., & Martinussen, R. (2001). Reconceptualizing ADHD. *Educational Leadership, 59*(3), 20–25.

Taylor, B., Pearson, P. D., Peterson, D., & Rodriguez, M. (2003). Reading growth in high-poverty classrooms: The influence of teacher practices that encourage cognitive engagement in literacy learning. *Elementary School Journal, 104*(1), 3–28.

Taylor, B. A., & Levin, L. (1998). Teaching a student with autism to make verbal initiations: Effects of a tactile prompt. *Journal of Applied Behavior Analysis, 31,* 651–654.

Taylor, R. L. (2006). *Assessment of exceptional students: Educational and psychological procedures* (7th ed.). Boston: Allyn & Bacon.

Tenenbaum, H., & Leaper, C. (2003). Parent–child conversations about science: The socialization of gender inequities? *Developmental Psychology, 39,* 34–47.

Tennyson, R., & Cocchiarella, M. (1986). An empirically based instructional design theory for teaching concepts. *Review of Educational Research, 56,* 40–71.

Terhune, K. (1968). Studies of motives, cooperation, and conflict within laboratory microcosms. In G. Snyder (Ed.), *Studies in international conflict* (Vol. 4, pp. 29–58). Buffalo, NY: SUNY Buffalo Council on International Studies.

Terman, L., Baldwin, B., & Bronson, E. (1925). Mental and physical traits of a thousand gifted children. In L. Terman (Ed.), *Genetic studies of genius* (Vol. 1). Stanford, CA: Stanford University Press.

Terman, L., & Oden, M. (1947). The gifted child grows up. In L. Terman (Ed.), *Genetic studies of genius* (Vol. 4). Stanford, CA: Stanford University Press.

Terman, L., & Oden, M. (1959). The gifted group in mid-life. In L. Terman (Ed.), *Genetic studies of genius* (Vol. 5). Stanford, CA: Stanford University Press.

Terry, S. (2006). *Learning and memory: Basic principles, process, and procedures* (3rd ed.). Boston: Allyn & Bacon.

Terwel, J., Gillies, R., van den Eeden, P., & Hoek, D. (2001). Cooperative learning processes of students: A longitudinal multilevel perspective. *British Journal of Educational Psychology, 71,* 619–645.

Terwilliger, J. (1997). Semantics, psychometrics, and assessment reform: A close look at "authentic assessments." *Educational Researcher, 26,* 24–27.

Tharp, R., & Gallimore, R. (1991). *The instructional conversation: Teaching and learning in social activity.* Washington, DC: National Center for Research on Cultural Diversity and Second Language Learning.

Thiede, K. W., & Anderson, M. C. M. (2003). Summarizing can improve metacomprehension accuracy. *Contemporary Educational Psychology, 28,* 129–160.

Thiede, K. W., Anderson, M. C. M., & Therriault, D. (2003). Accuracy of metacognitive monitoring affects learning of texts. *Journal of Educational Psychology, 95,* 66–73.

Thirunarayanan, M. O. (2004). The "significantly worse" phenomenon: A study of student achievement in different content areas by school location. *Education and Urban Society, 36*(4), 467–481.

Thoma, S., & Rest, J. (1996). *The relationship between moral decision-making and patterns of consolidation and transition in moral judgment development.* Paper presented at the annual meeting of the American Educational Research Association, New York.

Thorkildsen, T. (1996, April). *The way tests teach: Children's theories of how much testing is fair in school.* Paper presented at the annual meeting of the National Educational Research Association, New York.

Thorndike, E. (1924). Mental discipline in high school studies. *Journal of Educational Psychology, 15,* 1–2, 83–98

Thorndike, R. M. (2005). *Measurement and evaluation in psychology and education* (7th ed.). Upper Saddle River, NJ: Merrill/Prentice Hall.

Thornton, M., & Fuller, R. (1981). How do college students solve proportion problems? *Journal of Research in Science Teaching, 18,* 335–340.

Thrash, T., & Elliot, A. (2001). Delimiting and integrating achievement motive and goal constructs. In A. Efklides, J. Kuhl, & R. Sorrentino (Eds.), *Trends and prospects in motivation research* (pp. 3–21). Boston: Kluwer.

Tiedemann, J. (2000). Parents' gender stereotypes and teachers' beliefs as predictors of children's concept of their mathematical ability in elementary school. *Journal of Educational Psychology, 92,* 144–151.

Tisak, M. (1993). Preschool children's judgments of moral and personal events involving physical harm and property damage. *Merrill-Palmer Quarterly, 39,* 375–390.

Titsworth, S. (2004). Students' notetaking: The effects of teacher immediacy and clarity. *Communication Education, 53,* 305–320.

Tollefson, N. (2000). Classroom applications of cognitive theories of motivation. *Educational Psychology Review, 12,* 63–83.

Tomasello, M., & Slobin, D. I. (Eds.). (2004). *Beyond nature and nurture.* Mahwah, NJ: Erlbaum.

Tompkins, G. (2003). *Literacy for the twenty-first century* (3rd ed.). Upper Saddle River, NJ: Merrill/Prentice Hall.

Topping, D. H., & McManus, R. A. (2002). A culture of literacy in science. *Educational Leadership, 60,* 30–33.

Torff, B. (2005). Developmental changes in teachers' beliefs about critical-thinking activities. *Journal of Educational Psychology, 97*(1), 13–22.

Trawick-Smith, J. (1997). *Early childhood development: A multicultural perspective.* Upper Saddle River, NJ: Merrill/Prentice Hall.

Trawick-Smith, J. (2003). *Early childhood development: A multicultural perspective* (3rd ed.). Upper Saddle River, NJ: Pearson.

Triona, L., & Klahr, D. (2003). Point and click or grab and heft: Comparing the influence of physical and virtual instructional materials on elementary school students' ability to design experiments. *Cognition and Instruction, 2*(2), 149–173.

Troia, G. A., & Graham, S. (2002). The effectiveness of a highly explicit, teacher-directed strategy instruction routine: Changing the writing performance of students with learning disabilities. *Journal of Learning Disabilities, 35,* 290–305.

Trotter, A. (2000). Home computer used primarily for learning, families say in survey. *Education Week, 19*(30), 6.

Trotter, A. (2001a). Army's new cyber-school opens doors for online learners. *Education Week, 20*(16), 6.

Trotter, A. (2001b). New law directs schools to install filtering devices. *Education Week, 20*(16), 32.

Trotter, A. (2003). Simulated driver's ed. takes virtual twists and turns. *Education Week, 22*(19), 8.

Trotter, A. (2005). Tool helps Washington teachers write learning plans. *Education Week, 24*(23), 6.

Tschannen-Moran, M., Woolfolk-Hoy, A., & Hoy, W. (1998). Teacher efficacy: Its meaning and measure. *Review of Educational Research, 68*(2), 202–248.

Tucker, C., Zayco, R., Herman, K., Reinke, W., Trujillo, M., Carraway, K., Wallack, C., & Ivery, P. (2002). Teacher and child variables as predictors of academic engagement among low-income African American children. *Psychology in the Schools, 39,* 477–488.

Tuovinen, J., & Sweller, J. (1999). A comparison of cognitive load associated with discovery learning and worked examples. *Journal of Educational Psychology, 91*(2), 334–341.

Turiel, E. (1973). Stage transitions in moral development. In R. Travers (Ed.), *Second handbook of research on teaching* (pp. 732–758). Chicago: Rand McNally.

Turiel, E. (1998). The development of morality. In W. Damon (Series Ed.), and N. Eisenberg (Vol. Ed.), *Handbook of child psychology: Vol. 3. Social, emotional, & personality development* (5th ed., pp. 863–932). New York: Wiley.

Turnbull, A., Turnbull, R., Shank, M., Smith, S., & Leal, D. (2004). *Exceptional lives: Special education in today's schools* (4th ed.). Upper Saddle River, NJ: Merrill/Prentice Hall.

Twenge, J. M., & Campbell, W. K. (2001). Age and birth cohort differences in self-esteem: A cross temporal meta-analysis. *Journal of Personality and Social Psychology Review, 5,* 321–344.

Tyler, R. (1950). *Basic principles of curriculum and instruction.* Chicago: University of Chicago Press.

Tzuriel, D. (2000). Dynamic assessment of young children: Educational and intervention perspectives. *Educational Psychology Review, 12,* 385–435.

UCLA Center for Communication Policy. (2001). *Surveying the digital future: Year two.* Retrieved February, 2004, from http://www.ccp.ucla.edu

Urban Institute (2000). *American's homeless II: Populations and services.* Washington, DC: Author.

Urdan, T. (2001). Contextual influences on motivation and performance: An examination of achievement goal structures. In F. Salili, C. Chiu, & Y. Hong (Eds.), *Student motivation: The culture and context of learning* (pp. 171–201). New York: Kluer/Plenum.

U.S. Bureau of the Census. (2000). *Statistical abstract of the United States* (120th ed.). Washington, DC: U.S. Government Printing Office.

U.S. Bureau of the Census. (2001). Retrieved from www.census.gov/Press-Release/www/2001/cb01-158.html

U.S. Department of Education. (2000). *Digest of education statistics, 1999.* Washington, DC: National Center for Educational Statistics.

U.S. Department of Education. (2004). *Twenty-sixth annual report to Congress on the implementation of the Individuals With Disabilities Education Act.* Washington, DC: U.S. Government Printing Office.

U.S. Department of Education, Office of Special Education Programs. (2002). *Twenty-fourth annual report to Congress on the implementation of the Individuals with Disabilities Education Act.* Washington, DC: Author.

U.S. Department of Health & Human Services. (2001). *National survey results on drug abuse from the Monitoring the Future study. Vol. 1. Secondary school students.* Washington, DC: U.S. Government Printing Office.

U.S. Department of Health & Human Services. (2002). *Vital statistics of the United States.* Washington, DC: U.S. Government Printing Office.

U.S. Department of Justice. (1999). *Crime in the United States.* Washington, DC: U.S. Government Printing Office.

U.S. English. (2005). Retrieved from http://www.US.English.org

Valenzeno, L., Alibali, M., & Klatsky, R. (2003). Teachers' gestures facilitate students' learning: A lesson in symmetry. *Contemporary Educational Psychology, 28,* 187–204.

Valenzuela, A. (1999). *Subtractive schooling: U.S.-Mexican youth and the politics of caring.* Albany: State University of New York Press.

van Gelder, T. (2005). Teaching critical thinking: Some lessons from cognitive science. *College Teaching, 53,* 41–46.

van Gog, T., Paas, F., & van Merriënboer, J. (2004). Process-oriented worked examples: Improving transfer performance through enhanced understanding. *Instructional Science, 32*(1–2), 83–98.

van Lar, C. (2000). The paradox of low academic achievement but high self-esteem in African American students: An attributional account. *Educational Psychology Review, 12,* 33–61.

van Merriënboer, J., Kirschner, P., & Kester, L. (2003). Taking the load off a learner's mind: Instructional design for complex learning. *Educational Psychologist, 38*(1), 5–13.

van Meter, P. (2001). Drawing construction as a strategy for learning from text. *Journal of Educational Psychology, 93*(1), 129–140.

Vang, C. T. (2003). Learning more about Hmong students. *Multicultural Education, 11*(2), 10–14.

VanLeuvan, P. (2004). Young women's science/mathematics career goals from seventh grade to high school graduation. *Journal of Educational Research, 97*(5), 248–262.

Vaughn, S., & Bos, C. S. (2006). *Strategies for teaching students with learning and behavior problems* (6th ed.). Boston: Allyn & Bacon.

Vaughn, S., Bos, C., Candace, S., & Schumm, J. (2006). *Teaching exceptional, diverse, and at-risk students in the general education classroom.* (3rd ed.). Boston: Allyn & Bacon.

Vavilis, B., & Vavilis, S. (2004). Why are we learning this? What is this stuff good for, anyway?: The importance of conversation in the classroom. *Phi Delta Kappan, 86*(4), 282–287.

Veenman, M. V., & Spaans, M. A. (2005). Relation between intellectual and matacognitive skills: Age and task differences. *Learning and Individual Differences, 15,* 159–176.

Veenman, S. (1984). Perceived problems of beginning teachers. *Review of Educational Research, 54,* 143–178.

Venn, J. J. (2000). *Assessing students with special needs* (2nd ed.). Upper Saddle River, NJ: Merrill/Prentice Hall.

Verkoeijen, P. P., Rikers, R. M., & Schmidt, H. G. (2005). The effects of prior knowledge on study-time allocation and free recall: Investigating the discrepancy reduction model. *The Journal of Psychology, 139,* 67–79.

Vermeer, H. J., Boekaerts, M., & Seegers, G. (2000). Motivational and gender differences: Sixth-grade students' mathematical problem-solving behavior. *Journal of Educational Psychology, 92,* 308–315.

Verna, M., Wintergerst, A., & DeCapua, A. (2001, April). *College students benefit by employing second language learning strategies.* Paper presented at the annual meeting of the American Educational Research Association, Seattle.

Viadero, D. (2000). High-stakes tests lead debate at researchers' gathering. *Education Week, 19*(34), 6.

Viadero, D. (2003). Two studies highlight links between violence, bullying by students. *Education Week, 22*(36), 6.

Viadero, D., & Johnston, R. (2000). Lifting minority achievement: Complex answers. *Education Week, 19*(30), 1, 14–16.

Vidal, F. (2000). Piaget's theory. In A. Kazdin (Ed.), *Encyclopedia of psychology.* Washington, DC: American Psychological Association and Oxford University Press.

Villegas, A. (1991). *Culturally responsive pedagogy for the 1990s and beyond.* Princeton, NJ: Educational Testing Service.

von Károlyi, C., Ramos-Ford, V., & Gardner, H. (2003). Multiple intelligences: A perspective on giftedness. In N. Colangelo & G. Davis (Eds.), *Handbook of gifted education* (3rd ed., pp. 100–112). Boston: Allyn & Bacon.

Vosniadou, S. (2003). Exploring the relationships between conceptual change and intentional learning. In G. M. Sinatra & P. R. Pintrich (Eds.), *Intentional conceptual change* (pp. 377–406). Mahwah, NJ: Erlbaum.

Vosniadou, S., & Brewer, W. (1989). *The concept of the earth's shape: A study of conceptual change in childhood.* Unpublished manuscript, University of Illinois, Center for the Study of Reading, Champaign, IL.

Vygotsky, L. (1978). *Mind in society: The development of higher psychological processes* (M. Cole, V. John-Steiner, S. Scribner, & E. Souberman, Eds. & Trans.). Cambridge, MA: Harvard University Press.

Vygotsky, L. (1986). *Thought and language.* Cambridge, MA: MIT Press.

Wade-Steen, D., & Kintsch, E. (2004). Summary street: Interactive computer support for writing. *Cognition and Instruction, 22*(3), 333–362.

Wadsworth, B. J. (2004). *Piaget's theory of cognitive and affective development* (5th ed.). Boston: Pearson.

Walker, J. E., Bauer, A. M., & Shea, T. M. (2004). *Behavior management: A practical approach for educators* (8th ed.). Upper Saddle River, NJ: Merrill/Prentice Hall.

Walker, L., & Pitts, R. (1998). Naturalistic conceptions of moral maturity. *Developmental Psychology, 34,* 403–419.

Wallace, D. (2000). Results, results, results? *Education Leadership, 57*(5), 66–67.

Wallace, D., West, S., Ware, A., & Dansereau, D. (1998). The effect of knowledge maps that incorporate gestalt principles on learning. *Journal of Experimental Education, 67*(1), 5–16.

Wallace, R. (2004). A framework for understanding teaching with the Internet. *American Educational Research Journal, 41*(2), 447–488.

Walpole, M., McDonough, P. M., & Bauer, C. J. (2005). This test is unfair: Urban African American and Latino high school students' perceptions of standardized college admissions tests. *Urban Education, 40*(3), 321–349.

Walsh, D., & Bennett, N. (2004). *Why do they act that way?: A survival guide to the adolescent brain for you and your teen.* New York: Free Press.

Walton, S., & Taylor, K. (1996/97). How did you know the answer was boxcar? *Educational Leadership, 54*(4), 38–40.

Wang, M., Haertel, G., & Walberg, H. (1993). Toward a knowledge base for school learning. *Review of Educational Research, 63*(3), 249–294.

Warner, L., & Lynch, S. (2005). Classroom problems that don't go away. In K. Freiberg (Ed.), *Educating exceptional children 05/06* (7th ed., pp. 128–131). Dubuque, IA: McGraw-Hill/ Dushkin.

Wasley, P. A., Hample, R. L., & Clark, R. W. (1997). *Kids and school reform.* San Francisco: Jossey-Bass.

Watt, H. M. G. (2005). Attitudes to the use of alternative assessment methods in mathematics: A study with secondary mathematics teachers in Sydney, Australia. *Educational Studies in Mathematics, 58*(1), 21–44.

Waxman, H., Huang, S., Anderson, L., & Weinstein, T. (1997). Classroom process differences in inner-city elementary schools. *Journal of Educational Research, 91*(1), 49–59.

Wayne, A., & Youngs, P. (2003). Teacher characteristics and student achievement gains: A review. *Review of Educational Research, 73,* 89–122.

Webb, N., Baxter, G., & Thompson, L. (1997). Teachers' grouping practices in fifth-grade science classrooms. *Elementary School Journal, 98*(2), 107–111.

Webb, N., & Farivar, S. (1994). Promoting helping behavior in cooperative small groups in middle school mathematics. *American Educational Research Journal, 31*(2), 369–395.

Webb, N., Farivar, S., & Mastergeorge, A. (2002). Productive helping in cooperative groups. *Theory Into Practice, 41*(1).

Wechsler, D. (2003). *Wechsler intelligence scale for children* (4th ed.) San Antonio, TX: Psychological Corporation.

Weigel, D., Martin, S., & Bennett, K. (2005). Ecological influences on the home and the child-care center on preschool-age children's literacy development. *Reading Research Quarterly, 40*(2), 204–233.

Weiland, A., & Coughlin, R. (1979). Self-identification and preferences: A comparison of White and Mexican American first and third graders. *Journal of Social Psychology, 10,* 356–365.

Weiner, B. (1986). *An attributional theory of motivation and emotion.* New York: Springer-Verlag.

Weiner, B. (1992). *Human motivation: Metaphors, theories, and research.* Newbury Park, CA: Sage.

Weiner, B. (1994). Ability versus effort revisited: The moral determinants of achievement evaluation and achievement as a moral system. *Educational Psychologist, 29,* 163–172.

Weiner, B. (2000). Interpersonal and intrapersonal theories of motivation from an attributional perspective. *Educational Psychology Review, 12,* 1–14.

Weiner, B. (2001). Intrapersonal and interpersonal theories of motivation from an attribution perspective. In F. Salili, C. Chiu, & Y. Hong (Eds.), *Student motivation: The culture and context of learning* (pp. 17–30). New York: Kluer Academic/Plenum.

Weiner, L. (2000). Research in the 90s: Implications for urban teacher preparation. *Review of Educational Research, 70,* 369–406.

Weiner, L. (2002, April). Why is classroom management so vexing to urban teachers? *New Directions in theory and research about classroom management in urban schools.* Paper presented at the annual meeting of the American Educational Research Association, New Orleans.

Weinstein, C. S., & Mignano, A. J., Jr. (2003). *Elementary classroom management: Lessons from research and practice* (3rd ed.). New York: McGraw-Hill.

Weinstein, R. (1998). Promoting positive expectations in schooling. In N. Lambert & B. McCombs (Eds.), *How students learn: Reforming schools through learner-centered education* (pp. 81–111). Washington, DC: American Psychological Association.

Weinstein, R. (2002). *Reaching higher: The power of expectations in schooling.* Cambridge, MA: Harvard University Press.

Weiss, H., Mayer, E., Kreider, H., Vaughan, M., Dearing, E., Hencke, R., & Pinto, K. (2003). Making it work: Low-income working mothers' involvement in their children's education. *American Educational Research Journal, 40*(4), 879–901.

Weiss, I., & Pasley, J. (2004). What is high-quality instruction? *Educational Leadership, 61*(5), 24–28.

Weissberg, R., & Greenberg, M. (1998). School and community competence-enhancement prevention programs. In W. Damon (Ed.), *Handbook of child psychology* (Vol. 4). New York: Wiley.

Weissglass, S. (1998). *Ripples of hope: Building relationships for educational change.* Santa Barbara: Center for Educational Change in Mathematics & Science, University of California.

Wenglinsky, H. (1998). *Does it compute? The relationship between educational technology and student achievement in mathematics.* Princeton, NJ: Educational Testing Service. Retrieved March 6, 2002, from ftp://ftp.ets.org.pub/res/ technolog.pdf

Wenner, G. (2003). Comparing poor, minority elementary students' interest and background in science with that of their white, affluent peers. *Urban Education, 38*(2), 153–172.

Wentzel, K. (1996). Social goals and social relationships as motivators of school adjustment. In J. Juvonen & K. Wentzel (Eds.), *Social motivation: Understanding children's school adjustment* (pp. 226–247). Cambridge, England: Cambridge University Press.

Wentzel, K. (1999a). Social influences on school adjustment: Commentary. *Educational Psychologist, 34*(1), 59–69.

Wentzel, K. (1999b). Social-motivational processes and interpersonal relationships: Implications for understanding students' academic success. *Journal of Educational Psychology, 91,* 76–97.

Wentzel, K. (2000). What is it that I'm trying to achieve? Classroom goals from a content perspective. *Contemporary Educational Psychology, 25,* 105–115.

Wentzel, K. R., & Wigfield, A. (1998). Academic and social motivational influences on students' academic performance. *Educational Psychology Review, 10,* 155–175.

Wessler, S. (2003). It's hard to learn when you're scared. *Educational Leadership, 61*(1), 40–43.

Westwater, A., & Wolfe, P. (2000). The brain-compatible curriculum. *Educational Leadership, 58*(3), 49–52.

Whalen, C. K., Jamner, L. D., Henker, B., Delfino, R. J., & Lozano, J. M. (2002). The ADHD spectrum and everyday life: Experience sampling of adolescent moods, activities, smoking, and drinking. *Child Development, 73,* 209–227.

Wheeler, R. (1999). *The workings of language: From prescriptions to perspectives.* Wheeler, CT: Praeger.

White, E. B. (1974). *Charlotte's web.* New York: HarperCollins.

White, P., Sanbonmatsu, D., Croyle, R., & Smittipatana, S. (2002). Test of socially motivated underachievement: "Letting up" for others. *Journal of Experimental Social Psychology, 38,* 162–169.

White, R. (1959). Motivation reconsidered: The concept of competence. *Psychological Review, 66,* 297–333.

Wigfield, A. (1994). Expectancy-value theory of achievement motivation: A developmental perspective. *Educational Psychology Review, 6,* 49–78.

Wigfield, A., & Eccles, J. (1992). The development of achievement task values: A theoretical analysis. *Developmental Review, 12,* 265–310.

Wigfield, A., & Eccles, J. (2000). Expectancy-value theory of achievement motivation. *Contemporary Educational Psychology, 25,* 68–81.

Wigfield, A., Eccles, J., & Pintrich, P. (1996). Development between the ages of 11 and 25. In D. Berliner & R. Calfee (Eds.), *Handbook of educational psychology* (pp. 148–185). New York: Macmillan.

Wigfield, A., Guthrie, J., Tonks, S., & Perencevich, K. (2004). Children's motivation for reading: Domain specificity and instructional influences. *Journal of Educational Research, 97*(6), 299–310.

Wiggens, G. P., & McTighe, J. (2005). *Understanding by design* (2nd ed.). Alexandria, VA: Association for Supervision and Curriculum Development.

Wildavsky, B. (1999, September 27). Achievement testing gets its day in court. *U.S. News and World Report,* pp. 22–23.

Wilder, M. (2000). Increasing African American teachers' presence in American schools: Voices of students who care. *Urban Education, 35*(2), 205–220.

Wiley, D., & Harnischfeger, A. (1974). Explosion of a myth: Quantity of schooling and exposure to instruction, major education vehicles. *Education Researcher, 3,* 7–12.

Willard-Holt, C. (2003). *Differentiated constructivist pedagogy: Lessons from heterogeneous classrooms.* Paper presented at the annual meeting of the American Educational Research Association, Chicago.

Williams, C., & Zacks, R. (2001). Is retrieval-induced forgetting an inhibitory process? *American Journal of Psychology, 114,* 329–354.

Williams, J. (1992, April). *Effects of test anxiety and self-concept on performance across curricular areas.* Paper presented at the annual meeting of the American Educational Research Association, San Francisco.

Williams, R. L., & Eggert, A. C. (2002). Notetaking predictors of test performance. *Teaching of Psychology, 29,* 234–237.

Williams, S., Bareiss, R., & Reiser, B. (1996, April). *ASK Jasper: A multimedia publishing and performance support environment for design.* Paper presented at the annual meeting of the American Educational Research Association, New York.

Willingham, D. T. (2004). *Cognition: The thinking animal* (2nd ed.). Upper Saddle River, NJ: Merrill/Prentice Hall.

Willoughby, T., Porter, L., Belsito, L., & Yearsley, T. (1999). Use of elaboration strategies by students in grades two, four, and six. *Elementary School Journal, 99*(3), 221–232.

Wilson, B. L., & Corbett, H. D. (2001). *Listening to urban kids: School reform and the teachers they want.* Albany, NY: State University of New York Press.

Wilson, K., & Swanson, H. (1999, April). *Individual and age-related differences in working memory and mathematics computation.* Paper presented at the annual conference of the American Educational Research Association, Montreal, Canada.

Wilson, M., Hoskens, M., & Draney, K. (2001, April). *Rater effects: Some issues, some solutions.* Paper presented at the annual meeting of the American Educational Research Association, Seattle.

Winitzky, N. (1994). Multicultural and mainstreamed classrooms. In R. Arends (Ed.), *Learning to teach* (3rd ed., pp. 132–170). New York: McGraw-Hill.

Winn, W. (2002). Current trends in technology research: The study of learning environments. *Educational Psychology Review, 14,* 331–351.

Winne, P. (2001). Self-regulated learning viewed from models of information processing. In B. J. Zimmerman & D. H. Schunk (Eds.), *Self-regulated learning and academic achievement: Theoretical perspectives* (2nd ed.). Mahwah, NJ: Erlbaum.

Winner, E. (2000a). Giftedness: Current theory and research. *Current Directions in Psychological Science, 9,* 153–156.

Winner, E. (2000b). The origins and ends of giftedness. *American Psychologist, 55,* 159–169.

Winograd, K. (1998). Rethinking theory after practice: Education professor as elementary teacher. *Journal of Teacher Education, 49*(4), 296–303.

Winsler, A., & Naglieri, J. (2003). Overt and covert verbal problem-solving strategies: Developmental trends in use, awareness, and relations with task performance in children aged 5 to 17. *Child Development, 74,* 659–678.

Wolf, L., Smith, J., & Birnbaum, M. (1997, March). *Measure-specific assessment of motivation and anxiety.* Paper presented at the annual meeting of the American Educational Research Association, Chicago.

Wolfe, P., & Brandt, R. (1998). What we know. *Educational Leadership, 56*(3), 8–13.

Wolfram, W., Adger, C., & Christian, D. (1999). *Dialects in schools and communities.* Mahwah, NJ: Erlbaum.

Wolters, C. (1997, March). *Self-regulated learning and college students' regulation of motivation.* Paper presented at the annual meeting of the American Educational Research Association, Chicago.

Wolters, C. (2003). Understanding procrastination from a self-regulated learning perspective. *Journal of Educational Psychology, 95,* 179–187.

Wong, B. Y. L., & Donahue, M. (Eds.). (2002). *The social dimension of learning disabilities.* Mahwah, NJ: Erlbaum.

Wood, D., Bruner, J., & Ross, S. (1976). The role of tutoring in problem solving. *British Journal of Psychology, 66,* 181–196.

Wood, E., Motz, M., & Willoughby, T. (1998). Examining students' retrospective memories of strategy development. *Journal of Educational Psychology, 90,* 698–704.

Wood, E., Willoughby, T., McDermott, C., Motz, M., Kaspar, V., & Ducharme, M. (1999). Developmental differences in study behavior. *Journal of Educational Psychology, 91*(3), 527–536.

Wortham, S. (2004). The interdependence of social identification and learning. *American Educational Research Journal, 41*(3), 715–750.

Worthen, B. (1993). Critical issues that will determine the future of alternative assessment. *Phi Delta Kappan, 74,* 444–454.

Worthy, J., Moorman, M., & Turner, M. (1999). What Johnny likes to read is hard to find in school. *Reading Research Quarterly, 34,* 12–27.

Wright, S., & Taylor, D. (1995). Identity and the language of the classroom: Investigating the impact of heritage versus second-language instruction on personal and collective self-esteem. *Journal of Educational Psychology, 87*(2), 241–252.

Xu, S. (2002, April). *Opportunities and barriers: Teachers learn to integrate diverse students' popular culture into literacy instruction.* Paper presented at the annual meeting of the American Educational Research Association, New Orleans.

Yell, M. L., Robinson, T. R., & Drasgow, E. (2001). Cognitive behavior modification. In T. J. Zirpoli & K. J. Melloy, *Behavior management: Applications for teachers* (3rd ed., pp. 200–246). Upper Saddle River, NJ: Merrill/Prentice Hall.

Yeung, A. S., McInerney, D. M., Russell-Bowie, D., Suliman, R., Chui, H., & Lau, I. C. (2000). Where is the hierarchy of academic self-concept? *Journal of Educational Psychology, 92,* 556–567.

Yip, D. Y. (2004). Questioning skills for conceptual change in science instruction. *Journal of Biological Education, 38,* 76–83.

York-Barr, J., Sommers, W. A., Ghere, G. S., & Montie, J. (2001). *Reflective practice to improve schools: An action guide for educators.* Thousand Oaks, CA: Corwin Press.

Young, B. (2002). *Characteristics of the 100 largest public elementary and secondary school districts in the United States: 2000–01* (NCES 2002–351). U.S. Department of Education, National Center for Education Statistics. Washington, DC: U.S. Government Printing Office.

Young, B., & Smith, T. (1999). *The condition of education, 1996: Issues in focus: The social context of education.* Washington, DC: U.S. Department of Education. Retrieved October 1, 2002, from http://nces.ed.gov/pubs99/condition 99

Young, M., & Scribner, J. (1997, March). *The synergy of parental involvement and student engagement at the secondary level: Relationships of consequence in Mexican-American communities.* Paper presented at the annual meeting of the American Educational Research Association, Chicago.

Yussen, S., & Levy, V. (1975). Developmental changes in predicting one's own span of short-term memory. *Journal of Experimental Child Psychology, 19,* 502–508.

Zahorik, J. (1991). Teaching style and textbooks. *Teaching and Teacher Education, 7,* 185–196.

Zahorik, J. (1996). Elementary and secondary teachers' reports of how they make learning interesting. *The Elementary School Journal, 96*(5), 551–564.

Zambo, D. (2003). *Uncovering the conceptual representations of students with learning disabilities.* Unpublished doctoral dissertation, Arizona State University, Tempe.

Zanolli, K., Daggett, J., Ortiz, K., & Mullins, J. (1999). Using rapidly alternating multiple schedules to assess and treat aberrant behavior in natural settings. *Behavior Modification, 23,* 358–378.

Zeidner, M. (1998). *Test anxiety: The state of the art.* New York: Plenum Press.

Zhou, L., Goff, G., & Iwata, B. (2000). Effects of increased response effort on self-injury and objective manipulation as competing responses. *Journal of Applied Behavioral Analysis, 33,* 29–40.

Zimmerman, B. (2005, April). *Integrating cognition, motivation and emotion: A social cognitive perspective.* Paper presented at the annual meeting of the American Educational Research Association, Montreal, Canada.

Zimmerman, B., & Schunk, D. (2001). (Eds.). *Self-regulated learning and academic achievement: Theoretical perspectives* (2nd ed.). Mahwah, NJ: Erlbaum.

Zimmerman, B. J., & Schunk, D. H. (2004). Self-regulating intellectual process and outcomes: A social cognitive perspective. In D. Y. Dai & R. J. Sternberg (Eds.), *Motivation, emotion, and cognition.* Mahwah, NJ: Erlbaum.

Zins, J., Bloodworth, M., Weissberg, R., & Walberg, H. (2004). The scientific base linking social and emotional learning to school success. In J. Zins, R. Weissberg, M. Wang, & H. Walberg (Eds.), *Building academic success on social and emotional learning* (pp. 3–22). New York: Teachers College Press.

Zirpoli, T. J., & Melloy, K. J. (2001). *Behavior management: Applications for teachers.* Upper Saddle River, NJ: Merrill/Prentice Hall.

Zohar, D. (1998). An additive model of test anxiety: Role of exam-specific expectations. *Journal of Educational Psychology, 90*(2), 330–340.

Zook, K. (1991). Effects of analogical processes on learning and misrepresentation. *Educational Psychology Review, 3,* 41–72.

Zull, J. E. (2004). The art of changing the brain. *Educational Leadership, 62*(1), 68–72.

Zwiers, J. (2005). The third language of academic English. *Educational Leadership, 62*(4), 60–63.

AUTHOR INDEX

MATERIALS AND PRACTICE ASSESSMENTS TO HELP YOU PREPARE FOR YOUR LICENSURE EXAM

Correlation Guide for the Praxis II exam: Appendix A.

This guide lists in detail all of the topics covered on the Praxis II exam and shows you where in the book to find the material you'll need to understand to answer the Praxis questions that deal with each of those topics.

Practice answering assessments like those you'll find on your licensure exam.

STRATEGIES AND MATERIALS YOU CAN USE IN CLASSROOM TEACHING

Classroom Instruction